DATE DUE

PRINTED IN U.S.A.

Literature Criticism from 1400 to 1800

Guide to Gale Literary Criticism Series

For criticism on	Consult these Gale series
Authors now living or who died after December 31, 1959	*CONTEMPORARY LITERARY CRITICISM (CLC)*
Authors who died between 1900 and 1959	*TWENTIETH-CENTURY LITERARY CRITICISM (TCLC)*
Authors who died between 1800 and 1899	*NINETEENTH-CENTURY LITERATURE CRITICISM (NCLC)*
Authors who died between 1400 and 1799	*LITERATURE CRITICISM FROM 1400 TO 1800 (LC)* *SHAKESPEAREAN CRITICISM (SC)*
Authors who died before 1400	*CLASSICAL AND MEDIEVAL LITERATURE CRITICISM (CMLC)*
Authors of books for children and young adults	*CHILDREN'S LITERATURE REVIEW (CLR)*
Dramatists	*DRAMA CRITICISM (DC)*
Poets	*POETRY CRITICISM (PC)*
Short story writers	*SHORT STORY CRITICISM (SSC)*
Black writers of the past two hundred years	*BLACK LITERATURE CRITICISM (BLC)*
Hispanic writers of the late nineteenth and twentieth centuries	*HISPANIC LITERATURE CRITICISM (HLC)*
Native North American writers and orators of the eighteenth, nineteenth, and twentieth centuries	*NATIVE NORTH AMERICAN LITERATURE (NNAL)*
Major authors from the Renaissance to the present	*WORLD LITERATURE CRITICISM, 1500 TO THE PRESENT (WLC)*

ISSN 0740-2880

Volume 49

Literature Criticism from 1400 to 1800

Critical Discussion of the Works
of Fifteenth-, Sixteenth-, Seventeenth-, and
Eighteenth-Century Novelists, Poets, Playwrights,
Philosophers, and Other Creative Writers

Marie Lazzari
Editor

GALE GROUP

Detroit
San Francisco
London
Boston
Woodbridge, CT

STAFF

Marie Lazzari, *Editor*
Jelena O. Krstović , *Contributing Editor*
Pam Revitzer, *Assistant Editor*
Janet Witalec, *Managing Editor*

Maria Franklin, *Permissions Manager*
Kimberly F. Smilay, *Permissions Specialist*
Kelly A. Quin, *Permissions Associate*
Sandra K. Gore, *Permissions Assistant*

Victoria B. Cariappa, *Research Manager*
Patricia T. Ballard, Tamara C. Nott, Tracie A. Richardson,
Corrine Stocker, Cheryl L. Warnock, *Research Associates*

Gary Leach, *Graphic Artist*
Randy Bassett, *Image Database Supervisor*
Mike Logusz, Robert Duncan, *Imaging Specialists*
Pamela A. Reed, *Imaging Coordinator*

Contents

Preface vii

Acknowledgments xi

Preface

*L*iterature Criticism from 1400 to 1800 (LC) presents critical discussion of world literature from the fifteenth through the eighteenth centuries. The literature of this period is especially vital: the years 1400 to 1800 saw the rise of modern European drama, the birth of the novel and personal essay forms, the emergence of newspapers and periodicals, and major achievements in poetry and philosophy. *LC* provides valuable insight into the art, life, thought, and cultural transformations that took place during these centuries.

Scope of the Series

LC provides an introduction to the great poets, dramatists, novelists, essayists, and philosophers of the fifteenth through eighteenth centuries, and to the most significant interpretations of these authors' works. Because criticism of this literature spans nearly six hundred years, an overwhelming amount of scholarship confronts the student. *LC* organizes this material concisely and logically. Every attempt is made to reprint the most noteworthy, relevant, and educationally valuable essays available.

A separate Gale reference series, *Shakespearean Criticism,* is devoted exclusively to Shakespearean studies. Although properly belonging to the period covered in *LC,* William Shakespeare has inspired such a tremendous and ever-growing body of secondary material that a separate series was deemed essential.

Each entry in *LC* presents a representative selection of critical response to an author, a literary topic, or to a single important work of literature. Early commentary is offered to indicate initial responses, later selections document changes in literary reputations, and retrospective analyses provide the reader with modern views. The size of each author entry is a relative reflection of the scope of criticism available in English. Every attempt has been made to identify and include the seminal essays on each author's work and to include recent commentary providing modern perspectives.

Volumes 1 through 12 of the series feature author entries arranged alphabetically by author. Volumes 13 through 47 of the series feature a thematic arrangement. Each volume includes an entry devoted to the general study of a specific literary or philosophical movement, writings surrounding important political and historical events, the philosophy and art associated with eras of cultural transformation, or the literature of specific social or ethnic groups. Each of these volumes also includes several author entries devoted to major representatives of the featured period, genre, or national literature. With Volume 48, the series returns to a standard author approach, with occasional entries devoted to a single important work of world literature. One volume annually is devoted wholly to literary topics.

Organization of the Book

Each entry consists of a heading, an introduction, a list of principal works, annotated works of criticism, each preceded by a bibliographical citation, and a bibliography of recommended further reading. Many of the entries include illustrations.

- The **Author Heading** consists of the most commonly used form of the author's name, followed by birth and death dates. Also located here are any name variations under which an author wrote, including transliterated forms for authors whose native languages use nonroman alphabets. Uncertain birth or death dates are indicated by question marks. Topic entries are preceded by a **Thematic Heading,** which simply states the subject of the entry. Single-work entries are preceded by the title of the work and its date of publication.

- The **Introduction** contains background information that concisely introduces the reader to the author, work, or topic that is the subject of the entry.

- The list of **Principal Works** is ordered chronologically by date of first publication. The genre and publication date of each work is given. In the case of foreign authors whose works have been translated into English, the title and date (if available) of the first English-language edition is given in brackets following the original title. Unless otherwise indicated, dramas are dated by first performance, not first publication. Lists of **Representative Works** by different authors appear with topic entries.

- Reprinted **Criticism** is arranged chronologically in each entry to provide a useful perspective on changes in critical evaluation over time. The critic's name and the date of composition or publication of the critical work are given at the beginning of each piece of criticism. Unsigned criticism is preceded by the title of the source in which it appeared. All titles by the author featured in the text are printed in boldface type. Footnotes are reprinted at the end of each essay or excerpt. In the case of excerpted criticism, only those footnotes that pertain to the excerpted text are included. Criticism in topic entries is arranged chronologically under a variety of subheadings to facilitate the study of different aspects of the topic.

- Critical essays are prefaced by brief **Annotations** explicating each piece.

- A complete **Bibliographical Citation** of the original essay or book precedes each piece of criticism.

- An annotated bibliography of **Further Reading** appears at the end of each entry and suggests resources for additional study. In some cases, significant essays for which the editors could not obtain reprint rights are included here.

Cumulative Indexes

Each volume of *LC* includes a series-specific cumulative **Nationality Index** in which author names are arranged alphabetically by nationality. The volume or volumes of *LC* in which each author appears are also listed.

Each volume of *LC* includes a cumulative **Author Index** listing all of the authors that appear in a wide variety of reference sources published by The Gale Group, including *LC*. A complete list of these sources is found facing the first page of the Author Index. The index also includes birth and death dates and cross references between pseudonyms and actual names.

LC includes a cumulative **Topic Index** that lists the literary themes and topics treated in the series as well as in *Nineteenth-Century Literature Criticism*, *Twentieth-Century Literary Criticism*, and the *Contemporary Literature Criticism* Yearbook.

Each volume of *LC* also includes a cumulative **Title Index,** an alphabetical listing of all the literary works discussed in the series. Each title listing includes the corresponding volume and page numbers where criticism may be located. Foreign-language titles that have been translated into English followed by the tiles of the translation—for example, *El ingenioso hidalgo Don Quixote de la Mancha (Don Quixote)*. Page numbers following these translated titles refer to all pages on which any form of the titles, either foreign-language or translated, appear. Titles of novels, dramas, nonfiction books, and poetry, short story, or essay collections are printed in italics, while individual poems, short stories, and essays are printed in roman type within quotation marks.

A Note to the Reader

When writing papers, students who quote directly from any volume in the Literary Criticism Series may use the following general format to footnote reprinted criticism. The first example pertains to material drawn from periodicals, the second to material reprinted from books.

Eileen Reeves, "Daniel 5 and the *Assayer*: Galileo Reads the Handwriting on the Wall," *The Journal of Medieval and Renaissance Studies,* Vol. 21, No. 1, Spring, 1991, pp. 1-27; reprinted in *Literature Criticism from 1400 to 1800,* Vol. 45, ed. Jelena O. Krstović and Marie Lazzari, Farmington Hills, Mich.: The Gale Group, 1999, pp. 297-310.

Margaret Anne Doody, *A Natural Passion: A Study of the Novels of Samuel Richardson*, Oxford University Press, 1974, pp. 17-22, 132-35, excerpted and reprinted in *Literature Criticism from 1400 to 1800,* Vol. 46, ed. Jelena O. Krstović and Marie Lazzari. Farmington Hills, Mich.: The Gale Group, 1999, pp. 20-2.

Suggestions Are Welcome

Readers who wish to suggest new features, topics, or authors to appear in future volumes, or who have other suggestions or comments are cordially invited to call, write, or fax the editor:

Editor, *Literature Criticism from 1400 to 1800*
The Gale Group
27500 Drake Road
Farmington Hills, MI 48133-3535
1-800-347-4253
fax: 248-699-8049

Acknowledgments

The editors wish to thank the copyright holders of the excerpted criticism included in this volume and the permissions managers of many book and magazine publishing companies for assisting us in securing reproduction rights. We are also grateful to the staffs of the Detroit Public Library, the Library of Congress, the University of Detroit Mercy Library, Wayne State University Purdy/Kresge Library Complex, and the University of Michigan Libraries for making their resources available to us. Following is a list of the copyright holders who have granted us permission to reproduce material in this volume of *LC*. Every effort has been made to trace copyright, but if omissions have been made, please let us know.

COPYRIGHTED EXCERPTS IN *LC*, VOLUME 49, WERE REPRODUCED FROM THE FOLLOWING PERIODICALS:

Allegorica, v. VII, Summer. 1982. Reproduced by permission.—*Annali d' Italianistica*, v. 2, 1984. Copyright © 1984, Annali d' Italianistica, Inc. Reproduced by permission.—*Eighteenth-Century Life*, v. X, October, 1986. © 1986. Reproduced by permission of The Johns Hopkins University Press.—*Eighteenth-Century Studies*, v. 75, Summer, 1974. © 1974 by The American Society for Eighteenth-Century Studies. Reproduced by permission.—*English Language Notes*, v. XXVI, September, 1986. © copyrighted 1986, Regents of the University of Colorado. Reproduced by permission.—*Essays in Criticism*, v. XIV, April, 1964 for "John Gay: A Satirist's Progress" by Patricia Meyer Spacks. Reproduced by permission of the Editors of Essays in Criticism and the author.—*Forum Italicum*, v. 28, Spring, 1994. Copyright © 1994 by Forum Italicum. Reproduced by permission.—*JEGP: Journal of English and Germanic Philology*, v. LXV, 1966. Reproduced by permission.—*The New York Times Book Review*, December 15, 1946. Copyright © 1946 by The New York Times Company. Reproduced by permission.—*Orbis Litterarum*, v. 41. 1986. © 1986 Munksgaard International Publishers, Ltd. Reproduced by permission of the publisher and the author.—*Philological Quarterly*, v. 75, Summer, 1996 for "Dangerous Sissy: Gendered 'Lives,' John Gay and the Literary Canon" by Dianne Dugaw. Copyright © 1996 by The University of Iowa. Reproduced by permission of the author.—*Renditions*, v. 13, Spring, 1980. Reproduced by permission —*Studies in Philology*, v. LXXV, 1978. Copyright © 1978 by the University of North Carolina Press. Used by permission.—*Tamkang Review*, v. XIII, Summer, 1983: v. XII, Winter, 1986. Both reproduced by permission.—*Wascana Review*, v. 14, Fall, 1979. Copyright, 1979 The University of Regina, Canada. Reproduced by permission.

COPYRIGHTED EXCERPTS IN *LC*, VOLUME 49, WERE REPRODUCED FROM THE FOLLOWING BOOKS:

Alexander, Sidney. From an introduction to *The History of Italy*. By Francesco Guicciardini. Translated and edited by Sidney Alexander. Princeton University Press, 1984. Copyright © 1984 by Sidney Alexander. All rights reserved. Reproduced by permission.—Armens, Sven M. From *John Gay: Social Critic*. Octagon Books, Inc., 1966. Copyright 1954 by Sven M. Armens. Reproduced by permission of Octagon Books, a division of Farrar, Straus & Giroux, Inc.—Brown, Alison. From an introduction to *Dialogue on the Government of Florence*. By Francesco Guicciardini. Edited and translated by Alison Brown. Cambridge University Press, 1994. © in the translation and editorial matter Cambridge University Press 1994. Reproduced with the permission of Cambridge University Press and the author.—Calhoun, Winton. From *John Gay and the London Theatre*. University Press of Kentucky, 1993. Copyright © 1993 by The University Press of Kentucky. Reproduced by permission.—Domandi, Mario. From an introduction to *The History of Florence*. By Francesco Guicciardini. Translated by Mario Domandi. Harper & Row, 1970. Translation, Introduction, and Notes copyright © 1970 by Mario Domandi. All rights reserved. Reproduced by permission of HarperCollins Publishers. From "Translator's Preface" in *Maxims and Reflections of a Renaissance Statesman (Ricordi)*. By Francesco Guicciardini. Translated by Mario Domandi. Harper Torchbooks, 1965. Translation and Preface copyright ©

John Gay

1685-1732

English poet, dramatist, and essayist

INTRODUCTION

Despite an uneven, often controversial writing career, Gay was both beloved and admired by some of the greatest minds of his time. He secured his place in literary history with one of the most original dramatic works ever written, *The Beggar's Opera,* and ended his career by writing some of the least memorable plays of the era. Although Gay's reputation now rests mainly on the success of the *Opera,* he had long before achieved popular success with his poetry. His own works and collaborations with some of the best-known writers of his age brought him nearly unparalleled acclaim. Had he been more careful financially, he would have made more money than any other poet at that time. Gay, however, experienced many financial, personal, and professional disappointments.

Biographical Information

Gay was born in 1685 in the Devonshire town of Barnstaple. As a younger son in a large family, Gay was destined to apprenticeship in a trade. He left Barnstaple as a teenager, after receiving a basic grammar school education, and became an apprentice to a silk-mercer named Willet in London. He returned home in 1706, earlier than expected; his early release from his apprenticeship is often interpreted as a failure at trade. He began writing shortly afterwards, publishing his first poem, *Wine,* in 1708 (the year in which he met Alexander Pope), and a short essay on the flourishing trade in literary periodicals, *The Present State of Wit,* in 1711. Around 1708, he began working for Aaron Hill, a playwright and editor; by 1712, his first play, *The Mohocks,* was published. In 1713, Gay formed an association with a group of writers knows as the Scriblerians. Members of the Scriblerus Club included Dr. Arbuthnot, Bishop Atterbury, the dramatist William Congreve, Lord Oxford, Jonathan Swift, Thomas Parnell, and Pope. The same year, Gay obtained a position as secretary to the Duchess of Monmouth; after the death of Queen Anne in 1714, he found a job in the George I's Hanoverian court as secretary to Lord Clarendon. During his early years with the Scriblerians, Gay developed the literary and political preoccupations that would mark his brief career, toying with the pastoral in *Rural Sports* (1713), *The Shepherd's Week* (1714), and *Trivia* (1716), and experimenting with genre in such plays as *The Wife of Bath* (1713)

and *The What D'Ye Call It* (1715). By 1720, Gay was successful enough to put out two volumes of collected works, *Poems on Several Occasions.* He had among his patrons the German composer George Handel, with whom Gay had worked on the opera *Acis and Galatea,* and Robert Walpole, the prime minister whose position was becoming increasingly strong in the Hanoverian government. Against the advice of his friends, Gay invested all of his earnings in the South Sea company, which soon became embroiled in the biggest financial scandal in England's history, known as the South Sea Bubble. Gay lost his entire investment and became increasingly dependent on aristocratic support. He had some financial success with the publication of the immensely popular *Fables* in 1727, but he met with personal disappointment that year as well. On the death of George I, Gay had hoped to be rewarded for his loyalty and friendship with a good position in the court of George II and was not. The following year, Gay had his greatest success with *The Beggar's Opera.* The sequel, *Polly* (1729), was banned from performance by the government. Gay published it nonetheless, and its commercial success caused fellow dramatist Colley Cibber to suggest that Gay "had been a greater Gainer, by Subscriptions to his Copy, than he could have been by a bare Theatrical Presentation." He wrote a few more plays, none of them achieving the popularity or the quality of *The Beggar's Opera*. None were published during his lifetime. He died in December 1632.

Major Works

Gay's most famous work by far is his *Beggar's Opera,* whose place in the literary canon was confirmed by Bertold Brecht's twentieth-century adaptation, *The Threepenny Opera*. Gay's most important early works were poems that adapted the pastoral tone. His earliest works—*Wine, Rural Sports, The Fan*—were quickly forgotten, but his pastoral satire *The Shepherd's Week* demonstrated more of his promise. The poem is likely Gay's commentary on a dispute between poet Ambrose Phillips and Gay's friend Pope over the pastoral genre, but both in its realism and in its respect for rural life Gay's collection of eclogues surpasses mere parody. His next major poem, *Trivia,* uses the pastoral form, especially allusions to Virgil's *Georgics,* to draw a satiric picture of London city life. In vivid detail, Gay portrays the highest and lowest of city scenes, often juxtaposed for ironic effect. His most famous poetry, however, is his first collection of fifty *Fables,* another literary form that offered Gay the potent combination of rustic innocence and sharp satire. In them, Gay uses animal stories to highlight the misguided self-importance of man; yet although the work is satirical, it reflects the Augustan sensibility that the universe was ordered and coherent. Among his early plays, the so-called "Tragi-Comi-Pastroal Farce" *The What D'Ye Call It* most clearly indicates Gay's development as a dramatist, with its odd mixing of serious tragedy with social commentary. None of his plays, however, achieved the success or importance of *The Beggar's Opera*. A staunchly English opera performed during the height of Italian opera's popularity, the play was innovative both in its use of English ballads rather than foreign arias, and in its depiction of the lowest strata of London society. The hero Macheath is the swearing, whoring leader of a band of highwaymen, saved from hanging at the close of the play by the interjection of a "Player," who complains to the "Beggar"—the on-stage character of the playwright—that the opera needs a happy ending "to comply with the taste of the town." The heroine Polly is the virtuous, comically idealistic daughter of the merchant Peachum, whose business dealings reveal him to be no better than a criminal himself. Her goodness stands in stark contrast to the world of the play, in which Gay presents a darkly comic vision of the greed and self-interest of human nature, given free reign in a society which holds commercial values above all others.

Critical Reception

During his lifetime, Gay was widely considered one of the most gifted writers of his era. He was greatly admired by his friends Pope and Swift, and later eighteenth-century authors such as Oliver Goldsmith and Tobias Smollett spoke warmly of his "genius." Not long after his death, however, his reputation began to suffer. In particular, Samuel Johnson's characterization of him in *The Lives of the English Poets* (1779) as a poet "of a lower order" seems to have dogged his posthumous career through the twentieth century. The moralism of nineteenth-century criticism further darkened his reputation because of his tendency to depict the lowest realms of society. Only in the mid-twentieth century did scholars begin again to agree that Gay's works had a place among those of his Scriblerian friends, long considered "major" authors while Gay was nearly forgotten. In 1938, Phoebe Fenwick Gaye renewed the investigation into Gay's rightful place in the eighteenth-century literary canon, placing him on more of an equal footing with the authors such as Pope and Swift who were his contemporaries and friends. Later book-length studies by Adina Forsgren (1964) and Patricia Meyer Spacks (1965) further advanced Gay's cause, stressing Gay's skill as a poet and not allowing *The Beggar's Opera* to overshadow his other artistic and popular achievements. Many recent scholars have focused on Gay's blending of forms and his mixed use of classical and popular allusion, especially in his poem *Trivia*. Others, such as Carolyn Williams (1988) and Yvonne Noble (1988), have attempted to call attention to Gay's later drama, emphasizing his continued experimentation with genre and political satire following the success of the *Opera*. Gay's politics, especially in *The Beggar's Opera,* have been a consistent subject of critical interest; Sven Armen's often-quoted 1966 study of *John Gay: Social Critic* has been followed by the work of William A. McIntosh (1974), Peter Elfed Lewis (1976), and Winton Calhoun (1993), among others. As frequent twentieth-century revivals of *The Beggar's Opera* indicate, Gay's acute perception of the values of a commercially driven society continue to resonate with modern audiences.

PRINCIPAL WORKS

Wine [anonymous] (poem) 1708
To the Learned Ingenious Author of Licentia Poetica Discuss'd (poem) 1709
The Present State of Wit [anonymous] (essay) 1711
An Argument proving that the present Mohocks and Hawkubites are the Gog and Magog mention'd in the Revelation (satire) 1712
The Mohocks (drama) 1712

Rural Sports (poem) 1713

The Wife of Bath (drama) 1713; revised and altered edition, 1730

Reproof and Flattery [in the periodical *The Guardian*] (essay) 1713

The Fan (poem) 1714

The Shepherd's Week (poem) 1714

A Letter to a Lady (poem) 1714

The What D'ye Call It (drama) 1715

Two Epistles; One, to the Right Honourable Richard Earl of Burlington; The Other, to a Lady (poems) 1715

Trivia: or; The Art of Walking the Streets of London (poem) 1716

Three Hours after Marriage (drama) 1717

Acis and Galatea (libretto) 1719; first published 1732*

Poems on Several Occasions (poems, drama) 1720

A Panegyrical Epistle to Mr. Thomas Snow [anonymous] (poem) 1721

The Captives (drama) 1724

Newgate's Garland [anonymous] (ballad) 1725

To a Lady on her Passion for (Old China [anonymous] (poem) 1725

Fables (fables) 1727

The Beggar's Opera (drama) 1728

†*Polly* (drama) published 1729; first produced 1777

Achilles (drama) 1733

Fables [second volume] (fables) 1738

The Distress'd Wife (drama) 1734; first published 1743

The Rehearsal at Goatham (drama) 1754

Plays Written by Mr. John Gay (dramas) 1750

The Works of Mr. John Gay. 4 vols. (poems, satires, and dramas) 1770

Poetry and Prose 2 vols. (poems, satires, and essays) 1974

Dramatic Works 2 vols. (dramas) 1983

---

* Handel's *Acis and Galatea,* for which Gay provided the libretto, was privately performed in 1719 but not publicly performed until 1731.

†*Polly,* Gay's sequel to *The Beggar's Opera,* was long banned from the stage, and was not revived for its first performance until long after his death and the death of those who opposed it.

CRITICISM

G. C. Faber (essay date 1926)

SOURCE: "The Doubtful or Disputed Poems" in *The Poetical Works of John Gay,* edited by G. C. Faber, Oxford University Press, 1926, pp. xxiii-xxxiv.

[*In the following essay, Faber outlines his reasons for including or excluding several poems from his collec-* tion *of Gay's work. His analysis of the problem of authorship offers a concise overview of Gay's publishing history, his literary connections, and his literary style.*]

By far the most embarrassing problem, with which a conscientious editor of an eighteenth-century poet is confronted, is the problem of determining what he is to include as his author's. It is an embarrassing problem, and yet the labour spent upon it is for the most part unremunerative; for the pieces in doubt are generally of minor, if not of trifling, importance. However, a decision has to be made and supported; and this kind of detective work is not altogether without interest.

In order to clear the ground, we will begin by excluding from immediate consideration the following: (1) *Wine;* (2) pieces not hitherto printed in any collection of Gay's poems (of which more below); (3) the 'Gulliver' verses (discussed on p. xxxiv); (4) the *Poems from Gay's Chair,* which I have no doubt are deliberate forgeries,[1] (5) the Prologues to the *Three Hours after Marriage* and *Achilles,* which must needs be printed with the plays for which they were written, and are there discussed. We are left with a score of poems, long and short, which have been at one time or another attributed to Gay by his editors, and which may possibly or probably have been wrongly so attributed. They fall into four curiously definite groups, which we will examine in order.

The editions consulted are the late eighteenth- and early nineteenth-century editions, which helped to fix the tradition. They are: Potts, Dublin, 1770; Trade Edition, London, 1772; Bell, 1777; Trade Edition, London, 1779 (printed by J. Nichols; part of the series for which Johnson's *Lives of the Poets* were written, and published in 1781); Jeffery, 1795; Cooke, 1804; Park, 1808, with Supplement 1809. These all purport to be complete editions. No complete edition that I know of was published before 1770. Bell's edition of 1773 I have never seen; but I believe its text to be followed by that of 1777. I refer, in what follows, to all these editions by name, calling the 1772 edition 'Trade', and the 1779 edition 'Nichols'. Bell, it should be noticed, was among the publishers, for whom the Trade Edition of 1772 (but not that of 1779) was printed. . . .

I. The largest group consists of eleven pieces taken from Pope and Swift's *Miscellanies.* This famous collection of prose and verse by various hands, but mainly by Pope and Swift, appeared in five volumes from 1727 to 1735. We are only concerned with two out of the five; namely, *Miscellanies in Verse,* 1727, and *Miscellanies. The Third Volume,* 1732. The latter volume contained some verse, but more prose. No indication of authorship was given. In 1747 the *Miscellanies* were reissued.[1] The fourth volume of the reissue, 'consisting of verses by Dr. Swift, Dr. Arbuthnot, Mr. Pope, and Mr. Gay . . . 1747', is the one which we have to notice. It contains all the verse from the volumes of 1727 and 1732, together with two or three additional poems. As it formed part of a uniform edition of Swift's miscellaneous pieces, Swift's contributions had to be in some way distinguished from the others. Certain pieces are marked, both in the List of Contents and in the text, with a 'star'; and we are told that 'whatever are not mark'd with a star, are Dr. Swift's'. It does not, however, follow, that whatever is marked with a star, is *not* Swift's; and I own to a strong suspicion that Swift preferred not to recognize the legitimacy of some of his children.[2] The 1747 volume was reprinted in 1754 as volume vi of the fine demy 8vo edition of *The Works of Dr. Jonathan Swift,* issued by the same publisher, Bathurst.

Of these eleven pieces, seven were in the 1727 volume, namely **Molly Mog,** *Nelly, Quadrille,* **New Song of New Similies,** *Newgate's Garland, The Quidnuncki's, Ay and No.* All of these were included as Gay's by Bell, Nichols, Jeffery, Cooke, and Park; except that Park does not give *Ay and No.* Two more—*Epitaph of Bye-Words* and *Verses for a Picture*—come from the 1732 volume, and are given as Gay's by all five editions. The remaining two—*Bounce to Fop* and *Duke upon Duke*—were not printed in the *Miscellanies* till 1747. The first is given as Gay's by all five editions; the second only by Nichols and Cooke, and avowedly 'on conjecture only'. It is surprising that out of the mass of unclaimed material in the *Miscellanies* something was not chosen more in Gay's manner than this long and tedious ballad. It is certainly not by Gay, and is not mentioned by Underhill.

Eliminating *Duke upon Duke,* we are left with ten poems traditionally ascribed to Gay. Upon what authority? On that of John Bell or his editor. It was John Bell's four-volume edition of 1773 which fixed this tradition. I take the following from an apparently well-informed article by J. Yeowell in *Notes and Queries,* 2nd series, viii. 172:

> 'In 1773, Isaac Reed having several pieces by Gay not found in his collected *Works,* and wishing to help a necessitous relative named John Bailey, desired him to offer them to Mr. Bell, and turn them to the best use he could. Bell purchased them, and handed them over to the editor of his edition, who, not content with the additional pieces furnished by Isaac Reed, appears to have ransacked the Miscellanies and various Collections for others *supposed* to have been written by Gay. Among the doubtful pieces included in this edition may be mentioned the following: 1. **An Elegiac Epistle to a Friend.** 2. **A Ballad on Ale.** 3. Gondibert. 4. **The Story of Cephisa.** 5. **The Man-Mountain's Answer**

> to the Lilliputian Verses. . . . All these doubtful pieces, as well as **Molly Mog,** are omitted in the trade edition of Gay's Poems, 2 vols., 12mo, 1775; but Bell's edition appears to have been made the text for all the subsequent editions of the poet's works.'

I do not know from what source Mr. Yeowell derived his information,[3] but it bears the impress of accuracy. His conclusions, however, are obviously unsound. The five pieces he mentions are, in fact, the only entirely new pieces printed by Bell, and must almost certainly have been those 'furnished by Isaac Reed'. We shall return to them below. What does seem to be clear is that Bell's editor chose out of the *Miscellanies* the ten pieces we have now to consider; and that he had no special clue, denied to other editors, to help him in his search.

We must then, it seems to me, so far as pieces from the *Miscellanies* are concerned, reject the idea that the tradition initiated by Bell has any claim to be regarded as authoritative, and consider each piece purely on its own merits. **Molly Mog** is certainly, for the most part, Gay's (see p. 188). *Nelly* is usually given to Arbuthnot. He writes to Swift, under date October 14, 1718: 'Among other things I had the honour to carry an Irish lady to court, that was admired beyond all the ladies in France for her beauty. She had great honours done her. The hussar himself was ordered to bring her the king's cat to kiss. Her name is Bennet.' *Quadrille* is printed by Sir Walter Scott in his edition of Swift's *Works* (vol. xiii, p. 356), with the sub-heading 'Written by Mr. Congreve'. What authority he had for this ascription I do not know; Congreve is not mentioned in the volume of 1747 as a contributor to the *Miscellanies.* **The New Song of New Similies** is very possibly Gay's. **Newgate's Garland** and *The Quidnuncki's* are discussed at length below. *Ay and No may* be Gay's; I doubt it. The style is too rapid, and the addition of an explanatory note in the edition of 1754 suggests a different authorship. The *Epitaph on Bye-Words* is not at all in Gay's manner; no more are the *Verses for a Picture.* The latter is an attack upon Sir Richard Blackmore, who was a physician as well as a copious poetaster. Arbuthnot makes a sneering allusion to his poetic abilities in a letter to Swift (December 11, 1718), and probably wrote this cruel catalogue of his works. Last of the ten, *Bounce to Fop* is now generally supposed to be Pope's. Not only was it not printed till long after Gay's death; but (as Mr. Underhill points out) the name 'Lord Fanny' as applied to Lord John Hervey was originated by Pope himself in 1733 in his *Imitation of the First Satire of the Second Book of Horace.* It is an odd fact that twelve lines were added to this poem in Nichols's edition (1779); the editor perhaps had access to some information that Bell's editor had not. Mr. T. J. Wise has a copy of *Bounce to Fop* published in 1736, with 'by Dr. *S—T*' printed on the title-page. Whether Swift's or Pope's, it is certainly not Gay's.

To return to *Newgate's Garland* and *The Quidnuncki's*. I should not have found the two Broadside versions of *Newgate's Garland* (catalogued at the British Museum under 'Blueskin'), nor the Broadside of *The Quidnuncki's* (catalogued under 'Orleans'), without the help of Mr. F. Elrington Ball (*Notes and Queries,* 12th series, xii. 174). Mr. Ball says (*loc. cit.*) that the Broadside of *Newgate's Garland,* dated 1724-5, is 'in a volume of productions of the kind issued at Dublin'; and that the second Broadside of the same Ballad appeared 'in a Postscript to the *St. James's Post* of Nov. 28, 1725'. Starting with these supposed facts he advances with great confidence the theory that both *Newgate's Garland* and *The Quidnuncki's* (which latter piece is also in the volume of Broadsides described) are by Swift and not by Gay.

> 'The former is redolent of the atmosphere of the deanery at the period, and the latter foreshadows "Gulliver's Travels". But Swift had no part in the insertion of the *"Newgate Garland"* in the *St. James's Post,* for in its version as well as in the one in Gay's works, "honest Wild" is changed to "Jonathan", a name which Swift would naturally have avoided. My suggestion is that in some way Gay got hold of the Dublin broadsides and adopted them, after making alterations, very possibly with Swift's approval, as his own. That Swift helped him there is no question. To what extent is an inquiry on which Gay's admirers have not seen their way to enter.'

But, with all the respect of a pupil for his teacher, I cannot agree that the premises are correct. In the first place, a number of the Broadsides in the volume referred to are, in fact, London Broadsides, printed in London; and there is nothing to show that these particular Broadsides were not also printed in London. In the second place, the Ballad was not inserted in the *Post* for November 28, 1725, but was printed on the back of a single-sheet supplement to the *Post* for November 28, 1715. (There are two copies of this print in the British Museum.)

Against the hypothesis of Swift's authorship of the Ballad are the following considerations. First, that the incident that gave rise to it occurred in London and not in Dublin, and was a London and not a Dublin sensation. Second, that both pieces are starred in the 1747 edition of the *Miscellanies.* Third, that Wild was the prototype of Peachum in *The Beggar's Opera.*

It will make for clearness to recall briefly the circumstances. Jonathan Wild was the Moriarty of the Eighteenth Century. A master-criminal, a receiver of stolen goods on a huge scale, he posed as the guardian of public order. He had himself effected the arrest of his former tool, Joseph Blake. Blake attacked him during the trial, and succeeded in wounding him in the throat with a penknife. Blake was hanged on November 11, 1724; five days later the famous Jack Sheppard, who had also fallen foul of Wild, was hanged. Six months later, on May 24, 1725, Wild himself came to the scaffold.

The hypothesis, which I suggest covers all these facts, is this. Gay, soon after the occurrence of the assault on Wild, wrote to Swift, with whom he was in correspondence but whom he had not at that time met, sending him a copy of verses on a theme which was the talk of the town. This copy consisted of the first five stanzas of the Ballad. Swift replied, adding stanzas 6 and 7. Gay published the Ballad anonymously, including the additional stanzas. The Ballad caught on, and was speedily sold out. Later, when Wild himself came to trial, a revised version of the Ballad was hastily struck off on the only paper available at the moment, which happened to be a pile of ten-year-old supplements to the *Post,* printed on one side only.

Stanzas 6 and 7 differ curiously from the rest of the poem. In stanza 6 'you' is singular; elsewhere, it is plural. In stanza 7, 'thy' and 'thee' appear for the only time, and replace 'the' and 'you' in the original version. Why? Because, I suggest, in these stanzas Swift is speaking to Gay, his English correspondent, and has not in his mind the 'Gallants of Newgate' to whom Gay addressed himself in the first five stanzas. Strong colour is given to this view by the fact that stanzas 6 and 7 are omitted in the collected editions of Gay's poems.

As for *The Quidnuncki's,* I feel less certain of their parentage. The piece strikes me as imitative rather than original—as, indeed, very much the sort of thing that Gay might have written under Swift's powerful influence. But I am content to put it with the doubtfuls.

To sum up: I print **Molly Mog** and **Newgate's Garland** as Gay's; I omit *Duke upon Duke* and *Bounce to Fop;* the remainder I print in Appendix I.

II. The next group is a small one, and consists of two pieces only—***The Coquet Mother and Coquet Daughter*** and ***The Epistle to a Lady on her fondness for Old China.*** These two pieces are printed by Potts, 1770, among the 'Miscellanies' in the second volume (which generally corresponds to the second volume of Gay's **Poems upon Several Occasions**). They occupy the same position in the Trade edition of 1772. I find them also in an Edinburgh edition of the **Poems and Fables,** published in 1773. They are *not* in the 1762 edition of the **Poems on Several Occasions.** Every subsequent editor has included them without question. It is strange to find them stealing unannounced into Gay's works at so late a date.

It was only after this edition was in proof that I learned that they had previously been printed. Mr. T. J. Wise has a copy of Tonson's quarto *To a Lady on her passion for old China,* published in 1725. Another copy has been recently found in the British Museum—hitherto catalogued under 'Lady'. Beyond the association between Gay and Tonson, there is no further confirmation in this of Gay's authorship. But it is interesting to know that the piece had been separately published in Gay's lifetime, after the Quarto of 1720. *The Coquet Mother* I have now found in Steele's *Poetical Miscellany*—the Second (not the First) Edition, 1727, also published by Tonson. No author's name is given; but Gay contributed other pieces, one—*A Thought on Eternity*—unsigned but known certainly to be his, to the same volume.

Both pieces are thoroughly in Gay's manner; and I include them, without hesitation, in this edition.

III. The third group consists of pieces, other than those already mentioned, which are for the first time printed in Bell's edition. There are five of these; and all are named in the extract from *Notes and Queries* given above. Nichols and Cooke do not include them; but they are accepted by Jeffery and Park. A word about each. *Gondibert* is a continuation of Sir William Davenant's unfinished poem, published in 1651. I take the following note from Bell (1777):

> 'Though we do not pretend to give the following as the production of Mr. Gay, yet as we had them from a person of undoubted veracity, who assures us that they were found among his papers after his decease; and as many marks of correction were made in them, so there is little doubt that they have undergone the inspection of that celebrated Author. Considering these things, and that the imitation seemed too good to be lost, we have, on mature deliberation, given these Cantos a place in this Work, and have the greatest hopes that they will prove agreeable to our readers (*Gay's Works,* vol. iv, edit. 1773).'

It is not stated whether the manuscript was in Gay's hand-writing or not. But I think it is reasonable to argue that if it had been in the poet's hand it would undoubtedly have been printed as Gay's without more ado. It is a dull piece of narrative, and is probably no more than an exercise by a friend submitted to Gay for criticism. I do not think it necessary to encumber this edition with its eight hundred and thirty-four lines.

An Elegiac Epistle to a Friend, written by Mr. Gay, when he laboured under a Dejection of Spirits is a different matter. Like the three remaining pieces of this group, it is given by Bell without qualification as Gay's, and with them was undoubtedly printed from the papers supplied by Isaac Reed. Were they—like the *Poems from Gay's Chair,* at a later date—forgeries? It is entirely unlike any other poem of Gay's; but

this very unlikeness is strong evidence in its favour. I have no doubt that it was written by Gay, either in 1729 or in the last year of his life. He was already suffering from the internal disorder which killed him, and his letters reveal the depression of his spirits. It is in 1729 that he writes to Pope: 'I find myself in such a strange confusion and dejection of spirits, that I have not strength enough to make my will, though I perceive, by many warnings, I have no continuing city here.' He writes to Swift in May 1732: 'As for myself, I am often troubled with the colic. I have as much inattention, and have, I think, lower spirits than usual, which I impute to my having no one pursuit in life'; and to Pope in October 1732: 'I am frequently out of order with my colical complaint, so as to make me uneasy and dispirited, though not to any violent degree. . . . I begin to fear the illness I have so long complained of, is inherent in my constitution, and that I have nothing for it but patience.' Pope called his death in December, after a sudden and violent attack, 'unexpected'. But it is clear that Gay was, both in 1729 and in 1732, profoundly uneasy about his condition; so uneasy, indeed, that he followed Swift's advice and took hard exercise for three months in the summer of 1732, and was deeply disappointed to find himself no better.

The interest of this epistle is not merely biographical. Few would connect the names of Gay and Shelley. Yet these lines written in a dejection of spirits are curiously suggestive of the *Stanzas written in dejection, near Naples.* I cannot help thinking that the greater poet had them in his mind. And, lest this should be thought an utterly fanciful association of ideas, I will suggest, further, that the famous line in the *Ode to the West Wind,*

> I fall upon the thorns of life, I bleed!

was inspired by Gay's

> Full well I know, in life's uncertain road,
> The thorns of mis'ry are profusely sown.

Accepting the *Elegiac Epistle* as genuine, I am the less disposed to reject the *Ballad on Ale* and *Cephisa.* Both stand on the same footing; and both are quite in Gay's manner. There remains the *Man-Mountain's Answer to the Lilliputian Verses.* I believe this, too—as distinct from the other 'Gulliver' verses—must be from Gay's hand.[4]

I could write with more assurance upon the authenticity of this group, if I had been able to discover the four-volume edition of 1773, or the authority for Mr. Yeowell's statement quoted above.

An 'Advertisement' bound up in the wrong place in the British Museum copy of Jeffery's 1795 edition in six volumes is, however, evidently taken from the 1773 edition. It contains the following passage:

> With regard to the second volume, it comprises the poetical pieces of Mr. Gay not already inserted in those volumes that generally bear the title of his works. His translations and other little pieces are to be found for the most part dispersed in Garth's Ovid and in Swift's Miscellanies. As to the Poem called Wine, the Editor has already given his reasons for inserting it in a note at the bottom, and the **Story of Cephisa**, the **Elegiac Epistle to a Friend**, the **Man Mountain's Answer to the Liliputian** Ode, and the **Ballad on Ale** are inserted from no less an authority. As [to] the intrusion of Gondibert in this miscellany, if the apology already offered for it be not thought sufficient by the Critics, nothing further can be said here to excuse it, than to urge the good intentions of the Compiler, and his repeated hopes that it may prove agreeable to the generality of his readers.

It is curious that in Jeffery's edition these pieces are all printed not in the second but the fourth volume—where they were evidently printed in Bell's 1773 edition. (See the note quoted in Bell's 1777 edition, given above.) All six pieces are marked, in the List of Contents of volume iv, with an asterisk. *Wine* and *Gondibert* stand each on a different footing. But the remaining four rest, so far as external evidence goes, on exactly the same footing; so that if one be thought genuine, there is no reason for rejecting the others.

It may be noted here that Nichols's edition was the first collected edition of Gay's works to include four undoubtedly genuine small pieces and one important poem which had been already printed elsewhere. The four small pieces are: *The Epigrammatical Petition* (from a letter to Swift printed in Hawkesworth's edition, and also in *Additions to Pope*, 1776); *A Receipt for Stewing Veal* (from a letter to Swift, printed by Hawkesworth in 1766); *A Motto for an Opera* (from the *Additions to Pope*); the *Epigrammatical Expostulation* (from the pamphlet on *Mohocks and Hawkubites* by Pope and Gay, 1712); and, last but most important of all, *A Welcome from Greece*, Gay's congratulatory ode to Pope on the completion of his *Iliad*, first printed in the *Additions to Pope*, 1776. Jeffery has none of these; Park has the *Welcome from Greece*, but not the four short pieces.

We return now to the pieces that we excluded from immediate consideration [thus far].

(I) *Wine.* This poem was first included by Bell, and is given in all the subsequent editions named in this Preface. Bell's editor gives his authority for ascribing the poem to Gay. It is a letter from Aaron Hill to Savage, dated June 23, 1736 (Hill's *Works*, i. 339), in which he gives some particulars of Gay's life. Here is the relevant passage:

that poem you speak of, call'd **WINE**, he printed in the year 1710, as I remember: I am sure, I have one, among my pamphlets; but they lie . . . so . . . numerous, and . . . mix'd, that to distinguish any one of them . . . is a task of more labour, than consequence. Yet I will look for it, and send it you, if 'twill be of use, or satisfaction, to any gentleman of your acquaintance.

The date of *Wine* was 1708 not 1710; but this slip hardly invalidates Hill's testimony. Unnecessary doubt has been thrown on Gay's authorship of the poem.[5] It is involved and immature; but 'the minute touch of *Trivia*', as Austin Dobson well observes, is already evident in its concluding lines.

(2) *Pieces not hitherto printed in any collection of Gay's poems.* There are not many of these. No doubt hangs over the **Translations from Ariosto,** or the **Inscription to Mr. Tommy Potter,** or *My dear Belladine,* or *The Despairing Shepherd.* Four other pieces I have included in the Appendix of 'doubtfuls'.

(i) *Horace, Epod. iv. Imitated by Sir James Baker Kt.* Both the British Museum and Bodleian Catalogues treat Sir James Baker as a pseudonym of Gay's—I do not know on what authority. The piece, a libel on Lord Cadogan, was published as a Broadside together with *An Excellent New Ballad* beginning 'Of all the days in the Year'. The latter, a coarse and clumsy Jacobite ballad, is certainly not the composition of Gay. The Broadside can be dated with certainty. Cadogan received his barony in June 1716, and his earldom in May 1718. In the summer of 1717 he was maliciously accused of embezzlement by the Jacobites; Gay's friend Pulteney was concerned in the attack; and in July 1717 Pulteney took Gay with him to Aix. This combination of circumstances, together with the allusions in ll. 22-4 and 36, and the attribution of the piece to Gay, justify us in supposing that Gay may have written it in 1717 at Pulteney's instance.

(ii) *An Ode for the New Year* was attributed to Gay by a correspondent of *Notes and Queries* (2nd series, X. I). Gay and Cibber were enemies; the latter's appointment as Poet Laureate was resented and ridiculed by Gay's circle. But whether Gay wrote this singularly cruel attack on the Royal Family is perhaps more than doubtful.

(iii) The third piece, *The Banish'd Beauty,* has been maintained to be Gay's by no less an authority than Mr. T. J. Wise. I cannot myself agree with this view, for the reasons I shall briefly give; but—as with the *Poems from Gay's Chair*—I leave the verdict to the reader's judgement.

To my thinking the poem was written not by Gay, but by one of his friends. Gay would not have written of his own 'pointed numbers', nor have spoken of himself as 'much envied', nor have suggested that he might fail in kindness to his patroness, nor have developed an exhortation to himself at such length. The words 'at large' do not, surely, refer to this particular poem, but mean that Gay is exhorted to devote his talents generally to the service of the Duchess. The Macheath allusions, too, seem to me such as Gay neither would nor could have made. In **Polly** Macheath is, of course, put to death, and not reprieved. The criticism has often been made that this adds a dash of real tragedy to something essentially farcical. *The Banish'd Beauty* was, I think, written by one of Gay's friends, who felt this incongruity and thought Gay's satire would be more effective if it were more directly turned on Walpole. Lastly, the obscurity of the piece is alien to Gay's style.

(iv) Mr. Wise has brought to my notice *An Epistle to the most Learned Doctor W**d****d; from a Prude*, published in 1723. The Doctor is Dr. Woodward, the geologist, ridiculed by Pope, Arbuthnot, and Gay in *Three Hours after Marriage* (1717). He was an old butt of Arbuthnot's, who had so far back as 1697 attacked his views on the Deluge. In 1719 Arbuthnot, with as much coarseness as humour, pulled to pieces poor Dr. Woodward's *State of Physic and of Diseases*. Woodward had advocated the use of emetics.

I am inclined to think that Arbuthnot rather than Gay was the author of this epistle. 'The question of his literary work', says Aitken, 'is surrounded with difficulties, for he generally published anonymously, and took no trouble to secure fame through his writings . . . he was always ready to help his friends, and much of his work is therefore merged in the humorous writings of Swift, Pope and Gay, and others, and cannot now be distinguished.' But it must be admitted that in 1723 Gay was a good deal in Arbuthnot's company; and that, while Arbuthnot was undoubtedly the source of all the opprobrium heaped upon Woodward, Gay may have taken his cue from his friend. There is a remarkable parallelism between the opening passage of the *Epistle from a Prude* and lines 19-27 of the **Epistle to a Lady on her passion for old China,** which may be thought to support the theory of Gay's authorship. But, while the sentiment of the two passages is the same, the ideas the same, and the ridicule the same in intention, the expression in the **Old China** piece is infinitely more pointed and capable. The latter reads to me like the work of a professional writer—and by 1723 Gay was an old hand at this sort of thing; the former like the work of an amateur—such as Arbuthnot was, for all his wit and invention. The coarseness of the *Prude's Epistle* does not, perhaps, prevent it from being considered Gay's. But Gay was far less of an offender in this respect than most of his contemporaries. The indecency of his Tales is artistically necessary; it is pointed, rather than gross. That can hardly be said of the Prude's metamorphosis!

One more argument is worth mentioning. The simile of Mother Earth suddenly pushing up a Mountain suggests a hidden mock at Woodward's theory of the Deluge. (He held that the centre of the Earth was originally a cavity, full of water, which burst forth at the Flood.) This would be natural from Arbuthnot, but scarcely so probable from Gay.

It may also be noted that, if this piece is by Gay, the Ballad on *Nelly,* believed to be by Arbuthnot, may very well be Gay's. I have never felt certain that Gay did not in fact write that Ballad after hearing from Arbuthnot of the incident which it describes. Even if it be held that the Prude's Epistle is Arbuthnot's (as I believe it to be), the parallelism noted above goes to show that Gay did borrow Arbuthnot's ideas.

Of other pieces attributed to Gay, I ought perhaps to mention:

Yarhell's Kitchen: or, the Dogs of Egypt. An Heroic Poem. London, Lintott, 1713. This poem, a folio of 24 pages, has among the mottoes on the title-page this from Hudibras

—Till they're understood, all Tales
(Like Nonsense) are not true nor false.

The hidden meaning is not very difficult to fathom. Yarhell (the hero, who defeats the dogs of Egypt) is Harley; Ausan, the 'glorious Monster' who 'did invade this Isle', is William I (Nassau); the three Dogs, Haman, Touni, and Onnah are Walpole (who, like Haman, had fallen from his high estate), Godolphin (Touni is perhaps an allusion to Charles II's famous eulogy of G. 'never in the way and never out of the way'; but it may simply mean 'in and out of office'), and Marlborough (Onnah=Hanno).

Now Harley was the patron and friend of Prior, and the hand seems to be the hand of Prior rather than of Gay. The opening lines

I am the Bard; who whilom did rehearse
Pathetick Tales of Love in humble Verse:
Who solemn Hymns compos'd for Raree
    Shows;
And *Ghosts* and *Goblins* feign'd in tuneful
    Prose:
Who oft have made judicious Mobs rejoice,
Attentive to the Ragged *Siren*'s Voice:
Works gratefull unto Hawking Dames.—
But now the MUSE bids strike a higher
    String,
In peerless Numbers now—*Arms, and the Man
    I sing.*

seem to allude to Prior's literary record, and in particular to his prose *Dialogues of the Dead,* preserved unpublished at Longleat until Mr. A. R. Waller's Cambridge edition (1907). Mr. Waller does not, however, include *Yarhell's Kitchen* in his edition, nor even refer to it. A modern hand has pencilled 'By M. Prior' on the British Museum copy of *Yarhell;* and the motto from Hudibras (an author imitated by Prior in his *Alma*) helps to confirm what I should regard as a certain attribution.

The Fair Quakers: A Poem. London, 1713. [Wrenn Library Catalogue, University of Texas, 1920.] According to the Catalogue, however, this was the work of Hildebrand Jacob, on whom Gay pretended to father *The Mad Dog,* when he reprinted it separately in 1730. (See p. 125.)

A Tale of a Bottomless Tub. London, 1723. [Wrenn Library Catalogue.]

The Ball. Stated in a Dialogue between a Prude and a Coquet, Last Masquerade Night, the 12th of May. Printed for J. Roberts. 1724. A very long-winded affair.

A New Ballad. To the Tune of, London is a fine Town, &c. London 1726. [Wrenn Library Catalogue.]

The Pig, and the Mastiff. Two Tales. London, 1727. [Wrenn Library Catalogue.]

The Oak, and the Dunghill. A Fable. London, 1728. [Wrenn Library Catalogue.]

A Tale, being an addition to Mr. Gay's Fables, 1728. A quasi-satirical attack on Gay's hunt for a sinecure.

Ode after the Manner of the First of Horace Inscrib'd to the Right Honourable Horatio Walpole Esq. London, 1732. [Wrenn Library Catalogue.]

So far as I know, there is no evidence for any of these ascriptions.

One other piece is said to have been attributed by Pope to Gay—the dirty doggerel lines on Ditton and Whiston, from the *Miscellanies.*[6] I should have been inclined to give them to Arbuthnot, who in his Letters is for ever mocking at Whiston and his new method of determining longitude. Could Pope have made a mistake? I have not included them in this edition. If they are by Gay, there is a further argument for Gay's authorship of *Nelly*—Arbuthnot in each case sowing the seed in his friend's versatile mind. But a good deal of Pope's reported conversation in *Spence's Anecdotes* is known to be inaccurate.

(3) *The 'Gulliver' verses.* There is a pretty puzzle connected with the *Verses on Mr. Gulliver's Travels.* Pope, in a letter to Swift, under date March 8, 1726-7, writes:

You receiv'd, I hope, some commendatory verses from a Horse and a Lilliputian, to Gulliver; and an heroic Epistle of Mrs. Gulliver.

Pope here refers only to *three* pieces: namely the *Grateful Address of the Unhappy Houyhnhnms,* the *Ode to Quinbus Flestrin, the Man-Mountain,* and the *Epistle of Mary Gulliver.* The two latter, together with the *Lamentation of Glumdalclitch,* were published in pamphlet form, by Benj. Motte, with the title *Several Copies of Verses on Occasion of Mr. Gulliver's Travels,* 1727, price six-pence. A copy of this pamphlet is bound up in the Bodleian copy of the *Miscellanies.* The same three pieces (*Ode, Epistle,* and *Lamentation*) were also included in the *Miscellanies in Verse,* 1727. All four pieces were printed by Roscoe.

The *Ode, Epistle,* and *Lamentation* were printed by Bell as Gay's, together with yet another piece, **The Man-Mountain's Answer to the Lilliputian Verses.** Johnson and Cooke give the former three, but omit the *Answer.* Jeffery and Park follow Bell and print the *Answer,* which is a companion piece to the *Ode.*

Where did Bell get his additional poem from? I incline to the view that it must have been one of the additional pieces 'furnished by Isaac Reed', and that it was written by Gay in imitation of Pope's *Ode.* Otherwise it seems difficult to account for the facts (*a*) that Pope does not mention it to Swift, (*b*) that it was not printed in the Pamphlet or in the *Miscellanies,* (*c*) that it came into Bell's hands at all. This hypothesis also explains the inclusion by Bell of the other pieces, which were, in fact, by Pope. It is possible that the *Lamentation* was written by Gay; but I must admit that it is more in the style of Pope, and as it is easily accessible in Pope's works I do not include it in this edition.

(4) *The 'Poems from Gay's Chair'.* These are printed in Appendix V, where their origin is discussed at length.

Notes

[1] See Appendix V.

[1] The first volume of the reissue is called 'The Fifth Edition'.

[2] I am assuming that Swift, who died in 1745, had left indications of his own authorship, e.g. in marked copies of the original volumes. But, of course, the ascriptions may have been made without such direct evidence.

[3] Nichols's *Literary Anecdotes* contain a deal of information about Isaac Reed, one of the most celebrated bibliophiles of the eighteenth century. But there is nothing there to confirm Mr. Yeowell's statement.

[4] See below on the 'Gulliver' verses, p. xxxiv.

[5] *Notes and Queries,* 2nd series, viii. 145 and 175.

[6] 'The little copy of verses on Ditton and Whiston, in the third volume of the Miscellanies, was written by Gay.' Pope *loquitur.* Spence's *Anecdotes,* p. 201.

Phoebe Fenwick Gaye (essay date 1938)

SOURCE: "Chapter 18" and "Chapter 19," in *John Gay: His Place in the Eighteenth Century,* Collins, 1938, pp. 301-19; 320-45.

[*In the following excerpt, Fenwick Gaye focuses on the years 1727 and 1728, when Gay wrote and then premiered* The Beggar's Opera. *She pays particular attention to Gay's influential relationships with fellow Scriblerians Jonathan Swift and Alexander Pope, and to Gay's difficult relationship with the English court and government, including Prime Minister Robert Walpole.*]

> *"Amidst our hopes, Fate strikes the sudden wound."*
> GAY: 'A THOUGHT ON ETERNITY'

Early in [1727], Swift began to put into action his plans for coming to England. He had Irish plaids to discuss with Mrs. Howard, and medals to discuss with the Queen, the Miscellany of poems to discuss with the other Scriblerians—and all sorts of delicious prospects. He was sensible enough to know by now that plaids and medals were about as far as he could reasonably hope to go in Court favour. *The Tale of a Tub* had done its work too effectively for him to think that there was any longer a chance of his being transferred to an English Deanery. Even *Gulliver's* success could not atone for that. He knew, also, that Walpole had summed him up, after that unhappy dinner, and had decided not to bother with him further. Not only were his personal political hopes sunk, but his aspirations for Ireland were, it is all too clear, utterly baseless.

Even so, there was still plenty to attract the Dean in England. He wrote to Mrs. Howard:

> "I hope you will get your house and wine ready; to which Mr. Gay and I are to have free access, when you are safe at court. As to Mr. Pope, he is not worth mentioning on such occasions."

And Gay and Pope wrote one of their joint letters back to him. One can only suppose that the dying senator attitude was a catching one, for certainly in the part of the letter which was Gay's, Gay has it to perfection:

> "I believe 'tis my turn to write to you, though Mr. Pope hath taken all I had to say, and put it in a long letter. . . . I refused supping at Burlington House to-night in regard to my health and this morning I walked two hours in the Park. . . . The contempt of the world grows upon me, and I now begin to be richer and richer, for I could every morning I wake be content with less than I arrived at the day before. I fancy in time I shall bring myself into that state which no man ever knew before me, in thinking I have enough. I really am afraid to be content with so little, lest my good friends should censure me for indolence, and the want of laudable ambition. So that it will be absolutely necessary for me to improve my fortunes to content them. How solicitous is mankind to please others! "Yours most affectionately."

Interesting to see how Gay's mind like a chameleon's took on the hues of whatever friend he happened to be writing to—and all in the best of faith. He knew it would please Swift if he talked of having a contempt for the world. Swift's own advice was "Once kick the world, and the world and you will live together at a reasonable good understanding." Well, he was going to kick the world all right in the *Fables*—he had talked in an earlier poem of Courtiers being "monkeys in action, paroquets in talk," and now he would show them to be a perfect menagerie of wild beasts as well. What could please Swift more? . . . And to indicate his poetic impartiality he was including himself in the menagerie as a Hare. Meanwhile Gay and Pope worked together on the tattered remnants of Scriblerus—those snacks of verses with which the various members of the defunct Club had enlivened their evenings, so long ago. Swift, Pope, Parnell, Arbuthnot, Gay—they were all included. Later Pope wrote to Swift:

> "Our Miscellany is now quite printed. I am prodigiously pleased with this joint volume, in which methinks we look like friends, side by side, serious and merry by turns, conversing interchangeably and walking down hand in hand to posterity."

Doubtless Swift was prodigiously pleased too. Scriblerus had hitherto been only a warm memory, as potent but as ephemeral as a gulp of wine: now that he was between two covers there was a permanent record of days long past.

The *Miscellany* was published in March: in the same month Gay's *Fables* made their first appearance—and leapt into popularity with such spirit that they almost put *Gulliver* out of countenance. Their success, says one Editor, was "great, immediate and unqualified." Defoe brought out in the same year a pamphlet with the astounding title *Uses and Abuses of the Marriage Bed,* and perhaps nothing could better indicate the selling power of the *Fables* than the fact that they survived, and triumphed, even in the face of a publication with a title like that. The Prince and Princess of Wales read them, the Court read them, the Town read them—and old illiterate ladies in obscure parishes ordered parcels from Watts and Tonson and opened them with trembling eager hands. Infants lisped the sedate absurdities as they sat in their go-carts or rode upon the shoulders of footmen. William, the young Duke of Cumberland, and the favourite child of the Royal Family, for whose amusement the *Fables* had been invented, may even have gone so far as to cast his eyes over the woodcuts accompanying each fable and read with some degree of approbation:

> Accept, young Prince, the moral lay,
> And in these tales mankind survey;
> With early virtues plant your breast,
> The specious arts of vice detest.
> Princes like Beautys, from their youth
> Are strangers to the voice of truth . . .
> To those in your exalted station
> Each courtier is a dedication;
> Must I too flatter like the rest,
> And turn my morals to a jest?

Echo, backed up by the Duke of Cumberland, answers No, No, No! But Gay has buckled his sword on. *Fear not,* he reminds himself, *all men—even infant princes—are dedication-proof.* He has written the *Fables* with one ideal ahead of him—a better pension than £150 a year, and a better position than that of Lottery Commissioner. He clears his throat bravely and continues:

> But shall I hide your real praise,
> Or tell you what a Nation says?
> They in your infant bosom trace
> The virtues of your Royal race,
> In the fair dawning of your mind
> Discern you gen'rous mild and kind . . .
> Go on, the height of good attain
> Nor let a nation hope in vain.

Could anything sound more genuine and disinterested—except to those in the know? One of this number may have been Edward Young—who failed as usual to join in the general approbation and with most unclerical lack of charity wrote to a friend in Ireland: "Gay has just given us some Fables—50 in Number and about Five are tolerable." Dr. Johnson in his life of Gay is kinder, although he complains that from some of the fables "it will be difficult to extract any moral principle." He goes on: "They are, however, told with liveliness; the versification is smooth; and the diction, though now and then a little constrained by the measure or the rhyme, is generally happy."

There is no doubt that the volume was a best-seller and that people of all sorts bought it and read the first edition with an enthusiasm never equalled in the reading of the fourth or fifth or tenth or twentieth editions. Altogether, they have been the most re-printed of all

Gay's works. It is not difficult to see why. They were unique of their kind—they filled a cultural gap which La Fontaine had filled in France and Aesop in Rome: it was comparatively easy to be a classic when there were no other claimants to that particular classical niche: the *Fables* became a classic. The only one which need concern us, however, is the one chosen conspicuously to end the volume and so—its author hoped—linger suggestively in the minds of its readers. This is (perhaps because of its personal implication) the best of all.

The Hare and Many Friends

> Friendship, like love, is but a name,
> Unless to one you stint the flame.
> The child, whom many fathers share,
> Hath seldom known a father's care.
> 'Tis thus in friendships; who depend
> On many, rarely find a friend.
>   A Hare who, in a civil way,
> Complied with everything, like *Gay,*
> Was known by all the bestial train
> Who haunt the wood or graze the plain;
> Her care was never to offend,
> And every creature was her friend.
>   As forth she went at early dawn,
> To taste the dew-besprinkled lawn,
> Behind she hears the hunter's cries,
> And from the deep-mouth'd thunder
>   flies;
> She starts, she stops, she pants for breath;
> She hears the near advance of death;
> She doubles to mislead the hound,
> And measures back her mazy round,
> Till, fainting in the public way,
> Half-dead with fear she gasping lay.
>   What transport in her bosom grew,
> When first the Horse appear'd in view!
>   'Let me, (says she) your back ascend,
> And owe my safety to a friend.
> You know my feet betray my flight;
> To friendship every burdens light.'
>   The horse replied, 'Poor honest puss,
> It grieves my heart to see thee thus;
> Be comforted, relief is near,
> For all your friends are in the rear.'
>   She next the stately Bull implor'd;
> And thus replied the mighty lord:
>   'Since every beast alive can tell
> That I sincerely wish you well,
> I may, without offence, pretend
> To take the freedom of a friend.
> Love calls me hence; a favourite cow
> Expects me near yon barley-mow;
> And when a lady's in the case,
> You know all other things give place.
> To leave you thus might seem unkind,
> But see, the Goat is just behind.'

The Goat remark'd her pulse was high,
Her languid head, her heavy eye:
'My back, (says he) may do you harm;
The Sheep's at hand, and wool is warm.'

   The Sheep was feeble, and complain'd
His sides a load of wool sustain'd;
Said he was slow; confess'd his fears;
For hounds eat sheep as well as Hares.

   She now the trotting Calf address'd:
'Shall I, (says he) of tender age,
In this important care engage?
Older and abler pass'd you by;
How strong are those! how weak am I!
Should I presume to bear you hence,
Those friends of mine may take offence.
Excuse me, then! you know my heart;
But dearest friends, alas! must part.
How shall we all lament! Adieu;
For see the hounds are just in view.'

If reproach has ever been cast in more gentle language, then I have not come across it. There is no record of the book's reception by others in high places, but the Princess of Wales was quick to feel the aspersion. She assured Gay—through the usual telephonic exchange of Mrs. Howard—that on that happy day when George I should breathe his last she would "take up the Hare." She had also promised, a year earlier, to send Dr. Swift some medals. . . . Yet when Swift arrived back in England at the end of April, he had not yet received the medals. Did they too hang, in some mysterious way, on the decease of George I? If so, then both he and Gay could kick their heels in idleness. The King, for all they knew to the contrary, might live to be a hundred.

It was at this stage that Mrs. Howard kept them happy; no one knew better how to sound a restrained and reasonable note of optimism that all was for the best in the best of all possible worlds. Her optimism cannot often have been justified, but on this occasion it was. George I, who was on one of his periodic trips to Hanover, died suddenly at Osnaburg. (Nobody took better advantage of the situation than Thackeray who in a magnificently purple passage describes Robert Walpole galloping through the night along the road from Kensington to Richmond to announce the news to the new King.) The Tories must have been jubilant that night: they were certain that Walpole carried along the road with him not only the news of George I's death, but his own political death-warrant.

Unfortunately even certainties sometimes fail to come off. Everybody knows the almost comic readjustment of affairs—in which Walpole after a period of turbulent uncertainty emerged again as triumphant as Mr. Punch at the end of a Punch and Judy show. Mrs. Walpole went to the new Court and was cold-shouldered by all the Tories on her way in; but as she came

out, leaving a still omnipotent husband behind her, she declared she could have walked over their heads. It was all extremely entertaining for those who liked to catch the human monkey-house at a thoroughly lively moment. The Whigs therefore, entirely to their surprise, found themselves reinstated more firmly than before, all except Walpole who may have been shrewd enough to realise that the promise of an additional £100,000 a year to the royal purse from the Civil List had something to do with it. The Tories were as discomfited as ever. Almost the only person whose position was still unaffected, no matter which political party ruled the roost—was Mrs. Howard. George II moved with his Court to St. James's Palace and Mrs. Howard went with him, into a thoroughly comfortable suite. At this juncture that depression from Iceland, Mr. Howard, fades from the picture and is heard of little more. The triumph of near-virtue is supreme.

Although Walpole remained at the head of affairs, there was still a shred of hope for the place-hunters. Their new Majesties could not be expected to make any changes in official appointments until after the summer, but—at least in the smaller posts—they might be expected to please their own private inclinations. Swift, who had come over to England partly with the intention of going to Aix-les-Bains (on Arbuthnot's advice) and seeing what the waters there could do to cure his giddiness, was prevailed upon by Mrs. Howard to give up that idea. What actually passed in conversation is of course merely guesswork, but according to Swift we may gather that she gave some pretty strong hints that the men who stayed loyally on the spot were the ones who might hope to be remembered. It is also guesswork as to what precisely he hoped to achieve. But he took Mrs. Howard's advice, stayed in London and lived to regret it ever after.

Pope and Gay spent the late spring with Lord Harcourt in Oxfordshire acting, he described it, as his Merry Andrews, and chasing away those thoughts of depression which arose whenever he remembered the days of long ago. When they returned south Swift joined them at Twickenham. Lady Mary Wortley Montagu wrote to her sister:

> "Both Dr. Swift and Johnny Gay are at Pope's, and their conjunction has produced a ballad . . . which, if nobody else has sent you, I will."

The ballad may have been the still popular *Molly Mog* or, more likely, that first song from *The Beggar's Opera* which was then in the middle of composition. If it was this song, then Lady Mary was exaggerating as usual when she put it down equally to the Twickenham Triumvirate. Gay wrote the major part of it, and Swift and Pope, it is known, 'tightened up' the last couplet. It was all that they ever gave to *The Beggar's Opera*, beyond the attention and encouragement during composition, without which Gay would probably never have written that work. The play was a pleasant preoccupation and somehow it is nice to think of two such essentially unmusical men as Pope and Swift controlled, for a few short months in their lives, by the notes from a flute—notes sounding impudently through the cloistered rooms of Pope's house, or echoing like another blackbird among the bird-filled trees which hung over the river's edge.

Others besides Lady Mary Wortley Montagu were extremely interested in the Dean's stay at Twickenham. The Duchess of Queensberry, who could claim to be as haughty and overbearing in her own right as Swift ever was—and who had heard ecstatic descriptions of him from Gay—came over one day from Petersham to beard the lion in his friend's den, but, says history, he was "out of humour, and would only peep at her from behind the curtains." She went away disappointed. A more important visitor than the Duchess was M. Voltaire, exiled from France on account of his heretical opinions, and determined to meet the man whose heresy had upset religious opinion in England almost as much as he had upset it in France. Various apocryphal stories of that assemblage of wits have come down to us, the chief story being the one in which Mrs. Pope, horrified by the freedoms of Voltaire's conversation, left the table in a hurry. As, however, Mrs. Pope spoke no French and Voltaire's oral English was nowhere near as good as his written English, this seems unlikely. Another story is that Gay read over to him, in manuscript, a large part of *The Beggar's Opera:* this is certainly possible, for the time and the place and Voltaire were all together, and what poet does not seize the opportunity to read his works out loud when he has a new and distinguished audience? A Major Broome, who kept a manuscript journal at the time, declared that Voltaire said he "admired Swift, and loved Gay vastly." The distinction has the air of being a familiar one.

Apparently the news of the composition of *The Beggar's Opera* was now public property. Mrs. Howard was certainly privy to it, and also the Queensberrys. Dr. Arbuthnot as the only other musical man in Gay's circle would certainly know, and for a long time there was a suspicion that his daughter—probably the one who was as good-natured and idle as Gay himself—provided the author with a number of the Scots airs to which the verses were set. The marvel is that Martha Blount and Mrs. Pope and Swift's servant Patrick did not also claim to have had a hand in its composition. Everybody who was told of the Opera was interested, but nobody was very sanguine of its success. Just as by now the general conviction was that Walpole could not make a mistake or ever suffer a setback, so (in a much smaller way) the general conviction was that whatever Gay attempted

was bound—by the ill-luck which trailed him—to come off dubiously. And this in spite of the recent undeniable success of the *Fables.*

If ever a man could have been found to disagree with Stevenson that to travel hopefully is better than to arrive that man would have been Gay. He had been travelling hopefully for several years now—but in no sense could he be described as having arrived. Bolingbroke, when told of the Opera, was as encouraging as a mute at a funeral:

> "I wish John Gay success in his pursuit," he told Swift, "but I think he has some qualities that will keep him down in the world."

—a nasty back-hander from an expert in the art of giving back-handers. Gay was much too kind-hearted to reply but if he had thought of doing so there were several neat points to be made about Bolingbroke's *own* difficulty in rising out of a recumbent position.

But whatever Bolingbroke's opinion of the projected work—there was still immense fun to be got out of it at Twickenham, and beautiful memorable evenings in which the three friends would sit together—when Swift was at his most magnetic, Pope at his kindliest, and when Gay's own words were received with such instant appreciation that they sounded to him as if they were the wittiest words in the world. Doubtless there was the Dean's favourite claret to do honour to the situation: Pope may even have exceeded his usual thimbleful and risked the most excruciating headache in consequence: but that kind of evening does not require even the aid of wine to make it convivial. With such comradeship the glow comes from within: the wit is self-generated.

The house-party was split up, as before, by Swift's sudden departure for Ireland—unexplained but apparently inspired by his usual fears for Stella he left Pope a letter full of apologies and affection and Pope responded:

> "It is a perfect trouble for me to write to you, and your kind letter left for me at Mr. Gay's affected me so much, that it made me like a Girl. I cannot tell what to say to you; I only feel that I wish you well in every circumstance of life."

Swift certainly needed good wishes. It seemed to him that he was prejudicing his last chance by leaving England at such a time, yet Stella still came first. The stars in their courses fought against him and he was detained at Holyhead nearly a week waiting to cross, during which time he worked off his spleen in a diary left behind him when he *did* sail and which was for some reason returned by the landlady to Pope and Gay—not to him. Simultaneously as they received it the great moment arrived. The new appointments at the Court of George II were announced—and Gay found himself offered a position as Gentleman-Usher to the two-years-old Princess Louisa.

Bitter blows are no less bitter for having been in some degree expected. Obviously before the actual appointments were made—and even while Swift was still in England—a rumour had been set about that Gay might expect something of the kind. Swift declared that while walking and talking with Gay that year, he had often found him preoccupied and when the Dean put a sharp question to him, Gay answered quite beside the point with "Well, I am determined not to accept the employment of Gentleman-Usher." He was as good as his word—and of all the acts of his life none has made his editors more impatient. Most of them take the Johnsonian view that, as he had written verses for one Royal child, there was really nothing particularly unsuitable in that he should have been offered a virtual sinecure concerning another: furthermore, if it was money he wanted, then another £200 a year was not to be sneezed at, and he was a fool to sneeze at it. Only one biographer has a good word to say for the poet—Walter Scott. In his edition of Swift he writes of Gay: "He, with proper spirit, refused the appointment, and in **The Beggar's Opera** took a most ample satisfaction upon King, Queen and Ministers." But it is easy to see that Scott was in the minority—and to feel the usual exasperation at any one being so foolhardy as to throw away a good opportunity when it came knocking at the door.

Two hundred years' lapse may make one dull-witted—but what precisely *did* Gay expect of the Court? If he would not take a sinecure, what position *would* he have taken, or did he feel qualified to fill? The answer, most likely, would have been of the negative kind: he didn't know what he wanted but he knew what he did *not* want. He did *not* want to be 'mortified,' as he felt mortified by the offer of the post of Gentleman-Usher. Useless, at such a juncture, to have reminded him that the great Molière's position as Valet-de-Chambre to Louis XIV involved far more indignity than a gentleman-usher could ever have been called upon to undergo in an English Court. Primed all the summer by the company of Swift and Pope—swelled up to an unusually large sense of his own capacities, this usually modest man was being offered his chance at the psychological moment when he felt too grand to take it. He turned it down, shook the dust of the Court off his heels for ever and went down into the country with the sympathetic Queensberrys. But before he went he wrote to Swift:

> "The Queen's family is at last settled, and in the list I was appointed gentleman-usher to the Princess Louisa, the youngest princess, which upon account that I am far advanced in life, I have declined accepting; and have endeavoured in the best manner

I could to make my excuses by a letter to Her Majesty. So now all my expectations are vanished, and I have no prospect but in depending wholly upon myself, and my own conduct. As I am used to disappointments, I can bear them; but as I can have no more hopes, I can no more be disappointed, so that I am in a blessed condition."

Swift did not reply immediately, but Pope being made aware of the same news accepted it like the philosopher he was.

> "I have many years magnified in my own mind [he wrote to Gay] and repeated to you, a ninth beatitude, added to the eight in the Scripture, 'Blessed is he who expects nothing, for he shall never be disappointed!' I could find it in my heart to congratulate you on this happy dismission from all court-dependence; I dare say I shall find you the better and honester man for it many years hence; very probably the healthfuller and cheerfuller into the bargain. You are happily rid of many cursed ceremonies, as well as of many ill and vicious habits, of which few or no men escape the infection, who are hackneyed and trammelled in the way of a court. Princes indeed, and Peers (the Lackeys of Princes) and Ladies (the fools of Peers) will smile on you the less: but men of real worth and real friends will look on you the better. There is a thing, the only thing, which kings and queens cannot give you (for they have it not to give), liberty, and which is worth all they have; which, as I now thank God, Englishmen need not ask at their hands. You will enjoy that, and your own integrity, and the satis-factory consciousness of having *not* merited such graces from courts as are now bestowed on the mean, servile, flattering, interested and undeserving."

It is a wise and tender letter, and—a rarity in Pope's correspondence—a letter in which he meant every word he said. He commented to Swift on the situation:

> "Gay is a free-man, and I writ him a long congratulatory letter upon it. Do you the same: it will mend him, and make him a better man than a court could do."

It was not often that Swift took advice from other people but on this occasion he did just what Pope advised, and wrote to Gay:

> "I certainly approve your refusal of that Employment and your writing to the Queen. I am perfectly confident you have a keen enemy in the ministry. God forgive him, but not till he has put himself into a state to be forgiven. Upon reasoning with myself, I should hope they are gone too far to discard you quite, and that they will give you something which, although much less than they ought, will be (as far as it is worth) better circumstantiated. And since you already just live, a middling Help will make you just Tolerable."

But however well-intended, all this was cold comfort. Gay had turned down two hundred pounds a year which, although it was less than a royal groom drew, or a Maid of Honour, or a Lord of the Bedchamber, was still two hundred pounds a year. He had further shaken off the Court for ever: how then could he countenance, for a moment, Swift's deplorably-worded hope that he was not "discarded quite"—that he might still have something to make him "just Tolerable?" These were not the words of encouragement that he needed. He did his best, apparently, to make up on the swings what he had lost on the roundabouts by attempting to do a business deal on his own account—failed, and gave Arbuthnot matter for one of his best jokes. The Doctor wrote to Swift:

"There is certainly a fatality upon poor Gay. As for hope of preferment, he has laid it aside. He had made a pretty good bargain (that is, a Smithfield one) for a little place in the Custom-house, which was to bring him in about a hundred a year. It was done as a favour to an old man, and not at all to Gay. When everything was concluded, the man repented and said he would not part with his place. I have begged Gay not to buy an annuity upon my life; I am sure I should not live a week."

Meanwhile Gay, looking desperately about him for some kind of friendly encouragement, remembered Mrs. Howard. As the hart pants for the water-brooks so he panted for a letter of explanation from the woman who had all along invited him to hope. There are those who absolve Mrs. Howard completely of even the appearance of complicity in the business of having led Gay up the garden path—but for an innocent person the letter she did write him has a curious guilty ring:

"I hear you expect, and have a mind to have, a letter from me, and though I have little to say, I find I don't care that you be either disappointed or displeased. Tell her Grace (the Duchess of Queensberry) I don't think she looked kindly upon me when I saw her last; she ought to have looked and thought very kindly, for I am much more her humble servant than those who tell her so every day . . . I suppose she always uses those worst who love her best, Mrs. Herbert excepted . . . I cannot help doing the woman this justice, that she can now and then distinguish merit."

But to talk of distinguishing merit to a man whose merit had just been insufficiently distinguished was too thin ice even for as experienced a skater as Mrs. Howard. She hastened to change the subject. Letting bygones be bygones, she rushes immediately into the less embarrassing prospect of the future:

"So much for her Grace: now for yourself, John. I desire you will mind the main chance, and be in town in time enough to let the opera have play enough for its life, and for your pockets. Your head is your best friend: it would clothe, lodge and wash you, but you neglect it and follow that false friend your heart, which is such a foolish, tender thing, that it makes others despise your head that have not half so good a one upon their own shoulders; in short, John, you may be a snail or a silkworm, but by my consent you shall never be a *hare* again.

"We go to town next week; try your interest and bring the duchess up by the birthday. I did not think to have named her any more in this letter; I find I am a little foolish about her; don't you be a great deal so; for if *she* will not come, do you come without her."

But blandishments and invitations were of no avail. Gay had made his decision to cut out Court life and—surprisingly stubborn when it came to the point—nothing would induce him to go back on it. Later he was able to take some gloomy comfort from Swift's lines celebrating the whole affair:

"Thus *Gay,* the Hare with many friends,
Twice seven long years the court attends,
Who, under tales conveying truth
To virtue formed a princely youth.
Who paid his courtship with the crowd
As far as modest pride allowed,
Rejects a servile usher's place
And leaves St. James's in disgrace."

Nobody could be more righteously angry on a friend's behalf than Swift—and his sojourn in Ireland convinced him, the more he thought about it, that Gay had been cruelly and abominably misused. The fact that his own interests had been completely overlooked in the recent appointments is not referred to but his warmth on behalf of Gay is significant: now, as before, he was expending wrath and disappointment on his friend's case instead of his own. This let off steam quite as well, and did not harm his reputation. But if Swift suspected Walpole to be the Keen Enemy in the ministry who had foiled Gay at every turn, he knew at whose door to lay the blame for the blighting of his *own* ambition; and if she had hurt him, then she had also hurt Gay. In some of the bitterest lines he ever wrote he subsequently summed up Mrs. Howard: "If she had never seen a Court it is possible she might have been a friend."

. . . . .

"I have been behind the scenes, both of pleasure and business. I have seen all the coarse pullies and dirty ropes, which exhibit and move all the gawdy machines; and I have seen and smelt the tallow candles which illuminate the whole decoration, to

the astonishment and admiration of the ignorant audience."

A LETTER FROM LORD CHESTERFIELD TO SOLOMON DAYROLLES, FEB. 23, 1748

Early in January 1728, Colley Cibber was approached to know if he would accept Gay's new play *The Beggar's Opera* for production at Drury Lane. Not entirely unnaturally, he refused it. He had been mauled once by Pope and Gay in their *Three Hours After Marriage,* and there was no reason why he should now turn the other cheek. For much the same reason probably Aaron Hill, still Master of the Queen's Theatre in the Haymarket, turned it down. The old school tie might account for much in the way of influence, but on this occasion it did not extend to making one old Barumite—not notably successful—give publicity to another old Barumite whose *Fables* had recently put him in the best-selling class. Aaron Hill was never a bestseller. Besides, some one had recently rubbed salt in the wounds by making the odious comparison:

> "*Johnny*'s fine works at Court obtain renown.
> *Aaron* writes trash. He ne'er collogues the
>   town."

Impossible, after that, that Aaron should accept Johnny's opera for production. The play was subsequently accepted by Mr. Rich of the Lincoln's Inn Fields Theatre, but without enthusiasm. It is safe to say, in fact, that no roaring success ever started its career with so many buckets of cold water poured over it, at the outset, by friends and enemies alike. Half-way through January we have Pope writing to Swift:

> "John Gay's Opera is on the point of delivery. It may be called, considering its subject, a Jail delivery. Mr. Congreve, with whom I have commemorated you, is anxious as to its success, and so am I. Whether it succeeds or not, it will make a great noise, but whether of claps or hisses I know not. At worst it is in its own nature a thing which he can lose no reputation by, as he lays none upon it."

Pope was not exaggerating when he related Congreve's apprehension about the play. That expert dramatist had remarked gloomily at rehearsal that "it would either make a great hit or be damned confoundedly." This attitude of extreme caution percolated through Gay's entire acquaintance. Even the Duke of Queensberry— not a literary critic as a rule—gave as his verdict after reading it: "This is a very odd thing, Gay. I am satisfied that it is either a very good thing or a very bad thing." Fortunately however one of Gay's friends was stubbornly convinced that it was a Good Thing, and she was the Duchess of Queensberry. That she 'pushed' the play for all it was worth is obvious; and it is not

impossible that she may have crossed Mr. Rich's palm with silver before it was ever put on at all.

Rich was a queer customer; he had none of the prestige of the prolific Colley Cibber and the most that he could ever claim to have done for the English theatre was to introduce the Harlequinade to it. Colley Cibber was at least a pseudo-gentleman (no actor got nearer to gentility than that) but Rich, from what may be gathered, was not even pseudo. He was hasty, dirty, inaccurate, eccentric, and had a maddening habit of addressing every person as Mister. It was impossible that he should have discerned the potentialities of the piece he had just accepted, but he knew the Queensberrys to be wealthy and influential; he knew that the taste of the town was still entirely for "satires against the Government" and on this he probably decided to risk it.

There was no music to the play, in its original arrangement. It is even doubtful whether Gay meant the actors to do more than softly hum the airs of the songs. He had written them in song form because his natural taste ran to the neatness of lyric verse—and to make his task easier he had originally harnessed his inspiration to well-known tunes like *Packington's Pound* and *An Old Woman Clothed in Gray.* These were the ballad and country-dance tunes to which he had been brought up—tunes redolent of village-greens and tavern bars. They were to be found (by those who sought them there) in the tattered old Elizabethan and Stuart songbooks still available. The solo singing of them on a bare and unlighted stage, without any sort of accompaniment, must have made other persons beside Congreve gloomy at rehearsals. Then Rich showed that the Harlequinade was not the only idea he could produce. In the Memoirs of Cooke the actor we read:

> "To this opera there was no music originally intended to accompany the songs, till Rich, the manager, suggested it in the second last rehearsal. The junto of wits, who regularly attended, one and all objected to it; and it was given up till the Duchess of Queensberry, accidentally hearing of it, attended herself the next rehearsal, when it was tried, and universally approved of."

There is something that rings particularly true in that account: though many people are mentioned, including the anonymous junto of wits, nobody apparently dreamed of consulting the author. This piece of realism alone vouches for the veracity of the whole. Probably the Duchess of Queensberry, determined to have her own way in the matter, brought along with her to that almost final rehearsal the couple of fiddlers, the oboist and drummer who would, in all likelihood, have made up the orchestra. Dr. Pepusch, Rich's tame musical director, was called in at this point to take over the command of the musical side. In the short time at his disposal he "arranged the verses and wrote the overture" for the play. There his work ended. But the anxieties of production were not yet over. Mr. Quin, the principal actor and one of the few persons who, in Rich's opinion, could sing as well as act—suddenly turned down the part of Macheath. He had acted in other plays by Gay but throughout the rehearsals for this one he had felt that the gallant soap-bubble bravado of Captain Macheath did not come within his somewhat heavy range. The story is that just after he had decided to relinquish the part and struck producer and author and the Duchess of Queensberry dumb by this announcement—a voice was heard trolling some of the airs from one of the dressing-rooms. "There's your man," said Quin. The voice emerged as one Thomas Walker—an actor with the slightest of voices but with a most engaging personality. The exchange was made, and Walker took over the part which subsequently made him. After the heavy guns of Quin it was like having a mere catapult in action, but a catapult which succeeded in firing the highwayman's various points over into the auditorium with more ability and address than ever Mr. Quin's guns had done. Miss Lavinia Fenton, a young actress in her teens who had hitherto been entrusted with mere Abigail parts and walk-ons, at the salary of fifteen shillings a week, was given the part of Polly. She still had fifteen shillings a week. Rich could not have shown better how little he expected of the play.

The first night of the play was January 29, and *The Daily Journal* of February 1, describes it in these words:

> "On Monday was represented for the first Time, at the Theatre Royal in Lincoln's Inn Fields, Mr. Gay's new English opera, written in a manner wholly new, and very entertaining, there being introduced instead of Italian airs, above 60 of the most celebrated Old English and Scotch tunes. There was present then as well as last Night, a prodigious Concourse of Nobility and Gentry, and no Theatrical Performance for these many years has met with so much Applause."

This account, however, does not record how the play, before it turned into a *succès fou,* hung perilously in the balance. The manner was indeed so "wholly new" that neither the gallery nor the pit nor the nobility and gentry who had seats on the stage and in the sideboxes, knew quite how to take it. Add to this that the gallery and pit, always ill-mannered, began to boo and cat-call in the interval because no entr'acte (or 'second music' as it was called) was played. They were restored to good-humour temporarily by a 'bull' from the Irishman amongst the actors who, sent on to apologise before the curtain, begged them to be patient and remember that there was "never any music at an opera." Things went better thereafter. Here at last was a chance for the Duke of Argyll, charmingly complimented by Gay in his ill-fated **Letter to a Lady,** to return the

compliment. He was, says George Gilfillan, a playgoer "of taste and experience," and at this juncture he helped to restore confidence to the actors and the author's friends alike by exclaiming loudly (after a survey of the audience) "It will do. It *must* do! I see it in the eyes of them!"

Even so, it did not follow that what the eyes said the hands would reinforce. The applause did not begin until after the first eleven songs, when Polly's singing of the half-pathetic, half-comic lines:

> "O ponder well, be not severe;
>   So save a wretched wife
> For on the rope that hangs my dear
>   Depends poor Polly's life."

drew forth a spontaneous outburst of admiration. From then on, all was plain sailing. The play swept on to a triumphant conclusion. Mr. Walpole in a sidebox was observed to lead the applause. He was turning the tables on his enemies, as Bolingbroke had done at *Cato* so long ago—and by indicating his pleasure seeking to make the rest of the audience doubt their ears as to whether Gay had been 'getting at' the chief minister and his party all through the play or not. Bolingbroke had succeeded in misleading the audience as to which party Addison had intended to compliment by his couplet on Freedom in *Cato.* But *The Beggar's Opera* was very different stuff; no audience with even the smallest inkling of political opinion could fail to appreciate Gay's endless digs. It is a long worm that has no turning and the worm had turned at last.

Years earlier, Gay had written out a certain recipe for literary success:

> "Yet there are ways for authors to be great,
> With rancorous libels to reform the State."

Now, he was putting that recipe to the test. Gone was the 'squeamish' author who, because his natural friendliness forbade him to give offence to any man, wrote only harmless squibs. Mrs. Howard, time after time, had implored him to use his hard head, not his soft heart. Swift had asked his friends in their writings ever to give the world another lash on his account. Pope's whole doctrine was to attack dullness and hypocrisy by every weapon in one's armoury. His other friends Pulteney, Chesterfield, Bathurst, Bolingbroke and Burlington were all in league against the archenemy. Last—and up till then least in many estimates—now Gay, too, joined the fray, and the wit and audacity of his attack made all his other allies look silly.

Gay is, for most people, *The Beggar's Opera* and *The Beggar's Opera* alone. And *The Beggar's Opera* is one of those happy creations which needs no praise, no justification, no comparison with anything else. It triumphs because it *is*. Happy in the audacious hour of its birth, it remained the outstanding success in the eighteenth-century theatre—a play revived more frequently than any of its contemporaries and an almost unfailing 'mascot' in that it brought good luck and good audiences to every theatre in which it was played. William Hazlitt's review of a revival of the opera in 1815 contained the sentence, "All sense of humanity must be lost before *The Beggar's Opera* can cease to fill the mind with delight and admiration." He then tells an anecdote which, more than any of the superlatives which have piled up successively since 1728, 'fixes' *The Beggar's Opera* in character for ever. Apparently at some stage of that performance in 1815 an old gentleman in the audience was so overcome with gratification and excitement that he rose from his seat and roared out: "Hogarth, by God!" He was an even better critic than Hazlitt. For *The Beggar's Opera is* Hogarth: it has Hogarth's accurate eye for detail, his susceptibility and tenderness to beauty, his abhorrence—humorously conveyed—of crime and stupidity, his ability to present, with a few brilliantly sketched characters, an emotion or a situation common to all. The play has none of Swift's hurling angry rage—none of Pope's tittering malice—nothing of any writer but Gay; but it has more of Hogarth than any painter outside Hogarth ever had. As he is the most English of all English painters, then assuredly this is "the most English of all English Operettas."

It is curious that, with such an obvious affinity of spirit, Hogarth and Gay never seem to have "got together." Hogarth himself was affected by the opera's success as much as any one. He did a sketch in profile of the author. He painted Lavinia Fenton as Polly several times. He painted the scene on the stage where Macheath is in chains and Polly kneeling before him at least twice. He drew 'Benefit' tickets for Walker and for another actor. He cartooned the whole cast in the disguise of apes and donkeys and other creatures—as Gay had cartooned mankind in his *Fables*. He cartooned the triumphal entry of Rich (in Harlequin costume) into Lincoln's Inn theatre, when it was rebuilt—in a carriage drawn by satyrs and with a ribbon with the words GAY FOR EVER streaming victoriously across the theatre's façade. But for all that the artist and the poet never made common ground. Hogarth had not dealt kindly with Pope in his cartoon the *Temple of Taste,* and just possibly this may have affected Gay's attitude towards the artist. Whatever the cause—a meeting between them is never recorded.

If it can never be known what Gay and Hogarth thought of each other, Gay's and Walpole's opinions of each other are well known. Walpole, never one to waste words, had summed up Gay as "the fat clown." But Gay, in return, was as little tender as his nature al-

lowed him to be. Walpole might signify by his applause that he recognised the innocuousness of the whole performance, but it cannot have been pleasant to hear himself described as "Robin of Bagshot, alias Gorgon, alias Bluff Bob, alias Carbuncle, alias Bob Booty." Nor can he have appreciated overmuch being transformed into a highwayman and made to sing:

> "How happy could I be with either
> Were t'other dear charmer away!"

It has already been said that Gay was nothing if not topical. Miss Molly Skerrit, Lady Mary Wortley Montagu's dear friend, had been living secretly with Walpole until 1728. During this year she began to live with him openly. Mrs. Walpole was still, however, alive—and *How happy could I be with either* had therefore tremendous point. But it was not the words so much as the whole implication of the opera which set Walpole by the ears. For years the press and the Opposition had been impotently belabouring both him and the Government with every opprobrious epithet they could lay hands on—but here came a man with a handful of popular songs and country dances and a fantastic tale about a handsome highwayman and laughingly exhibited his songs and his tale and said to the world *Behold the Government!* The thief-taker, modelled on Jonathan Wild, sang at the outset:

> "And the statesman because he's so great
> Thinks his trade as honest as mine."

The thief-taker's wife answered him patly:

> "My daughter to me should be, like a court
>   lady to a
> Minister of State, a key to the whole gang."

This was bad enough, but worse followed. Polly the young heroine, looking as neat and innocent as a fresh-plucked daisy, remarked, two seconds after her entry, "a woman knows how to be mercenary, though she has never been to a court or an assembly." The same strain of cynicism and contempt runs through every character in the play. Highwaymen and whores, it might be supposed, were not in a position to discuss ethics but Gay made Captain Macheath declare that, as for tearing Polly from him "You might sooner tear a pension from the hands of a courtier." Even the Gang, in their haunt at Newgate, hammer the point home:

> *Matt Harry*　Who is there here that would betray
> 　　　　　　　him for his interest?
> 　　　　　　　　Show me a gang of courtiers that
> can say as much.

Peachum and *Lockit* return to the charge with—"In one respect indeed, our employment may be reckoned dishonest, because, like great statesmen, we encourage those who betray their friends" . . .

> Lockit   "When you censure the age
>   Be courteous and sage
>   Lest the Courtiers offended should
>   be:
>   If you mention vice or bribe
>   'Tis so pat to all the tribe
>   Each cries 'That was levelled at
>   me.'"

Small wonder that at this point the delighted house turned with one accord to see how Walpole was taking it in his side-box. He was smiling as imperturbably as ever, a villain, villain smiling damnèd villain to the assembled Tories. Not then, or at any time afterwards, was he incautious enough to betray any personal resentment at the criticism of himself and his *régime* in *The Beggar's Opera. The Craftsman* with joy might declare that the opera was "the most venomous *allegorical Libel* against the G———t that hath appeared for many years." Walpole still gave no sign of thinking so.

The criticism in the play was all the more effective since it was not overdone. If the satire had been laid on more heavily it must have failed through over-emphasis. But Gay had no more written *The Beggar's Opera* with the principal object of downing Walpole than he had written it, as many supposed, to make mock of the prevalent rage for Italian music. The Newgate subject had been in his head ever since Swift had first suggested it in 1715. Ten years later the exploits of Wild and Sheppard had made Newgate indubitable news, and in celebrating them in the *Newgate's Garland* that magnificent inspiration had come into Gay's head—of making comparisons between the corruption on Hounslow Heath and in prison and corruption in the Government. He might have illusions about highwaymen. He had none about the Government, or the Court where he had wasted so many years.

The Beggar's Opera, first and foremost, was an amplified *Newgate's Garland.* And, again like Hogarth, he had exhibited the vice and beastliness of some of his characters by setting their darkness against the light of the others. Students of Gay's technique will find a particularly interesting example in *Polly,* who makes her first entrance with all the brazen brisk impudence of a Restoration heroine, sings one thoroughly sophisticated song—and proceeds to change slowly thereafter into the natural lovely *Polly* that we know. In her the perpetual clash in Gay's nature between the pure lyric spirit he had been endowed with and the sophistication of the century he had inherited, fought a final battle. The lyric spirit won to the play's great advantage. Dryden had once declared with poetic insight of the work of that other poet Chaucer: "There is the rude sweetness of a Scots tune in it, which is natural and pleasing, though not perfect." So, had he been alive, might he have found in Gay's work not the rude but the tender, thready sweetness of an English flute. . . . No character of Gay's creation is so indubitably his—no one has songs fuller of poetry, than Polly with her *I like a ship in storm was tost, O Ponder well, be not severe, The turtle thus with plaintive crying, O what pain it is to feel, Thus when the Swallow, seeking prey, Cease your Funning,* and *No power on earth can e'en divide the Knot that sacred Love hath tied.*

Mr. Courthope, in his life of Pope, is one of the few who have esteemed Gay's work really justly. "Beyond all his contemporaries," he writes, "with the exception of Pope, he was by nature a poet, in the sense that he had an intuitive perception of the way in which whatever subject he selected ought to be treated in verse." I would go further and say that, because of his lyric gift, he could occasionally aspire to a buoyant melodic level which Pope never reached. Such occasions were admittedly rare, but in all Polly's songs the lyric note is sustained. Again, "Gay's happiest songs," says W. F. Bateson, "are pure poetry." The line *Over the Hills and Far Away* from one of the songs has been called the most characteristic line in English poetry. It has much of Gay in it, in that it is both effortless and simple—so simple that it is a line that seems to have developed itself naturally as it went along, as a stream develops, winding its way between the banks. Impossible, one would think, that any one ever deliberately *composed* such a line—and yet Gay was the first to put it into words. . . . In *Dione,* never published till after his death, fragments here and there again echo the true Gay—like a blackbird, wakened by a false warmth in October, suddenly essaying again the flute-notes with which he had filled the month of May:

> "May no rude winds the rustling branches
>   move
> Breathe soft, ye silent gales, nor wake my
>   love.
> Ye shepherds, piping homeward on the way,
> Let not the distant echoes harm your lay;
> Strain not, ye nightingales, your warbling
>   throat,
> Make no loud shake prolong the shriller note
> Lest she awake; O sleep, secure her eyes
>   That I may gaze, for if she wake, she
>   flies."

Even from the heart of *Trivia*'s gentle tripping stanzas, pure poetry may be unearthed:

> "Let elegiac lay the woe relate,
> Soft as the breath of distant flutes, at hours
> When silent evening closes up the flowers;
> Lulling as falling water's hollow noise . . ."

In the *Shepherd's Week* is a song of praise, as simple and as natural as the song of a bird:

> "My Blouzelinda is the blithest lass,
> Than primrose sweeter, or the clover-grass,
> Fair is the king-cup that in meadow blows,
> Fair is the diasie that beside her grows,
> Fair is the gilliflow'r, in gardens sweet,
> Fair is the mary-gold, for pottage meet.
> But Blouzelind's than gilliflow'r more fair,
> Than daisie, mary-gold, or king-cup rare."

Still more the songs in *Acis and Galatea,* "O Ruddier than the cherry" and the lesser-known but still lovelier:

> "Love in her eyes sits playing
>   And sheds delicious Death
> Love on her lips sits straying
>   And warbling in her breath."

No more interesting commentary on the times could be found than the fact that apart from taking Polly Peachum completely to their hearts the audiences had no comment to make on her—and that the character who *did* arouse comment and criticism was the dashing Captain Macheath. Everybody adored Polly, although they knew she was too good to be true. The trouble with Macheath, on the other hand, was that he was far too true to be good. Just as the best publicity for a *risqué* turn at a variety hall in these days is for a bishop to declare the whole thing to be disgusting, so *The Beggar's Opera* received the same 'lift' from a Dr. Herring, a cleric who, soon after the start of the Opera's run, devoted a whole sermon to preaching against it. Had the play needed any extra boosting this would have been the move most calculated to supply it: but it was splendidly, triumphantly self-sufficient. It laughed at Dr. Herring and did not need his censure. Nevertheless the question as to the morality of the Macheath character continued to occupy the public mind until the time of Dr. Johnson, when the Doctor after some such discussion "collecting himself as it were," says Boswell, "to give a heavy stroke, remarked: 'There is in it such a labefaction of all principles as may be injurious to morality!'" Labefaction or not, the stories as to the pernicious influence of Macheath upon young and plastic minds abounded in those early days. Young men with good homes who had gone to the Opera came out, it was said, transformed characters and made a bee-line immediately for Hounslow Heath and a highwayman's career. One young man could not even wait till he got there before beginning the life of a malefactor, but from a spirit of pure emulation took a gold watch off the first passer-by he encountered on leaving the theatre.

Gay's opera was singularly free of the dull smuttiness which marked contemporary plays, and to which virgins and grandmothers were accustomed to listen without batting an eyelid; but because Gay refused to be smug and sententious in his depicting of vice—and even made it humorous—the minority amongst his audience declared that he was a frightful danger to morality. A little controversy of this sort, helped on by Dr. Herring's diatribe, lent additional impetus to a play already progessing easily on its own momentum. As for the influence that Macheath and Polly between them exerted on the public—there are many anecdotes available. The best concerning Macheath has about it a certain nineteenth-century smugness completely missing from the character as drawn by Gay: "Walker, the original Macheath, was not a singer by profession, but his acting as the gallant highwayman was so excellent that his society was eagerly sought by all the dissipated young gentlemen of the day, *among whom he acquired habits of intemperance by no means favourable to the performance of his professional duties.*" (The italics are mine.) Concerning Polly, Lavinia Fenton woke, like Walker and Gay, to find herself famous overnight. If she had lived now she would have immediately been employed to advertise silk stockings and patent foods: as it was her portrait appeared instead on fans and miniature screens and her 'sayings,' genuine and apocryphal, were collected and published in book-form to divert the crowd. Very few voices were raised against the young actress but the Reverend Edward Young (never one for exercising the Christian virtue of charity in his letters, as we have seen) managed to comment less enthusiastically than the rest. Perhaps he was swollen just then with the importance of having been appointed Chaplain to the King. However that may be his comment, to his friend Tickell, was "Gay's *Beggar's Opera* has a Run, which is well for him. He might run, if his Play did not." He could also point out the mote in Miss Lavinia Fenton's eye.

> "Polly," he wrote to the same friend " . . . is the *publica cura* of our noble Youth; she plays her Newgate part well. It shows the Advantage of being born and bred in the Mint; which was really the case. She, 'tis said, had raised her Price from one Guinea to 100, tho' she cannot be a greater whore than she was before."

To turn to the musical aspect: nothing is more curious than that a play originally written as we know without any intention of an orchestral accompaniment, should have succeeded in killing the Italian opera so thoroughly that it was driven out of England for many years. This was the most astounding by-product of *The Beggar's Opera....* Mrs. Pendarves, afterwards Swift's friend Mrs. Delany, gives us the best bird's-eye view of the whole affair. Handel's new opera had been put on almost simultaneously with *The Beggar's Opera.* Mrs. Pendarves, who had an unusually educated musical sense for an Englishwoman, wrote to her sister in January:

"I like it extremely, but the taste of the town is so depraved, that nothing will be approved of but the burlesque. *The Beggar's Opera* entirely triumphs over the Italian one."

"Burlesque," had she known it at that early stage, was particularly applicable—for Gay had not confined himself entirely to old ballad-tunes and tunes of country dances. Handel himself had had rude hands laid upon him and his solemn march in *Rinaldo* was forced to accompany the impudent libretto of the tavern song:

"Let us take the road
Hark! I hear the sound of coaches."

That was another occasion, on the first night, when the audience, in the colloquial phrase, was 'bit.' Purcell, also, was made to do service, and his *Britons, Strike Home* marvellously changed into the less patriotic sentiment, "Since I must swing I scorn to wince or whine." But it was not so much the individual songs in **The Beggar's Opera** which killed the Italian opera as the overwhelming effect of a skilful collection of native music falling, with all its plaintive simplicity, upon ears weary of the rigidly traditional cadenzas of the Italian school. In February Mrs. Pendarves continued her Jeremiad to her sister. Only a month had passed since the first night of **The Beggar's Opera;** but it had done its work once for all. Mrs. Pendarves wrote:

"The opera [meaning the Italian opera] will not survive after this winter: I wish I was a poet worthy the honour of writing its elegy. I am certain, excepting some few, the English have *no real taste for music;* for if they had, they could not neglect an entertainment so perfect of its kind for a parcel of ballad singers. I am so peevish about it that I have no patience."

A fortnight later, however, the spell overcame Mrs. Pendarves as it overcame practically all other opposition; by now she had seen Gay's play and she wrote:

"I desire you will introduce **The Beggar's Opera** at Gloster; you must sing it everywhere *but at church,* if you have a mind to be *like the polite world.*"

Meanwhile the exuberant author wrote to Swift:

"I have deferred writing to you from time to time till I could give you an account of **The Beggar's Opera.** It is acted at the Playhouse at Lincoln's Inn Fields with such success, that the Playhouse has been crowded every night. To-night is the fifteenth time of acting and it is thought it will run a fortnight longer. I have ordered to send the play to you at the first opportunity. I made no interest either for approbation or money, nor has anybody been pressed to take tickets for my benefit; notwithstanding which I think I shall make an addition to my fortune of

between 6 and 7 hundred pounds. I know this account will give you pleasure, as I have pushed through this precarious affair without servility or flattery.

"As to my favours for great men, I am in the same state you left me, but I am a great deal happier as I have no expectations. The Duchess of Queensberry has signalised her friendship to me this season in such a conspicuous manner that I hope for her sake you will take care to put your fork to its proper uses, and suffer nobody for the future to put their knives into their mouths. . . . Lord Cobham says that I should have printed it in Italian over against the English, that the ladies might have understood what they read. The outlandish (as they call it) opera has been so thin of late that some have called that **The Beggar's Opera,** and if the run continues I fear I shall have remonstrances drawn up against me by the royal academy of music. As none of us has heard from you of late, every one of us are in concern about your health. I beg we may hear from you soon. By my constant attendance on this affair I have almost worried myself into an ill state of health, but I intend in five or six days to go to our country seat at Twickenham for a little air . . . I would write more but as to-night is my benefit I am in a hurry to go about my business."

The author's benefit night, in which all the evening's takings came to him, was commonly every third night of the run. As the usual run was anything from three days to a fortnight, but seldom longer, the manager and proprietors of the theatre found this an adequate arrangement. Rich, however, appears to have seen fairly early on that **The Beggar's Opera** was going far to exceed the usual run and that therefore the author would get more than what he considered a fair share of the takings. After the first two weeks, therefore, Gay stopped drawing a profit from every third night, and some other arrangement was come to. He was not a good manager of his own business affairs, however much he may have thought he was.

The man who *had* a good business head, without any doubt, was Jacob Tonson. Soon after the publication of **The Beggar's Opera** in book form in February, Messrs. Tonson and Watts, who were jointly responsible for publishing it, bought (for under a hundred pounds) the complete copyright of both **The Beggar's Opera** and the **Fables,** the two productions of Gay's which, above all his others, went on selling merrily well into the middle of the eighteenth century.

The news of Gay's success came to Swift at a time when he most sorely needed some brightening contact with his friends in London. Gay had written that none of the Dean's acquaintances had heard from him for a very long time. The reason was not far to seek. Stella had, ever since Swift's last return from London, been slowly sinking. She died the day before **The Beggar's**

Opera was produced, and Swift in an agony of mind and spirit not often given to mortal man to bear had withdrawn himself out of sight of the windows through which the light from the church would come, when her funeral service was conducted. And as he withdrew his physical presence so he sought also to withdraw his mental one. In the "character" of Stella which he sat down to compose the night she died dispassion triumphed as it had always done over passion, and he wrote that she had every virtue but that she was "a little too fat." It is not the language of a lover or a priest; it is a more terrible spectacle—the Dean being honest with himself and proving to himself that he could see the flaw even in Stella. The motive is transparent. Admit the flaw, and he knew that the memory could not hurt him so much; it was a trick familiar to him from his youth.

Upon the inevitable loneliness in which he found himself after Stella's death, Gay's letter with its cheerful chatter of success and happiness fell like a missive from another world. He grasped at it desperately: he dragged his mind back out of the dark recesses where it still went groping, aching after Stella, and forced it to concentrate, instead, on affairs in London. Stella was dearer to him far but she was dead. Let the dead bury their dead. He wrote to Gay mentioning no word of Stella, and congratulating him heartily upon his good fortune:

> "I beg you will be thrifty and learn to value a shilling . . . get a stronger fence about your £1,000, and throw the inner Fence into the Heap, and be advised by your Twickenham Landlord and me about an Annuity. You are the most refractory, honest, good-natured man I have ever known; I could argue out this Paper . . .

> "Will you desire my Lord Bolingbroke, Mr. Pulteney and Mr. Pope to command you to buy an annuity with the Thousand Pounds? . . . Ever preserve some spice of the Alderman and prepare against Age, and Dullness, and Sickness, and Coldness or death of Friends. A whore has a resource left, that she can turn bawd; but an old decayed Poet is a creature abandoned. . . . Lord, how the schoolboys at Westminster and university lads adore you at this juncture! have you made as many men laugh, as Ministers can make weep?"

And finally, paying the most generous compliment in his power:

> "*The Beggar's Opera* has knocked down Gulliver; I hope to see Pope's dullness [the Dunciad] knock down *the Beggar's Opera*."

Swift could do more than give Gay good advice. He boosted *The Beggar's Opera* in *The Intelligencer*—a paper which he and Sheridan had recently started in Dublin. It was a congenial task:

> "This comedy contains . . . a satire which, without enquiring whether it affects the present age, may possibly be useful in times to come; I mean where the author takes the occasion of comparing the common robbers of the public and their several stratagems for betraying, undermining and hanging each other, to the several arts of the politicians in times of corruption.

> "This comedy likewise exposes, with great justice, that taste for Italian music among us, which is wholly unsuitable to a northern climate and the genius of the people, whereby we are overrun with Italian effeminacy and Italian manners. An old gentleman said to me, that many years ago, when the practice of an unnatural vice grew frequent in London, that many were persecuted for it, he was sure it would be the forerunner of Italian operas and singers; and then we should want nothing but stabbing, and poisoning, to make us perfect Italians."

Swift's article was typical of the eulogy of the time and Gay—who had never consciously intended it—must have been amused to find himself quite suddenly the champion of English music. True, he had asked in the *Epistle to Paul Methuen:*

> "Why must we climb the Alpine mountain's sides
> To find the seat where Harmony resides?
> Why touch we not so soft the silver lute,
> The cheerful haut-boy and the mellow flute?"

But the question had been merely rhetorical. Dozens of other wits, besides himself, had made mock of that so-essentially mockable thing, the Italian opera. Young and Gay did not often think alike on the same subjects but Young had written of the smart audiences:

> "Italian musick's sweet because 'tis dear,
> Their vanity is tickled, not their ear."

and earlier still, Steele and Addison had used every weapon of ridicule in vain against the musical seasons of Bononcini and Attilio. Hogarth had done in pencil what the rest had done in verse and prose. All to no avail. It had been left to John Gay to pelt the foreign opera out of England "with lumps of Pudding" as an Italian complained—*Lumps of Pudding* being the air to which the last song in *The Beggar's Opera* was set.

The triumph was as complete as it could well be. Even Colley Cibber (who had immediately set to and written *Love in a Riddle* in direct imitation of *The Beggar's Opera,* and seen it flop like a hamstrung elephant) gave credit where credit was due. He said handsomely that Gay was a good-natured, honest man, and added, "I will grant . . . that in his *Beggar's Opera* he hath more skilfully gratified the publick taste, than all the brightest authors that ever went before him." Not that every one was as large-minded as Colley Cibber. An anonymous—and obviously Whig—writer in the *Daily Post,* for instance, made a violent attack on what he described as *the Twickenham Hotch-Potch.* This article drew a sad contrast between virtue unrewarded in previous times, and vice triumphant in the present:

"Thus have I set before the Readers' Eyes (it ran) in as short a Method as I could, the cruel Treatment that so many extraordinary Men have received from their countrymen for these last hundred Years. If I could now shift the scene and show them also the Penury and Avarice changed all at once into Riot and Profuseness, and more, squandered away upon four objects (an impertinent *Scotch*-Quack, a Profli-gate *Irish*-Dean, the Lacquey of a superannuated Dutchess, and a little virulent Papist) than would have satisfied the greater Part of those extraordinary Men, the Readers to whom these creatures should be altogether unknown, would fancy them prodigies of Art and Nature."

It is all very obscure and ungrammatical—and one is tempted to think that if it is true that Walpole paid out £50,000 a year to Whig press propagandists, then he might have got better value for his money. Such abuse, however, would not stop *The Beggar's Opera* or make people forget *Gulliver,* or rub out Pope's unfinished *Dunciad.* The stars in their courses may have fought against Scriblerus, but now despite Walpole and all he could do, the Scriblerians were coming into their own. Meanwhile the "Lacquey of a superannuated Dutchess" wrote jubilantly again to Swift:

"I have got by all this success between seven and eight hundred pounds and Rich (deducting the whole charge of the House) hath clear'd already near four thousand pounds. In about a month I am going to the Bath with the Dutchess of Marlborough and Mr. Congreve, for I have no expectations of receiving any favours from the court. I would not have talk'd so much upon this subject or upon anything that regards myself but to you; but as I know you interest yourself so sincerely in whatever concerns me, I believe you would have blamed me if I had said less. Your Singer owes Dr. Arbuthnot some money— I have forgot the sum but I think it is Two Guineas, the Dr. desired me to let you know it. I saw him last night with Mr. Lewis at Sir William Wyndham, who if he had not had the gout would have answered your letter you sent him a year and a half ago; he said this to me a week since, but he is now pretty well again and so may forget to write."

The Irish bull quality of the last sentence is Gay all over. He goes on hopefully:

"I have bought two pair of Sheets against your coming to town, so that we need not send any more to Jervas upon that account. I really miss you every day, and I would be content that you should have one whole window to yourself and shall long to have you again. I am, dear sir,
    "Yours most affectionately."

The underlying formality of the letters between Pope and Swift and Gay is important: throughout their lives they had a genuine respect for each other. Such formality contrasts oddly with Bolingbroke's assumption of easy *bonhomie:*—"Adieu, dear Swift, with all thy faults I love thee entirely—make an effort and love me with all mine." This was not the way to the Dean's heart, but Bolingbroke never learnt it.

Pope, too, wrote to tell Swift of the opera's progress:

"Mr. Gay's opera has been acted near Forty days running, and will certainly continue the whole season. So he has more than a Fence about his Thousand Pound. He will soon be thinking of a Fence about his Two Thousand." He seems, however, to have had an inkling that Gay was going to be as stubborn as usual about the matter of the annuity, for he adds:—"Shall no one of us live as we would wish each other to live? Shall he have no annuity, you no settlement on this side, and I no Prospect of getting to you on the other?"

If there was an answer to that, it was not in Swift's power to give it. He could not solve these conundrums, he could only wish, like Pope, that matters were otherwise. Meanwhile, London's Longest Run had come to an end (after taking in total receipts, close on ten thousand pounds) and the irresponsible author was off to Somerset again with Congreve and his young Duchess—thundering in a coach over the treacherous Hounslow Heath—clinging to his hat across the windy Wiltshire downs and so, after three days' travelling, to Bath. . . . Martha Blount, writing to Swift, was far less shrewish than usual when she said: "Mr. Gay's fame is increasing, but his riches are in a fair way of diminishing. He is gone to the Bath."

Donald Bond (essay date 1947)

SOURCE: Introduction to "The Present State of Wit" by John Gay, *Augustan Reprint Society,* Ser. I, No. 3, May 1947, pp. 1-5.

[*In the following essay, Bond discusses the possible political biases revealed in Gay's review of the periodicals circulating in London coffeehouses of the early eighteenth century. With some attention to Gay's treatment of Joseph Addison and Richard Steele, Bond suggests that this early work may indicate Whig leanings that predate Gay's association with the more Tory-sympathetic Swift and Pope.*]

Gay's concern in his survey of *The Present State of Wit* is with the productions of wit which were circulating among the coffee-houses of 1711, specifically the large numbers of periodical essays which were perhaps the most distinctive kind of "wit" produced in the "four last years" of Queen Anne's reign. His little pamphlet makes no pretence at an analysis of true and false wit or a refining of critical distinctions with regard to wit in its relations to fancy and judgment. Addressed to "a friend in the country," it surveys in a rapid and engaging manner the productions of Isaac Bickerstaff and his followers which are engrossing the interest of London. In other words it is an early example of a popular eighteenth-century form, of which Goldsmith's more extended *Inquiry into the Present State of Polite Learning* is the best known instance. . . .

Gay is writing, he tells us, without prejudice "either for Whig or Tory," but the warm praise which he extends to Steele and Addison makes his pamphlet sound like the criticism of one very close to the Whigs. Though Gay is ordinarily associated with the Tory circle of Swift and Pope, he was in 1711 still in the somewhat uncertain position of a youngster willing to be courted by either group. His earliest sympathies were if anything on the side of the Whigs, in spite of the turn of events in the autumn of 1710. Gay's interests in these early years are nowhere so well analysed as in the early pages of W. H. Irving's *John Gay: Favorite of the Wits* (Durham, N.C., 1940): cf. the title of the second chapter: "Direction Found—the Year 1713." Even as late as 1715 Swift apparently thought of him as a Whig (Swift's *Letters,* ed. Ball, II, 286, cited by Irving, p. 91).

One need not be surprised, then, to find Gay eulogizing Captain Steele as "the greatest scholar and best casuist of any man in England," an essayist whose writings "have set all our wits and men of letters on a new way of thinking." Swift's reaction is well known. "Dr. Freind was with me," he writes to Stella on May 14th, "and pulled out a two-penny pamphlet just published, called, **The State of Wit,** giving a character of all the papers that have come out of late. The author seems to be a Whig, yet he speaks very highly of a paper called the *Examiner,* and says the supposed author of it is Dr. Swift. But above all things he praises the *Tatlers* and *Spectators;* and I believe Steele and Addison were privy to the printing of it. Thus is one treated by these impudent dogs" (*Journal to Stella,* ed. J. K. Moorhead, Everyman's Library, p. 168).

In addition to the *Tatler* and *Spectator* Gay discusses a dozen other periodical publications which are of some interest to-day. Dr. King's "monthly *Philosophical Transactions,*" mentioned in the third paragraph, had begun as a parody of the Royal Society's publications, but they had failed to hold the public interest, in spite of the wit of the author of the *Art of Cookery:* "though that gentleman has a world of wit . . . , the town soon grew weary of his writings." King's *Useful Transac-*

tions in Philosophy had in fact run to only three numbers in the early months of 1709. The *Monthly Amusement* of John Ozell, mentioned in the following paragraph, which Churton Collins erroneously considered to be not a periodical but "simply his frequent appearances as a translator" (p. xxxii)—a statement repeated by Lewis Melville in his *Life and Letters of John Gay* (London, 1921, p. 12)—ran for only six numbers, from April to September 1709. Gay's statement that it "is still continued" may refer to the better known *Delights for the Ingenious; or a Monthly Entertainment for the Curious of Both Sexes* (edited by John Tipper) which was currently appearing in 1711.

As to the political papers Gay's observations are moderate in tone. Defoe's *Review* (1704-13) and *The Observator* (1702-12), begun by John Tutchin, are noticed in rather supercilious fashion. *The Examiner* (1710-14) is damned with faint praise: though "all men, who speak without prejudice, allow it to be well written" and "under the eye of some great persons who sit at the helm of affairs," Gay's admiration is reserved for its two chief opponents, Addison's short-lived *Whig Examiner* (1710) and *The Medley* (1710-12).

The real hero of the pamphlet, however, is Richard Steele, with his coadjutor Mr. Addison, "whose works in Latin and English poetry long since convinced the world, that he was the greatest master in Europe of those two language." The high praise which Gay lavishes upon this pair—comparable in their own field, he says, to Lord Somers and the Earl of Halifax—is eloquent testimony to the immense interest aroused by their two papers in the London of 1709-12. There is no need to review here the particulars of Gay's eulogy, but one or two points may be noted. In the first place, Gay's remarks are not extravagant when compared with other contemporary testimony. Many of these tributes were brought together by Aitken in his monumental biography of Steele, and since 1889 other contemporary sources have been published which give corroborating support. Hearne first mentions the *Spectator* on April 22, 1711, in a comment on No. 43, and even this crusty Tory and Jacobite notes in his diary: "But Men that are indifferent commend it highly, as it deserves" (*Remarks and Collections,* ed. Doble, III, Oxford, 1895, p. 154). The published reports of the Historical Manuscripts Commission, too, contain many contemporary references (see, e.g., *Manuscripts of the Hon. Frederick Lindley Wood* (1913), p. 247; *Manuscripts of the Marquess of Downshire,* I (1924), 889). It is interesting to observe, further, that Gay makes no reference to the political prejudices of the *Spectator* though it was not without criticism at the time for its meddling in politics. *The Plain Dealer* of May 24, 1712, for example, objected to the publication of No. 384 (the reprinting of the Bishop of St. Asaph's Introduction to his *Sermons*) and hinted at a "Mercenary Consideration" behind this sorry attempt to "propagate ill Principles."

Gay's attitude on this point would be another reason for Swift's dislike of the pamphlet.

The "continuations" of the *Tatler* are given due attention by Gay, as well as three of its imitators: *The Grouler* (6 numbers, 1711), *The Whisperer* (one number, 1709), and *The Tell Tale,* which may be *The Tatling Harlot* (3 numbers, 1709), or, as Churton Collins conjectured, *The Female Tatler* (1709-10). Gay's postscript makes an agreeable reference to *The British Apollo* (1708-11), which has "of late, retreated out of this end of the town into the country," where "it still recommends itself by deciding wagers at cards, and giving good advice to shopkeepers and their apprentices," an interesting comment in view of Gay's own possible connection with this journal (cf. Irving, pp. 40-56). It is these casual remarks, as well as the more extensive critical comments on the present state of "wit," which give Gay's pamphlet a permanent interest. . . .

Patricia Meyer Spacks (essay date 1964)

SOURCE: "John Gay: A Satirist's Progress," in *Essays in Criticism,* Vol. XIV, No. 2, 1964, pp. 156-70.

[*In the following essay, Spacks considers the strengths and weaknesses of Gay's satiric efforts, concentrating on his satiric epistles and the* Fables. *Comparing Gay primarily to Pope, Spacks suggests that Gay's recognition of his own feelings may have blunted the point of some of his satire.*]

Several years ago, in 'The Muse of Satire', Maynard Mack, reminding us that 'all good satire . . . exhibits an appreciable degree of fictionality', isolated three distinguishable 'voices' characteristic of the *personae* in Pope's formal satires: those of the satirist 'as *vir bonus,* the plain good private citizen', as *ingénu,* and as hero, or public defender. The 'total dramatic development of any one of [Pope's] formal satires is', Mr. Mack concluded, 'to a large extent determined by the way they [the voices] succeed one another, modulate and qualify one another, and occasionally fuse with one another'.[1]

The illumination of satiric technique in Mr. Mack's essay also clarifies, indirectly, the achievement and limitations of other eighteenth-century satirists. A case in point is John Gay, who has been considered, apart from his triumph in *The Beggar's Opera,* merely a second- or third-rate Pope. Ian Jack barely mentions Gay in his book on Augustan satire; James Sutherland treats him kindly and perceptively, but not as a serious satirist. 'If Gay was not an earnest moralist', Mr. Sutherland writes, 'neither was he a determined satirist. We may suspect that his satirical tone was acquired mainly from living among satirists in a satirical age. We can see him occasionally in his letters working himself up

to a fashionable indignation with the age in which he lives, but there is no conviction in his protests.'[2] Yet Gay's persistent attempts at satire deserve more attention; his weaknesses and his strengths are worth understanding.

Gay's principal satiric poems are a group of verse epistles, five 'eclogues', and the fables, fifty published in the first series (1727) and sixteen much longer, quite different ones issued posthumously in 1738. The fables, once Gay's most popular work (always excepting *The Beggar's Opera*), went through more than three hundred and fifty editions, including translations into Urdic and Bengali. They are, however, hardly read today—and their neglect, it might be added, is undeserved. Gay's poetry, indeed, has been far too generally neglected. At the moment there is actually no edition of the poems in print, although a new one is being prepared in America.

The satiric methods employed in the widely different forms of verse Gay attempted of course themselves vary widely; one feels the poet seeking a congenial mode of expression. In the epistles and eclogues, his satiric thrust is seldom sharp. We may find the wit of the Popean satirist, his epigrammatic condensation, even his energy—yet as satires these works are strangely unconvincing. In the epistles particularly, the poet (the fictional poet who speaks) seems to feel himself all too deeply involved in the world he nominally criticizes. There is no separation between satirist and target: if he objects to feminine hypocrisy, he simultaneously observes the significant fact of masculine lust, and himself as an instance of it ('**To a Young Lady, with Some Lampreys**'). He may use an entire poem ('**To a Lady on her Passion for Old China**') to define human weakness, but conclude by approving of it: the greatest good possible in an irrational world, he suggests, is the willing acceptance by women of their feminine frailty, because the alternative breakage of a lover's 'faithful heart' is the most dreadful destruction possible. Of course Gay himself is the lover in this case—that is part of the joke. But the limitation of perspective the poet deliberately assumes by taking this rôle makes it impossible for him to denounce his fellows. The attitude toward humanity defined by virtually all the epistles is constant: the poet observes and understands human weakness, finds it comic though pathetic, and because of his own lively sense of pleasurable involvement in the general irrationality cannot be bitter or fierce. The satirist's function is to censure, to lash; Gay does neither. 'Life is a jest and all things show it': the famous first line of his self-epitaph suggests the tone of much of his early satire.

The voice of the poet, in other words, is predominantly that of the *ingénu,* the *naïf.* This can be a valuable resource for the satirist, a means of revelation: the child looks at the king and remarks, 'But Mama, he doesn't have any clothes on' (see Mack, p. 230). But the fresh perspective provided by the innocent's point of view must be supported by some more authoritative voice, and the modulation from innocence to authority which Pope could manage so masterfully was apparently too difficult for Gay. Except, notably, in 'The Birth of the Squire', a piece almost completely successful in its own terms, Gay rarely achieved the high tone of defender of the right; struggling toward such heights, he falters again and again. In the satiric poems preceding the *Fables* we may discover isolated passages of genuine brilliance, but most of these pieces leave the reader strangely dissatisfied. The satiric ineptitude which we repeatedly sense is above all the result of inadequate perspective. Gay's major problem was to find an appropriate stance, a public rôle which would make satire fully possible. The consequences of his early failures to accomplish this suggests as vividly as Pope's successes the importance of the *persona* in eighteenth-century satiric verse.

Unlike Pope, Gay seems to have chosen typically a *persona* much like his own character—or perhaps he simply used the same *persona* in his life and his poetry. His contemporaries record the image of him as gentle, easy going, rather feckless, dependent on others for guidance (his most recent biographer, however, insists on Gay's sound practical sense); Gay employs the identical image in such a poem as the 'Epistle to Pulteney', where he presents himself as merely the ordinary Englishman, a combination of *naïf* and 'plain good man'. He disarms criticism by forestalling it:

> Yes, I can sagely, when the times are past,
> Laugh at those follys which I strove to taste.
>
> (ll. 3-4)

His tone is dominated by puzzled annoyance at the idiosyncrasies of the French; if such annoyance produces no biting denunciation, it yet allows a good deal of insight. The poet describes himself as the constant butt of French sophisticates: his clothes are, by French standards, poorly tailored; he is ridiculously ignorant of the business of *amour;* when he complains because the opera audience sings with the musicians, his neighbour reproaches him for not loving music. His sketch of Parisian society seems shaped more by innocent confusion than by malice; its vigour derives from the very simplicity of the viewpoint the poet has assumed. Gradually one is forced to realize that in this society men have been reduced—have reduced themselves— to things. Descriptive details underline the horrifying yet comic fact. The wit who lacks scarlet plumes must be forlorn; however Apollo-like his utterance, he cannot win approval while he 'wants th' assurance of brocade and lace' (l. 54). Women, who judge men by their apparel, also treat themselves as objects. Corinna 'pawns her person for the sharper's loan' (l. 88), thus

winning the poet's ironic praise for her integrity in paying debts of honour. Madame 'puts on her Opera face' (l. 94) as she dons her gown; her brilliant cheeks resemble not real flowers, but the silken rose on her dress. 'Crowds of rustling manteaus' (l. 134) throng the Tuilleries; it is merely incidental that there are men inside them. A fop is identifiable not by his face but by his embroidery; 'embroider'd youth' (l. 187) inhabit the Opera stage and are admired for their gold-clocked stockings. Clothes, more important than men, provide the ultimate standard of judgment; men and women, in this world, can be no more than their clothes.

It is a clockwork society, this sophisticated world:

> But hark! the full *Orchestra* strikes the
>   strings;
> The Hero strutts, and the whole audience
>   sings.
>
> (ll. 191-2)

Sexual activity is as mechanized as musical endeavour. When a woman's charms, evaluated like her clothes, grow 'cheap by constant use', she begins to sin 'for scarves, clock'd stockings, knots and shoes' (ll. 171-2). Sex is anything but natural. Women regulate their promiscuity by formal principles:

> She scorns th' ignoble love of feeble pages,
> But with three Abbots in one night engages.
>
> (ll. 175-6)

This is unconvincing enough, but the poet, seeking emphatic images, is hardly concerned with realism. The society he depicts, with wonder, itself seems to have little to do with reality. Even its contacts with nature are artificial: love arbitrarily flies the town for the woods in the springtime, but grass is merely a temporary and meaningless alternative to velvet couches.

So far, one can find little to deprecate in Gay's satiric powers. We may complain that his utterances occasionally have more authority than his naïve rôle should permit:

> He dresses, fences. What avails to know?
> For women chuse their men, like silks, for
>   show.
>
> (ll. 59-60)

—but the satiric vigour and economy of such a couplet surely justify themselves. We may note the general lack of bite in the satire, its constant awareness of the genuine comedy of Parisian vices—but this, too, is of course an acceptable satiric mode. The real difficulty appears only in what Mr. Mack calls the 'antithesis layer', the account of the poem's positive standards. The problem of rôle in Gay is almost always involved with that of values: not knowing, apparently, quite what he stands for, the poet has difficulty in assuming a firm position.

His characteristic inability to trumpet forth the call to virtue is vividly demonstrated in the **'Epistle to Pulteney'**. Here is the image of British rectitude which he opposes to that of French frivolity:

> Happy, thrice happy shall the monarch reign,
> Where guardian laws despotic power restrain!
> There shall the ploughshare break the stubborn
>   land,
> And bending harvests tire the peasant's hand:
> There liberty her settled mansion boasts,
> There commerce plenty brings from foreign
>   coasts.
>
> (ll. 247-52)

This is in some general sense relevant to the discussion it follows: it opposes to the mechanized chaos of France an eighteenth-century vision of 'natural' hierarchical order in England. Yet it is unconvincing, inadequate, and confusing. Pope concludes his 'Epistle to Burlington' with a not entirely dissimilar vision of national glory; his exalted tone exemplifies what Gay vainly tried to achieve. But Pope's exaltation is *earned,* as Gay's is not. The positive images which Pope finally offers reflect and comment on the negative ones that have preceded them; the energy with which he has denounced the misuse of riches justifies the intensity with which he praises the proper employment of wealth. It is quite otherwise with Gay. The relation of man to nature has been hardly at all a theme of his poem; that of kings to subjects is even more remote from the main subject. And the final glorification of commerce is worse than irrelevant: a poet can hardly afford to praise commercial success as a goal while deriding the activities of a society based on materialistic standards. Gay does not seem to perceive the relation between commerce and materialism. He partly accepts the standards he condemns; as a result, he cannot approach the authoritative passion of the true satirist.

Gay's apparent confusion about the nature of satiric authority can be documented in all the epistles and in most of the eclogues as well. Typically his vacillation about rôles is related, as in the Pulteney epistle, to the problem of determining the appropriate poetic attitude toward material success. Writing about patronage, in the **'Epistle to the Right Honourable Paul Methuen, Esq.'**, he is capable of satiric brilliance when he manages to maintain the dispassionate pose of the commentator. He lists the techniques which will help an author 'to be great':

> Or if you chuse more sure and ready ways,
> Spatter a Minister with fulsome praise:
> Launch out with freedom, flatter him enough;
> Fear not, all men are dedication-proof.
>
> (ll. 19-22)

Here his sure metaphors are used with freedom and verve; his scorn of the flatterer is more than ordinarily convincing. But, after all, Gay could not quite preserve his distance from such a subject. He falls into the old naïve pose when such a pose is singularly inappropriate:

> Yet let not me of grievances complain,
> Who (though the meanest of the Muse's train)
> Can boast subscriptions to my humble lays,
> And mingle profit with my little praise.
>
> (ll. 41-4)

This is naïveté in the service of the very values the poem nominally deplores. Gay here makes the 'innocent' assumption that money is, in effect, the ultimate criterion of artistic as well as commercial value. Irony may be intended, but since the poem neither offers nor implies any *other* real criterion of artistic success, it is highly unconvincing. And so, as a consequence, is Gay's mockery of the unprincipled scramble for patronage. Later in the poem he lapses into adolescent self-esteem, nominally praising Burlington's taste, but actually admiring, by implication, his own sophistication in recognizing it (ll. 65-8). That sophistication is placed in question, however, when he makes a flattering comparison between Raphael and the contemporary artist William Kent—thus reminding one unavoidably of the Frenchman he mocks in the Pulteney epistle for equating Raphael and Rigaud. Indeed, the poem as a whole makes one suspect that naïveté is no rôle for Gay, that it represents, rather, his actual nature. And such a suspicion is fatal to the pretensions of a satirist.

One reason Gay is an exceptionally interesting object of study is that—unlike most of his contemporaries— he typically wrote directly about his own literary problems. He does so not self-consciously, not like modern poets who obsessively multiply poems about writing poems, but from a sort of fatality, without, one would guess, being fully aware of what he was doing. So it is, at any rate, that he inevitably turns to the subject of poets and their relation to men of business. In the epistle to Methuen he had explored it almost inadvertently, and with unfortunate results. In the epistle **'To My Ingenious and Worthy Friend, W[illiam] L[owndes], Esq., Author of that Celebrated Treatise in Folio Called the "Land-Tax Bill"**', he investigates the metaphorical equivalents between poet and man of business. Poets, he points out, who write with no desire for money, win fame for their artistic creation; how much greater should be the fame of the composer of a bill which raises millions of pounds a year. Throughout the poem, Gay treats the parliamentary bill as a work of literature. Lowndes, neither poet nor historian, has the genius of the satirist:

> Satyr is thy talent; and each lash
> Makes the rich Miser tremble o'er his cash.
>
>   (ll. 30-31)

The lash which Gay himself was unable to wield, he is quite able to recognize. But what are the implications for the artist of a society in which the only 'satire' truly felt is that which affects men's pockets? This question Gay avoids; his epistle trails off without facing the real issue.

He returns to the question in the **'Panegyrical Epistle to Mr. Thomas Snow'**, published separately in 1721, where the ambiguities of his attitude emerge fully. Snow, a goldsmith, had made a fortune buying and selling shares of the South Sea Company; Gay had lost most of his small fortune in the South Sea Bubble. In the light of these events, the poet sees the contrast between poet and man of business as one between the romantic and the realist. Snow, whatever his sins (and he is described at the outset as an essentially demonic figure) is pre-eminently a realist. The South Sea Company dealt in imaginary profits; the profits Snow gained from it are genuine. The search for wealth in Peru yielded few results; Snow's shop is a far richer Peru. Unlike such lesser money lenders as 'Vulture' Hopkins (attacked by Pope in the 'Epistle to Bathurst'), Snow has nothing to do with merely 'ideal debts'. To him is opposed the typical poet, 'Who live[s] on fancy, and can feed on air' (l. 20), 'Who ne'er enjoy'd a guinea but in dreams' (l. 22), who contemplates 'millions of imaginary gold' (l. 24). The poet is the type of the eternal victim, a man of 'fancies wild' (l. 25); Snow is one whose 'judgment scorns poetic flights' (l. 28), and in this difference lies the central meaning of the epistle.

The conflict of values between unworldy poet and realistic man of business is symbolically presented in a little fable about life in an insane asylum—an asylum explicitly defined as the retreat of genuine wisdom from a mad world. (Indeed, the tale is really the converse and corollary of Dryden's 'Great wits are sure to madness near allied'.) Two of the inmates are a poet and a banker, counterparts of the anonymous poet who appeared earlier and of Snow himself. The banker occupies himself with elaborating and contemplating an imaginary estate, which he offers the poet the dubious privilege of buying for ten thousand pounds. When the poet accepts this offer, the banker, in a moment of lucidity, realizes that both his estate and

the payment the poet will give are imaginary. Presumably he assumes that the poet will come to the same realization, but he sees the opportunity for earning a genuine penny anyhow. 'Give me a Penny', he commands, 'and thy Contract's void' (l 65). The poet, who has a penny no more than he has ten thousand pounds, is indignant; scorning the notion that he should 'compound' his debts, he makes ten notches in a skewer and cries defiantly, 'There, take my Tally of Ten Thousand Pound' (l. 71).

If this fable defines the eternal struggle of realist and romantic, it does little to clarify Gay's attitude toward either. The poet 'wins' in the little story—wins because in a world unconnected to actuality, the inhabitant with the least awareness of reality must triumph: the poet is well adapted to life in an insane asylum. Although he is clearly the moral superior of the banker, he, too, is mocked. His indignation, his cry of defiance, derive from some obscure notion of honour, equally ridiculous within and outside the context of an asylum. Context alone makes the banker ludicrous: his limited concern with concrete actuality becomes meaningless in a madhouse. But has anything really been said about the value of such standards in another setting? Gay seems this time to have dealt with the problem of the poet's stance by refusing to assume any position at all. His story must stand in its own terms, with all its ambiguities; and however valuable we have discovered ambiguity to be, ambiguity of standards is a dangerous luxury for satirists.

In some of his epistles, then, Gay attempted to write about the problem of standards and was as unable to resolve his position as he had been when he seemed less fully aware of the difficulty. In the first series of **Fables,** however, he turned his attention directly to the root difficulty—and by so doing largely solved it.

This first group of fables do not seem, at first glance, the sort of poems to deal with the artistic difficulties of achieving appropriate perspective. They were written as part of Gay's continuing attempt to find patronage, dedicated to the six-year-old Duke of Cumberland, and nominally intended for his instruction and amusement. Yet their relation to Gay's other poetry is much like that of **The Beggar's Opera** to his other plays. The fables, like the opera, exploit themes and images that had long preoccupied their author, but do so with crucial differences.

The explicit subjects of these tales, like their characters, are varied. If the court vices of flattery and treachery are targets, so are many other sorts of human weakness; the 'characters' range from dunghills to elephants to angels. But dunghills and angels, stories of the court and stories of the farmyard, all shed a comic light on man and his pretentions and emphasize both the impossibility and the dreadful necessity of achieving proper perspective. The problem of perspective is treated as a metaphysical rather than a practical issue; recognizing its metaphysical implications, Gay solves his immediate artistic problem.

In the imaginary world of these fables, failure of perspective is universal. A hag complains that she is thought a witch because she keeps cats; her cats, with a different but equally limited point of view, reply that they lose credit because of their association with her (Fable XXIII). A tame monkey urges his fellows to 'reform' by copying him in the corruption he has learned at court; the monkeys, lacking better standards, thus become as evil as men (Fable XIV). Turkeys complain that the chief sin of man is gluttony; an ant who has just escaped the turkey's beak makes the obvious comment that it is all a matter of point of view (XXXVIII). Two monkeys at a fair interpret what they have seen as the attempts of humanity to imitate them (XL); horses understand the universe as one in which men serve them (XLIII); fleas tell man he was made for their need (XLIX); an owl defines human limitation by man's failure to understand the profundity of owls (XLI). Animals, in the typical mode of the fable, provide both analogues for human evil and commentary on it. They frequently assert their own moral superiority to men, but in doing so they usually demonstrate their essential identity of nature.

> Man then avoid, detest his ways,
> So safely shall prolong your days.
> When services are thus acquitted,
> Be sure we pheasants must be spitted.
> (XV, ll. 43-6)

The pheasant's argument, based on her observation of human ingratitude, is that of self-interest; she is as selfish as the men she detests. A fox on his deathbed, all appetite gone, repents his sins of murdered poultry and urges his sons to do the same, on the grounds that they will be safer if they give up plunder. His appetite returns; his children insist that reform is useless, given the bad reputation of foxes; he hears the cluck of a chicken and commands, 'Go, but be mod'rate in your food;/ A chicken too might do me good' (XXIX, ll. 49-50). Only self-interest has motivated him throughout; self-interest has produced his various limitations of viewpoint, as well as the different ones of his children. He is no hypocrite, this fox—but he is easily self-deceived.

The fox, like most of the other figures Gay employs, is not a flattering image for mankind. He is not even the wily trickster familiar from Aesop and fairy tales, but a mere dodderer, ineffectual and petty. Yet although Gay seems to deny mankind all dignity, he does not deny his victims sympathy. The characteristic tone which dominates the tale of the fox is gentle, amused—

and sympathetic. This is the special note of Gay's satire; no one could call *him* a monkey ladling out boiling oil on the passers-by. Yet satire is not necessarily less serious for being gentle. The mode which Gay discovered in writing fables proposes the creation of awareness rather than the accomplishment of reform. Reform, indeed, is hardly possible for that sin of blindness which obsessed Gay; such sin is part of the fallen nature of man, and is clearly perceived by the poet as such. Gay tries to make man aware of his limitations; meanwhile, human unawareness is supremely comic. A bookseller finds himself confronted with a Greek-reading elephant. Overwhelmed by his opportunity, he urges the beast to make use of his talents:

> Learn'd Sir, if you'd employ your pen
> Against the senseless sons of men,
> Or write the history of *Siam*,
> No man is better pay than I am;
> Or, since you're learn'd in *Greek*, let's see
> Something against the Trinity.
> (X, ll. 61-6)

At the same time that we are invited to recognize the 'senselessness' of this particular example of mankind, we are forced laughingly to admire his business enterprise. He is quite convincingly human, a comic-pathetic example of man's obsessive self-interest and consequent self-limitation. The typical union of comedy and lightly touched pathos in Gay's characters—foxes and sheep as well as men—makes his fables seem rather more complex than traditional representatives of the form, and a good deal more interesting. Our attitudes toward even the most lightly-sketched character is seldom allowed to be single; Gay appears to have sensed the positive value of the quality of ambiguity which had earlier weakened his work.

Once Gay had dealt with social evils; now he considered evils more general still. If he wrote of patronage or foppery, he felt obliged to assume in relation to these phenomena a specific rôle which was likely to be either unsteady or inadequate; the poet's impulse to sympathy was altogether out of place in social satire. But the fact that he himself was involved in the universal human weakness of limited perception could be taken as given; it was equally clear that he possessed the *awareness* of limitation which could give him satiric authority. In these early fables he almost never wavers in wielding that authority. The form itself provided built-in perspective and power: an author's relation to turkeys and monkeys can hardly present such problems as those involved in dealing with contemporary bankers. The poet's attitude is implied by his choice of genre. Characters in a fable are in a special way the author's creation, product of his artifice—like those in pastoral. He has complete control over them. Even though the animals are analogues for men, they clearly belong to a fairy tale world, and the men who also appear in the fables seem little more than analogues for animals. The sympathy which Gay offers them has nothing to do with individuals, or with the nature of his own immediate society; it is based simply on his awareness of the universality of the human plight. That awareness makes him superior; he can even play jokes on his readers.

One of the most dexterous techniques of these fables is Gay's manipulation of the reader's point of view to involve him in the central action. A case in point is Fable V, **'The Wild Boar and the Ram'**. It begins with a 'pathetic' image:

> Against an elm a sheep was ty'd,
> The butcher's knife in blood was dy'd;
> The patient flock, in silent fright,
> From far beheld the horrid sight . . .
>
> (ll. 1-4)

The conventionality of the language ('patient flock', 'horrid sight') reassures us that no special reaction is demanded. But the issue is made moral rather than sentimental when a 'savage Boar' (l. 5) standing near-by mocks 'the fleecy brood' (l. 6) for their cowardice in failing to take revenge on the men who treat them so cruelly. A ram replies that the sheep's revenge is of a subtler kind. Violence, he explains, always brings vengeance upon itself; man's destruction of sheep produces 'The two chief plagues that waste mankind' (l. 24): sheepskin supplies parchment for the 'wrangling bar' (l. 25) of law, and drums to call men to war.

A sharp change of feeling is demanded of the reader in the course of these few lines. The initial sentimental vignette prepares us to offer easy, temporary sympathy to the suffering sheep; when the boar's voice intervenes, however, it seems perfectly logical: we are willing to believe, in terms of the fairy tale world of the fable, that sheep deserve vengeance if they are capable of taking it. And to whatever extent we have any reaction at all to the problems of these highly improbable animals, we participate in the boar's scorn for sheepish passivity. 'The heart that wants revenge is base', cries the boar (l. 14); we recognize and readily approve the accents of conventional heroism. Sheep are, after all, emblems of the eternal victim—a 'fleecy brood', destined to be sheared and slaughtered.

But the poetic justice of the dénouement requires a shift of perspective about values as well as about the place of sheep in the universe. The 'patience' of the sheep, established in the third line and emphasized by the tone of the ram's utterance, so different from the boar's rabble-rousing vehemence, has its ultimate effect in furthering the impatience and violence of mankind. Man's destructiveness, then, is essentially its own

punishment; the sheep's serenity, its own reward. The sheep—'silly sheep', as they are so often termed in pastorals—are, after all, the true wits: wits in conception and in expression. This is the joke of the poem, but also its 'lesson'. And the shock of reversed perspective extends to the reader, to whatever degree he finds himself participating, even temporarily, in the values of the boar.

This fable exemplifies the virtues of Gay's best ones in its economy (twenty-eight lines for the whole story), its wit, its expert quick characterization. Here Gay demonstrates his fine ear for speech, his ability to parody, his unerring control of his characters, his awareness of the complexity of his chosen theme. These skills he exercises again and again, with a light, sure touch. His lively sense of incongruity operates brilliantly: he sketches an elephant 'wrinkling with a sneer his trunk', makes a rose talk like a character in *Through the Looking-Glass,* composes heroic speeches for a rooster and describes his demise in splendid mock-heroic vein. Sometimes he goes to the trouble of stating an explicit moral for his tales:

> Restrain your child; you'll soon believe
> The text, which says, we sprung from *Eve.*
>
> (XX, ll. 1-2)

But the moral seldom has much to do with the actual tale, although the conjunction of sober-sounding morals and irreverent tales was enough to reduce at least one nineteenth-century critic (anonymous, but himself an author of more respectable fables) to apoplectic rage. Often Gay states no moral at all, but leaves his reader to arrive at sometimes startling conclusions. Occasionally, unfortunately, he takes the conventional course: explains his moral, then writes a story which genuinely illustrates it. His fables of this sort are almost always disappointing. But over and over, in richly varied ways, the poet explores his eighteenth-century theme: man presumptuous, proud, blinded by his pride; or, conversely—but really the same—man limited in perspective, unable to see himself clearly, and consequently able to be proud. Man, Gay realized, could see very little; these fables were designed to make him see more. And if he did not *wish* to see more (Gay thought he might not: see Fable XVIII, **'The Painter Who Pleased No body and Everybody'**)—at any rate, such satire as Gay had now discovered how to write justified itself by its sheer good spirits.

Gay attempted, disastrously by all artistic standards, to repeat the success of **The Beggar's Opera** with **Polly**; he likewise followed the first series of fables with a second. The second group are far less interesting; they take themselves a good deal more seriously, are more orderly and restrained, much longer and much duller than their predecessors. And they are more concerned with topicality than with universality. Their preambles are longer than the fables themselves; in these introductory sections, although we find flashes of Gay's superb ability to characterize in a phrase, to define the atmosphere of a social situation, the tone wavers frequently as the poet reveals his old unsureness about the proper stance of a satirist. In the first group of fables he had faced directly his satiric problems and achieved an individual mode of satiric statement. In the second series he demonstrated that he did not realize what he had achieved. The achievement itself is one of the most revealing (and neglected) illustrations in the eighteenth-century canon of the sources of satiric power.

Notes

[1] The essay is reprinted in *Studies in the Literature of the Augustan Age,* ed. Richard C. Boys (Ann Arbor, Michigan, 1952). The quotations here used are from pages 223, 228 and 229.

[2] 'John Gay', reprinted in *Eighteenth-Century English Literature,* ed. James L. Clifford, A Galaxy Book (Oxford, 1959), p. 138. Mr. Sutherland makes the same point about Gay in his *English Satire.*

Adina Forsgren (essay date 1964)

SOURCE: "The Shepherd's Week," in *John Gay: Poet "Of a Lower Order,"* Natur Och Kultur; Broderna Lagerstrom AB, 1964, pp. 105-167.

[*In the following excerpt, Forsgren examines Gay's pastoral poems in both their political and their literary contexts, discussing* The Shepherd's Week's *connections not only to classical antecedents, but to Spenser's* Shepherd's Calendar *and his peer Pope's pastorals, including "Windsor Forest." Forsgren maintains that the period of peace following the treaty of Utrecht during the reign of the Stuart Queen Anne was an important influence in the revival of pastoral poetry during the early eighteenth century.*]

The Shepherd's Week contains elements which would justify its place not only in this volume. But as its quality of a political *Gelegenheitsgedicht* has hitherto been overlooked by critics, the poem will be treated of in this context.

Gay's Eclogues pay homage to the period of peace after Utrecht and to those who were responsible for it, by picturing Queen Anne's Tory millennium. The poet thereby facetiously made use of the expression Golden Age both as a term of criticism of pastoral poetry and as a notion which in its conventional sense was alien to "modern" doctrines of progress and cyclic changes, in particular adhered to by Whig Augustans.

The famous *Guardian* rules for serious English pastoral poetry are of about the same importance for **The Shepherd's Week,** as Addison's precepts concerning Georgics for **Wine,** to some extent for **Rural Sports** and for others of Gay's poems which will be treated of later on. No more than Swift in *The City Morning* did Gay form "fields, or nymphs, or groves where they [were] not"[1], although the contrast was not driven as far as in **Wine,** for instance. The rural scene was here preserved as a prerequisite for pastoral poetry. As so often, Gay imitated the genre in the comic mode, picturing the "image of the times" in all its aspects, in this poem in combination with idealized pastoral characters. In the case of pastoral poetry, the "image of the times", English "modern" Eclogues about the busy period of peace after Utrecht, was an anomaly, whether in the light of the "neoclassic" school of pastoral criticism with its imitation of the Golden Age, or the "rationalistic" school with its generalized representation of the ease and tranquillity of a shepherd's life.

Gay killed at least two birds with one stone and indulged in laughter both at solemnity in criticism and at Augustan "high seriousness" and ambitious "modern" aspirations. In the field of pastoral poetry, the aspirations found an outlet in the amount of praise bestowed on Philips's *Pastorals,* which by implication purported to be and were interpreted by admirers as innovations. They supposedly played the same pioneering part as Theocritus' *Idylls* for the whole Kind and as *The Shepherd's Calendar* for Spenser and his epic poem, English poetry not far removed from its "infant state". Gay's Eclogues, on the other hand, are demonstratively and conspicuously imitative with echoes and borrowings from classical models. They are also related to low verse, yet no "country-scraper['s]" songs, but the most complicated products of "Art". This double nature of the poems is indicated in the Proeme, where Gay introduces himself as a simple rustic bard, but also reveals himself as a connoisseur of both criticism and the new philosophy. At the same time, more subtly than Philips's, the poems call to mind Elizabethan pastoral poetry.

Previous Criticism

Before entering on a detailed analysis of the poems to prove the above argument, it will be useful to make a survey of the abundant criticism that has hitherto been devoted to **The Shepherd's Week.**

Gay's purpose in writing his Eclogues has been discussed by a number of critics. Some, like Goldsmith,[2] Dr. Johnson,[3] Southey,[4] Aikin,[5] and later on Austin Dobson,[6] Kerlin,[7] Homer Smith,[8] find that Gay went beyond his original intention of burlesque or parody of some sort of pastoral poetry. Goldsmith concluded that "Gay has hit the true spirit of pastoral poetry". Dr. Johnson praised the reality and truth to nature. Aikin could not decide whether *The Shepherd's Week* was "jest or earnest". The discussion long turned upon the question whether Gay ridiculed the conventional, "refined" form of the genre or the anglicized type, as it was represented in the period by Ambrose Philips's *Pastorals.* Pope was originally responsible for the view that his own quarrel with Philips, which originated in the exaggerated praise of his rival's poems by the Whig poets, was what induced Gay to write *The Shepherd's Week.*[9] Pope's editor Warburton passed it on as correct, adding that

> the object of [the ridicule] was ill understood by those who were strangers to the quarrel. These mistook the Shepherd's Week for a burlesque of Virgil's Pastorals.[10]

In our own times, Professor Sherburn's investigation of Pope's early literary activities has given new support to the poet's interpretation of the aim and purpose of *The Shepherd's Week,* and a number of critics have adopted this view.[11]

However, the "strangers to the quarrel" have also had their followers. One of them was Edmund Gosse, who found that for

> the first time since the reign of Elizabeth, a serious attempt was made to throw to the winds the ridiculous Arcadian tradition of nymphs and swains, and to copy Theocritus in his simplicity.[12]

Gay has also in recent times been thought to parody Virgil, "for his burlesques are nearer to the Latin than many of the serious imitations".[13] Although acknowledging the difficulty of ascertaining the object of ridicule, Professor Foster Jones found that the

> strictness with which the poems adhere to the Virgilian type without any apparent artificiality makes them one of the most successful attempts at putting new wine into old bottles offered by the eighteenth century.[14]

According to Professor Bond, Gay burlesqued "the eclogue mould", but "did not imitate Philips' eclogues closely enough for parody."[15] Two later writers on pastoral poetry also follow this line. Gay has been compared with Diaper in *Nereides* as an innovator of the genre,[16] and *The Shepherd's Week* looked upon as a variation of the conventional pastoral poem.[17]

In the opinions of those who have investigated Gay's life and works, both views are reflected. Professor Irving inclines towards the latter theory and believes that "Gay may have encouraged Pope to think" that he ridiculed Philips, but that the fundamental idea for the poems may have been suggested by the *Guardian* papers on pastoral poetry, and that the poet also had

burlesque of *The Bucolics* in mind.[18] The most recent critic of Gay's poetry is of the opinion that *The Shepherd's Week* was

> meant to . . . point up the incompatibility of describing British rural matter (actual country scenes and life) in the strict form of the Vergilian eclogue.[19]

The main support for this statement is the discussion in an article by Dr. Trowbridge, who by means of biographical and internal evidence, the latter obviously directed against Professor Bond's view, arrives at the conclusion that

> in parallel echoes, Gay's poems follow up Pope's ironical criticism of Philips's in No. 40 of *The Guardian* and that therefore *The Shepherd's Week* was designed as a burlesque of Philips's *Pastorals.*

Any other hypothesis, "a realistic picture of country life", "a burlesque of pastoral poetry in general" or "a Virgilian parody", is said to provide insufficient explanation. The poem can be understood and enjoyed "only against the background of controversy in which it originated".[20] One or two things may, however, be observed concerning the arguments for Gay's indiscriminate aversion to the poets at Button's coffee-house. In the light of more recent research, it is obvious that at the time Gay must have been on friendly terms with Steele.[21] After the main event of the following year, the performance and the publication of *The What D'Ye Call It* (1715), he was still patronized by Addison, who subscribed generously to *Trivia* and received the poet's particular thanks.[22] Besides, part of what has been adduced as biographical evidence rather illustrates more general tendencies in Gay's production.[23] Some of the internal evidence is perhaps also a little doubtful.[24]

The variation of opinions among critics about Gay's purpose in writing his Eclogues seems partly to have been caused by some uncertainty as to the real character of Ambrose Philips's *Pastorals.*[25] This problem has been disentangled by Professor Congleton, who has drawn the line between the "neoclassic" and the "rationalistic"-empirical schools of pastoral criticism, which were prevalent in late 17th and early 18th century England.[26] The former school, after Rapin[27] and with Chetwood as its first English representative, based its principles on ancient authoritative precedence in criticism and poetical practice. Pastoral poetry should convey an image of shepherds living in the Golden Age, reflect the affluence, contentment, and innocence of that age in a simple though not rustic language, in the manner of Virgil rather than of Theocritus. The more "modern" school, after Fontenelle, discarded ancient authority and applied a psychological method, took the demands of the poet's audience into account, so to speak. It was the "Native Laziness" in the reader and his love of "some motion" that made the poet succeed with idealized pastoral poetry, "a kind of half Truth", about the tranquillity and ease of a shepherd's life seasoned with the "Passion[s]" of love. Theocritean "Country Matters" were condemned.[28] Yet an actual poem written according to the "modern" notions might not be very different from the Golden Age images that the "neoclassic" critics recommended,[29] just as, for a comparison, the Sublime was very much the same, whether according to Longinus or to Dennis. It was the methods of attaining to the critical principles that differed. In the case of pastoral poetry, Aristotelian poetics was obviously at the fountain head of both schools.[30]

The famous *Guardian* essays on pastoral poetry[31] belong to the "rationalistic" school, although there is in fact also a sprinkling of "neoclassic" notions.[32] To Fontenelle's reason why pastoral poetry pleased, the author of the paper No. 22 also added two others, more typically English perhaps, namely the reader's love of the countryside and his "secret approbation" of natural goodness.[33] In contrast to both French critics, No. 28 gave the palm to Theocritus in preference to Virgil. But for the specific usage of English pastoralists, the fourth paper, No. 30, departed from foreign theories and, in the spirit of Addison about the "clime" in a Georgic,[34] advised poets how they could "lawfully deviate from the ancients." "The difference of the climate" had to be considered, and also such things "of a changeable kind" as the customs, "theology",[35] dress, and sports of the characters, whom the essayist persistently calls shepherds. The pastoral poems on which he based his precepts and to which he resorted for examples, were those by Spenser and Ambrose Philips. In *The Guardian,* No. 40, however, Pope ironically compared Philips's *Pastorals* with his own, thereby seemingly adopting the views of the preceding *Guardian* papers, but in reality defending his own "neoclassic" principles. Finally, Gay's views of this problem are deduced by Professor Congleton from the Proeme to *The Shepherd's Week,* which is read as consistently ironic in the manner of Pope's essay. Gay is said to have pronounced himself in favour not only of a simple though not rustic diction and conventional pastoral names, but also of "Golden Age shepherds", such as those used by Pope, and of descriptions of "such decorous prospects as are to be found in the classical idyls and eclogues".[36]

The most recent contributor to the discussion about the aim of *The Shepherd's Week* has approached the problem from a new angle. Dr. Ellis has demonstrated some similarities with and borrowings from the *Wit and Mirth* volumes which can be detected in Gay's Eclogues, and also pointed to some passages in the poetry of the period where the names of Ambrose Philips and D'Urfey are linked together as of equal rank.[37]— D'Urfey was the principal poet represented in Playford's song-books and had the reputation of being an unlearned and popular writer, a gay and harmless song-

ster.[38]—Dr. Ellis concludes that Gay intended to insult Philips by ostensibly making D'Urfey the object of his parody, a "trick for escaping the responsibility of ridiculing Philips", and that he "did not intend to encourage, but rather to hinder, the growth of a native poetry about the peasant".[39]

Finally, Professor Dobrée has emphasized the genuine pastoral spirit, the "humour and lightheartedness which carries back" to Elizabethan poetry.[40]

The Shepherd's Week in the Light of Gay's Earlier Productions and of Contemporary Pastoral Poetry

Can the result of the investigations referred to above— Gay's parody of Virgil, his ridicule of Philips directly or by way of D'Urfey, his support of conventional pastoral poetry with its "decorous prospects" against "the growth of a native poetry about the peasant"—be reconciled with the tendencies that can be distinguished in the poet's early productions? Before writing his Eclogues, Gay had already ridiculed solemnity in criticism and high-flown pretensions at genius and inspiration. Against high Kinds, heroic loftiness, and Augustan "high seriousness", he had set his own low Kinds and low subject matter. By way of close imitation, he had adapted classical poems and themes to his own time, produced the "image of the times". He had echoed and followed the mode of older English poetry, and *The Shepherd's Week* was not the first poem where he echoed, borrowed from, or at least indirectly availed himself of the realism of low poetry or even prose. **Wine, The Mohocks, Araminta,** even **Rural Sports** and **The Fan** are evidence of this. Gay's view of pastoral poetry may have been the conventional. The genre was what it was even to him. But the fact remains that he never wrote conventional pastoral poems like Walsh's or Pope's. Even in his pastoral songs, the few "shades" and "streams" which occur, are mixed with realistic details.[41] The plays which contain pastoral elements, **The What D'Ye Call It** and **Dione,** are in varying ways non-conventional. Besides, Gay had already displayed a taste for experiments and new schemes, not only in **Wine** and **Rural Sports,** but also in **Panthea,** a fashionable lady's rural Elegy,[42] in **Araminta,** an urbanized version of a classical Elegy, and in **A Contemplation on Night,** a "modern" version of the conventional descriptions of night. The two latter poems are particularly relevant examples of how Gay, probably in 1712 and 1713 respectively, varied conventional forms, raised traditionally low characters or brought old themes up to date, so to speak. In the two Elegies, in particular, Gay heeded Prior's admonition to the "Translators" in his own "artful" manner and without resorting to the freedom of a D'Urfey, whose originality Prior seemed to prefer.[43] If Gay had expressed his reaction against yet another edition of *Ovid's Epistles,* he might be expected to respond in a similar way to outworn forms of pastoral poetry. There was indeed a need for rejuvenating the pastoral genre.

Among the most common types of the Kind, were the translations and imitations of "the Greeks and Romans", the apparent immediate occasion of *The Guardian,* No. 30. The *Miscellany Poems,* I and II (1702), contain versions of *Idylls* by Dryden, Duke and Bowles, and translations of Virgil's *Eclogues* by Caryll, Tate, Creech, Dryden, Duke, Chetwood, and three or four others. Although the 1716 edition changed in the direction of a more popular taste, it still reprinted most of the translations. An expert in the Virgilian elegiac Kind, though not always close to the pattern, was Robert Gould. His *Works* might alone have been sufficient to provide a Tickell and a Trapp with the material for their "perusals" of pastoral poems with "fifty lean flocks, . . . an hundred left-handed ravens, besides blasted oaks", and "withering meadows". Although Gould professed his disbelief in the "Tales" of the Ancients and "an Age of Gold", in "Flow'ry Shades" and "faithful Swains",[44] and although he consistently eschewed the conventional apotheosis, he filled one hundred and twelve octavo pages with *Funeral Elegies* and seventy pages with *Funeral Eclogues,* the latter, dialogues between Damon and Alexis, Menalcas and Strephon, Amyntor and Doran, etc. There was indeed reason for Trapp's exclamation, "Who can bear those Crowds of Pastorals, . . . daily publish'd in *Latin* and *English,* upon the Death of Princes, or Friends?"[45] Undergraduates also seem to have written Eclogues, perhaps with a secret hope of future glory.[46]

Less learned frenchified beaux, however, practised the pastoral song,[47] which was so common that Ned Ward ironically called it "the inimittable Song of O Happy Groves",[48] not imitations of Virgil or Theocritus, but pastoral poems in the French manner which were condemned in *The Guardian,* No. 28, as "a run of numbers, commonplace descriptions of woods, floods, groves, loves, &c." Their extreme popularity appears from No. 1 of the *Delights for the Ingenious,* for instance, where the editor[49] encourages his readers to collaboration and tries to smoothe their way by printing poems "designed as a Pattern chiefly, of the Kinds of Verse, and of such Subjects that generally please the most sort of Readers". The "pattern" for pastoral poetry is *The Parting,* of which I quote the first stanza.

> CHLOE once in Face and Mind,
> The best and brightest of her Kind,
> In Rural Gardens, Groves and Glades,
> Flow'ry Fields and verdant Shades,
> Did all her softer Hours improve
> With Wit, and Innocence, and Love;
> Then, *Thyrsis* wrapt in Joys Divine,
> Was ever Passion bless'd like Thine!

The subsequent contributions are all dialogues—the pastoral Kind had been defined as a sub-species of the "Dramatick"—and all the "actors" are Strephons and Celias, Damons and Dorindas, Daphnes and Sylvias or similar characters. Gould's volumes contain thirty-one pastoral songs with Celias, Myrtillos and their usual companions. The genre was common in the *Wit and Mirth* volumes and other Playford music-books, in publications like *The Diverting Post* (1704-06) and on the broadsheets. In the ballad collections, the foreign shepherds recur with such persistency that J. W. Ebsworth, editor and co-editor, respectively, of *The Bagford Ballads* and *The Roxburghe Ballads,* could even maintain that the Strephons were more frequent than the Damons and the Coridons, none of them individualized, even by Dryden.[50] The "inimittable Song" indeed grew so threadbare that the "purling stream" and the "shady grove" became catch-words for country-scenery even in prose,[51] just as meaningless as the "lean flocks" and the "track of light in the skies" of the funeral Elegy.

"Neoclassic" Pastoralists, "Country-Scraper[s]" and Their "Prelude[s]"

If we call to mind Gay's early practice, it is really not possible to assume that, even without the challenge of the Pope-Philips controversy, the poet should have chosen to write pastoral poetry in concession to conventions as outworn as has been sketched above. It was in his view of the problem of imitation versus "original composition" that Gay was "neoclassic". To him the difference was between learned pastoral poems and those of the "country-scraper". Pope and himself represented the former school, whereas Philips and D'Urfey provided examples of the latter. In both categories of pastoral poetry, names, scenery, etc. could either be conventional or English, as in fact they were.—D'Urfey at least edited a number of conventional pastoral lyrics.—On the other hand, even Pope half-heartedly had his eye on Northern plains and groves and introduced some English names of "shades" and "streams" in the manner of the translators of *L'Art poétique* and *Le Lutrin.*[52]

As Dr. Ellis has shown, D'Urfey and Philips were regarded by the Scriblerians as "two of a kind",[53] but not, it must be emphasized, just because both wrote indigenous pastoral poetry. D'Urfey was more or less condescendingly represented as an original lyric poet, by Prior, for instance, and by Steele in *The Tatler,* No. 1, where his style and manner are said to be "wholly new and unknown to the ancient Greeks and Romans".[54] He was indeed the unlearned "sonneteer" *par excellence*—at the same time, it should be noticed, an expert angler—tolerated, sometimes even liked by learned poets, as long as he stuck to his catches and ditties, his *"Fish-hooks, Baits,* and *artificial Flies".*[55] No wonder that he was patronized by Steele, who had a taste for things non-heroic. In his *Pastorals,* Philips rather cautiously set out to continue the part of "country-scraper" that he had played earlier,[56] like the "sonneteer", contemptible to strict neo-classicists of the school of Rapin, because relying on genius or "Wit" and "a lucky hit" more than on learning. Philips's way of mentioning Theocritus, Virgil and Spenser in his Preface and his declaration by way of implication that he intended to imitate country scenery,[57] Nature, rather than other poets' "groves" and "streams", indicate that he regarded himself as an innovator within the Kind. His style was also simple, and he actually invited comparison with D'Urfey when he called his poems "ditties".[58] Partly, however, against his rôle of originator, Philips fell into the usual rut of servile imitation. That is why Pope's ridicule in *The Guardian,* No. 40, of *The Third Pastoral* after Virgil's *Eclogue V* and of *The Fifth* after Strada was particularly apt.[59] Pope himself, though not professedly an "original composer", was shortly to be rebuked for his "Imitations" by another member of the other school.[60]

The persistent eulogies of Philips's *Pastorals* from the quarters of Whig poets[61] to the exclusion of Pope's did, however, not just imply praise or inattention, respectively, of isolated productions. What gave an added point to this taking of sides was the fact that the pastoral genre was considered to be the "prelude to Epic", a notion of which Philips had reminded his readers in the Preface to his *Pastorals.* In praising their friend then, the Whig poets at Button's made clear that they expected him to fulfil a promise of "something greater", as Addison expressed it. Gay, it will be remembered, had early hailed Pope as a pastoral poet with the same prospects of a greater future that could now be read between the lines of the encomiums of Philips.[62]

It was about this time, in particular, that Horace's advice to poets to choose subjects "equal to [their] strength"[63] seems to have been adopted as the leading principle of Scriblerian friends in contrast to the aspirations of their antagonists towards Aristotelian high Kinds. This is obvious not only from Gay's productions, indirectly from **Wine** and **Rural Sports** and directly from the *Guardian* essay on dress (1713) and the later *Epistle to Burlington* (1715), but also from Swift's *First Ode of the Second Book of Horace Paraphras'd* (1714) and Parnell's *Bookworm* (1714).[64]

So that although ridicule of Philips was part of Gay's game in *The Shepherd's Week,* the point was not only directed against the Whig poet's *Pastorals,* but also and mainly against the patriotic pretentiousness of the whole party supporting them, and that was Gay's game more than Pope's at this time. Like the essays on genius by the two friends,[65] **The Shepherd's Week** and *The Guardian,* No. 40, have a similar aim, namely to argue *against* pretentious "scribbler[s]" and "country-scraper[s]" and *for* learned, "artful" poetry. But in both cases, Gay is not only the more cheerful critic. In

contrast to Pope's, his ridicule is also more positive and in itself a defence for the modest "little Taste", in this poem, low pastoral characters and rural matter, a close observation of details and a cheerful mood as opposed to solemnity in criticism, conventions, and sentimental features in pastoral poetry. Pope had discreetly pointed to Virgil as his model and written "downright poetry". Philips had compared himself to the great pastoralists and produced insipid poems and slavish imitation. Gay, however, frankly introduced himself as a rustic bard, an 18th century Autolicus, a Bowzybeus,[66] and thus disclaimed any promise for the future, although in fact he really brought his poetical career to a climax.

Cheerful Bowzybeus and His Criticism

In interpreting the prefatory pieces to **The Shepherd's Week,** the tone of the whole poem with its lightness and gaiety must be taken into consideration. Gay was still a hopeful young man, who had yet to meet the really serious disappointment in his poetical and diplomatic career. Both the Proeme and the Prologue reveal such a boyish cheerfulness and such a delight at playing the game of disguise, the part of the simple bard, that it is difficult to believe that our *"Loving Countryman"* could have kept up an attitude of cool irony behind the mask of the rustic swain. Moreover, this was not the only occasion on which Gay played the part of a fancy character. He seems to have been so thoroughly familiar with some ballad figures that they took on general characteristics, which could be applied to himself and his friends. In the Suffolk collection of manuscripts, for instance, there is an unpublished letter from Gay to somebody he calls "your Grace",[67] possibly the Duke of Queensberry, or perhaps "Duke" Disney. He addresses his friend "Most Honour'd Roger", and calls himself "a Timothy Tim". Lady Jekyll is "a Tim", and "the Duchess of Queensberry is so too", although sometimes she has her "Ralph Days".[68] Gay also talks of some common friends, the "Rigadoon[s]" and of a certain "Society of Tips". The dancing-masters he obviously knew through some Italian woman.[69] Gay looks upon his addressee as an "ignorant Caxton Roger just come out of the Country" and promises to tell him the names of his "Friends & Relations" when they meet again. The whole spirit of the letter is that of the Proeme to **The Shepherd's Week,** and one is sometimes more true to one's character in disguise than in one's own clothes.

Although the main tone of Gay's naive Preface is raillery, it is possible to read it in a straightforward way, if one remembers the double nature of the author. Our *"Loving Countryman"* is actually half learned and half of the mould of the writers employed by Thomas Cross and the Playfords, and the Proeme partly profound and partly naive. Like other pastoral poets—Guarini, Fletcher, Ben Jonson, Spenser—Gay defended his innovation. One of his models was naturally the Dedicatory Epistle and the Argument prefixed to *The Shepherd's Calendar*,[70] the only English pastoral poems of importance in the general discussion on the genre from Dryden onwards. There are even in Gay's Preface verbal echoes like "travail", "gallimawfry", "more rumbling than rural". But the language is not just a "richly flavored Elizabethan diction".[71] It is also appropriately the circumstantial language used, for instance, in contemporary vulgar advertisements about "excellent Pills" for the "Green-sickness" or about fortune-telling according to the "most Noble Art of Christian Astrology",[72] the sort of language, realistic details not abstractions, which for its comic effects was sometimes resorted to in mock-Prefaces.[73] That Gay paid attention to advertisements is obvious from a letter to Parnell, March 26 [?], 1716, where he mentions *The Bookworm* and says that at Button's, "Gentlemen have been made to void Worms for advertisements by Mr John Moore's worm powder". Then follows a long poem dedicated to Mr. John Moore "of the celebrated Worm Powder".[74]

In defending his Eclogues, Gay first of all makes fun of solemn quarrels between critics of pastoral poetry. In his "preface meet", Gay, or Bowzybeus, as he calls himself in the Prologue,[75] describes the reactions of imaginary critics, just as he was to do in the Preface to **The What D'Ye Call It.**

> GREAT marvell hath it been (and that not unworthily) to diverse worthy wits, that in this our Island of Britain, in all rare sciences so greatly abounding, more especially in all kinds of Poesie highly flourishing, no Poet (though otherways of notable cunning in roundelays) hath hit on the right simple Eclogue after the true ancient guise of Theocritus, before this mine attempt.

The opinion is noted with some surprise by the poet Bowzybeus, and rightly, for his swains and maidens had appeared on many of the broadsheets that were peddled along country lanes or brought home to cottages from nearby fairs. Yet, like any other writer of "A New Ballad", he knows no rival *"travailing in this plain high-way of Pastoral"*. But John Gay remembers Fontenelle's aversion to Theocritus well enough to quote the passage from *Idyll I* that the French critic found particularly "gross".[76] He is sufficiently learned to quote from the Greek, but his prose version shows that he also knows Creech's translation.[77] The incorrect number of the *Idyll* is perhaps a gleeful dig at Philips's unsuccessful *Third Pastoral*.[78] To the simple taste of Bowzybeus, it is not only the recent *"rout"* about the Golden Age that seems *"idle"* and futile. He has also discovered that poems written according to the principles of the "neoclassic" school are not very different from those supposedly written after the theories of the "rationalistic" critics. What *The Guardian*

has allowed as lawful deviations, Gay, the rustic bard, considers to be a loose garment thrown over the same sort of character, which is not to his taste, whether in *"Gothic"* disguise or not.[79]

> *Verily, as little pleasance receiveth a true homebred tast, from all the fine finical new-fangled fooleries of this gay Gothic garniture, wherewith they so nicely bedeck their court clowns, or clown courtiers, (for, which to call them rightly, I wot not) as would a prudent citizen journeying to his country farms, should he find them occupied by people of this motley make, instead of plain downright hearty cleanly folk, such as be now tenants to the Burgesses of this realme.*

In order to underline the fact that he has seen through the cheat, Gay makes the last few lines of this passage echo "neoclassic" Dryden's description of Virgil, as he appears to him in the *Pollio* and the *Silenus*.[80]

Gay or Bowzybeus goes on to convey his own idea of Eclogues—and here the double-natured poet certainly expresses his own conviction.—They must be such, *"as nature in the country affordeth"*. As regards the characters or *"the manners"*, they must also be *"meetly copied from the rustical folk"* in the poet's beloved *"native country Britain"*. Where the scenery is concerned, the *"gentle reader"* can expect *"a picture, or rather lively landscape of* [his] *own country"*. For an illustration, Gay quotes the simile in which Milton expresses the sudden delight of the Serpent at seeing Eve in the Garden of Eden.

> As one who long in populous city pent,
> Where houses thick and sewers annoy the air
> Forth issuing on a summer's morn to breathe
> Among the pleasant villages and farms
> Adjoin'd, from each thing met conceives
>   delight;
> The smell of grain or tedded grass or kine
> Or dairie, each rural sight, each rural sound.[81]

I do not think this is plain irony.[82] But it is significant that the poet borrowed one of Milton's pictorial similes, as he did on other occasions. Perhaps, for a contrast with Pope and Philips, this was Gay's way of humbly confessing that he made no promise for the future, and that his Muse was not fit for the high Kinds, but rather for descriptions.—Like the other English critics of pastoral poetry, Gay or Bowzybeus has his opinion of Spenser, whom he also loves as *"a bard of sweetest memorial"*. He is familiar with Dryden's and Pope's[83] disapproval of Spenser's verse and of the allegory à la Mantuan in pastoral poetry, as well as with the discussion about Spenserian names, the observation or neglect of decorum,[84] and the use of dialect.[85] To Bowzybeus, of course, Spenser's names are what *"liketh* [him] *best"*. Unlike Philips, however, the rustic bard did not add French-sounding names in his poems, but names from more congenial sources. Furthermore, the problem of the existence of the pastoral wolf was so famous in the period that it had even been referred to by La Fontaine.[86] Pope, who ironically praised Philips's unrealistic allusion to a wolf, could support himself on *July* and *November*,[87] but our *"Loving Countryman"* gleefully quotes from *September.*

> Well is known that since the *Saxon* King
> Never was wolf seen, many or some
> Nor in all *Kent* nor in christendom.

Bowzybeus, related as he almost is to Hogarth's signpainter and with no notion of the Idea, has, and should have, an exaggerated respect for decorum, as is shown by his opinion about the wolf, Sunday sports, rustic names, the English landscape *at the proper season".*

Queen Anne's and Bowzybeus's "Modern" Golden Age

It is in the passage on the language used by Bowzybeus's *"ploughmen"* and damsels that Gay displays his Scriblerian spirit and reveals the true character of his poems. In a naively and comically detailed style, he paraphrases Ben Jonson's succinct description of Spenser's pastoral diction, "no language".[88] Then he swerves round from the reference to this diction as such to the importance that was attached to it by the Renaissance poet.[89] Like E.K., Gay has provided *"glosses and explanations of uncouth pastoral terms".* But these are widely different from the *"glosses"* in *The Shepherd's Calendar.* They are realistic, concrete words, which indicate the character of Gay's Eclogues as "modern" poems.[90] This passage links up with another in the Proeme, which is equally significant and important. To Bowzybeus, the *"gallimawfry"* about an Arcadian Golden Age is nothing but *"idle trumpery (only fit for schools and schoolboys)",*[91] the same sort of *"trumpery"* in fact as the ancient deities that Addison had relegated to schoolboy learning.[92] After Bowzybeus has rejected the idealized pastoral poem, whether picturing the Golden Age state of things before the "decay" that the Ancients presupposed or the more "modern" halftruth of rural ease, he emits his unreserved opinion of the former conceit, which now suddenly takes on a different connotation and of which, he says,

> *I avow, I account nothing at all, knowing no age so
> justly to be instiled* Golden, *as this of our* Sovereign
> Lady Queen ANNE.

Nobody really believed in either Arcadia or a Golden Age in the sense of the age of Saturn any longer.—Gay made common cause with Addison[93] and Philips[94] in this respect, as appears, for instance, in *Damon and Cupid* or in the Prologues to **The Wife of Bath** and **Dione.**[95]—On the contrary, the idea of progress was common among "modern" Augustans. Shaftesbury's whole philosophy of optimism counteracted the old notion of decay,[96] and so did the activities of "modern" experimental philosophers and antiquarians.[97] Poets sang of the golden future, as for instance Dennis in *A Poem upon the Death of Queen Anne* (1714), which contains the most undisguised homage to the notion of a future British Golden Age. Even the last passage of *Windsor-Forest* prophesies Albion's future "golden days". The same notion in literary criticism had recently been expressed by Oldmixon in *The Muses Mercury*,[98] and Shaftesbury looked forward to the glory of the British Muses, who only wanted "repose of arms" to arrive at perfection.[99] The concept also affected pastoral poetry, although the author of *The Guardian,* who accepted the conventional idealization and even resorted to Arcadia for illustration, obviously assumed that the lawful deviations were timeless.[100] Hobbinol in Philips's *Sixth Pastoral* lays "*Albion*'s Golden Days" in the days of Elizabeth, but he is corrected by Lanquet, who is appropriately progressive. Shepherds are happier now because Anna regins.

> O ever may she reign!
> And bring on earth the golden age again.[101]

The Shepherd's Week provided the triumphant answer to similar desires, as far as the English ploughman was concerned. The Golden Age is now on earth, now that the "repose of arms" is a fact, unfortunately for the Whigs under Tory supremacy. Like Virgil, the shepherd poet leaves his pipe and his flocks for the Court, rid of his particular fears.

> Of soldier's drum withouten dreed;
> For Peace allays the shepherd's fear
> Of wearing cap of Grenadier.[102]

> (ll. 46-48)

The whole Prologue is Bowzybeus's own panegyric to the Queen and her ministers in gratitude for peace, Queen Anne's Golden Age, the poet's own time and not only his "clime". As in most of the peace poems, Oxford gets his share of praise,

> *Oxford,* who a wand doth bear,[103]
> Like *Moses,* in our Bibles fair.

It befits the ballad poet to fetch his comparison from the Bible. It is, however, Bolingbroke who receives the main part of the peace poem eulogy. He is praised for his steadfastness to Tory principles, incarnated in the combination of "Church and Queen", a little surprising perhaps in the case of St. John, the deist, but natural to the simple poet as the two foremost objects of his veneration.—Learned poets referred to the Queen's interest in religion by describing the lofty spires of the City churches that she ordered to be built.—The usual description of the progress of trade follows. But the whole of this panegyric passage is more charming, more genuinely affectionate, though at the same time respectful, than any other addressed to St. John.

> Lo here, thou hast mine Eclogues fair,
> But let not these detain thine ear.
> Let not affairs of States and Kings
> Wait, while our *Bowzybeus* sings.
> Rather than verse of simple swain
> Should stay the trade of *France* or *Spain,*
> Or for the plaint of Parson's maid,
> Yon' Emp'ror's packets be delay'd;
> In sooth, I swear by holy *Paul,*
> I'd burn book, preface, notes and all.
>
> (ll, 87-96)

The only other peace eulogy that can vie with the cheerfulness of Gay's poem is, not unexpectedly, the Preface to volume V of *Wit and Mirth* (1714). "Doctor Merriman" refers to the happy events of the preceding year and recommends his "incomparable Pills" as a remedy against the "quarrelsome Disposition" that blood and slaughter have produced in mankind.[104] The *"Pills"* will now heal possible breaches between the parties and cement unity. Bowzybeus, Gay's *alter ego,* was the kind of writer who contributed to the gay atmosphere of the Playford song-books, and the learned poet himself assumed a similar conciliatory attitude in his relationship with Whig and Tory friends, took the same cheerful view of divergences in criticism and politics, and was consequently as averse to lofty panegyric as to fierce satire.

The dedication of **The Shepherd's Week,** not to the Lord Treasurer and fellow Scriblerian, but to the chief peace negotiator was certainly not just mercenary. St. John and Gay were in a way kindred souls, and Bolingbroke's affection for "gentle Gay" survived the poet's death.[105] Besides, St. John seems, at least in later years, to have had an inclination for the Horatian manner of living, if we may believe the sincerity of his letter to Lord Bathurst[106] or of his rural taste manifested in the way he decorated his country house with pictures of rustic tools.[107] But he was also and above all a decided supporter of the "modern" observers and experimenters as against the followers of "metaphysical pneumatics" and "ontology",[108] and would therefore particularly appreciate Gay's Eclogues, which are "modern" in the peculiar sense that the word had in the period.

According to the *Guardian* rules, like Fontenelle's deduced by way of a "modern" method, pastoral poetry ought to picture a rural scene of perfect ease and tranquillity, where innocence, simplicity, and joy abound.[109] Both the "neoclassic" and the "rationalistic" critics rejected the "too much business and employment"[110] of the countryside. Fontenelle had also repre-

sented the state of idleness, the demand of the senses, as a relief from "that presumptuous Tyrant of the Mind".[111] In France, both Ancients and Moderns could be said to cultivate the "Tyrant of the Mind". But the followers of Bacon and Newton in England opposed the dominance of Aristotelian metaphysics in a different way. They relied on experiment and observation, from the collected result of which conclusions were to be drawn about higher things. Not abstract Cartesian thinking, but industry, "mechanics", practical arts, husbandry, manual work and the evidence of the senses were their means of gradually arriving at the higher secrets, the mysteries of the existence of all things, body and soul as well as the universe. In reality, however, the final aim was sometimes lost sight of and very often certainly unheard of by many of those who enthusiastically and with painful detail reported discoveries, experiments and observations to the secretary of the Royal Society. Such details were appropriately condemned by critics and eschewed by poets who, according to Aristotelian principles for idealization in serious Kinds, only represented "a kind of half Truth". When, on the other hand, "Mechanicks" were admitted into the supposedly high Kinds and sublime style, as when in one of his Epics, Blackmore too meticulously described an angel's garment, that was designated as "Bathous".[112]

But poems about the countryside in Queen Anne's Golden Age, comic poems, images as up-to-date and as "modern" as the critical methods if not the poetry of the "rationalistic" school, could not picture a rural scene of ease and idleness, but had to represent industry, the low "Country Matters" which Fontenelle in particular despised, and the "too much business' that all the critics rejected. This was in accordance with what really happened, after the Peace Treaty, in particular. In a number of peace poems, the farmer had been praised happy for being able to carry on his work undisturbed by the ravages of war. Ease and "tranquillity" was not an ideal state of things in post-war England. It is perfectly logical then that in Gay's Prologue, Oxford is praised for providing opportunities for the industry of farmers and weavers, and that in **Saturday,**[113] a Theocritean description of English reapers, the same theme as in **Rural Sports,** but brought down to the level of rustic Bowzybeus, not "beheld" by the poet, corresponds to the picture of the return of the Golden Age in Virgil's *Eclogue IV.*

It is also logical that Gay's "Eclogues", as he himself calls his poems, purport to imitate Theocritus's rusticity, English country occupations—not gentlemanly this time—but industrious swains and dairy-maids ploughing, haymaking and reaping the harvest, thrashing, tending the pigs and making butter and cheese. Bowzybeus, the rustic bard, is basically similar to the Greek bucolic poet, about whom Lady Mary Wortley Montagu wrote that he was not "a romantic writer" and that if he had been born in England, he would have written Idylls about "thrashing and churning".[114] To Gay, the learned poet, however, the "image of the times" implied a comic genre picturing the details of various aspects in the period, among other things also the activities of pedants and experimental philosophers, in their way as "modern" as the aspirations toward English Augustan high Kinds and originality. As this aspect of **The Shepherd's Week** has not at all been dealt with in the previous criticism, it will receive a fairly extensive treatment here, particularly as it is entirely Scriblerian.

"Modern" and Low Pedantry

The most conspicuous "modern" features in **The Shepherd's Week** are the footnotes. According to the Prologue, notes "profound", most probably in the sense of "belonging to *Bathous*", were suggested by St. John. To the Scriblerians, such Bentleian pedantry deserved ridicule, and Gay thoroughly served the common cause by equating Bowzybeus and "modern" cranks.[115] Most of the words commented upon[116] are denoted as "Old Word" or "S[axon]" in contemporary dictionaries,[117] one of which particularly shows the influence of "modern" philosophy. "Husbandry, Gardening, Confectionary, Cookery" are enumerated among the "Arts and Sciences" together with "Divinity, Law, Philosophy".[118] In accordance with the etymological information and with the character of the poems, Gay's derivations of words annotated are "Saxon", "*ancient* British", or "Dutch". Sometimes the Virgilian *Eclogues* on which Gay's poems were modelled.[119] **Monday** is a regular singing-contest like Virgil's *Eclogues III* and *VII* or Theocritus's *Idylls V* and *VIII*. **Tuesday,** a love-lament, is reminiscent of *Eclogue II* and part of *Idyll III*. The first song of *Eclogue VIII* seems to have provided the framework for **Wednesday.**—Two of Ovid's elegiac Epistles were, however, certainly also in Gay's mind, as is evidenced by imitative passages and the fact that the lament comes from women.[120]—**Thursday** is a *Pharmaceutria* and corresponds to *Eclogue VIII*, the second song, more than to *Idyll II*, the first song. Gay's version of the lament for Daphnis, Virgil's *Eclogue V*, is **Friday.**—Two shepherds lamenting the loss, though not death, of their mistress is, however, also treated of by Calpurnius in *Ecloga Nona*, or Nemesianus's *Eclogue II*.—Finally, **Saturday** is perhaps the most obvious and the cleverest imitation of Virgil, *Eclogues IV* and, mainly, *VI*. One passage is clearly an imitation of Mantuanus, whose rustic realism is also akin to Gay's. Into these moulds, Gay poured "modern" and other low subject matter from various sources, some of it certainly as he himself had observed it. All the poems are heavily sprinkled with echoes and borrowings, which in a masterly, truly neo-classical way, Gay adapted to his own and Bowzybeus's "modern" Eclogues. His footnotes, again in the "modern" manner, provide the clues to some of the classical passages imitated.[121]

There is some "modern" and Scriblerian subject matter in **Monday,** for instance. The wagers staked by the conventional shepherds, the "beechen cups" in *Eclogue III*, the goat and lamb, calf and pipe in the *Idylls,* Spenser's and Pope's more elaborate bowls in *August* and in *Spring,* all that is left aside for not only an "oaken staff" à la Philips's, but also a realistically described tobacco-pouch. In **Friday,** Bumkinet refers to the autumn as the cyder-brewing season. The reason seems to be that cyder and tobacco were among the useful products supposed to be unknown to the Ancients and sometimes facetiously held to be among the advantages of the Moderns.[122] The swing and the see-saw in the passages that Gay added in 1720, are Scriblerian playthings, which were allowed to Martin because they gave him "an early notion of the sciences"[123] They served Gay for an appropriate rustic version of the flaw in the innocence of a shepherd's character.[123] Lobbin Clout hung "the slacken'd cord" on "two near elms"

> Now high, now low my *Blouzelinda* swung.
> With the rude wind her rumpled garment rose,
> And show'd her taper leg, and scarlet hose.
>
> (ll. 104—6)

Rustic Cuddy allowed himself similar innocent mischief when on "the plank" across "the fallen oak", he "pois'd" himself "against the tott'ring maid".

The delightful comparisons in the same Eclogue, **Monday,** could even suffer scrutiny by "modern" philosophers.

> Leek to the *Welch,* to *Dutchmen* butter's dear,
> Of *Irish* swains potatoe is the chear;
> Oats for their feasts, the *Scottish* shepherds grind,
> Sweet turnips are the food of *Blouzelind.*
> While she loves turnips, butter I'll despise,
> Nor leeks nor oatmeal nor potatoe prize.
>
> (ll. 83—88)

Cuddy's "landlord" eats roast-beef and the squire hare, the parson likes pudding and his wife fat capon, whereas Buxoma loves white-pot.

According to his own version of the law of decorum, Gay skilfully makes use of "modern" nutritional physiology. His distribution of the alimentary details follows Arbuthnot's prescription that "general Rules about Diet without Regard to particular Constitutions are absurd". The famous doctor recommended, for instance, milk and fresh eggs, "Decoctions and Creams or Gellies of well fermented Bread" to persons with "weak Fibres".[124] So what, in Cuddy's loving eyes, could better suit his Buxoma, to him the daintiest of creatures, than white-pot, which, according to the contemporary *Dictionarium Anglo-Britannicum* by Kersey, was "a Mess of Milk with Eggs, fine Bread, Sugar, &c bak'd in an Earthen Pot". Similarly, in addition to the historic explanation why leek is the Welsh national emblem, there was a "modern" scientific theory which might support a physiological connection between the symbol and the national character. Leek was among the vegetables that "excite[d] a momentary Heat and Fever",[125] and "Taffy" was notoriously "hot and dry". As for Blouzelinda's turnips, the cultivation of these vegetables was an achievement of the Moderns, and a vegetarian diet seems to have been recommended by the new philosophers. In D'Urfey's Opera *Wonders in the Sun,*[126] for instance, philosophers eat turnips and carrots, and King had ridiculed the use of turnips for food.[127] Cornelius Scriblerus, on the other hand, forbade Martin's nurse to eat beef, because it would spoil the understanding of Martin[128]—That the words for food are important for the interpretation of Gay's poem is indicated by the fact that they were italicized in the first two editions of **The Shepherd's Week.**

The contents of the two stanzas referred to in **Monday** have no direct classical counterparts. Alimentary details belonged to Horace's Kinds, not to Eclogues. But in a simple "artless" form they are typical of Bowzybeus's repertoire, as for instance, the following lines.

> While you eat goose and capon, I'le feed on
>   beefe and bacon,
>   And piece of hard cheese now
> and then;
> We pudding have, and souse, always ready in
>   the house.[129]

Gay's details are, however, arranged in a perfect Virgilian Eclogue comparison, in the manner of Dryden's translation.

> The Poplar is by great *Alcides* worn:
> The Brows of *Phoebus* his own Bays adorn.
> The branching vine the jolly *Bacchus* loves.
> The *Cyprian* Queen delights in Mirtle groves.
> With Hazle, *Phillis* crowns her flowing Hair;
> And while she loves that common Wreath to
>   wear,
> Nor Bays, nor Mirtle Bows, with Hazle shall
>   compare.[130]

Silenus's song in *Eclogue VI* was, however, the most rewarding for Gay's "modern" adaptation in **Saturday.** It had been the object of much discussion among critics for its non-pastoral sublimity. Fontenelle had made fun of "honest Silenus" and his "hearty Carouse" and also disapproved of the way in which Virgil had represented "philosophical Notions", the creation of the universe, according to were famous ballad figures, sometimes speaking Somerset dialect.[131] The Index to

the Roxburghe collection has at least ten titles about "West-Country" nymphs and lovers, weddings and wonders. Moreover, a Western lass, Gillian, who speaks "Zumerset", is a prominent character in D'Urfey's play *The Bath, or, The Western Lass.* Another evidence of Gay's dualistic decorum is his use of proverbs, "modern" as well as low. Dr. Bentley was notorious for his predilection for that stylistic device. John Ray published *A Collection of English Proverbs* (1670), and representatives of the Ancients had ridiculed the practice of their antagonists.[132] Proverbs and "wise-saws" were, however, of old recognized as belonging to a low style. As regards pastoral poetry, Fontenelle had, of course, discarded both "trivial Comparisons" and "clownish proverbial sayings", because used by "real Shepherds".[133] But *The Guardian* recommended them as one of the ways in which the pastoral poet might "lawfully deviate from the ancients", obviously after Philips's example.[134]

Antiquarian pedants concerned themselves not only with linguistic problems, Anglo-Saxon and Middle English, but with the English past in its various aspects, even with Scandinavian history and literature.[135] The research of "modern" pedants into old customs, ancient as well as English, for instance, was made fun of by William King and the Scriblerians.[136] King ridiculed certain treatises on the "plays of the Grecian boys", which were supposed to correspond to English children's games.[137] For his description of homely rustic sports in **Monday,** Gay was obviously indebted to King's "Playford Letters", Playford, of course, being the name not only of an imaginary "modern" scholar, but of the patron of song-writers like Bowzybeus. Gay perhaps also had his eye on Budgell, who in *The Spectator,* No. 161, September 4, 1711, had compared cudgel-playing with Roman sports and referred to White Kennet for the relationship between country wakes and ancient love-feasts.[138] In his Eclogue, Gay represents the homely games as a field of achievement, in which rustic Colin and his companions excel. On the other hand, Lobbin Clout's blindman's buff probably reminded learned readers of how the Italian shepherdess Amaryllis, eyes bandaged, was left alone with her Myrtillo in a similar amorous situation.[139]

"Modern" Natural Philosophy

There are also in Gay's poems allusions to the theories and the "learning" of the "modern" scientists. But these will best appear in comparisons of passages in **The Shepherd's Week** with corresponding lines in Gay's classical models, of which the reader will be reminded in passing. The rustic subject matter is in the spirit of Theocritus, but the outer mould in which it is cast was borrowed from other classical poets as well. Professor Jones and Dr. Bragg have identified there is a reference to a quotation from Chaucer, also in keeping with "modern" principles, as Chaucer was looked upon as the first refiner of the English language, which was supposed to have been in a state of progress up to the time of Waller and Dryden and to be subjected to those changes according to "modern" cyclic theories to which Gay alludes in the Proeme. A source of reference which Gay indicates, is *"Ray. F.R.S."*. It is from his *Collection of English Words* that the long footnote to 1. 89 in *Wednesday* is lifted and quoted literally.[140] The derivation of "Dight" is also taken from Ray, his section "North Country Words". The note to "Dumps" in *Wednesday* is in the real spirit of Martinus Scriblerus and his father Cornelius. There is one foreign and one native theory of derivation, the latter supposed to have been put forward by the "English *Antiquaries*", who *"have conjectured that* Dumps . . . *comes from the word* Dumplin, *the heaviest kind of pudding that is eaten in this country, much used in Norfolk . . ."* This is perhaps an echo from current theories about aliments and probably again from *"Ray"*, who included Norfolk dumplings in his *Collection of English Proverbs*.[141] Dirge" is annotated in a similar dual way with one Latin and one "Teutonic" origin. This time the quotation is literal except for the addition of the adjective "popish", meaning foreign, but also a term used in low anti-Jacobite argumentation.[142]

The playful preference for the "Teutonic" antiquaries is, of course, in keeping with the "modern" Englishness of *The Shepherd's Week*. Gay took his inspiration for this device from *A Journey to London* (1698), where William King, detractor of and learner from pedants, opposed his "Mr. Shuttleworth" to "M. Baudelot" in Lister's *A Journey to Paris*. The Frenchman was preparing a dissertation on a Greek marble with a list of the members of the Erecteis tribe killed by the Athenians, whereas the English pedant was ready to publish a report on a stone from Scotland with "a catalogue . . . of the most principal persons that were killed at *Chevy Chase*."[143] King's original intention seems to have been ridicule of pedantry on the whole. But it is worth observing that in *Miscellanies in Prose and Verse* (1709), he introduced a new edition of his *Journey* by representing it "as a vindication of [his] own country" against France, the enemy.[144] Similarly, in his rustic poems about the Tory Golden Age after the war with France, Gay appropriately gave the preference to the "Teutonic" school, so to speak, really native explanations.[145]

To the supporters of "ancient" philosophy as well as to gentlemanly learned persons, some of the objects of the antiquarian interest, such as ballads,[146] seemed too insignificant to deserve serious attention. A common way of ridiculing the Moderns was therefore to imply that their learning was vulgar. Gay consistently carries out the principle of this double-natured decorum in his allusions to "modern" pedantry. In the footnotes, for instance, words like "ken", "doff", "don", which are represented as the object of the study of scholars, could

at the same time also be recognized by readers as vulgar and naturally belonging to the vocabulary of Bowzybeus. The latter two are typical broadside ballad words. Both "modern" and low is also the footnote to 1. 21 in *Tuesday*, "Kee, *a West-Country Word for* Kine *or* Cows". Ray's *Collection* contains "South-Country" and "North-Country" words, but the "West-Country" lads and lasses "Epicurus's System".[147] Chetwood had tried to read Christian notions into the song and vindicated Silenus's drunken "Flights".[148]

The Flights is exactly the sub-title of *Saturday*, a fact which in itself may be an indication that Gay was familiar with the dispute. He now efficiently brought Virgil's sublimity down to earth. "Modern" experimental philosophy provided the material for his version of the classical poet's passage about the causation and origin of things. The whole song reads like a table of contents in an issue of *The Philosophical Transactions*. At least one paper can be identified with certainty. William Derham, one of the most prominent members of the Royal Society, had reported on the "Migration of Birds" in "Letter", No. 313 (1708),[149] and King had referred to this in his *Useful Transactions*.[150] The nightly movements of owls, the sleeping habits of "bat and dormouse", the blindness of puppies, the mysteries of comets and glow-worms mentioned in *Saturday*, were all in the line of subjects treated in detail in the letters to the Royal Society. Richard Waller had actually reported on the "Flying Glow-Worm" in the *Transactions*,[151] with King's subsequent ridicule, not so much of the glow-worm "volant",[152] it seems, as of the style in which it was presented to the readers. *"Our swain"*, says Gay in a facetious footnote, *"had possibly read* Tusser, *from whence he might have collected these philosophical observations."* What the poet wants to say is, as in the case of some of the foot-notes, the proverbs and the ballads, that these *"philosophical observations"* were simple enough to be within the knowledge and understanding of "swains" and "huntsmen" and hardly deserved their epithet.[153] At the same time then such things as glow-worms and the *"Will-a-Wisp"* were within the range of a ballad poet's subject matter. The mention of the crude old Georgic is probably an allusion to what obviously seemed, even in Gay's time, a curious relationship, that between the useful arts and the new philosophy. Tusser was probably chosen because a new edition of his art of husbandry had appeared in 1713 under the title of *Tusser Redivivus*. The whole passage in *Saturday* is a clever "modernization" of Virgil, with some ridicule directed against exaggerated and blind-folded pedantry among the many amateur supporters of "modern" philosophy.

It has been said that Bowzybeus's song burlesques Blackmore's *Creation,* and, in particular, the song of Mopas in *Prince Arthur*.[154] *Eclogue VI* must, however, be the origin of both songs, the subject matter of which is as philosophical as that of *Creation*. Blackmore, perhaps after Chetwood, combined the ancient Epicurean theory in Virgil with biblical notions and produced a "modern" version of the passage just as sublime as Virgil's. Both Gay and Blackmore imitated Virgil's, or rather Dryden's form. The following passage is a quotation from the English paraphrase of the *Silenus.*

> He sung the secret Seeds of Nature's Frame,
> How Seas, and Earth, and Air, and active
>   Flame,
> Fell through the mighty Void . . .
>
> ———
>
> From thence the birth of Man the Song
>   pursu'd,
> And how the World was lost, and how
>   renew'd.
>
> ———
>
> He sung the lover's fraud . . . [155]

All the elements in Mopas's song are to be found in Virgil's poem, chaos, orbs, vapours, earth, sea, plants, living things. Silenus was a sufficiently important figure in the criticism of the period to have provided the model for both Mopas and Bowzybeus. Moreover, in his *Eclogue VIII,* Diaper follows the same pattern in Proteus's song of "the World's first Birth" from "Chaos" and "Globules", making use of Epicurean atomic notions, Cartesian vortices, Newtonian gravity. Lines beginning "How", "He sung" also occur, and Gay echoes the last line.

> When ruddy to the Waves, sunk the declining
>   Day[156]

in

> 'Till, ruddy, like his face, the sun descends.
>   (1. 128)

The two serious poets make use of the physico-theology of the period, while in the comic manner, Gay resorts to the low *"material things"* of the experimental philosophy.

The inscription on Blouzelinda's tombstone in *Friday,*

> *Here* Blouzelinda *lyes—Alas, alas!*
> *Weep shepherds—and remember flesh is grass,*
>   (ll. 91-92)

is yet another "modernized" version of Virgil, in this case the epitaph on Daphnis in *Eclogue V.* Prior's *Hans Carvel*[157] probably inspired the wording, but the contents are "modern" and Epicurean.[158]

Finally, the "ALPHABETICAL CATALOGUE of *Names, Plants, Flowers, Fruits, Birds, Beasts, Insects,* and other mate-*rial*[!] *things mentioned in these Pastorals"* with which Gay closes *The Shepherd's Week,* is perhaps the most important evidence of the "modernness" of his Eclogues. His predecessors are here not classical poets, but Spenser and William King.[159] Gay certainly intended his Catalogue to serve a similar purpose in *The Shepherd's Week* as Spenser his Glossary in *The Shepherd's Calendar.* Just as Spenser emphasized the importance of his contribution of old English words to enriching the language not only of pastoral poetry, so Gay pointed to the significance of concrete words for lending colour to rural poetry. The use of dialect words was in the tradition of Renaissance critics,[160] but the use of words for *"material things"* was in the spirit of the English Moderns. The Baconians had created the antithesis between the things material, the concrete world of the new philosophy, and the "empty words" of the schoolmen; between, on one hand, manual work and the evidence of the senses, and, on the other hand, the work of the mind and abstractions. The understanding of Martinus, we know, a Modern to the point of perversion, "was so totally immers'd in *sensible objects,* that he demanded examples from Material things of the abstracted Ideas of Logick."[161]

Gay's Use of "Modern" Ballads

In order to appreciate the use of "Fables . . . Modern" in *The Shepherd's Week* in combination with echoes of the new philosophy, it may be useful to recall the position of the ballad in the early 18th century. By the time of the publication of Philips's first four *Pastorals,*[162] the admiration for the "venerable ancient Song-Enditers"[163] had already begun to assert itself,[164] supported as it was by some congenial new or revived notions and ideas. Among these were the Longinian rehabilitation of genius in competition with learned "Art", of simplicity—even the "country-scraper['s]"—in rivalry with "artfulness", together with the activities of the English antiquaries, some of whom collected ballads, among other things.[165] Although more distantly, the appreciation of old songs was connected with the "modern" theory of cyclic changes, the Whig political principle of progress, and perhaps Augustan pride. It thus came to counteract the "ancient" notions of decay and even of imitation of classical poetry. Detractors of "modern" notions in general, but in particular of antiquarian pedantry, therefore often represented ballads as fit for the low taste of their antagonists, supposedly the same as that of the unlearned, learning, of course, consisting of classical knowledge. Grub Street and the new philosophy were not far apart.[166] In one of the parodies of Addison's ballad criticism, for instance, "the Polite *Woodwardius*" is said to have shed tears "upon reading some of the most pathetical Encounters of Tom Thumb." In his company are Tom D'Urfey and John Dunton.[167] Even before Addison had praised *Chevy Chase,* King had written about that ballad as suitable for the ped-antry of his "Mr. Shuttleworth".[168]

This relationship between ballads and the unlearned, in a double sense, was resorted to by Gay in **Saturday**, where with subtle playfulness, he expressed his scep-ticism about the serious admiration for the native genre and about the use of ballad "fables", as if they repre-sented an English Golden Age. The poet probably owed part of his inspiration for the trick to Fontenelle, who disliked the whole of Silenus's song, not only the "philosophical notions", but also the ancient "fables".[169] Where Silenus tells the stories of Phaeton's sisters, Scylla, Pasiphae and Taurus, Bowzybeus entertains the merry reapers with ballads, that is to say, English "fa-bles", two of which Addison had praised in rivalry with ancient poetry[170] and two of which had recently been used in serious plays.[171] When the ballad-singer intoned *Chevy Chase*,[172] as Gay writes, he appropriate-ly "raised his voice" to "louder strains", as if to inti-mate the heroic quality of the song. The counterpart of the story of Pasiphae and the bull is Denham's song about the Quaker and the mare, *All in the Land of Essex*,[174] and *"Wantley's Dragon"*[175] is perhaps intend-ed to correspond to Scylla and the "howling monsters" which girded her waist. There is *"Taffey Welch"*[176] and *"Sawney Scot", "Lilly-burlero"*[177] and the *Irish Trot"*[178] *"Bateman"*[179] and *"Shore"*,[180] *"The bow'r of Ro-samond"*[181] and *"Robin Hood"*[182] and the song which significantly describes "how the *grass now grows where* Troy town *stood"*.[183] It is a catalogue of ballads, sim-ilar to those hung on the walls of Baucis's and Philem-on's cottage in Swift's poem, some of them "vulgar", others "traditional", "Fables . . . Modern", but also fit to entertain maidens and swains.

The view of the English past as pre-Augustan was per-haps the reason why ballads were more or less face-tiously linked with Greek poetry, the products of sup-posed natural genius. In Fontenelle's *New Dialogues of the Dead*, Anacreon is called a "petty Ballad-maker" or in Hughes's translation, "a little Scribbler of Sonnets".[184] *The Muses Mercury* accused Perrault, another French Modern, of treating Homer as "a common Ballad-mak-er"[185] and when in *A Journey to London,* William King called *Chevy Chase* "a noble Pindaric", the intention was plainly derogatory. Similarly, Addison's compari-son of D'Urfey to Pindar is rather condescending.[186] It was, however, with a true flair for business that Curll adopted this method when he advertised the second edition of Theocritus's *Idylliums* as "Love-Dialogues, &c".[187] This sort of "modern" advertising method, though in the reverse, was continued by the author of the Pref-ace to *A Pill to Purge State-Melancholy* (1715), who pushed his "Dittys" by referring to ancient Kinds as ballads, shepherd's songs or "Love-Sonnets", the "Ploughman's Ditty's", and "Catches".[188] So why—that is the conclusion—be ashamed of publishing a collec-tion of broadside ballads?[189]

Broadside verse was what actually became of the medieval "Balades", "Compleyntes, Roundelets, Dities, Rondils" in which Chaucer's Franklin excelled. When they were removed from the list of the recognized Kinds, they did not altogether disappear, nor did they all develop into something more Augustan. Like so many other fashions and currents of taste, they ended up at the bottom of the scale of aesthetics and of so-ciety. The unlearned writers of broadsheet ballads as well as the "sonneteer" of the period, Thomas D'Urfey, used the old appellations without much discrimination of their inherent qualities. Sub-titles like "A New Son-net" and "An Excellent New Ditty", "A Doleful Ditty" and "A Pleasant Pastoral Sonnet" are common in all ballad collections, and there are titles like *The Swain's Complaint, The Milke-Maid's Dumps* and *The Lyke-Wake Dirge,*[190] none indicating the form, though some the mode or the manner. In D'Urfey's Opera *Don Quixote,* a shepherd and a shepherdess sing a "Dirge". When in *The Second Pastoral,* Philips referred to Colinet's poem as "sonnets" and "ditties", he seriously aimed at the effect of the "venerable ancient Song-Enditers". But in the case of **The Shepherd's Week,** the words "sonnet", "madrigal", "ballads", "rounde-lays", "catches",[191] have different semantic values. Play-fully following the habits of broadsheet poets and his fellow-"sonneteer", but with a thorough knowledge of classical Kinds, Gay in his disguise called his love-laments after the model of *Eclogues II* and *VIII* and Ovid, **Tuesday; or, The Ditty** and **Wednesday; or, The Dumps. The Spell** and **The Flights** are the "home-bred" versions of the classical *Pharmaceutria,* respec-tively the *Pollio* and the *Silenus,* both sublime. Finally, the funeral Elegy is a **Dirge.**[192] The duality of the genre is thus facetiously but openly announced.

Themes Otherwise Anglicized and Brought Down to Earth

Sometimes homely songs and classical poems were interrelated, the former perhaps imitations of imitations, rather than of originals. In other cases, themes proba-bly imitated human nature in general. There was some justification for the "modern" comparison of ballads with classical Kinds. Passages in Gay's poems some-times seem indebted to both. But in each case, they retain their own peculiar quality of gentle and delicate mock-pastoral with charming details, an earthy but agreeable realism, set off for a contrast in particular against melancholy or sublime themes in similar genres.[193] Like Alexis in *Eclogue II,* for instance, Nell in *The Countrey-Farmer* tempts her beloved with gifts and the prospect of her accomplishments.[194] The de-scriptions of the latter recall similar passages in **Tues-day.** Marian's "wailings" in Gay's poem are also rem-iniscent of one of D'Urfey's songs about "Sawney".[195] But the woman's reproachful reminder, so to speak, is at the same time typical of *Heroides.* The following quotations may serve to illustrate this relationship. The first is from *Tuesday,* the second and third are from the two songs.

> Whilom with thee 'twas *Marian*'s dear
>   delight
> To moil all day, and merrymake at night.
> If in the soil you guide the crooked share,
> Your early breakfast is my constant care.
> And when with even hand you strow the
>   grain,
> I fright the thievish rooks from off the plain,
> In misling days when I my thresher heard,
> With nappy beer I to the barn repair'd;
> Lost in the musick of the whirling flail,
> To gaze on thee I left the smoking pail;
> In harvest when the Sun was mounted high,
> My leathern bottle did thy drought supply;
> When-e'er you mow'd I follow'd with the
>   rake,
> And have full oft been sun-burnt for thy sake;
> When in the welkin gath'ring show'rs were
>   seen,
> I lagg'd the last with Colin on the green;
> And when at eve returning with thy carr,
> Awaiting heard the gingling bells from far;
> Strait on the fire the sooty pot I plac't,
> To warm thy broth I burnt my hands for haste.
> When hungry thou stood'st *staring like an
>   Oaf,*
> I slic'd the luncheon from the barley loaf,
> With crumbled bread I thicken'd well thy
>   mess.
> Ah, love me more, or love thy pottage less!
>   (ll. 49-73)

> And I'le [churn the] milk, and thou shalt
>   mowe,
> I'le card and I'le spin, while you harrow and
>   sowe,
> And call upon Dobbin with Hey-ye-woe!
>
> I gave him fine Scotch Sark and band, I put
>   them on
>   with mine own
>   hand;
> I gave him Honey and I gave him Land;
> ———
> I robb'd the groves of all their store and
>   nosegays
>   made to give Sawney one.

Ovid's Oenone and Paris lay on leaves and flowers and on straw in the shade, all of which the woman recalled after her lover left her.

> When you rose up to hunt, I shew'd you
>   Game,
> Surpriz'd the Infant Savage and his Dame:

> Companion of your Sports, the Toils did
>   place,
> And chear'd the swift pac'd Hounds upon the
>   Chace.[196]

In the burlesque version, the lovers meet in the stable and "on a Truss of Hay". After Paris has left her, Oenone remembers how her admirer has been promoted from the stable "to the table".

> Did I not teach you then to lay a Cloath?
> There's no Man but must have his first
>   Beginning,
> Who learnt you then to fold your Table-
>   Linnen?
> Did you not often when the Cloath was spread
> Just in the middle put your Salt and Bread?
> [You did not know how to fill a glass]
> Did I not show you how to broach your
>   Drink?
> And tilt the Vessel when 't began to sink?[197]

Man and woman are the same at all times, and Gay knew both Ovid, Radcliffe, D'Urfey and his fellow-creatures. Besides, another contemporary pastoralist who tried to vary the conventional pattern, had just produced yet another version.

> Oft have I wound in Plaits the yielding Reed,
> And plac'd the well-wrought Garland on your
>   Head.
> Oft have I choicest Fish with Labour caught
> And the sweet Prey to you a present
>   brought.[198]

Another of *Ovid's Epistles* was certainly in Gay's mind when he wrote **Wednesday.** *Phillis to Demophon* invited burlesque, at least the English translation of the passage that describes the maiden's hesitation before the lover's leap

> Hard by, where two huge Mountains guard the
>   Way,
> There lies a fearful, solitary *Bay;*
> Oft I've resolv'd, while on this Place I've
>   stood,
> To throw my self into the raging Flood,
> Wild with Despair, and I will do it still,
> Since you continue thus to use me ill.
> And when the kinder Waves shall waft me
>   o'er,
> May thou behold my Body on the Shore[199]
> Unburied lye; and though thy Cruelty
> Harder than Stone, or than thy self should be,
> Yet shalt thou cry, astonish'd with the Show,
> Phillis, *I was not to be follow'd so.*
> Raging with Poisons would I oft expire,
> And quench my own by a much happier Fire.
> Then to revenge the Loss of all my Rest,

Would stab thy Image in my tortur'd Breast.[200]

The last choice is hanging, and then Phillis composes her own epitaph. Surely, Prior was right, even for a joke, to prefer D'Urfey to such translations. But by combining the realism of songs and ditties with this classical theme, Gay produced an English picture of womanly irresolution set off against a background of pigs, curs, and the village pond.

> A sudden death shall rid me of my woe.
> This penknife keen my windpipe shall divide.
> What, shall I fall as squeaking pigs have dy'd!
> No—To some tree this carcass I'll suspend.
> But worrying curs find such untimely end![201]
> I'll speed me to the pond, where the high
>   stool
> On the long plank hangs o'er the muddy pool,
> That stool, the dread of ev'ry scolding quean;
> Yet, sure a lover should not dye so mean!
> There plac'd aloft, I'll rave and rail by fits,
> Though all the parish say I've lost my wits;
> And thence, if courage holds, myself I'll
>   throw,
> And quench my passion in the lake below.[202]
>
> (ll. 100-12)

Virgil's sublime passages were treated by Gay in the same irreverent manner as the theme of the forsaken lover's melancholy end. *Friday* is a proper Answer, particularly in this respect, to the many conventional imitations of *Eclogue V,* of which *The Guardian* complained. In all those that copy the traditional pattern, the lament for the dead shepherd is followed by the apotheosis, which is usually indicated by another shepherd pointing to the sun breaking through a streak in the clouds. Spenser's Dido in *November* really becomes a goddess in the Elysian Fields. There were also some 18th century variations, such as Congreve's in *The Mourning Muse of Alexis,* where a flame from the tomb of the dead shepherdess extends to heaven and fixes in the firmament as a new star.[203] Philips's Albino, whose death is accompanied by no heathen paraphernalia, looks down "from above", more like a representative of the new English Christian-Platonic supernatural. But Gay performs the transition from sorrow to rejoicing through a wholesale reversal of the conventional pattern. In the delightful funeral scene, correct after Virgil and Rapin, but realistic and more elaborate even than Mantuan's,[204] the deification is negligently hinted at in passing in the parson's sermon.

> He said, that heaven would take her soul, no
>   doubt.
>
> (l. 141)[205]

The louts "wail'd", it is true, and in a cumulative comparison, which is rustic, but basically similar to that which accompanies the vows of Virgil's shepherds, they swore to praise Blouzelinda "for ever". In reality, however, these mortal swains remember their promises and their grief only

> 'Till bonny Susan sped a-cross the plain;
> They seiz'd the lass in apron clean array'd,
> And to the ale-house forc'd the willing maid;
> In ale and kisses they forget their cares,
> And Susan Blouzelinda's loss repairs.
>
> (ll. 160-64)[206]

The address to D'Urfey in *Wednesday* is another de-sublimed Virgilian passage and imitates the panegyric to Pollio in *Eclogue VIII.* Pollio's consulship was supposed to bring back "the reign of Saturn", and as in Gay's period D'Urfey was the most prolific writer of pastoral poems about contemporary shepherds, the implication is obviously that Queen Anne's reign was the new Golden Age.

The most conspicuous example of anti-sublimity is *Saturday,* an imitation of *Eclogues IV* and *V,* which most critics considered too sublime for the pastoral Kind. Gay starts with an invocation.

> SUBLIMER strains, O rustick Muse, prepare;
> Forget a-while the barn and dairy's care;
> Thy homely voice to loftier numbers raise,
> The drunkard's flights require sonorous lays.
>
> (ll. 1-4)

The "loftier numbers" were indeed efficiently brought down to earth in Gay's rustic and "modern" versions of the Golden Age and of the "causes of things" and in the catalogue of English "fables"[207]. Just as Rapin had justified Silenus's song as the subject matter of pastoral poetry by saying that the audience were shepherds, so Gay in his turn could "answer" Virgil's most sublime Eclogue with a ballad-singer's repertoire and allege as his excuse that Bowzybeus sang to maidens and swains, whose literary craving was actually satisfied with Dunton's and Cross's broadsheets.

Devices from Low Literature

The concrete realistic quality of **The Shepherd's Week** was achieved not only by means of borrowings from and allusions to the productions and the activities of experimenters and antiquaries, by the description of *"material things"* observed and by a purposeful choice of models, realistic and sublime passages in Theocritus, Virgil, Ovid and Mantuan for imitation and parody, respectively. In accordance with their sub-titles, Gay's poems also contain general characteristics of and details from the sort of literature that could be supposed to be familiar to Bowzybeus, the rustic bard. The naming of the Eclogues after the days of the week, for instance, is not just in the manner of Spenser, as Gay pretended. The calendar motif had deep roots in popular literature with, perhaps after Hesiod, certain days propitious and others not, for certain sorts of work or important events.[208] Gay had been anticipated in applying it to loving and wooing both by William Basse[209] and an anonymous ballad poet.[210] Like Philips, Gay gave his characters pastoral names that had been used by Spenser and his immediate followers, Basse and Wither, as well as by Abel Evans and D'Urfey. But whereas Philips added French-sounding names to the native ones, Gay drew on English sources. Blouzelinda is obviously an invention in the spirit of D'Urfey,[211] whereas Hobnelia, Buxoma, Sparabella, Grubbinol, Bumkinet, Lubberkin recall contemporary coinages like Basketia, Thirsto, Drowtho in King's *The Furmetary* and Tarbox, Lowbell, two of the characters in the rustic anti-masque of D'Urfey's *Cynthia and Endimion*.[212] They are pastoral, but at the same time in the comic English tradition that Gay followed in some of his plays.

The examples of superstition in ***Thursday*** are also thoroughly low and Northern, if not English, as appears, for instance, from a comparison with Lansdowne's version of the *Pharmaceutria*. If they have a literary source, it could only be the chap-books. Flinging hemp-seeds or peels over one's head or shoulder,[213] putting peascods over or under one's door,[214] throwing apple and orange peels, so that they form a certain letter of the alphabet, turning round in a circle,[215] counting the spots of a lady-bird, listening to the first cuckoo in spring[216] are all more or less well-known as means for simple and popular divination. Midsummer Eve and May Day are perhaps more important in Scandinavia, but the 14th of February is still a thoroughly English "Day", although the Valentine wooing has now become commercial as much as romantic. Gay's story about Hobnelia's visit to the "pothecary's shop" in order to buy *"golden flies"* is obviously, on the other hand, an "image of the times".[217] For one or two of the descriptions of traditional spells as well as for the picture of the fortune-telling gypsies in ***Tuesday,*** Gay might have found support in respectable old English poetry,[218] although the latter colourful passage was perhaps directly inspired by one of the *Spectator* essays.[219]

> Last *Friday*'s eve, when as the sun was set,
> I, near you stile, three sallow gypsies met.
> Upon my hand they cast a poring look,
> Bid me beware, and thrice their heads they shook,
> They said that many crosses I must prove,
> Some in my worldly gain, but most in love.
> Next morn I miss'd three hens and our old cock,

> And off the hedge two pinners and a smock.[220]
>
>   (ll. 73-80)

As opposed to the Naiads and Nymphs, to Venus and Diana in Pope's *Pastorals*,[221] the "theology" of ***The Shepherd's Week*** is indeed English, ingeniously adapted to the simplicity of swains and maidens, and just as proper for Queen Anne's Golden Age as the "hobthrushes, fairies, goblins, and witches" that the *Guardian* essay, No. 30, recommended. Like *The Spectator* about Sir Roger's credulity, but unlike older English poetry about "gypsan" ladies, the description of Marian's experiences could also teach a sophisticated town reader something about the folly of trusting to palmistry in love-affairs and other forms of superstition.

Among the characteristics of low poetry in ***The Shepherd's Week*** are some stylistic features, such as burthens, cumulative comparisons and similes, repetitions and absurdities, which, however, belong to both ballads, *Idylls* and *Eclogues*. Ballads sometimes have series of comparisons or incremental repetitions with little regard to decorum or even to contents.[222] But Gay used all these ornaments artistically. Even a burthen was made into a product of "Art",[223] and his comparisons in ***Monday*** are woven into intricate "figures", reminiscent of poems by Bolton,[224] Quarles, and Henry King.[225] Certain stock phrases, elements and themes are borrowed from ballads, others from contemporary songs. One of the instruments which Sparabella considers as a means by which to shorten her unhappy life is the "pen-knife", that is to say, the "wee pen-knife" or "little pen-knife" of Scottish ballads,[226] the "Poynard" of a later song.[227] The "nuncupative" testament in *Friday* is another ballad element,[228] which has no classical counterpart, but which occurs, for instance, in Spenser's *Daphnaida* in a highly idealized form. It was popular enough to be used in burlesque satire.[229] A serious version occurs in *The Bride's Buriall,* which was "kept in print from the time of James I down to the [19th] century",[230] and which was also published in Philips's *Collection of Old Ballads*. Its testament does not actually contain more than one item, but Blouzelinda's will is full of comic realistic detail. She gives directions for the care of her poultry and the "sickly calf" and then shows her mother

>   yonder shelf,
> There secretly I've hid my worldly pelf.
> Twenty good shillings in a rag I laid,
> Be ten the Parson's, for my sermon paid.
> The rest is yours—my spinning-wheel and
>   rake,
> Let Susan keep for her dear sister's sake;
> My new straw-hat that's trimly lin'd with
>   green,[231]
> Let *Peggy* wear, for she's a damsel clean.
> My leathern bottle, long in harvests try'd,

Be *Grubbinol's*—this silver ring beside:
Three silver pennies, and a ninepence bent,
A token kind, to *Bumkinet* is sent.
Thus spoke the maiden, while her mother
    cry'd,
And peaceful like the harmless lamb she
    dy'd.[232]

(ll. 119—32)

Various details, such as the incident with Susan and her garter in *Saturday* and the "stool", "the dread of ev'ry scolding quean", in *Wednesday,* were borrowed by Gay from less serious "ditties".[233] The fairs with their rope-dancing, mountebank performances and glittering "pedlars stalls" described in *Saturday,* were trivial events, which were depicted in street ballads and which were among the specialities of artists like Hogarth and D'Urfey.[234] The *Wit and Mirth* volumes contain a number of songs about haymakers and reapers, refreshing themselves from a "Leather Bottle", like Colin Clout in *Tuesday,* or saluting a maid's mother in the language of Gay's Hobnelia, "[I] doft my Hat".[235] There are threshers and gallant swains, industrious maidens[236] and girls with "ruddy Cheeks and Nut-brown Hair",[237] although there were similar creatures in older English literature as well. An admirer attacking a maiden's virtue, as in *Wednesday,* is the slightly varying subject matter of the popular *Northern Ditty,* beginning "Cold and Raw",[238] but the theme is, of course, not D'Urfey's invention. In a similar genre, but in a different mode of imitation, it occurs, for instance, in William Browne's *The Shepherd's Pipe.*[239] By means of the italicized quotations in *Friday*[240] and *Saturday,* the list of ballads and songs at the end of the latter Eclogue, and the tribute to D'Urfey in *Wednesday,*[241] Gay drew the reader's attention to his familiarity with low poetry. The learned part of the audience were perhaps expected to remember a line in *Eclogue VIII,* part of the model for the latter passage, "a te principium, tibi desinam". As a confession of indebtedness to low poets in general, it was literally true.

Relationship with Earlier English Poetry

It is not only for its subject matter, but also for its tone of mirth and gaiety that *The Shepherd's Week* is indebted to songs, in particular D'Urfey's. But its "spice of humour and light-heartedness", it has been said, also "carries back to Nicolas Breton and earlier Elizabethans."[242] For a number of the borrowings we can also look beyond D'Urfey, which to some extent diminishes the value attached to the evidence and the conclusions that have been drawn from similarities with contemporary songs.[243] Lobbin Clout's vow in *Monday* for instance,

Ah Blouzelind! I love thee more by half,
Than does their fawns, or cows the new-fall'n
    calf.

(ll. 15-16)seems to echo a passage in Fletcher's
The Faithful Shepherdess.

I love thee better than the careful ewe
The new-wean'd lamb, that is of her own
    hew.[244]

The importance to lovers of having a sweet breath in the days of neglected dental care was reflected in poetry before Gay's time. Thomas Overbury's milkmaid has a breath "like a new made Haye-cocke",[245] and Hero was thought to smell of flowers when "'twas the odour which her breath forth cast".[246] Again, Greene's Carmela in *Menaphon* "wiped her mouth with her white apron before kissing",[247] whereas with Blouzelinda the same gesture implies content with the lover's boldness. The "cocked haye" serves for a pastoral shady grove in Spenser's *November,*[248] but also and more appropriately in Gay's *Monday* with its early summer pictures of primroses, king-cups and daisies. Like Alexander Barclay, Gay could mix a georgic element into his Eclogues. But whereas Virgil's husbandman observes how the heifer "looks up to heaven" and "snuffs the breeze", Cloddipole can tell a shower by noticing the heifer's tail, just as, in Elizabethan times, Alcon could "save a penny in almanacks" because of his cow, whose "verie taile was a kalender". His little boy could foretell a storm, "if she had but set vp her tayle".[249]

Furthermore, English country sports, wrestling, pitching the bar and throwing "the weightie fledge", were traditional elements in English pastoral poetry from Barclay's and Ben Jonsons's time.[250] The haggard face of Marian, resembling "ashes, leather, oatmeal, bran and chalk", is described in a comically expanded echo from *The Knight's Tale,*[251] and when Gay compared the "wan complexion" of Clumsilis to "the withered leek", he again resorted to a good old English simile, used by Greene in *Doron's Eclogue* and by Sidney in *A Remedie for Love.*[252] Another favourite old tag is "blubber'd", about pouting lips and a face drenched with tears.[253] The description of Love as "some bloody butcher's son" harks back to Shakespeare more than to Theocritus or Virgil.[254] Glow-worms had raised the curiosity of people before the time of the "modern" pedants, a fact which was reflected in poems before *Saturday,*[255] and the "green gown" is a tag in ditties, not only D'Urfey's,[256] but it also belongs to poetry and plays by Robert Greene, Ben Jonson, Browne, Herrick.[257] The "hundredth psalm" among the ballads in *Saturday* alludes to the metaphor with which Mrs. Ford illustrates the incompatibility of Falstaff's "disposition" with "the truth of his words", "the Hundredth Psalm to the tune of Green Sleeves".[258]

The italicized phrases in *Friday*—*"Hang sorrow", "wash sorrow from thy soul", "cast away our care"*— are all quotations from drinking-songs,[259] literal or rendered with just that slight variation which shows that

Gay was familiar enough with the cheerful songs of tavern-hunters to quote from memory. But a hundred years earlier, a kindred spirit had availed himself of the same printer's device to emphasize his light-hearted mood. It is in fact not only this *carpe diem* echo that *A Christmas Carroll* has in common with *The Shepherd's Week.* George Wither's descriptions are as low and as rustic as Gay's, though of a different season, door-posts decorated with ivy and holly, meat roasting in ovens and turning on spits, lads playing on "a Bag-pipe and a Tabor", and

> Brisk *Nell* hath brought a Ruffe of Lawne,
> With droppings of the Barrell.

The characters in *The Shepherd's Week* may seem indebted to D'Urfey's lads and lasses, but they are also descendants of Overbury's happy milkmaid, of Tusser's ideal housewife,[260] of Lucy in *Friar Bacon and Friar Bungay.*

> Into the milk-house went I with the maid,
> And there amongst the cream-bowls did she
>   shine,
> As Pallas, 'mongst her princely housewif'ry:
> She turn'd her smock over her lily arms,
> And div'd them into milk to run her cheese.

It is the King who describes Lucy, whereas Blouzelinda's obituary is spoken by simple Bumkinet.

> If by the dairy's hatch I chance to hie,
> I shall her goodly countenance espie,
> For there her goodly countenance I've seen,
> Set off with kerchief starch'd and pinners
>   clean.
> Sometimes, like wax, she rolls the butter
>   round,
> Or with the wooden lilly prints the pound.
> Whilome I've seen her skim the clouted
>   cream,
> And press from spongy curds the milky
>   stream.
>
>   (ll. 55-62)

. . . . .

To sum up—as on previous occasions or in similar circumstances, Gay wrote "something [lower]" than other contemporary poets of some renown, here pastoralists of various kinds. *The Shepherd's Week* was certainly suggested by the *Guardian* papers and is related to them in a way similar to that in which there is a relationship between Addison's "Essay on the Georgics" and other poems by Gay. But the Eclogues need not therefore be interpreted as directly ridiculing either poets, poetry or poetical characters. As in so many other cases, they reveal Gay's taste for experimenting, for writing something different, something non-conventional, and at the same time, they disclose his attitude towards altercations among literary critics, too serious perhaps in the opinion of Gay, who knew that rules do not make a poet.

Gay demonstrated his position both where the pastoral genre, the notion of the Golden Age and the veneration for ballads were concerned. In respect of the ballad, the poet neither condemned nor unduly venerated it, whether popular or traditional. As a merry young man, flute-player and partaker in country-dancing, he could don the ballad-singer's leathern jacket as naturally as Dr. Corbett. As he showed, not only in *The Shepherd's Week,* respectable and "artful" poetry could profit from the realistic and colourful picturesqueness of the vernacular genre. The tenets of both "neoclassic" and "rationalistic" serious criticism of pastoral poetry are treated irreverently and with naive common sense by the unlearned rustic bard, Gay's *alter ego.* Some fun is directed against the "rationalistic" as well as "neoclassic" notion of the ease and tranquillity of shepherds, some also against exaggerated "modern" pedantry and the supposedly vulgar preoccupation with the details of natural science. As against both the "ancient" concept of a Golden Age and the "modern" notion of a Golden future, Gay facetiously set his simple eulogy of Queen Anne's Golden Age.

The "modernity" of the subject matter is obvious in the emphasis on industry, low from an "ancient" point of view, in the philosophical passages with borrowings from the productions of the English "Moderns"[261] and in the substitution of a partly purposeful selection of ballad fictions for "ancient" stories in the passage imitating the *Silenus.* But the most important feature is the glossary. Like Spenser's obsolete words in Glosses, Gay's words for *"material things"* are collected in a Catalogue and their use emphasized as a novelty, indeed a change from the "purling streams" and the "shady groves". Here Gay is certainly serious. The taste for concrete and pictorial rustic subject matter must have been on the increase, witness not only Philips's and Evans's *Pastorals,* but also a poem called *The Smock-Race at Finglass* in Steele's Miscellany and rural songs and ballads printed in the later editions of the Dryden Miscellanies.

Some of Gay's subject matter à la Theocritus and Mantuan was certainly the result of direct observation. Sometimes it seems to have been inspired by or borrowed from, and was in any case related to that of ballads and other low productions as well as older English, and, from a neo-classical point of view, not very respectable poetry. It was not the first time that Gay profited from or manifested his relationship with low verse and prose. The reason why his indebtedness sometimes seems to lie both with the latter and with older English poetry, is perhaps that the broadside quality of poetry must have been the link that kept the

16th and 17th century tradition of song and pastoral poetry alive during a period when conventional imitation of classical poems was practised by poets and poetasters.

The low subject matter of varying origin is formed into learned and "artful" Eclogues, imitating and echoing Virgil, Theocritus, Ovid. As might be expected, it is in particular the sublime and melancholy passages in the models that are brought down to earth and common sense by way of parodical realistic Answers. As the poems represent the "image of the times", Queen Anne's Golden Age, they may be characterized as "Comi-Pastoral" Eclogues, as usual a mixed Kind. In this mock-genre, the use of abundant comic detail is correctly justified. But the "true spirit of pastoral poetry" is due above all to Gay's dairy-maids, who are raised to fulfil the requirements for pastoral characters.[262] Like the happy angler in **Rural Sports,** they are typically English and admirably suited in poems that celebrated the period of peace after the wars with France.

Gay was of the same school of "Art" as Pope and undoubtedly admired the latter's poems. But he never wrote anything that resembled his friend's *Pastorals.* Like most young gentlemen of the period, he did write pastoral songs, but they all contain realistic details.[263] The difference between Philips's *Pastorals* and **The Shepherd's Week** is, the mode of imitation apart, the extreme "artfulness" of the latter poem with its close imitation and its wealth of echoes and borrowings. Gay did not anglicize a Kind in the sense intended by Addison and the *Guardian* critic of pastoral poetry. He mixed Kinds, Comedy and pastoral Eclogue, relied on precedents in English poetry and borrowed from classical poetry and low verse.

Gay was probably amused at the pretensions of Philips and his friends in alluding to the *Pastorals* as a prelude to Epic, poems which were copies rather than imitations or, conversely, pretended to originality, in reality the "country-scraper['s]" simplicity. **The Shepherd's Week** serves the same purpose as Pope's *Guardian,* No. 40. But as in the case of the essay on genius, the touch of ridicule is light, and we are at the same time led to enjoy the poet's low things. By referring to Milton and quoting one of the epic poet's colourful similes, Gay seems to have disclaimed promises about the future similar to Philips's and Pope's and declared in the spirit of Horace that his genius was "of a lower order", capable of description and not fit for epic invention. Yet in contrast to Philips and even more than Pope, Gay consistently followed his own genius and in the *Fables* really achieved "something greater", something of a character that may be said to have been foreshadowed in his Eclogues. The old shepherd in the introductory Fable who draws his wisdom from nature, the life of plants and animals, seems to have been

anticipated in the character of cheerful Bowzybeus, Gay's *alter ego* in **The Shepherd's Week.**

> That *Bowzybeus* who could sweetly sing,
> Or with the rozin'd bow torment the string;
> That *Bowzybeus* who with finger's speed
> Could call soft warblings from the breathing
>   reed;
> That *Bowzybeus* who with jocund tongue,
> Ballads and roundelays and catches sung.[264]

. . . . .

The same tendencies as in the early works are manifested in Gay's complimentary poems, both in **An Epistle to a Lady,** like **Rural Sports** a counterblast to panegyric on a public event, and in other Epistles of a more private character.[265] The familiarity and the "Art" of the former poem are in efficient contrast to the lofty genres and the supposedly inspired products published on the same occasion, this time the arrival in England of the new royal family from Hanover. The hollowness of the eulogy was the more conspicuous since to the British in general the event was at once more negligible and less welcome than the Peace Treaty in the preceding year. To Gay personally, it meant the end of his diplomatic mission and of his success at court. The Whigs were back in power. Even more than before, then, the poet had reason to protest against poetic loftiness and inspiration.

All the Epistles are of the Horatian variety, but constructed after different models, such as the Ovidian contention between a high and a low Kind—directly or by way of Cotton's imitation—travel accounts, a river trip after Ariosto, even "punctual History". In neither of them is there anything of the "sort of inspiration" which Mr. Spectator could find characteristic of an Epistle by a Whig poet or which an earlier Whig warbler had demurely, but deliberately aimed at in an epistolary eulogy of Marlborough. Instead there is plenty of "Art" and learning. In **An Epistle to a Lady,** Gay even demonstrated directly the threadbareness of what was supposed to be inspired panegyric, but was in reality outworn convention. The charming informal welcome addressed to a friend in the poem to Pope was intended to set off the supposedly enthusiastic, but in fact coldly ceremonial celebrations of the arrival of Kings and plenipotentiaries. Its background matter, part of which had been relegated to low taste by one of the representatives of the "high seriousness", must have been designed as a contrasting effect. Other Epistles are travellers' accounts of insignificant things observed—a lady's jewels and her cosmetic art, a female barber's gewgaws and "*Honiton's*" "finest lace",[266] commonplace scissors and elbow-chairs, "stony lanes" and "shrubby heaths"—all of which counterbalance reports of more dignified sights. The subject matter is sometimes low enough to carry the reader's thought to simple songs and prose tales, periodicals and travel books. Borrowings are often obvious or the source even indicated. Now and then the relationship with older English prose or poetry is apparent. In particular the longer Epistles display characteristics which in some form or other are to be found in the rest of Gay's poetry.

Notes

¹ *Tatler,* No. 9, April 30, 1709.

² *The Beauties of English Poesy,* ed. Oliver Goldsmith, 2 vols., London, 1767, I, 133. Reference in Congleton, op. cit., p. 146.

³ *Lives,* II, 282.

⁴ Prose passage prefixed to *English Eclogues,* in *Poetical Works,* 10 vols., London, 1837-38, III, 2.

⁵ Congleton, op. cit., p. 136.

⁶ In his article on Gay in the *DNB.*

⁷ R. T. Kerlin, *Theocritus in English Literature,* Lynchburg, Virg., 1910, p. 57.

⁸ *Pastoral Influence in the English Drama,* Philadelphia, 1898, p. 456.

⁹ Letter to Caryll, June 8, 1714, Pope, *Correspondence,* I, 229. Quoted, for instance, by Sherburn, *Alexander Pope,* p. 121.

¹⁰ Pope, *Works,* ed. Elwin and Courthope, 10 vols., London, 1871-89, I, 234.

¹¹ *Alexander Pope,* pp. 114 ff.—Cf. H. G. de Maar, *A History of Modern English Romanticism,* Oxford, 1924, pp. 105-6; C. Kerby-Miller, editor of *The Memoirs of . . . Martinus Scriblerus,* New Haven, 1950, p. 221; Edna L. Steeves in her edition of *The Art of Sinking in Poetry,* New York, 1952, p. xv; Smithers, op. cit., p. 325, to mention a few examples.

¹² Op. cit., in Spenser, *Works,* ed. Grosart, III, xliii.

¹³ Elizabeth Nitchie, *Vergil and the English Poets,* New York, 1919, p. 173.

¹⁴ R. F. Jones, "Eclogue Types in English Poetry", *JEGP,* XXIV, 1925, p. 49.

¹⁵ Op. cit., pp. 110-12.

¹⁶ Diaper, *Complete Works,* pp. xxxviii-xxxix.

¹⁷ R. A. Brower, *Alexander Pope, The Poetry of Allu-sion,* Oxford, 1959, p. 24.

¹⁸ *John Gay,* pp. 82-83.

¹⁹ Armens, op. cit., p. 161.

²⁰ H. Trowbridge, "Pope, Gay, and *The Shepherd's Week*", *MLQ,* V, 1944, pp. 81 ff.

²¹ Steele inserted praise of *The Fan* in *The Englishman* in December, 1713, when we know that Gay was writing his Eclogues.—Letter from Pope to Swift, December 8, 1713, Pope, *Correspondence,* I, 200. Quoted by Irving, *John Gay,* p. 82.—In the same month, Steele published four poems by Gay in his *Poetical Miscellanies*—Imprint 1714, but published on Dec. 29, 1713, according to R. Blanchard, *The Occasional Verse of Richard Steele,* Oxford, 1952, p. xviii.—*The Shepherd's Week* was advertised in several issues of *The Lover.* Moreover, Gay's publisher was this time not Lintott, but Ferdinand Burleigh, who also published *The Englishman* and *The Lover,* a fact which may diminish the evidence of the advertisements, but which, on the other hand, may indicate that Steele helped Gay to find a publisher.—R. Blanchard, ed., *Richard Steele's Periodical Journalism,* Oxford, 1959, p. 271.

²² Letter from Gay to Addison [1716?], Addison, *Letters,* pp. 449-500.

²³ Gildon's attack on Gay concerns the triviality of the subject matter of *The Fan.* The Dedication of *The Mohocks* was intended not only to support Pope, but also to express Gay's own opinion about Dennis's preoccupation with the Sublime and the high Kinds. *The What D'Ye Call It* does not only ridicule Philips's and Addison's Tragedies, but rather the solemnity of Tragedy in general.—Cf. the contemporary *Complete Key to the Last New Farce The What D'Ye Call It,* London, 1715, and Irving, *John Gay,* pp. 112-14.—The play, a Kind mixed beyond identification, has a social aim . . . with low characters *"copied"* after nature in contrast to the noble characters of Tragedy imitated after Nature. For the Preface, see pp. 47 and 187 ff.

²⁴ Gay described English flowers not only in *The Shepherd's Week,* but also and earlier in *Panthea,* a fact which takes away the point from the suggestion that these sort of descriptions parody similar elements in Philips's poems. Names like Lightfoot do not seem to have been very unusual in poetry of this kind. Abel Evans has Whitefoot in No. VIII of his *Pastorals.*—*A Select Collection of Poems,* ed. J. Nichols, 8 vols., London, 1780-84, V, 98. The poems are dated 1707, 1709, 1710, 1719 and 1726. Reference in Jones, "Eclogue Types in English Poetry", p. 50.—The so-called "inane exclamations" in *Thursday* (ll. 5-6) may parody lines in Philips's *Pastorals,* but the common source may also be the Theocritean complaint, for in-

stance, in Creech's translation, of which there was an edition in 1713.

> Ah me! unhappy me! what pains I bear?
> Ah me! undone! yet you refuse to hear.

The Idylliums of Theocritus, p. 23.—Finally the "pseudo-simplicity" passage in *Monday* (ll. 103-10), which is supposed to support Pope's ridicule of similar lines in his rival's *Sixth Pastoral,* was added as late as 1720. By then the original controversy must have fallen into oblivion, but not the general principles which the poems of the two antagonists represented.—Both Philips's and Gay's passages, showing transgressions in the innocence of the characters and actually paralleling the Aristotelian tragic "flaw", again have a common source, a convention which probably originated in the bathing scene in Tasso's *Aminta* (III, i). Fontenelle's use of it in his *Eclogue VIII* had been criticized by Chetwood for offending against the French critic's own second rule that characters should be innocent.—"A Preface to the Pastorals", in Dryden, *Works,* XIII, 335.—It was thus enough in the limelight to be imitated by Philips, commended in the latter's version by *The Guardian,* No. 23, and later added by Gay.

[25] Cf. for instance, also W. H. Williams in the Introduction to Gay's *Trivia,* London, 1922, p. xiv, where Philips's poems are said to belong to the "conventional" type, the "artificiality" of which Gay "intended to ridicule", and Diaper's editor, who calls Pope and Philips "adherents to the formal pastoral eclogue".—*Complete Works,* p. xxviii.

[26] Congleton, op. cit., pp. 75 ff., in particular.

[27] *A Treatise de Carmine Pastorali.* See Congleton, op. cit., pp. 53 ff.

[28] Quotations from Fontenelle, *Of Pastorals,* pp. 282, 284 and 279. See Congleton, op. cit., pp. 65 ff.

[29] Cf. Congleton, op. cit., pp. 70-71, and Introduction to Pope, *Pastorals,* in *Poems,* I, 16.

[30] Apart from the general idealization, cf. Rapin's classification of pastoral poetry, as *"Epicks of an inferior rank".—A Treatise de Carmine Pastorali,* p. 18.—Cf. also his *Reflections,* p. 71.

[31] Nos. 22, 23, 28, 30, 32.—Congleton, op. cit., pp. 87 ff.—They are ascribed to Tickell by J. E. Butt, "Notes for a Bibliography of Thomas Tickell", *Bodleian Quarterly Record,* V, 1928, p. 302. Quoted by Sherburn, *Alexander Pope,* p. 118 n. 4, and Congleton, op. cit., p. 324 n. 46.—Cf. however, Trapp, *Lectures on Poetry,* p. 178; R. E. Tickell, *Thomas Tickell,* pp. 26-27; and Ellis, op. cit., p. 209 n. 39.—Cf. below p. 113 n. 3.

[32] No. 22, the third paragraph, and No. 32, the second paragraph.

[33] This seems very much in the spirit of Steele.

[34] Cf. p. 62 supra.

[35] Cf. *Spectator,* No. 523, by Addison, warning poets not to celebrate the peace treaty with ancient fictions.

[36] Congleton, op. cit. pp. 200 and 180.

[37] Ellis, op. cit., pp. 203 ff.

[38] Loc. cit.; Cf. also Day, *The Songs of Thomas D'Urfey,* pp. 29 ff., and the same writer's Introduction to *Wit and Mirth: or, Pills to Purge Melancholy.*

[39] Op. cit., p. 212.

[40] *OHEL,* VII, 141.

[41] Cf. below p. 206.

[42] Cf. below pp. 180-81, 194 ff.

[43] *A Satyr on the Modern Translators* (1685), in *Literary Works,* I, 19-24. Reference in the Introduction to *Eloisa to Abelard,* in Pope, *Poems,* II, 275 n. 2.

[44] *The Works of Mr. Robert Gould,* 2 vols., London, 1709, I, 156.

[45] *Lectures on Poetry,* pp. 179-80. Quoted by Congleton, op. cit., p. 111.

[46] Marion K. Bragg, *The Formal Eclogue in Eighteenth Century England* (University of Maine Studies, Second Series, No. 6), Orono, 1926, p. 57.

[47] The popular taste for pastoral song was shared by Steele, although the admixture of light raillery was really what appealed to him, as in his praise of Lady Winchilsea's *Pastoral Dialogue,* published in "a collection of the best pastorals that [had] hitherto appeared in England", Philips's and Pope's included. (This seems to speak against Steele's authorship of the *Guardian* essays, at least the one praising Philips).—*Tatler,* No. 10. Quoted by R. Blanchard, ed., *The Occasional Verse of Richard Steele,* p. xvi.—Pope's *January and May* was also in this volume VI of *Poetical Miscellanies,* London, 1709. The reference to it in *The Guardian,* No. 30, need therefore perhaps not necessarily have been intended to insult Pope, as is thought by D. A. Fineman, "The Motivation of Pope's *Guardian* 40", *MLN,* LXVII, 1952, pp. 24 ff.—Probably after the footnote to No. 10 in Chalmers's edition of *The Tatler,* Dr. Ellis in op. cit., p. 208, ascribes the *Pastoral Dialogue* to Mrs. Singer. But in vol. VI of *Poetical*

Miscellanies, p. 225, the poem is said to be "By the Author of the Poem on the Spleen". Elizabeth Singer's *Pastoral* appeared in vol. V of the same Miscellany, 1704, pp. 378 ff., and is a mixed version of *Idyll VIII, Ecl. III* and Fontenelle's *Ecl. VIII*, plus, it seems, Mrs. Singer-Rowe's own additions.

[48] [Ned Ward,] "Of the Beaus Club", *The Secret History of Clubs*, London, 1709, p. 143.

[49] John Tipper, the almanac-maker, according to W. Graham, *English Literary Periodicals*, New York, 1930, p. 146.—On the copy in the Bodl. Lib., Hope Adds 1190, is added in ink "Thos Walden".

[50] *Roxb. Ballads*, V, 127; *Bagf. Ballads*, II, 496.

[51] Cf. Gay's letter quoted below p. 194 n. 3; a letter to Mrs. Howard in *Suffolk Letters*, I, 12; and *Spectator*, No. 37, for instance.

[52] It is typical that it was Rowe who in this respect criticized Ozell in his prefatory "Account of Boileau's Writings, and this Translation" prefixed to *Boileau's Lutrin*.

[53] Op. cit., p. 207.

[54] Prior, *A Satyr on the Modern Translators*. Quoted by Ellis, op. cit., p. 203. For Steele, see p. 204. Cf. also p. 212.

[54] *The Craftsman*, No. 146, April 19, 1729. Cf. also *The Guardian*, No. 67.

[56] Cf. supra pp. 24-25.

[57] Pointed out by Congleton, op. cit., p. 86.

[58] In *The Second Pastoral*, in *Poems*, p. 15.

[59] Cf. also *Poems*, p. xxii.

[60] Dennis, *A True Character of Mr. Pope, and His Writings* (1716), in *Critical Works*, II, 104.

[61] See Sherburn, *Alexander Pope*, p. 118.

[62] Cf. supra pp. 50-51.

[63] *Ars Poetica*, ll. 38-39.

[64] Parnell refuses to accept Dennis's Tragedies and "Philips' rustic strain" among the venerable books, Homer, Virgil, Tasso, with which he builds his "sacred alter".—Mentioned by Sherburn, *Alexander Pope*, p. 121, and both poems by Ellis, op. cit., pp. 206-7, though not with quite the same purpose as here.

[65] Cf. supra pp. 36-38.

[66] The ballad-singer in *Saturday*.

[67] *The Suffolk Papers*, II, 59, Brit. Mus. Add. MSS 22626.

[68] Roger is generally a lusty ballad character, as for instance, in D'Urfey's *Roger's Delight* (1687-88), *Roger's Renown*, both in *Roxb. Ballads*, VII, 210 ff. and 236 ff., and *Roger Twangdillo*, in *Wit and Mirth*, II, 1707, 1712, pp. 225 ff.—Ralph seems to be less cheerful. Cf. *The Winchester Wedding*, in *Roxb. Ballads*, VII, 208. According to Chappell, op. cit., II, 495. this ballad appeared in D'Urfey's *Several New Songs*, 1648. It is also in *The Dancing Master* of 1686 and in *Wit and Mirth*, I, 1707, p. 22.—Cf. *The Ballad of Tom and Will* in *Miscellany Poems*, III, 1706, pp. 250 ff. about two similar characters.

[69] This may have been the circle of acquaintances that Martha Blount wished Mrs. Howard would persuade Gay to leave, because they "so ill deserve[d] his compay".—*The Suffolk Papers*, I, 9 v (not published).

[70] E. R. Wasserman, *Elizabethan Poetry in the Eighteenth Century* (Illinois Studies in Language and Literature, No. 32), Urbana, 1947, p. 144.

[71] Loc. cit.

[72] *The Bagford Collection for the History of Printing*, Nos. 243 and 231.

[73] Cf. Will. King, "The Publisher to the Reader" prefixed to *The Art of Cookery* (1708), for instance, or his Preface to *Joan of Headington, Useful Miscellanies* (1712), in *Original Works*, III, 41 ff. and 3 ff.—The latter Preface is mentioned by Professor Sutherland in his Introduction to *The Dunciad*, in Pope, *Poems*, V, xl.

[74] C. J. Rawson, "Some Unpublished Letters of Pope and Gay, and Some Manuscript Sources of Goldsmith's *Life of Thomas Parnell*", RES, New Series, X, 1959, pp. 380 ff.

[75] St. John, to whom the poems were dedicated, obviously approved of Gay's "sonnets" or "madrigals" and suggested that they should be printed

> With preface meet and notes profound
>
> 　　　　　　　　　　　　　(1.83)

It seems that in the Prologue, Gay related things as they had happened. Queen Anne, for instance, was in reality dangerously ill about Christmas 1713, and the Court ladies are mentioned by name. It is not unlikely that Arbuthnot and Bolingbroke had something to do with the swain's "hying" to court.

[76] Ll. 87-88; Fontenelle, *Of Pastorals,* p. 278.

[77] *The Idylliums of Theocritus,* p. 6.

[78] Cf. supra p. 118.

[79] Cf. Trapp, *Lectures on Poetry,* p. 186, and later Aikin, who disapproved of the "mixed pastoral". Congleton, op. cit., p. 136.

[80] "Dedication of the Pastorals", in *Works,* XIII, 323.

[81] *P. L.,* IX, 445-51. *Monday,* 1.71, "in a gamesone mood" echoes *P. L.,* VI, 620.

[82] For Swift on the "neoclassic" side, see Congleton, op. cit., p. 84.—Swift, however, repeatedly demonstrated his aversion to conventions, as in *Apollo's Edict* (unless this poem only refers to Tickell), the *Town Eclogue,* the "unprintable" poems. He did not write either much imitative poetry or conventional pastoral poems. As for the hint to Gay to write Quaker and Newgate Pastorals (Congleton, loc. cit.), that was certainly suggested by Fontenelle's *Of Pastorals.*

[83] Although not yet published, Pope's "Discourse" was written at an early date (Pope, *Poems,* I, 13), and Gay may have seen it. Besides, the discussion about pastoral poetry was certainly not only carried on in writing.

[84] *Guardian,* No. 40 (names), Nos. 40 and perhaps 30, and Pope's "Discourse", for various aspects of pastoral decorum.

[85] Theocritus's Doric was accepted by all critics. Spenser's dialect was approved of by the "rationalistic" but not the "neoclassic" school.

[86] Fable X, vi.

[87] Ll. 56 and 136. Cf. Pope's later commentary to *Summer,* in *Poems,* I, 78.

[88] Ll. 151—53.

[89] *Timber, or Discoveries,* in *Ben Jonson,* VIII, 618.—There is also in this passage of Gay's an echo from "modern" Fontenelle's *Dialogues of the Dead.* In the Dedication, Fontenelle addresses Lucian and maintains that he works with his own materials on Lucian's "Ground-plat" or "Plan".—*New Dialogues of the Dead,* trans. J. D[ryden], London, 1683, A2, and *Fontenelle's Dialogues of the Dead,* trans. J. H[ughes], p. xlvi— Gay, of course, says that he works with old material.

[90] Cf. Jones, *The Triumph of the English Language,* pp. 117 and 211.

[91] Cf. below pp. 131 ff., 142-43.

[92] The notions of the Golden Age and "Arcadie" were much in the limelight not only through the *Guardian* essays, Nos. 22, 32 and 40, but also through a Rapin-inspired article in *The Rhapsody,* No. 6, Jan. 15, 1712, and the French critic's own *Discourse,* which was prefixed to Curll's much advertised new edition of Theocritus's *Idylls,* published in February, 1713.

[93] *Spectator,* No. 523, about peace poems.

[94] Addison acquired "a very great distaste of the Golden Age" through his experiences of rustic lodgings during his Grand Tour.—*Letters,* p. 36.

[95] *A Reflection on Our Modern Poesy.*—Savages are said to have left their caves in order to seek "fitter *Dwellings*".—Cf. supra p. 39 n. 3.

[96] *Poetical Works,* pp. 184, 328, 368.

[97] J. B. Bury, *The Idea of Progress,* London, 1924, pp. 218-19.

[98] See Jones, *Ancients and Moderns,* in particular pp. 191 ff.

[99] For June, 1707, pp. 127 ff.

[100] *Advice to an Author* (1710), in *Characteristics,* I, 141-42, 145.

[101] Nos. 30 and 32. Cf. supra pp. 111-12.

[102] Cf. also *The Third Pastoral,* a funeral Elegy on the death of the young Duke of Gloucester and directed to the Queen.—According to the Bodl. Lib. catalogue, *The Pastorals* were published in four different editions in 1710, the year of crisis for the Whigs, perhaps as yet another reminder of the peacefulness of the British Isles in spite of the Whig war.

[103] The theme of pressing is met with in several ballads, some dating from the wars of William of Orange, such as *The Young Women and Maidens' Lamentation,* in *Roxb. Ballads,* VII, 117, others published in *Wit and Mirth,* for instance, IV, 1709, 1712, pp. 102, 117, 134.—In *The What D'Ye Call It,* Gay made use of the same theme.

[104] The white staff of the Lord Treasurer.

[105] The Queen is praised as the "Compassionate and tender Mother", who by the Peace has "establish'd her own Glory and the Welfare of her People".

[106] Bolingbroke, *Fragments, or Minutes of Essays,* in *Works,* VIII, 165. Bolingbroke refers to "our friend Gay's Fly, in his Fables" as an example of "the principle of continuity".

[107] *Works,* IV, 162.

[108] Myra Reynolds, *The Treatment of Nature in Poetry from Pope to Wordsworth,* Chicago, 1896, p. 6.

[109] Bolingbroke, *Letters, or Essays, Addressed to Alexander Pope, Esq.,* in *Works,* V, 83.

[110] *Guardian,* No. 22.

[111] Quotation from Rapin, *A Tratise de Carmine Pastorali,* p. 28.

[112] *Of Pastorals,* p. 282.

[113] *The Art of Sinking in Poetry,* p. 62.

[114] Ll. 7-12.

[115] Letter to Pope, April 1, 1717, Pope, *Correspondence,* I, 398. Quoted by Kerlin, op. cit., p. 61.

[116] Bentley's *Q. Horatius Flaccus Ex Recensione & cum Notis atque Emendationibus,* Cambridge 1711, 310 pages of text and 410 pages of notes and index, was ridiculed in "Notes upon Notes" in *The Odes, Epodes, and Carmen Seculare of Horace, in Latin and English; with a Translation of Dr Ben-ley's Notes,* London, 1712-13.—Mohocks are mentioned in Part V, for instance.

[117] Supposedly imitating Theocritus's Doric. Cf. p. 143, n. 1, below.

[118] For instance, Edw. Phillips, *The New World of Words,* 6th ed. J[ohn] K[ersey], London, 1706.

[119] Preface to J. Kersey, *Dictionarium Anglo-Britannicum,* London, 1708.

[120] Jones, "Eclogue Types in English Poetry", p. 49 n. 23; Bragg, p. cit., p. 56.

[121] Cf. below pp. 148-52.

[122] As Gay did not indicate the sources otherwise than as "Virgil" and "Theocritus", the numbers and lines are supplied here, together with some more echoes, in particular a group from the *Idylls,*

Monday, 23 ff. 83-94, 117-18, 120

Wednesday, 5-8, 9-18, 18, 25, 37, 59-62, 67-72

Thursday, 64, 127, 66, 93, 109, 123, 131

Friday, 15, 84, 90, 93, 153

Saturday, 22, 40, 43, 47, 51 ff., 97, 112, 117

Monday, 49-56, 59-70, 72

Geo., I, 375 ff.

Ecl., VII, 61-64; *III,* 106-7, 109

Ecl., VIII, 2-4, 6-7, 12-13, 16, 26, 27, 28

Id., II, 23-24, 58

Ecl., VIII, 83, 102, 77-78, 95-96, 107

Ecl., V, 10-11, 38-39, 42, 45-47 and 50-51, 76-78

Ecl., VI, 16, 22, 25-26, 29-30, 31 ff., 45-46, 74

Id., XI, 20; *XII,* 3-8; *VIII,* 41-48, 72-73

Tuesday, 41-44, 15-18, 73-78

Wednesday, 49-50

Thursday, 127-28

Saturday, 7-12

Id., II, 88-89; *X,* 1-6; *III,* 31-33

Id., VI, 34-38

Id., II, 48-49

Id., X, 51

[123] Will. King, *Dialogues of the Dead,* IX, in *Original Works,* I, 171.—Cf. p. 32 supra.

[124] Kerby-Miller, op. cit., p. 111.

[125] Cf. supra pp. 109—10 n. 5.

[126] *An Essay Concerning the Nature of Aliments and the Choice of Them According to the Different Constitutions of Human Bodies,* London, 1731, pp. 71-72.

[127] Ibid., p. 53. Cf. also Kerby-Miller, op. cit., pp. 106 and 210—11.

[128] This Opera, called by Gay in his footnote the *World in the Sun,* was probably a source of inspiration for *The Beggar's Opera.* In the "World of the Sun", a courtier is considered low, but a "Cut-purse" is an ingenious person, who is entitled to a pension when

attacked by palsy in his hands. The mildest person, not a tyrant as on the earth, is chosen King in the "Kingdom of Birds".

[129] *The Transactioneer,* II, in *Original Works,* II, 37.

[130] Kerby-Miller, op. cit., p. 106.

[131] *God Speed the Plough* (c. 1665), in *Roxb. Ballads,* VI, 521.

[132] *Ecl. VII,* ll. 84—90, in *Poems,* II, 900-01.

[133] Cf. Ellis, op. cit., pp. 209 and 210, where Gay's echo of the ballad in *The Guardian,* No. 40, is pointed out, but not its "modernity". That Steele with his low taste was led to accept Pope's praise of it as genuine, is perhaps less surprising if we remember that by the time of the fourth edition of *Miscellany Poems* (1716), verse like *The West-Country Bachelor's Complaint,* not unlike the "ancient ballad" that Pope quoted as a ludicrous example, had become respectable enough to be published in that anthology. For other ballads in the same Miscellany, see Friedman, op. cit., p. 130.

[134] Preface to Bentley, *A Dissertation upon the Epistles of Phalaris,* London, 1699.—Cf. also King, *Dialogues of the Dead,* I, and *The Transactioneer,* I, in *Original Works,* I, 147, and II, 41-42.

[135] *Of Pastorals,* p. 293.

[136] Rapin in fact also considered proverbs "fit for a *Shepherd*'s mouth"—*A Treatise de Carmine Pastorali,* pp. 67-68.

[137] For Sir William Temple in this respect, see Hustvedt, op. cit., p. 48.—An extract from *Hervarer Saga* was published in its original form and with an English translation in vol. VI of *Miscellany Poems,* 1716, pp. 387 ff.—William King quoted from the Swedish scholar Scheferus, from whom the interest in Lapland songs must have spread.—*Remains of . . . William King,* p. 51.—*Lapponia* was published in Latin in 1673 and in English in 1674.—Curiously enough, the volume about Sweden and Lapland, among other countries, by the Frenchman De la Mottraye was illustrated with engravings by Hogarth, the realist, who hardly left London. But perhaps no more surprising than that William Kent illustrated *The Faerie Queene.*—A. de la Mottraye, *Voyages and Travels,* 3 vols., London, 1723, II, No. XXXVIII. Cf. Antal, op. cit., p. 85.

[138] Kerby-Miller, op. cit., pp. 109 ff., and for King, pp. 221-22.—Gay's lines on hot-cockles in *Monday* are quoted p. 226 without further comment.

[139] Ibid, pp. 221-22. It is No. V of *Useful Transactions,* in *Original Works,* II, 83. For the Playford letters as one of the sources for Ch. V of the *Memoirs* and for the theory of authorship, see Kerby-Miller, op. cit., p. 222.

[140] The reference is to Kennet's *Parochial Antiquities,* London, 1695, pp. 610 and 614.

[141] Guarini, *Il Pastor Fido,* II, v, 2.

[142] 2nd 3d., London, 1691, p. 143.

[143] There may be an allusion to Walpole from Norfolk, who had been impeached in 1712 and had many a ballad written on him, even supposed, like *Lilliburlero* James II, to have sung him out of office.—Preface to *A Pill to Purge State-Melancholy.*—A dumpling is thrown against the monster of war in *Yarhell's Kitchen,* London, 1713, and seems in the satire of the period to be an emblem of the English. Cf. also *A Learned Dissertation on Dumpling,* London, 1726. For the authorship, see G. A. Aitken, *The Life and Works of John Arbuthnot,* Oxford, 1892, p. 111. In the *CBEL* the pamphlet is ascribed to Henry Carey.

[144] "Cowell's Interpreter", which is the source indicated, is *A Law Dictionary: or, the Interpreter of Words and Terms Used either in the Common or Statute Laws,* etc. First Published by the Learned Dr. Cowel . . . , London, 1708.—Gay probably found it in his friend William Fortescue's chambers.

[145] *Original Works,* I, 200.

[146] Ibid., I, 187.

[147] The English "modernness" of the charming "nosegays" in the comparisons in *Monday* was probably also suggested by King's *Dialogues of the Dead* and *A Journey to London,* where English rosemary is held up against gaudy French tulips, carnations and jonquils.—*Original Works,* I, 172 and 203.—"Sprigg'd rosemary" could be naturally introduced by Gay into his funeral Elegy, "rosemary . . . for remembrance". For Gay's awareness of the gradation of flowers, cf. his treatment of the poetical rose in Fable I, xlv.

[148] Cf. below pp. 143 ff.

[149] *Of Pastorals,* pp. 286-87.

[150] "Preface to the Pastorals", in Dryden, *Works,* XIII, 334.

[151] *The Philosophical Transactions,* London and Oxford, 1665 et seq., XXVI, 123.

[152] No. III, in *Original Works,* II, 114-15, but with the wrong number.

[153] Letter, No. 167 (1685), XV, 841 ff.

[154] *The Transactioneer,* II, in *Original Works,* II, 42.—King's reference is to No. 240 (1698), XX, 167 ff., a report from New England about glowworms and other insects and birds.

[155] This is also in the spirit of King, whose Gentleman answered the Virtuoso's zeal for Jamaica pepper by saying that every "kitchen-girl about the town" was familiar with that spice.—*The Transactioneer,* I, in *Original Works,* II, 10.—The reference is to No. 192 of *The Philosophical Transactions.*

[156] J. R. Moore, "Gay's Burlesque of Sir Richard Blackmore's Poetry", *JEGP,* L, 1951, pp. 83-89.

[157] *Poems,* II, 895 ff.

[158] *Complete Works,* pp. 34-36, 304-5.

[159] L. 50.

[160] Lucretius, II, 67 ff. Cf. Pope's *Essay on Man,* III, 15 n., in *Poems,* III, i, 93. Cf. also Arbuthnot, *An Essay Concerning . . . Aliments,* p. 23, "All Animals are made, immediately or mediately of Vegetables, that is by feeding on Vegetables, or in Animals that are fed on Vegetables, there being no Process in *infinitum.*"—Cf. also Bolingbroke, *Works,* VIII, 231.

[161] King provided the model for "modern" subject matter. His *Journey to London* has an Index similar to Gay's Catalogue.—The Catalogue is called a "mark of Scriblerus" by C. F. Burgess, who does, however, not indicate its real character.—'Scriblerian Influence in "The Shepherd's Week" ', *N&Q,* CCVIII, 1963, p. 218.

[162] Emma F. Pope, "Renaissance Criticism and the Diction of *The Faerie Queene*", *PMLA,* XLI, 1926, pp. 575 ff., in particular, p. 588.

[163] Kerby-Miller, op. cit., p. 119.

[164] In *Oxford and Cambridge Miscellany Poems* (1708), according to Miss Segar in her Introduction to *The Poems of Ambrose Philips,* p. xix.

[165] Cf. Philips's use of the verb "endite" in *The Second Pastoral.*

[166] Cf. supra pp. 25 and 39-40. *Chevy Chase* had already been printed in *Miscellany Poems,* 1702, according to Hustvedt, op. cit., p. 60.

[167] Bagford and Wanley, for instance. See supra p. 65.

[168] For the importance of *The Works of the Learned* for the Scriblerians, see Kerby-Miller, op. cit., pp. 14-15.

[169] W. Wagstaffe, *A Comment upon the History of Tom Thumb,* London, 1711.—Mentioned in Hustvedt, op. cit., p. 73.—"Woodwardius" is, of course, the supposed model for Dr. Fossile in the Jonsonian Comedy, *Three Hours after Marriage,* by Gay mainly, Pope and Arbuthnot, ed. R. Morton and W. M. Peterson (Lake Erie College Studies, No. 1), Painsville, 1961, and ed. J. Harrington Smith (Augustan Reprint Society Publications, No. 91-92), Los Angeles, 1961.

[170] Cf. supra p. 133.

[171] *Of Pastorals,* pp. 286-87.

[172] One of them, *The Children in the Wood (Wit and Mirth,* II, 1707, 1712, p. 116), was imitated in a "modern" version about "Audenard", in *Wit and Mirth,* IV, 1709, p. 328. King made Orpheus play it in *Orpheus and Eurydice* (1704). Cf. also *The Guardian,* No. 41. Gay echoed the first line in Polly's song, "Air XII", in *The Beggar's Opera.*

[172] Addison's *Rosamond* appeared in its 3rd edition in 1713.

[173] *Wit and Mirth,* III, 1707, 1712, p. 82.—Part of Gay's almost literal borrowing (ll. 103-08) from the ballad is one of the "thoughts" that Addison praised in *The Spectator,* No. 74, and part echoes King's satire of the pedant in *A Journey to London,* the dissertation on the "old stone of Scotland" with the old pindaric where words like "stumps" were printed in "black letters". One recognizes the discussion on the style of ballads.—"Witherington" still seems to be remembered by English people as the man who "fought upon his stumps".

[174] *Wit and Mirth: An Antidote against Melancholy,* London, 1682, p. 14. Later editions seem to have dropped it in favour of another song on a similar Quaker theme.—Ellis, op. cit., p. 211, refers for these and the following ballads to the numbers of items in Day and Murrie, *English Song-Books.* Where possible, the references in this volume are to the early editions of *Wit and Mirth.*

[175] *A True Relation of the Dreadful Combat between More of More-Hall and the Dragon of Wantley,* in *Wit and Mirth,* I, 1707, 1712, p. 1. Cf. also *Roxb. Ballads,* VIII, 415.

[176] *Cousin Taffy,* in *Wit and Mirth,* III, 1707, 1712, p. 188, or *Of Noble Race was Shinking,* in *Wit and Mirth,* I, 1707, p. 311, and "Air XXXI" in *The Beggar's Opera.*

[177] See De Sola Pinto and Rodway, op. cit., p. 71; *Bagf. Ballads,* II, 370; and Chappell, op. cit., II, 568. It is "Air XLIV" in *The Beggar's Opera.* Cf. also *Roxb. Ballads,* IX, 792.—For *"Sawney",* see below p. 148 n. 4.

[178] Kidson, op. cit., p. 74.

[179] *A Warning for Maidens; or, Young Bateman*, in *Roxb. Ballads*, III, 194 and Chappell, op. cit., I, 196.— As an example of "the Miraculous" and in order not to disappoint female readers, "who, like the Justice in the *What d'ye Call it*, doubtless expect in such a Collection a Competency of Ghosts", Ambrose Philips includes it in his vol. I, 261.

[180] Probably *The Woeful Lamentation of Jane Shore, a Goldsmith's Wife in London, Sometime King Edward the Fourth's Concubine*, in *A Collection of Old Ballads*, I, 147.—Rowe's Tragedy *Jane Shore* was published in the beginning of the year 1714.—*A New Ballad of King Edward and Jane Shore* is a burlesque, in *Wit and Mirth*, III, 1707, 1712, p. 20. Cf. *Roxb. Ballads*, VIII, 421.

[181] *Fair Rosamund* by Th. Deloney, in *Roxb. Ballads*, V, 667 and *Wit and Mirth*, V, 1714. *A Collection of Old Ballads* has two versions, I, 1 and I, 11.—The "bow'r" is made much of in both the ballad and the Opera.

[182] For the numerous ballads about this hero and literary references, see Chappell, op. cit., II, 387, and *Roxb. Ballads*, II, 419-49 and IX, 481-539.—*A Collection of Old Ballads* contains eleven ballads about Robin Hood.

[183] *An Excellent Ballad, Intituled, The Wandering Prince of Troy*, the first stanza of which ends "and Corn now grows where *Troy* Town stood".—*Wit and Mirth*, III, 1707, 1712, p. 15. For the story of the ballad, see *Roxb. Ballads*, VI, 547, where it is called *The Wandering Prince of Troy; or Queen Dido*. It is "Air XLV" in *Polly*.

[184] *New Dialogues of the Dead*, p. 21, and *Dialogues of the Dead*, p. 13.—For a survey of Renaissance and neo-classical criticism of Homer, see E. N. Tigerstedt, *Engelsk nyhumanism och nyklassicism under 1700-talet* (Humanistisk Kultur, No. 7), Stockholm, 1963, Ch. 1.

[185] January, 1708.

[186] *Guardian*, No. 67.

[187] *The Evening Post* for February 10-12 and 21-24, 1713.

[188] Mentioned by Ellis, op. cit., p. 204.

[189] This Preface anticipated or was even the model for those to *A Collection of Old Ballads*. But the editor, Ambrose Philips, was at least half serious, in spite of what he assured his readers in the Preface to the third volume.

[190] Cf. *Roxb. Ballads*, I, 331, 337, 564, 611; II, 345; IV, 409; VII, 24.

[191] *Wednesday*, 1. 8; *Thursday*, 1. 73; *Friday*, 1. 75; *Saturday*, 1. 28.

[192] *The Squabble* for the singing-contest seems to echo the chorus in *The Queen's Health; or, New Gillian of Croydon*, "Then hey for the Squabble in Spain".—*Wit and Mirth*, 1719, I, 146. The tune is "Mall Peatley", a country dance, and the same that Gay used for "Air XVIII" in *Achilles*. *Gillian of Croydon*—to William III—is in *Wit and Mirth*, II, 1707 and 1712, and is not an alteration of the former, as was thought by Chappell, op. cit., I, 289 and II, 778, but rather vice versa.

[192] Cf below pp. 151 ff., 200. ff.

[194] *The Countrey-Farmer; or, The Buxome Virgin* (*Roxb. Ballads*, III, 363) was sung to "a New Tune, called New-Market", which Chappell (op. cit., II, 562) thinks is D'Urfey's "To Horse, Brave Boys", one of the songs mentioned in *Wednesday*.

[195] In *The Virtuous Wife* (1680) and *Wit and Mirth*, I, 1707, p. 133. It is "Air XXX" in *Polly*.—This song begins "*Sawney* was tall and of noble Race". There are two other "Sawneys", one in *Wit and Mirth*, II, 1707, 1712, p. 242, and one in I, 1707, p. 237, the latter by Motteux, according to Chappell, op. cit., II, 612.

[196] J. Cooper's translation in *Ovid's Epistles* (1712), p. 90.

[197] Radcliffe, *Ovid Travestie*, pp. 70-71.

[198] Diaper, *Nereides*, I, 13-16. The editor quotes this passage in comparison with Gay's, but without mentioning the common source. Op. cit., p. xxxix.

[199] These lines and a similar passage in *Leander to Hero, Ovid's Epistles*, pp. 71-72, and also *Tatler*, No. 82, seem to have provided ingredients for the ballad in *The What D'Ye Call It*.

[200] Op. cit., pp. 38-39.

[201] Cf. this couplet with *Id. XXIII*, ll. 50 ff.

[202] Cf. "quench" in the quotation from *Phillis to Demophon*, l. 3 from the bottom.

[203] Cf. the ending of *The Rape of the Lock*.

[204] *Eclogue III*, in *The Bucolicks of Baptist Mantuan*, tr. Th. Harvey, London, 1656, p. 24.

[205] The following line echoes Browne's *Britannia's Pastorals*, II, v.—

The glasse of Time had well-nye spent the
    sand
It had to run.

[206] There is some warrant for this realistic ending in *Ecl. II*, 1. 73.—Cf. Ned Ward's description of rustic "noisy Revels" at wakes, where swains and "tann'd Trulls" dance round Maypoles and then repair to the ale-house orchard for "March-Beer", apple-pie and cheese.—*Nuptial Dialogues and Debates,* 2 vols., London, 1710, I, 144.

[207] Cf. supra pp. 125 ff., 140-41, 143 ff.

[208] Cf. for instance, J. S., *The Shepherd's Kalender: or, The Citizen's and Country Man's Daily Companion,* London, n.d., in the Bodl. Lib. catalogue dated c. 1715.

[209] *Pastorals.* Mentioned by Tucker Brooke as anticipating Gay, in A. C. Baugh, ed., *A Literary History of England,* New York, 1948, p. 503.

[210] *A Week's Loving, Wooing and Wedding,* in *Roxb. Ballads,* VII, 136.—Cf. also D'Urfey's poem *Collin's Walk through London and Westminster* (1690).

[211] From Rosalinda and Blouzabella, the latter in D'Urfey's *Italian Song Call'd Pastorella; made into an English Dialogue,* in *Wit and Mirth,* III, 1707 and 1712, p. 309.

[212] The first line of Collin's song in that Opera was echoed by Gay in his ballad in *The What D'Ye Call It.*

    'Twas when the Sheep were shearing.

[213] *Mother Bunch's Closet Newly Broke Open,* 2 pts., ed. G. L. Gomme, London, 1885, I, 18.—The editor says in the Introduction that Part I is dated 1685.

[214] Ibid., II, 29.

[215] L. C. Wimberley, *Folklore in the English and Scottish Ballads,* Chicago, 1928, pp. 362-63.

[216] The trick in *Thursday,* ll. 15-24, is described in an edition in the Bodl. Lib. (Douce p. 164) of *Mother Bunch's Closet Newly Broke Open,* n.d. and n. p., I, 24. See also II, 14 and 15.

[217] There are advertisements about "Golden Pills", the "Golden Unction" and other universal remedies, even for love-sickness, in the *Bagford Collection for the History of Printing,* Nos. 92, 228, 243. Cf. also advertisements about fortune-tellers and many a "Student in Astrology". Those dated are from the early 18th century.

[218] Th. Campion, *Songs from Lute Books,* in *The Ox-*

ford Book of Sixteenth Century Verse, pp. 841-42; *Volpone,* IV, i; *Othello,* III, iv; *The Sad Shepherd,* II, iii; *The Gipsies Metamorphos'd; Th.* Middleton and W. Rowley, *The Spanish Gipsie;* and later, Prior's version of *Henry and Emma.*—Cf. below p. 187.

[219] No. 130. Cf. also rules for palmistry in J. S., *The True Fortune-Teller,* London, 1686.

[220] L. 80 echoes *The Gipsies Metamorphos'd,* ll. 248-49.

[221] Addison in *The Spectator,* No. 523, obviously criticizes Pope's "theology".

[222] Gummere, op. cit., pp. 117 ff.

[223] The first line of the burthen in *Thursday* echoes *A&C,* V, ii, 307.

[224] *Palinode.* Cf. ll. 69-80 in *Panthea.*

[225] *Hos ego versiculos* and *Sic Vita,* in *The Oxford Book of Seventeenth Century Verse,* ed. H. J. C. Grierson and G. Bullough, Oxford, 1951, pp. 339 ff. and 359. Cf. also pp. 183 ff.

[226] *The Cruel Mother* and *Clerk Colvill,* for instance. Quoted by Wimberley, op. cit., pp. 254 and 286.

[227] *The Song of Philander* in two song-books from the 1680's, according to Chappell, op. cit., I, 279 ff., and in *Wit and Mirth,* II, 1707, p. 252.

[228] Hodgart, op. cit., p. 32.

[229] The hare bequeathes her body to her tormentors.—*Roxb. Ballads,* VII, 87.—A young man gives "toil and travel" to poor folk and "Hearts of Flint" to rich men.—*Wit and Mirth,* IV, 1709, p. 34.—There is a translation of one in *The Muses Mercury* for October, 1707.

[230] *Roxb. Ballads,* I, 186 ff.

[231] Cf. this line and also 1. 95 in *Tuesday* with the famous letters from Stanton Harcourt in August, 1718. See Sutherland, op. cit., p. 74.

[232] Echoes *The Bride's Buriall,* "And like a Lamb departed Life."—The quotation is from Philips's *Collection,* I, 234. For the authorship of the *Collection,* see Friedman, op. cit., p. 147 n. 72.

[233] Cf. *Wit and Mirth,* I, 1707, pp. 125, 249; II and III, 1707, 1712, pp. 180 and 25; *Have among You! Good Women,* in *Roxb. Ballads,* I, 435, and *Cucking a Scold,* in *The Pepys Ballads,* ed. H. E. Rollins, 8 vols., Cambridge, Mass., 1929, I, 454.—One of the Roxburghe ballads (IV, 355) is illustrated with a woodcut repre-

senting a "stool".

234 *Wit and Mirth,* I, 1707, 1712, p. 254; II, 1707, p. 171; IV, 1709, pp. 86 and 89; *Roxb. Ballads,* VIII, 235; *The Diverting Post,* No. 14, 1705.

235 *Wit and Mirth,* II, 1707, 1712, p. 148, beginning "All in a misty Morning" and "Air XXX" in *The Beggar's Opera.*

236 *Wit and Mirth,* I, 1707, pp. 293 and 327.

237 *Wit and Mirth,* I, 1707, p. 220.

238 Ellis, op. cit., p. 212.

239 VII, 43—45.—Cf. also *Roxb. Ballads,* IV, 385 and VII, 279.—*The Northern Ditty* was printed in *Wit and Mirth,* II, 1707, 1712, p. 163, and is "Air III" in *The Beggar's Opera.*

240 For *"wash sorrow from thy soul",* see p. 162 n. 1; *"o'er hills and far away",* "Air XVI" in *The Beggar's Opera,* in *Wit and Mirth,* IV, 1709, pp. 99 and 102, and in *Roxb. Ballads,* V, 316 ff. For *"Gillian of Croydon",* see p. 148 n. 1. *Patient Grissel* was one of the best known "Fables . . . Modern" and appeared both as play, Tale and ballad. Mentioned among the popular entertainments in, for instance, *An Ancient Song of Bartholomew-Fair,* in *Wit and Mirth,* II, 1707, p. 171.

241 Ellis, op. cit., p. 211.

242 Dobrée, *OHEL,* VII, 141.

243 Cf. supra p. 112.

244 Francis Beaumont and John Fletcher, *Works,* ed. A. Glover and A. R. Waller, 10 vols., Cambridge, 1905-12, II, 406.

245 *The Overburian Characters* (Percy Reprints, No. 13), ed. W. J. Paylor, Oxford, 1936, p. 56.

246 Marlowe, *Hero and Leander,* I, 22, in *Poems,* ed. L. C. Martin and in *Works and Life,* ed. R. H. Case, 6 vols., London, 1930-33, IV, 29.

247 *Life and Complete Works,* ed. A. B. Grosart, 15 vols., London, 1881-86, VI, 141.

248 L. 12.

249 Greene and Lodge, *A Looking Glass for London and England,* I, iii, 356-60, in Greene, *Plays and Poems,* ed. J. C. Collins, 2 vols., Oxford, 1905, I, 155.

250 *The Sad Shepherd,* I, iv, 48-50; Barclay, *Eclogue I,* ll. 323-27; Browne, *Britannia's Pastorals,* I; The theme

is in the *Geo.,* II, 527 ff.

251 Ll. 1302 and 1364.

252 Reference in G. Kitchen, *A Survey of Burlesque and Parody in English,* Edinburgh and London, 1931, p. 72 n. 1.

253 Spenser, *Daphnaida;* Marlowe, *Dido,* V, i, 133; Ph. Fletcher, *Piscatory Eclogues,* III, 4; Drummond, *Phyllis, on the Death of Her Sparrow;* Crashaw, *To Pontius,* also Prior, *A Better Answer.*

254 *LLL,* IV, iii, 8; *Ecl. VIII; Id. III.*

255 *MND,* III i, 173; *Pericles,* II, iii, 43; *The Duchess of Malfi,* IV, ii; *The Sad Shepherd,* II, viii, 57; Greene, *Doron's Eclogue;* Marvell, *The Mower to the Glow-Worms;* Carew, *To . . . Sandys.*

256 Cf. Ellis, op. cit., p. 211.—*Wit and Mirth,* I, 1707, pp. 22 and 252; II, 1707, 1712, pp. 145, 210; Chappell, op. cit., I, 312 n. 1, hardly gives the adequate explanation of the expression.

257 *George-a-Greene, the Pinner of Wakefield,* II, iii, 374; *The Sad Shepherd,* I, iv. 51; *The Shepherd's Pipe,* III, 54; *Corinna's Going a-Maying.*—Cf. also *Spectator,* No. 365.

258 *MWW,* II, i.—It is not a gibe at Blackmore, as is thought by J. R. Moore, op. cit., pp. 86 ff.

259 Playford, *The Musical Companion,* London, 1673, p. 9; Brome, *Songs and Other Poems,* p. 138; *The Muses Mercury* for June and December, 1707; Chappell, op. cit., II, 689 and 777, says there are several versions of the song he reprints.—Gay's song in *The Mohocks* echoes a drinking-song in *Wit and Mirth,* I, 1707, p. 204; "Air XIX" in *The Beggar's Opera* is also a drinking-song.

260 *Th. Tusser 1557 Floruit His Good Points of Husbandry,* ed. D. Hartley, London, 1931, pp. 169-70.

261 Cf. the "Dissection of a *Beau's* HEAD and of a *Coquette's* HEART" in No. 275 of *The Spectator.*

262 Cf. below pp. 183 ff.

263 Cf. below p. 206.

264 *Saturday,* ll. 23-28. Even Blouzelinda may represent a realistic shepherdess, if one may judge from a letter to Gay from Pope, 23 Sept., 1714, *Correspondence,* I, 255.

265 For two of the lesser Epistles, see Armens, *John Gay,* pp. 106 ff. and 114 ff.; and for a more detailed

treatment of four of the longer ones, with consideration of the aspect of the "lower order", see Adina Forsgren, "Some Complimentary Epistles by John Gay", *Studia Neophilologica,* XXXVI, 1, 1964.

[266] For the history of lace-making, see J. R. W. Coxhead, *The Romance of the Wool, Lace and Pottery Trade in Honiton,* 1957, Cf. Thomas Fuller, *The History of the Worthies of England,* 2 vols., London, 1811, I, 272, where, under the heading of "Manufactures" for Devon, "Bone-lace" is the only item.

Patricia Meyer Spacks (essay date 1965)

SOURCE: "Early Masks and Models" in *John Gay,* Twayne Publishers; Inc., 1965, pp. 17-40.

[*In the following excerpt, Spacks examines Gay's earliest poetry, demonstrating how the poet developed both his voice and his major artistic concerns. Although his early work is uneven, Spacks argues, it prefigures his more successful efforts at marrying the pastoral form with a more sophisticated tone, and adapting traditional genres to new uses.*]

Not until 1713, when he was twenty-eight years old, did John Gay begin to discover models which made extended poetic expression possible for him. He then described himself, in the first version of *Rural Sports,* as having "courted Bus'ness with successless Pain,/ And in Attendance wasted Years in vain." For about eleven years he had struggled to make his way in London, having come from the provinces (Barnstaple, in Devon) as an apprentice to a silk mercer. When, around 1708, he became secretary to Aaron Hill, a minor playwright and magazine editor who briefly managed Drury Lane theater, he entered for the first time the literary world he yearned to be part of. Before 1713, however, he had published only one long poem, *Wine* (a work apparently too poor, in his opinion, to include in the collected poems seven years later), and a farcical play, *The Mohocks,* which he had been unable to get produced.

His vision of success, then as later, had to do with approval more than with accomplishment. For the patronage of the great he would dance attendance, never feeling that his rewards were adequate, yet always hopeful of winning some appointment, the symbol of success, or a gift, tangible sign of approval, or the warm glow of general admiration in which a poet might bask. His poetic resources were not impressive: a grammar school education, a first-hand knowledge of the country (which would not, in the early eighteenth century, provide a great deal of respectable poetic subject matter), a comparatively superficial and recent knowledge of the life of the town, and, of course, a strong desire to be a poet.

The path he should follow must have seemed rather clearly defined. A man who, in our own time, sets out to be a poet has above all the problem of originality: if he can readily be dismissed as an imitator, or as essentially indistinguishable in technique and subject from his contemporaries, he is unlikely to win recognition. He must, at the very least, follow Pound's dictum and "make it new." He must offer his own insights, make his voice seem a *special* one. In early eighteenth-century London the poetic situation was spectacularly different. Pope was soon to offer his famous definition in the *Essay on Criticism:*

> True wit is nature to advantage dressed:
> What oft was thought, but ne'er so well
>   expressed.

The idea that a poet need say nothing new, need only say something true, well, was a commonplace of the age. Moreover, the "imitation" was itself a highly respected literary form: a young man could versify in English some Latin model, changing allusions for the sake of topicality, and the results would be recognized as fresh poetry.

Gay's first problem, then, was to choose appropriate models. Not only did he value classical sanctions for his utterances, he needed a point of view: to select a specific Latin model was to determine the poetic stance he would adopt, the perspective from which he would approach his material. And the problem of perspective was always to be crucial for John Gay, whose tolerance and amiability apparently made it difficult for him to assume the authority of a commentator on the human scene.

In 1713 the first version of *Rural Sports* was published and also *The Fan;* early the next year *The Shepherd's Week* appeared. These three poems, with the earlier *Wine,* comprise a sequence of increasingly elaborate attempts to employ respectable models; despite their obvious weaknesses, they also demonstrate some of Gay's important poetic resources. *Wine,* his first published work, soon forgotten even in its own time, nonetheless tells us a good deal about our poet. It was in conception actually third-hand: a parody of Milton which imitated two far more successful pieces in the same vein, John Philips' *Splendid Shilling* and *Cyder.* "The merit of such performances begins and ends with the first author," commented Dr. Johnson of *The Splendid Shilling.* "He that should again adapt Milton's phrase to the gross incidents of common life, and even adapt it with more art, which would not be difficult, must yet expect but a small part of the praise which Philips has obtained; he can only hope to be considered as the repeater of a jest."[1] *Wine,* which generally has been dismissed as only a repeated jest, can make few claims to real poetic merit, yet it demonstrates certain un-Miltonic characteristics which foretell a good deal about Gay's later poetry. The problems it manifests, although here more blatantly displayed, are those which were persistently to plague its author.

The piece is a burlesque account of the virtues of wine, considered as "the source/Whence human pleasures flow." In the first 186 lines Gay explains the emotional values of drinking, its importance to trade, its inspirational effect on poets, its association with the classical past; roughly the last hundred lines of the poem detail the progress of a modern evening of drinking.

When the burlesque mask drops, as it frequently does, the reader becomes suddenly conscious that Gay is not merely joking. He praises wine for checking "inglorious, lolling ease"—which, biographies and contemporary letters frequently assert, was his own besetting temptation; he describes how wine stimulates the circulation of the blood (11. 42-44); he even recounts, in emotively colored language, the end of the night of drinking and the stumbling trip homeward:

> Thus we the winged hours in harmless mirth
> And joys unsullied pass, till humid night
> Has half her race perform'd; now all abroad
> Is hush'd and silent, nor the rumbling noise
> Of coach or cart, or smoky link-boy's call
> Is heard—but universal Silence reigns:
> When we in merry plight, airy and gay,
> Surprised to find the hours so swiftly fly,
> With hasty knock, or twang of pendent cord,
> Alarm the drowsy youth from slumb'ring nod;
> Startled he flies, and stumbles o'er the stairs
> Erroneous, and with busy knuckles plies
> His yet clung eyelids, and with stagg'ring reel
> Enters confused, and mutt'ring asks our wills;
> When we with liberal hand the score
>   discharge,
> And homeward each his course with steady
>   step
> Unerring steers, of cares and coin bereft.
>   (11. 256-72)

If the language and tone help to ridicule the "drowsy youth," for example, they do not entirely obscure the poet's real sympathy for him; the same language defines the precise nature of the drinkers' state, "of cares . . . bereft." Such sections reveal a use of elevated Miltonic diction for two contradictory purposes: to mock low concerns by treating them with high language, but also, at other moments, to dignify such matters by the language the poet applies to them. If he burlesques in the mode of Philips, he also praises in the mode of James Thomson, who in *The Seasons* was to elevate rural concerns partly by employing the language of Milton.

Miltonic diction here provided John Gay not with one perspective but with two; and the apparent lack of conviction in **Wine** comes partly from the resultant division of emphasis. The unmistakable note of sincerity dominates when Gay deals honestly with real reactions and feelings, speaking not of the artificial mythological associations of wine-drinking, but of its genuine effects—genuinely, if a trifle shamefacedly, perceived as valuable. *Wine* asserts—clumsily, deviously, yet vividly—the value of companionship, of talk, of vigor, of life itself. And the assertion that life was intrinsically interesting and valuable, although that assertion was often heavily disguised, was to become Gay's major poetic theme.

Equally significant in relation to Gay's later development is the extraordinary sense of vigor and movement which **Wine** frequently projects. Correlatives of this feeling of energy are not far to seek. Many of the ideas in the poem emerge through images of movement. **Wine** proceeds by a series of visions of rising, soaring, falling, sailing, clashing, fighting. Gay's muse is to soar with "no middle flight" (1. 13); the wine raises the "drooping fronts" of its drinkers (1. 42), who lift the glass so that the wine may glide "swiftly o're the Tongue" (1. 47). As a result, "The circling *Blood* with quicker motion flies" (1. 48). The repulsed lover, encouraged by wine, "*Storms* the Breach, and *Wins* the Beauteous Fort" (1. 67). The British seaman finds himself "plowing the Ocean" (1. 71), while his ship "Rides tilting ore the Waves" (1. 72). Wine stimulates the poet's muse until

> aloft she towres
> Born on stiff *Pennons,* and of Wars alarms,
> And *Trophies* won, in loftiest Numbers sings.
>   (11. 106-08)

It enflames sluggish minds with generous fires (1. 112), engages the quickened soul (1. 113), causes yet another muse to soar aerial (11. 122-23), heightens wit (1. 144). Examples can be lavishly multiplied; the dominant tone of the poem is that of abounding energy.

This fact is surprising, when one considers the nature of Miltonic blank verse, particularly as perceived by its eighteenth-century imitators. In contrast to the heroic couplet, which was the poetic norm of the early 1700's, blank verse seemed a leisurely and comparatively undisciplined form. It did not demand the obvious control of the couplet; it did not encourage a verse of elaborate tensions and balances. When James Thomson, a few years after Gay, used Miltonic blank verse for serious purposes in *The Seasons,* Dr. Johnson was able to make a dramatic point by reading aloud only every other line. The effect, listeners agreed, was as coherent as blank verse could be expected to be. Moreover, Miltonic blank verse provided a particularly tempting model because its devices seemed to the unwary so obvious and so easy to imitate: the rolling Latinate words, the thunderous lists of exotic names, the convoluted grammatical constructions. All these techniques, obviously, would encourage a slow and ponderous pace, a tone the opposite of energetic.

And Gay uses them all, if only to parody them; they can be demonstrated within a few lines of *Wine*. The poet speaks, for example, of the sources of wine:

> Whether from *Formian* Grape depress'd,
> *Falern*
> Or *Setin, Massic, Gauran* or *Sabine,*
> *Lesbian* or *Caecuban.* . . .
>
> (11. 141-43)

The invocation of grape names mocks Milton's sonority and grandeur. Four lines later occurs a striking example of tortured construction and Latinate diction:

> But *we,* not as our Pristin sires, repair
> T'*umbrageous* Grot or Vale, but when the Sun
> Faintly from Western Skies his rays oblique
> Darts sloping, and to *Thetis* wat'ry Lap
> Hastens in Prone Career. . . .
>
> (11. 146-50)

Yet such passages, interesting for their expertise in parodying an old-fashioned mode, are so interspersed with moments or sequences of sheer enthusiasm that the total effect of *Wine* depends less on them than on a totally contradictory image of youthful life. The lines quoted above continue, "with Friends select/Swiftly we hie to Devil *Young* or *Old.* . . . " The Devil was a famous tavern of Gay's time; the jauntiness of the pun on "going to the devil" is thoroughly characteristic of Gay.

Wine, hardly a good enough poem to justify detailed critical examination, is a significant portent. Its confusions of attitude and emphasis, its alternations between vigor and mechanical imitation, reveal the poet's divided mind; its concern with feeling and its respect for simple pleasures suggest some of his central interests; its poetic skill and its ineptitudes indicate the difficulties of evaluating the work of John Gay.

II

Rural Sports demonstrates problems similar to those of *Wine,* but it is a far more interesting poem. In it Gay returned to the classics for a model to be used straightforwardly. Virgil's *Georgics* echo always behind the poem, which contains a lengthy tribute to its Virgilian source; moreover, as a modern critic has thoroughly demonstrated, Gay's drastic revision of *Rural*

Sports in 1720 must have been at least partially intended to emphasize its georgic aspects.[2] In many ways Gay follows his master closely: in his stress on the theme of seasonal progression, in his emphasis on the contrast between city and country life, in his detailed instructions about how to pursue the activities he describes, in his concern with the welfare of animal life (to the very worm on the fish hook), even, as Aden points out (pp. 231-32), in the "magisterial tone" which he frequently adopts. But however closely it imitates a model, *Rural Sports* is peculiarly Gay's own—the more so, perhaps, for the sense of tradition it conveys. In it we can see clearly his early mastery of poetic techniques which later dominate poems of quite a different kind.

Rural Sports is dedicated to Pope—a young and rural Pope, not yet come to town from Windsor Forest. "You, who the sweets of rural life have known,/Despise th' ungrateful hurry of the town" (11. 1-2). The dedication has, in the context of the poem as a whole, profound appropriateness. It is used most immediately, however, as a preamble to some lines of conventionalized self-pity: Gay envies Pope his capacity merely to enjoy himself and the muse in his rural retreat, and he contrasts Pope's lot with his own, as "Long in the noisie town . . . immur'd" (1. 11).

The organization of the poem is simple. After the opening passage, Gay indicates certain general advantages of country living, including the fact that the country provides an appropriate environment in which to read the *Georgics.* He suggests the progress of the day and then that of the seasons, moving thus into his central subject: the sports appropriate to various seasons. Spring is sacred to fishing, whose techniques and excitements the poet thoroughly displays. Autumn calls him to hunting, depicted in almost equal detail. And the poem concludes with a lengthy panegyric on the joys of country living, in which the "happy fields" are finally "The kind rewarders of industrious life" (1. 437).

This sort of subject matter could be dull enough; it provided material for many "set piece" descriptions in well-forgotten eighteenth-century poems. And *Rural Sports* has its dull stretches. That these do not dominate the poem is due to the peculiar complexity of Gay's vision, manifested in his close attention to language. For an example, let us examine the uses of the word *air* within a comparatively short section of the poem. In line 111, "Millions of worlds hang in the spacious air." Later comes a metaphoric couplet: "So the gay lady, with expensive care,/Borrows the pride of land, of sea, and air" (11. 187-88). A few lines after: "The scaly shoals float by, and seiz'd with fear/Behold their fellows tost in thinner air" (11. 217-18). Then the fish, drawn to shore, "lifts his nostrils in the sick'ning air" (1. 250); and, finally for our purposes, when Gay turns to hunting he describes the greyhound pursuing the hare and observes that the outwitted dog "snaps deceitful air with empty jaws" (1. 293).

It becomes obvious, looking at these excerpts in conjunction with one another, that Gay speaks of air each time in a radically different sense. Each individual sense, moreover, is fairly complicated in itself. The line about "millions of worlds" provides a momentary God's-eye-view of the universe. Its poetic effect depends first on the word *hang,* implicitly reminiscent of the Miltonic vision of the world suspended by a golden chain from heaven, but expanding that vision. "Spacious air" is also vital to the line, with its suggestion that infinite space can be perceived as a comfortable rather than as a frightening fact. The universe suggested is an ordered one, and the poet's joy at that fact is apparent.

How different is the vision of air implied by the gay lady's borrowing from it. By the conjunction of land, sea, and air, we are reminded faintly once more of the ordered universe—but reminded also of the sense in which human pride and vanity substitute a frivolous for a cosmic order. Land, sea, and air are for the lady essentially differentiated not at all; all merely gratify vanity, and the universe previously implicitly perceived as dominated by heaven is now reduced to a tiny system revolving around a single bedizened belle.

In the next reference, we move even farther from a divine perspective—to the fishes' view, in which water is the true air and the air which human beings breathe is frightening because "thinner." Its frightening quality is more explicit when it becomes "the sick'ning air": the element of death to a fish although of life to a man. And the dog's point of view makes it "deceitful" because of its very emptiness: air is now important because of what it does *not* contain, at a given spot in a given moment, rather than because of what it *does* contain ("millions of worlds").

We have been given, then, five different ways of considering air, all of which rely on various human preconceptions—if only to reverse or to expand them. Each attitude toward air is interesting in itself; each is appropriate to its moment in the poem. But the attitudes are even more revealing in relation to one another. The gay lady's perspective becomes more significant because we have previously been reminded of a more inclusive, more important way of looking at our natural environment; the fishes' point of view, with its reversal of the human, carries subtle ironic force when we have been reminded of the possibility that normal standards can be reversed, or seriously limited, even within the human world. For the fish and for the dog, air is significant in what it lacks (life-giving water, rabbits to kill); for the human being it is important in what it offers, but what it offers can be perceived in many different ways (as the element of life, the stuff of

vanity, objects for philosophic contemplation). Gay has, in effect, put all these attitudes side by side. We discover through them that the concerns of a poem of limited theme have widened a good deal.

Of course, normally we do not consider such curious conjunctions of meaning, for **Rural Sports** does not insist on them; certainly the reader would not ordinarily work out these implications in such detail. Yet the effect of expansion can operate even without conscious recognition of it, by the sheer power of repeated instances. These references to air are by no means the only examples of Gay's technique of placing different uses of a word side by side for consideration. Some instances are more obvious than others, but the cumulative effect is inescapable. If we are told about birds that "death in thunder overtakes their flight" (1. 342)—an economical way of suggesting the extent to which the arbitrary intervention of man in the animal world must seem to the animals themselves merely one more inexplicable natural phenomenon: thunder or guns, it's all the same—a few lines later we learn that "The jocund thunder wakes th' enliven'd hounds" (1. 368). In this case, the thunder is that of the huntsman's horn, welcomed by the dogs but the signal of potential destruction to the game. The earlier use of the word must influence the later; we are reminded once more of the importance of point of view: the extent to which (and this is a minor but meaningful theme of the hunting passages) one's attitude toward hunting must depend upon whether one is hunter or hunted. Similarly, we hear about the "subtle hare" (1. 294), and then, a bit later, about the "subtle dog" (1. 309). Both animals are equally skillful, equally sagacious, to use one of Gay's own words, but their modes of cleverness are opposed: the result of subtlety in the dog must inevitably be the destruction of the hare in all its subtlety.

The ultimate effect of repeated variations of this sort is not merely to convince us that Gay is sympathetic to animals. It is rather to suggest a breadth of perspective vital to **Rural Sports.** Speaking of the hunting of larks, Gay explains that the birds are enticed to come near the ground by rays of light reflected from a "twinkling glass." He summarizes,

> Pride lures the little warbler from the skies:
> The light-enamour'd bird deluded dies.
> 　　　　　　　　　(11.360-61)

This statement may recall the earlier description of "female pride" (1. 178), the gay lady who "Borrows the pride of land, of sea, and air" until she becomes merely a "glittering thing" (1. 189). Her pride consists in her unwillingness to accept her natural state; by failing to be properly herself, trying to be more, to plunder the universe for the sake of her vanity, she reduces herself below the level of humanity to that of mere "thingness." Similarly, the bird leaves his proper station, rejects the light of the skies, to come down to earth for a lesser gleam, enamored of light as the lady is of "Furs, pearls, and plumes." As a result he dies; the lady is more deviously destroyed.

The connection between lady and bird is implicit not merely in the word *pride,* but also in the concepts invoked. The question of perspective here becomes particularly important. Gay sees the bird from the same point of view as that with which he contemplates ladies, and the lady with the same eye he turns on birds. At his best, he manages to make this poem, in its consideration of merely rural concerns, significantly concerned also with the central problems of life. Judgment and skill, hope and fear, treachery and faithfulness are involved in these sporting affairs as in more important ones, and Gay usually remembers this fact. Hunting is not seen as an image of human life; rather, the poet's consciousness of a broader scheme of judgment, a broader realm of affairs, informs his treatment of comparatively trivial concerns.

In the best passages of **Rural Sports,** however, there is no indication that the poet considers country pursuits trivial and city ones important, and no clear indication of the reverse system of values. When he speaks of fly fishing, Gay mentions the necessity of making the flies in such a way "That nature seems to live again in art" (1. 208). His vision of the actual occupation of fishing is of moments in which "all thy hope hangs on a single hair" (1. 210). Both these statements, although they have perfectly literal force in the context, suggest also an expanded area of reference and invite the reader to make connections to other realms of experience. Gay's characteristic method, in short, is that of expansion: he places ideas, insights, words into meaningful conjunctions, implicit or explicit.

It is a method quite different from that of Virgil. Far more consistently and more forcefully than **Rural Sports,** the *Georgics,* with *work* as their subject, insist that each detail is more meaningful than the nominal subject matter (the concerns of the farmer) would suggest. But Virgil conveys significance primarily through *deepening* rather than expanding. Bees and horses and bulls are important, ultimately as well as initially, as beings *in themselves*—not as analogues for human problems. Their importance, to be sure, derives largely from the fact that Virgil perceives them so clearly in their proper roles in the cosmic scheme of things. He deals always with a hierarchical universe. Perceiving clearly a cosmos in which the gods have their place, man has his, cows theirs, he realizes intensely the ultimate importance of each individual participant in the total scheme. If his discussion of bees, for example, leads one to feel that the lives of the bees have lessons for men, it is only because the bees are fulfilling their functions with perfect propriety, perfect order; and one

is made conscious of the fact that man does not always function with equal order and propriety. The total scheme, with its ultimately supernatural sanctions, is always implicit in each individual observation.

Gay, on the other hand, although he is capable, as we have seen, of making reference to a cosmic scheme, is not predominantly conscious of any particular system of order. His perspective varies, and its variations are themselves important; moreover, breadth of perspective provides a technique for redeeming the apparent triviality of sports—play—as a subject. One of Gay's favorite methods of "broadening" is to suggest the contrary-to-fact, the technique that Keats employed so brilliantly in, for example, "La Belle Dame Sans Merci":

> The sedge is withered from the lake,
> And no birds sing

—which suggests simultaneously the bleak present and the more luxuriant past. Gay uses the device so frequently that it becomes a dominant mannerism. "No warbling cheers the woods" (1. 95); "no rude gale disturbs the sleeping trees" (1. 97); "No swelling inundation hides the grounds" (1. 125); the rapid surface of the brook is "unknown to weeds" (1. 142); the bosom of the fisherman "glows with treasures yet uncaught" (1. 146). And so on, particularly in the first canto of the poem. The actual fact and its hypothetical opposite are suggested at once; Gay reminds us repeatedly that he is aware of contradictory possibilities. And when he convincingly evokes the sense of these possibilities, **Rural Sports** is most successful.

But the poem is not, as a whole, so successful as these comments may suggest. If Gay occasionally manages to infuse his Virgilian imitation with a truly felt personal vision, more often his insights seem uncontrolled, his verbal conjunctions random collocations of meaning rather than significant, selected juxtapositions. Toward the end of the poem, Gay offers a fairly lengthy treatment of the lot of the rural maid:

> What happiness the rural maid attends,
> In cheerful labour while each day she spends!
> She gratefully receives what heav'n has sent,
> And, rich in poverty, enjoys content.
>   (11. 410-13)

The paradox ("rich in poverty") is all too easy, but the passage continues to yet more distasteful sentimentalities, as it systematically contrasts the lot of the country maiden with that of the "courtly dame." The advantage is all on the side of the country girl, who is neither hypochondriac nor melancholy, who never yearns for "glaring equipage," who does not carelessly lose her reputation or wear out her beauty at midnight masquerades. "If love's soft passion in her bosom reign," Gay observes comfortably, "An equal passion warms her happy swain" (11. 426-27). The explicit comparison between rural and urban values finds all good in the country, all evil in the town; the poet can come to such conclusions only by insistent dwelling on the superficial. His is a determined refusal to look beneath the surface.

That Gay was capable of looking beneath surfaces the rest of the poem frequently suggests. But that he was capable of rejecting his own insights is perhaps ultimately more significant. The convention of rural bliss was as readily available to him as that of civilized sophistication, and he chose to rely on it as an easy resolution to his poem. One is reminded of Rasselas's sister, in Dr. Johnson's moral fable: after discovering that shepherds are in actuality brutish, stupid, and malicious, she yet remains unaccountably convinced that true bliss is to be found in the pastoral life; she and some selected maiden friends will tend their sheep in luxuriant grasslands forever free from storms, indulging the while in the pleasures of polite conversation.

Gay retreats from reality in a similar fashion at the end of *Rural Sports;* he prefers the country to the town not for genuine reasons, as he did at the beginning of the poem, but for illusory ones. And the reader is thus caused to wonder about the integrity of the piece as a whole. The breadth of perspective which the poem offers, potentially valuable as a source of complexity, may be, after all, merely a mode of avoiding commitment. The brilliant patterns of language, economy of sentence structure, pieces of perfect selectivity do not add up to anything richly coherent or totally meaningful. The verdict finally on *Rural Sports* must be that it offers instance after instance of genuine poetic power and skill, that it is clearly the work of a man capable of being a poet—but also of a man who had not yet found his proper subject and mode, who sometimes unfortunately relied on fashionable convention rather than on honest feeling.

III

With *The Fan,* his next published poem, Gay came no closer to finding his own subject matter and tone— indeed, he moved farther away from his true note. A long poem containing a series of Ovidian episodes in a pseudo-mythological framework, *The Fan* seems now unutterably trivial and almost unreadable. "I am very much recreated and refreshed with the News of the advancement of the *Fan,*" wrote Pope in August, 1713, "which I doubt not will delight the Eye and Sense of the Fair, as long as that agreeable Machine shall play in the Hands of Posterity. I am glad your *Fan* is mounted so soon, but I wou'd have you varnish and glaze it at your leisure, and polish the Sticks as much as you can."[3] Reading the poem, it is hard to tell whether Gay

varnished and polished too little or too much. At any rate, *The Fan* suffers badly by comparison with *The Rape of the Lock,* written at approximately the same time, which deals infinitely more expertly with the concerns and values of polite society.

Gay's next literary endeavor was far more successful, by contemporary and by modern standards. *The Shepherd's Week* is still frequently anthologized, still thought to be essentially representative of its author, and still a subject for controversy. The success of the poem and its representative qualities are clearly related to the positive aspects of Gay's poetry that we have discovered in his earlier works; and the controversy points to some of the central problems in evaluating Gay as poet and as thinker.

The dispute over *The Shepherd's Week,* to outline it in the simplest terms, has to do with defining the literary traditions that Gay here employs and—more crucially—with understanding his attitudes toward them. The matter was not clear at the time of the poem's first publication; and, although it has been clarified to some extent in the two and a half centuries since that time, there is still room for question. The most strongly supported theory is the one with Pope's authority behind it: Gay wrote his pastorals to defend Pope and to attack Ambrose Philips.

The Pope-Philips quarrel over the proper criteria for pastoral was one of the most famous and fierce literary disputes of the early part of the eighteenth century: it focuses for us the whole question of what traditions a poet should properly employ in writing about the country, and in what way it is proper for him to employ them. Philip's pastorals were published first in 1708; Pope's, in 1709; both later appeared in the same volume of Tonson's *Miscellany.* At the beginning, there was no opposition between the two men; indeed, Pope writes to his friend Henry Cromwell quite generously about his rival's verse, summing up: "In the whole, I agree with the Tatler, that we have no better Eclogs in our Language."[4] The trouble started over a series of essays which appeared in the *Guardian* in April, 1713.[5] Usually attributed to Thomas Tickell (although there is some possibility that they were written by Steele), these essays set up a series of criteria for pastoral poetry and illustrate excellence in the genre almost entirely by examples from Philips' pastorals, ignoring Pope. Angered by the omission, Pope submitted anonymously to the *Guardian* his own essay on pastoral, which purports to continue the praise of Philips by criticizing adversely the eclogues of Pope himself. The criticism is, of course, satiric; the paper (*Guardian* No. 40) makes Philips look ridiculous. Pope quotes, for example, some extraordinarily bad verses:

> Ah me the while! ah me! the luckless day,
> Ah luckless lad! the rather might I say;

Ah silly I! more silly than my sheep,
Which on the flowery plains I once did keep.

Then he comments, devastatingly: "How he still charms the ear with these artful repetitions of the epithets; and how significant is the last verse! I defy the most common reader to repeat them, without feeling some motions of compassion."

Gay was, of course, a friend and admirer of Pope's; and at this time he was much involved in the activities of Pope, Swift, and the Scriblerus Club. In a letter to John Caryll (June 8, 1714), Pope explains his annoyance with Philips on the grounds that Philips had held back subscription money actually due to Pope. He then says, quite explicitly, "It is to this management of *Philips,* that the world owes Mr. *Gay's Pastorals.*"[6] Hoyt Trowbridge has demonstrated the extent to which Gay's poems may be taken as detailed parodies of Philips,' echoing point by point the criticisms of Philips implied by Pope's *Guardian* paper.[7] Pope objects to Philips' obsolete language, his use of undignified rustic names, his violations of decorum (as in the listing in conjunction of flowers that actually bloom only at different seasons of the year), his use of platitudinous proverbs, his pseudo-simplicity, and his inanity.[8] All these aspects of Philips' poetry are echoed by Gay; some are explicitly commented on in his ironic proem. Professor Trowbridge sums up by observing that Gay's "purpose is to reveal the artistic fatuity of Tickell's pastoral theory and of Philips' practice; . . . if, as Tickell claimed, the rules of pastoral were to be drawn from the practice of Philips, this was the sort of poem which must result. This idea, implicit in Gay's proem and consistently applied in the eclogues themselves, is the organizing principle of *The Shepherd's Week.* It is this idea which gives the poem a coherent artistic plan" (88).

This argument is both logical and convincing. But arguments of almost equal force have been presented for the theory that Gay was actually satirizing Sir Richard Blackmore, that his central target was Thomas D'Urfey, and that he was really satirizing no one at all. Blackmore, a doctor who by his own confession composed his poems of interminable length in his head while doing his medical rounds, was a favorite target of early eighteenth-century wits. The very image of dullness, he was an obvious butt because of his self-importance, because of the extent to which he had won undeserved fame, and because of his political and moral ideas were sharply opposed to those of Pope, Swift, and their circle. Most generally admired among Blackmore's works were his *Creation,* a long poem praising God through the wonders of His creation, and his "Song of Mopas," from *Prince Arthur,* which has a similar theme. John Robert Moore has shown how Blackmore's favorite structural devices and his important themes are systematically parodied in **"Saturday,"** the final

poem of *The Shepherd's Week.*[9] And here, too, the evidence is impressive and the suggested connections illuminating. The same might be said of the demonstration by William D. Ellis, Jr., that Gay may have wished to attack the popular song writer Thomas D'Urfey, who is explicitly mentioned in *The Shepherd's Week.*[10] Ellis points out that "ballad material, much like that for which D'Urfey gained his popularity," helped to supply the fable of three of Gay's eclogues" (**"Tuesday," "Wednesday,"** and **"Thursday"**) (211); that the members of the Scriblerus Club were concerned to attack D'Urfey (206-07); and that there are in **"Saturday"** explicit references to the song writer.

Yet critics who have recorded their admiration of *The Shepherd's Week* have tended to justify the poem not as a satiric work, but as a straightforward, accurate, and at times moving rendition of rural actuality. Thomas Purney, writing on pastoral as early as 1717, "believes that Gay gave a true picture 'of the Fellows and Wenches in the Country, and put down every thing' just as he 'observ'd them act.'"[11] Dr. Johnson, who records the history of the Pope-Philips controversy and Gay's share in it, concludes: "But the effect of reality and truth became conspicuous, even when the intention was to shew them groveling and degraded. These Pastorals became popular, and were read with delight, as just representations of rural manners and occupations, by those who had no interest in the rivalry of the poets, nor knowledge of the critical dispute."[12] And the recent volume on the early eighteenth century in the Oxford History of English Literature observes that *The Shepherd's Week* was Gay's "first durable contribution to the poetic canon," apparently mainly because in the poem Gay "is firmly contemporary and realistic."[13]

These theories, to be sure, are not really incompatible with one another. It is quite probable that Gay began writing his pastorals in the service of the Pope-Philips dispute; that he included with the satire of Philips some digs at that even more vulnerable pastoral poet, D'Urfey; that the satire on Blackmore was incidental; and that, in spite of all these satiric purposes, the poem rests on a firm foundation of clearly perceived and precisely rendered actuality. This explanation is probable not only because each critical theory seems individually convincing, but because Gay in his early poetry wavered so conspicuously among various perspectives, searched several literary traditions, and incorporated as many points of view as he conceivably could in, for example, *Rural Sports.* The existence of widely divergent explanations of the origin and effect of *The Shepherd's Week* is critically significant as well as historically interesting: it suggests once more the extent to which Gay achieved poetic effects not merely by imitating a model but by bringing traditional material into meaningful conjunction with quite different systems of values. That *The Shepherd's Week* is so much more successful than **Rural Sports** may be partly explained by the fact that in it the conjunctions seem systematically controlled and ultimately purposeful.

The Shepherd's Week presents an image of rural life radically different from that at the end of **Rural Sports,** but one in the long run more appealing. Five of the six eclogues concern love, traditional subject for pastoral, with frequent verbal parody-echoes of Virgil pointed out by Gay's own notes. (William Henry Irving, indeed, believes that in the beginning the poem was intended as "burlesque of Vergil rather than ridicule of Philips."[14]) Gay's maidens are of quite a different sort from Virgil's; this was, after all, an important point of the joke. "Thou wilt not find my shepherdesses idly piping on oaten reeds," Gay writes in his proem, "but milking the kine, tying up the sheaves, or if the hogs are astray driving them to their styes."[15] He presents the notion of working shepherdesses as a jest, implicitly inviting his readers to recall the girls in Virgil's pastorals, who do nothing more serious than pelt their swains with apples; inviting them also to perceive how ridiculous were Philips' attempts to bring realism to the superbly artificial form of the pastoral. Yet, when Gay combines these two contradictory concepts of art, the result is frequently not ridiculous at all.

The idea of work is of primary importance in these poems, and not merely as a joke. As the shepherds in the first eclogue contend in praising their mistresses, each points out that his beloved makes toil sweeter, so that with her near, "Ev'n noon-tide labour seem'd an holiday" (1. 66). Cloddipole, who is to judge between them, finally refuses to make a choice—not, like the judge in Virgil's third eclogue, because the contestants are too equal, but because the time for singing and for playing at judgment is past:

> But see the sun-beams bright to labour warn,
> And gild the thatch of goodman *Hodges'* barn,
> Your herds for want of water stand adry,
> They're weary of your songs—and so am I.
>
> (11. 121-24)

The really meaningful context for action and for judgment throughout these pastorals is that of pastoral responsibility: the sun warns the swains to labor; the proper activity for shepherds is tending their sheep. Gay does not present his shepherds and shepherdesses milking the kine *instead of* idly piping, as he promises in the proem: the point is rather that he first shows them piping and singing, and then offers country work as a more meaningful alternative.

Similarly, in the second eclogue, **"Tuesday, or, The Ditty,"** the result of Marian's unrequited love for Colin Clout is the loss of her ability to work well. She is, before Colin turns his affections elsewhere, the ideal country maiden—ideal, like Blouzelinda in **"Friday,"** because responsible and expert at her work. But as a result of love the maid becomes "witless" (1. 17), and this adjective is not casually employed. Such terms as *witless* and *silly* are used frequently throughout these pastorals; almost invariably they point to genuine value judgments. Marian complains:

> Ah! woful day! ah, woful noon and morn!
> When first by thee my younglings white were
>   shorn,
> Then first, I ween, I cast a lover's eye,
> My sheep were silly, but more silly I.
>
> (11. 25-28)

This is obviously a parody of the same passage from Philips that Pope had chosen to make fun of. But it is more than parody. Philips' swain utters a perfectly conventional complaint, ludicrously unaware of its literal force. Marian's complaint, on the other hand, is a genuine commentary on the destruction of personal value involved in giving up "all busy heed." The context in which she recognizes her silliness is that of sheep shearing (compare Philips' vision of sheep browsing "flowery plains"), and the judgment she makes of herself is perfectly accurate: it is also Gay's judgment. But it is not inevitable: Gay does not suggest that the country maiden *must* be as silly as her sheep. On the contrary, **"Tuesday"** systematically sets up a series of contrasts between present and past which establish a vision of the rural ideal quite different from the romantic one of **Rural Sports.** Marian asserts her own superiority to Colin Clout's other sweetheart on the grounds that she is willing to work harder for Colin's sake; she recollects the glories of the past (11. 49-72) in terms of shared work. The poem is resolved with a ludicrously matter-of-fact image:

> Thus *Marian* wail'd, her eyes with tears
>   brimfull,
> When Goody *Dobbins* brought her cow to
>   bull.
> With apron blue to dry her tears she sought,
> Then saw the cow well serv'd, and took a
>   groat.
>
> (11. 103-36)

Sven Armens comments on this passage, "The necessity of fulfilling her daily tasks does afford some release for her grief-stricken existence. . . . Love is only a part of her life. When it vanishes, the country maid has something else of value left, a useful role as a contributing member of her society."[16] This analysis fails to point out that the "useful role" is partly a joke: the cow-bull episode places matters of love in a new perspective. **"Friday,"** the dirge for Blouzelinda, ends with the grief-stricken shepherds consoling themselves for the loss of one maiden by finding another; **"Thursday,"** the complaint and spell-casting of lovelorn Hobnelia, is resolved by the quite effortless seduction of the girl. Love and sex are, in this world, much the same; relations between men and women bear a conspicuous resemblance to those between cow and bull.

A reader may have ambivalent feelings about this fact. On the one hand, he is invited to look at these youths and maidens from the superior perspective of civilized sophistication, to laugh at them because of *their* conspicuous lack of sophistication—and, for that matter, even of civilization. But there is also the implicit juxtaposition of these country characters with the more romantically conceived ones of traditional Virgilian pastoral, and the advantage in this comparison is partly on the side of Gay's characters. If they are uncouth, they recognize and accept what they are; inasmuch as they are men and women of integrity, they are not ultimately comic.

In reading these poems we can never afford to be unaware that the comedy may turn at any moment back upon the reader. The worldly reader may laugh at these characters, but they might as readily laugh at him: they are more honest than he. The view of "civilized" life which Gay offers in *Trivia,* the fables, and the town eclogues frequently reminds us that beneath the facade of civilization men and women often resemble bulls and cows as much in the city as in the country; the difference is that in the city they ignore rather than accept the realities of mating animals.

The realism of the country is heavily stressed throughout *The Shepherd's Week.* In **"Wednesday, or The Dumps,"** Sparabella, mourning her lost lover, decides finally to commit suicide. She is deterred, however, by her vanity:

> This penknife keen my windpipe shall divide.
> What, shall I fall as squeaking pigs have dy'd!
> No—to some tree this carcass I'll suspend.
> But worrying curs find such untimely end! . . .
>
> (ll. 101-14)

Finally she decides to throw herself in the lake, "if courage holds" (l. 111); but by this time it is nightfall:

> The prudent maiden deems it now too late,
> And 'till to-morrow comes defers her fate.
>
> (ll. 119-20)

The comedy here derives from the disproportion between the girl's exaggerated and romanticized sense of tragedy and her underlying realism, which makes her find constant excuses for deferring her fate, and which will obviously always prevent a dramatic denouement

for her situation. But again, the comedy cuts two ways. We laugh at the maiden because she does *not* commit suicide; we would not laugh at her if she actually did kill herself. We are all too willing to accept seriously the posturings of sentimental self-dramatization. If Sparabella is ridiculous because of the gap between her image of herself and the actuality, more sophisticated readers may be equally ridiculous in their willingness to accept romantic poses as adequate bases for structuring actuality.

"Friday, or, The Dirge," also depends heavily on the tension between reality and romantic illusion. It is in some ways a genuinely moving dirge; it has moments of sharp perception and true feeling. Blouzelinda is mourned not as an idealized creature but as a girl who worked honestly and well, and for whom love was part of the natural pattern of life. At one point a mourning shepherd in conventional fashion invites nature to mourn her loss—yet his plea is not quite conventional after all.

> Henceforth the morn shall dewy sorrow
>   shed,
> And ev'ning tears upon the grass be spread;
> The rolling streams with wat'ry grief shall
>   flow,
> And winds shall moan aloud—when loud they
>   blow.
> Henceforth, as oft as autumn shall return,
> The dropping trees, whene'er it rains, shall
>   mourn;
> This season quite shall strip the country's
>   pride,
> For 'twas in autumn *Blouzelinda* died.
>
> (ll. 33-40)

These lines, which broadly parody common pastoral convention, also sum up the shepherd's real perception. Even in his grief, he has not lost sight of natural realities: he does not allow himself to believe that the normal order can be distorted as a result of one human death. Nothing will change except the interpretation of events. The dew that normally falls in the morning and evening, the streams that normally flow, the wind that blows and the trees that drip—all can now be explained in a different way; but the facts themselves have in no way been altered. The eclogue begins with Bumkinet's evocation of the bleakness of autumn, before he has learned of Blouzelinda's death; he can thus comment, "Yet e'en this season pleasance blithe affords" (l. 7). The same Bumkinet speaks later of the mourning of nature: only his perspective is different. To be sure, toward the end of his dirge he invites the fields to show "rueful symptoms" by substituting weeds for flowers as an emblem of the loss of beauty in Blouzelinda's death (ll. 83-88), but this momentary comic deviation from realism (in a passage, incidentally, closely imitated from Virgil) is immediately compensated for by Bumkinet's matter-of-fact adjuration to the swains to make sure that they spell properly the inscription on Blouzelinda's gravestone.

The inscription itself, with its reminder that "flesh is grass," (1. 92) is of central importance not only to this eclogue but to the entire series. It works in two ways: it insists on the ultimate unimportance of the lives of these people, in all their transience; but also it insists that human life participates meaningfully in the natural cycle. Flesh quite literally becomes grass which is eaten by cows which must be tended by yet other human beings; at every point in the cycle, man is directly involved with nature, and his acceptance of his responsibilities is also an acceptance of his place in the natural order. So Blouzelinda on her deathbed worries about the welfare of her poultry and her calf; so the mourners at her grave are conscious of the fact that the preacher talks somewhat too long, and they retreat from mourning to cider, because "Excessive sorrow is exceeding dry" (1. 152). The point is not merely that these are insensitive country bumpkins, although we are indeed from time to time invited to think so; it is also that these particular sorts of insensitivity imply the recognition that sentimentality over the dead is not so important as the duties—and even the pleasures—of the living.

But surely Gay would laugh at so heavy-handed and serious a treatment of his shepherds and shepherdesses, who retain their vividness finally as a result of their charm. When Cuddy describes his Buxoma as

> Clean as young lambkins or the goose's down,
> And like the goldfinch in her Sunday gown
>   **("Monday,"** 11. 51-52),

he provides a strong poetic evocation of her appeal; when dismal Sparabella cries out,

> Sooner shall scriech-owls bask in sunny day,
> And the slow ass on trees, like squirrels, play,
>   . . .
> Than I forget my shepherd's wonted love
>   **("Wednesday,"** 11. 69-70,72),

we enjoy her imagery although we may not altogether accept her grief.

The charm of these characters is far more important than any philosophical significance we may posit for them. But what is its ultimate effect? Professor Trowbridge comments on this point: "Like Shakespeare's artisans, shepherds, and squires, Gay's rustics have a certain naïve charm, but from the sophisticated urban point of view which Gay (like Shakespeare) expected in his readers, these dairymaids and swineherds are ludicrous—delightful but absurd."[17] But the matter is more complicated. If Gay really mocks Philips and D'Urfey and Blackmore and Virgil, while he conveys directly and convincingly the actualities of country existence—if he does all these things successfully, his effects must be extraordinarily various. Surely he can simultaneously deride Philips' "realism" and Virgil's artifice, Blackmore's pretentiousness and D'Urfey's rusticity, only by choosing for himself some middle position. That hypothetical midway norm is never directly embodied in the poem, but it is implicit; and it allows Gay to criticize the city through the demonstrated standards of the country, inasmuch as these standards involve real values, as well as to criticize the country by the implicit standards of the city. He pretends, as Professor Trowbridge points out, to assume "the character and attitudes of a rustic bard" (86), and he does so in order to mock the rustic bard. Yet he uses his persona also as a convenience for exposing the genuine values that the country has to offer. The pure nostalgia which dominates and frequently weakens **Rural Sports** has here been combined with the sophistication which unsuccessfully seeks to find expression in **The Fan;** the skill at parodying conventional forms while expressing personal perceptions through them which we noted even in **Wine** has now found more appropriate subject matter. And the complexity which makes **The Shepherd's Week** interesting seems a direct product of the tension between the point of view of the country man and the more fashionable perspective which contradicts it, both points of view incorporated in the poet. Gay has here found a mask which does not entirely obscure his own features: uncomfortable in the total guise of sophisticate, unwilling to commit himself completely to the unfashionable posture of a lover of the country, he adapts many voices to his own use. Mocking Ambrose Philips, imitating Virgil, parodying the unrealistic conventions of pastoral, he seems for the first time to have succeeded in saying what he wanted to say. Later in his poetic career he would want to say more—and then, too, his problem would be to find the proper voice with which to say it.

Notes

[1] Samuel Johnson, "J. Philips," *Lives of the English Poets,* ed. George B. Hill, 3 vols. (Oxford, 1905), II, 284-85.

[2] John M. Aden, "The 1720 Version of *Rural Sports* and the Georgic Tradition," *Modern Language Quarterly,* XX (1959), 228-32.

[3] Pope to Gay, Aug. 23, 1713, *The Correspondence of Alexander Pope,* ed. George Sherburn, 5 vols. (Oxford, 1956), I, 188.

[4] Oct. 28, 1710; Pope, *Correspondence,* I, 101.

[5] The essays were in Numbers 22, 23, 28, 30, and 32 of the *Guardian.*

[6] Pope, *Correspondence,* I, 229.

[7] Hoyt Trowbridge, "Pope, Gay, and *The Shepherd's Week,*" *Modern Language Quarterly,* V (1944), 79-88.

[8] *Ibid.,* pp. 84-86.

[9] John Robert Moore, "Gay's Burlesque of Sir Richard Blackmore's Poetry," *Journal of English and Germanic Philology,* L (1951), 83-89.

[10] William D. Ellis, Jr., "Thomas D'Urfey, the Pope-Philips Quarrel, and *The Shepherd's Week,*" *Publications of the Modern Language Association,* LXXIV (1959), 203-12.

[11] J. E. Congleton, *Theories of Postoral Poetry in England, 1684-1798* (Gainesville, Fla., 1952), p. 93.

[12] Samuel Johnson, "Gay," *Lives of the English Poets,* II, 61.

[13] Bonamy Dobree, *English Literature in the Early Eighteenth Century* (Oxford, 1959), p. 141.

[14] William Henry Irving, *John Gay, Favorite of the Wits* (Durham, N.C., 1940), p. 83.

[15] *The Poetical Works of John Gay,* ed. G. C. Faber (London, 1926), p. 29. The whole poem is highly illuminating and well worth reading.

[16] Sven M. Armens, *John Gay, Social Critic* (New York, 1954), p. 167.

[17] Hoyt Trowbridge, *op. cit.,* p. 84.

Patricia Meyer Spacks (essay date 1965)

SOURCE: "The Beggar's Triumph," in *John Gay,* Twayne Publishers; Inc., 1965, pp. 145-61.

[*In the following excerpt, Spacks suggests that in* The Beggar's Opera *Gay developed a dramatic form that ideally suited both his artistic voice and his political concerns. Spacks also looks at the* Opera's *less successful sequel,* Polly, *to illuminate the reasons for the* Opera's *popular and critical acclaim, in both the eighteenth and twentieth centuries.*]

It is, of course, for *The Beggar's Opera* that Gay is remembered in the twentieth century, even among people with no particular interest in eighteenth-century poetry or drama. The play was revived in a rather romanticized London production with great success in 1926; its music was later adapted and presented by Benjamin Britten; in 1963 the Royal Shakespeare Company produced it once more, with great attention to realistic detail, and with a vivid sense of the play's topicality in modern England, once more riddled with scandal in high places. Made into a movie starring Laurence Olivier, *The Beggar's Opera* still returns to art theaters; it has been reissued in formats ranging from an inexpensive student paperback to a splendid reproduction of the 1729 edition; a new recording recently presented all its music and much of its speech.

Probably nothing, however, has brought Gay's work so much to popular attention as the fact that *The Beggar's Opera* was the basis for Bertolt Brecht's *Threepenny Opera,* which relied on it for broad plot structure, for many of its characters, and even for some of its music. The Brecht play, which had a record-breaking run off-Broadway, seems lively and singularly relevant; it has led some readers to new awareness of comparable qualities in Gay's opera, which conveys so highly sophisticated a structure of qualifications that its subject almost seems to be the nature and necessity of qualification in life. In its awareness of the immense difficulty of civilized existence, it speaks directly to our own time.

The relevance of *The Beggar's Opera* to the twentieth century was underlined by its most recent London production, a Brechtian version in which slight textual alterations stressed the applicability of Gay's satire to such modern phenomena as the Profumo affair (*e.g.,* "I, Madam, was once kept by a Tory."). In a "preview" published in the *Manchester Guardian* the day before the play's London opening, Philip Hope-Wallace speculated about the modern effect of the comedy. "Will anyone be shocked now?" he asks, and concludes that it is "a question of age perhaps." "I should think," adds Hope-Wallace, "this indestructible old bag of other men's tunes and its comedy within a comedy would be exactly to modern taste and once again become the talk of the town."[1]

He was, however, rather too optimistic. Although the play's audiences were clearly amused and refreshed by the satiric energy of the "opera" in Peter Wood's production, which employed an elaborate and ingenious set, stylized action, broad parody, and deliberate techniques of "alienation," the newspaper critics were less enthusiastic. They revived the issues of the eighteenth century: the *Sunday Times* commentator, alone in liking the play, praised Polly, like his predecessors two hundred years before, as "an unquenchable sunbeam in a world of tumultuous shadows."[2] Other critics returned to the question of morality. "Morality does not suit an eighteenth-century comedy," wrote David Pryce-Jones, "particularly one so sensitive as *The Beggar's Opera,* where all the lessons to be learnt are implied and all the criticism is self-contained."[3] Kenneth Tynan had similar objections: "What should be implied is shrieked aloud."[4] The problem remains: how can moral satire be made clear and convincing without becoming too blatant? Gay solved that problem largely through his conception of the play; the modern producer, by trying to stress through setting (the play takes place on a prison ship), realistic costume, and stylized action the indictment of social conditions implicit in *The Beggar's Opera,* apparently made that indictment less palatable.

In considering the *Fables* we discovered that the nature of their form helped Gay to achieve success. The same is true of *The Beggar's Opera:* the special variety of dramatic form that Gay here chose was maximally useful in solving the problems that plagued him. He had long experimented with various uses of disguise in drama; now he developed a form almost completely dependent on disguise. He could actually introduce himself directly into his play, given the disguise (and a very significant one it is, considering his preoccupation with money) of beggar.

The importance of this mask as a distancing device becomes apparent when we compare the Introduction of *The Beggar's Opera* with that of its sequel, *Polly.* The first words of the Beggar in the earlier play are these: "If Poverty be a Title to Poetry, I am sure Nobody can dispute mine. I own my self of the Company of Beggars; and I make one at their Weekly Festivals at St. *Gile's.* I have a small Yearly Salary for my Catches, and am welcome to a Dinner there whenever I please, which is more than most Poets can say" (I, 135). The charm of this speech comes chiefly from the fact that the poet thinks of himself *mainly* as beggar, only secondarily as poet; from this perspective he can treat the financial need characteristic of poets with saving irony. He does not appear to take himself or his poetry very seriously; extolling the pleasures of beggarhood, he thus makes a telling comment on the difficulties of being a poet (his point, of course, is that the beggar is *more* independent than the typical poet). But he manages to avoid pathos and distasteful self-concern: his self-esteem is, for a change, appealing rather than unattractive.

His counterpart in *Polly,* on the other hand, is called not *beggar* but *poet.* The disguise is much thinner, and the language of the character reflects his greater closeness to the actual nature of the author: "A Sequel to a play is like more last words. It is a kind of absurdity; and really, sir, you have prevailed upon me to pursue this subject against my judgment. . . . I know, I must have been looked upon as whimsical, and particular, if I had scrupled to have risqued my reputation for my profit; for why should I be more squeamish than my betters? and so, sir, contrary to my opinion, I bring *Polly* once again upon the stage" (II, 3). This is Gay speaking virtually in his own voice. After the wit of the first sentence, the speech degenerates into a sort of

apology which upon analysis becomes increasingly distasteful. The point seems to be that the author *is,* in fact, offering this play for the sake of personal profit, but that his mode of admitting this is intended to remove all onus from him. He retains the rather unpleasant tone of moral superiority with no evidence of any real claim to such elevation. One important effect of the series of disguises in *The Beggar's Opera* is to make all pretensions to superiority into jokes; nothing in *Polly* reveals the Poet's claim as ludicrous. But the joke is necessary; the perspective it provides is a major—perhaps *the* major—source of strength in *The Beggar's Opera.*

Of course the disguise of Beggar for the author is only the first of many masks in *The Beggar's Opera;* all serve similar purposes of implicit commentary. The other disguises in the play are more complicated and less obvious than the introductory one, and they are difficult to define. Is one to say, for example, that Macheath is essentially an aristocrat in the disguise of a highwayman? Or is it more accurate to say that the highwayman in the play disguise themselves to themselves as aristocrats? Here is a sample of dialogue among Macheath's gang:

> *Ned:* Who is there here that would not dye for his Friend?
> *Harry:* Who is there here that would betray him for his Interest?
> *Matt:* Show me a Gang of Courtiers that can say as much.
> *Ben:* We are for a just Partition of the World, for every Man hath a Right to enjoy Life.
> *Matt:* We retrench the Superfluities of Mankind. The World is avaritious, and I hate Avarice. A covetous fellow, like a Jack-daw, steals what he was never made to enjoy, for the sake of hiding it. These are the Robbers of Mankind, forMoney was made for the Free-hearted and Generous, and where is the Injury of taking from another, what he hath not   the Heart to make use of?
>
> (I, 163-64)

These are aristocrats indeed: honorable, loyal, governed by principle; and if the principles seem to partake largely of rationalization, surely this fact makes the gang seem no less *aristocratic.* We get a different, but equally convincing, view of the highwayman as aristocrat from the Peachums, who, as William Empson has demonstrated, represent the bourgeois perspective in the play.

> *Mrs. Peachum:* I knew she was always a proud Slut; and now the wench hath play'd the Fool and married, because forsooth

she would do like the Gentry. Can you
support the Expense of a Husband, Hussy,
in gaming, drinking and whoring? . . .
If you must be married, could you introduce
no-body into our Family but a
Highwayman? Why, thou foolish Jade, thou
wilt be as ill-us'd, and as much neglected,
as if thou hadst married a Lord!

Peachum: Let not your Anger, my Dear, break
through the Rules of Decency, for the
Captain looks upon himself in the
  Military Capacity, as a Gentleman by his
Profession.

(I, 149)

Earlier, before the marriage is revealed, the Peachums
discuss Macheath's wealth and prospects. They agree
that he keeps good company and associates with the
gentry, but this tendency is a weakness: he cannot
expect to win at the gaming tables without the education of a fine gentleman. "What business hath he to
keep Company with Lords and Gentlemen?" Mrs. Peachum concludes: "he should leave them to prey upon
one another" (I, 142). To be aristocrats means, then, in
this world, *not* to be men of honor and principle, but
to be men who prey on one another.

William Hazlitt, assuming the identity between aristocrat and gentleman, finds Macheath heroic indeed:

Macheath should be a fine man and a gentleman,
but he should be one of God Almighty's gentlemen,
not a gentleman of the black rod. His gallantry and
good-breeding should arise from impulse, not from
rule; not from the trammels of education, but from
a soul generous, courageous, good-natured, aspiring,
amorous. The class of the character is very difficult
to hit. It is something between gusto and slang, like
port-wine and brandy mixed. It is not the mere
gentleman that should be represented, but the black-
guard sublimated into the gentleman. This character
is qualified in a highwayman, as it is qualified in a
prince. We hope this is not a libel.[5]

This image of Macheath as nature's nobleman is appealing, but the play will not allow us to rest content
with it. Just at the point where we may be tempted to
say that the highwaymen are true aristocrats, the nobility false ones, we discover that Macheath, for example,
despite his prating of honor, is as capable of treachery,
as proud of his seductions and their ultimate effect in
populating Drury Lane (the resort of prostitutes) as his
"betters" could conceivably be.

Similarly, our vision of Polly is made to fluctuate wildly.
Eighteenth-century audiences wept and applauded at
Polly's song, "Oh ponder well! be not severe," respond-
ing to its pathos and to her as a pathetic heroine. She

has, to be sure, all the postures of the traditional romantic lead: her frequent evocations of the idea of
love, her parroting of the notions of playbooks (although, to be sure, her admission of their source rather
tempers the potency of such notions), her quite unjus-
tified faith in Macheath's loyalty and her unwillingness to betray him—all these characteristics are conventionally admirable. But the first words of this Polly, who insists on her sentimentality and her virtue,
spoken to her father, are, "I know as well as any of the
fine Ladies how to make the most of my self and my
Man too. A Woman knows how to be mercenary,
though she hath never been in a Court or at an Assembly. We have it in our Natures, Papa" (I, 147).

This is not, to be sure, a direct statement of Polly's
own feelings: she wishes at the moment to obscure her
actual marriage to Macheath by pretending to conform
precisely to her father's standards. But she has the
lesson a bit too pat for comfort: it is easy to suspect
that she really partakes of these values. After all, the
truth is that she *does,* as she claims, have such visible
marks of the captain's favor as a watch. The song she
sings immediately after this speech ("Virgins are like
the fair Flower in its Lustre") emphasizes the commodity view of virginity; when, later in the play, Polly
comes into contact with Lucy, who has loved not wisely but too well, her sense of superiority rests on the
fact that she has been smart enough to make a better
bargain than Lucy: marriage for virginity. William
Empson documents her feverish interest in hanging,
the extent to which she seems almost to desire what
she most fears, Macheath's death by hanging, the only
form which death takes in this play.

All this is not to say that Polly lacks charm; she is, of
course, the play's most appealing character. But it is
the nature of this play that its most charming personages are frequently undercut, while its least attractive
figures have moments of such moral clarity that we
can hardly reject them. Thus the senior Peachums,
underhanded, self-seeking, treacherous as they are, can
convince us momentarily that the evils they abundantly
demonstrate are merely natural concomitants of good
business practice: they have the airs, the language, the
self-esteem of successful businessmen; and our moral
detestation of them cannot be quite secure—particularly if we perceive their resemblance to modern representatives of the business world. All the characters of
The Beggar's Opera could be transferred to a new
plot about the participants in a television quiz-show
scandal with little change in their natures or their comments. The play leaves us with no secure stance; in
place of one perspective from which to view the characters, it offers many. These characters do not come on
stage in the casing of a mummy or a crocodile. They
are disguised even *from themselves;* they do not know
what they really are. As a consequence it becomes
difficult for us to know what they are. This is a far

more subtle use of the disguise motif than Gay ever made before or later; it dramatizes the almost metaphysical implications of the device.

II

If the shifting self-disguises (Polly as her father's daughter, as sentimental heroine, as wronged wife; Macheath as honorable gentleman, as dishonorable seducer; the Peachums as practical business people, as despicable profiteers in vice) afford one mode of constant qualification in the play, another is provided by the patterns of imagery which run through songs and prose alike. William Empson has discussed brilliantly and in some detail the imagery of hanging and its ramifications. Two other themes of the imagery are almost equally obvious: money and animals. And the three patterns in conjunction provide interesting commentary on one another.

The image of human beings as animals, a favorite of Gay's, becomes in **The Beggar's Opera** a subtle and complicated device. Lockit's direct summary of the motif is well-known: "Lions, Wolves, and Vulturs don't live together in Herds, Droves or Flocks.—Of all Animals of Prey, Man is the only sociable one. Every one of us preys upon his Neighbour, and yet we herd together.—*Peachum* is my Companion, my Friend—According to the Custom of the World, indeed, he may quote thousands of Precedents for cheating me—And shall I not make use of the Privilege of Friendship to make him a Return?" (I, 196). In tone and emphasis this speech is wonderfully characteristic of the play. It parodies the note of self-satisfaction we hear so often in these characters: Lockit is smug over the "superiority" of man, demonstrated by his sociability, to other vicious animals with an immediate exposition of precisely what this sociability means in practice. But the play provides many more specific statements of the similarity between men and animals.

It seems—although there are many exceptions—that the women in the play are somewhat more likely to think of love in animal terms, while the men connect love directly with money. Mrs. Peachum sees the "simple Maid" as a moth, constantly playing about the flame until, if she is not made a wife, her honor's singed. ("If Love the Virgin's Heart invade" [I, 143]). Polly describes the virgin as a flower, with her lovers as bees and butterflies ("Virgins are like the fair Flower in its Lustre" [I, 147]). Later, in a sentimental song, she likens herself to a turtledove ("The Turtle thus with plaintive crying" [I, 156]). Again, immediately after Macheath, masculine and money-oriented, has compared his love for her to that of a miser for his shilling, she compares hers for him to that of a boy for his sparrow ("The Miser thus a Shilling sees" [I, 162]). Jenny Diver, one of the trulls, sees Macheath as a cock attended by hens ("Before the Barn-door crowing" [I, 171]).

All these images, with the possible exception of Polly's boy-sparrow one, are comparatively innocent, although in the total context of the play they seem less so than we might expect. Gradually, though, the connections between human love and the animal world become increasingly sinister. Macheath, betrayed by women, shifts the bird imagery to a new realm: "Women are Decoy Ducks; who can trust them! Beasts, Jades, Jilts, Harpies, Furies, Whores!" (I, 173). When Lucy confronts her betrayer, Macheath, in prison, she sings a song which makes him the trapped rat and her the good housewife who throws it to the dog or cat ("Thus when a good Huswife sees a Rat," [I, 177]). Polly, still dwelling on bird imagery, compares herself to a female, Macheath to a male swallow, in a song whose point, Empson suggests, is that she is eagerly awaiting Macheath's death ("Thus when the Swallow, seeking Prey" [I, 186]).[6] Then Lucy sees herself as a fox, Macheath as another ("I like the Fox shall grieve" [I, 193]). The final two songs in this sequence of animal lyrics are worth quoting in full. The first is sung by Lockit to Peachum, as he suggests that Macheath can be trapped by keeping an eye on Polly:

> What Gudgeons are we Men!
> Ev'ry Woman's easy Prey.
> Though we have felt the Hook, agen
> We bite and they betray.
> The Bird that hath been trapt,
> When he hears his calling Mate,
> To her he flies, again he's clapt
> Within the wiry Grate.
>
> (I, 201-02)

The second is sung alternately by Polly and Lucy:

> *Polly:* A Curse attends that Woman's Love.
>   Who always would be pleasing.
> *Lucy:* The Pertness of the billing Dove,
>   Like tickling, is but teazing.
> *Polly:* What then in Love can Woman do?
> *Lucy:* If we grow fond they shun us.
> *Polly:* And when we fly them, they pursue:
> *Lucy:* But leave us when they've won us.
>
> (I, 209)

The songs comment tellingly on the sentimentality of some of the previous uses of bird imagery. Lockit's lyrics are particularly explicit, juxtaposing the image of men as "poor fish" to be hooked by women with an even more sinister picture of female birds as decoys to trap the males. All attempts to glamorize the notion of human beings as animals or birds must ultimately fail; this is degrading imagery, and Lockit, for the moment at least, sees it quite explicitly as such. (It is also Lockit, incidentally, who provides the most menacing animal image of the play: "Like Pikes, lank with Hunger, who miss of their Ends,/They bite their Companions, and prey on their Friends" [I, 197].) Polly and Lucy, from the opposite, feminine, point of view, perceive the same truth: they may try to romanticize their roles, but the actuality is hard and inescapable.

The pattern of animal imagery, in other words, provides its own commentary. Moving in general from benign to vicious images, it also moves from the un-self-conscious, romantic, and conventional to a more cynical and analytical use of the same sort of material. And the later usages reflect back on the earlier ones, causing us to feel that innocence in this world (whatever innocence Polly truly had at first) can be equated only with ignorance, that romanticism is a resource only for those who know nothing of reality.

The notion of human beings as animals is further illuminated by frequent metaphorical and literal remarks about money. Love and money are, of course, closely related: Filch's first song establishes the nature of the relationship:

> 'Tis Woman that seduces all Mankind,
> By her we first were taught the wheedling
>   Arts:
> Her very eyes can cheat; when most she's
>   kind,
> She tricks us of our Money with our Hearts.
> For her, like Wolves by night we roam for
>   Prey,
> And practise ev'ry Fraud to bribe her Charms;
> For Suits of Love, like Law, are won by Pay,
> And Beauty must be fee'd into our Arms.
>
> (I, 139)

This song not only summarizes the masculine point of view toward "love," as it exists in the world of the play; it also suggests the relation between human emphasis on money and the notion of human beings as animals. Men become wolves, Filch says quite explicitly, because of the feminine demand for money. And since, as other songs and comments in the play make abundantly clear, virtually *every* human enterprise depends upon money, it is quite apparent that man can hardly escape reduction to animality.

Mrs. Peachum is the only woman in the play who states explicitly that women themselves are commodities of equivalent value to money. She sees the maid as "like the golden Oar,/Which hath Guineas intrinsical in't"; the precise value of the ore is unknown until it is minted. The wife, on the other hand, is "like a Guinea in Gold,/Stampt with the Name of her Spouse"; although she no longer has the advantage of being of incalculable value, she acquires a new benefit: that of being an accepted medium of exchange, "current in

every House" (I, 145). "The first time a Woman is frail, she should be somewhat nice methinks, for then or never is the time to make her fortune" (I, 151). This is Mrs. Peachum's morality, and, if no other woman quite states it, there is little evidence that anyone has an essentially different standard. Polly sees Macheath as her "treasure"; she also seems to have had a good sense of the value of her virginity, though she would not use such crass terms as her mother.

"You might sooner tear a Pension out of the Hands of a Courtier, a Fee from a Lawyer, a pretty Woman from a Looking-glass, or any Woman from Quadrille.—But to tear me from thee is impossible!" This is Macheath's idea of a fitting protestation of love to Polly (I, 160), who, in the play's comedy, accepts it quite blandly as such. More consistently than anyone else, he connects love with money. His metaphor of Polly as the shilling, himself as the miser, seems surprising: more often he values women in terms of guineas: "A Man who loves Money, might as well be contented with one Guinea, as I with one Woman" (I, 166). And again, "I must have Women. There is nothing unbends the Mind like them. Money is not so strong a Cordial for the Time" (I, 167).

Hazlitt may include Macheath's "amorousness" among his virtues, but this particular aspect of the captain's high regard for women is hardly attractive. The trulls he has sent to Drury Lane share his values: one praises another because, "Though her Fellow be never so agreeable, she can pick his Pocket as cooly, as if Money were her only Pleasure. Now that is a Command of the Passions uncommon in a Woman!" (I, 170). After one of them betrays the captain (for money), they argue over their "accounts": how many hanged men should be laid to the credit of each (I, 174). Macheath himself is greeted in prison by Lucy, whom he has seduced and left pregnant; one of her songs to him ends:

> Whoever steals a Shilling,
> Through Shame the Guilt conceals:
> In Love the perjur'd Villain
> With Boasts the Theft reveals.
>
> (I, 178)

And there is justice in her complaint. Macheath convinces her that he plans to marry her, but she is unable to soften her father's heart. Macheath suggests that in such a case a bribe is indicated: "Money well tim'd, and properly apply'd, will do any thing" (I, 184). His next song elaborates the point, concluding that the way to win a woman is to offer her money: "That Reason with all is prevailing" (185). "In the Account of Love you are in my debt," Macheath tells Lucy (192). "Owe thy Life to me," Lucy replies. But as Macheath points out a bit later, "Death is a Debt,/A Debt on demand" (217)—and a gentleman always pays debts of this sort, if not those of love.

Of course these examples in the play do not even begin to exhaust the discussion of money, its function and its effects. But the ways in which money is connected with love—or with what passes for love in the play—are particularly indicative of the total corruption of the world described here. Filch makes a living by "helping the Ladies to a Pregnancy against their being called down to Sentence" (198)—by eighteenth-century law pregnant women could not be hanged. Sven Armens comments accurately on this fact: "Here sexual intercourse, which can be the warm expression of true love, has been most thoroughly debased. Even lust itself has been undermined. Love is moral and practical; lust is immoral and impractical; but begetting illegitimate children in order to cheat justice combines immorality with a sort of practicality. This is sex as simply business for all concerned; a breed farm for criminals represents the complete perversion of the chivalric code of courtly love."[7]

Except for Polly, sex seems to be hardly more than business for anyone in the play; even Lucy, who claims to be desperately in love, is capable of bargaining over her sexual rights. The Peachums consider their daughter a business asset; Polly herself can deal with her virginity as a commodity; Macheath makes little distinction between the pursuits of love and of money; Lockit thinks of love and money as equivalent material for bargaining. The money-love imagery sums up and emphasizes the nature of a society completely dominated by money—for frequent references in the play insist that lawyers, courtiers, doctors—all the world—care only for money; and Lockit and Peachum, those companions in crime, fall out before our eyes over their profits.

"Money well tim'd, and properly apply'd, will do any thing." "Of all Animals of Prey, Man is the only sociable one." Considered in conjunction, these two thematic statements explain and reflect upon one another. The cause of man's preying and of his sociability, as expounded in this play, is money. Or, conversely, the reason that money will do anything is that man is an animal of prey. his prey is only incidentally other human beings, ultimately it is money. Fierce punitive measures dispose of the weak, the poor, the unlucky in such a society: this brings us to the matter of hanging, the source of the third major pattern of imagery. Love, death, and money; human beings reducing themselves to a sub-animal level—it sounds a somber play indeed. And of course it *is* somber—but funny as well; for the involved structure of cross-commentary, keeping the reader constantly a little off-balance, forces him to see the ridiculous as well as the horrible aspects of each situation.

The ending of the play is a perfect instance of the way in which this particular double view (of the world as both horrifying and ridiculous) is maintained. Macheath is about to be hanged when the player of the Introduction protests to the beggar-author that an opera must end happily. The beggar agrees to cry a reprieve for Macheath; the player approves: "All this we must do, to comply with the Taste of the Town" (223). Sven Armens summarizes the implications of this piece of action by observing, "The moral of the play is dismissed as the town in its ethical degradation dismisses morality."[8] True enough—here is the horror: that the "town" which witnesses the play is a society of the same sort as that depicted in the play equally corrupt, equally perverted in values, and that honest drama, which shows "that the lower Sort of People have their Vices in a degree as well as the Rich: and that they are punish'd for them" (224), is consequently impossible. But it is equally true (and of course Sven Armens elsewhere demonstrates his awareness of the play's comic aspects) that the superb inconsequence of the ending accords tonally with the general lightheartedness of the play as a whole, lightheartedness which persists, paradoxically, despite the bitterness, the intense cynicism reiterated by the ending. It is quite proper to laugh at these matters—if one can retain the perspective of an outsider and fail to realize that he also is being condemned. And it is proper also to abhor and denounce the world depicted: the one response is incomplete without the other.

III

An obvious aspect of **The Beggar's Opera** which we will in the main have to ignore is its music. Most operas, even comic operas, hardly exist for the average reader outside their stage productions; their music supplies justification or compensation for the improbabilities of their plots, their eccentricities of language and meter. It is a measure of how remarkable Gay's accomplishment was that his play has such vivid life even on the printed page, its songs self-justified by the charm of their lyrics. But the music of **The Beggar's Opera** adds an extra dimension to the play on stage—and Gay used this resource, too, in his elaborate structure of cross-commentary.

The commentary comes from the relation of Gay's lyrics to the original words attached to the music. Almost all the songs in the play are traditional tunes (hence the name of the genre created by this work: *ballad opera*), and the lyrics originally connected with them would have been familiar to the early audiences. A recent edition of the play has printed texts of the early songs side by side with Gay's versions,[9] and some comparisons are instructive. Many have been pointed out by Professor Bronson in the essay previously cited. In general, they intensify the same implications we have discovered already. When Mrs. Peachum sings of how maids are like gold ore, wives like gold guineas, she sings to a tune which earlier had words insisting that:

> We're just like a Mouse in a Trap,
> Or Vermin caught in a Gin;

We Sweat and Fret, and try to Escape
And Curse the sad Hour we came in.

Thus the imagery of money is in effect placed in conjunction with that of animals—the precise metaphor of the mouse in a trap is to be used later by Lucy. The song, "'Tis Woman that seduces all Mankind" goes with a tune whose words describe a masculine seducer who loves and leaves his victims: if listeners are conscious of the traditional version, they are by this very fact prevented from having a simple view of the situation. Macheath's sentimental song, "Pretty Polly, say," is based on a piece beginning "Pretty Parret say"—and this in itself is adequate comment on the captain's sentimentality. (Indeed, the view of Polly as parrot sheds light on her apparent complexity: her ideas are second-hand, derived from diverse sources; she recites whatever seems appropriate in a specific situation.) The lyric beginning. "No power on earth can e'er divide/ The knot that sacred Love hath ty'd" must be considered in conjunction with its predecessor:

Remember Damon you did tell,
In Chastity you lov'd me well,
But now alas I am undone,
And here am left to make my Moan.

So much for professions of everlasting and sacred love!

These sketchy examples should be enough to emphasize once more the consistency with which Gay insisted upon keeping his readers and audiences simultaneously conscious of different—often radically different—perspectives on the action, the characters, the very language of his play. *The Beggar's Opera* is a work of enormous sophistication, unprecedented in Gay's literary career and never again to be equaled or even approached by him. When he attempted immediately to duplicate his success by reusing the same characters in *Polly,* the result was a literary—although by no means a financial—fiasco. And perhaps the best way to conclude a discussion of *The Beggar's Opera* is by a brief examination of its sequel, which demonstrates by its failure to employ them how valuable the devices of the earlier play are.

IV

The early history of *Polly* is more interesting than the play itself. The comedy was finished late in 1728. Although it was far more innocent politically than *The Beggar's Opera,* in December its performance was prohibited on vague political grounds by the lord chamberlain. (As Gay himself put it, "I am accused, in general terms, of having written many disaffected libels and seditious pamphlets."[10]) W. E. Schultz suggests the probability that the prohibition depended not so much on the content of the play as on the fact "that the report of a new play bearing Gay's name was . . .

unfit for the comfort of the Walpole circle."[11] At any rate, the play could be printed if not acted, with the prospect of the added sales that censorship always seems to bring. Within a year 10,500 copies had been sold of two large quarto editions.[12] Estimates of Gay's actual proceeds vary wildly: Schultz believes that the playwright may have made £3,000;[13] James Sutherland suggests £1,000.[14] At any rate, immediate pirated editions reduced his receipts: the first piracies appeared within three or four days after the original publication of *Polly,* early in April, 1729, and by June there were injunctions for piracy against seventeen printers and booksellers.[15] Evidently a good many others felt, with Gay, that a sequel to *The Beggar's Opera* could hardly fail.

But, whatever its receipts, the play remains a failure. *The Beggar's Opera* presents us with a world in which *everyone* is corrupt: we may discern differences of degree, but no real distinctions of kind. Filch, the youth who makes his living by causing pregnancies, has his moments of charm; Polly, that delightful heroine, has hers of unpleasant calculation. In *Polly,* on the other hand, society splits into heroes and villains; there is no doubt at all where one's sympathies are to lie. Polly has become a model of virtue; we are expected to take with entire seriousness her protestations of undying love to Macheath, although at the end of the play, having discovered Macheath's full villainy, she appears ready to marry a noble savage who is also, conveniently, a prince.

Her speech at this juncture is characteristic of her language throughout: "I am charm'd, prince, with your generosity and virtue. 'Tis only by the pursuit of those we secure real happiness. Those that know and feel virtue in themselves, must love it in others. Allow me to give a decent time to my sorrows. But my misfortunes at present interrupt the joys of victory" (II, 78). It is almost inconceivable that Gay could offer us such speech with no ironic perspective, but here and throughout the play he does exactly that. The Indians are without exception noble, so their language must be noble, too; the pirates, invariably villainous, talk always like villains.

Macheath has now painted himself black (a convenient symbol), named himself *Morano,* and taken up with Jenny Diver, who managed to be transported with him. He is no longer the model of the highwayman-gentleman, having been morally destroyed by his unworthy love. When at the end he is finally hanged, we could hardly wish for a reprieve (indeed, one is actually granted, but too late): he has become so conventionally detestable that we find him both boring and distasteful and feel well rid of him. ("If justice hath overtaken him," says the Indian prince to Polly, with superb lack of logic, "he was unworthy of you" [II, 76].) The only interesting villain in the play is a minor one, Ducat, the plantation owner who originally buys Polly to be his concubine and who at the very last hopes still to make a profit from her. In Gay's depiction of him alone (and occasionally of Mrs. Trapes, a transplant from *The Beggar's Opera*), we find touches of the poet's old satiric insight.

It is significant that these minor figures should be the most successful characters in the play, for they are also the two who have the closest relation to eighteenth-century actuality. Ducat is struggling to follow the model of the English gentleman; Mrs. Trapes, his tutor, guides him in his progress in vice. Given this much relation to real society, these characters seem more meaningful than their companions; the Indians, the pirates, Macheath himself, certainly Polly, do not have much to do with reality, although the playwright frequently insists that Macheath and his band are allegorical representatives of the viciousness inherent in English society. In *The Beggar's Opera,* on the other hand, although the atmosphere is permeated with a delicious sense of unreality (we don't believe for a moment that highwaymen or "fences" ever talked like that; we don't believe in the action; the sudden shift at the ending is a surprise but not a shock, considering that none of the action has caused the suspension of disbelief), the total effect depends fundamentally on our constant, steady conviction that everything that happens on stage has its direct analogue on higher levels of society. Lacking the power to convey this conviction, *Polly* can only seem an essentially frivolous and meaningless exercise.

There's no use flogging a dead horse, and *Polly* is a very dead one indeed. Yet it provides a dramatic illustration of how precarious was the balance Gay established in *The Beggar's Opera.* Lacking that balance all other devices must fail. The imagery in *Polly* comes from the same realms as that of its predecessor; the songs are based on similar originals. But nothing works in *Polly,* and certainly no two devices work together. The difference between hackwork and comic drama informed by a vision can seldom have been so clearly demonstrated as in the relation between *The Beggar's Opera* and its sequel.

Notes

[1] "Archetype Musical," *The Guardian,* July 15, 1963, p. 7.

[2] J. W. Lambert, "Beggars Behind Bars," *The Sunday Times,* July 21, 1963, p. 32.

[3] Review of *The Beggar's Opera, The Spectator,* July 26, 1963, p. 110.

[4] Review of *The Beggar's Opera, The Observer,* July 21, 1963, p. 23.

[5] William Hazlitt, *On the English Stage,* under date July 27, 1826; quoted by William Eben Schultz, Gay's Beggar's Opera, Its Content, History, and Influence (New Haven, Conn., 1923) p. 274.

[6] William Empson, "The Beggar's Opera: Mock-Pastoral as the Cult of Independence," Some Versions of Pastoral (Norfolk, Conn., 1960), p. 218.

[7] Sven M. Armens, *op. cit.,* p. 141.

[8] *Ibid.,* p. 141.

[9] John Gay, *The Beggar's Opera.* A Faithful Reproduction of the 1729 Edition (Larchmont, N.Y., 1961).

[10] Preface to *Polly,* quoted by Schultz, *op. cit.,* p. 211.

[11] Schultz, *op. cit.,* p. 213.

[12] James R. Sutherland, "'Polly' Among the Pirates," *Modern Language Review,* XXXVII (1942), 291.

[13] Schultz, *op. cit.,* p. 220.

[14] Sutherland, "'Polly' Among the Pirates," p. 291.

[15] See *ibid.,* pp. 292-93.

Martin C. Battestin (essay date 1966)

SOURCE: "Menalcas' Song: The Meaning of Art and Artifice in Gay's Poetry," in *JEGP: Journal of English and Germanic Philology,* Vol. LXV, 1966, pp. 662-79.

[*In the following essay, Battestin calls for a new understanding of Gay's use of the pastoral in his poetry, suggesting that Gay's skill with form and artifice reflect an Augustan aesthetic akin to that of Pope.*]

For Gay, no less than Pater, art was necessary because life was deficient in form. This is the essential point, not only about the manner of Gay's verse—that "delicate and sophisticated craftsmanship," as Professor Sutherland has remarked, producing *objets* as precious and frail as Chelsea china[1]—but about Gay's meaning as well. His best known poems—the *Fables, The Shepherd's Week, Rural Sports, Trivia*—are characteristically witty and finely wrought, apparently frivolous and fragile. It is perhaps not surprising that Dr. Johnson should dismiss their author as lacking the "*mens divinior,* the dignity of genius,"[2] or that this estimate should have survived through nearly two centuries. One of the very best of modern critics, though delighting in what he calls Gay's "artistic coquetry," regrets that he wanted "the moral earnestness" of his friends Swift and Pope, that his goodness is that of "a witty child . . . who has read about or even seen the world, the flesh, and the devil, without ever experiencing their desperate allure."[3] Since Professor Armens' more recent study,[4] however, it is no longer possible to dismiss Gay quite so easily on these grounds—to see him, as we had grown accustomed to seeing him, as an affable dabbler in verse, in life as a sort of ineffectual and improbably indolent Puck. If life was a jest to Gay (as his epitaph assures us it was), the joke was too often grim and disconcerting, cracked in a "biting" spirit akin to that of Swift's Jove.

Form and artifice are the distinguishing features of Gay's verse, as they are of the Augustan mode in general. These poets prized the virtues of elegance and proportion, the virtues of a highly mannered art, not because of any easy complacency about the eventual triumph of sanity and decorum, but because they everywhere saw the forces of Chaos and Dark Night threatening to overwhelm them. Such is Pope's meaning in the grotesque apocalypse of *The Dunciad,* where, in parody of classical and Christian poems that celebrate the establishment of Order, Dulness and her legions undo the work of creation. Though Pope is the greater poet (perhaps even because he is), Gay's verse is more clearly representative of this basic assumption both of the Augustan aesthetic and of the Augustan world view. In *Trivia,* especially, we will find embodied the controlling paradox of this mode: the idea—seldom openly expressed but nearly always implied in the poetry itself—that in the poem, as indeed in life, Nature must be made to imitate Art.

Of all the poetic kinds, the one most suited to this theme—and the one in which Gay worked most comfortably—is that of the pastoral. "The first Rule of Pastoral," as Pope more than once insisted, is that "its Idea should be taken from the Manners of the *Golden Age,* and the Moral form'd upon the Representation of Innocence."[5] Fundamental here is the contrast between an Age of Gold nostalgically evoked and an Age of Iron all too present, between a bright, ideal world—ordered, healthy, virtuous—and a world fallen, sick, depraved. A variation on this theme is the constant motif of Gay's poetry: the contrast between the country and the town. Under Gay's hand, however, this conventional thematic polarity of the pastoral (and of the related mode of the georgic) takes on a further significance—one already perhaps implicit in this most stylized, most self-consciously formal of the genres. The art of the pastoral poet, like that of Virgil's husbandman, does not imitate Nature as she actually appears in this degenerate world, but rather subdues and improves her, restoring her as far as possible to her original perfection. In that ideal state, to adapt a remark of Sir Thomas Browne's, Nature was not at variance with Art, nor Art with Nature, "they being both servants of his Providence."[6] In Eden, the perfect handiwork of God, Art and Nature were one; the extreme artfulness of the pastoral style is, in effect, an attempt to express this fact. In Gay's idiom the familiar antitheses of this mode—the country versus the town, the ideal versus the real—are constantly being rendered, not in the conventional terms of the natural as opposed to the civilized worlds, as is commonly asserted, but rather in terms symbolizing the basic opposition in this fallen world between Art and Actuality.

By reading the pastoral motif too literally, by seeing Gay's poetry as a celebration of the Natural as opposed to the Artificial and Civilized, the accepted critical view has prevented an appreciation of the peculiar quality and true significance of Gay as a poet. It has committed the ultimate violence upon the poetry by proposing, in effect, a separation between its manner and meaning which is absolute. One reason for this confusion is that we have regarded only what the poem (in certain conventional passages) *says,* and not at all attended to what it *is.* A further problem is the ambiguity of the terms *natural* and *artificial,* which may have both positive and pejorative connotations in Gay. As they are typically used in the pastoral, these words suggest, respectively, the simplicity, purity, and innocence of the Golden Age as opposed to the duplicity and affectation introduced after the Fall in the service of human greed and vanity: these are the "subtil arts"[7] of city whores and pickpockets and politicians, or the "art" of the painted belle, Sylvia, which repairs "her roses and her charms."[8] Alternatively, and more essentially in Gay, art is the sum of every human virtue: it is the affirmation of civilization in the face of vulgarity and savagery; it is the hard-earned means by which the man of reason and sensibility—the poet and the gentleman—disciplines the wilderness in nature and in himself. With the triumph of art the human situation, however grim in actuality (one thinks, for example, of *Trivia* and *The Beggar's Opera*), is seen as ultimately comic, because the human mind has learned to cope with it, to transcend it. This is not to say that the poet, like the meretricious painter of *Fable XVIII,* enacts a lie by showing deformity in the likeness of beauty; it is rather that in imitating the actual, he asserts by his manner the redeeming values of form and harmony.

The country in Gay's poetry is important, then, primarily as a symbol of an ideal order irrevocably lost in actuality, but attainable through art. Gay's Age of Gold is not to be sought after in time or in space, or in any easy retreat into rural or primitive regions; the Devonshire of his youth was no Eden, and it is likely to have been dull. The ideal in Gay's poetry is found rather in that curious discrepancy between his subject matter, which can be gross and sordid enough, and his elegant, witty manner. It is an ideal achieved, aesthetically, in the poem itself, in which all the devices of artifice—the polished, balanced couplet, the music and symmetry of the line, the circumlocution of the diction, the allusion to myth and to the classics—conspire to triumph over the messy and intractable and too often tragic stuff of life. It is achieved, ethically and socially, in what he refers to as the strict payment of "due civilities,"[9] in those polite rituals of courtesy and charity which enable us not to exalt, but to vanquish, the natural man. It is achieved, in other words, by attaining the condition of art. Form, decorum are *everything;* they are the ultimate values, for they enable us to survive and function in a world too often hostile and unmanageable.

Variations on this theme occur throughout Gay's poetry. Consider, for instance, the functional art of the "skilful angler" in **Rural Sports** (1720), a poem usually said (I think mistakenly) to celebrate the Natural as opposed to the Artificial. The angler, who is also Gay the poet, has left the noisy, noxious city behind, if only temporarily. Now in "a calm retreat" (I, 23) in the country, he must with care and judgment select the "proper bait" (I, 160), and then "Cleanse them from filth, to give a tempting gloss" (I, 167); with his eye on Nature to improve upon her, he fashions his lure with such patient dexterity "That nature *seems* to live again in art" (I, 208; italics mine). There is a correct procedure for casting, for playing the fish, and for drawing him to shore "with artful care" (I, 249). Perhaps the closest modern analogue to Gay's meaning in this poem occurs in Hemingway's story, "Big Two-Hearted River." Having crossed the burned-over land and "left everything behind," Nick Adams found his own "good place" to fish in the woods.[10] In both the poem and the story, the art of fishing and the purity of the style serve the same function, affording a means of controlling experience, of imposing on life an order and a discipline that it does not *naturally* have. There are rules to be observed, limits to be self-imposed, a ritual to be performed. One does not stray into the swamp, where, as Nick Adams observes, "fishing was a tragic adventure" (p. 231); nor does one, in Gay's words,

> wander where the bord'ring reeds
> O'erlook the muddy stream, whose tangling
>   weeds
> Perplex the fisher. . . .
>
> (I, 259-61)

It is not Nature that Gay (or Hemingway) celebrates, but nature controlled and subdued, set in order by art and artifice.

Despite the burlesque tone, and despite the coy assurances that he means *"to set before thee . . . a picture, or rather lively landscape of thy own country, just as thou mightest see it"* (Proeme, p. 29), Gay in the "trim" eclogues of **The Shepherd's Week** (1714) is not primarily interested in mocking Ambrose Philips or in depicting the authentic life of the English countryside—the twin purposes critics usually attribute to these poems. His shepherds and shepherdesses do fill their songs with homely references to the business of their daily lives, but Gay's highly mannered verse has refined away every crudeness, every trace of actuality; his English swains remain the conventional, idealized figures of the pastoral. Arcadia has been translated into Devon. Like Gay's own polished couplets, his rural lasses are "tidy" and "clean," dressed in "kerchief starch'd" and sporting straw-hats "trimly lin'd with green."[11]

Again conventionally, these shepherds are poets—poets, moreover, who understand the lesson that Gay's own verse imparts: "Numbers, like Musick, can ev'n Grief controul."[12] In **"Friday; or, The Dirge,"** Gay involves his shepherd-poets in situations that are emblematic of the relationship between the artist and the rude, recalcitrant material of life. In the first of these, Bumkinet and Grubbinol retire to a sheltered vantage point from which, having gained the necessary detachment from the business of life, they may mourn the death of Blouzelinda, and "with trim sonnets *cast away our care*" (l. 16). In the second, Grubbinol recalls the ceremonies of her burial:

> With wicker rods we fenc'd her tomb around,
> To ward from man and beast the hallow'd
>   ground,
> Lest her new grave the Parson's cattle raze,
> For both his horse and cow the church-yard
>   graze.
>
> (ll. 145-48)

In like manner, the artifice of the verses to follow fences us off from the incursions of nature, by a refining process removing us from its rough force and coarseness, turning bulls into fragile china figments:

> While bulls bear horns upon their curled
>   brow,
> Or lasses with soft stroakings milk the cow;
> While padling ducks the standing lake desire,
> Or batt'ning hogs roll in the sinking mire;
> While moles the crumbled earth in hillocks
>   raise,
> So long shall swains tell *Blouzelinda*'s praise.
>
> (ll. 153-58)

The meaning of art and artifice in Gay, however, is more clearly represented in the preceding poem, which may be seen as a comic dramatization of the poet's function. In **"Thursday; or, The Spell"** Hobnelia uses magic to lure her errant lover "from the faithless town" (l. 88). The verse itself—with its frequent alliteration, its repetitions and antitheses—imitates the formal, circular movement of her dance and incantatory refrain:

> *Hobnelia,* seated in a dreary vale,
> In pensive mood rehears'd her piteous tale,

Her piteous tale the winds in signs bemoan,
And pining eccho answers groan for groan.
  I rue the day, a rueful day, I trow,
The woful day, a day indeed of woe!
When *Lubberkin* to town his cattle drove,
A maiden fine bedight he hapt to love;
The maiden fine bedight his love retains,
And for the village he forsakes the plains.
Return my *Lubberkin,* these ditties hear;
Spells will I try, and spells shall ease my care.
  *With my sharp heel I three times mark the
    ground,*
  And turn me thrice around, around, around.

                            (ll. 1-14)

Like his comic shepherdess, Gay employs his own potent forms and incantations to discipline the wayward circumstances of life.

In proposing the identity of form and meaning in Gay, I do not at all wish to imply that he was the advocate and exponent of any empty aestheticism. The meaning is that art, of a highly conscious and deliberate sort, is necessary not only to the making of the poem, but also to the shaping of Gay's hero, who is not the natural, but rather the truly *civilized,* man. The artist, in life as in poetry, is supremely skilful, for he has learned to control, even to transform, his material; he is not the victim of life, but its master. An awareness of this fact will help to reveal that Gay's verse has precisely that "third dimension," that "prismatic depth," which it has been said to lack.[13] The superficiality of Gay's verse is illusory; it exists because the poetry itself is the substantiation of Gay's belief that art must order, refine, simplify—that the poem must not (as T. S. Eliot has averred that it must) itself reflect the dominion of Chaos and Dark Night in this fallen world, but that it must redeem this world, introducing elegance and form, harmony and humor, in the very absence of these things. According to Addison, Virgil in the *Georgics* "breaks the clods and tosses the dung about with an air of gracefulness."[14] The image applies equally well to Gay in his mock-georgic, *Trivia,* a poem that stands as a kind of extended parable of the relation between actuality and art.

Despite Professor Sutherland's insistence that "if we want the actual movement and stench and uproar of the London streets" we must go to Ned Ward, not to Gay,[15] the notion still prevails that Gay's motive in *Trivia* is "mild satire" of London life, and that his method is a detailed and photographic "realism."[16] The usual comparison is with Hogarth in such works as *Gin Lane.* Gay's purpose, however, is not at all to photograph the squalor and the crowded alleys of midwinter London; he has no desire to make us *feel* the crush of the mob or the biting chill of the weather; he does not wish us to smell the stench of Fleet-ditch or to witness the filth of the kennels. His subject matter, his material, may be the same as that of Hogarth; but thrust deliberately between us and the reality, removing us from it, insulating us against it, are Gay's tone and his style—with his music and elevated diction, the correctness of his numbers, and those neat couplets patting everything into place, smoothing things over, rendering them, as it were, harmless.

The point can be clearly seen, I think, if we place side by side passages from *Trivia* and from Swift's own burlesque georgic, *A Description of a City Shower;* the subjects are identical, but the treatment and effect are entirely opposite. Here is Swift:

  NOW from all Parts the swelling Kennels
    flow,
And bear their Trophies with them as they go:
Filth of all Hues and Odours seem to tell
What Street they sail'd from, by their Sight
  and Smell.
They, as each Torrent drives, with rapid Force
From *Smithfield,* or St. *Pulchre*'s shape their
  Course,
And in huge Confluent join at *Snow-Hill*
  Ridge,
Fall from the *Conduit* prone to *Holborn-
  Bridge.*
Sweepings from Butchers Stalls, Dung, Guts,
  and Blood,
Drown'd Puppies, stinking Sprats, all drench'd
  in Mud,
Dead Cats and Turnip-Tops come tumbling
  down the Flood.[17]

This is realism. The grossness of the imagery, the cacophony of the closing triplet with its final, ponderous alexandrine, function pitilessly to make the reader confront the muck and horror of actuality—almost, indeed, to overwhelm him with it. Listen now to Gay:

  But when the swinging signs your ears
    offend
With creaking noise, then rainy floods impend;
Soon shall the kennels swell with rapid
  streams,
And rush in muddy torrents to the *Thames*. . .

Then *Niobe* dissolves into a tear
And sweats with secret grief: you'll hear the
  sounds
Of whistling winds, e'er kennels break their
  bounds;
Ungrateful odours common-shores diffuse,
And dropping vaults distill unwholesome
  dews,
E'er the tiles rattle with the smoaking show'r,
And spouts on heedless men their torrents
  pour.

                  (I, 157-60, 168-74)

A crucial difference here is Gay's tone, which departs radically from Swift's and reflects a very different attitude toward the material. The sense of outrage is gone. Instead, the extravagance of Gay's method implies a certain wry detachment; the poet is aloof, arch if not exactly comic, as if he were sure of his ability to dispel the curse of the scene's noisome reality. Gay's lines—with their predominantly ordered rhythm of regular iambics and with their ostentatious use of the devices of allusion, alliteration, and assonance—call attention to themselves: not to *what* is being described, but to *how* it is being described. They call attention, in other words, to the conscious art of the poet. With respect to the principle that in a successful poem "The *Sound* must seem an *Eccho* to the *Sense*," Swift's treatment looks to be superior; certainly if Gay were trying for an Hogarthian effect, for "realism," one can say only that he bungled the job egregiously. Gay's manner in this passage is, however, precisely the embodiment of his meaning in this poem: which is that, though life can be hideous, art offers us a way of coping with it.

Trivia; or, The Art of Walking the Streets of London (1716) will of course remain interesting and useful as one of our chief documents of London life in the days of Anne and George I; however, as far as Gay's thematic intention is concerned, the symbolic meaning of the city is paramount. Together with the title and the Virgilian epigraph (which I shall discuss later), the exordium of the poem provides the necessary clues. Gay begins by declaring his subject and his very practical purpose; he then proceeds to celebrate the votaries of the Muse:

> Through winter streets to steer your course
>   aright,
> How to walk clean by day, and safe by night,
> How jostling crouds, with prudence to decline,
> When to assert the wall, and when resign,
> I sing: Thou, *Trivia*, Goddess, aid my song,
> Thro' spacious streets conduct thy bard along;
> By thee transported, I securely stray
> Where winding alleys lead the doubtful way,
> The silent court, and op'ning square explore,
> And long perplexing lanes untrod before.
> To pave thy realm, and smooth the broken
>   ways,
> Earth from her womb a flinty tribute pays;
> For thee, the sturdy paver thumps the ground,
> Whilst ev'ry stroke his lab'ring lungs resound;
> For thee the scavenger bids kennels glide
> Within their bounds, and heaps of dirt
>   subside.
> My youthful bosom burns with thirst of fame,
> From the great theme to build a glorious
>   name,
> To tread in paths to ancient bards unknown,
> And bind my temples with a Civic crown;

> But more, my country's love demands the
>   lays,
> My country's be the profit, mine the praise.

These lines suggest Gay's broadly allegorical intention. As in an overture, the dominant motifs of "the great theme" are sounded, to be developed in the body of the poem. The season is winter; the streets of London are the setting: together they will come to represent the inimical conditions of life itself, the natural and man-made forces opposing the wayfarer who seeks to pass without injury or stain through the City of this World. As the subtitle and the four lines of the proposition imply, there is an art of life to be mastered before the pilgrim can thread the labyrinth; so, like those other practical artists who "smooth the broken ways" and keep filth within bounds, the poet includes himself among the followers of the Muse.

The poem takes its title from the Roman name for Diana or Hecate, whose shrine was situated at the meeting of three roads; it is Trivia, goddess both of virgin forests and of the underworld, whom Gay invokes to conduct him safely through "the muddy dangers of the street" (I, 194), just as Aeneas had been guided by her priestess through the infernal regions of Dis. Gay's characterization of London transforms the brawling town into something analogous to Virgil's underworld—into another Babylon, the City of this World, corrupt, treacherous, contaminating, where on every side "smutty dangers" (II, 36) threaten to besmirch the traveler who has not mastered "the Art of Walking the Streets." London is Gay's emblem for actuality, for Life itself. Patterns of recurring images function cooperatively to give the town this symbolic character. The poem opens, as we have seen, with a metaphor comparing the "winding alleys" and "perplexing lanes" of the city to a maze, through which the muse must safely conduct the poet. In Book II (ll. 77-90) the figure is resumed and its implications extended: the "doubtful maze" that bewilders the innocent peasant who has strayed into London from a better country, is now associated with "the dang'rous labyrinth of *Crete*," the story of which, etched on the walls of the temple of Phoebus by Daedalus himself, Aeneas had read at the entrance to the underworld.

The quality of life that waits within these streets is as predatory and violent, as monstrous, as that which Theseus found. Coaches clash in a snarl of traffic, provoking "the sturdy war" (III, 36); the drivers lash each other and grapple in the mud of the street. Chaos and brutality prevail:

> Forth issuing from steep lanes, the collier's
>   steeds
> Drag the black load; another cart succeeds,
> Team follows team, crouds heap'd on crouds
>   appear,

And wait impatient, 'till the road grow clear.
Now all the pavement sounds with trampling
    feet,
And the mixt hurry barricades the street.
Entangled here, the waggon's lengthen'd team
Cracks the tough harness; here a pond'rous
    beam
Lies over-turn'd athwart; for slaughter fed
Here lowing bullocks raise their horned head.
Now oaths grow loud, with coaches coaches
    jar,
And the smart blow provokes the sturdy war;
From the high box they whirl the thong
    around,
And with the twining lash their shins resound:
Their rage ferments, more dang'rous wounds
    they try,
And the blood gushes down their painful eye.
And now on foot the frowning warriors light,
And with their pond'rous fists renew the fight;
Blow-answers blow, their cheeks are smear'd
    with blood,
'Till down they fall, and grappling roll in
    mud.
So when two boars, in wild *Ytene* bred,
Or on *Westphalia*'s fatt'ning chest-nuts fed,
Gnash their sharp tusks, and rous'd with equal
    fire,
Dispute the reign of some luxurious mire;
In the black flood they wallow o'er and o'er,
'Till their arm'd jaws distil with foam and
    gore.

                                (III, 25-50)

The utter capitulation to rage and swinish brutality
characterizes the spiritual condition of the citizens.

Equally significant are the recurrent references in the
poem to filth of all kinds—mud, offal, soot, ashes,
grease, blood. It is not merely that this filth exists in
the town, but that it threatens constantly to bespatter
and befoul the wayfarer, just as the moral corruption in
which the city wallows threatens to soil and stain his
spirit:

          oft in the mingling press
The barber's apron soils the sable dress;
Shun the perfumer's touch with cautious eye,
Nor let the baker's step advance too nigh. . . .
The little chimney-sweeper skulks along,
And marks with sooty stains the heedless
    throng;
When small-coal murmurs in the hoarser
    throat,
From smutty dangers guard thy threaten'd
    coat:
The dust-man's cart offends thy cloaths and
    eyes,

When through the street a cloud of ashes flies;
But whether black or lighter dyes are worn,
The chandler's basket, on his shoulder born,
With tallow spots thy coat; resign the way,
To shun the surly butcher's greasy tray,
Butchers, whose hands are dy'd with blood's
    foul stain,
And always foremost in the hangman's train.
    Let due civilities be strictly paid.

                                (II, 27-30, 33-45)

Considering the character of the world that Gay describes, that last exclamation is a more than perfuncto-
ry appeal. In this world deceit and duplicity, sham and
gaudy surfaces prevail. Very little is what it appears to
be. The lost, looking for a guide, have their pockets
picked; ballad-singers like "*Syrens* stand / To aid the
labours of the diving hand" (III, 79-80); the link-man's
torch, meant as a beacon, serves as a lure to trap the
unwary; beggars turned thieves use their crutches to
fell their victims; whores, promising love, spread infection. In contrast to the honest walker are the riders,
rich by rapine and fraud, who loll in coaches, their
gaudy insignia belying the rottenness within: "The tricking gamester insolently rides, / With *Loves* and *Graces*
on his chariot's sides" (I, 115-16). Civility and charity
are the moral virtues that the poem recommends in the
face of pride and inhumanity so widespread as to suggest the ignoble savagery of Hobbes's natural man.
Amidst the weak and the poor, the walker practices
benevolence while "Proud coaches pass, regardless of
the moan / Of infant orphans, and the widow's groan"
(II, 451-52). The piling up of such scenes and images
is relentless, and the ultimate effect is to present the
city as the very type and habitation of moral disorder,
depravity, and disease.

In Book III the horror of the spectacle darkens with
nightfall, and there is less relief from Gay's levity
of tone. Threatened from above by falling shop windows and "dashing torrents" (III, 205) from gutters,
and from below by the filth of the streets, the wayfarer finds himself like Ulysses "Pent round with
perils" (III, 178), calling for aid in vain. He is cautioned to avoid the fate of Oedipus, archetypal victim of the *tri-via,* who came to grief "Where three
roads join'd" (III, 217): "Hence wert thou doom'd
in endless night to stray / Through *Theban* streets,
and cheerless groap thy way" (III, 223-24). The
scenes that follow recapitulate the themes that have
characterized the city throughout—the corruption of
innocence and the triumph of deceit and misrule:
whores use their "subtil arts" to despoil the Devonshire yeoman of his money, his health, and his virtue; the cause of justice and order finds its hopeless
champions in the ineffectual watchman and the mercenary constable, who attends only to "the rhet'rick
of a silver fee" (III, 318). Rakes kindle riots, bea-

cons are extinguished—the city is given over completely to disorder and darkness.

The grim tableau culminates, however, in a scene that places this spectacle of worldly folly and vice within the larger contexts of history and eternity, asserting the ultimate victory of divine justice. As with Gay's method throughout, the local and particular image is given universal significance by the use of analogy and allusion. The total darkness—in which the chariots of the town's proud riders have been broken, to sink in the gulph of common-shores—is interrupted by the outbreak of fire in the city. Here Gay's allusive technique serves to relate this conflagration both to those which signalled the destruction of Sodom and Troy, and to the lurid prodigies that presaged the fall of Caesar. The "blazing deluge," the tiles descending "in rattling show'rs" (III, 359-60), recall God's judgment against the iniquitous cities of the plain (Genesis 19:24). As the burning building "sinks on the smoaky ground" (III, 386), Gay's final simile (shifting the frame of reference from past to future time) envisions the fiery collapse of still another city, this time Naples:

> So when the years shall have revolv'd the date,
> Th'inevitable hour of *Naples'* fate,
> Her sapp'd foundations shall with thunders shake,
> And heave and toss upon the sulph'rous lake;
> Earth's womb at once the fiery flood shall rend,
> And in th'abyss her plunging tow'rs descend.
> (III, 387-92)

The imagery brings to mind the infernal fires and the holocaust that will signal the world's final hour. Gay's reassuring burlesque tone is subdued by these vivid reminders of the precarious grandeur of empires and the certain doom of the cities of this world.

To render the meaning of the city clear, the penultimate paragraph universalizes Gay's depiction of "the perils of the wintry town" (III, 394), likening his own experience and didactic intent to those of other bold travelers, from the deserts of Arabia to the frozen wastes of Greenland, who have witnessed the savagery of man and the hostility of nature:

> Thus the bold traveller, (inur'd to toil,
> Whose steps have printed *Asia*'s desert soil,
> The barb'rous *Arabs* haunt; or shiv'ring crost
> Dark *Greenland*'s mountains of eternal frost;
> Whom providence in length of years restores
> To the wish'd harbour of his native shores;)
> Sets forth his journals to the publick view,
> To caution, by his woes, the wandring crew.
> (III, 399-406)

Barbarism and bitter weather are the conditions of life in this world. The winter streets of London are Gay's symbol for this fact.

It is conventional to say that Gay's answer to the corruption and artificiality of the town is the purity and naturalness of the country. This contrast, which certainly appears elsewhere in his poetry, is found in *Trivia* as well: "On doors the sallow milk-maid chalks her gains; / Ah! how unlike the milk-maid of the plains!" (II, 11-12). As we have already seen, however, references to the country in Gay do not function as they do in a primitivist or romantic work (in Smollett's *Humphry Clinker,* let us say, or in Wordsworth's "Michael"), to recommend a return to rural regions. They serve rather to establish a *symbolic* antithesis to the meanings of the city that we have previously discussed, keeping just at the back of our minds—as of the thoughts of Gay's wayfarer through life—the memory of a better country left behind, a distant Eden forever lost. In the same way, the fact that *Trivia* is a mock-georgic establishes a continually implicit comparison between Virgil's happy husbandmen and the sordid denizens of the town. If the pastoral is a symbolic mode, an artful imitation of the Golden Age, *Trivia* reflects its opposite, the Age of Iron—the Age, more specifically, of Georgian England. To read *Trivia* as an assertion of natural values as against the values of art and civilization is to miss the point. These are *winter* streets; Gay's choice of the harshest, darkest season was quite deliberate. Nature, as she appears in *Trivia,* affords no refuge from the grim conditions of life; she is rather *part* of them and very nearly as pitiless as the town itself—drenching the traveler with winter rain, making him wince with the biting cold. The imprudent walker who has not learned "to know the skies" (I, 122) runs the danger of succumbing to the malevolence of the weather—of being "Surpriz'd in dreary fogs or driving rain" (I, 124), of having to gasp for breath in "suffocating mists" (I, 125) that blot out the sun, of being threatened by "the piercing frost . . . the bursting clouds . . . the drenching show'r" (I, 130-32). Significantly, the Mall lies "in leafy ruin" (I, 27), and the Thames, frozen over, reflects the death of every vital force.

Gay's answer to the "smutty dangers" and bitter climates of life is, then, not an escape into rural regions, not a return to Nature. More constructively, it is rather an assertion of the redeeming value of art and artifice in enabling us to cope with the shock of experience, to wrest from the dominion of Chaos and Dark Night a measure of grace, a private terrain where order and joy prevail. In this sense the art of the poem is not merely decorative, but completely functional: it is as useful in helping us to survive as the "art" referred to in Gay's subtitle, or as those practical artifacts which, following Virgil, he celebrates at length in Book I—shoes, surtouts, umbrellas—implements devised by men as protection against a hostile environment. Something like this is the meaning of the *Georgics,* I, where the invention of every art is said to have been occasioned by the fall of Saturn and the end of the Golden Age: before the Fall, as Virgil asserts, Nature and Man were in complete harmony; now art is necessary to enable us to control a harsh and inimical world. It is our one way of reclaiming a part at least of our former relationship to an ideal order. It is the Muse who enables Gay, through winter streets, "to walk clean by day, and safe by night," who conducts him "securely" through the labyrinth. Gay includes himself among the other votaries of Trivia, because—like the paver, whose "art / Renews the ways" (II, 309-10), and the scavenger, who "bids kennels glide / Within their bounds"—the poet smooths and disciplines the crude material of life.

Gay's redaction of the *Georgics* includes the burlesque of Virgil's account of the invention of implements for subduing and cultivating the earth; the travesty is not the less appropriate to his theme for being comic. The mock-myth of Vulcan's invention of pattens, for example, symbolizes precisely Gay's conception of the function of art. Spying Patty, the country girl in whom he saw for the first time "Sweet innocence and beauty meet in one" (I, 244), Vulcan, the artificer god, descends to earth in the guise of a blacksmith to woo her. Winter weather threatens to despoil the mortal girl of her health and beauty, until the god, who once fashioned the invulnerable shield of Achilles, forges another practical artifact designed to ease her way along muddy country lanes that prove as treacherous in their way as the streets of London:

> Yet winter chill'd her feet, with cold she
>   pines,
> And on her cheek the fading rose declines;
> No more her humid eyes their lustre boast,
> And in hoarse sounds her melting voice is
>   lost.
>   This *Vulcan* saw, and in his heav'nly
>   thought,
> A new machine mechanick fancy wrought,
> Above the mire her shelter'd steps to raise,
> And bear her safely through the wintry ways.
> Strait the new engine on his anvil glows,
> And the pale virgin on the patten rose.
> No more her lungs are shook with drooping
>   rheums,
> And on her cheek reviving beauty blooms.
>
>   (I, 267-78)

As functional as the "mechanick fancy" of Vulcan, the art of Gay's poet lifts us, so to speak, out of the mire that threatens to overwhelm us, and restores the bloom of the fading rose on the cheek of innocence. Equally relevant is the burlesque myth depicting the genesis of

the bootblack's "beneficial art" (II, 152), whom the gods make

> useful to the walking croud,
> To cleanse the miry feet, and o'er the shoe
> With nimble skill the glossy black renew.
>
>   (II, 154-56)

Trivia and her fellow deities aid "the new japanning art" (II, 166)—"The foot grows black that was with dirt imbrown'd" (II, 209). The bootblack joins Gay's paver and crossing-sweep, as well as the poet himself, in the company of those whose function it is to introduce a measure at least of order and beauty in the face of squalor.

A crucial passage in the development of this theme occurs in Book II, where Gay and his friend William Fortescue stroll along the Strand passing sites formerly inhabited by men of taste, but now claimed by the forces of vulgarity. Only the name Arundel, famed connoisseur and collector of art, remains to mark the street where once his mansion stood as a monument to an aesthetic ideal:

> Where *Titian*'s glowing paint the canvas
>   warm'd,
> And *Raphael*'s fair design, with judgment,
>   charm'd,
> Now hangs the bell'man's song, and pasted
>   here
> The colour'd prints of *Overton* appear.
> Where statues breath'd, the work of *Phidias*'
>   hands,
> A wooden pump, or lonely watch-house
>   stands.
> There *Essex*' stately pile adorn'd the shore,
> There *Cecil*'s, *Bedford*'s, *Viller*'s, now no
>   more.
>
>   (II, 485-92)

In a world thus given over to barbarism and depravity, one sanctuary alone remains, one bastion against the ugly and the vulgar: the Palladian house of Richard Boyle, third Earl of Burlington, whose good taste Pope would later compliment in his *Moral Essays* (IV). This is Gay's Palace of Art, embodying in the correctness of its outward form and in the works of art cherished within its walls, the aesthetic ideal which the poem itself asserts:

> Yet *Burlington*'s fair palace still remains;
> Beauty within, without proportion reigns.
> Beneath his eye declining art revives,
> The wall with animated picture lives;
> There *Hendel* strikes the strings, the melting
>   strain

Transports the soul, and thrills through ev'ry
  vein;
There oft' I enter (but with cleaner shoes)
For *Burlington*'s belov'd by ev'ry Muse.
                              (II, 493-500)

Here alone, where Beauty and Proportion reign, can the wayfarer find a refuge from the mud of winter streets.

While Gay in such passages "often [as Addison said of Virgil in the *Georgics*] conceals the precept in a description, and represents his Countryman performing the action in which he would instruct his reader,"[18] the poem is itself the substantiation of the theme. Gay's tone and that ostentatious artificiality of style that we have remarked, never permit the actual world to intrude, even though that world—grim, unpredictable, violent—is his subject. A splendid illustration of this triumph of manner and artifice is the story of Doll, the ill-fated apple-woman. In itself the situation Gay describes is horrid: one day, as Doll is hawking pippins on the frozen Thames, the ice opens and swallows her, cutting off her head. (One can imagine what Hardy would have done with this!) But Gay's treatment cancels out the horror, transforming a grotesque and potentially tragic accident into a formal object of comic harmony and grace:

> 'Twas here the matron found a doleful
>   fate:
> Let elegiac lay the woe relate,
> Soft as the breath of distant flutes, at hours
> When silent evening closes up the flow'rs;
> Lulling as falling water's hollow noise;
> Indulging grief, like *Philomela*'s voice.
>   *Doll* ev'ry day had walk'd these
>   treach'rous roads;
> Her neck grew warpt beneath autumnal loads
> Of various fruit; she now a basket bore,
> That head, alas! shall basket bear no more.
> Each booth she frequent past, in quest of gain,
> And boys with pleasure heard her shrilling
>   strain.
> Ah *Doll*! all mortals must resign their breath,
> And industry it self submit to death!
> The cracking crystal yields, she sinks, she
>   dyes,
> Her head, chopt off, from her lost shoulders
>   flies;
> Pippins she cry'd, but death her voice
>   confounds,
> And pip-pip-pip along the ice resounds.
> So when the *Thracian* furies *Orpheus* tore,
> And left his bleeding trunk deform'd with
>   gore,
> His sever'd head floats down the silver tide,
> His yet warm tongue for his lost consort

cry'd;
Eurydice with quiv'ring voice he mourn'd,
And *Heber*'s banks *Eurydice* return'd.
                              (II, 375-98)

The mock formality of Gay's "elegiac lay"; the too delicious repetition of the liquid *l* sounds in "Lulling as falling water's hollow noise"; the forced exclamation of grief ("That head, alas!") and the strained platitudes on mortality; Doll's ludicrously abbreviated cry resounding across the ice; the absurdly incongruous allusions to Philomela and to Orpheus—every touch conspires to turn pathos into laughter, to remove us from any involvement in the scene. By his skill as a craftsman and rhetorician, Gay has transformed the grotesque into the exquisite, imposing on the chaos of life a certain form and comic grace. In such passages, having managed to make life conform to the principles of art, he holds it up at arm's length, as it were, for our admiration and diversion. Like the magic of Hobnelia or the art of the paver, Gay's style, his manner, continually controls or remakes the crude material of experience, no matter how terrifying and intractable. What occurs in Gay's best poems is not the imitation of Nature or reality, but its metamorphosis, leaving the object still recognizable—witness Doll's fate or the city shower or the bull in the **"Friday"** eclogue—but harmless; and not merely harmless, but aesthetically pleasing. Gay's characteristic tone of impish laughter has cost him the serious attention of more than one reader in our time, as it appears to have done in his own, because we have not seen that, far from being frivolous or irrelevant, the note he strikes is that of a hard-won affirmation: the poet's assertion of the redeeming value of his art. Gay does not imitate reality; because he is its master, he mocks it.

For his epigraph to **Trivia** Gay chose the opening line of Virgil's *Ninth Eclogue*: "*Quo te Mœri pedes? An, quo via ducit, in Urbem?*" (which Dryden renders: "Ho *Mœris!* wh[i]ther on thy way so fast? / This leads to Town"[19]). The theme and the situation in Virgil's poem help, I think, to illuminate Gay's own meaning. The shepherd Mœris and his friend, the poet Menalcas, have been dispossessed of their pastures, and very nearly deprived of their lives, by the soldiers of the emperor. Mœris is journeying toward the town, bearing forced tribute to his oppressors. Lycidas, who hails him, is at first surprised:

> Your Country Friends were told another
>   Tale;
> That from the sloaping Mountain to the Vale,
> And dodder'd Oak, and all the Banks along,
> *Menalcas* sav'd his Fortune with a Song.
>   (ll. 11-14)

Like the song of Menalcas, the poetry of John Gay makes, so to speak, this same attempt to redeem the land. Menalcas, "in these hard Iron Times" (l. 16), failed; in *Trivia* at least—and in those other poems we have been considering—Gay succeeded.

Notes

[1] James R. Sutherland, "John Gay," in *Pope and His Contemporaries: Essays Presented to George Sherburn,* ed. James L. Clifford and Louis A. Landa (Oxford, 1949), pp. 201-14. This excellent essay is of fundamental importance to a critical appreciation of Gay's poetry.

[2] Samuel Johnson, *The Lives of the Most Eminent English Poets* (London, 1781), III, 136.

[3] Maynard Mack, "Gay Augustan," *Yale University Library Gazette,* XXI (1946), 6-10.

[4] Seven M. Armens, *John Gay: Social Critic* (New York, 1954). Since the present essay was written and submitted for publication, welcome signs have appeared suggesting that Gay's poetry is at last beginning to receive the serious critical attention it deserves. Two recent studies are especially noteworthy: Adina Forsgren, *John Gay, Poet "of a Lower Order": Comments on His Rural Poems and Other Early Writings* (Stockholm, 1964); and Patricia Meyer Spacks, *John Gay,* Twayne's English Authors Series (New York, 1965).

[5] Alexander Pope, *The Guardian,* No. 40 (27 April 1713); 1747 ed., I, 257. See also Pope's *Discourse on Pastoral Poetry.*

[6] Sir Thomas Browne, *Religio Medici,* Pt. I, sec. 16; *Works,* ed. Geoffrey Keynes (London, 1928), 1, 22.

[7] *Trivia,* III, 263. My quotations from Gay are from *The Poetical Works of John Gay,* ed. G. C. Faber (Oxford, 1926).

[8] *The Tea-Table: A Town Eclogue,* l. 38.

[9] *Trivia,* II, 45.

[10] *The Short Stories of Ernest Hemingway* (New York, 1953), pp. 210, 215.

[11] See "Friday; or, The Dirge," ll. 58, 76, 125, 126.

[12] *An Epistle to Her Grace, Henrietta, Dutchess of Marlborough,* l. 3.

[13] Mack, p. 8.

[14] Joseph Addison, "An Essay on Virgil's Georgics," *Works* (London, 1761), 1, 244.

[15] Sutherland, p. 205.

[16] See, for example, Armens, pp. 4-5, 9-10, 74; and George Sherburn, "The Restoration and Eighteenth Century (1660-1789)," in Albert C. Baugh, ed., *A Literary History of England* (New York, 1948), p. 919.

[17] *The Poems of Jonathan Swift,* ed. Harold Williams (Oxford, 1937), 1, 139, ll. 53-63.

[18] Addison, I, 238-39.

[19] *The Works of Virgil,* trans. Dryden (London, 1697), p. 41.

Sven M. Armens (essay date 1966)

SOURCE: "The Beggar's View of Courtly Love," in *John Gay: Social Critic,* Octagon Books, 1966, pp. 128-54.

[In the following excerpt, Armens considers Gay's view of relationships between men and women in the context of Restoration and early eighteenth-century stereotypes of feminine vanity and the expectation of marital infidelity. Armens focuses on The Beggar's Opera *and* Achilles, *but connects Gay's dramatic work to his earlier pastoral poems. Armens also discusses Gay's relationships with particular women.]*

Love, usually considered the most basic of the passions, offers a good measure for examination and judgment of a society. Attitudes toward sex and the ideals of relationship between men and women are necessarily basic fodder for the satirist and the social commentator. Of them Gay makes good use. Much of his thought was devoted to such examination, and his judgments on sex conduct and love are expressed in all his works.

It is fair to assume that Gay was an expert in the psychology of the feminine mind, for it is certainly true that he had gained the allegiance of many women, including the noblest duchesses of the court. When the performance of **Polly** (later published in 1729) was suppressed, the ladies showed their response to his appeal by rallying to his support. An anonymous friend made the matter the subject of a mocking poem entitled *The Female Faction; or, The Gay Subscribers.* As quoted by Mr. Underhill, it runs:

> Thrice happy poet! whose unrivall'd lays
> Can hosts of Ladies in thy Quarrel raise,
> For thee, their Features do they cease to prize,
> And lose in Rage the Lustre of their eyes!
> On thy blest Lot, accept, without disdain,
> A Brother Bard's Congratulating Strain.[1]

Gay was well able to view in all aspects the usages of Augustan courtly love. In a sense his relationship to the noble duchesses recalls the medieval courts of love, and we can picture him as a sort of Chrétien de Troyes reading a lay to Marie de France or as an Andreas Capellanus prescribing precise rules of devotion for lovers at the mercy of female judges.

There was, however, an intrinsic difference between courtly love in an earlier day and in the Augustan period. Basically life and manners were in eighteenth-century London different from the chivalric mode of living in medieval Provence. The beloved lady was no longer the mistress of a feudal manor but a figure in town society. She was not actually regarded as a singular goddess or inspiration but was only referred to as such in words that she and the lover regarded as no more than conscious artifice. The eternal devotion of Jaufre Rudel had given way to the rule of unfaithfulness in the love game of the Restoration and Augustan periods. All concepts of loyalty were limited to marriage, though observance of marital fidelity was considered "Puritanical" and sneered at by the sophisticated husbands and wives embroiled in fashionable love pursuits.

The town fine lady who was the object of the new courtly love was honored by the foolish and despised by the wise in the Augustan period. She is depicted by Addison—with accents reminiscent of the satire of the Augustan period of Rome—in *Spectator,* No. 73, the best description of the type:[2]

> An *Idol* is wholly taken up in the Adorning of her Person. You see in every posture of her Body, Air of her Face, and Motion of her Head, that it is her Business and Employment to gain Adorers. For this Reason your *Idols* appear in all publick Places and Assemblies, in order to seduce Men to their Worship. The Playhouse is very frequently filled with *Idols;* several of them are carried in Procession every Evening about the Ring, and several of them set up their worship even in Churches. They are to be accosted in the Language proper to the Deity, Life and Death are in their Power; Joys of Heaven and Pains of Hell are at their disposal, Paradise is in their Arms, and Eternity in every Moment that you are present with them. Raptures, Transports, and Extasies are the Rewards which they confer: Sighs and Tears, Prayers and broken Hearts are the Offerings which are paid to them. Their smiles make Men happy; their Frowns drive them to despair. (p. 277)

As to the fashionable lover, the following description of his code of behavior may be compared with the *De arte honeste amandi* of Andreas Capellanus to show the difference between medieval lover and eighteenth-century gallant, who

must be well born; he must dress well but not ostentatiously; he must be poised and witty, so that he is never out of countenance; he must be skilled in making love, whether to women of the town, to married women, or to young ladies of his own rank, and he may conduct several love-affairs simultaneously, provided his head is always master of his heart. He must not boast of his amours, however, and he must be discreet: it is unpardonable to betray the confidence of any woman of his own class. If he is so weak as to entertain a serious passion he must conceal the fact by an affectation of indifference or by overacted and conventional protestations of devotion. If he is married he must not show any jealousy of his wife, nor may he let it be seen that he is in love with her. The fashionable lady is his counterpart, except that she has somewhat less freedom in love. Ideally she should be perfectly familiar with the world of intrigue without allowing herself to become involved in it; if she is a widow, or is married to an uncongenial husband, she may indulge in illicit love, provided she is not found out. In any case she will not expect complete constancy from her husband.[3]

These are the fine ladies and gentlemen who set the standards and manners of the worldly society of the town—the social leaders who devote themselves to being "in vogue." Their foibles, petty deceits, and vanities are amusing to the urbane gaze of Gay. But does he think them entirely harmless? He does not.

Instead he pillories them by showing their reflections distorted in characters of low life. He accepted the premises that the wealthy set the fashions and that, because the wealthy are not "virtuous," they often establish false standards of taste in dress, amusement, and morality. These are imitated by those lower in the social scale, and because the basis of being "in vogue" is self-interest, not to imitate the selfishness of the rich and powerful is to be vulgar. In *The Beggar's Opera,* Lockit (a warden in Newgate prison) berates his daughter, Lucy, because she let Macheath escape from prison for love rather than for a bribe:

> Thou wilt always be a vulgar slut, Lucy—If you would not be look'd upon as a fool, you should never do any thing but upon the foot of interest. Those that act otherwise are their own bubbles. (p. 517)

Self-interest is fashionable, and the same ideas color all society from the noble lord to the highwayman. Macheath, in vowing constancy to Polly Peachum, employs burlesque analogies to bribery, vanity, and gambling, all typical symbols of social success:

> Is there any power, any force that could tear me from thee? You might sooner tear a pension out of the hands of a Courtier, a fee from a Lawyer, a pretty woman from a looking-glass, or any woman from *Quadrille.* (p. 500)

The contrast between social vulgarity and true moral vulgarity is heightened throughout the play by incidents and references showing what is supposedly fashionable or polite. In these Gay's irony operates at its best. Lucy Lockit is effusively polite as she plies her rival, Polly Peachum, with poisoned gin. She excuses her previous jealous passion by saying, "I was so over-run with spleen [high-society melancholia or neurotic depression], that I was perfectly out of my self. And really when one hath the spleen, everything is to be excus'd by a friend" (p. 524). The glass of "Strong-waters" offered as a gesture of renewed friendship is another symbol of gentility and is accompanied with the boast, "Not the greatest lady in the land could have better in her closet, for her own private drinking." Polly also from time to time shows a liking for the foibles of the fine ladies. And the prostitute, Jenny Diver, assumes one of the favorite poses of the fine lady—that of the prude. Macheath greets her:

> What! and my pretty Jenny Diver too! As prim and demure as ever! There is not any Prude, though ever so high bred hath a more sanctify'd look, with a more mischievous heart. Ah! thou art a dear artful hypocrite. (p. 504)

It is unnecessary to belabor the point that the duchess and the whore may be alike in more ways than one. Nothing could show better the cynical aspect of Gay's view of Augustan love.

Imitation of the vogue can lead to more hypocrisy and distortion than this. In *The Beggar's Opera,* Peachum has black-listed[4] Bob Booty (a parody of Robert Walpole), an old customer, because Bob was devoting himself too much to females and not providing Peachum with enough profits. Mrs. Peachum objects, and Peachum replies:

> What a dickens is the woman always a whimp'ring about murder for? No gentleman is ever looked upon the worse for killing a man in his own defence; and if business cannot be carried on without it, what would you have a gentleman do? (p. 490)

Mrs. Peachum then obsequiously murmurs, "If I am in the wrong, my dear, you must excuse me, for no-body can help the frailty of an overscrupulous Conscience." Peachum comforts her by appealing, not to her gentleness, but to her gentility; we can almost picture him putting a loving arm about her shoulders as he assures her that "murder is as fashionable a crime as man can be guilty of."

There is another side of the coin. Whether Gay is praising the true love of Polly, Cylene, and the rural wife or mocking the debased loves of Jenny, the Ducats, and the city fine lady, he is always voicing his firm belief in certain elements as absolutely necessary to love and marriage. These key attributes are devotion, faithfulness, cheerfulness, self-sacrifice, and the ability to create a home environment in which children may be reared virtuously. Such characteristics are simply, easily comprehensible to common sense, and supposedly basic to the benevolent spirit with which Gay thought mankind to be imbued.

Much of the laughter in *The Beggar's Opera* and *Polly* springs from farcical situations created by lust and lack of honor in love. Yet through the two, Polly, continually tempted and continually noble, represents continuing faithfulness to the beloved. She rebels against the vicious social code her parents advocate, which includes exploiting a lover for his money and then betraying him; she marries Macheath even when she knows he may soon be executed; she suffers transportation to the West Indies for him; she risks the loss of her honor; absurdly enough, she even becomes a soldier. Her initial aim was the honest completion of her love through marriage, but the normal fulfillments of marriage in a home and children were frustrated by Macheath's transportation. Later, he, as the pirate chief Morano, is not only unfaithful but evil; he contracts a bigamous marriage with Jenny, the genteel prostitute. His ambition and lust for money destroy his earlier good-natured charm and thwart Polly's loyalty. But love as usual is quite blind. The reins of judgment slip easily from Polly's hands. Despite all the ill-treatment he heaps on her, she still thinks that "my love . . . might reclaim him." This hopeful illusion illustrates an archetypal mode of futility. Gay laughs at his ridiculous Polly, but his account of her undeviating faithfulness shows, behind the mockery, his sentimental admiration for honest devotion in affairs of love.

Much more seriously presented is the heroine of *The Captives,* which is cast in the somewhat outmoded form of the heroic drama.[5] Cylene, the female captive, is a typical, angelic heroine, filled with loyalty and self-sacrifice in a manner to meet the tasteless demands of Gay's audience. Her husband, Sophernes, is a captured Persian prince, like Dryden's Almanzor, but Sophernes is shadowed into total eclipse by his wife's exalted virtue. Her devotion, indeed, seems as endless as some of the monologues. Although the moral force of the play is vitiated by its sentimentality, *The Captives* does fulfill the purposes of the exemplary drama.[6] The key scene (IV, vii) is laid in a dank dungeon. Cylene, by a ruse, has entered Sophernes' cell to give up her life so that he may reassert the rights of the Persian people. After a tender moment of recognition and renewal of affection, Cylene tricks her husband into an oath that he will grant her whatever she will ask. After he swears, she says,

> I thank thee. Thou hast given me all my
>   wishes,
> For now thy life is safe; and sav'd by me.

Here, take this veil; this shall secure thy
  flight,
With this thou shalt deceive the watchful
  guard.
O blest occasion! fly, my Lord, with speed;
I never wish'd to part till now.

(ll. 77-82)

He, of course, objects, refusing to save his life at the
expense of hers. But she is adamant and threatens
suicide until he consents to go and leave her. The last
two speeches of the scene, though by no means great
poetry, touchingly evoke genuine tragic love in a way
reminiscent of Shakespeare's *Othello* and *Romeo and
Juliet*:[7]

> *Cyl.* From thy dear hands I take the galling
>   chains.
> Lest danger intercept thee, haste, be gone;
> And as thou valuest mine, secure thy life.
> Thou hadst no hope. Who knows but my
>   offence
> May find forgiveness! 'tis a crime of love;
> And love's a powerful advocate to mercy.
> *Soph.* O how I struggle to unloose my heart-
>   strings,
> That are so closely knit and twin'd with thine!
> Is't possible that we may meet again?
> That thought has filled my soul with
>   resolution.
> Farewell: may Heaven support thee, and
>   redress us!

(ll. 116-126)

Thus true and lasting love can be demonstrated in Gay's
works, but far more often does he offer pictures of the
distortions of love in town. In **The Beggar's Opera** we
are offered no sample of successful marriage like that
of the Persian captives. Instead, marriage is constantly
being viewed as an encumbrance. Peachum avers that
"there is nothing to be got by the death of women—
except our wives." Macheath, confronted by both Polly and Lucy, sings,

> One wife is too much for most husbands to
>   bear
> But two at a time there's no mortal can bear.

Thieves and gentlemen share this distaste for the married state, and alike they seek fulfillment of the psychi-
cal and physical needs of love outside the moral bounds
of matrimony. Possibly the gay lovers of Restoration
comedy and of the Augustan courtly love game were
truly in love, but the fact that their love never reached
its natural fulfillment in marriage gave to it a certain
air of spiritual prostitution. How far this immorality
could go is shown in Peachum's attitude toward the
marriage of his daughter Polly:

> You know, *Polly*, I am not against your toying and
> trifling with a customer in the way of business, or
> to get out a secret, or so. But if I find out that you
> have play'd the fool and are married, you jade you,
> I'll cut your throat, hussy. Now you know my mind.
> (p. 493)

Mrs. Peachum, whose usual honeyed and motherly tones
only emphasize her basic viciousness, is of the same
mind as her husband. When Polly confesses that she
has indeed been honorable enough to marry Macheath
instead of fleecing him, Mrs. Peachum denounces her
with rage:

> I knew she was always a proud slut; and now the
> wench hath play'd the fool and married, because
> forsooth she would do like the Gentry. Can you
> support the expense of a husband, hussy, in gaming,
> drinking and whoring? have you money enough to
> carry on the daily quarrels of man and wife about
> who shall squander most? There are not many
> husbands and wives, who can bear the charges of
> plaguing one another in a handsome way. If you
> must be married, could you introduce no-body into
> our family, but a highwayman! Why, thou foolish
> jade, thou wilt be as ill us'd, and as much neglected,
> as if thou hadst married a Lord! (p. 494)

She is angry primarily because she feels that she has
been cheated in a business deal; her daughter's virginity was a valuable business asset, now stolen by Macheath. Polly's offer of an excuse shows her primitive
and basically natural impulses, the innocence of a
country girl:

> I did not marry him (as 'tis the fashion) cooly and
> deliberately for honour or money. But, I love him.
> (p. 495)

The absurdity of this explanation makes Mrs. Peachum
faint. Polly and Mr. Peachum revive her with a cordial,
and she is able to deliver herself of a businesslike rule
for chastity that summarizes Gay's idea of deceit in
love:

> Yes, indeed, the sex is frail. But the first time a
> woman is frail, she should be somewhat nice
> methinks, for then or never is the time to make her
> fortune. After that, she hath nothing to do but to
> guard herself from being found out, and she may do
> what she pleases. (p. 495)

Nevertheless, Polly has already been married, and Mr.
and Mrs. Peachum must make the best of a bad bargain. Peachum immediately conceives a plan for gaining profit. "Where," he asks Polly, "is the woman who
would scruple to be a wife, if she had it in her power
to be a widow whenever she pleas'd?" He suggests

that she get all that Macheath has and then contrive to have him "peach'd the next Sessions" so that she can arrive at complete possession. Polly exclaims in horror, "What, murder the man I love!"—and her father answers, "Fye, *Polly!* What hath murder to do in the affair? Since the thing sooner or later must happen, I dare say, the Captain himself would like that we should get the reward for his death sooner than a stranger." In this suggestion he carries self-love to a true extreme for he attributes to another an altruism that would be to his own benefit. Such ludicrous cynicism primarily is intended to burlesque the egocentricity of town love.

Macheath himself is offered as almost the perfect example of self-love. When Peachum and his wife resolve to "peach" Macheath anyway, Polly, true to the standards of sentimental heroines of play books and romances, is ever faithful to her love, and warns the intended victim of the plot. He goes into hiding, but his own moral code depends entirely on self-gratification. The Augustan lover *par excellence,* he has no intention of being true to Polly. In the tavern scene (II, iii), he declares that he "loves the sex" and says that if it were not for him and the recruiting officers, Drury Lane (a favorite hangout for prostitutes) would be uninhabited. He boasts that he has made promiscuity a fine art. In Act II, Scene IV, he as the "maker" greets many of his "creations"—various types of prostitutes:

> Dear Mrs. *Coaxer,* you are welcome. You look charmingly today. I hope you don't want the repairs of quality, and lay on paint.—*Dolly Troll!* kiss me, you slut; are you as amorous as ever, hussy? You are always so taken up with stealing hearts, that you don't allow your self time to steal any thing else.— Ah *Dolly,* thou wilt ever be a Coquette!—Mrs. *Vixen,* I'm yours, I always lov'd a woman of wit and spirit; they make charming mistresses, but plaguy wives.—*Betty Doxy!* come hither, hussy. Do you drink as hard as ever? You had better stick to good wholesome beer; for in troth, *Betty,* strong-waters will in time ruin your constitution. You should leave those to your betters. . . . Mrs. *Slammekin!* as careless and genteel as ever! all you fine ladies, who know your own beauty, affect an undress.—But see, here's *Suky Tawdry* come to contradict what I was saying. Every thing she gets one way she lays out upon her back. Why, *Suky,* you must keep at least a dozen Tally-men. *Molly Brazen!* (*She kisses him.*) That's well done. I love a free-hearted wench. Thou hast a most agreeable assurance, girl, and art as willing as a turtle. (p. 504)

In such company as this Macheath is at home and jovial, with poor "bitten" Polly forgotten. Fundamentally corrupt worldliness is shown bare in the philosophical discussion among "the ladies" on the question of being kept (p. 506); it is agreed that the "best sort of keepers" are the most generous. The attitude is the same as that of Mr. and Mrs. Peachum—money is the standard

for measuring love. And since Peachum is a munificent briber when the occasion demands, it is not surprising that Jenny and Tawdry, when kissing Macheath, betray him to the constables by beckoning in their "boss" (Peachum).

Town love is nothing but a round of betrayals, and Macheath is himself adept at the game. When brought into Newgate, he is immediately confronted with Lucy Lockit, whom he previously seduced with the promise of marriage. But to him, as to the finest town gallant, promises mean nothing. Before Lucy comes in, he soliloquizes:

> What signifies a promise to a woman? does not man in marriage itself promise a hundred things that he never means to perform? Do all we can, women will believe us; for they look upon a promise as an excuse for following their own inclinations. (p. 508)

To Lucy he recalls the promise, appealing to her tenderness as her husband-to-be and assuring her of the value of his word as a "man of honour." Lucy flares at him. "Tis the pleasure of all you fine men to insult the women you have ruin'd," she says, and adds, "I could tear thy eyes out." But Macheath soon convinces her, at least momentarily, that he has not married Polly (although he has) and that he will make an "honest woman" of Lucy—and Lucy longs more for that label than for actual marriage itself.[8] Macheath denies Polly not because he loves her less, but only because he loves no one but himself.[9] He would be quite willing to marry Lucy too, since he is not averse to bigamy, but unfortunately for him Polly comes to Newgate to visit him, and there is a showdown among the three. Macheath denies his marriage and his love for Polly, because Lucy is in a better position to help him escape from Newgate and from hanging.

Polly sings once more of true and lasting love:

> No power on earth can e'er divide
> The knot that sacred Love hath ty'd.
> When parents draw against our mind,
> The true-love's knot they faster bind.
>
> (p. 515)

Macheath, the courtly gamester, instead sings:

> How happy could I be with either,
>   Were t'other dear charmer away!

Actually, of course, he loves neither—only himself— and soon demonstrates the fact. After Lucy helps him to escape, he is promptly captured again, this time in the bed of Mrs. Coaxer, who, with her bawd, Mrs. Trapes, has laid a new trap for him. There is further betrayal in Lucy's attempt to poison Polly, an attempt which fails because Polly, startled at seeing Macheath again in custody, drops the glass of poisoned gin. Thus both girls are frustrated—the more so when, in Scene xv four more wives are brought in by the jailer to claim Macheath, each "with a child a-piece." He pictures himself in song:

> Thus I stand like a Turk, with his doxies
>   around;
> From all sides their glances his passion
>   confound;
> For black, brown, and fair, his inconstancy
>   burns,
> And the different beauties subdue him by
>   turns.

> (p. 532)

He thus swaggers on the stage, a symbol of virile and in one sense "natural" man, as promiscuous as the beasts and as selfish. He must satisfy his all-consuming sexual drive at whatever cost to others. Such is the fine example of Augustan courtly lover, who does not devote himself to one woman, whether Idol or no, but makes of love a mere pastime. Gay puts Macheath before us and expects us to laugh at Macheath's immense potency; perhaps he even expects us to envy him; but most assuredly he does not want us to admire him.

Macheath's thorough selfishness in sexual matters is, however, outmatched by that of the despicable Filch, the thieves' apprentice who has turned into a childgetter. Lockit greets him in Act III, Scene iii, with a fitting reference to a creature lower in the chain of being than a human:

> Why, boy, thou lookest as if thou wert half starv'd;
> like a shotten Herring. (p. 519)

Filch replies:

> One had need have the constitution of a horse to go through the business.—Since the favourite Childgetter was disabled by a mishap, I have pick'd up a little money by helping the ladies to a pregnancy against their being call'd down to sentence.—But if a man cannot get an honest livelihood any easier way, I am sure, 'tis what I can't undertake for another Session. (p. 519)

Here is a ludicrous, bawdily funny figure. Yet behind him loom shadows. A society with conditions so bad as to make Filch plausible enough to be funny is open to sharp criticism. Here sexual intercourse, which can be the warm expression of true love, has been most thoroughly debased. Even lust itself has been undermined. Love is moral and practical; lust is immoral and impractical; but begetting illegitimate children in order to cheat justice combines immorality with a sort of practicality. This is sex as simply business for all concerned; a breed farm for criminals represents the complete perversion of the chivalric code of courtly love. Gay's irony touches a high point when he has Lockit say of the professional childgetter:

> Truly, if that great man should tip off, 'twould be an irreparable loss. The vigor and prowess of a Knight-errant never sav'd half the ladies in distress that he hath done.

> (p. 519)

The satire on society and sex in *The Beggar's Opera* thus ranges from catlike gentleness to outright savagery. It ends on a note of compounded mockery. What happens to Macheath, that symbol of distorted love in urban civilization, provides a key to the standards of that civilization's view. The beggar (Gay as the satirist) claims that the moral—that punishment is meted out only to the poor—demands Macheath's death. The Player insists that this ending would not "comply with the taste of the town" (p. 531). Gay (as pretended cynic) succumbs to the Player. The moral of the play is dismissed as the town in its ethical degradation dismisses morality.

In discussing the attack in *The Beggar's Opera* on evil social attitudes with the solemnity the subject deserves, it is sometimes easy to forget that the manner of presenting social criticism is that of burlesque and good-natured farce. Indeed if a veil of comic humor were not drawn between the audience and the attitudes and actions in the drama, the play would be simply a distressing and unpleasant indictment of a society more fit for a grim sociological report than for theatrical entertainment. But the laughter is there to soothe and alleviate the ferocity of the social attack. *The Beggar's Opera* well illustrates the perceptive remark by T. S. Eliot in his essay on Philip Massinger that great farce has "the ability to perform that slight distortion of all the elements in the world of a play or a story, so that this world is complete in itself." Gay's farce-created world gives latitude for all sorts of absurdities in sex relationships.

His last play, *Achilles,*[10] has in a way even more ribaldry than *The Beggar's Opera*. It deals with the period when Achilles is in forced hiding. His mother, Thetis, knowing that he is doomed to die at Troy, wishes to put him in some refuge where none can find him and persuade him to join the Greek forces going to attack the Trojans. She decides to disguise him as a girl and put him in the palace of Lycomedes. This shameful doffing of his sex is contrary to Achilles' code of honor, but he has no choice, for he has sworn to obey his mother. We find him living, sullen and wrathful, disguised as the Lady Pyrrha among the many daughters of Lycomedes and Theaspe. Thus a young and virile man is spending all the hours of day and night in company with young and lovely girls. The possibilities of the situation are obvious. When you add the fact that Lycomedes is a confirmed lecher, who immediately attempts to seduce his ward, the Lady Pyrrha, the comic possibilities are much increased. Gay exploits them to the full.

The lustful hopes of Lycomedes give rise to some of the broader strokes of humor in the play. The king employs one of his great ministers, Diphilus, as a go-between, but the Lady Pyrrha firmly repulses all the suggestions of Diphilus. The minister then reports to the king that the Lady is merely playing the coquette (one of the regular roles of the Idol) and is really ambitious for the power that being the king's mistress will give her:

> *Lycom.* But, dear *Diphilus,* I grow more and more impatient. *Diph.* That too by this time is her Case.— To save the Appearances of Virtue, the most easy Woman expects a little gentle Compulsion, and to be allow'd the Decency of a little feeble Resistance. For the Quiet of her own Conscience a Woman may insist upon acting the Part of Modesty, and you must comply with her Scruples.—You will have no more trouble but what will heighten the Pleasure. (p. 613)

The king is deceived by this persuasion and goes in person to approach Pyrrha. When "she" refuses his proposals, he tries to use force. The result is that he is violently thrown down, with the breath thoroughly knocked out of him. Justice thus farcically triumphs, virtue is exonerated in an unreal situation.

Theaspe, the queen, is meanwhile concerned about her husband's wandering fancy and determines to frustrate his intentions by marrying Pyrrha to her nephew, Periphas. She broaches the subject to Pyrrha, who is with "her" favorite "sister," Deidamia. Pyrrha stalls for time. "She" says that Periphas will be welcome when he returns from the siege of Troy, renowned for martial deeds. The inverted relationships throw a comic but dismal light on self-seeking human motives.

At the outset of the disguise, Achilles has already expressed his opinion that he cannot live among the girls without causing trouble. When Thetis expresses the hope that he will remember his disguise and fears that he, "among the ladies, might be so little Master of [his] passions as to find [himself] a Man," Achilles replies with a song of little consolation:

> The Woman always in Temptation,
>   Must do what Nature bids her do;
> Our Hearts feel equal Palpitation,

> For we've unguarded Minutes too.
>   By Nature greedy,
>   When lank and needy,
> Within your Fold the Wolf confine;
>   Then bid the Glutton
>   Not think of Mutton;
> Can you persuade him not to dine?
>
>   (Air III; p. 599)

His intention of being a wolf among sheep he thoroughly justifies by making Deidamia pregnant. Achilles and Deidamia are then faced with their different conceptions of honor:

> *Ach.* Was there ever a Man in so whimsical a Circumstance!
> *Deid.* Was there ever a Woman in so happy and so unhappy a one as mine!
> *Ach.* Why did I submit? why did I plight my Faith thus infamously to conceal my self?— What is become of my Honour?
> *Deid.* Ah *Pyrrha, Pyrrha,* what is become of mine!
> *Ach.* When shall I behave my self as a Man!
> *Deid.* Wou'd you had never behav'd yourself as one! (p. 619)

Achilles, a pompous, military boor at heart, is unable to see the desperation of Deidamia, who has lost her own honor without being able to explain how, and prates of his own dissatisfaction:

> For Heaven's sake, *Deidamia,* if you regard my Love, give me Quiet.—Intreaties, Fondness, Tears, Rage and the whole matrimonial Rhetorick of Woman to gain her Ends are all thrown away upon me; for, by the Gods, my dear *Deidamia,* I am inexorable. (p. 620)

The masquerade of Achilles is exposed by Ulysses, who comes disguised as a merchant to the palace. He unpacks two bundles of goods, one of lovely silks, one of armor; all the others look at the silks, but Pyrrha begins to examine the armor. "She" is therefore unmasked, and Achilles is able to marry Deidamia and go off to war, a man of honor once more.

In *Achilles* Gay takes the opportunity to make sharp and even misogynistic comments on female motives and wiles. The play is studded with prose epigrams against women, reminiscent of Pope's best satire. The clean conciseness of Gay's thrusts give an acid tone to his criticism of the female mind and temperament. Their fundamental enmity for each other is reflected in the speech addressed to Achilles:

> You are so very touchy, *Pyrrha,* that there is no enduring you.—How can you be so insociable a

Creature as to deny a Friend the Liberty of laughing at your little Follies and Indiscretions? For what do you think Women keep Company with one another?

(p. 600)

Diphilus, the procurer and cynic, expresses a very low opinion of the chastity and honesty of women in general:

Things of this Nature shou'd be always transacted in Person, for there are Women so ridiculously half-modest, that they are asham'd in Words to consent to what (when a Man comes to the Point) they will make no Difficulties to comply with. (p. 612)

And indeed the women in the play display all sorts of unpleasant traits—obstinacy, prudery, ambition, jealousy, and snobbery. Far from being charitable toward a sister's fall from chastity, they delight in it:

Lesb. Now, dear *Artemona,* can any Woman
      alive imagine that
Shape of hers within the compass of common
      Modesty?
Art. But how can one possibly have those
      Suspicions?
Phil. She is a Woman, Madam; she hath
      Inclinations and may
have had her Opportunities that we know
      nothing of.

(p. 628)

One can even feel sympathy for Periphas, when he offers the conventional objection of the courtly lover to matrimony. Addressing Theaspe, he says:

How cou'd you, Madam, imagine I had any Views of this kind!—What, be a Woman's Follower with Intention to marry her! Why, the very women themselves wou'd laugh at a Man who had so vulgar a Notion of Galantry, and knew so little of their Inclinations.—The Man never means it, and the Woman never expects it; and for the most part they have every other view but Marriage.

(pp. 622-623)

Later in a soliloquy he carries the theme farther, bringing forth a military metaphor in speaking of the battles of marriage:

Had I so little Taste of Liberty as to be inclin'd to marry; that Girl is of so termagant a Spirit!—The bravest Man must have the dread of an eternal Domestic War.—In a Tongue-combat Woman is invincible, and the Husband must come off with Shame and Infamy; for though he lives in perpetual

Noise and Tumult, the poor Man is only ridiculous to his Neighbours.—How can we ever get rid of her?—*Hercules* conquered the seven-headed *Hydra,* but his Wife was a venom'd Shirt that stuck to him to the last. (p. 624)

All of this is offered in **Achilles** in sportive vein, with the convincing unreality of farce. The mockery of fashionable attitudes toward sex is light. Even the attempt of Lycomedes to force his attentions on Pyrrha is little more than straight burlesque.

In **Polly,** however, a similar situation is treated comically but with an underlying serious vein of criticism of the truly vicious. Clearly, the immorality cultivated by "the vogue" is not entirely a laughing matter. The Ducats, representative of the wealthy but ignorant bourgeoisie, epitomize all that is cheap and vulgar in the *nouveaux-riches.* Mr. Ducat is a rich planter; born in the Indies, he has no knowledge of town ways but a great desire to learn them. Who then is chosen as instructress? Mrs. Trapes, a transported bawd, who has learned her principles by imitating the "great" of London. Witness her advice to Ducat:

Though you were born and bred and live in the *Indies,* as you are a subject of *Britain* you shou'd live up to our customs. Prodigality there, is a fashion that is among all ranks of people. Why, our very younger brothers push themselves into the polite world by squandering more than they are worth. You are wealthy, very wealthy, Mr. *Ducat;* and I grant you the more you have, the taste of getting more should grow stronger upon you. 'Tis just so with us. But then the richest of our Lords and Gentlemen, who live elegantly, always run out. 'Tis genteel to be in debt. Your luxury should distinguish you from the vulgar. You cannot be too expensive in your pleasures. (p. 539)

She reinforces this recommendation of extravagance, debt, and showy luxury by singing an air praising the manners of the polite world and the custom of ignoring the rights of any but yourself. Mrs. Trapes is, in short, telling Ducat to make himself into a ruthless wastrel. Fundamentally, fashionable gentility compels the rich to spend their money in such ways as to transform harmless foibles into dangerous vices. They should use their wealth to gain power so that they in turn will be imitated and by this imitation spread corruption.[11] Mrs. Trapes sings finally,

Morals and honesty leave to the poor,
As they do at London.

Ducat is persuaded that he must squander money on the "superfluities" of life—first of all on a beautiful mistress. Poor Ducat, shamefaced, has confessed that he is still having sexual relations with his wife and that she is "unreasonable enough to expect to have [him]

always to herself." Mrs. Trapes sets out to improve this unfashionable state of affairs. "Keep mistresses," she says. To help him find one, she suggests that he take advantage of her "fresh cargo of ladies just arrived," because

> We are not here, I must tell you, as we are at *London,* where we can have fresh goods every week by the waggon. My maid is again gone aboard the vessel; she is perfectly charm'd with one of the ladies; 'twill be a credit to you to keep her. I have obligations to you, Mr. *Ducat,* and I would part with her to no man alive but your self. If I had her at London, such a lady would be sufficient to make my fortune; but, in truth, she is not impudent enough to make herself agreeable to the sailors in a publick-house in this country. By all accounts, she hath a behaviour only fit for a private family. (p. 541)

Ducat is convinced, and says that "if we can agree upon the price I'll take her into the family." He is congratulated by Mrs. Trapes on his wish to spend money on a real "delicacy."

The "delicacy" turns out to be Polly, who thinks that Mrs. Trapes (her father's old friend) is going to get her an honest job as servant to Mrs. Ducat.

Ducat at first balks at the price of a hundred pistoles, but Mrs. Trapes attacks him with sophistic reasoning:

> *Trapes.* Mr. *Ducat.* Sir. . . . I had many a stratagem . . . to inveigle her away from her relations! she too herself was exceeding difficult. And I can assure you, to ruine a girl of severe education is no small addition to the pleasure of our fine gentlemen. I can be answerable for it too, that you will have the first of her. I am sure I could have dispos'd of her upon the same account for at least a hundred guineas to an alderman of *London;* and then too I might have had the disposal of her again as soon as she was out of keeping; but you are my friend, and I shall not deal hard with you. . . .

> *Ducat.* But, dear Mrs. *Dye,* a hundred pistoles say you? why, I could have half a dozen negro princesses for the price.

> *Trapes.* But sure you cannot expect to buy a fine handsome christian at that rate. You are not us'd to see such goods on this side of the water. For the women, like the cloaths, are all tarnish'd and half worn out before they are sent hither. Do but cast your eye upon her, Sir; the door stands half open. (p. 546)

It is not the reasoning of the bawd but a view of Polly that convinces Ducat:

> *Ducat.* I'll have her. I'll pay you down upon the nail. You shall leave her with me. Come, count

your money, Mrs. *Dye.*

> *Trapes.* What a shape is there! she's of the finest growth.

> *Ducat.* You make me mis-reckon. She even takes off my eyes from gold.

> *Trapes.* What a curious pair of sparkling eyes!

> *Ducat.* As vivifying as the sun. I have paid you ten.

> *Trapes.* What a racy flavour must breath from those lips!

> *Ducat.* I want no provoking commendations. I'm in youth; I'm on fire! twenty more makes it thirty; and this here makes it just fifty.

> *Trapes.* What a most inviting complexion! how charming a colour! In short, a fine woman has all the perfections of fine wine, and is a cordial that is ten times as restorative.

> *Ducat.* This fifty then makes it just the sum. So now, Madam, you may deliver her up.

(p. 547)

Fortunately for Polly, Mrs. Ducat is jealous, and "will have none of [Ducat's] hussies about [her]." When Polly rejects Ducat's advances, she finds she has an ally and is firm, though Ducat makes her status appallingly clear to her:

> *Polly.* 'Tis barbarous in you, Sir, to take the occasion of my necessities to insult me.

> *Ducat.* Nay, hussy, I'll give you money.

> *Polly.* I despise it. No, Sir, tho' I was born and bred in England, I can dare to be poor, which is the only thing now-a-days men are asham'd of.

> *Ducat.* I shall humble these saucy airs of yours, Mrs. *Minx.* Is this language from a servant! from a slave!

> *Polly.* Am I then betray'd and sold!

> *Ducat.* Yes, hussy, that you are; and as legally my property, as any woman is her husband's, who sells her self in marriage. . . . Your fortune, your happiness depends upon your compliance. What, proof against a bribe! Sure, hussy, you belye your country, or you must have had a very vulgar education. 'Tis unnatural. . . . Besides, hussy, your consent may make me your slave; there's power to tempt you into the bargain. You must be more than

woman if you can stand that too.

Polly. Sure you only mean to try me! but 'tis barbarous to trifle with my distresses.

Ducat. I'll have none of these airs. 'Tis impertinent in a servant, to have scruples of any kind. I hire honour, conscience and all, for I will not be serv'd by halves. And so, to be plain with you, you obstinate slut, you shall either contribute to my pleasure or my profit; and if you refuse play in the bed-chamber, you shall go work in the fields among the planters. I hope now I have explain'd my self.

(pp. 551-552)

Polly is nearly helpless, the victim of poverty and of her own loyalty to Macheath. Yet, as "rural" heroine, she sturdily defends her honor:

My freedom may be lost, but you cannot rob me of my virtue and integrity: and whatever is my lot, having that, I shall have the comfort of hope, and find pleasure in reflection.

(p. 552)

She is saved by circumstance. At just the right moment news comes that the pirates have invaded the island. Polly gets the aid of Mrs. Ducat, who is glad to get rid of her, and escapes to the jungle. Dressed as a soldier, she sets out to find her wandering husband. Ducat, the forsaken and despised slave-owner, is left to the consolation of his servant, Damaris:

But you [Ducat] are too rich to have courage. You should fight by deputy. 'Tis only for poor people to be brave and desperate, who cannot afford to live.

(p. 553)

Beneath the glitter of this ridicule of Ducat is bitter comment on the ugliness to which sexual relations can be reduced. The references to the slave trade are by no means incidental. Polly is sold, with Ducat as buyer, Mrs. Trapes as seller, and Mrs. Trapes's parlor the auction block. The fashionable Idol could play with love and dispense her favors whimsically, with only a little danger of losing her reputation; she is protected by wealth and position. But the girl of lower class, caught by the "rules" of courtly love, finds herself in the slave mart. When love becomes a commodity, so does the girl unfortunate enough to be caught in the immoral business of flesh selling. The resultant effects on the psychology of all concerned and on society itself are lamentable.

Gay's works can be seen as fairly full commentary on the distortions of love that characterize "town" life. Just how much this was based on earlier literary models, just how much on Gay's burning social views, just how much on Gay's own personal life and attitudes—here is a question that cannot easily be settled.

Gay was a bachelor. He seems never to have found a woman with whom he thought he could establish a relationship satisfactory enough for marriage. It may be that he vainly sought the image of the mother he lost at the age of nine—a woman who could make real the idealistic picture of contentment around a Devonshire hearth such as he described in *Rural Sports.* Possibly, however, he considered such scenes of happiness with a rural mother and frolicking children as unreal and unattainable—only a dream into which he could retreat.

He may, on the other hand, simply have felt that his economic status was too insecure for marriage. He did not have the income necessary to support a "lady." He might have married a rich widow, such as Mrs. Drelincourt, but probably had scruples against it, since such a match would have had a touch of the mercenary in it. The "affair" with Mrs. Drelincourt, which lasted from 1727 to 1731, was no more than a remote attachment, a blossom that never opened despite Swift's encouragement.[12] Nothing came of it whether because Gay was repelled by the problems of wealth and independence involved or because he felt that she did not meet the demands of his dreams. After all, a bachelor in his forties does not accept the idea of marriage easily.

Finally there is the question of the author's relationship to the beautiful and captivating Duchess of Queensberry.[13] He knew her well and possibly was so in love with her that, although she was unattainable, he could not bear the thought of marrying anyone else. Certainly he was in her company most of the time. They enjoyed one another's wit and cleverness and used to write joint letters to mutual friends, Swift, Pope, Mrs. Howard, and others. Manuscripts of these letters[14] show that the Duchess and Gay wrote alternately, the one taking up a paragraph where the other had left off. Such intimacy between a member of the nobility and a man of letters was unusual and not in accord with the ordinary standards of decorum of the day. The very writing of the letters implies physical as well as mental closeness.[15]

The age was certainly licentious, as it appears in records, such as the letters of the observant and gossipy Lady Mary Wortley Montagu. Gay, though fat, was a handsome man with an individual charm, highly attractive to women. He shared with the Duchess many interests in which the stolid Duke could not participate. But do these facts imply that poet and lady were lovers? Not in the light of other circumstances. Though

Gay was financially competent at the period when he came to stay for long visits at the Queensberry home and thus not actually dependent upon his host, he was not such a man as to betray his obligations as a guest. It is true that it was the Duchess who was banished from court for protesting too vehemently against the suppression of **Polly,** but the Duke also took Gay's part and threw his influence to the support of the poet then and on other occasions. Gay seems to have been a truly devoted friend of the Duke, who valued the writer's business ability and entrusted him with the management of many financial affairs. "Honest" John Gay was not the man to indulge in an affair with a friend's wife behind his back; as this chapter has shown, such an act would have been directly contrary to his deep-felt views of love and friendship. There seems to have been no blemish on his relations with the Duke and Duchess. They erected for him a monument with words engraved upon it that seem, even with allowance for the exuberant idealization in epitaphs, to betoken heartfelt love for a man who was to them both

> The warmest friend;
> The most benevolent man:
> Who maintained
> Independency
> In low circumstances of fortune;
> Integrity
> In the midst of a corrupt age
> And that equal serenity of mind,
> Which conscious goodness alone can give,
> Through the whole course of his life.

Their respect for his character and his abilities seems to have been unbounded. It seems to be reflected in further words on the monument:

> Favourite of the Muses,
> He was led by them to every elegant art;
> Refin'd in taste,
> And fraught with graces all his own;
> In various kinds of poetry
> Superior to many,
> Inferior to none,
> His words continue to inspire,
> What his example taught,
> Contempt of folly, however adorn'd;
> Detestation of vice, however dignified;
> Reverence of virtue, however disgrac'd.[16]

This is a gentle epitaph indeed for a man who dealt somewhat ungently with the faults and foibles of his day. He knew the evils of courtly love game conventions in high society and the savage difficulties of love among the poor and the criminal. These evils he mocked with the seeming cynicism of a man who has become doubtful as to human morality. Yet the flow of wit and the mordant criticism were instinct with a kindliness and an integrity that made his strictures on love in his

day palatable to contemporaries and to generations afterward until the present.

Notes

[1] Quoted in note 1, pp. lxviii-lxix, of the introduction to his edition on Gay's poems. The anonymous poet goes on to name Gay's famous partisans: the Duchess of Marlborough, the banished Duchess of Queensberry, the Duchess of Bedford, and Lady Essex. In addition, the powerful Mrs. Howard, who was not mentioned in this poem, must certainly not be overlooked.

[2] In Gregory G. Smith, ed., *The Spectator by Joseph Addison, Richard Steele, and Others,* I, 275-279.

[3] In George Nettleton and Arthur E. Case, eds., *British Dramatists from Dryden to Sheridan* (Boston, 1939), p. 151. The deviations from this norm, by age, class, wit, or beauty are the common topics satirized in the comic roles of Restoration comedy by dramatists who, unlike Wycherley, were the upholders of the decorum of the courtly love game.

[4] To be black-listed by Peachum or Lockit was tantamount to an actual sentence of death, because their protection against the law was necessary for survival in this society.

[5] Gay wrote in his dedicatory letter to Princess Caroline that its chief aim was to show virtue rewarded and distress relieved (Faber, p. 434). The conventional themes of love and war are expressed in a prosy blank verse, not in the usual couplets of Dryden's heroic dramas. Gay's tragedy, however, has its full share of the bombast characteristic of the earliest heroic plays.

[6] Dr. John Harrington Smith's definition of exemplary comedy, in *The Gay Couple in Restoration Comedy* (Cambridge, Mass., 1948), p. 261, is fully as applicable to this type of late heroic drama. The definition is derived from two principles implicit in Jeremy Collier's criticism of the stage: " . . . that the code of human behavior expressed in comedy (or tragedy) ought to be better than the code in effect in life; and that comedy should devote itself to recommending these higher ideals by framing characters who should exemplify them and by punishing or chastening their opposites."

[7] It is perhaps pertinent to note that there are certain signs of influence of Shakespeare upon Gay. He uses Shakespearean epithets in his descriptions; he often refers to Shakespearean characters; he employs dramatic situations which seem to be derived from Shakespearean drama; and, of course, his love for the country is similar to that of the rural Shakespeare of *As You Like It*. Undoubtedly his knowledge and appreciation were augmented by helping Pope in his editing of Shakespeare's plays.

8 Cf. Laetitia Snap in Fielding's *Jonathan Wild.*

9 Polly says of him: "The Coquets of both sexes are self-lovers, and that is a love no other whatever can dispossess" (p. 525).

10 This farce was produced in 1733, one year after Gay died. According to Faber (p. 594), there were no really extensive revisions in the text after the author's death.

11 An example of this logic occurs in I, ix, when Ducat muses, "Family divisions, and matrimonial controversies are a kind of poor man's riches. The whole mode of keeping mistresses and maintaining separate households for estranged wives is held up to scorn in the conclusion of Ducat's soliloquy: "For the poor people [such as the contented and useful parents in *Rural Sports,* for example] are happy out of necessity, because they cannot afford to disagree."

12 Swift to Gay (June 29, 1731), Ball, *The Correspondence of Jonathan Swift, D.D.,* IV, 233-234.

13 Fable II: xvi, would seem to indicate that the Duchess was Gay's Laura, the lady of his few poetic eulogies, primarily because Gay in his tributes to Laura praises her moral virtues and reasoning ability, as well as her beauty—virtues which he has ascribed to the Duchess. See also George Sherburn, "The Duchess Replies to the King," *Harvard Library Bulletin,* VI (1952), 118-121.

14 In the British Museum (Add. MS. 4806).

15 In one of these joint letters (August 20, 1730, Melville, p. 120) to Mrs. Howard, Gay writes, "Now she says I must write you a long letter; but to be sure I cannot say what I would about her, because she is looking over me as I write. If I should tell any good of her, I know she would not like it, and I have said my worst of her already."

16 Mrs. Howard wrote of Gay two years after his death in a similar manner: " . . . it is a sort of pleasure to think over his good qualities: his loss was really great, but it is a satisfaction to have once known so good a man." (Quoted in Irving, *Favorite of the Wits,* p. 297.)

Works Cited

Gay, John, *The Poetical Works of John Gay; Including Polly, The Beggar's Opera; and Selections from the other Dramatic Work.* Edited by Geoffrey Faber. Oxford edition. London, 1926. Unless otherwise specified, this is the edition referred to in all page and line references of the text and footnotes of this study.

Ball, F. Elrington, ed., *The Correspondence of Jonathan Swift, D.D.* 6 vols. London, 1913.

Irving, William Henry, *John Gay, Favorite of the Wits.* Durham, N.C., 1940.

Melville, Lewis [Lewis S. Benjamin], *Life and Letters of John Gay.* London, 1921.

Smith, Gregory G., ed., *The Spectator by Joseph Addison, Richard Steele, and Others.* 4 vols. London, 1907.

William A. McIntosh (essay date 1974)

SOURCE: "Handel, Walpole, and Gay: The Aims of *The Beggar's Opera,*" in *Eighteenth-Century Studies,* Vol. 75, No. 4, Summer, 1974, pp. 415-33.

[*In the following essay, McIntosh disputes commonly held assumptions about Gay's satiric targets in* The Beggar's Opera. *McIntosh suggests that Gay's cordial relationship with Handel and his treatment of music in his own work contradicts the notion that Gay was attacking Italian opera, and that evidence of specific, personal attacks on Walpole is very weak. Instead, he proposes that the object of Gay's satire is society itself.*]

> I have deferr'd writing to you from time to time till I could give you an account of the ***Beggar's Opera.*** It is acted at the Playhouse in Lincoln's Inn fields, with such success that the Playhouse hath been crowded every night; to night is the fifteenth time of Acting, and 'tis thought it will run a fortnight longer.
>
> John Gay, 1728[1]

Gay's Letter to Swift, written some two weeks after ***The Beggar's Opera*** opened on 29 January 1728,[2] might have seemed to some an extraordinary boast. The expectation that his play would equal its already unprecedented run was, however, well founded. At a time when a dozen consecutive performances of a play were all but unheard of, ***The Beggar's Opera*** was produced without interruption no fewer than sixty-two times.[3] After more than a week's run (the usual interval signaling a play's success) the *Daily Journal* reported that at Lincoln's Inn Fields "no one third Part of the Company that crowd thither to see [the play], can get Admittance."[4] Even after the close of the 1727-28 season ***The Beggar's Opera*** was acted an additional fifteen times at the Haymarket Theatre by a semiprofessional company.[5] Indeed, it was not until the 1732-33 season that audiences were drawn to ***The Beggar's Opera*** with promises that one of the afterpiece's actresses would dress in boy's clothing or that "Signora Violante will perform her surprising Entertainments on the Rope [6 September 1732]."[6]

The remarkable success of *The Beggar's Opera* is perhaps matched only by critical misprisions of the play. To be sure, a great deal of scholarship has gone into studies of *The Beggar's Opera,* but from our vantage point some two and a half centuries later we seem no closer to coming to grips with it than Herring, Burney, or Hawkins. The precise circumstances occasioning *The Beggar's Opera,* or the purpose of the play itself, may never be understood fully, but before any substantial answers to either of those questions can be formulated, it is necessary to clear the air—to put into proper perspective if not altogether dismiss, a number of critical assumptions which heretofore have impeded a productive study of the play. To borrow from James Sutherland: *The Beggar's Opera* "has suffered, in fact, from the most damaging kind of criticism that gives with one hand and takes away with the other."[7] The purpose of this paper, then, is not to assert a set of conditions that led Gay to produce *The Beggar's Opera,* or even to suggest what he is up to in the play itself; instead, my intention is to scrutinize, and, where possible, to set aside the critical commonplaces that surround the play, to dispense with the notion that Gay's ostensible purpose in writing *The Beggar's Opera* was the dissolution of Handelian opera, and to open a path for subsequent studies of the play less overgrown than the one this study has had to follow.

I

> . . . A set of Quaker pastorals might succeed, if our friend Gay could fancy it, and I think it a fruitful subject; pray hear what he says. I believe farther, the pastoral ridicule is not exhausted, and that a porter, footman, or chairman's pastoral might do well. Or what think you of a Newgate pastoral among the whores and thieves there?
>
> Jonathan Swift, 1716[8]

Swift seems to have been enthusiastic about his proposal for a Newgate pastoral, and many discussions of *The Beggar's Opera* point to his suggestion as being the motivation behind the play.[9] Few, however, take into account that Swift's letter was sent to Pope, not Gay, or that more than eleven years passed before Gay wrote *The Beggar's Opera.*[10] In fact, according to Pope, Gay gave up the idea of a Newgate pastoral in favor of a comedy. Spence quotes Pope as saying: "This [decision of Gay's] was what gave rise to *The Beggar's Opera.* He began on it, and when first he mentioned it to Swift, the Doctor did not much like the project."[11] The issue here is not that Swift favored the pastoral form over comedy. More to the point is that Swift was urging a variety of humor that has as its basis an unlikely turn of one kind or another. What could be more bizarre than a pastoral in which a Quaker bacchanal is celebrated, if not a picture of thieves and whores frolicking like shepherds and nymphs? It is exactly that

sort of humor that prompted Swift's "Ode on a Lady's Dressing Room" in which the lovely coquette is portrayed void of any cosmetic charms and perched upon a chamber pot.

Such incongruities delighted the members of the Scriblerus Club, and one may find in the *Memoirs of Martin Scriblerus* the essential burden of *The Beggar's Opera.* In his endeavors "to find out the Seat of the Soul," Martinus discovered that

> Calves and Philosophers, Tygers and Statesmen, Foxes and Sharpers, Peacocks and Fops, Cock-Sparrows and Coquets, Monkeys and Players, Courtiers and Spaniels, Moles and Misers, exactly resemble one another in the conformation of the *Pineal Gland.* He did not doubt likewise to find the same resemblances in Highwaymen and Conquerors.
>
> (XII. 29-35)[12]

There is little difference in Martinus' record of his discoveries and the epigrammatic remarks of Gay's Beggar, who says: "Through the whole piece you may observe such a similitude of manners in high and low life, that it is difficult to determine whether (in the fashionable vices) the fine gentlemen imitate the gentlemen of the road, or the gentlemen of the road the fine gentlemen" (III.xvi)[13] The comic ethos amounts to a portrayal of the incongruous, the antecedents of which have some peripheral relationship to Swift's suggestion of a Newgate pastoral, but less tenuous is the play's connection with the Scriblerian activity of 1726-27.[14]

All of that is not to imply *The Beggar's Opera* was not prompted by other considerations, but it should, if nothing else, evoke a more cautious approach to critics such as Hawkins, who reduces the occasioning of the play to a purely personal level. Of Gay, Sir John writes: "The motive for writing the piece, and for the many acrimonious expressions and bitter invectives against statesmen, lawyers, priests, and others, contained in it, was the disappointment of Mr. Gay in his application for preferment at court."[15] But Gay was capable of the same sorts of analogies Hawkins refers to long before he lost his place at court. In late summer of 1723 Gay wrote the following to Mrs. Howard:

> I cannot indeed wonder that the Talents requisite for a great Statesman are so scarce in the world since so many of those who possess them are every month cut off in the prime of their age at the Old Baily. How envious are Statesmen! and how jealous are they of rivals! A Highway-man never picks up an honest man for a companion, but if such a one accidentally falls his way; if he cannot turn his heart He like a wise Statesman discards him. Another observation I have made upon Courtiers, is, that if you have any friendship with any particular one you

must be entirely governed by his friendships and resentments not your own.[16]

More than four years passed before Gay's hopes for an important position at court were dashed by his appointment as Gentleman-usher to the two-year-old Princess Louisa. After declining the post he wrote to Swift, "As I am us'd to disappointments I can bear them, but as I can have no more hopes, I can no more be disappointed, so that I am in a blessed condition."[17] Though Gay's tone is not one of delight, it suggests a kind of resignation, and nothing more. Nor does Swift's reply to his friend. He writes, "I entirely approve your refusal of that employment, and your writing to the Queen. I am perfectly confident that you have a firm enemy in the Ministry [viz. Walpole]. God forgive him, but not till he puts himself in a state to be forgiven."[18]

Gay, remember, had finished *The Beggar's Opera* sometime in October of 1727, which, we see, was a crucial period in his political life. It seems unlikely indeed that a man who had hopes of obtaining a significant position at court would jeopardize his chances by insulting the one man who could help him. His friendship with the Scriblerians would have made his political life difficult enough without his taking up the torch against the Ministry. One might argue that to ease his spleen Gay revised *The Beggar's Opera* after losing the appointment, but time has to be taken into account. *The Beggar's Opera* is not simply another eighteenth-century comedy—though without its music the play might pass for one easily enough—but instead a fairly complex dramatic piece that required some degree of musical collaboration, and more important, rehearsal. At the very latest it would have had to have been to Rich by the new year, and before that some time was lost when Gay took the play to Cibber.[19] In short, Gay had perhaps less than two months to alter the play, and, as will be discussed more fully in another section of this paper, if any alteration did take place it was to weaken, not intensify, the sting of *The Beggar's Opera*.

To summarize, then, the play seems to have been occasioned by Gay's desire to produce a comedy of incongruities, built around his long-held notion of the impingement of the rapacious and base on polite society. That Gay would draw the parallels he does between high and low life is no surprise; nor is his opting for a dramatic vehicle. What does remain puzzling, however, is the dramatic form he chose.

Many commentators[20] take Gay's use of the ballad opera as an explicit jab at Italian opera in general, and Handelian opera in particular. That question is discussed fully in the following section, but there can be no doubt whatever that Gay's selection of a musical mode was influenced by the immense popularity of Italian opera. There was, however, a long tradition of the use of

dramatic song on the English stage from which Gay must have drawn; indeed, his use of music in *The Beggar's Opera* more closely matches Shakespeare's in *The Tempest* than either of *The Tempest*'s revisions set by Purcell and Arne. Nor was Gay the first to bring a ballad opera to the eighteenth-century theatre. There are at least three plays produced earlier in the century that may be classified as ballad operas.[21] Of those, Gay's play has greatest kinship with Thomas D'Urfey's *Wonders in the Sun* (1706.) Burney records that D'Urfey's play ran for five nights before closing,[22] which was a satisfactory performance record, if a disappointment to D'Urfey. Gay could expect a comparable run for his own play for novelty's sake alone. His friends were not so confident. According to Spence, Pope, speaking for himself and Swift, remarked: "When it was done neither of us thought it would succeed. We showed it to Congreve, who, after reading it over, said, 'It would either take greatly, or be damned confoundly.'"[23]

The motivation behind Gay's writing a ballad opera may never be plumbed, nor can the reasons for its staggering success compared with the barely adequate run of D'Urfey's ballad opera be understood completely. Of one thing we can be certain: Both the comic ethos and the dramatic form of *The Beggar's Opera* number Gay among the great wits of the eighteenth century. As Dr. Johnson so aptly observed: "Whether this new drama was the product of judgment or luck, the praise of it must be given to the inventor."[24]

II

In the year 1727, Violent Parties were formed, between the 2 famous Singers, Faustina and Cuzzoni; and in the Election for Directors Faustina's Party carried it. These Animosities were very prejudicial to the Interest of the Academy, and the Houses began to grow thinner upon it. *The Beggar's Opera* appearing soon after, gave such a Turn to the Town, that Operas were generally neglected.

The Earl of Shaftesbury, 1760[25]

Charles Burney quotes Cromwell as saying that Italian opera, "being in an unintelligible tongue . . . cannot corrupt the morals of the People,"[26] but owing to its absolute power on the English stage during the first three decades of the eighteenth century, it managed, as Shaftesbury implies, to corrupt itself absolutely. The rivalries between singers, the castrati, flamboyant and idiotic props, libretti of the most pathetic sort, and a host of other absurdities elicited growing sentiments against the opera that ranged from the amusing, if highly subjective, satires of Addison to the gloomy declamation of Arthur Bedford.[27] Gay was no less aware of the foibles of Italian opera than the rest of London, and the entirety of *The Beggar's Opera* is filled with satiric barbs directed at it. But most critics who have not taken Dr. Johnson's remark that "this play [is] written in ridicule of the musical Italian drama,"[28] as sufficient comment have gone off on tangents of ingenuity that all but blast Gay out of the water.

Those critics who have fantasized an enmity between Handel and Gay, or even an intense hatred for Italian opera on Gay's part,[29] not only have failed to understand Gay's play, but also have distorted historical fact. It has been observed elsewhere that there is no evidence to suggest that Handel was annoyed with Gay after the appearance of *The Beggar's Opera.*[30] In fact, there is considerable evidence to show that Handel was not upset, and even more to demonstrate the existence of a pleasant association of that great master and the Scriblerians. There is nothing in the writings or letters of Handel that indicates he was smarting from Gay's "attack," and it is interesting to note that he had entered into a new partnership with "gay" John Rich by August of 1734.[31] During the early 1720s Handel, Gay, Pope, and Arbuthnot had all gathered at Canons with the Duke of Chandos, and apparently that company was an harmonious one. One late-eighteenth-century writer records their relationship thus:

> [Pope] heard the performances of Handel with perfect indifference, if not impatience. Gay was pleased with music without understanding it, but forgot the performance when the notes ceased to vibrate. Arbuthnot, on the contrary, who was a judge of music, and a composer, felt the merits of Handel, and conceived an esteem of him, which he afterwards displayed under the most trying circumstances.[32]

Handel's association with Gay's circle had begun a decade before the Canons period. Aaron Hill, Gay's friend and classmate under Robert Luck,[33] approached Handel with the idea of *Rinaldo,* and it was at Hill's instance and under his supervision that Paolo Rolli completed the libretto that Handel set. Some five years later, in 1716, Gay's *Trivia* recalled his time with Handel and the others at Burlington's palace:

> There *Hendel* strikes the Strings, the melting Strain
> Transports the Soul, and thrills through ev'ry Vein;
> There oft' I enter (but with cleaner Shoes)
> For *Burlington*'s belov'd by ev'ry Muse.[34]

In 1719 Handel brought out his first setting of Gay's masque, *Acis and Galatea,*[35] and the following year, along with his partner in opera, Heidegger, he was among the subscribers to Gay's poems.[36] It was also in 1720 that Handel completed his first English oratorio, *Esther.* When it was performed at Canons on 29 August of that year, the audience heard Handel's settings

of airs written for *Esther* by Arbuthnot, Pope, and Gay.[37] During the 1725 revival of *The What D'ye Call It,* Handel's "'Twas When the Seas Were Roaring" was performed,[38] and he was delighted when Gay used it again in *The Beggar's Opera.* Perhaps most telling of all is this exchange between Pepusch and Handel, recorded by Hibbert after *The Beggar's Opera* was produced:

> Pepusch: I hope, sir, you do not include me among'st those who did injustice to your talents.

> Handel: Nod at all, nod at all, God forbid! I am a great admirer of the airs of *The Beggar's Opera,* and every professional gentleman must do his best to live.[39]

Handel is not being magnanimous; nor should he have been. An opera, even a ballad opera, drawing together the works of Purcell, Clarke, Bononcini, Eccles, would have been remiss to have excluded Handel's.

It has been argued that Gay's attack on opera was merely another manifestation of his difficulties at court—that because opera enjoyed the support of the crown Gay felt it had to be destroyed.[40] Such a circumstance is unlikely indeed. And even if the assertion were correct, it should be noted that Handel's difficulties with the court were very much like Gay's. He was actively and viciously opposed by the Prince of Wales for several years, and by 1729, Hawkins reports, was himself completely at odds with the court.[41]

Those who supported opera, and particularly that of Handel, continued their support despite the growing canon of ballad operas. Handel was not at all put off by the appearances of his music in *Polly,* 1729,[42] as evinced by his subscription to Gay's collected works in 1730.[43] Nor was he deterred from reviving *Rinaldo* in 1731. For a form which was supposed to have been driven from the stage, composed by a man who was supposed to have been forced away from opera, *Rinaldo* did remarkably well. It was performed at the Haymarket Theatre no fewer than six times in less than a month.[44] Finally, and significantly, Handel continued, after its initial London performance in 1731, to revive *Acis and Galatea,* "which in every Respect charms, to this Day, Persons of all Ranks and Capacities,"[45] up to his death in 1759. That Handel gave up the composition of opera is undeniable, but that the appearances of *The Beggar's Opera, Polly, Achilles,* or any of the others were responsible is as untenable as the assertion that John Gay led the crusade out of animus towards a man who had been his friend for two decades.[46]

Among recent commentators, C. F. Burgess is perhaps most adamant in his arguments that Gay was militantly against Italian opera.[47] Gay's oft quoted letter is frequently cited as evidence of his antipathy towards opera, and it is worth looking at again here. On 3 February 1722/23 he writes to Swift:

> As for the reigning Amusement of the town, tis entirely Musick. Real fiddles, Bass Vials [sic] and Hautboys not Poetical Harps, Lyres, and reeds. Theres [sic] nobody allow'd to say I sing but an Eunuch or an Italian Woman. Every body is grown now as great a judge of Musick as they were in your time of Poetry. And folks that could not distinguish one tune from another now daily dispute about the different styles of Hendel, Bononcini, and Attillo. People have now forgot Homer, and Virgil & Caesar, or at least they have lost their ranks, for in London and Westminster in all polite conversation's Senesino is daily voted to be the greatest man that ever liv'd.[48]

A close reading of that passage suggests that Gay is talking about people, not music. His sarcasm is leveled at the "great judges" of music *and* poetry; moreover, he is concerned here with the fickle nature of polite society, not with that society's longing for opera. Swift's views are another matter altogether; however, it is important to remember that Swift, not Gay, wrote:

> [*The Beggar's Opera*] likewise exposeth with Great Justice that unnatural Taste for Italian Musick among us, which is wholly unsuitable to our Northern Climate, and the Genius of the People, whereby we are overrun with Italian-Effeminacy, and Italian Nonsense.[49]

That is not to say that Gay was not disgusted with certain features of the opera. Any sensible and sensitive person must have been. But the passage extracted from his letter to Swift is his most fully developed comment on the subject of opera, excepting *The Beggar's Opera,* and that will carry the argument only so far.

Addison's four *Spectator* essays[50] have also been cited as proof of Gay's opposition to Italian opera.[51] First, it must be remembered that the most recent of Addison's attacks was printed on 3 April 1711, scarcely more than a month after the triumphal opening of *Rinaldo*.[52] Four years earlier Addison had been humiliated by the financial and artistic disaster of his own opera, *Rosamond*.[53] None of that, however, has anything whatsoever to do with John Gay. When *The Beggar's Opera* was written, Addison had been dead for some eight years. Further, it is not certain that Steele shared Addison's vehement feelings against the new opera; none of the four *Spectator* numbers in question bears Steele's mark. And there is no reason to believe that Steele, even granting that he agreed with Addison, urged them on Gay. He was not one of Gay's intimates, and at the time *The Beggar's Opera* came to the stage was, himself, ill.[54]

That Gay hated the foreignness of Italian opera is a misconception at best; at worst it is the result of putting Swift's words into Gay's mouth.[55] If the foreign flavor of the opera is what bothered Gay, how ironic it is that he should bring to the English stage a variety of the German *Singspiel*.[56] Excepting only those done by Carey,[57] every ballad opera, including *The Beggar's Opera,* was arranged and orchestrated by a German. Perhaps even more ironic is that the intentionally simple English melodies of *The Beggar's Opera* were to become bravura concert pieces that grew more florid with each production of the play. Burney laments:

> But either from the ambition of the singer, or expectations of the audience, Music is not suffered to remain simple long upon the stage; and the more plain and ancient the melodies, the more they are to be embellished by every new performer of them. The tunes in *The Beggar's Opera* will never appear in their original simple garb again.[58]

From Burney's comments, then, it would seem that the actions of ballad opera stars had become mirrors of Faustina and Cuzzoni, or, if not, that the audiences became not unlike those that flocked to Covent Garden and Haymarket for the opera. Perhaps it was the good fortune of Gay, Swift, and even Handel to have been laid to rest before a Dublin revival of *The Beggar's Opera* on 2 January 1765. The part of the swaggering Macheath was taken by Ann Catley, but to make matters worse, all the music had been "newly improved" and ornamented by a young Italian composer, Tommaso Giordani.[59]

There is a tradition that on the opening night of *The Beggar's Opera* the audience took Pepusch's overture to be the first sounding, but when no second music was forthcoming, the audience all but lost control. To silence the crowd, the comedian Jack Hall was sent out to explain that there would be no further soundings, but the hush that fell over the audience when he appeared so unnerved him that he blurted out: "Ladies and Gentlemen, we—we beg you will not call for First and Second Music, bec-because you know—there is never any music at all to an opera."[60] Perhaps it was Jack Hill's *faux pas* that began the whole gruesome tradition of reading *The Beggar's Opera* as a brutal satire designed to destroy Italian opera. Surely Gay never intended to do more than offer, as Bukofzer wisely suggests, a few good humored parodies for the amusement of the friends of *opera seria*.[61] Given the sorts of straws that have been grasped by some, one wonders why someone has not attempted to establish a link between the cage of sparrows Addison lampoons in the fifth *Spectator* and the over thirty references to birds, beginning with Polly's name, that Gay includes in his play. The point, simply, is this: if lampoon is to be appreciated it must first be recognizable. The Lucy-Polly conflict may very well allude to the bickerings of

Faustina and Cuzzoni. Or does it, as many have suggested, recall a quarrel (of which there is no record) between Lady Walpole and Maria Skerrett, Sir Robert's mistress?[62] If one must choose, the former is certainly the more plausible. Notwithstanding the assertion that *everyone* knew of Walpole's philandering, the prime minister never took it to the stage; Faustina and Cuzzoni, quite literally, aired their linen before the public, and few in Gay's audience would have failed to make the connection between the two famous singers and the play's two female leads. But that sort of parody hardly constitutes a vicious attack on opera; moreover, those who followed opera were not charmed with the antics of the two prima donnas, and would have been as pleased with the joke as a Jonathan Swift.

If Gay had wanted opera off the stage he would not have relied merely upon a singers' war, or the speeches of the beggar at the beginning and end of the play (I. intro. & III. xvi), for they are too subtle. Such techniques almost always produce laughter, but rarely do they produce anger. If the death of opera was Gay's goal, he could have secured it easily enough. Macheath, instead of a rich tenor, could have been played by a squeaking castrato; Peachum, instead of dealing in contraband would have kidnapped young boys for the opera; Gay might have demanded the same sort of musical treatment of his songs from Pepusch as they actually received from Giordani four decades later. But Gay did none of those things. There are swipes at opera in his play, but swipes are not death blows. To look for more is to spoil the fun; to see more is to see something that does not exist.

III

> Does Walpole think you intended an affront to him in your opera? Pray God he may, for he has held the longest hand at hazard that ever fell to any sharper's share, and keeps his run when the dice are changed.
>
> Jonathan Swift, 1728[63]

One of the most significant contributions to the study of Walpole's being satirized in *The Beggar's Opera* was made some years ago by Jean Kern, who ends once and for all the myth that the Peachum-Lockit quarrel is a parody of a similar disagreement between Walpole and his brother-in-law, Townshend.[64] The Walpole-Townshend row, if anything, was a parody of the quarrel that had been acted out on stage more than a year before. Walpole is among the targets of the play's satire, but the extent to which he is ridiculed must, as Professor Kern's example suggests, be approached with some caution. Gay did not, in fact, nurture a long hatred for Walpole, and from the presence of his name on the list of Gay's subscribers in

1720[65] it seems that the prime minister was nominally cordial towards Gay.

Walpole, of course, was not a beloved figure, and it is well known that the first organized opposition to him can be traced to the Scriblerian activities of the period 1726-1729.[66] I have already established that Gay had sufficient reason to be at odds with Walpole by 1727, but he was no fool and not about to risk a head-on collision with so powerful an adversary.[67] Even Walpole could tolerate the references to himself in "Robin of Bagshot, alias Gorgon, alias Bluff Bob, alias Carbuncle, alias Bob Booty," and there are numerous reports of his calling for an encore of the air (XXX) that ends with the line: "That was levelled at me."[68] What he could not tolerate, though, would be an allusion to his dalliances. And if the Polly-Lucy argument is intended to embarrass Walpole, how cleverly Gay has covered himself. The obvious analogue is the operatic rivalry, and it is behind that similarity Gay could take refuge. If the burden of *The Beggar's Opera* is an attack on the Walpole government, it necessarily must have been camouflaged; and what better subterfuge than the burlesque of an opera?

In the amount of criticism received, opera was second only to the Ministry; Handel, second only to Walpole. And the association between the two men, at least as far as the public could tell, was strong. On three occasions it was Walpole who arranged pensions for Handel,[69] though neither man held any affection for the other. As late as 1733, well after Handel's rift with the court, they were connected in print. On 15 June 1733 *The Craftsman* carried this epigram:

> Quoth W————e to H————l, shall
>   We Two agree,
>   and Excise the whole Nation?
> [Handel:] Si, caro, Si.
> Of what use are Sheep if the Shepherds can't
>   sheer them
> At the Haymarket I, you at Westminster?
> [Walpole:] Hear him.
> Call'd to order, the seconds appear'd in their
>   place;
> One fam'd for his Morals, and one for his
>   Face.
> In half they succeed, in half they were crost:
> The Excise was obtained, but poor *Deborah*
>   lost.[70]

If the orientation of *The Beggar's Opera* is political, there are, subterfuge notwithstanding, few substantial allusions to Walpole. The Peachum-Lockit parallel does not exist; the Polly-Lucy conflict is tenuous at best. More to the point, perhaps, is the parody of Walpole's having to choose between his wife and mistress in Macheath's "How Happy Could I Be with Either" (Air XXXV),[71] but even that would have meaning to only a very few. Gay's allusion in Robin of Bagshot is transparent, but there is never the sort of clearly defined allegorical schema to the play that allows positive identifications to be made.[72]

It has been noted that the mode of political satire is established by the overture before the play ever begins.[73] Pepusch incorporated into his overture a tune known as "Walpole." That title was not so well known as an earlier one, "The Happy Clown," and when the same tune appears in *The Beggar's Opera* as "I'm Like a Skiff on the Ocean Tossed" (Air XLVII), it is printed under its original and best known title, "One Evening Having Lost My Way." When Lucy sings the air, it is set in G major with a time signature of 6/8. The overture, however, is written in the key of B-flat major with a time signature of 12/8. First, it is unlikely that the audience even heard the overture through its own din; second, it is doubtful that the air would have been recognized, for Pepusch treats it in fugal form in the allegro section of his French overture, and the tempo, even when the tonic melody can be followed, is considerably faster than the tempo at which it was supposed to have been sung.[74] Only a trained musician could have recognized the melody in the amount of time it took the orchestra to play it, and an extraordinary pair of ears would have been needed to have heard it played at all on the two oboes, two violins, and harpsichord for which that part of the overture was scored.

Taken altogether, the political satire of the play is hardly so potent as to conclude that it brought about Walpole's downfall.[75] Gay no more had that in mind than the dissolution of Italian opera. It was Swift who saw Walpole as damned, not Gay, whose own views, like those of Pope, were mixed; "both lunched with and satirized Sir Robert."[76] Gay had been hurt, but not to the point of wanting to destroy himself, and to have gone farther than all concrete evidence indicates he went would have spelled his end. Even so, it seems he struck closer to home than he had intended, or, perhaps, the joke simply had worn itself out. Despite the façade of good cheer, one cannot but pity the writer of these lines:

> By the beginning of my letter you see how I decline in favour, but I look upon it as my particular distinction, that as soon as the Court gains a man I lose him; tis a mortification I have been us'd to, so I bear it as a philosopher should.[77]

IV

But the best of all was Sir William Ashurst, who sat in a box, and was perhaps one of the first judges who ever figured away at *The Beggar's Opera,* that strong and bitter satire against the professions, and particularly his.

Hannah More, 1778[78]

More studies of *The Beggar's Opera* would do well to take up Sir William's standard, for it is in its treatment of the professions, especially law, that the play's most pointed and consistent satire exists. Exactly what Gay is attempting, or why he is attempting it, remains a mystery. Hawkins' suggestion, which was quoted earlier, seems to be off the mark, as do the many that have followed it. No one has taken into account the tradition of legal satire carried on by the later Jacobean and Caroline playwrights for the benefit of their Inns of Court coterie. Nor has there been any explanation for Gay's dark, almost twentieth-century view of humanity. Certainly that was the feature of the play that attracted Brecht's attention.

On no fewer than eleven occasions there are explicit references that call the legal profession into question.[79] Each of those is put into the mouth of one of the play's low-life figures, as if some sort of vindication through balance and antithesis were intended. Every vile act in the play is justified by the vilification of polite society or one of the professions.

> The gamesters and lawyers are jugglers alike
> If they meddle, your all is in danger:

sings Jenny Diver to Macheath an instant before giving him the Judas-like kiss that allows him to be taken off in chains. Peachum's masterminding of the release of several members of his gang is followed by Filch's air, which observes:

> For suits of love, like law, are won by pay
> And beauty must be fee'd into our arms.

Peachum and his wife plot the undoing of Macheath, and that is sealed with an air containing these lines:

> If lawyer's hand is fee'd, sir,
> He steals your whole estate.

And the pattern repeats itself time and again throughout the play.

The morality of the play, or lack of it, prompted a number of attacks, most famous of which was Bishop Herring's sermon against *The Beggar's Opera.* If only for its splendid polemic, a portion of Swift's answer to the Bishop is worth quoting. "Upon the whole," he writes,

> I deliver my judgment That nothing but servile Attachment to a Party, Affectation of Singularity, lamentable Dullness, mistaken Zeal, or studied Hypocrisy, can have the least reasonable Objection against this excellent moral Performance of the Celebrated Mr. Gay.[80]

In fact, Swift never answers the critics of the play's morality; perhaps he dared not. The world of Gay's play is a world of enormities, but so, too, is the world that watches it. After the rabble has cried its reprieve, the beggar steps forward and remarks:

> Had the play remained as I first intended, it would have carried a most excellent moral. 'Twould have shown that the lower sort of people have their vices in a degree as well as the rich, and that they are punished for them. (III. xvi)

Like the beggar, we know that there is no morality in the liberation of Macheath, but like Gay, we know too that there is no morality in his being hanged by men who belong on the scaffold with him. Gay does not, like almost all his contemporaries in drama, give us romp, which is tied up by the meting out of a brand of inefficacious poetic justice in the last scene. *The Beggar's Opera* is no thesis play, but neither is it mere frolic. Gay wants to entertain, and in that he succeeds most excellently. But if his treatment of society and the professions evokes laughter, it also evokes a feeling of uneasiness among those laughing. We are placed in the uncomfortable position of having to come to terms with two worlds. The world within the play is crowded with criminals on every level, but so is the world without. What we do with that second world is our own affair. What Gay himself would have done with it—indeed, what he already had done with it—is manifestly obvious in his letters.

In the preceding pages I have discussed the events and attitudes that occasioned *The Beggar's Opera,* set aside the notion that the aim of the play was the dissolution of Italian opera, and suggested a more cautious view of the play's political satire. I have suggested that the dominant force in *The Beggar's Opera* is its professional and social satire, and that its function is essentially didactic. Finally, I have implied that in working towards a stage didactic that proffers something other than pap, Gay is unique among his contemporaries. This paper does not pretend to do more than open the door to subsequent investigations, whose starting point should not be with the tired clichés put away here, but instead with a kind of drama unique in its time, the work of "a natural man, without design, who spoke what he thought, and just as he thought it."[81]

Notes

[1] C. F. Burgess, ed., *The Letters of John Gay* (Oxford, 1966), pp. 70-71. Hence-forth cited as *LJG.*

[2] Emmett L. Avery, *The London Stage, 1700-1729* (Carbondale, Ill., 1960), II, 956.

[3] Ibid., p. 931.

[4] Ibid., p. 958.

[5] Ibid., p. 931.

[6] Arthur H. Scouten, *The London Stage, 1729-1747* (Carbondale, Ill., 1961), I, 231 f.

[7] James Sutherland, "John Gay" in *Pope and His Contemporaries,* ed. James L. Clifford and Louis A. Landa (Oxford, 1923), p. 122.

[8] From a letter to Pope, dated 30 August 1716, quoted in William E. Schultz, *Gay's Beggar's Opera* (New Haven, 1923), p. 122.

[9] See, in addition to Schultz, p. 122: Lewis Melville, *The Life and Letters of John Gay* (London, 1921), p. 41; and Oscar Sherwin, *Mr. Gay* (New York, 1923), p. 96, for example.

[10] The exact date of the play's completion is unknown; however, on 22 October 1727 Gay wrote Swift: "My opera is already finished." See Burgess, *LJG,* p. 69.

[11] Quoted in Schultz, pp. 122-23.

[12] Notice that in the series of juxtapositions the animals are cited first, except in the courtier-spaniel comparison, which lowers the courtier to the level of the other beasts (Charles Kerby-Miller, ed., *The Memoirs of Martinus Scriblerus* [New Haven, 1950], p. 137).

[13] This and all subsequent citations refer to Edgar V. Roberts, ed., *The Beggar's Opera* (Lincoln, 1969).

[14] Kerby-Miller, p. 57, points to three periods of Scriblerian activity: 1714, 1716-18, and 1726-27. Though the authorship of the *Memoirs* is generally attributed to Pope and Arbuthnot, Gay no doubt had access to, if not a part in, this final version from which the quoted passage is taken.

[15] Sir John Hawkins, *A General History of the Science and Practice of Music* (1776; rpt. ed. anon., 3 vols., London, 1875), II, 875.

[16] Burgess, *LJG,* p. 45.

[17] Ibid., pp. 68-69. The date of the letter is 22 October 1727.

[18] F. Elrington Ball, ed., *The Correspondence of Jonathan Swift,* 6 vols. (London, 1911-14), III, 431.

[19] Schultz, p. 1.

[20] See especially: Arthur V. Berger, "*The Beggar's Opera,* the Burlesque, and Italian Opera," *Music and Letters,* 17 (April 1936), 93-105; Edmund M. Gagey, *Ballad Opera* (New York, 1937), pp. 18 f.; Max Goberman, "Mr. John Gay's *The Beggar's Opera,*" *Music*

Review, 24 (April 1963), 3-12; W. J. Lawrence, "Music and Song in the Eighteenth-Century Theatre," *Musical Quarterly,* 2 (April 1916), 67-75; and Schultz, p. 139 f.

[21] See George Tufts, "Ballad Operas: A List and Some Notes," *Musical Antiquary,* 4 (January 1913), 61-86.

[22] Charles Burney, *A General History of Music from the Earliest Ages to the Present Period* (1789; rpt. ed. Frank Mercer, 2 vols., London, 1935), II, 657.

[23] Quoted in Schultz, p. 125.

[24] Samuel Johnson, *Lives of the Poets,* Vols. VIII and IX of *The Works of Samuel Johnson,* 16 vols. (rpt., Troy, N. Y., 1903), IX, 308.

[25] From his *Memoirs of Handel;* quoted in Otto Erich Deutsch, *Handel* (London, 1955), pp. 844-45.

[26] Burney, p. 677.

[27] Arthur Bedford, *The Great Abuse of Musick* (1711; facs. rpt., New York, 1965), p. 196. Bedford regards the fallen state of music in London as retributive. He writes: "Our *Purcel* was the Delight of the Nation, and the Wonder of the World, and the Character of Dr. *Blow* was but little inferior to him. But when we made not that use thereof which we ought, it pleas'd *God* to shew his Resentment, and put a Stop to our Progress, by taking away our *Purcel* in the Prime of Age, and Dr. *Blow* soon after. We all lamented our Misfortunes, but never consider'd them as Judgments for the *Abuse* of this *Science;* so that instead of growing better we grew worse and worse. Now therefore *Musick* declines as fast as it did improve before."

[28] Johnson, p. 303.

[29] Gagey, p. 18, suggests that *The Beggar's Opera* was an attempt to force Handelian opera off the stage; Schultz, p. 139, calls the play Gay's effort to kill Italian opera.

[30] Bertrand H. Bronson, *"The Beggar's Opera"* (1941; rpt. in *Facets of the Enlightenment,* Berkeley and Los Angeles, 1968), p. 77.

[31] Erich H. Müller, ed., *The Letters and Writings of George Frideric Handel* (London, 1935), pp. 32-33.

[32] John Christopher Smith (1799) quoted in William H. Irving, *John Gay Favorite of the Wits* (Durham, 1940), p. 284.

[33] Ibid., p. 11.

[34] It is worth noting that Gay's allusion to Handel's

music transporting the soul is tied to the Pythagorean concept of spiritual transmigration that leads ultimately to a kind of apotheosis, and it is a compliment of the highest sort. There is a rich tradition of this notion in English thought, and Gay is drawing from it. Cf. Dryden's "Alexander's Feast" ("With ravish'd ears the monarch hears"); cf. also, Morrison C. Boyd, *Elizabethan Music and Musical Criticism,* 2nd ed. (Philadelphia, 1962), pp. 5, 11, 35.

[41] Hawkins, p. 876.

[35] Deutsch, p. 99.

[36] Ibid., p. 121.

[37] Irving, p. 184.

[38] Deutsch, p. 179.

[39] Quoted in Irving, p. 242.

[40] Schultz, p. 139.

[42] *Polly* incorporates two of Handel's minutes from the *Water Music* and a third piece, the March from *Scipione.*

[43] Percy M. Young, "Handel the Man" in *Handel: A Symposium,* ed. Gerald Abraham (London, 1954), p. 3.

[44] 6, 10, 20, 24, 27 April; 1 May 1731 (Deutsch, pp. 273-74). Likewise, *Julius Caesar,* the most Italianate of Handel's operas, was revived successfully in 1730 (performed eleven times between 17 January and 31 March) and again in 1732 (for four performances between the 1st and 12th of February). For a complete listing of Handel's numerous operatic revivals and premières during this general time frame, see Deutsch, pp. 252-302.

[45] John Christopher Smith, 1740, quoted in Deutsch, p. 493.

[46] For a number of informative discussions of Handel's leaving opera for oratorio see: Manfred F. Bukofzer, *Music in the Baroque Era* (New York, 1947), pp. 331 f.; Winton Dean, *Handel's Dramatic Oratorios and Masques* (London, 1959), pp. 33 f.; and E. D. Mackerness, *A Social History of English Music* (London, 1964), pp. 102 f.

[47] See esp., C. F. Burgess, "The Genesis of *The Beggar's Opera,*" *Cithara,* 2 (November 1962), 11. Henceforth, *Cithara.*

[48] Burgess, *LJG,* p. 43.

[49] From *Intelligencer* number 3 in *Satires and Personal*

Writings by Jonathan Swift, ed. William A. Eddy (London, 1932), p. 266. Swift was a frequent commentator on musical tastes, and himself no small judge of music if his work with his Dublin choir is any indication of his musical abilities. It seems, however, that even though he is clearly opposed to Italian music in the passage cited, he is no less concerned with human folly associated with it than Gay. That can be illustrated further by his satires on two *English* musical forms: the birthday ode and the ode to music. For respective examples, see Deutsch, p. 246 and Robert M. Myers, "Neo-Classical Criticism of the Ode for Music," *PMLA,* 62 (June 1947), 399 f.

[50] See *Spectators* 5, 13, 18, and 29.

[51] Burgess, *Cithara,* p. 11.

[52] 24 February 1711 (Deutsch, p. 34).

[53] 1707 (Schultz, p. 136).

[54] It is unlikely, therefore, that he encouraged Gay one way or another. He died the following year.

[55] For a contrary view, see Berger, p. 105.

[56] The similarities of that form and the ballad opera are suggested by Alan Rich, *Music: Mirror of the Arts* (New York, 1969), p. 175.

[57] J. S. Manifold, *The Music in English Drama* (London, 1956), p. 137.

[58] Burney, p. 1000.

[59] W. J. Lawrence, "Tommaso Giordani: An Italian Composer in Ireland," *Musical Antiquary,* 2 (October 1910), 99-107.

[60] Quoted in W. J. Lawrence, "Music and Song in the Eighteenth-Century Theatre," p. 69.

[61] Bukofzer, p. 332.

[62] Gagey, p. 45.

[63] Eddy, p. 437. From Swift's letter to Gay, 26 February 1728.

[64] See Jean B. Kern, "A Note on *The Beggar's Opera,*" *PQ,* 17 (October 1938), 411-13, for a complete explanation.

[65] Irving, pp. 177-78.

[66] Kerby-Miller, p. 177.

[67] That was a prudent decision on his part. For example, a publisher, Haynes, was prosecuted by Walpole for printing a letter that suggested certain parallels between *Richard II* and the ministry. See James J. Lynch, *Box, Pit, and Gallery* (Berkeley, 1953), p. 248. It is a tribute to Gay's circumspect treatment of politics in *The Beggar's Opera* that the whole affair ended with nothing more than the suppression of *Polly.*

[68] For instance, see Gagey, p. 40; Schultz, pp. 186-88; and Ulrich Weisstein, "Brecht's Victorian Version of Gay," *CLS,* 7 (September 1970), 319.

[69] Joseph E. Ceci, "Handel and Walpole in Caricature," *Musical Times,* 92 (January 1951), 20.

[70] Quoted in Ceci, pp. 17-18.

[71] Schultz, pp. 155-56.

[72] Burgess proposes this allegory: Newgate=Whitehall; Macheath=George II; Lockit=Townshend; and Peachum=Walpole. Discounting Townshend altogether, what would have been the point of having Macheath double for the king? If called on to explain himself to the prime minister, Gay could not hope to satisfy Walpole with the assurance that it was not Walpole but the king he was satirizing. And Newgate is more than an analogue for Whitehall; rather it is a microcosm for all of polite society. Cf. C. F. Burgess, "Political Satire," *Midwest Quarterly,* 6 (April 1965), 265-76.

[73] See Bukofzer, p. 332.

[74] The original setting of the ballad showing a time signature of 6/8 is recorded in William Chappell, *Popular Music of the Olden Time* (1859; rpt., ed. anon., New York, 1965), II, 675.

[75] That, however, is precisely Schultz's assertion, p. 197. But if Gay brought Walpole down, it took him from 1728 to 1742 to do it.

[76] Sven M. Armens, *John Gay Social Critic* (New York, 1954), p. 192.

[77] Gay to Swift, 18 January 1731/32, Burgess, *LJG,* p. 119.

[78] Quoted in Schultz, p. 200.

[79] I, i, ii, iv, ix, xiii; and Airs I, II, XI, XXIV, LVII, LXVII.

[80] Eddy, p. 267.

[81] Alexander Pope on John Gay, quoted by Dr. Johnson, p. 307.

Peter Elfed Lewis (essay date 1976)

SOURCE: *"The Beggar's Opera* as Opera and Anti-Opera," in *John Gay: "The Beggar's Opera,"* Edward Arnold, 1976, pp. 8-23.

[*In the following excerpt, Lewis connects Gay's opera to concurrent developments in the Italian opera then performed in London, demonstrating specific sources from several operas, including those of Handel. Lewis concludes that Gay's approach to* The Beggar's Opera *reflects concern with the popularity of foreign opera, but does not indicate a condemnation of the genre itself.*]

Today **The Beggar's Opera** is usually regarded as one of the very few great English plays of the eighteenth century and as one of the major literary works of the Augustan period; yet the title asserts unequivocally that it is an opera. This apparent discrepancy poses the question—what kind of opera? To Gay's contemporaries, the title of his work would at first have seemed as incongruous (although for a slightly different reason) as those of the mock-heroic poems, *The Rape of the Lock* and *The Dunciad,* by his friend Pope. Writing for an élite educated in the classics, Pope knew that the words 'The Rape of' would bring to mind 'The Rape of Leda' or 'The Rape of Helen' or 'The Rape of Lucretia', myths and stories about events that had wide-ranging repercussions of epic proportions, such as the Trojan War. 'The Rape of' produces expectations that are dashed by the rest of Pope's title referring to a lock of hair. Similarly *The Dunciad* recalls Homer's *Iliad* and Virgil's *Aeneid,* but Pope's title indicates that his poem is an inverted epic, not of heroes but of dunces. By the time Gay wrote *The Beggar's Opera* in 1727, 'opera' in England had become virtually synonymous with Italian opera, a theatrical form characterized by great dignity and seriousness and peopled with mythological figures or personages of high rank from the distant past. That an 'opera' could be a 'beggar's' consequently amounted to a contradiction in terms. Gay's very title more or less announces that he is turning Italian opera upside down, that his own opera is both a burlesque of the Italian form and a radically new kind of English opera, indeed the first comic opera, since before Gay most operas were devoid of levity and none sported such a flippant and unlikely title as **The Beggar's Opera.**

In order to appreciate the rationale behind Gay's opera, it is necessary to know something about the history of opera in England during the preceding three-quarters of a century. Towards the end of the Interregnum, it was possible to get round the Puritan ban on the staging of plays by presenting in private houses dramatic works which featured musical accompaniment throughout. These established a form, the English dramatic opera, that survived the reopening of the theatres in 1660 following the restoration of the monarchy. After 1660, however there was no need for the music to be sustained throughout in order to evade prosecution, and the all-sung pattern of the Interregnum operas, in which every word had to be set to music, was abandoned. In form, though not of course in content, the dramatic opera of the Restoration period resembles the modern musical more closely than modern opera, which derives from Italian opera. The music is intermittent rather than continuous and some of the dialogue is spoken rather than sung, but the musical sections, although embedded within the framework of a spoken play, are usually much more important than the non-musical sections. As far as content goes, on the other hand, English dramatic opera resembles Italian opera in that the world it presents is elevated and heroic rather than realistic. Early in the eighteenth century the popularity of dramatic opera waned, and even though a few English operas continued to hold the stage after 1710, the genre was rapidly supplanted by Italian opera.

Not long after the 1705 production of *Arsinoe,* the first Italianate opera to be staged in England, a vogue for Italian opera was developing. What did more than anything else to accelerate this development was Handel's visit to London in 1710 and his subsequent decision to stay there. Handel, a prolific composer of genius but also something of an opportunist, arrived at exactly the right time. He was immediately commissioned to write an Italian opera and obliged with *Rinaldo* (1711), the first of many popular successes he supplied to English audiences. From 1710 the new Queen's Theatre was the home of Italian opera in England and became known as the Opera House. Furthermore, leading Italian singers were paid enormous sums to perform in London and, as 'stars', were figures of widespread public interest. In the year in which **The Beggar's Opera** was written, for example, the personal feud between the two leading ladies of Italian opera in London, Faustina Bordoni and Francesca Cuzzoni, provided a considerable amount of off-stage entertainment, especially as on one occasion it erupted on stage into mutual punching, scratching and hair-pulling.

The snobbish vogue for Italian opera and the idolizing of its principal performers soon produced a hostile reaction from some English intellectuals, who laughed at the male castrati singers, at the temperamental behaviour of the prima donnas, at the convention of recitative, at the lavishness of operatic productions, and at the fact that operas were sung in a language which was incomprehensible to most of the audience. To some extent such mockery can be put down to patriotic bias, but neo-classical critics like Addison and Dennis genuinely believed that the vogue for Italian opera posed a threat to the orthodox dramatic forms of tragedy and comedy as well as to the vitality of English music. One of the charges levelled against Italian opera was that its appeal was very superficial, delighting the ear and the eye but failing to supply the intellectual stimulus and spiritual nourishment afforded by the English dramatic tradition since the Elizabethans.

Gay himself was musical and did not dislike Italian opera in the way that his more doctrinaire neo-classical contemporaries did. Indeed, he even provided Handel with an operatic libretto, *Acis and Galatea,* about ten years before he wrote *The Beggar's Opera.* But during the 1720s he became alarmed at the ever-increasing popularity of Italian opera and its effect on English drama and music. 'As for the reigning Amusement of the town, tis entirely Musick,' he complains in a letter to Swift (3 February 1723), adding that 'folks that could not distinguish one tune from another now daily dispute about the different Styles of Hendel, Bononcini, and Attillio'. Just as Jane Austen objected much less to the Gothic novel *per se* than to the excessive seriousness with which it was taken by impressionable members of the reading public, Gay condemns not Italian opera but the completely uncritical theatregoers who had turned it into a fashionable cult. Jane Austen nevertheless felt that a corrective was necessary, and in *Northanger Abbey* wrote a book that is both a burlesque of Gothic fiction and a realistic novel in its own right. In conceiving *The Beggar's Opera* Gay did something very similar. He set out to combine burlesque of Italian opera with the creation of a rival form, a comic and distinctly English form of opera that quickly became known as ballad opera. This dual purpose explains the considerable difference between *The Beggar's Opera* and the few previous burlesques of Italian opera, which are aimed at very specific targets and do not attempt to transcend burlesque. Gay deliberately avoids direct parody and close burlesque because this might well have prevented him from achieving a self-sufficient 'opera' capable of standing as an independent work of art.

Musically, there are two great differences between *The Beggar's Opera* and Italian opera. Firstly, much of Gay's work consists of orthodox dramatic dialogue without any musical accompaniment, whereas all the words in Italian opera are sung; in this respect *The Beggar's Opera* resembles the English dramatic opera of the Restoration more closely than Italian opera. Secondly, apart from the Overture, the music for *The Beggar's Opera* was taken from pre-existing sources, whereas an Italian opera was an entirely new musical creation. For the sixty-nine songs in the play, Gay himself selected the melodies, most of which were well known. Forty-one of the airs have broadside-balled tunes (this explains the term 'ballad opera') but others have tunes by such distinguished contemporary composers as Purcell and Handel; Air XX is actually sung to the music of a march in one of Handel's greatest operatic successes, *Rinaldo.* What Gay did—and this was his most daringly original stroke—was to put new wine into old bottles, substituting his own words for

the familiar ones, though retaining and modifying phrases here and there. This gamble might have failed disastrously, but Gay did it so well that in no time at all dramatic hacks were churning out inferior imitations. In the years immediately following 1728, ballad operas and ballad farces darkened the air; and although Italian opera continued to be popular, it now had to compete with a new vogue. Whatever Gay may have thought of the progeny his masterpiece spawned, he had certainly succeeded in restoring English opera. Today 'opera' seems the wrong word, but in the case of *The Beggar's Opera,* the large number of songs together with their vital dramatic importance distinguish it from plays of the seventeenth and early eighteenth centuries containing incidental music and songs. There is nothing incidental about Gay's memorable songs, and to many people they are the glory of the work.

As has been noted, Gay's burlesque of Italian opera is for the most part indirect and non-parodic, but his burlesque purpose explains many features of *The Beggar's Opera.* In order to maintain a superficial resemblance to Italian opera, Gay adopts several of its formal characteristics, such as a three-act structure instead of the five-act structure invariable in full-length tragedies and comedies. Again, following the example of Italian opera and departing from the customary practice of orthodox drama, he dispenses with both prologue and epilogue, the conventional and completely detachable speeches preceding and following a tragedy or comedy that were often contributed by someone other than the author. Operas did not open with a prologue but with an instrumental overture, and Gay specifies that an overture should be played for *The Beggar's Opera.* For the first production, J. C. Pepusch, a German composer of theatre music, provided a suitable overture featuring the melody Gay chose for Air XLVII. Although Gay's use of speech instead of recitative is a significant departure from operatic practice, his actual lay-out of the airs corresponds to that of arias in an Italian opera. The sudden switching from speech to song and back again without any attempt to justify the interpolation of an air on realistic grounds, as is often done in orthodox drama, recalls the alternation of recitatives and arias in opera. There is a further correspondence to Italian opera in that not all of Gay's airs are solos, some being duets, one being a trio, and a few involving a chorus.

Gay goes to some pains to draw attention to these and other operatic parallels in his Introduction, which precedes the Overture and which is an essential part of his design in a way that the conventional prologue was not. In this short scene, the supposed author of the opera, the Beggar, explains his work to one of the actors, the Player, and claims that although written to celebrate the marriage of two English ballad singers it is to all intents and purposes an orthodox opera. Instead of announcing explicitly in his own voice that he is about to burlesque Italian opera, Gay chooses the much subtler satiric method, perfected by Swift, of adopting a 'mask' or 'persona', that of the Beggar, and speaking indirectly through him. The Beggar's seriousness is really Gay's sleight of hand; his words are undermined from within so that we do not take them at their face value. Gay's irony can be fully appreciated only in the light of what is to follow, but his gibe at Italian opera is unmistakable when the Beggar says, 'I hope I may be forgiven, that I have not made my Opera throughout unnatural, like those in vogue; for I have no Recitative.' The Beggar appears to be apologizing for not making his opera 'throughout unnatural', but by implication these words carry their own qualification and disapproval. Gay is clearly invoking the Augustan aesthetic yardstick of nature as a measure for exposing the limitations of Italian opera. The further implication that 'Recitative' in particular is unnatural is a complaint often levelled against Italian opera at the time. According to Addison, English audiences were at first 'wonderfully surprized to hear Generals singing the Word of Command, and Ladies delivering Messages in Musick' (*The Spectator,* no. 29).

The rest of the Beggar's speech can also be interpreted at two levels. He is pleased with himself for using 'the Similes that are in all your celebrated Operas', and the ones he lists do appear in *The Beggar's Opera:* 'The Swallow' in Air XXXIV, 'the Moth' in Air IV, 'the Bee' and 'the Flower' in both Air VI and Air XV, and 'the Ship' in both Air X and Air XLVII. What Gay implies, however, is that such similes have been rendered inexpressive in Italian opera by having been worked to death; after all, they are 'in all your celebrated Operas', which is more or less true since simile arias were exceedingly popular. Gay himself tries to revitalize them, to rinse them clean, by employing them in an unconventional context. The Beggar also seems to be proud of his 'Prison Scene which the Ladies always reckon charmingly pathetick'. As his words suggest, a prison scene was almost a *sine qua non* in an Italian opera and usually occurred at a high point of the dramatic action so that as much emotional appeal as possible could be wrung from it. The irony here lies in the fact that not just one poignant scene but almost half of *The Beggar's Opera* takes place in a prison, and in addition that the prison is not some historically or geographically remote one with romantic associations, but Newgate prison in the heart of London, exactly as it was at the time with all its petty corruptions and abuses. As regards 'the Parts', the Beggar's self-congratulation at achieving 'a nice Impartiality to our two Ladies, that it is impossible for either of them to take Offence' carries a more immediately topical irony, referring as it does to the current quarrel between Francesca Cuzzoni and Faustina Bordoni over operatic roles. In some Italian operas there are two heroines who are rivals for the hero's affections, and to avoid

causing friction, composers like Handel had to ensure that there was no obvious imbalance between the two parts. Nevertheless, even if they could not actually 'take Offence', Francesca Cuzzoni and Faustina Bordoni tended to treat an opera in which they appeared together as a singing contest, vying with each other vocally instead of working as part of a team. This satirical reference to the prima donnas also serves to draw attention to the operatic parallel: *The Beggar's Opera* itself has two heroines, Polly Peachum and Lucy Lockit, who are rivals for the affections of the hero, Macheath. Indeed, the rivalry between Polly and Lucy alludes to that of the prima donnas and to that of the operatic roles they performed.

The Beggar claims that except for using speech instead of recitative his work 'must be allow'd an Opera in all its forms'; but by means of irony and by explicit references to beggars, to ballad singers, who were not particularly reputable, and to the notorious London parish of St Giles-in-the-Fields, the resort of thieves, highwaymen and prostitutes, Gay indicates throughout the Introduction that the content of *The Beggar's Opera* is totally unlike that of Italian opera. While in many respects Gay does adhere to the 'forms' of Italian opera, the world he presents is the very unoperatic one of St Giles-in-the-Fields. He completely inverts Italian opera, with its classical, mythological or similarly elevated narratives and its exotic atmosphere, by setting *The Beggar's Opera* very firmly in the criminal underworld of contemporary London. Theatregoers in 1728 would have recognized immediately that two of the major characters, Peachum and Macheath, were based on the best-known underworld figures of the early eighteenth century, Jonathan Wild and Jack Sheppard, both of whom had been executed less than four years before the first production of the work. One of the locations is the city's principal criminal prison, and death by hanging or transportation to the colonies is the fate that seems to await most of the characters. For them, the year is divided not into seasons but into the various sessions of the city's criminal court, the Old Bailey. Instead of a typical operatic hero such as Handel's Rinaldo, Gay provides the leader of a gang of highwaymen, Macheath, who is called 'Captain' but has no legitimate claim to the rank. And instead of two typical operatic heroines like the high-born Rossane and Lisaura in *Alessandro,* the opera which Handel wrote for Faustina Bordoni's London début in 1726, Gay supplies Polly Peachum, the daughter of an organizer of crime and a receiver of stolen goods, and Lucy Lockit, the daughter of the very corrupt chief jailor of Newgate. The sustained tussle between Polly and Lucy over Macheath is a low-life equivalent of that between Rossane and Lisaura over Alessandro (Alexander the Great) and of almost identical love-battles in other Italian operas, as well as being a satirical allusion to the real-life tension between the two sopranos who played these operatic rivals. Of the other characters in *The*

Beggar's Opera almost all the men are criminals of one sort or another and almost all the women are whores. Just as Jane Austen's characters in *Northanger Abbey* are anti-types of the stereotyped figures of the Gothic novel as well as self-sufficient novelistic characters, Gay's characters are anti-types of operatic stereotypes as well as self-sufficient dramatic characters. **The Beggar's Opera** is undoubtedly true to its title in that it controverts every normal operatic expectation. The nobility of character, dignity of conduct, and refinement of both sentiment and language characteristic of Italian opera are largely replaced by the attitudes, behaviour and idiom of the underworld.

However, Gay cleverly exploits, for burlesque as well as for other purposes, the discrepancy between operatic expectations and what he provides, especially in his treatment of his 'operatic hero' Macheath; thus he ensures that the burlesque level is not lost sight of behind the layers of social and political satire. In some ways Macheath acts and sounds like an operatic hero. The first words he *speaks*, 'Suspect my Honour, my Courage, suspect any thing but my Love' (I.xiii), have a distinctly heroic note, and Polly's reply, with its unquestioning assumption that her highwayman-husband is on a par with Hercules or Alexander the Great, makes the burlesque parallel explicit: 'I have no Reason to doubt you, for I find in the Romance you lent me, none of the great Heroes were ever false in Love.' Polly's father, even at the moment of arresting Macheath in II.v, makes an identical connection between his son-in-law and the sort of men normally presented as operatic heroes: 'Your Case, Mr Macheath, is not particular. The greatest Heroes have been ruin'd by Women.' Lucy too acknowledges the 'heroic' status of Macheath, as in her first remark on visiting him in the condemned cell: 'There is nothing moves one so much as a great Man in Distress' (III.xv). In his dealings with his gang, Macheath clearly sees himself as the equivalent of a military leader like Alexander and actually behaves with the magnanimity expected of an operatic hero. He claims to be brave, loyal, fair-minded, and generous: 'Is there any man who suspects my Courage? . . . My Honour and Truth to the Gang? . . . In the Division of our Booty, have I ever shown the least Marks of Avarice or Injustice?' (II.ii). And in III.iv, when two members of his gang are short of money after failing to steal anything, he keeps his word by digging into his own pockets: 'I am sorry, Gentlemen, the Road was so barren of Money. When my Friends are in Difficulties, I am always glad that my Fortune can be serviceable to them.' Here as elsewhere he addresses members of the gang as 'Gentlemen', insisting that they are all honourable: 'I have a fixt Confidence, Gentlemen, in you all, as Men of Honour, and as such I value and respect you' (II.ii) and 'But we, Gentlemen, have still Honour enough to break through the Corruptions of the World' (III.iv). In all such passages, the mock-heroic incongruity between the crim-

inals who act, speak, and are spoken about, on the one hand, and the conduct and the sentiments expressed, on the other, registers as ironic burlesque.

Gay's use of familiar melodies, especially simple ballad tunes, as opposed to the elaborate arias of Italian opera is the musical equivalent of his making an operatic hero out of Macheath rather than someone like Alexander. The fact that the criminal characters of **The Beggar's Opera** burst into song in the manner of operatic figures in itself creates burlesque humour; and while it is unlikely that Gay intended to parody any specific arias, he does occasionally enhance the burlesque by making the hackneyed similes mentioned in the Introduction by the Beggar express attitudes, especially towards love, which are not found in the relatively chaste world of Italian opera. The simile of 'the Moth', for example, appears in Air IV, 'If Love the Virgin's Heart invade', in which Mrs Peachum reflects that if her daughter, like any other girl, 'plays about the Flame' and loses her virginity, she may end up as a whore—'Her Honour's sing'd, and then for Life, / She's—what I dare not name.' Gay also links operatic simile, in this case 'the Flower', with the fate of deflowered virgins in Polly's song about her politic motives for retaining her virginity, Air VI, 'Virgins are like the fair Flower in its Lustre'; this is intended to reassure her father that she knows how to 'grant some Things, and refuse what is most material', although she has in fact secretly married Macheath. In each of these songs the operatic simile is burlesqued by being made to convey non-operatic subject matter, but it is simultaneously rinsed clean in order to express a truth about the realities of contemporary life. The girl who succumbed to her sexual desires premaritally was, like the moth in the flame, quite likely to destroy herself. If she was known to have lost her virginity, she might well be cast out of the society that had nurtured her, and left to her own resources which usually meant prostitution. In Polly's song, Gay clarifies the severity of a social code that demanded such a penalty for a momentary human failing, and also conveys the fragility of virginity and the sense of sadness at its loss, by means of the very image which he is burlesquing. It is Gay's inspired juxtaposition of a natural garden and Covent Garden, which was a red-light district as well as London's vegetable, fruit, and flower market, that makes this possible. The cut flower ('once pluck'd, 'tis no longer alluring') being sent by the gardener to the market at Covent Garden signifies the deflowered virgin being virtually forced by society to the other Covent Garden, the flesh-market of the brothels ('There fades, and shrinks, and grows past all enduring, / Rots, stinks, and dies, and is trod under feet').

In other airs the discrepancy between what the simile normally conveys in opera and what it conveys in **The Beggar's Opera** is much less marked or even nonexistent; but because of the incongruity between the conceited linguistic idiom of opera and the unoperatic singer as well as the popular tune, the burlesque effect is still recognizable. Lucy's outburst of distress in Air XLVII, 'I'm like a Skiff on the Ocean tost', when she believes that Polly is 'sporting on Seas of Delight' with Macheath and decides on a plan of revenge as the only way to appease her jealousy, employs 'the Ship' simile mentioned by the Beggar in the Introduction; this therefore takes the form of an operatic cliché, for such outbursts of distress and jealousy were fairly common in Italian opera. Other airs, especially Polly's most tender expressions of devoted love for Macheath, also have operatic antecedents. Air XXXIV, 'Thus when the Swallow, seeking Prey', is the most obvious case since the Beggar points it out in speaking of the simile of 'The Swallow'; but Air XIII, 'The Turtle thus with plaintive crying', which is sung when Polly discovers that her parents are determined to arrange Macheath's execution and which features the conventional comparison of lovers to turtle-doves, is very similar. Shortly afterwards, Macheath and Polly are alone together for the first time in the play, and this scene (I.xiii), in which they declare their love for each other before having to part, contains no less than five airs, including three duets. The marked preponderance of song in itself indicates a parallel to operatic love scenes, and in his fine essay on the play, Bertrand H. Bronson tentatively suggests that Gay may have had in mind a scene between parting lovers in Handel's *Floridante* (1721); one of the duets (Air XVI) in particular bears some resemblance to the impassioned avowals of everlasting love by Elmira and Floridante. . . .

Bronson argues that several other situations in *The Beggar's Opera* may have specific operatic sources. The way in which Macheath is arrested in a tavern (II.V) could be based on the attempt on Ptolemy's life in a seraglio in Handel's *Giulio Cesare* (1724), and the quarrel between Peachum and Lockit (II.X) possibly owes something to another scene between arguing fathers in Handel's *Flavio* (1723). In the latter case, however, the main source is the quarrel between Brutus and Cassius in Shakespeare's *Julius Caesar* and the similarity to the operatic scene may be no more than a coincidence. Whether Gay intended these very specific situational correspondences remains hypothetical. However, especially in the closing stages of *The Beggar's Opera* there are several unmistakable though general parallels with Italian opera, and these culminate in the *coup de théâtre* when the two characters from the Introduction, the Beggar and the Player, enter to produce a happy ending out of apparent catastrophe.

First of all there is Lucy's attempt to eliminate her rival, Polly, by poisoning her (III.vii-x). Having helped Macheath to escape from Newgate, Lucy is tormented by 'Jealousy, Rage, Love and Fear' because she believes, wrongly, that he is with Polly. Lucy has 'the Rats-bane ready', and when Polly comes to visit her at Newgate, Lucy suggests that they have a drink to cheer themselves up. But at the moment when Lucy forces a glass containing the poison on Polly, the recaptured Macheath is brought back to the prison and Polly is so shaken at the sight of him in chains that she drops the glass and spills its contents. Gay undoubtedly bases this episode on a popular feature of a number of contemporary Italian operas, the scene set in a prison in which one of the principal characters narrowly escapes death in the form of a cup of poison. These incidents take various forms, but in several of Handel's operas produced not long before *The Beggar's Opera,* the hero seems doomed to die by drinking a cup of poison yet is saved as a result of a last-second intervention during which the cup is upset. In *Radamisto* (1720), for example, the heroine Zenobia is forced by Tiridate to take a bowl of poison to her condemned lover, Radamisto himself, who is shackled and awaiting execution; but when she reaches him, she offers to drink it herself and is prevented only by the sudden entrance of Tiridate who knocks the bowl out of her hands. An almost identical scene occurs in *Floridante.* In *Radamisto* and *Floridante,* the gesture is one of heroic self-sacrifice, and the treatment is intensely emotional. In *The Beggar's Opera,* the action is a cunning and unheroic attempt to commit murder under the pretence of friendship, and the treatment verges on the comic. This whole episode has a further burlesque significance in that it resembles the encounters between rival operatic heroines, such as Rossane and Lisaura in *Alessandro,* where they attempt to discuss their relationships with the hero.

The burlesque parallel continues in the scenes following Macheath's return to Newgate. The kind of prison scene in Italian opera that 'the Ladies always reckon charmingly pathetick', to use the Beggar's phrase, is the one outlined above in which a woman visits her lover or husband who is awaiting death; the greater his suffering and her grief, the more 'charmingly pathetick' the scene would be. Earlier in *The Beggar's Opera* (II.xiii), Gay provides a counterpart to such scenes by exposing the imprisoned Macheath simultaneously to Polly and Lucy, each of whom regards herself as his wife. The result, a comic confrontation between a rake and two of his women, one of whom, Lucy, is pregnant by him, is the antithesis of the decorous intensity of operatic prison scenes; it also travesties the situation of a hero like Alessandro, who is faced with an almost impossible choice between Rossane and Lisaura. Macheath, under verbal bombardment from both Polly and Lucy, responds in the rollicking and impudent Air XXXV, 'How happy could I be with either', by deciding to ignore both of them. The operatic parallel is considerably reinforced by Gay's subsequent use of two duets in this scene. In Air XXXVI, 'I'm bubbled' ('bubbled' means 'deceived'), the vocal line passes back and forth between Polly and Lucy just as it does between the singers of operatic duets, especially rival heroines; but the situation from which the song arises, their discovery of Macheath's duplicity in making identical promises to both of them, is unlike anything to be found in Italian opera. Air XXXVIII, 'Why how now, Madam Flirt?', in which Polly and Lucy attack each other verbally, differs in that the vocal line does not alternate throughout; instead Lucy sings the first stanza and Polly the second. Of particular interest here is the fact that the monosyllabic words at the end of the third line of each stanza, 'Dirt' and 'made', must be sung in melismatic or coloratura style, each word running for seventeen notes and occupying almost three bars. Such ornate, bravura singing is standard in operatic arias but very rare in folk songs and ballads, and is the only sustained example in *The Beggar's Opera,* where Gay usually fits one syllable to one note of music. That Gay should draw such attention to the operatic parallel in this song is doubly significant since nowhere else is the rivalry between Polly and Lucy so bitterly and vulgarly expressed. The contrast between matter and operatic manner is therefore exceptionally pronounced, and this in turn highlights the undignified personal behaviour of Francesca Cuzzoni and Faustina Bordoni in comparison with the dignified roles they took in operas. Off stage the prima donnas behaved as Polly and Lucy do on stage.

In the closing scenes Gay again brings Polly, Lucy, and Macheath together in Newgate after Lucy's attempt to poison Polly (III.xi). This encounter between the highwayman and his two 'wives' is less obviously a travesty of 'charmingly pathetick' prison scenes, but the continuing competition between the women for Macheath's attention, especially when it takes the form of a duet in Air LII, 'Hither, dear Husband, turn your Eyes', sustains the operatic burlesque. The way in which one voice takes over from the other like an echo in the second half of the song (''Tis Polly sues. / 'Tis Lucy speaks') imitates a feature of many operatic duets. As before, Macheath's predicament as expressed in Air LIII, 'Which way shall I turn me?—How can I decide?', is the essentially comic one of a philanderer, who is expert at handling one woman at a time, becoming helpless and retreating into silence when face to face with two of his conquests; again it alludes to the dilemma confronting Alessandro and some other heroes. If John O. Rees is correct in interpreting this scene as a mock-heroic version of the classical myth called The Judgment (or Choice) of Hercules, the burlesque resemblance to opera is greatly enhanced since Hercules was a very suitable candidate for operatic treatment (see bibliography). In the myth, Hercules is confronted by two goddesses, Virtue and Pleasure (or Vice), and has to decide between them. This subject was popular with creative artists from the Renaissance onwards because it allowed them to present a metaphysical and moral conflict as a dramatic and concretely-realized situation; in the eighteenth century it was treated by several poets and composers in England,

including Handel. The symmetrical arrangement of Gay's characters, with Polly and her father on one side of Macheath, and Lucy and her father on the other, is very similar to the usual formal organization of painted versions of the myth and could well be modelled on them; but it would be wrong to push the parallel too far by identifying Polly with Virtue and Lucy with Pleasure.

As an interlude before the scene changes to the condemned cell, Gay specifies 'A Dance of Prisoners in Chains' at the end of III.xii. This plainly grotesque dance is a low-life counterpart to the dignified ballet dancing that had been incorporated in many operas since the seventeenth century, and the completely arbitrary way in which it is introduced is itself a comment on the frequent insertion of dances into operas with little or no dramatic justification. The burlesque intention is much more obvious here than in the 'Dance a la ronde in the French Manner' in II.iv, but although this may sound more formal and operatic, it is not performed by deities in a temple or by aristocrats in a court but by Macheath and eight whores in a tavern near Newgate. It too is introduced in a gratuitous way when Macheath hears harp music: 'But hark! I hear musick. . . . E'er you seat your selves, Ladies, what think you of a Dance?'

When the scene does change to the condemned cell (III.xiii), Macheath sings a soliloquy to music taken from no less than ten different songs so that the ten airs, LVIII-LXVII, coalesce into an extended piece of singing. Nowhere else in the play does Gay use fragments of tunes and nowhere else does one air follow another without any speech intervening. Of the ten airs, one consists of one line, six consist of two lines, two consist of four lines, and only the final one of eight lines is of average length. Despite the Beggar's initial claim that his opera contains 'no Recitative', Macheath's segmented utterance and abrupt changes of tune, interrupted only when he pours himself stiff drinks, is not unlike operatic recitative, especially as it concludes with a full-length air in the same way as recitative prepares the way for an aria. In opera such rapid changes of thought and emotion as Macheath's can be encompassed only in recitative, never in arias. From Gay's scrupulous avoidance before this of anything resembling recitative, one would expect the bulk of Macheath's monologue to be spoken; so the startling use of song is extremely effective in bringing home the operatic parallel. At the level of burlesque, Macheath's 'recitative and aria' is a mockery of those sung by operatic heroes in prison. Instead of exhibiting courage and fortitude while awaiting execution, like Floridante in Handel's opera who even welcomes death as a deliverance, the much more human Macheath drinks heavily in a not very successful attempt to go to the gallows bravely and concentrates his thoughts on alcohol and women.

The one sung trio, Air LXVIII, 'Would I might be hang'd!', occurs at what might be called the most 'charmingly pathetick' moment when Polly and Lucy visit Macheath in the condemned cell just before he is about to be taken to Tyburn to be hanged (III.xv). Since these three characters are on stage together in a number of scenes, there are several opportunities for trios; Polly and Lucy actually sing duets in front of Macheath, but only here do all three share an air. Gay is again following operatic precedent, because it is common in opera for the principal characters (if there are three) to join in a trio at the climax of the work. The cowardly but credible behaviour of Macheath, who has run out of alcohol ('I tremble! I droop!—See, my Courage is out'), is the antithesis of, for example, Floridante's operatic heroics in the face of death, and the yearning of both Polly and Lucy to share Macheath's fate on the gallows ('Would I might be hang'd! / And I would so too!') is a comic transformation of the attempts by self-sacrificing operatic heroines to kill themselves in order to save their lovers' lives. Gay's choice of tune for this 'Hanging Trio' could hardly have been better since 'All you that must take a Leap' was a ballad about the execution of two criminals. The burlesque effect is greatly intensified at this point by the sudden arrival of four more of Macheath's 'wives', each accompanied by a child, so that he is confronted by no less than six of his 'wives' and four of his children. Gay deliberately plunges what in opera would be intended to be a profoundly moving climax to the level of farce. Ironically, only in this ludicrous situation does Macheath acquire the moral strength of an operatic hero and welcome death as a deliverance: 'What—four Wives more!—This is too much.—Here—tell the Sheriffs Officers I am ready.' The travesty of opera could hardly be taken further, yet Gay does just that in the next scene.

As Macheath is led away, the action is interrupted and the dramatic illusion shattered by the entry of the Player and the Beggar (III.xvi). This is a low-life equivalent of the device known as the *deus ex machina,* common in heroic drama, tragicomedy and opera after the Restoration, and involving a surprise intervention or unexpected discovery that produces a virtually magical transformation at a stroke. No matter how closely Italian operas approached tragedy, happy endings were *de rigeur,* and the contrived dénouements necessitated by this convention were particularly vulnerable to hostile criticism. At the end of *Arsinoe,* for example, Dorisbe stabs herself melodramatically after being rejected in love, but in no time at all she participates in the finale, explaining that her wound is not serious. In opera after opera the villain redeems himself at the end of the third act, and however diabolically he has behaved throughout, he suddenly becomes penitent and is reconciled with the other characters. In *The Beggar's Opera* the Player prevents the law taking its natural course by expostulating to the Beggar about Macheath's

imminent execution. To the Player's surprise, the Beggar admits that he is 'for doing strict poetical Justice' with Macheath executed and all the other characters hanged or transported. But he gives way in the face of the Player's irrefutable argument:

> *Player* Why then, Friend, this is a down-right deep Tragedy. The Catastrophe is manifestly wrong, for an Opera must end happily.
>
> *Beggar* Your Objection, Sir, is very just; and is easily remov'd. For you must allow, that in this kind of Drama, 'tis no matter how absurdly things are brought about.—So—you Rabble there—run and cry a Reprieve—let the Prisoner be brought back to his Wives in Triumph.
>
> *Player* All this we must do, to comply with the Taste of the Town.

The play can then end with a song and a dance to celebrate Macheath's release. What is so ingenious about this episode is that it allows Gay to criticize explicitly Italian opera and its fans, to burlesque by means of Macheath's reprieve the miraculous reversals of fortune and character with which operas frequently end, and at the same time to secure a fitting conclusion to what is, after all, a comedy. *The Beggar's Opera* demands a non-tragic ending, and in rescuing Macheath, Gay makes a virtue of necessity—indeed, several virtues. There is even a political innuendo in Macheath's unexpected escape from death; during the difficult situation following George I's death in 1727, Sir Robert Walpole surprisingly avoided political extinction by promising the new king, George II, more money for the royal family. The burlesque is given an added pungency by the completely arbitrary nature of Macheath's reprieve, which is in no way earned and is not accompanied by any moral transformation. His promise of fidelity to Polly, 'I take Polly for mine . . . And for Life, you Slut,—for we were really marry'd' (III.xvii), cannot be taken too seriously considering the value of his earlier promises, not to mention his condescending though admittedly affectionate use of 'Slut'.

Today, Gay's burlesque of Italian opera seems much less significant than his social satire, which is more immediately accessible to us, and criticism of the play understandably concentrates on such literary qualities as irony and imagery. Nevertheless, Gay aimed to create an original type of opera by turning the conventions of Italian opera upside down so that he was simultaneously poking fun at them, and this attempt lies behind the overall structure of *The Beggar's Opera* and the detailed organization of many of its parts. The continuing popularity of the work means that it is possible to enjoy it without being aware that it burlesques Italian opera, just as it is possible to enjoy *Northanger Abbey* without knowing anything about the Gothic novel; but the subtlety and skill of Gay's design cannot be fully appreciated without grasping the extent to which he uses, *mutatis mutandis,* stock operatic features and situations. *The Beggar's Opera* is much more than a mock-opera, but at one level that is what it is. In addition, it is ultimately impossible to separate the social satire from the operatic burlesque since they are two sides of the same coin. . . . To the literary critic, Gay's use of language is so absorbing that it is easy to forget that he wrote the play for the theatre and for part-musical performance. But the main reason that *The Beggar's Opera* appealed so much to theatregoers in 1728 and has held the stage ever since is not that it is a literary masterpiece, but that it is a lively and unconventional musical comedy, a kind of opera.

Howard Erskine-Hill (essay date 1977)

SOURCE: "The Significance of Gay's Drama," in *English Drama: Forms and Development-Essays in Honor of Muriel Clara Bradbrook,* edited by Marie Axton and Raymond Williams, Cambridge University Press, 1977, pp. 142-63.

[*In the following essay, Erskine-Hill considers the whole of Gay's dramatic corpus to illuminate Gay's experimentalism and the development of his most famous work,* The Beggar's Opera. *Erskine-Hill focuses on Gay's tendency to mix and subvert familiar generic forms to create entirely new types of theatre.*]

John Gay's comedy *The Distress'd Wife* is the last and least-known of his full-length plays. Among those but once reprinted since the eighteenth century, it is a useful vantage-point from which to view Gay's dramatic achievement. The great original success of *The Beggar's Opera,* and continuing attention paid it in our time, have obscured the interest of the other plays, the relation of these to the *Opera,* and the larger significance of the canon.[1] I want to consider these matters, and to convey to the reader the experimental combination of forms, idioms and attitudes, and the humour and humanity, to be found in most of Gay's work for the theatre.

Gay wrote just two plays which espoused the formal dramatic orthodoxies of his time: his blank verse tragedy *The Captives* (1724) and *The Distress'd Wife* (written but probably not completed in his last years, and published in 1743). Only in the latter did Gay ever practise the form of the so-called Restoration comedy of manners. Yet this form was the most prominent and successful in Gay's lifetime; it had the approval of the great Congreve, had been flexibly adapted by Farquhar to the rendering of provincial life, and, stylised as it may seem to us with the hindsight of the eighteenth- and nineteenth-century novel, it was the literary realism of its age.[2] In *The Distress'd Wife,* as in other plays in the tradition of the comedy of manners, the language of the drama has a plausible relation with its fiction, judged by realist criteria. A terse, pointed and mainly polite prose is to be found in much of Gay's drama, but only here would it have been accepted by a contemporary audience as approximately the idiom they might hear in the specified setting.

The Distress'd Wife throws into relief the non-realist origins of all Gay's earlier drama. If we look at the earliest, *The Mohocks. A Tragi-Comical Farce* (1712), we infer from the subtitle an attraction towards parodic form. Indeed the farce comprises three kinds of literary language, of which the least conspicuous, the idiom of *beau* Gentle ('I vow and protest Gentlemen, I just now came from my Lady *Pride*'s in the City' I.ii.181-2[3]), derives from the fopling figures of the comedy of manners. Most conspicuous is the mock-epic manner of the Mohocks themselves, a seemingly innocent amalgam of the more elevated blank verse of Milton and Dryden, interspersed with Rochesterian echoes:

> Thus far our Riots with Success are crown'd,
> Have found no stop, or what they found
>   o'ercame;
> In vain th' embattell'd Watch in deep array,
> Against our Rage oppose their lifted Poles . .
>
> May constant Impotence attend his Lust;
> May the dull Slave be bigotted to Virtue;
> And tread no more the pleasing Paths of Vice
>   (I.i.1-4, 51-3)

High style goes with high-handedness and licence, homely with the humble and lawful. But the latter idiom, like the Mohocks' in I.i, undergoes extreme exaggeration, and Gay goes to school to Shakespeare (not for the last time in his plays) to strike the right note of lubberly yet warm farce. Dogberry, Verges and the Watch, and the mechanicals of *A Midsummer Night's Dream,* are all suggested by Gay's Watch, while Peter Cloudy is allowed one near-Falstaffian moment:

> d'ye see, Mr. Constable, here is this Pole, Mr. Constable—I'll engage that this Pole—Mr. Constable, if it takes a *Mohock* in the right Place—it shall knock him down as flat as a Flounder, Mr. Constable—Pole is the word, Sir—I, one Night, Mr. Constable, clap'd my Back against the Watch-house, and kept nine *Mohocks,* with their Swords drawn, at Pole's length, broke three of their Heads, knock'd down four, and trim'd the Jackets of the other six.
>
>   (I.ii.93-8)[4]

Each kind of language is exaggerated so as to make us aware, not just of a social decorum of high and low styles, but of the problem of style itself; it is as if the boldly discrepant styles of *1* and *2 Henry IV,* or Dryden's *Don Sebastian,* have been drawn, in comic game, so far apart that each questions not only the others but itself. In this respect **The Mohocks** derives not from the relatively mimetic mode of the comedy of manners, but the critical farce of Buckingham's *Rehearsal.* Yet with a difference. The manner of Buckingham's Bayes is reductive farce, while Gay's first scene enters with verve into the vein it mocks: mock-epic to Buckingham's burlesque. Buckingham's commentators are terse and dry compared with the child-like muddling of Gay's Watch. And while in *The Rehearsal* Bayes is hardly received into the gentlemanly milieu of Smith and Johnson, the Mohocks are eventually assimilated into the ignominious deference of the Watch. The movement of the piece is one of descent from the high style and pretensions of the Mohocks in 1.1 to the point at the end where the Emperor declares (aside): 'Faith, 'tis high time for us to sneak off' (I.iii.108). **The Mohocks** is in this way similar to *Mac Flecknoe* or Rochester's *Disabled Debauchee:* all three works have a calculated movement from high to low, and from it their, admittedly various, comedy in large measure arises.

But the movement of the piece focuses on something not yet mentioned: on sex—on the intent of the Mohocks to ravish, cuckold and castrate, and on the happy survival of Joan and Peter Cloudy's marriage. The warm and virtuous bawdry of Peter's plea to Abaddon:

> my Ears or my Nose is wholly at your
>   Worship's Service; but pray, good, dear,
>   loving Sir, don't let poor *Gillian* lose her
>   only Comfort
>
> (I.ii.141-3)

may suggest a *double entendre* in Gillian (Joan's) later reproach that Peter 'throws away upon two Wenches in one Night, [*Weeping*] what with good Huswifery would have satisfied his poor Wife for a Fortnight' (I.iii.102-4), and certainly constitutes the prosperous outcome of the piece. The bubble of high language and high action has been pricked; the Mohocks fall to fearful and undignified men, like the Watch; Peter and Joan are intact; and the final dance concludes the comic form of the farce.

The happy note of **The Mohocks** is maintained in the intrigue and disguise of Gay's next play, **The Wife of Bath** (1713). But this is comedy of intrigue and disguise with a difference. While in his Prologue Gay insists that men and women in Chaucer's day were not more innocent than those of his own time—'They knew the World as well as You and I'—his play differs from any contemporary model. It ignores realistic illusion by presenting itself happening, as it were, in the interstices of the famous *Canterbury Tales,* in an inn on the pilgrims' road to Canterbury. It is avowedly 'literary'

in the sense that it offers the audience the pleasure of seeing on stage characters such as the Franklin and the Wife of Bath.[5] The poet Chaucer himself appears in the intrigue, where he uses his poetic skills to gain the woman of his choice. And though the style of the play is certainly more homogeneous than the contrasting exaggerations in **The Mohocks,** there are within it very sharply distinct idioms of both prose and verse.

The fopling type is again the most obvious connection with seventeenth-century comedy, and it is in relation to this type that the varieties of the rest of the play are best displayed. The idiom of the poetaster Frank Doggrell is effectively juxtaposed with the blunt English bawdry of the Wife of Bath and the distinctly pre-Waller lyricism of Chaucer. Doggrell is the successor of *beau* Gentle and the speaker of the most self-consciously polite and modern idiom of the play:

> My Name is originally of *French* Extraction, and is
> written with a D, and an Apostrophe—as much as
> to say, *De Ogrelle,* which was the antique Residence
> of my Ancestors. (p. 2)

At the end of the play, tricked into marriage with a woman's woman, he becomes the frank Doggrell he has always resisted being. The Wife of Bath can then exclaim that his new wife's 'Great Uncle, in the Fifty Ninth Degree, was Groom of the Privy Stool to *William* the Conqueror—ha, ha, ha—' (p. 62).

This contrast, within the range of Restoration comedy, is the basis for others best demonstrated from the characteristic lyrics of the play. Here is the vein of the sophisticated D'Ogrelle (read aloud by Chaucer in a bored voice):

> *STANZAS, upon a Fair Lady making me*
> *Happy.*
>
>   Ye Gods! did Jove e'er taste such
> Charms,
>   When prest in fair Alcmena's Arms,
>   O ye Immortal Pow'rs . . .
> *Dogg.* Hold, hold, Sir,—Mark the Harmony,
>   Sir;—and the easie Cadence that falls
>   through the whole Stanza.
>
> (p. 45)

Here is the Wife of Bath: 'The Maiden and the Batchelor,/Pardie . . . are simple Elves' (p. 27); or again:

> There was a Swain full fair,
>   Was tripping it over the Grass,
> And there he spy'd with her Nut-brown Hair,
>   A Pretty tight Country Lass.
>   Fair Damsel, says he,
>   With an Air brisk and free . . .
>
> (p. 55)

And here is the lyric incantation of Chaucer the feigned Magus:

> Swiftly, swiftly haste away,
> And my inverted Wand obey:
> Let no hurly-burly rise;
> Nor Storms the Face of Heav'n disguise;
> Let the Winds in silence lye,
> Nor dreadful Lightnings streak the Skye . . .
>
> (p. 39)

These are more various literary idioms than simply rude and polite. The polite Restoration is assimilated into the vein of Doggrell, and Gay uses his medieval setting to tap different and older literary sources (in Chaucer's lines we may note the Shakespearean 'hurly-burly' and faint reminiscence of the Dirge in *Cymbeline*) by means of which the polite is placed. Different styles almost seem to call themselves in question, and not only through song. Even that prose which, with greater or lesser degree of bluntness or affectation, is the shared idiom of most characters becomes comically problematic when spoken by Canterbury pilgrims:

> *Myrtilla.* Love naturally flows into Poetry. I admire, Sir, that your Muse was never so obliging as to throw away a few tender things upon the Lady to whom you are so generous as to bestow your Heart.
>
> *Chaucer.* Really, Madam, I never write Elegy.
>
> (p. 47)

It would have sounded quite different in the milieu of *The Distress'd Wife*.

The Wife of Bath has been regularly dismissed.[6] It has been said that Doggrell is a mere mouthpiece for Gay; how can this be true of a character whose affectation the comedy progressively deflates? It has been said that most of the figures are *roles* not personalities; by this criterion much early Shakespearean and Jonsonian comedy could be condemned. It has been said that its plot is 'broken-backed', the interest 'continually divided between the Florinda-Merit and Chaucer-Myrtilla episodes'.[7] It has indeed a double and not very streamlined plot, but intrigue and disguise bring the two parts farcically together. Thus Doggrell, pressed but unwilling to marry Florinda (who prefers Merit), pays court to Myrtilla (who is about to take the veil). Lured into thinking he has enjoyed a liaison with Myrtilla (it was the Wife of Bath disguised as a nun), he is further tricked into the belief that he has achieved clandestine marriage with Myrtilla (it was Myrtilla's maid disguised as a nun). Chaucer wins Myrtilla through disguise as an astrologer. It may be seen that Doggrell and the Wife of Bath, one as gull and the other as plotter, bring together the two strands of the play. It can also be seen that their liaison formally joins the downright and the affected in idiom and outlook, as we find when she asks him next morning how he got on:

> *Dogg.* Ah, Madam,—the most lovely of her Sex! kind, tender and obliging!—to find her pretty Lips the very Fountain of Wit, threw me in a perfect Extasie;—Harmony dwells in her Voice, and *Zephyrs* wanton in her Breath
>
> *Wife.* Was you thereabouts my Man of Might,—'twas I advised you, my Lad . . . a rare Pupil i'fackins!—Her Breath sweet as balmy *Zephyrs!* 'Slidikins,—I begin to think my self young again—
>
> (p. 54)

This comedy of juxtaposition is admirably built up to the successful theatre of the conclusion. Doggrell, still congratulating himself on his good fortune, resolves to keep cool in the face of Franklin's wrath—'I'll hum a Tune, and receive the Storm with all the Patience of an ancient Philosopher'. He hums a very Popean pastoral while Franklin rages up and down:

> *Dogg.* Fa, la, la, la . . .
>   For *Damon* stay'd;—*Damon* the loveliest Swain;
> *Frank.* Bred up a Child under my own Wing, as a Body might say—
> *Dogg.* And she the fairest Nymph of all the Plain.
> *Frank.* Mad! stark staring Mad!—Why *Frank,* Sirrah
> *Dogg.* Thus she complains, while all the Feather'd Throng,
> *Frank.* Death, and Confusion!
>
> (pp. 59-61)

Doggrell doubly invites his come-uppance when he warns the Wife not to be familiar with his spouse (the maid Busy) and thus learns the latter's true identity:

> *Dogg.* Oh most egregious Error! Embarrass'd with a Chamber-maid, when I bid fair for a Countess!
> *Frank.* Dal te ral, tal lal [*Sings*]
>
> (p. 62)

Doggrell's glittering bubble is burst, and Franklin can sing his 'Dal te ral' to D'Ogrelle's earlier 'Fa, la, la'.

The play concludes in reconciliation. Jack hath his Jill. Merit wins Florinda, Chaucer Myrtilla, Doggrell, reconciled to Busy, can congratulate Chaucer, and the Wife seems likely to marry Franklin: 'Give me thy

Hand then, old *Nestor*—I will defy the World to shew another such like Couple, in the decline of their Age. Ours is a meer *Italian* Autumn, that even excells the Spring in its variety of Beauty' (p. 63). In this atmosphere 'all turn Mediators' and the comedy ends with a dance more inclusive than *The Mohocks'*. But again the comic form has been a process of deflation. Again (though to a lesser degree) the drama has been rich in linguistic contrast, though too happy to scourge fools out of their humour. Doggrell loses Myrtilla but not his *beau* idiom, and the play, self-consciously literary as it is, manages to slip free from the patterns of Restoration comedy (which it nevertheless makes use of in part) and sail simply towards a sweeter final reconciliation than any other drama by Gay.

The pastoral mode in **The Mohocks** was the confused prose of the Watch. This was succeeded in **The Wife of Bath** by that of Franklin's servants Anthony and William (II.i), but another version of pastoral in the play was the strain of Doggrell's Popean eclogue in IV.iii. That couplet vein, considerably fraught with workaday particulars and earnest incongruity, becomes the chief mode of Gay's next play, **The What D'Ye Call It: A Tragi-Comi-Pastoral Farce** (1715). Again it is worth pausing upon the title. **What D'Ye Call It** comments wittily on the subtitle—what indeed?—but also alludes to Shakespeare. It carries *As You Like It* and . . . *What You Will* a step further (as Mr P. E. Lewis has pointed out), while the subtitle reminds us of *Hamlet* (II.ii.424-30). Parodic sophistication is thus announced more conspicuously than before, and this is further stressed by the way the couplet vein of the play itself is set off by the more or less realistic rustic prose of a substantial induction. Alerted by Gay's Preface (lines III-14) we easily connect Gay's rustics preparing their play with the mechanicals in *A Midsummer Night's Dream* (see III.i.195 for the probable source of Gay's Peascod). In a sense the real pastoral of the play is the induction, contrasting almost as strongly with the verse of the play itself as the prose of the Watch contrasted with the hyperbolical vein of the Mohocks. We are again alerted to the relative arbitrariness of literary forms and decorums.

The induction also makes it clear that the play is a piece to order. As Sir Roger demands of his steward: 'And is the play as I order'd it, both a Tragedy and a Comedy? I would have it a Pastoral too; and if you could make it a Farce, so much the better—and what if you crown'd all with a spice of your Opera?' (lines 43-7). Sir Roger is the strongest link between induction and play, since his role as master is the same in each. He has ordered: now he can preside. By Sir Roger's 'hint' the play has so fitted the parts to his own tenants that 'ev'ry man talks in his own way!' (lines 53-5). He, Sir Humphry and Justice Statute sit at the table throughout the first act (perhaps throughout the play) with pipes, tobacco and tankard, and, appropriately enough, never speak without drinking. Their mastery gives them the advantage of being inside and outside the action at the same time; they propose for themselves the best of both worlds, with claret into the bargain.

The couplet vein of **The What D'Ye Call It** is quite remarkable. It has astonishing pace and verve; Gay deploys it in expressive variety of form and tone with the brilliance of a virtuoso, and a very notable subtlety of effect. Its most conspicuous feature, burlesque, is indeed responsible for some of the funniest moments, but the laughter is not dismissive. There are points when Popean pastoral is allowed its overt emotion:

> KITTY
> Dear happy Fields, farewell; ye Flocks, and you
> Sweet Meadows . . .
>
> (II.viii.1-2)

When she turns to her rake, 'Companion of my Cares', anyone familiar with Gay's age of burlesque and mock-epic prepares to laugh at the low and ludicrous to come; yet what follows is not simply funny:

> 'Tis to thy Help I owe this Hat and Gown;
> On thee I've lean'd, forgetful of my Work,
> While *Tom* gaz'd on me, propt upon his Fork.
>
> (II.viii.6-8)

We have only to compare this with Pope's burlesque of Ambrose Phillips in *Guardian* 40 to realise that Gay's humour does not preclude a real pathos in Kitty's artless literalism, which also has the merit of giving us a precise picture. When, in the next line, a more elevated note is regained—

> Farewel, farewel; for all thy Task is o'er—

rake, hat, gown and fork are taken up by the emotive pastoral vein to which they delicately lend substance.

Or let us look at the most famous and funny burlesque moment, brilliantly successful on the stage: Timothy Peascod's dying speech as he prepares to be shot for desertion. The literary joke comes over first as the couplet rhetoric ('O Fellow-Soldiers, Countrymen and Friends' II.i.5) plunges on into artless detail:

> I play'd at Nine-pins first in Sermon time:
> I robb'd the Parson's Orchard next; and then
> (For which I pray Forgiveness) stole—a Hen.

(But these crimes are not merely low and ludicrous if we remember eighteenth-century penalties.)

> I. COUNTRYMAN.
> Come, 'tis no time to talk.—
>   II. COUNTRYMAN.
> . . . Repent thine Ill,
> And Pray in this good Book.—[*Gives him a
>   Book.*]
>   PEASCOD.
> . . . I will, I will.
> Lend me thy Handkercher—*The Pilgrim's Pro*
>   [*Reads and weeps.*]
> (I cannot see for Tears) *Pro - Progress*—Oh!
> - *The Pilgrim's Progress - Eighth - Edi -t- on
> Lon-don-prin-ted - for - Ni-cho-las Bod-ding-
>   ton*
> *With new ad-di-tions never made before.*
> - Oh! 'tis so moving, I can read no more.
>   [*Drops the Book.*]
>
>   (II.i.12-14, 21-30)

I have spoken of Kitty's artless literalism; here we have literalism specifically pointed. What is it that we laugh at? Certainly the banal details of the imprint and the idea that Tim should call them moving. But we see that in this situation anything would move him; he weeps really for his own death. To do this is not purely risible by any means. Gay has used the exaggerations of farce to create a most peculiar blend of hilarity and pity. At the same time the buoyant song of the couplets, every sob in place, runs its course like a nimble athlete taking each obstacle in his stride to complete his lap. Altogether a strange sense of the separateness of the constituent elements is achieved: printed object distinct from the emotions it appears to evoke, pity distinct from laughter, couplet-form distinct from potential disorder of laughter or tears. This is highly sophisticated and self-conscious farce. It warrants every term of the subtitle.

Sir Roger, however, wanted not merely a tragi-comi-pastoral farce, but 'a spice of your Opera' as well. Here too Gay keeps the promise of his induction. In II.viii Mrs Bicknell, playing Kitty, sung the ballad ''Twas when the seas were roaring' which Gay also published separately, and which Handel may already have set. It is the climax of Gay's lyric performance in the drama. Kitty's situation is first intimated in the induction ('Ay, I have felt Squire *Thomas*'s love to my cost'); in the play itself, in ways we have already seen, her situation is lyrically if humorously expounded, but in the ballad it is raised to a pure lyric intensity. This is another of Gay's salient formalistic contrasts, and may be thought to bring farcical rusticity to the brink of the tragic:

> All melancholy lying,
>   Thus wail'd she for her dear;
> Repay'd each blast with sighing,
>   Each billow with a tear;

> When, o'er the white wave stooping,
>   His floating corpse she spy'd;
> Then like a lily drooping,
>   She bow'd her head, and dy'd.
>
>   (II.viii.55-62)

Not without its own exaggeration, this operatic moment effectively puts Kitty beyond the reach of patronising laughter. (Her final lines in this scene seem to me to be funny in a purely 'literary' way—parodying Belvidira's madness at the end of *Venice Preserved*—and not to affect her status as a dramatic figure.)

One of the effects of Gay's writing is that we sympathise with as well as laugh at the rustics.[8] This is endorsed by the speech Gay liked enough to copy out and send to Parnell on 29 January 1715 ('O Tyrant Justices . . .')[9] and indeed by the structure of the play as a whole. Like **The Beggar's Opera, The What D'Ye Call It** is suddenly checked before the end: its fictionality is suspended, 'what's our Play at a stand?' and the parson refuses to mount Sir Roger's 'stage *pro tempore*' to marry Kitty and Filbert. Hurried parleying induces him to marry the two in the parlour—'So natural!' as the unsuspecting Sir Roger says—and thus the play is turned against the despotic patron who had ordered tragedy, comedy, pastoral and farce altogether, yet also a drama so like the existing order of things that each could talk in his own way. Kitty, the steward's daughter, whom Squire Thomas had seduced in real life, but who was only to be married to him (playing Thomas Filbert) in fiction, is now by the contrivance of the steward married to him in fact. Thus art turns unexpectedly on the patron; it refuses to be both acceptably fictional and acceptably factual: conscious of fact, it turns back upon fact to rectify it, and thus paradoxically vindicates its independence as fiction. Like **The Wife of Bath, The What D'Ye Call It** ends with marriage, here promoted by that 'plaguy dangerous thing' a stage play, but the concluding dance excludes Sir Roger who has stormed off in a passion.

The What D'Ye Call It was Gay's first stage success. We know something of how it was played and what people thought. Gay considered it to be 'out of the way of the Common Taste of the Town' (Gay to Caryll, 3 March 1715) and at first it bewildered. Some could sit through a performance and still not agree with the majority that it was meant to be funny. Pope's anecdote about the deaf Henry Cromwell who, 'hearing none of the words and seeing the action to be tragical, was much astonished to find the audience laugh' tells us that the play was performed in tragic manner, at least in part, as the frontispiece to the editions (insufficient evidence on its own) also suggests.[10] Gay himself was especially pleased with the performances of Penkethman as Peascod, Mrs Bicknell as Kitty and Miss Younger as the little girl Joyce. It is probable that the overall theatrical effect was mock-heroic, not burlesque, and that manner and gesture remained dignified even when the words were low. Some of the surreal touches—the chorus of sighs and groans, and the ghost of the unborn child—would not of course have been so apparent to the audience as to the reader. One way and another the play made people uneasy; they felt it was getting at something but didn't know what. Griffin and Theobald read it as a 'jest upon the tragic poets'; others, noting the authorship, thought it a 'satire on the late war' (the impressment of country folk for military service).[11] Each response holds a part of the truth, but the brilliance of Gay's achievement lies most in his having evolved from a hint in *Hamlet* a dramatic structure which dissolves the hierarchy of dramatic forms, disorients by making its audience sympathise where they also ridicule, and, integrally with these effects, promotes a most unhierarchical marriage.

Griffin and Theobald thought Pope had a hand in *The What D'Ye Call It,* and a phrase in one of Gay's letters suggests some assistance from Pope and Arbuthnot.[12] With his next play, *Three Hours After Marriage* (1717) they certainly assisted, and were regarded and lampooned as confederates. With Cibber playing Plotwell, Penkethman Underplot and Mrs Bicknell Phoebe Clinket, *Three Hours* was performed on seven consecutive nights at Drury Lane to a tumultuous and controversial reception. On the second night, as a 'neutral' member of the audience recorded, 'the play was acted like a ship tost in a tempest'; the evidence is, however, that by the time Cibber got the play withdrawn the favourable party was prevailing, and general applause being given.[13] While there were extrinsic reasons for the play's excited and in part hostile reception, there were intrinsic ones also, for the play is perhaps the most avant-garde comedy of eighteenth-century England.

Gay called *The What D'Ye Call It* a farce, but *Three Hours* a comedy.[14] The later play has not less of the absurd than the former, yet the designation reliably suggests a close relation with seventeenth-century comedy. It is in that pattern that the play seems to be set at the start, and to focus on the hasty marriage of a woman of the town to the elderly doctor and collector Fossile, a figure descended from Congreve's Foresight, and probably a lampoon on the contemporary Dr Woodward. Stock expectations concerning young wives, old husbands and prolific cuckoldry have been aroused when Phoebe Clinket, Fossile's niece and a poetess, enters, pens stuck in her hair, and preceded by her maid bearing a writing desk on her back. The first lines she recites concern the imminent death of Nature (p. 5), and proceed, as Ian Donaldson rightly observes, to deploy an image from Horace's *De Arte Poetica* and Ovid's *Metamorphoses* traditionally associated with

natural confusion and literary enormity. Pope was later to give the allusion brilliant setting in *The Dunciad*.[15] 'A rare Affected Creature' (as Mrs Townley calls her), Phoebe is an extension of the Doggrell figure into the realms of near-fantasy. The juxtaposition of a standard comedy-of-manners setting with (as it turns out) a tragedy on *The Universal Deluge* is the first of the surreal effects of this drama.

The recitation of *The Universal Deluge* is next mingled, in most effective stage farce, with the efforts of Plotwell and Mrs Townley to communicate surreptitiously with one another under cover of reciting their parts:

> *Town.* [As Pyrrha]   Thou seest me now
>   sail'd from my former Lodgings
>   Beneath a Husband's Ark
> . . .
> *Plotw.* [As Deucalion] Through all the Town
>   with Diligent Enquiries, I sought my
>   *Pyrrha—*
> *Clink.*   Beyond all Patience! the
>   Part, Sir, lies before you; you are never
>   to perplex the *Drama* with
>   Speeches *Extempore.*
> *Plotw.*   Madam, 'tis what the top-
>   Players often do.
>
>   (p. 16)

The comedy works outwards from the intermingling of two orders of fiction (Deucalion's Flood unnervingly penetrating the world of Townley and Plotwell) to reflect upon the relation of fiction and fact. The whole sequence is working up to the open recognition that it is Colley Cibber, a 'top-Player', who is thus made to admit his own practice. The audience, having perceived that the part of Deucalion really discloses Plotwell, suddenly sees that the part of Plotwell really discloses Cibber, there on the stage playing Plotwell playing Deucalion. In this way the drama comically explores the very idea of dramatic fictions.

In the admirable scene that follows, the tragedy, now feigned to have been written by Plotwell lest its female authorship inhibit its reception, is submitted for the approval of Sir Tremendous (Dennis) and two players. Its opening (Phoebe Clinket now reads) discloses an immense flood with cattle and men swimming, steeples rising above the waters and 'with Men and Women perching on their Weather-Cocks'. Sir Tremendous perceives an improbability:

> *Sir Trem.* Begging your Pardon, Sir, I believe
>   it can be proved, that Weather-cocks are
>   of a modern Invention.
>
>   (p. 21)

As anachronism after anachronism is excised (to the protests of Phoebe that 'Were the Play mine, you should gash my Flesh, . . . any thing sooner than scratch my Play' p. 22) the pace madly accelerates:

> *Sir Trem.* Such Stuff! [*strikes out.*]
>   abominable! [*strikes out.*] most execrable!
> *1st Play.* This Thought must out.
> *2nd Play.* Madam, with Submission, this
>   Metaphor.
> *1st Play.* This whole Speech.
> *Sir Trem.* The Fable!
> *Clink.* To you I answer—
> *Sir Trem.* The Diction!
> *Clink.* And to you—Ah, hold, hold—I'm
>   butcher'd, I'm massacred. For Mercy's
>   Sake! murder, murder! ah [*faints.*]
>
>   (p. 24)

The sequence farcically asks the question: what is a play? Everything is struck *out.* What can be left? Only a metaphysical emptiness. But the play has no existence outside the disordered imagination of its author, hence the propriety of her fainting at the moment she does. The scene, with a kind of *Alice Through the Looking Glass* logic, comically exposes the notions of dramatic *'Vray-semblance'* and neo-classical regularity.

A later scene, the most celebrated or notorious of the play, is even richer in farcical humour and sophisticated literary awareness. Here Plotwell and Underplot woo Mrs Townley, the first disguised as a Mummy, the second as an Alligator:

> *Plotw.* Thus trav'ling far from his *Egyptian*
> Tomb,
>   Thy *Antony* salutes his *Cleopatra* . . .
>   [*Underplot in the Alligator crawls
>   forward, then rises up and embraces her.*]
> *Under.* Thus Jove within the *Serpent*'s scaly
> Folds,
>   Twin'd round the Macedonian Queen.
> *Townley* Ah! [*shrieks.*]
> *Plotw.* Fear not, Madam. This is my evil
>   Genius *Underplot* that still haunts me. How
>   the Devil got you here?
>
>   (pp. 58-9)

As in the earlier scene, the pace soon accelerates to what F. W. Bateson has well called 'a crescendo of absurdity'[16].

> *Plotw.* Madam, I am a Human Creature. Taste
>   my Balsamick Kiss.
> *Under.* A Lover in Swaddling-Clouts! What is
>   his Kiss, to my Embrace?

> *Plotw.* Look upon me, Madam. See how I am
>   embroider'd with Hieroglyphicks.
> *Under.* Consider my beautiful Row of Teeth.
> *Plotw.* My Balmy Breath.
> *Under.* The strong joints of my Back.
> *Plotw.* My erect Stature.
> *Under.* My long Tail.
> *Townley* Such a Contest of Beauty! How shall
>   I decide it?
>
>   (p. 60)

In this scene Gay is closer to Jonsonian comedy (we may remember Volpone rising from his bed to woo Celia, and the uncasing of Sir Politic Would-Be) than in any other of his plays. The logic in the fantasy works wonderfully, the two disguises expressing different amorous advantages, Plotwell having the sweet kiss, the erect stature and the embroidered garb, Underplot the embrace, the strong back and the long tail. Plotwell is the polite lover, Underplot the bawdy seducer. The names of the two lovers convey not only different roles within dramatic fictions, but different aspects of them; here again the drama thinks about the composition of dramas. The Mummy has the conventional stiffness and sweetness of the overplot, the Alligator the underplot's propensity to rise vigorously from below and carry away the interest. (The farce is so fertile here that when, on the fourth night of performance, Penkethman playing Underplot fell backwards into the Mummy-case and got stuck, the audience may have seen some point in it; certainly the fifth-night audience demanded a repetition.[17])

Gay brought this stage *Dunciad* to resolution with perhaps the most adroit and suggestive of all his concluding reconciliations. Mrs Townley is reclaimed by a previous husband; Fossile who desired posterity without a wife, can keep her baby. Phoebe Clinket, in a beautifully conventional end-of-comedy speech, puts it thus:

> *Clink.* Uncle, by this Day's Adventure, every
>   one has got something. Lieutenant
>   *Bengall* has got his Wife again. You a
>   fine Child; and I a Plot for a Comedy; and
>   I'll this Moment set about it.
>
>   (p. 80)

What will this comedy be like? Very much, no doubt, like what the audience has just seen. Thus the fantasies of *Three Hours After Marriage. A Comedy* bend back to link with the fantasies of *The Universal Deluge. A Tragedy,* like a serpent biting its own tail. If, before, we thought the mad imagination of Phoebe Clinket was 'placed' in the play, Gay in the concluding lines removes that assurance. Have we not, perhaps, been witnessing her new comedy?

Gay's next two dramas mark a break from the sophisticated literary combinations we have been exploring. ***Dione. A Pastoral Tragedy*** (published in 1720 but never performed) is straightforward in a way the earlier plays are not. 'Pastoral Tragedy' has, of course, none of the comic paradox of the subtitles of ***The Mohocks*** or ***The What D'Ye Call It,*** and works entirely within one literary mode: the pastoral eclogue in couplets, expanded in such a way as to comprise a sustained action. The skilful and often moving quality of the verse has often been noted. ***The Captives*** (1724), a relative success in the theatre, is in some ways similar. Written in the muted and flexible blank verse deriving from *All For Love, The Mourning Bride* and *Cato,* this tragedy never questions its own conventions by combination or contrast. In one important respect, however, these two plays mark an advance on what has gone before, and a development to be sustained in Gay's future drama. While the dramatic figures of the earlier plays were on a diminutive scale, capable of being easily manipulated into ingenious and surprising patterns by the dramatist, the chief figures of ***Dione*** and ***The Captives*** are on a full human scale, and are sufficiently sustained in a single dramatic mode as to induce a measure of identification on the part of the audience. Dione in particular, who has the cruelly ambiguous role of Viola in *Twelfth Night*—disguised as a man commissioned to woo for another the man she is herself in love with—certainly invites this interest, while in ***The Captives*** something of the same is true of the imprisoned prince Sophernes, his wife Cylene, and Phraortes the king. It is further notable that both these plays are studies of fidelity in love. In ***The Captives,*** too, it is corruption in high places that menaces a fidelity which could survive even military defeat and capture. Gay has built up the sketchy magistrates of ***The Mohocks,*** and the petty but believable tyrant Sir Roger in ***The What D'Ye Call It,*** into the figure of Phraortes the gullible though good king. Perhaps for the first time in Gay's drama, certainly the last, authority effectively aids fidelity.

In several ways, then, these little-known plays point ahead to the best known. To turn from ***The Captives*** to ***The Beggar's Opera*** (1728) is by no means to be returned simply to the manner of the experimental farces and comedies, for the human scale is maintained, as is the preoccupation with fidelity. Yet ***The Beggar's Opera*** is a return to a mixed dramatic form. And here it is necessary to affirm what is perhaps still a minority view about the ***Opera,*** expressed by Bertrand Bronson in what seems to me the best criticism we have on a drama by Gay.[18] 'There is little probability that Gay intended a serious attack on Italian opera . . . ***The Beggar's Opera*** may more properly be regarded as a testimonial to the strength of opera's appeal to John Gay's imagination than as a deliberate attempt to ridicule it out of existence'. This makes sense if we remember ***The What D'Ye Call It.*** The farce became

operatic when Kitty sang ''Twas when the seas were roaring', which Handel set. (The setting is used again in the ***Opera,*** II.ix.) The effect of that song was to set Kitty's experience in a new light, to release from a diminutive and sometimes ridiculous figure a lyrical emotion which the structure of the drama could not otherwise have conveyed. If it mocked operatic form it did so in a context where every dramatic form was mocked. The life of ***The Beggar's Opera*** lies also in its deployment of contrasting but equally valid and equally questionable modes. It does not follow *The Rehearsal* in mocking one mode to endorse another.

This point may be referred to the parting of Polly and Macheath at the end of Act I. While many of the airs are taken from high opera, Purcell, Handel, Buononcini and others, these settings happen to be popular. But when Macheath sings:

> Were I laid on Greenland's Coast,
> And in my Arms embrac'd my Lass;
> Warm amidst eternal Frost,
> Too soon the Half Year's Night would pass
>
> (I.xiii.31-4)

it is not apparent that the choice of 'Over the Hills and far away' is ridiculing either Italian operatic form, operatic form, or the reality of the lovers' emotion. It may, certainly, be building on the English Dramatic Operas to create a more popular English operatic mode than had existed before: that is to claim something different. In this instance the poetry too—'Warm amidst eternal Frost'—has an affirmative intensity denied by the terse, polished, worldly idiom of Macheath's preceding prose: 'You might sooner tear a Pension out of the Hands of a Courtier, a Fee from a Lawyer, a pretty Woman from a Looking-glass, or any Woman from Quadrille' (I.xiii.27-9). ***The Beggar's Opera*** is most obviously a mixed form because Gay has abandoned recitative, thus leaving himself free to employ much highly unoperatic colloquialism. Having thus, in the song, established a mode strikingly different from the prose of a cynical world, Gay is able, in Polly's symmetrical response, to hint at a prospect from the world of crime and punishment: transportation.[19]

> Were I sold on *Indian* Soil,
> Soon as the burning Day was clos'd,
> I could mock the sultry Toil . . .
>
> (I.xiii.35-7)

The operatic plighting of troth, and the corrupt world of robbers and receivers, are momentarily held side by side in the song. That is not all. Contemporary responses to Gay's drama show how ready audiences were to detect literary allusion.[20] Bronson's suggestion that this scene remembers the parting of the lovers

Floridante and Elmira in Handel's *Floridante* (1721) is eminently plausible, but it is surely clear from the way Gay's scene itself works that it is hardly 'ridiculing it out of existence'.

In *Three Hours After Marriage* we noticed how a part of the comedy arose from the contrast of different levels of fiction with what a historical actor (Cibber) actually did. In the famous quarrel of Polly and Lucy (II.xiii) a similar effect is achieved, if not quite with the outrageous practicality which used the actor in question to admit his own fault on stage. The quarrel in the *Opera* unmistakably alludes to the notorious stage quarrel of the two rival singers Faustina and Cuzzoni, in Buononcini's *Astyanax* (1727). Equally certain is the allusion to Handel's *Alessandro* (1726) which had been written to give each of the two celebrities an equally good part, as Lisaura and Rossane vie with each other for the great conqueror's love. A contemporary witness of the *Opera* detected an allusion to the same *matter,* though in this case in the form of the earlier drama by Lee.[21] Once again three levels of 'reality' play off against one another: Faustina and Cuzzoni, whose real quarrel broke the fiction of *Astyanax;* Polly and Lucy (were Miss Fenton and Miss Egleton really quarrelling, the first audience could have wondered); and the rival lovers in Handel and Lee, an allusion which, as Bronson observes, 'makes something of an Alexander out of Macheath'.[22]

The relation between prose and song is the whole art of the *Opera,* and is of course far more various than these instances suggest. If its chief feature is the contrast between the prose of familiar corruption—'Indeed, indeed, Brother, we must punctually pay our Spies, or we shall have no Information' (II.x.39-41)—and the lyric of high intensity or tenderness—the *Twelfth Night*-like vein of 'Love with Youth flies swift away,/ Age is nought but Sorrow' (II.iv.37-8)—there are plenty of songs whose mordant satiric pace reinforces our sense of the world that the prose renders. There are moments too when the roles are reversed, as at that politically crucial point where the buoyant singing about court treachery to the tune of Lillibullero is succeeded by Macheath's ringing avowal: 'But we, Gentlemen, have still Honour enough to break through the Corruptions of the World' (III.iv.6-17). For the moment (it will not be sustained) Macheath has moved into the part of the true patriot, *Craftsman,* or Tory satirist, dedicated to saving his country by bringing down corrupt government.[23]

Perhaps it may be said that while Gay's earlier comedies playfully use different conventions to question and undermine one another, in the *Opera* an equally analytic and experimental skill deploys them to question and make one another good. This may be one mark of the *Opera*'s relatively greater stature. Yet nobody who compares *The What D'Ye Call It* with the *Opera* can

fail to see certain formal similarities. In each a 'criminal' about to be executed attempts to face death with courage only to break down (Peascod by attempting to run away, Macheath by drinking until his 'Courage is out'). In each he is confronted by mistress and 'base-born child'—in the *Opera* to an almost farcical degree. In each play the extreme artifice of the main action is thrown into relief through being set in a wider framework—Sir Roger and the steward, the Beggar and the player—and in each case the drama comes to an unexpected yet supremely fit conclusion as inner and outer fictions collide. The conclusion of the *Opera* is problematic in that it is a 'happy' ending in which every problem raised by the drama is conspicuously unsolved. Peachum and Lockit are not 'brought to the gallows', the fate of Polly and Lucy remains in suspense, Macheath sneakingly acknowledging his marriage in an aside to Polly, but putting off its public announcement.

Much recent criticism of Gay has stressed his importance as a social critic and as one of that courageous group of satirists who assailed the Hanoverian court and the Walpole régime. I am far from dissenting from this view, though my present argument has been of a different kind. It is, however, necessary to bring this issue into focus as we turn to Gay's last works for the theatre, *Polly* (published 1729), *Achilles* (1733), *The Distress'd Wife* and *The Rehearsal at Goatham* (published 1754). 'John Gay: Lightweight or Heavyweight?' is a question that has recently been posed.[24] The dichotomy is misleading. It associates 'serious' with the grave, earnest and even ponderous, and links 'entertaining' with the trivial. Gay is a serious critic both of life and art, but what makes his criticism tell is precisely his deft and lighthearted manner. A devastating reflection in the buoyant gaiety of a song, or the turn of a swift sentence—these are his means, but not his only means. His light but mordant touch is the effect also of the protean nature of his dramatic structures. The carefully poised instability of his comic form, as I have tried to display it, lends lightness to his reflections: a moral parallel or a political allusion is suddenly perceived, only to be whisked away as the kaleidoscope of his perspective is deftly thrown into a new configuration.

With *Polly,* however, Gay does move in the direction of a more straight-forward kind of moral play. The action of *Polly* is not fully framed, like that of the *Opera;* it has an induction of Poet and Players but they never reappear at the end. We are thus led into the central fiction, culminating in the execution of Morano (Macheath), and the union of the faithful Polly to the virtuous Indian prince Cawwawkee, as into a truth-telling mode that is never challenged. It is in this respect closer to *The Captives* than *The What D'Ye Call It, Three Hours* or the *Opera*. There is good evidence that in *Polly* Gay sought to create a more stable moral fiction than the *Opera*, with a clear and firm conclusion.[25] Polly, virtuous and faithful, true to the now unromantically criminal Macheath to his death, can finally be joined to a virtue worthy of her own. This does not mean, in my view, that **Polly** is drastically inferior to the **Opera.**[26] It is rather a kind of moral *riposte* to the **Opera** and to be judged as such. Macheath is here the criminal hero of unglamorous middle age; not an Alexander of the underworld but the Antony of an opulent West, Jenny his Cleopatra, tempting him to abandon the empire of the Indies for love ('Let us seize the ships then, and away for *England*' II.ix.58-9). Polly is his suffering Octavia. This parallel, explicit more than once, is the governing metaphor of the play. The **Opera** gave us the old world, **Polly** the new; in the **Opera** Polly is threatened with poisoning by Lucy, in **Polly** with seduction by Jenny; in the **Opera** suspense over Macheath's death is ended by a reprieve, in **Polly** by execution; in the **Opera** the conclusion is indeterminate, in **Polly** it is clear.

The 1730 revision of *The Wife of Bath* is another sign of Gay's move away from an experimental, formally self-questioning drama. A full discussion of the changes would be of interest,[27] but it is clear from the conversion of Franklin into Plowden, Chaucer into Sir Harry Gauntlet, and the excision of the more archaic and interesting poetry, such as Chaucer's spell and the Wife's ballad of love-making, that Gay now wished to bring his early play closer to the comedy-of-manners form. This version perhaps deserves Allardyce Nicoll's judgement that *The Wife of Bath* 'owes more to the dramas of the time of Charles II than to any others'[28] and is the less interesting for it.

Gay's course towards a plainer moral form of drama is interestingly complicated by his last opera, *Achilles* (posthumously performed in 1733). The truth-bearer is now not Dione or Polly in men's clothing but the youthful Achilles in woman's clothing, placed in that disguise in the corrupt court of Lycomedes by Thetis, to keep him from the Trojan War. The form is that of situational farce, the theme fidelity to a purpose. Achilles is, as it were, the Manly, the Plain Dealer in a world of gossip and intrigue. And the shock at hearing Gay's polite modern prose in the mouths of the Canterbury Pilgrims is outdone by the same parlance being given to a Homeric hero and his divine mother:

> *Ach.* Were I allow'd to follow my Inclinations, what wou'd you have to fear? - I
>   shou'd do my Duty, and die with Honour. - Was I to live an Age I cou'd do no
>   more.
> *Thet.* You are so very obstinate, that really, Child, there's no enduring you. - Your
>   Impatience seems to forget that I am a Goddess . . .
>
>   (I.i.52-6)

True to himself, Achilles as Pyrrha gets a court lady with child and rebuffs with great violence the amorous advances of the king. In a well-contrived resolution, Ulysses disguised as a merchant precipitates the definitive betrayal of Achilles's masculine and martial character. The comic conclusion is a celebration of honesty to Nature—

> Nature breaks forth at the Moment unguarded;
>   Through all disguise she herself must betray—
>
>   (III.xii.79-80)

the dance celebrates both Achilles' marriage and his departure for the Trojan War, and marks also the fall of the corrupt minister Diphilus whose 'paltry flattery' brought about the king's humiliation at Achilles' hands. The quite *recherché* unrealism of the opera's action lightly and charmingly endorses the heavyweight virtues embodied in Achilles. Though the quality of the songs is notably inferior to those of *The Beggar's Opera* and *Polly,* Gay's third and final opera is a work of real merit, and considerable stage potential.

And so we return to *The Distress'd Wife,* and come to *The Rehearsal at Goatham.* Both plays labour their moral judgement, and while the idea of the latter had possibilities for experimental farce, these are undeveloped in the rough dramatic sketch about the censorship of *Polly* which has come down to us. *The Distress'd Wife* is more considerable, and the first act has an overt moral desperation quite new in the drama of Gay. Viewed as a whole the relative realism of its mode falls into the pattern of a fable of false stewardship and marital betrayal. There is no combination or questioning of modes. Sir Thomas, a country gentleman whose wife entangles him in the web of court deception and connives with his treacherous steward to gamble away his inheritance, struggles to preserve his integrity and be master of his household again. (In the context of the Tory writers' assault on Walpole and Queen Caroline the political implications are reasonably clear.)[29] Gay's last plays are serious works at least, and each contains speeches which help us appreciate what is implied in the dazzling formalistic indirection of his earlier drama.

> *Sir Headstrong.* [on the innocent Romantic puppet-show at Goatham]:
> Such audacious Wretches should starve, who, because they are poor,
> are so insolently honest in every thing they say, that a rich Man
> cannot enjoy his Property in quiet for 'em.
> *Pother.*   We must keep these Wretches down. 'Tis right to keep Mankind in
> Dependance.
>
>   (pp. 37-8)

This exchange may stand, in summary, for 'John Gay: Social Critic'.[30] It underlines Gay's true pastoral perspective upon power and wealth, which his plays repeatedly though never steadily or continuously offer their audience. Gay is not proposing an alternate social structure; he may hardly be thought to oppose hierarchy as such, yet no part of the operation of hierarchy escapes his radical mockery and free judgement. But Gay the social critic is part only of Gay the dramatist. Here is the culminating speech of the strong first act of **The Distress'd Wife,** Sir Thomas in soliloquy:

> Where shall one look for Honesty?—Who hath it?—
> Or of what use is it to the Owner?—'Tis a Restraint
> upon a Man's Fortune; 'tis a Curb upon Opportunity,
> and makes either a Publick or private Trust worth
> nothing. What's its Reward?—Poverty—Is it among
> the Rich? No. For it never keeps Company with
> Avarice, Luxury and Extravagance.—Is it among
> the Vulgar? No. For they act by Imitation—Who
> can one Trust?—If I trust my servant I tempt him.—
> If I trust my friend I lose him.—If I trust my Wife,
> for the quiet of the Family She looks upon it as her
> Duty to deceive me.
>
> 'Tis then our selves, who by implicit Trust,
> Tempt Servants, Friends and Wives to be
>   Unjust.
>
> (pp. 21-2)

This is a little more complicated than the exchange from **The Rehearsal at Goatham.** Gay writes here with understanding of a person who cannot relate truth and falsity in a single coherent picture of society. In the Falstaffian self-interrogation on Honesty (cf. the soliloquy on Honour in *1 Henry IV*) there lurks a deeper paradox concerning the complicity of the judging mind in what it judges. The possibility of a moral life seems questioned. The soliloquy asks the question: 'Where shall one look for Honesty?' and touches on the question: 'How shall one look for Truth?' It may be thought that it is dubiety on this score which underlies the formal experimentation, the contrasting and questioning of modes, and the kaleidoscopically shifting perspectives of Gay's best comedy. Far from seeing man in 'One clear, unchanged and universal light' (*An Essay on Criticism,* line 71), these plays are aware that the thing perceived depends on the approach of the perceiver; Kitty in **The What D'Ye Call It** is tragicomi-pastoral, farcical and operatic. As the genre is applied so the truth will be found. The writer who feels this must, like Gay, seek to construct his plays out of several genres, making them work together while yet letting the audience sense the separateness of the constituent parts, as versions of reality.

Gay stands in a special place in English drama. The sixteenth and seventeenth centuries had exhausted the available dramatic forms, in the sense that an early eighteenth-century dramatist could not but be aware of their full and successful exploitation in the hands of his predecessors. Though the comedy of manners was by no means dead, as the drama of Sheridan, Goldsmith and Boucicault attests, English drama was not to find new forms until the Irish playwrights of the twentieth century. This may account for the restless character of Gay's dramatic achievement—'Will he, alone, not imitate himself?' asks the Prologue to *Achilles*—and its curious Janus-faced position. On the one hand it seems *fin-de-siècle:* the amused, sophisticated parody of greater masters, the lively farce after the great century's drama was done. On the other hand, as Gay seems to have recognised, his restless combination of different forms, idioms and subjects was innovatory, and to that extent it is not absurd to detect a modernistic indeterminacy in some of his best drama. Gay was after all one of the Scriblerus Club, whose deep humanistic respect for classical forms combined with an inventively parodistic freedom in their handling to produce *A Tale of a Tub* and *The Dunciad,* those formally problematic and multi-perspectived masterpieces.

I don't wish to weaken a case which may already seem to be verging on the wildly anachronistic, but I suggest that Gay's peculiar dramatic achievement can helpfully be seen in the light of some remarks of Serenus Zeitblom on the early work of Leverkühn in Mann's *Dr Faustus:* '. . . this disillusioned masterpiece . . . already bore within itself the traits of parody and intellectual mockery of art, which . . . so often emerged in a creative and uncanny way . . . All the superficial lot simply called it witty and amusing. In truth parody was here the proud expedient of a great gift threatened with sterility by a combination of scepticism, intellectual reserve, and a sense of the deadly extension of the kingdom of the banal'.[31] Needless to say, Gay is no Leverkühn, Schönberg or Mann. The grandiosity of Zeitblom's formulation is inappropriate to England's least pretentious writer. These qualifications made, Mann's words do, I suggest, help us to recognise something of the larger significance of Gay's theatre, corresponding to the *fin-de-siècle* face of modernism. Gay's gift and situation had something in common with Leverkühn's 'great gift'. But it is to another great twentieth-century German author we must turn for applicable words expressive of the other face of modernism: Brecht developing some remarks on **The Beggar's Opera** and *The Threepenny Opera.* 'The new school of play-writing must systematically see to it that its form includes "experiment". It must be free to use connections on every side; it needs equilibrium and has a tension which governs its component parts and "loads" them against one another'.[32] This well describes some of Brecht's most famous plays (not just *The Threepenny Opera*). It would be a good description of the best drama of Gay. It makes it clear that Brecht did not just find in **The Beggar's Opera** the raw material for a new kind of play. It means rather that, surprising as it may seem, there are some radical affinities between the eighteenth-century and the twentieth-century playwright.

Notes

[1] Mr P. E. Lewis has written: 'Another look at John Gay's *The Mohocks*', *Modern Language Review*, LXII (1968), 790-3; 'Gay's burlesque method in *The What D'Ye Call It*', and 'Dramatic burlesque in *Three Hours After Marriage*', *Durham University Journal*, LX (1967-8), 232-9 and LXIV (1971-2), 13-25. These are helpful studies. I differ from them in thinking that the category of literary burlesque alone is insufficient for the explication and appreciation of Gay's drama. Mr. Lewis's very well judged critical study of *The Beggar's Opera* (1976), published by Edward Arnold appeared too late for inclusion in my discussion.

[2] I am speaking of the lifetime of Gay (1685-1732). This is not yet the period of Richardson and Fielding, but it may be thought that the fictions of Defoe merit the term 'realism'. Without doubt certain scenes in Defoe evoke the word 'realistic' but it is doubtful if the same is true of his fictions as a whole. Where they reach beyond a limited subjectivity (Crusoe or Moll) it is in the direction of a providential and ultimately metaphysical order. Restoration comedy, on the other hand, offers something of a secular and objective scrutiny of a number of different individuals in a social pattern, which I take to be a requisite of realism.

[3] With the exception of *The Beggar's Opera* and perhaps of *Three Hours After Marriage* none of Gay's plays has been satisfactorily edited. In quotation I have: (i) used John Gay, *The Beggar's Opera*, ed. P. E. Lewis (Edinburgh, 1973), the best modern edition of the *Opera;* (ii) cited the accessible *Poetical Works of John Gay*, ed. G. C. Faber (Oxford, 1926) for all other plays whose complete texts are included in that volume; and (iii) in the case of the plays not so included (*The Wife of Bath, Three Hours After Marriage, The Distress'd Wife* and *The Rehearsal at Goatham*) cited the first editions, giving page references. I have sometimes reversed the founts in Gay's use of Italic, and regularised abbreviations of characters' names.

[4] The debt to *Much Ado About Nothing* has been noted by W. H. Irving, *John Gay: Favorite of the Wits* (Durham, North Carolina, 1940), p. 66 and F. S. Boas, *An Introduction to Eighteenth-Century Drama, 1700-1780* (Oxford, 1953), p. 169.

[5] Gay and Pope were both working in the aftermath of Dryden's revival of interest in Chaucer. See Irving, *John Gay*, pp. 77-8 for the immediate context of the comedy.

[6] The play exists in two versions, 1713 and 1730; it is radically revised in the later version. F. W. Bateson, *English Comic Drama, 1700-1750* (Oxford, 1929), p. 82 and P. M. Spacks, *John Gay* (New York, 1965), pp. 131-2, are especially contemptuous.

[7] The judgement of Irving, *John Gay,* p. 79, who is, however, much the most interesting critic on this play.

[8] Bateson, *English Comic Drama*, p. 83, has well said that 'the parody itself becomes creative and develops into a miniature comedy of sentiment of singular attraction'—though this oversimplifies—and Boas, *Eighteenth-century Drama*, p. 173, notes that Kitty's grief finds 'moving expression' in the ballad.

[9] *The Letters of John Gay*, ed. C. F. Burgess (Oxford, 1966), pp. 17-18.

[10] Pope to Caryll, 3 March 1715; *Letters of John Gay*, p. 19.

[11] Benjamin Griffin and Lewis Theobald, *A Complete Key to the Last New Farce The What D'Ye Call It* (London, 1715); Pope to Caryll (see n. 10 above).

[12] Gay to Parnell, 29 January 1715 (see n. 9 above).

[13] George Sherburn, 'The fortunes and misfortunes of *Three Hours After Marriage*', *Modern Philology*, XXIV (1926-7), 102-5; this essay is an admirable account of the play's performance and reception.

[14] Gay to Parnell (see n. 9 above) and the title-page of *Three Hours After Marriage.*

[15] Ian Donaldson, *The World Upside-Down: Comedy from Jonson to Fielding* (Oxford, 1970), pp. 185-6. Donaldson's chapter on Gay in this book is much to be recommended.

[16] Bateson, *English Comic Drama,* p. 87.

[17] Sherburn, *'Three Hours After Marriage',* p. 102.

[18] B. II. Bronson, *'The Beggar's Opera',* first published in *Studies in the Comic* (Berkeley, 1941); reprinted in *Restoration Drama: Modern Essays in Criticism,* ed. John Loftis (New York, 1966), pp. 298-327; see p. 314. As Bronson observes, the significance of Gay's having written the libretto for Handel's *Acis and Galatea* cannot be forgotten.

[19] This is observed by William Empson, *Some Versions of Pastoral* (London, 1950), pp. 241-2.

[20] This is clear from the suspicious/hostile attitude of Griffin and Theobald in *A Key . . . to The What D'Ye Call It,* and from the appreciative attitude of a paper

on *The Beggar's Opera* submitted to *The Craftsman* on 23 April?1728, by 'W.B.' The whole paper is of great interest for the contemporary reception of the *Opera,* and especially its recognition that an allusion to another author is not necessarily a mockery of him. W.B. writes of 'pleasant Parallells with some of our most celebrated Dramatic Authors, who at ye same Time must not be understood to suffer by this jocular Treatment, no more than ye great Virgil by Cotton's Travesty, or the mightiest Homer by Dr Swift's exquisite pleasantry in his Battel of Books . . . At ye Quarrelling Scene of Peachum and Lockit, I could not help thinking on Brutus and Cassius, but without lessening my Respect for those Ancient Heroes, or the incomparable Shakespear, and Porcia must likewise excuse me, if I remembered her, when Polly sends Filch to the Old Bailey to learn what he coud of Macheath.

The Rival Queens seem Rivald again in Polly & Lucy who contend as earnestly for their little Robbr as Statira & Roxana did for the Great Plunderer of the World'. (Cholmondeley (Houghton) MSS. 74. 48. These are the papers of Sir Robert Walpole at present deposited in the Cambridge University Library.) *The Craftsman* was close to the Scriblerus Club writers, and such literary criticism as was submitted to it may be thought to have some authority.

[21] Nathaniel Lee, *The Rival Queens, Or The Death of Alexander The Great* (London, 1677), alluded to in the *Craftsman* MS. cited above.

[22] Bronson, *'The Beggar's Opera',* p. 309.

[23] I am indebted for this valuable insight to Mr J. S. Bull, of the Department of English Literature, University of Sheffield.

[24] Arthur Sherbo, 'John Gay: lightweight or heavyweight?', *The Scriblerian* (November 1975).

[25] Gay's standard, though plausible, affirmation to Swift concerning the moral seriousness of *Polly* (Gay to Swift, 18 March 1729; *Letters,* p. 78) is interestingly endorsed by what his patroness, the Duchess of Queensberry, told Mrs Larpent on the occasion of the opera's first performance on 19 June 1777. Mrs Larpent, described by one who has studied her papers as 'a rather dull, puritanical young lady' noted in her journal that she was 'extremely pleased to go with the Duchess of Queensberry to see this Opera, which from the protection she gave its author Gay, & from the spirit of those times, occasioned her dismission from Court . . . the moral [of the opera] is nothing remarkably pointed, altho' the Duchess told me, that on Gay's being accused of immorality in the end of ye Beggar's Opera, some Nobleman (I really think Lord Bath but I am not certain) said "Why Gay you have only *transported* him

pursue him, & bring him to punishment -" & see says she "how finely he has wrought out the tale".' (L. W. Conolly, 'Anna Margaretta Larpent, The Duchess of Queensberry and Gay's *Polly* in 1777', *Philological Quarterly,* LI.4 (October 1972), p. 956).

[26] Most critics consider it so; see especially Irving, *John Gay,* pp. 270-1 and Spacks, pp. 159-61. The trouble is that, because *Polly* is a narrative continuation of the *Opera,* it has been assumed that Gay wished to write a formally similar work, and that since *Polly* is not formally similar it must be a failure.

[27] Irving, *John Gay,* pp. 78-80 offers some comparative remarks.

[28] *A History of Early Eighteenth-Century Drama* (Cambridge, 1925), pp. 157-8. In half a sentence, however, Nicoll considers it 'a good comedy'.

[29] For this theme in the attack on Walpole, see my book, *The Social Milieu of Alexander Pope* (London, 1975), pp. 243-59, especially p. 244.

[30] The phrase is the title of the study by Sven Armens (New York, 1954).

[31] Thomas Mann, *Doctor Faustus,* translated from the German by H. T. Lowe-Porter (London, 1949), pp. 151-2.

[32] *Brecht on Theatre,* edited and translated by John Willett (London, 1964), p. 46.

Dianne S. Ames (essay date 1978)

SOURCE: "Gay's *Trivia* and the Art of Allusion," in *Studies in Philology,* Vol. LXXV, No. 2, 1978, pp. 199-222.

[*In the following essay, Ames makes a case for Gay's often-unrecognized skill with classical allusion, comparing his* Trivia *with John Dryden's translation of Virgil's* Georgics. *Ames argues that Gay's burlesque, with its unassuming tone, better approximates the classical originals.*]

Few studies of John Gay's poetry accord him the full praise he merits as a master of the poetry of classical allusion. Recently, in "John Gay: Lightweight or Heavyweight?" (*Scriblerian,* VIII [1975]), Arthur Sherbo has even indicated that in the last five years there has, in fact, been an hiatus in Gay scholarship altogether. And yet, Sherbo's 1970 essay, "Virgil, Dryden, Gay, and Matters Trivial" (*PMLA,* LXXXV), like Martin Battestin's earlier "Menalcas' Song: The Meaning of Art and Artifice in Gay's Poetry" (*JEGP,* LXV [1966]), had made a compelling plea for our recognition of Gay's emulation—in *Trivia*—of Vergil's *Georgics.* These claims for Gay I should like to extend by enlarging upon the poet's complementary powers as an allusive poet and as a satirist of the decline of culture. For, when read closely, Gay's *Trivia* discloses an advocacy of Scriblerian causes quite as fervent as Pope's or Swift's.[1] Indeed, some readers may even become persuaded with me that *Trivia* ranks among the most sophisticated and most accomplished exemplars of neoclassical allusiveness.

Though the officious advertisement and proem of *Trivia* allege the poem to be a sort of *vade mecum* for the instruction of London pedestrians, the fatuousness of Gay's advice—for instance, the index entry, "feet, their use"—soon makes it clear that we will learn from *Trivia* how to exercise our minds rather than our legs. Gay frustrates the reader's expectations of learning anything practical from *Trivia,* and substitutes entertainment and satire. He adopts the guise of a kind of Martinus Scriblerus whose enthusiasm is greater than his taste, and says of himself, in the poem's motto, *"Non tu in trivi-is, indocte, solebas / Stridenti miserum stipulâ disperdere carmen?"* ("Was it not you, Master Dunce, who at the crossroads, used to murder a sorry tune on a scrannel straw?")[2]

Most of the humor of *Trivia* proceeds from carefully bungled or splendidly mangled imitations of the English Augustan canon of Latin poets: Vergil, Horace, Ovid, and Juvenal.[3] Gay seems to subscribe to a principle of inept decorum, based on the generally understood merits of these poets: he copies Vergil to teach, Horace and Martial to moralize, Juvenal to rave, and Ovid to Indulge Fancy. In attempting to do justice to all the *auctores,* he seems to do justice to none. There is method in the mad eclecticism, for all that various critics have found *Trivia* unaccountably heterogeneous. At a loss to account for the principle of unity in the poem, Sven Armens, for example, terms Gay ambivalent, and even Patricia Spacks underestimates his skill, as Battestin has shown.

One can see how *Trivia* might be particularly perplexing, since Gay's strategy is to strain the generous provisions of the georgic for digression and variety beyond the limits of reason and taste. Even at its most conservative, the georgic is a relatively free form like satire, which is by definition a hodgepodge.[4] It may consist of a series of pictorial sketches, political allusions, and philosophical and mythological digressions, arranged casually within the flexible framework of a didactic treatise.

Gay makes a point of abusing this license, however, by making sequential material clash with the vengeance of *concordia discors.* For one thing, Vergil's *res rusticae* are inimical to the *"res urbicae"* of the Latin satirists. For another, the purity of Vergil's much

acclaimed high style can only be muddied by infusions of their *genus humile.* For a third, his pedagogic approach is hardly apposite to the characteristic attitudes of the others. Of course, the satirists themselves vary: Martial treats the annoyances of city life with epigrammatic succinctness, while Juvenal castigates its vices with "savage indignation," and Horace is by turns indifferent towards and mildly annoyed with it.

The mercurial tones and intentions as well as the protean subjects that result from this practice can only perplex those hoping to find Gay's personal voice among the many in the poem. In fact, he conceals it so well behind the masks of his models that the reader is left only with many small reflections of him in the polish of *Trivia*'s couplets.[5] Furthermore, Gay's imitations are not random Latinisms, as Sherbo's article suggests, but precisely those Latin set-pieces most flogged by the pens of schoolboys and scribblers. In this he proves himself a stylistic virtuoso. The great stylist could, like Vergil, "raise" any subject no matter how intrinsically "low" to a high level of art, and "toss dung about with an air of gracefulness."[6] Gay was commended in his own time for this ability in terms of "invention" and "imagination" and the assumption of many that "scanty Subjects are the best Touchstones of Genius and Inspiration."[7] He revivifies the hackneyed themes and set-pieces of the poetry of his era, especially those drawn from the ancients because they were the most tired of all, and he numenizes, that is, makes wonderful, the most pedestrian subjects and events. Discussion of Gay's version of the most popular Latin set-pieces follows. I shall provide examples of his imitation of the style of each of the *auctores,* in their longer set-pieces (section I) and popular similes and anecdotes (section II), and I shall illustrate his synthesis of several allusions in one passage (section III).

I

To begin at the beginning, we might consider the proem of *Trivia* as an attempt to emulate Vergil. The proem of the *Georgics* provides a useful example of Vergil's characteristic style. He begins the *Georgics* with an air of unaffected dignity:

> Quid faciat laetas segetes, quo sidere terram
> vertere, Maecenas, ulmisque adiungere vites
> conveniat, quae cura boum, qui cultus
>   habendo
> sit pecori, apibus quanta experientia parcis,
> hinc canere incipiam.
>
> (1. 1-5)

(What makes the crops joyous, beneath what star,
Maecenas, it is well to turn the soil, and wed vines

to elms, what tending the kine need, what care the herd in breeding, what skill the thrifty bees—hence shall I begin my song.)

Dryden, whose translation of the *Georgics* helped establish its reputation and made it accessible to a wide audience, also taught readers to expect majestic verse from a georgic. To this end, he preserves the syntax of the original but "improves" the diction:

> What makes a plenteous Harvest, when to turn
> The fruitful Soil, and when to sowe the Corn;
> The Care of Sheep, of Oxen, and of Kine;
> And how to raise on Elms the teeming Vine:
> The Birth and Genius of the frugal Bee,
> I sing *Maecenas,* and I sing to thee.
>
> (1. 1-6)

Dryden does not tolerate a phrase as humble as *apibus quanta experientia parcis* ("how great the skill of the thrifty bees"); he amends this to "the Birth and Genius of the frugal Bee," which is elegant but misleading since Vergil does not trace the origin of bees, only the origin of their *mores.* "Plenteous Harvest," "fruitful Soil," and "teeming Vine" enhance the topics of Vergil with florid epithets—quite a liberty since Vergil, like most Latin poets, rarely used them.[8] It is a change in the direction of affectation, and Dryden's *Georgics* seem somewhat over-refined.

Gay's unassuming version,

> Through winter streets to steer your course
>   aright,
> How to walk clean by day, and safe by night,
> How jostling crouds, with prudence to decline,
> When to assert the wall, and when resign,
> I sing: Thou, *Trivia,* Goddess, aid my song . . .
>
> (1. 1-5)

comes closer to the lucid simplicity of Vergil's middle style. Yet Gay no less than Dryden shows by his diction that he is rising to the occasion. "Decline" and "assert" carry some of the force of their parent verbs in Latin (*adserere* is essentially a legal term meaning "to lay claim to as a slave," while *declinare* means "to shun"). Moreover, Gay's ability to shift from the middle to the high style by incorporating Latinisms is indicated by the different tones of a phrase like "to steer your course aright" and "with prudence to decline." The integration of such nuances gives *Trivia* the suppleness of the *Georgics* themselves, and testifies to Gay's attention to the variety as well as the harmony of his verse. These nuances also testify, on numerous occasions, to the originality of Gay's georgic. He is not dependent on Dryden for major assistance: the borrowing of single words, after all, is not so signifi-

cant when they are consistently used in ambitiously long adaptations of the *Georgics,* adaptations whose syntax and couplets are Gay's own.

Trivia's high burlesque skirts Dryden's high style, but Gay insures that the cheerful lameness of his topic will belie the lofty tone of the telling. Vergil's style endows Gay's burlesque of trivial subjects with the kind of "grave and serious air" that, according to Addison, gives the reader an extra measure of "agreeable entertainment."[9] For instance, in the five-line apostrophe to the muse of *Trivia,* a passage pendant to the argument, Gay makes something literal of one of Vergil's "grave and serious" metaphors from the corresponding 37-line passage of the *Georgics,* and this reduction to the absurd precipitates a cluster of witticisms about roads. In *Trivia, da facilem cursum* ("grant me a smooth course," I. 40) becomes:

> . . . Thou, *Trivia,* Goddess, aid my song,
> Thro' spacious streets conduct thy bard along;
> By thee transported, I securely stray
> Where winding alleys lead the doubtful way,
> The silent court, and op'ning square
>   explore,
> And long perplexing lanes untrod before.
>
> (1. 5-10)

Gay's version of the major set-piece of the *Georgics,* the so-called "praises of Italy" (2. 109-76), exhibits some of the finest qualities of the high burlesque of the era. Vergil's grand style at its most august commemorates the end of civil war and the advent of Augustus' *pax Romana.*[10] Augustan Italy is said to outvie marvels like Arabia's incense-bearing sand (*totaque turiferis Panchaia pinguis harenis,* 2. 138), and to be free of prodigies like the crop of men bristling with helmets and lances (*galeis densisque virum seges horruit hastis,* 2. 142). Though Gay tempers the loftiness of his diction somewhat by domesticating Vergil's exotic place-names and eschewing the marvelous, he achieves high seriousness by combining the pathetic style with personification:

> Not that I wander from my native home,
> And (tempting perils) foreign cities roam.
> Let *Paris* be the theme of *Gallia's* muse,
> Where slav'ry treads the street in wooden
>   shoes;
> Nor do I rove in *Belgia's* frozen clime,
> And teach the clumsy boor to skate in
>   rhyme . . .
> Let others *Naples'* smoother streets rehearse,
> And with proud *Roman* structures grace their
>   verse,
> Where frequent murders wake the night with
>   groans,
> And blood in purple torrents dies the stones;

Nor shall the Muse thro' narrow *Venice* stray,
Where *Gondolas* their painted oars display.
O happy streets, to rumbling wheels unknown,
No carts, no coaches shake the floating town!

(1. 83-100)

Gay's representation of Naples' predicament—shrieks in the night, rivers of blood—exploits the rumors circulated about that city for pathos, evoking sensations of pity and horror. Similarly, visions of intangible colossi—"slav'ry treads the street" or elsewhere "liberty and justice guard the land" (3. 150)—are sublime and evoke a sense of wonder as efficaciously as does the marvelous in "the praises of Italy."[11] Furthermore, the symmetry of the passage (two lines for Belgium and Paris, four for Naples and Venice), along with its perfectly uniform heroic couplets and extended periods, gives it a dignity comparable to Vergil's treatment and superior to versions of "the praises of Italy" in the occasional verse of the scribblers. At the same time, the concluding couplet raises a ridiculous question, and so re-establishes the burlesque.

In rendering the best known set-pieces of the Latin satirists, Gay is often at pains to follow a course opposite to that I have just outlined: he raises rather than lowers the tone of his source to suit the generally Vergilian cast of *Trivia*. For example, the epigram Martial addressed to his patron, Sparsus, contains a notable statement of the theme of *rus in urbe* ("the country in the town"). Gay anglicizes the passage and modifies it to suit the situation and pretensions of his own patron, the Earl of Burlington.

For Martial, to have "the country in the town" within the confines of a villa is the ultimate luxury of the rich:

tu, Sparse, nescis ista nec potes scire,
Petilianis delicatus in regnis,
cui plana summos despicit domus montis,
et rus in urbe est vinitorque Romanus
(nec in Falerno colle maior autumnus)
intraque limen latus essedo cursus,
et in profundo somnus et quies nullis
offensa linguis, nec dies nisi admissus.

(12.57. 18-25)

(You, Sparsus, know nothing of these things, and cannot know, luxurious as you are in your Petilian domain whose ground floor looks down on the hill tops, and where you have the country in the town, and a Roman for your vine-dresser—not on Falernian hills is there a greater crop—and within your boundary a broad drive for your curricle, and unfathomed depths of slumber, and a stillness broken by no tongues, and no daylight unless you let it in.)

The principal benefits of the country, those extolled in the Latin poetry of retirement (good food, ample shade, peaceful quiet), are artfully maintained at Sparsus' villa—in the midst of the din, glare, and mediocre provisions of an urban environment. A triumph of art, perhaps; but, from most other points of view, merely sensual.

Gay's oasis of the sensibility, the *locus amoenus* of Burlington House, stands in approximately the same relationship to the rest of London as the Petilian villa did to Rome. The *summum bonum* to which the arts are directed at Burlington House, however, is far more uplifting to the soul:

Yet *Burlington's* fair palace remains;
Beauty within, without proportion reigns.
Beneath his eye declining art revives,
The wall with animated picture lives;
There *Hendel* strikes the strings, the melting strain
Transports the soul, and thrills through ev'ry vein. . . .

(2. 493-8)

While the arts at the Petilian villa are ultimately enervating, those at Burlington House are stimulating. The greatest music of the era delights the ear, the finest Italian paintings the eye, and the punctiliously symmetrical architecture of Burlington's protégé, William Kent, the mind. Gay goes beyond traditional satire's facile antithesis of the city and the country to rhapsodize on the cultural advantages of urbanity itself. This attitude is actually perfectly attuned to Vergil's view of culture in the *Georgics*. To him the rightful domain of culture was the city, which became *"pulcherrima"* only by labor and art. To Gay, as to his patron and Vergil, the proper realization of *urbs* was not *rus* but the cultivation of *urbanitas*.

As Gay improves upon Martial's theme, so he improves on his style. By declining to imitate Martial's familiarity, his audacious opening reproach (*nescis ista nec potes scire*), and his colloquial interjections, Gay rises above the "low" style. Not for this protégé the guise of an iconoclastic vulgarian. Gay's compliment to his patron is remarkably free of impertinence. He confines himself to acknowledging merit where it is due; he praises the man by extolling the works he has collected and commissioned. His reference to Burlington is thus deferentially oblique; he uses a nominative and personification ("declining art revives") where Martial uses the vocative. The result is elegant and in keeping with the dignity of Vergil's allusions in the *Georgics* and elsewhere to Maecenas, his patron and afterwards the exemplar of patronage.

Gay's compliment is also free of fawning. Gay disdains to stoop to the boorish flattery of Martial, who exclaims something to the effect of "You do have a long driveway, Sparsus" (1. 23). His self-discipline in this regard—and certainly for a former draper's apprentice the restraint is remarkable—may be attributed to his silent avowal of the epicurean and stoical motto, *nil admirari,* of a spirit more kindred to his own than either Martial's or Vergil's. Like Gay, Horace shared a well-bred relationship with his patron; he knew his place but could impose on Augustus' good humor with grace. Hence the affectation of *nil admirari* in his satires, with its transparent complacency and easy scorn for obsequiousness. In a like manner, Gay, while deferring to Burlington, jests offhandedly when he condenses his gratitude for fifteen years' privilege of residence at Burlington House into the meiotic aside, "There oft' I enter (but with cleaner shoes)" (2. 499).

Horace's philosophical satire pervades *Trivia* to good comic effect, for Gay claims for his pedestrian a life of refined ease and moderation like that which Horace claims for himself. His cultivation of this satirist's characteristic style produces another series of those passages I have characterized as "beautifully flawed." Take, for example, Horace's saucy boast:

> Hoc ego commodius quam tu, praeclare
>   senator,
> milibus atque aliis vivo.
>   Quacumque libido est,
> incedo solus; percontor quanti holus ac far;
> fallacem Circum vespertinumque pererro
> saepe Forum; adsisto divinis. . . .
>   Haec est
> vita solutorum misera ambitione gravique;
> his me consolor victurum suavius ac si
> quaestor avus pater atque meus patruusque
>   fuissent.

> (In this and a thousand other ways I live in more comfort than you, illustrious senator. Wherever the fancy leads, I saunter forth alone. I ask the price of greens and flour; often toward evening I stroll round the cheating Circus and the Forum. . . . Such is the life of men set free from the burden of unhappy ambition. Thus I comfort myself with the thought that I shall live more happily than if my grandfather had been a quaestor, and my father and uncle likewise.)[12]

The epicurean side of Horace's philosophy shines through the smug irony of *commodius quam tu vivo:* Gay makes such assertions of complacency often, as when he enumerates the modest luxuries of the market-place, which afford the pedestrian kingly pleasures (2. 539-64).

Gay also extorts comic dues from the Horatian stoicism typical of the English Augustans, who claimed to prefer the tranquility and liberty of anonymity to fame. For example, he scorns with the vituperation of Juvenal seven wretches who sacrificed their self-respect to ambition but concludes:

> If purchas'd at so mean, so dear a rate;
> O rather give me sweet content on foot,
> Wrapt in my virtue, and a good *Surtout!*
>   (2. 588-90) .

This image of a Malvolio flouncing self-righteously off the stage with a sweep of his cloak is a perversely witty paraphrase of Horace's

> . . . resigno quae dedit et mea
> virtute me involvo probamque
>   Pauperiem sine dote quaero.

> (I renounce her [Fortune's] gifts, enwrap me in my virtue, and woo honest Poverty, undowered though she be.)[13]

This whimsical yoking of virtue and a surtout, of Horace and Juvenal, and of *Trivia's* concerns with those of the twenty-ninth ode of the third book, ends Book II, and leaves us with a ridiculous image of the priggishness of the bourgeois stoic.

Though Gay's verse is most at ease with sentiments of this sort, the poet also tries his hand at rendering the celebrated *saeva indignatio* of Juvenal. With Juvenal's account of the cruelty of bullies from the third satire in mind, Gay tells, among other vicious pranks, how the scowrers murdered a matron by rolling her down Snow Hill in a barrel (3. 321-34). This urban atrocity lends *Trivia* tones as somber as those in Vergil's description of a plague in the *Georgics.*

In general, however, Gay only pretends to the virulence of Juvenal in order to strike poses of comic severity. After all, the lighter vein of Juvenal's raillery, as when he upbraids the conspicuously unearned affluence of the parasites and flatterers of Rome, is better suited to *Trivia.* Juvenal's lawyer Matho rides in specious glory, elevated in his sedan chair above trudging poets of principle:

> . . . nam quis iniquae
> tam patiens urbis, tam ferreus, ut teneat se,
> causidici nova cum veniat lectica Mathonis
> plena ipso . . .
>   (1. 30-3)

> (For who can be so tolerant of this monstrous city, who so iron of soul, as to contain himself when the

brand-new litter of lawyer Matho comes along, filled
with his huge self . . .)

Ever the guardian of the class consciousness of his
patrons, even in regard to the dispensation of charity,
Gay impugns the *nouveaux riches* and the misers recently risen from the back alleys of London:

> The tricking gamester insolently rides,
> With *Loves* and *Graces* on his chariot's sides;
> In sawcy state the griping broker sits,
> And laughs at honesty and trudging wits. . . .
>   (1. 115-8)

Though he himself was surely the most pampered protégé of his age (despite his grumblings about Queen
Caroline's slighting him), Gay cannot resist a reference to "trudging wits," a reference which recalls Juvenal's delightfully clever stance of mawkish self-pity
in *Satura* I. One must also recognize that resonances
of Juvenal in matters of morality give Gay's judgments
the proverbial universality of statement found in English Augustan satire. Gay has little sympathy for the
devils of a modern economy and implies that those
who profit above their station have always had the
scorn of honest satire.

In his satiric attacks on the mediocre poetry characteristic of the "trudging wits" of Grub Street, those who
might naively scribble a line like "Wrapp'd in my virtue, and a good *Surtout!*," Gay chose to fight fire with
fire, and this meant that later generations thought his
blaze was like his fuel, small, and dubbed him a "poet
of a lower order." Satirists have always been liable to
the imputation that the matter of their verse confines
their works to the category of *misera carmina,* songs
of the humble, domestic, personal sphere.

Perhaps the principal way in which Gay's art transcends imputations of this kind is through his genius
for the "fairy way of writing." The ability to create
supernatural figures has not recently been considered
as a chief accomplishment of Gay's; and yet it may
well be. After all, Addison's revolutionary statement
of the aesthetic of fanciful writing (*Spectator* 411-21)
antedates the first edition of *Trivia* by four years, and
Gay's chief addition to the second edition (1720) is
another myth. Moreover, the classical poet who was
most valued for his accomplishments in this style, Ovid,
was Gay's most frequent model throughout his career;
critics of the late eighteenth century, in fact, faulted
him for being excessively Ovidian.[14]

Gay consistently chooses the example of Ovid, even
over Vergil, when he wants to delineate the passions
or fabricate a myth. As a result, his Ovidian supernatural machinery gilds prosaic London with enchanting
numina as affecting and thought-provoking in their way

as Collins's and Gray's. At the same time, these myths
are inspired, technically speaking, by the somber Aristaeus *epillion* of the fourth *Georgic.*[15] *Trivia*'s versions,
consequently, benefit considerably from a little amorous levity from Ovid.

Trivia's myths (properly *aitia,* or origin myths) would
be at home among the fanciful love stories of the
Metamorphoses because in both works, when a deity
spies a comely mortal, love and inventions follow. In
Trivia, the gods' intervention on earth produces two of
the most unexceptional features of London street life,
the patten and the bootblack. The success of Vulcan's
courtship of Patty is less dependent on the marvelous
than on the advice of Ovid's witty guide to wooing,
the *Ars Amatoria.* As that guide predicts, Patty enjoys
Vulcan's blandishments and wears his presents. Presents given to humor an ailing lover are said to be the
most seductive; hence, the patten that saves Patty from
rheum-inducing mud wins Vulcan's suit. Gay's explanations follow Ovid's own, and he captures Ovid's
gently insidious tone by incorporating a truism like
*delectant etiam castas praeconia formae; / virginibus
curae grataque forma sua est* (1. 623-4).[16] Thus, with
Ovid in hand, Gay satisfies the formal dictates of the
aition and transforms the Vergilian myth in the process: he derives the lowly patten from Patty's name in
an amorous myth domesticated to suit the commonness
of his matter.

Gay's modification of Vergil's Aristaeus *epillion* in
the second edition of *Trivia* takes greater liberties with
the *aition,* going beyond Vergil's diminution of the
epic to an *epillion* to undercut even the sobriety of
this. The result is a "mock-epillion," not a mock-epic,
for the emphasis is clearly on the supernatural rather
than the human level of the action—something that
would not occur in epics and their burlesque counterparts. Although *Trivia*'s burlesque *epillion* concerns
the origin of the bootblack and contributes a host of
classical deities to watch over "happy Augusta," its
principal deity is a comic goddess of the sewers. Cloacina had had a shrine in the Roman Forum and had
graced Roman coins, for, humble though her province
was, she represented Rome's major feat of technology:
a monumentally complex drainage and sewage system.
Although Gay would have had access to the conventional iconographic representation of Cloacina on antique coins—especially given the fact that such coins
were the major representatives of the Roman pictorial
tradition at the time—Gay makes of her a comic grotesque:

> With wither'd turnip tops her temples
>   crown'd;
> Low reach'd her dripping tresses, lank, and
>   black
> As the smooth jet, or glossy raven's back;
> Around her waste a circling eel was twin'd,

Which bound her robe that hung in rags
  behind.

(2. 196-200)

The bard of the streets brings Cloacina's attributes more into line with her sphere of operation in London's common-shores and her rank in the vulgar echelon of deities. Her attributes, turnips and eels, mimic the grand baroque ones assigned by Cesare Ripa to the deities in his authoritative *Iconologia*—thunderbolts, spears, and so forth. Much as the fashions of love at court filtered down to the society of valets and ladies' maids, Cloacina imitates her "betters," Vulcan and Vergil's Cyrene, the dignified water spirit who won the favor of Apollo and bore the demigod, Aristaeus, by him. Cloacina pursues her beloved scavenger in the guise of a cinder wench.

The diminution and domestication of the Aristaeus *epillion,* moreover, is perfectly consistent with rococo spoofs of baroque treatments of myths. For every baroque allegory of the arts in which a handsome Apollo holds court among the muses (e.g., Nicolas Poussin's), a rococo version portrays a peevish cupid in his place being mollified by his mother, *deshabillée* (e.g., Watteau's). Likewise, in place of the matronly compassion of a baroque Cyrene for the dolorous lamentations of Aristaeus, and her exhortations to him to ply his "art" in Dryden's translation of the *Georgics, Trivia* shows us the bastard bootblack muttering his complaints to the muddy waters of his mother's commonshore as well as her comic efforts to secure him a suitable "art" from the gods.

The distinction between the baroque mode and the rococo, between Dryden and Gay's georgics, is the difference between high tone and *bon ton.* Works possessing the former, akin as it is to the heroic mode, inspire awe and encourage virtue; works having the latter, witty and irreverent as they are, chiefly amuse. The difference is also that between the *Georgics* and the *Metamorphoses,* which has itself been called a mock-georgic. For example, while Aristaeus wins his boon only after a herculean struggle with Proteus in the *Georgics,* in the *Metamorphoses* and in *Trivia* the gods dispense their favors liberally. Thus Diana, Neptune, and Vulcan, as they fostered the fortunes of many a shepherd in the *Metamorphoses,* become protectors of a humble bootblack in *Trivia:*

Each Power contributes to relieve the poor:
With the strong bristles of the mighty boar
Diana forms his brush; the God of day
A tripod gives, amid the crouded way
To raise the dirty foot, and ease his toil;
Kind *Neptune* fills his vase with fetid oil
Prest from th'enormous whale; The God of
  fire,

From whose dominions smoaky clouds
  aspire,
Among these gen'rous presents joins his part,
And aids with soot the new japanning art. . . .

(2. 157-66)

As always, Gay's whimsical sense of decorum is delightful, and the periphrasis of "japanning art" for a shoeshine is a winning stroke of wit.

II

The skittish wit of *Trivia,* now high burlesque and now low, at worst produces a discursive and episodic structure, and at best affords an engaging succession of pleasantries. After all, an equal emphasis on the effectiveness of the parts of a work can be a virtue rather than a fault when it is expressive of variety (*varietas*) and contributes to a general refinement of execution. In any event, one ought not to expect too much formal unity from *Trivia* because, as I have said (n. 3), georgics are inherently miscellaneous and satire is generically a hodge-podge.

In his mock-georgic Gay, instead of building up to a sublime stroke, chooses to entertain us with many small surprises. For this reason, juxtaposition governs the order both of long and short set-pieces. Having already discussed the long adaptations, I will now turn to the small ones. The snippets of didacticism from Vergil and Martial, the mock-heroic similes and short bathetic parodies not only break the flow of the narration but also stand out from it in defiant whimsicality. Each allusion is meant to be recognized. Dryden once said, "to copy the best authors is a kind of praise"; in this way, Gay pays homage to the *auctores* and his contemporaries alike by giving them cameo roles to play in *Trivia.*

Gay's adaptations of Vergil's omens have the quality of propriety about them. Like Gay, Vergil adapted his technical sources selectively, disclaiming responsibility for the whole body of horticultural lore with the explanation, *non ego cuncta meis amplecti versibus opto* ("not mine the wish to embrace all the theme with my song"). For example, from Aratus' *Phenomena,* a dry and exhaustive compendium of astronomical lore, Vergil selected a few promising weather signs, some already recognized as mere superstitions in his own time—but imaginative enough to merit poetic treatment. He improves on Aratus' prosaic omen of the lamp:[17]

ne nocturna quidem carpentes pensa puellae
nescivere hiemem, testa cum ardente viderent
scintillare oleum et putris concrescere fungos.

(1. 390-2)

(Even at night, maidens that spin their tasks have
not failed to mark a storm as they saw the oil
sputter in the blazing lamp, and a mouldy fungus
gather on the wick.)

Vergil not only creates a genre scene, he enhances the
images in an exceptional way, exceptional because vivid
epithets are rare. He changes plain "snuff" to "mouldy
snuff" and plain "lamp" to "blazing lamp." In his version of the prognostication, Gay uses precisely the same
technique: "E're winter sheds her snow, or frosts con-
geal, / You'll see the coals in brighter flame aspire, /
And sulphur tinge with blue the rising fire. . . ." (1.
134-6). That is, he uses a verbal, "rising," to lend
movement to a noun, just as Vergil did with *ardente*.
He also preserves the Latin connotations of *aspirare*
("to climb up, exhale") to enhance his image of burning coal. He advances the passage another step in the
direction of vividness by changing to the vocative,
"you'll see. . . ." Gay thus achieves in miniature a
delightfully absurd imitation of the *Georgics*.

Martial's epigrams also lend themselves to such cam-
eo-like effects. The short epigrams, particularly those
of Books XIII and XIV, arrest the reader's attention
with their insistent imperatives. Since they are in the
nature of labels for articles of merchandise, they admirably suit the commercial atmosphere of the street
scenes in *Trivia,* populated as they are by vendors of
all sorts. For instance, Gay's "True *Witney* broad-cloth
with its shag unshorn, / Unpierc'd is in the lasting
tempest worn" (1. 47-8) is at face value a precise delineation of a type of cloth. Yet the curious phrasing of
"shag unshorn" marks it as one of Martial's epigrams,
his "Laena":

tempora brumali non multum levia prosunt:
calfaciunt villi pallia vestra mei.

(14. 136)

(In the winter season smooth coverings do not much
avail: my shaggy hair makes warm your outer
garment.)

Trivia is studded with such epigrammatic gems as
Martial's *villi mei.*

The index singles out these imitations in miniature
rather than the long set-pieces so that the reader may
know how much the poet congratulates himself on the
aptness of his allusions while being capable of measuring out only pipkins of wit. Many of the entries refer
to figures from the *Metamorphoses* familiar to the
grammar schoolboys of the time: Scylla and Charyb-
dis, Theseus, Glaucus, Phaeton, and Orpheus. Others,
like the references to Pythagoras and Oedipus drawn
from Vergil and Sophocles, show the poet's pretensions to Latin learning and a knowledge of the Greeks.

Gay uses his Ovidian similes primarily for high burlesque. They clash with their lowly topics, and make
him seem the overgrown schoolboy for attempting such
dubious analogies. For example, a periwig drooping
with rain is like the snakey tresses of Alecto when
charmed by Orpheus and also like the merman's beard
in Book XIII of the *Metamorphoses:*

. . . thus hung *Glaucus'* beard, with briny dew
Clotted and strait, when first his am'rous view
Surpriz'd the bathing fair; the frighted maid
Now stands a rock, transform'd by *Circe*'s
aid.

(1. 205-8)

Here Gay incorporates the two main elements of Ovid's
poetry, metamorphosis and *amor,* to grace a reference
to a soggy periwig; even the dullest reader could catch
the humor of this impropriety.

More obscure and more bathetic is Gay's version of
the classical age's "original sin." According to Epicurus' theory of the four ages of history, the contentment
of agricultural man was disrupted when the first sailor
took ship and brought home corrupting luxuries. It is
an event as auspicious as Prometheus' gift of fire to
man, and so Horace, in the third ode of the first book,
muses on the first hero in this fashion:

illi robur et aes triplex
　　circa pectus erat, qui fragilem truci
commisit pelago ratem
　　primus, nec timuit praecipitem Africum

decertantem Aquilonibus . . .
quem mortis timuit gradum,
　　qui siccis oculis monstra natantia,
qui vidit mare turbidum . . .

(ll. 9-19)

(Oak and triple bronze must have girt the breast of
him who first committed his frail bark to the angry
sea, and who feared not the furious southwest wind
battling with the blasts of the north . . . What form
of Death's approach feared he who with dry eyes
gazed on the swimming monsters, on the stormy
sea . . .)

Gay surrounds his ludicrous version of the passage
with a foil of mundane verse, the better to juxtapose
nonsense with sense. Ten lines of information about
oyster bars lead the reader into the following luxurious
nonsense:

The man had sure a palate cover'd o'er
With brass or steel, that on the rocky shore
First broke the oozy oyster's pearly coat

And risqu'd the living morsel down his
throat.[18]

Gay undoubtedly delighted in the knowledge that this
passage would be censured by the naive as an outrageous Jacobean conceit. To the educated ear, the pre-
ciousness of the bathos and the cloying showiness of
a phrase like "the oozy oyster's pearly coat" would
double the pleasure of the jest.

III

Despite the skill with which Gay imitates single authors, he is most splendid when managing a complex
synthesis of several authors, as in the opening of Book
II of *Trivia.* Here he combines ancients with moderns,
paying homage to his friend Swift's *A Description of
a Morning* (1711), the *Spectator,* Martial, and Vergil.[19]
Because this passage is rather long, I would prefer to
discuss Gay's skill at such syntheses with an example
more succinct and illustrative of the cunning tension
of these "hodge-podges," *Trivia*'s citified version of
Groundhog Day. Here Gay expostulates on an old
maxim of Latin doggerel concerning the prognosti-
cating power of St. Paul's festival. The medieval
quatrain has the forceful and mnemonic simplicity of
those Latin rhythms determined by stress rather than
quantity:

clara dies Pauli bona tempora denotat anni
si nix vel pluvia, designat tempora cara;
si fiant nebulae, pereunt animalia quaeque;
si fiant venti, sedignat praelia [sic] genti.

(If the day of Paul be clear, it designates good
weather for the year; if there is snow or rain, it
indicates bad weather; if there are clouds, all animals
will perish; if there are winds, it means wars for
man.)[20]

William Chambers says that these "monkish" verses
are found very frequently in medieval manuscripts; Gay
could have learned them in Latin class.[21]

In any event, in one of his customary cock-eyed associations, Gay links *dies Pauli* with Luna of the *Georgics:*

Si vero solem ad rapidum lunasque
sequentis
ordine respicies, numquam te crastina fallet
hora neque insidiis noctis capiere serenae.
luna revertentis cum primum colligit ignis,
si nigrum obscuro comprenderit aëra cornu,
maximus agricolis pelagoque parabitur imber:
at si virgineum suffuderit ore ruborem,
ventus erit; vento semper rubet aurea Phoebe.

(1. 424-31)

(But if you pay heed to the swift sun and the moons,
as they follow in order, never will to-morrow's hour
cheat you, nor will you be ensnared by a cloudless
night. Soon as the moon gathers her returning fires,
if she encloses a dark mist within dim horns, a heavy
rain is awaiting farmers and seamen. But if over her
face she spreads a maiden blush, there will be wind;
as wind rises, golden Phoebe ever blushes.)

The combination is the more daring for the yoking of
incongruous meters, mythologies (the pagan and the
Christian), and qualities of verse. On behalf of tasteless eclecticism, Gay sacrifices no allusiveness and
allows resonances of the humble and the great to coexist in disarming harmony:

How, if the festival of *Paul* be clear,
Plenty from lib'ral horn shall strow the year;
When the dark skies dissolve in snow or rain,
The lab'ring hind shall yoke the steer in vain;
But if the threat'ning winds in tempests roar,
Then war shall bathe her wasteful sword in
    gore.

(1. 177-82)

The opening line captures some of the asperity of the
doggerel's *clara dies Pauli,* but the rest is eighteenth-
century opulence. The first of Gay's improvements on
the original is perhaps the most ambitious, plain *bona
tempora denotat anni* being wrought into "Plenty from
lib'ral horn shall strow the year." Here Gay has introduced a third allusion: he imports an Horatian figure,
so that the voice of the *auctor* may be juxtaposed with
that of the "monk," and by succeeding him, pleasantly
surprise. The reader recalls Horace's

. . . hic tibi copia
manabit ad plenum benigno
ruris honorum opulenta cornu.

(In this spot shall rich abundance of the glories of
the field flow to the full for thee from bounteous
horn.)[22]

The line's pictorial features appeal to the reader's
imagination. *Benigno cornu,* accurately rendered as
"lib'ral horn," is the major attribute of the iconographic figure of Plenty. Given the name and an attribute, a
reader trained in "the pleasures of the imagination"
could visualize Plenty, probably in a standard pose from
mythological or historical painting.

Pereunt animalia quaeque provides the occasion for a
different sort of picture. The blunt Latin phrase, by a
process of association, recalls an image of the plague
from Book III of the *Georgics* to the "chemick fancy"
of the poet:

. . . it tristis arator,
maerentem abiungens fraterna morte iuvencum,
atque opere in medio defixa relinquit aratra.

(3. 517-9)

(Sadly goes the plowman, unyokes the steer that sorrows for his brother's death, and amid its half-done task leaves the share rooted fast.)

Like Vergil's hind, Gay's has yoked his steer in vain. The bard of the streets was not about to neglect one of Vergil's most pathetic images.

The result of the combination of the doggerel, Vergil, and Horace is at once pictorial and auditory. The effect on the ear is like four-part harmony, all the subordinate voices adding nuances to the melody line, the part of Gay. The synthesis also illustrates the grace and proficiency with which Gay gives order to a chaotic variety of sources, making the tension of the parts the strength of the piece.

With so thorough a mastery of long and short imitations, of close paraphrases and ludicrous distortions, and of ingenious syntheses, Gay's allegedly homely *olio* exceeds expectations. We are not taught the lessons we expected to hear; we learn to love good poetry instead, because we cannot help admiring Gay at his best and deploring his victims' worst. Gay's satire has the vitality Dryden demanded from satirists—and none of the faults he deplored: the "perpetual dearth of wit" and the "barrenness of good sense and entertainment." The main ingredient in Dryden's recipe for a good satire, "entertainment," is ultimately Gay's. The elegance, vigor, scholarship, and good humor with which Gay manages his complex synthesis make him an exemplar of humanistic poetics and give the lie to the poem's apologetic motto: Gay is not *indocte* and his poem is not a *miserum carmen*. **Trivia** is a highly successful exercise in the art of classical allusion.

Notes

[1] For a discussion of *Trivia*'s affinities with Opposition politics as well, see Isaac Kramnick's *Bolingbroke and His Circle* (1968), pp. 226-7.

[2] I consider this motto a particularly brilliant éclat of Gay's wit since the lines (*Eclogues* 3.26-7) are quoted by Dryden in *A Discourse Concerning the Original and Progress of Satire* (1693) as an example of Vergil's ability to write sharper satires than either Juvenal or Horace (*Of Dramatic Poesy and Other Critical Essays*, II, 131; hereafter *ODP*) because Vergil here lashes the proverbial bad poet. The allusiveness of the reference to a dunce (*indocte*) ought not to be lost on us either, given the Scriblerians' creation of Martinus Scriblerus and the *Dunciad*. The translation of the Latin

is H. Rushton Fairclough's (Loeb Classical Library, London, 1967). All translations from the Latin are from Loeb Library editions, unless otherwise stated. The edition of Gay's *Trivia* used in this paper is *The Poetical Works of John Gay,* ed. G. C. Faber (London, 1926).

[3] As Robert Ogilvie points out in *Latin and Greek: A History of the Influence of the Classics on English Life from 1600 to 1918* (1964), at the time Gay was in school and during his early career, Petronius, Catullus, Tibullus, and Propertius were not much read, hardly translated. Aside from the appearance of Catullus, Tibullus, and Propertius in *Miscellaneous Poems and Translations* (Oxford, 1686), there were only three other editions of Catullus (1707, 1719, 1795), three of Tibullus (1720, 1759, 1792), and one of Propertius (1782). There were two editions of Petronius, one of them reprinted four times. The "major" poets, on the other hand, were frequently translated, and those translations were reprinted several times. Thomas Creech's *Odes, Satyres and Epistles of Horace* (1684) appeared in print six times before 1730, and this was only one of six translations of these works on the market. *The New Cambridge Bibliography of English Literature,* Volume 2, lists more than eighty printings of Horace, some fifty of Ovid, seventeen of Juvenal, and twelve of Martial. Though it passes over Gay, Howard D. Weinbrot's *The Formal Strain: Studies in Augustan Imitation and Satire* (Chicago, 1969) is a useful study of the imitation of the classics.

[4] Dryden, in fact, takes pains to defend the cause of thematic unity in satire, as he rebuts the accepted definitions: "the very word *satura* signifies a dish plentifully stored with all variety of fruites and grains" (*ODP* 2.145); "And if variety be of absolute necessity in every one of them [satires], according to the etymology of the word" (*ODP* 2.146); "that *olla,* or hotchpotch, which is properly a satire" (*ODP* 2.146).

[5] I disagree with Sherbo's conclusions about the references in the index to *Trivia*. I do not believe "author" and "walker" refer to different persons, for I take the citations in the index to be comic—and hence unreliable. Gay fills the index with synonyms to achieve a false image of variety and to intimate the compiler's pedantry. The absurdly wide variety of references seems to me a parody of variorum machinery, much like that of the *Dunciad Variorum* and other Scriblerian parodies of ridiculous scholarship.

[6] Addison's compliment to Vergil's skill appears in the "Essay on Virgil's Georgics," which prefaced Dryden's translation of 1697.

[7] This aesthetic commonplace appears in the preface to Joseph Mitchell's *The Shoe-Heel: A Rhapsody* (1727). The passage is worth quoting in full since Mitchell's

defense of burlesque poetry is much like those now current (e.g., de Sola Pinto, *The Common Muse*)—particularly in cases where we deplore the motives of the poet:

> It must be own'd, that to raise Flowers and Fruits on a barren soil, requires a masterly Skill: Every Poet is not equal to such an arduous Task. One might describe the *Seasons,* and Sing of *Heroes,* not amiss, who yet cou'd not make any Thing of a *Shilling,* or a *Shoe-Heel.* Had Boileau never sung the *Lutrin,* Pope a *Lock of Hair,* and Garth the *Dispensary,* perhaps the World had never bestow'd on them that Applause, which they are now deservedly possessed of. Imagination and Invention are the Soul of Poetry; and scanty Subjects are the best Touchstones of Genius and Inspiration.

[8] L. P. Wilkinson, *The Georgics of Virgil: A Critical Survey* (Cambridge, England, 1969), p. 9.

[9] Addison [or William Somerville?], "Preface," *Hobbinol, or the Rural Games* (1740).

[10] Wilkinson describes the historical context of the *Georgics, c.* 89 B.C., as a "wave of popular enthusiasm heightened to hysteria by relief at the final end of twenty years of the civil wars" (*loc. cit.,* p. 163).

[11] We may also compare the sublimity of this poetic device to the grand manner of Sir James Thornhill's heroical wall paintings of the same period. In the mural programs at the Royal Naval College, Greenwich, for example, personifications of national virtues join with deities from classical mythology, British worthies, and the reigning monarchs, to celebrate Britannia's glory.

[12] Horace, "Satires" 1.6.110-4, 128-31, *Satires, Epistles, Ars Poetica* (London: Loeb Library, 1926), tr. H. Rushton Fairclough.

[13] Horace, "Odes" 3.29.54-6, *The Odes and Epodes* (London: Loeb Library, 1927), tr. C. E. Bennett.

[14] Ovid's *Metamorphoses* had provided seventeenth-century schoolboys like Gay with their main excursion into ancient mythology and the fabulous, and they retained their fondness for him as adults. Dryden, for example, said of Ovid that he was "certainly more palatable to the reader than any of the Roman wits" ("To the Right Honourable My Lord Radcliffe," *ODP* 2.163).

[15] An *aition* is a myth which accounts for the origin of some art or article. *Epillion* means "little epic," and in the *Georgics* it is the form given to the *aition* of the "Bugonian method" of restoring beehives. Aristaeus' bees die because he caused Euridice's death. His mother Cyrene has him sacrifice a cow, and soon after, a bee-like insect's larvae hatch. Although in the *Aeneid* Vergil

has Orpheus bring Euridice safely out of hell, she dies in the *Georgics.* Wilkinson points out that, just as the bees die because of Aristaeus' lust, so normal intercourse is made to seem debilitating in the *Georgics.*

[16] Similarly, Gay's "tho' flatt'ry fail, / Presents with female virtue must prevail" renders Ovid's

> Vere prius volucres taceant, aestate cicadae,
> Maenalius lepori det sua terga canis,
> Femina quam iuveni blande temptata repugnet:
> Haec quoque, quam poteris credere nolle,
>   volet.
>
>   (1. 271-4)

> (Sooner would birds be silent in spring, or grasshoppers in summer, or the hound of Menalus flee before the hare, than a woman persuasively wooed resist a lover: nay, even she, whom you think cruel, will be kind.)

The imputation that Patty's virtue is bought is also in perfect keeping with the philosophy of the *Ars Amatoria.*

[17] Wilkinson translates Aratus' version (*Phenomena,* ll. 976 ff.) in this way: "If on a misty night snuff gathers on the nozzle of a lamp; or if in winter its flame now rises steadily, now emits sparks like light bubbles in rapid succession . . ." (p. 186).

[18] *Trivia* 3. 195-8. For this and other borrowings from Horace, see Caroline Goad's *Horace in the English Literature of the Eighteenth Century* (New Haven, 1918).

[19] Just as Gay admits in the poem's advertisement that the idea for *Trivia* came from Swift, so he honors his friend in the text by beginning Book II with images reminiscent of *A Description of a Morning* (1711). Gay "vergilianizes" these images by borrowing from Vergil's "O fortunatos" set-piece (*Georgics* 2. 458-68). The image of the drummers sounds suspiciously like that of *Spectator* 364, as W. H. Williams points out in the annotations to his 1922 edition of *Trivia.* Gay may also owe a debt to Martial's epigram on a Roman morning (12.57) and to Horace's schoolboys (*Satires* 1.6.74).

[20] This translation is my own. Chambers discusses the festival in Vol. I, 157, of *The Book of Days* (London, 1864). Another translation may be found in Williams.

[21] The verses appear, for example, in Thomas Hunt's *Abecedarium scholasticum: or the grammar-scholars abecedary* (1671). Here they are incorporated, in an English version, in a longer entry for Januarius (p. 78):

If Saint *Paul* be fair and clear,
It betides an happy year:
If the winds do blow aloft,
Then wars shall vex the Realm full oft;
And if it chance to snow or rain,
Then dear shall be all kinds of grain.

[22] Horace, "Odes" 1.17.14-16 in *The Odes and Epodes.*
Goad suggests other possible sources as well (p. 121).

Charles E. Beckwith (essay date 1986)

SOURCE: "The Languages of Gay's *Trivia,*" *Eighteenth-Century Life,* Vol. X, No. 3, October, 1986, pp. 27-43.

[*In the following essay, Beckwith considers the classical antecedents of Gay's* Trivia, *including Virgil's* Georgics, *to explicate Gay's "mock" effects. Beckwith finds that despite its pointed satire, the poem's mock tone makes possible an overall sense of positivity about the dynamic nature of city life.*]

> You can deny, if you like, nearly all abstractions: justice, beauty, truth, goodness, mind, God. You can deny seriousness, but not play.
>
> Johan Huizinga

In Gay's *Trivia* (1716; II, 99-220 added in *Poems on Several Occasions,* 1720) a number of possible "meanings"—mock georgic, satire, moral didacticism, straight reportage of journalism, pastoral yearnings, apocalyptic vision—have attracted one reader or another;[1] but I think it might better be read as a game of languages, that is a game with meaning itself. Such a way of reading has the initial advantage of equalizing the lines of the poem at one starting point, so that we will not be too readily seduced by heightened or apparently insistent statements, or those that seem to cluster around some theme, or the literal and predicative; and mock work is especially susceptible to such seduction toward atomistic treatment. We get the hang of the work right away, begin to ask what lies beyond the joke, and fix on what appear to be thematic lines, spots of density, or other pointers—ignoring their modifying context.

A characterizing remark about mock pastoral (by Martin Price in *To the Palace of Wisdom*) reminds us that

> the mock form cuts both ways: if it protects the "pastoral vision" from a misguided literalism, it also convicts the pastoral forms of a high-minded vacuity by offering a world of robust energy.[2]

Each side in this face-off, each valid yet wanting, forces on the other a context the other would prefer to do without; each reveals some absurdity in the other. Yet in some larger view, or reality, they complete one another, though their absurdities remain absurdities. Their forced joining is at once significant and inescapably comic, all ragged and compromised as it is: a natural metaphor for experience or life itself.

The joining, and the metaphor, occur in the listener's mind; the joke itself is discursive, one side presenting its case, the other then undercutting it. But jokes are characteristically brief, economical, and above all strategic; even in their discursiveness they suggest simultaneity. This would suggest the pun as the ideal joke-structure; and if we can escape the trap of sound alone we can discover or invent what amounts to complex puns of situations, or values, or realities. The result, among other things, is to patch an inherent flaw in the joke-structure, its necessary discursiveness or chronology. The mind joins the first and second parts of a joke-pun and adjusts the incompleteness of each part in light of the other.

Mock work advances in such ways too. In **"Friday"** of **The Shepherd's Week** Gay provides an example which also shows his very great skill and tact in the management of tones so important to this kind of operation. He describes the death and obsequies of Blouzelinda the country wench with surprising leisure and attention to pathetic circumstance; it is only after some forty lines of a genuinely touching scene that he returns to the mock. And the return itself is not abrupt. He eases back with a few lines of graceful transition:

> With wicker Rods we fenc'd her Tomb
>   around,
> To ward from Man and Beast the hallow'd
>   Ground,
> Lest her new Grave the Parson's Cattle raze,
> For both his Horse and Cow the Church-yard
>   graze.[3]
>
>   (ll. 145-48)

This is charming and funny; and it is, if we will, an undercut. But it equally illustrates the blend of tones, and of realities, that mock work can effect beyond the typical joke structure. And through such devices as ambiguity, allusion, calculated word choice ("Beast"), ironic tone, reticence, insinuation, the mock work can achieve lines, passages, ultimately whole pieces, simultaneously mock and not-mock. In this way it moves on from the more mechanical two-part "similic" structure of the discursive joke form toward something like real metaphor in the text itself.

All this may be simply one way of redescribing that quality of double-saying so well known in Gay. Throughout *Trivia* he has a manner of regularly infusing into moods, tones, and references a light tinge of excess, deficiency, indecorum or other distortion, giving the whole a subdued running effect of the uncertain and the quizzical. Empson described one of his types of ambiguity as an outward sign that the mind of the poet was making itself up on the spot.[4] This shifting, off-center touch of Gay's insinuates a sense of theme being questioned, variegated, and so continually re-created, on the spot. The constant slight modulation of tone induces a sense that something additional and tangential is being suggested. It is inconclusive and teasing, as such *silex scintillans* would naturally be. Indeed we could call it part of the mock-maneuver to play upon the reader's or (even more) the critic's susceptibilities, enticing him to try conclusions about the work that the whole work will not support, since it is likely to be subverting them somewhere else. The key, if there is one, to the "meaning" of *Trivia,* if it has one, lies rather, I think, in the relation of its other-saying levels to the more evident substantive—the literal and predicative—body of the poem.

For such a distinction we usually bring in terms like "style" and "rhetoric," "tone" and "gesture," "device." But in their effect they function as greater and lesser languages. If all stylistic elements affect meaning, they all make meaning; and the meaning they make is more often than not likely to be inconsistent in some way and degree with the literal meaning. This typically happens in all poetry, of course, but in poetic mock work it assumes a special importance. The initial face-off that mock is suggests right away the idea of mutual ironic scrutiny, which in turn suggests that all positions, points of view, assumptions of value might be up for scrutiny in the ensuing work. Then if a mind like Gay's falls upon such considerations, a range of variety in mock, mock upon mock, mock and not-mock intertwined and interchanged, can emerge. *The Shepherd's Week* and *Rural Sports* disclose some odd features of that interesting and undervalued mind: a fascination with the relation between literary forms and the realities they are presumed to represent (as in *Rural Sports* where we may be unsure whether he is looking at the scenery or periphrasing the *Georgics*—no doubt both, but he has taken pains to tell us that he is *in* the country *and* with a copy of the *Georgics*); a companion fascination with the relation between language and physical detail; at the same time a very great alertness, a hyper-alertness, to physical detail in itself, I think beyond that of any other Augustan poet; a cautionary awareness of the absolute difference between physical detail and language, language forms, literary forms; yet a sense of the pressure, the seductiveness, so to call it the gravitational pull, of physical detail. Add to this a sense of delicacy and featness, again beyond that of any other Augustan poet, this time excepting Pope; an attuned and attunable ear; and that so-humorous and quizzical imagination variously evident in *Rural Sports* and much more in *The Shepherd's Week.*

Such a mind is capable of turning everything into an array of languages, while withholding commitment from all of them. Gay was also heir to a social and cultural sense of language variability, as well as more specifically to several categories of language in the more traditional senses when he came to the writing of *Trivia.*

Not many studies have been made of the words in *Trivia,* however, either by themselves or in relation to their contexts; and those that have do not pursue the matter anything like as far as the poem will bear. One suggestive study, the best of its kind that I know ("Virgil, Dryden, Gay and Matters Trivial," by Arthur Sherbo, *PMLA* 85 [1970]: 1063-71), resurrects a useful figure: since a great many of Gay's words, it reminds us, derive meaning and shades of meaning from Latin, Virgil or other Roman poets, and from Dryden's translation, *Trivia* should be read like a palimpsest. And it rightly rebuked earlier critics who, eager to make a point, gave the work only a surface or a selected reading.[5]

Without quibbling over metaphors, I would prefer the figure of a series of overlays or transparencies, since those earlier layers, and the latest, should all be read at once, and all through each other. The exemplary word offered in Sherbo's article is the word "doubtful" in the line, "And in the doubtful Day the Woodcock flies" (I, 234). The phrase "doubtful Day" refers to daybreak, and is ratified by Virgil. Sherbo cites Ovid, but a related use is in *Georgics* I, 252—*dubio caelo*—though "dubio" there modifies not daybreak but weather. It is in Dryden too, but drawn from Milton where it means the uncertain outcome of a battle.[6] These facts are then used to suggest that the opinion of Spacks (p. 44) who gives the word moral force (since this is the day on which the milkmaid Patty may be seduced), is thereby somehow cancelled or damped.

But surely our reading must accommodate all senses. The immediate context adds to the semantic interest of the detail, as does the traditional literary context. The woodcock's reputation for gullibility is proverbial, and appears often in literature: twice in *Hamlet,* where the first time it refers to a "green girl" in danger (so her father thinks) of seduction.[7] Well enough, but this moral meaning should not cancel or damp the historical and literary. Each meaning qualifies the others, producing that kind of jointure and metaphor with its attendant complex of feeling that I have been describing. We do feel for poor Patty, though not without some censure (we may feel unqualified pity for a woodcock in a springe, but human beings have not the right to behave like woodcocks), which Gay reinforces: "Presents with female Virtue must prevail" (I, 280). But all that feeling is tempered and distanced, purged of sentimentalism, by our awareness of the verbal craft of the thing, which contrives with the simplest means a metaphor with so many levels of affiliation: uncertain weather, uncertain battle, moral vulnerability. It takes us right away from any literalizing of Patty's troubles by making us see them in the ironic light of artifice, made more ironic by the presence of so much artifice in so little room. At the same time it qualifies the artifice with a transient touch of pathos, achieved through the same means.

Below such specifics is what we might call a running pattern of the latinate, an undercurrent of distancing quasi-allusion, literary and historical. Before examining the effect of its latinate roots, let us examine an early line that describes the approach of winter, the often-noted "all the Mall in leafy Ruin lies" (I, 27). The word "ruin" just pricks the attention, partly because it has a touch of wrongness: thc Mall is in ruin only with respect to the leaves, and even those will be replaced in the spring. It is at the least an arresting word in that context, which ties the two nouns, "ruin" and "Mall," together, and reduces the real object of ruin to an adjective, "leafy." If we then begin to think of the themes of revival, reparation, cyclicism, or, say, the high cost of preserving and continuing life, we may feel some embarrassment at loading such a freight of meaning on one word, even if its use and context are provocative. Yet as it happens the word recurs some four or five times in a range of deepening contexts. First comes a kind of preparation in the form of several comic ruins: the ruin of wigs by the rain, or a suit by chandler's wax, or stockings by a fall on the ice, and so on. Then near the end of Book II the word reappears: "The Sun's beamy Ruin gilds the Plains" (l. 538)—the reference is to the adventures of Phaeton. "Beamy" makes the word oddly ambiguous, as well as implying a ruin beyond the nature we know, a cosmic ruin. Gay remains reticent and non-commital—it is part of his game—and moves on to three other stages or kinds of ruin, mixing, in three kinds of proportion, the natural and unnatural or accidental: the "ruin'd Nose" of a victim of syphilis (III, 304), the "pitchy Ruines" of a shipwreck (III, 350), and the "smoky Ruin" of London itself (III, 372), together suggesting other kinds of ruin, cosmic or moral or whatever. He then draws in the threatened ruin of Naples, a feared recurrence of the historical ruin of Pompeii. Might the combination suggest the physical-moral disruption of nature, or perhaps the ruin of the world in an apocalypse both physical and moral? And if so, what does that make of this mock work?—a symbolic representation of the disruptive impact of urban culture on the human psyche? the eternal nature-nurture struggle? Heavy going for a mock work; but the little suggestive pattern is there, though suggestion may be all we get.

Yet there is one more meaning of "ruin," which Gay's first readers would have known and appreciated. It is (as John Chalker reminds us in *The English Georgic*, p. 163) the Latin *ruina,* a falling-down; and though it

may also mean destruction, that secondary meaning need not, should not, be leaped at or read to the exclusion of the original, i.e., a *mere* falling-down with no necessary implication of destruction. Such an exclusive leap would distort the theme by leading our minds too soon away from the mere procession of the seasons, a mere operation of nature. The other examples are all examples of ruin in the derived sense: yet this neutral and "innocent" meaning helps stabilize over-dramatic and over-thematic readings toward a more neutral and artificial effect. Still (*pari passu*), this literal meaning may generate, in its contexts, its own theme: those other "ruins" obey natural impulse (even Phaeton with his urge toward emulation, and his ambition to assume a functional part in the operations of nature). It is, of course, they all are, nature gone wrong: but nature still.

Does the word then emerge with a single (however complex) final or dominant "meaning"? Yes, in a way: but it is not what we usually mean by meaning. Rather it is a kind of dynamic, all these meanings in opposition, so that the whole makes up a withheld finality, meaning on the verge of resolution but remaining on the verge: mock meaning.

The general latinate base in **Trivia** is then "overlaid" with Virgil's Latin and the *Georgics,* a monument that **Trivia** decorates: sometimes with the usual reductive burlesque, sometimes with more subtle parody, sometimes with serious imitation, and sometimes with a form of adaptation or extrapolation of Virgil that cxtcnds an implicit theme or develops an explicit one further. One distinctive passage which shows how in his hands the scope of statement and significance grows is Gay's manipulation of Virgil's instructions (*Georgics* I, 351-460) in how to judge the weather by *certis signis* (I, 133-74). It is an important passage in Virgil, which in a cumulative series sets out the natural and cosmic signs so significant to farmers. In **Trivia** it opens up that specially effective attribute of the mock, the mock that is at the same time not mock, or that shifts back and forth, so that the determination of mock or not-mock at any given moment may be difficult or impossible. Gay begins with a straightforward imitation of Virgil in a comparable tone:

> The changing Weather certain Signs reveal.
> E'er Winter sheds her Snow, or Frosts
>   congeal,
> You'll see the Coals in brighter Flames aspire.
>   (I, 133-35)

This is a nearly literal rendition of Virgil; but as the passage unfolds, a sophisticated mock begins to insinuate itself. Like Virgil, Gay next shows frisking fawns as signs of spring, and imitates quite directly Virgil's *haud equidem credo* with "not that their Minds with greater Skill are fraught"; but where Virgil's point is that they do not have knowledge from on high (leaving implicit the comparison with humans), Gay draws the animal-human comparison more literally: "The Seasons operate on every Breast; / 'Tis hence that Fawns are brisk, and Ladies drest" (I, 151-52). This often-observed passage is a graceful maneuver, a blend of model and mock so finished as to produce a third level of expression, a comic meta-mock. The pairing of creatures of vanity with those of nature is also a serious comparison, or something like an equation, of nature and nurture; the animals and ladies are ultimately one. And far from being satiric, the lines are comic, mocking on the surface, and overmatch Virgil in scope and thematic suggestion.

The passage then continues the verbal game with a pun that is yet not quite a pun, overlaying model and mock: "But when the swinging Signs your Ears offend / With creaking Noise, then rainy Floods impend" (I, 157-58). This joke Gay likes so much that he returns to it in a later and more mimetic context, where, talking about finding one's way in the city, he says "Be sure observe the Signs, for Signs remain,/Like faithful Landmarks to the walking Train" (II, 67-68). Although this kind of trick is not so clearly repeated in **Trivia,** it can stand as a paradigm of Gay's shuttling between mock and not-mock, at moments blending them to produce what I have called meta-mock. By itself it is of course no pun; the context (i.e., the passage of *certis signis* in Book I) produces the pun-like effect. As to the weather, swinging shop signs do provide the city man with the most immediate sign of change. But their movement is natural too, since it is caused by the rising wind; or so to say, the natural and artifical are brought into harmony, which we are always reminded is one point of serious georgic. And like all good puns this one is not just a play of sound, but is both a *res* and a *verbum* play.

If we wish to load it with "interpretation," we may brashly say: the "signs" are now ours, not nature's; we have affiliated them wholly with the city, with the needs of city man. Signs, shop signs, do remain, they do serve as landmarks, they do indicate rising wind and so direct us to look for shelter, they do facilitate business. And business is to the city as agriculture to the country; so, handy-dandy, which now is the mocker, which the mocked? Or we may say that it all reminds us of our deeper affiliation with nature, which we sever, or attempt to sever, at high cost, perhaps a cost we cannot afford. Or, on the very edge of commitment, perhaps we remember what the work is. It is likely that many lines will resist our ironic gaze: the praise of Burlington, lament over the decay of noble houses, or dire warning against drink and whores. Surely all these are "meant." But even they might yield some mockery if we remember both the context

within the poem and that provided by Virgil and other forebears. Praise of a patron, nostalgia for better times, blight of crops and murrain of cattle are stock features of the georgic; and of course every comparison implies a contrast, of what-ever kind and whatever degree. Burlington / Maecenas; noble houses / the whole long Empire of Rome; drink and whores / blight and murrain—these are perhaps contrasts as much as parallels.

Common sense might balk us here: Gay poured all kinds of observation and feeling into this often miscellaneous poem, and some must be genuine or "sincere." Besides, he seems nothing like the steel-nerved craftsman who would or could keep all his material at such distance, or play such a consistent game. But he is tough and tensile enough to deserve a fair test, especially if we note his way of parrying feeling with feeling, or backing away into a *non sequitur,* or devising little verbal tricks. Here is a small example of the sort of thing often taken to exhibit Gay as a "pastoralist" longing for the country and country virtues, health and all the rest:

> On Doors the sallow Milk-maid chalks her
>   Gains;
> Ah! how unlike the Milk-maid of the Plains!
> (II, 11-12)

Here, with a *cri de coeur,* speaks the real Gay? But surely this type of passage is obligatory in a mock georgic. Wherein, though, is it "mock"? Perhaps in its inversion and reduction of the famous line of the farmer's happiness (*Georgics* II, 458), *O fortunatos nimium;* perhaps in its sentimentalism, quite absent from Virgil; or in its casual, throwaway manner, again quite unlike Virgil, whose own passage is a set-piece; or its triteness; perhaps even in the lineup of "sallow," "milk," and "chalks," a little touch of characteristic absurdity.

Though Virgil of course provides the centerpiece of this poem, Gay extends his pattern of allusion to other Roman writers. Except for some rather obvious uses of Juvenal ("Here the brib'd Lawyer, sunk in Velvet, sleeps" II, 579), these have not been much commented on. The best brief notice I have seen (by Dianne S. Ames), not only usefully cites a number of allusions to Horace, Ovid, and Martial, but shows even more usefully how Gay renders them in "carefully bungled or splendidly mangled" form appropriate to the subversive decorum of mock work. One example will suggest all: for Horace's *mea virtute me involve* we have Gay's "perversely witty" "Wrapt in my Virtue, and a good Surtout!" (II, 590).

Ames makes another contribution to our awareness of what Gay is doing. She rigorously holds to the rhetorical view, skirting the moral or didactic or emotional content of the work as such, as well as the putative personal. So we learn of the *aitia* and *epillia* of the work, the *numina* of the Ovidian machinery, the *varietas* of the whole, in imitation of the inherently miscellaneous georgic genre: refreshing terms for Gay's work at so long last. Of course this kind of approach, like any approach, can be overdone, perhaps here is: but if we know or are reminded that, say, the seduction of Patty is both a burlesque of Jove's amours and of the origin myths in the *Georgics,* rather than (or in addition to) the bitter satire that "Presents with Female Virtue must prevail" may suggest (itself also a burlesque of the outcome of Jove's activities—as is, indeed, the very choice of Vulcan, the artificer for other gods but famous for his own ill success), or that the episode of Cloacina is a burlesque of the Aristaeus episode in the *Georgics* and not (or not only) a tasteless bit of scatology or sentimentalism or both, it will help us read a work so thoroughly and beautifully artificial.

A language that provides a different kind of overlay is that of Dryden's translation of the *Georgics.* More than the earlier influences, static and heritable, Dryden's language is for Gay alive, still part of a growing tradition. And it serves Gay in a language crisis of a special kind. He is not a new hand at mock work when he comes to *Trivia: Rural Sports* (not mainly a mock work, but with hints and touches), *The Fan,* and *The Shepherd's Week*—even that shaky achievement *Wine*—have been brought off with differing degrees of success, and of course *The Shepherd's Week* is a small masterpiece. But the genre of each of these handed him a certain prepared style, tone, and ambience, and point of view, and he could count on his readers' recognition of them. With *Trivia* he is on new ground; and also the victim of some bad luck. The city streets were only the city streets, with as yet no tradition, no genre, no appropriate tone or serious poetic ambience. The raw presence of the city, its nakedness, made it difficult to calculate an approach, and presented some real dangers. The gravitational pull of lived reality, the pressing "there-ness" of city detail, surely was felt by Gay as a new kind of problem for literary expression; yet the city had to be concretely and pervasively in the poem, or the point of the subject Gay had chosen was lost. Virgil's language, and his scenes and situations, imposed on the blunt factuality of the city, might be enough: but these might also produce a rather thin and mechanical, above all a too-obvious, mock effect.

There were also literary pressures, or pseudo-literary, toward thinness and mechanical effect, toward the gimmick—which was the bad luck. A "literature" of the city had begun, as early as Greene's cony-catching pamphlets. But it produced casual travelogue or crude journalism, whose effect lay in the mere tale or picture, with a salting of smart remarks: the likes of D'Urfey's *Collin's Walk through London and West-minster* or the effusions of Tom Brown and Ned Ward (with the last of whom Gay compares himself, ironically, at the end of *Trivia*). And from another direction came more bad luck, a prose example of gimmick-mock, the often revised but seldom improved *Scarronides* or *Virgil Travesty* of Charles Cotton. Thin stuff indeed, which runs one single low-burlesque joke ("A Trojan true as ever pist") doggedly through many lines. To a rising poet that kind of work opened a pit before his talent, or a literary death in the form of a one-shot poem.

Gay had to avoid both the gimmick-trap and the mimetic-trap, device-style or no-style. The first might bring him under the dead weight of georgic machinery: imitate this, next imitate that. . . . And the second might turn the poem into a piece of journalism, with the promise of a merely antiquarian survival if any. But a mock poem had to begin, at least, on the reductive level, which unelaborated easily becomes a gimmick; and a mock georgic had to be mimetic. Here Dryden's language came in, as a buffer between model and mock, and a tempering of mere circumstantiality and blunt fact.

It has been noticed (by Ames most recently) that Dryden applies a certain elegance to Virgil's text that goes beyond Virgil's comparatively plain style. Perhaps to fulfill, self-consciously, his role as inaugurator of the Augustan mode, perhaps in reflection of the modern disparity between Virgilian attitudes and contemporary rustic realities (the kind of disparity that raised issues between Pope and Ambrose Philips in the next generation), he takes it upon himself to "heighten" Virgil's language: for *aerii mellis caelestia dona,* for example, he has "aerial honey, and ambrosial dews"; for *fetu nemus omne gravescit,* "till with the ruddy freight the bending branches groan," and so on. He thus incorporates into the *Georgics* a style of his own, to suit the needs both of translation and of the growing poetic mode (it is not, or not wholly, a matter of his metaphraseperiphrase-imitation distinction). Though the core of literal meaning is there, the tone and gesture are Dryden's, and the aureate vocabulary. His aplomb (the late W.K. Wimsatt's word, perfect for Dryden) is evident in every line. He is among other things providing a saving ambience for the raw and the "low" in the English countryside, which would insistently press in, even if all the scenes and references were from the ancient and Italian model. That the language Gay applied to the city was prepared by Dryden for the country, and is therefore in a sense misapplied, fits of course the false decorum which is a feature of the mock. But it also supplies something more positive. Dryden's heightened, distanced, elegant but supple and responsive, ultimately a warm and beautifying language, retains that feel when Gay uses it to gild the cityside. Tracking its forebears this way makes us see *Trivia* more and more as a succession of allusive forms: and of course allusion is a natural enough impulse in mock work, which is all a kind of allusion. However, there are comparatively few of the typical Augustan obligatory allusions, such as clear echoes of Homer and Milton.

In *Trivia*, more subtly, there is a parade of small ambiguities, contradictions, confrontations in which the lines of force move in different directions, producing an aura of irony and reticence suffusing the whole poem. Lines like

> Hands, that stretch'd forth invading Harms prevent (I, 52)
>
> And the Streets flame with glaring Equipage (I, 114)
>
> Hov'ring, upon her feeble Knees she bends (I, 141)
>
> Turnips, and half-hatch'd Eggs, (a mingled Show'r) (II, 224)
>
> Fair Recluse, who wanders Drury Lane (II, 282)
>
> The Rabble part, in Shoals they backward run (III, 84)
>
> That bruises oft' the Truant School-Boy's Heel (III, 118)
>
> To shun the Hurries of the publick Way (III, 128)

form a network of sensitive and delicate, perhaps unconscious, touches upon feelings not appropriate to the mock but incorporating a sense of pathos and pity, yet comic too, and quite without sentimentality.

The accumulating effect is rich, but the risk is always there of foreshortening or failure of tone:

> Her head, chopt off, from her lost Shoulders flies:
>
> Pippins she cry'd, but Death her Voice confounds,
>
> And pip-pip-pip along the Ice resounds.
>
> (II, 390-92)

Perhaps the funniest passages in *Trivia,* but surely also the ugliest. Over-extended, the tone breaks. Yet the excesses of technique may themselves be thematic. These lines have valuable reverberations: the mingled comic and tragic, better still the absurd and the horrifying; the appearance of death in the triviality of events; the unnaturalness of events against a larger naturalness. Gay seems to have been rather taken with the experiment. He pursues the disjunction of feeling in a comparison of Doll, the killed apple-woman, with Orpheus:

> His sever'd Head floats down the silver Tide,
>
> His yet warm Tongue for his lost Consort

> cry'd;
>
> *Eurydice,* with quiv'ring Voice, he mourn'd.
>
> And *Heber's* Bank *Eurydice* return'd.
>
> (II, 395-98)

A greater strain than the mock can possibly bear. Yet it illustrates that probing of the limits of mock that makes Gay so effective in his much more frequent successes. And the Doll-Orpheus passage is partly redeemed by the lines which follow, a cool and lyrical transition back to the once again distanced city streets:

> But now the western Gale the Flood unbinds,
>
> And black'ning Clouds move on with warmer Winds
>
> (II, 399-400)

—so nature moves on, and so does the city. Whether the excursus succeeded or not, it was a risk worth taking.

Another, that has seemed to many a failed risk, is the infamous Cloacina adventure (II, 99-220). This may appear a real lapse of taste, reflecting the "muddy mind" of Swift, as one critic put it, and a true excrescence on the poem; Johnson wished away both it and the Patty-Vulcan episode.[8] That it appeared not in the first editions of *Trivia* but only in the version in *Poems on Several Occasions* four years later, may suggest that Gay had unworthy second thoughts or that he yielded too passively to Swift. (He had said of the whole poem at the beginning, "I owe several Hints of it to Dr. *Swift*.")[9]

Yet the episode follows the mock logic of inversion; it inverts the classic theme of divine intervention in human affairs. Could there be a deity of sewage? Well, it would oversee an inexorable human function; and in Gay's time sewage happened to be a mounting urban concern. Gay's note tells us that a statue of an unknown goddess, found in a Roman sewer, was dubbed Cloacina. Perhaps a broad world-view, broader (even) than the Augustan, might hold that all human acts are at root divinely inspired or are divine functions; or, to turn it all around, what do the filth and crassness of the amours between Cloacina and her lover, a collector of excrement (which resulted in the birth of a lad who later became a smudge-faced shoeboy), tell us of the amours of the Greek pantheon, their brutality and unconcern, their disposition toward "heady riots, incest, rapes," as Marlowe describes the carvings in the crystal pavement of Venus' temple in *Hero and Leander,* his own mock undertaking? Gay's goddess shows tender feeling for her lover and for her offspring. And the offspring has a Dickensian *claritas,* learns to perform a wholly useful act to make a living, and is distinctly humanized. We are reminded again of a world of robust energy pitted against high-minded vacuity.

Such an episode, parodying both the georgic form and the convention of divine intervention, tests Gay's ability to balance tones, and comments on the restrictions of the georgic tone. Beyond all this, it explores through example the central georgic problem of how to achieve a balance of harmony between the expressive and the mimetic modes. The mock conception enables Gay to be more daring than Virgil, and for a moment more capacious; but if he is not to be merely reductive, he must derive from the game-playing something more on the side of the valid and the positive, with respect both to the theme and to artifice. The most effective mock work does not match positive with negative, but positive with positive (though usually disguised as negative). The Cloacina episode, a fantasy with a grotesque figure in its center, develops a series of oppositions or confrontations: between model and mock, between the conventional-expressive and the mimetic, between the raised version of the classical georgic and the humanistic revelations of life. It is as if to say that deities a modern age can produce and support are as removed from those of the classical pantheon as Cloacina from Aphrodite. Cloacina not only, however, has her own claim as goddess and mother to our serious attention, but she can cope with more (the modern city, forced by mere numbers to live daily with common shores and the fact of the brown lover's cart and its nightly sound, its "pleasing thunder" as Gay ironically calls it), and can produce, right through her ostensible disadvantages, an emotion both valid in itself and scoring over the rather tightly limited emotions appropriate to the decorum of classical georgic.

Appropriately, the episode mingles its tones. In the midst of its comic fantasticality—"With wither'd Turnip Tops her Temples crown'd" (II, 196) and "Around her Waste a circling Eel was twin'd" (199)—appear lines which arrest the emotion attending these with quite others. This goddess

>　　　　　　　　　　sought no Midwife's
> Aid,
> Nor midst her Anguish to Lucina pray'd;
> No chearful Gossip wish'd the Mother Joy.
> 　　　　　　　　　　(II, 137-39)

And capping this Dickensian sympathy is a masterful, pathetic line: "Alone, beneath a Bulk she dropt the Boy" (140).

I have spoken of various minglings in *Trivia:* of tones, attitudes, themes, and languages. One last language,

diffuse throughout the poem, is I think the key to the whole: a pervasive catachresis, that symbolizes both the inversion that mock necessarily is, and the distorted, confused and finally fragmented, constructions upon experience that the city may thrust upon us. At the beginning this language is unobtrusive, an occasional poetic fillip adding charm and freshness; but after a while it becomes clear that such off-center modification is forming another pattern. Out of dozens of possible examples I select a representative handful: "Dirty Show'rs" (I, 92) blacken the canals of Belgium—clean of course when they were rain from heaven, dirty as they fall off the pavement, though still called "showers." Blood "in purple torrents" (I, 96)—like rain or the effect of rain—flows in the streets of Rome, and "muddy torrents" (I, 160) flow from the kennels—clean, simple rain hardly exists in this poem, so much of it about rain.

But then the rain pelts the tiles with a "smoaking Show'r" (I, 173), an odd sort of conjunction of unlike or contrary elements that soon gets repeated more oddly, with Patty's milkpail that "smoaks upon her Head" (I, 238). Here is something new, distortions more wrenched: and we soon see that a game of such misapplied or slant-epithets has begun, which builds as the poem progresses. On the one hand, ever more fantastical "showers" occur: at a pillorying, "Turnips, and half-hatch'd Eggs, (a mingled Show'r) / Among the Rabble rain" (II, 223-24); from "on high" (II, 267) where masons are working, "Mortar and crumbled Lime in Show'rs descend" (II, 269); the fish market gives off "Spirts of scaly Rain" (III, 106). On the other, the showers blend with, in effect are confused with, and finally give over to, fire—and a foreshadowing of the triumph of fire ("Threat'ning with Deluge this *Devoted* Town" as in Swift's *City Shower*), also with misapplied epithets, comes along early with streets that "flame with glaring Equipage" (I, 114), and goes on through ribbons that "glow" (II, 263), a "bright Chariot" (II, 573), or one "that with [a] blazon'd Scutcheon glows" (II, 577), or still another, where "flames a Fool" (II, 581). It is but a slight distortion if any that the "Flambeau gilds the Sashes of *Pell-Mell*" (III, 158), but it keeps before us the idea of potential destruction in the figure of the whore whose "tawdry Ribbons glare" (III, 269), whose "artful Blushes glow" (III, 272), and who "darts" her leers from "Sarsnet Ambush" (III, 281). Even thunder in this deluge-threatened town comes on in distorted form, as from the charivari-drums with their "Vellom-Thunder" (II, 17-18), the rumbling of carts—particularly the "pleasing Thunder" of Cloacina's "brown Lover's Cart" (II, 125-26)—a door-knocker which (wrapped because of a funeral) "Forbids the Thunder of the Footman's Hand" (II, 468), and most grotesquely of all, the hogshead in which the "Mohocks" roll a matron for their sport, a "rolling Tomb" which "O'er the Stones thunders" (III, 331-33). When a real fire begins (III, 353), there comes a reversal of the "smoking Show'r"; the fire flows and spreads like water, a "blazing Deluge" (III, 359), and a "fiery Tempest" that "pours along the Floors" (III, 373-74).

Such catachrestical shifts form a running pattern in this poem of disruption, a special move or series of moves in the game of substitution and inversion that mock work in general plays. So when we puzzle over the meanings of *Trivia,* we need to think of the alternating or standoff game. This is not to say that the poem does not harbor serious meanings; clearly there are serious emphases and accumulations, like the fire and water mixture, which pushes inexorably toward metaphor. And in talking about verbal games we ought not to forget the substantive root or base of the counters in such games; the words themselves in their references. The bulk of these in *Trivia* are references mimetically to the city; it is then a natural conclusion to see verbal distortions and misapplications as expressing—and in their juxtapositions and confrontations as symbolizing—the confusions of that new disoriented world, the world of the city and "modernity." The term was unknown to Gay, but not, apparently, the idea, inasmuch as he reflects on how the city's organization, activity, and concentration of poverty, crime, and all that kind of "infection" invade our psychology. That "infection" is the right evaluative term is verified in Gay's description of the fire: "From Beam to Beam, the fierce Contagion spreads" (III, 357), "contagion" not being a word applied to fire in Virgil, but which Gay derived from Dryden's description of the Great Fire in *Annus Mirabilis.*

It is also a more straightforward city georgic—mock with respect to Virgil's *Georgics* and its world of reference, but serious with respect to its own. Gay learned the impossibility of genuine modern country georgic from John Philips' *Cyder;* that is, the impossibility of transposing the verbal world of Virgil to the physical reality of our daily life. But a tone and style, inevitably mixed and full of contradictions, false starts, undercuttings and disappointments, might be devised which would fit lived reality. It would be, above all, a shifting and inconclusive tone: the tone of a serious joke. After the Miltonic climax of the fire—now elevated by Gay into the light that involved Rome at Caesar's fall, then into the fate of Naples when Vesuvius erupts for the last time—"Earth's Womb at once the fiery Flood shall rend, / And in the Abyss her plunging Tow'rs descend" (III, 391-92) (a couplet comparable in tone and reference to the last lines of *The Splendid Shilling* about the ship plunging into the vast abyss), Gay imperturbably continues (as Philips does not)—"Consider, Reader, what Fatigues I've known" (III, 393)—abruptly drawing back to the mimetic, thus enforcing the ambiguity and saving the mock. Gay's *Wasteland* "Falling towers"—Rome, Naples, London—are "Unreal."[10]

It is all there in *Trivia*—the satire, the moralizing, the pastoral longings, even the "apocalypse," along with the workaday reduction of Virgil—all there in a dynamic, in a sense an explosive, mixture. The "positive" tone is there too, the quality that matches our need for meanings that will save us from the apparent negativism or mere foolery of it all. Another possible or potential theme, a note struck quite forcefully, is that while something is now amiss—in the city and perhaps the world—order, perhaps not cosmic or natural, but an order which would serve our turn, may still be found. Handel's "melting Strain" (II, 497), Burlingston's "fair Palace" (II, 493), are also products of the city. The odds are still against order: the malaise of the modern world; the decline of tradition, expressed in the melancholy lines about the decay of great houses ("*Cecil*'s, *Bedford*'s, *Villers'*, now no more" [II, 490]); the growth of vulgar and hedonistic taste. Strong odds. The poem ends with no great sense of revival or recovery, but with several positives nevertheless: for the city, "a world of robust energy" struggling to shape itself and everywhere expressive of life, a life more in tune, after all, with nature than with inherited forms ("'Tis hence that Fawns are brisk, and Ladies drest"); for the poem, a Chaucerian breadth of unassuming observation, tolerance, good humor, and above all an art and artifice that "fixes" and distances its vision (Battestin, chap. 4).

"Perspective," it has been said, "is almost the subject of the poem" (Spacks, p. 52). To me it *is* the subject, or as close to a subject as we shall ever get. We may shy away from commitment to such a word, seeming to represent a mere point of view rather than a position, or worse still a kind of total relativism. But everything seen in perspective is, after all, seen; all that is valued is valued, however many countervalues, also valued, supervene; all that is, is. To offer nothing as final is not to offer nothing. It is more like offering an opportunity, through observation, to see more, and to hope to see all; only the observer must be one on whom, as James prescribed, nothing is lost. It has been suggested that the theme of Chaucer's greatest mock work, the *Nun's Priest's Tale,* is "the virtue of seeing."[11] We could not do better than to take that as the theme of *Trivia* too.

I began by speaking of a "game" of languages. A similar point is made (by Professor Price in *To the Palace of Wisdom*):

> The mock form is the most studied use of conflicting languages, and it becomes, with satire, the form in which Augustan writing finds its greatest range.

(p. 251)

He also puts the point more generally:

The Augustans maintain the iridescence of the image of man; they deliberately create perspectives that shimmer into each other and apart again.

(p. 250)

"Iridescence" is to me a striking and suggestive word, as is "shimmer," to describe the joke form that *Trivia* makes into a game, and that at bottom mock work itself is.

Notes

[1] Gay's work in general has until fairly recently been dealt with in rather literalistic or "unilevel" fashion: he writes city satire or country pastoral, or on occasion alternates between them in clearly noticeable divisions of emphasis (as in *Rural Sports*); mock pastoral (in *The Shepherd's Week*) that turns out to be "real" pastoral with a superficial, perhaps negligible, overlay of mock (Johnson's famous remark in his Life of Gay is that "the effect of reality and truth became conspicuous"); a mock georgic which is "really" a guide to the city of London; and so on.

Trivia, just because of its guide-book circumstantiality (which is indeed very "real"), has been held most firmly under the reducing lens. A characteristic treatment of this sort is that of W.H. Williams in the introduction to his ornate reprinting of the 1st edn. (London: Daniel O'Connor, 1922): "*Trivia,* which began as a burlesque of the 'Arts,' developed . . . into an original poem, containing a series of picturesque scenes, the harvest of a quiet eye, which had been fascinated by the panorama of the London streets" (pp. xiv-xv). And such a view persisted. Even as recently as 1953 the late brilliant critic and theoretician, W.K. Wimsatt, called the poem "mainly good advice on how to walk the streets of London" and adds, "I believe . . . *Trivia* is a poem highly prized by historians of the city" (*ELH* 20 [1953]; rpt. in *Hateful Contraries* [Lexington: Univ. of Kentucky, 1965], pp. 149-64; Wimsatt's remarks are on p. 156 of this rpt).

Of course the presence in the poem of two or more contributing elements—georgic burlesque, city description, pastoral asides—has been noted; but usually one has been taken as the main matter with the others functioning as vehicles or "decorations," as if Gay were, say, using Virgil to float his travelogue. There is a whole book on Gay which in effect does this; it deserves honorable notice as a serious inquiry, but takes almost exclusively a moralistic line, presenting Gay as a kind of apocalyptic revealer of the evils and ills, physical and moral of London, through whose sermons runs a thread of pastoral longing (Sven Armens, *John Gay Social Critic* [N.Y.: Columbia Univ., 1954]; see chap. 3, "The Beggar's Milieu: *Trivia*"); in turn, the travelogue is used as a series of texts for lessons in sin

and virtue, and the whole is a remarkable instance of over-emphasis on what is undoubtedly a valid element in the poem.

The idea of an ironic intermingling or blend of elements, producing a unique expressive effect, and the idea of the subtle craft involved in this interinanimation, were slow in coming. An early recognition, a rather general overview but emphasizing Gay's craftsmanship rather than his imputed moral or pastoral obsessions, is James Sutherland's "John Gay" (in *Pope and His Contemporaries, Essays Presented to George Sherburn,* ed. James A. Clifford and Louis A. Landa [Oxford: Clarendon, 1949], pp. 201-14). There followed no immediate rush to critical judgment; but the awareness of Gay as an artist, and one who strove, not for the kind of "atomism" that *Trivia* may appear to represent, but for a complex unity, was soon planted. A sense of Gay's pervasive irony, as an element of his craft, also appeared. A characteristic title is C. F. Burgess' "The Ambivalent Point of View in John Gay's *Trivia*" (*Cithara* 4 [1964]: 53-65), which shows satire, sympathy, burlesque and travelogue, as working together, not just existing side by side, or alternately. Alvin B. Kernan in "The Magnifying Tendency: Gay's *Trivia*" (pp. 36-50 of *The Plot of Satire* [New Haven: Yale Univ., 1965]), notes that the level of expression in *Trivia* is not realism or direct moralizing but "stylistic inflation and amplification" in order to achieve a heightened satire. Gay's wit and sense of ambiguity are discussed in Patricia Spacks' book for the Twayne series, *John Gay* (N.Y.: 1965), but she comes out rather heavily on the side of his moralizing. The general drift remained toward stylistic analysis, however. An important turn in the direction of Gay's active use (not just acknowledgment) of Virgil and other sources for allusion, including the latinate style that was a heritage of the seventeenth century, is represented by a few pages of *Trivia* in John Chalker's *The English Georgic* (London: Routledge & Kegan Paul, 1969), pp. 163-79. Chalker notes the force of individual words which inject a nuance of irony through the disparities between the Latin and English senses, or which emphasize the Latin over the English senses. This kind of language play was an element hardly noticed in Gay, the study of which was to turn out to be remarkably fruitful.

Perhaps the two most important critical contributions to the understanding of Gay's art—as distinguished from his assumed didactic or satiric positions—are "Virgil, Dryden, Gay, and Matters Trivial," by Arthur Sherbo (*PMLA* 85 [1970]: 1063-71), and "Gay: the Meanings of Art and Artifice," chap. 4 of Martin Battestin's *The Providence of Wit* (Oxford: Clarendon, 1974). In a magisterial argument, Sherbo demonstrates with convincing thoroughness that both Virgil's Latin and Dryden's latinate translations infuse Gay's words with complex meanings; and that *Trivia* must be read as a composite (his word is "palimpsest") of original

Latin meanings, Virgil, Dryden, and Gay's own skillful strategic manipulation of these vocabularies. And Battestin with equal force and greater subtlety shows Gay as always a maker who distances assumed reality, non-verbal reality, and remakes it through style into the special and perdurable reality of art.

More circumscribed but significant studies, sharing the general position that Gay should be seen as a blender of sources, an ironist, a dealer in ambiguities, and an artist who always (Sherbo's words) knew what he was doing, have continued to appear. Christine Rees, in "Gay, Swift, and the Nymphs of Drury Lane" (*Essays in Criticism* 23 [1973]: 1-21) anticipates one of Battestin's main points when she says that Gay's "charm of manner insinuates the fiction rather than the truth." Dianne Ames' spirited and scholarly study of Gay's deliberately distorted allusions, as well as the special rhetorical structures she employs in *Trivia,* ("Gay's *Trivia* and the Art of Allusion," *Studies in Philology* 75 [1978]: 199-22), is most important. The expressive function of allusion, this time stressing Gay's use of Horace, is discussed at some length in "Gay's 'Roving Muse': Problems of Genre and Intention in *Trivia*" (*English Studies* 62 [1981]: 259-70), by Eugene Kirk, which concerns itself chiefly with the deliberately "blurred boundaries" between source-genres, particularly those of georgic and formal verse satire. A final noteworthy piece is "The Wolf in the Fold: John Gay in *The Shepherd's Week* and *Trivia*" (*Studies in English Literature* 23 [1983]: 413-23, by Anne McWhir), who writes on the relation between "realism" and literary realism, notes Gay's repeated undercuttings of his own ostensibly sincere admonishments, and concludes with Gay's characteristic maneuvers that "trick us with benevolent webs of words."

The general direction of all such commentaries, combining scholarship and critical subtlety in equal measure, we may expect to see continued: it is that of discovering in Gay an artist of subtle awareness with a fund of usable learning who produced works more finished and complex than criticism for a long time was able to perceive, and that belie their apparent simplicity and blandness of surface.

[2] Martin Price, *To the Palace of Wisdom* (N.Y.: Doubleday, 1964), p. 254.

[3] *The Shepherd's Week,* "Friday," 11. 145-48. The edn. cited throughout is *John Gay: Poetry and Prose,* ed. Vinton A. Dearing with the assistance of Charles E. Beckwith (Oxford: Clarendon, 1974).

[4] "An ambiguity of the fifth type occurs when the author is discovering his idea in the act of writing, or not holding it all in his mind at once, so that, for instance, there is a simile which applies to nothing exactly, but lies half-way between two things when the author is

moving from one to another" (William Empson, *Seven Types of Ambiguity,* 3rd ed. [N.Y.: Meridian, 1955], p. 175). Though Empson is talking about a different kind of poetry, this is no bad way of describing, or beginning to describe, mock work.

[5] Sherbo cites Armens; Alvin Kernan, who makes some extensive remarks on *Trivia* in chap. 2 of *The Plot of Satire* (New Haven: Yale Univ., 1965); and unnamed "others" (p. 1064).

[6] *Paradise Lost* I, 104: "In dubious Battel on the Plains of Heav'n." Dryden uses the term a half dozen or so times, usually in this sense of uncertain as to outcome (as in the example here from Virgil, which Dryden renders [*Georgics* I, 172] "dubious months uncertain weather bring"); but with only one exception (*Britannia Rediviva,* 1. 122: "Fain would the fiends have made a dubious birth"), they all occur in his translations of Ovid and Virgil. That he first got the word from Milton, however, is suggested by his using it at least twice when "dubious," in whatever grammatical form, does not occur in the original, e.g. in Ovid's *Metamorphoses* (I, 318-19), "hic [i.e., Mount Parnassus] ubi Deucalion . . . adhaesit" (Dryden [I, 421]: "High on the summit of this dubious cliff"), or in the *Georgics* (III, 291-92), "sed me Parnasi deserta . . . raptat amor" (Dryden [III, 457-58]: "the commanding Muse my chariot guides, / Which o'er the dubious cliff securely rides.")

[7] Polonius to Ophelia in *Hamlet,* I, iii, 101: "Affection? Pooh, you speak like a green girl," and 115: "Ay, springes to catch woodcocks."

[8] The phrase, "Swift's muddy mind," is W. H. Irving's in *John Gay Favorite of the Wits* (Durham: Duke Univ., 1940), p. 127. He is voicing an objection not merely of his own, however, but that of Joseph Warton, in his *Essay on the Genius and Writings of Pope,* 4th edn., 2 vols. (London, 1782) 2:251: "The fable of Cloacina is indelicate. I should think this is one of the hints given him by Swift. . . ." Johnson, in his Life of Gay, says, "some of his decorations might be wished away"; but his two objections are on different grounds, only one of them moralistic. The Patty-Vulcan episode (I, 223-82), in which the god seduces Patty the milkmaid with a gift of nail-shod shoes, then called "pattens" (a real type of 18th-c. shoe for wet weather), could have been a mere mortal event, and so was "useless and apparent falsehood." But the Cloacina episode is "nauseous and superfluous," as well as being subject to the same objection to "supernatural imposition." (*Lives of the English Poets,* ed. George Birkbeck Hill, 3 vols. [Oxford: Clarendon, 1905], II:284.)

[9] "Advertisement" following title and epigraph of *Trivia.*

10 Eliot's lines in "What the Thunder Said" (sec. V. of *The Wasteland,* 11. 374-77) are: "Falling towers / Jerusalem Athens Alexandria / Vienna London / Unreal."

11 Charles Muscatine, *Chaucer and the French Tradition* (Univ. of California, Berkeley, 1957), p. 242.

Carolyn D. Williams (essay date 1988)

SOURCE: "The Migrant Muses: A Study of Gay's Later Drama," in *John Gay and the Scriblerians,* edited by Peter Lewis and Nigel Wood, Vision Press; St. Martin's Press, 1988, pp. 163-83.

[*In the following essay, Williams examines Gay's depictions of women in light of the works of other Scriblerians, especially Pope and Swift. Williams suggests that the unevenness of Gay's later works in part stems from his attempts to translate into dramatic representations topics better addressed in prose or poetry.*]

One of Pope's epitaphs on Gay tells only half the truth:

> Favourite of the muses,
> He was led by them to every elegant art:
> Refined in taste,
> And fraught with graces all his own:
> In various kinds of poetry
> Superior to many,
> Inferior to none.[1]

The muses were, in fact, cruelly capricious in their favours, alternately wafting Gay to pinnacles of brilliance and leaving him to flounder through a slough of well-intentioned tedium. They decreed that his masterpieces should be inimitable—even by Gay himself. Most exasperating of all was their habit of slipping away without letting him know they had gone: the man who could proudly offer *Polly* as a sequel to *The Beggar's Opera,* or follow *Fables II,* clearly found it difficult to assess the quality of his own output.

The unevenness of Gay's work, combined with the apparently effortless elegance of his successes, gave the impression that everything came by chance. Dr. Johnson, doubtless perplexed by this haphazard performance and annoyed by the necessity of reading (or finding excuses not to read) so much that was second-rate, treated Gay as a minor figure who happened to please the public taste from time to time. According to Johnson, the success of *The Shepherd's Week* was partly accidental: 'the effect of reality and truth became conspicuous, even when the intention was to shew them groveling and degraded.' He dismissed *The What D'Ye Call It* as beneath critical attention: 'Of this performance the value certainly is but little; but it was one of the lucky trifles that give pleasure by novelty.' Inevitably, *The Beggar's Opera* became 'this lucky

piece'. *Trivia* confronted Johnson with a degree of excellence he was unable to ignore: 'To *Trivia* may be allowed all that it claims: it is spritely, various, and pleasant.' But Johnson still found a way to imply that Gay did not deserve all the credit: 'The subject is of that kind which Gay was by nature qualified to adorn.' In other words, Gay could not help writing *Trivia,* because that was what he was born for. Johnson gives the impression that he would have rated Gay more highly if he had been a more consistent writer, even if that consistency had been achieved at the expense of originality. He quoted with approval the female critic who relegated Gay to 'a lower order', but the real problem was Gay's inability to stay at one level long enough to be assigned to any order at all.[2]

Efforts to overthrow Johnson's verdict culminated fifty years ago with the publication of William Empson's *Some Versions of Pastoral* (1935), after which it has been possible to take Gay seriously without undue critical embarrassment. Some of his works, especially *The Beggar's Opera,* have received a great deal of respectful attention; and his tercentenary provided a welcome opportunity for making up deficiencies in other areas. However, a natural tendency to concentrate on Gay's best work has only increased general bewilderment at the muses' flighty conduct. In order to understand Gay properly, it is necessary to find out what he was trying to achieve when he was writing badly. 'Badly', of course, is a relative term when applied to Gay: even *Dione* displays some fugitive lyrical charm. Still, no one would attempt to deny that some of his works are better than others. The standard of his drama is particularly prone to fluctuation, exemplified most clearly by his failure to consolidate the position he gained by *The Beggar's Opera.* John Fuller sees Gay's later drama as the result of a pious but regrettable sacrifice of wit to responsibility:

> Like Pope, Gay 'stoop'd to Truth', but his growing preoccupation with sexual mores and with political corruption may seem at times a poor exchange for the imaginative riches of Scriblerian farce and burlesque.[3]

I should like to argue for a broader definition of 'Scriblerian' to encompass Gay's later drama, and help to account for its patchiness by showing that its faults and virtues owe just as much to Scriblerian influences as his earlier work. Gay's problems are a question of manner rather than matter: sexual mores, after all, loom large in such successes as *The What D'Ye Call It* and *Three Hours after Marriage,* and combine with political corruption to dominate *The Beggar's Opera.* Nor can it be reckoned an un-Scriblerian activity to follow Pope (not to mention Swift and Arbuthnot) into the realms of serious moral satire. Gay's troubles arose when he attempted to deal with common Scriblerian preoccupations in a way that was unsuited to his chosen form. An examination of *Polly, Achilles* and *The Distress'd Wife* will show where his difficulties lay.

Achilles, posthumously produced in February 1733, was condemned for tedium: an article in the *Daily Courant* (16 February 1733) charitably maintained that it was an unfinished piece, completed by a committee of Gay's friends, since 'Mr. *Gay* could not *deviate* into so much *Dulness'.*[4] Exception was also taken to the vulgarity (sometimes amounting to indecency) of the lyrics. This often caused more offence in the playhouse than in the closet, where readers could enjoy low humour without having their own virtue or gentility called into question. The most conspicuous deficiency of *The Distress'd Wife,* another posthumous production, is the character drawing. As a comedy of manners, it arouses expectations of realism and consistency that are disappointed in audience and readers alike. In a letter to Elizabeth Young (28 September 1743), James Thomson observed that Lady Willit's 'Affectations are drawn so monstrous, they are not the Affectations of a Woman of Sense and Wit but of a Fool.' Miss Friendless's acceptance of the aging Lord Courtlove distressed Thomson who had 'expected, from her sensible and serious Turn, that she would have disdained the Proposal, and rather lived in a Cottage with some Person she loved'.[5] Fuller detects a 'touch of primitivism'[6] in these cavils, but even in these days of post-structuralist sophistication, traditional character criticism still haunts the theatre, refusing to be exorcized by repeated incantations that the text's the thing. However unscrupulously the dramatist uses a character as a moral exemplum or a convenient plot device, the actor insists on investing the part with a recognizable human identity, as does the theatrically minded reader of plays. *Polly* was a special case: it was banned before rehearsal in December 1728 and not performed until 1777. This may not have been an unqualified disaster for Gay. One can only imagine how an uninitiated first-night audience, all agog for the highly publicized sequel to the longest running show in history, would have responded to Macheath's impenetrable blackface disguise, Polly's transvestite heroics, and the interminably self-righteous noble savages. But one would much rather not.

In each instance, Gay required his cast to give bodily form to notions that were plausibly expressed in other Scriblerian texts (his own included) but which looked disconcertingly flimsy on stage. Idealistic moral, economic and political theory abounded; so did predictable diatribes on corrupt practice. Nominally happy endings were contrived by proposing impracticable solutions to insoluble problems. This made life awkward for the actors, and worse for the actresses, who carried the additional burden of exemplifying Scriblerian ideas about women. The Scriblerians were not conspicuously misogynist, by contemporary standards; they were capable of feeling, and expressing, genuine admiration for the virtues, charms and intellectual achievements of individual women. But they tended to view the sex as a whole with a mixture of suspicion and contempt that reflected the most drearily conservative doctrines of female inferiority—except for the occasions when they added a further twist of their own devising. And Gay, as usual, took his colour from his company.

However inadequate Pope's *Epistle to a Lady* (1735) may seem as an account of women in general, there is no disputing its accuracy as a survey of women in Gay's drama:

> In Men, we various Ruling Passions find,
> In Women, two almost divide the kind;
> Those, only fix'd, they first or last obey,
> The Love of Pleasure, and the Love of Sway.
>   That, Nature gives; and where the lesson
>   taught
> Is but to please, can Pleasure seem a fault?
> Experience, this; by Man's oppression curst,
> They seek the second not to lose the first.
>   (207-14)[7]

Gay's women employ various subversive strategies to gain their ends; the most commonly effective is the cultivation of an attractive surface, as enjoined in *Achilles* by the court lady Artemona:

> Think of Dress in ev'ry Light;
>   'Tis Woman's chiefest Duty;
> Neglecting that, our selves we slight
>   And undervalue Beauty.
> That allures the Lover's Eye,
>   And graces every Action;
> Besides, when not a Creature's by,
>   'Tis inward Satisfaction.
>   (III, viii, 7-14)[8]

The end of the song suggests that most women are so consumed by vanity that beauty has ceased to be a means and become an end in itself.

Achilles provides a hospitable niche for this idea, since the plot hinges on the notion that preoccupation with finery is a distinguishing sexual characteristic. The young warrior prince Achilles, disguised as a girl at the behest of his mother, who wishes to keep him out of the Trojan War, is living at the court of Scyros. In order to expose him, Ulysses and Diomedes assume the rôle of merchants, peddling cloth, jewels, weapons and armour. The girls are fascinated by the adornments; the boy blows his cover by seizing a sword. If Achilles had shared his companions' concern with fashion, or any of the girls had been capable of taking an intelligent interest in Bronze Age metallurgy, the scheme would have misfired. An apparent exception to the feminine rule is Deidamia, Achilles's bedfellow, who is so worried by other matters that she pays hardly any attention to the merchants' wares. This anxiety, however, is still articulated in terms of dress; she is afraid that Achilles's indifference to clothes will betray his sex and consequently ruin her reputation—which cannot, in any case, last much longer, since her pregnancy is becoming visible to observant eyes, despite her attempts to hide it under her gown.

Achilles and *The Distress'd Wife* show women attending to their chiefest duty in a woefully unbusinesslike manner. Lady Willit in the latter play runs up huge bills without caring that her husband will be unable to pay them: 'Was there ever a Man, who grew to be of any Consequence, who did not run out?—Would you have Credit, and not make use of it?' (I, ii, 58-61). Incurring debt was regarded as antisocial; George Lillo makes this point in *The London Merchant* (1731), when the exemplary Mr. Thorowgood instructs his apprentice

> to look carefully over the files to see whether there are any tradesmen's bills unpaid and, if there are, to send and discharge 'em. We must not let artificers lose their time, so useful to the public and their families, in unnecessary attendance. (I, i, 55-9)[9]

Prompt payment was not a virtue required only from the bourgeoisie; William Darrell, gentleman and Jesuit, inveighed against debtors in *The Gentleman Instructed* (1704), a conduct book ostensibly directed to the nobility:

> Now when a Creditor must be eternally upon the Trot to come up to his Debtor, and ply at all the *Coffee-houses* for Intelligence of his Haunts, the Irons cool at home, Trade sinks, Work is at a Stand, and a Bankrupt treads upon his Heels. For how shall a Merchant pay his Debts, who receives none? Now, Sir, here is *lucrum cessans* on the one hand, and *damnun emergens* on the other, and in the Sight of God you stand responsible for both: They will be put to your Accounts, and you must either repair 'em here, or suffer for 'em hereafter.[10]

Lillo and Darrell condemned debt as a general evil; the specific link between women and irresponsible expenditure appears more characteristic of Swift, who expresses his usual views with only a slight increase of his customary venom when he takes on the mask of the projector in *A Modest Proposal* (1729):

> . . . the Body of a plump Girl of fifteen, who was crucified for an Attempt to poison the Emperor, was sold to his Imperial *Majesty's prime Minister of State,* and other great *Mandarins* of the Court, *in Joints from the Gibbet,* at Four hundred Crowns. Neither indeed can I deny, that if the same Use were made of several plump young girls in this Town, who, without one single Groat to their

Fortunes, cannot stir Abroad without a Chair, and appear at the *Play-house,* and *Assemblies* in foreign Fineries, which they never will pay for; the Kingdom would not be the worse.[11]

Scriblerian economics also underlie another constant in female consumerism as perceived by Gay: women prefer imported goods to native manufacture. As Artemona observes in *Achilles:* 'There must be something pretty in every thing that is foreign' (III, x, 64-5). In the same play, Philoe rejects a length of cloth, even though she likes the design, because it is locally made. She is like the women of quality in eighteenth-century Dublin 'who seldom wear any of our own Goods, Except impos'd on them under the Name of Foreign Works'.[12] The tastes of Artemona, Philoe and Lady Willit are typical of the female extravagance condemned by Swift in his *Answer to Several Letters from Unknown Persons* (1729):

> Is it not the highest Indignity to human nature, that men should be such poltrons as to suffer the Kingdom and themselves to be undone, by the Vanity, the Folly, the Pride, and Wantonness of their Wives, who under their present Corruptions seem to be a kind of animal suffered for our sins to be sent into the world for the Destruction of Familyes, Societyes, and Kingdoms; and whose whole study seems directed to be as expensive as they possibly can in every useless article of living, who by long practice can reconcile the most pernicious forein Drugs to their health and pleasure, provided they are but expensive; as Starlings grow fat with henbane: who contract a Robustness by meer practice of Sloth and Luxury: who can play deep severall hours after midnight, sleep beyond noon; revel upon Indian poisons, and spend the revenue of a moderate family to adorn a nauseous unwholesom living Carcase.[13]

Unfortunately for Gay, a playwright cannot indulge his imagination as freely as a pamphleteer; in bringing these creatures on stage, he did not realize that his audience expected to see women, and Swift had provided him with a formula for monsters.

Of course, the Scriblerians were not the first to take this view of women: it had long been proverbial that 'far fetched and dear bought is good for ladies.' Lady Dainty shows similar proclivities in Colley Cibber's comedy, *The Double Gallant* (1707), but she is provided with a discerning friend who refuses to share her perverse tastes:

> *Lady Dainty.* How came you, dear *Sylvia,* to be reconcil'd to any thing in an *India* House: You us'd to have a most barbarous inclination for our own odious Manufactures.
>
> *Sylvia.* Nay, Madam, I am only going to recruit my *Tea Table:* As to the rest of their

Trumpery, I am as much out of humour
with it as ever. . . .

Lady Dainty. Well, thou art a pleasant
Creature, thy distast is so diverting!

Sylvia. And your Ladyship is so expensive,
that really I am not able to come into it.

Lady Dainty. Now, 'tis to me prodigious!
how some Women can muddle away their
Money upon Houswifry, Children, Books,
and Charities, when there are so many well-
bred Ways, and foreign Curiosities, that
more elegantly require it—I have every
Morning the Rarities of all Countries
brought to me, and am in love with every
New thing I see. (III)[14]

Cibber makes many of his most telling dramatic effects by juxtaposing different types of women; Scriblerian satire usually reaches the conclusion that all wom-
en are the same.

This is not to say that any one woman will be recognizably herself from one moment to the next: *'varium
et mutabile semper/femina'* (Virgil's *Aeneid*, IV, 569-
70). Pope's *Epistle to a Lady* expresses this paradox:

Nothing so true as what you once let fall,
'Most Women have no Characters at all'.
Matter too soft a lasting mark to bear,
And best distinguish'd by black, brown, or
   fair. . . .
   Come then, the colours and the ground
   prepare!
Dip in the Rainbow, trick her off in Air,
Chuse a firm Cloud, before it fall, and in it
Catch, ere she change, the Cynthia of this
   minute.

(1-4, 17-20)[15]

If women are such shifting—not to say shifty—characters, how can their mental processes be recorded? *The
Rape of the Lock* (1714) takes an appropriately indirect
approach, working by allusion—almost by allegory.
According to David Fairer, the poem 'is concerned
with the imagination as a glorious, amoral, irresponsible and alluring thing, a paradoxical cluster of adjectives as apt for Belinda as for the sylphs'.[16] To say that
the sylphs represent Belinda's imagination is not far
from saying that they represent Belinda. Pope's language suggests that they are spectacular, impalpable,
and not too reliable:

Loose to the Wind their airy Garments flew,
Thin glitt'ring Textures of the filmy Dew;
Dipt in the richest Tincture of the Skies,
Where Light disports in ever-mingling Dies,
While ev'ry Beam new transient Colours
   flings,

Colours that change whene'er they wave their
   Wings.

(II, 63-8)[17]

Dramatists have made theatrical capital from female
unpredictability for centuries, despite the danger that
the 'infinite variety' which sounds so enchanting when
Enobarbus describes its effect on Cleopatra's admirers
might degenerate into maddening indecisiveness when
it actually appears on stage. Forced to rely on the talents of a flesh-and-blood performer, unaided by a glam-
orizing aura of sylphs, they take certain precautions to
ensure that their women do not appear merely demoment-
ed. It is easy for narrative poets, such as Dryden in
Cymon and Iphigenia (1700), to work on the assumption that it is a woman's privilege to change her mind:

Then impotent of Mind, with alter'd Sense,
She hugg'd th' Offender, and forgave th'
   Offence,
Sex to the last.

(366-68)[18]

Dramatists, however, have no opportunity for explaining developments with helpful asides *in propria persona*. They try to make sure that their characters' words
and actions are self-explanatory, which accounts for
their reluctance to show behaviour that has no apparent explanation at all. Women who vacillate on stage
often do so on purpose, as a means of manipulating the
men who are supposed—officially, at any rate—to
control their destiny. Hippolita, in Wycherley's *The
Gentleman Dancing-Master* (1672), pretends to change
her mind in order to test her lover's sincerity. Milla-
mant, the supreme exponent of inconsistency as sexual
strategy, uses her lightning-swift changes of mood to
keep Mirabel off balance, perplexed, and duly besotted
in Congreve's *The Way of the World* (1700).

When a dramatist shows a woman who is genuinely
unable to make up her mind, her confusion often serves
as a distress signal, to indicate an anxiety that she is
unable to discuss with the other characters. The audience is usually put in possession of enough information to interpret her behaviour correctly, even when
she does not appear to be aware of its significance
herself. Lady Lurewell in Farquhar's *Sir Harry Wildair*
(1701) is a typical case: exacting, capricious, and thoroughly unreasonable, she makes life miserable for
herself and her entire household, but is unable to define the cause of her discontent:

Lady Lurewell. Oh, Mr. Remnant! I don't
know what ails these stays you have made
me; but something is the matter, I don't like
'em.

Remnant. I am very sorry for that, madam.

But what fault does your ladyship find?
Lady Lurewell. I don't know where the fault
lies; but in short, I don't like 'em; I can't
tell how; the things are well enough made,
but I don't like 'em.

Remnant. Are they too wide, madam?
Lady Lurewell. No.
Remnant. Too strait, perhaps?
Lady Lurewell. Not at all! they fit me very
well, but—Lard bless me! can't you tell
where the fault lies?

(II, i, 58-70)[19]

The fault lies with her recent marriage to Colonel Standard. The new stays, with their association of close restraint on the female physique, represent the marriage bond; her dislike shows that she has not yet reconciled herself to the adjustments she will have to make in her way of life. The stays do fit her, however, and there is no objective reason why she should not be perfectly comfortable: Colonel Standard is a good match and they are destined, after a few ups and downs, to live happily ever after. The audience might not be able to decode all these subtleties at first hearing, but they have certainly been fed enough data to be able to deduce that the lady's troubles are marital, not sartorial, in origin.

Lady Willit, on the other hand, produces virtuoso exhibitions of dithering for dithering's sake, as in a scene with her maid Fetch:

Lady Willit. BLESS me!—How can any Mortal
be so awkward! [Fetch *combing her Hair.*]—Dost
think I have no Feeling?—Am I to be flea'd alive?—
Go—begone. [*going.*] Come hither. [*returning.*]—
Who do you think is to dress me?—Tell 'em I'll
have the Tea-kettle ready this Instant. [*going.*]—Is
the Wench distracted?—What, am I to sit all Day
long with my Hair about my Ears like a Mermaid?
[*returning.*]—Now, I'll be sworn for't, thou hast
not spoke for the Tea-water all this while, though I
order'd it an Hour ago.
Fetch. Not by *me,* Madam.
Lady Willit. So you tell me I lye—that's all.
[*going.*]—What is the blundering Fool a doing?—
Am I to be dress'd to Day or no? [*returning.*]—Bid
the Porter bring me up the Book of Visits.—Why
don't you go? [*going.*]—Must I bid you do the same
Thing a thousand Times over and over again?—I
am to have no Breakfast to Day, that I find you are
determin'd upon.

(II, i, 1-17)

The first outbreak might be attributed to her natural agitation on learning that her husband means to take her back to the country, but Fetch's repeated protests imply that this is her normal *modus operandi:*

If it be not an unreasonable Request from a Servant,
I could wish your Ladyship would know your own
Mind before you speak;—'twould save you a great
many Words, and me a great deal of Trouble. (IV,
iv, 6-9)

A realistic interpretation might account for her behaviour by reference to various inner conflicts deducible from the text, such as the tension between her envy of Lady Frankair's flair for adultery and her fear of following her example. But Gay offers no explicit endorsement of this reading. Lady Willit's paranoid tone, if taken literally, could only issue from a neurotic state far too painful to be contained within the bounds of comedy. It is hard to resist the conclusion that Lady Willit dithers chiefly because Gay intends to make her a compendium of fashionable female failings.

This suspicion is confirmed by comparison with the girls in ***Achilles.*** The chief difference is that Lady Willit's condition is indistinguishable from mental illness, whereas Artemona and her companions appear to be labouring under some form of mental handicap. The moral is that all fine ladies are mad or stupid, as a just consequence of their selfishness, frivolity and affectation. Philoe suffers from the same sort of absent-mindedness as Lady Willit:

Servant. The Anti-chamber, Madam, is crowded
with Trades-People.
Philoe. Did not I tell you that I wou'd not be
troubled with Those impertinent Creatures?—But
hold—I had forgot I sent for 'em—Let 'em wait.

(III, ix, 8-12)

When her mind is present, it serves her no better:

Ulysses. We have things of all kinds, Ladies.
Philoe. Of all kinds!—Now that is just what I wanted
to see.

(III, x, 19-21)

The precision of 'just' is ridiculously nullified by the hopelessly vague 'all kinds', so that the two halves of her speech cancel each other out. Language is similarly mistreated by Lesbia: 'This very individual Pattern, in a blue Pink, had been infinitely charming' (III, x, 52-3). Her words are debased coinage. To provide an equivalent for her ideas, she either pays out too many (hence the tautology of 'this very individual') or chooses an inappropriately high denomination (the extravagance of 'infinitely'). As for the 'blue Pink', it has the same self-negating quality as Philoe's utterance, suggesting that there may not be an idea behind it at all. It might refer to a pink so deeply tinged with blue that it verges on mauve, but the overall satiric tendency of the dialogue suggests that Gay was endeavouring to create a touch of exuberant nonsense, analogous to the modern 'sky blue pink with orange spots on'. All in all, Gay's brand of girl talk is far from convincing.

This is disappointing because elsewhere he writes about women and their clothes with sympathy, precision and infectious delight. Even the notion that ladies are mindless creatures, activated by forces of nature, can appear charming in a descriptive passage that does not require the reader to think in terms of individual women:

> The Ladies gayly dress'd, the *Mall* adorn
> With various Dyes, and paint the sunny Morn;
> The wanton Fawns with frisking Pleasure
>> range,
> And chirping Sparrows greet the welcome
>> Change:
> Not that their Minds with greater Skill are
>> fraught,
> Endu'd by Instinct, or by Reason taught,
> The Seasons operate on every Breast;
> 'Tis hence that Fawns are brisk, and Ladies
>> drest.
>
>   (***Trivia,*** I, 145-52)[20]

A similar connection between female fashion and organic life appears in *The Fan:*

> Should you the rich Brocaded Suit unfold,
> Where rising Flow'rs grow stiff with frosted
>> Gold;
> The dazled Muse would from her Subject
>> stray,
> And in a Maze of Fashions lose her Way.
>
>   (I, 241-44)

The spontaneous vitality implied by 'unfold', 'rising' and 'grow', all associated with burgeoning vegetation, gives the impression that these flowers, worked to please the ladies, have been called into being by the natural laws that control the growth of real plants: not such an improbable hypothesis, if the same laws also govern the ladies' fancy. The use of 'frosted'—another natural process at work—strengthens the impression that fashion develops of its own accord without conscious human intervention, a phenomenon to be celebrated by the poet with the same respectful admiration as a sunset or a storm at sea. Then 'Gold' returns to the manufactured, inorganic reality, inviting the reader to participate with Gay in an ironic reappraisal of the relationship between nature and artifice.

If the poet handles his subject so felicitously, why does the dramatist blunder? Once more, the muses have been repelled by sound Scriblerian principles. 'Th'inconstant Equipage of Female Dress' (*The Fan,* I, 230) exemplifies the moral instability that Swift, Pope and Arbuth-

not saw as a threat to civilization. Gay's court ladies are devoid of values; even aesthetic standards are unknown to them. 'Unless you have any thing that is absolutely new and very uncommon,' warns Artemona, 'you will give us and your selves, Gentlemen, but unnecessary Trouble' (III, x, 1-3). Taking novelty as a criterion of merit reduces every statement to nonsense sooner or later, as Swift demonstrates in *A Tale of a Tub.* He claims 'an absolute Authority in Right, as the *freshest Modern,* which gives me a Despotick Power over all Authors before me', but his work is avowedly 'calculated for this present Month of *August,* 1697',[21] and not published till 1704, which discredits it on its own terms. The quest for novelty was traditionally perceived as a symptom of political decadence as well as intellectual chaos. In *Catiline* (1611) Ben Jonson associated it with the fall of Rome:

> Can nothing great, and at the height
> Remaine so long? but it's owne weight
> Will ruine it? Or, is't blinde chance,
> That still desires new states t'advance,
> And quit the old? Else, why must *Rome,*
> Be by it selfe, now, over-come? . . .
> They hunt all grounds; and draw all seas;
> Foule every brooke, and bush; to please
> Their wanton tasts: and, in request
> Have new, and rare things; not the best!
>
>   (I, 531-36, 569-72)[22]

Diomedes, playing up to the ladies in ***Achilles,*** declares that 'Novelty is the very Spirit of Dress' (III, x, 13) but this is a contradiction in terms. 'Spirit' is a life-giving force, an eternal, unchanging essence: novelty cannot be the spirit of anything. It bestows an illusion of life that may keep the carcase twitching for a little while, but cannot preserve it from corruption. And the characters are as void of life as the ideas they represent.

Corruption—both sexual and political—is a key issue in Gay's drama, and he often links them so closely that they become indistinguishable. Women are potential bribes in political deals, such as Lady Willit's attempt to gain Lord Courtlove's patronage by offering him the hand of Miss Sprightly. They are also vulnerable to direct political manipulation. Some, like Miss Friendless and Polly, are offered as instances of incorruptibility, but doubts are raised by Miss Friendless's decision to secure independence by marrying Lord Courtlove (marriage being the only form of independence to which a woman of the period could reasonably aspire) and the prudential thrust of Polly's arguments in favour of virtue as a sound investment. They suggest that it is woman's chiefest duty to keep an eye to the main chance:

> Frail is ambition, how weak the foundation!
>   Riches have wings as inconstant as wind;

My heart is proof against either temptation,
Virtue, without them, contentment can find.

(***Polly,*** III, xv, 38-41)

Most women, like Mrs. Ducat, are blatantly out for
whatever they can get:

I will have my humours, I'll please all my
  senses,
I will not be stinted—in love or expences.
I'll dress with profusion, I'll game without
  measure;
You shall have the business, I will have the
  pleasure.

(***Polly,*** I, viii, 9-12)

Her maid, Damaris, employs the language as well as
the skills of the politician in the cause of female sol-
idarity:

I am employ'd by master to watch my mistress, and
by my mistress to watch my master. Which party
shall I espouse? To be sure my mistress's. For in
hers, jurisdiction and power, the common cause of
the whole sex, are at stake. (I, x, 3-7)

Women were commonly supposed to be natural Jacobites, but the Scriblerians appear to have believed that
every woman was at heart a Whig: not an Old Whig,
or an Opposition Whig, but an unscrupulous Walpolean
Whig, venal from her laced shoes to her powdered
hair. Women were ambitious and materialistic; money,
power and influence at court lay in the gift of the
Whig government. Another inducement to she-Whig-
gery was the widespread female tendency to prefer the
town to the country. The expensive, glamorous amusements of London society were a dangerous distraction
from the responsibilities of the landed gentry who were
the natural upholders of the Tory interest. Only an
exceptional woman, whose inborn proclivities were
suppressed by common sense and a virtuous education,
could be trusted. Dr. Arbuthnot showed the two types
in action in *Law is a Bottomless-Pit,* one of the pamphlets constituting *The History of John Bull* (1712),
where Bull's first wife (the Whig-influenced Godolphin ministry) is a precursor of Lady Willit, while her
successor (Harley's Tory ministry) behaves more like
Martha Blount. The first was 'an extravagant Bitch of
a Wife . . . a luxurious Jade, lov'd splendid Equipages,
Plays, Treats and Balls, differing very much from the
sober Manners of her Ancestors, and by no means fit
for a Tradesman's Wife'. The second was 'a sober
Country Gentlewoman, of a good Family, and a plen-
tiful Fortune; the reverse of the other in her Temper'.[23]

Gambling provided a powerful analogy between sexual and political temptation. Barter in ***The Distress'd***

Wife hints that Lady Willit's virtue is endangered by
this pursuit:

Barter. Does she game as deep as ever?
Sir Thomas. You know she does.
Barter. And can you be so unreasonable as to put
her out of the
Way of so *innocent* an Amusement?

(I, i, 61-4)

There is no need for more than a hint, when the danger
is defined so clearly, time and again, in the literature
of the period, a good example being the predicament
of Lady Gentle in Cibber's *The Lady's Last Stake*
(1707). A wife who lost heavily might be tempted to
pay her debts of honour with her body rather than
confess her extravagance to her husband. The masculine equivalent, endangering public virtue, was specu-
lating on the stock market, according to George Berkeley in his *Essay Towards Preventing the Ruin of
Great Britain* (1721):

Money is so far useful to the public as it promoteth
industry, and credit having the same effect is of the
same value with money; but money or credit
circulating through a nation from hand to hand
without producing labour and industry in the
inhabitants, is direct gaming.[24]

Barter rejects Lord Courtlove's offer of inside information from government sources with a crushing rebuke:

But then one exorbitant Fortune of this sort hath
made at least a thousand Beggars.—'Tis the most
fraudulent, the most pernicious Gaming, under a
more specious Denomination; and those who practise
it, disgrace the Profession of a Merchant. (IV, xiv,
47-51)

It is unlikely that eighteenth-century merchants were
quite so highly principled off stage, but Gay was prepared to sacrifice credibility, yet again, to moral edification.

Scriblerian ideals, however, were not always a deter-
rent to the muses. Even Gay's habitual hostility to
Walpole, which slows down the action so badly in
Polly, is turned to good theatrical account when government espionage is used to provide the catastrophe
of ***The Distress'd Wife.*** Although the play opens with
Sir Thomas Willit's resolution to give up his quest for
a government employment and return to the country,
he does not act on his decision until he accidentally
reads a letter directed to Lady Willit, revealing that she
has been getting money from his steward on the sly. A
blunder by the Post Office brings about his enlightenment: the Clerk in the Inland Secretary's Private Of-

fice has opened the letter and neglected to seal it again. Intercepting the mail of suspected criminals and political opponents was longstanding government practice; according to Barter, ''Tis a Grievance that is become so general, that no Particular will take it upon him to complain' (V, iv, 27-8). Pope and Swift were both convinced that their correspondence was subjected to these flattering attentions and said so in their letters.[25] Dr. Johnson thought Pope was suffering from an inflated sense of his own importance: 'All this while it was likely that the clerks did not know his hand.[26] Whatever the true state of affairs, it must have given the Scriblerians great satisfaction to envisage government policy defeated by its own weapons. It would have given them even greater satisfaction to know that John Lefebure, who became Foreign Secretary to the Post Office around 1718 and held that key post until his death in 1752, was a Jacobite mole.[27] This was one of many sardonic flourishes with which life has insisted on embellishing Scriblerian irony.

The Scriblerian attitude to humour was also a healthy influence on Gay's drama, encouraging him to uphold the tradition that comedy ought to be funny. The Scriblerian collaboration, *Three Hours after Marriage,* represents a reaction to the encroaching vogue for sentimentality: so do *Achilles, The Distress'd Wife* and even parts of *Polly.* Comparison between *The Distress'd Wife* and Cibber's *The Provoked Husband* (1728) shows Gay to advantage in this respect. Cibber based *The Provoked Husband* on Sir John Vanbrugh's unfinished *A Journey to London.* According to Robert D. Hume, *The Provoked Husband* is 'an important and undervalued play', which offers highly effective solutions to the marital problems under examination; Gay, on the other hand, 'was to end his *The Distress'd Wife* (1734) by having an extravagant wife hauled off to the country, an unsatisfying ending to a weak play'.[28] Cibber certainly treats his subject more seriously, in the main plot at least, attempting a convincing reconciliation between husband and wife, but not everyone was impressed. Henry Fielding gave his opinion in *Tom Jones* (1749):

> The Puppet-show was performed with great Regularity and Decency. It was called the fine and serious Part of the *Provok'd Husband;* and it was indeed a very grave and solemn Entertainment, without any low Wit or Humour, or Jests; or, to do it no more than Justice, without any thing which could provoke a Laugh. The Audience were all highly pleased. A grave Matron told the Master she would bring her two Daughters the next Night, as he did not shew any Stuff; and an Attorney's Clerk, and an Exciseman, both declared, that the Characters of Lord and Lady *Townly* were well preserved, and highly in Nature. (XII, 5)[29]

Gay's comedy offers no obeisance to provincial respectability. He tries to maintain, and even intensify,

the comic force of Vanbrugh's original sketch. Vanbrugh gives the town-loving wife, Arabella, a sensible friend who tries to persuade her that it is possible to enjoy both the town and the country, with due moderation:

> *Clarinda.* I would entertain my self in observing the new Fashions soberly, I would please my self in new Cloaths soberly, I would divert my self with agreeable Friends at Home and Abroad soberly. I would play at Quadrille soberly, I would go to Court soberly, I would go to some Plays soberly, I would go to Operas soberly, and I think I cou'd go once, or, if I lik'd my Company, twice to a Masquerade soberly.
>
> *Lady Arabella.* If it had not been for that last Piece of Sobriety, I was going to call for some Surfeit-water. (II, i, 167-74)[30]

Even with the surfeit-water to wash it down, Cibber found this dose of sobriety excessive, and reduced it drastically. Gay strikes a blow for laughter by removing the sensible friend altogether and substituting the effervescent Miss Sprightly, who has her own very strong reasons for preferring country life, but makes no attempt to confute Lady Willit. What the play loses in coherence it gains in vitality. James Thomson objected that 'Miss Sprightly's Wit is affected, and has not that amiable Softness and gentle Character which ought to recommend the Sprightliness of your Sex.'[31] This is high praise: a persual of the sentimental melodrama *Edward and Eleanora* (1739), in which Thomson indulged to the full his taste for female softness, will confirm the reader's good opinion of Miss Sprightly.

The muses entertained no objection to morality, so long as it was compatible with good drama. It was when Gay forgot his need of them that they repaid his neglect by sneaking off. In an age of scholarly, cultivated gentleman dramatists, Gay had to remember how important it was to be a man of the theatre as well. He was always sure of attaining a reasonable degree of success when he kept established dramatic precedent in view; he achieved his masterpieces when he narrowed and sharpened his focus still further, to concentrate on the idea of theatre itself. Gay is at his best when he explores, and apparently defies, the nature of dramatic convention. *The What D'Ye Call It* and *The Beggar's Opera* engage the audience's emotions from within a framework that seems calculated to alienate them. He is not a conjuror, relying on concealment and illusions, but a magician, who can get his effect while leaving his apparatus in full view. This is a typically Scriblerian trick: *A Tale of a Tub* makes its point with a pyrotechnic display of controlled pointlessness; *The Dunciad* celebrates, in great poetry, the conditions that, according to its author, make great poetry impossible.

Gay was the only Scriblerian to bring this technique to the stage, which explains the paradox that he was never more Scriblerian than when he was most himself. ***Achilles*** and ***The Distress'd Wife*** are, in structural terms, conventional dramas; even ***Polly,*** despite the promise of the Introduction, dwindles into a straightforward ballad opera, lacking the ironic complexities provided in ***The Beggar's Opera*** by the re-entry of the Beggar and the Player at the end. His later material was just as rich in Scriblerian associations, but he lacked the independent perspective that had previously enabled him to take command of his form. Christopher Smart understood the necessity, for all the Scriblerians, of the clear view that precedes the satiric kill. His observations would have made a more appropriate epitaph than Pope's:

> Let Eliada rejoice with the Gier-eagle who is
>   swift and of great penetration.
> *For I bless the Lord Jesus for the memory of*
>   *GAY, POPE and*
> *SWIFT.*[32]

Notes

[1] Quoted in *The Poetical Works of John Gay* (London, 1804 (C. Cooke)), I, 13. This inscription, although never finally used, was commonly quoted. See Theophilus Cibber, *The Lives of the Poets of Great Britain and Ireland,* 5 vols. (London, 1753), IV, 258.

[2] Quotations from Johnson from George Birkbeck Hill (ed.), *Lives of the English Poets* (Oxford, 1905), II, 269, 271, 276, 283-84, 282.

[3] 'Introduction', John Fuller (ed.), *John Gay: Dramatic Works,* 2 Vols. (Oxford, 1983) I, 2.

[4] Quoted in *DW,* I, 58.

[5] Alan Dugald McKillop, *James Thomson: Letters and Documents* (Lawrence, Kansas, 1958), p. 168.

[6] *DW,* I, 65.

[7] F. W. Bateson (ed.), *Epistles to Several Persons (Moral Essays),* 2nd edn. (London and New Haven, 1961), p. 67. Vol. III, ii of the Twickenham Edition of *The Poems of Alexander Pope.*

[8] Act, scene, and line references are to the texts of Gay's plays in *DW,* from which all quotations are taken (roman for italics in Airs).

[9] William H. McBurney (ed.), *The London Merchant* (London, 1965), p. 12.

[10] *The Gentleman Instructed in the Conduct of a Virtuous and Happy Life,* 5th edn. (London, 1713), III, 374.

[11] Herbert Davis (ed.), *The Prose Writings of Jonathan Swift* (Oxford, 1939-75), XII, 113-14.

[12] *Dublin Intelligence,* 14 January 1729.

[13] Davis, XII, p. 80.

[14] *The Double Gallant; or, The Sick Lady's Cure,* 2nd edn. (London, 1707), pp. 27-8.

[15] Bateson, pp. 46, 49-50.

[16] 'Imagination in *The Rape of the Lock*', *EC,* 29 (1979), 54.

[17] Geoffrey Tillotson (ed.), *The Rape of the Lock and Other Poems,* 3rd edn. (London and New Haven, 1962), pp. 163-64. Vol. II of the Twickenham Edition of *The Poems of Alexander Pope.*

[18] James Kinsley (ed.), *The Poems of John Dryden* (Oxford, 1958), IV, 1750.

[19] A. C. Ewald (ed.), *The Dramatic Works of George Farquhar* (London, 1892), I, 259.

[20] Line references are to the texts of Gay's poems in Vintar Dearing (ed.), with the assistance of Charles E. Beckwith, *John Gay: Poetry and Prose,* 2 Vols. (Oxford, 1974), from which all quotations are taken.

[21] Davis, I, 81, 26.

[22] C. H. Herford and Percy Simpson (eds.), *Ben Jonson* (Oxford, 1925-52), V, 452-53.

[23] Alan W. Bower and Robert A. Ericson (eds.), *The History of John Bull* (Oxford, 1976), pp. 12-13, 16.

[24] A. A. Luce and T. E. Jessop (eds.), *The Works of George Berkeley Bishop of Cloyne* (London, 1948-57), VI, 71.

[25] See George Sherburn (ed.), *The Correspondence of Alexander Pope* (Oxford, 1956), III, 431-32 (Pope and Bolingbroke to Swift, 15 September 1734); IV, 231-32 (Pope to the Earl of Orrery, 27 March 1740); and Harold Williams (ed.), *The Correspondence of Jonathan Swift* (Oxford, 1963-65), V, 119-20 (Swift to Pope and Bolingbroke, 8 August 1738).

[26] Hill, III, 211.

[27] See Eveline Cruickshanks, *Political Untouchables: The Tories and the '45* (London, 1979), p. 47. For details of Post Office procedure, see Kenneth Ellis, *The Post Office in the Eighteenth Century* (London,

1958), p. 64; for the official version of John Lefebure's career, see ibid., pp. 66-7.

[28] 'Marital Discord in English Comedy from Dryden to Fielding', *Modern Philology,* 74 (1976-77), 263.

[29] Martin C. Battestin and Fredson Bowers (eds.), *The History of Tom Jones* (Oxford, 1974), II, 637-38.

[30] Bonamy Dobrée (ed.), *The Complete Works of Sir John Vanbrugh* (London, 1927), III, 150.

[31] McKillop, p. 168.

[32] Karina Williamson (ed.), *The Poetical Works of Christopher Smart,* I (*Jubilate Agno*) (Oxford, 1980), p. 26.

Yvonne Noble (essay date 1988)

SOURCE: "Sex and Gender in Gay's 'Achilles,'" in *John Gay and the Scriblerians,* edited by Peter Lewis and Nigel Wood, Vision Press; St. Martin's Press, 1988, pp. 184-215.

[*In the following essay, Noble argues that Gay's later drama registers the paradoxical position of women in a patriarchal society, with an emphasis on contemporary constructions of rape. Noble concludes that while Gay was not necessarily "feminist," his work nonetheless reflects the voice of the oppressed.*]

At a time of unparalleled academic interest in the relationship (which is to say, discrepancy) between sex and gender, John Gay emerges as an extremely interesting writer, distinctively conscious and candid, able through his characteristic duple forms and modes to render the simultaneous state of authenticity and inauthenticity in which those who do not embody the norm are condemned to dwell. Little interested in party politics, uninterested in social theory, Gay was acutely aware of the transactions of oppression between individuals; he is able through these duple forms and modes to force those who would be intractable to preaching to take account of the unvoiced suffering even in their own circle. Gay's last work, the seemingly frivolous ballad opera *Achilles,* confronts in this way the serious issue of rape.

Achilles, which had just gone into rehearsal when Gay died, features its hero throughout dressed in the clothes of a girl. How is this figure to be read? Much current writing would presume that a figure like this, particularly in a work of burlesque, must at least trivialize its subject or at worst serve a retrograde and conservative function by embodying a mockery of woman to mollify the anxieties, and reinforce the prejudices, of men.[1] While by no means denying the applicability of such

insightful analysis to the theatre of Gay's time—for indeed, the pronounced sexism of the period cries out for analysis of this sort[2]—I would nevertheless like to widen the realm of interpretation by suggesting quite a different possibility for Gay's travesty subject. I propose that Gay selected this Achilles as his subject precisely because the figure could open up interesting questions of gender-identity[3] and be used to undermine one of the key tenets of male dominance—the principle that women's sexual desire corresponds to men's—exactly at its most reinforcing point of textual authority in classical literature. My reading will locate an important significance of the figure of Achilles by reference to classical contexts it invokes, in a current of meaning flowing from Gay to those of his auditors who could recognize that context. This study will therefore also chart a little more of that relatively neglected side of Gay's artistry, his relation to and transformation of the literature of antiquity, through which he moves with grace, wit, fondness, and good acquaintance.[4]

Achilles is based upon the episode in which the hero, disguised as a girl, is concealed on the island of Scyros among the daughters of King Lycomedes. His mother, the sea-goddess Thetis, has learned by a prophecy that her son can have a long, uneventful life in obscurity or a short life of great glory if he joins the Trojan War; understandably Thetis seeks to preserve her son. The Greeks, on the other hand, discover that they cannot win without Achilles and therefore mount an expedition to find him. Ulysses, in the guise of a merchant, prepares a stock of women's gear amid which he places a suit of armour together with arms. When Ulysses displays these wares to the maidens of Scyros, Achilles is found out, tricked by the lure of the arms into revealing himself.

One epigraph to the printed *Achilles* (1733) directs us to Ovid's *Metamorphoses* for the classical source being represented or evoked. The passage occurs in Book XIII, as a part of a speech by Ulysses, debating against Ajax after Achilles's death in order to claim the hero's armour. Ulysses brings up the episode in order to demonstrate that the Greeks would not have had the services of Achilles except for Ulysses's cleverness—and he includes the gibe that his opponent Ajax was completely taken in by Achilles's disguise. (Gay alludes to this point in making Ajax avid to duel for 'Pyrrha' in Act III.[5]) Besides schoolboy exposure to Ovid's poem, Gay would have encountered the passage as one of Dryden's *Fables* (1700, reprinted 1713, 1721), an excerpt later collected into Garth's edition of the *Metamorphoses Englished* (1717, 1720, 1727) to which Gay also contributed work; this translation obtained new currency in 1732—the year *Achilles* was written—as the English part of a sumptuous illustrated Latin-English folio of Ovid's poem, containing a visual representation of the disguised Achilles in the recognition scene.[6] Accompanying other work by Gay, the passage appears as translated by Theobald in the rival English *Metamorphoses* edited by Sewell (1717 [1716], 1724 (reissued 1726)). Such repeated editions and reprintings imply a wide public thoroughly familiar with the stories, whom a writer like Gay could assume he was addressing. Book XIII—the pair of speeches—was also often translated by itself, and Gay would have had particular reason to notice two of these versions: one in 1708 with Ulysses's speech translated by his schoolfriend and early London mentor Aaron Hill[7], and a modernized burlesque version in 1719 put out by his pseudonymous namesake and bane, 'Joseph Gay' (later to be immortalized as a pursuable phantom by Pope in the *Dunciad* games).[8] Of course, it would not have taken someone else's work to put John Gay's mind running on burlesque, and the low-life treatment by 'Joseph Gay' is rather coarse, but certain features might have stimulated his imagination, particularly the wife supplied for the first time for Lycomedes and the garb and kit of a Scottish peddler that Ulysses assumes.[9]

Gay incorporates into his ballad opera, however, many aspects of the legend that were well-known in antiquity but do not figure in the *Metamorphoses,* with its focus upon concealment and disclosure.[10] These include such memorable features as the clandestine amour with King Lycomedes's daughter Deidamia, Achilles's engagement in women's work (spinning), the presence of a group of daughters (or court maidens), the use of a trumpet call as part of Ulysses's ruse, and Achilles's adoption of the name 'Pyrrha'. The first two can be found elsewhere in Ovid (*Ars Amatoria*), in Statius, and in (pseudo-) Bion. Lycomedes's daughters are in Statius and in Bion, as well as in a number of minor writers, and the trumpet call occurs in Statius and others. From Statius, Gay could draw the psychology of awareness: 'Conscious of her and Achilles's concealed guilt, Deidamia is tormented with anxiety and thinks her sisters are aware but not mentioning what they suspect or know.'[11] The idea that the intrigue began as a result of the couple's having been assigned the same bed or bedchamber derives, by contrast, not from Statius but from Bion and Ovid (*Ars Amatoria*). To know that Achilles was called 'Pyrrha', Gay must have had first-hand or at least indirect access to the less familiar writers, Apollodorus, Hyginus and Sidonius.[12]

But as my review of the English versions of the *Metamorphoses* tale suggests, Gay could draw upon not only his own familiarity with the classical story, but also that of his readers, even the unlearned. Thus it is important to review, with the content of his likeliest sources, how widely they could have been known. Of the Bion—the fragmentary *Epithalamius of Achilles and Deidameia*—I have found no translation into English until long after Gay's death.[13] I believe, nevertheless, that Gay must have known this fragment, which occurs among a group of idylls often associated with those of

Theocritus, of whom he composed a full-scale imitation in *The Shepherd's Week* and whom he cites there many times by name. In the Bion fragment the story of the love affair is told in the same Doric style that Theocritus uses and that Gay approximates with clattering rhymes, low country lore, and archaisms. In Bion such a version answers the call made by a rustic for 'a pretty (Sicilian) love-song such as Polyphemus sang to Galatea'; Gay's mind would have seized on this text, for he wrote exactly that song himself—**'O ruddier than the Cherry!'** for Handel's *Acis and Galatea* (II, 17-27).[14] Treating Achilles, Bion's singer stresses the clear male selfhood within the ostensibly feminine beauty, then paints in detail the lover's conduct in the early stages of courtship:

> Achilles alone hid among the girls, the daughters of Lycomedes, and he learned woolworking instead of arms, and with white arm he sustained a maiden's task, and he appeared like a girl; for he actually became girlish like them, and just such a blossom blushed on his snowy cheeks, and he walked with the walk of a girl, and he covered his hair with a veil. But still he had the heart of a man and the passion of a man, and from dawn to night he sat beside Deidamia, and sometimes he kissed her hand, and many a time he raised up her fair weaving and he praised her patterned web; and he did not eat with any other companion, and he did everything in his eagerness to share her bed; and he even spoke a word to her: 'The other sisters sleep with one another, but I sleep alone and you girl sleep alone, we two maiden companions, we two fair; but we sleep alone in our separate beds; but that wicked crafty Nysaia cruelly separates me from you. For I do not you. . . .'[15]

As for Statius's version of the story, it was certainly known by part of Gay's audience, for one critic, 'Atex' Burnet, writing before the printed edition of *Achilles* (with its Ovid epigraph) was published, unhesitatingly declared Statius—that is, his *Achilleid*—to be Gay's source.[16] This work had been published in an English translation by Sir Robert Howard among his *Poems* in 1660. Many common details—for example, Achilles's insisting upon a ceremony to confirm his marriage to Deidamia—make it clear that Gay knew Statius's poem. The general currency of this classical author may be indicated by recalling the place of translations from his earlier epic, the *Thebaid,* among Pope's juvenilia and earliest publications. In Book I of the *Achilleid* Statius treats Achilles's time in Scyros at length. Here, Achilles agrees to put on the woman's garment only after he has been kindled by the sight of Deidamia. The poet slowly builds with psychosomatic details—tightenings of the scalp, flushes of the skin, impulsive movements checked by bashfulness—the representation of the force of sexual feeling within an inexperienced adolescent boy. Achilles constantly hovers near Deidamia, keeping his presence known by little gaucheries. In

Deidamia, similarly, Statius depicts the special psychological state of a nubile virgin, who encourages Achilles's courtship without allowing herself consciously to know the circumstances in which she is placed; whenever Achilles tries to explain his deception, she will not allow him opportunity to do so. After many days of restraint, combined with the loss of his old male activities and the frustrations of his new rôle, finding himself near the girl in the dark one night in a sacred grove, 'He gains by force his desire, and with all his vigour strains her in a real embrace.'[17] Statius conveys that this act, while not wholly unpremeditated, largely flows from a compulsion more powerful than the lad at his stage of understanding and of physical development can control. Deidamia, who has had no idea that there was a man nearby, is of course frantic and terrified. When these stresses have abated, however, their mutual attraction draws them to continue a secret liaison as lovers and to protect each other. Deidamia achieves considerable mastery over her circumstances, for, with the assistance of her nurse, she manages to conceal her pregnancy, her lying-in, and her growing child, and to prevent Achilles impetuously giving himself away many times to Ulysses's searching eyes; Achilles, in turn, immediately his identity is revealed, also confesses their situation and asks (successfully) to marry her. In short, while Statius does not condemn the rape, and even uses it in his narrative as an index of his hero's masculinity, he also presents it as an index of his hero's immaturity.

Sustaining the sexual dynamic I have already described, Statius renders the disclosure of Achilles's true self at the sound of the alarm as the unleashing of even more irresistible natural power concentrated within the taut form: standing motionless amid the panic, Achilles simply grows huge and dominant: as his womanly garments fall away, *he* (his whole body) erects:

> *illius intactae cecidere a pectore vestes,*
> *iam clipeus breviorque manu consumitur*
>   *hasta,*
> *—mira fides!—Ithacumque umeris excedere*
>   *visus*
> *Aetolumque ducem: . . .*
> *immanisque gradu, ceu protinus Hectora*
>   *poscens,*
> *stat medius trepidante domo: Peleaque virgo*
> *quaeritur.*
>
>   (I, 878-81, 883-85)

From his breast the garments fall away untouched, now the shield and puny spear are swallowed up by his hands—marvellous to believe!—his head and shoulders loom up above those of Ulysses and Diomede: . . .

Mighty of limb, in combat stance, as if he could summon Hector, he stands amid the panic-stricken house: and the girl-that-was for whom they search [they will never find].[18]

Achilles in legend enacts the tragic impossibility of escaping one's destiny. At the moment Statius treats in this passage, the ties of life—the long life Thetis has sought for him, the inane alternative symbolized in his inappropriate raiment—are sloughed away by the true heroic reality that declares itself. Not accidentally is this heroic manifestation expressed by likeness to the declaration one part of a man's body can make of exemption from qualifying circumstance and personal uncertainty. Throughout the Scyros episode Statius makes plain, both explicitly and symbolically, the relationship between male sexual, and heroic military, potency, and grounds them both in irresistible nature. Gay takes over Statius's themes, but recasts into questions his certainties.

Of all the classical treatments of Achilles and Deidamia, however, Ovid's *Ars Amatoria* would have been the most familiar and most influential. Throughout the history of secular classical education, the confident, urbane advice to men by the writer of the *Ars Amatoria* on how to obtain and retain women's love must have been devoured by schoolboys after hours when it failed to find a place in the formal curriculum. Since Gay's time, bowdlerism has successfully prevented many readers from becoming aware of Ovid's full text.[19] Gay's contemporaries, by contrast, could choose among many candid translations of Book I by Thomas Heywood (1650, 1662, 1672, 1677, 1682, 1684), Francis Wolferston (1661), Thomas Hoy (1682, 1692), or Dryden (1709, 1712, 1716, 1719). They could also read the advice applied to modern times—in the coarse anonymous *Art of Love* (1701, reissued slightly revised in 1702 as *The Poet Banter'd*) or in William King's elaborate adaptation (1708, reissued 1712), where quite witty burlesque elements sometimes conceal the onset of the bowdlerizing impulse.[20]

It was Ovid in the *Ars Amatoria* who introduced the idea that Achilles raped Deidamia (setting for his successor Statius the problem he so brilliantly solved of accounting for the rape).[21] The story is brought in as an illustration in a context I shall describe later. Ovid's narrator is a bully, interested in understanding others' psychology only in order to achieve an ascendancy: he therefore mocks Achilles for dressing as a woman and for spinning. But, for him, Achilles asserts his true nature not as a hero in warfare but as a man in rape. Manliness is staked upon sexual conquest.

Thus, while the account in the *Metamorphoses* focuses on Achilles as an object of concealment and disclosure, other sources concentrate upon the significance of the figure while in disguise, as he shares the education, occupations, indeed one of the beds, of the daughters of Lycomedes. Achilles's love affair with Deidamia, confirmed in her pregnancy,[22] testifies to the hero's genuine manliness despite his appearance. The figure—or idea—of the disguised Achilles spinning doubles with that of Hercules in similar garments engaged at the same task, and therefore indicates that what is represented is not man, or mere man, but hero, in displacement. Depending on the treatment, the image could suggest a wide range of possible values, from debasement through latent power to the enhancement of one's power by encompassing the attributes of the Other. These parts of the legend share an interest in the question of gender-identity and its relation to 'true' identity and to the ability to act effectively in the world.

The Achilles-in-Scyros story therefore held many interesting themes for Gay to explore. He would have met the figure of Achilles in petticoats early in his studies and had reason to be reminded of the figure over and over in the intervening years. Furthermore, the figure would in itself have appealed to Gay, whose imagination repeatedly created figures in cross-gendered disguise. In his plays such figures partly reflect common theatre conventions, but for Gay they also reflect his wider imaginative habitation in double forms—burlesque- or mock-modes—and his fascination with duple or liminal figures, such as pregnant maidens or castrati. Gender disguise can be found also in his poetry and translations. Particularly striking is the early passage in his **Epistle to Burlington** (circulating in manuscript in 1717, printed 1720) in which he candidly and without any suggestion of oddity describes his pleasure in finding himself in women's clothes. He and his squires have ridden four days on horseback; at an inn they have the chance to strip to the skin, and have all their clothes laundered; the maid gives them women's nightgowns to sleep in:

> The Maid, subdu'd by Fees, her Trunk
>   unlocks,
> And gives the cleanly Aid of Dowlas Smocks.
> Mean time our Shirts her busy Fingers rub,
> While the Soap lathers o'er the foaming Tub.
> If Women's Geer such pleasing Dreams incite,
> Lend us your Smocks, ye Damsels, ev'ry
>   Night!
>
> (103-8)

The idea of fingers touching the clothes from the outside combines with the reverie induced by comfort, relaxation, passivity, the sensation of unfamiliar but agreeable garments felt from the inside, and the strange but not unpleasant disruption of the attributes of sexual identity. Day returns the dreamers to the certainty of their masculinity, 'We rise; our Beards demand the Barber's art' (109), but allows them to reassume their reverie with all the elements I have mentioned—the

stroking fingers, the sensation to the skin, the comfort, relaxation, passivity, the pleasing disruption of sexual norms:

> A Female enters, and performs the part. . . . .
> Smooth o'er our Chin her easy Fingers move,
> Soft as when *Venus* stroak'd the Beard of
>   *Jove.*
>
> (110, 113-14)[23]

The composition of the immediate predecessor to **Achilles** among Gay's ballad operas may help to explain why Gay thought later of Achilles as a subject. In that work, **Polly,** Gay had put his heroine into breeches. Quite apart from any imaginative predispositions, Gay would have arrived at this feature by the same process that led him to write **Polly** in the first place: to follow up on the unprecedented success of **The Beggar's Opera.** Polly Peachum had become a celebrity—there were 'biographies' of her, books of her sayings, engraved portraits, her face on screens and fans—and the actress who embodied her had capped the glamour with a flourish by setting up with a duke. How natural to feature Polly in a sequel and to put her into disguise as a man, at once greatly extending the character's scope for action and the actress's scope for display.

For his next ballad opera Gay would easily think of reviving the travesty in reverse, and Achilles-in-Scyros would readily follow to mind—already associated, furthermore, with modernization and with burlesque. For Polly-in-breeches Gay had written a scene based upon the story of Potiphar's wife. As **Polly** had not been performed, Gay carried the idea over to his new piece and rewrote the scene with the sexes reversed. Adding a jealous wife for Lycomedes and taking over the two elements—love affair and disclosure—from the classical story, Gay had the material for his text. This material he then structured to raise questions about the relation of gender to personal identity.

A noticeable feature of his structure is that during the greater part of **Achilles** no other character present is aware that the person called Pyrrha is anything but the young woman she seems. The exposition is set out for the audience in dialogue between Achilles, already disguised, and Thetis, who then departs. Until II, x, the drama then deals with the feminine-gendered Pyrrha, whose treatment and circumstances the audience must evaluate in terms of the smouldering male consciousness that must endure them. The nature of what Gay achieves here can be made clearer by comparing his plotting with that of Paolo Rolli for Handel's last opera, *Deidamia* (1741). As soon as possible in Act I, Rolli establishes that both Lycomedes and Deidamia are aware that their guest Pyrrha is Achilles—Lycomedes has promised his friend Peleus, Achilles's father, that he will conceal his son. Without my delaying to set out the obvious male ruling-class affiliation of the heroic mode, we might notice that the goddess Thetis, whom antique plots were able to tolerate, if only to thwart, is obliterated in Rolli's heroic plot in favour of her mortal, but male, spouse: Lycomedes can be bound, against the claims of Ulysses, by an oath to Peleus, as he cannot by a promise to a female, a mother. Rolli can concentrate the action of his drama upon the efforts of his principal, Ulysses (for Ulysses, not Achilles, was *primo uomo*), to discern the evidences of heroic manliness in the lineaments of a nymph who hunts exceptionally well, and who fails to respond to the gestures of courtship, but who, in the end, cannot resist a helmet and shield.[24] Ulysses, the 'subject', or viewing mind, achieves mastery over the 'object', which has an existence and a true nature independent of him that can be 'dis-covered', and that, by the right test, he can force it to disclose. In this ontology, a person's nature inheres in his or her sexual identity, which informs all aspects of behaviour and taste; it therefore cannot be long concealed from the discerning eye. Rolli's position is precisely Ovid's: 'She, not discover'd by her Mien or Voice,/ Betray'd her Manhood by her manly Choice' (*Metamorphoses*, translated by Dryden).[25] With Ulysses as subject, Achilles does not simply *manifest* himself like Statius's hero; not self-directed and irresistibly powerful, he is beckonable, controlled.

Unlike Rolli, Gay holds off till the last moment—the tenth scene of the final act—before allowing Ulysses's configuration of reality to take hold of his play. Ulysses, observing the discernible behaviour of '*Achilles . . . handling and poising the Armour*', sees in it first the outward manifestations of the hero's nature—'That intrepid Air! That Godlike Look!'—then the heroic nature itself—'His Nature, his Disposition shews him through the Disguise.' 'Son of *Thetis,* I know thee', he declares, and Achilles acknowledges himself (III, x, 81-90). But the finale, which Gay gives to Ulysses and his point of view, in fact undercuts the value, and the grounds, of the discovery:

> Nature breaks forth at the Moment unguarded;
>   Through all Disguise she her self must
>   betray. . . .
>
> Thus when the Cat had once all Woman's
>   Graces;
>   Courtship, Marriage won her Embraces:
> Forth lept a Mouse; she, forgetting Enjoyment,
>   Quits her fond Spouse for her former
>   Employment.
>
> Nature breaks forth at the Moment unguarded;
>   Through all Disguise she herself must
>   betray.
>
>   (III, xii, 80-1, 84-9)

Here is a reality, a 'something' that can 'break forth', as the essence of 'catness' leaps out of the woman's clothes to pursue the mouse, when stressed by the irresistible temptation specific to its nature, which for the hero is the armour. Yet the 'something' is controlled neither by its own integrity (it can 'betray' itself), nor by its male master; it responds no more readily to guile than to random contingency. The hierarchical status of what Ulysses has discovered—the heroic male warrior—is discredited by his being equated with a female domestic beast in pursuit of her 'former Employment', while man-the-subject-discerner is left embarrassed at not being able to discriminate at all, even in the intimacy of marriage, between the image of woman concealing the nature of cat, the image of woman concealing the nature of hero, and the image of woman concealing the nature of woman (if, for such subjects, the latter distinction can be known).

Following *Achilles* backwards from this final wobbly affirmation of a knowable inner essence to its beginning, we find a series of progressively external definitions of identity that occupy more and more of the play time (or text) the earlier, and more external, they are. The speech preceding the finale, 'We may for a while put on a feign'd Character, but Nature is so often unguarded that it will shew itself.—'Tis to the Armour we owe *Achilles*' (III, xii, 77-9), suggests in its last phrase that the heroism lodges not in the man but in the armour. In one sense, Ulysses's clothing-trick brings out a distinction between Achilles and the maidens, but in another sense it is a distinction without a difference: some are attracted by costumes of one sort, some by costumes of another sort, but all are the same in being attracted by costumes. Rather than there being an innate, hierarchical difference, there may be no meaningful difference at all—Gay's irreverent presentation certainly supports the latter notion. His point is explored in the Prologue 'Written by Mr. *GAY*' (nevertheless attributed by some to Pope).[26]

> To Buskins, Plumes and Helmets what
>   Pretence,
> If mighty Chiefs must speak but common
>   Sense? . . .
> And whatsoever Criticks may suppose,
> Our Author holds, that what He [Achilles]
>   spoke was Prose.
>
>   (17-18, 23-4)

The questions of diction and criticism—particularly if they are raised by the translator of the *Iliad* and the *Odyssey*—invoke the debate between Ancients and Moderns, with the indication that if Gay's Achilles 'speaks prose',[27] as he does (even while the Prologue 'speaks couplets'), correspondingly what is *embodied* or *dressed* in the epic verse will be absent, too. Once, 'Buskins, Plumes and Helmets' were put on by real warriors and corresponded to real danger, real courage: they signified grandeur and magnanimity as opposed to triviality and mean-spiritedness. Now they have no function except as costumes put on by actors or opera singers. But the first line hints by its metonymy that, even in the past, heroes—'Buskins, Plumes and Helmets'—were no more than their costumes and that their virtue had no more existence than now. Thus can be read Ulysses's summation: ' 'Tis to the Armour we owe *Achilles*' (III, xii, 79).

Institutionalized distinctions in virtually all cultures testify that for most people the essence of personal identity lodges in the sex organs and in their expression of fertility and potency. Gay uses the Deidamia plot to set forth sexuality's claim to be the lodgment of true identity. For him love-making—sex—is naturally a matter of mutual pleasure and desire understood to lead to pregnancy: 'I have copied Nature, making the Youths Amorous before Wedlock, and the Damsels Complying and Fruitful' (preface, **The What D'Ye Call It**, 90-1). In the verse of Air III of **Achilles**—with a hint of Statius's outlook—Gay suggests the danger of attempting to repress the power of sexual energy in the metaphor of a foolish shepherd who would pen up a hungry wolf within the fold, while the tune Gay chooses for this air reinforces the theme by recalling that paragon of vainly-pent sexual energy, Macheath, in the condemned cell of Newgate Prison singing Air LXV to the same strains, 'But can I leave my pretty Hussies,/ Without one Tear, or tender Sigh?' (**The Beggar's Opera,** III, xiii, 18-19).

There are a few jokes that play upon the sense of the hidden male organ, particularly when Lycomedes's guards begin to search Pyrrha for a 'Dagger . . . You will find . . . some where or other conceal'd' (II, v, 9-10), but direct references like these to Achilles's sex are few. Gay is far more interested in the question of how sexual identity can be known indirectly: he sets up the Achilles-Deidamia plot as flowing from Theaspe's incorrect judgement about Achilles's sexual identity. This has induced her to demand that her daughter be 'scarce ever from her [Pyrrha]; they have one and the same Bed-Chamber' (I, viii, 83-4). Other lines in Theaspe's same speech indicate further ways of knowing on this plane of identity—direct verification of the organ (Deidamia 'insists upon it that I have nothing to fear from *Pyrrha;* and is . . . positive in this Opinion' [I, viii, 76-8], recalling Thetis's fear 'that when you are among the Ladies you shou'd be so little Master of your Passions as to find your self a Man' (I, i, 85-7), and indirect indication through the symptoms of pregnancy, here morning sickness ("There must be some Reason that *Deidamia* hath not been with me this Morning' (I, viii, 86-7).

In Gay's original text the subplot that presents this plane of the question of identity may have been introduced directly in dialogue between the two lovers[28], even so, there, as in the published version, this subplot (and the plane it presents) are set aside until very late in the play (the last scene of Act II or, in Burnet, several scenes into Act III), where they occupy a brief, discreet segment of the text. It is important to notice that Gay, utterly in contrast to Statius, does not dramatize the love-making. Nor does he exploit the long-standing analogy of penis to weapon of warfare or conquest, hero to sexual conqueror, even disregarding Statius's striking representation of this theme. What interests him principally is the eloquence of indirect testimony, as expressed in the shape of not the man's but the woman's body, which makes the male presence 'monstrously evident' (III, vii, 56-7)[29]: 'That she [Deidamia] hath all the outward Marks of Female Frailty must be visible to all Woman-kind' (III, vii, 65-6), say her sisters. Sexed—female—body here speaks to sexed (or gendered?) female eye.

Deidamia is defined by, and defines Achilles by, his sex, but he defines manhood by behaving publicly—and being recognized—as manly:

> *Achilles.* When shall I behave my self as a
>   Man!
> *Deidamia.* Wou'd you had never behav'd
>   yourself as one!
>
>   (II, x, 9-10)

A whole repertory of gestures—long strides, swearing, 'aukward Behaviour'—define men as different from women (II, x, 72, 85-6; I, i, 75). Air XXXVI captures the process of rationalization by a man, Achilles, who finds it difficult to behave as women so easily do: soon the impossible attainment begins to be disqualified as merely a manifestation of a 'natural variousness'; then that nature begins to be disqualified as one that a man, with his integrity of being, would not wish to have:

> Your Dress, your Conversations,
>   Your Airs of Joy and Pain,
> All these are Affectations
>   We never can attain.
> The Sex so often varies,
>   'Tis Nature more than Art:
> To play their whole Vagaries
>   We must have Woman's Heart.
>   (II, x, 76-83)

In the first act the difference between men and women is asserted over and over in the dialogue between Thetis and Achilles, not precisely themselves a woman and a man but very conscious of their several natures—divine and heroic—that they feel they debase by pretending to be women (I, i, 30-2, 67-8). Here Gay approaches the issue at the heart of the old legend about the heroic destiny that cannot be gainsaid. Manliness longs to define itself as an immutable inner essence residing in 'the Heart of a Man' (I, i, 14-15), but the language keeps pressing the residence of manly reality outward, to the minds of other manly men with whom one interacts in public deeds—who know one's 'character', recognize one's 'honour', the worth of one's 'Word', remember one's 'glory', preserve one's 'Fame' (I, i). Embroidery, the reading of romances, preoccupation with dress, the spleen (I, ii), are the gendered occupations of 'the Life of a Woman' (I, i, 52), which is not to live as something distinct—womanly—but as something *not manly,* not truly or fully existent and therefore debased: manly 'Character' is opposed to womanish 'Infamy', 'Honour' to 'Cowardise', 'Death with Fame' to 'Life with Shame', one's 'Word' to the pleasure of breaking promises, integrity of being to natural variousness, sword to tongue, duty to country to obedience to mama, resolution to pity, freedom to captivity (I, i, Air XXXVI; III, iii, 18-19, Airs L, XXXIII). In short, whatever one's qualities of generosity, courage, resolution, confidence, one cannot be a 'Man' unless one is recognized to be so by other 'Men', and to be visible requires definition against the contrasting background. 'Honour' is in the recognition; it is for this reason that Achilles becomes dishonoured by his disguise: 'my Honour is already sacrific'd to my Duty. That I gave you when I submitted to put on this Womans Habit' (I, i, 30-2).

Dependency upon the recognition of others for the empowerment of one's identity is only a step away from our final category, in which the reality *arises out of* how we are apprehended by others. Deidamia fears that Achilles will seem to her sisters to be a man because 'whenever I look upon you, I have always the Image of a Man before my Eyes' (II, x, 97-8). The greater part of *Achilles* is given to investigating the reality of this kind of identity wherein what Achilles *is* is only what he is believed to be by Lycomedes—a young girl. When Deidamia sees in Pyrrha the image of a man, she discerns what she *knows* but also projects what she *desires;* for Lycomedes, however, Pyrrha is his desire alone.

The Lycomedes plot is the most interesting part of *Achilles,* for it is entirely Gay's own contribution to the legend; he emphasizes its importance by giving it the greater part of his dramatic time. Its basis is the stock situation in theatre—soon to become the stock situation in the novel as well—in which the young heroine is exposed to unwelcome sexual advances from a man, usually older or of a higher social position, whom she ought to be able to look to for protection. This plot comes into *Achilles,* we have noticed, from *Polly,* where Gay used it in its 'Potiphar's wife' variant. His adding the twist of the travesty to the scene moves its concern from the question of sex to the

question of gender and stresses how largely the harassment is a function of power rather than of true sexual desire. In Gay's version of the Achilles plot (unlike Rolli's), Thetis, pretending to be 'a distress'd *Grecian* Princess' (I, i, 68), asks Lycomedes to allow her 'daughter Pyrrha' to share the education and pastimes of his girls. Lycomedes does not believe the reasons Thetis gives for making her request, but, when his aide Diphilus flatters his vanity by suggesting that the 'most delicious Piece' he admires might be 'had' (I, v, 3, 12), he cannot find any other explanation for the girl's being left behind than that the women hope that he will make the girl his mistress. In other words, the girl exists for him only as a blank onto which he projects his own fantasies; he cannot summon up the thought that she might have a mode of being beyond his awareness or imagination. Though he can see clearly that Pyrrha's behaviour—for example, her vehemently denouncing Diphilus as 'a Pimp, a Pandar, a Bawd' (II, i, 34)—is not overtly encouraging, he eagerly accepts Diphilus's construction that the girl's language is a matter of 'ill-breeding' and her attitude an 'affectation' covering 'Modesty' (II, iv, 31), which therefore expresses the receptiveness he desires: 'She had all the Resentment and Fury of the most complying Prude' (II, iii, 19-20).

Lycomedes begins his effort to possess the girl by sending an agent to attempt to buy her with gifts. Next he offers the presents personally. Next he tries to beguile her with flattery. He declares his passion. Indifference and resistance become imperatives for aggressive love-making:

> To save the Appearances of Virtue, the most easy Woman expects a little gentle Compulsion, and to be allow'd the Decency of a little feeble Resistance. For the Quiet of her own Conscience a Woman may insist upon acting the Part of Modesty, and you must comply with her Scruples. (II, iii, 36-41)

When the last tactics seem not to work, he quickly turns to trying rape:

> When the Fort on no Condition
>   Will admit the gen'rous Foe,
> Parley but delays Submission;
>   We by Storm shou'd lay it low.[30]
>   (II, iv, 65-8)

the burlesque battle this conceit introduces functions in comic terms to release the tension in the scene. We must not leap to the supposition, however, that the playwright thereby trivializes the kind of oppression he has been dramatizing. As Pyrrha, Gay's underdog is endowed with precisely the invincible power that Lycomedes's whole attitude presupposes—and that the very idea of Hero embodied in Achilles presupposes—

to be utterly absent in women (i.e., non-men): 'Am I so ignominiously to be got the better of! . . . By a Woman!' (II, iv, 99, 101). Humiliated, Lycomedes takes the still-all-too-familiar recourse of blaming the victim:

> *Achilles:* Who was the Aggressor, Sir?
> *Lycomedes:* Beauty, Inclination, Love.
>
> (II, v, 24-5)

When Lycomedes becomes finally convinced that the girl cannot become his own possession, he does not enlarge his perception of her from object to person, but merely comes to look upon her as something disturbing to be got rid of. Candidly stating what most people act upon but do not admit to themselves about someone whom they have injured, he declares: 'Her Presence just now wou'd be shocking.—I cou'd not stand the Shame and Confusion' (II, viii, 30-1). He therefore joins in with his wife's plans to marry her off to the (as it happens, uninterested) man of their choice.

'When shall I appear as I am', says Achilles to himself, to be able to 'extricate my self out of this Chain of Perplexities!—I have no sooner escap'd being ravish'd but I am immediately to be made a Wife' (II, x, 65-8). He is clear that these torments occur because he is gendered as female, even though he may not realize the link between the intended marriage and the failure of the attempted rape. Gay's plot makes explicit how, in a society with a double standard, women are forced to destroy each other: Queen Theaspe, whose status derives from her husband, looks through his eyes to see the object of his desire ('I can see her [Pyrrha's] Faults, Sir. I see her as a Woman sees a Woman. The Men, it seems, think the aukward Creature handsome' (I, vi, 16-18). She confirms the men's deduction as to why Pyrrha has been left behind: 'The Woman, no doubt, depends upon it, that her Daughter's Charms are not to be resisted' (I, vi, 97-8). She is attuned to proclivities in her husband before he is even aware of them; she feels jealousy, well-placed, but before the event. Diphilus is able to use her jealousy as an argument to persuade Lycomedes to pursue the affair; the evidence that women are (merely) objects of men's desire comes, then, not just from the men but also from other women's jealousy and anxiety.

The young girl is therefore perceived in sexual terms by the persons she must look to for protection. By the travesty Gay makes this quite clear: Achilles's attractiveness to young men, presumably by virtue of his felt qualities of heroism and leadership, is, because of his gender, interpreted as the sexual charm of a belle (by Diphilus, II, v, 96-7, by Theaspe II, vi, 13-14). His enthusiastic admiration, when Theaspe asks him how he likes Periphas, for the man's wonderful 'Impatience . . . to serve . . . at the Siege of *Troy*' (II, ix, 9-10), she misreads in the same way. The predicament for women

in an oppressive society is that young girls require protection, but because of hypocrisy and the double standard it is *assumed* that they are being put forward not for protection but for advantage through covert sex. It is the inexperienced and little-aware girl who has the greatest chance for advantage, while, for men, experience, wealth, and self-confidence offset the natural attractions of youth. What is 'experience' for 'experienced women' is the coming to awareness of the arrangements and how they work, but, as Gay shows, that very awareness acts to propel the oppression forward upon other women.

What a woman must do—and is entitled to do—in the face of unwelcome attentions Gay expresses through Parthenia in **Dione.** Gay supports her point of view by arranging his plot so that her wishes can be fully met, and in order to do so he was obliged to cast his play as a tragedy, for him not at all a comfortable mode.[31] Because of her exceptional beauty Parthenia persistently finds herself attracting men's desire; a man puts the argument to her: 'What heart is proof against that face divine?/ Love is not in our power' (I, iii, 11-12). But she refuses to accept that someone else's desire should obligate her when she had done nothing to encourage it:

> If e'er I trifled with a shepherd's pain,
> Or with false hope his passion strove to gain;
> Then might you justly curse my savage mind,
> Then might you rank me with the serpent
>   kind:
> But I ne'er trifled with a shepherd's pain,
> Nor with false hope his passion strove to gain:
> 'Tis to his rash pursuit he owes his fate,
> I was not cruel; he was obstinate.
>
> (I, iii, 13-20)

And she goes on with what one might call a Whig feminist credo:

> Why will intruding man my peace destroy?
> Let me content, and solitude enjoy;
> Free was I born, my freedom to maintain,
> Early I sought the unambitious plain.
>
> (I, iii, 25-8)

She sternly advises that her suitor be 'Bid . . . his heart-consuming groans give o'er, . . . be wise,/ Prevent thy fate' (I, iii, 37, 39-40). Lycidas's disregard of her insistence that he take responsibility for his own life (or, his disregard of the autonomy of *nature*) brings death to himself and Dione but leaves Parthenia unmated and unharassed, as she had wished.

By the time of **Achilles** the question of women's right—or desire—to live unmolested had become a topical issue through the sensational Charteris case, which had dramatized the social factors as blatantly as can be imagined. Colonel Francis Charteris had amassed a huge fortune by graft, gambling, close-dealing and chicanery. He had been censured before the House of Commons for taking pay-offs as an officer. He was known by his male visitors to run his household of maid-servants as a brothel.[32] He had been found guilty in Scotland of raping a woman at pistol-point on a public road, but had been pardoned by George I. In February 1730 he was found guilty of raping a recently hired serving-maid in his London house and was sentenced to hang. Vast quantities of his property, which had become forfeit, were then seized by various public officials, and in due course bought back by his son-in-law, the Earl of Wemyss, for very large sums. On 10 April he was pardoned by George II. Charteris was a well-known public figure, whose life had touched many of both sexes and all social classes in various parts of Great Britain, and his case attracted great interest. Day-to-day details, particularly between the trial and pardon, were widely reported and reprinted in the numerous London newspapers, and there flourished a complement of ballads, 'lives', portraits, and journalistic commentary.

Charteris's defence declared that the woman had been sleeping with him for many nights and that she had many times joked with other servants about his being impotent.[33] Some people (Addison, for example) preferred to fancy that this was true, in order to secure the piquant irony that Charteris 'having daily deserved the GIBBET for what/he *did,*/Was at last condemn'd to it for what he *could*/not *do'*.[34] Implicit in Charteris's defence—and accepted, though perhaps not faced, by those who liked the irony—was the idea that the rape charge was false. This is not far from the idea that *all* rape charges are false, that there is in fact no such thing as rape—'The late King [George I], as likewise Queen Elizabeth', Viscount Percival observes, predicting Charteris's pardon as early as 28 February, 'would never suffer a man condemned for a rape to be executed, as not believing it possible for to commit the crime unless the woman in some sort consented'.[35] The physical vulnerability of the woman's body to the man's invasion is opposed to the legal vulnerability of the man to the woman's accusation. In Charteris's instance the sex difference was underscored as a class difference, not only between master and serving-maid, but also between jurymen and Privy Council. Satirical editorials began to comment that, inasmuch as members of the upper class did not count rape a crime but instead something called 'gallantry', those with money and influence ought to be licensed to do it freely; this would spare useless trials, clarify social distinctions, and teach the lower classes—particularly lower-class women—their place.[36]

Gay followed this case—in fact he wrote to Swift just at the moment that Charteris was about to be pardoned:

> today I dine with Alderman Barbar the present Sheriff who holds his feast in the city. Does not Chartres' misfortunes grieve you, for that great man is like to save his life and lose some of his money, a very hard case![37]

Gay's thoughts run as they do because Barber had been one of the three officials involved in the seizure of Charteris's forfeited goods, payment for which was still being negotiated,[38] and he was doubtless looking forward to talk of the case at the dinner. Gay probably heard other stories about Charteris from the Duke of Queensberry, whose mother is said to have been cheated of several thousand pounds by him at cards in a single evening.[39] After the pardon, interest in Charteris did not fade; rather, he became a symbolic figure of public corruption for artists of greater imaginative scope: Swift compares him to the recently-appointed English Dean of Fern in Ireland, who was indicted for rape on 6 June; *The Craftsman* and other political writers establish him as a satirical surrogate for Robert Walpole; Hogarth depicts him leering at Moll Hackabout, just disembarked from the York coach; Pope cites him in the *Epistle to Bathurst* as evidence that wealth is no index of moral worth.[40] All these works appeared in the period between Charteris's pardon and the opening of *Achilles* in February 1733.

The context in 1730 also generated Fielding's *Rape upon Rape,*[41] which, targeting its satire against the venal Justice Squeezum and his associates, builds a plot out of false charges of rape, accusations of false charges of rape, and charges of conspiracy to bring false charges of rape. For Fielding rape is rather more a term of utterance than a frightening and opprobrious reality:

> But, Ladies, did not you too sympathize?
> Hey! pray, confess, do all your Frowns arise
> Because so much of *Rape* and *Rape* we bawl?
> Or is it, that we have no *Rape* at all?
>
> Indeed, our Poet, to oblige the Age,
> Had brought a dreadful Scene upon the Stage:
> But I, perceiving what his Muse would drive at,
> Told him the Ladies never would connive at
> A downright actual *Rape*—unless in private.[42]

'Jokes about rape', writes Ian Donaldson, 'characteristically imply that the crime may not in fact exist; that it is a legal and social fiction, which will dissolve before the gaze of humour and the universal sexual appetite.' Fielding validates his knowing implication by having a woman speak the lines quoted, thus exposing the 'disparity between a woman's words and her actual desires' that such jokes presume.[43] Fielding discounts 'rape' by locating it as an encounter between men and women of the same high and sophisticated social class. Fielding's outlook is that of a man of this class, classically educated, confident, forward, whose social and financial ascendancy encourage him and his fellows to understand that the desires of others correspond to their own.

Gay began to formulate *Achilles* sometime in the wake of the Charteris case. Certainly, even if we resist accepting the partisan impulse to which *The Daily Journal* and *Achilles Dissected* attribute its genesis, we must acknowledge that it arises out of the temporal context in which people, certainly the people in Gay's circle, knew the configuration of sexual desire among persons at Court—the King, the Queen, Mrs. Howard, Lord Hervey (the Vice Chamberlain)—and knew that symbols inviting identification with Walpole's administration would be read in a partisan way. The duel between Ajax and Periphas, for example, could recall that between Pulteney and Hervey in January 1731 over the former's putting into print innuendos about the nature of Hervey's passion for Stephen Fox.[44] Since *The Beggar's Opera,* as Gay was well aware, the theatre had become more and more explicitly partisan and satirical of Walpole and the Court.

However much *Achilles* may have arisen out of this context, and whatever invitation it could be perceived to offer party journalists to politicize its genesis, intention and meaning, the fact is that, for Gay, public corruption was always less interesting and acutely felt than the tyranny of one individual over another. In the figure of the travesty Achilles, Gay saw a means—in a light context that would not be resisted—to signal to men of Fielding's background and mentality an indirect but telling point about themselves in their personal conduct. To the legend, Gay added Lycomedes's pursuit of Pyrrha. Lycomedes's attempted rape of Pyrrha, the culmination of this extensive part of *Achilles,* invokes by inversion, for the classically-aware segment of his audience, the rape of Deidamia *by* Pyrrha in Ovid's version, where the idea of rape was added to the old tale. One might wish to argue, in fact, that the epigraph from Ovid's *Metamorphoses* on the title page of *Achilles* be construed as a significant misdirection to the right author but the wrong text.

What I have not mentioned so far is the context in which Ovid invokes the tale. Many of my readers will be surprised to learn that what is today called 'date-rape' has for generations of 'gentlemen' been sanctioned by classical authority. In *Ars Amatoria* Ovid, the sophisticated instructor of the inexperienced young man, assures him that he need have no hesitation in raping his girl if she does not readily yield:

> oscula qui sumpsit, si non et cetera sumit,
>   haec quoque, quae data sunt, perdere dignus

> erit.
> quantum defuerat pleno post oscula voto?
>   ei mihi, rusticitas, non pudor ille fuit.
> vim licet appelles: grata est vis ista puellis:
>   quod iuvat, invitae saepe dedisse volunt.
> quaecumque est veneris subita violata rapina,
>   gaudet, et inprobitas muneris instar habet.
> at quae, cum posset cogi, non tacta recessit,
>   ut simulet vultu gaudia, tristis erit.
>   (I, 669-78)[45]

Henry Fielding himself (though years later) was to put out a 'modernization' of the Ovid with quite a close translation of these particular lines:

> Now when you have proceeded to Kisses, if you proceed no farther, you may well be called unworthy of what you have hitherto obtained. When you was at her Lips, how near was you to your Journey's End! If therefore you stop there, you rather deserve the Name of a bashful 'Squire than of a modest Man.

> The Girls may call this perhaps Violence; but it is a Violence agreeable to them: for they are often desirous of being pleased against their Will: For a Woman taken without her Consent, notwithstanding her Frowns, is often well satisfied in her Heart, and your Impudence is taken as a Favour; whilst she who, when inclined to be ravished, hath retreated untouched, however she may affect to smile, is in reality out of Humour.[46]

To support this advice Ovid adduces various instances of women who came to dote on their rapists, most importantly 'the well-known story, worth repeating nevertheless' (*fabula nota quidem, sed non indigna referri* (I, 681)) of Achilles and Deidamia. As rhetorically Ovid claims ascendency over his pupil by the skilful anticipatory blocking action of the terms *rusticitas* and *pudor* (I, 672), which pressure the young man to act as he directs, so does he sustain his posture by daring to mock even Achilles, in his disguise, who conceals his manhood behind a skirt (*veste virum longa dissimulatus* (I, 690)) and who messes about with spindles and wool. But, he observes, Deidamia certainly found out that he was a man (*vir, viri*)—and it was by force (*vis, vim, vires*):

> haec illum stupro comperit esse virum
> viribus illa quidem victa est, ita credere
>   oportet:
> sed voluit vinci viribus illa tamen.
>   (I, 698-700)

She wanted to be conquered by force, and afterwards when he was going off to Troy she kept begging him to stay. As Fielding puts it:

> He ravished her, that is the Truth on't; that a Gentleman ought to believe, in favour of the Lady: but he may believe the Lady was willing enough to be ravished at the same time.[47]

Gay calls up this passage—the example, the very advice (in lines already quoted)—and by moving Achilles from agent to recipient enforces a reassessment of the advice from within the consciousness of the woman whom Ovid keeps silent until she has been subdued. The burning male consciousness of Achilles invites his fellow Fieldings, or Ovids, to recognize what it might be to suffer and be silent, while, for those of Gay's audience gendered female, the concealed power replots Ovid's tale so that the would-be rapist becomes the booby object of ridicule. Alas that it takes a John Gay to be able both to see what Ovid's attitude implies for women and to express to men what he sees. The characteristic duality of his symbols, his forms and his modes reflects the dependency of his life and both enables him to speak and withholds what he would say. While, through Gay's comedy, women who are sexually harassed become empowered by the representation of Pyrrha, at the same time the figure of Pyrrha must suggest that to become empowered they must become what they cannot become, a hero and a man.[48]

My argument is not that Gay is a feminist *per se,* but that the predicament of women represents one mode of the wider condition of dependency, the dynamics and abuses of which Gay knew all too well in his own life, and which he probes in terms of many kinds of social relationships in his writing. Many other modes of dependency, not touched upon in this paper but well worth attention, can be found in the very piece we have been considering. Gay's duples, such as Pyrrha/Achilles, enable him to render the dependent's unresolved adherence to, and rage against, the social system in which he or she is both sustained and suppressed. Gay's art can make us hear simultaneously the voice (or the eloquent silence) of acquiescence *and* the voice of rage, as the inner ears of dependents hear. And by the very means of something apparently inconsequential—a burlesque, a ballad opera—perhaps Gay beguiles some of the powerful to hear the double voices, too.

Notes

[1] For example, Sue-Ellen Case, 'Classic Drag: The Greek Creation of Female Parts', *Theatre Journal,* 37 (1985), 317-27, or David Mayer, 'The Sexuality of Pantomime', *Theatre Quarterly,* 4, 13 (1974), 60, 63.

[2] John Harold Wilson noticed in 1958 the sexual dimension added to 'page' or 'breeches' parts (such as Shakespeare's Rosalind and Viola) when after the Restoration they came to be played by women. He points out (quoting Mandeville's *The Fable of the Bees,* Remark P) that they provided a unique, sanctioned public opportunity for men to look at women's legs and thighs in an era when skirts came to the floor (*All the King's Ladies: Actresses of the Restoration* (Chicago, 1958), p. 75). Quite apart from consideration of the practice of cross-casting, he finds that, out of about 375 new or altered plays first produced in London between 1660 and 1700, eighty-nine contained rôles for women dressed as men (p. 73). New parts of this sort continued to be written after the turn of the century, as we see, for example, in *The Recruiting Officer* (the most performed play of the period before *The Beggar's Opera*) or in Gay's *Dione* and *Polly.*

The advent of actresses at the Restoration had quite different consequences for travesty of the opposite kind. Actors who before the Commonwealth had been trained to play women found difficulty now in getting parts, and few new rôles calling for men to appear as women were written; R. C. Sharma finds only one, in Farquhar's *The Constant Couple,* within the plays he surveys (*Themes and Conventions in the Comedy of Manners* (New York, 1965), p. 184). In theatre the scope of female travesty tended to dwindle to the occasional rôles that could be played as a comic 'dame', a representation, Mayer points out, that projects considerable hostility to, and ambivalence about, women (see note 1). (Opera, incidentally, has quite a separate history during this period with respect to travesty.)

In this theatrical context Gay's travesty rôle of Achilles seems modally unique, projected along a psychological plane that burlesques women no more than men. Whatever comic latitude the actor may feel he is invited to take throughout most of the play, he must embody an attractive person fit to be a hero, and one of the young marrying couple, at the end. The ideas of youth and manliness combined with the idea of the dependent young girl suggest quite different psychological features from those of the dame. We do not know whether Gay gave indications about casting and in any event he was dead before the play was worked out in rehearsal, but the actor so cast, Thomas Salway, seems to support the resonance I suggest. Apparently in his mid-twenties, he counted as a singer in Rich's company (he was a tenor); from his rôles he appears to have been capable of slapstick, comedy and second-line romantic parts (Edward A. Langhans, draft of 'Salway', to be published in the *Biographical Dictionary of Actors* [& c.] *1660-1800,* ed. Philip H. Highfill, Jr., *et al.*).

[3] See, for example, Phyllis Rackin's insightful study of the figure in an earlier period, 'Androgyny, Mimesis, and the Marriage of the Boy Heroine on the English Renaissance Stage', *PMLA,* 102 (1987), 29-39, which unfortunately appeared too late for me to use in preparing this essay.

[4] Little critical attention has been given to *Achilles.* Contemporary party journalists—a reviewer in the *Daily Courant* (16 February 1732/33) and an 'Atex Burnet' (see note 16)—pretended to discover in it a satire of George II's household and of Walpole. Howard Erskine-Hill, touching upon the work briefly but approvingly in 'The Significance of Gay's Drama', sees the disguised Achilles as the 'truth-bearer' giving moral weight to the form of farce (Marie Axton and Raymond Williams (eds.), *English Drama: Forms and Development: Essays in Honour of Muriel Clara Bradbrook* (Cambridge, 1977), pp. 160-61). Seven M. Armens finds Gay non-judgemental—ribald, comical, light—about the men's sexual politics that form the plot of *Achilles,* but sees the work as 'studded' with 'sharp and even misogynistic comments' about women (*John Gay: Social Critic* (New York, 1954), pp. 142-46). In his valuable study, 'John Gay's *Achilles:* The Burlesque Element', Peter Lewis sets forth the burlesque relationships of the work to heroic drama, Italian opera, and sentimental comedy (*Ariel,* 3 (1972), 17-28). But none of these critics address the aspects of *Achilles* I wish to consider.

[5] This is the only source that gives Ajax as Ulysses's companion; Statius and Philostratus have Diomede (and Argytes, noticed but unnamed by Philostratus, to blow the trumpet); Hyginus indicates, but does not name, one or more companions; Apollodorus indicates no companions (for references, see note 10).

[6] T. Folkma, sculp. (1722), 'Achilles disguised like a Woman, is discovered by Ulysses', S. le Clerc, invent., *Ovid's Metamorphoses* (Amsterdam, 1732), p. 419.

[7] Published for the same bookseller (William Keble) and advertised in the same notice that announces publication of Gay's *Wine* (*Daily Courant,* 22 May 1708). Ajax's speech is by Nahum Tate.

[8] *Ovid in Masquerade, being, A Burlesque upon the xiii*[th] *Book of His Metamorphoses, containing the Celebrated Speeches of Ajax and Ulysses. . . .* By Mr. Joseph Gay. London: for E. Curll, 1719 [1718]. Foxon enters the item under John Durant de Breval, but advises caution, 'since the pseudonym Joseph Gay was also used by Francis Chute'.

[9] Also circulating would have been the seventeenth-century translations of the passage in George Sandys's *Ovid's Metamorphosis English'd* (1626, 1628, 1632, 1638, 1640, 1656, 1664, 1669, 1678, 1690); and in two versions of Book XIII: *Wisdoms Conqvest* (1651), sometimes assigned to Thomas Hall; and P[atrick] K[er]'s *Logomachia* (1690).

[10] The Achilles-in-Scyros story is told or alluded to in the following classical texts: *Greek:* Apollodorus, *The Library,* III, xiii, 8; Bion (or Pseudo-Bion), II; Eurip-ides, *Skyrioi;* Paulus Sileniarius (*Greek Anthology*), V, 255; Pausanias, I, xxii, 6; Philostratus the Younger, *Imagines,* I; *Latin:* Horace, *Odes,* I, 8; Hyginus, *Myths,* XCVI; Ovid, *Ars Amatoria* (hereafter *AA*), I, 681-704, *Metamorphoses* (hereafter *M*), XIII, 162-70; Pliny, *Natural History,* XXXV, 134; Seneca, *Troades,* 212-15, 343-44, 570-71; Sidonius, *Carmina,* IX, 140-43; Statius, *Achilleid,* I, 5-6, 142, 270-72, 283-381, 533-35, 560-674, 709-960.

[11] *sed opertae conscia culpae/cuncta pavet tacitasque putat sentire sorores* (*Achilleid,* I, 562-63; Loeb edition of *Statius,* ed. J. H. Mozley (London and New York, 1928)).

[12] *Deidamia and the Love Affair:* not in *M* (but as intrigue mentioned by Sandys (1632 only), Ker); *as intrigue:* Apollodorus, Philostratus, Seneca; *as rape:* *AA,* Statius; Bion's 'stolen joys/espousals' could be read as either, according to whether they are considered 'unknown to others' or 'stolen from Deidamia'; Sidonius's language is coy, but seems to allude to Statius's *mise en scène. Achilles Spinning:* not in *M;* in *AA,* Statius, Bion. *The Group of Lycomedes's Daughters;* not in Ovid (but mentioned by Sandys); in Statius, Bion, Philostratus, Hyginus, Pausanias (also reporting Polygnotus), Sidonius. *The Trumpet:* not in Ovid; in Statius, Apollodorus, Hyginus.

[13] Eric Arthur Barker rejects its attribution to Bion (*Oxford Classical Dictionary* (1949), p. 138). This piece is not in the following volumes that might have contained it: Thomas Stanley, *Poems* (1651); Theocritus, *Idylliums,* trans. Creech (2nd edn., 1713); Moschus and Bion, *Idylliums,* trans. Cooke (1724); Thomas Cooke, *Tales* (1729).

[14] Act, scene, and line references are to the texts of Gay's plays in John Fuller (ed.), *John Gay: Dramatic Works,* 2 vols. (Oxford, 1983) [*DW*], from which all quotations are taken (roman and italic reversed in predominantly italic passages such as Airs).

[15] The fragment breaks off at this point; 'A veritable cliffhanger', remarks Professor Peter Westervelt of Colby College, to whom I am grateful for providing a literal translation where the Loeb edition (*The Greek Bucolic Poets,* trans. J. M. Edmonds (London and New York, 1919), pp. 398-401) was seduced into a false Spenserian style.

[16] *Achilles Dissected: Being a Compleat Key of the Political Characters In that New Ballad Opera, Written by the late Mr. Gay. An Account of the Plan upon which it is founded. With Remarks upon the Whole . . . To which is added, The First Satire of the Second Book of Horace, Imitated in a Dialogue between Mr. Pope and the Ordinary of Newgate* (London, 1733), p. 1; Burnet's identity is unknown, despite his being

confused sometimes with the author of the accompanying poem, Guthry, or with Tom Burnet.

[17] Loeb translation: *vi potitur votis et toto pectore veros/ admovet amplexus* (I, 642-3); translations from Latin, when not otherwise credited, are my own.

[18] *Pelea virgo,* 'the daughter of Peleus', is whom Thetis asked to leave behind; Achilles is Peleus's son. But in ending the passage with these words, Statius's principal opposition is not of female child to male child, but of what is lesser than man (woman), hence shameful, to what is greater than man (hero), hence awesome.

[19] Observe, for example, the actively misleading language of even quite recent scholars in describing Achilles's rape of Deidamia in Statius and Ovid: 'The event [Ulysses's disclosure of Achilles] was told . . . at some length by Statius in his *Achilleid.* The courtship of Deidamia was recorded by Bion and by Ovid in his *Art of Love'* (Wilmon Brewer, *Ovid's Metamorphoses in European Culture,* rev. edn. (Francestown, New Hampshire, 1978), II, 1419); 'Gay's principal source [for *Achilles*] seems to have been Statius, but the story also appears in Bion and Ovid' (John Fuller, 'Introduction', [*DW,* I, 59]). Fuller gives no citations for Bion and Ovid and no indication that the Scyros episode is treated *twice* in Ovid, and he discusses the treatment of the love affair in these authors no further.

[20] King 'endeavour[s] . . . to give Readers of both Sexes some Ideas of the Art of Love; such a Love as is innocent and virtuous'; to this end, he manipulates Ovid's text, which he prints in blocks as footnotes, rearranging the material and taking occasion to omit a number of lines; furthermore, he neglects to translate some of the Latin he actually prints. Ovid's advice that prompts the Achilles story is entirely omitted, as is the rape (although King does recount the rape of the Sabines); here it is Deidamia who initiates the affair, which King represents as the consequence of avoiding military service: 'Thus whilst we Glory's Dictates shun,/ Into the Snares of Vice we run' (*The Art of Love: In Imitation of Ovid De Arte Amandi* (London, 1708— dated by Foxon, who also records the reissue, which I have not seen), pp. vii, 59-64). Gay would have been aware of this edition, for the announcement of its publication follows immediately on the page of the *Daily Courant* the announcement of his own *Wine* (22 May 1708). By 1711, at least, Gay knew King, whose destitute plight he mentions with compassion in *The Present State of Wit,* Vintan Dezring (ed.), with the assistance of Charles E. Beckwith, *John Gay: Poetry and Prose,* 2 vols. (Oxford, 1974) [*PP*], II, 449). If he also knew King's text, Gay must have enjoyed its burlesque, which has affinities with themes he would develop in *The What D'Ye Call It*—when Deidamia's pregnancy is about to be discovered, Achilles runs off

into the army in order to avoid punishment. For *Achilles* Gay may have taken hints from King's modernization for Thetis's instructions to her son concerning women's dress, posture, movement and mannerisms (which have their source in Statius, not Ovid) and for the substitution of embroidery work for spinning.

[21] Ovid may have received the rape from a lost Greek tradition (as represented by papyrus Hypothesis, cited by T. B. L. Webster, *The Tragedies of Euripides* (London, 1967), pp. 95-6).

[22] The child was called Neoptolemus or Pyrrhus; he appears in *The Iliad* as Achilles's son, even if the Scyros episode does not. Shortly before arriving at the Scyros tale in his speech in the *Metamorphoses,* Ulysses mentions Pyrrhus of Scyros as Achilles's son (and therefore logical recipient of the contested armour if it is to be awarded on the grounds of kinship), but Ovid does not clearly connect his origin to the time Achilles dwelt in disguise. Statius of course treats these connections in the episode fully.

[23] *PP,* I, 206 (Commentary, II, 581). The classical sources Gay associates with his garb and reverie are worth noticing, all together forming an imaginative cluster that could have influenced the choice and shaping of *Achilles;* Dearing (*PP,* II, 583) observes that it is not Venus (*Aeneid,* I. 229ff.) but Thetis, appealing on behalf of Achilles (*Iliad,* I, 501), who holds Zeus 'under the chin'.

[24] I have not been able to see the 1741 libretto; my knowledge of the plot of *Deidamia* is taken from the summary by Edward J. Dent ('The Operas', in Gerald Abraham (ed.), *Handel: A Symposium* (London, 1954), pp. 59-62), and from Winton Dean's broadcast commentary accompanying a B.B.C. radio performance (ca. 1974) of which I heard an imperfect transcription.

[25] Samuel Garth (ed.), *Ovid's Metamorphoses* (London, 1717), p. 443; Ovid has *decepterat omnes . . . sumptae fallacia vestis: arma . . . anima motura virilem* (XIII, 163-66), the last phrase being translated literally as 'to tempt a manly mind' by Sandys, *Wisdoms Conqvest* and Theobald.

[26] Burnet, who of course took the view that a number of writers were involved in finishing *Achilles,* is the first to state that the '*Prologue . . .* was written by Mr. Pope' (p. 2); Norman Ault provides an extensive argument to support this attribution ('The Prologue to *Achilles*', *New Light on Pope* (London, 1949), pp. 215-21). Fuller accepts Ault's argument and deploys Ault's evidence in a series of footnotes (*DW,* II, 390). Maynard Mack, however, in his review of Ault's book finds the argument unconvincing (*Philological Quarterly* 29 (1950), 291), and, *pace* Ault, John Butt places it among the less plausibly attributable to Pope of the 'Poems of

Doubtful Authorship' considered for volume VI of the Twickenham Pope (Norman Ault and John Butt, (eds.), *Minor Poems,* (London and New Haven, 1964), p. 457).

[27] This alludes to Dennis's description of Pope's *Homer* as a translation in which 'there are Twenty Prosaick Lines, for One that is Poetical.' 'Where the Original is pure, the Translation is often barbarous,' he writes: 'In short, the HOMER which LINTOTT prints, does not talk like HOMER, but like POPE' (*Remarks Upon Mr. Pope's Translation of Homer* (London, for E. Curll), 1717, pp. 10-12).

[28] The considerable differences in the *dramatic structure* of the performed *Achilles* described by Burnet in *Achilles Dissected* and the version appearing in the printed edition do imply that rearrangements and perhaps rewriting of this aspect of the work may have taken place in rehearsal and during the run. *Achilles* opened on 10 February; Burnet's pamphlet is dated 12 February (leaf B1ʳ), but one should note that it extracts (at length) the review appearing in the *Daily Courant* of 16 February; *Achilles* was published on 1 March (*Grub-street Journal*). One song, probably (as Fuller points out (*DW,* II, 391)) from the end of III, ii, with the lines

> Hercules's *Shirt*[-a]
> *Which burnt him all to—Dirt*[-a],
> *And set him all on a Fire-a,*
> [*Contriv'd by his Deianira*]

(*Daily Courant,* with bracketed variants from Burnet), may have been cut in response to their ridicule. Scholars of Gay have noticed this song (if not its variants), but no commentator, so far as I am aware, has discussed the changes in structure. The structure Burnet describes is as follows: Act I: 'our young Hero burns for his Deidamia, and she sighs for her Achilles'; Lycomedes desires Pyrrha; Act II: Lycomedes's pursuit of Pyrrha and Theaspe's jealousy; Act III: Lycomedes's attempted rape of Pyrrha; duel between Ajax and Periphas; revelation of Deidamia's sexual knowledge of Pyrrha's masculinity; Ulysses's disclosure of Achilles's identity (pp. 2-5). In the revised version the Lycomedes plot is disposed of before the Deidamia plot is begun, and several of the climaxes are moved back from Act III to increase the dynamics of Act II. These alterations do not affect the main argument of this paper, which attributes the exploration of sex and gender identity in the work to Gay and which finds greatest interest in the part of the story that Gay added, the Lycomedes plot, which in Burnet's version occupies even more of the play than the version we read.

[29] 'Thus Ladylike he with a Lady Lay,/ Till what he was her belly did bewray' (Heywood, tr., *AA* (1650 edn.), p. 30); see also King translation, *AA* (1708), p. 63.

[30] Some earlier translators anticipate Gay in making the implicit analogy explicit in their diction: 'Yet will she fight like one would loose the field' (Heywood, p. 29); 'Who e'er retreats, when he thus far has gone;/ How almost was He Master of the Town!' and 'The Siege [of a Royal Virgin] much safer, . . . by Force, he won the Field' (Hoy translation, *AA* (1682), pp. 40, 41). For the use of this metaphor in Ovid and elsewhere in antiquity, see Molly Myerowitz, *Ovid's Games of Love* (Detroit, 1985), pp. 205-6, n. 78.

[31] The play was never performed and has attracted few readers. Shortly after *Achilles* opened, however, an operatic adaptation set by Johann Friedrich Lampe using Gay's plot of *Dione* and some of his dialogue for the recitative ran briefly from 23 February 1733 (Fuller, *DW,* I, 36; *The London Stage 1660-1800,* Part 3 (1729-1747), ed. Arthur H. Scouten (Carbondale, Ill. 1961), p. 273.

[32] *Diary of Viscount Percival, Afterwards First Earl of Egmont*—Historical Manuscripts Commission, *Manuscripts of the Earl of Egmont,* I (London, 1920), 75 (28 February 1730).

[33] *The Proceedings at the Sessions of the Peace, and Oyer and Terminer, for the City of London, and County of Middlesex held At Justice-Hall in the Old Bailey, on Friday the 27th of February . . . upon a Bill of Indictment found against Francis Charteris, Esq; for committing a Rape on the Body of Anne Bond, of which he was found Guilty* ((London), 1730). A fuller version of the trial appears in *Select Trials, for Murders, . . . at the Sessions-House in the Old-Bailey. . . . Vol. II: From the Year 1724, to 1732, Inclusive* (London, 1735), pp. 339-51; this text also covers subsequent events beyond his death in 1732 by collating and reprinting the newspaper coverage. A brief notice of Charteris's life by Pope can be found as annotation to the *Epistle to Bathurst,* l. 20 (F. W. Bateson (ed.), *Epistles to Several Persons (Moral Essays),* 2nd edn. (London and New Haven, 1961), pp. 85-6—vol. III, ii of the Twickenham Pope). A fuller summary occurs in the *Dictionary of National Biography.* A good modern account, directed towards his meaning for Hogarth, can be found in Ronald Paulson, *Hogarth: His Life, Art, and Times* (New Haven and London, 1971), I, 244-51.

[34] 'An Epitaph' (beginning, 'Here lieth the body of Colonel/Don Francisco'). It was printed in the *London Magazine,* 1 (April 1732), 39, in the *Gentleman's Magazine,* 2 (April 1732), 718, and also in the Pope-Swift *Miscellanies, The Third Volume* (1732), with the *Select Trials* (1735) (n. 33), and as part of Pope's footnote (*Epistle to Bathurst,* l. 20n (n. 33)), where its attribution to Arbuthnot is made.

[35] *Diary,* I, 75.

[36] *Grub-street Journal* (12 March and 9 April 1730).

[37] C. F. Burgess (ed.), *The Letters of John Gay* (Oxford, 1944), pp. 90-1 (31 March 1730).

[38] For the seizure: *Daily Courant* (28 February), *London Evening Post* (26-28 February), *Daily Post* (28 February), *Monthly Chronicle* (27 February). For the payment: *Daily Journal* (31 August). Sheriff Barber's share was £1,650.

[39] E. Beresford Chancellor, *Col. Charteris and the Duke of Wharton—The Lives of the Rakes,* III (London, 1925), 62-3.

[40] 'An Excellent New Ballad: or, The true Eng—sh D—n to be hang'd for a R-pe', *The Poems of Jonathan Swift,* ed. Harold Williams, 2nd edn., II (Oxford, 1958), 516-20; it appeared in the *Grub-street Journal* of 11 June 1730. *The Country Journal; or, the Craftsman,* 8 August 1730, and *An Answer To One Part of a late Infamous Libel, intitled, Remarks on the Craftsman's Vindication of his two honourable Patrons; In which The Character and Conduct of Mr. P. is fully Vindicated In a Letter to the most Noble Author* (London, 1731), pp. 43-4, sometimes attributed to William Pulteney. 'A Harlot's Progress', Plate 1; the painting of the series may have been finished in September 1731; the prints were published on 10 April 1732 (Ronald Paulson, comp., *Hogarth's Graphic Works* (New Haven and London, 1965), I, 141, 144). The *Epistle to Bathurst* was published on 15 January 1733.

[41] Bertrand A. Goldgar, *Walpole and the Wits: The Relation of Politics to Literature, 1722-1742* (Lincoln, Neb., and London, 1976), pp. 105-10.

[42] 'Epilogue. Spoken by Mrs. Mullart', *The Coffee House Politician; or, the Justice Caught in his own Trap* (London, 1730) leaf A3ʳ; italic and roman reversed. *Rape upon Rape; or, the Justice Caught in his own Trap* opened on 23 June 1730 and was immediately published (*London Evening Post,* 23/25 June). When the play reopened in November its title was softened to *The Coffee House Politician; or, the Justice Caught in his own Trap;* the text was reissued under this title with altered front matter, including revision of the epilogue. The quotation is from this revised epilogue.

[43] Donaldson, *The Rapes of Lucretia: A Myth and its Transformation* (Oxford, 1982), pp. 87-9, which also treat other flippant references to rape in English plays of the period. Donaldson's thoughtful and intelligent study provides a valuable consideration of the theme of rape in literature and art.

[44] See Romney Sedgwick, 'Introduction' to John, Lord Hervey's *Some Materials towards Memoirs of the Reign of King George II* (London, 1931), I, xxii-xxx, and Robert Halsband, *Lord Hervey: Eighteenth-Century Courtier* (Oxford, 1973), pp. 108-18, 144. It is plausible that Gay might have been led to think of a 'Master-Miss' at Court as a comic subject, in the context of gossip about Hervey in 1731, perhaps in banter with political friends. In *Achilles Dissected,* Burnet, already having indicated that Gay's Lycomedes might not have been '*ignorant of the sex of* ACHILLES', insinuates that 'the *Duel* fought between that Hero AJAX and a *Great* LORD, [is] a plain Representation of what lately happened between a *Little* LORD and a *Great* COMMONER' (pp. 12, 13); Gay's version of the duel (if it is that) belatedly lags after the immediate spate of satires inevitably following the event—*An Epistle from Little Captain Brazen, to the Worthy Captain Plume, The Countess's Speech To her Son Roderigo, The Duel; A Poem, Pulteney: or, the Patriot,* and others—which had laid the ground for comic interpretation. One might note that Hervey, writing of *Achilles* to the Duke of Richmond on 17 February, singles out Ajax as 'the only part that has the least pretence to humour', though rather more owing to the actor Hall than Gay, in an otherwise dull piece (The Earl of Ilchester (ed.), *Lord Hervey and His Friends: 1726-38* (London, 1950), pp. 162-63).

[45] Latin texts of *AA* are conflated from A. S. Hollis's edition of Book I (Oxford, 1977), pp. 26-7, and J. H. Mozley's Loeb edition, rev. G. P. Goold (1979), pp. 58, 60.

[46] Fielding, *Ovid's Art of Love Paraphrased, and Adapted to the Present Time. With Notes. and A most Correct Edition of the Original. Book I* (London, 1747), p. 75. The 1760 edition of this work, which bears the title *The Lovers Assistant, or, New Art of Love,* is edited by Claude E. Jones as Augustan Reprint 89 (Los Angeles, 1961). See Ovid, *The Erotic Poems,* trans. Peter Green ((Harmondsworth), 1982), for an excellent modern translation.

[47] Fielding, p. 79.

[48] Gay's indirection, or a blunter social sanction, seems to have got his message across to Fielding to some degree by 1747, for he prefaces his treatment of the Achilles passage with a disclaimer (however ironic) for modern times: 'Ravishing is indeed out of fashion in this Age; and therefore I am at a loss for modern Examples; but ancient Story abounds with them. . . . Though the Story of *Deidamia* was formerly in all the *Trojan* News-Papers, yet my Readers may be pleased to see it better told' (p. 77).

Calhoun Winton (essay date 1993)

SOURCE: *"The Beggar's Opera* in Theatre History" and "The Opera as Work of Art," in *John Gay and the*

London Theatre, University Press of Kentucky, 1993, pp. 87-108; 109-27.

[*In the following excerpts, Winton examines the history of the writing and reception of* The Beggar's Opera, *focusing on Gay's close relationships with Pope and Swift. Winton suggests that Gay's innovative use of both classical works and English popular ballads created a uniquely English genre from the then-popular Italian opera.*]

Hearing of Stella's illness, Swift had departed for Dublin in September 1727. Before he left he had read scenes from **The Beggar's Opera,** which was finished, if we can trust the text and dating of Gay's letter to him,[1] by late October 1727. How long had it been in active preparation, one may ask, actually in the stage of composition, and what influenced Gay in writing it?

Many years before, in the Scriblerian days of 1716, Swift had written to Pope about what Gay might do: "what think you of a Newgate pastoral, among the whores and thieves there?"[2] Swift presumably meant a pastoral poem, a comic urban pastoral of the sort he himself wrote in "Description of the Morning." **Trivia** itself is close to a Newgate pastoral poem at times; the scene in that work quoted earlier of the apprentices' football game is a kind of **Shepherd's Week** episode in urban dress. Gay was certainly capable of writing a Newgate pastoral if he wished to do so.

His instinct was for the stage, however, as Swift's was not. Gay had been writing ballads intended for or employed in stage performance off and on over the years, as we have seen; most recently and importantly **"Newgate's Garland"** for Thurmond's pantomime, *Harlequin Sheppard* in 1724. He had been in and around music for a long time, from his years as an apprentice, from the days of Aaron Hill and the *British Apollo,*[3] and especially from the beginning of his association with Handel. An eighteenth-century legend, which I have not been able to verify, says that Gay could play the flute, that is, what we could call the recorder.[4] Although there is no reason to believe that he had musical training, he was on the other hand a most sophisticated listener with considerable experience at adapting words to musical settings. He had a good poetic ear and a good musical ear; the combination does not occur so frequently as one might suppose. As far as the musical side of his experience is concerned, he was fully ready by 1727 to compose a ballad opera, a genre that he was in the process of inventing.

As for literary "influences," that happy hunting ground of scholars who believe that playwrights write plays by surrounding themselves with books, from which they make appropriate selections, as for these, in spite of assiduous searching, not much has turned up. Richard

Brome's *A Jovial Crew, or The Merry Beggars,* a Caroline comedy that was revived frequently after the Restoration and that the Drury Lane company had been playing for more than twenty years, has often been mentioned as it features songs and deals with beggars. But it has nothing whatever to do with **The Beggar's Opera** (which after all includes only one beggar: the author poet). Set in the country and full of rural jokes, jollity, and folklore, *A Jovial Crew* is much closer to **The Wife of Bath** in spirit than to the **Opera.** It was adapted in 1731 as a ballad opera, after the success of Gay's work, and had a long stage life of its own, but the influence is all the other way around.[5] Christopher Bullock's *A Woman's Revenge, or A Match in Newgate,* produced in 1715—Bullock was one of the actors who defected from Drury Lane to Rich's company that year—depicts bawds and criminals in Newgate, but the parallels of plot and character are not at all convincing, and neither *A Jovial Crew* nor *A Woman's Revenge* resembles the **Opera** in language, of dialogue or song. It is entirely possible, however, even probable, that Gay as an ambitious dramatist *saw* both of these plays, as an aspiring cinematographer today would screen every film he could lay hands on. With the London repertory theatres, one could see most of the standards every season or two, recognizing that the form in which one saw a particular play was that which the managers had given it: Nahum Tate's adaptation of *Lear* with a happy ending, for example.

To correct impressions of drama altered for the play-house, one could buy the play in its original form. Printed versions of almost all the plays produced on the London stage were available at the booksellers, soon after or during opening night. In imitation of the 1709 Rowe edition of Shakespeare, collected editions of plays were also becoming increasingly common—even pirated editions from The Hague, with London on the title page. All this was catering for the rising literacy rate in London and the provinces, and the evolving provincial and colonial book trade that supplied a growing literate public.[6] The books were available to Gay if he had wished to use them.

Beyond that, though, on the subject of literary influence, beyond his own important participation in *Harlequin Sheppard,* one comes back to the astute comment of Gay's most recent biographer: "All we need to say is that a succession of such plays no doubt forced him to recognize the possibilities of the subject and to speculate on his own ability to handle it."[7]

It was probably in the summer of 1727, with Swift and Pope at hand to remind him of reality, when Gay finally understood substantial preferment was not likely to come in his direction. After the king's sudden death in June some persons were out of employment and others were in. One person most securely in was Sir Robert Walpole, who was cultivating the new queen and making himself indispensable to the new king.[8] As Irving has pointed out, Gay's friend Henrietta Howard, the king's mistress, the classic Other Woman, did not stand to be much help to him with the king's wife. Pope himself called on Walpole in August, and Pope was in touch with his and Gay's good friend, William Fortescue, who saw the first minister frequently. Pope and Fortescue were both sensitive men, good readers of others' intentions. They must have known that Walpole was not going to bestir himself on Gay's account and that without Sir Robert's acquiescence, at the least, little in the way of place or profit was going to be his.

Pope's and Swift's attitude toward Gay's place-seeking perhaps differed somewhat at this particular juncture. Swift had committed himself in *Gulliver's Travels* as a satirist of Walpole's political methods—and everyone recognized what he was up to.[9] Pope was still trimming his sails a bit in 1727; in fact, as recently as 1725 he had accepted a two-hundred pound grant from the Treasury, that is, from Walpole's government though technically from the King,[10] which he kept discreetly quiet about. Both Swift and Pope, however, still hoped that Gay might receive something from the Court and were angered when he was, as he and they thought, fobbed off with the appointment as Gentleman Usher to the baby princess. Why, asks Bertrand Goldgar, a scholar who has studied this issue carefully, were Gay and his friends so shocked that he did not find favor? After all, Gay had no family connections, not much money, little political acumen. "The answer seems to be . . . that as 'men of wit' they regarded patronage as their due and honestly expected those in power to support them regardless of 'party,' and as humanists they expected poets, the teachers of virtue, to play some role in the circles of power."[11] Such dreams of influence might possibly have proved true when Robert Harley was a Scriblerian and also Lord Treasurer—though Swift the realist was capable of a good deal of self-deception when it came to practical politics—but it was certainly not true in 1727.[12] Fortunately, as his friends recognized, Gay possessed artistic talent that in proper combination with circumstance could amount to genius, and he was about to make use of that talent.

Some time in that early summer of 1727, then, Gay probably began working seriously on **The Beggar's Opera.** The *Fables* had occupied him through the spring, and, as we have seen Fable 50, **"The Hare and many Friends,"** itself reflects his conviction that friends in high place would not help him in the day of trouble. It was time to help himself. He may have written the work rapidly, and even though Pope and Swift were around it was not to be a collaborative effort. Pope, speaking to Spence a few years later, was careful to underline that fact: "He began on it, and when first he mentioned it to Swift the Doctor did not much like the project. As he carried it on he showed what he wrote to both of us, and we now and then gave a correction or a word or two of advice, but 'twas wholly of his own writing. When it was done, neither of us thought it would succeed. We showed it to Congreve, who after reading it over, said, 'It would either take greatly, or be damned confoundedly.'"[13]

By October he had apparently finished the **Opera.** It was an odd kind of work he had produced, not much like anything else in the drama, but the genius that informs it is distinctly a Scriblerian kind of genius, combining social satire, political satire, and literary burlesque, as Pope was combining the same ingredients just at this time in the first version of *The Dunciad,* and as Swift had recently done in *Gulliver's Travels.* The three works are utterly different, but they are recognizably kin, too.

Once he had written it, he was faced with getting the piece onto the stage. It was tough going to have a new play produced in one of the two patent theatres in those days, even for an experienced dramatist like Gay.[14] Drury Lane, which had produced his earlier plays and whose actors and actresses he consequently knew well, was the obvious place to start. Because of its subsequent astonishing success, the first production of **The Beggar's Opera** is so beclouded with theatre gossip, partisan comment, and *parti pris* recollection as to make certainty about what actually happened almost impossible to come by. Colley Cibber always appears center stage as the Dunce who turned down the hit of the century for Drury Lane, in a fit of pique or vanity. But Cibber was only one of three managers there; Wilks and Barton Booth must have turned it down, too, or at least have agreed with Cibber's decision. Why did they do so?

Naturally Cibber does not dwell on, or even mention the decision in his *Apology,* which must constitute a principal source, maddeningly organized and discursive though it be, for what was going on in the London theatres during his lifetime. There is no evidence at all, however, there or elsewhere to support the contention that the Drury Lane managers in general or Cibber in particular were displeased with Gay at this time. They had, after all, kept his pastoral turkey **The Captives** running for seven performances in 1724, against the strenuous competition of Lincoln's Inn Fields. **The What D'Ye Call It** was in their repertory, ready to make money for them when audience taste for farces returned. On balance the three managers probably regarded Gay with about the same enthusiasm as that with which they regarded living dramatic authors in general, that is to say, guarded, lukewarm. Dead writers were preferable because one did not have to pay them for author's benefit nights or listen to their annoying complaints about the production. John Gay, in their eyes, was a typical living author; no better than the rest, perhaps, but no worse.

Nor is there much to say for the supposition, frequently voiced, that Tory political satire in the *Opera* frightened the Whiggish triumvirate of managers. The *Opera* was swept up after its production into the political storm, along with everything else written by Gay and the other Scriblerians, but this was later, in the period between 1728 and 1730 to which Bertrand Goldgar has given the title, "The Triumphs of Wit," the triumphant wit being that of the Scriblerians, of course.[15] In truth, *The Beggar's Opera* does not embody much specific political satire, Tory or Whig. Received opinion is always difficult to counter or alter, but in this case received opinion wants changing. The biographer W. H. Irving, so right on so many judgments about Gay is simply mistaken when he asserts that "Gay proposed to make his play somewhat of a theatrical *Craftsman*," that is, a vehicle of propaganda for the Tory and dissident Whig opposition.[16]

It was later converted into such a vehicle, as we shall see, by among others Swift in *The Intelligencer* and by *The Craftsman* itself, but this was after the fact, several weeks after the opening. There are, to be sure, political references salted here and there through the play that would have drawn laughs. Peachum's reference, for example, in I.iii, to "*Robin of Bagshot, alias Gorgon, alias Bluff Bob, alias Carbuncle, alias Bob Booty.*" This bit of verbal exuberance—note its resemblance to the list of aliases seen earlier in the Introduction to *Harlequin Sheppard*—is invariably footnoted heavily, and explained in ponderous academic lectures as a reference to Robert Walpole, which of course it is. But the dialogue that follows effectively draws the teeth of the satire:

> Mrs. *Peachum.* What of *Bob Booty,* Husband? I hope nothing bad hath betided him. You know, my Dear, he's a favourite Customer of mine. 'Twas he made me a Present of this Ring.
>
> *Peachum.* I have set his Name down in the Black-List, that's all, my Dear; he spends his Life among Women, and as soon as his Money is gone, one or other of the Ladies will hang him for the Reward, and there's forty Pound lost to us for-ever. (I.iv.1-7)

So much for Bluff Bob, who has one line of dialogue in the entire opera. If Gay intended Bob Booty for political satire with Walpole as the satiric victim he was remarkably inept in his dramaturgy. And likewise with Macheath, who is also often said, following *The Craftsman*'s guidance, to represent Walpole. The male lead, the hero, who enjoys to the end the steadfast love of both Lucy Lockit and Polly Peachum? Macheath as Walpole as satiric victim? The identification will not bear dramatic analysis. In *Polly,* it can be argued; but not in *The Beggar's Opera.*

The script presented to the three managers, assuming it resembled the version that finally appeared in print, had almost nothing in it to frighten Cibber and his colleagues, nothing that would have sent a Court Whig out of the theatre at the first interval. And in point of fact the Court Whigs paid to see *The Beggar's Opera* when it was produced, along with everyone else. It was not topical satire that kept the Drury Lane managers from accepting Gay's proposal. What then was it?

An informed guess is that the script Gay showed Cibber, Wilks, and Booth impressed those theatre professionals as being too out-of-the-way, too experimental, too nonstandard for commercial success. It was a what-d'ye call it. They had a point: *The Beggar's Opera* is out-of-the-way, experimental, and nonstandard. That is part of its glory: its dazzling originality; it is as original in its own way as *Gulliver's Travels* or the *Dunciad*. But the very originality must have worked against its chances with the managers, who could have said: "Interesting, yes. Original, no doubt about that. But risky. Will it take?" Leo Hughes has made the cogent suggestion that they may have been right, "that the history of Gay's ballad opera—and therefore of ballad and comic opera in general—might have been different if Cibber and his partners at Drury Lane had accepted the play."[17] The Drury Lane audience did not expect or relish novelty: one went to Lincoln's Inn Fields for novelty. The audience at Drury Lane had greeted the realistic pantomime *Harlequin Sheppard,* which included Gay's satirical ballad, with "a universal hiss." It is entirely possible that they might have hissed *The Beggar's Opera,* too, as being out of place at Drury Lane.

Another aspect that may have discouraged Cibber and his colleagues is also a part of the *Opera*'s glory: its musicality. The title proclaims it to be an opera. Opera is what was being produced at the King's theatre in the Haymarket, at enormous expense, opera in Italian, but opera all the same. Drury Lane employed music and musicians—though less than had been so twenty years earlier—and had even been venturing hesitantly into pantomime, as we have seen, in response to Rich's success with the form at Lincoln's Inn Fields. The company could accommodate the occasional song but to take on a piece with at least one song in every scene may have seemed daunting to a group of actors and actresses who had been together for a quarter-century or more and who were beginning to look their age. The music was not difficult, Gay could have told them, mostly popular tunes, but even so there was a great deal of it, and Drury Lane, the managers may have decided, was simply not a musical theatre, not a place for an opera, a beggar's or anyone else's.

Finally, and perhaps most important, the Drury Lane company was flourishing in the autumn of 1727, while Lincoln's Inn Fields wilted. The Coronation took place on 11 October, with all its pageantry. *Everyone* who was Anyone was in Town. Competition at the two theatres was fierce. Like duellers, on 4 November *both* houses played Rowe's old warhorse favorite, *Tamerlane,* toe to toe, as it were. Challenging simultaneously Italian opera at the King's Theatre and pantomime at Rich's house, Drury Lane mounted a production of *Henry VIII* in honor of the recent succession of George II, which incorporated important elements of spectacle as Benjamin Victor reported: "on the Account of their present Majesties Coronation, a pompous representation of [Henry's] Ceremony was introduc'd into that play."[18] With copious advertising, *Henry VIII* became the hit of the new season. The King, Queen, the Princess Royal, and Princess Carolina attended a performance on 7 November and, according to *The British Journal* of 11 November, "seemed very well pleased with the Performance."

Fighting Shakespeare with Shakespeare, Rich ran *The Jew* [i.e., *The Merchant*] *of Venice* against *Henry VIII* on 13 November and grossed only eighty-six pounds plus shillings, just thirty-six pounds over the house charges of about fifty.[19] The *Daily Post* reported that day that *Henry VIII* "with the magnificent Coronation of Queen Anna Bullen, . . . still continues to draw numerous Audiences, which is owing to the Excellency of the Performance, and the extraordinary Grandeur of the Decorations."[20] *Macbeth,* with Quin in the title role, grossed a meager thirty-one pounds at Lincoln's Inn Fields on 17 November, not even enough to pay the house charges. In desperation Rich mounted a pantomime *Harlequin Anna Bullen* in December, which fizzled.[21] The money poured into Drury Lane. It was in this prosperous context, then, that the managers read Gay's script of **The Beggar's Opera,** and told him no. It was a decision they would soon come to regret.

At some point in the negotiations for production, Gay's friends Catherine and Charles Douglas, Duke and Duchess of Queensberry, seem to have come to his assistance. A likely time would have been after the Drury Lane managers had turned him down. Gay would find that the Queensberrys did not at all resemble those fair-weather friends of the Hare in **"Fable No. 50,"** who abandoned him to the hunter in his day of trouble. They were both young, he not yet thirty and she even younger, and they had been married only since 1720. Catherine Douglas was a Hyde, second daughter of the fourth Earl of Clarendon and granddaughter of the historian. Charles had succeeded his father, the second duke, in 1711, and had inherited estates in England and vast acreage in the border country of Scotland, along with the pink sandstone castle at Drumlanrig built by his grandfather, the first duke. This young noble couple would prove to be Gay's loyal, lifelong friends, ready to stand by him even if friendship cost them considerably in terms both social and financial.[22]

Precisely what **The Beggar's Opera** cost the duke and duchess, if anything, before its opening is difficult to assay. The duchess may have guaranteed some or all of the costs of production to John Rich; the evidence for this is uncertain.[23] Robert D. Hume, writing of young Henry Fielding's entry into the theatrical world, is skeptical about the potential influence of the nobility on theatre managers. Authors, he writes "cadged introductions and recommendations from . . . persons of social distinction—though whether such recommendations really helped is doubtful."[24] Still, Rich was in dire financial straits and a guarantee might conceivably have attracted his eye, which was on the main chance as always. Benjamin Victor, a principal source for information about the production, does not refer to any subsidy. He notes, however, that the Drury Lane managers "peremptorily rejected this Opera." "Nay, it was currently reported that the happy Manager [Rich], who perform'd it, gave it up after the first Rehearsal, and was with some Difficulty prevailed on to make the Trial."[25] Rich may or may not have been reluctant to take the **Opera** on, but he certainly would have *appeared* reluctant if the duchess had agreed to foot the bill. Any difficulties in rehearsal would have allowed him to raise the ante, like a Peachum from Gay's opera. Rich also had the continuing problem of competition from Drury Lane to nag his days and nights. The other house had followed up its triumph with *Henry VIII* by reviving Vanbrugh's *The Provok'd Husband,* as edited and altered by Cibber. Critics protested, but audiences loved it: beginning 10 January 1728 it ran for twenty-eight nights successively, an unprecedented hit. This was enough in itself to make any rival manager nervous. Could the unknown comic opera by Gay face up to this sort of competition? Rehearsals continued.

Lavinia Fenton, destined for theatrical immortality, was selected to play Polly Peachum, though she had barely two years' experience on the stage. Rich had cast Fenton as Cherry in *The Beaux Stratagem* during the previous season; she had also played Ophelia and appeared as an entr'acte singer and dancer. Someone right for the ingenue part of Cherry who could sing would be right for Polly as well. Thomas Walker, strictly a journeyman actor to this date, was chosen for the part of Macheath instead of James Quin, the leading actor of the company, who apparently rejected the role.[26] The other parts Rich filled out with the regulars of his company, not a distinguished group of actors, but adequate. As its stage history affirms, adequate actors will do well in **The Beggar's Opera,** good actors will do superbly.

But this was in the future. Right down to opening night there was every reason for Rich and his company to have second thoughts about presenting a new production. Drury Lane's *The Provok'd Husband* was demolishing competition. The premiere of John Sturmy's

Sesostris grossed only sixty pounds on opening night (17 January) at Lincoln's Inn, dragged on for a second author's benefit of forty-seven pounds on the 23rd and closed forever on the 27th of January 1728.[27] *The Beggar's Opera* was next up. It was not a promising atmosphere for Gay's new play.

The author and his friends were naturally apprehensive. Congreve's judgment (that "It would either take greatly, or be damned confoundedly") was scarcely an opinion to calm Gay's nerves, and the tension communicated itself to Congreve, too. Pope wrote Swift: "John Gay's Opera is just on the point of Delivery. It may be call'd (considering its Subject) a Jayl-Delivery. Mr. Congreve (with whom I have commemorated you) is anxious as to its Success, and so am I; whether it succeeds or not, it will make a great noise, but whether of Claps or Hisses I know not. At worst it is in its own nature a thing which he can *lose* no reputation by, as he lays none upon it."[28] This is a friend talking to a friend about another friend, but one guesses that Gay longed more fervently for his opera's success than was evident to Pope. The theatre had been the locus of his principal literary ambitions for more than fifteen years; he had, he felt, been publicly humiliated by the Court. What better way, what *other* way to settle accounts than by writing a successful play?

About six o'clock on the night of Monday, 29 January 1728, as was the custom, the author appeared at the theatre, hoping for the best. Pope, and an entourage of friends also turned up at Lincoln's Inn Fields, along with, the *Daily Journal* later reported, "a prodigious Concourse of Nobility and Gentry."[29] Gay had of course peddled tickets genteelly to all his friends; this was also customary. Seated in their box seats, Gay and his associates awaited the verdict of the Town with trepidation, as the orchestra launched into the overture, composed and conducted by the competent musical director of Lincoln's Inn Fields, Dr. John Christopher Pepusch. As Pope later recalled it to Spence:

> We were all . . . in great uncertainty of the event, till we were very much encouraged by overhearing the Duke of Argyle, who sat in the next box to us, say, "It will do—it must do! I see it in the eye of them." This was a good while before the first act was over, and so gave us ease soon, for that Duke, beside his own good taste, has as particular a knack as any one now living in discovering the taste of the public. He was quite right in this, as usual. The good nature of the audience appeared stronger and stronger every act, and ended in a clamour of applause.[30]

Benjamin Victor's recollection confirms the tension, and also confirms that indecision on the part of the audience so torturing to a cast, especially on opening night: "On the first Night of Performance, its Fate was doubtful for some Time. The first Act was received with silent Attention, not a Hand moved; at the End of which they rose, and every Man seemed to compare Notes with his Neighbor, and the general Opinion was in its Favour." This must have been about the time the Duke of Argyle delivered the memorable aside that Pope and Gay picked up in the next box, but "silent Attention" is not enough. Victor continues: "In the second Act they broke their Silence, by Marks of their Approbation, to the great Joy of the frighted Performers, as well as the Author; and the last Act was received with universal Applause."[31] Act II opens with the great tavern scene, the musical and dramatic strategy of which will be discussed in the following chapter. Act I closes with the quiet love duet of Macheath and Polly, "Parting," as Gay's stage direction indicates, "and looking back at each other with fondness; he at one Door, she at the other" (I.xiii.70-73). It is a notably understated act closing, one that does not draw much applause in modern productions. Victor's recollection accords with the dramatic logic of the *Opera.*

In the first week Gay's fortune was assured. On Thursday 1 February the *Daily Journal* reported succinctly on "Mr. Gay's new English Opera, written in a Manner wholly new, and very entertaining, there being introduced, instead of Italian Airs, above 60 of the most celebrated old English and Scotch tunes. . . . [N]o Theatrical Performance for these many Years has met with so much Applause." The opposition newspaper, *The Craftsman,* which would soon undertake its explication of the *Opera*'s latent political comment, contented itself in the initial week with recording on 3 February for the first time that witticism that has become standard: The *Opera* "has met with a general Applause, insomuch that the Waggs say it has made *Rich* very *Gay,* and probably will make *Gay* very *Rich.*"[32] It is worth reiterating that the re-education campaign of the opposition, the program of finding and pointing out specific political propaganda, did not begin until *The Beggar's Opera* was securely established as a hit.

By 15 February Gay was feeling sufficiently confident to write Swift a letter that signalizes his triumph and also reflects the deep satisfaction he was receiving from that triumph. It is worth quoting in full:

> Dear Sir / I have deferr'd writing to you from time to time till I could give you an account of the **Beggar's Opera**. It is Acted at the Playhouse in Lincoln's Inn fields, with such success that the Playhouse hath been crouded every night; to night is the fifteenth time of Acting, and 'tis thought it will run a fortnight longer. I have order'd Motte to send the Play to you the first opportunity. I made no interest either for approbation or money nor hath any body been prest to take tickets for my Benefit, notwithstanding which, I think I shall make an addition to my fortune of between six and seven hundred pounds. I know this account will give you

pleasure, as I have push'd through this precarious Affair without servility or flattery. As to any favours from Great men I am in the same state you left me; but I am a great deal happier as I have no expectations. The Dutchess of Queensberry hath signaliz'd her friendship to me upon this occasion in such a conspicuous manner, that I hope (for her sake) you will take care to put your fork to all its proper uses, and suffer nobody for the f[uture] to put their knives in their mouths.

Gay's comment on the generosity of the duchess is apparently the ultimate source of later speculation about her subsidizing rehearsals, but it could refer to many other manifestations of the noble lady's warm heart. The advice to Swift on minding his table manners is of course a delightful aside between old friends. Gay continues:

> Lord Cobham says that I should [have] printed it in Italian over against the English, that the Ladys might have understood what they read. The outlandish (as they now call it) Opera hath been so thin of late that some have call'd that the Beggars Opera, & if the run continues, I fear I shall have remonstrances drawn up against me by the Royal Academy of Musick. As none of us have heard from you of late every one of us are in concern about your health. I beg we may hear from you soon. By my constant attendance on this affair I have almost worried myself into an ill state of health, but I intend in five or six days to go to our Country seat at Twickenham for a little air. Mr. Pope is very seldom in town. Mrs Howard frequently asks after you, & desires her compliments to you; Mr. George Arbuthnot, the Doctor's Brother is married to Mrs. Peggy Robinson. I would write more, but as to night is for my Benefit, I am in a hurry to go out about business. / I am Dear Sir / Your most affectionate / & obedient Servant / J. Gay[33]

"I have push'd through this precarious Affair without servility or flattery." It is as if Gay is seeking to underline his independent action to Swift, whom he knew to have been skeptical about his search for preferment.

Gay sold the copyright to John Watts, for an unknown but no doubt substantial sum. Watts was by then the leading publisher of dramatic authors. He began publishing editions on 14 February, "To which is Added, The MUSICK *Engrav'd on* COPPER-PLATES," as the title page of the first edition indicated. Watts must have had to push his engravers and printers hard to produce the edition just sixteen days after the opening but it was well worth the effort: edition followed edition, in varying states which have puzzled bibliographers ever since.[34]

Gay's remark to Swift about this being his benefit night and having to see about his business may stem from the slim returns of the first author's benefit, which dipped mysteriously from opening night (£169 to £161), then leaped to £175 on the fifth night. On his benefit night on 8 February the take was again down to £165, even though the *Daily Journal* that day commented the show "meets with that universal Applause, that no one third Part of the Company that crowd thither to see it, can get Admittance." These were spectacular receipts—the opening of *Sesostris* in January, it will be remembered, grossed only sixty pounds, barely enough to cover the house charges. Although Rich's books are difficult to interpret, it may be that he was at first skimming some off the top for his own use, as it were, before reporting the gross on benefit nights to Gay. This, then, would account for Gay's anxious attention to business on benefit night: so that he could verify the totals himself.[35]

Rich was shoehorning that happy third part of the crowd into every square inch of space he could clear. On the 23rd of March, for example, the *Opera* grossed £194, with 238 spectators in the boxes, *98*(!) on the stage, 302 in the pit, 65 in the slips (extensions of the boxes), 440 compressed into the first gallery, 196 in the second gallery, and 2 paying customers in a category not yet explained by scholarship, but the comfort of which imagination can conjure up: "pidgeon holes."[36] A total of 1,341 in the audience. For comparison, a year earlier on 13 March 1727 Rich had taken in £133 for a performance of *Hamlet* with Quin in the title role playing to 891 in the audience—7 on the stage and no one in pidgeon holes. A routine performance of *The Beggar's Opera* came out 50 percent ahead, in terms of both audience and receipts.

Precisely how much came to Gay of these receipts is impossible to say: his own estimate in mid-February to Swift of between six and seven hundred pounds may or may not be accurate. If he had his wits about him and insisted on additional benefit nights or some similar arrangement, it is on the low side. The figure to precise pounds, shillings, and pence that is quoted so confidently by both his latest biographer and editor has no relationship to reality, however, and will not be given further life here.[37]

Consecutive performances of the *Opera* continued through February and early March. On 22 February the Royal Family attended a command performance: their entourage took up twenty-eight box seats, plus a place for a Yeoman of the Guard in the pit.[38] The company performed it on the 7th of March and gave it a brief rest, offering James Carlisle's *The Fortune Hunters,* "Carefully Revis'd, with Fenton as Nanny." The star system was working: receipts for the revival were a most satisfactory £131. But the temptations of the *Opera*'s gross were too much, and it was back on the stage the following Monday. Drury Lane, meanwhile, was attempting to counter Gay's success, which had overshadowed even the bonanza of *The Provok'd Husband.* In a rare deviation from previous form, the Drury Lane managers produced a new play: young Henry Fielding's *Love in Several Masques.* This intrigue comedy was given its first performance on 16 February 1728, in the very teeth of the *Opera*'s success and ran only four nights, "neither a success nor a fiasco."[39] After this Cibber and his colleagues returned to the tried and true, running repertory standards: *Hamlet, The Funeral, The Way of the World, The Man of Mode.* The success of Gay's *Opera* would soon shake both Drury Lane and Lincoln's Inn Fields out of their extreme conservatism by encouraging competition for new work, but that was still in the future.

Now Rich could watch the money roll in, and the Opposition could be about showing how *The Beggar's Opera,* correctly interpreted, represented a frontal attack on Sir Robert Walpole and his ministry. Swift wrote Gay on 26 February, in reply to Gay's account of the *Opera*'s success: "Does W[alpole] think you intended an affront to him in your opera. Pray God he may, for he has held the longest hand at hazard that ever fell to any Sharpers Share and keeps his run when the dice are changed."[40] The strength of Swift's feeling about Walpole is not in dispute, but this letter, which is frequently cited as proof that Gay *did* intend an affront to Walpole in the *Opera,* seems on the contrary to be evidence that he did not. Swift had read at least part of the *Opera* in manuscript; he asks Gay if Walpole thinks that Gay intended an affront. Surely if Swift had known that Gay intended an affront he would have written "knew you intended" or "believed you intended." The comment appears to be, rather, a query set off by *The Craftsman*'s famous blast of 17 February—which Swift could have seen by 26 February. Swift seems to be telling Gay that Walpole may have taken offense where no offense was intended, and that Gay should be happy about it.

The sequence of events that the opposition set in motion to convince the public that the *Opera* was anti-Walpole propaganda is interesting in its own right as an effective use of the print medium in politics. How far Gay himself was involved is a matter for conjecture, but his financial interests were at least carefully protected, and there is every reason to believe that he knew what was going on. *The Craftsman,* after its initial, good-humored comment about Rich and Gay on 3 February, waited until the opera was well established, the printed edition had been placed on sale, and Gay had received his benefit for the fifteenth performance to publish on 17 February the richly ironic letter by "Phil. Harmonicus" to *The Craftsman*'s putative editor, "Caleb D'Anvers." Harmonicus identifies *The Beggar's Opera* as "the most venemous [sic] *allegorical Libel* against the G[overnmen]t that hath appeared for many Years past." He explains that Macheath represents Walpole, and that Peachum and Lockit *also*

represent Walpole and his brother Horatio. "Harmonicus" demonstrates how to read the *Opera* for innuendo, of which he finds plenty.

A few weeks later, in the middle of March, Harmonicus's letter was republished as part of a little guide or do-it-yourself kit for Walpole-bashing, appended to the "second edition" of Christopher Bullock's *Woman's Revenge.*[41] Bullock, one of a family of actors, had died in 1722 but his widow Jane was the highest paid female actor on the Lincoln's Inn payroll in the late 1720s and republication of the play may have brought her some copy money. What the customers presumably wanted, however, was the reprinted letter, here appearing as *A Compleat Key to the Beggar's Opera,* by "Peter Padwell of Paddington, Esq;" a "Town Pastoral to Mrs. Polly Peachum"—a verse satire with Walpole the satiric victim—and, significantly, Gay's **"Newgate's Garland."** The opening lines of the **"Garland's"** last stanza with a reference to William Wood and the Irish coinage scandal, which Swift had celebrated in *The Drapier's Letters,* would have evoked echoes in Dublin:

> What a Pother has here been with *Wood* and
> his Brass,
> Who would modestly make a few Half-pennies
> pass?

Perhaps they did evoke such an echo. Jonathan Swift in the other island was about to reinforce the attacks on Walpole, with his own satiric touch. Swift employs a somewhat different strategy from that of the "Key," although also an ironic one, for his Irish audience in an essay published in the Dublin *Intelligencer* in May 1728. The essay is to be seen in the context of Swift's pamphlet battles with the Walpole ministry and their Irish representatives, of which the *Modest Proposal* (1729) would be the crowning jewel. Swift simply coopts Gay for his side. He, Swift, writes satire, he contends, only for personal satisfaction. "If I ridicule the Follies and Corruptions of a *Court,* a *Ministry,* or a *Senate,* are they not amply paid by *Pensions, Titles,* and *Power:* while I expect, and desire no other Reward, than that of laughing with a few Friends in a Corner?" He continues, "My Reason for mentioning *Courts,* and *Ministers* (*whom I never think on, but with the most profound Veneration*) is, because an Opinion obtains, that in the **Beggar's Opera** there appears to be some Reflections upon *Courtiers* and *Statesmen,* whereof I am by no Means a Judge."[42]

Unlike Phil. Harmonicus, Swift does not spell out the Reflections for his audience. Rather, he contends that Gay's merit and his fourteen years' attendance at Court have been overlooked and he has "failed of Preferment," which of course was true. "It must be allowed, That the **Beggar's Opera** is not the first of Mr. Gay's Works, wherein he hath been faulty, with Regard to

Courtiers and *Statesmen.* For to omit his other Pieces, even in his Fables, published within two Years past, and dedicated to the Duke of Cumberland, for which he was promised a Reward, he hath been thought somewhat too bold upon the *Courtiers.*" Swift here sends the readers of the **Fables** back to their volumes, to seek out innuendoes that to that moment no one had recognized. After a discussion of recent attacks on the morality of the **Opera,** Swift in his inimitable backhanded manner focuses attention on the transvaluation of values dramatized in the work: "This *Comedy* contains likewise a *Satyr,* which without enquiring whether it affects the present Age, may possibly be useful in Times to come. I mean, where the Author takes the Occasion of comparing those *common Robbers of the Publick,* and their several Stratagems of betraying, undermining and hanging each other, to the several Arts of *Politicians* in Times of Corruption" (p. 36). Times of Corruption. Not *these* times, not the present Age, of course. It is the rhetorical device of praeteritio, saying by affecting not to say; one of Swift's favored techniques. "Disingenuous," Bertrand Goldgar has termed Swift's arguments in *The Intelligencer.*[43] Disingenuous they are, but ingenious.

Benefiting from the political guidance of *The Craftsman* and Swift, audiences now knew when to laugh and when to glance significantly at politicians in the theatre boxes. It all added to the fun, and Gay had provided the perfect cue with Lockit's song in Act II:

> When you censure the Age,
>   Be cautious and sage,
> Lest the Courtiers offended should be:
>   If you mention Vice or Bribe,
>   'Tis so pat to all the Tribe;
> Each crys—That was levell'd at me.
>
>   (II.x.21-26)

By this time vendors were selling mezzotint engravings of Lavinia Fenton and Thomas Walker as Polly and Macheath; Gay sent Swift, at Swift's request, a pair of these predecessors of publicity shots. Gay was in an ebullient mood, writing the Dean in March:

> On the Benefit day of one of the Actresse's last week one of the players falling sick they were oblig'd to give out another play or dismiss the Audience, A Play was given out, but the people call'd out for the **Beggar's Opera,** & they were forc'd to play it, or the Audience would not have stayd. I have got by all this sucess between seven & eight hundred pounds, and Rich, (deducting the whole charges of the House) hath clear'd already near four thousand pounds. In about a month I am going to the Bath with the Dutchess of Marlborough and Mr. Congreve, for I have no expectations of receiving any favours from the Court.[44]

The two lovers and Gay found a production of the **Opera** playing in Bath when they arrived there. Swift as an author was annoyed at the disproportionate size of Rich's bonanza, writing Gay that "I think that rich rogue Rich Should in conscience make you a present of 2 or 3 hundred Guineas." It was time for Gay to provide for himself: "Ever preserve Some Spice of the Alderman [i.e., financial acumen] and prepare against age and dulness and Sickness and coldness or death of friends. A whore has a ressource left that She can turn Bawd: but an old decayd Poet is a creature abandond."[45] With the politicization of the **Opera** Gay must himself abandon all hope of preferment, as he knew. The Government wisely chose not to attempt to refute the innuendoes—that would have been fulfilling Lockit's prediction in his song—but decided to move against the work on moral and aesthetic grounds. Dr. Thomas Herring, chaplain at Lincoln's Inn, preached a sermon in March against the morality of *The Beggar's Opera,* contending that the favorable presentation of criminals in the work would encourage crime.

Pope and Gay recognized that Herring's sermon was a political plant—Swift said as much in his *Intelligencer* essay—but his contentions were taken seriously, then and later. Daniel Defoe, perhaps still smarting from his encounter with the Mohocks, complained in a pamphlet that "Every idle Fellow, weary of honest Labour, need but fancy himself a *Macheath* or a *Sheppard,* and there's a Rogue made at once."[46] Samuel Johnson felt compelled to refute such criticism in his "Life of Gay" in *Lives of the Poets:* "The play, like many others, was plainly written only to divert, without any moral purpose, and is therefore not likely to do good; nor can it be conceived, without more speculation than life requires or admits, to be productive of much evil. Highwaymen and housebreakers seldom frequent the playhouse."[47]

The next chapter will examine the moral content, if any, of *The Beggar's Opera,* but it is a fact that, Johnson to the contrary notwithstanding, many people continued for a long time to brood about its tendency to deprave. A biographer of Gay writing in the 1820s presented a long discussion of Herring's sermon, concluded that he was correct, and regretfully summed up Gay's career after the **Opera**'s success this way: Gay "had a pleasing turn for poetry," but "unhappily falling into the hands of Swift and Pope and their set, he was promoted into a walk, which rendered his talents a snare to himself, and in general a nuisance to his fellow creatures. . . . Let his example prove a warning to others, and it will not have been in vain."[48]

Another line of attack on *The Beggar's Opera* by the government's followers was aesthetic: that the opera was a debased form of entertainment. This could be and sometimes was associated with the charge of immorality. The *London Journal* of 23 March 1728, for example, viewed the declining interest in opera as a symptom of failing aesthetic taste: "I would not be thought here to speak with any Prejudice or Ill-will to the **Beggar's Opera,** in which I am willing to allow there is a great deal of true low Humour." Just what the audiences, unfortunately, wanted. These charges were perhaps motivated primarily by politics, but they had a residual sting and no doubt some persuasive effect.

Those of the aristocracy who took a dim view of the stage found their opinions amply confirmed that spring. The Duke of Bolton attended a performance of the **Opera** on Monday, 8 April, when Gay also had a box seat there.[49] The Duke came to the next two performances and brought his duchess to the **Opera** on Saturday 13 May. On 22 June The Craftsman reported, "To the great Surpize of the Audience, the Part of _Polly Peachum_ was performed by Miss WARREN, who was very much applauded; the first Performer being retired, as it is reported, from the Stage." Retired indeed: "The D[uke] of Bolton," Gay informed Swift, "I hear hath run away with Polly Peachum, having settled 400£ a year upon her during pleasure, & upon disagreement 200£ a year."[50] Lavinia Fenton was "now in so high vogue," Gay had written Swift, "that I am in doubt, whether her fame does not surpass that of the Opera itself."[51] Lavinia had struck paydirt; eventually the duke would make her his duchess, but these were unseemly doings, even for the nobility. A good many individuals, in all classes, felt that the theatre was no better than it should be. Perhaps some kind of systematic censorship was in order.

The _Daily Journal_ got the matter right when it wrote of "Mr. Gay's new English Opera" in the issue of 1 February 1728. Like all great works of art, **The Beggar's Opera** possesses differing meanings for different members of the audience—every audience; its significance will not be exhausted in any single discussion. However, the three terms used by the _Journal_, new, English, and opera, provide convenient guideposts to what it was that Gay delivered to the reluctant—and soon to be gay—John Rich.

There is nothing entirely new in the theatre, of course. Readers of this book will remember that the use of music, popular and/or traditional music, was a strategy Gay had adopted at the very beginning of his dramatic career, with the songs in **The Mohocks,** and had continued in most of his later plays except for his tragedies. He had worked with—and learned from—Handel on _Acis and Galatea._ Handel's setting for "'Twas when the Seas were roaring" from **The What D'Ye Call It** was being reprinted for popular sale—Gay would employ the tune again in the **Opera.** Most recently he had written a ballad for performance in the pantomime _Harlequin Sheppard,_ sung to an old favorite tune, "The Cut-Purse," or "Packington's Pound," which he would

also use again in the **Opera.** One imagines Gay humming tunes to himself as he wrote. Music was never far from the center of his artistic creativity.

Notes

[1] Pope edited the letter extensively before publishing it: see The Correspondence of Alexander Pope, ed. George Sherburn, 5 vols. (Oxford: Clarendon, 1956), 2:454-56.

[2] Pope, *Correspondence,* 1:360.

[3] See Rosamond McGuiness, "The British Apollo and Music," in Journal of Newspaper and Periodical History 2 (1987): 9-19. I am indebted to Yvonne Noble for this reference.

[4] This has been an especially frustrating inquiry. Both Fiske and Irving assume it as fact, without providing documentation. I have no quarrel with the assumption but would feel more secure if I knew of a contemporary reference to Gay's playing the flute.

[5] See Fiske, *English Theatre Music,* 105.

[6] See Shirley Strum Kenny, "The Publication of Plays," in London Theatre World, 309-36; and John Feather, The Provincial Book Trade in Eighteenth-Century England (Cambridge: Cambridge Univ. Press, 1985), 44-68.

[7] William Henry Irving, John Gay Favorite of the Wits (Durham: Duke Univ. Press, 1940), 236.

[8] J. H. Plumb, Sir Robert Walpole The King's Minister (London: Cresset, 1960), 157-61.

[9] Betrand A. Goldgar, Walpole and the Wits (Lincoln: Univ. of Nebraska Press, 1976), 51: "from the beginning [Gulliver's Travels'] political allusions were obviously understood."

[10] Public Record Office [of Great Britain], T. 29/25, p. 26: "200£ to Mr. Pope as his Mat Encouragemt to his translacion of Homers Odyssey and to the Subscripcons making for the same." Other Treasury documents having to do with this gift are in T. 60/12, p. 391; and T. 52/52/33, p. 324.

[11] Goldgar, 67.

[12] In addition to Goldgar, see Maynard Mack, The Garden and the City (Toronto: Univ. of Toronto Press, 1969), 116-28.

[13] Joseph Spence, Observations, Anecdotes, and Characters of Books and Men, ed. James M. Osborn, 2 vols. (Oxford: Clarendon, 1966), 107.

[14] To appreciate just how tough, see Robert D. Hume's tables in *Henry Fielding and the London Theatre* 1728-1737 (Oxford: Clarendon, 1988), 15, 105.

[15] Goldgar, 64-86.

[16] Irving, 238.

[17] Hughes, *The Drama's Patrons* (Austin: Univ. of Texas Press, 1971), 102.

[18] [Benjamin Victor], *Memoirs of the Life of Barton Booth, Esq;* (London: John Watts, 1733), 13. "Pompous" was of course a term of praise with Victor.

[19] Figures are based on Rich's accounts in the Harvard Theatre Collection, shelfmark fMS Thr 22, from which the *London Stage* statistics are drawn. This account book includes much information not published in *LS* and there are discrepancies between the information it contains and the published figures.

[20] Not seen. Here as quoted in *London Stage.*

[21] The Rich accounts (n. 19) show that after the first night the bill with the pantomime made the house charges only once.

[22] Biographical information from G. E. C[okayne]., *Complete Peerage England, Scotland, Ireland . . .*, rev. ed., 12 vols., by V. Gibbs, H. A. Doubleday, G. H. White, and R. S. Lea (London: St. Catherine Press, 1910-59) and personal observation.

[23] Schultz, 2, accepts the eighteenth-century legend much too uncritically, and he has been followed by scholars, including Fuller, since. Cooke's *Memoirs of . . . Macklin* (pub. 1804), on which this story and other *Opera* legends are based, is shot through with demonstrable error and must be used with great caution. See the article on Macklin in *Biographical Dictionary.*

[24] Hume, *Henry Fielding,* 21.

[25] Benjamin Victor, *The History of the Theatres of London and Dublin,* 3 vols. (London: T. Davies, 1761-71) 2:153.

[26] This, too, is part of that tangle of theatrical gossip which surrounds the *Opera,* but it does seem likely that Quin could have had the role if he wanted it. He took it in a 1730 revival.

[27] Here and elsewhere shillings and pence are eliminated in totals from Rich's accounts (which record them to the halfpenny).

[28] Pope, *Correspondence,* 2:469.

[29] *Daily Journal,* issue of 1 February.

[30] *Anecdotes,* 107-8.

[31] Victor, 2:154.

[32] *The Country Journal: Or, The Craftsman;* copy used here and hereafter in the microfilm series of Early English Newspapers.

[33] *The Letters of John Gay,* ed. C. F. Burgess (Oxford: Clarendon, 1966), 70-71.

[34] Including the most recent editor, John Fuller, who adopts the novel technique of discussing "some of the significant variants" (*Dramatic Works,* 374) without, however, specifying which some. This, it goes without saying, is worse than discussing *none* of the significant variants, because it presents the unwary user a bibliographical minefield: that undiscussed significant variant may be of the highest significance. P. E. Lewis, *The Beggar's Opera* (Edinburgh: Oliver and Boyd, 1973), strives valiantly but does not succeed in discriminating among the differing states of the first editions and declines to introduce the music into his edition, saying (42) that "is a task for a musicologist." A critical edition of the *Opera,* with music, is a prime desideratum. Dr. Yvonne Noble has one in preparation.

[35] There is no other apparent correlation with, say, day of the week, for the mysterious fluctuations in receipts. Common sense suggests that Rich was packing every possible body into every performance, and this is corroborated by the *Daily Journal*'s statement.

[36] I accept the *London Stage* totals here, though they do not seem to add up correctly for the box and stage attendance when one divides the reported cash totals by the admission price. The fragile condition of the account book, which has so far made any kind of duplication impossible, inhibits detailed study.

[37] Fuller, 1:46, following Irving, 254. See Appendix B.

[38] The places of the Royal Family and entourage are all carried as "orders" in Rich's accounts, a puzzling category omitted from the *London Stage* calculations. Free seats?

[39] Hume, *Henry Fielding,* 26-33.

[40] Pope, *Correspondence,* 2:475.

[41] Schultz, 368, cites the Book List for March in the *Monthly Chronicle,* which I have not seen, as authority for the publication date of 14 March. The play itself appears to be a reissue of the 1715 edition with new prelims and, of course, the appended anti-Walpole

material.

[42] Swift, *Irish Tracts, 1728-1733,* ed. Herbert Davis (Oxford: Basil Blackwell, 1955), 34.

[43] Goldgar, 70.

[44] *Letters,* 72.

[45] Pope, *Correspondence,* 2:482.

[46] *Second Thoughts Are Best* (1729), quoted in Paula Backscheider, *Daniel Defoe His Life* (Baltimore: Johns Hopkins Univ. Press, 1989), 518. It is interesting that Defoe associates Sheppard with Macheath, in view of Gay's ballad on Sheppard.

[47] *The Lives of the Poets,* ed. G.B. Hill (Oxford: Clarendon, 1905), 2:278.

[48] James Plumptre, "Life of John Gay," Cambridge University Library, Manuscript Add. 5829. Plumptre dates his summary comment September 19, 1821.

[49] From Rich's account book, which sometimes names ticket holders.

[50] *Letters,* 76.

[51] Pope, *Correspondence,* 2:479.

Dianne Dugaw (essay date 1996)

SOURCE: "Dangerous Sissy: Gendered 'Lives,' John Gay and the Literary Canon," in *Philological Quarterly,* Vol. 75, No. 3, Summer, 1996, pp. 339-60.

[*In the following essay, Dugaw asserts that late-eighteenth-century and nineteenth-century notions of class and literary propriety led to a reluctance on the part of Gay's contemporaries to consider him a significant contributor to the literary culture of his era.*]

John Gay's reputation tumbled as literary criticism metamorphosed in the eighteenth century from a descriptive project to a determinant of taste and values. His own era judged him a prominant figure, an author who sparked controversy and emulation. By the nineteenth century Gay's "official" stature shrank. At the same time, English literary historiography took the form it still holds today. The two phenomena are not unconnected. The changing narratives that successively represented Gay's "life" and his "character" disclose the social, moral, and ideological imperatives that have shaped the valuing of authors and texts from the satiric sensibility of the early Georgian age to the Modernism of the twentieth century. Critiques of Gay open a window onto the historiography of English letters. Analy-

sis of them shows how ideas about gender have shaped the authorial canon of English literary history with patterns of exclusion as well as of "excellence."

Samuel Johnson, moralist of his age, brought to English literature and its authors a quest for personal character and worth based on an idea of heroic manliness. Johnson found in Gay a negative lesson: a man womanishly trivial, childishly dependent, a "poet of a lower order." The history of Gay's literary reputation illuminates how commentators, especially after Johnson, enlisted the valences of gender that intersect with what we currently term "sexual orientation" in their presentation of authors as biographical subjects. These elements appear differently in the earlier period than in the later. Critics since the eighteenth century have extended the "queering" of Gay's character and life that began in Johnson's era. By the twentieth century, critics dismissed a decadent, feminized Gay presented through a "Life" contemptible in its *un*manliness and indolence. The terms and emphases of this dismissal reflect similar evaluations rendered to find other writers unworthy of high regard. The trajectory of Gay's "Lives" supplies a model for how biographical and personal assessments serve the dismissal of unsuitably "unmanly" writers—a category that of course includes all women.

Today Gay is "minor." Critical studies of him and editions of his work are shorter and fewer than those of "major" authors. Commentary about him has in many cases emphasized, even assumed, his dependence upon other writers. Around him on the shelves of the library reside "bigger" names—authors studied with heavily annotated multi-volume editions, long critiques, and probing biographies. Here are his friends, Swift and Pope; his elders, Milton and Dryden; his adversary, Defoe. John Gay and his work have not commanded the same scholarly review. Eighteenth- and nineteenth-century appraisals of the poet map a fascinating history to this review as the applause and contentious critique of his own era gave way to uneasy questioning and eventually outright disparagement.[1]

Our own era seems perplexed by Gay, with assessments more tentative and hopeful than fixed. Presently our view is under reconstruction, as recent scholars argue for his greater accomplishment, significance, and respectability.[2] His ironic sensiblity resonates with our own. The social bent of his satire has sparked the imaginations of key twentieth-century writers: Bertolt Brecht who penned his admiring reworking of Gay, *Dreigroschenoper (The Threepenny Opera)* in the 1920s, and Vaclav Havel with his *Zebrácká Opera (Beggar's Opera)* of the 1970s. With seemingly postmodern self-consciousness, Gay's writing exposes the gaps and ironies of attempts to convey experience and its meanings in language, as well as the unavoidably political dynamics of these representations.

John Gay's satire insists that meaning is unstable and relational, exposing through parody the socially determined, and determinant, nature of art's representations.[3] Gay interrogates injustice, conflict, exploitation, and value in burlesques set up to expose the dynamic between those wielding power and acting upon it, and those deprived of it and acted upon. In other words, Gay's art articulates the *politics* of relational individualism that stands at the core of the capitalist modern world, particularly as expression itself always remains inscribed within this politics. At our late-century moment of reflexivity, deconstruction, and cyberspace, we can appreciate Gay's art perhaps more than any audience since his time; we too inhabit a world of (sometimes alarmingly) contingent, rather than absolute, forms and values.

Gay's often controversial poems and plays were subject to critique in his own time, that Georgian era when depreciation had its heyday. Nonetheless, his success was obvious. *The Beggar's Opera* remained in production every year for a century and spawned nearly 200 imitations. His farce, *The What-d'Ye-Call-It,* continued to play through the century. Eighteenth-century publishers brought out editions of his plays and poems for all ranks: lavish editions for the wealthy, duodecimos and chapbooks for common readers. The initial acclaim and polemical responses that met Gay's work on its own satiric terms, however, gave way in the latter part of his century to a didactic resistance that shifted attention from the poet's works to his life and person. This essay traces in eighteenth- and nineteenth-century "Lives" of Gay the increasingly moral and fictionalizing attention given to Gay's biography, his character, and finally his body.

Within a generation, the sensibility of Gay's era, rooted in a profound and comic irony, gave way. The discordant critiques of Tory satire—inherited from Dryden and present in the works of Swift, Delarivier Manley, Gay, and others—yielded to a view of art as an expressive (and stable) signifier.[4] Literature became the creation of striving individuals—increasingly understood as gendered—within the context of an expanding and determining empire. The literary canon we have inherited emerged from this mid-eighteenth century reimagining of the function and nature of literature.[5] The transformation of John Gay's reputation reveals some of the assumptions embedded within this cultural project of establishing art's "seriousness" and its function as the product and shaper of persons of a lofty mind. Tracing Gay's reputation from his own first third of the eighteenth century, into the Age of Johnson, and finally through the Victorian Era, we find increasingly fictionalized critiques. In them Gay becomes a dangerous and unheroic model, a threat to an ethical code whose reference is as biographical as it is aesthetic. The story of Gay's reputation discloses the gendered and sexualized underpinnings of this system of literary value.

1. "The Envy of the Playwrights": Gay's Importance to His Times

Eighteenth-century commentators assumed the importance of Gay's writing. Early in the century, while his works drew extensive comment, his life received little or none. John Mottley is the supposed author of "A Compleat List of all the English Dramatic Poets, and of All the Plays ever printed in the English Language to the Present Year 1747";[6] Mottley's account of Gay is complimentary and respectful. His "Compleat List" is a survey that presents dramas not as literature to be read but as staged works forming a public and ongoing theatrical tradition. Plays appear with brief remarks about their character and performance history. Notably, the "Compleat List" focuses entirely on the works, spending almost no time at all on the lives or even the characteristic sensibilities of particular authors. Nevertheless, Mottley's comments and especially the size of his entries reveal his weighting of authors. Of the ninety playwrights from Mottley's own era—the reigns of Anne, George I, and George II—only Cibber, Fielding, and Mottley himself are accorded longer entries than that for Gay (who died early in the reign of George II). Of the 184 writers from the era immediately preceding Gay's—the reigns of Charles II, James II, and William and Mary—only the discussions of Dryden and Behn extend beyond the three pages allotted to Gay. For the period before Cromwell's closing of the theaters, only Shakespeare and Jonson occupy more attention. In Mottley's history of the "English Dramatic Poets" Gay was a major figure.[7]

Other critics at mid-century and after remark on the excellence and popularity of Gay's work. In 1745 William Ayre finds Gay unexcelled in the pastoral.[8] In *Lives of the Poets of Great Britain and Ireland* (1753), Theophilus Cibber conveys the prevailing admiration. With a sweep, his discussion of Gay proclaims:

> As to his genius it would be superfluous to say any thing here, his works are in the hands of every reader of taste, and speak for themselves.[9]

Oliver Goldsmith praises Gay with the commonplace apogee for writers of pastoral that "he more resembles Theocritus than any other English pastoral writer whatsoever."[10] The editor of a 1772 edition describes *The Beggar's Opera* as "an unrivalled master piece" and accords *The Fables* "the same rank of estimation."[11] *Biographia Dramatica* (1782) says that *The What-d'-Ye-Call-It,* almost forgotten today, "became so popular that it excited the envy of the playwrights."[12] In his *History of England* (1790), Tobias Smollett praises Gay's "genius for pastoral" and his fables which "vie with those of La Fontaine, in native humour, ease, and simplicity."[13] These commentators assume Gay's importance among influential authors ancient and modern. Moreover, they focus on his works, not his life.

Not all eighteenth-century responses to Gay were praising. Throughout the period his satire, along with that of his colleagues Swift and Pope, sparked heated discussion. A moral outcry at *The Beggar's Opera*'s mock-heroic underworld of highwaymen and whores followed the play's first run.[14] Indeed, the social tenor of Gay's satire, its sensitivity to the emerging politics of class, caught the attention of critics from the start. Futhermore, the politics in Gay's ongoing targeting of Robert Walpole's Whig ministry was not lost on his contemporaries. At least one later commentator remarked on its panache. A 1770 Dublin editor suggests Gay's political audaciousness, with notable reference to the context of social and economic class:

> There is scarcely, if at all, to be found in history an example, where a private subject, undistinguished either by birth or fortune, had it in his power, to feast his resentment so richly at the expense of his sovereign.[15]

Already in 1746 Eliza Haywood located the troubling social politics readable in Gay: "a constant Strain runs through it [*The Beggar's Opera*], of putting the whole Species pretty much upon a Level."[16] Certainly Gay's satiric preoccupation with power in relationships is rooted in awareness and exposure of what since the nineteenth century has been termed social and economic "class." The characterization of Gay as "womanish" and "queer" follows upon this uneasiness with his reading of class. Both take place at precisely that mid-century time when English politics and culture shifted irretrievably away from a Tory world of satire and wit, a world increasingly seen—in gendered terms—by a "manly" Whig hegemony as foppish and decadent.

At mid-century, the remarks of the clergyman Joseph Warton disclose an ambivalence toward Gay that foreshadows later responses. While placing him in then-accepted fashion among poetry's elite ("such as possessed the true poetical genius"), Warton responds with a perplexed discomfort at the destabilizing class politics that Haywood noticed. Despite his respectful ranking of the poet, the troubled Warton finds little to commend when he turns to specific works. His response is a moral one. Admitting that he "could never percieve [sic] that fine vein of concealed satire supposed to run through [*The Beggar's Opera*]," he says:

> [T]hough I should not join with a bench of Westminster Justices in forbidding it to be represented on the stage, yet I think pickpockets, strumpets, and highwaymen, may be hardened in their vices by this

piece; and that *Pope* and *Swift* talked too highly of its moral good effects.[17]

Uncertain how to read the burlesque, Warton fears its dangers for a class of people indelicate as well as threatening. He misses the ironic social reversals at the heart of Gay's satire: pickpockets, strumpets, and highwaymen stand in for prime ministers and politicians, tradesmen and kings. At the same time, he responds uneasily to the slippage of social categories that such reversals make imaginable.

As eighteenth-century commentary focused on the characters of authors as well as the nature and importance of their works, Gay's life assumed greater importance. Accounts by early commentators—in accordance with the then-current practice of discussing writers' works rather than their lives—gloss over or elevate the poet's ambiguous social rank.[18] Born in Barnstaple in 1685 into a Devonshire trading family, Gay was the orphaned younger son of a younger son. As recent scholars point out, his financial prospects were from the beginning precarious, and his education, if solid, was gained only in a provincial grammar school.[19] Indeed, almost the only records we have from the future poet's early years are connected with his unfinished tenure as an apprentice to a London draper.[20] The facts are these: Sometime as a teenager, the orphaned John Gay went from his hometown of Barnstaple to London, apprenticed to one Willet, a silk mercer in the Strand. In the summer of 1706, about halfway through the usual term, he was released and returned to Devon. Little else is certain.

Recently David Nokes has seen in the apprenticeship and other facts of the poet's biography evidence suggesting that Gay indeed was (as we now say) gay. Nokes states: "During his early years in London, Gay had been employed as a draper's apprentice at Willet's shop in the New Exchange, an area notorious as a favourite haunt of sodomites."[21] Nokes suggests—his prose suggesting some squeamishness of his own—that Gay's friends and Pope in particular closeted this information, their "guilty secret" as he calls it. "When Pope was approached by Richard Savage in 1736 for biographical information about Gay's early life," Nokes observes, "he was keen to draw a veil over this period. 'As to his being apprenticed to one Willet, etc.,' he protested, 'what are such things to the public? Authors are to be remembered by the works and merits, not accidents of their lives.'"[22]

Nokes' research and his biographical "outing" of Gay fit into a tradition of critical attention to the poet's personal life. By the end of the eighteenth century wary and ever more negative readings of Gay's character began to accumulate. As we shall see, the apprenticeship episode supplies a measure of the growing importance of Gay's "life" to his reputation and also demonstrates a change in the values enlisted to interpret that "life."[23] Moreover, Nokes' uneasy and anachronistic psychologizing of Gay's life in terms of "secret homosexual tendencies" puts his biography directly in the tradition of Gay's "lives" that I am tracing here: presentations of Gay increasingly colored by terms that project-sometimes subtly, sometimes not so subtly—delineations of "manliness' and "womanliness." Applying to his subject a psychology based upon gendered traits, Nokes thus finds in his explicitly (and negatively) queered Gay a "painful sense of inferiority" (364) and "anxieties about his own sexuality" (329). According to Nokes, these stem from the poet's failure as a (normal) "predatory male" and his "basic psychological" discomfort at being an "emasculated one," an "honorary female" (340). Such disapproving feminizing of Gay's character is a traceable thread in the history of accounts of his life and one that is not evident from the beginning.

The first commentators on Gay's life invariably see in his youthful engagement and then failure as a silk mercer's apprentice a mark of superiority, strength, and genius. They move quickly over the provinciality and apparent financial precariousness in Gay's background, and justify his leavetaking. The Ayre account of 1745 is quick to see Gay's gentlemanly love of books beneath his failure at the "Slavery" of trade:

> [H]e grew so fond of Reading and Study, that he frequently neglected to exert himself in putting off Silks and Velvets to the Ladies. . . . Not being able to go thro' this Slavery, and doing what he did in the Shop with a mind quite bent another Way, his Master seldom put him forward to serve, but some other, who had the Business more at Heart: By Degrees Mr. *Gay* became entirely to absent himself from the Shop, and at last, by Agreement with his Master, to withdraw from it, and retire into the Country.[24]

The 1760 preface to the **Plays** published by the Tonsons describes Gay's apprenticeship as a "station not suiting his liberal spirit," likewise casting his leavetaking in an approving light:

> Having thus honourably got free from all restraint, he followed the bent of his genius, and soon gave the public some admirable proofs of the character for which he was formed by nature.[25]

A 1770 Dublin edition of his works depicts his departure from the mercer's shop in similar terms. Characterizing Gay as "an original poetic genius," the biographer says approvingly:

> [H]aving thus purchased the ease of his mind, he indulged himself freely and fully in that course of life, to which he was irresistibly drawn by nature. Genius concurred with inclination; poetry was at once his delight and his talent.[26]

This version of the curtailed apprenticeship serves a portrait of the poet's innately genteel genius. As we shall see, however, new attitudes applied to the same facts in a short time produced a different tale.

2. "Poet of a Lower Order": An Unheroic Gay in the Age of Johnson

Samuel Johnson's considerations of poets' works and lives created criticism of a new kind, which conferred on the individual writer a moral heroism that until well into this century undergirded the literary canon. In *The Lives of the English Poets* (1779), Johnson took up with keen, if sometimes perplexed attention the interplay of a writer's works and of *his* life (the masculine pronoun is definitional).[27] The individual poet became an exemplary lesson: Johnson articulated a moral ideal of autonomous, forceful, and prevailing manliness. Necessarily excluding women from serious discussion, the new criterion introduced questions of character framed by gender: How "manly" are the poet's life and works?

Johnson's apotheosis of the individual writer ennobled private life and thus fit the emerging sensibility of an increasingly privatized and nationalized modern world.[28] His view stands utterly at odds with the parodic and relational ethos that underpins the satire of John Gay. Moreover, this late-century criticism served a new cultural function: where earlier commentary had articulated prevailing performance practice (and the taste it implied), Johnson's opinions formed and led assessments of aesthetic merit and inferiority. His declarations about Gay, like his opinions of others treated in the *Lives,* echo through the remarks of subsequent writers of prefaces, biographical dictionaries, and works of literary commentary.[29]

Johnson begins with a qualified and chary discussion of Gay's poetry and drama. Although the sixteen-page account is not Johnson's most damning portrait, his disaffection emerges—and with explicit reference to gender. "As a poet he cannot be rated very high," Johnson declares, "He was, as I once heard a female critick remark, 'of a lower order.' He had not in any great degree the *mens divinior,* the dignity of genius."[30] Early in the discussion, however, the poet's "life," or rather Johnson's version of it, becomes a charged and determining presence. Johnson the moralist delineates faults in Gay's person and habits—pliancy, dependence, awkwardness—which take over the discussion. A charge of failed personal heroism permeates his account of John Gay.

The life as "moral tale" structures Johnson's reading of the works. However, from the outset Johnson and Gay display not only different but *competing* moral agendas. Gay, the satirist, for his part sees a world that human beings negotiate relationally and in terms of power—that is, politically—at every turn. By contrast, Johnson is a moralist of the individual, and of an ostensibly depoliticized individual at that. As Jeffrey Plank has recently observed, literature in Johnson is, at least overtly, "separated from politics."[31] For Johnson morality transcends the dynamics of the social and the political. Of course, from our vantage point, Johnson's individual seems altogether political: with his morality of personal striving and reason, he fittingly reflects the socio-economic currents and nationalist ideology of Hanoverian England. Plank identifies Johnson's method in the *Lives* as a "recombination" of the poetic device of inserting an "inset narrative as a moral tale in descriptive poetry" (335). Both the writers and their works serve a didactic purpose.[32]

The "moral" in Gay's "life" emerges in the telling as Johnson shapes the poet's biography. In the first ten paragraphs he takes up the known facts: Gay's parentage; his early schooling and apprenticeship; his service to the Duchess of Monmouth; his writing of *The Shepherd's Week* and other early "trifles"; the poet's failure to gain court patronage. Johnson's account of the apprenticeship story embroiders tellingly on what little is known:

> How long he continued behind the counter, or with what degree of softness and dexterity he received and accommodated the Ladies, as he probably took no delight in telling it, is not known. The report is that he was soon weary of either the restraint or servility of his occupation, and easily persuaded his master to discharge him.[33]

Johnson, in notable contrast to earlier writers, uses the possessive pronoun to identify the young and future poet with "his occupation." Even more significant, Johnson's language feminizes the "pliant" Gay, suggesting in the latter's "accommodation" the "softness and dexterity" of the very "Ladies" he served. Such gendering, as we shall see, dominates subsequent descriptions of Gay.

As Johnson renders it, Gay's "life" supplies an "unheroic" caveat: pliancy, awkwardness, eagerness to please, and success through luck cannot lead to great literary production. From this point in the account Johnson's fictionalizing increases as he infers from known events the imagined "hopes," thoughts, and feelings that create for the poet a character that serves the intended lesson. He finds in Gay,

> . . . a man easily incited to hope and deeply depressed when his hopes were disappointed. This is not the character of a hero; but it may naturally imply something more generally welcome, a soft and civil companion. Whoever is apt to hope good from others is diligent to please them; but he that

believes his powers strong enough to force their own way, commonly tries only to please himself. (2:272)

The remainder of the account presses home the homily. Johnson scoffs that Gay "had been simple enough to imagine that those who laughed at the *What d'ye call it* would raise the fortune of its author" (2:272). Later he retells an account of Gay's awkwardness at court, describing how the poet, "advancing with reverence, too great for any other attention, stumbled at a stool" (2:274). A subsequent paragraph ends accusingly: "[Gay] is said to have been promised a reward, which he had doubtless magnified with all the wild expectations of indigence and vanity" (2:274). Projecting into the mind of his subject "magnifications" and "expectations," Johnson castigates his protagonist as a dangerous example: "This is not the character of a hero."

Not surprisingly, given their competing ethical visions, Johnson saw nothing of morality in Gay's work. *The Beggar's Opera* he describes as "without any moral purpose" (2:278). Of the fables he says:

> For a Fable he gives now and then a Tale or an abstracted Allegory; and from some, by whatever name they may be called, it will be difficult to extract any moral principle. (2:283)

However, Gay's satires, especially the fables, insistently question the configurations and delusions of human power, not least of which delusions is moral expression.[34] Indeed, with conscious self-implication, it is often moralizing per se about which Gay moralizes. Exposing the inherent self-deception in pontification, Gay targets the danger of imagining morality in absolute terms apart from specifics governed by social relation, context, and power.

Johnson's blindness to the moral seriousness of *The Beggar's Opera* and *The Fables* fits with his dismissal of Gay's use of the pastoral as the site for interrogations of power.[35] The conclusion to Johnson's "Life of Gay" discloses the critic's blindness to both the politics of the pastoral as well as the politics embedded in his own moral viewpoint.

> There is something in the poetical Arcadia so remote from known reality and speculative possibility, that we can never support its representation through a long work. A Pastoral of an hundred lines may be endured; but who will hear of sheep and goats, and myrtle bowers and purling rivulets, through five acts? Such scenes please barbarians in the dawn of literature, and children in the dawn of life; but will be for the most part thrown away as men grow wise, and nations grow learned. (2:285)

This closing scene of "wise men" and "learned nations" looking with superior satisfaction on "barbarians" and "children" resonates like a parodic image from one of Gay's fables. It is little surprise to find Samuel Johnson an unsympathetic reader of John Gay. How could this moralist *fail* to rebuke the fabulist who playfully imagines the absurdity of didactic assurance like Johnson's own—from a Monkey who moralizes after "seeing the world"?

> Hear and improve, he pertly crys,
> I come to make a nation wise.
>
> **(Fable** 14)

The two writers offer inimical moral readings of the world and its creatures. For Samuel Johnson, both the works and the unheroic character of John Gay supply a negative model for "wise men" intent upon building "learned nations." Were Gay asked to comment on Johnson as a model, one can imagine him fabling of a monkey "come to make a nation wise."

3. "The Little Fat Poet": Censuring a Feminized Gay

Johnson's negative assessment of Gay in *The Lives of the English Poets* tremendously influenced subsequent criticism and biography. In particular, later editors enlisted Johnson's didactic reading of the character and works of Gay to counter the widespread and dangerous popularity of his poems and plays among readers of the lower ranks whose behavior became the concern of educators. Gay's writing and character came to represent not only an individual warning but also the failed sensibility of his witty and decadent satiric age.

Commentators after the 1780s almost invariably contend with Johnson's verdicts, engaging his language and assessment even when they disagree. Gay's admirers testify to the sway of Johnson's taste by objecting to it as a reference point. In 1790 the flippant author of *The Bystander; or, Universal Weekly Expositor by a Literary Association* questions Johnson's own character, inferring that his dismissal of Gay stems from a dour envy:

> . . . though *Oliver* [Johnson], in compliance to a lady, will not allow him to have been more than of the *lower order*—which expression one would think the *world* has imitated—yet I will venture to say if he himself could have boasted half his lyric merits, he would have maintained a much higher rank in poetic fame.[36]

In a 1796 edition of the **Fables,** William Coxe complains:

> Johnson certainly did not sufficiently estimate the poetical works of Gay. . . . Though Gay cannot be classed among the highest ranks in the Temple of Fame, yet he certainly does not deserve to be placed in the lower order.[37]

The "Life of the Author" appended to a 1794 *Poetical Works of John Gay* counters Johnson using his terms: "[Gay's] compositions, though original in some parts, are not of the highest kind." The anonymous editor then goes on to complain that "The estimate of his poetical character, as given by Dr. Johnson, is, in some instances, too severe to be approved by readers uncorrupted by literary prejudices."[38] This objection to a tainting "literary prejudice" comments suggestively on the (then in-process) formation of a national literary history and canon, and Johnson's role in this emerging cultural project.

Subsequent critics and historians extended Johnson's moral agenda. As Gay's works entered the stream of literature especially printed for the instruction of youth of various classes, the poet's early biography took on a new homiletic significance, especially the anecdotal history of his apprenticeship. In new editions of Gay's "life" and works, this "biographical" incident metamorphoses further, and with pointed application to the new market for instructional literature for children and for the lower-classes.[39]

Popular editions from the end of the century extend Johnson's warning tone. Far from giving evidence of Gay's genius, the apprenticeship episode signals the moral lapse of an individual of a particular class. Following Johnson's lead, biographers identify the young Gay with the job of apprentice and suggest that poetry is no excuse for shirking one's duties. In a telling maneuver, two accounts shift the reader's perception of the event from Gay's point of view to that of the unnamed silk mercer. A "Life of the Author" of 1793, for example, describes Gay's leavetaking with the following sentence: "Of an occupation ill suited to his talents he soon became weary, and easily procured a discharge from his master, to whom he was like to be of little service."[40] An 1801 version supplies the feelings of apprentice and master, sympathy clearly residing with the latter:

> . . . the accommodating nature of moving behind a counter became disgusting. His consequent want of attendance and assiduity gave much dissatisfaction to his master, which procured his release on easy conditions, long before the expiration of his term of servitude.[41]

Voicing concern for correct behavior in apprentices, this account adds to Johnson's legacy of biography as a moral tale a farther purpose: instruction for a lower-class audience through school editions and cheap popular prints.

The identification of Gay with a perplexing and barbarous past—an idea already raised by both Warton and Johnson—added to the criticism of both his work and his life. Gay represented not only a failure of personal character but of the moral and aesthetic sensibility of his age as well. His works continued to be enjoyed, especially **The Beggar's Opera, The Fables,** and **Trivia.** However, by the late eighteenth century expurgated versions appeared, trimmed of their "savage," "heathen," and "indelicate" elements.[42] The Library of Standard Music published **The Beggar's Opera** in the 1830s with *"the objectionable poetry altered."*[43] James Plumptre's remarks of 1823 capture the tone of this trimming. In his preface to a school edition, Plumptre declares to "the Special and Sub-committees of the Society for promoting Christian Knowledge" that he has relieved the fables of "a very considerable portion of alloy" so that "nothing should appear inconsistent with the faith, the conversation, and the practice of a Christian."[44] In an unpublished manuscript, Plumptre makes the point even more bluntly: "[Gay] was promoted into a walk, which rendered his talents a snare to himself, and in general a nuisance to his fellow creatures. . . . Let his example prove a warning to others, and it will not have been in vain."[45]

In his 1849 edition of *Select Works of the British Poets,* John Aikin identifies Gay as an epitome of his indelicate Augustan times. Aikin passes over the poetry and drama with dispatch to focus on the character of both poet and era. Despite a "sweetness of disposition," Gay "was indolent and improvident;"[46] the success of **The Beggar's Opera** indicates "a coarseness in the national taste which could be delighted with the repetition of popular ballad-tunes, as well as a fondness for the delineation of scenes of vice and vulgarity" (283).

Later in the century, presenting a sampling of works by Addison, Gay, and Somerville, Charles Cowden Clarke similarly critiques Gay with scarce mention of the works at all.[47] Focusing his "reading" on the poet himself, Clarke (1875) declares briskly: "Gay's works lie in a narrow compass, and hardly require minute criticism" (158). The fables Clarke understands entirely in terms of Gay's character: "He understands animals, because he has more than an ordinary share of the animal in his own constitution" (159).

The most influential Victorian critic of Gay was William Makepeace Thackeray, whose lecture in "The English Humourists" (1853) is remarkable in its concurrent attention to and trivializing of the poet's person.[48] With a breezy tone Thackeray reads Gay as Johnson's "playfellow of the wits."

> In the portraits of the literary worthies of the early part of the last century, Gay's face is the pleasantest perhaps of all. It appears adorned with neither periwig nor nightcap . . . and he laughs at you over his

shoulder with an honest boyish glee—an artless sweet humour. He was so kind, so gentle, so jocular, so delightfully brisk at times, so dismally woebegone at others, such a natural good creature that the Giants loved him. (587)

Thackeray describes Gay's physical attributes in terms that diminish him and make this "natural good creature" utterly frivolous.

As Thackeray continues, Gay becomes, in the Johnsonian manner, an object of personal critique and warning. His habits and indeed his body itself become the critic's curious fixation:

> But we have Gay here before us, in these letters— lazy, kindly, uncommonly idle; rather slovenly, I'm afraid; for ever eating and saying good things; a little, round, French abbe of a man, sleek, soft-handed, and soft-hearted. (590)

Thackerary's discussion consistently passes over the works in favor of a critique of his subject's presumably "lazy," "idle," "slovenly" character. With this insistent gaze upon the poet's person, finally even his body, Thackeray constructs a caricature of the kind more often found in criticism of women writers. His imagined Gay is suggestively "sleek, soft-handed, and soft-hearted."

In turn, Thackeray dismisses the "morality" of Gay's **Fables,** arguing not from the texts themselves, but from their imagined failure to improve the infant prince to whom Gay dedicated them in 1727. Thackerary enlists the figure of this prince, grown to manhood to be "The Butcher of Culloden" in 1745, as a measure of morality in Gay's poems:

> Mr. Gay's Fables, which were written to benefit that amiable prince, the Duke of Cumberland, the warrior of Dettingen and Culloden, I have not, I own, been able to peruse since a period of very early youth; and it must be confessed that they did not effect much benefit upon the illustrious young prince, whose manners they were intended to mollify, and whose natural ferocity our gentlehearted Satirist perhaps proposed to restrain. (591)

The contrast between the naturally ferocious warrior prince and the soft, "gentle-hearted Satirist" continues the text's feminizing of Gay.

As this novelistic depiction proceeds, Thackeray adds to his portrait a further projection of class and ethnic otherness, imagining the poet as a "Savoyard" performer in a figurative circus:

> . . . but the quality of this true humourist was to laugh and make laugh, though always with a secret

kindness and tenderness, to perform the drollest little antics and capers, but always with a certain grace, and to sweet music—as you may have seen a Savoyard boy abroad, with a hurdy-gurdy and a monkey, turning over head and heels, or clattering and piroueting in a pair of wooden shoes, yet always with a look of love and appeal in his bright eyes, and a smile that asks and wins affection and protection. Happy they who have that sweet gift of nature! It was this which made the great folks and Court ladies free and friendly with John Gay—which made Pope and Arbuthnot love him—which melted the savage heart of Swift when he thought of him—and drove away, for a moment or two, the dark frenzies which obscured the lonely tyrant's brain, as he heard Gay's voice with its simple melody and artless ringing laughter. (591-92)

Thackeray's discussion has little connection with the satirist or his work. This simile of the dancing dark-skinned boy hoping for "affection and protection" from such (men) as are "lonely tyrants" proceeds from the same aesthetic and moral promontory from which Johnson looked out over "barbarians" and "children." In his trivializing fiction of Gay, Thackeray speaks from the position of Johnson's wise and manly writer. The sexualized effeminacy and racial inferiority of his "Gay" make strikingly explicit the troubling larger implications of Johnson's view.

Late nineteenth-century commentators turned biographical description into stridently personal attack on the poet's habits and appearance. Austin Dobson in 1899 recast a now familiar anecdote with added emphasis on Gay's supposed passivity:

> In his boyhood . . . it must be assumed that Gay's indolence was more strongly developed than his application, for his friends could find no better opening for him than that of apprentice to a London silk mercer.[49]

A few pages later, Dobson reiterates the by now familiar images of women and children:

> He was thoroughly kindly and affectionate, with just that touch of clinging in his character, and of helplessness in his nature, which, when it does not inspire contempt . . . makes a man the spoiled child of men and the playfellow of women. (271)

Placing Gay in the company of women, Dobson at the same time feminizes him as "kindly and affectionate," "clinging" and "helpless."

Duncan Tovey's essay of 1897 dismisses Gay with a striking fixation on his body. Tied to the material, Gay is "unsuited for high themes": "This plump Artaeus had no strength but when he touched earth."[50] Once again Gay's works are bypassed as the poet, now be-

come an objectified body, stands only in the company of others to whom he owes whatever work he has:

> "Let us lend friend Gay a hand," we can fancy these greater gods [Swift, Pope, &c.] saying, bursting in upon the little fat poet who is racking his brains in that most painful of all tasks, the quest of things sprightly or naive. (117)

With the overdetermined bodily imagery of "the little fat poet . . . racking his brains," Tovey fully trivializes his fictionalized Gay's "quest" with the adjectives "sprightly" and "naive," words customarily reserved for women and children.

Tovey explicitly conflates character and works in the construction of literary reputation when he proposes that:

> We may . . . treat [Gay's] memory with the good-humoured indulgence which his friends extended to his life. (137)

This sweeping dismissal contrasts sharply with the prestige accorded Gay by such Georgian writers as Cibber, Mottley, and even the troubled Warton. Tovey's portrait stands in a long line of highly inferential—indeed fictionalized—treatments of Gay's biography.[51]

The story of Gay's "Lives" discloses the concern with moral biography in eighteenth- and nineteenth-century English literary history. A long tradition of ethical controversy has followed Gay's work and reputation. Particularly after Johnson, this discourse proceeded from a focus on Gay's character as a negative example. Indeed, the telling of his life transformed to meet didactic needs, as the variants of the apprenticeship episode show. Moral uneasiness about Gay solidified in the nineteenth century, in part owing to the potentially threatening facts of his popularity and the plebeian rank of a good many of his readers. Gay's character became feminized, an "unheroic" and dangerous model. His works required censure, alteration, and careful sifting. This tradition of dismissal supplies an important context for our perceptions of Gay today. Indeed, he supplies a case in point for examining the ways biography, character, and life have been turned to the service of literary history and its gallery of reputable authors and works.

The story of Gay's "lives" discloses the interbraiding of gender and moral biography in the literary history we inherit from the eighteenth and nineteenth centuries. Not only does this story bring us to reconsider John Gay in light of the diverging reputations and cultural valences he accrued for different audiences and different generations of critics. In addition, it opens a window onto the politics—notably the politics of gender and sexuality—that frames and determines what from the past we remember, and what we eclipse and forget. The literary "lives" of John Gay is a case study in English literary history that invites us to investigate the conceptual legacies of that history, and, even more important, to articulate the unspoken assumptions that it has bequeathed to our very ways of seeing.

Notes

[1] William Irving offers a sketchy overview of Gay's reputation in the last chapter of *John Gay, Favorite of the Wits* (Duke U. Press, 1940), 292-316.

[2] See David Nokes, *John Gay, A Profession of Friendship* (Oxford U. Press, 1995); Calhoun Winton, *John Gay and the London Stage* (U. Press of Kentucky, 1993); and Peter Lewis and Nigel Wood, eds. *John Gay and the Scriblerians* (London: Vision Press; New York: St. Martin's, 1988).

[3] See Dianne Dugaw, "The Female Warrior, Gay's *Polly,* and the Heroic Ideal," Chapter 8 in *Warrior Women and Popular Balladry, 1650-1850* (Cambridge U. Press, 1989; paperback edition, U. of Chicago Press, 1996), 191-211. See also, Dianne Dugaw, "Folklore and John Gay's Satire," *SEL* 31 (1991): 515-33.

[4] For discussion of this shift with regard to women writers, see Catherine Gallagher, *Nobody's Story* (U. of California Press, 1994).

[5] For discussion of this overarching cultural phenomenon, see William Weber, *The Rise of the Musical Classics in Eighteenth-Century London* (London: Clarendon Press, 1992).

[6] Mottley's account is an appendage of well over two hundred pages attached to Thomas Whincop's *Scanderberg; or, Love and Liberty: A Tragedy* (London: W. Reeve, 1747), 87-320.

[7] Gay's near contemporaries, of course, considered the writing of plays to be more significant than later commentators found it.

[8] Gay is here favorably contrasted with Pope: "It is plain that Mr. Pope esteem'd himself a Writer only of that Sort of Pastoral which painted the Golden Age. Mr. Gay, on the contrary leaves that behind, and gives his Shepherds and Shepherdesses a Turn altogether modern and natural." Some pages later (184), it is said that comedy was "his natural Genius." See William Ayre, *Memoirs of the Life and Writings of Alexander Pope,* 2 vols. (London: Printed for the Author, and Sold by the booksellers of London and Westminster by his Majesty's authority, 1745), 2:129. It has been argued that Edmund Curll is the author of these *Memoirs.* See Ralph Straus, *The Unspeakable Curll* (London: Chapman and Hall, 1927), 194-97 and 312.

[9] Theophilus Cibber, et al., *The Lives of the Poets of Great Britain and Ireland,* 5 vols. (London: Printed for R. Griffiths, 1753), 4:259. This work was compiled mainly by Robert Shiels with revisions and additions by Cibber.

[10] Oliver Goldsmith, *Works,* ed. J. W. Gibbs, 5 vols. (London, 1884-86), 5:156. His 1758 review of *The Beggar's Opera* observes that "so sweet and happy a genius as Mr. Gay possessed of could achieve anything." See Oliver Goldsmith, *The London Chronicle; or, Universal evening post,* 4, no. 278 (Oct. 7-10, 1758).

[11] John Gay, *The Beggar's Opera . . . to Which is Prefixed the Life of the Author* (Glasgow: np, 1772), 7. This editor observes, with admiration, that these works are "universally read" and "represented."

[12] David Erskine Baker (continued from 1764 to 1782 by Isaac Reed), *Biographia Dramatica, A new edition carefully corrected, greatly enlarged, and continued from 1764 to 1782,* 2 vols. (London: Printed for Mess. Rivingtons, &c., 1782), 2:401. Reed notes that this "good-natured burlesque" was still "frequently performed" in 1782.

[13] Tobias Smollett, *The History of England from the Revolution to the Death of George II,* 5 vols. (London: T. Cadell and R. Baldwin, 1790), 2:460.

[14] Most twentieth-century discussion of the debate about morality and Gay has focused on *The Beggar's Opera.* See Winton, op. cit., 109-27. See also William E. Schultz, *Gay's Beggar's Opera: Its Content, History and Influence* (Yale U. Press, 1923).

[15] John Gay, *The Works . . . to Which is Added an Account of the Life and Writings of the Author,* 4 vols. (Dublin: James Potts, 1770), 1:vii.

[16] [Eliza Haywood], *The Parrot* (London: T. Gardner, 1746), No. 9, P2 verso. The lines of the play she quotes underscore the extent to which her discomfort stems from concepts of class and the social order. She says: "The late witty and ingenious Mr. *Gay . . .* tells us, I very well remember, *"Your little Villains must submit to Fate, / That great Ones may enjoy the World in State."* I SHOULD be extremely sorry indeed to be assured that this Piece of Satire were as *just* as it is *severe.*"

[17] Joseph Warton, *An Essay on the Genius and Writings of Pope,* 5th ed., 2 vols. (London: W. J. and J. Richardson, &c., 1806), 1:245-46. Warton's discussion was first published in 1756.

[18] Later commentators often follow this assertion of the "gentlemanliness" of Gay's background. Cf. Irving, 5-14.

[19] See Nokes, op. cit., 16-35.

[20] Irving contextualizes this skeleton of a story with discussion of trade in Barnstable and in Gay's family. See op. cit., 17-27.

[21] David Nokes, "The Smartness of a Shoe-Boy: Deference and Mockery in Gay's Life and Work," *TLS*, January 20, 1995, 13-14. For discussion of Gay in terms of sexual orientation, see Nokes' *John Gay*, 42-50. Nokes cites John Dunton's "The He-Strumpets," a poem describing Willets' clientele as "Men worse than goats / Who dress themselves in petticoats . . . / These doat on men, and some on boys, / And quite abandon female joys" (42).

[22] Nokes, "Smartness of a Shoe-Boy," 13. Nokes proposes that "the urgent attempts of Pope and Swift to suppress and sanitize the details of Gay's early private life would seem to confirm a suspicion that there was something they wished to conceal more shameful than a mere background in trade" (*John Gay*, 44). This "something" Nokes believes to be that Gay was "at least a latent homosexual" (50). Whatever the poet's affectional life and sexual expression, Nokes' comments stand squarely within the tradition I trace here of discussing Gay in terms of "manliness" and a gendered identity.

[23] What we know of Gay's life has been significantly shaped by anecdotal traditions connected to Swift and Pope. In these accounts, Gay is routinely mentioned, typically as a lesser figure who functions to enhance the stature of his friends. It is reasonable to be skeptical of the retrospective downsizing of Gay in these memoirs. On the shaping of Gay's life by Pope and Swift. see Nokes, *John Gay*, 36ff.

[24] Ayre, op. cit., 2:97.

[25] John Gay, *Plays . . . to Which is Added an Account of the Life and Writings of the Author* (London: J. and R. Tonson, 1760), iii-iv.

[26] John Gay, *The Works . . . to Which is Added an Account of the Life and Writings of the Author*, 4 vols. (Dublin: James Potts, 1770), 4:ii.

[27] Samuel Johnson, *Lives of the English Poets*, ed. George Birkbeck Hill, 3 vols. (Oxford: Clarendon Press, 1905). Commissioned by his publishers, Johnson's three-volume *Lives* should be seen in the context of the general eighteenth-century preoccupation with retrospective collecting and cataloguing in dictionaries, memoirs, collections, and checklists of various sorts. Johnson infused this codifying impulse with a compelling morality. For discussions of Johnson and biography see William H. Epstein, *Recognizing Biography* (U. of Pennsylvania Press, 1987), especially chapter 4, "Patronizing the Biographical Subject: Johnson's *Life of Savage*," 52-70. (For a survey of biographical scholarship in general, see pp. 1-12.) See also Park Honan, "Dr. Johnson's Lives" in *Authors' Lives: On Literary Biography and the Arts of Language* (New York: St. Martin's Press, 1990), 17-25.

[28] On heroism and writing in the eighteenth century, see Michael McKeon, "Writer as Hero: Novelistic Prefigurations and the Emergence of Literary Biography" in William H. Epstein, ed., *Contesting the Subject: Essays in the Postmodern Theory and Practice of Biography and Biographical Criticism* (Purdue U. Press, 1991), 17-41. See also Robert Folkenflik, "The Artist As Hero in the Eighteenth Century," *Yearbook of English Studies* 12 (1982): 91-108.

[29] By the first decade of the nineteenth century, Johnson's "Life" was already being reproduced—without attribution—in disparate publications of Gay's works. See, for example, editions of *The Fables . . . With the Life of the Author* published in Vienna by R. Sammer in 1799 and in Dublin by William Porter in 1804.

[30] Johnson, op. cit., 2:282. All subsequent quotes are from this edition.

[31] Jeffrey Plank, "Reading Johnson's *Lives:* The Forms of Late Eighteenth-Century Literary History," in Paul Korshin, ed., *The Age of Johnson: A Scholarly Annual*, vol. 1 (New York: AMS Press, 1989), 351.

[32] As Plank observes, Johnson's "lives" may counter, sometimes even parody authors' works. He points to Milton and Pope as examples, noting that "the life of Milton is thus a parody of *Paradise Lost, Paradise Regained*, and *Samson Agonistes*. . . . If the life of Milton is a moral tale that parodies the epic and the epic hero . . . then the life of Pope is a moral tale that demonstrates the superiority of the moral tale to the mock epic for the dealing with the figure of the poet" (343-44).

[33] Johnson, op. cit., 2:267-68.

[34] See Jayne Lewis, "Risking Contradiction: John Gay's *Fables* and the Matter of Reading," chapter 6 in *Fables and the Foundations of Literate Culture in England, 1652-1740* (Cambridge U. Press, 1996).

[35] As Annabel Paterson shows, the pastoral up to the Romantic era conventionally carried moral and political implication. See *Pastoral and Ideology* (U. of California Press, 1987). See also Sven Armens, *John Gay, Social Critic* (New York: King's Crown Press, 1954) and William Empson, *Some Versions of Pastoral* (London: Chatto and Windus, 1935).

[36] *The Bystander; or, Universal Weekly Expositor by a Literary Association* (London: H. Thomas, 1790), 195.

[37] William Coxe, "Life of Gay," in John Gay, *Fables, Illustrated with Notes and the Life of the Author* (London: T. Cadell, jun. and W. Davies, 1796), 65-66.

[38] *The Poetical Works of John Gay . . . to Which is Prefixed the Life of the Author* (Edinburgh: Mundell and Son, 1794), 262.

[39] Gay's works were widely popular across class lines from the beginning. Their appropriation by those marketing children's literature—for example, the Bow Churchyard printshop of William and Cluer Dicey— both contributed to and resulted from this popularity. Eventually moral reformers involved themselves in the promulgation of literature for lower-class people and children. The cautionary presentation and editing of Gay's works traced here is best understood in the context of this larger development in the field of popular literature as a whole. See Dugaw, *Warrior Women,* 140-42.

[40] John Gay, *Fables . . . with a Life of the Author,* 2 vols. (London: J. Stockdale, 1793), 2:163-64.

[41] John Gay, *Poems . . . with the Author's Life* (Poughmill: George Nicholson, 1801), i.

[42] See the editor's remarks about the fables in *Poems by John Gay . . . to Which is Prefixed, A Sketch of the Author's Life* (Manchester: G. Nicholson, 1797), 2.

[43] *The Beggar's Opera . . . the Objectionable Poetry Altered . . . with New Symphonies and Accompaniments for the Piano-forte,* by John Barnett (London: Library of Standard Music, [183?]). See also a series of letters by the clergyman, John Lettice on "the defective morality" of Gay's *Fables* published in *European Magazine* in 1815 and 1816. Cf. "Letters on Gay's Fables," *European Magazine* 68 (1815): 17-18, 114-15, 213-14, 325-26, 407-8, 505-6, and 69 (1816): 29-30, 119-21, 218, 314-15, and 415-16.

[44] John Gay, *A Selection from Fables . . .* Selected by James Plumptre (Huntingdon: T. Lovell, 1823), iii and ix-x. Plumptre cites both Johnson and Lettice as authorities.

[45] Plumptre wrote an unpublished biography of Gay (Cambridge University Library, Manuscript Add. 5829) from which Winton quotes, op. cit., 107.

[46] John Aikin, *Select Works of the British Poets* (London: Longman, Rees, &c., 1849), Alr.

[47] Charles Cowden Clarke, ed., *The Poetical Works of Joseph Addison; Gay's Fables; and Somerville's Chase* (London: Cassell Petter and Galpin, [1875]).

[48] William Makepeace Thackeray, "The English Humourists of the 18th Century: A Series of Lectures delivered in England, Scotland, and the United States of America" [1st edition 1853], in *Henry Esmond, The English Humourists, The Four Georges,* vol. 14 of *The Oxford Thackerary,* ed. George Saintsbury (Oxford U. Press, 1908).

[49] Austin Dobson, *Miscellanies* (New York: Dodd, Mead, and Co., 1899), 241.

[50] Duncan C. Tovey, "John Gay" in *Reviews and Essays in English Literature* (London: George Bell and Sons, 1897), 136.

[51] Arthur Salmon included an admiring chapter on Gay in his *Literary Rambles in the West of England* (London: Chatto and Windus, 1906), 72-86. In a letter of 1906, he voiced his dilemma of going against the prevailing current saying, "You may be surprised to hear that the *Times* reviewer censured me for including this writer at all in my book; but to my mind he is a most interesting literary character, and my fear is that I hardly did him justice." (From MS Postcard to E. L. Gay, September 6, 1906 in Harvard University, Widener Library copy of Salmon's *Literary Rambles.*)

I am grateful to the William Andrews Clark Memorial Library and the Center for 17th and 18th Century Studies at the University of California, Los Angeles for support of this project. I also extend heartfelt thanks to Jayne Lewis, Rachel Fretz, and especially Amanda Powell for their help in the planning and writing of this essay.

FURTHER READING

Bibliography

Price, Cecil. "Gay, Goldsmith, Sheridan, and Other Eighteenth-Century Dramatists." In *English Drama (excluding Shakespeare): Select Bibliographical Guides,* edited by Stanley Wells, pp. 199-212. Oxford: Oxford University Press, 1975.

> Bibliographic essay provides a short overview of earlier works on Gay; includes citations for general reference.

Biographies

Dearing, Vinton A. "The Life of Gay." In his *John Gay: Poetry and Prose,* pp. 1-16. Oxford: Oxford University Press, 1974.

> Dearing follows Gay's literary and court career, connecting events in his personal life to the works he

was writing when they occurred.

Irving, William Henry. *John Gay: Favorite of the Wits.* Durham, N.C.: Duke University Press, 1940, 317 p.

    The first important modern biography of Gay. Attempts to distance Gay from his earlier reputation as a second-class writer.

Melville, Lewis [pseudonym for Benjamin, Lewis S.]. *Life and Letters of John Gay (1685-1732), Author of "The Beggar's Opera."* London: Daniel O'Connor, 1921, 163 p.

    This biography of Gay focuses on his friendships with Swift and Pope and his relationship with various ladies at court, in the context of his major works.

Nokes, David. *John Gay: A Profession of Friendship.* Oxford: Oxford University Press, 1995, 553 p.

    Examines Gay's life and works in the context of his culture and in light of late-twentieth-century developments in literary criticism. Advances the hypothesis that Gay was homosexual.

Underhill, John. "Introductory Memoir." In his *Poems of John Gay,* pp. xi-lxix. London: George Routledge and Sons, 1893.

    Reflects the nineteenth-century view of Gay as lazy, unrealistic, and only moderately talented.

Warner, Oliver. *John Gay.* London: Longmans, Green and Co., 1964, 40 p.

    A brief biography focusing on Gay's literary career; maintains the notion that Gay was undisciplined and his artistic output uneven at best.

Criticism

Bender, John. "The Novel and the Rise of the Penitentiary: Narrative and Ideology in Defoe, Gay, Hogarth, and Fielding." *Stanford Literature Review* 1, No. 1 (Spring 1984): 55-84.

    Discusses Gay's depiction of Newgate prison in the context of legal and social developments of the eighteenth century.

Burgess, C. F. "Political Satire: John Gay's *The Beggar's Opera.*" *The Midwest Quarterly* 6, No. 3 (April 1965): 265-76.

    Argues that Gay attacks Walpole in his depiction of the unethical merchant Peachum, and suggests that Macheath represents George II.

———. Introduction to *The Letters of John Gay.* Oxford at the Clarendon Press, 1966, pp. xi-xxiv.

    Provides a brief introduction to Gay as revealed through his letters.

Forsgren, Adina. "Some Complimentary Epistles by John Gay." *Studia Neophilologica* 36, No. 1 (1964): 82-100.

Discusses Gay's adaptation of both classical and contemporary models of epistles, especially those of Horace.

———. "Lofty Genii and Low Ghosts. Vision Poems and John Gay's 'True Story of an Apparition.'" *Studia Neophilologica* 40, No. 1 (1968): 197-215.

    Argues that Gay's poem was a Scriblerian response to Whig versions of history.

Fuller, John. "Introduction." In his *John Gay: Dramatic Works,* pp. 1-76. Oxford: Clarendon Press, 1983.

    Provides a substantive overview of Gay's dramatic career, demonstrating the development of his social criticism and his experimentalism.

Klein, J. T. "Satire in a New Key: The Dramatic Function of the Lyrics of *The Beggar's Opera.*" *Michigan Academician* 9, No. 3 (Winter 1977): 313-21.

    Suggests that the ballads of *The Beggar's Opera* do not serve to advance the plot but to provide the play's moral commentary.

Lewis, Peter Elfed. "Gay's Burlesque Method in *The What D'ye Call It.*" *Durham University Journal* 60, No. 1 (December 1967): 13-25.

    Considers Gay's farce as part of the development of the dramatic burlesque genre, concluding that the play was an important artistic achievement for Gay.

———. "John Gay's 'Achilles': The Burlesque Element." *Ariel* 3, No. 1 (January 1972): 17-28.

    Interprets Gay's play as an effective attack on Italian opera and heroic drama, despite its dramatic weaknesses.

———. "The Beaux' Stratagem and The Beggar's Opera." *Notes and Queries* 28, No. 3 (June 1981): 221-24.

    Claims that Gay drew from George Farquhar's 1707 comedy in writing *The Beggar's Opera.*

Preston, John. "The Ironic Mode: A Comparison of *Jonathan Wild* and *The Beggar's Opera.*" *Essays in Criticism* 16, No. 3 (July 1966): 268-80.

    Draws parallels between Henry Fielding's satiric method in his earliest novel and Gay's depiction of Macheath in his *Opera.*

Rees, Christine. "Gay, Swift, and the Nymphs of Drury Lane." *Essays in Criticism* 23, No. 1 (January 1973) 1-21.

    Focuses on Swift's and Gay's depiction of women in the context of the Augustan conflict between Art and Nature.

Teske, Charles B. "Gay's ' 'Twas When the Seas Were Roaring' " and the Rise of Pathetic Balladry." *Anglia* 83 (1965): 411-25.

    Examines Gay's ballad in its original setting, his farcical *The What D'Ye Call It,* to contradict its reputation as a serious sentimental art song.

Wiggins, Gene. "The Uneasy Swain: Folklore in John Gay." *Tennessee Folklore Society Bulletin* 66, No. 3 (September 1980): 45-62.

Reviews Gay's use of folklore to conclude that the poet worked to conceal the extent of his knowledge with a pretense of satirical sophistication.

Francesco Guicciardini

1483-1540

Italian historian, diplomat, statesman, and political writer.

INTRODUCTION

Guicciardini is known today chiefly for his friendship with Niccolò Machiavelli and for his masterwork, *Storia d'Italia,* (1561-65; *History of Italy*). Guicciardini's literary reputation has undergone numerous reexaminations over the centuries. Many early commentators, for example, found his attitude toward history and politics cold and cynical. Today, however, his writings are admired largely for their close attention to detail and their vivid evocation of Renaissance Italy.

Biography

Much of what is known about Guicciardini can be found in his two-volume diary or *Ricordanze* (1515, 1528). He was born in the city-state of Florence to an aristocratic family. He pursued a law degree at 15 and graduated with a doctorate in civil law in 1505. In 1508 he married Maria Salviati, possibly in order to connect himself with her politically influential powerful family. At about this time, he began work on the *Storie Fiorentine* (1509; *History of Florence*). Although left unfinished, this *History* reveals Guicciardini's devotion to Florence as well as to his own aristocratic class. Written after the ouster of the Medici and during the initial tenure of the Florentine Republic, it is also critical of the tyranny of the Medici family. Guicciardini attained increasingly important posts in the Republic. From 1512 to 1513, he served as ambassador to Spain. During this time he started writing a book of political aphorisms known as the *Ricordi* (1580; *Maxims and Reflections of a Renaissance Stateman).* He also wrote a political treatise, *Discorso di Logrogno* (1512; *Discourse of Logrogno*) and worked on his *Relazione di Spagna* (1512-13; *Report from Spain*). The *Report from Spain*—an examination of that country's ancient history and of its Renaissance status—stands as an example of the attention to detail that appears in much of Guicciardini's writing. While Guicciardini was still in Spain, the Florentine Republic fell and was replaced once again by the rule of the Medici. On returning to Florence, Guicciardini was appointed by the Medici Pope Leo X to several influential posts: the governorship of Modena (1516) as well as of Reggio and Parma (1517). Impressed with his work as governor, Leo X made him commissioner of the papal

armies in 1521. It was during this time that Guicciardini met Machiavelli. The two men became friends, and their work has frequently been compared by critics who see in both writers a loyalty to Florence linked with a reliance on *realpolitik*. Guicciardini's ambitions carried him successfully through another ouster of the Medici and a reinstatement of the Florentine republic in 1527. When the Medici returned to power in 1530, he expected to continue to rise under the leadership of Cosimo Medici. This time, however, the hoped-for advancement did not occur. Disappointed, Guicciardini withdrew from politics and spent the rest of his life working on his *History of Italy.*

Principal Works

None of Guicciardini's works was published during his lifetime, but critics believe that none except for the *History of Italy* was in fact intended for publication. This *History* and the *Maxims and Reflections of a Renaissance Statesmen* (which Guicciardini worked on from 1512 to 1530), are regarded as his two most significant contributions to Renaissance literature. Critic Mark Phillips describes the *Maxims* as "clear and direct" but skeptical lessons on the dos and don'ts of social and political life. The *History of Italy,* on the other hand, is written in a "grave," more complex style. It is the work of a man in retirement facing the closing years of his life, and it looks on the domestic affairs of Italy as well as its European encounters from 1492 to 1534 in a pessimistic light.

Critical Reception

The critical reception of Guicciardini's works has been various. Some of his own Italian contemporaries hated him for his support of the tyrannical Medici family. In fact, Guicciardini himself disapproved of the Medici's brutality, but believed that their power guaranteed the survival of his own aristocratic class. For this attitude he has been condemned as cynical and opportunistic, sharing the same cold adherence to *realpolitik* as his friend Machiavelli. By contrast, Renaissance Englishmen who read Geoffrey Fenton's translation of Guicciardini's *History of Italy* were impressed with the Italian historian's work. Indeed, portions of the *History* appear in English historian Raphael Holinshed's *Chronicles.* The French essayist Michel de Montaigne, however, deplored what he saw as the *History's* overly complicated and convoluted style and worried that Guicciardini's failure to provide examples of virtuous and rational conduct was a sign that the historian himself was "corrupted." Interest in Guicciardini's writings was revived in the nineteenth century when Giusep-pe Canestrini published his collected works, or *Opere inedite* (1857-67). Once again Guicciardini came under criticism for his aristocratic prejudices, and was at that time compared unfavorably to the more plebian Machiavelli. One nineteenth-century student of Guicciardini's works—Francesco De Sanctis—revealed mixed views that were not uncommon in reaction to the Renaissance historian: De Sanctis admired Guicciardini for his formidable intelligence but criticized him for his coldness. Twentieth-century critics have tended to be less judgmental. Mario Domandi, for example, applauds the fact that Guicciardini was able to separate ethics from politics in his *Maxims.* And Sidney Alexander considers Guicciardini distinctly mo-dern for his focus on the individual rather than the group in his histories. Finally, several critics have praised the anecdotal quality of Guicciardini's works, and others have pointed out that he could be both rational and passionate in his assessment of Florentine politics.

PRINCIPAL WORKS*

Storie florentine [*History of Florence*] (unfinished history) 1509

Discorso di Logrogno [*Discourse of Logrogno*] (essay) 1512

Relazione di Spagna [*Report from Spain*] (diplomatic report) 1512-13

Ricordanze. 2 vols. (diary) 1515 and 1528

Dialogo del reggimento di Firenze [*Dialogue on the Government of Florence*] (essay) 1524

Considerazioni sui "Discorsi" del Machiavelli [*Observations on Machiavelli's "Discourses"*] (essay) 1530

Storia d'Italia [*History of Italy*] (history) 1561-65

Ricordi [*Maxims and Reflections of a Renaissance Statesman*] (aphorisms) 1580

Opere inedite. 10 vols. [published by Giuseppe Canestrini] (collected works) 1857-67

Le cose fiorentine [*Florentine Affairs*] (unfinished history edited by Roberto Ridolfi) 1945

*Because none of Guicciardini's works was published during his lifetime, all dates (except those for the *Storia d'Italia, Ricordi, Opere inedite,* and *Le cose fiorentine*) indicate the approximate time of completion of the work rather than a publication date.

CRITICISM

Cecil Grayson (essay date 1965)

SOURCE: Introductory Notes to *Francesco Guicciardini: Selected Writings,* edited and introduced by Cecil Grayson, translated by Margaret Grayson, Oxford University Press, 1965, pps. xxv, 59-60, 127-28.

[*In the following brief notes, Grayson describes the contents, physical appearance, and publication history of Guicciardini's* Ricordi, Considerations on the "Discourses" *of Machiavelli, and* Ricordanze.]

Introductory Note: Ricordi

Guicciardini made three redactions of this work. Although he began to collect together certain maxims as early as 1512, the main body of the collection, in a manuscript now lost, was put together sometime before 1525, re-copied, enlarged, and corrected in 1528, and further revised in 1530. In this process he made no fewer than 606 formulations for a total of 276 maxims, of which in the final version he discarded 55. The history of the growth and elaboration of the *Ricordi* has been reconstructed by R. Spongano in his excellent critical edition published by the Accademia della Crusca, Florence, in 1951 (Sansoni). The present translation, based on this edition, is confined to the 221 *ricordi* of the final redaction.

The **Ricordi** in one form or another were printed several times in the sixteenth century, and translated early into French, Dutch, and Spanish. The first English translation did not appear until 1845 (by Emma Martin, *The Maxims of Fr. Guicciardini,* London); a further translation was made by N. H. Thomson, **Counsels and Reflections of Fr. Guicciardini,** London, 1890. But in these, as in Italian editions before Spongano's edition of 1951, some degree of confusion, or at best parallelism, between the various redactions was inevitably present. On the diffusion, translation, and influence of this work, see V. Luciani, *Fr. Guicciardini and his European Reputation,* New York, 1936 (Italian translation brought up to date, Florence, 1949) Chapter X. . . .

Introductory Note: Considerations on the "Discourses" of Machiavelli

Machiavelli composed his *Discourses* between 1515 and 1518 in three books, dealing respectively with the internal politics, the expansion, and the contribution of individuals to the greatness of the Roman Republic. Ranging over a far wider area of historical and political interest and example than these general themes and his principal source would suggest, they represent the most mature reflection of Machiavelli on his long experience of contemporary affairs and continual reading of histories. After his death they were published for the first time in 1531 by Blado in Rome.

Guicciardini began his **Considerations** in Rome in 1530, where he probably had access to the autograph copy on which the Blado edition was based. He evidently intended to comment on more than thirty-eight chapters from the three books, but the work remained unfinished, and was unknown and unpublished until the nineteenth century. The present translation (the first complete translation into English) is based on the text published by R. Palmarocchi in vol. VIII *(Scritti Politici e Ricordi)* of Guicciardini's **Opere** (Bari, Laterza, 1933, pp. 3-65), which we have also followed in numbering the chapters according to the relevant number of the *Discourses* and in adding the title of each chapter from Machiavelli's work.

For a full appreciation of this work, the **Considerations** and the *Discourses* should ideally be read together. Machiavelli's *Discourses* have, however, been translated into English in recent years by Fr. L. J. Walker, London, Routledge & Kegan Paul, 1950 (though the translation is not always reliable, the notes, in vol. II, are very full and include copious reference, often with translations, to Guicciardini's **Considerations**). This fact, as well as reasons of space (in general each *Discourse* is much longer than its *Consideration*) and the

character of the present series, determined the limitation of our notes to an indication for each *Consideration* of the essential argument and examples of Machiavelli's text commented on by Guicciardini. Much that Machiavelli wrote in these *Discourses* was ignored by Guicciardini for one reason or another: some indication of the major 'omissions' is given in the notes. With their help and through Guicciardini's comments it is possible to perceive Machiavelli's views, and to appreciate the difference of approach of the two writers to the history of the past and of their own times. . . .

Introductory Note: Ricordanze

The **Ricordanze** here translated are in fact two separate records of Guicciardini's life and personal affairs: the first compiled between April 1508 and December 1515 and covering the period 1482-1515; the second written between July 1527 and February 1528, covering the period 1506-27. They exist in different holograph books, the second having the following descriptive title:

> This book belongs to messer Francesco di Piero Guicciardini and is entitled Debtors and Creditors A; it was begun on 1 July 1527, because the other books I had started in the past, I had left behind and could not continue, as I was abroad for eleven years without a break.

From pp. 3-150, Debtors and Creditors;

From p. 150 to end, Ricordanze.

Although the second record repeats some few items of the first they are in the main very different in their material content, the one chiefly social-political, the other commercial-financial. Although they overlap slightly materially and chronologically, and though they are incomplete, together they give a remarkably coherent picture of the personality, interests, and concerns of Guicciardini the lawyer, citizen, husband, father, and business man.

The **Ricordanze** were not intended by the author for publication. The first part was published for the first time by Canestrini in 1867, and the second by P. Guicciardini in 1930. The present translation (the first into English) is based on the edition of R. Palmarocchi in vol. IX *(Scritti autobiografici e rari)* of Guicciardini's **Opere,** Bari, Laterza, 1936, pp. 53-98. The last three pages of the second part have, however, been omitted here. They contain an inventory of the silver plate which Guicciardini had made while he was in Romagna in 1524 or had acquired in earlier years for household purposes. As they are made up almost entirely of details of weights, alloys, makers' names, etc., it was felt that these pages might be dispensed with in the present translation.

Notes have been added to the text with the prime object of clarifying some of the financial transactions. The reader is reminded that the dates in the text are in Florentine style, the year beginning on 25 March. . . .

Nicolai Rubinstein (essay date 1965)

SOURCE: Introduction to *Maxims and Reflections of a Renaissance Statesman (Ricordi)*, by Francesco Guicciardini, translated by Mario Domandi, Harper Torchbooks, 1965, pp. 7-32.

[*In the following essay, Rubinstein provides an overview of Guicciardini's eighteen-year endeavor known as the* Ricordi, *and points out the differences in Guicciardini's work from that of his contemporary and colleague, Machiavelli.*]

I

In the history of Renaissance thought, Guicciardini's ***Ricordi*** occupy a place of singular importance. Few works of the sixteenth century allow us so penetrating an insight into the views and sentiments of its author as these reflexions of the great Italian historian, written down over a period of eighteen years. Like Machiavelli's *Prince,* the ***Ricordi*** form one of the outstanding documents of a time of crisis and transition; but unlike the *Prince,* they range over a wide field of private as well as public life. In doing so, they reveal the man as well as the political theorist.

. . . . .

In January 1512, Francesco Guicciardini left Florence for the Spanish court as ambassador to the king of Aragon. It was Francesco's first major appointment, and one that was remarkable on account of his youth: "No one could remember at Florence that so young a man had ever been chosen for such an embassy," he writes in his diary.[1] Born in 1483, Franceso, after studying law in Florence, Ferrara, and Padua, had become a successful lawyer in his native city, and had already been elected to minor posts in the republic. As a member of an ancient patrician family, he now followed in the footsteps of his father, grandfather, and great-uncle, who all had held high positions in the government and diplomatic service of Florence. During the fifteenth century, his family had raised their political status by supporting the Medici, and Jacopo and Luigi, Francesco's grandfather and great-uncle, had belonged to Lorenzo the Magnificent's inner circle. Francesco's father Piero, although less active in public life, continued to hold office under the new republican regime. Thus when, in October 1511, the Council of Eighty elected Francesco ambassador to Spain, the future may well have seemed mapped out for the young lawyer. Service to the state was in the tradition of the Florentine aristocracy, and this embassy would normally have been the first of many high offices in the republic; but Francesco's career was changed by a sequence of political events. During his absence in Spain, the Spanish and Papal forces advanced on Florence, since 1494 a loyal ally of France, and forced her to recall the Medici, who restored their political supremacy and abolished the republican institutions that had been set up in 1494. In 1513, Lorenzo the Magnificent's son Giovanni became Pope Leo X and placed Florence under Papal control. A side-effect of Florence's new dependency on Rome was that individual Florentines might be appointed to posts in the Papal administration. Guicciardini was one of these. After his return to Florence in 1514, he had been elected a member of the Eight of Ward, and then of the *Signoria;* but soon much wider opportunities opened up for him outside his native city. In 1516, Leo X made him governor of Modena, and in 1517, of Reggio. It was the beginning of a long and distinguished career in the Papal administration, first under Leo X, and then under the second Medici Pope, Clement VII.

When Guicciardini left for Spain, he had already written two historical works: his family memoirs and an unfinished ***History of Florence*** from 1378 to his own time. In this history he had voiced his views on the respective merits of the Medicean and the republican regime; and his strictures on these, and particularly on the government of Piero Soderini, who became head of the republic in 1502, doubtless reflected the attitude of many aristocrats. During his stay at the Spanish court, he composed a discourse on the reforms by which, in his view, the republican regime could be improved and saved: "I had nearly finished writing it," he notes in his manuscript, "when I heard the news that the Medici had entered Florence."[2] The same manuscript also contains his report on Spain, as well as a collection of twenty-nine maxims, preceded by the note: "In the year 1512, while I was ambassador in Spain."[3] This is the second of the two earliest collections of his ***Ricordi;*** the first, which consisted of thirteen maxims, was also written in Spain. Both collections are introduced by an entry which provides a kind of title—the present one was probably adopted only after Guicciardini's death—as well as an explanation of the origin of the reflections contained in them: "Although leisure alone does not give birth to whims, it is indeed true that there can be no whims without leisure." Composed in the relative leisure of his Spanish embassy, about half of these earliest *ricordi* deal with the political conditions of a city-republic, and several of them with questions discussed in the ***Discourse of Logrogno,*** and in that on Medicean reforms written shortly afterwards; they almost read like by-products of his thinking on the contemporary problems of his native city, for which there was no place in his treatises. After his return from Spain, Guicciardini wrote many new *ricordi,* and in 1528, "during the great leisure I then had," he made another collection of them, containing 181 reflections; this had probably been preceded by an earlier one, which is no longer extant. In May 1530, when his enforced leisure was drawing to an end, he began to compile his final collection of 221 *ricordi.*

In rearranging—usually with greater or lesser changes of their wording—earlier *ricordi,* in combining or omitting others, and in adding new ones, Guicciardini clearly applied to his various collections some principles of order. Yet basically the **Ricordi** remain what they had been from the beginning, namely, reflections on a large number of questions based on Guicciardini's personal experience rather than on any theoretical plan. Thus the successive collections reflect Guicciardini's attitudes to changing situations. The earliest are full of references to the political problems of the republican regime in Florence, which foundered in 1512. But then the horizon widens: the stage is now set in the Papal State and in Italy at large, at a time of crisis, when the entry of European powers into Italian politics had profoundly upset long-established patterns of political behavior; and the writer is no longer the unexperienced ambassador of the Florentine republic, but the successful Papal governor, used to positions of high responsibility and great danger. Finally, the scene shifts back to Florence; having been appointed in 1526 Papal lieutenant-general with the army of the League of Cognac against Charles V, Guicciardini helped protect his city from the army of German mercenaries which threatened it in 1527; and he returned to Florence, where, after the sack of Rome by that army, the Medici had once more been expelled and the republican regime restored. Suspect owing to his close association with them, he fled in September 1529 to the Papal court. From there he followed the city's staunch resistance against the besieging imperialist army, which ended in August 1530 with Florence's capitulation, and with the fall of its last republican regime. It was in May of the same year that Guicciardini had begun the final collection of his *ricordi*—at a time, as he writes in the first of them, when the Florentines had "fought off these armies from their walls for seven months, though no one would have believed they could do it for seven days." (C 1) [The letters C, B, Q¹, and Q² refer to various series of Guicciardini's *Ricordi*.].

Like the first collections of *ricordi,* those of 1528 and 1530 belong to periods when the circumstances of Guicciardini's life provided him with the leisure in which to dedicate himself to study and writing. In 1528, he began his second, equally unfinished **History of Florence** (the so-called **Cose fiorentine**); probably in 1530, he wrote his **Observations on Machiavelli's Discourses.** Like many other statesmen before and after him, Guicciardini used such periods of enforced leisure to meditate on past and present events, to analyse or justify his part in them, and to search for theoretical solutions of contemporary problems. They also gave

him an opportunity to sift and collect observations jotted down at random during periods of intense activity: all but ten of the 181 *ricordi* of the collection of 1528 had been composed before 1525. Indeed, while sustained literary efforts demanded prolonged periods of freedom from public activities, the literary form of the brief observation or maxim lent itself particularly well to a life dominated by political business.

One may ask why Guicciardini undertook to compile the successive selections of these maxims—a work that involved a great deal of rewriting and rearranging. Like his diaries and family memoirs, they were hardly intended for publication; even the last of these collections, that of 1530, contains references to his family which were clearly meant for its members.[4] The keeping of diaries and commonplace books was a Florentine tradition of long standing, and Guicciardini himself dedicated his family memoirs of 1508 to his descendants. Such writings often included advice of a moral or economic character, along the lines of the treatises on practical wisdom and on household government which were so popular in fourteenth- and fifteenth-century Florence. On a vastly superior intellectual level and with a much wider perspective, Guicciardini's **Ricordi** could serve a similar purpose. Nor is this only a matter of the use to which the *ricordi* could be put. Several of them contain views that were common property of Florentine Renaissance society and that could also be found expressed, in a simpler and homelier form, in such handbooks of practical advice as Paolo da Certaldo's *Libro di buoni costuni,*[5] or in Giovanni Rucellai's *Zibaldone.*[6] But times had changed: the guidance which Rucellai gave his sons around the middle of the fifteenth century presupposed a vigorous civic society whose structure was still basically intact. Guicciardini, on the other hand, writes in a time of crisis and disillusionment, when ancient traditions and institutions had been uprooted or swept away, and when individual self-reliance and self-preservation, by means fair or foul, were at a premium. His **Ricordi** show his reactions to the changing contemporary world, as well as to his personal vicissitudes and problems. In this close relationship with his life of action and his everyday experience, they also reflect an outstanding characteristic of his political thinking.

For Guicciardini's political ideas did not originate primarily from theoretical study, but from his reactions to the political situations that confronted him; and if he owed a debt to earlier political thought, it was to that which was embodied in Florentine political tradition rather than to that expounded in classical or medieval philosophy. Although acquainted with Plato's and Aristotle's political theories, as anyone who had received a humanist education in Florence at the end of the fifteenth century was bound to be, he disclaimed any scholarly ambitions—"According to my father's wishes," he says in his diary, "I pursued, in my early youth, literary studies, and apart from Latin, I acquired a little Greek, which, however, because of different occupations, I forgot after a few years."[7] He often inveighs against abstract theorizing and the mechanical application of the political doctrines of antiquity to modern situations. This close connection between political fact and theory is already shown in his first *History of Florence,* of c. 1509, where the examination of political conditions and developments, first under the Medici and then under the new republican regime established in 1494, led him to formulate general judgments on political questions. Conversely, when in 1512 he tried to give to his views on the political problems of the republican regime a systematic form, he was concerned with questions that had direct relevance to the political situation of contemporary Florence. While criticisms of republican politics in general, and of the Gonfalonier of Justice Picro Soderini in particular, which we already find in the *History of Florence,* are repeated and elaborated, they are now accompanied by constructive proposals, such as the limitation of the Gonfalonier's powers and the creation of an aristocratic senate on the Venetian model. Although as a practical program of reform, the *Discourse of Logrogno* was obsolete by the time Guicciardini had finished writing it, it retained its importance as the first comprehensive and systematic formulation of his views on what constituted good republican government for Florence. The basic assumptions underlying these views are, firstly, that in Florence no good government can exist unless the aristocrats are given a prominent, though not an exclusive, share in it, thus at the same time satisfying their rightful claims and giving power to those who are, by upbringing and status, qualified to wield it; and, secondly, that such government could be established and safeguarded by a judicious combination of constitutional elements. While the former view reflects traditional attitudes of the Florentine patriciate, the latter testifies to the deep-rooted Florentine belief in the effectiveness of institutional policies and reforms. That this belief might occasionally be backed by references to Aristotle's teachings only shows that the *Politics* could once again be read as a practical manual of city-state politics. But Guicciardini's conclusion that the best constitution for Florence was a mixture of monarchical, oligarchical, and democratic elements, while influenced by Aristotle's doctrine of the mixed constitution, is arrived at through an examination of the political conditions of contemporary Florence; if anything, it was this objective and empirical examination of the historical development and present structure of Florentine politics which incidentally confirm for him the validity of Aristotle's theory.

After the Medici restoration, Guicciardini turned his attention to the question of how best to secure the new regime, first in a brief discourse composed while he was still in Spain, and subsequently, in 1516, in a longer one. To accuse him of opportunism would be easy enough; indeed, like so many of his compatriots, including the republican Machiavelli, Guicciardini was, from the beginning, eager to serve the new masters. Yet irrespective of personal interests and commitments, these two discourses reveal a striking continuity of approach to the problem of good government. In the first, Guicciardini shows himself opposed to a regime exclusively founded on the support of partisans, and in favour of giving the people, "which had tasted, during eighteen years, the sweetness of the republican way of life,"[8] as large a share in government and administration as possible; in the second, he criticizes the Medici for having disappointed their followers and estranged the masses, and urges them to rely on the help and advice of a group of loyal citizens, "whom they ought to encourage to speak freely the truth."[9] While accepting Medici supremacy, Guicciardini thus remains loyal to his aristocratic ideals, and to his belief in a balanced form of government which he had expressed in the *Discourse of Logrogno.* Moderation is, in fact, the keynote of all three of these discourses, a moderation that finds its most emphatic expression in his unqualified condemnation of those men who were advising the Medici to assume absolute power: "they could not take a more pernicious decision."[10]

Nor did Guicciardini's long and distinguished service under two Medici popes lead him to modify substantially his views on what constituted good government for Florence. Some time before the death of Leo X in December 1521, he began yet another treatise on this subject, which he completed under the next Medici Popc, Clement VII, in 1525 or 1526. The *Dialogue on Florentine government* is a far more ambitious work than the preceding ones; in it Guicciardini is no longer concerned with immediate reforms but with a systematic enquiry into the problem of the ideal government for Florence, based on an evaluation of the two constitutions the city had experienced in his own time. His critical comparison between the Medicean regime before 1494 and the republican regime that followed it is, on balance, favourable to the former; and yet the picture of an ideal Florentine constitution, which he draws in the second book of the *Dialogue,* resembles the pattern he had outlined before the fall of the republic in 1512. Guicciardini is clearly at pains to justify so remarkable, and in view of his career surprising, a loyalty to his republican sympathies, as is shown by the three different versions of his preface. The work, he points out, is only meant as an intellectual exercise; it expresses the opinions of the interlocutors of the dialogue, not his own; it is not intended for publication (although in the earliest version of the preface, he still visualizes that this might be possible "before I reach old age"). Did he begin composing the *Dialogue* at a time when, under the rule of Cardinal Giulio de' Medici after 1519, Florentines with republican leanings, among them Machiavelli, were hoping against hope that the Medici might soon be prepared to liberalize their rule? The discovery, in 1522, of a conspiracy against the Medici regime dashed these hopes, and in the following year Cardinal Giulio became Pope Clement VII and imposed his will on Florence with greater determination than ever. *Qui s'excuse, s'accuse:* in the end, Guicciardini had to admit, in no uncertain terms, to the possibility of a clash between his loyalties to the Medici and to his native city. But in this event, he insists, his choice would be clear: his first duty would lie with his city.[11]

Whatever the problem of personal loyalties, there certainly is no ambivalence in the constitutional theory he expounds in the *Dialogue.* Despite the advantages which the Medici regime had brought Florence, Guicciardini emphatically does not consider it the ideal form of government, not even in its relatively mild form under Lorenzo the Magnificent. This he is now more certain than ever to have found in a mixed constitution incorporating a variety of checks and balances; a constitution which, while democratic by virtue of a great council similar to the one established in 1494, and monarchical in respect of the head of the state, appointed, like the Gonfalonier of Justice Piero Soderini in 1502, for life, has as its central element an aristocratic senate. Elected for life, the senate was to hold "the balance between despotism and popular license," and was at the same time designed "to keep satisfied the most capable and best-qualified citizens."[12] At the beginning of the *Dialogue,* Guicciardini insists that he is not concerned with theory but with facts, not with whether a constitution is good in itself, but with what its effects would be in a given historical situation; consequently, the doctrines of political philosophers are irrelevant to his inquiry into the best regime for contemporary Florence.[13] It might be argued, with some justification, that Guicciardini, while pragmatically rejecting past theory, ends up by formulating one himself, and that his own theory contains a claim to absolute validity that is not so different from the claims of political philosophers such as Plato.[14] However, it should be remembered that Guicciardini's approach to politics had from the beginning been empirical and pragmatic rather than theoretical; that his search after an ideal constitution was exclusively concerned with Florence; that his conclusions, however close they sometimes came to Aristotelian concepts, were based on the historical development of that city; and, finally, that he himself made no claim to their universal applicability.

When, in May 1527, the Medici having been once more expelled from Florence, the republican regime was restored for the last time, it was so in a form that was even further removed from Guicciardini's ideals than the one it had possessed until 1512. His personal misfortunes undoubtedly deepened his disappointment over the new regime; having lost, after the sack of Rome and Clement VII's imprisonment in Castel Sant' Ange-

lo, his post as the Pope's lieutenant-general in the army of the League, he was, after his return to Florence, burdened with heavy taxes, and, despite his vast political and diplomatic experience, bypassed in the appointments to civic offices. The problem of divided loyalties, of which he had been so keenly aware in his *Dialogue on Florentine Government,* now proved to have more drastic effects on his life than he could have foreseen when he wrote that work. While he had then put the loyalty to his city above that to his Papal employer, he now forcibly appeared to the republican radicals of 1527 as the faithful servant of two Medici Popes, to the extent of being accused of having, as early as 1512, plotted the Medicean restoration. He found some comfort in the reflection that "the suspicion with which the people regards you, because it considers you a supporter of the Medici, will pass away, and the time will come, and perhaps sooner than you imagine, when you will be held in high esteem"; and that it will then be easier to convince the people "that you are not opposed to a free government."[15] But despite his friendship with the head of the state, the Gonfalonier of Justice Niccolò Capponi, these hopes proved vain. Capponi's fall from office in April 1529, when it was discovered that he had been secretly negotiating with the Pope, compromised Guicciardini's position further; and when the Papal and imperial army was advancing on Florence, he fled, in September 1529, to the Papal court. Here may have been a plan to arrest him, together with other friends of the Medici, as he asserted after his flight; in fact, he was condemned in his absence as a rebel. He returned to Florence after the city's capitulation and the restoration of the Medici in August 1530, as Papal representative, and in this capacity, he took a leading share in the persecution of Clement's republican enemies. It was not surprising that he should now support the Medicean regime more wholeheartedly than he had done after 1512. True, despite the ruthless advice he gave the new rulers, in his memoranda of 1530-32, on how to establish their power permanently, he still warned, as he had done in 1516, against the creation of a principality.[16] Yet he materially helped Duke Alessandro de' Medici to consolidate, in 1532, his new princely authority, and later enjoyed great influence under him. After Alessandro's assassination in 1537, when there was a good chance of restoring the republic, Guicciardini was instrumental in securing Cosimo I's succession to the ducal throne. But even now, his vain attempt to impose limitations on Cosimo's authority showed both his belief in constitutional safeguards and his dislike of extreme forms of government. If he had hoped to guide the young ruler, he was soon disillusioned, and virtually retired from public affairs, devoting the last years of his life—he died on 22 May 1540—to his greatest work, the *History of Italy.*

Just as his first *History of Florence* grew out of his researches into the history of his family, also his last work has autobiographical overtones, its original nucleus being an account of his lieutenantship with the army of the League of Cognac. From his family memoirs, Guicciardini had turned to the history of his city; from that of the war against Emperor Charles V after 1525, he turned to the history of his country, beginning with the origins of the foreign invasions which had changed its destiny. Nor does his narrative stop at the frontiers of Italy: that country having become the chief stage for the conflicts between France and the Habsburgs, Guicciardini's *History of Italy* time and again assumes the character of a history of Europe.

This extension of Guicciardini's subject reflects, in its turn, the broadening of his personal experience of contemporary affairs. While his juvenile *History of Florence* shows his knowledge of and concern with the politics of his city, the *History of Italy,* written about thirty years later, reveals the vast and manifold experience of an Italian statesman and diplomatist who for many years had been in close touch with the inner counsels of Italian politics, and who more than once had taken a leading part in shaping them. But while the years spent in high office and in the midst of far-reaching political and military events had immeasurably widened and deepened Guicciardini's experience of public affairs, they had also brought him many disappointments; and the pessimistic overtones of his *History of Italy* bear witness to the impact of Italy's misfortunes on the intellectual development of an Italian historian and patriot in an age of crisis.

The development of Guicciardini's views on Italy coincides largely with the time of his friendship with Machiavelli. The two men shared the same views on a number of subjects; yet this went hand in hand with fundamental disagreements. Their intellectual relationship was of the nature of a long debate between equals, rather than of one-sided or mutual influence; while Guicciardini accepted some of the ideas which Machiavelli had put forward in his political works, *The Prince* and the *Discourses,* he strongly rejected others. Dating back to Machiavelli's brief visit, in 1521, to Modena, where Guicciardini was Papal governor, the friendship between the two men became closest in the last years of Machiavelli's life. During the disastrous development of the war of the League of Cognac, Machiavelli was in charge of Florentine fortifications, and went on frequent missions to the Papal lieutenant-general in the dramatic months when the army of German *Landsknechte* was advancing south; and their Florentine and Italian patriotism, their strenuous efforts to help defend both their city and their country from the foreign invaders, brought them nearer to one another than ever. "Io amo messer Francesco Guicciardini, amo la patria mia più dell' anima," writes Machiavelli a few weeks before his death in 1527:[17] "I love Francesco Guicciardini and I love my fatherland more than my own soul."

Foremost among the attitudes the two men shared, besides their patriotism, was an objective and non-ethical approach to politics, which has earned Guicciardini the epithet of "the first of the Machiavellians."[18] Where their views differed, as in the question of the applicability of precedents from Roman antiquity to modern times, or in that of the intrinsic goodness or evil of human nature, Guicciardini's objections were largely bound up with his distrust of Machiavelli's tendency to theorize and to draw what he would consider to be sweeping conclusions from inadequate evidence. These objections to some of Machiavelli's basic theories appear already, together with a good deal of similarity in judgment, in the *Dialogue on Florentine Government.* A few years later, he formulated them systematically in his unfinished *Observations on the "Discourses" of Machiavelli,* written probably in 1530, when that work was being prepared for printing. That Guicciardini should have felt the urge to clarify his views on Machiavelli's political philosophy is significant in that it shows how deeply Machiavelli's ideas affected him. For us, the *Observations* have the additional significance that Guicciardini was writing them about the time when he was engaged in compiling the final selection of his *Ricordi.*

II

While the *Observations* provide Guicciardini with an opportunity to state his own views in critical examination of those of Machiavelli, the *Ricordi* are free from any limitation to a specific subject. The harvest of an active life by a profound and subtle mind, they reflect the vicissitudes of that life as well as the development of his thought. Written over a period of about eighteen years, stretching from his first high office to his involuntary retirement from a great public career, they reveal, both in the addition of new maxims and in the alteration of earlier ones, the development of his views and the effect on them of changing external circumstances. That some of these views should also be expressed in the political treatises written during that period is not surprising.[19] In fact, many *ricordi* could have formed the subject of systematic discussions; however, Guicciardini chose to leave them in the lapidary form of reflections. Adverse to abstract theory which was not based upon experience, he considered himself, when writing down his meditations on a wide variety of subjects, primarily a man of action; and when he finally withdrew from public life, he chose history and not philosophy as his principal field of activity.

While it would thus be futile to expect to find systematic order in the *Ricordi,* it would be equally mistaken to deny them any form of organization. A comparison between the different collections he made of them, and particularly between the two last ones of 1528 and 1530, shows Guicciardini attempting, however loosely, to arrange his reflections in groups, with one *ricordo* often leading up to another. Taken together, these groups of *ricordi* cover a number of fairly well-definable topics, while a few themes, such as that of the function of reason in human action, run through the entire work. Guicciardini's basic assumption, that experience was a more reliable source of knowledge than deductive theory, affected in its turn both the subject matter of single *ricordi* and the modifications and additions made in the successive collections. Many of the *ricordi* have a direct bearing on the political situation of the day and on Guicciardini's attitude to it; others reflect his experience in peace and war as a high-ranking administrator. Thus, most of the earliest reflections refer, as we have seen, to the Florentine republican regime which fell in 1512. These are included in the collection of 1528, which Guicciardini compiled in the year after the republican restoration, but are nearly all omitted from the last collection of 1530 (C), which Guicciardini began at a time when he was an exile from the Florentine republic. The collection of 1528 (B) is headed by the following remark: "Written before 1525 in other notebooks, but copied in this one at the beginning of the year 1528, during the great leisure I then had, together with most of those [*ricordi*] that follow in this notebook." There has been some scholarly discussion about the meaning of the first words in this sentence; and it may well be that they partly refer to an intermediate collection, made between 1512 and 1525, of which the manuscript is lost.[20] At the same time, there can be no doubt that two of the notebooks mentioned by Guicciardini are identical with the two earliest extant collections of *ricordi* of 1512 (Q[1] and Q[2]): of the first twenty-three *ricordi* of B, all but one are, with greater or lesser modifications, taken over from the earliest collections, which contained thirteen and twenty-nine *ricordi* respectively. This combination of an earlier and a later stratum in the 1528 collection is reflected in a change of subject matter which takes place after the first twenty-three *ricordi:* there is a marked shift from civic problems related to the Florentine republic, to questions concerning diplomacy (B 24), the conduct of war (B 28), and the administration of the Papal State (B 29)— in other words, to questions that would have a direct bearing on Guicciardini's experience, first as ambassador in Spain, and then as Papal administrator. Similarly, the final collection, which Guicciardini began to compile in May 1530, opens with a long new *ricordo* on the siege of Florence by the Imperialists, which at that time had lasted seven months (C 1). In this reflection, Guicciardini considers the impact of faith on the resistance put up by the Florentines, which had prolonged the struggles beyond all rational expectation; and several of the newly added *ricordi* in that collection deal with the intervention of imponderable factors in the course of events, which often renders rational prediction futile,[21] or specifically discuss the effectiveness of religious belief in political and military affairs.[22] Although meditations along similar lines can

also occasionally be found earlier,[23] the dramatic events which Guicciardini was witnessing during the months of Florence's heroic resistance provided him with fresh evidence for the fallibility of reason in foretelling the vagaries of individual and collective action.

But if new experiences could confirm as well as refute previously held opinions, they could also modify them in details or bring about qualifications or changes in emphasis. Such changes could affect the form as well as the content of single *ricordi;* and changes in form were for Guicciardini a matter of intellectual clarity and penetration rather than of stylistic elegance. A comparison of the different versions of single *ricordi* shows his efforts to achieve conciseness and lucidity of expression. In the process some *ricordi* might be ruthlessly omitted, new ones added, or several *ricordi* fused into one. It is not always easy to determine whether, in a given case, changes are caused by this striving after concise and lucid formulation or by Guicciardini's having modified his views on the subject. Thus C 41 combines into one, four or five earlier *ricordi* on the necessity of harsh and cruel measures, *severità,* in government. Was this because his view on this question had mellowed, as the editor of the ***Ricordi*** suggests,[24] or simply because Guicciardini wished to avoid repetition? At the same time, clarity and brevity of statement did not necessarily imply for him finality of judgment. The tentative, almost groping character of many of the *ricordi* seems to reveal a search after truths that might elude precise and rigid formulations. The same reluctance to commit himself definitively may also help to explain apparent inconsistencies, such as his wavering between an optimistic belief in the fundamental goodness of human nature, and a pessimistic conviction that, in reality, most men are wicked (C 134, 201). The *ricordo* stating that "there are more bad men than good" (C 201) is added to the collection of 1530, doubtless under the influence of Guicciardini's recent personal experiences; yet while this may reveal a significant shift in his view on this matter, equally significant is his retention of the optimistic belief in human goodness (C 134), a belief that already appears in the first collection of 1512 (Q[1-2] 4) and, in almost identical terms, in the ***Discourse of Logrogno,***[25] that is voiced again in the ***Dialogue on Florentine Government,***[26] and is included in the collection of 1528 (B 3), where it is further stressed by the addition of a new *ricordo,* equally taken over in 1530, to the effect that of a man who prefers evil to goodness "you may surely say that he is a beast, not a man" (B 4, C 135).

There is perhaps no better example of Guicciardini's reluctance to commit himself than his discussion of the question of the validity of general rules of conduct— and hence, ultimately, of the *ricordi* themselves. "Read these *ricordi* often, and ponder them well," warns the ninth *ricordo* of the final collection. "For it is easier to know and understand them than to put them into practice." Guicciardini adds to the corresponding reflection of the collection of 1528 the explanation that this difficulty in carrying out rules of conduct is due to man's failure to let knowledge guide his actions—"for very often, men will not act on their knowledge" (B 100). From the beginning, Guicciardini had voiced his doubts about the existence of generally valid rules of action. Already in the second collection of 1512 he had said of rules *(regole)* that "they are written in books"; but "exceptional cases are written in your discretion" (Q² 12). This *ricordo* is included in an expanded form in the collection of 1528, together with a new one to the same effect (B 35, 121), which is then omitted in that of 1530. In the final version, Guicciardini insists even more strongly that discretion *(discrezione),* the pragmatic judgment of each case on its own merits, may, in the end, matter far more than theoretical rules; for "in nearly all [things], one must make distinctions and exceptions, because of the differences in their circumstances" (C 6). Similarly, he adds in 1530 to a *ricordo* of 1528 the observation that "you cannot always abide by a fixed rule of conduct" (C 186), and emphasizes even more strongly the superiority of discretion over theory: "In this, as in all other matters, you must be able to distinguish the character of the person, of the case, of the occasion; and for that, discretion is necessary. If discretion is not given by nature, it can rarely be learned from experience. It can never be learned from books." Rules, experience, discretion—these are, for Guicciardini, three possible guides of action; and while experience proves time and again superior to theory, often natural "tact" only will suffice. Guicciardini evidently does not see any inherent contradiction between such casuistic pragmatism and the claim that his maxims contained useful guidance. The limited applicability of general rules, owing to the innumerable exceptions to which in practice they are subject, does not deprive them altogether of their validity, just as the power of fortune does not entirely prevent reason and free will from influencing man's destinies.

Accordingly, Guicciardini sees the question of the usefulness of general rules of conduct as part of the wider problem of the place of reason in the sphere of human action. One of the principal themes of the *Ricordi,* this wider question plays a key role in Guicciardini's, as in Machiavelli's, thought. In spite of Guicciardini's deepening scepticism on this subject, he again appears reluctant to commit himself definitively. Thus in C 137—a new *ricordo* added in 1530—he voices much the same confidence in the superiority, in politics, of reason over ignorance, which had been an underlying theme of his *Dialogue on Florentine Government.* Yet in the preceding *ricordo,* equally added in 1530 and referring to the siege of Florence in that year, he points out that "it sometimes happens that fools do greater things than wise men" (C 136). This, he says, is due to the fact that the wise men take little account of fortune, whose effects can sometimes be

"incredible"; and he inserts, after these two new *ricordi,* an earlier one from the collection of 1528 that adds a determinist note: "Neither fools nor wise men can ultimately resist what must be" (C 138, B 80). Fundamentally a rationalist, Guicciardini is increasingly convinced of the limitations of reason in the conduct of human affairs, without, however, abandoning his aristocratic belief in the superiority of knowledge over ignorance. Indeed, his very scepticism regarding the effectiveness of reason is largely based on a rational analysis of past and present events. In the great debate on the respective role of *fortuna* and *virtù,* of fortune and individual initiative, which so strikingly reflects the intellectual and political crisis of early sixteenth-century Italy, Guicciardini consequently adopts a less optmistic approach than his friend Machiavelli, although it must be added that also Machiavelli's attitude to this problem was, in the long run, more tentative and liable to change than might appear from the reading of *The Prince.* But for Guicciardini, who sometimes tends to oversimplify Machiavelli's views in order to make his own position clearer, Machiavelli stands for the belief in the effectiveness of reason and hence in the possibility of an exact political science; and he comments scathingly that "in affairs of state, you should guide yourself not so much by what reason demonstrates a prince ought to do, as by what he will most likely do, according to his nature or habits. Princes will often do what they please or what they know, and not what they should" (C 128). This observation, if accepted, would demolish the very foundations of *The Prince* as a guide to political action; just as, on a different plane, Guicciardini's scepticism about the relevance for contemporary politics of examples from Roman antiquity strikes at another basic assumption of Machiavelli's political theory.[27]

For Guicciardini, as for Machiavelli, the problem of *fortuna* and *virtù* applied both to the interpretation of historical events and to the conduct of personal affairs. If in his historical writings Guicciardini might observe the working of fortune in history, in the **Ricordi** he concentrates on its place in human affairs in general. In so far as fortune's power limited the predictability of events, it severely handicapped any attempt to lay down valid rules of conduct. "If you consider the matter carefully, you cannot deny that Fortune has great power over human affairs. We see these affairs constantly being affected by fortuitous circumstances that men could neither foresee nor avoid," he says in *ricordo* 30. Guicciardini's scathing criticism of astrological claims to predict events contrasts with the deep-rooted Renaissance belief in that "science" (C 57, 207): "How wisely the philosopher spoke," he observes in *ricordo* 58, "when he said: 'Of future contingencies there can be no determined truth'"; and he sums up his view on this matter in *ricordo* 23: "The future is so deceptive and subject to so many accidents that very often even the wisest of men is fooled when he tries to predict it."

Accordingly, it is prudent, "although a future event may seem inevitable, never [to] depend upon it completely" (C 81); just as it is futile *(fallacissimo)* to hope to learn—as Machiavelli had been trying to do—from the past for the future: for "every tiny, particular circumstance that changes is apt to alter a conclusion" (C 114). What matters, in the end, is once more discretion *(discrezione)*—the discerning judgment of each event on its own merits.

With such reservations and uncertainties, which in their turn form an essential part of his rational philosophy based on experience, Guicciardini presents in the *Ricordi* the elements of a theory of conduct. The central topic of this work is the preservation and aggrandizement of the individual and his family in a society dominated by conflicting bids for power and wealth. Guicciardini's exclusive concern is with man as a political animal who would renounce power only if forced to do so (C 17), but the scope of whose actions is constantly determined by his relations with his fellow men. Hence the importance of a proper understanding of the political and social conditions in which man has to act; and accordingly, Guicciardini's comments on contemporary society and politics have time and again direct relevance for the problems of individual behavior. For Guicciardini, the social and political background was that of early sixteenth-century Italy, in which the survival of much of the varied pattern of earlier Renaissance politics went hand in hand with the decline of long-established institutions and with sudden military and political changes. There can have been few Italians of his generation who possessed so wide a knowledge of that society as Giucciardini, who was equally at home at princely courts and republics, and who was intimately familiar with the intricacies of contemporary diplomacy, with the ups and downs of politics and wars, and with the rise and fall of governments. His reflections reveal him as an unbiased and detached observer—a quality that is particularly striking in his *ricordi* on the Church and the Papacy. This high-ranking Papal administrator could still include, in his collection of 1528, a *ricordo* dating back to 1512 in which he expressed his hope that he might see, before he died, "the world delivered from the tyranny of these wicked priests" (B 14, Q² 17); and although he omits it from his final collection of 1530, he expands it in branding "the avarice and the sensuality of the clergy" in another *ricordo* of 1528 (C 28, B 124).

His condemnation of the Church remains unaffected by his refusal to draw personal consequences from it: "the positions I have held under several popes have forced me, for my own good, to further their interests. Were it not for that, I should have loved Martin Luther more than myself" (C 28). For if Guicciardini considers knowledge of the contemporary world necessary for rational individual behavior, he also considers it a postulate of enlightened self-interest which demands

the acceptance of that world as it is. Guicciardini's attitude on this matter comes close to that of Machiavelli, to the extent of sometimes adopting the conditional device with which Machiavelli introduces some of the chapters of *The Prince:* if men were good, this counsel would be wrong; but since most of them are wicked, you have to act toward them as they would act towards you.[28] But not only is Guicciardini far more moderate in the conclusions he draws from such premises, as when he admits the necessity of harsh measures because most men are "either not very good or not very wise," while at the same time expressing his preference for a middle path between *severità* and *dolcezza* (C 41). He is also concerned with giving advice to the subject or citizen rather than to the despotic ruler—that is to men like himself who, although they might be placed in positions of great responsibility and power, would also have to know how to be subject to the rule of others.

We have seen that, in the collection of 1530, nearly all the early maxims on republican politics are omitted. Their place is taken by reflections on the behavior of subjects and princes and their mutual relations. While this shift reflects the vicissitudes of Guicciardini's career, as well as his final estrangement from the republican cause, it also doubtless reveals his growing conviction that the future belonged, in Florence as in most of Italy, to monarchy; and his attitude towards change, like that toward society, shows a pragmatic acceptance of it, whatever his views on its desirability. He advises resolutely against taking an active part in trying to bring about a change of government, "unless he do it out of necessity, or because he hopes to be head of the new government" (C 51); and he condemns participating in conspiracies, not because they are objectively wrong, but because they endanger the lives of the conspirators (C 19, 20). Yet he can speak with evident distaste of tyranny (a term which Machiavelli studiously avoids in *The Prince*) and with admiration of the valor of republican Florence in resisting her enemies.

The man for whom Guicciardini writes his rules of conduct is no longer, like his Florentine forbears, protected by long-established institutions and traditions, as a member of a tightly-knit community; born into a world of conflict and change, of dissolving traditions and fresh opportunities, he has to meet its challenges with a new sense of self-reliance. In order to defend and assert himself against the selfishness of his fellowmen, Guicciardini wants him to act as if he were surrounded by enemies. Although he might prefer to trust them, he must meet them with suspicion, for "men are so false, so insidious, so deceitful and cunning" (C 157); although he would like to be frank and honest toward them, he must simulate and hide his intentions (C 104);[29] although lying is morally reprehensible, he has to practice it (C 37). He must exaggerate his own power (C 86) and cover up his weaknesses (C 196), and above all he must be secretive (C 49); although it is desirable enough to "discuss things with pleasant, loving familiarity," it is prudent not to speak of one's own affairs, "except when necessary" (C 184). His is a harsh world in which revenge on one's enemies is sweet, and may be necessary (C 72, 74), and in which true security consists in a situation in which your enemies, although they wish to do so, are unable to harm you (C 27).

Guicciardini takes it for granted that political power is desirable (C 16);[30] and while deploring indiscriminate egotism, he makes success in this world depend upon enlightened self-interest (C 218).[31] The trouble is that men do not always appreciate where their true interest lies: "to think it always resides in some pecuniary advantage rather than in honor, in knowing how to keep a reputation, and a good name." Indeed, it is desire for honor and glory that both ennobles and sanctions political ambition: the craving after power for its own sake is "pernicious and detestable" (C 32). Such craving, he adds in the final version of 1530, is common among princes. He thus draws, in the light of long years of experience of princely courts and politics, a distinction between the ordinary man and the ruler that retains some of the civic sentiment of the earliest version of this *ricordo* (Q[1-2] 2).[32] But also his notion of honor, *onore,* is not devoid of civic Florentine overtones: in Florentine administrative terminology, *onori* were the highest posts in the city's government, which did not carry salary, in contrast to the salaried offices of the territorial administration, the *utile*. Thus Guicciardini's declaration, in a *ricordo* of 1528 and 1530 (C 15) that he had always desired "*onore e utile, like all men,*" retains, despite its universal applicability, some of the subtle Florentine distinction between the different motives for seeking positions in the state: social ambition and public-spiritedness, and desire for economic gain.

Reputation *(reputazione)* is one of the basic concepts of the *Ricordi;* time and again, Guicciardini reverts to the desirability of acquiring and preserving it, and to the difficulties in achieving this. "Do not strive harder to gain favor than to keep your good reputation," he says in a new *ricordo* of 1530; for "when you lose your good reputation, you also lose good will, which is replaced by contempt" (C 42). A good name is more important than great wealth (C 158); like Machiavelli, he considers keeping up appearances essential for preserving one's reputation and furthering one's interests: "one of the greatest pieces of good fortune a man can have," he says in a passage that could have been written by the author of *The Prince,* "is the chance to make something he has done in his own interest appear to have been done for the common good" (C 142). But unlike Machiavelli, Guicciardini is thinking of the ordinary member of the sophisticated and self-seeking Renaissance society rather than of the prince; and unlike him he points out, in a *ricordo* retained in all collections, that in the long run only those good appearances which are based on fact will last (C 44).[33] At the same time, he admits in a late *ricordo* that contrary to what he had thought in his youth, such superficial accomplishments as "knowing how to play, dance, and sing, and such trivialities" may help create a good impression, especially at the courts of princes, "for the world and the princes are no longer made as they should be, but as they are" (C 179). Guicciardini, who disliked frivolity[34] and cherished a patrician sobriety, clearly found the sixteenth-century courtier uncongenial; yet he accepts him as part of a new age.

As so many of his *ricordi,* his reflections on reputation and honor are intensely personal; in them Guicciardini, having been compelled to withdraw from public affairs after the collapse of his career in Papal service, looks back on the motives and aims of his past life; and the charges of fraud that formed the legal pretext for his trial and condemnation by a Florenntine court in March 1530 lend to some of the last *ricordi* an additional sense of apologia which echoes the two discourses he wrote in his self-defense in 1527.[35] In this, as in other respects, the final collection of the *ricordi* appears, in retrospect, almost like a political testament: although Guicciardini doubtless hoped that the period of enforced leisure would be no more than an episode in his public career, it actually proved a turning point in his life. After a term as Papal governor of Bologna between 1531 and 1534, a post he lost on the death of Clement VII, he retired more and more to private life and devoted his last years to his greatest historical work, the **History of Italy**. Written down over a period of eighteen years, the **Ricordi** not only express Guicciardini's views on a large number of questions, but also contain the materials for a self-portrait. Some of his self-analysis reminds one of Montaigne: "I have been of a very easy-going nature" (C 132); "I have always been resolute and firm in my actions" (C 156); "like all men, I have pursued honor and profit" (C 15). He scorns frivolity and vanity (C 200), despises ignorance (C 168), and ridicules self-deception (C 122). Ideally he would wish to be able to "do or carry out things perfectly, that is, to have them free of the slightest defect or disorder" (C 126); but he realizes how difficult it is to achieve this. In spite of his doubts concerning the effectiveness of reason in the conduct of human affairs, he has learnt to control his actions by thought (C 83). While he recognizes, like Machiavelli, the power in political life of religious faith, his attitude towards ecclesiastical ritual borders on agnosticism (C 124);[36] what really matters, he says in a late *ricordo,* are not fasts and prayers but Christian charity, "to harm no one, and to help everyone as much as you can" (C 159). At heart a moderate, he admires courage but despises injudicious bravery (C 70, 95), and would like to temper severity with kindness, vengeance with clemency.[37] In the last *ricordo* of the collection of 1528, which he omitted from that of 1530, he accepts and expands Petrarch's verdict on the Florentines: "They are by nature lively and acute rather than grave and mature" (B 181)—qualities that he may well have claimed as his own and that were in fact shared by the Florentine patriciate to which he belonged by birth. For however much his public career had endowed him with an Italian rather than a Florentine perspective, he remained deeply attached to his native city, as well as to the aristocratic attitudes of his class. Adverse to revolutions and prepared to accept existing regimes whatever their nature, he never quite abandoned his belief in reforms from within; thus he says in a *ricordo* of 1528 and 1530: "Whenever a country falls into the hands of a tyrant, I think it the duty of good citizens to try and cooperate with him, and to use their influence to do good and avoid evil" (C 220). Loyalty, to his city or to his masters, clearly mattered a great deal to him;[38] but so did honor, and few *ricordi* have so immediate a ring of personal commitment as the one in which he speaks of his lifelong desire for it: "A man who esteems honor highly will succeed in everything, since he takes no account of toil, danger, or money. I have experienced it myself, and therefore I can say it and write it: the actions of men who do not have this burning stimulus are dead and vain" (C 118).

Notes

[1] "Ricordanze," in Francesco Guicciardini, *Scritti autobiografici e rari,* ed. R. Palmarocchi (Bari, 1936), p. 69.

[2] Francesco Guicciardini, *Dialogo e discorsi del reggimento di Firenze,* ed. R. Palmarocchi (Bari, 1932), p. 218, n. 1 (the discourse on pp. 218-59). Shortly afterwards, he wrote a second discourse (ibid., pp. 260-66), this time on the reforms to be adopted by the Medici.

[3] Raffaele Spongano, *Ricordi, edizione critica* (Firenze, 1951), p. xvi, n. 1.

[4] See C 39: *"nostro padre"* instead of *"mio padre"* in the corresponding *ricordo* B 66.

[5] Ed. A. Schiaffini (Florence, 1945).

[6] Ed. A. Perosa (London, 1960).

[7] *Scritti autobiografici,* pp. 53-54.

[8] *Dialogo e discorsi,* p. 265.

[9] Ibid., p. 271.

[10] Ibid., p. 281.

[11] Ibid., 3-6, 295-301.

[12] Ibid., p. 118.

[13] Ibid., pp. 13 ff.

[14] See V. de Caprariis, *Francesco Guicciardini. Dalla politica alla storia* (Bari, 1950), pp. 80 ff.

[15] "Consolatoria" (Sept. 1527), in *Scritti autobiografici,* pp. 179, 180.

[16] *Opere inedite,* ed. G. Canestrini (Florence, 1857-67), II, 373. Cf. F. Gilbert, "Alcuni discorsi di uomini politici fiorentini . . . ," in *Archivio Storico Italiano,* XCIII, 2 (1935), 3-24.

[17] Letter of April 16, 1527, to Francesco Vettori, in Machiavelli, *Lettere,* ed. F. Gaeta (Milan, 1961), p. 505.

[18] R. Ridolfi, *Vita di Francesco Guicciardini* (Rome, 1960), p. 214.

[19] To give three examples, which could be easily multiplied: C 134, on the basic goodness of man, which goes back to the earliest collection of 1512, appears also in the *Discourse of Logrogno* of that year and again in the *Dialogue on Florentine Government* (*Dialogo e discorsi,* pp. 225, 55); C 97 ("che e pochi e non e molti danno communemente el moto alle cose"), which is also contained in B 30, corresponds to a view stated twice in that *Discourse* (pp. 238, 242); the statement, in C 48, that "tutti [gli stati] . . . sono violenti" by origin, already in B 95, can also be found in the same *Discourse* and in the *Dialogue* (pp. 222, 163).

[20] This is the thesis of the editor of the *Ricordi,* R. Spongano; see his preface, pp. xvi ff. The biographer of Guicciardini, Roberto Ridolfi, did not consider it to be definitively proven; see his *Vita,* pp. 485-6.

[21] See C 81, 116, 117, 136, 166, 180.

[22] See C 124.

[23] See B 28, 127.

[24] P. x. I am not certain that he is right in believing that B 12 had been used for this *ricordo.*

[25] Op. cit., p. 225.

[26] Op. cit., p. 55.

[27] See C 110. Cf. also the *Dialogue on the Government of Florence,* op. cit., p. 68, and the *Considerazioni intorno ai Discorsi di Machiavelli sopra la prima Deca di Tito Livio,* in *Scritti politici e Ricordi,* ed. R. Palmarocchi (Bari, 1933), p. 11.

[28] See, e.g., *The Prince,* ch. 16, 18; cf. C 5, 41, 48, 157.

[29] See also C 37 and 133.

[30] See also C 17.

[31] Added in 1530.

[32] At the same time, the final version omits the reference to the public good from that of 1512.

[33] Cf. Q^{1-2} 3, B 2.

[34] See also C 167, 200.

[35] "Consolatoria" and "Defensoria," in *Scritti autobiografici,* pp. 165-90, 249-81; C 204 clearly refers to the charges of fraudulent practices.

[36] See also C 92.

[37] See above, pp. 141.

[38] See above, pp. 98.

Mario Domandi (essay date 1965)

SOURCE: Translator's Preface to *Maxims and Reflections of a Renaissance Statesman (Ricordi),* by Francesco Guicciardini, translated by Mario Domandi, Harper Torchbooks, 1965, pp. 33-38.

[*In the following essay, Domandi asserts that Guicciardini's* Maxims, *like the writings of his colleague Machiavelli, should be commended for separating politics from ethics.*]

If Guicciardini's **Ricordi** has been as well known as Machiavelli's *Prince,* they would surely have competed for the reputation of being the most immoral piece of political prose of the early Cinquecento. The great critic Francesco DeSanctis, whose liberal-nationalism generally predisposed him to see the excellence of neglected or little known Italians, called Guicciardini's book of political maxims "the corruption of Italy, codified and exalted to a rule of life."[1] It is easy enough to understand why these cynical, wordly-wise *ricordi,* with their constant and clear appeal to self-interest, might have given offense. But to take Guicciardini to task for divorcing political action from ethics is to miss the point of his particular contribution to the history of political thought. For it was precisely the virtue of his works, and those of his friend Machiavelli, that they finally and completely removed politics from its moorings in ethics and philosophy.

In Guicciardini's world of thought, political and social action is not to be determined by super-temporal eth-ical, theological, or religious principles; rather, it should be based on self-interest (*el particulare),* and on reason. To be sure, both require taking cognizance of the demands of honor; but not any longer the chivalric sort of honor. Guicciardini understands honor in the Florentine sense of a duty performed without pay, for which one receives recognition and homage. Honor, in other words, is not an abstraction against which life is molded and measured, but a pragmatic notion, a force like all others, of great—perhaps even primary—importance, but not qualitatively different from the others. And among these others, Guicciardini exalts experience and native ability as necessary prerequisites of proper political action. When these qualities are found properly combined in an individual, they produce discretion, that wonderful virtue which enables a man to see the way things are, and to act accordingly.

Guicciardini speaks so often and so emphatically of the need for experience, that we might be tempted to see in him the seeds of empiricism. But a careful reading of these *ricordi* will show that for him the opposition of reason and experience, of which later generations made so much, simply did not exist. When he tells us (C 12) that the similarity of proverbs in all countries is due to the fact that people everywhere have the same, or similar, experiences, he is simply establishing the *homogeneity* of experience, which makes it possible to deal with matters consistently, rationally, and universally. For him, experience and reason are simply the two sides of the same coin. He says explicitly (C 10) that native intelligence, no matter how great, can get nowhere without the help of experience. On the other hand, learning imposed on weak minds not only does not better them but tends to hurt them (C 47). In *ricordo* B 160 he tells us it is right to act according to rational principles even if things turn out wrong, and warns us not to be proud of success if it came about by chance. And then, in B 70, he again tells us that experience teaches a great deal, and more to large minds than to small. In short, not only is there no polarity—not to speak of hostility—between reason and experience, but they are in fact inseparable, the indispensable prerequisites for knowledge and discretion.

Guicciardini constantly reminds us that Fortune, that irrational and whimsical character, can never be left out of consideration. We can almost see him sighing as he writes: "Although cleverness and care may accomplish many things, they are nevertheless not enough. Man also needs good Fortune." (C 30) The value of all those lessons learned from reason and experience would seem to be rendered nugatory by the power of blind Fortune over human affairs. But here, too, the inconsistency is only apparent. Knowledge and discretion may not be sufficient to assure success in human affairs, but they are certainly necessary. Like Machiavelli, though less directly, Guicciardini uses mind to restrict the force and the effectiveness of Fortune's blows. "Remember this," he warns, "whoever lives a life of chance will in the end find himself a victim of chance. The right way is to think, to examine, and to consider every detail carefully, even the most minute. Even if you do, it takes great pains to make things come out right. Imagine how things must go for those who drift." (C 187) Clearly, the lesson that Guicciardini wanted his descendants to learn from his *ricordi* was that the forces governing life, especially political life, are knowable and, to a large degree, controllable; and that such knowledge and control require effort, talent, experience, mind—and Fortune.

. . . . .

Recent students of Guicciardini's **Ricordi** have been more concerned with the dispute concerning their textual tradition than with their intellectual content. The dispute arose only some thirty years ago, and has already produced a number of very learned, highly detailed studies on both sides. There certainly is no need to go into the minutiae of evidence each side has adduced. But the problem poses an interesting challenge to the scholar-detective, and merits being presented here at least in its general outlines.

Basing himself on the autograph manuscripts, Guiseppe Canestrini first published the **Ricordi** in 1857, under the title *Ricordi civili e politici.*[2] Canestrini presented the two series as one, numbered sequentially and with the second series first. The Guicciardini family archives contain two autograph manuscripts of the *ricordi,* subsequently called B and C, the first containing 181 *ricordi,* the latter 221; and two autograph notebooks *(quaderni),* subsequently called Q 1 and Q 2, containing twelve and twenty-nine *ricordi* respectively. All twelve in Q 1 are repeated in Q 2. There is no doubt that both notebooks were written at the time of Guicciardini's embassy to Spain, in 1512. At the head of the series we call B, in Guicciardini's own hand, there is a note telling us they were "written before 1525 in other notebooks, but copied in this one at the beginning of the year 1528, during the great leisure I then had, together with most of those that follow in this notebook." In *ricordo* B 138, Guicciardini mentions the date at which he is writing, which is February 3, 1523 (Florentine style, i.e., February 3, 1524, our style). And before *ricordo* B 172, he wrote: "Supplement begun in April, 1528." As for series C, it was definitely written in 1530, during and after the siege of Florence. It contains 221 *ricordi,* using 127 from B (combining some, re-casting them all), five from A (about which series more in a moment), and adding ninety-one new ones.

To recapitulate: Guicciardini wrote and re-wrote his *ricordi* several times, changing them, polishing them, and rejecting some versions altogether. If we consider the notebooks Q 1 and Q 2 together, there are three autograph manuscripts of the **Ricordi:** these notebooks of 1512, containing twenty-nine *ricordi;* the manuscript of 1528 (B), containing 181 *ricordi,* 171 of which were written before 1525, and ten added in April, 1528, presumably at the time when Guicciardini was transcribing the whole series from another manuscript which no longer exists; and a manuscript of 1530 (C) containing 221 *ricordi,* ninety-one of which were new, and the rest re-casts of earlier versions.

The dispute arose when Roberto Palmarocchi published his edition of the **Ricordi,**[3] giving the first and second series (B and C) in their chronological sequence, and numbered separately. At about the same time, Michele Barbi published an article[4] in which he tried to show that aside from Q 1 and Q 2, there were really three versions of the **Ricordi,** which he baptized A, B, and C. A, of course, was that manuscript from which Guicciardini copied B in 1528, but which is nowhere to be found. Barbi arrived at his conclusion by comparing the autograph manuscript B with various printed versions and manuscripts of the **Ricordi** dating from the latter half of the sixteenth century, conserved in various libraries throughout Italy. The origin of these copies seems clear. One of the manuscripts *Biblioteca Riccardiana* 3.2967) mentions that "Piero Guicciardini, son of Nicholò, gave a copy of these 'admonishments' *(avvertimenti)* to Don Flavio Orsini . . . much to the dismay of the Guicciardini."[5] That very probably happened in 1561. Fifteen years later, a printed edition of the **Ricordi** appeared in Paris, published by Corbinelli.[6] And in 1582, another appeared in Venice, published by Fra Sisto.[7] Many of the extant manuscripts, on the other hand, are hard to date; but they are of the latter half of the sixteenth century, some of the seventeenth, and one may be as early as 1562, just one year after Piero made a gift of the original. The entire dispute revolves around the question whether Piero's gift was simply a copy of B, or another manuscript from which Guicciardini copied B. Barbi, and Raffaele Spongano after him, fervently affirm the existence of A.[8] They point out that the motto and the first twenty-three *ricordi* of B are, with only one exception, re-writes of the twenty-nine *ricordi* in Q 2. And the *ricordi* from B 24 to B 171 correspond nearly completely to the first 147 of the *ricordi* in A (which contains in all 161). What could be more logical than to suppose that Guicciardini sat down in April, 1528 with Q 2 and A before him, and transcribed both into B making only a few changes, and adding ten new *ricordi?*

To Palmarocchi, the matter did not seem quite so logical at all. If things are as Barbi claims, he asks, why is it that B 172 (the first of the supplement begun after April, 1528) appears as A 155? Furthermore, he says, "If it is true that A 1 corresponds to B 24, it is also true that five [actually, six] of the first twenty-three *ricordi* in B are also to be found in A, though in a different order."[9] He finally points out that of the final eleven *ricordi* in A none except 155 is to be found in B, but that many re-appear in C. If B had been transcribed from Q 2 and A, it hardly seems likely that Guicciardini would have omitted the last eleven *ricordi* of A, only to pick some of them up two years later, when writing C.

In 1951, Raffaele Spongano published his critical edition of the **Ricordi,** which is a masterpiece of erudition. By comparing all the manuscripts, several of which he uncovered, by making the most detailed linguistic and editorial analysis of the various versions, he succeeds in showing that a manuscript A did indeed exist. His presentation, if not iron-clad, is most convincing. But since I proposed only to outline the problem and not to solve it, and since an even modest attempt to present Spongano's case would require going into the minute details I promised to avoid, I feel justified in stating only his conclusion, without the proofs. Suffice it to say, then, that on the basis of present evidence, it would seem that Guicciardini wrote four versions of his **Ricordi.**

Nevertheless, the text of A differs so little from B that it would hardly have been worth reproducing it here. I have translated C, B, and Q 2, and given them in that order, which is the reverse of the chronological. C is the most mature, the most thought-out version. It seemed to me that it should be read first so that the others might be measured against it. To facilitate comparisons, I have included a table of correspondences among the various versions. I have also added a few footnotes in the hope that they will illuminate the text.

I wish to thank my colleagues and friends Carlo Ascheri and Eduardo Saccone for their invaluable help in penetrating to the meaning of some of Guicciardini's hard, terse language. For all errors, I am, of course, solely responsible.

Notes

[1] Francesco DeSanctis, *Storia della letteratura italiana* (Napoli, 1873), II, p. 118.

[2] Francesco Guicciardini, *Opere inedite,* ed. Guiseppe Canestrini (Firenze, 1857-67, 10 vols.), II, pp. 81-224.

[3] Guicciardini, *Ricordi,* in: *Scritti politici e Ricordi,* ed. Roberto Palmarocchi (Bari, 1933).

[4] Michele Barbi, "Per una compiuta edizione dei Ricordi civili e politici del Guicciardini," in: *Studi di filologia italiana,* III, pp. 163-196.

[5] Raffaele Spongano, *Ricordi, edizione critica* (Firenze, 1951), p. XXI, n. 1.

[6] Under the title *Più consigli et avvertimenti di M. Fr. Guicciardini Gentilhuomo fior. in materia di re publica et di privata* (Paris, 1576).

[7] Under the title *Considerazioni civili sopra l'Historie di M. Francesco Guicciardini e d'altri historici. Trattate per modo di discorso da M. Remigio Fiorentino* (Venezia, 1582).

[8] So, too, does the excellent critic Mario Fubini, in "Le quattro redazioni dei *Ricordi* del Guicciardini," in: *Studi sulla letteratura del Rinascimento* (Firenze, 1948), pp. 138-207.

[9] Palmarocchi, *Scritti politici e Ricordi,* p. 372.

Sidney Alexander (essay date 1969)

SOURCE: Introduction to *The History of Italy,* by Francesco Guicciardini, translated and edited by Sidney Alexander, Princeton University Press, 1969, pps. xxv, 59-60, 127-28.

[*In the following excerpt, Alexander compares Guicciardini's writing style to that of several twentieth-century writers, asserting that Guicciardini's style is modern because it focuses on the individual in history.*]

"If we consider intellectual power [the **Storia d'Italia**] is the most important work that has issued from an Italian mind." The judgment is that of Francesco de Sanctis, surely himself one of the foremost Italian minds. But like a great many classics, Guicciardini's **History of Italy** (published for the first time in 1561, twenty-one years after the author's death) is more honored in the breach than in the observance. Which is a pity, for if not every word need be read, surely a great many of them should be read, not only for the light they cast on a dark time in Italian (and European) history but for the light they cast on the processes of history. For most readers (I do not speak of professional historians) the chief interest here resides not in the details of treaties long since crumbled into dust, or the shed blood of dynasties, but rather in the perennial mystery of human behavior.

Francesco Guicciardini might be called a psychological historian—for him the motive power of the huge clockwork of events may be traced down to the mainspring of individual behavior. Not any individual, be it noted, but those in positions of command: emperors, princes, and popes who may be counted on to act always in terms of their self-interest—the famous Guicciardinian *particolare.*

Guicciardini's style is Jamesian, Proustian—that is to say, his basic meanings reside in his qualifications. His mind portrays itself in its *sfumatura:* the conditions, the exceptions, the modifications, the qualifications with which the author weighs every human act and motivation. He had not read, of course, but he was a fellow Florentine of Leonardo da Vinci who wrote (in mirror-writing in his arcane notebooks) that slashing attack on the *abbreviatori*—those impatient abbreviators of anatomy who do not realize that "impatience, mother of folly, praises brevity," and that "certainty is born of the integral cognition of all the parts. . . ."

So Leonardo over his cadavers and messer Francesco over the bleeding body of Italy—there is indeed a similarity in the stance of both men: a distrust of systems, a scorn for theory, a reliance upon experience, a surgical dispassion, a moon over a battlefield. So with lunar indifference the vegetarian da Vinci designs war chariots for the Sforza and serves Cesare Borgia, the enemy of his country. And so Francesco Guicciardini, who favors a republic, is for many years the faithful servant of Medici tyrants. The scientific temperament can lead to schizophrenia: makers of atomic bombs can work for one side or the other. There is the public mask and the private face; what decides is self-interest:

> I know no man who dislikes more than I do the ambition, the avarice, and the lasciviousness of the priesthood: not only because each of these vices is odious in itself, but also because each of them separately, and all of them together, are quite unsuitable in men who make profession of a life dedicated to God. . . . And yet the position I have served under several popes has obliged me to desire their greatness for my own self-interest; and were it not for this, I would have loved Martin Luther as myself. . . . [1]

Truth resides therefore in the specific instance, in the *particolare,* in the clash of egotisms as these work themselves out in great events. And yet, his cold surgical eye fixed on this cause, cautious Francesco Guicciardini does not conclude that he has isolated *the* cause. No historian was ever less monomaniacal. Even though he would seem to have tracked the motive power down to its source in individual behavior—more especially individual ambition—ultimately all is mystery, for all rests in the hands of Fortuna. And the lady has aged; she is more implacable than the goddess of Fortune whom Machiavelli felt could still be taken by assault, the lady who yielded at least 50 percent of the time to man's intervention. Guicciardini's Fortuna is more impersonal, distant; no one can ever predict how she will act, whether favorably or unfavorably; the world has become very bleak indeed. Man acts, always in terms of self-interest; he attempts, if he is wise, to weigh all possibilities with reason and a clinical knowledge of human behavior; he will preserve his dignity, his honor (the sole quality which the fickle goddess cannot sully); but what ultimately ensues is beyond all calculation.

> If you had seen messer Francesco in the Romagna . . . with his house full of tapestries, silver, servants thronged from the entire province where—since everything was completely referred to him—no one, from the Pope down, recognized anyone as his superior; surrounded by a guard of more than a hundred landsknechts, with halberdiers and other cavalry in attendance . . . never riding out with less than one hundred or one hundred and fifty horse; immersed in governing bodies, titles, "Most illustrious lords," you would not have recognized him as your fellow citizen . . . but considering the importance of his affairs, his boundless authority, the very great domain and government under him, his court and his pomp, he would have seemed on a par with any duke rather than lesser princes. . . .

Thus Francesco Guicciardini depicts himself, to the life, as he appeared and behaved at the time when he was governor of the central Italian province of the Romagna. Like his contemporary and fellow Florentine Niccolò Machiavelli—but on a much more exalted level—he had always been an active participant in the politics he wrote about; and all his writings, like Machiavelli's, are the fruits of enforced idleness. Guicciardini's **History,** his last and greatest work, was the compensation of a man of action removed against his desire from the scene. Like Niccolò after 1512, a brain-truster out of work, messer Francesco after 1537, no longer *persona grata* to the Medici back in power after the siege, retires to his villa in the green hills of Santa Margherita in Montici above his native Florence and commences for the third time to write a history of his epoch.

But now his vision has broadened. He is fifty-five years old; he has seen much, experienced much, been confidant and adviser to three popes; now the great spider must cast his web much wider than in his earlier attempts at writing the traditional humanistic history of his city-state. Now the youthful **Florentine History** must become the **History of Italy** (a title itself never applied by Guicciardini), and since Italy has become the cockpit where Hapsburg Charles V struggles with Valois Francis I, Holy Roman Emperor versus Most Christian King, Guicciardini's **Storia d'Italia** becomes perforce the history of Europe. Since Thucydides no vision had ranged so far. As in a Greek tragedy, after the prologue of Laurentian peace and prosperity, the fates begin to spin out the tragic succession of events from the French invasion of Charles VIII in 1494 to the death of Pope Clement VII in 1534, years dense with dramatic happenings and calamities which seem to confirm Guicciardini's disenchanted convictions.

On the surface he seems to be following the conventions of the chroniclers; patiently telling his story year by year; draping, like any good Renaissance humanist, his actors in togas; imitating—like Biondo, like Machiavelli—the classical historians, especially Livy and

Tacitus; inventing stage speeches uttered by his captains on the eve of every battle; intending to deal exclusively with what was considered the true business of the historian: politics and war.

Intending, I say, for the greatness of the *Storia* is where it deviates from its set models, as a novel is successful only when the characters talk back to their creator and go their own ways against the author's will. Imitation of the ancients is first supplemented and then superseded by meticulous documentation from municipal archives (many of which Guicciardini had simply taken home to his villa from the Palazzo dei Signori); the text is rewritten more than seven times and not for stylistic concerns alone.

And as Guicciardini examines his world, the tumultuous world of the end of the fifteenth and the first three decades of the sixteenth century, his history, almost against the author's will, begins to comprehend far more than mere dynastic politics and wars. The discovery of the new lands misnamed America; the invention of those terrifying weapons called cannon; the first appearance of syphilis; the threat of the Turks and the greater threat of Martin Luther whose Christ-centered theology reduces the Church as Copernicus' heliocentric astronomy had reduced the earth; the history and huckstering of the Swiss, most dreaded mercenary soldiery of Europe; battle pieces full of gallantry and butchery; the incredible corruption of the Borgia and the martyrdom of Savonarola; the origins of Church claims to secular power; a brilliant picture gallery of Renaissance popes; the sack of Rome; the siege of Florence; the amatory complications of Henry VIII—all this and more we find in a richly orchestrated narrative wherein are embedded many of the famous maxims or *Ricordi* which the historian had been secretly writing all his life for his own edification. But now, confined to instances rather than abstracted in the void, how much more resonant are these scathing pessimistic opportunistic observations!

He is the master of the fillip; in the solemn Ciceronian periods of his rhetoric, how his irony flickers: a dragon's tail. "So that as a result of reverence for their way of life, the holy precepts which our religion contains in itself, and the readiness with which mankind follows—either out of ambition (most of the time) or fear—the example of their prince, the name of Christian began to spread marvelously everywhere, and at the same time the poverty of the clerics began to diminish."

Vanity vanity, Guicciardini seems always to be saying; and yet his art offers the comfort of a true discovery, a light placed in focus, a scientific examination carried to its limits. His capacity to reveal the psychology of single personages by relating them to the logic of events is truly extraordinary. His profiles are constructed from within, just as are his plots, crimes, wars, treaties, grave

and dramatic moments in Italian history. The master builder always, he never loses command of his grand design.

But with all his fine discriminating political sense, his absence of dogmatism, his openness to the lessons of experience, his extraordinary sensitivity to the play of interests, there is something inhuman about the ice palace of this greatest of Italian historians. The irony is that Guicciardini, who abjures all system building, has fallen victim to a reductive fallacy that equally distorts the range and variety of human behavior. Although (unlike Machiavelli) he believes that man is essentially good, in practice he depicts him as almost invariably bad. Hence his psychological portraiture is all nuance and monochrome. Here are his comments on Piero de' Medici in exile asking advice of the Venetian senate:

> Nothing certainly is more necessary in arduous deliberations, and nothing on the other hand more dangerous, than to ask advice. Nor is there any question that advice is less necessary to wise men than to unwise; and yet wise men derive much more benefit from taking counsel. For, whose judgment is so perfect that he can always evaluate and know everything by himself and always be able to discern the better part of contradictory points of view? But how can he who is asking for counsel be certain that he will be counseled in good faith? For, whoever gives advice (unless he is bound by close fidelity or ties of affection to the one seeking advice) not only is moved largely by self-interest, but also by his own small advantages, and by every slight satisfaction, and often aims his counsel toward that end which turns more to his advantage or is more suitable for his purposes; and since these ends are usually unknown to the person seeking advice, he is not aware, unless he is wise, of the faithlessness of the counsel.

An almost mathematical exposition of ethical relations, an algebra of behavior. Who has ever put it so neatly? But isn't the very precision, almost predictability, of this world without ideals itself an intellectual construction, cleaving to experience and yet remote from it? Throughout the *Storia* such Guicciardinian structures glimmer, subtle spider webs of psychological analysis on the rich green field of sheer storytelling. . . .

None of Guicciardini's writings were issued during his lifetime. Only in 1561 were the first sixteen books of the *Storia* (out of twenty) published in Florence, and three years later the last four appeared separately in Venice. Many others followed this first edition, all of them, however, based not directly on the manuscripts but on the expurgated Torrentino text of 1561 which had appeared while the Council of Trent, the general staff of the Counter-Reformation, was in full session. Hence, in all these editions certain passages considered injurious to the Roman pontiffs were truncated, especially in Book Four, wherein Guicciardini traces the origin of Church claims to temporal power. Finally in a magnificent edition dated from Freiburg,[2] Guicciardini's **History** was published in its entirety according to the manuscript conserved in Florence, the final version which had been revised and corrected by the author himself, containing the mutilated passages. The **Ricordi** had various partial editions between 1576 and 1585; his other writings were extracted from the family archives and published in the second half of the nineteenth century.

Within the very sixteenth century that saw its first publication, the **History of Italy** was swiftly translated into French, Latin, Spanish, German, Flemish, as well as the first English "translation" by Geffray Fenton of which I will speak later. According to Roberto Ridolfi, whose brilliant biography and Guicciardini studies have done more than anything else to see the record straight, in the same Cinquecento Italian editions alone, both integral and partial, counted almost one hundred. Obviously poor messer Francesco is another of those not infrequent cases of posthumous literary success.

The English version by Sir Geffray Fenton, an Elizabethan literatus, first published in London in 1579, is most curious. Fenton knew no Italian and his "translation"—considered his major work and greatly successful in his time—was derived not from Guicciardini's original text but from the foreign language Fenton knew—namely French. Fenton based his work on the 1568 French version of Chomedey; what we have therefore is a translation of a translation! As Paolo Guicciardini has pointed out in his *Le Traduzioni Inglesi della Storia Guicciardiniana* (Olschki, Firenze, 1951) Fenton's dependence on the French version is proved by the fact that he maintained in his English text the spellings of proper names used by Chomedey instead of adopting, which would have been more logical, the Italian spellings. Thus we have Petillane for Pitigliano, Triuulce for Trivulzio, Francisquin Cibo for Franceschetto Cibo, Ceruetre for Cerveteri, etc.

Furthermore I have discovered that Fenton indulges throughout his text (which is remarkably faithful considering that it is second hand) in numerous excisions, paraphrases, omissions, ellipses, and revisions, frequently in the interest of courtly bows to the English ruling house. In any case, to render it available to the modern reader, Fenton's knotted Elizabethan English would require a translation, in which case we would have a translation of a translation of a translation!

The only other integral English version of the **History of Italy** is that by Austin Parke Goddard, published in ten volumes in London over the years 1753 to 1756. Goddard was expert in Italian, had studied and resided in Italy for many years at the invitation of Cosimo III,

the Grand Duke of Tuscany, who was a friend of his family. Furthermore, aside from his expertise in the language, Goddard's intentions were scrupulously to adhere to Guicciardini's phraseology rather than redo it "in a very elegant Style."

But unfortunately the road to paraphrase is paved with good intentions. Goddard extracts wholesome lessons from Guicciardini and then puts them into courtly periwigged English. What he has accomplished for the most part is a good, sometimes sparkling paraphrase of the **Storia d'Italia,** clothing it in the opulent Gibbonsonian style of eighteenth-century historical rhetoric. Much more serious are Goddard's frequent variations of meaning, reinterpretations, polite omissions, invented gallantries—a general transformation of Guicciardini's feeling-tone from solemn Latinate obliquity and acerbity to a very English mixture of manners and morals.

Hence we have the unusual situation that since Guicciardini's classic was first published more than four hundred years ago, the only two integral versions in English of his work are both disqualified as true translations—one because it was not based on the original Italian text, the other because it is a paraphrase.[3]

There is a theory and practice of translation in our day which, in an effort to avoid the archaicism and "no-language" of translatese, leaps to the other extreme and gives us Romans of antiquity who talk pure Hemingwayese.

But I should say that a true translation, while rendering available to the modern reader the speech of another time and culture, will also preserve the savor of that speech, the flavor of that time. A pinch of antiquity must be added. A good translation of a sixteenth-century text should be redolent of its period. It should bring us back there; we should not only understand it, we should be permeated by it in a kind of historical osmosis, research through the pores. To render Guicciardini in clear modern English available to the modern reader may be admirable pedagogy but it is not the art of translation.

I have called Guicciardini a Proustian historian—that is, a vision and a logic manifested in a certain kind of language. The stylistic challenge I set myself therefore was more than searching for English equivalents that would avoid archaicism on the one hand and clear modern English (which is archaicism in reverse) on the other. I have tried instead to re-create an English that would be faithful to the literal meanings of the text, and yet convey Guicciardinian involutions, his Ciceronian periods, his Proustian *longueurs*—an English that would convey in the twentieth century the flavor of a personalized Latinate Italian style of the sixteenth century.[4]

Enmeshed in this web, one found that one was searching the processes of Guicciardini's thought. Sometimes one had to cut the interminable sentences, balanced like some incredible trapeze act, clause upon (and within) clause, often a page high. Sometimes one had to clarify Guicciardini's casual way with antecedents and pronouns, substitute proper names for his strings of ambiguous he's and him's. (Those scholars who claim that Guicciardini never writes other than crystal-clear merely betray thereby their ignorance of the text.) Great monuments are not marred by scratches, even Homer nods (or makes us), and Guicciardini's marvelous rhetoric is not without its faults of overelaboration, density, impenetrable thickets.

The true translator must only clear up as much of this Sargasso Sea as is absolutely necessary to make for passage. But to clarify what was ambiguous in the original is not translation but explication. The job of the translator is not to make clear that which was not clear, but to render in another tongue (and sometimes another century) the same degree and kind of ambiguity wherever this occurs.

Guicciardini's chief literary fault is his prolixity—the inevitable outcome of his obsessive search for detail, his quest for truth by amassing all particulars—which gave rise to the legend of the Laconian (condemned because he had used three words where two would do) who was offered his freedom if he read entirely through Guicciardini's interminable account of the siege of Pisa, but who pleaded—after attempting a few pages—that he be sent instead to row in the galleys.

I hope the reader will be able to savor in these pages (from which most of the siege of Pisa has been cut) something of Guicciardini's extraordinary qualities as a historian. Scholars debate whether Francesco is more *res* than *verba,* but I should say that if there is a discrepancy between his hard skeletal thinking and the rhetorical artifices in which it is shrouded, this literature is very important. To transform it into simple modern English is to destroy those obliquities which are the very mark of the man: his intellectual clarity, his astuteness, his diplomatic visor glinting at all times.

The present version consists of more than half of the original enormous text and, in view of what I have indicated with regard to Fenton and Goddard, may justly claim to be the first extended English translation that is not a paraphrase or derived from a secondary source. Selections have been made from all twenty books, so organized as to present a running and coherent narrative from first to last, tied with bridge passages wherever necessary. In the light of Thoreau's "If you are acquainted with the principle, what do you care for a myriad instances and applications?" I have excised only repetitive episodes—thus a few battles serve as the models for Guicciardini's descriptions of many battles; a few examples suffice for his thirty or so invented set speeches.

Guicciardini's **History of Italy** has been pillaged for the past four hundred years as the chief source of Renaissance history and politics. Now the modern reader will be enabled for the first time in English to go to the source itself, and experience immersion in a world remote perhaps in time but discouragingly up-to-date so far as man's political behavior is concerned.

Notes

[1] The entire quotation from the *Ricordi,* second series, No. 28, reads:

> Io non so a chi dispiaccia più che a me la ambizione, la avarizia e le mollizie de' preti: sì perché ognuno di questi vizi in sé è odioso, sì perché ciascuno e tutti insieme si convengono poco a chi fa professione di vita dependente da Dio; ed ancora perché sono vizi sì contrari che non possono stare insieme se non in un subietto molto strano. Nondimeno el grado che ho avuto con più pontefici, m'ha necessitato a amare per el particulare mio la grandezza loro; e se non fussi questo rispetto, arei amato Martino Luther quanto me medesimo, non per liberarmi dalle legge indotte dalla religione cristiana nel modo che è interpretata ed intesa communemente, ma per vedere ridurre questa caterva di scelerati a' termini debiti, cioè a restare o sanza vizi o sanza autorità.

[2] This edition, dated 1774-76, was actually published in Florence; the fiction of its having been printed in "Friburgo" was obviously intended to deceive the censor. This is the first edition, after the *editio princeps,* to be based on the Codex Mediceo Palatino, and the first to restore almost all the passages Bartolomeo Concino, the Secretary of Duke Cosimo I, had expurgated in the original edition which Agnolo Guicciardini, the historian's nephew, had dedicated to the Duke (*see* Alessandro Gherardi, ed. *La Storia d'Italia,* Firenze, 1919, I, p. clxxviii).

[3] More serious is the fact that both Fenton and Goddard omit practically all of the famous forbidden passages—the sections in Book III concerning the incestuous loves of the House of Borgia; Book IV on the effect of the new discoveries of Columbus and the Portuguese on interpretations of Sacred Scripture; Book X on Cardinal Pompeo Colonna inciting the people of Rome to rebel against the papacy; as well as numerous Guicciardinian anticlerical ironies such as his remark that the Holy Ghost must have inspired the cardinals in the election of Adrian VI, etc.

Neither Fenton nor Goddard, of course, could make use of most of these omissions since they were restored only in the "Friburgo" edition which appeared *after* their works. Available to them in print were two suppressed sections of the *Storia* published in a Protestant pamphlet in Basel (Pietro Perna, 1569). The 1618 Fenton in my possession declares on the title page: "The third Edition, diligently revised, with restitution of a Digression towards the end of the fourth Booke, which had bene formerly effaced out of the Italian and Latine copies in all the late Editions." None of the other cuts, however, are restored. Goddard prints two of the scandalous passages from Books III and IV in an appendix but flatly declares them spurious (Paolo Guicciardini, *Le Traduzioni Inglesi della Storia Guicciardiniana,* pp. 12-15, 24, Olschki, Florence, 1951; and Vincent Luciani, *Francesco Guicciardini and His European Reputation,* pp. 35 ff., K. Otto, New York, 1936).

⁴ Luciani, *op. cit.,* p. 35: "A gifted translator would attempt to render in the foreign tongue the serious majestic level of the Italian." This follows an acute and detailed analysis of the various inadequacies—both scholarly and artistic—of Fenton and Goddard.

Mario Domandi (essay date 1970)

SOURCE: Introduction to *The History of Florence,* by Francesco Guicciardini, translated and edited by Mario Domandi, Harper & Row, 1970, pp. xiii-xxxvii.

[*In the following excerpt, Domandi examines the structure, style, and purpose of Guicciardini's* History of Florence *and notes that the work stresses the importance of rational thought. (Note: Only those footnotes are included which pertain to this particular excerpt.*]

After lying in the Guicciardini family archive for 350 years, the *History of Florence* was edited and published for the first time by Giuseppe Canestrini, as the third volume of his *Opere inedite di Francesco Guicciardini.*²² The original manuscript, bearing no title, is a continuous narrative, without division into books or chapters. The only attempts at subdivision of the material are evidenced by dates put in the margin of the text at the beginning of each year, starting in 1494 and ending in 1508. The manuscript ends abruptly in the middle of a sentence, while Guicciardini is describing the siege of Pisa. Judging from his tone throughout, it would seem that Pisa was close to but not yet at the point of surrender. Since the city fell on June 8, 1509, we may guess that Guicciardini finished writing shortly before that date. About two thirds of the way through the manuscript, he refers to the date February 23, 1509, as "today" (p. 201). An indication that he stopped writing shortly after that date is provided by the fact that the entire manuscript, which was probably copied from a draft or notes, seems to be written in the same handwriting—a very careful hand, showing some traces of haste only in the last few pages.²³

In the most enlightening piece yet written on the *History of Florence,* Nicolai Rubinstein investigated, among other things, the available evidence for dating the work, and concluded that it was probably begun in the spring of 1508, at the same time that Guicciardini started work on his *Family Memoirs* and his *Remembrances.*²⁴ That enables us to say that the *History of Florence* was probably written in about a year, between spring 1508 and spring 1509. It is possible to argue that he was working on it even later—any time up to January, 1512, when he left Florence to go as ambassador to Spain; but that would seem to be contradicted by the sameness of the handwriting. Furthermore, as Palmarocchi points out, if that much time had passed after the date he mentions as "today," it is legitimate to assume that he would have filled the many blanks he left for names and dates.²⁵

The only argument in favor of assuming that he wrote any part of it after the conquest of Pisa seems to be provided by the nature of the last few pages—those pages which Palmarocchi noticed were written in a more hurried hand. The quality of the narrative changes there. The minute details Guicciardini gives on Pisan affairs, and his precise knowledge of the exact role played by so minor a figure as Filippo di Puccierello, suggest that he may have received a first-hand report from someone close to the scene. Since his father-in-law Alamanno was commissary at Pisa and had been in touch with Filippo di Puccierello, we might hazard the guess that Guicciardini heard those details from Alamanno, whom he visited in Pisa very soon after its capitulation. But it is only a guess.

Some twenty years later, at a time of enforced leisure, Guicciardini started work on a second history of Florence, the *Florentine Affairs,* Though the work was intended to cover much the same ground as the first *History of Florence,* we find no mention of the juvenile work. Why he should have gone about writing a second *History,* ignoring the first and using very different sources, will probably always remain an open question. But to infer, as has been done, that he did it because he may have been conscious that the first was more a "political pamphlet" than a genuine work of history is not warranted by a close examination of the work before us.²⁶ Without doubt, he is very concerned in this *History of Florence* with the political and legal institutions of the city. He is looking for the reasons for the city's weakness and lethargy in his time, and he believes he has discovered them by tracing historically how one-man rule, beneficial though it was in the hands of a Lorenzo, led to the inheritance of power by succession, putting the state into the hands of a madman like Piero, who plunged the city into the abyss (p. 36). The tyranny of Piero de'Medici in turn gave rise to a popularly based republic, with all the attendant weaknesses and defects that Guicciardini so assiduously points out.

Under both forms of government, the aristocrats did not enjoy as much political power as their training, experience, and breeding would warrant. For that reason, they were very dissatisfied with the Great Council, the most jealously guarded of popular-republican institutions; and for that reason, such prominent leading citizens as Alamanno Salviati were willing to support Piero Soderini, another aristocrat, as gonfalonier for life. They knew it would be folly to try to attack the Great Council itself; instead, they preferred to set one of their number in a permanent position of power in the government, in the belief that he would bring about a renewal of aristocratic influence. Their hopes were dashed by Soderini's subsequent mistrust of them, and his reliance on men of lesser rank dependent upon him—among them, Niccolò Machiavelli. Guicciardini's enmity toward Soderini, the traitor to his class, is clear and undisguised. But he displays it by depicting Soderini's role in the many foreign and internal political crises that faced Florence at the time, and by showing how the counsel of the aristocrats was often right but went unheeded. Though he does it reluctantly and with many qualifications, he gives the gonfalonier his due: he tells us that Soderini reduced taxes, straightened out the city finances, and caused the Monte to pay more interest than usual (p. 248). In describing the dispute over the question whether to send the ambassadors to Emperor Maximilian, a matter to which Guicciardini devotes several pages, and in which his father and his father-in-law as ambassadors-elect were among the strongest opponents of the gonfalonier's views, he relates the miserable end of the emperor's great plans, admitting in effect (though not explicitly) that Soderini was right in not wanting to send them. And, as a final example, in the controversy with Lucca, the wise men were against an attack on Viareggio. But when the gonfalonier had it done despite them, he writes: "It became clear that the attack, though carried out against the wishes of the wisest citizens, was nevertheless a good idea; and this showed that to act very cautiously, to be afraid, and to try to foresee everything is at times as harmful as it is useful. . . ." (p. 287).

Professor Rubinstein's conclusion as to the simultaneous beginning of the *Family Memoirs* and the *History of Florence* constitutes another basis from which to evaluate the nature and intent of the two works. The *Memoirs,* biographical sketches of the Guicciardini family from the fourteenth century to 1493, make use of many of the same documents used in the *History,* which traces the city's political development from 1378 to 1509. But it is clear that although the two works cover much the same ground and use many of the same sources, the *Memoirs* were intended to be a record, perhaps even an exaltation of the Guicciardinis' political and personal achievements, meant for family use; whereas the *History* was almost surely meant to be seen by others, and perhaps even for publication. In the *Memoirs,* Guicciardini proudly portrays the impor-

tance of his ancestors to the Medici régime; but in the *History* he underplays that relationship, even while he stresses the contribution of his family to the city's government throughout the years. That would be understandable only if he meant the work to be seen in republican Florence, where the Medici were in bad odor, but not if he were writing for his family or for posterity. There are other unmistakable signs of attempts at historical objectivity. Francesco loved his father "more ardently than children generally love their fathers," and he usually portrays him in the best possible light. Still, in relating the struggle between the Panciatichi and the Cancellieri, he tells us that the Florentine supporters of the Panciatichi, among them his father, "moved slowly . . . stayed under cover, and in fact proceeded with caution" (p. 187). And later, when discussing the harsh measures taken by the Signoria against Filippo Strozzi in 1508, he says that the Priors, "especially Luigi Guicciardini . . . were censured for allowing themselves to be led by him [Soderini]" (p. 300). Though the singling out of his elder brother may in part be ascribed to sibling rivalry, Francesco probably felt it was dictated by the demands of historical objectivity.

Certainly the distribution of chronological emphasis in the *History of Florence* is very uneven. More than half the period the book means to cover, that is, from the Revolt of the Ciompi (1378) to the Peace of Lodi (1454), is treated in eight pages. The next fifteen years, to the death of Piero de'Medici in December, 1469, are afforded more extensive treatment in thirteen pages. From then on, starting with the rule of Lorenzo, the narrative is still more detailed; and after 1494, Guicciardini covers the story year by year. Indeed, he tells us explicitly that he intends to treat the period after 1454 "in more detail and tell what I know, since no one has written any history that covers the period extending from the Peace of Lodi to the present" (p. 8). And the closer he gets to his own time, the more detailed the narrative becomes.

These differences in chronological emphasis give rise to the question of Guicciardini's sources. Professor Rubinstein's study of the *Family Memoirs* and the *History of Florence* reveals that "although the young historian may on occasion have consulted the records preserved [in the archives of the Commune] or extracts from them, he certainly did not do so as a rule."[27] He probably relied more heavily on letters, diaries, and other documents in his family archive. Moreover, his father Piero, his father-in-law Alamanno, his relatives (his mother Simona was the daughter of Bongianni Gianfigliazzi), and other friends, all aristocrats involved in the governments of Lorenzo, Piero, and then of the republic, undoubtedly passed on enormous amounts of detailed information orally—which would account both for his emphasis on more recent events and for his intimate knowledge of the positions taken by leading citizens on the various issues that came up. This also accounts for the fact that the *History of Florence* contains details that sound like trivia or down-right gossip. Guicciardini knows at what time of night Lorenzo went forth to visit his mistress, when he returned, and who was with him. He knows which Florentines found refuge in the Capponi bank when the Pisans rebelled (because his father was among them); or that Alessandro Manelli's wife, who was murdered, was an evil and dishonest woman. He reports not only who accepted a post, but also who turned it down and why. The careful reader of the *History* can often guess where Guicciardini is using a written source and where he is repeating what he heard from "people worthy of faith" (p. 70).

A final indication of the historical-mindedness of Guicciardini in this work is to be noted in the joy he takes in detailed narration. He must have had little documentary evidence or few first-hand reports for some of the battles and campaigns he describes, but his delight in those narratives is nevertheless full and clear. When he does have written evidence or a reliable witness, as in the case of the war against Pope Sixtus and King Ferrante, where he had the reports of his grandfather Jacopo, who was commissary, or in the case of the Pisan campaign, where his father-in-law was commissary, he takes great relish in describing at length the preparations, movements of troops, plots, and expenditures of money. This fascination with the sequence of events, the delight in their depiction, and the love of accurate, detailed reporting are the hallmarks of a historical mind.

The social and political attitudes reflected in Guicciardini's *History of Florence,* written when he was about twenty-six years old, are the same as those reflected in the *History of Italy,* written shortly before his death. There is, to be sure, an inevitable mellowness in the later work, a surer eye, less cockiness, and a more balanced sense of the importance of events; but the cast of mind has not changed, and the prejudices are the same. Politically and personally, he is always an aristocrat; and intellectually, a firm believer in the power of mind to shape history.

One of the faults he persistently points out in the Medici is that they did not give aristocrats their due place in government, but rather preferred to favor men of low rank whom they could trust.[28] He is scornful of Cosimo for thinking that expensive clothes can make "vile men noble" (p. 4); and he reflects the anger of his class when he recalls that Bartolomeo Scala, son of a miller from Colle, became Gonfalonier of Justice (p. 75). Nevertheless, he cannot be accused of advocating a pure oligarchy, either in this or in his other works. He is arguing for a state in which important affairs are directed by competent men; and for him that normally means the aristocrats. He puts it very succinctly: "The wise citizens . . . saw themselves being divested of

reputation and power; and that hurt them not only because of self-interest, but also because the city is sure to suffer when men of quality do not have, I will not say tyrannical power, but at least the rank they justly deserve" (p. 220). He never suggests that the people should be completely excluded from government; but he stresses that things will go wrong if they are in complete control.

His thoughts on tyranny are analogous. Cosimo and Lorenzo are both highly praised for their contributions to Florentine grandeur, and for their virtues, the one as a canny banker and creator of Medici power, the other as a magnificent patron of the arts and a brilliant mind. Guicciardini knows Florence prospered in their time and that the masses were happy. But aristocrats were not given a fair share of political power under the Medici; nor was the city really free, which fact alone would make the Medici worthy of censure. Moreover, when a family usurps political power and then passes it on by inheritance, it will inevitably come into the hands of someone like Piero de'Medici, who then ruins the city. What Guicciardini derives from his study of Florentine history is the system of checks and balances he expounds in his various treatises on government: a government in which the people would have a share through the Great Council; the aristocracy would make itself felt through a powerful senate; and the advantages of continuous one-man rule would be preserved in the long-term office of gonfalonier or in a Medici prince. Such an ideal could be used to criticize the realities of both Medicean and republican Florence, as it is in this *History;* but it is nonetheless a republican ideal, well within the boundaries of Florentine political traditions.

Guicciardini's remarkable ability to look at even the most turbulent events dispassionately and rationally earned him, among other things, the epithet "First of the Machiavellians." When examining the results of the Pazzi conspiracy, in which Giuliano de'Medici was killed and Lorenzo came within an ace of losing his own life, Guicciardini writes: "And yet, he [Lorenzo] gained so much reputation and profit from it that the day may be called a lucky one for him," because it removed his brother, with whom he would have had to share power, and it consolidated his hold on the régime. Guicciardini's detachment is not due to any unwillingness to moralize—he can preach loudly when events bear out some pet principle of his. Rather, it derives from his mental habit of looking at history with an eye for explanations: events and appearances are viewed as the results of a series of causes, and then as the causes of a further series of effects.

Guicciardini considers history a manmade process which, if closely studied, will reveal its laws and its operating mechanisms. This fundamental rationalism is not at all contradicted by his reliance on fortune as another key to the understanding of events. So far as the *understanding* of history is concerned, these two forces, reason and fortune, work together to explain everything. To cite an example: when King Ferrante of Naples found time to recover his strength after the defeats he suffered at the hands of the rebellious barons and Jean d'Anjou, Guicciardini says the king was able to keep his throne "either because they [the barons] secretly wanted to prolong the war, or because fortune, favoring King Ferrante, blinded them to their opportunity" (p. II). Their secret but self-defeating wish to prolong the war would be a rational explanation; their temporary blindness would be due to fortune. But either one explains the facts.

A little later, he contrasts reason and fortune again, but uses them together to explain things. In the war following the Pazzi conspiracy, the Florentines achieved some notable successes at first, but then began to lose. "Victory seemed at hand; but then fortune changed, bringing that glory and happiness to the enemy which by reason should have been ours" (p. 43). By "reason," Guicciardini means that the Florentines had calculated all the military factors and dealt with them intelligently. What they failed to consider were factors that had nothing to do with the war directly, namely, the consequences of the hostility and bad blood between two of their hired captains, which ultimately forced them to divide their army. Fortune favored the enemy by making them stronger through a set of circumstances which they, the enemy, had not created. Still, here too, reason and fortune do not contradict each other but serve together to explain what happened.

The relationship of fortune and reason is not nearly so friendly when we move from the interpretation to the making of history. On this point Guicciardini's views are unequivocal, not only in this but in all his works. "Remember this," he writes in his *Ricordi*, "whoever lives a life of chance will in the end find himself a victim of chance. The right way is to think, to examine, and to consider every detail carefully, even the most minute. Even if you do, it takes great pains to make things come out right. Imagine how things must go for those who drift."[29] The sense of this *Ricordo*, as of so many others, is incorporated in his depiction of men and events in the *History of Florence.* He understands that fortune may restrict, contradict, or thwart the aims of human mental effort; but that does not lessen man's obligation to try.

Not only does he demand compliance with the dictates of reason; he scoffs at anyone who takes credit for success due to fortune. When the Florentine people censured their commissaries for failing to follow up a military victory that would probably have led to the surrender of Pisa, he defends the commissaries on the grounds that the "victory would have been more due to chance than to reason" (p. 113). Conversely, to act according to reason justifies a man even if the results are bad. In the **Consolatoria,** written after the disastrous war he had advised Pope Clement to undertake, he writes to himself: "Even less ought you to feel troubled because you promoted a war that proved so unsuccessful . . . if it was an error, it was of judgment, not of will. Nevertheless, in view of the way things then stood, the advice was good. Advising cannot be based on results."[30] Fortune is blind; she operates according to laws men cannot understand, if indeed they can be called laws at all. But men have vision, and the things they deal with are illuminated through reason.

The world of history is subject to, but not exhausted by, the laws of reason. Unlike the world of mathematics, conditions and circumstances change in history, so that laws cannot be uniformly applied. The control of events requires reason, experience, effort, and pertinacity. Together, these give birth to discretion, that wonderful quality which enables a man to see how a particular situation is constituted, even if it deviates from the general rule. To be sure, the best laid plans of the most penetratingly discreet man may work out wrong, because of unforeseeable changes in circumstances, or because of bad fortune. But that only goads Guicciardini on to understand each historical occurrence in its particularity, to be added to the storehouse of experience, which will then have a general relevance. For he presupposes that there is a meaning, a logic, a generally rational and knowable matrix behind events, even if one of the elements of that matrix should be chance. If there is any difference between the young Guicciardini of the **History of Florence** and the more mature writer of the **History of Italy,** it resides only in the greater degree to which the later work ascribes the outcome of events to folly and fortune rather than to reason. But the obligation to act rationally remains the same: "We must not surrender, like animals, a prey to fortune; rather, we must follow reason, like men."[31]

Notes

[22] I have used the more recent edition by Roberto Palmarocchi (Bari, 1931). Both Canestrini and Palmarocchi divided the text into chapters, but their divisions are not the same. Palmarocchi changed the title from Canestrini's *Storia fiorentina dai tempi di Cosimo de'Medici a quelli del gonfaloniere Soderini* to the plural *Storie fiorentine dal 1378 al 1509,* which he considered more consonant with sixteenth-century usage. Guicciardini uses the Florentine style of dating, which begins the year on March 25, not January 1. In this translation, all dates are in the modern style.

[23] Palmarocchi edition, p. 351.

[24] Nicolai Rubinstein, "The *Storie fiorentine* and the *Memorie di famiglia* by Francesco Guicciardini," *Rinascimento,* IV (1953).

[25] Those lacunas have been filled in in this edition, and are indicated by square brackets or footnotes.

[26] Vittorio de Caprariis, *Francesco Guicciardini: Dalla politica alla storia* (Bari, 1950), argues that the *History of Florence* is "not a work of history . . . but a book of political criticism," p. 61.

[27] Rubinstein, *op. cit.,* p. 219.

[28] Nicolai Rubinstein has shown that the rise of "new families" under Cosimo was by no means as spectacular as Guicciardini suggests. See Rubinstein, *The Government of Florence Under the Medici* (Oxford, 1966), pp. 66 ff.

[29] *Maxims and Reflections [of a Renaissance Statesman (Ricordi)],* p. 135.

[30] *"Consolatoria," Scritti autobiografici,* p. 188.

[31] *Maxims and Reflections,* p. 135.

Mark Phillips (essay date 1977)

SOURCE: "The Historian's Language," in *Francesco Guicciardini: The Historian's Craft,* University of Toronto Press, 1977, pp. 174-83.

[*In the following essay, Phillips examines the writing style displayed in Guicciardini's* Storia d'Italia (The History of Italy), *concluding that the style is complicated, cool, and "mannered," but that it can also be passionate when called for by the subject matter; additionally, Phillips observes that Guicciardini's writing is a good example of the ambiguity found in humanism.*]

In the present century, when extended prose narrative is by far the dominant literary form, historians have largely abandoned their commitment to story-telling. In the sixteenth century, on the contrary, the art of prose narrative was still in its infancy, but historians were among its leading practitioners. The historian's craft is literary as well as analytic. Guicciardini's extraordinary intellectual achievement cannot be separated from the way in which his great book works upon the reader. The vast chronological scheme of the *Storia d'Italia,* its preoccupation with the decline and fall of Italy, its hesitations over the limits of historical understanding, all these are absorbed by the reader as part of the discipline, so to speak, imposed by the author. We respond to his style and tone, to his sense of decorum and of audience, and in so doing we learn to accept and comprehend the larger dimensions of his story.

Guicciardini's language is his signature. Complex, mannered, coldly impressive, it is uniquely his own and uniquely suited to his task. The reader who is familiar with the simpler diction and less elaborate periods of a contemporary historian like Nerli, or who comes to the *Storia d'Italia* from the more energetic rhythms of Machiavelli's prose is immediately struck by the elaborateness and complexity of Guicciardini's slower moving sentences. His style, says the most ambitious of his translators, is 'Jamesian, Proustian— that is to say, his basic meanings reside in his qualifications.'[1] Rather than arranging themselves, his sentences complicate themselves as they proceed, spinning a web of qualifying phrases as if to catch hold of those tiny distinctions the *Ricordi* so insist on. At times these sentences stretch continuity and attention to the breaking point. But, unlike the prose of traditional stylists who also indulge in lengthy periods, Guicciardini's is not clarified to the ear by rhetorical conventions of symmetry and balance. The ear, in fact, seems to be ignored in favour of the silent eye. These slow sentences are the evidence of Guicciardini's strained effort to collect together in a single structure the many elements necessary to describe a single event. And as his descriptions are typically both exactly precise and yet open-ended, in that he so often presents us with simultaneous motivations to choose among, so his sentences have to carry on a number of arguments at once. Thus, these structures do not close with the satisfying resolution (however long delayed for rhetorical effect) of the Ciceronian period. Their complexity is not resolved within the sentence, but is frequently carried across the formalities of punctuation so that Guicciardini seems to write in paragraphs rather than in sentences. Sometimes indeed a single sentence can be a paragraph in length, but more often sentences are strung together with conjunctions which make no more break between two sentences than between two phrases. Not until the whole complex of motives and events is assembled and examined can the interconnections of the prose be cut and work on a new assembly begun.

This style has been described as 'labyrinthine,' but that suggests confusion rather than control. On the contrary, for all its complexity, Guicciardini's prose sometimes has the airless clarity of bright days in winter:

> Certainly nothing is more necessary when making difficult decisions than asking advice; on the other hand nothing is more dangerous. No doubt wise men are less in need of advice than fools; nevertheless the wise derive much more profit from taking it. Who is so universally wise that he can always know and judge everything on his own, and in conflicting arguments can always see the better cause? But what certainty has the man who seeks advice of being faithfully advised? The one who gives the advice, if he is not particularly fond of or faithful to the one who asks, is not only moved by considerable interest but for any small convenience of his own, for any slight satisfaction, will often give such advice as will bring about the result most

profitable or pleasing to himself. As the one who asks advice is usually unaware of these purposes, he does not realize—if he is not very prudent—the unreliability of the advice. This is what happened to Piero de' Medici.[2]

The elaboration here is less labyrinthine than Ptolemaic; and we recognize still the paradox-haunted (or paradox-loving?) author of the **Ricordi.**

Guicciardini's style is shaped by his task. Analytic often to the point of bloodlessness, it conveys no colours, paints no landscapes, and attempts very little physical characterization of any kind. His is a language that gathers and sifts. Corio can take seven pages off from his rambling history of Milan to describe Pope Alexander VI's elaborately colourful coronation.[3] Machiavelli, equally vivid but in a suitably grimmer vein, describes at length the furious mutilation of two men by a mob that tore, bit, and even tasted the flesh of its victims.[4] For nearly two thousand pages, however, Guicciardini goes directly at his task. I have noted only one aesthetic reference—praise for the beauty of the Certosa di Pavia—in all those pages. Nerli quotes verses and Corio quotes Latin, but for Guicciardini, and from him, there are no distractions. A few spare similies comparing events to fires, seeds, and diseases are unsparingly repeated. Even the colloquialism of the **Storie fiorentine** is gone. What is left is the unremitting intellectual pressure that we feel sentence by sentence and page by page. This is our reward in place of all the verses, metaphors, and colourful description of other narrators.

But I do not want to exaggerate; certainly along with intellectual pressure there is passion too. Perhaps the most notable eruption is the one which greets the death of Alexander VI, the Borgia pope. His body, poisoned by his own wine, is described as black, bloated, and ugly ('nero, enfiato e bruttissimo') and all the populace came to see him dead:

> All Rome thronged with incredible rejoicing to see the dead body of Alexander in St. Peter's, unable to satiate their eyes enough with seeing spent that serpent who in his boundless ambition and pestiferous perfidy, and with all his examples of horrible cruelty and monstrous sensuality and unheard-of avarice, selling without distinction sacred and profane things, had envenomed the entire world. And nevertheless he had been exalted by the most unusual and almost perpetual good fortune from early youth up to the last days of his life, always desiring the greatest things and always obtaining more than he desired.[5]

Here the full force of Guicciardini's grand strain, usually reserved for momentous events, is directed at a single head; even so the historian is immediately drawn into a wider reflection on the illusoriness of men's opinions and the paradox of earthly success:

> A powerful example to confound the arrogance of those who, presuming to discern with the weakness of human eyes the depth of divine judgements, affirm that the prosperity or adversity of men proceeds from their own merits or demerits: as if one may not see every day many good men unjustly vexed and many depraved souls unworthily exalted; or as if, interpreting it in another way, one were to derogate from the justice and power of God, whose boundless might cannot be contained within the narrow limits of the present, and who—at another time and in another place—will recognize with a broad sweep, with rewards and eternal punishments, the just from the unjust.[6]

The pope is all the more a monster for being, contrary to humanist precept, an *esempio* (example) of vice rewarded. And some of the passion with which Alexander is condemned carries over into the denunciation of those who judge too simplistically. In the sweep and dignity of the final lines, however, any quality of personal anger is forgotten. Here, in language that is as unusually simple and bare as the condemnation of Alexander was uncharacteristically purple, we have a rare glimpse of Guicciardini moving to a higher moral vision of history. Momentarily at least, history becomes inviolate, an event occurring in the eye of God, and so not to be judged foolishly by childish notions of reward and punishment. In the name of a remoter God, Guicciardini dismisses the whole didactic tradition of Florentine historiography from Villani on.

Moments like this are crucial in a great book. They demonstrate the author's range and power and therefore help to establish his authority. Thus although it is far more typical of Guicciardini to tack against the wind than to run before it, the grand strain is still characteristic. And this passage is characteristic in another way. Seldom in the **Storia d'Italia** is the smooth flow of the narrative interrupted by an authorial presence. Even in this intervention, Guicciardini speaks with the objective majesty of history itself. Similarly, throughout the history the author remains impersonal and aloof. We might have expected just the opposite from the opening sentences of the book, which announce the author's intentions and begin with an emphatic 'I': 'I have decided to write about the events which have taken place in Italy within our memory . . .' But it is as though once having taken the decision to set this world in motion the author feels it unnecessary to refer to himself again.[7] Occasionally the first line will find an echo in programmatic statements announcing that it is now necessary that we be told of the background to one situation or another, but these interruptions are few and impersonal. He never stops to chat as others do, never takes us aside for a confidence or addresses us rhetorically. The author does not identify himself with Florence, much less with the historical character Francesco Guicciardini, papal lieutenant. In this respect as in others Guicciardini reminds us of

Thucydides, a historian equally involved in the events he narrates and equally absent from his own narrative. By contrast, Nardi slips (not quite noiselessly) between triple roles as author, witness, and actor, so that his history in places takes on added characteristics of chronicle or memoir.[8]

And yet Guicciardini's implicit presence is felt everywhere in the history. Neither his individual sentences nor the line of his narrative unfolds with the effortlessness or natural logic of more classical works. The wilfulness of his structures and of his style reveal his effort to control the elements of his analysis and to qualify and make as precise as possible the truth as he finds it. The author reveals his presence in this, even while he studiously effaces his personality. Guicciardini's order, then, is an imposed order that implicitly acknowledges the limits of reason and the fragmentary nature of experience.

Matching this veiled author, isolated in some cold tower of the imagination that appears to allow him equally clear sight of events in all corners of Italy, is an equally isolated reader. This stands in sharp contrast to the *campanilismo* of the **Storie fiorentine,** a loyalty which united the historian to his audience in implicit understanding. In that early work 'we,' 'us,' and 'our' came easily to Guicciardini in the unself-conscious intimacy of his identification with Florence. In the **Storia d'Italia,** however, the potential readership is enormously widened and the individual reader is so much more alone.[9] As noted earlier, this late history implies not so much an audience as a reader. Like the first person singular, the first person plural appears prominently in the opening lines of the book and then disappears. The foreigners, says Guicciardini, have been brought in 'by our princes themselves' and thus from the start he identifies his readership with Italy rather than with Florence. But there can be no question of the wider identity fully substituting for the narrower. It would be centuries before such a reference could create bonds of sympathy between a writer and his unknown reader that could supplant the closed circle of city walls. Italy is still an unemotional abstraction, though the loss of independence had strengthened a sense of a common culture and a common fate. It is generally accepted that Guicciardini made a great leap when he abandoned the municipal horizons of earlier historical writing, but the implications of this 'progress' are not often examined. The extensiveness of his research, the complexity of his narrative, and not least the cold dispassionateness of his presence are all implied. Something is lost as well as won in Guicciardini's development from historian of Florence to historian of Italy.

Perhaps it is useful to see Guicciardini's use of classical conventions in the same light. If Guicciardini had projected himself to a great height in order to achieve an Italian perspective, he was able to support himself in that thinner atmosphere by borrowing two major conventions of classical historical writing. I have previously down-graded the discussion of rhetorical speeches and annalistic narrative because I do not regard the first as being disfunctional or the second as structurally very important. But there is another side to these classical borrowings that we should consider. By shaping nearby events with the canonical forms of a revered past, Guicciardini, like his humanist predecessors, gained a sense of perspective without which his narrative could not have been so vast and so measured. He could not always remain distant from the great changes of his lifetime, but in the lofty and serious tone of classicism he could find composure.

Gravity is the desired effect. Many of the characteristics we have observed amount to the search for a style that will lend dignity to the story. Guicciardini is impressed with the momentousness of the events he describes and through the formality and artificiality of his language he impresses us with the same idea. But if the dignity of the language is never lost, the same cannot be said of its decorum. Certainly there are times when we feel its presence strongly, as in the majestic rhetoric of the opening pages. There the grandeur of the theme dwarfs anything personal, ironic, or eccentric. But as we read further we observe the restless complexity of Guicciardini's narrative. There is nothing decorous in its rapidity, nor anything classical in its lack of straight lines. And this criss-cross geography also has its analytic and moral counterparts. In Bruni or even in Machiavelli events have definite causes and clear significance. In their histories there is a kind of narrative space which is rational and open. The motives behind an event, the event, and the significance of the event are carefully aligned on clear orthogonals that converge on a moral or political lesson as on a vanishing point. We saw that Guicciardini too used this technique in his early history. The story of the Pazzi plot was clearly told, and then its significance was elaborated, first for Florentine government and then for the politics of conspiracy in general. The straight lines of this progressive abstraction were equally evident in the portrait of Lorenzo, where good and bad characteristics could be defined easily because they were moral abstractions that did not depend on the specific historical context. These clear categories were then matched up with all the balance and care of an attentive hostess's seating arrangements.

We have already seen how the portraiture of the late history is transformed. The simple linearity of the early work is gone and with it a kind of ease and hopefulness. By comparison the new character study is a tangle in which radical changes of viewpoint are compressed into a few pages. Where clarity was the hallmark of the first, illusion and reality become the theme of the second, and irony its mood. That ease in which a single formula could define a man is lost, and now we are impressed by the difficulties of judgement, the illusiveness of expectation, and the incapacity of rulers. The writing is much more compressed and its scheme is more dynamic. The whole exercise depends on a kind of tension between the personalities of the two popes. And when Leo dies, Clement's single character is described in terms of internal contradictions which now replace the external ones. In its concreteness as well as in its complexities, the dual portrait distinguishes itself from its predecessor. Clement and Leo are not fitted into a pre-existing space which has been defined by universal standards of conduct. Rather they are judged by historical standards of success or failure which can only be clarified by the progress of the narrative itself. Hence we have the irony that the abstemious and intelligent Clement is revealed in time to be a failure in concrete historical terms, though abstractly he is certainly more virtuous than the lazy, pleasure-seeking Leo.

Similar observations can be made about the motivation and explanation of events. Here again we see a cluttering of narrative space. In Giovanni Villani's chronicle earthly events directly reflect divine providence and astrological influence. Thus even though his history lacks the lucidity the humanists would give to historical writing, it has a moral unambiguousness because there is always a direct and simple relationship between the event and the moral world which it reflects. The humanists bring to history a more sophisticated morality as well as more classical techniques of narrative. In a sense narrative was freed to respond to its own needs because human events no longer were required to mirror a non-historical world. Nonetheless, their didacticism was as strong as Villani's, and this very didacticism, located now within history rather than cutting across it, help to confer additional clarity on events. The moral and political lessons that humanist history teaches tie events together into well-understood units and give the reader a core of meaning to follow. But in Guicciardini the vestiges of didacticism have no such effect, and a multiplicity of overlapping explanations attaches to events. There are, of course, lessons in the *Storia d'Italia,* the wickedness of princes and the instability of human affairs being the most explicit. But the meaning of these 'salutiferi documenti' is meditative rather than didactic, passive rather than active. They enlighten the reader, but do not arm him. In this they are consistent with the prudential and paradoxical character of the *Ricordi,* many of which indeed show up as maxims in the history.

What are the consequences of our knowing these lessons? In the public sphere there can be none. Guicciardini offers us an understanding that is private to the political individual, though the subject is fully public. He alerts us to the complexity of history and politics, demanding prudence, foresight, rationality, humility in the face of Fortune. Himself a private man once again,

he writes without a public commission. Addressing no single polity or recognizable collective group, Guicciardini speaks to a reader somewhat removed from the public forums of humanism, and unlike Bruni he neither makes a public celebration of the past nor prescribes for the future. As individual readers we are left to draw our own conclusions. History becomes a meditation.

In short, the *Storia d'Italia* lacks the public spirit, the composure, or the clarity that we expect from a work written in the classical spirit. There is grandeur but there is not simplicity. There are too many questions and too few lessons, too many objects and not enough space, too much irony and too little certainty, too much movement and too little repose, too much strain and very little ease. In all these respects Guicciardini has severely modified the traditions of humanism, though his continued dependency is equally obvious.

It is not fanciful to recognize in this some analogy to the anticlassical strain in the contemporary visual arts, usually called 'Mannerism.' New subjects call for experiment in form. Guicciardini broached a vast new subject and endowed history with a special kind of truthfulness. Just as Machiavelli helped to divorce politics from traditional moral codes, so Guicciardini simultaneously undermined both the moral and political uses of history which had been at the basis of the humanist historiography. Adopting Walter Friedlaender's description of classicism in his famous essay on the classical and anticlassical in sixteenth-century art, we can say that humanist historiography too was 'idealistically heightened and ethically stressed.'[10] It too sought an idealized space expressing 'a higher reality purified of everything accidental.' It too produced 'an unambiguous, constructed space in which equally unambiguous fixed figures move and act.' Of course, history can never purify itself of everything accidental in the sense that art can, but it can engage in a constant comparison of the accidental with the eternal, of the particular with the universal. The didacticism of the humanists provides that essential link between history as the study of particulars and a higher and normative world of ethical politics. Once that link is cut, as it is in Guicciardini, history is set free to pursue the particular *ad infinitum,* with not entirely happy results. Guicciardini's history has the 'freer and apparently more capricious rhythms' of Mannerist painting because it too has lost its obligation to the universal. His observation has an obsessive edge to it that comes from a tendency to equate particularily with truth. But his particulars are so concrete because his abstractions are so vague. Abstractions and higher forces remain, but they no longer constitute a unifying element. Ethics linger as ironies. Somewhere a remote God judges. Fortune enters history more frequently than ever, but only to complicate it. The most universal element in the history, it is the most inscrutable.

The humanist historian, and to a lesser degree the chronicler as well, had two functions, both of them public: his task was to commemorate and to teach. Guicciardini's lessons are few and negative, and the story he commemorates is a tragedy that never becomes heroic. More a modern than a Greek drama, it is filled with petty men and wasted opportunity. The grandeur of the history lies entirely in its vast scope, which is the historian's own contribution. Only he has been able to unify so many incidents into so large a story. And the creation is all the more personal as it corresponds to the boundaries of no recognized polity. To whom then would he commemorate these deeds? Not a historian by virtue of any public office or responsibility, he writes for posterity and to satisfy some private desire. And as he meditates on the vast story, he finds nothing in it that constitutes a public lesson except the mutability of history and the selfishness of power.

Notes

[1] Sidney Alexander, introduction to his translation of the *History of Italy*, p. xvii. On Guicciardini's style, see G. Getto, 'Note sulla prosa della *Storia d'Italia* di Francesco Guicciardini,' *Aevum*, XV, 1941, pp. 141-223.

[2] Trans. Grayson, *History of Italy*, p. 174. 'Niuna cosa è certamente più necessaria nelle deliberazioni ardue, niuna da altra parte più pericolosa, che'l domandare consiglio; nè è dubbio che manco è necessario agli uomini prudenti il consiglio che agli imprudenti; e nondimeno, che molto più utilità riportano i savi del consigliarsi. Perché chi è quello di prudenza tanto perfetta che consideri sempre e conosca ogni cosa da se stesso? E nelle ragioni contrarie discerna sempre la migliore parte? Ma che certezza ha chi domanda il consiglio d'essere fedelmente consigliato? Perché chi dà il consiglio, se non è molto fedele o affezionato a chi 'l domanda, non solo mosso da notabile interesse ma per ogni suo piccolo comodo, per ogni leggiera sodisfazione, dirizza spesso il consiglio a quel fine che più gli torna a proposito o di che più si compiace; e essendo questi fini il piú delle volte incogniti a chi cerca d'essere consigliato, non s'accorge, se non è prudente, della infedeltà del consiglio. Così intervenne a Piero de' Medici.' *Storia d'Italia*, I, pp. 93-4.

[3] Bernardino Corio, *Storia di Milano*, ed. E. De Magri (Milano, 1855), p. 464 ff.

[4] See Machiavelli's account of the expulsion of the Duke of Athens from Florence in Chapter 37, Book II of the *Storie fiorentine*. Machiavelli's interest in physical characterization is discussed by Peter Bondanella in his recent *Machiavelli and the Renaissance Art of History* (Detroit: Wayne State University Press 1973). He fails to recognize, however, that this is not a new feature but a direct borrowing from Villani.

[5] Trans. Alexander, *History of Italy*, p. 166. 'Concorse al corpo morto d'Alessandro in San Piero con incredibile allegrazza tutta Roma, non potendo saziarsi gli occhi d'alcuno di vedere spento un serpente che con la sua immoderata ambizione e pestifera perfidia, e con tutti gli esempli di orribile crudeltà di mostruosa libidine e di inaudita avarizia, vendendo senza distinzione le cose sacre and le profane, aveva attossicato tutto il mondo; e nondimeno era stato esaltato, con rarissima e quasi perpetua prosperità, dalla prima gioventù insino all'ultimo dì della vita sua, desiderando sempre cose grandissime e ottenendo più di quello desiderava.' *Storia d'Italia*, II, pp. 97-8.

[6] Trans. Alexander, *History of Italy*, p. 166. 'Esempio potente a confondere l'arroganza di coloro i quali, presumendosi di scorgere con la debolezza degli occhi umani la profondità de' giudici divini, affermano ciò che di prospero o di avverso avviene agli uomini procedere o da' meriti o da' demeriti loro: come se tutto dì non apparisse molti buoni essere vessati ingiustamente e molti di pravo animo essere esaltati indebitamente; o come se, altrimenti interpretando, si derogasse alla giustizia e alla potenza di Dio; la amplitudine della quale, non ristretta a' termini brevi e presenti, in altro tempo e in altro luogo, con larga mano, con premi e con supplici sempiterni, riconosce i giusti dagli ingiusti.' *Storia d'Italia*, II, p. 98.

[7] Even this opening is brief and 'objective' when compared to the apologies with which historians like Corio, Bembo, or Vettori preface their work. And one of the principal tendencies in the revisions of the 'Commentary' text is the suppression of the first person.

[8] See Nardi, *Istorie della Città di Firenze* (Florence 1858), especially his account of his role in the 'Friday tumult' of 1527, an incident we have already looked at in terms of Guicciardini's self-description (*Istorie*, II, p. 116ff). The very rare occasions on which he reveals his identity are interesting. The first self-reference that I have found marks his appointment at a very young age as Florentine ambassador to Spain: ' . . . imbasciadore Francesco Guicciardini, quello che scrisse questa istoria, dottore di legge, ancora tanto giovane che per l'età era, secondo le leggi della patria, inabile a esercitare qualunque magistrato . . .' (*Storia*, III, 154-5). A quarter of a century later his pride at his youthful appointment was still uncontainable and spills over into this self-display, while his much larger historical role as papal governor and lieutenant is covered with suitable anonimity. Not modesty, of course, but decorum governs this decision. A second such intrusion, motivated by filial piety, is his identification of Piero Guicciardini as his father: 'gl'imbasciadori fiorentini, tra' quali fu Piero Guicciardini mio padre . . .' (*Storia*, II, 134). In the sixteenth book he marvels over why Ieronimo Morone allowed himself to be taken in by the Marquis of Pescara and captured since he remembers

well that Morone had told him that there was not a man in Italy more faithless or more evil than Pescara. Since these late books are not fully revised, however, it is likely that Guicciardini would have brought this observation into line with his usual practice.

[9] One ironic indicator of this expanded readership is the way in which readers with local loyalties up and down the peninsula took offense with Guicciardini's views and rose to defend their cities. And to this category we might add the attacks of the Florentine exiles and the censorship of offensive passages by the Church. Apparently Guicciardini was able to offend everybody equally. For this literature, see V. Luciani, *Francesco Guicciardini and his European Reputation.*

[10] W. Friedlaender, *Mannerism and Anti-Mannerism in Italian Painting* (New York: Schocken 1965), pp. 6-8.

Sheila ffolliott (essay date 1982)

SOURCE: "Francesco Guicciardini's *Report from Spain:* Introduction," *Allegorica,* Vol. VII, No. 1, Summer, 1982, pp. 60-2.

[*In the following essay, ffolliott describes the* Report from Spain *as a genre of writing new to the Renaissance, and observes that this report reveals much about the Florentine Republic's relationship with Spain at a particular point in history.*]

The *Report from Spain* was written by the Florentine lawyer and historian Francesco Guicciardini (1482-1540) while he was Ambassador at the Court of King Ferdinand in 1512-1513 on behalf of the Florentine Republic.[1] It is a unique document never before wholly translated into English: a distillation of Guicciardini's Spanish experience about which he also wrote a travel diary and numerous letters.[2] It is significant in being, according to Vincent Luciani, author of the most thorough account of Guicciardini in Spain, the most complete judgment of the Spanish character by an Italian author of the sixteenth century.[3] It is also one of the earliest contemporary portraits of Ferdinand of Aragon.

In spite of initial doubts about taking the assignment, since it would mean a loss of revenue from his law practice, the prestige value of the assignment prevailed, the young Guicciardini undertook it, and the records show that he was well paid.[4] Ferdinand, who interested himself in affairs on the Italian peninsula, had just allied himself with the Venetian Republic and the pope in the so-called "Holy League," designed to serve the interests of the Church which in this case meant driving the French out of Italy.

Not authorized to negotiate, Guicciardini was asked to remind the King of his obligations to Florence. "What

a ticklish job it must have been for an ambassador from the country most loyal to France (Spain's enemy) to ask for Spain's help against Pope Julius (Spain's ally), whose armies were led by Raymond de Cardona (the Spanish Viceroy in Naples)."[5] While Guicciardini was in Spain the Florentine Republic fell and the Medici regained control of the city with the resulting shift in political allegiances. The fact that the initial rationale for his mission no longer existed when it ended does not lessen the significance of the document which he produced for readers desiring a profile of Spain and the Spanish just after the death of Queen Isabella.

The ambassadorial report is a new genre of writing which developed during this period, the extensive collection of those of the Venetian ambassadors being the best known.[6] These documents are frequently consulted by historians today interested in the insights they offer, and Guicciardini's has been used by historians interested both in Spain and in the historian's own later career and political philosophy. This report combines, as Mark Phillips has noted, observations on geography, history, economics, political analysis, the military, and social organization.[7] It was written with the premise that its readers wanted to know what to expect from King Ferdinand. Guicciardini has provided them with the material which he thinks they need in order to make that decision. He tries to provide a picture of how the King's mind works and insights into traits of his character, and he includes the background necessary to place these remarks into their proper contexts. Therefore, in addition to the character analysis of the King, he describes his habits, the way in which his court functions, and the peculiar characteristics of the geography and history of the country which he believes to be relevant to its contemporary situation.

This was Guicciardini's first exposure to the workings of a royal court. He relates the history of how Ferdinand and Isabella gained control over their territories and subjects as an example of how the Florentine Republic ought to expect them to act in future. He describes their income and its sources in great detail.[8] His report is peppered throughout with value judgments: towns are ugly, the people are not industrious or learned. He attributes much of what has happened in Spanish history to what he perceives as being the national character of its people. He notes, for example, their fondness for simulation and ceremony and their adherence to a code of behavior known as the "Hidalgo." His observations in the report illustrate his abilities as a keen observer, but he is quite clearly culturally biased: Spain and the Spanish are seen as being far behind Italy and the Italians.

For Guicciardini himself the Spanish years were important in exposing him to a world wider than that of Tuscany and its environs. Before leaving the Italian peninsula, he had written his *History of Florence.*[9]

While in Spain, in addition to the letters, travel diary, and report already mentioned, he wrote the **Discorso di Logrogno,** a treatise on the ideal government for the Florentine state, and he began writing his **Ricordi,** the political maxims which he would continue to write for the rest of his career.[10] The latter writings are more general observations on politics and human nature. Guicciardini's humanist education is visible in the pages of this report. He refers to Spain's ancient history in describing the origins of place names and demonstrates his familiarity with Livy and other ancient historians. He sees a definite connection between historical events, even in antiquity, and the present condition of Spain.

The report is a useful gem for the information which it contains and synthesizes into a profile of Spain during the years just after the discovery of the New World and just prior to its assumption into the Habsburg domain under Charles V.

Notes

[1] The best biography of Guicciardini is that of Roberto Ridolfi, *The Life of Francesco Guicciardini,* trans. Cecil Grayson (New York: Knopf, 1968). I would like to thank Professor Judith Brown and John F. d'Amico for their invaluable assistance in completing this study.

[2] J. H. Robinson, *Readings in European History* (New York, 1906), II, p. 24. The "Relazione di Spagna" and the Spanish correspondence are in *Opere inedite di Francesco Guicciardini* (Florence: Cellini, 1864), Vol. VI.

[3] Vincent Luciani, "Il Guicciardini e la Spagna", *Publications of the Modern Language Association,* LVI (1941) p. 1001.

[4] He was paid three florins per day plus a stipend of three hundred florins. See Richard Goldthwaite, *Private Wealth in Renaissance Florence* (Princeton: Princeton University Press, 1968), p. 137.

[5] Francesco Guicciardini, *The History of Florence,* trans. and intro. by Mario T. Domandi (New York: Harper and Row, 1970), p. xx.

[6] E. Albèri, ed. *Relazioni degli ambasciatori veneti al Senato* (Florence, 1839).

[7] Mark Phillips, *Francesco Guicciardini: The Historian's Craft* (Toronto and Buffalo: University of Toronto Press, 1977), p. 9.

[8] For comparisons with wealth in contemporary Florence where the valuations are given in florins, which are equivalent to ducats, see Goldthwaite, op. cit., for tables.

[9] Francesco Guicciardini, op. cit.

[10] Francesco Guicciardini, *Maxims and Reflections of a Renaissance Statesman,* trans. by Mario T. Domandi with an intro. by Nicolai Rubenstein (New York: Harper and Row, 1965).

Peter Bondanella (essay date 1984)

SOURCE: "Francesco Guicciardini in Modern Critical Literature," *Annali d'Italianistica,* Vol. 2, 1984, pp. 7-18.

[*In the following essay, Bondanella traces the publication history of Guicciardini's writings, noting that while some of his editors have been interested in the moral content of his work, others have concentrated on his style and method.*]

Guicciardini's place in Italian and European literary history owes as much to extraliterary factors as it does to a reasoned assessment of the merits of his works. Given the peculiar publication history of his works, a comprehensive view of Guicciardini's contributions to Italian Renaissance culture was perhaps not even possible until only very recently. It is too often forgotten that Guicciardini's critical reputation was originally based upon a small portion of his total work—only the **Storia d'Italia** was ever published in its entirety during the Renaissance. The *editio princeps* appeared in Florence in 1561, followed in rapid succession by translations in Latin and all the major European languages. Thus, Guicciardini's reputation rested solely upon his magisterial history of Italy from the time of its publication until the mid-nineteenth century, and critics or scholars remained unaware that other works of great interest were yet to be discovered in the Guicciardini family archives and to be edited for publication. These would include all of Guicciardini's voluminous correspondence, his **Ricordi,** his **Considerazioni sui "Discorsi" del Machiavelli,** his several discourses on Florentine government, and two historical works—**Le cose fiorentine** and **Storie fiorentine.** In short, before the nineteenth century, Guicciardini's stature as a major writer was impossible to analyze accurately.

The publication of the ten volume edition of Guicciardini's almost complete works by Giuseppe Canestrini between 1857 and 1867 set the stage for an immediate and radical reevaluation of Guicciardini's importance to Renaissance culture, although the implications of these archival discoveries have become clearly evident only during the last decade. I say almost complete because an early historical work, **Le cose fiorentine,** had yet to be discovered by the dean of Guicciardini scholars, Roberto Ridolfi, and would remain unknown until the mid-twentieth century. Canestrini's edition appeared at a fateful moment, during the height of the Risorgimento and its struggle to unify a modern Italy. Guicciardini's hitherto unpublished works represented a gold mine of information about Italy's most glorious historical epoch, and it was only natural that Italians of the last century would wish to reexamine their traditions in the light of their recent struggle for national independence and unification. Particular attention was paid to the Renaissance during this period of national soul-searching, for educated Italians needed an answer to a vexing question: How had Italy fallen from the cultural, political, and economic hegemony over Europe in the Renaissance to a position of servility and dependence? What flaw of national character made this tragedy possible? The answer to this complex question was to influence Guicciardini's critical reputation for almost a century.

In response to Canestrini's discoveries, two early interpretations appeared in France and in Italy which would continue to dominate the critical literature for some years to come: a French book by Eugene Benoist,[1] and a critical essay entitled "L'uomo del Guicciardini" by Francesco De Sanctis (1865), the thesis of which was later incorporated into the immensely influential *Storia della letteratura italiana* (1870-71).[2] While Benoist's study is one of the first to examine all of Guicciardini's writings, it nevertheless pronounces a negative judgment on them. In fact, he agrees with Montaigne's earlier pronouncement that Guicciardini must have had some serious personal flaw to see only self-interest in the mechanisms of human history. It was De Sanctis' judgment which was to carry more weight.

De Sanctis admits that the **Storia d'Italia** must be considered one of the most important works ever written by an Italian in terms of its intellectual power; he nevertheless bases much of his influential opinion of Guicciardini upon a reading of the **Ricordi**. And in raising this collection of philosophical maxims to a position ranking alongside Guicciardini's major historical work, De Sanctis signals the path for several generations of critics. However, De Sanctis views Guicciardini from the perspective of the Risorgimento. In his opinion, the Italians of the High Renaissance (and he considered Guicciardini a perfect representative of his times and his class) abandoned spiritual values, the love for liberty or freedom, and the desire to sacrifice themselves for a noble cause; in the place of these high ideals was self-interest, Guicciardini's *particulare.* Guicciardini, like Machiavelli, wanted to see Italy freed from the clutches of the priests and foreigners, but unlike Machiavelli he was incapable of following his ideals when they clashed with his self-interest. If Machiavelli's exhortation at the conclusion of *Il principe* to free Italy from the barbarians was taken (erroneously) to signify a precursor to the Risorgimento's unification of Italy under a Savoy dynasty, Guicciardini's attitude did not suit a generation tested by prison, exile, and war to achieve political independence. De Sanctis viewed Guicciardini's perspective not only as a personal defect in his character but as a flaw in the na-

tional character as well: fools such as Machiavelli were too few, while the "wise" men such as Guicciardini were too many; and while individuals such as Guicciardini may prosper, a nation of such people can only meet with disaster.

While De Sanctis established a point of view on Guicciardini's works which employed the writer's motives and biographical information to call into question the morality of his ideas, other scholars abroad were more interested in Guicciardini's place in the development of historiography. In particular, the German scholars Leopold von Ranke[3] and, later, Eduard Fueter[4] attempted, with remarkable success, to place Guicciardini in a broader framework which analyzed his achievements somewhat more dispassionately than had De Sanctis. In their writings we witness the first phase of interest in Guicciardini's contributions to Renaissance historiography, a scholarly topic which has been revived in recent years.

In the first half of the twentieth century Guicciardini scholarship was characterized by several developments: an increasingly complex perspective on the composition of the two major works, the **Ricordi** and the **Storia d'Italia;** a major reconsideration of Guicciardini's critical fortune in European culture; the publication of important critical editions of Guicciardini's writings; and the appearance of a number of general works which aimed at a synthesis of the writer's life and works. In 1926, for example, Andréi Otetea published a French monograph on Guicciardini's life and writings which, although now rendered somewhat unreliable due to recent archival discoveries, was for its time a rather valuable study.[5] Other equally general interpretations, although less reliable and less useful today, include works by Luigi Malagodi[6]—a somewhat shallow biographical treatment of Guicciardini, now rendered obsolete—Vito Vitale,[7] and Ugo Spirito,[8] who produced an interesting comparison of Guicciardini with Machiavelli, continuing this always fascinating argument which had entered the critical literature with De Sanctis.

None of these studies, however, made as original a contribution to the critical literature as that of an American, Vincenzo Luciani, whose *Francesco Guicciardini and his European Reputation* presented a monumental overview of Guicciardini's reception within Italy and abroad—a work which remains even today the single indispensable treatment of the topic.[9] Luciani's book finally received an Italian translation over a decade after its initial appearance in English, and it has been a standard work for any scholar interested in Guicciardini since that day. A model for scrupulous scholarship, comprehensive treatment, and careful erudition, this study constitutes one of the best examples of a type of research, a writer's reception abroad, which is no longer so popular today.

Luciani's analysis of the complexities behind the growth of Guicciardini's European reputation made a greater original contribution to our knowledge about the Florentine writer than did the various general works on his life and writings; however, philological discoveries and theories about the composition of Guicciardini's two major works made perhaps the most lasting impression upon this century's scholarship. In the case of Guicciardini's *Storia d'Italia,* Roberto Ridolfi's important treatment of the work's genesis and composition would lay the groundwork for any future treatment of the evolution of Guicciardini's historiography.[10] According to Ridolfi's thesis, the work was begun around 1534 (and not in 1528-29 as Benedetto Varchi claimed) as a less comprehensive narrative of historical events ocurring between 1525-26. Three manuscripts of this "false start" exist, and the material was later incorporated into Book XVI of the historical work that was eventually published. Then Guicciardini began dictating to his secretary a different history, which returned to 1490 as a starting point and of which several versions exist in manuscript with autograph corrections. Finally, the last copy (presently in the Biblioteca Laurenziana) was dictated in 1539 after the author suffered a serious attack of apoplexy. Although the last four books were completed without receiving a final revision, the entire work stands as a completed and unfragmentary whole and was, unlike all Guicciardini's other works, very definitely intended for publication. His death in 1540 hindered these plans, but the papers were saved by the family until the eventual publication in 1561 of the first printed edition of the history which made its author famous.

The problems surrounding the composition of the *Ricordi* are even more complex and their suggested solutions even more uncertain and debatable. Unlike the history of Italy, this work was never completed for publication during Guicciardini's lifetime (indeed, we are uncertain whether he ever intended it to see the light of day). Moreover, his maxims were collected in a bewildering series of manuscripts, one of which was apparently given away in 1561 by a relative, causing some of the maxims to appear in print during the sixteenth century. It is largely due to the work of Michele Barbi[11] and Mario Fubini,[12] later followed closely by the magnificent editorial work of Raffaele Spongano,[13] that we have come to understand the history of the composition of the *Ricordi.* Two notebooks in Guicciardini's hand (known as Q1 and Q2) contain some 29 maxims. A more comprehensive autograph manuscript, manuscript B, retains the Q2 maxims in their original order with a total of 181 *ricordi.* The final version, C, contains 221 maxims and dates from 1530; 91 maxims in it are completely original and are not contained in B. The result of the scholarly efforts by Barbi, Fubini, and Spongano was to prove that another manuscript (A) once existed, which is no longer extant but was probably a version of the one given away by a family member in 1561.

The controversy over Guicciardini's methods of composition had important consequences for the preparation of critical editions of his various writings (most of the autograph manuscripts of which, with a few notable exceptions, are conserved in the family archives in Florence). By the end of the war in 1945, a number of major critical editions had been prepared under the direction of Roberto Palmarocchi, whose scholarly work was particularly important for Guicciardini's minor dialogues or treatises and his autobiographical writings.[14] In addition, there appeared an important edition of the *Storia d'Italia* edited by Costantino Panigada.[15] Even more useful an undertaking was the beginning of a complete edition of Guicciardini's voluminous correspondence, edited by Roberto Palmarocchi and Pier Giorgio Ricci, which began to appear in 1938 and is still in the process of reaching completion.[16] But the greatest surprise was Roberto Ridolfi's discovery of a hitherto unknown work, an incomplete history of Florence which Ridolfi entitled *Le cose fiorentine.*[17]

This discovery changed entirely the way scholars looked at Guicciardini's intellectual development. This work, begun around 1527, almost two decades after the composition of his earlier *Storie fiorentine,* was left unfinished when Guicciardini turned to work on his masterpiece, the *Storia d'Italia.* As far as we can tell, the narrative was to have begun around the Ciompi revolt and to have continued until around 1494. While the first Florentine history owes a great debt to the medieval chronicles of the city, this second effort reveals that Guicciardini was profoundly influenced by humanist views of historiography. In particular, Ridolfi's research and the resulting critical edition demonstrated the extent to which Guicciardini employed new and more modern historical methodology than any of his contemporaries, Machiavelli included. Rather than continuing a single narrative source, Guicciardini sifted patiently through both primary and secondary sources, having archival materials at his disposal. In brief, his writing was far closer to the kind of work we now call historical research than that of any other man before his lifetime.

Guicciardini studies since 1945 have been characterized by a number of new critical perspectives, which slowly shifted from a predominantly Italian perspective to a wider, European or even trans-Atlantic one. For the purposes of this survey article, we may distinguish several specific areas in which the greatest contributions have been made during this period: work on Guicciardini's biography and his immediate family; the analysis of Guicciardini's minor works and their place in the genesis of the greater history and his maxims; Guicciardini's place in the tradition of humanist historiography; Guicciardini's style; and finally (and not the least in importance), translations of Guicciardini's various works.

Through the efforts of several tireless workers engaged in the Guicciardini family archives (especially Roberto

Ridolfi), we now know far more about Guicciardini's life and his immediate family circle than ever before. Ridolfi's *Vita di Francesco Guicciardini,* which first appeared in 1960, was translated into English in 1968 and has recently been revised and reissued in Italian. Ridolfi's work established a masterful critical biography which remains the single most important research tool for any serious scholar.[18] Ridolfi's life of Guicciardini may be less compelling than his companion volume on Machiavelli, but it is a gold mine of information, ideas, and perspectives no scholar can afford to ignore. The late Conte Paolo Guicciardini, a worthy descendant of the Florentine historian, was most active in organizing the family archives (where most of Guicciardini's papers and manuscripts are still conserved), making them available to scholars, and publishing a number of quite useful works on his ancestor which were based upon the extensive holdings of Guicciardini translations and editions in the Guicciardini family library. In particular, his two volumes on English and French translations of the *Storia d'Italia* remain of value. Perhaps even more intriguing is a discussion of the history of the Guicciardini family palazzo (on Via Guicciardini next to the Palazzo Pitti), with a minutely detailed account of its many alterations and a description of its library and archives.[19]

Archival studies of the family documents have revealed a good deal of interesting historical information, since the Guicciardini family archives are among the most completely preserved in Florence. In 1953, Nicolai Rubinstein published an important article which established clear links between the traditional family diaries composed by the patrician families of Florence (including Francesco's family) and Guicciardini's first attempts at the composition of history in the *Storie fiorentine.*[20] Even more interesting data arose from a major analysis of private wealth in Renaissance Florence by Richard A. Goldthwaite.[21] This comparative study of four major patrician families provides a very detailed description of how the various members of the Guicciardini family made their fortunes, how their riches were invested, and how their wealth fluctuated over the course of time. A briefer but excellent article several years later by Randolph Starn furnishes a useful supplement to Goldthwaite's groundbreaking work by focusing upon the economic relationships between Francesco and his brothers.[22]

While attention was being focused upon Guicciardini's biography and family background with fresh discoveries from the archives, two Italian works and one German study offered rich hypotheses concerning the development of Guicciardini's thought and new documentation on the political and cultural context of his works. In an important book, Vittorio De Caprariis moved away from the traditional emphasis upon the *Ricordi* and examined the slow progression in Guicciardini's life from minor political dialogues and trea-

tises or urban histories to the *Storia d'Italia.*[23] De Caprariis was perhaps the first scholar to direct our attention to the fact that Guicciardini was a serious political thinker with concrete proposals for constitutional changes in Florence and that his subsequent fame as a historian was more the result of a "conversion" from politics to history brought about by the course of events rather than by choice. In much the same vein, Raffaello Ramat published another masterful overview of Guicciardini's works, emphasizing their political content and Guicciardini's efforts to reconstruct the Florentine constitution.[24] For Ramat, however, the *Ricordi* remain a crucial moment in the intellectual formation of the historian. In fact, the *Storia d'Italia* represents an enlargement of the negative vision of the maxims, a grandiose work which gives historical credibility to the cynical principles collected in the writer's private notebooks never intended for publication. For Ramat, the structure of the *Storia d'Italia* consciously presents the fate of Renaissance Italy in a tragic light, and it is this stoic perspective upon human history which constitutes Guicciardini's originality.

Without any doubt, however, the most important book from the decade immediately following the war must be considered Rudolf von Albertini's *Das florentinische Staatsbewusstsein im Übergang von der Republik zum Prinzipat* (1955), which received an Italian translation only in 1970 and remains still unavailable in English.[25] With a masterful sense of perspective, von Albertini traced the evolution of the city of Florence from the rule of Lorenzo de' Medici and Savonarola through the republic of Machiavelli and Soderini to the establishment of a Medici dynasty. In the process, von Albertini provided the most exhaustive analysis to date (including an appendix of documents of approximately 200 pages) of the constitutional debates and political issues which motivated all historians or political theorists of the period, Guicciardini included. As a result of von Albertini's study, much of which had traditionally passed for original thinking in the works of a Machiavelli or a Guicciardini, for example, was now seen as part of a larger constitutional debate in which other voices had interesting, if not so celebrated, points of view. Furthermore, von Albertini's comprehensive survey of the interrelationship between the historical events and the many treatises, histories, discourses, and dialogues the period produced enabled the scholar to distinguish true originality from mere reflections on preexisting traditions in political philosophy. Without his work, the studies of Felix Gilbert or J. G. A. Pocock—to mention only a few scholars who followed in his footsteps—would have been impossible.

Following von Albertini's lead, a number of important studies by F. Gilbert, Emanuella Lugnani Scarano, and J. G. A. Pocock focused upon Guicciardini's relationship to the political crises of his times and their influences on his various historical or political writings.

Gilbert's *Machiavelli and Guicciardini: Politics and History in Sixteenth-Century Florence* may, in some respects, be said to represent a worthy successor to De Sanctis' earlier juxtaposition of these two great Florentine writers.[26] Gilbert viewed the period which produced both writers as one of recurrent political crises, to which each theorist responded in profoundly different ways. Gilbert's interpretation of Guicciardini thus results from a wider vision of sixteenth-century Florentine and European politics. Primarily interested in Guicciardini's progress from his early works to his mature historical masterpiece, the *Storia d'Italia,* Gilbert believes that Guicciardini was the first important historian to reject using history to demonstrate general rules of conduct. Since history did not reveal a pattern for him, the historian could turn his attention to factual correctness and, more importantly, to constant change. As a result, history began to take on its own, independent meaning. Thus Guicciardini serves as both the last great expression of classical historiography and the first great work of modern historiography.

Interested as he was in Guicciardini's role as historiographer, Gilbert paid little attention to the minor political treatises, dialogues, and maxims. These too-often neglected "minor" works, as well as the *Ricordi,* were treated in much greater detail, following von Albertini's lead, by E. Lugnani Scarano in several important articles,[27] in a major new critical edition of Guicciardini's writings,[28] and in a volume she contributed to the prestigious critical history of Italian literature published by Laterza.[29] The article on the *Dialogo del reggimento di Firenze,* by far the most penetrating and lengthy study devoted to one of Guicciardini's minor works, discovers in it great originality, in particular a striking depersonalization of political theory with a parallel heightened attention to the role of social institutions. While the dialogue fails to predict the rise of a hereditary principality in Florence under the Medici, it nevertheless employs historical data in an attempt to fashion political institutions to suit changing times, and in this sense it is one of the most original works of the period. In Scarano's second and equally lengthy examination of the various stages of the maxims and their relationship to Guicciardini's other works, her findings trace accurately the various stylistic and philosophical shifts in Guicciardini's writing and thinking, all of which are mirrored in the different versions of the *Ricordi.* In particular, Scarano sees a progression in the revision of the maxims towards a maximum of autonomy for the individual maxim and an increasing abstraction of thought (as opposed to practical advice or historical hypotheses). Thus, following Gilbert's view of the *Storia d'Italia* as a work of contemplation rather than of action, Scarano concludes that the *Ricordi* follow the same pattern: they reflect Guicciardini's state of mind as he moved from concrete, practical political treatises suggesting institutional reforms to a more pessimistic and philosophical view of

history as an end in itself, since history revealed no didactic patterns of any significant use to the contemporary politician. For Scarano, then, Guicciardini becomes one of the most modern of all Renaissance writers in his renunciation of action and his philosophical pessimism. In addition to these excellent scholarly essays, Scarano provided the texts of the minor works along with the more famous maxims and the history of Italy in an easily accessible edition. Her volume in the Laterza history of Italian literature devoted to Guicciardini and the other political thinkers of the period managed to expand the role normally devoted to Guicciardini in literary histories.

If Gilbert and Scarano aimed to set Guicciardini and his works within broader Italian political and historical contexts, *The Machiavellian Moment: Florentine Political Thought and the Atlantic Republican Tradition* by J. G. A. Pocock represents one of the most ambitious attempts at synthesis in the last several decades of Renaissance scholarship.[30] By "Machiavellian moment," Pocock means not only the historical period in which Machiavellian theories appeared but also, in a broader sense, the epoch when early modern Europeans saw the republic, and the citizen's role in it, as a major problem in historical understanding. This "problem" arose in a specific moment in time during which the republic confronted its temporal finitude, while attempting to remain stable in a context of constantly changing historical events. What is most remarkable about Pocock's book is that he convincingly demonstrates that Florentine republican thinkers, such as Machiavelli, Guicciardini, and Giannotti, began a chain of ideas which would influence republican theories not only in England (James Harrington) but also in colonial America (Jefferson, Adams). Moreover, the Machiavellian tradition (of which Guicciardini was an important element) was always a major republican aspect in English or American political theory, even though it has been consistently overlooked in favor of the social contract theories established by Hobbes and Locke. Pocock sees Guicciardini's early *Discorso di Logrogno* and the later *Dialogo del reggimento di Firenze* as crucial documents in the history of the intellectual tradition, particularly in regard to the formation of new definitions of political liberty and the author's discussions of how the various social classes may be represented in different institutions of the state.

So much important material unearthed in the archives and so many novel intellectual perspectives are at the basis of several recent studies which attempt to draw together these various materials within a single work. Two such attempts at a general synthesis include my own *Francesco Guicciardini*[31] and *Francesco Guicciardini: The Historian's Craft* by Mark Phillips.[32] My brief monograph on Guicciardini seeks to provide a synthesis of what was known about Guicciardini to the date of publication and to offer a guide to all his works.

In particular, my contention is that Guicciardini's literary style has been long overlooked (although generally admired), and thus the monograph tries to turn the discusion towards such topics as the structure of the maxims, the portrait sketch in the historical writings, and the like. M. Phillips provides an even closer reading of the major and minor texts by Guicciardini. His work begins with the assumption that histories are a literary genre and that historical writing is essentially narrative rather than informative or rhetorical. Taken together, then, these two studies afford the reader a compendium of biographical or historical data now regarded as accurate by most Guicciardini scholars along with a perspective on Guicciardini's qualities as a stylist that political historians often overlook. Both books reflect an even more general tendency in the literature on political writings of the period, especially Machiavelli's, that has recently focused a great deal of attention upon the various rhetorical strategies, terminologies, and narrative techniques of writers usually considered only for their political theories. This perspective has yielded some impressive results, such as the very suggestive recent article by Joseph Markulin on the form of Guicciardini's maxims and the very notion of a book,[33] or several of the essays contributed to this special Guicciardini issue.[34] Finally, mention must be made of a major survey by Erich Cochrane, *Historians and Historiography in the Italian Renaissance,*[35] as ambitious in its attention to detail and to the countless variety of Renaissance histories as Pocock's work was in its chronological sweep. Cochrane returns, in a sense, to the historical tradition established by the German scholars of historiography in the nineteenth century (Fueter, in particular). His comprehensive analysis of the various forms of history written in the Italian Renaissance now makes it possible to set Guicciardini against a clearer picture of his intellectual context, his peers, and the methodologies of historiography current in his day.

One could not accurately assess Guicciardini's critical reputation today without paying some attention to the various translations which have recently appeared. Outside of Italy, there is little question that Guicciardini's reputation (even among historians who normally know Italian well) has improved as adequate texts in English translation have become available. Unlike so many of the thoroughly unreliable translations of Machiavelli's works (some still reprinted from nineteenth-century and early twentieth-century editions), Guicciardini's fate among his translators has been remarkably fortunate. All of the translators of Guicciardini have been well versed in the language of the period as well as in its history. As a result, most of the existing translations of Guicciardini are excellent. Cecil Grayson's anthology of the **Storia d'Italia** and of the **Storie fiorentine** (regrettably now out of print) offers selections from these two major historical works.[36] An even more remarkable collection of Guicciardini's works, edited by Cecil

Grayson and translated by Margaret Grayson, *Selected Writings,* included not only the **Ricordi** but also the much rarer **Ricordanze** and the **Considerazioni sui 'Discorsi' del Machiavelli,**[37] all in their entirety. It, too, is now out of print. The late Mario Domandi produced two superb translations—one of the maxims (which included not only the final C version but also the other earlier versions as well),[38] and another of the complete **Storie fiorentine.**[39] Both volumes contained impeccable annotations and critical introductions (the edition of the maxims is still available in an inexpensive paper edition). Finally, mention must be made of Sidney Alexander's excellent partial translation of the **Storia d'Italia.** Profusely illustrated and handsomely printed, it was recently reissued by the Princeton University Press.[40] Thus, American students and scholars have access to excellent translations of the maxims and the most important sections of the **Storia d'Italia** in paperback editions that are reliable as well as readable.

While important archival discoveries may still surprise us in the future, there is little question that the major outlines of Guicciardini's career and works are now clear. Perhaps Guicciardini's writings will never arouse the passionate controversy that has always attended the study of Machiavelli, but the debate over the significance of Guicciardini's historical methodology, his political ideology, and his narrative style remains far from terminated today.[41] It is in this regard that the special issue of *Annali d'Italianistica* devoted to Guicciardini represents an important and very timely reassessment of Francesco Guicciardini's significance for Italian Renaissance culture.

Notes

[1] *Guichardin: Historien et homme d'état italien au XVIe siècle* (Marseille: Librairie Générale, 1862).

[2] See Francesco De Sanctis, *Saggi critici* (Bari: Laterza, 1963), 3:1-25; or his *Storia della letteratura italiana* (Milano: Feltrinelli, 1970), 493-550; for an excellent reconsideration of De Sanctis' judgment of Guicciardini by the foremost Guicciardini scholar of this century, see Roberto Ridolfi, "L'uomo Guicciardini cento anni dopo 'L'uomo del Guicciardini,'" *Studi guicciardiniani* (Firenze: Olschki, 1978), 225-43.

[3] Leopold von Ranke, *Zur Kritik neuerer Geschichtsschreiber* (Leipzig: Reimer, 1824).

[4] Eduard Fueter, "Guicciardini als Historiker," *Historische Zeitschrift* 78 (1897); and *Geschichte der neueren Historiographie* (München: Oldenbourg, 1911; Italian trans. Napoli, 1943-44).

[5] *François Guichardin: Sa vie publique et sa pensée politique* (Paris: Picart, 1926).

[6] *Guicciardini* (Firenze: La Nuova Italia, 1939).

[7] *Francesco Guicciardini* (Torino: UTET, 1941).

[8] *Machiavelli e Guicciardini* (Firenze: Sansoni, 1945).

[9] (New York: K. Otto, 1936); Italian trans., *Francesco Guicciardini e la fortuna dell'opera sua* (Firenze: Olschki, 1949).

[10] "La genesi della *Storia d'Italia,*" *La bibliofilia* 40-(1938); revised as *La genesi della 'Storia d'Italia'* (Firenze: Olschki, 1939), and reprinted in *Opuscoli di storia, letteratura e di erudizione* (Firenze: Bibliopolis, 1942), 175-201. The definitive and revised version of this key essay can now be found in Ridolfi's *Studi guicciardiniani* 79-130, together with Ridolfi's collected essays on Guicciardini.

[11] "Per una compiuta edizione dei *Ricordi politici e civili del Guicciardini,*" *Studi di filologia italiana* 3-(1932):163-96.

[12] "Le quattro redazioni dei *Ricordi* del Guicciardini (contributo allo studio della formazione del linguaggio e dello stile guicciardiniano)," *Civiltà moderna* 13-(1941):105-24, 247-71.

[13] *Ricordi,* ed. critica (Firenze: Sansoni, 1951).

[14] *Dialogo e discorsi del reggimento di Firenze* (Bari: Laterza, 1932); *Ricordi* (Bari: Laterza, 1933); *Scritti autobiografici e rari* (Bari: Laterza, 1936); *Scritti politici e ricordi* (Bari: Laterza, 1933); *Storie fiorentine* (Bari: Laterza, 1931).

[15] *Storia d'Italia,* 5 vols. (Bari: Laterza, 1929).

[16] *Carteggi di Francesco Guicciardini,* eds. Roberto Palmarocchi and Pier Giorgio Ricci (Napoli: Istituto Storico Italiano, 1938-), 17 vols. to date. The remaining volumes of this vast undertaking will be edited by Pierre Jodogne, and details may be found in his essay "La ripresa dei lavori intorno ai carteggi di Francesco Guicciardini," *La bibliofilia* 83(1981):161-64.

[17] *Le cose fiorentine ora per la prima volta pubblicate* (Firenze: Olschki, 1945).

[18] *Vita di Francesco Guicciardini* (Roma: Belardetti, 1960; rev. ed. rpt. Milano: Rusconi, 1982; Eng. trans. New York: Knopf, 1968).

[19] Paolo Guicciardini, *Le traduzioni inglesi della storia guicciardiniana* (Firenze: Olschki, 1951); *Le traduzioni francesi della storia guicciardiniana* (Firenze: Olschki, 1950); and P. Guicciardini and Emilio Doni, *Le antiche case ed il palazzo dei Guicciardini in Firenze* (Firenze: Olschki, 1952).

[20] "The *Storie fiorentine* and the *Memorie di famiglia* by Francesco Guicciardini," *Rinascimento* 4(1953):171-225.

[21] *Private Wealth in Renaissance Florence: A Study of Four Families* (Princeton: Princeton Univ. Press, 1968).

[22] "Francesco Guicciardini and His Brothers," in Anthony Molho and John A. Tedeschi, eds., *Renaissance Studies in Honor of Hans Baron* (Dekalb: Northern Illinois Univ. Press, 1971), 409-44.

[23] *Francesco Guicciardini: Dalla politica alla storia* (Bari: Laterza, 1950).

[24] *Il Guicciardini e la tragedia d'Italia* (Firenze: Olschki, 1953).

[25] (Bern: Francke AG Verlag, 1955; Ital. trans. Torino: Einaudi, 1970.)

[26] (Princeton: Princeton Univ. Press, 1965; rev. ed. New York: Norton, 1983.)

[27] "Il dialogo *Del reggimento di Firenze* di Francesco Guicciardini," *Giornale storico della letteratura italiana* 145(1968):232-92, 523-60; and "Le redazioni dei *Ricordi* e la storia del pensiero guicciardiniano dal 1512 al 1530," *Giornale storico della letteratura italiana* 14(1970):181-259.

[28] *Opere di Francesco Guicciardini,* 3 vols. (Torino: UTET, 1970-81).

[29] *Guicciardini e la crisi del Rinascimento,* Letteratura italiana Laterza, 23 (Bari: Laterza, 1979).

[30] (Princeton: Princeton Univ. Press, 1975.)

[31] (Boston: Twayne, 1976.)

[32] (Toronto: Univ. of Toronto Press, 1977.)

[33] "Guicciardini's *Ricordi* and the Idea of a Book," *Italica* 59(1982):296-305.

[34] See especially the articles dealing with Guicciardini's style by P. M. Forni, F. Chiappelli, and also N. S. Struever.

[35] (Chicago: Univ. of Chicago Press, 1981.)

[36] *The History of Italy and History of Florence* (New York: Washington Square, 1964).

[37] (Oxford: Oxford Univ. Press, 1965.)

[38] *Maxims and Reflections (Ricordi)* (New York: Harper & Row, 1965; rpt. Philadelphia: Univ. of Pennsylvania Press, 1972).

[39] *The History of Florence* (New York: Harper & Row, 1970).

[40] *The History of Italy* (New York: Macmillan, 1969; rpt. Princeton: Princeton Univ. Press, 1984).

[41] For a rather different assessment of Guicciardini criticism in the last century, see the recent review article by Marco Santoro, "Guicciardini nel quinto centenario della nascita: Problemi e prospettive," *Forum Italicum* 17(1983):278-87.

Donald J. Wilcox (essay date 1984)

SOURCE: "Guicciardini and the Humanist Historians," *Annali d'Italianistica*, Vol. 2, 1984, pp. 19-33.

[*In the following essay, Wilcox places Guicciardini within the tradition of Renaissance humanist historians but stipulates that Guicciardini's writings differ from the rest thanks to his understanding both of individual psychology and of the complex, changing connections between historical events.*]

Guicciardini's relation to the tradition of humanist historiography remains problematic despite considerable study over the past thirty years. Early attempts to dissociate Guicciardini were flawed by misunderstanding of the fundamental traits of humanist historiography. In 1950, Vittorio De Caprariis accepted a long-standing interpretation of the humanists when he saw them as pale and inaccurate reflections of the vernacular chroniclers, lacking interest in detail or critical method that would make them good sources for modern historians.[1] De Caprariis stressed Guicciardini's departure from the humanists and saw in the *Storia d'Italia* the qualities of careful research and attention to detail that have given the work such a reputation among positivist historians. De Caprariis acknowledged that some of Guicciardini's earlier works, such as his first history of Florence, resembled the humanist histories, but he felt that they were works of political theory rather than true history.

De Caprariis' tendency to evaluate the humanists from the perspective of modern historical standards made their relation to Guicciardini's work intrinsically hard to grasp. In 1965, with Felix Gilbert's *Machiavelli and Guicciardini,* we come to a new perspective. Gilbert asked what the humanists themselves regarded as the important goals of historical writing. Basing his analysis partly on the humanist historians but more directly on such writings as Pontano's *Actius,* which formulated a theoretical basis for historical writing, Gilbert showed that the differences between humanist histories and modern ones lay in a different conception of the goals of history. Pontano, who drew on such classical authors as Cicero, saw history as moral and literary in its aims. He saw the historian primarily as an artist and a teacher, not a researcher. History should entertain, teach, and inspire its readers to right conduct.[2]

Because of these goals the humanists were only secondarily interested in the detailed analysis and comparison of primary sources that constitute the basis of modern historiography. Most chose to follow one source at a time, adding details from other sources or public records only when necessary to strengthen a particular moral lesson or to create a certain literary effect. Their interest in classical models was thus not an unfortunate diversion from true history; it was an essential ingredient in the fulfillment of their aims. As part of their desire to entertain and inspire, they looked to classical models to organize and present their material. In light of Gilbert's understanding of the humanists, many of Guicciardini's characteristic traits, such as his adoption of annalistic form, his use of set battle pieces, and his inclusion of orations, were all consonant with humanist historical theory.

These similarities of approach notwithstanding, Gilbert found that in many ways the *Storia d'Italia* departed from humanist canons of historical writing. Instead of the straightforward and clear moral lessons that Pontano prescribed, Guicciardini presented a complex and paradoxical picture of the events in which the traditional moral virtues were no longer valid supports to a successful political life. Where the humanists had used these virtues and vices to characterize individuals, Guicciardini considered self-interest to be so important that it over-powered all other considerations and became the primary characteristic of human nature (Gilbert 292). Gilbert did not argue that Guicciardini abandoned the moral function of history. On the contrary, he felt that the *Storia d'Italia* raised it to a new plane. Aware that self-interest had introduced a calculating and analytical element into any description of the past, Guicciardini at the same time acknowledged the power of fortune, of unpredictable and uncontrollable circumstances that brought the schemes of self-interested princes to naught. This realization produced not despair but a reaffirmation of the individual's value. Guicciardini sought to give his readers perspective on the ambitions and temptations of the world: "Thus although Guicciardini did not share the humanist view that history exemplifies general rules or guides man's behavior, he returned to the humanist concept of the moral value of history: history appeals to man to become conscious of his own intrinsic value" (Gilbert 300).

Gilbert assessed Guicciardini largely on the basis of humanist historical theory, but practicing historians during the fifteenth century implemented this theory in distinctive ways. My own study of the Florentine humanist histories of Bruni, Poggio, and Scala confirmed their compliance with the theories they found among classical authors, but it also revealed certain aspects of their work that could not be deduced from the theory. In particular, the inclusion of moral lessons did not lead to explicit moralizing or to a reliance on traditional moral categories. In fact they adopted a less moralizing tone than their chronicle sources and tried more often than not to avoid direct condemnation of personal vice.[3] To make history morally didactic the humanists did not moralize; instead they introduced an analytical element that was largely absent from their chronicle sources. They explained the political consequences of different types of behavior through an analysis of the psychological realities that underlay the political process. By this analysis they showed that all acts had consequences. Moral decisions depended on an awareness of all significant historical factors. Thus for the humanists all actions became morally significant, not just those that illustrated traditional virtues and vices.

Since the moral purpose of history was fulfilled by political analysis, that aspect of Guicciardini's work does not separate him from the humanists. It is instead the later historian's refusal to fix on a single analytical perspective that distinguishes him, a refusal that gives prominence in his narrative to sensory details and concrete images. Mark Phillips studied Guicciardini in light of this complex perspective that weakens the didacticism. Acknowledging the affinities between the analytical perspective of the *Storia d'Italia* and that of the humanist histories, Phillips saw less confidence in the moral lessons of history than did Gilbert and less of that concern for the individual dignity that redeemed him in Gilbert's eyes:

> The humanists bring to history a more sophisticated morality [than the chronicles] as well as more classical techniques of narrative. In a sense narrative was freed to respond to its own needs because human events no longer were required to mirror a non-historical world. Nonetheless, their didacticism was as strong as Villani's and this very didacticism, located now within history rather than cutting across it, helped to confer additional clarity on events. The moral and political lessons that humanist history teaches tie events together into well-understood units and give the reader a core of meaning to follow. But in Guicciardini the vestiges of didacticism have no such effect, and a multiplicity of overlapping explanations attaches to events. There are, of course, lessons in the *Storia d'Italia,* the wickedness of princes and the instability of human affairs being the most explicit. But the meaning of these "salutiferi document" is meditative rather than didactic, passive rather than active. They enlighten the reader but do not arm him.[4]

Gilbert and Phillips effectively documented the profound and complex influence of the humanist tradition on Guicciardini's *Storia d'Italia.* They showed that the influence cannot be dismissed as a purely formal or superficial one. It permeated his analysis, narrative technique, and deepest conceptions of his craft, and yet its results did not bring universal assent. The very complexity and paradoxical quality of his relationship with the humanists have preserved among many scholars a skepticism about the role of humanism in determining the structure and substance of the *Storia d'Italia.* Emanuella Lugnani Scarano argued in a recent study that Guicciardini's significance lay in the rejection of humanist norms of historical writing. She quoted with approval Fueter's characterization of him as the first analytical historian and saw the humanistic traits as stylistic elements that interfered with the important features of the work.[5] Furthermore, this interpretation appeared in the most recent general work on Italian Renaissance historiography, Eric Cochrane's *Historians and Historiography in the Italian Renaissance.* Cochrane minimized the influence of humanism, limiting it to the most formal of rhetorical devices. He even considered the format of the work—a study of all the political and military events in the various parts of Italy during a given period of time—to be without precedent, ignoring Flavio Biondo's *Decades,* which had so deeply influenced the later Florentine humanists, including Machiavelli.[6]

All these interpretations treat the Florentine humanist tradition in more or less static terms. This approach has the effect of exaggerating the role of Bruni, undoubtedly the most important and widely read of the Florentine humanist historians. The histories of Scala and Poggio lack the analytical rigor, the breadth of research, the interest in public documents, and the republican fervor that characterize Bruni's work. To look at the three works without regard for their context is to make such a judgment inevitable. Yet the context should not be ignored. The subsequent histories of Florence were not simply pale imitations of Bruni's; their authors had other goals and sought to modify his work in such a way as to achieve them. In the process they created a dynamic tradition of Florentine history, one whose coherence is not entirely clear from the histories themselves. That coherence becomes evident, however, in light of the achievements of Machiavelli, who wrote explicitly in the tradition of Bruni and Poggio and whose work represents a synthesis of trends clearly perceptible in fifteenth-century humanism.

Poggio and Scala departed from Bruni's historical method in two major ways. First, they introduced into the analytical structure questions and perspectives not part of Bruni's political-psychological approach. Second, they added to the *res gestae* sensory details and tangible elements which Bruni had excluded.[7] These changes were carried on by Machiavelli to produce a narrative in which personalities played a greater role than they had in Bruni's history and in which the narrative became more dynamic and expressive of real change.

With great single-mindedness Bruni had interrelated the psychological and political elements of the past into a single explanation of the roots of Florence's strength. His concern sprang from his commitment to republican institutions and his conviction that these institutions could be defended intellectually through constructing a picture of Florence's past. To teach these political lessons Bruni excluded other ones, especially those associated with traditional morality or with divine judgment. Later humanists were more concerned with these traditional virtues and vices. They tried to combine them with Bruni's political analysis to produce a narrative that would be useful and morally didactic to a readership less imbued with republican values.

Poggio's treatment of the Ciompi revolt shows clearly this difference. Bruni described the Ciompi revolt in purely political and psychological terms, tracing the spread of discontent and rebellion down through Florence's social classes. He sought to use the revolt to draw lessons about the difficulty of controlling rebellions once they begin.[8] When Poggio described the Ciompi revolt, he addressed that element of civil dissension, but he also expanded his analytical framework to include the issue of divine judgment, thus suggesting that the revolt may have been punishment for Florence's war with the papacy. He adduced in support of his point of view the fact that the eight in charge of the war all died in a brief time.[9]

Poggio did not intend these interpretations to exclude one another. He offered them as alternative views in the minds of those who lived through the revolt. Each view had a distinctive didactic effect, and both served the historian in putting his narrative to a variety of uses. He may have been unable to resolve the alternatives into one coherent picture, but that is less important than his accepting this ambivalence. He felt that the story took on added depth and richness—and thus greater truth—through the variety of views that it comprehended. This variety in turn led to the second major way in which Poggio departed from Bruni's model, the inclusion of sensory details and tangible features.

Bruni subordinated all other considerations to his analysis, excluding from his account any tangible details which might detract from its dignity or blur in the reader's mind the theoretical picture of the past. He thus ignored myriad details in the chronicle sources that were available to subsequent historians, should they wish to include them. Poggio told his story in more concrete terms. He gave detailed accounts of minor troop movements and foraging expeditions where Bruni was only interested in issues of strategy and tactics.[10]

Yet Poggio's narrative, while including tangible details that were not strictly necessary to convey the analytical lessons, exhibited little sensory value. It concentrated on the psychological and moral impact of events. When Giangaleazzo sent a flotilla of burning ships against a bridge on the Po, Poggio ignored the visual aspects of the event to concentrate on the spectators' impressions,[27] and his battle descriptions used indirect and general language to portray the actual clash of the troops (214). It is the third chancellor-historian of Florence, Bartolommeo Scala, who extended the attention Poggio payed to tangible elements into a genuine concern with the sensory impact of historical events. He evoked the odor of lilies to describe the origin of Florence's name, the sight of corpses floating in the cistern where Totila had thrown them, and even the visual effects of an eclipse.[11]

The elements in the development of Florentine humanist historiography during the fifteenth century—new didactic interests and more tangible subject matter—seem to lack focus when seen in themselves. It is easy to see how they are related, but not to grasp the overall effect. That becomes clear when Machiavelli is seen as a part of this tradition. His history of Florence carried on both these trends. More stongly committed to Bruni's political analysis than the late fifteenth-century humanists, he nevertheless added several other perspectives, highlighted by the prefaces he wrote for the early books.[12] He took from the chronicle sources many details ignored by the humanists and integrated them into the narrative, giving his account a vitality and immediacy that theirs lacked.

In Machiavelli's work these characteristics produced an important result that constituted a major event in Western historiography. Machiavelli presented a new approach to change, one that expressed change through concrete events in the narrative and tied it with the personalities in the historical drama.[13] This achievement had remained embryonic in former humanist historical writing. The humanists avoided the simple moral characterization of the chronicles, but their concentration of psychological realities left the personalities one-dimensional, without deep interaction with the historical events. The character traits and the events remained on separate planes, without any real influence on one another. Poggio, for instance, characterized individuals by dominant traits which rose and fell with events but suffered no real change in relation to one another. He defined Giovanni Visconti, for instance, by ambition, and treated specific events by describing their effects on this trait. The conquest of Genoa increased it; the realization that he could conquer no more decreased it (Poggio 198, 207). Even Visconti's death is described as a decrease in ambition.[14] But Poggio portrayed no dynamic relation between the Milanese leader's character and the events, which, in the narrative, did not cause Visconti to take on other traits and feelings, nor did his feelings give new directions or important dimensions to the events.

Bruni achieved a higher degree of subtlety in portraying Giangaleazzo as a devious character with hidden motives, but the greed that underlay his conduct overshadowed the subtlety, and the motives themselves did not take on specific substance. Nor did Giangaleazzo undergo change. Fraud and deceit remained his basic political tools, from his first usurpation of Milan by tricking his uncle (9:239) to the final oration of Bruni's history, where the Florentines stressed to the Venetians the dangerous contrast between Giangaleazzo's deed and words (12:285-87).

Machiavelli added complexity to his humanist presentation of character. He saw both a greater variety of motives and a more intricate relation between historical events and personal character. Where Bruni and Poggio saw constant states of character behind Visconti policy, Machiavelli saw change: "Costui [Giangaleazzo] credette potere divenire re di Italia con la forza, come gli era diventato duca di Milano con lo inganno."[15] Where Bruni found in Michele di Lando's *virtus* the cause of the city's salvation from the tumult of the Ciompi, Machiavelli gave to this virtue such specific traits as prudence, kindness, and goodness (3.17:152), but described his specific behavior in ways that seem more illustrative of cruelty or unrestrained anger than of virtue.[16]

This interplay between character and events gave to Machiavelli's narrative a dynamic quality that the humanists' lacked, since it allowed him to portray a meaningful interrelationship between the events and the psychological states that underlay them. Machiavelli, however, did not present his individuals developmentally. Though events had a definite impact on their psychological states in the sense that a given character had meaning only through specific acts, the character itself did not change. That was the achievement of Guicciardini, whose narrative built upon the previous development of Florentine historical writing to create individuals who experienced real change and whose character was meaningfully enmeshed with the events. For the humanists, constancy and change were real parts of the narrative only at the level of general events, where psychological states changed in such a way as to reflect general historical patterns. For Guicciardini constancy and change permeated the individuals; only through them did the events become dynamic.

Discussions of Guicciardini's treatment of individuals have tended to focus on his description of the Medici. The characterization of Lorenzo, which begins the *Storia d'Italia,* provides insight into Guicciardini's changing interpretation of politics, as he moves from the Lorenzo of his earlier works. The two Medici popes interacted with one another during their own lives;

consequently, they gave Guicciardini an opportunity to explore the differences among characters and show how these differences affected the historical process in different ways.[17] The following analysis will focus on his treatment of Alexander VI and Julius II. With those popes he was first of all confronted with characters more historical than the later ones, more removed from his own time and without the degree of personal contact he enjoyed with the Medici. At the same time, they were directly involved in the story, unlike Lorenzo, whom he used as a symbol of a more peaceful time.

The popes' status as elected princes was important to Guicciardini as he endowed individuals with the psychological dimensions the humanist had found in political realities. Their elections depended on the perceptions of the electors and thus connected them more immediately than hereditary monarchs with general characteristics of the time in which they were elected. But as princes they made personal decisions that effected change directly. To explain their elections Guicciardini brought together these personal and political factors; he combined inherent psychological characteristics, the memory of past events, and the reputation created by their previous behavior.

In Alexander's case Guicciardini introduced the historical context by observing that Alexander could not have succeeded in his simony without help from such corrupt members of the curia as Ascanio Sforza.[18] He raised the issue of reputation by describing the effect of Alexander's election on others. King Ferdinand of Naples, who did not even cry at the death of his children, shed tears at the election of such a pope, who would bring ruin to Italy and Christendom. Only after raising these issues of historical context and reputation did the historian present the inherent character of the new pope. "Perché in Alexandro sesto . . . fu solerzia e sagacità singolare, consiglio eccellente, efficacia a persuadere meravigliosa, e a tutte le faccende gravi sollecitudine e destrezza incredibili; ma erano queste virtù avanzate di grande intervallo da' vizi: costumi oscenissmi, non sincerità non vergogna non verità non fede non religione, avarizia insaziabile, ambizione immoderata, crudeltà più che barbara e ardentissima cupidità di esaltare in qualunque modo i figliuoli i quali erano molti" (1.2:12). This mixture of political virtues and private vices would hardly fit into any conventional schema of character. Because he already grounded the traits in their historical context and indicated the reputation they had produced, they remained attached to the events. Alexander's virtues and vices are not simply external means to explain what happens—as Bruni had used Giangaleazzo's viciousness—nor are they mere grounds for moral condemnation. They are part of the story as a whole, as real as the events themselves.

But Alexander is not simply a collection of general traits wedded to historical circumstances. He is also an individual, whose reality cannot be fully explained by what has happened to him, and whose personality possesses inherited traits. One of the most important precipitating factors in the quarrels which eventually brought the French into Italy was Fernando's attempt to secure control over some castles that had been in the possession of one of Innocent VIII's children. Fernando sought these castles partly because he remembered the long history of troubles with the papacy over the border between his land and theirs, but he was also moved by "il timore che in Alessandro non fusse ereditaria la cupidità e l'odio di Calisto terzo pontefice, suo zio" (1.3:16).

Guicciardini used a similar technique to introduce Julius II, describing first the election and singling out its salient feature, in this case the rapidity and near unanimity of the decision (6.5:565). As with Alexander, Guicciardini then gave concrete form to this peculiarity by describing the impression other people had of the new pope. Although many were surprised at the easy election of a pope reputed to be so difficult and restless, Julius had during his long cardinalate displayed a magnificence and a greatness of spirit which accumulated for him a reputation not only as a man of great power and authority but also as a defender of the dignity of the Church. This reputation made more effective the promises he made to his supporters. Just as Alexander's greed and obscenity took on historical substance in the reaction of his enemy Ferrante, so Guicciardini validated the picture of Julius by quoting his most bitter enemy, Alexander: "Perché [Julius] aveva lungamente avuto nome tale d'uomo libero e veridico che Alessandro sesto, inimico suo tanto acerbo, mordendolo nell'altre cose, confessava lui essere uomo verace" (6.5:566).

Two features are particularly significant in Guicciardini's use of individuals. First, he brought the process of real change into the substance of the personality of his individuals. By contrast, in Machiavelli's history men work real change through personal intervention in the course of events, but they themselves do not undergo important changes. Secondly, through the description of individuals, Guicciardini integrates moral and political elements into a single narrative. Both features arise from his initial integration of psychological traits with historical contexts, and both carry on developments within the humanist historical tradition.

The humanists took emotions the vernacular chroniclers had limited to individuals and ascribed them to groups, thus giving a new explanation and pattern to political change. Especially useful in this regard were the emotions of fear and hatred. Bruni explained the overthrow of Walter of Brienne in 1343 as a change among the Florentines of fear into hatred.[19] Machiavelli followed Bruni in interpreting the overthrow through the same change in psychological states, although he

embedded this change more fully into the context of concrete events (2.26-27:108-15). In the *Prince* Machiavelli wrote on the relation of these two emotions, and showed that a prince should be feared but not hated. But with both Bruni and Machiavelli the change remained generalized in the sense that its most fundamental psychological aspects were not connected to specific people. The individuals did not change, only the political unit did.

Guicciardini returned these psychological states to the individuals, but by fully integrating their emotions and motives in the historical context he maintained the reality of change at both levels. His technique can best be seen in his explanation for changes during the pontificate of Julius II, a pope whose dramatic political reversals, especially his abandonment of the League of Cambrai, startled his contemporaries and fundamentally upset the diplomatic order of Italy. In the **Storia d'Italia** Julius' policy is not inexplicable; it revolves around changing states of feeling, each responding to historical circumstances. Constancy and change become inseparable parts of a single personality, whose mutation reinforces integrity and whose identity transcends any abstract collection of traits or specific set of historical circumstances.

The foundation of Julius' personality lies in that greatness of soul with which Guicciardini explained his election to the papacy. By avoiding the specific vices and virtues he had ascribed to Alexander, Guicciardini made it possible to include within this greatness of soul a number of conflicting feelings, in particular hatred and fear, which were particularly useful. Since fear and hatred have specific objects, he could attach them directly to actual historical situations. In this manner Guicciardini created a dynamic picture of Julius' soul in which changes are real but comprehensible within a specific context. At one point early in his pontificate, Julius, after long negotiations, finally agreed to release Caesar Borgia from prison and openly proclaimed the release in consistory. One would expect him to observe his promise. "Ma altra era la mente del pontefice; il quale . . . avea in animo di prolungare la sua liberazione, o per timore che, liberato, operasse che 'l castellano di Furlì negasse di dare la rocca o per la memoria delle ingiurie ricevute dal padre e da lui o per l'odio che ragionevolmente gli portava ciascuno" (6.10:597).

Three factors take shape within the *animo* of Julius to produce the emotion of fear which directly explains his conduct. First, his fear is stimulated by an immediate danger—the loss of Forlì. Second, it is grounded in memories of events that are unspecified in this passage but remain fixed in the reader's mind from the previous narrative of Alexander's reign. Third, he fears another psychological state in the *animi* of others, a hatred that is a reasonable response to the relationship between the Borgia and the Della Rovere.

Julius' greatness of soul constitutes his basic reality, never changing and always providing the integrity and constancy of his personality. Apparent departures from this trait are explained by specific historical circumstances which hid or delayed it, but never destroyed it. All marvelled when Julius, with such a reputation for ambition and restlessness, proved so passive in hesitating to join Louis' attack on the Venetians: "Ma in Giulio era intenzione molto diversa; e deliberato di superare l'espettazione conceputa, aveva atteso e attendeva, contro alla consuetudine della sua pristina magnanimità, ad accumulare con ogni studio somma grandissima di pecunia, acció che alla volontà che aveva di accendere guerra fusse aggiunto la facoltà e il nervo di sostenerla" (7.1:634). Here Guicciardini showed Julius' will, which preserved its inherent ambition and great designs, but manipulated the external circumstances in preparation for expressing its true object.

But the emotions that dominate Julius' *animo* are fear and hatred. In his description of the pope's career, Guicciardini presented his complex and often contradictory policy as a relationship between these emotions, either within his own soul, or between Julius and other political elements. The historian used fear and hatred to present the dramatic changes in Italian politics during the war of the League of Cambrai. He saw them changing within Julius' soul, as the original fear of the French produced hatred, an emotion whose strength overcame his fear and led him to focus all of his energies on driving the French out of the peninsula.

In his earliest relations with the French, Julius was affected most by fear and suspicion. When he broke off talks and went back to Rome, he did so partly because of the renewal of his suspicions of the Cardinal of Rouen and partly because of the fear the king would not receive him if they met ("forse concorrendo l'una e l'altra cagione" 7.5:659). Julius' fear and suspicion did not remain unmixed with hatred for long. When Bologna was reinforced against his will, he blamed the king and, "transportato non meno dall'odio che dal sospetto," he accused the king of exciting the disturbances in Genoa as a pretext to attack the pope (7.7:670). But at this point the growing hatred for the king did not yet have the strength to overcome other fears. The memory of ancient quarrels between popes and emperors and the realization that the causes for those quarrels still existed, made him fear the Emperor Maximilian. Dissuaded from an open break with Louis, he incited Maximilian against the Venetians to increase the power of the League (8.1:723).

Throughout the formation of the League, fear of the French remained an important factor in Julius' decisions, conflicting with his animosity to the Venetians: "Maggiore dubitazione era nel pontefice, combattendo in lui, secondo la sua consuetudine, da una parte il desiderio di ricuperare le terre di Romagna e lo sdegno contro a' viniziani e dall'altra il timore del re di Francia" (8.1:727). Fear and suspicion of the French induced Julius to receive the Venetians after the battle of Ghiradadda and to consider pardoning them (8.7:761-62). But soon important changes occurred in the relation among these emotions in the pope's soul. Gradually hatred overcame his fear of the French, and, inspired by this hatred, Julius embarked on a new policy of reconciliation with the Venetians and explusion of the French from Italy.

Guicciardini showed the specific historical circumstances that first brought Julius to hate the French more strongly than he feared them. The first issue where Guicciardini addressed the change was a quarrel between Julius and Louis over the appointment to the see of Provence. Julius seemed to acquiesce in the settlement, but the quarrel had caused an important change: "Queste erano le cagioni apparenti degli sdegni suoi: ma per quello che si manifestò poi de' suoi pensieri, avendo nell'animo più alti fini, desiderava ardentissimamente, o per cupidità di gloria o per occulto odio contro al re di Francia o per desiderio della libertà de genovesi, che 'l re perdesse quel che possedeva in Italia" (8.12:800). A fundamental change in policy is intimated here, one that would throw Italy into chaos and realign the relations among the major powers. Guicciardini traced the change to a psychological state of hatred, mobilized by the quarrel but developing out of a previous series of events in which Julius had been led to fear the French.

Julius' change of policy was the direct result of transforming fear into hatred. In describing his reaction to the French support of Ferrara against the pope, Guicciardini gave full expression to this interpretation: "Aveva il pontefice propostosi nell'animo, e in questo fermati ostinatamente tutti i pensieri suoi, non solo di reintegrare la Chiesa di molti stati, i quali pretendeva appartenersegli, ma oltre a questo di cacciare il re di Francia di tutto quello possedeva in Italia; movendolo o occulta e antica inimicizia che avesse contro a lui o perché il sospetto avuto tanti anni si fusse convertito in odio potentissimo, o la cupidità della gloria di essere stato, come diceva poi, liberatore di Italia da' barbari" (9.5:849). Here Guicciardini combined constant emotions such as the love of glory with the historical context of the long record of quarrels with the French. The historical circumstances transformed fear into hatred; that psychological change altered the political relationships among the Italian powers. Political and personal change are brought together, founded on psychological states and tied to historical events.

Though transformation of fear to hatred explains his permanent hostility to the French, the vagaries of Julius' policy are too many to be so easily traced. Instead Guicciardini showed his behavior in the last years of his pontificate as a mixture of conflicting emotions, of which hatred for the French was always the foremost, but in which fear of the Emperor or of specific military threats often produced dramatic reversals and attempts to secure peace. At times he seemed to have no fear of the consequences of his actions. All marvelled that at a moment when he was threatened with a council and the armies of both the French and the Germans were in Italy, he should alienate himself from the Emperor (9.11:924). At other times fear became a more decisive factor. After the loss of Bologna, fearing that the victorious army might follow up its advantage, he asked for peace, "combattendo insieme nel petto suo la paura la pertinacia l'odio e lo sdegno" (9.18:937). His final pact with Aragon, a move which brought into Italy a power that would eventually dominate the peninsula, was the result of such a combination: "Dunque il pontefice, rimossi tutti i pensieri dalla pace, per gli odii e appetiti antichi, per la cupidità di Bologna, per lo sdegno e timore del concilio e finalmente per sospetto, se differisse più a deliberare, di essere abbandonato da tutti, [formed the pact]" (10.5:969).

Within the context of a constant hatred for the French, Julius' behavior emerges from Guicciardini's narrative as reflecting a constant struggle between hatred and fear, one in which historical circumstances determined the victor. After the battle of Ravenna, the pope listened to the various alternatives "con somma ambiguità e sospensione, e in modo che si potesse facilmente comprendere, combattere in lui da una parte l'odio lo sdegno e la pertinacia insolita a essere vinta o a piegarsi, dall'altra il pericolo e il timore" (10.14:1044). Events which Guicciardini characterizes as a turn in the wheel of fortune (10.14:1046) determined the results. With the removal of foreign troops from Romagna, the pope abandoned his fear, settled matters in Rome, called his own council, and moved to achieve his long-desired ends.

Constancy and change thus permeate the historical process at all levels in the *Storia d'Italia.* Individuals are presented in such a way as to reflect within themselves the psychological changes the humanists used in order to explain general political events. But the individuals remain dynamic. Beyond the state of hatred or fear lie other related feelings, which cause a wavering condition determined by external events, some of which are unpredictable while others fall into rational patterns of political discourse. Guicciardini blends the contingent with the analytical and the political with the moral in order to produce a historical narrative that fulfills the promise of the preceding century of historians.

By means of the second feature of his treatment of individuals, Guicciardini combines political analysis with traditional moral consideration within a single historical process. Here again, as was the case with his integration of personality into the process of change,

he carried on developments within the humanist tradition and brought them to new levels of realization. One of the moral issues he felt most deeply about was the ecclesiastical corruption that was so evident an element in the world around him. He used the personalities in his narrative to castigate this corruption, while at the same time analyzing its political effects. Ecclesiastical corruption was a moral scandal to be deplored in categorical terms; practical considerations, however, could not be ignored, since corruption was also a factor in Italy's political weakness and played a role in determining the course of the Italian wars.

The combination of these factors is clearest in his treatment of Alexander VI, whose personal immoralities and political successes fascinated and repelled Guicciardini. The Borgia pope's career raised vividly in his mind the question of the relationship between the personal and political facets of Alexander's character and the general scene of Italian life. In discussing how Alexander used his spiritual power, Guicciardini stressed that no one with Alexander's character and reputation could have acquired the papacy if the spiritual functions had been fulfilled and respected in the preceding period. At the same time, the historian felt that Alexander's obscene habits and greed for his children further eroded the spiritual position of the office in significant ways.

Guicciardini saw that the decline in spiritual power had a definite historical context. In speaking of Alexander's attempt to secure the support of the French to reassert papal control over Romagna, he reviewed the history of the states of the Church. In a long digression he explained how the popes, beginning with Peter, had gradually accumulated political power, first in order to support their spiritual functions, then as an end in itself. We learn that the most marked degeneration of spiritual power occurred in the period after the return of the popes to Rome from Avignon, when they could barely exist in Rome without help from secular rulers. After the return, succeeding popes gradually lost their memory of former troubles and began to live more as secular princes than as popes, reveling in luxury and private vice, pursuing the interests of their families at the expense of the spiritual interests of Christendom, and fomenting wars over secular gains rather than bringing peace (4.12:427-28).

Alexander was partly the victim of this general historical background and partly the cause of further decline in papal authority. To demonstrate this point, Guicciardini introduced into his narrative a variety of details which might not have concerned him had his focus been exclusively on political analysis. With his great talents at dissimulation and persuasion, the pope made use of all the traditional ceremonies and observances of the papacy. When he finally welcomed Charles VIII into the Vatican, he observed the customary marks of respect, allowing the king to kiss his cheek and present the water at the pontifical mass. He even commissioned a painting of the meeting to be hung in the Vatican (1.17:118-19). Receiving the victorious Consalvo di Cordova after the taking of Ostia, Alexander honored him with the traditional rose bestowed by the popes each year as a special mark of honor (3.11:311). Neither event fits easily into the Brunian model for history with its narrow focus on political happenings, though Poggio and Scala could easily have mentioned them. Here the ceremonies allowed Guicciardini to expand his scope to include his concerns about the misuse of the spiritual powers of the papacy.

Alexander's observance of the trappings of papal ceremony, however, could not overcome the scandal of his private life or his wanton disregard for moral issues. Guicciardini reinforced this point by describing the popular rumors around specific policies or actions of Alexander. When Prince Diem, the Sultan's brother, died after having been given over to Charles VIII, who wanted to use him in a crusade against the Turks, Alexander was believed to have poisoned him, either because the pope did not like being forced to surrender Diem due to his envy at Charles' glory, or because he feared that a successful crusade would create a movement to reform. At this point, Guicciardini comments that the affairs of the Church, "allontanatesi totalmente dagli antichi costumi, facevano ogni dì minore l'autorità della cristiana religione, tenendo per certo ciascuno che avesse a declinare molto più nel suo pontificato; il quale, acquistato con pessime arti, non fu forse giammai, alla memoria degli uomini, amministrato con peggiori" (2.3:156).

In the foregoing analysis Guicciardini employed the psychological and political tools of the humanists to show the effects of Alexander's behavior on his ability to use his spiritual powers. The result is clear and the events show the effects. When Alexander demanded that Charles either leave Italy or appear before him under threat of spiritual punishment, Guicciardini observed that the pope was following a course of action adopted by earlier popes. Adrian I had condemned Desiderius in the same fashion; at this time, however, "mancata la riverenza e la maestà che dalla santità della vita loro ne' petti degli uomini nascevano, era ridicolo sperare da costumi e esempli tanto contrari gli effetti medesimi" (2.11:116).

The ambiguity of Guicciardini's treatment is complex. On the one hand, Charles' disrespect arose only partly from Alexander's misdeeds, since it also depended on the papal abuse over the preceding century he had described earlier. On the other, Guicciardini was acutely aware that Alexander's sins were not always punished. He was surprised and shocked by the pope's success in his endeavors and the frequency with which people ignored his deviousness and trickery. As the pope's

body was carried through Rome, people flocked to see it, "non potendo saziarsi gli occhi d'alcuno di vedere spento un serpente che con la sua immoderata ambizione e pestifera perfidia, e con tutti gli esempli di orribile crudeltà di mostruosa libidine e di inaudita avarizia, vendendo senza distinzione le cose sacre e le profane, aveva attossicato tutto il mondo. Nondimeno era stato esaltato, con rarissima e quasi perpetua prosperità, dalla prima gioventù insino all'ultimo dì della vita sua, desiderando sempre cose grandissime e ottenendo più di quello desiderava" (6.4:555).

The combination of analysis and fortune that is so prominent a feature of the *Storia d'Italia* is thus also part of the development of humanist historiography. Guicciardini wedded the analytical concerns of Bruni to the interest in traditional moral categories found among the humanist historians of the late fifteenth century. He incorporated these into a single narrative style, organized along traditional annalistic lines, but conveying a complex web of personal and political realities. By bringing the personal and political elements of the story together with common psychological terms, expressed through concrete and vivid personal acts, he presented a narrative of change which supports his explicit description of human affairs as a sea swept by the winds.

Seen against the background of developments within the previous century and a half of humanist historical writing, Guicciardini takes on some familiar traits but loses none of his orginality and historical greatness. The categories of analysis which lie behind his explanation of events are those that would have been familiar to his readers and had been used by previous historians in their effort to broaden the basis of humanist history. Guicciardini's use of these categories, however, added a portrayal of individuals and a sense of change beyond anything previously achieved in that tradition and created also a new narrative structure which conveyed his insight into the dynamic quality of history.

Notes

[1] Vittorio De Caprariis, *Francesco Guicciardini: Dalla politica alla storia* (Bari: Laterza, 1950).

[2] Felix Gilbert, *Machiavelli and Guicciardini: Politics and History in Sixteenth-Century Florence* (Princeton: Princeton Univ. Press, 1965), 203-35.

[3] Donald Wilcox, *The Development of Florentine Humanist Historiography in the Fifteenth Century* (Cambridge: Harvard Univ. Press, 1969), 40-41.

[4] Mark Phillips, *Francesco Guicciardini: The Historian's Craft* (Toronto: Univ. of Toronto Press, 1977), 181-82. See also Phillips, "Machiavelli, Guicciardini,

and the Tradition of Vernacular Historiography in Florence," *American Historical Review* 84 (1979):86-105.

[5] Emanuella Lugnani Scarano, *Francesco Guicciardini,* La letteratura italiana: storia e testi, IV, Il Cinquecento: Dal Rinascimento alla Controriforma (Bari: Laterza, 1973), 4.2:245, 315.

[6] Eric Cochrane, *Historians and Historiography in the Italian Renaissance* (Chicago: Univ. of Chicago Press, 1981), 302-3.

[7] For a detailed discussion of these characteristics of the later humanist historians, see Wilcox, chapters 4, 5, and 6.

[8] "Cavenda vero maxime videntur principia seditionum inter primarios cives," Leonardo Bruni, Aretino, *Historiarum Florentini Populi Libri 12,* ed. E. Santini e C. di Pierro in *Rerum Italicarum Scriptores* (Città di Castello: S. Lapi, 1934), 19.3:224.

[9] Poggio Bracciolini, *Historia Florentina,* ed. J. Recanati, in *Rerum Italicarum Scriptores,* ed. L. Muratori (Milano: 1731), 20: 242-43.

[10] See for example his description of the expedition of the Britons into the Vallombrosa, Poggio 213.

[11] Bartolommeo Scala, *Historia Florentinorum* (Roma: 1677), 5, 35, 93.

[12] On the meaning of these prefaces see Felix Gilbert, "Machiavelli's *Istorie fiorentine:* An Essay in Interpretation," in *Studies on Machiavelli,* ed. Myron Gilmore (Firenze: Sansoni, 1972), 75-99.

[13] See Mark Phillips, "Machiavelli," and Donald Wilcox, "The Renaissance Sense of Time," in *Classical Rhetoric and Medieval Historiography,* ed. Ernst Breisach (Medieval Institute, forthcoming).

[14] "Mors peropportuna inanes curas illius et dominandi appetitum diremit," Poggio 209.

[15] Niccolò Machiavelli, *Istorie fiorentine,* in *Tutte le opere di Niccolò Machiavelli,* eds. Francesco Flora and Carlo Cordiè (Milano: Mondadori, 1960), 3.25:163. References are to book, chapter, and page.

[16] For example he turned the fury of the mob onto the hated official Nuto and stabbed several members of a delegation that came to negotiate with him in the Palazzo della Signoria.

[17] For an intelligent analysis of these individuals see Phillips, *Francesco Guicciardini* 157-68.

[18] Francesco Guicciardini, *Storia d'Italia,* ed. Silvana Seidel Menchi (Torino: Einaudi, 1971), 1.2:11. References are to book, chapter, and page.

[19] "Superante iam odio metum," 6:164.

Nancy S. Struever (essay date 1984)

SOURCE: "Proverbial Signs: Formal Strategies in Guicciardini's *Ricordi,*" *Annali d'Italianistica,* Vol. 2, 1984, pp. 94-109.

[*In the following essay, Struever suggests that Guicciardini presented his* Ricordi *as a set of proverbs in order to express important ethical ideas in a traditional and therefore intimate, accessible form.*]

As long ago as 1939, Felix Gilbert demonstrated the usefulness of a textual analysis of the moral-political discourse of the Renaissance. He argued that a fundamental political reorientation can be diagnosed in the alterations in the genre of advice or counsel, for example, in reading Machiavelli's *Prince* as a transformation of medieval and humanist "Mirrors for Princes."[1] Since then, of course, Quentin Skinner, appealing to the initiatives of analytic philosophy of language, has advocated a more sophisticated project: the formal redescription of the *Prince* as a series of "speech-acts." Yet the fundamental assumption remains the same: for both Gilbert and Skinner, the structure of political rhetoric reveals rhetoric as politics, discourse as action.[2] Since a traditional exercise in the definition of Florentine political thought has been the comparison of Machiavellian and Guicciardinian achievement, it seems to follow that a formal analysis of Guicciardini's political rhetoric would be useful. I shall argue that the *Ricordi,* the collection of observations, exhortations and maxims which presents a telling example of the state of the art of political and moral advice in Florence in the early sixteenth century, is central to the vital Guicciardinian difference. I shall also claim that the strength and unity of his differential contribution relates to the proverbial form of the *Ricordi.*

A major focus of modern scholarship on the *Ricordi* has been the definitive establishment of the texts of the five successive redactions of the maxims. These redactions, available in the 1951 critical edition of R. Spongano, include two very early lists of maxims of 1512, the second adding 16 new *ricordi* to the original 13; a much larger collection of 161 maxims, retaining only 8 from the 1512 lists, was produced in the period 1523-25; a fourth redaction of 1528, which contains all of the *ricordi* of 1512 as well as all of the previous collection, plus 12 new *ricordi;* and the final redaction of 1530 which contains 91 new *ricordi* plus 130 from earlier collections, many of them radically revised. The concern with the redactions has been a concern with progressive change in the text. The central issue, of course, is the direction and force of the intellectual movement between versions, an issue E. Scarano Lugnani addresses in her monograph, *Guicciardini e la crisi del Rinascimento*.[3] First, she notes the deepening of the political theoretical interests in the third redaction, accompanied in places by the elimination of "municipal" interests, the specifically Florentine references of the early *ricordi*. The municipal concern returns in the fourth redaction of 1528, an urban interest which, she speculates, reflects Guicciardini's preoccupation with the contemporary Florentine political crisis. The fifth redaction represents a radical transformation on the plane of internal organisation as well as in selection of content; the tone is now "exquisitely" theoretical and contemplative. Thus, for example, where there had been a nourishing reciprocity between example and rule in the third version, in the fifth collection, according to Lugnani, the maxim absorbs totally the illustrative event, depriving it of any autonomous interest; the concrete and particular event is now *mere* example.

I wish to argue, however, the essential unity of the *Ricordi,* a unity grounded in the constraints of proverbial form.[4] My interest lies in characterizing Guicciardini's exploitation of the *ricordi* form as both a cognitive tactic and a moral act: my premise is that "proverb" and "maxim" represent a meta-discursive strategy, a sign system or code which reorients the reader to political-moral reality.[5] Lugnani has raised the issue of the relation of the *Ricordi* to Guicciardini's major texts in claiming that it is in the *ricordi* of 1523-25 that the major themes of Guicciardini's mature work, specifically the *History of Italy,* are first isolated. My claim is that the proverbial form dominates the *Ricordi,* where it is employed by Guicciardini to both intensify and enlarge political consciousness and moral sensitivity, and thus makes a heavy contribution to the thematic structure of Guicciardini's history.[6]

But first, any analysis of Guicciardini's use of the *ricordo* form must begin with his self-conscious statements about the *Ricordi* as discursive practice. In these statements the *ricordo* takes its place in a semantic field composed of proverb ("proverbio" 97), saying ("detto" 163), rule ("regola" 111), and maxim ("massima" 192). The congruence of the *ricordo* and proverb form is attested by the instances where the *ricordi* are simply versions of proverbs. This is the case in *ricordo* 136, a restatement of the classical tag "Audaces fortuna iuvat"; or 138, a reissue of "Ducent volentes fata, nolentes trahunt"; and 163, an updating of "Magistratus virum ostendit." Or, a *ricordo* may attempt either to correct an "antico proverbio" (96), or to make a strong and concrete case for its validity (33, 54, 116, 144).

Then, Guicciardini appeals to a proverb to criticise the proverbial strength of the *Ricordi* as practice; in *ricordo* 210 he begins, "'Poco è buono' dice el proverbio" ("'Less is more,' says the proverb,") and then raises the question whether he has diluted his message by producing too many *ricordi*. Verbosity must contain nonsense, he says, while economy is easily digested: a selection ("fiore") might have been better.

Here Guicciardini recognises economy as formal value. And certainly it is the case that any account of the proverbial form must stipulate the criterion of economy. In the proverb, a skeletal prose purveys skeletal premises; it is a severe statement of guarded expectations of human behavior. The simplicity of form is designed to obtain sophistication of response; the minimum of descriptive effort is to achieve a maximum of critical response, by means of the elimination or reduction of naive assumptions and superfluous inferences. Where the proverb is preceptive, it is designed to limit the exposure of designated action to the least possible amount of speculative damage. Proverbial effect relates to the piquancy of stating broad imperatives in a language of narrow surprises; general assent or inclusive attitudes are constituted by means of incisive raids upon a domain of cherished beliefs and shared moral truisms. Used within the context of serious investigation, the preferred use of proverb is as a folk wisdom which subverts folk cant.

But if a primary attribute of the proverbial form is economy, a primary value of a collection of proverbs is richness. Just so, Terence Cave has emphasised the complementarity of the criteria of *brevitas* and *copia* in sixteenth-century literary theory and practice; Erasmus' *Adagia,* indeed, is "a stylish example of the marriage of *copia* and *brevitas*" (20-21). Brevity in the adage "Festina lente" is described as "gem-like"; that is, a small compassable unit which is both enduring and resettable, a relocatable brilliance.[7] Complementarity of brevity and richness, or *unitas* and *varietas,* invests the single proverb as well. In a contemporary humanist collection of proverbs, Filippo Beroaldo claims that proverbs are "similar to laws, in that a narrow text gives rise to the widest possible interpretation; contained by the greatest brevity, they unfold the most fruitful meaning."[8]

And thus the generative complementarity of *brevitas* and *copia* affects the cognitive strategy of the proverbial form. At issue, of course, is the fit of the proverbial form in the general argument of the receiving text, and thus the relation of general and specific, rule and experience. Within the context of his inclusive political-historical project, Guicciardini wishes to give a pragmatic (useful) account of events; he is constrained, because he starts with obdurate and resistant events, to argue backwards, to search, as the rhetorician searches, for general lines of argument, *topoi,* which will account for the events. Aristotle specified in his *Rhetoric* that maxims can function as major premises in an argument; they supply a general or common meaning which can be applied to specific events in conclusions.[9] The proverbial tactic is one of epistemological clarification and deconstruction; as major premiss, it dismantles other, less economical premisses. The proverbs accomplish "home truths" by eschewing claims with systematic or academic resonances; proverbial tactics evince a distrust of syllogistic chains of propositions, lengthy argumentative development.

Proverbial form, then, qualifies generality and the relation of rule and example, instantiation and maxim. But whereas Lugnani claimed that the redactions evince a development in the direction of generality where maxim "swallows" event, Hess has characterised the aphoristic relation of universal and individual in Guicciardini as a tension: they subsist in a dialectical mode in the sense that each is incomplete without the other.[10] Further, one must note Guicciardini's pervasive tendency to focus on the reception or consumption as well as the production of maxim; proverbs "address" a unified body of producers/consumers. In *ricordo* 79, the unity of meaning must be subordinated to the variety of use. Specific circumstances of application may constrain a total reversal of import; thus the proverb "el savio debbe godere el beneficio del tempo" may stipulate either *celerità* (decisiveness) or procrastination. The relation of general to specific is certainly not a straightforward one in which genus exhaustively explains species. The proverbial appeal is to a wisdom, which, while it might cohere with the propositions developed in a formal Aristotelian or scholastic matrix, claims a diffuse collective origin. It specifies a domain of informal and irregular acts of invention and judgment, and provides, therefore, space for thought-experiment. Just as Cicero insists that the domain of juridical oratory is created by the fact that laws are not omnicompetent, and thus judges have discretion, so Guicciardini privileges the cases which cannot be decided by reference to law only, but require a jurisprudential strategy, a manner of adjudicating a variety of opinions (111, 113). The relation of species to species, of exemplary to imitative act, is equally aporetic: "to judge by example is very misleading," because tiny differences in contributing circumstances can cause great variations in effects (117, 114). The potential imitator of exemplary events, then, operates in a realm of contingency, judging, and reckoning "giornata per giornata" (114).

The *Ricordi* represent a deliberate strategy for gaining a different purchase on civil issue, a use of proverb to enter and change political debate. At the same time, the proverbs represent a direct and simple edifying address: both affirmations and subversions make unequivocal calls on judgment and act. For the proverb aims for the broadest popular recognisability; proverbial generality appeals to a continuity with traditional memory, and gives a suggestion of cross-cultural validity. The proverb, Guicciardini claims in *ricordo* 12,

has universal application because it is a universal phenomenon; all nations have the same proverbs, even if expressed in different words, because they express the same resolution of similar experiences. And the verbal form of the proverb is of such rigidity that Guicciardini's *ricordi* confuse; the reader hesitates whether to judge them as newly-minted or obscurely archaic expressions (82, 140). The proverb is easily counterfeited; "artificial" proverbs, by virtue of the simplicity and rigidity of form, have the same force as "real" ones.

What I now claim is that a focus on this proverbial strategy enables a revision of one of Lugnani's characterisations of the *Ricordi* and the reinforcement of a second. First, Lugnani sees in the changes that took place between the early and late redactions a rejection of Florentine, municipal interests. My hypothesis is simply that Guicciardini's proverbial strategy represents the endurance, not cancellation of this municipalist motive. That is to say, the invocation of proverbial authority is at the same time an invocation of the communal wisdom familiar to, indeed, identified as, the collective possession of small-scale societies. The archetypal proverb is an appeal to a shared residual knowledge, which is the firm possession of unlettered or literate inhabitants of a social network. The attribute "communia" of proverbs is a shared assumption of both Guicciardini's *Ricordi* and contemporaneous humanist collections; indeed, the notion of communality underwrites a continuity between "learned" and "popular" forms.[11] Then, Fubini (153ff.) notes that the successive redactions of the *Ricordi* demonstrate a progressive movement towards a more generic "literary" expression; yet, while removing local "Florentine" expressions, the author retains the originary vulgar force, and though he discards "Florentinity" he discards "Latinate" usage as well. Guicciardini is not so much repudiating municipalism as removing parochialism in order to raise urbane instruction to a more general, and therefore accessible, plane. Proverbs, the form and content of the *Ricordi,* both strengthen the Florentine claim to special wisdom and appeal to a general audience's nostalgia for small communal identity. A very specific instance of this appeal would be, of course, Guicciardini's tactic of attributing a saying to his father (44, 45); indeed, he also cites a source, Pope Leo, as attributing a saying to *his* father (25). Generality does not specify cosmopolitanism but intimacy and informality.

As we observe the intimate and informal quality of the social relations which are often the object of Guicciardinian investigation, we notice at once that a very high proportion of the *Ricordi* deal with the production and reception of "benefits," namely, not only the material rewards but also the offices, good will, trust, and advice which are the currency of civil society. Here, I might add, is a clear instance where Guicciardini does not appear as anti-classical, for there are very strong parallels with the theory and practice of benefits Seneca adumbrated in his *De Beneficiis*. Like Seneca, Guicciardini depicts a network of benefits as constituting the most important social bonds: "quae maxime humanam societatem alligat."[12] Both the Senecan and Guicciardinian initiatives focus on personal rather that institutional transactions; the choices depicted are not primarily choices of public policy, but of private, for example, familial needs. Thus, when Guicciardini intones "nothing is more precious than friends" (14), he refers to a thick discursive matrix where one's reputation, and thus power, is continuously assessed, voted up or down.

The *Ricordi,* then, stipulate and explain a peculiar domain of civil interest, but, most importantly, they indorse a particular tone and point of view in defining ethical values in this domain as well; to use the proverb is to engage in a peculiar type of moral work. Indeed, the strong appeal of the proverbial account relates to its moral claims; recall that Aristotle remarked that the maxim invests a speech with moral character: "There is moral character in every speech where the moral purpose is conspicuous, and maxims always produce this effect, because the utterance of them amounts to a general declaration of moral principles (1395b). Further, as Aristotle noted, the use of maxims has powerful effect because it authenticates the popular morality: "The maxim is a general statement, and people love to hear stated in general terms what they already believe in some particular connection" (1395b). This statement by no means establishes the superiority of general rule to specific insight. Indeed, the proverbial strategy in an interesting way undermines the project of the construction of an exhaustive set of eternal moral rules.[13]

Thus, proverbial universality is an appeal to shared capacity or possession and not ontological order. Further, while Guicciardini depicts and appeals to a heavy, vital, social network which is both confrontational and omnipresent, he also enjoins a peculiarly negative, almost quiescent moral capacity. This, I think, is the motive of Lugnani's claim that the *Ricordi* are cognitive and not preceptive in tone (73). Recall that in *ricordo* 9 Guicciardini asks his audience to read his maxims often and hold them in mind, for they are easier to understand than to observe. They must become a habit of mind, always fresh in the memory; in an earlier version he remarks that habit will insure that use will then seem as rational as it is easy (B11). Guicciardini's initiative is designed to shape attitudes or stances, rather than alternative policies (170, 176); when he enjoins his readers to hold a maxim deep in their hearts ("avessino bene nel cuore," 196), he wishes to induce a mental state of cognitive alertness. In the relations of rule and example (110), of book and experience (186), in his emphasis on discretion ("discrezione" 6), on thoughtfulness ("pensare" 83, B25), on reflection (152, 187, 215), he describes as desideratum a passive and

receptive frame of mind, flexible and open to the variations of experience (10), the mixed nature of things (213). His skeletal prose construes a simple armature, a perceptive screen; proverbial injunctions enjoin a sieving activity which need not produce a formula for heroic results.

"Cognitive" is not equivalent to "academic," of course; the emphasis on discretion and flexibility is also a deemphasis of book learning, ("dottrina," "libri" 186); reasoning not reading strengthens reflective capacity (187, 208). And his insistence on the bankruptcy of hindsight (22) and the impossibility of foresight or prophecy (23, 57, 58, 114, 176, 182, 207, 211) contribute to construing proper mentation as an almost empty readiness.

Further, proverbial constraints, in forcing epistemological pessimism, limit moral possibility. The *Ricordi,* which radically demarcate the domain of the real from that of the ideal, the realm of "is" from that of "ought," also contribute to the attenuation of the preceptive drive. In *ricordo* 128 and 179, what "ought to be" is not the proper object of cognition and investigative scrutiny, and therefore ceases to be a topic in the schooling of the will as well.[14] The pessimism enjoins a still further refinement of the definition of the "real"; "real" becomes "the perception of the real." The *ricordi* which deal with benefit concern the success or failure of the benefit given to induce the receiver to *perceive* the benefit as gain (40, 42, 43, 44, 86); the benefit must operate in a domain of gratitude and ingratitude, of reputation of liberality or miserliness (42, 158, 185, 217), of designations of respect or offense (B148, B153).

We may detect in the proverbial strategy a general moment of interiorisation. If the proverbs describe or stipulate spiritual capacity, they also deal with goals as spiritual achievements. "Honor" becomes not so much a public charge as a private possession; true integrity of reputation is an assessment by the individual of his own attitudes and accomplishments. The *Ricordi* also define a temporal dimension to moral competence and public reputation. Memory is an enabling capacity; the *Ricordi* are useful, available in so far as they are remembered (9); benefits and offenses exist in a domain of memory (24, 25, 62, 130, 150, 207). Reputation, the vital ingredient of success, is shared memory, a consensual remembrance (42, 158, 217, 218). But Guicciardini, like Seneca, develops a phenomenology of memory which distinguishes function and dysfunction. Not simply benefit, but the memory of benefit creates social bonds; the moralist who engages in "healing souls and maintaining faith in human affairs," Seneca claims, also has the duty of "engraving upon minds the memory of services" (*De Beneficiis* I.iv:6). Similarly, ingratitude, as destroying bonds, is a social evil; Guicciardini attacks the "malcontenti" as distorting political equations (131).[15]

Intimate domain and moral initiative are entwined, then; the *Ricordi* aim to provide a reflective command of intimate social relations; Guicciardini employs the proverbial form to generate a peculiarly thick description of moral competence within an informal social context. The specific and interesting locus of moral insight is the domain of benefits, a Senecan domain where benefits are a recalcitrant necessity: they are, on the one hand, the essential social cement or glue, and, on the other, extraordinarily hard to give and receive. Pessimism is, of course, constrained by the formal criterion of brevity; moral optimism requires an elaborate argument. Like Seneca, Guicciardini premises the essential fragility of human nature, its susceptibility to evil motives and forces: "malos esse nos, malos fuisse, —invitus adiciam, et futuros esse."[16] But also like Seneca, Guicciardini enjoins purity of motive: a benefit entered into a calculus of loss and gain is not a benefit; the benefit lies in the generosity ("benevolentia") of intention.[17]

Discussions of virtuous purity are circumscribed by the de-reification tactics of the *Ricordi.* His few direct references to virtue concern the sphere of will and affect; at one point he describes the extreme satisfaction one gains from the repression of illicit desire (B17). Positive attributes are attributes of manner; Guicciardini does, at the end of the collection, produce a list of characteristics of a virtuous mode: "cioè fargli con ragione, con tempo, con modestia, e per cagione e con modi onorevoli" (217). There is, to be sure, ambiguity: one *ricordo* maintains that true merit lies in action rather than disavowals of inaction (129); another will, with infinite caution, claim that the greatest good is to harm no one (139).

"Harmlessness" denotes moral parsimony. And, in gene-ral, proverbial form represents and imitates proverbial capacity. The economy and elegance of the prose state, without excess, the economical premisses of the true state of affairs as a state of affective artifice. That is to say, the maxims are quintessentially proverbial as deconstructive of moralism, rather than reinforcing it, as humanist collections seem. The proverbial initiative, as spare and necessitous, inculcates habits of mind rather than political roles; it subverts law and inefficient ways of discussing moral issues; it insists on the limitation of the will, while addressing an audience from which it expects reasonable behavior; it underlines the importance of perception and reputation, and thus underscores the necessity of dissimulation and reticence as well as of frankness and liberality. The enunciation of proverb questions or even subverts the status of proverbial rule, which applies as hedge and constraint; every general injunction imposes a burden of specific and therefore difficult use. Indeed, the strategy denies fixed rules of action at the same time as it attempts to fix the potential to observe and reflect.

The issue which remains to be discussed is: What is the place of the *Ricordi* in Guicciardini's work as a whole? I have already cited Lugnani's remark that the major concepts of the *History of Italy* made their first appearance in the *Ricordi;* I have tried to make the case that the dominant proverbial form was at the same time a cognitive tactic and a moral strategy. Indeed, this choice of mode illumines the place of Guicciardini's work in Florentine political and historical thought as well. I shall claim that we must see the *Ricordi* as the product of a double initiative in Florentine moral-political inquiry, an initiative both traditional, in its proverbial appeal to a social wisdom of time immemorial, and revolutionary, partaking of the radical innovations of Machiavellian political analysis.

Or, the initiative may be judged traditional, radical, and classical. While he makes few references to classical protagonists or authors in the *Ricordi,* Guicciardini mentions Tacitus three times (C13, 18; B101); in *ricordo* 18, his observation that Tacitus spoke as much to the issue of how subjects can live under tyranny as to how tyrants can maintain their rule, is, I would argue, as much a summary of Guicciardini's program as of that of Tacitus.[18] Just so, Machiavelli's *Prince* recapitulates this agenda: it is as much addressed to the task of accommodation to the failure of republican possibilities as to that of constructing a principate. Guicciardini, like Machiavelli, employs the shock tactics of depicting the current political dilemmas of tyranny in rich, compelling, and Tacitean detail. But in Guicciardini there is a specific commitment to the use of the proverbial form in order to authenticate a *modus vivendi,* a potential of endurance for a reader now defined as Tacitean subject rather than Ciceronian citizen. Certainly the careers of both Machiavelli and Guicciardini reflect the imperative that the subject with a capacity for generous endurance must embrace the role of counsellor. Guicciardini, when he claims that the subject of a principate has greater opportunities than the subject of a republic (107), describes these opportunities specifically as those of proverbial prudence.

The central assumption of the *Ricordi,* I have argued, is that the dominant matrix of all civic activity, both political and moral, is one of intimate obligation and benefit. By the relocation of virtuous activity within this intimate network of social bonds, Guicciardini is justifying the fundamental importance of a domain of intimate relations which persists within, or even encloses, the new political power structures. One of the tasks of the *Ricordi* is to refine and correct the distinction of public and private spheres by placing the public domain within the matrix of affect and then subordinating political action to the affective network.[19] From this follows the transformation of the notion of "public" into "public perception": the politician functions in a realm of perceptions, reputations, deceptions, and self-deceptions. The very simple republican definitions of political space of earlier Renaissance "Civic Humanism" are effaced by this strategy; further, many maxims make specific contributions to the definition of the peculiarity of the princely domain.[20] Here the coherence of "public" and "political" entirely breaks down. The *Ricordi* stress not only the web of dissimulation which invests courtly activity, but insist on the opacity of the court to civic framework, of the palace to the forum: "often there is such a dense cloud or a thick wall between the palace and the market place that the human eye is unable to penetrate it" (141).[21]

This proverbial version of contextual challenge coheres with the notion of proverbial response; the account stipulates the isolation of the prince in a difficult environment, and thus severely circumscribes the possibilities of action of both prince and subject, immersed in an ambiance of opinion and affect, deception and interest.[22] The prince must use benefit and punishment as both spur and bridle (B3), but use must be related to affective reality. Like Seneca, Guicciardini emphasises disparities in the phenomenology of memory: because of habits of self-deception (165), the subjects of a prince tend to overemphasise their own merit (26, 52); therefore, while their memory of benefits granted tends to be fleeting (24, 203), their resentments of injury are durable (23, 150). And because of their feckless optimism, hope is stronger than fear as motive (5, 62, 173). Thus Guicciardini also recommends to the prince evasiveness and time gaining tactics (36).[23]

Then, Guicciardini offers counsels of affective prudence to counsellors as well as to the prince; the subject also must recognise that he has to operate within a realm of affective reality (151, 154). Guicciardini recalls Castiglione when he recommends to the subject the virtues of a prudential stylishness; intensely private graces and accomplishments may be the means to political achievement; deft gentility may gain the ear of the prince for the community good (179, 220). Thus proverbial strategy, by assuming an intimate politics, stresses the omnicompetence of proverbial wisdom; the same tactics control personal affairs and policy decisions (197, 198). The very existence of disinterested public motive is impugned by Guicciardinian cynicism; expressions of an ideology of liberty, he claims, are more likely expressions of self-interest (66). Both proverbial omnicompetence and the omnipresence of dysfunctional affect blur the definitions of public and private. Where a *topos* of civic humanist history, such as Leonardo Bruni's *History of Florence,* was the necessity for separation of public and private interests and the condemnation of the private use of public power, Guicciardini recommends the talent of "His Catholic Majesty" in representing actions for his own interests as actions for the common good (142).

In contrast, J. G. A. Pocock is probably correct in seeing Machiavelli as "Civic Humanist" in his retention of a well-defined public political sphere.[24] There are, to be sure, broad similarities in Machiavellian and Guicciardinian strategies: they share, obviously, premisses of the fragility and mobility of human affairs. However, they agree not so much on a simple premiss of the evil of human nature as on a complicated awareness of the necessity of dissimulation. Their emphasis on the dominant matrix of perception is at the same time a focus on agility, on the capacity to master perception, on the uses of frankness as well as deception, on the usefulness of reticence, but, above all, on the importance of discretion. Discretion, here, is the product of deliberation and interior dialogue; both Machiavelli and Guicciardini have "intellectualist" proclivities. *Ricordo* 83, which presses meditation on political actors, is of a piece with Machiavelli's letter to Guicciardini, which deplores the lack of opportunity for "thinking" as opposed to both action and talk.[25]

But I will claim that Guicciardini's *Ricordi,* as a rich instantiation of proverbial strategy, provide a more tough-minded account of political history and political possibility than Machiavelli's *Prince.* Machiavelli teaches by example. The *Discourses* as well as the *Prince* can be seen as a tissue of narrative paradigms, and the paradigms often isolate Machiavelli on the high ground of policy decisions, forcing him to draw inferences from one complex political situation in order to make sense of another. One of the difficulties of the *Prince,* then, is the presence of naive injunctions to imitate involuted, even tortuous, policies. It is true that this in effect often subverts imitative response by denying his reader simple models or exemplars. But while his accounts often leave the reader little to imitate, this dialectic of imperative and subversion makes his style difficult, if not repellant. Guicciardini has a more sophisticated notion of imitation, and thus a more suggestive conception of the relation of exemplar to image and of general rule to specific use.[26] Guicciardini emphasised the pertinence of receptive frame; his notions of exemplarity and instantiation require of the reader "a good and perspicacious eye" (117), habits of close attention to detail, and a taste for variety and surprise. It would seem that it is in clear contrast to Machiavelli that Guicciardini exclaims: "How wrong it is to cite the Romans at every turn. For any comparison to be valid, it would be necessary to have a city with conditions like theirs, and then to govern it according to their examples" (110).[27]

It would seem, then, that Guicciardini's "classicism" is peculiar as well. While Machiavelli attempts a thorough integration of classical Roman and vernacular Italian examples, Guicciardini's *Ricordi* read classical texts as a vernacular wisdom. Thus the *Ricordi* represent, on the one hand, a manifestation of municipalism, i.e., Florentine patriotism, and, on the other hand, recapitulation of a proverbial strategy used by those hard-pressed Romans, Tacitus and Seneca.[28] And certainly there are important differences between "normal" humanist modes of classical appropriation and Guicciardinian tactics of use. The contemporaneous discourse on proverbs of Beroaldo and Polydore Vergil shares the fundamental humanist assumption that there is nothing so humble or ordinary that cannot be rendered splendid by oratorical ornament. And Polydore Vergil's second collection, the *Adagiorum Liber,* displays the humanist passion for discourse analysis; here he accounts for proverbs as verbal strategies, figures of speech: metaphor, allegory, *allusio, hyperbole, scomma.*[29] Both the ornamental and analytic initiatives attest a basic humanist commitment to "manipulation." A compendious late Renaissance collection by Grynaeus responds to the challenge of accessibility; proverbial wisdom, organised under the *topoi,* the commonplaces of argument, becomes instantly useful to the reader as writer.[30] And in the most manipulative of all strategies, Henri Estienne's work *Les Premices* not only organises proverbs under commonplaces but engages in an elaborate double discourse; to demonstrate use, "proverb" becomes the active verb "proverbialise"; his aim is to write "proverbs epigrammatizez," or rather, "epigrammes proverbializez."[31]

It would not do, then, to overemphasise a discontinuity between classical or "learned" and popular proverb. Indeed, Stackelberg detects a general trend of "proverbialising" *sententiae* in the late Renaissance; the aphorism, which began as a learned, specifically medical maxim, is presented increasingly in "unsystematischen, unpedantischen, und kurzgefassten Darstellungsweise."[32] Certainly, the late Renaissance collectors treat Guicciardini and Machiavelli as well as Tacitus and Seneca as quintessentially proverbial.[33] The homogeneity of tone of proverbial wisdom is rooted in the homogeneity of premiss of the nature of political behavior. Tacitus, Seneca, and Guicciardini teach the importance of an enduring intimate community, the face-to-face encounters within an imperial or princely context, tyrannical or not. The basic constraint of proverbial omnicompetence constrains a description of response to occasions of the widest possible distribution: that is, to the ordinary give-and-take of individuals forced to use objects and services as signs. Proverbs teach skills for close encounters; since princely encounters are necessarily invested with intimacy, they teach political survival as well. The *Ricordi* share procedures with Roman imperial satires and letters, histories and essays, while they eschew another classical strategy: that of the formal exercise which relates to political policy and structures to a general logico-ontological system. Seneca and Guicciardini prefer informal investigation, a presentation of a heterogeneous group of insights as explanatory of the variety of experience; the "authority" of the writer derives from a bond with an assumed collective wisdom.[34]

To be sure, it is somewhat suspicious to attribute an "anthropologising" consciousness to Guicciardini in the light of the current historical fashion of explaining the behavior of Renaissance Florentine elites, indeed, of all classes by reference to modern anthropological constructs. But my emphasis on the proverbialising moment in the *Ricordi* is a claim for the wit and perspicacity of Guicciardini's conflation of reading, experience, and counsel.[35] The *Ricordi* must be placed within the general context of the production and reception of counsel in the sixteenth century.[36] And again, we should observe the coherence of humanist and Guicciardinian proverbial strategies. First and most importantly, all strong initiatives recognise the imperative of investigating a social paradigm and fabricating a notion of community which takes account of the severe constraints of a "courtly" environment. Thus the humanist Beroaldo insists on personal interdependence as fact: the *prudentia* of the prince in the matter of wisdom; counsel is a matter of discursive exchange, rather than solipsist construction.[37] At the same time, for Beroaldo as well as Guicciardini the task of counseling is complicated by the difficult as well as useful intimacy of the court. A *topos* of the texts of counsel is the attack on the flattery which infects the relation between prince and courtly subject; Beroaldo thus describes adulation: " . . . veluti gangrena serpens latissime intra limina potentiorum . . ." (*De Optimo Statu* n.p.). And surely, when Guicciardini, citing Tacitus again (B101), refers to Tiberius' rating of the deplorable Roman patriciate, he focuses on the dangers of the politics of intimacy. When Guicciardini represents the isolation of a prince (141), the latter appears as isolated in a crowd.

This, of course, is the state of affairs which the proverb, as communal wisdom for communal use, addresses. Beroaldo makes a specific connection between "proverbial" and "political"; advice to princes, he claims, is easily couched in proverbial terms (*De Optimo Statu* ciiiv.v). But where Beroaldo goes on to invoke an abstract understanding of ideal political forms, the claims the *Ricordi* make, as proverbial, are those on a residual, shared experience of intimate relations. Discretion is as much a condition as a result of reading. Thus Hess describes Guicciardini's advice as requiring intimate response: as "diario di esperienza," it demands a series of immediate and naive reactions from life.[38]

The appeal of the proverbial mode is a much less simple, direct, and didactic approach than it at first appears. In all evaluations of moral discourse, one must make a distinction between useless moralism and true moral work. Both Machiavelli and Guicciardini efface moralism by new and rigorous varieties of moral work which allow neither the cheerful truism nor smug casuistry to survive as valid stratagem. Like Machiavelli, Guicciardini is thoughtful but not academic. There is no attempt either to teach a programme of canonic moral texts or to place one's own work within a tradition of systematic commentary. The perspicuity of Guicciardini's project, however, lies in a proverbial capacity to repel attempts to stray from intimate experience in the formulation of political insight, a capacity which subverts intellectual as well as political solipsism.

Notes

[1] Felix Gilbert, "The Humanist Concept of the Prince," *JMH* 11(1939):449-83.

[2] Quentin Skinner, "'Social Meaning' and the Explanation of Social Action," in *Philosophy, Politics, and Society,* fourth ser., eds. P. Laslett et al. (Oxford: Blackwell, 1972), 144-45. An intriguing Derridian effort is that of Michael McCanles, *The Discourse of "Il Principe,"* Humana Civilitas 8 (Malibu: Undena Publications, 1983); a neo-Aristotelian reading can be found in E. Garver, "Machiavelli's *Prince:* A Neglected Rhetorical Classic," *Philosophy and Rhetoric* 17(1980).

[3] "Le cinque redazioni dei *Ricordi,*" in *Guicciardini e la crisi del Rinascimento* (Bari: Laterza, 1979), 61ff. Francesco Guicciardini, *Ricordi,* ed. R. Spongano, Autori classici e documenti di lingua pubblicati dall'Accademia della Crusca (Firenze: Sansoni, 1951). All Italian citations, unless otherwise noted, will be from the primary, or C version of Spongano; all English translations will be those of M. Domandi, *Francesco Guicciardini: Maxims and Reflections of a Renaissance Statesman* (New York: Harper & Row, 1965).

[4] G. Hess, "Guicciardini und die Anfänge der moralistischen Literatur," in *Gesellschaft-Literatur-Wissenschaft: Gesammelte Schriften (1938-1966),* ed. H. R. Jauss and C. Muller-Daehn (Müchen: 1967), claims that a focus on the successive versions is necessarily a focus on the issue of the *Ricordi* as "eine eigene, neuartige Form von literarischer Aussage . . ." (15). "'Inhalt' und 'Ordung' sind demnach wenig wichtig. Worauf es ankommt, lässt sich am ehesten an der Struktur (oder Form) des Aphorismus erkennen" (18).

[5] Recall that Kenneth Burke begins his project of relating literature to life with the proverb, as strategy for dealing with, naming situations, as originary instance of literary activity as social action; he asks, "Could the most complex and sophisticated work of art legitimately be considered somewhat as 'proverbs writ large'?" "Literature as Equipment for Living," *The Philosophy of Literary Form: Studies in Symbolic Action* (Baton Rouge: Louisiana State Press, 1941), 296. "Strategy," of course, is the key construct of Burkean rhetorical analysis. Burke, I think, would claim that for Guicciardini to begin with proverb would indicate Guicciardini was getting down to brass tacks in political speculation; here Guicciardini enjoins "realistic," not simply "self-gratifying" strategies (298).

On proverb or adage in the Renaissance see R. L. Colie, *The Resources of Kind: Genre-Theory in the Renaissance* (Berkeley: Univ. of California Press, 1973), esp. ch. 2, "Small Forms: *Multo in parvo,*" 32ff.; Terence C. Cave, *The Cornucopian Text: Problems of Writing in the French Renaissance,* (Oxford: Clarendon Press, 1979), ch. 1, *"Copia"* and N. Z. Davis, *Society and Culture in Early Modern France: Eight Essays* (Stanford: Stanford Univ. Press, 1975), ch.8, "Proverbial Wisdom and Popular Errors."

[6] See M. Fubini's seminal discussion of the stylistic and thematic importance of the *Ricordi,* "Le quattro redazioni dei *Ricordi* del Guicciardini: Contributo allo studio della formazione del linguaggio e dello stile guicciardiniano," *Studi sulla letteratura del Rinascimento* (Firenze: La Nuova Italia, 1971), 126-77. Fubini cites E. Fueter's dismissal of the *Ricordi* as neither stylistically nor theoretically as interesting as La Rochefoucauld's *Maxims* only to confute it (126); further, Fubini emphasises *unity in progress:* the later redactions develop a more "generic and literary" expression, but do not lose or diminish the insights of earlier redactions of the proverbs (143ff.).

[7] Fron Margaret M. Phillips, *Erasmus on his Times: A Shortened Version of the Adages of Erasmus* (Cambridge: Cambridge Univ. Press, 1967), 3.

[8] P. Beroaldus, *Proverbiorum Libellus* (Venezia: 1498), xxxvi r: "Ad haec habent proverbia quiddam simile legibus; quarum scriptum angustum et interpretatio latissima. Siquidem summa brevitate conclusa: intellectum uberiorem complectuntur."

[9] Aristotle, *Rhetorica,* tr. W. Rhys Roberts (Oxford: Oxford Univ. Press, 1946), 1393b.

[10] G. Neumann, "Einleitung," *Der Aphorismus: Zur Geschichte, zu den Formen und Möglichkeiten einer literarischen Gattung* (Darmstadt: Wissenschaftliche Buchgesellschaft, 1976), cites Hess, "Guicciardini und die Anfänge der moralistischen Literatur," and comments that in the aphorism the relation is essentially problematical; the aphorism is a "Konfliktform des Erkennens zwischen einzelnem Faktum and generalisierender Aussage. Die 'Ricordi' Francesco Guicciardinis leben aus der Dialektik von *caso* und *regola,* von Situation und Leitsatz: Aus ihrem Spannungsfeld entspringt dem Leser die politische Einsicht" (7).

[11] Thus P. Beroaldus: "Vulgares sententiae sunt proverbia. Vulgares scriptores sunt Virgilius et Cicero. Quid enim magis in ore vulgi est, quid usu populari magis detritum? Docti indoctique, urbani et rustici, opifices omnes . . . ," "Oratio proverbiorum," *Opuscula quae in Hoc Volumine Continentur . . .* (Venezia: 1508), lvi r. See also the prefatory letter to Polydore Vergil's *Proverbiorum Libellus* (Venezia: 1498). The

attribute "communis" is, of course, medieval as well: G. Vecchi, "Il 'proverbio' nella pratica letteraria dei dettatori della scuola di Bologna," *Studi mediolatini e volgari* 2(1954):283-302 cites two medieval definitions: "Premittendum est generale proverbium, id est communis sententia, cui consuetudo fidem attribuit, opinio communis assensum accommodat. Incorrupta veritatis integritas adquiescit . . . ," from Matthew of Vendôme, *Ars Versificatoria,* in E. Faral, *Les Arts poétiques du XII et du XIII siècle* (Paris: Champion, 1924), 284, and "Proverbium est sermo brevis communi hominum opinione comprabatus . . . ," from Bene di Firenze, *Candelabrum* 288.

[12] Seneca, *De Beneficiis, in Moral Essays* III.I.iv:2, tr. J. W. Basore, (Cambridge: 1975); the list of benefits I used is Seneca's, I.ii:4. I do not think it is necessary to make a case that Guicciardini "read" Seneca, although the proverb of 138 is Senecan: Senecan texts permeated Florentine culture. R. Sabbadini claims Seneca's philosophical works as "notissime," *Le scoperte dei codici latini e greci ne' secoli XIV e XV: Nuove ricerche* (Firenze: Sansoni, 1914), 250.

[13] S. Cavell attacks a naive moralism which insists that "the concept 'good' is simply application of a general principle to individual cases" (cf. P. Foot, "Moral Beliefs," in *Theories of Ethics,* ed. P. Foot [Oxford: Oxford Univ. Press, 1967], 85). Cavell eschews the search for moral "rules": "No rule or principle could function in a moral context the way regulatory or defining rules function in games. It is as essential to the form of life called morality that rules so conceived be absent as it is essential to the form of life we call playing a game that they be present . . . ," *The Claim of Reason* (Oxford: Oxford Univ. Press, 1979), 307; cited in Richard Rorty, *Consequences of Pragmatism* (Minneapolis: Univ. of Minneapolis Press, 1982), 185.

[14] The notion of the proverb as eschewing cognitive optimism and thus moral simplicity is medieval as well; see Vecchi, "Il 'proverbio,'" (286), where he cites Boncompagni di Firenze's definition: "Proverbium est brevis verborum series obscuram in se continens sententiam," *Palma,* in C. Sutter, *Aus Leben und Schriften des Magisters Boncompagno* (Freiburg: Mohr/Siebeck, 1894), 103.

[15] Seneca, *Ad Lucilium Epistulae Morales,* tr. R. Gummere (Cambridge: 1970), LXXXI.24: "At contra sapientia exornat omne beneficium ac sibi ipsa commendat et se adsidua eius commemoratione delectat. Malis una voluptas est et haec brevis, dum accipiunt beneficia, ex quibus sapienti longum gaudium manet ac perenne."

[16] Seneca, *De Beneficiis* I.x:3; see *Ricordi* 41, 134, 135, 201.

[17] Seneca, *De Beneficiis* I.vi:1; *Ep.* LXXXI.21; see *Ricordi* 11, B43.

[18] "Insegna molto bene Cornelio Tacito a chi vive sotto a' tiranni el modo di vivere e governarsi prudentemente, così come insegna a' tiranni e modi di fondare la tirannide."

[19] See, for example, *Ricordi* 1, 71, 93, 175, 191, 193, 195, 196, 198.

[20] See *Ricordi* 2, 4, 53, 77, 88, 90, 94, 128, 130, 131, 153, 154. See N. Rubinstein's account of "Civic Humanism" in "Le dottrine politiche nel Rinascimento," in *Il Rinascimento: Interpretazioni e problemi,* eds. M. Boas-Hall et al. (Bari: Laterza, 1979), 183-237. Note that Rubinstein comments on Guicciardini's distrust of "liberty."

[21] " . . . spesso tra 'l palazzo e la piazza è una nebbia sì folta o uno muro sì grosso che, non vi penetrando l'occhio degli uomini. . . . "

[22] See *Ricordi* 38, 53, 88, 90, 94, 98-101, 103, 132, 170, 174, 184, 186, 195, 200.

[23] A close reading of both the *De Beneficiis* and the *Ep.* LXXXI will reveal many parallels with the Guicciardinian account of benefit exchange. It is intriguing that K.-D. Nothdurft, in *Studien zum Einfluss Senecas auf die Philosophie und Theologie des zwölften Jahrhunderts,* Studien und Texte zur Geistesgeschichte des Mittelalters 7 (Leiden: Brill, 1963), has pointed out that the early "Mirrors for Princes" and their sources, e.g., William of Conches' *Moralium Dogma Philosophorum,* also employed the central passages from the *De Beneficiis* to describe the princely situation. One could say Guicciardini transforms the *Fürstenspiegel* by employing fresh Seneca to refurbish old Seneca; see Nothdurft, esp. 101ff.

[24] *The Machiavellian Moment: Florentine Political Thought and the Atlantic Republican Tradition* (Princeton: Princeton Univ. Press, 1975).

[25] Niccolò Machiavelli, *Lettere* (Milano: Feltrinelli, 1961), 451.

[26] I have discussed another revision of Machiavelli an exemplarity in "Pasquier's *Recherches de la France:* The Exemplarity of His Medieval Sources" (paper read at the Medieval Academy, April, 1983). Felix Gilbert notes the lack of *exempla* in the *History of Italy,* in *Machiavelli and Guicciardini: Politics and History in Sixteenth-Century Florence* (Princeton: Princeton Univ. Press, 1965), 282.

[27] "Quanto si ingannono coloro che a ogni parola allegano e Romani!—Bisognerebbe avere una città con-

dizionata come era loro, e poi governarsi secondo quello essemplo: el quale a chi ha le qualità disproporzionate è tanto disproporzionato, quanto sarebbe volere che un asino facessi el corso di uno cavallo."

[28] The connection of Senecan wisdom and proverbial form is medieval; typical of the medieval *florilegia* which employ the strategy of distilling Senecan texts into lists of aphorisms is *Les Proverbes Seneke,* a late thirteenth-century text, embedded in a chronicle; see E. Ruhe, *Les Proverbes Seneke le philosophe: Zur Wirkungsgeschichte des Speculum historiale von Vinzenz von Beauvais und der Chronique dite de Baudouin d'Avesnes,* Beiträge zur romanischen Philologie des Mettelalters 5 (München: Hueber, 1969).

[29] *Polydori Vergilii Urbinatis Adagiorum Liber* (Basilea: 1521), 3.

[30] J. J. Grynaeus, *Adagia, id est: Proverbiorum, proemiarum et parabolarum omnium . . .* (1629).

[31] H. Estienne, *Les Premices, ou le I livre des proverbes epigrammatizez, ou, des epigrammes proverbializez . . .* (1584).

[32] J. von Stackelberg, "Zur Bedeutungsgeschichte des Wortes 'Aphorismus,'" in *Der Aphorismos* 210n.

[33] Stackelberg cites G. Canini d'Anghiari, who translated B. Alamos de Barrientos' *Tacito Español* (Madrid: 1614), and who also produced *Aforismi politici, cavati dall' historia d'Italia di M. F. Guicciardini* (Venezia: 1625), in "Bedeutungsgeschichte" (214).

[34] See the review essay of E. Brucker, "Tales of Two Cities," *AHR* 88(1983):599-618.

[35] This is in opposition to M. Gagneux's rather reductive Marxist reading of Guicciardini as simply spokesman for his class; see "Idéologie et opportunisme chez François Guichardin, in *Ecrivains et le pouvoir en Italie à l'époque de la Renaissance,* Centre de recherche sur la Renaissance italienne, eds. A. Rochon et al. (Paris: Université de la Sorbonne Nouvelle, 1973), 155-242. Dale Kent's work in the fifteenth-century letters of the Medici archive, for example, would seem to reveal similar "anthropological" investment in the reciprocal bonds of gratitude and benefit between patron and client, with similar constraints and moral rationalisations, and thus would substantiate Guicciardini's account as perspicacious ("The Dynamic of Power in Cosimo de' Medici's Florence," unpublished paper).

[36] On the history of the career and role of the intellectual as counselor in Renaissance Italy see F. Gaeta, "Dal comune alla corte rinascimentale," and A. A. Rosa, "La Chiesa e gli stati regionali nell'età dell'assolutismo", *Letterratura italiana: I. Il letterato e le istituzioni,* ed. A. A. Rosa (Torino: Einaudi, 1982); on Guicciardini see esp. Rosa, 267-69.

[37] P. Beroaldus, *Libellus de Optimo Statu & Principe,* in *Opusculum Eruditum . . .* (Bologna: 1497), n. p. "Sit igitur princeps non solum ipse preditus prudentia verum etiam consiliarios prudentes habeat: quibus bene consulentibus credere possit. Nemo enim per se unquam solus ita sapit: Nemo ita circumspectus ac sagax: Nemo ita lineus est ut non aliquando labet atque cecutiat." This notion of the counseling situation recalls N. Elias' construct of "figuration" as "a structure of mutually oriented and dependent people. . . . they exist . . . only as pluralities, figurations," *The Civilizing Process: The History of Manners,* tr. E. Jephcott (New York: Urizen Books, 1978), 261.

[38] G. Hess, "G. und die Anfänge der moralistischen Literatur" (27); "Bei der zeitlichen Nähe zu Montaigne—und der Nähe romantischer 'Tagebücher'—lag es wohl nahe, den Bekenntnischarakter der *Ricordi* zu betonen und sie als 'diario di esperienza,' als 'storia e confessione' des Ich zu deuten" (17). To be sure, Colie felt that intimate exchange was an attribute of all Renaissance "mini-genres," but her originary example was Erasmus' *Adagia,* a text which continually requires the reader to make connections and supply contexts and functions (*Resources of Kind* 35ff.). And perhaps we can reconcile the "privacy" of the *Ricordi,* demonstrated in the thinness of its publication history, with its intrusive, interventionist nature if we see privacy as related to demanding intimacy. Frank Whigham, *Ambition and Privilege: The Social Tropes of Elizabethan Courtesy Theory* (Berkeley: Univ. of California Press, 1984), ch. 1, claims that "Guicciardini's ultrapragmatic family *Ricordi,* unpublished during the Renaissance, have the status of a concealed weapon. . . . " Whigham also regards as central Burke's definition of literary strategy as proverbial strategy.

Salvatore DiMaria (essay date 1994)

SOURCE: "Divine Order, Fate, Fortune and Human Action in Guicciardini's *Storia d'Italia,*" *Forum Italicum,* Vol. 28, No. 1, Spring, 1994, pp. 22-40.

[*In the following essay, DiMaria argues that Guicciardini's* Storia d'Italia *reflects the spirit of the times; that is, Guicciardini acknowledges the large part that fortune plays in an increasingly complex world even as he asserts that individuals have a measure of power over events.*]

The decades of relative calm and political stability preceding the death of Lorenzo de' Medici (1492) undoubtedly contributed to the humanist belief in one's ability to influence the course of human affairs. The prevailing mood of self-assurance and self-determination promoted the belief that the individual could indeed build, to use a Machiavellian metaphor, the necessary dikes to withstand the flood of adverse Fortune, when and where it struck. However, soon after Lorenzo's death, Italy became host to a series of devastating wars which were to involve much of western Europe. The socio-political instability, the inhibiting apprehensions, and the depreciation of human life brought on by war eventually began to erode one's confidence in the ability to foresee and act upon new developments. Machiavelli himself, who in *The Prince* (1513) had given the individual a fifty-fifty chance against the unexpected and unforeseeable ways of Fortune, seems to have lost some of that optimism by the time he finished writing the *Istorie Fiorentine* (1522). He ended his narration rather abruptly with a foreboding description of the times that were to follow Lorenzo's death.[1]

In this atmosphere of turmoil and uncertainty the changes were too rapid and far-reaching for people to still believe in their ability to help shape world events. The balance of the fifty-fifty equation had clearly shifted in favor of Fortune, which became more predominant as the times grew increasingly unstable. This is not to say, however, that individuals abandoned altogether the prerogative to act or, more specifically, the efforts to shape the course of their lives. The extent to which he continued to see himself as an influential force needs to be seen in relation to other major forces thought to be at work in the world of the Renaissance. One can reasonably expect to find a reflection of this relationship in the works and views of those who experienced, observed and recorded human actions and aspirations within the context of the times. Such is the case with Guicciardini's writings, in particular his last and major work the *Storia d'Italia* (1537-40) which, given its breadth and wealth of details, represents an encyclopedic window on those events that characterized life in Italy in the four decades following Lorenzo's death, 1494-1534. Not surprisingly, the *Storia* begins with a description similar in tone to Machiavelli's conclusion of the *Istorie*. In fact, with reference to those "seeds that ruined" early sixteenth-century Italy, Guicciardini proposes to dwell on the trials and tribulations brought upon mortals either because of "l'ira giusta d'Iddio" or because of the wickedness of others. With respect to these "others," he intends to show that much of human suffering was largely caused by the deeds of thoughtless individuals moved by ambition or lack of prudence.[2] He further proposes to show that all woes were also precipitated by the instability of Fortune whose capriciousness undermined a world previously thought to be somewhat more stable or, at least, changing within rational expectations. And so, in the first paragraph of this voluminous work Guicciardini identifies God, Fortune and man as the major forces which motivate the world of the *Storia.*

It is not unusual for Guicciardini, at least in the *Storia,* to invoke God, Fortune or human beings in order to explain the cause or outcome of major events. For instance, following the French defeat of the Neapolitan forces in 1495, Don Federigo of Aragon, speaking on behalf of his nephew Ferdinand of Naples, tells Charles VIII that the French victory was willed by "Dio la fortuna e la volontà degli uomini" (II, 3:222). The cause for the great fire which in 1513 swept through Venice is attributed either to "l'ira del cielo o i casi fortuiti che dependono dalla protestà della fortuna" (XII, 5:1160). Heaven and Fortune are also seen as the source of the 1521 resumption of hostilities between France and the Empire, which made Italy once again the stage for long and destructive wars. Guicciardini comments rather sarcastically that it seemed as if "Il cielo il fato proprio e la fortuna" were either envious of Italy's tranquility or fearful that it might once again regain its old prosperity (XIV, 1:1333).

While it is rather obvious that the world of the *Storia* is essentially governed by God, mortals and Fortune, a legitimate question continues to vex scholars regarding the specific role these powers are thought to have in the actual development of the narrated events. In the ensuing discussion I propose to identify the place and function of these forces by examining the author's and, in some instances, his personages' perception of them. By so doing, I intend to define their respective sphere of influence and, at the same time, determine which force is behind the outcome of given events, thus elucidating the dynamics of the narrated world. This, in turn, will help put in clearer perspective Guicciardini's view of the world, as it will reveal whether, or to what extent, he sees individuals in control of their own affairs or simply controlled by superior and ineluctable powers. The inquiry, thus, assumes ontological dimensions, for it proposes to explore man's view of his condition as perceived by Guicciardini in the context of the Italian Renaissance. In the end, I hope to show that contrary to the established view orginally proposed by Roberto Palmarocchi, in Guicciardini's apprehension of the world, the individual represents a significant force in the shaping of human events.

Before examinning the place God, Fate, Fortune and humans occupy in Guicciardini's narrative, one must first confront the difficult task of defining the actual domain of these forces. Guicciardini's world-view is not to be found in any neatly couched theory or specific treatise, for, as Roberto Palmarocchi points out, he is mainly a pragmatist, constantly subjecting his views to practical considerations.[3] Accordingly, he does not proceed from theories or definitions concerning, say, God's place or Fortune's role in the world; he simply comments on the role they played in given events. But, since all situations are not the same, his view of their role shifts considerably, thus escaping definition. In the *Storia,* for instance, Guicciadini writes that "con la prudenza gli uomini possono prevenire le cose destinate" (I, 15:179). But later in the same work he acknowledges that "i consigli umani non bastano a resistere alla fortuna" (V, 15:562). Speaking of the imprisonment of the Milanese ambassador Ieronimo Morone, he concedes that "nessuno rimedio è contro a' mali determinati" (XVI, 10:1581). And, with reference to Leo X's ascent to the papacy (1513), he states that it seemed God was already beginning to approve of this pontificate in that the schismatic cardinals, Santa Croce and San Saverino, submitted to the authority of the new Pope (XI, 8:1096). Elsewhere, however, he warns against believing that God helped so and so because he was good, and that so and so experienced misfortunes because he was wicked, for the opposite is often true (**Ricordi**, 92C, 147C).[4]

Adding to this confusion is the fact that a term such as "fortuna," which in Guicciardini appears with a frequency unparalleled in Renaissance authors, is not always employed with the same connotation, as we shall see. Furthermore, no indication is ever given as to the specific domain of these forces, whether they operate independently of one another or are subordinated in a hierarchical order, i.e. God, Fate, Fortune, Man. At other times, they are seen as contributing somewhat equally to the development of a particular event. At other times, the cause of an event is traced to one or two of them. And in some cases there is even doubt as to which force is behind a given situation. Such is the case in the surrender of Serezanello, a small Florentine stronghold whose defenders frustrated for days all French efforts to capture it. But to the greatly embarrassed French help came in the person of Piero de' Medici, who simply handed over to them the small fortress. Guicciardini characterizes the episode by noting that "era destinato che, o per beneficio della fortuna o per ordinazione di altra più alta podestà [. . .] a tale impedimento sopravenisse rimedio immediato" (I, 14:172).

The allusion to God ("alta podestà") as having an active role in human affairs brings us to consider Guicciardini's apprehension of the Divine. The scholarship surrounding Guicciardini's religious beliefs is sharply divided between those who believe him pious and those for whom he is a pagan. Francesco Sarri, perhaps the most outspoken proponent of Guicciardini's religiosity, has hardly had any impact upon the resolution of the issues.[5] However, although his argumentation is often biased, and, at times, even superficial, the evidence he brings forth is so overwhelming that he seriously undermines the position of those who, like Otetea, see Guicciardini as "irréligieux," and an unbeliever ("nie le miracle"). Indeed, Guicciardini's works exhibit too many pious references to the Divine to corroborate Otetea's charge of paganism: "Guichardin était un païen."[6] A more balanced view is that Guicciardini is neither saintly nor a pagan, but a man raised in both the Christian beliefs of his ancestors and the worldly ideas of the Renaissance, especially those ideals that elevated the individual to the status of a *deus in terris*. Such a secular view was obviously incompatible with the strong belief in a strong Divine presence on earth, and the paradox became a significant trait of the Renaissance. For, if on one hand, individuals—so proud of their free-will and so confident in their intellectual prowess—believed in their ability to control that which was human, they still needed to turn to God for matters pertaining to the Hereafter. This explains, at least in part, why in Guicciardini's works the presence of God is neither pervasive nor as rare as has been recently claimed.[7] A cursory glance at the **Ricordanze** may be enough to confirm Guicciardini's frequent mention of the Divine. The work opens with an invocation of the Lord, the Virgin Mary and other saints. The loss of close relatives and friends is accepted in the name of God: "piacque a Dio." Speaking of his daughter's death, he hopes that the Lord will preserve his other children. In "A se stesso," a short note reminding himself of his duties towards both God and his fellow man, he thanks God's Grace for his high standing and good reputation among his peers.[8] He takes credit for his brilliant defense of Parma after due tribute to God ("doppo lo aiuto di Dio").[9] The **Dialogo del reggimento di Firenze** is replete with references to the Divine: "For the love of God . . . God knows . . . by the Grace of God . . . may it please God," and so on. And the autobiographical writings of 1527, especially the **"Defensoria,"** abound with pious expressions, such as "God be my witness . . . may God help me . . . praise the Lord . . . God most just Judge," etc.[10]

Admittedly, this overwhelming reference to the Divine is mostly ceremonial. One should be careful not to be swayed by religious fervor, as in the case of Sarri, and accept these and other similar appeals *prima facie*. This type of invocation, though reflecting the Christian environment of one's religious upbringing, is largely formulaic, peculiar to common speech and therefore void of any meaningful indication of actual faith.[11] Guicciardini's true religious spirit can be found more readily in his frequent appeals to God's judgement, the ultimate Justice which no human can escape. For instance, he cannot accept the idea that God's justice would permit Ludovico Sforza's heirs to enjoy a prosperous rule of Milan, which Ludovico had "maliciously" usurped from its rightful ruler, young Francesco Sforza (**Ricordi**, 91C). He considers Liverotto da Fermo's gruesome death an expression of Divine Jusice, as it took place exactly one year after Liveretto's brutal murder of several prominent citizens, including his own uncle.[12] And the Marquis of Pescara's sudden death is suggested as evidence of God's justice, which could not allow such an "insidious" man to enjoy the fruit of his evil deeds. (XVI, 11:1586). Alexander VI's simoniacal procurement of the papacy did not escape the contempt of his contemporaries nor the eventual but ineluctable "giudizio divino" (I, 2:93; VI, 4:584). Guicciardini calls the Pope's ignominious death a powerful example of God's justice which "in altro tempo e in altro luogo, con larga mano, con premi e con supplici sempiterni, riconosce i giusti dagli ingiusti" (VI, 4:584). The nuns and the Roman women being raped by soldiers during the Sack of Rome might find comfort in the assurance that the perpetrators will not escape "i giudizi di Dio" (XVIII, 8:1759).

It is important to note that pronouncements of faith such as these, while attesting to deep religious beliefs, tend to reveal a strong conviction that God does not interfere in mortal affairs, not even to prevent the most nefarious deeds. Indeed, religious rhetoric aside, in Guicciardini's view of the human condition, the Divine is no longer perceived as the source of good and evil befalling mankind, but as a transcendental power confined largely to the realm of the Hereafter, where one day He will judge all humans and their actions. To be sure, there are many narrated instances where God's intervention is attested to by alleged miracles, or other supernatural occurrences. Among the omens foreboding Lorenzo de' Medici's death, for instance, people reported seeing a comet, a bull with flaming horns, wolves howling, and lions slaying a beautiful lion. Some even saw an arrow hit the lantern in the cupola of Santa Liperta causing stones to fall towards the Medici's residence (**Storie Fiorentine,** p. 99)[13] There are countless other situations, particularly in the **Storia,** where individuals bring God into almost every aspect of their lives: they go to war in the name of God, attribute to His Will events beyond their control, invoke His Name to explain the unintelligible, pray for His intervention to extricate themselves from difficult situations, and find comfort in the idea that their cause will one day prevail before the Ultimate Judge. These appeals, however, whether proceeding from religious beliefs or other psychological imperatives, such as fear, are not to be confused with Guicciardini's own views. He is simply presenting, not endorsing, historical characters with all their beliefs, fears, hopes and superstitions.[14]

At times, he goes beyond his avowed task of objective representation and proceeds to lay bare the futility of these hopes. Such is the case of Charles VIII who, finding himself in desperate straits in Taro in 1495, invoked the help of Saint Denis and Saint Martin, France's most revered protectors. In the end, if he did manage to escape almost sure defeat, it was not thanks to his patron saints, but rather to Fortune which caused many of the enemy soldiers to abandon battle in pursuit of rich loot (II, 9:254-6). The unexpected election of Adrian VI to the Papacy (1522) was largely due to impulse rather than forethought. The cardinals, hard pressed to explain why they had chosen a man so "barbaro" and so removed from the intricate realities of Rome, attributed their extravagance to the Holy

Spirit's failure to inspire them, as if the Holy Spirit, Guicciardini comments sarcastically, refused to visit the hearts and minds of such corrupt men (XIV, 12:1404). Also, Francis I, in announcing his decision to cross the Alps to conquer Milan in 1524, tells his soldiers that God, in His infinite justice, had finally opened the way for them to claim what was rightfully theirs (XV, 9:1491). A few pages later (p. 1523), as if to underscore the belief that God does not interfere in earthly affairs, Guicciardini describes the tragic failure of the expedition: in February 1525, only five months after claiming God's consent, the French were routed, and the king himself taken prisoner. And, in urging Clement VII to take immediate action either by accepting or rejecting Charles V's suggested alliance, Guicciardini reminds the Pontiff that God helps those who help themselves: "a chi non si aiuta né Dio suole, né la fortuna può aiutare."[15]

But the notion of the Divine as existing outside the *ordo rerum* does not imply that God is altogether removed from human reality. He may be distant, but He is definitely not absent. He is still the last refuge and comfort of those in despair. His name is constantly invoked as the ultimate explanation of the inexplicable. And, most importantly, He is still thought of as that superior power "che muove tutto" (**Ricordi,** 211C). It is, indeed, as the Prime Mover behind the order of things that Guicciardini perceives God's presence in the world. In this apprehension, Divine action is closely identified with the role Guicciardini assigns to "fato," "destino" or, at times, "cielo" (the Heavens). "Le cose del mondo," Guicciardini believes, "non stanno ferme, anzi hanno sempre progresso al cammino a che ragionevolmente per sua natura hanno a andare e finire" (**Ricordi,** 140B). Although he does not use the word "fato" either in this "Ricordo" or in its elaboration (**Ricordi,** 71C), it is reasonable to assume that the phrase "per sua natura" (more often "per ordine della natura") refers to a supernatural power which foreordains the course of things.[16] Such a view of progression in the world comes close to Alberti's definition of Fate as the "cursum rerum in vita hominum"—the actual course of human events.[17] Under its sway things happen, change or move in a somewhat orderly fashion, such as the cycle of life itself. Its ineluctable course leads the willing and drags the unwilling to their destined path: "Ducunt volentes fata, nolentes trahunt" (**Ricordi,** 138C).

One may see Fate at work in the case of Vitellozzo who "non potè fuggire il fato di casa sua, di morire di morte violenta, come erano morti tutti gli altri suoi fratelli, in tempo che avevano già nell'armi grande esperienza e riputazione, e successivament uno dopo l'altro, secondo l'ordine dell'età" (V, 11:545). In 1512, following the Sack of Prato, the Gonfaloniere Piero Soderni, either because of his natural timidity of fearing the return of the Medici or simply led by "fato," adapted a political strategy that was to be the cause of his personal downfall as well as the ruin of Florence (XI, 4:1067). With regard to Julius II's health, Guicciardini wonders whether the Pope's sudden recovery was due to his physical strength or simply because he was destined "da fati" to cause further harm to Italy (X, 4:1098). In a similar way Guicciardini notes that the Cardinal was destined by Heaven to great "felicità" (X, 16:1043). The "felicità" is of course the Papacy, as Clement was led "da' fati" to the priesthood (XI, 8:1098). In a similar way Guicciardini anticipates Ludovico Sforza's inescapable doom when he attributes the duke's refusal to strengthen his defenses against the French either to lack of prudence or to avarice or simply to the fact that no one can resist "i consigli celesti" (IV, 8:442). Also, with reference to the 1527 Sack of Rome, Guicciardini comments that the city was "destinata per ordine de' cieli" to the greatness as well as to frequent calamities (XVII, 8:1758).

The association of "fato" with a preordained course of events points to Guicciardini's idea of Fate in the Boethian sense of a "providentially ordered and ordained *dispositio*."[18] The Jesuit Antonio Passovino, commenting on Guicciardini's treatment of Fate and Fortune, reiterates the traditional difinition of Fate as the expression of God's will: "fatum nihil aliud esse intelligendum quam sanctionem et vocem divinae mentis."[19] It is important to stress here that such characterization of Fate does not constitute Divine intervention in worldy affairs; it simply points to the existence of a cosmic order in motion, to the ineluctable course of the Providential plan. It is out of this conviction that Passovino charges Guicciardini with reducing "Providential" Fate to the level of whimsical and erratic Fortune by attributing to both powers the outcome of wars and other human deeds.[20] Passovino's reaction, however, is hasty and unfounded. Guicciardini may indeed attribute an event to both Fate and Fortune. This association, however, does not imply similarity between the two forces, it only suggests that they both contributed, each within the realm of its powers, to a particular outcome. Thus, the proposition that the "Heavens, Fortune and Fate conspired against Italy" simply denotes that each of these agents contributed within the its respective sphere of influence to Italy's ills. In other instances, he merely observes that an occurrence was due to either caso/fortuna or fate, expressing his uncertainty as to whether it was fortuitous or predetermined. The cardinal of Pavia was led either by "caso" or "fato" in his tragic selection of untrustworthy wsoldiers (IX, 17:926). The 1503 French defeat at the Garigliano river was due either to fortune (the weather) or "fato avverso" (VI, 7:612).

But though appearing together and, at times, even exhibiting similar characteristics, the two terms are never used interchangeably. For instance, Guicciardini believes that Maximilian's opportunity to enhance the prestige of the House of Austria by choosing a wealthy and powerful successor to the Imperial throne, namely Charles V, is an "occasione portatagli dall'ordine della natura e della fortuna" (XIII, 11:1308). As used here, "ordine della natura" is synonymous with Fate in that it implies that Charles was destined by birth and wealth to be an emperor. Fortuna, instead, suggests the coincidence of Charles' availability at a time when a new emporer was needed: he was in the right place at the right time. The latter, then, is accidental, while the former is predetermined; both, however, are unforeseeable. Also, in an important speech regarding the 1509 defense of Padova against the threatening armies of the League of Cambrai, Lionardo Loredano makes an eloquent distinction between Fate and Fortune. Having noted that Fate had led Venice to lose so much in so short a time, the Doge exhorts his disheartened fellow Venetians to seize the opportunity and stand up against "fortuna." Their resolve, he insists, will not only erase their shame, it will also show that the Serenissima's misfortunes did not issue from their cowardice, but from "una certa fatale tempesta [alla quale né il consigno né la costanza degli uomini può resistere]" (VIII, 10:792). In Loredano's view, then, one can stand up against adverse Fortune, but no one can resist Fate. With reference to the French's failure to attack Milan while it was poorly defended, Guicciardini writes that adverse fate blinded the French, as it had done in the past, preventing them from seizing such a golden opportunity (XV, 3:1455). Here, Fate points to the ineluctable course one is destined to follow, whereas Fortune is a mere coincidence, a temporary situation, an opportunity one may or may not exploit.

Thus, although Fate and Fortune share the element of unpredictability, they are actually quite distinct. The first is perceived as a foreordained course of events, hence a *causa per se;* the latter is seen more as a *causa ex accidenti,* a fortuitous event. But in Guicciardini's parlance fortuitousness is not Fortune's only characteristic, as the term takes on different connotations, albeit always associated with the unexpected. He uses it most liberally in the general sense of plain "luck." There are countless situations, especially in the *Storia d'Italia,* in which individuals are said to be determined or unwilling to "try their luck," particularly in battle.[21] In this popular use Fortune is but a commonplace indicating risk, and uncertainty. In other contexts, it may signify one's wealth or prosperity. And in some instances, it is employed to connote the influence of constellations, that is the astrological element incorporated into the conception of Fortune.[22]

In many cases, Fortune is identified with the occurrence of natural phenomena, such as rain. Thus, Piero de' Medici's plan to take Florence was thwarted by Fortune, as a heavy rain caused him to reach the city too late for a surprise attack. The slow advance allowed the defenders to organize an effective resistance, turning away Piero's beleaguered forces. Guicciardini notes that Piero would have succeeded had Fortune not made up for his adversaries' ineptitude (III, 13:375). In the war against Pisa, Fortune was contrary to Paolo Vitelli's ill-fated decision not to engage the enemy until summer. When summer came, the hot winds blowing from nearby marshes infested his entire army with disease, crippling his plans definitively. This and other misfortunes placed Paolo in jeopardy with his Florentine employers, who ultimatey sentenced him to death (IV, 11:458). Also, Prospero's brilliant idea to dig trenches to defend Milan was aided by Fortune in the form of a great snowfall which provided enough cover for the digging to proceed unhindered by enemy fire (XIV, 13:1410). And, in the 1527 Sack of Rome, Borbone's assault on the city was assisted by Fortune, as a thick fog rendered his troops almost invisible to the otherwise vigilant defenders (XVIII, 8:1756).

In addition to being perceived as a blind, casual, and indomitable force of nature, Fortune is often personified as the agent actively shaping, or at least interfering with, human events: it smiles upon Charles VIII (I, 10:158); it prevents Ferdinando from exhibiting his "virtù" (II, 3:222); it takes pleasure in the mistakes of the Papal captains by bringing about more confusion within their ranks (XIII, 8:1296); and, looking with a benign eye upon Clement's and the Emperor's military affairs, it interrupts the ominous planning of their captains (XIV, 7:1373). Paolo Vitelli's predicaments are largely due to ill fortune (IV, 10:458); the Duke of Nemours failed to regroup because he had adverse fortune (V, 15:562); Bentivoglio never experienced the bitterness of Fortune (VII, 11:71); Trivulzio was always persecuted by Fortune's fickleness (III, 10:1306), and its "ruota" turns in favor of Julius II (X, 1:935). Its *modus operandi,* then, is the traditional arbitrariness, constant changes, and the erratic spinning of the wheel, beneficial to some and ruinous to others.

Though still the personification of unforeseeable and uncontrollable forces befalling mankind, Fortune is no longer the whimsical goddess or the scholastic "ministra" of Providence, that is, a power proceeding from a supernatural or divine order. In Guicciardini it is perceived as an accidental *concursus causarum* whose origin is to be found mainly in the realm of human actions and ambitions. In the words of Mario Santoro, the source of events giving rise to Fortune lies "nella dimora dell'oumo e della società umana."[23] And, with reference to both *Storie Fiorentine* and the *Storia d'Italia,* Vito Vitale perceptively observes that in Guicciardini all historical causes "sono ricondotte alla volontà e all'azione umana."[24] This view of Fortune, reminiscent of the Albertian notion that people often make their own Fortune, though rare in the *Storie Fiorentine,*[25] pervades the entire *Storia d'Italia,* starting with the assertion that Italy's ills were brought on largely by Ludovico Sforza's decision to invite the French into Italy. Guicciardini labels the duke's action "the seed and origin of all the ills" that were to be visited upon Italy in the following four decades (I, 2:94). But Ludovico never intended his deed to give rise to all these calamities. He merely wished to secure his rule of Milan which, he feared, was being undermined by Florence and Naples. For a time he felt in total control of the events he put in motion, boasting of having Fortune "sotto i piedi," of being Fortune's "figliolo," and of steering "ad arbitrio" the affairs of Italy (III, 4:319-20). However, his action interacted with the expansionist aspirations of the French, it produced an uncontrollable course of events with dramatic consequences for individuals both near and far. Indeed, the events of the French invasion elicited responses from those it affected which, in turn, prompted others to react, starting a never ending chain of unpredictable events. Ludovico did not and could not have foreseen that his attempt to defend himself would bring about his ultimate downfall, that is, his "mala fortuna" (IV, 14:483).

Similarly, Charles VIII's expansionistic passions, stirred by Ludovico's invitation, dominated the affairs of France for almost 40 years. The series of events that engaged the energy and resources of three successive French kings began with Charles' decision to come to Italy in order to assert his rights to the Kingdom of Naples. However, as he proceeded to fulfill his ambitions, he aroused the hopes or fears of many who reacted either by opposing or joining him. Furthermore, his deeds paved the way for his successor Louis XII, who added Milan to the list of French claims. And when Francis I succeeded Louis (1515) not only did he share Louis' "inclinazione," he also found himself bound to pursue France's aggressive policy in Italy. The pressure to stay the military course came mostly from all the "young nobles, and from the glorious memory of recent French victories" (XII, 10:1184). But the dreams of conquest and glory, which Guicciardini appropriately calls "sfortunata cupidità (VI, 10:619), turned into a series of misfortunes for all three kings and for all of France: Charles barely escaped with his life in 1495 after Taro; Louis suffered the loss of Naples and the "ruina" of his army, including the loss of many great men and young nobles (VI, 1:569); and Francis I, with a great number of his generals and French nobles either dead or captured, was himself taken prisoner in 1525 (XVI, 1:1529). Shocked and in "smisurato dolore," France was ultimately forced to accept a humiliating peace treaty.

The pattern that emerges thus far leads one to conclude that both Ludovico's misfortunes and France's series of disasters were not determined by a supernatural power, but mostly by the deeds of individuals interacting or reacting—either in response or casually—with the actions of others.[26] As the chain of events grew exponentially, it became an unmanageable force on an erratic course, giving rise to Fortune, that is, fortuitous situations beneficial to some, and disastrous to others. Its positive or adverse impact depended largely on which side of that fortuitous event the individual chose or happened to stand.[27] Fortune was "benigna" to Charles VIII, in that enemy fortresses surrendered to him rather quickly, allowing him to conquer the whole kingdom of Naples in just a few days (II, 2:221-22). The surrender was, in turn, catastrophic to the king of Naples, as it brought on his downfall. In the 1503 battle of Garigliano, Louis XII's troops were soundly defeated due in part to the "iniquita della fortuna" in the form of a severe winter (VI, 7:606). The bad fortune of the French throughout this campaign is frequently mentioned as the cause for the success of the Spanish, especially for allowing Consalvo to enjoy "il favor della fortuna" (p. 568), and for providing him with good "occasione" (p. 572). And during the war of Urbino in 1517, Fortune, together ("congiunta") with the inept management of the Papal forces, stirred a brawl between Italian and German soldiers, causing the command to separate the forces by nationality and to suspend all military operations (pp. 1275-6). The "mala fortuna" that brought total ruin to Cardinal Francesco Soderini, as he was tried for high treason against the Church, presented Cardinal de' Medici, the future Clement VII, with the opportunity to rise in power and prestige at the papal court (XV, 3:1448).

In one form or another, good or bad, Fortune is so predominant and so frequently invoked in the *Storia* that it has prompted several critics, including Felix Gilbert, to espouse Palmarocchi's view that Guicciardini, unlike other humanists, projects a world almost totally under the sway of Fortune, in which the individual is no longer believed to have that fifty-fifty percentage of autonomy proposed by Machiavelli: "Ognun vede come il Guicciardini, a differenza di altri umanisti, riconsca alla fortuna un predominio quasi assoluto e non dia alla virtù dell'individuo neppure quella percentuale di autonomia che le assegnava Machiavelli."[28] He bases his view on selected narrative instances in which Fortune is invoked to explain the outcome of certain events. He also takes into account Guicciardini's own comments about the impact Fortune has on worldly affairs. The merit of Palmarocchi's otherwise well-grounded argument is somewhat undermined by his swift conclusion that Guicciardini "ammette che una forza estranea all'individio accompagni, modifichi e spesso annulli la sua libertà d'azione."[29] This rather dim view of mankind under the sway of an all powerful Fortune fails to take into account that in Guicciardini all too often Fortune is not a force "estranea" to the individual, but immanent in personal behavior; not a force that controls human actions, but one which results from them.

A case in point is King Ferdinand of Naples who, intent upon preserving the Pope's support in the face of the French threat, blames his "mala fortuna" for the strained relations with Rome. By "mala fortuna," here, the king refers to Ludovico Sforza's efforts to discredit him with the Pope. The duke had indeed warned Alexander VI to regard Ferdinand as a threat, reminding him that in the past the Aragonese had never hesitated to occupy the Holy city. But although Ludovico was responsible for poisoning the relations between Naples and Rome, Ferdinand's "mala fortuna" was actually unleashed by his own doing. The duke merely exploited the king's short-sighted approval of the sale of Cibo's Roman strongholds to the Orsini, avowed enemies of the Pope. In discussing that sale, Guicciardini warns that Ferdinand's support was a poor "deliberazione" in that it was to give rise to grave consequences. In fact, it not only offended the Pope by showing total disregard for his authority, it also threatened the security of the Papal territories. More importantly, it reinforced Ludovico's suspicions of the king, whose actions were always suspect to the duke (I, 3:98). When Ferdinand tried to repair the damage, to defend against Fortune as it were, it was already too late, for by removing the cause, Guicciardini comments, one does not necessarily remove the effects (I, 3:104). It would have helped Ferdinand to heed the saying: "it is prudent to consider every detail, however insignificant, for little things are often the causes of major events," (*Ricordi*, 82C).

This is not to say that misfortunes always arise from one's own doing; often the source of Fortune lies in the actions of others. For instance, Fortune was "avversa" to the Duke of Nemours in his attempt to re-group his forces scattered near Bari (V, 15:562). But the adversity attributed to Fortune can actually be traced back to Louis d'Ars' decision to go alone to the rendez-vous rather than joining forces with the Duke of Atri. As a result, Atri proceeded by himself, careful not to run into the Spanish forces en route to Matera. But Atri never reached the main body of the French forces, as a large Spanish contingent, responding to a rebellion in nearby Rutigliano, changed course, and accidentally fell upon him, annihilating his smaller army, and taking him prisoner. In the ensuing battle (1503), Nemours found himself at a fatal disadvantage, for he had to fight with his ranks "diminished," without the support of Atri's forces (p. 565). Thus, the adversity of Fortune invoked to explain the Duke's defeat and subsequent death is, at least in part, the direct result of a costly decision by one of his captains.

Where Fortune is the product of human actions, it is not unreasonable to suppose that it is within human power to prevent it or, at least, guard against it. In his youthful works, in particular the *Storie Fiorentine* (1508-9), Guicciardini himself had shared in the humanist belief that humans could actually oppose Fortune with their prudence, roughly the equivalent of Machiavelli's "virtu." But eventually, Mario Santoro has argued, he lost confidence in human prudence, having experienced first-hand its insuffiency vis-a-vis the preponderance of Fortune. He expressed his dismay in the 1527 personal writing, an introspection of his unhappy role in the war that led to the infamous Sack of Rome. But, if the crisis brought him face to face with the limits of prudence, it never really extinguished his belief in human actions as the measure of one's *dignitas*. Mario Santoro points out that Guicciardini, having acknowledged the absolute dominance of Fortune, has come to believe that human dignity rests not in the outcome of one's actions, but in having acted wisely.[30] The strength of this rather stoic argument lies primarily in Guicciardini's often-noted view that individuals, like actors, should not be judged by the role they are assigned to play, but rather by how well they play it (**"Consolatoria,"** 508-9). This same belief informs his justification of Clement VlI's politics throughout the war, whereby he argues that the Pope should not be judged by the result of his deeds, but by "le ragione che lo mossono, perche da queste, non dallo evento, s'ha a fare giudicio della prudenzia o imprudenzia sua."[31]

The emphasis on one's prerogative to act tends to free her/him from the yoke of that "forza estranea" and, at the same time, redeems humans from the gloomy condition painted by Palmarocchi. However, this redemption is somewhat illusory, for, as long as individuals are seen as responsibile only for having acted well, the outcome of their doing remains within the power of forces beyond their control ("estranea"), reducing their actions to mere form, an empty gesture. It is important to recognize, at this point, that the view of mortals as powerless in the face of an all-powerful Fortune derives its authority largely from the autobiographical writings, in which a dejected Guicciardini tries to recall and explain his responsibilities in a calamitous war that enveloped his beloved Florence, along with the entire Italian peninsula. In fact, both the image of the individual as an actor and the assessment of the Pope's conduct betray Guicciardini's personal crisis and, in particular, his need to defend his role as Clement's political and military adviser. It is out of this concern that he calls attention to the reasons that justified Rome's fateful decisions, attributing to circumstances the outcome of those decisions, that is, the failure of the Pope's (and his own) policies.[32] The subjective nature of these writings tends to undermine the soundness of the view that one's *dignitas* or self-worth is to be found not in the motive or scope of his/her actions but in the way s/he acted. Accordingly, the validity of Santoro's suggestion must be weighed against evidence from later works, such as the *Storia,* where it is more likely that a self-assured Guicciardini, having rebounded from his crisis, will express a more objective and balanced view of humankind and the world.

To be sure, in the *Storia* there are numerous authorial reflections on the overwhelming power of Fortune as well as legions of narrated events whose outcome is attributed solely to Fortune. But there is also a host of cases in which both humans and Fortune are said to have contributed to the outcome of an event. Ferdinand of Naples managed to keep his kingdom thanks to his prudence and good fortune (I, 6:131). The French could have easily taken Francete (1496), but either because of lack of prudence or bad fortune they lost a great opportunity, (III, 7:334). The Doge tells the Venetian Senate that impending calamities often fail to materialize either because of Fortune or because of prudence (III, 4:318). Alviano, a great man of arms, never won a major battle, either because of *mala fortuna* or because of his rash decisions (XII, 17:1223). At the river Oglio, the allies escaped grave danger partly because of Fortune and partly because of the enemy's imprudence. Also, their decision to move their camp to higher ground was made with prudence and with the aid of Fortune (XIV, 8:1376). The entire French campaign, in particular its defeat at Bicocca (1522), was partly due, as Marshal Lautrech will report to Francis I, to adverse fortune, but mostly to lack of prudence: "parte per colpa sua, parte per negligenza e imprudenti consigli di quegli che erano appresso al re, parte, se è lecito dire il vero, per la malignità della fortuna" (XIV, 14:1418). During the Sack of Rome, the assault on San Pietro in Valle succeeded either because of Fortune or because of the defenders' imprudence (XVIII, 12:1779). And, in pointing out the difference between Lorenzo the Magnificent's brash trip to Naples in 1479 and his son Piero's "imprudent" visit to Charles VIII in 1494, Guicciardini notes that one should not be guided by past examples, for situations may reoccur only if the same Fortune and prudence exist (I, 14:173). Thus, he clearly perceives both forces as having a role in determining the course of human events.[33]

Guicciardini's view of human beings as an active force in the development of worldly affairs, and, hence, as partly responsible for their consequences, is not at all surprising if one considers that, especially in the *Storia,* human prudence or imprudence is invoked perhaps as frequently as Fortune in explaining the outcome of events. All too often, in fact, either prudence or imprudence is perceived as the only force behind human failures or success. Speaking of Pisa's self-proclaimed independence from Florence and the turmoil that followed, Guicciardini comments that had the Florentines consulted with the Pisans, as they had in the past, things would have turned out differently. But, as often happens in cases of emergency, he continues, people tend to lose "la prudenza con la quale arebbono potuto impedire le cose destinate" (I, 15:179). The French loss of Calabria in 1496 was due to negligence and imprudence (II, 7:341). Guicciardini attributes the fiasco of the whole campaign to Charles VIII's "negligenza" and short-sightedness as well as to the corruption of his advisers (III, 7:344). And, the series of setbacks culminating in the fateful battle of Pavia are traced back to the ineptitude of the French. The cause of Lautrech's retreat toward Milan is said to be the imprudence of the French advisers, acting either out of negligence or "incapacita" (p. 1379). The main reason for the allies' easy access into Milan proceeded from the negligence of the French (p. 1385). And, looking back at the allies' conduct of the war, especially with regard to Milan, Guicciardini notes that the Pope and his allies could have taken advantage of the situation by attacking the beleaguered imperial armies defending the city. But Clement failed to take the initiative, as he was too "confused," always lacking the necessary resolve to exploit favorable fortune or to resist it whenever it was unfavorable (XVI, 11:1587-92). With reference to the allies' ineptitude, Guicciardini notes that it was typical of allied forces to lack the necessary flexibility to take advantage of good Fortune or to resist it when it turns unfavorable (p. 1588).[34]

The postulate that prudence or imprudence is often the cause of one's failures or success suggests a view of humankind as responsible for the outcome of their own actions. This not only underscores the belief that the individual can, at times, oppose or prevent Fortune, it also reveals that Fortune itself is not so "predominant" as to reduce an individual to a mere "good actor." In sum, while acknowledging Fortune's dominant role in the world, Guicciardini never ceases to believe in one's ability to help control, determine or influence the outcome of worldly affairs. In his apprehension of the human condition, then, mortals figure as one of the forces that shape the course of the world.

Rather than the absence of humanist optimism, lamented by Palmarocchi, one finds in Guicciardini a world in which the individual strives to assert influence against the frustrations inherent in a constantly changing reality or Fortune itself. The need to change or "mutare" with the times, advocated by Machiavelli, has become more difficult, as the dynamics informing the rapid developments of war-torn Italy are no longer confined to regional politics. Now, events of great consequences are often set in motion by individuals from different cultures and distant lands.[35] In Guicciardini, there is the subtle apprehension that in such a fast-changing and growing world, the individual is becoming more and more aware of human limitations. But if humans cannot fully determine what happens in their world, they can still play a role, admittedly diminished, in shaping its course. Indeed, human *dignitas* does not lie merely in having acted well, but, more pointedly, in one's role as a significant force in the development of human events.

Notes

[1] N. Machiavelli, *Istorie Fiorentine,* a cura di Franco Gaeta (Milan, 1962), p. 577, concludes: "subito morto Lorenzo, cominciarono a nascere quegli cattivi semi i quali, non dopo molto tempo [. . .] rovinorono e ancora rovinano la Italia." For a discussion of Machiavelli's pessimism vis-à-vis this aspect of the *Istorie,* see Salvatore Di Maria, "Machiavelli's View of History: the Istorie Fiorentine," in *Renaissance Quarterly,* XLV, no. 2, (Summer, 1992), 248-270.

[2] All quotations from the original are from the edition of Emanuella Lugnani Scarano, F. Guicciardini, *Storia d'Italia,* in *Opere,* (Turin, 1981, rp. 1987), Il-lll. To provide the reader with quick access to the text, each quotation is followed by book, chapter, and page number; numbers up to 1045 are from the second volume. All translations are my own.

[3] R. Palmarocchi, *Studi guicciardiniani* (Florence, 1947), p. 38.

[4] F. Guicciardini, *Ricordi,* in *Opere,* a cura di Emanuella Lugnani Scarano, (Turin, 1970), I.

[5] F. Sarri, "Guicciardini e la religione," in *Francesco Guicciardini nel IV Centenario della morte (1540-1940).* Supplement I of *Rinascita* (Florence, 1940). Besides Sarri, both L. Malagoli, *Guicciardini* (Florence, 1939), and V. De Caprariis, *Francesco Guicciardini. Opere* (Milan, 1953) argue for a religious Guicciardini. Also, M. Santoro, *Fortuna. ragione e prudenza nella civiltà letteraria del Cinquecento* (Naples, 1967), p. 311, notes that in this tumultuous period Guicciardini "sente affiorare nella sua coscienza la presenza di Dio."

[6] A. Otetea, *Francois Guichardin. Sa vie publique et sa pensée politique* (Paris, 1926), p. 318. For an informed discussion of this view see Palmarocchi, op. cit., p. 45.

[7] M. Phillips, *Francesco Guicciardini: The Historian's Craft* (Toronto, 1977), p. 26, noting the expanded role of Fortune in the *Storia,* in contrast to the earlier *Storie Fiorentine,* writes that "God is never invoked as an explanation in the later work."

[8] In De Caprariis, op. cit., pp. 17, 20.

[9] Ibid., *Per la difesa di Parma.* p. 57.

[10] The *Dialogo* as well as the autobiographical writings "Consolatoria," "Accusatoria," and "Defensoria" are in Scarano's, op. cit., I.

[11] De Caprariis, op. cit., p. 12, argues that these religious expressions are not mere formulas, but evidence of Guicciardini's actual faith. With reference to the expression "A Dio piaccia," he notes: "Questa—come altre notazioni simili—non è solo generica formula, ma è indizio di un'anima tutt'altro che sorda alle risonanze religiose." He reiterates this same belief in a similar comment to "A se stesso," p. 23: "Questo bra-

no concitato—come i numerosi accenni alle *Ricordan-ze*—fa avvertiti che il problema della religiosità guic-ciardiniana non è riducibile al facile schema che si ode ripetere ogni giorno più o meno orchestrato e si giova di pochi *Ricordi,* male interpretandoli." With reference to "A se stesso," De Caprariis observes that Guiccia-rdini was not the atheist people thought he was: "non fu l'ateo, l'uomo senza religione che si è creduto per molto tempo" (p.x).

[12] Sarri, op. cit., p. 166, erroneously states that the victim was Cesare Borgia.

[13] See, *Storie Fiorentine,* in Scarano's, op. cit. I. In the *Storia* there are several instances of visions and pre-monitions (I, 9, 153-4), ghosts (1, 18:194), supersti-tions (V, 15:567; V1, 7:608), and miracles (X, 9:995). These means of explaining the unknown (see, Ricordi, 123C), far from representing Guicciardini's own be-liefs, constitute the vox populi which helps provide an objective representation of man with all his fears and superstitions.

[14] Here are a few, but typical examples of this frame of mind: the Milanese ambassador begs Charles VIII to answer God's call and cross the Alps into Italy: "Dio è quello [. . . che] vi chiama, Dio è quello che vi mena" 1, 4:113). Charles attributes to "la volontà di Dio" his own decision to return to Italy in 1496. The ferocious Mottino exhorts his troops to battle, assuring them that God is on their side: "con l'aiuto del sommo Dio" (X1, 12: 1115). Cardinal Sedunense harangues his Swiss soldiers to go out and kill the French with the help of God "che con giusto odio perseguita la superbia dei francesi" (XII, 15:1212). For a discussion, see Salvatore Di Maria, "Narratorial Strategy in Guic-ciardini's *Storia d'Italia," Stanford Italian Review,* vol 9, (Winter, 1991), pp. 115-132.

[15] F. Guicciardini, "Proposta di alleanza di Carlo V a Clemente VII," in *Scritti politici e ricordi,* a cura di Roberto Palmarocchi (Bari: Laterza, 1933), 161.

[16] The notion of "natura" as an extension of fate is not altogether uncommon. Hanna F. Pitkin, *Fortune is a Woman: Gender and Politics in the Thought of Niccolò Machiavelli* (Berkeley, 1984), p. 167, con-trasting Machiavelli's view of fortune and nature, notes that nature "is usually said to determine birth and death; [. . . it] tends to mean what one starts with or from; [. . . it] tends to be connected with what is fixed or long-range or, if changing, then cyclical like the seasons and the tides. [. . it] is the permanently given from which we begin."

[17] L. B. Alberti, *Fatum et fortuna,* in *Prosatori latini del Quattrocento,* a cura di Eugenio Garin, (Milan, 1952), p. 656. At the end of the dream-vision the phi-losopher concludes that fate is nothing but the course of human events which proceeds according to its own order: "Fatum didici esse aliud nihil quam cursum re-rum in vita hominum, qui quidem ordine suo et lapsu rapitur."

[18] V. Cioffari, *Fortune and Fate: from Democritus to St. Thomas Aquinas* (New York, 1935), p. 86. J.G.A. Pocock, *The Machiavellian Moment* (Princeton, 1975), p. 39ff, discusses in more details Boethius's concept of Fate, especially in its relation to Fortune and Prov-idence.

[19] Quoted by Palmarocchi, op. cit., p. 45.

[20] Ibid.: "fato atque fortunae, quae nihil est, saepe tri-buit exitus bellorum ac regnorum conversiones." For a survey of the concept of Fate as well as Fortune see, besides Cioffari, H. R. Patch, "The Tradition of the Goddess Fortuna in Medieval Philosophy and Litera-ture," *Smith College Studies in Modern Languages,* III, 4 (July, 1922), pp. 179-235.

[21] There are, indeed, dozens of instances in which Fortune is used in the commonplace acceptance of plain luck: "tentare. . . . seguitare la fortuna, mettere in potestà . . . a discrezione . . . in arbitrio della fortuna, fare esperienza della fortuna, commettersi alla fortu-na," and other similar phrases.

[22] In the "Consolatoria," p. 508, for example, Guiccia-rdini writes that our "persona" is given us by Fortune: "la persona che sostegnamo nel mondo è quella che ci è data dalla fortuna."

[23] Santoro. op. cit., p. 306.

[24] V. Vitale, *Francesco Guicciardini* (Turin, 1941), p. 285.

[25] For a discussion of the limited role of Fortune in this youthful work see Santoro, op. cit.

[26] Ibid., pp. 305-6, Santoro writes that for Guicciardini Fortune is "il complesso delle circostanze in cui l'uomo di volta in volta si trova ad agire," adding that these circumstances are to be identified "con le azioni indi-viduali che direttamente o indirettamente interessavano il campo di inchiesta." He goes on to observe that "le radici degli eventi e delle circostanze che concorre-vano a formare il territorio della 'fortuna' erano nella dimora dell'uomo e della società umana."

[27] Patch, "The tradition," p. 185, explains that for St. Thomas "Good and bad fortune depend merely on the way fortune suits individual taste and desire."

[28] Palmarocchi, op. cit., p. 43. Palmarocchi's view is echoed by F. Gilbert, *Machiavelli and Guicciardini: Politics and History in Sixteenth-Century Florence*

(Princeton, 1965), p. 288, for whom the "master of the events of history is Fortuna." Gilbert, without distinguishing between Fate and Fortune, concludes: "The strongest, most permanent impression which the *History of Italy* imparts—and was meant to impart—is that of the helplessness and impotence of man in the face of fate." Santoro, op. cit, p. 312, finds Palmarocchi's study lacking in historical perspective in that it fails to trace the gradual development of Guicciardini's concept of Fortune.

[29] Ibid., p. 44.

[30] Santoro, op. cit., p. 290, with reference to Pontano's view of the binary opposition Prudenza-fortuna, writes: "Ma il Guicciardini, che aveva sperimentato più lungamente e duramente la impossibilità per l'uomo di contrastare con la 'fortuna,' ricorreva ad una soluzione del tutto diversa: non interessavano le 'occasioni' e le condizioni in cui l'uomo si trovasse a svolgere la sua attività; interessava il modo con cui l'uomo di volta in volta si comportasse."

[31] F. Guicciardini, "Giustificazione della politica di Clemente VII," in *Scritti politici e ricordi,* p. 198.

[32] Upon leaving his post as Papal adviser, a dispirited Guicciardini returned to Florence, where his name was smeared by accusations of fraud and disloyalty. It was under these trying circumstances that he wrote the "Consolotaria," the "Accusatoria" and the "Defensoria." Commenting on these works, Emanuella Lugnani Scarano, *Opere,* 1, p. 49, notes that especially the "Consolatoria" "vuole essere un tentativo di reagire alla prostrazione psicologica che quei fatti hanno determinato."

[33] Cf. *Ricordi,* 110C and 117C

[34] The direct responsibility individuals often bear in the outcome of events argues rather convincingly against Pocock's suggestion that Guicciardini's concept of prudence may be identified with one's ability to adapt to events, to maneuver rather than to act. With specific reference to the *Dialogo del Reggimento di Firenze,* Pocock, op. cit. p. 238, contrasting Machiavelli's concept of virtù with Guicciardini's idea of prudence, notes that for Guicciardini prudence is "the steersman's or doctor's power to observe events and accommodate oneself to them, rather than seeking to shape or determine them; his is a politics of maneuver rather than action." Pocock reiterates this definition of prudence when he compares Machiavelli's and Guicciardini's man, as depicted in the *Prince* and on the *Ricordi:* "Machiavelli's individual is a ruler seeking to shape events through virtù in the sense of audacity, Guicciardini's a patrician seeking to adapt himself to events through prudence" (p. 269).

[35] Underscoring the international dimensions of the events narrated in the *Storia,* Guicciardini writes, that the year 1494 "aperse la porta a innumerabili e orribili calamità, delle quali si può dire che per diversi accidenti abbia di poi partecipato una grande parte del mondo" (I, 6:131). He also laments the swift changes and the instability affecting Italian cultural and political life, when he traces back to Charles VIII's all the ills befalling the peninsula: "i semi di innumerabili calamità, di orribilissimi accidenti, e variazione di tutte le cose: perché dalla passata sua non solo ebbono mutazioni di stati, sovversioni di regni, desolazioni di paesi, eccidi di città crudelissime uccisioni, ma eziandio nuovi abiti, nuovi costumi, nuovi e sanguinosi modi di guerreggiare, infermità sino a quel dì non conosciute [. . .] altre nazioni hanno devastata l'ìtalia" (I, 9:157). Giuliano Procacci, "La 'fortuna' nella realtà politica e sociale del primo Cinquecento," *Belfagor,* VI, n. 4 (July, 1951), pp. 407, 421, discusses Guicciardini's concept of Fortune within the context of this instability.

Alison Brown (essay date 1994)

SOURCE: Introduction to *Dialogue on the Government of Florence,* by Francesco Guicciardini, edited and translated by Alison Brown, Cambridge University Press, 1994, pp. vii-xxviii.

[*In the following excerpt, Brown provides a close assessment of Guicciardini's* Dialogue, *compares his work to that of his colleague Machiavelli, and concludes that while Guicciardini preferred freedom to tyranny, he was ultimately a practical man who believed in realpolitik.*]

The year 1509 . . . marks Francesco's initiation into the life of politics, when he was summoned for the first time to a consultative meeting of citizens, or *pratica* (see Glossary). In 1511, aged only 28, he was elected Florentine ambassador to Spain, and it was there, at Logrogno, that he wrote the **Discourse** which anticipates in many respects his reform scheme in Book II of the **Dialogue [on the Government of Florence]**. It offers a blueprint for the reform of the republican regime headed by Piero Soderini, completed (if we are to believe its date, '27 August 1512') just before the collapse of this regime at the hands of the Spanish at the end of August, and several weeks before he would have heard about it. The same period of relative leisure also inspired the first of three versions of reflective **Ricordi** or **Maxims,** which he twice revised during similar periods of enforced leisure, in 1528 and 1530. Kept well-informed by his family of the new situation in Florence, and of 'who stood highest in Medici favour', he was allowed to return home in January 1514.

Far from being disadvantaged by the fall of the republican regime and restoration of the Medici, Francesco found himself on his return favoured by a series of offices, initially in Florence and later in the Papal States. He was happy to accede to Lorenzo di Piero de' Medici's wish that he, rather than his elder brother, should take his father's place as one of the Seventeen Reformers in 1514. The following year he was appointed a member of the Eight of Ward and then a member of the Signoria, and in December that year he was appointed a consistorial advocate by the Medici pope Leo X. These interim years of office in Florence produced two more political writings on Florentine government, *On the Government of Florence after the Medici Restoration in 1512* and *On How the Medici Family Should Secure Power for Themselves.* Both realistically accept that, since self-preservation is the objective of government, the Medici will have to protect themselves against popular opposition by building up a group of partisans who will have more to lose than gain by a change of regime: 'so that utility, indeed necessity, and not just love' will ensure their support (*Del governo,* p. 266). The second piece, written in 1516, shows early traces of the influence of Machiavelli's *Prince*—as Gennaro Sasso has pointed out[1]—in its 'digression' about the problem of ruling new states and reference to Cesare Borgia and Francesco Sforza. Accepting that the Medici are now 'bosses' *(padroni)* of Florence, it suggests that they could avoid the problems experienced by Lorenzo il Magnifico by feeding their friends in Rome, not Florence, 'now that they have the pontificate in their hands' (*Del modo,* pp. 273, 279): prescient advice in view of the reward he himself received from them later that year.

Francesco's first papal appointment marked another turning-point in his life, as he may himself have recognised at the time. For this was the moment when he apparently had his first horoscope written, anticipating by some months his appointment as papal Governor of Modena in the summer of 1516, when it said he began to enjoy 'wealth and office in a very alarming and difficult position'. The following year he was appointed Governor of Reggio as well as Modena, in 1521 papal Commissary General in the war against the French, in 1524 President of the Romagna under the new Medici pope Clement VII (the year in which he possibly had a second horoscope prepared), and in 1526 papal Lieutenant General of the War of the League of Cognac.

It was during this period of his life, more precisely between August-November 1521 and, at the earliest, April 1524, that Francesco wrote the *Dialogue on the Government of Florence.* It is dated in its second preface (B; see p. xxv below), which states that it was begun 'at the time of Leo, when I found myself in the position of his Commissary General in the imperial and papal army in the war against the French', and was finished 'now that I have been appointed by Clement Governor of all the cities in the Romagna, which are extremely disturbed and full of infinite difficulties

because of the uprisings that followed Leo's death'. So it belongs to the period when Florentines were optimistic about a return to a more republican government. After the death in May 1519 of Lorenzo, Duke of Urbino, Florence's Captain General and the last legitimate descendant (with Leo X) of Lorenzo the Magnificent, the Florentines had been consulted by the well-liked cardinal Giulio de' Medici about how their city should be governed. Since Giulio was popular in Florence and known to be fond of the city, they were evidently confident that he would treat their suggestions seriously and introduce constitutional reform. So it seems likely, as Giovanni Silvano has suggested,[2] that—far from being written after the moment for a republican restoration had 'gone forever', in Pocock's words—Guicciardini's *Dialogue* shared the same very practical purpose as Machiavelli's *Discourse on the Government of Florence after the Death of Lorenzo de' Medici* and other blueprints proposed at this time.

The situation was transformed in a paradoxical way by two events. The first was the abortive plot to kill Giulio de' Medici in 1522, which alienated Giulio and, instead of reducing Medici power in Florence, increased it. The second was Giulio's elevation to the papacy as Clement VII in November 1523. By initially strengthening the Medici's position in Florence, these events must have increased the fear Guicciardini had already expressed (in prefaces A and B, pp. 2, 5, nn. 4 and 19) of alienating his patrons through his republicanism. Yet, at the same time, the growing and openly-discussed posibility of revolution in Florence, now governed by the unpopular cardinal Silvio Passerini and the young Medici bastard Ippolito, raised a worse spectre for Guicciardini of being victimised by the republican regime as a Medicean—and possibly suffering the same fate as Bernardo del Nero, his *alter ego,* who was executed for his Medici sympathies. So whereas the first preface (A) expressed the hope of publishing the *Dialogue,* 'before I grow old', despite the danger of doing so with Florence 'under the shadow of the Medici government' (in A and B), its final preface (C) disclaims any political relevance or intention to publish (p. 4 and nn. 4, 14). The final preface also adds a flattering reference to Piero Soderini's republican government. Instead of suggesting that he might be thought ungrateful to the Medici in writing the *Dialogue,* he now alludes to Xenophon and Aristotle in order to suggest his political detachment (since Xenophon's loyalty to Athens was evidently not compromised by his biography of Cyrus, nor Aristotle's loyalty to Alexander the Great by his *Politics* (p. 4)); and at the same time he removes names from the text to modify his earlier more trenchant comments on both regimes. Far from being detached, however, these cosmetic adjustments to the text and its convoluted preface suggest that the *Dialogue* was both relevant and potentially dangerous in the later 1520s.

In May 1527, a year after Guicciardini was appointed Lieutenant General of the papal army, Rome was sacked by imperial troops and the Medici regime in Florence fell. Losing his position, Guicciardini retired to his villa outside Florence, where he wrote two imaginary orations which accurately forecast what was to happen two years later, the *Accusatoria,* in which he accuses himself of crimes against the state before a session of the Court of Forty, and the *Defensoria,* in which he defends himself. Increasingly isolated as the republican government in Florence became more extreme, he began his second history of Florence, the *Cose fiorentine,* as well as a third version of his *Maxims.* The Treaty of Barcelona between Clement and Charles V in June 1529 obliged the Emperor to restore the Medici to Florence. Threatened with imprisonment and banishment by the republican government, Guicciardini fled from Florentine territory; despite acting as mediator between Florence and the Pope, however, he was accused of contumacy and banished as a rebel. His *Considerations on the 'Discourses' of Machiavelli* was written as he travelled as an exile to Rome, whence he returned as papal emissary to restore order in Florence after its final capitulation in August 1530. Rewarded with the Governorship of Bologna—but not the Romagna, as he had hoped—Guicciardini finally retired to Florence after the death of Clement VII in September 1534. Before then, however, he had been responsible for helping to establish Alessandro, the illegitimate last descendant of the elder Medici line, as Duke of Florence in 1532. In January that year he had repeated to the Pope the advice he had given Leo X in 1516: that the Medici should not establish a principate but strengthen their partisans in the city, among whom he now openly included himself (*Discourse* of 30 January 1532, p. 455). A *balìa* was created (as he had recommended) and in April 1532 it appointed him one of the Twelve Reformers who made Alessandro Duke of Florence. Later he became one of Alessandro's closest advisers and was principally responsible for defending him against the exiles' charges of tyranny in 1535-6, asserting not only that Alessandro's ducal title was legitimate, since it had been granted by the delegated authority of a Florentine *parlamento* with imperial consent, but that his behaviour was 'most holy and his government free and pious'.[3]

The equivocation of Guicciardini's political stance is reflected in the *Dialogue on the Government of Florence,* whose republican idealism seems equally at odds with its political pragmatism and *realpolitik.* The problems Guicciardini faced in the 1520s in writing what Sasso calls 'this brief but complex' work[4] make it, as we have seen, deliberately ambiguous and difficult to decode. For if we adopt a republican reading and identify Guicciardini with the idealism of Book II, we would interpret del Nero's defence of Medici tyranny in Book I as Guicciardini's safeguard against the danger of alienating his papal employers; whereas if we identify Guicciardini with del Nero's position in Book I, we would read Book II as his protection against a possible republican restoration. Revisions to the first draft suggest that he modified criticism both of the Medici and of the republican regimes. After 1527, however, the republican restoration and his banishment as a rebel in 1529 made the parallel between his position and del Nero's very evident. Perhaps, as Sasso has suggested,[5] it was already in Guicciardini's mind when he was writing the *Dialogue.*

It purports to represent a discussion held in the villa of Bernardo del Nero just after the revolution of November 1494, which replaced the 'narrow' regime headed by Piero de' Medici with a more 'open' regime, under the control of a Great Council of some three-and-a-half thousand members. Bernardo del Nero, the former Medici supporter beheaded in 1497 for failing to reveal a pro-Medicean conspiracy, defends the Medici regime against the charges of the other younger participants, who in varying degrees all represent republican opposition to the Medici. Piero Capponi, a key figure in the downfall of the Medici and in the new regime, is a representative of the old mercantile aristocracy of Florence, the so-called *ottimati,* or optimates, who had governed Florence since the 1380s; Pagolantonio Soderini and Piero Guicciardini (the author's father) participate as citizens who played an influential role in consultative discussions after 1494, Pagolantonio as a leading Savonarolan and Piero Guicciardini as a more cautious supporter of the Savonarolan regime and also, as Ficino's pupil, the 'academic' voice in the *Dialogue.*

Ever since Cosimo de' Medici's return from exile in 1434, the Medici party had been narrowing the basis of power in Florence. It was gradually undermining the authority of the old-established councils of the People and Commune by replacing them with other, smaller councils, or by using special legislative powers, or *balìa,* to bypass them altogether. At the same time it controlled elections to offices through the use of select scrutineers, or *accoppiatori.* This regime was overthrown in November 1494, as a reaction against the Medici's growing autocracy and the incompetence of Piero de' Medici when faced with the French invasion. It was replaced initially by a government controlled by twenty optimates (among them, Piero Capponi); and then, after the intervention of the Dominican monk Savonarola, by a more open regime drawn from members of an enlarged Great Council of major office-holders over four generations, which became a potent symbol of the new republican regime. The *Dialogue* thus claims to represent a discussion about the rival merits of liberty, or open government, and restricted, or narrow government, based on 'the actual conversation' once held by its participants. Yet in approaching it, we must remember that del Nero, 'almost like an oracle' (p. 3), is allowed to enjoy the benefit of foresight in predicting the outcome of the 1494 revolution some 30 years after the events he describes. And since the argument for liberty is presented by members of the oligarchy which had replaced the guild regime in 1382 and had collaborated closely with the Medici after 1434, the issues are inevitably less clear-cut—and more interesting—than the antilogical form of the *Dialogue* initially suggests.

The *Dialogue* opens with a general discussion about the nature of revolutions and how to judge them. Whereas del Nero as a Medicean argues that such political upheavals always do more harm than good to a city, Soderini defends the 1494 revolution by distinguishing it from other types of political change, which he condemns for their factionalism. What he condemns are changes or *alterazioni* like those of 1433 and 1434 (when Cosimo de' Medici was exiled and restored to power), or those of 1466 and 1478 (following the Pitti and Pazzi Conspiracies), which simply transferred power within the ruling elite or increased its political control. Quite different, he argues, are revolutions or *mutazioni* that transform 'one species of government into another' (p. 7), such as the 1494 overthrow of the Medici regime, which restored liberty to the people. Although historians still argue about the extent to which the 1494 revolution in Florence differed from earlier changes, we can all today readily understand the issue at stake: the merits and demerits of overturning restrictive or 'narrow' governments in the name of popular freedom.

Soderini's suggestion that del Nero is also secretly pleased by the restoration of liberty in Florence encourages del Nero to define his position and social status. Unlike the other speakers, he does not belong to one of the old optimate families, 'not being of noble birth nor surrounded by relatives' as they are, nor is he well-educated. Instead, he is a self-made man who has become their political equal through his own efforts and through the patronage and friendship of the Medici. This serves to alert us to the fact that his approach to politics is going to be far from traditional. We should not be misled by the fact that it is he who first introduces the traditional scholastic argument that, of the three types of government—of the one, the few and the many—government of one man when good is the best. For he does so only to undermine it by insisting, against the scholar Piero Guicciardini, that in fact governments must be judged by results, not by principles.

Judging only by results, del Nero is able to argue that there is no difference between legitimate and illegitimate regimes *ex titulo* (one of Bartolus of Sassoferrato's two types of tyranny) since their claim to power is irrelevant to their ability to rule. In this way he destroys one of the time-honoured definitions of tyranny as the worst of the six types of government according to the scholastic typology. He then proceeds to replace this old typology with new simplified terms that can

easily be understood 'by the man in the street' (p. 12; they are discussed more fully on pp. xxv-xxvi below). But his distinction between what he colloquially calls 'broad' and 'narrow' government is not only easily comprehensible to all levels of Florentine society. It also enables him usefully to gloss over the old distinction between optimate government 'of the few' and Medici one-man government. According to his classification, instead of being different types altogether, the difference is simply one of degree.

Equally novel is his attack on Capponi's argument, based on Florence's long history and reputation as a free commune, that free and open government is the city's natural form of rule and therefore the best for it. On the contrary, del Nero responds, free communes were not introduced 'to allow everyone to participate in government', but simply 'to safeguard the laws and the common good', which is best achieved by one man, if he is good (p. 17). And far from being natural to the city, he continues, Capponi's much-vaunted freedom and equality is in fact no more than a slogan, used as a means of social advancement by the outs to get into power, and then discarded by them once they have achieved their objective (pp. 36-7). By distinguishing between civil and political liberty, and then by reductively defining liberty and equality as techniques for social advancement, del Nero offers a radical attack on the republican myth, which he then uses to undermine Capponi's patriotic defence of communal 'freedom' and noble virtue.

After this innovative introduction, which marks del Nero's importance in the *Dialogue,* the remainder of the first book is devoted to a discussion of the pros and cons of Medici government according to the three headings proposed by Capponi: the administration of justice, the distribution of honours and offices (which includes an interesting discussion of methods of taxation), and foreign policy. While Capponi condemns the Medici on each count for their favouritism and self-interest, del Nero defends them on the grounds that knowing favouritism is preferable to ignorant incompetence, and the Medici's successful self-interestedness preferable to the factionalism and disorder created by the optimates' destructive competition for honour and glory, what Sasso calls a 'Hobbesian' free-for-all.[6] Although not obviously original, since much of the material is familiar from Guicciardini's *History of Florence,* the interest of this long discussion lies in its combination of the general and the specific—its illustration of general political arguments (for example, popular government's lack of secrecy and expertise) with specific Florentine examples. Particularly interesting is its overall account of the Medici patronage, or 'Big Boss', system of government, which is marked by favours or 'considerations' *(rispetti)* paid to friends and 'satellites' *(satelliti),* 'jobs for the boys' *(pascere gli amici),* corrupt practices *(aggiramenti),* organised gangs and chiefs *(capi)* in the countryside, and control of enemies through marriage and tax manipulation.

Del Nero's portrait of Lorenzo de' Medici in the *Dialogue* has been described by Felix Gilbert and Nicolai Rubinstein as Lorenzo's 'posthumous image', which became the source of the 'mythic Golden Age' Lorenzo.[7] But what is striking is its often unflattering realism and the amount of agreement between del Nero and his republican critics about Lorenzo's role. As del Nero comments, there was a danger that 'we'll find ourselves agreeing too closely with each other' (p. 58). Describing Lorenzo pragmatically as a man who knew his job, because 'this was the trade in which he'd set up shop', del Nero provides the most telling evidence of Lorenzo's abuse of power in admitting that he gave offices to men who then 'obeyed his signals', kept careful watch on people's behaviour, so that 'pleasing him acted as a reward and being in his bad books served as a punishment', and used taxes 'as a stick to beat people with' (pp. 23, 54, 49). So when Capponi proceeds to describe Lorenzo's malpractices in greater detail, it is no surprise to find that nearly all of them can be substantiated by other evidence. We know that Lorenzo influenced legislation and elections on behalf of friends and supporters, brought pressure to bear on the decisions of the Mercantile Court (see Bibliographical note, p. xxxvi) and the criminal court of eight citizens, the Eight of Ward, and enjoyed special powers and privileges, like the right to bear arms, which were denied to other citizens. Lorenzo also signed military contracts and treaties single-handed and laid 'his hands on communal funds' as Capponi puts it (p. 30), incurring a debt with the communal Monte of over 22,000 florins by the time of his death.

It seems likely that many details of this portrait were supplied to Guicciardini by his father and grandfather Jacopo, or were contained in family papers—such as Lorenzo's personal intervention in the surrender of Pietrasanta in 1484, when Jacopo was Florentine commissary, or his use of communal money, which Jacopo as a Monte treasurer would also have known about. Thus we find ourselves presented, not with opposing images of Lorenzo, but with a single and convincingly realistic image of the political broker and power-monger, a man familiar to all our participants. Far from dismissing it as a flattering myth, we should read this dialogic portrait as an accurate picture of Lorenzo, his two faces, far from being merely a literary construct, betraying the optimates' ambivalence towards the man they both collaborated with and resented. The truth was, as they all knew, that their own prosperity to a large extent depended on Lorenzo's dominance.

When the argument is resumed the following day and del Nero is persuaded to describe his ideal government, we expect something more innovative than what we are given, which is a blueprint for a government on the Venetian model: a life Gonfalonier at its head, a life senate of 150 men, in whom real power is vested, an executive magistracy of ten, with an elected advisory *pratica,* and a Great Council, as well as an appeal court of forty. Most of its features—with the exception only of the senate, which was briefly introduced after Soderini's fall in September 1512—had in fact been introduced by the reforms of 1502. It was then, after lengthy debate about the rival merits of a life head of state or a life senate, that the two-monthly office of Gonfalonier of Justice was transformed into an elective life office and the Quarantia established as a court of appeal in place of the Great Council (p. 124, n. 316). It is Soderini, rather than del Nero, who first presents the argument that in all states, both classical and contemporary, "it is always the virtue of a few people that counts', for only a few are capable of attaining true glory and honour (p. 91). But because del Nero's scheme closely resembles the government Guicciardini proposed in his Logrogno *Discourse* of 1512, 'On how to order the popular government', especially in its desire for government to be in the hands of 'men of worth', *uomini da bene,* represented by a senate drawn from old optimate families like his own, it has been taken to represent not only the views of del Nero and the other disputants, but Guicciardini's too. As Pocock points out,[8] it is here that del Nero approximates most closely to aristocratic values in accepting ambition and the desire for honour as virtues—provided they are exercised and rewarded in a public arena. His argument climaxes in a paean of praise for optimate government, where the ruler freely steps down to allow the best men to win true honour and glory through exercising public offices for the good of their country, the *Dialogue* concluding with the hope that del Nero's 'lucid and wise' discourse will enlighten the whole city and be acted on in the speakers' lifetime (p. 168).

This reading of the *Dialogue* as a republican tract that reflects Guicciardini's own optimate ideals has met with widespread approval. In simultaneously providing a career structure open to talent and restricting power to a small elite, it reassures us about Guicciardini's republicanism and at the same time is consistent with the early-modern trend towards greater elitism. In 1459 the Signoria of Florence had been renamed 'priors of liberty' instead of 'priors of the guilds', since this title (the law states) had suggested that 'humble and abject people, the lowest of the low' had 'worked their way into government'. The guilds were subsequently given a reduced role in government, which became restricted to fewer longer-term and more experienced citizens, ruling in the interests of the rich banking and merchant class. Guicciardini's blueprint reflects these trends in its disparagement of 'workshop' values and its attempt to deprive tradespeople of an active role in government, which he wanted to be limited to experts, wise men ruling in the interests of the state as a whole.

Yet there are problems in accepting this as the only reading of the *Dialogue.* This is partly because of the difficulty of accepting its republican rhetoric at face value. As the leading ideology of the day, piously invoked by the government in prefaces to laws and two-monthly orations on justice, its claim to provide wise, impartial government was belied by the self-interest of rich banking and merchant optimates like Guicciardini himself, as his discussion of taxation can serve to illustrate. Fearing that the people will 'overburden the better-off' and that a tax or *catasto,* based on a written return of all sources of wealth, would be 'dishonest' if it forced merchants to publicise their 'true state of affairs', del Nero prefers the Medici's arbitrary methods of assessment, which, though dangerous if used as 'a stick to beat people with', nevertheless operated in the best economic interests of the merchant class—and therefore, as he would claim, of the state as a whole (pp. 49-50).

Such a reading also fails to do justice to the *Dialogue*'s apparent novelties and the ambiguity of del Nero's role in it. It is difficult to reconcile the unconcealed admirer of the Medicean system in Book I with the republican sage in Book II, or to explain his radicalism in both books. For after undermining the old distinctions between good and bad government in Book I, del Nero further erodes the moral basis of political power towards the end of Book II, where he outspokenly argues that, 'for reason of state', political power inevitably depends on unchristian actions like murdering prisoners of war and placing bounties on human heads. Here, and in his later defence of Alessandro de' Medici's rule, Guicciardini is as iconoclastic as Machiavelli in arguing for a divorce between the worlds of politics and religion. Perhaps not surprisingly, del Nero warns the other disputants against publicising his views on Christian morality and on the difficulty of living in the world 'without offending God', for 'we can cope with this argument among ourselves, but we shouldn't however use it with others, nor where there are more people' (p. 159).

So there is no easy or straightforward republican reading of the *Dialogue.* Few historians today accept De Caprariis' 'Crocean' suggestion that the contrast between Books I and II represents Guicciardini's retreat 'from politics to history',[9] but by emphasising its political relevance as a whole, they exacerbate the problem of defining what its purpose was. In view of Guicciardini's difficult situation, it is interesting to note that on two occasions (in the preface and in the first draft of the beginning of Book II) Piero Guicciardini is described as a passive participant in the discussion, who 'won't want to let himself be understood' (pp. 3, 83, n. 228). So if Guicciardini wished to protect himself, then of course the ambiguity of the Ciceronian dialogue form, which presents both sides of the political debate without concluding in favour of either,

served his purposes very well. He was not influenced only by humanist models, however. As a lawyer as well as a humanist by training, he was skilled in adversarial techniques, and it is likely that his legal career, as Osvaldo Cavallar has suggested,[10] exercised an important influence on his political thinking. We know that his admiration for the adversarial court and for the practice of publishing arguments in advance provided models for his projected government, to enable citizens to arrive at the truth and win fame and reputation by 'presenting themselves well'. And on the evidence of the two orations he wrote in 1527, one accusing himself of imagined charges of malpractice, the other defending himself, it was his habitual practice to argue both sides of the question and to formulate his ideas as opposites, as when he suggests that 'everyone necessarily either loves liberty or he loves the tyrant, and if he loves one, he must hate the other' (*Oratio accusatoria,* p. 219). So if the *Dialogue* purposely offers an open choice, it would perhaps be wrong to impose on it a single reading or interpretation.

An open reading also has the advantage of making the *Dialogue* accessible to a wide audience, as a discussion of political principles instead of simply one of Florentine politics. Yet in accepting it, as in accepting the 'safe' republican reading, we risk missing the more dangerous implications of the work that Guicciardini apparently wanted to conceal by using the ambiguous dialogue form. For just as his two-faced portrait of Lorenzo concealed a single coherent image of the man, so his dialogue about politics in Books I and II may conceal a more pragmatic and integrated argument than either of the above approaches indicates. So without attempting to suggest a single or uniform interpretation, we may be able to discover the prevailing direction of its argument by clarifying some of its special features.

In the first place, it is clear that Guicciardini's preferred government is not a hereditary aristocracy limited to the optimates, as it might appear, but rather a meritocracy. Florentine history had amply demonstrated that the weakness of aristocratic government lay in its factionalism and competitiveness, from which the optimate regime of 1382-1434 (idealised by Capponi) was saved only by external wars and reaction to the Ciompi revolt. So although political power in Guicciardini's model is concentrated in the hands of a life senate of 150 men, who exercise the key political, financial and judicial functions in the state, final legislative power rests in the hands of the popular Great Council, which also appoints to other offices. At the same time, the practical authority of the senate and its executive of Ten is moderated both by the life Gonfalonier and by a *pratica,* or *junta,* chosen from the senate by outside electors. Life membership of the senate is won not by birth but by previous performance in administrative offices and public debate. For as Guicciardini says in his *Considerations on the 'Discourses' of Machiavelli:* 'the optimates must not be drawn always from the same lines and families, but from the whole body of the city . . . and a senate must be elected to deal with difficult matters, containing the flower of the prudent noble and rich men of the city'.[11]

There is no better way to illustrate what Guicciardini meant by this than by considering Bernardo del Nero's role in the *Dialogue.* One reason for being chosen as Guicciardini's *alter ego* could have been, as Sasso has suggested,[12] his fate in being victimised as a Medicean in 1497, which Guicciardini may have feared would be his own fate, and which he tried to avert through the argument of the *Dialogue.* In birth and social status, however, as Giovanni Silvano has been the first person to stress,[13] del Nero was very different from Guicciardini: not an optimate at all but an artisan, a second-hand clothes dealer, whom Guicciardini had earlier listed as one of Lorenzo de' Medici's clients who owed his position to Lorenzo's patronage alone. Although called 'extremely cruel and extremely ambitious' before his execution in 1497, there is no doubt he was a man of ability and judgement, who enjoyed important political offices in the Medici, as well as in the republican, regime. He was also well-read—although, as he says in the *Dialogue,* ignorant of Latin. Like Socrates in Plato's dialogues, he is clearly intended to represent the practical wisdom of the common man. So if he and another Medici upstart, the unpopular Antonio di Miniato Dini, are described in the *Dialogue* as 'wise men' (pp. 3, 72 (notes), 126) and del Nero is also 'a man of worth', its ruling elite is certainly not intended to be closed but open to all men of talent, to whom it offered access to the top honours.

At the same time it is not a popular government either, despite del Nero's origins and the important role in Guicciardini's argument of the Great Council (consisting of all the citizens, now defined as the major office-holders over four generations). In Book I, he had criticised the new Great Council for encouraging tradespeople and workers to enter the government, as he had in the Logrogno *Discourse.* There, following the example of the Romans, he had wanted the members of an enlarged Great Council to appoint to offices without being qualified to exercise them (pp. 224-5). In Book 11 of the *Dialogue* he allows the Great Council to approve all laws without discussion and appoint to all offices (apart from the Gonfaloniership and the senate, which are to be nominated by the senate and then approved by the Great Council; and ambassadors, commissaries and the Ten of War, to be appointed by a special electoral council or *junta*). But he deprives it of any other powers, 'because I don't trust the judgement of the people, nor would I ever recommend them being allowed to decide any affair of importance' (p. 153). He also disparages them for loving the tyrant's 'festivals, jousts and public games', as well as the

magnificence of his house and court, 'which are the things that appeal to the lowest classes' (p. 160). In his *Maxims* (C 140, Appendix, p. 174 below), as well as in the *Considerations* (pp. 102-6), he describes the common people as 'a mad animal gorged with a thousand and one errors and confusions'. So although Guicciardini valued the people's role in curbing the senate, and pragmatically recognised that 'now that they have had a taste of the Great Council . . . And so set their hearts on their free government . . . there's no hope of getting them to forget it' (Maxim 38, p. 172 below), he otherwise had a low opinion of their ability.

Guicciardini's negative view of the people is reinforced by comparing his views with Machiavelli's. Although Machiavelli is alluded to only once in the *Dialogue,* for arguing that the excellence of Rome's army depended on its excellent administration, he is present throughout *in absentia*—providing the 'other' voice in the dialogue through Piero Guicciardini, who scrupulously presents 'the authentic thought of his great fellow-citizen'.[14] Whereas Machiavelli's model is Rome, Guicciardini's is Venice. Whereas Machiavelli admires Roman conflicts, the role of the tribune of the plebs, and the militia, Guicciardini thought the conflicts were destructive, the tribunes far less effective than the kings in protecting the people and advancing their rights, and the militia successful only because it was established under its kings, well-disciplined and highly reputed—which would not be the case if Florence were to establish a citizen militia. Since the tribunate (in Florence, the office of Captain of the People, abolished in 1477) and the militia were symbols of popular government, Guicciardini's hostility to them marks him as antipopular by comparison with Machiavelli.

The remaining figure in Guicciardini's government is the elected head of state or life Gonfalonier. Although in the *Dialogue* this figure is subordinate to the senate, which is the real centre of power, in the Medicean state (as in Machiavelli's 1520 blueprint) the position is of course occupied by the Medici themselves. After his experience of Piero Soderini's life office, we cannot know how confident Guicciardini was of the life Gonfalonier's capacity to control the optimates (especially since he attributes Soderini's fall in his *Oratio accusatoria,* p. 228, to his 'negligence, or patience or pusillanimity'), or of their capacity to control a powerful Gonfalonier. It is revealing, perhaps, that he refers to the life Gonfalonier as 'a boss or patron . . . not a lord who rules, but someone who being a fixture will necessarily devote the thought and care to the city's affairs that bosses give to their own affairs' (p. 101), since these are the terms Guicciardini uses to describe Lorenzo's role in the city, not Soderini's. He knew, too, that because of their wealth and status in Rome, the Medici could not realistically be exiled from Florence for ever, so he proposed what he describes as his 'new way of doing things', that is, recalling them to Florence once the republic was firmly established (p. 167).

Guicciardini's description of the life Gonfalonier's role as a boss or patron, not a lord, also suggests that he was aware of the later distinction made between the spheres of public and private interest. It may be objected that since he does not use this vocabulary, we cannot legitimately use it either. However, both Guicciardini and Machiavelli do use the public/private antithesis to contrast constitutional or public authority with private ambition and favouritism. And it is clear from Machiavelli's reiteration of this antithesis in his writings that he uses the words public and private to make exactly the distinction Guicciardini makes in the *Dialogue* between the Medici's constitutional authority and their private use of partisans, chiefs and favourites. Thus Machiavelli contrasts Neri Capponi's public route to power with Cosimo's 'public and private' route, through friends and 'partisans' (*Florentine Histories,* bk. II, ch. 2); and in the *Discourses* (bk. 1, ch. 16) he recognises that one of the great weaknesses of republican government is its inability to win the support of grateful partisans, since everyone expects rewards and honours as his due without any sense of obligation to the government. It was perhaps with this weakness in mind that Guicciardini on several occasions after 1512 and 1530 urged the Medici to create partisans in Florence to solidify their authority through bonds of obligation. In contrast to Machiavelli, however, who consistently condemns this fusion of public and private interest, Guicciardini seems precociously aware that it may be necessary, in order to recreate the stability achieved by Lorenzo de' Medici's semi-public, semi-private role in Florence.

Such other clues as we have suggest that the direction of Guicciardini's thought was towards the concentration of power in a strong head, whether this head was a senate or a prince. These clues include his new political vocabulary, which glossed over the old distinction between good and bad government, his tough views about the reality of power, and his conviction that 'in Florence power must necessarily either be held by one man alone or pass totally into the hands of the people'. They also include his admiration for monarchy in Rome, as well as his later support for Alessandro's rule in Florence, and his frankly-admitted enjoyment, in his self-accusation, of his own magnificence and 'unbounded authority' as papal governor, having 'received more favours from the Medici than any other citizen' (*Oratio accusatoria,* pp. 207, 209-10; cf. Maxim C 107, p. 173 below). Because affairs of state, the 'serious matters', are confined to the senate, which acts as mediator, we should perhaps hesitate to call his government 'mixed' in balancing power equally between its three constituent parts. Yet at the same time it is novel in insisting that all these parts contribute to government

in varying degrees. Reading the *Dialogue* as a whole, we can see that Guicciardini, like Machiavelli in his 1520 *Discourse,* realistically acknowledges the need for power to be concentrated in the hands of a single head, the Medici—'during their lifetimes', as Machiavelli put it—or a senate of wise men. Despite loving liberty and republicanism more than tyranny, he did business with both types of regime, like del Nero, who must remain the key to an integrated understanding of the *Dialogue.*

Texts and editions

There are two surviving manuscripts of the *Dialogue,* both in the Guicciardini family archives in Florence (described by R. Ridolfi, *L'Archivio della famiglia Guicciardini,* Florence, 1931). One, the first draft, is entirely autograph (A). The second is a later version in a secretary's hand (B), which has been corrected by the author (C), making C the definitive version. The dialogue has been published in three editions, by G. Canestrini in Guicciardini's *Opere inedite* (vol. 11, Florence, 1858), by R. Palmarocchi (Bari, 1932), who provides a full critical edition with alternative readings from A and B, and most recently by E. L. Scarano (UTET, Turin, 1970). In my translation I have followed Palmarocchi, adopting his nomenclature and his use of C for the printed text, and quoting variant readings from A and B where they throw light on C or provide interesting evidence of changes of thought. From this point of view, the earlier versions of the preface (Palmarocchi, pp. 295-301, printed in an Appendix by Scarano, pp. 475-83) are particularly valuable, and for this reason they have been described in expanded footnotes to the preface. The reader should not to be deterred either by the Jamesian convolutions of the preface, nor by its bulky footnotes, since both are untypical of what follows.

Language and concepts

There was at the time a long-standing debate in Florence about how to translate Florentine political terminology into Latin—should new words be invented or classical words used instead, and, indeed, should Latin be used at all? By writing his *Histories* and this *Dialogue* in Italian, not Latin, Guicciardini was already departing from the practice of most humanist scholars, as he was in rejecting scholastic terminology to define types of government in this *Dialogue.* After introducing this terminology, which distinguishes between six types of good and bad government of 'the one, the few or the many' (kings, aristocracies and polities ruling for the common good, tyrants, oligarchies and democracies ruling for their own self-interest), and more broadly between oligarchy and democracy, representing wealth and poverty (pp. 10-13), Guicciardini purposely discards it in favour of new words which more accurately describe his view of Florentine political history. This he saw not so much as a cycle of con-stantly-changing regimes, according to the classical formulation, but rather as a series of subtle and con-stantly-changing shifts in the balance of power be-tween openness, *largezza,* and narrowness, *strettez-za.* Thus at one end of the scale, the 1290s guild regime and the 1490s Savonarolan regime could be seen to represent broad or open government, while the oligarchic government in Florence from 1382-1434, as well as the almost one-man government under Lorenzo de' Medici, represent narrow or 'very narrow' government. Because of the imprecision and fluidity of the political situation at this time, these words offered a sliding-scale which was not only conveniently mobile but was also non-moral, thus avoiding the need to distinguish clearly between republican, oligarchic and tyrannical government. Yet the significance of Guicciardini's use of these words has been largely lost, tanks to translators and com-mentators who have either attempted to force them into ill-fitting classical clothing (*stato stretto* has been translated as 'despotism', or 'absolutism', as well as optimate government)—or else, more com-monly, have left them untranslated. It is important, however, to respect Guicciardini's language by avoid-ing scholastic terminology and adopting his 'new' but vulgarly colloquial words—such as *largo* and *stretto,* which had popular religious and sexual, as well as political, connotations, and were readily understood by the man in the street. Hence I have nearly always translated *stato largo* or *libero* as a broad or free regime/government, *stato stretto* as a narrow one. Just because they do not belong to a typology familiar to us, they convey the novelty and effect intended by Guicciardini.

Guicciardini uses three other words, fortune, humours and virtue (*fortuna, umori* and *virtù* in the Glossary), which together help to define his mental world. Al-though it is Capponi who distinguishes himself from the other participants in the ***Dialogue*** for having prac-tically no learning, 'apart from a bit of astrology picked up from his father' (pp. 10-11), Guicciardini himself—despite the whiggish rationalism of the ***Di-alogue*** and his numerous maxims about 'the madness of those who believe in astrology' (Maxims C 23, 57, 58, 114, 207 and B 170)—was evidently more influ-enced by popular astrology than we might think. In Anthony Parel's convincing account of Machiavelli's cosmos,[15] Machiavelli believed that the cyclical pat-tern of history was caused by the influence of the unchanging planets on cities and men, change being introduced by the play of fortune, which affects coun-tries and people differently according to their humours and temperament. Although differing in emphasis, Guicciardini's account of the cycle of history in the ***Dialogue,*** in which 'everything which exists at present has existed before' (p. 16), resembles Machiavelli's, as does his account of the natural life-cycle of cities,

which are difficult to reform when old (pp. 140, 148-9, 153), his frequent use of bodily and medical anal-ogies (pp. 41, 62, 97-9, 157), and his attempt to find the right government for Florence 'after considering the nature, the quality, the conditions, the inclina-tions—in a word, the humours of the city and its cit-izens' (p. 97). We know from the ***Dialogue*** that his own father had a 'melancholic, balanced and happy disposition, according to Marsilio Ficino' (p. 11), and he evidently agreed with Machiavelli about the im-portance of being born at the right time, 'when your own special virtues or qualities are valued' and on the virtual impossibility of changing one's nature 'according to the times', to escape fortune's thrall (Maxim 31, pp. 171-2; cf. pp. 81 and 141, and Max-im 216, p. 174 below). For fortune is 'just as influ-ential as many believe', or at least 'quite powerful in ensuring that things are born in time to enjoy the right company and occasion to be able to achieve their effect' (pp. 139, 148). Anyone who tries to es-cape the power of fortune through change and revo-lution incurs her anger, 'in whose dominion these things lie' (p. 84). And although fortune can bring success and prosperity if she smiles on the city, her cornucopia is not unlimited and can be used up (pp. 139, 148-9, 90). He also talks of the impossibility of 'escaping one's fate', of the natural cycle of human affairs and, 'as you others like to say, of fate, which very often has more force than men's reason or pru-dence' (pp. 3, 140, 79-80); and of 'the dispositions of the heavens and destiny' being more important than counsel in bringing about Piero de' Medici's fall (p. 10).

Guicciardini's use of the words fate and fortune sug-gest that he shared the same view of the world as Machiavelli. Yet his emphasis on the particular and the exceptional enabled him to avoid the determinism of Machiavelli's rules and generalisations, nor does he apparently share the paganism that Parel attributes to Machiavelli. For although he was as critical of the Roman Church and its clergy as Machiavelli, he did not rule out the power of God's providence in influ-encing events. On one occasion he refers to 'fortune, or God's goodness', on another to Italy's situation after the French invasion being 'more or less in the hands of God', and elsewhere he states that 'God loves liberty.' (pp. 135, 70, 91). Despite finding it difficult to accept that goodness and evil were not rewarded and punished by God, he still thought it impossible that 'divine justice', or God (as the first draft A has it), would allow the Medici exiles to be put to death as outlaws, when they themselves had killed no one (p. 163; cf. Maxims C 91, 92). His view of man's natural goodness and virtue also differs from Machiavelli's. Virtue, or individual merit, which can bring success independently of fortune, is for Guic-ciardini a moral or civic quality, closely associated with the performance of deeds that benefit the republic, rather than Machiavellian ability or prowess. It remains difficult to know how Guicciardini reconciled these different elements in his cosmos. Despite his lucidity of thought and expression, his penetrating but sceptical comments on the world suggest that his beliefs are as unfathomable as his God, whom he describes, in the words of the Bible, as 'a profound abyss' (Maxim C 92, quoting from Romans 11:33). It is this combination of qualities that makes him one of the most important and challenging writers in the early-modern period.

Notes

[1] G. Sasso, 'Machiavelli and Guicciardini', in *Per Francesco Guicciardini. Quattro studi,* Rome, 1984, pp. 94-5.

[2] Gli *uomini da bene* di F.G: coscienza aristocratica e repubblica a Firenze nel primo '500', *Archivio storico italiano* 148 (1990), pp. 856-60; J. G. A. Pocock, *The Machiavellian Moment: Florentine Political Thought and the Atlantic Republican Tradition,* Princeton, 1975, p. 221.

[3] J. Nardi, *Istorie di Firenze,* Florence 1858, II, pp. 335-74 at p. 350; G. B. Busini, letter to B. Varchi (30 May 1550), in *Lettere,* ed. G. Milanesi, Florence, 1860, p. 220.

[4] *Per Francesco Guicciardini,* p. 183; cf. Silvano, 'Gli *uomini da bene',* p. 861.

[5] *Per Francesco Guicciardini,* pp. 189-94; cf. pp. 172-9.

[6] *Ibid.,* p.19.

[7] See Bibliographical note below.

[8] Pocock, *The Machiavellian Moment,* pp. 248-251, 258-261.

[9] See Bibliographical note below.

[10] O. Cavallar, *Francesco Guicciardini Giurista. I Ricordi degli Onorari,* Milan, 1991, pp.

[11] *Selected Writings,* ed. C. and M. Grayson, Oxford, 1965, p. 65.

[12] See note 5 above.

[13] 'Gli *uomini da bene',* pp. 862-3.

[14] Sasso, *Per Francesco Guicciardini,* p. 105.

[15] *The Machiavellian Cosmos,* New Haven and London, 1992; cf. Pocock, *Machiavellian Moment,* pp. 31-48.

FURTHER READING

Biographies

Bondanella, Peter E. *Francesco Guicciardini.* Boston: Twayne Publishers, 1976, 160 p.

 Contains a biographical chapter and a timeline of Guicciardini's life and works, as well as primary and secondary bibliographies.

Luciani, Vincent. *Francesco Guicciardini and His European Reputation.* New York: Karl Otto & Co., 1936, 437 p.

 Provides a brief biography of Guicciardini, comparing him to Machiavelli, as well as a bibliography of other biographies and of his writings, plus descriptions of his critical reception in Europe over the years.

Ridolfi, Roberto. *The Life of Francesco Guicciardini,* translated by Cecil Grayson. London: Routledge and Kegan Paul, 1967, 338 p.

 The standard biography of Guicciardini's life, works, and times, first published in 1960 in Italian.

Criticism

Alexander, Sidney. "On Translating from Renaissance Italian." In *The World of Translation,* with a new introduction by Gregory Rabassa, pp. 15-26. New York: PEN American Center, 1987.

 Discusses the difficulties Alexander encountered while translating Guicciardini's *Storia d'Italia* into English.

Centuori, Walter. "Francesco Guicciardini's Concept of Government, Part I: His Critics (1862-1950)." *Filologia E Letteratura* XVI, No. 61 (1970): 360-72.

 Discusses the positive and negative reactions to Guicciardini's works since they were published in a multivolume edition by Canestrini in the nineteenth century.

Di Maria, Salvatore. "Divine Order, Fate, Fortune, and Human Action in Guicciardini's *Storia d'Italia.*" *Forum Italicum* 28, No. 1 (Spring 1994): 22-40.

 Discusses *Storia d'Italia* as a response to the "atmosphere of turmoil and uncetainty" in which Guicciardini lived.

Gilbert, Felix. *Machiavelli and Guicciardini: Politics and History in Sixteenth-Century Florence.* Princeton, N.J.: Princeton University Press, 1965, 349 p.

 Outlines the historical and political atmosphere of Renaissance Florence and assesses the place of Machiavelli's and Guicciardini's political thought within this context.

Gottfried, Rudolf B. *Geoffrey Fenton's "Historie of Guicciardin."* Bloomington: Indiana University Publications, 1940, 42 p.

Analyzes the Elizabethan fascination with Guicciardini in the context of Geoffrey Fenton's late-sixteenth-century English translation of the *Storia d'Italia*.

Hale, John R. "Introduction." In *Guicciardini: "History of Italy" and "History of Florence,"* edited and abridged by John R. Hale, pp. vii-xlvii. New York: Twayne *History of Florence*.

Markulin, Joseph. "Guicciardini's *Ricordi* and the Idea of a Book." *Italica* 59, No. 4 (Winter 1982): 296-305.

Looks for indications that Guicciardini was trying to impose an organizing principal on the seemingly discontinuous collection of maxims in three published versions of the *Ricordi*.

Moulakis, Athanasios. "Francesco Giucciardini and His Reputation as a Writer." In *Republican Realism in Renaissance Florence: Francesco Giucciardini's "Discorso di Logrogno,"* pp. 27-39. Boston: Rowman and Littlefield, 1998.

In this chapter of his full-length study of Giucciardini, Moulakis describes the author's reputation as having fallen victim to the changing attitudes to history and politics over the centuries. He also asserts that Giucciardini's works nevertheless deserve to be read as primary sources of Florentine history, thanks to his engaging writing style and perceptive sense of events.

Phillips, Mark. *Francesco Guicciardini: The Historian's Craft*. Toronto: University of Toronto Press, 1977, 192 p.

Examines the structure and themes of Guicciardini's

works of Italian history in an effort to make these works more accessible to modern readers. A chapter from this study is included in the entry above.

————. "Reappraising 'Guicciardinian Man': Changing Contexts of Judgment on Guicciardini Since De Sanctis." *Rivista Di Studi Italiani* 1, No. 2 (December 1983): 13-29.

Looks at the work of three generations of Guicciardini specialists and discusses how their moral assessments of his writings differ from one another.

————. "Francesco Guicciardini: The Historian as Aphorist." *Annali d'Italianistica* 2 (1984): 110-22.

Analyzes the aphoristic style of the *Ricordi* as well as the aphorisms which appear in *Storia d'Italia* and concludes that Guicciardini relied on aphorisms to convey a deeper meaning in his texts. This volume of *Annali d'Italianistica* is devoted to critical essays on Guicciardini, three of which are reprinted in the entry above.

Zimmermann, T. C. Price. "Francesco Guicciardini and Paolo Giovio." *Annali d'Italianistica* 2 (1984): 34-52.

Suggests that while historians Guicciardini and Giovio were completely different temperamentally and stylistically, Guicciardini might nevertheless have been influenced by some of Giovio's ideas on historical events. This volume of *Annali d'Italianistica* is devoted to critical essays on Guicciardini, three of which are reprinted in the entry above.

P'u Sung-ling

1640-1715

Chinese short story writer, novelist, poet, songwriter, and essayist.

INTRODUCTION

P'u is regarded as a monumental figure in Chinese literature for his entertaining collection of supernatural and satiric folk tales, *Liao-chai chih-i* (partially translated as *Strange Stories from a Chinese Studio*). This collection contains many masterpieces of short narrative written in a highly allusive, traditional Chinese style.

Biographical Information

P'u was born into a merchant's family in Tzu-ch'uan, Shantung, near the end of the Ming dynasty. During his lifetime, the Manchus of northern China overthrew the Ming empire. P'u aspired to a scholar's life at an early age. After completing his prefectural examination with high honors in 1658, P'u undertook the more difficult provincial exam, which would enable him to enter government service. P'u never attained this goal despite repeated attempts throughout his life. Some biographers believe that his failure to pass was due to the clash of his humanitarian sensibility with the elitism of the ruling Manchus, rather than any deficiency in scholarship. P'u earned his living largely as a teacher, factotum, and scribe. In 1670 he became secretary to the magistrate in the southern province of Chiang-su; two years later he obtained a job with a wealthy friend, with whom he and his family resided for over thirty years.

Major Works

Historians believe that P'u began compiling and writing stories early in life but are not certain of exact dates. It is known that he visited many notable landmarks and amassed numerous regional stories whenever he traveled. In 1679 P'u composed a preface for his collection *Strange Stories*, indicating that the work was completed, or nearly so. For approximately eighty years *Strange Stories* circulated in manuscript until an admiring scholar undertook its publication. P'u's stories belong to the genre *ch'uan-ch'i*, a short narrative form that originated during the T'ang dynasty (618-907 A.D.). In *Strange Stories* P'u successfully revived this early literary tradition, producing works of compact, semi-poetic prose embroidered with esoteric allusion.

Critics note, however, that P'u surpassed his T'ang predecessors through a greatly refined style and innovative fusion of social criticism with entertainment. Largely drawn from imaginative folk tales and legends, his stories contain ghosts, fairies, and various birds and animals symbolizing both the ruling and ruled classes. In this carefully masked social criticism, P'u protested the harsh Manchu domination of the Chinese. His stories depict a dualistic world in which forces of evil, though initially triumphant, are ultimately overcome by forces of good.

Critical Reception

Scholars have observed that in *Strange Stories* P'u wrote unevenly, at times liberating his narrative from reference to antecedent works, writers, and events, while at other times overloading it with these elements. And although P'u has been criticized by Maoist critics for failing to acknowledge that the Manchu system itself was the fundamental cause of injustice and cruel abuse, other scholars note the frequently sharp satirical commentary found in *Strange Stories*. In addition, despite the otherworldly features and romantic sensibility of the tales, critics unanimously commend the realistic effect of *Strange Stories* and credit P'u for his ability to develop fantastic situations into readily visualized and even believable scenes. Known as a serious writer to few people beyond a small circle of scholars and writers in his day, P'u attained enormous status in the centuries after his death because of the enduring intellectual and aesthetic appeal of the tales, many of which were imitated by later Chinese writers or adapted to the stage.

PRINCIPAL WORKS

Liao-chai chih-i [Strange Stories from a Chinese Studio, partial translation, 1880] 1765
†*Hsing-shih yin-yuan chuan [Marriage as Retribution*, partial translation, 1984] (novel) 1870
Liao-chai chih-i wei-k' an kao 1936
Liao-chai ch'uan-chi. 2 vols. (essays, poetry, short stories, and songs) 1936

*Exact dates remain unestablished for much of P'u's work. *Liao-chai chih-i* is believed to have been in near-final form in 1679, though scholars agree that later additions and emendations to the collection were made.

†*Hsing-shih yin-yuan chuan,* according to some sources, may have appeared in book form as early as 1728, though this too has not been conclusively verified.

CRITICISM

Herbert A. Giles (essay date 1908)

SOURCE: Introduction to *Strange Stories from a Chinese Studio,* Boni and Liveright, 1925, pp. xi-xxiii.

[*A highly regarded English sinologist, Giles, through his numerous lectures and publications in the late eighteenth and early nineteenth centuries, was instrumental in conveying the rich variety of Chinese culture to the English-speaking world. In 1880 Giles translated and published* Strange Stories from a Chinese Studio, *the first and most extensive translation of P'u's* Liao-chai chih-i. *In the following introduction, originally written in 1908, Giles comments on P'u's stature in Chinese literature. In his text Giles also includes a 1679 essay by P'u and an 1842 essay by T'ang Mêng-lai.*]

The barest skeleton of a biography is all that can be formed from the very scanty materials which remain to mark the career of a writer whose work has been for the best part of two centuries as familiar throughout the length and breadth of China as are the tales of the "Arabian Nights" in all English-speaking communities. The author of **Strange Stories** was a native of Tz -ch'uan, in the province of Shan-tung. His family name was P'u; his particular name was Sung-ling; and the designation or literary epithet by which, in accordance with Chinese usage, he was commonly known among his friends, was Liu-hsien, or "Last of the Immortals." A further fancy name, given to him probably by some enthusiastic admirer, was Liu-ch'üan, or "Willow Spring"; but he is now familiarly spoken of simply as P'u Sung-ling. We are unacquainted with the years of his birth or death; however, by the aid of a meagre entry in the *History of Tz -ch'uan* it is possible to make a pretty good guess at the date of the former event. For we are there told that P'u Sung-ling successfully competed for the lowest or bachelor's degree before he had reached the age of twenty; and that in 1651 he was in the position of a graduate of ten years' standing, having failed in the interim to take the second, or master's, degree. To this failure, due, as we are informed in the history above quoted, to his neglect of the beaten track of academic study, we owe the existence of his great work; not, indeed, his only production, though the one by which, as Confucius said of his own "Spring and Autumn,"[1] men will know him. All else that we have on record of P'u Sung-ling, besides

the fact that he lived in close companionship with several eminent scholars of the day, is gathered from his own words, written when, in 1679, he laid down his pen upon the completion of a task which was to raise him within a short period to a foremost rank in the Chinese world of letters. Of that record I here append a close translation, accompanied by such notes as are absolutely necessary to make it intelligible to non-students of Chinese.

AUTHOR'S OWN RECORD

"Clad in wistaria, girdled with ivy:"[2] thus sang Ch'ü-P'ing[3] in his *Falling into Trouble.*[4] Of ox-headed devils and serpent Gods,[5] he of the long-nails[6] never wearied to tell. Each interprets in his own way the music of heaven;[7] and whether it be discord or not, depends upon antecedent causes.[8] As for me, I cannot, with my poor autumn firefly's light, match myself against the hobgoblins of the age.[9] I am but the dust in the sunbeam, a fit laughing-stock for devils.[10] For my talents are not those of Kan Pao,[11] elegant explorer of the records of the Gods; I am rather animated by the spirit of Su Tung-p'o,[12] who loved to hear men speak of the supernatural. I get people to commit what they tell me to writing and subsequently I dress it up in the form of a story; and thus in the lapse of time my friends from all quarters have supplied me with quantities of material, which, from my habit of collecting, has grown into a vast pile.[13]

Human beings, I would point out, are not beyond the pale of fixed laws, and yet there are more remarkable phenomena in their midst than in the country of those who crop their hair;[14] antiquity is unrolled before us, and many tales are to be found therein stranger than that of the nation of Flying Heads.[15] "Irrepressible bursts, and luxurious ease,"[16]—such was always his enthusiastic strain. "For ever indulging in liberal thought,"[17]—thus he spoke openly without restraint. Were men like these to open my book, I should be a laughing-stock to them indeed. At the crossroad[18] men will not listen to me, and yet I have some knowledge of the three states of existence[19] spoken of beneath the cliff;[20] neither should the words I utter be set aside because of him that utters them.[21] When the bow[22] was hung at my father's door, he dreamed that a sickly-looking Buddhist priest, but half covered by his stole, entered the chamber. On one of his breasts was a round piece of plaster like a *cash*;[23] and my father, waking from sleep, found that I, just born, had a similar black patch on my body. As a child, I was thin and constantly ailing, and unable to hold my own in the battle of life. Our own home was chill and desolate as a monastery; and working there for my livelihood with my pen,[24] I was as poor as a priest with his alms-bowl.[25] Often and often I put my hand to my head[26] and exclaimed, "Surely he who sat with his face to the wall[27] was myself in a previous state of existence"; and thus I referred my non-success in this life to the influence of a destiny surviving from the last. I have been tossed hither and thither in the direction of the ruling wind, like a flower falling in filthy places; but the six paths[28] of transmigration are inscrutable indeed, and I have no right to complain. As it is, midnight finds me with an expiring lamp, while the wind whistles mournfully without; and over my cheerless table I piece together my tales,[29] vainly hoping to produce a sequel to the *Infernal Regions.*[30] With a bumper I stimulate my pen, yet I only succeed thereby in "venting my excited feelings,"[31] and as I thus commit my thoughts to writing, truly I am an object worthy of commiseration. Alas! I am but the bird, that dreading the winter frost, finds no shelter in the tree; the autumn insect that chirps to the moon, and hugs the door for warmth. For where are they who know me?[32] They are "in the bosky grove, and at the frontier pass"[33]—wrapped in an impenetrable gloom!

From the above curious document the reader will gain some insight into the abstruse, but at the same time marvelously beautiful, style of this gifted writer. The whole essay—for such it is, and among the most perfect of its kind—is intended chiefly as a satire upon the scholarship of the age; scholarship which had turned the author back to the disappointment of a private life, himself conscious all the time of the inward fire that had been lent him by heaven. It is the keynote of his own subsequent career, spent in the retirement of home, in the society of books and friends; as also to the numerous uncomplimentary allusions which occur in all his stories relating to official life. Whether or not the world at large has been a gainer by this instance of the fallibility of competitive examinations has been already decided in the affirmative by the millions of P'u Sung-ling's own countrymen, who for the past two hundred years have more than made up to him by a posthumous and enduring reverence for the loss of those earthly and ephemeral honours which he seems to have coveted so much.

Strange Stories from a Chinese Studio, known to the Chinese as the ***Liao Chai Chih I,*** or more familiarly, the ***Liao Chai,*** has hardly been mentioned by a single foreigner without some inaccuracy on the part of the writer concerned. For instance, the late Mr. Mayers states in his *Chinese Reader's Manual,* p. 176, that this work was composed "circa A.D. 1710," the fact being that the collection was actually completed in 1679, as we know by the date attached to the "Author's Own Record" given above. I should mention, however, that the ***Liao Chai*** was originally, and for many years, circulated in manuscript only. P'u Sung-ling, as we are told in a colophon by his grandson to the first edition, was too poor to meet the heavy expense of block-cutting; and it was not until so late as 1740, when the author must have been already for some time a denizen of the dark land he so much loved to describe, that his aforesaid grandson printed and published the collection now universally famous. Since

then many editions have been laid before the Chinese public, the best of which is that by Tan Ming-lun, a Salt Commissioner, who flourished during the reign of Tao Kuang, and who in 1842 produced, at his own expense, an excellent edition in sixteen small octavo volumes of about 160 pages each. And as various editions will occasionally be found to contain various readings, I would here warn students of Chinese who wish to compare my rendering with the text, that it is from the edition of Tan Ming-lun, collated with that of Yü Chi, published in 1766, that this translation has been made. Many have been the commentaries and disquisitions upon the meaning of obscure passages and the general scope of this work; to say nothing of the prefaces with which the several editions have been ushered into the world. Of the latter, I have selected one specimen, from which the reader will be able to form a tolerably accurate opinion as to the true nature of these always singular and usually difficult compositions. Here it is:—

T'ANG MÊNG-LAI'S PREFACE

The common saying, "He regards a camel as a horse with a swelled back," trivial of itself, may be used in illustration of greater matters. Men are wont to attribute an existence only to such things as they daily see with their own eyes, and they marvel at whatsoever, appearing before them at one instant, vanishes at the next. And yet it is not at the sprouting and falling of foliage, nor at the metamorphosis of insects that they marvel, but only at the manifestations of the supernatural world; though of a truth, the whistling of the wind and the movement of streams, with nothing to set the one in motion or give sound to the other, might well be ranked among extraordinary phenomena. We are accustomed to these, and therefore do not note them. We marvel at devils and foxes: we do not marvel at man. But who is it that causes a man to move and to speak?—to which question comes the ready answer of each individual so questioned, "*I* do." This "*I* do," however, is merely a personal consciousness of the facts under discussion. For a man can see with his eyes, but he cannot see what it is that makes him see; he can hear with his ears, but he cannot hear what it is that makes him hear; how, then, is it possible for him to understand the rationale of things he can neither see nor hear? Whatever has come within the bounds of their own ocular or auricular experience men regard as proved to be actually existing; and only such things.[34] But this term "experience" may be understood in various senses. For instance, people speak of something which has certain attributes as *form,* and of something else which has certain other attributes as *substance*; ignorant as they are that form and substance are to be found existing without those particular attributes. Things which are thus constituted are inappreciable, indeed, by our ears and eyes; but we cannot argue that therefore they do not exist. Some persons can see a mosquito's eye, while to others even a mountain is invisible; some can hear the sound of ants battling together, while others, again, fail to catch the roar of a thunder-peal. Powers of seeing and hearing vary; there should be no reckless imputations of blindness. According to the schoolmen, man at his death is dispersed like wind or fire, the origin and end of his vitality being alike unknown; and as those who have seen strange phenomena are few, the number of those who marvel at them is proportionately great, and the "horse with a swelled back" parallel is very widely applicable. And ever quoting the fact that Confucius would have nothing to say on these topics, these schoolmen half discredit such works as the *Ch'i chieh chih kuai* and the *Yü ch'u-chii,*[35] ignorant that the Sage's unwillingness to speak had reference only to persons of an inferior mental calibre; for his own *Spring and Autumn* can hardly be said to be devoid of all allusions of the kind. Now P'u Liu-hsien devoted himself in his youth to the marvellous, and as he grew older was specially remarkable for his comprehension thereof; and being moreover a most elegant writer, he occupied his leisure in recording whatever came to his knowledge of a particularly marvellous nature. A volume of these compositions of his formerly fell into my hands, and was constantly borrowed by friends; now, I have another volume, and of what I read only about three-tenths was known to me before. What there is, should be sufficient to open the eyes of those schoolmen, though I much fear it will be like talking of ice to a butterfly. Personally, I disbelieve in the irregularity of natural phenomena, and regard as evil spirits only those who injure their neighbours. For eclipses, falling stars, the flight of herons, the nest of a mainah, talking stones, and the combats of dragons, can hardly be classed as irregular; while the phenomena of nature occurring out of season, wars, rebellions, and so forth, may certainly be relegated to the category of evil. In my opinion the morality of P'u Liuhsien's work is of a very high standard, its object being distinctly to glorify virtue and to censure vice; and as a book calculated to elevate mankind, it may be safely placed side by side with the philosophical treatises of Yang Hsiung[36] which Huan Tan[37] declared to be so worthy of a wide circulation.

With regard to the meaning of the Chinese words **Liao Chai Chih I,** this title has received indifferent treatment at the hands of different writers. Dr. Williams chose to render it by "Pastimes of the Study," and Mr. Mayers by "The Record of Marvels, or Tales of the Genii"; neither of which is sufficiently near to be regarded in the light of a translation. Taken literally and in order, these words stand for "Liao—library—record—strange," "Liao" being simply a fanciful name given by our author to his private library or studio. An apocryphal anecdote traces the origin of this selection to a remark once made by himself with reference to his failure for the second degree. "Alas!" he is reported to have said, "I shall now have no resource (*Liao*) for my old age"; and accordingly he so named his study,

meaning that in his pen he would seek that resource which fate had denied to him as an official. For this untranslatable "Liao" I have ventured to substitute "Chinese," as indicating more clearly the nature of what is to follow. No such title as "Tales of the Genii" fully expresses the scope of this work, which embraces alike weird stories of Taoist devilry and magic, marvellous accounts of impossible countries beyond the sea, simple scenes of Chinese everyday life, and notices of extraordinary natural phenomena. Indeed, the author once had it in contemplation to publish only the more imaginative of the tales in the present collection under the title of "Devil and Fox Stories"; but from this scheme he was ultimately dissuaded by his friends, the result being the heterogeneous mass which is more aptly described by the title I have given to this volume. In a similar manner, I too had originally determined to publish a full and complete translation of the whole of these sixteen volumes; but on a closer acquaintance many of the stories turned out to be quite unsuitable for the age in which we live, forcibly recalling the coarseness of our own writers of fiction in the eighteenth century. Others, again, were utterly pointless, or mere repetitions in a slightly altered form. From the whole, I therefore selected one hundred and sixty-four of the best and most characteristic stories, of which eight had previously been published by Mr. Allen in the *China Review,* one by Mr. Mayers in *Notes and Queries on China and Japan,* two by myself in the columns of the *Celestial Empire,* and four by Dr. Williams in a now forgotten handbook of Chinese. The remaining one hundred and forty-nine have never before, to my knowledge, been translated into English. To those, however, who can enjoy the **Liao Chai** in the original text, the distinctions between the various stories in felicity of plot, originality, and so on, are far less sharply defined, so impressed must each competent reader be by the incomparable *style* in which even the meanest is arrayed. For in this respect, as important now in Chinese eyes as it was with ourselves in days not long gone by, the author of the **Liao Chai** and the rejected candidate succeeded in founding a school of his own, in which he has since been followed by hosts of servile imitators with more or less success. Terseness is pushed to extreme limits; each particle that can be safely dispensed with is scrupulously eliminated; and every here and there some new and original combination invests perhaps a single word with a force it could never have possessed except under the hands of a perfect master of his art. Add to the above, copious allusions and adaptations from a course of reading which would seem to have been co-extensive with the whole range of Chinese literature, a wealth of metaphor and an artistic use of figures generally to which only the writings of Carlyle form an adequate parallel; and the result is a work which for purity and beauty of style is now universally accepted in China as the best and most perfect model. Sometimes the story runs along plainly and smoothly enough; but the next moment we may be plunged into pages of abstruse text, the meaning of which is so involved in quotations from and allusions to the poetry or history of the past three thousand years as to be recoverable only after diligent perusal of the commentary and much searching in other works of reference. In illustration of the popularity of this book, Mr. Mayers once stated that "the porter at his gate, the boatman at his midday rest, the chair-coolie at his stand, no less than the man of letters among his books, may be seen poring with delight over the elegantly-narrated marvels of the **Liao Chai**"; but he would doubtless have withdrawn this statement in later years, with the work lying open before him. During many years in China, I made a point of never, when feasible, passing by a reading Chinaman without asking permission to glance at the volume in his hand; and at my various stations in China I always kept up a borrowing acquaintance with the libraries of my private or official servants; but I can safely affirm that I never once detected the **Liao Chai** in the hands of an ill-educated man. In the same connection, Mr. Mayers observed that "fairytales told in the style of the *Anatomy of Melancholy* would scarcely be a popular book in Great Britain"; but except in some particular points of contact, the styles of these two works could scarcely claim even the most distant of relationships.

Such, then, is the setting of this collection of ***Strange Stories from a Chinese Studio,*** many of which contain, in addition to the advantages of style and plot, a very excellent moral. The intention of most of them is, in the actual words of T'ang Mêng-lai, "to glorify virtue and to censure vice,"—always, it must be borne in mind, according to the Chinese and not to a European interpretation of these terms. As an addition to our knowledge of the folk-lore of China, and as a guide to the manners, customs, and social life of that vast Empire, my translation of the **Liao Chai** may not be wholly devoid of interest. It has now been carefully revised, all inaccuracies of the first edition having been, so far as possible, corrected.

Notes

1 Annals of the Lu State.

2 Said of the bogies of the hills, in allusion to their *clothes,* Here quoted with reference to the official classes, in ridicule of the title under which they hold posts which, from a literary point of view, they are totally unfit to occupy.

3 A celebrated statesman (B.C. 332-295) who, having lost his master's favour by the intrigues of a rival, finally drowned himself in despair. The annual Dragon Festival is said by some to be a "search" for his body. The term *San Lü* used here was the name of an office held by Ch'ü-P'ing.

4 A poem addressed by Ch'ü-P'ing to his Prince, after his disgrace. Its non-success was the immediate cause of his death.

5 That is, of the supernatural generally.

6 A poet of the T'ang dynasty whose eyebrows met, whose nails were very long, and who could write very fast.

7 "You know the music of earth," said Chuang Tzu; "but you have not heard the music of heaven."

8 That is, to the operation of some influence surviving from a previous existence.

9 This is another hit at the ruling classes. Hsi K'ang, a celebrated musician and alchemist (A.D. 223-262), was sitting one night alone, playing upon his lute, when suddenly a man with a tiny face walked in, and began to stare hard at him, the stranger's face enlarging all the time. "I'm not going to match myself against a devil!" cried the musician, after a few moments, and instantly blew out the light.

10 When Liu Chüan, Governor of Wu-ling, determined to relieve his poverty by trade, he saw a devil standing by his side, laughing and rubbing its hands for glee. "Poverty and wealth are matters of destiny," said Liu Chüan; "but to be laughed at by a devil—," and accordingly he desisted from his intention.

11 A writer who flourished in the early part of the fourth century, and composed a work in thirty books entitled *Supernatural Researches.*

12 The famous poet, statesman, and essayist, who flourished A.D. 1036-1101.

13 "And his friends had the habit of jotting down for his unfailing delight anything quaint or comic that they came across."—*The World* on Charles Dickens, July 24, 1878.

14 It is related in the *Historical Record* that when T'ai Po and Yü Chung fled to the southern savages they saw men with tattooed bodies and short hair.

15 A fabulous community, so called because the heads of the men are in the habit of leaving their bodies, and flying down to marshy places to feed on worms and crabs. A red ring is seen the night before the flight encircling the neck of the man whose head is about to fly; at daylight the head returns. Some say that the ears are used as wings; others that the hands also leave the body and fly away.

16 A quotation from the admired works of Wang Po, a brilliant scholar and poet, who was drowned at the

early age of twenty-eight, A.D. 676.

[17] I have hitherto failed in all attempts to identify the particular writer here intended. The phrase is used by the poet Li T'ai-po and others.

[18] The cross-road of the "Five Fathers" is here mentioned, which the commentator tells us is merely the name of the place.

[19] The past, present, and future life of the Buddhist system of metempsychosis.

[20] A certain man, who was staying at a temple, dreamt that an old priest appeared to him beneath a jade-storfe cliff, and, pointing to a stick of burning incense, said to him, "That incense represents a vow to be fulfilled; but I say unto you, that ere its smoke shall have curled away, your three states of existence will have been already accomplished." The meaning is that time on earth is as nothing to the Gods.

[21] This remark occurs in the fifteenth chapter of the Analects or Confucian Gospels.

[22] The birth of a boy was formerly signalled by hanging a bow at the door; that of a girl, by displaying a small towel—indicative of the parts that each would hereafter play in the drama of life.

[23] See Note 2 to No. II.

[24] Literally, "ploughing with my pen."

[25] The *patra* or bowl, used by Buddhist mendicants, in imitation of the celebrated alms-dish of Shâkyamuni Buddha.

[26] Literally, "scratched my head," as is often done by the Chinese in perplexity or doubt.

[27] Alluding to Bôdhidharma, who came from India to China, and tried to convert the Emperor Wu Ti of the Liang dynasty; but, failing in his attempt, because he insisted that real merit lay not in works but in purity and wisdom combined, he retired full of mortification to a temple at Sung-shan, where he sat for nine years before a rock, until his own image was imprinted thereon.

[28] The six *gâti* or conditions of existence, namely:—angels, men, demons, hungry devils, brute beasts, and tortured sinners.

[29] Literally, "putting together the pieces under the forelegs (of foxes) to make robes." This part of the fox-skin is the most valuable for making fur clothes.

[30] The work of a well-known writer, named Lin I-ch'ing, who flourished during the Sung Dynasty.

[31] Alluding to an essay by Han Fei, a philosopher of the third century B.C., in which he laments the iniquity of the age in general, and the corruption of officials in particular. He finally committed suicide in prison, where he had been cast by the intrigues of a rival minister.

[32] Confucius (*Anal.* xiv.) said, "Alas! there is no one who knows me (to be what I am)."

[33] The great poet Tu Fu (A.D. 712-770) dreamt that his greater predecessor, Li T'ai-po (A.D. 705-762) appeared to him, "coming when the maple-grove was in darkness, and returning while the frontier-pass was still obscured";—that is, at night, when no one could see him; the meaning being that he never came at all, and that those "who know me (P'u Sung-ling)" are equally non-existent.

[34] "Thus, since countless things exist that the senses *can* take account of, it is evident that nothing exists that the senses can *not* take account of."—The "Professor" in W. H. Mallock's *New Paul and Virginia*.

This passage recalls another curious classification by the great Chinese philosopher Han Wên-kung. "There are some things which possess form but are devoid of sound, as, for instance, jade and stones; others have sound, but are without form, such as wind and thunder; others, again, have both form and sound, such as men and animals; and lastly, there is a class devoid of both, namely, *devils and spirits.*"

[35] I have never seen any of these works, but I believe they treat, as implied by their titles, chiefly of the supernatural world.

[36] B.C. 53-A.D. 18.

[37] B.C. 13-A.D. 56.

Carl Glick (essay date 1946)

SOURCE: "Oriental Otherworld," in *The New York Times Book Review,*" December 15, 1946, p. 20.

[*In the following excerpt from a review of* Chinese Ghost and Love Stories, *translated by Rose Quong in 1946, Glick somewhat misleadingly describes this partial collection of Pu's stories as retold folk tales.*]

In old China no story was considered worthy of being published until it had been told and retold by word of mouth for generations. Then, when its popularity was assured, and the telling had been so perfected that each word and every line had meaning, the story was ready to be printed. So around 1680. Pu Sung-Ling collected some 400 of the best-known and best-loved folk tales and, immortalized them by retelling them in his own poetic style. For a long time the manuscript was passed around among his friends, and finally in 1740 it was published by his grandson. It is considered one of the Chinese classics. Pu Lung-Ling called his book, **Liao Chai Chih Yi,** which roughly translated means. "Strange Stories from the Refuge of My Study." And that's what they are: fanciful, humorous, and strange stories of the love between mortals and ghosts, of foxes turned into beautiful girls, of happenings in the otherworld, and of all manner of unusual and weird adventures.

Chun-shu Chang and Hsueh-lun Chang (essay date 1980)

SOURCE: "P'u Sung-ling and His 'Liao-chai Chih-I'—Literary Imagination and Intellectual Consciousness in Early Ch'ing China," in *Renditions,* Vol. 13, Spring, 1980, pp. 60-81.

[*In the following essay, the critics provide a thematic overview of P'u's* Strange Stories.]

I

One of the major tasks of an historian is the search for and depiction of the spirit of an age. But the spirit of an age is forever elusive and tantalizing. This is particularly so if the historian follows only the traditional politico-socio-economic approach in his research and analysis. The gist of the spirit of an age is what Raymond Williams has called "the structure of feeling" and it is nowhere more manifest than in the imaginative literature of an age. Therefore, unless an historian uses literary works as one of the major sources in his studies, he never feels the presence of a "living" age in his mind, and hence misses a critical part of his understanding of the age under study. Through the ideas, emotions, and imaginations of creative literature one feels the spirit of an age unfolding in front of his eyes. Furthermore, the conditions, values, aspirations, and consciousness of a society can become alive again through the fiction and drama of an era.

The age of the Ming-Ch'ing dynastic transition, during the mid and late seventeenth century, is a good example of the need for this type of study. Our comprehension and appreciation of this critical age in Chinese history would be far from complete and, in fact, greatly hindered, without a thorough understanding of the rich fiction and dramatic writings of that era. Our venture on the short stories by P'u Sung-ling (1640-1715), in a collection entitled **Liao-chai chih-i** (Tales of the Unusual from the Leisure Studio), is intended to illustrate this point.

Among the popular literary works of the early Ch'ing period, P'u Sung-ling's **Liao-chai chih-i** is one of the most widely read. Its main manuscript was completed in 1679, but for many decades this collection of short stories was circulated in manuscript form only. Not until 1766 was it first printed and published. Within a short period it gained a wide circulation in imperial China. Since then, as its English translator Herbert Giles rightly pointed out, it has been as familiar throughout the length and breadth of China as have the tales of *The Arabian Nights* in all English-speaking communities [Introduction to *Strange Stories from a Chinese Studio,* 1929]. "Almost in every household there is a volume of this collection," recorded one Chinese writer in the middle of the nineteenth century. Even Chi Yün (1724-1805), the chief editor of the great *Complete Library of the Four Treasuries* (*Ssu-k'u ch'üanshu*), recognized the literary power of the **Liao-chai chih-i,** although he did not approve of its writing style [*Yüeh-wei ts'ao-t'ang pi-chi,* 1934].

The **Liao-chai chih-i** is the best-written collection of short stories from the early Ch'ing period. In its traditional popular edition, the collection includes 431 short stories, many of which are ghost stories, fox-fairies, and other fantasies that make the outlook of the book very much similar to the tales of *The Arabian Nights.* However, it is of a much more serious nature. The author makes it rather plain in his preface that he wrote the book for the purpose of venting his excited feelings of distress and frustration. What we gather from reading these stories are the author's strong feelings toward the injustices of his day. Many tales in the book, beneath the cover of ghosts and fairies, actually aim at attacking, exposing, and satirizing the society of his time. Yet, at the same time, other stories conform with the established values of the society. Their contradiction in ideas appears throughout the book. To obtain a better understanding of such a book, the author's social and family background should first be taken into consideration.

P'u Sung-ling, a native of Tzu-ch'uan District of Shantung, was born into a once-prosperous landlord-merchant family. Scholars have long suggested that P'u's ancestors were not Chinese, and that he may have been descended from P'u Shoukeng—the famous Arab who served both the Sung and the Yüan dynasties and accumulated incredible wealth in the thirteenth century—or from Turkish or Mongol peoples. Recent studies have demonstrably proved that P'u's ancestry was Islamic. However, no records of P'u Sung-ling's days indicate that members of the P'u clan were then still Moslems. P'u Sung-ling's own account of his family background reads, in part, as follows:

> My father P'u Min-wu showed talent in his youth and was fond of study; he followed T'ao and Teng in his literary style but failed to pass the first-degree examination. As the family was poor, he gave up

study and went in for trade; and in about twenty years became well off. But when he was over forty and had no son, he stopped trying to make money and stayed at home to study, never leaving his books, so that even well-learned scholars could no longer equal the erudition and depth of his scholarship. He helped the poor, contributed to the building of temples, and neglected his own estates. Then his first wife gave birth to three sons, his second wife to one; and when they reached their teens he taught them himself. Since there were many mouths to feed and little money coming in, however, our family gradually grew poor.

["Shu Liu-shih hsing-shih," *P'u Sung-ling chi,* ed. by Lu Ta-huang, 1962]

P'u's family lived near the eastern coast, where commerce had been highly developed since ancient times, and his father had engaged in trade; P'u was naturally influenced by this urban background. Many heroes and heroines in his stories are merchants and prostitutes, and he did not show any of the traditional Confucian disrespect for them. On the other hand, when P'u Sung-ling was born, his father had already retired from urban life and was living as a country squire. His father was fond of study; the fact that he failed to obtain any degree must have been a lifelong regret for him. And he taught his sons to study. All his life P'u Sung-ling, a holder of an elementary degree, was haunted by the desire to be successful through the imperial examination system.

The combination of merchant-landlord family background and varied ideological orientations is one of the key factors that cause a sharp conflict of ideas in P'u Sung-ling's writing. For example, there is the conflict between free marriages and the traditional marriages arranged by parents through the medium of go-betweens; the conflict between ideas of fatalism and ideas of retribution; the conflict between his hatred for the examination system and his helpless longing for position and wealth through this system; the conflict between individualism and conformism; and the conflict between Confucianism and Taoism.

The life of P'u Sung-ling can be summed up with a simple description: he lived a poor and frustrated man. Many of his poems describe or reflect his extremely poor living conditions. As an unsuccessful scholar who obtained only the elementary degree, he made his living as a private tutor all his life, except for one period in 1670-1671 when he was an invited guest and private secretary. When he was an old man, his son wrote about him: "My father is now seventy-four; only in the recent four years has he not taught as a private tutor" [*P'u Sung-ling chi*]. The life of a private tutor was lonely and boring; the income was small; and he had to be separated from his family most of the time. P'u Sung-ling once wrote a long satirical drum-song (*ku-*

tz'u) to describe the life of a private tutor and concluded it with "If I could have any choice, I would not want to be the master of children" [*P'u Sung-ling chi*]. But fortune never fell upon him, and year after year he failed in all higher (provincial) examinations, after being granted the first degree at the age of nineteen. The lonely life of a private tutor and his frustration at failing examinations led him to commit his thoughts to writing. His voluminous writings include not only his famous short stories—represented by the celebrated collection *Liao-chai chih-i*—but also a considerable variety of other works: volumes of classical poems and lyrics, and essays of more than sixteen forms; three musical plays; six drum-songs and fourteen narrative folksongs (*li-ch'ü*); extensive popular instructions on almost all basic aspects of daily country life—such as rites, rituals, morality, calendar, wedding customs, popular worship, medicine, plants and animals, agriculture, and silkworm rearing; learned commentaries on religious matters (Taoism, Buddhism, popular beliefs); discussions on the colloquial usage of the Chinese language; and so forth. However, of all these works, only the *Liao-chai chih-i* has brought P'u Sung-ling fame and popularity. The rest received little attention until recent time. Some of them still remained in hand-copied manuscript form at the time of their discovery; some were represented only by their short prefaces; and some, except for their titles, were completely lost. But the fact that P'u Sung-ling was such a productive, versatile writer and scholar provides us with new insights into his mind. He was a man of broad interests and knowledge, a scholar of admirable erudition. An examination of his writings reveals a remarkable range of intellectual pursuits: literature, classics, biographies, politics, history, social customs, folklore, law, language, philosophy, technology, science, medicine, and religion.

Although P'u Sung-ling was ahead of his time in many of his ideas, particularly his conscious use of various types of colloquial literature for expressing his moral, social, and political ideas, he was also conditioned by the prevailing ideals and values of his time. He spent much of his time writing the so-called "Pretended Memorials" (*i-piao*)—memorials to the throne that were written in the name of high-ranking officials but never made known to the emperor or the officials. These memorials, altogether seventy-nine, constitute a noticeable portion of P'u's writings. But, written in stock style, as a whole they demonstrate nothing but his feverish longing for official position and success. Some of P'u's narrative folksongs and short stories also show his constant indulgence in pornographic subjects and details. It seems clear that P'u Sung-ling was typical of the frustrated intellectuals who were searching with all their intellectual resources for the relevance and meaning of their life in a trying age of dynastic transition.

P'u Sung-ling's times made a significant impact upon

him and his works. P'u belonged to the first generation under the new Manchu regime. He was born in 1640, four years before the Manchu conquest, and grew up in the turbulent period when the Ming resistance force were still active in South China. However, in 1659, the last Southern Ming remnant regime in South China under Emperor Yung-li (1646-1659) was driven out to Burma by the Ch'ing forces, and the last strong Southern Ming loyalist forces under Cheng Ch'eng-kung (Koxinga, 1624-1662) and Chang Huang-yen (1620-1664) suffered disastrous defeat by the Manchu armies. With these defeats, the hope of restoring the Ming regime was gone forever. It was just the year before that P'u, at nineteen, participated in the district examination and won distinction. Also about this time, P'u started to write the short stories that were to be put into a collection later named *Liao-chai chih-i*. The main manuscript of the *Liao-chai* was completed in 1679. Thus the creative period of the book lies in the twenty years from about 1660 to 1679. The period itself is an important factor in the creation of the *Liao-chai*. It was a period characterized by a tense political atmosphere within the Chinese empire, before the Manchu's high-handed policy changed to one of appeasement of defiant Chinese scholars, as expressed by the special *Po-hsüeh hung-tz'u* examination in 1679. The newly established regime still faced various resistance forces and rebellions. Under the circumstances, being much more sensitive to and conscious of its alien rule, the court launched a literary inquisition and persecution of Chinese scholars, as in the cases of Chuang T'ing-lung and Chuang T'ing-yüeh in 1661-1663, Chin Sheng-t'an in 1661, Shen T'ien-fu and Lü Chung and Hsia Lin-ch'i in 1667; as a result, hundreds of scholars were killed. This "reign of terror" overshadowed the academic world for a long, long time. Under such circumstances, it was natural for men of letters to retreat to a world of fantasy to express their realistic feelings through an imaginative world of ghosts and fairies.

Although we are not writing a literary history and do not propose to give an intrinsic treatment in an artistic sense, we should point out that the literary style of the short stories of the *Liao-chai* follows a combination of the styles of *chih-kuai* stories of the Six Dynasties (220-589) and *ch'uan-ch'i* tales of the T'ang period (618-907). Only in the *Liao-chai* did the artistic and thematic achievements reach their maturity, compared with similar attempts of earlier periods—such as the Ming dynasty Ch'ü Yu (1341-1427)'s *Chien-teng hsin-hua* (New Tales of Wick-trimming Hours), which influenced the writing of the *Liao-chai*. It also should be noted here that the romantic spirit of P'u Sung-ling, as well as those of his contemporary dramatists, such as Hung Sheng (1645-1704) and K'ung Shang-jen (1648-1718), were influenced by the romantic movement of the late Ming, called the movement of "ardent Zen" (*k'uang-Ch'an yun-tung*). The impact of this movement upon

the popular literature as a whole is seen in two characteristics, individualism and sentimentalism. The individualism, as represented by Li Chih (1527-1602) and others, provoked general reaction among scholars who were strongly opposed to the threat of moral and social anarchy in Li Chih's thought; however, in the world of letters its romantic spirit satisfied the individual writer's yearning for freedom in pursuing a happier life. The sentimentalism, with its emphasis on love as the most essential element in life, is represented by the dramatist T'ang Hsien-tsu (1550-1617), under whose influence the style of Ming drama passed on to Hung Sheng and K'ung Shang-jen in the Ch'ing period.

The outlook of the *Liao-chai* is, as Lu Hsün once pointed out, a collection of strange stories. The strange stories at the end of the Ming dynasty are usually so brief and absurd that they seem incredible. But the stories of the *Liao-chai* contain such detailed descriptions and normal incidents that even flower-spirits and fox-fairies appear humane and approachable. Yet, just as we forget that they are not human beings, the author introduces some peculiar happenings to remind us that they are supernatural after all.

Among the short stories in the *Liao-chai,* the largest portion consists of love stories. If we try to group the rest of the collection according to their themes, they can be divided into three major categories: stories that exposed the corruptions of the bureaucracy; stories intended chiefly as a satire upon the civil service examination system and upon the scholarship of the age as a whole; and stories that reflected the anti-Manchu feelings of the Chinese people. Of course, some of the stories are for other purposes or merely for amusement, such as some ghost stories that emphasize only the thrill of horror. Since it is not our intention to give an intrinsic treatment of the writing in an artistic sense, we shall examine in this study the stories according to the four major themes that represent the author's thought: love, bureaucratic corruption, scholarship and the examination system, and anti-Manchu sentiments.

II

The love stories in the *Liao-chai* are very colorful; they reveal a world of fantasies in which love becomes the symbol of passion, and outruns time and space. Some of the love stories deal strictly with mortals—men and women. Others deal with men and ghosts, men and goddesses, men and fox-fairies, or men and the spirits of insects, birds, flowers, and trees. The reason for the existence of this fantastic world is obvious. The author realized that in the real life of the traditional society, true love between men and women was so rare and so hard to find that he had to create another world to satisfy his yearning for happiness. However, the author never forgot the reality; he used these incredible romances to depict real human society.

As pointed out before, under the influence of the romantic movement of the late Ming, the author created his heroes and heroines as rebels, somewhat defiant of convention and alienated from their society. They represented the author's protest against the social ethics of his day. One of P'u's characteristic protest is his concept of feminity. Protesting against the prevailing idea of "A woman without talent is a woman of virtue," the author embodies his heroines with so much wisdom, courage, talent and wit that they sometimes surpass the men in the stories. In the story of **"Yen Shih"** (The Daughter of the Yen Family), the young woman whose husband was frustrated by constant failures in the civil service examinations disguised herself as a man and took the examinations. She succeeded in all examinations and finally won the highest degree, *chin-shih* (doctor). There are many talented girls in the world of the *Liao-chai*: the expert surgeon Miss Chiao-nu in the story of **"Chiao-nu"**; the learned sisters in the story of **"Hsien-jen tao"** (The Island of Fairies); the maiden poet Hsiang-yü in the story of **"Hsiang-yü"** (The Flower Maiden Hsiang-yü); and the expert lady fencer in the story of **"Hsia-nü"** (The Lady Knight-errant), to name only a few.

Another important aspect of these love stories is the author's emphasis on devotion. There are many love stories in which the heroes are faithful to their beloved: the honest and devoted scholar, Feng, in the story of **"Hsin Shih-ssu niang"** (Hsin Shih-ssu Niang, the Fox-lady); the foolish lover, Sun Tzu-ch'u, in the story of **"A-pao"** (Miss A-pao); the faithful scholar, Huang, in the story of **"Hsiang-yü"**; the book worm, Lang Yü-chu, in the story of **"Shu-chih"** (The Bookworm); the brilliant and affectionate young scholar, Wang Tzu-fu, in the story of **"Ying-ning"** (Ying-ning, the Laughing Girl), and so on.

On the other hand, the heroines in these love stories show not only deep devotion but also courage and endurance. The story of **"Ya-t'ou"** (Ya-t'ou, the Faithful Girl) is a good example. In the story, a young girl, Ya-t'ou, falls in love at first sight with a poor scholar, Wang Wen. But Ya-t'ou's mother is a greedy woman who wants Ya-t'ou to become a prostitute to make money. The two young lovers elope to another town and make an honest living by keeping a small shop, but the mother later finds out where Ya-t'ou lives and forces her to come home. To separate the two young lovers, the mother moves the family north and demands that Ya-t'ou to change her mind. Ya-t'ou refuses, and is beaten almost to death. She is asked again and again, and she refuses repeatedly; each time she refuses, she suffers a more severe punishment. But nothing can change her deep devotion for Wang Wen. Finally, her mother gives up and imprisons her. Only after eighteen years of separation do the two lovers finally have a happy reunion.

Another typical love story is **"Hsiang-yü."** In this story, the heroine is a beautiful maiden transformed from the spirit of a flower, a white peony, that grows in the courtyard of a temple. Her lover, the scholar Huang, happens to live in a nearby cottage. They meet and fall in love. One day the white peony is picked by a traveller who passes by the temple, and as a result, the flower maiden Hsiang-yü also dies. Huang mourns over her death so sincerely that he at last moves the Flower Goddess, who then allows the spirit of the white peony to revive. It takes Huang one year to water and take good care of the peony plant before its spirit finally is embodied again as Hsiang-yü.

The theme of this story is very simple; yet the author recounts it in such an exuberant, concise, and classic style that it delights its readers as a true story. Moreover, it also carries a message to the readers: If one concentrates one's emotion, one can reach the spiritual essence of things; the spirit of flowers can thus be related to the soul of man.

In the story of **"A-pao,"** the hero is A-pao's foolish lover, Sun. Sun is so crazy about A-pao that he cuts off one of his fingers when he is told that she wants him to do so. A man of extremely simple nature, Sun always readily believes in people and does what he is told. After he has done a number of crazy things, he finally wins the girl's heart. The author is so sympathetic with this simple but honest man that at the end of the story he makes the following comment:

> Only those who are crazy have both the will and the perseverance that are necessary to succeed in life. Whoever is crazy about writing may become a successful writer; whoever is crazy about art may become a successful artist. Only the unsuccessful are not crazy at all!

This belief in "craziness" actually represents the force behind the author's drive towards imaginative writing. It is manifested not only in the "crazy" devotion of the love stories, but also in extreme devotion to objects in other stories in the *Liao-chai*. For example, in the story of the crazy bookworm, **"Shu-chih,"** the poor scholar loves his books to the point of being crazy about them, and then becomes crazy to the point of being bewitched by them. Nevertheless, the author's sympathy with this crazy bookworm is obvious; he arranges a happy development for him by having a beauty from a book conduct an incredible romance with him. Another example of this lies in the story of the stone-lover of **"Shih Ch'ing-hsü"** (A Stone from Heaven). The story is about a man who is so crazy about a piece of strange stone that he chooses to die for it rather than part with it. The strange stone returns its master's affection by crushing itself into a hundred pieces rather than allowing itself to be taken away from its master. Here again, the message is identical to the one in the story of the Flower Maiden.

Not only flowers and stones have "love and affection." Animals, such as birds, also have it. In the story of **"Ko-yi"** (The Strange Dove), the man who is fond of doves one day receives a pair of unusually beautiful white doves from the fairy of the doves. After two years, this pair of white doves gives birth to six doves. One day a high-ranking official visits this man and admires his doves. To please this high-ranking official, the man gives him two white doves as a precious present. But the official, who has no fondness for doves, turns them over to the cook and then eats them. As a punishment for this man's betrayal of their trust, the rest of the white doves leave him and fly away. The message is that love should be perfect; anything less than perfect love is unacceptable. The doves stayed with the man only because the man loved them; once they found that the man treated them as less than a devoted friend, they left him forever.

Similiar search for perfection is seen in the creation of the many idealized heroines in the *Liao-chai.* There is a remarkable contrast here between the real and the ideal. In reality, the women in the traditional society were pitiable. Submitted to the ideology of male supremacy, they were weak and incapable of taking care of themselves, both mentally and physically. In addition the women, who lived in a large, compound family, tended to be tricky, jealous, and quarrelsome; they fought with each other to win the favor of their men. In the idealistic world the heroines were strong and talented; they were simple, charming, passionate, and courageous; they dared to defy their parents and their society with the great courage to face their fate. The aboved-mentioned Ya-t'ou in the story of **"Ya-t'ou"** is an example. In the story of **"Ying-ning,"** the sunny character of the irresistible Ying-ning gives another unforgettable example: she is pure and innocent, witty and full of life, and her lovely face that beams with laughter all the time makes people forget about all their worries. In a word, Ying-ning represents everything opposite to the traditional image of a girl.

One may say that in the world of *Liao-chai,* most of the heroines were girls transformed from goddesses, fox-fairies, and ghosts, and thus it was much easier for them to be brave and independent. But is it not exactly because the author was dissatisfied with the real human situation that he himself escaped to the loving world of fantasy?

III

The second category of stories includes those that expose the corruption and injustice of the bureaucracy. The most explicit example is the story of **"Meng-lang"** (A Dream of Wolves). The story is about an old man who has a bad dream about his older son, a magistrate of a distant district. In his dream, the old father visits his son's *yamen* and finds that it is thronged within and without by wolves, some sitting and some lying, while a great heap of white bones is piled in the courtyard. Then the old man sees his son changed into a tiger hounded by two warriors in gilded mail. Awake and worried, the old man sends his second son to visit his older brother. The younger brother goes to see the magistrate brother and stays with him for a few days; in the magistrate's *yamen,* he sees nothing but corruptive runners and bribe-givers who stream in from morning till night. The younger brother begs the magistrate with tears to mend his way, but is only scoffed at by the latter, who says, "What do you know of official life? Promotion depends upon a man's superiors and not upon the people. If your superiors approve of you, you are a good official; but if you love the people, how can you please those above you?" Unable to persuade the magistrate, the younger brother returns to tell his father about all that has occurred. Soon, news comes that the magistrate has been promoted to a post in the Ministry of Civil Officials. Before long, it is reported that the older brother, the former magistrate, has been killed by robbers on his way to his new post. It is also reported that before his head was cut off, the former magistrate begged the robbers for his life but the robbers said: "We are here to avenge the wrongs of the people of the whole district, not just to take your money."

The theme of this story is very clear, as the author commented on it at the end of the story: Many officials in this world are tigers, and their subordinates wolves. Even if an official is not a tiger, his subordinates may be wolves; and some officials are worse than tigers.

If the story of **"A Dream of Wolves"** symbolizes hatred for corrupt officials, a similar theme is fully elaborated in a remarkable short satire, **"Ts'u-chih"** (The Cricket)—officials only try to please their superiors and never care about the people. In this story, the crickets become favorite pets in the palace, for the royal family likes to watch them fighting with each other. To please the royalty, all the officials in the empire send their running-dogs to the countryside to look for strong crickets that can fight bravely. Thus the tribute of crickets becomes a ladder to success in the officialdom. In the story, Ch'en Ming's rise from obscurity shows how a cricket can affect a man's destiny. As a poor and unsuccessful scholar, before he finds the right cricket, he is scolded, beaten and extorted by local petty officials. But after he finds the right cricket, fortune smiles on him and everything comes his way. The right cricket makes him a rich and powerful official. Here P'u Sung-ling clearly says that in the eyes of officials, the lives of people are worth less than the life of a cricket.

In the story of **"Han Fang"** the author satirizes officials who use every pretext to rob the people, just as he narrates how ghosts extort money from the people while on their way to hell. In the story, Han Fang's parents are very sick; as a poor farmer, Han can do nothing but go to a nearby temple to pray for them. Heaven hears his prayer and sends a local deity to help him. The local deity tells Han Fang that the Jade Emperor (Supreme God) in Heaven has summoned all evil ghosts to report themselves to Hell; while on their way, some of the evil ghosts cannot help extorting money from the people they meet. Han's parents are among those preyed upon by these evil ghosts. The only way to cure this is to put a yellow paper on the bed and say aloud: "I will report you to the Jade Emperor if you do not stop bothering us." So Han Fang does as he is told, and his parents are immediately cured. At the end of the story, we read the following comment by the author:

> In either the thirty-third or thirty-fourth year of K'ang-hsi [1694 or 1695], as I recall it, the authorities decreed a new grain tax, which they called the "Voluntary Contribution." The different prefectures and districts also levied additional sums for themselves. Moreover, at that time, as a result of flood, the seven districts of North Shantung had a very poor harvest; so it was exceptionally difficult for the peasants to pay up. Han-lin Compiler T'ang of our district, who happened to visit Li-chin [district], saw about a dozen arrested men on the road and stopped to ask what their offense was. "The authorities are taking us to the district city to make us pay the 'Voluntary Contribution'," they told him. The peasants did not know what the "Voluntary Contribution" meant, and thought it the name for some new form of labor conscription or extortion! This is laughable, but sad too.

There are many other stories in the *Liao-chai* that expose the corruption and tyranny of the officials. In the story of **"Hung-yü,"** a discharged censor, Sung, fancies a poor scholar's wife. First, Sung attempts to buy her from her husband; he is refused. Then he sends several scoundrels to the poor scholar's house. Both the scholar and his father are beaten on the floor while the scoundrels take away the young wife and leave the baby crying in bed. Badly wounded, the old man dies. The scholar then appeals to the authorities for justice, but is turned down several times, for although discharged from office, Sung still had powerful influence over the local authorities.

In the story of **"Mei-nü"** (The Daughter of the Mei Family), an innocent girl is forced to hang herself because a petty official accepts a small amount of cash and lets the girl's reputation be spoiled by a scoundrel. The story begins one night when the girl's father catches a thief and sends him to the authorities. The thief bribes the jail warden with three hundred coins; the warden releases the thief and announces that the accused merely had an affair with the daughter of the accuser. Thus, for the small amount of three hundred coins, the greedy jail warden causes the death of an innocent girl. In

those days, a girl's chastity was more important than her life.

Perhaps the most forceful satire of all is the story of **"K'ao-pi ssu"** (The Bureau of Frauds). The head of the Bureau of Frauds in the world of the dead is portrayed as a greedy, cruel hypocrite called Hsü-tu Kuei-wang (The Empty-stomach Ghost King) who institutes the most evil practice of requiring all dead degree-holders to cut a piece of their rump as a tribute to him. Only those who can make a costly bribe can be excused from this painful exploitation. P'u Sung-ling then describes the details of the cruel torture of cutting rump and the horrible cries of the victims. Thus the world of exploitation of helpless scholars by cruel, corrupt superiors was a world of horror. In the story, a scholar finally appeals to Hades; the latter, who usually represented the opposite of justice in traditional thinking, actually grants justice to the poor scholars by punishing the head of the Bureau. One may raise the question: Why not appeal to the Supreme God, who was the symbol of justice in traditional times? The answer given by the author was a simple one: "The Supreme God of Heaven was far in the blue sky; where can He be found and told about our grievance? Only Hades, in the world of ghosts, is near and can be the possible access to justice." In a word, evil officials can be checked only by evil means; true justice is beyond reach.

IV

Related to the corruption of the bureaucracy was the whole system of imperial civil service examinations. Many stories in the *Liao-chai* reveal the dark side of this system and form the third category of the *Liao-chai* collection. Being a victim of this system, P'u Sung-ling attacked it most vigorously. Yet he never questioned the existence of this system, he only exposed and ridiculed its many abuses. There are two central themes in this category of stories: the corrupt and incompetent examiners on the one hand and the ill fate of the mass of *hsiu-ts'ai* (holders of the elementary degree) on the other. We shall choose a few stories to elaborate on these themes.

In the story of **"Ssu-wen lang,"** the author made up a story of Hades to satirize the injustice of the examination system. In the world of ghosts, a minor office known as a clerk in charge of writings in the office of God of Literature is temporarily filled by a deaf boy. As a result, the writings which show real talent cannot be found. In the mortal world, the examiners were even worse. The author uses a blind monk to exaggerate his criticism: "Although I am blind, I still can use my nose to tell good writing from bad; but those [the examiners] are not only blind but they also have lost their [sense of] smell."

In the story of **"Chia Feng-chih,"** Chia is a learned scholar, but he fails the examination every time. He is told that his thought is too profound and his writing too smooth and lucid, and that he has to learn the current stale style in order to pass the examination. But he is too honest a scholar to make himself accept this advice. He fails again and again, until one year he is forced by a spirit to write the examination paper in a stale, ridiculous style. Not only does he make it this time, but he passes the examination with the highest honor. He is so ashamed of what he has written that whenever he thinks of it, his face becomes flushed. Burdened by this sense of shame, he eventually leaves home for the seclusion of the mountains.

In the story of **"Yü Ch'ü-wo,"** the author uses a ghost named Yü Ch'ü-wo to express his criticism of the examination system. The ghost Yü once says to a mortal friend T'ao Sheng-yü: Those who are successful through all examinations know nothing about historical classics. When they are young, study is only a stepping-stone to an official career. Once they pass the examinations and become officials they never study again. After their appointment as officials, having spent more than ten years in taking care of official writing, even the "men of letters" cannot know anything of real learning. But it is from among these half-educated bureaucrats that examiners are chosen; how could they be expected to advance the talent?

While many stories in the *Liao-chai* ridicule the examiners of the examination system, even more describe the general disposition of the poor scholars as a whole. In this regard, the author obviously had mixed feelings. On the one hand, he praised the honest, self-respected and learned scholars who held on to their beliefs, such as Chia Feng-chih in the story of **"Chia Feng-chih"**; Wang P'ing-tzu in the story of **"Ssu-wen lang"**; and T'ao Sheng-yü in the story of **"Yü Ch'ü-wo."** On the other hand, the author satirized the vanity, love of money, and self-importance of scholars who were products of the examination system. For example, in the stories of **"Ishui hsiu-ts'ai"** (A Scholar from I-shui), and **"Yü-ch'ien"** (The Money-rain), the scholars' love for money is sharply deplored. In the story of **"Hsien-jen Tao,"** the ignorant but self-esteemed, egoistic scholar becomes the laughingstock among the fairies. In the story of **"Chai-p'ing kung-tzu"** (A Young Gentleman from Chia-p'ing), the young gentleman, although handsome and good mannered in his physical appearance, is empty and ignorant inside. In the story of **"Hsü Huang-liang"** (A Continuation of the Huang-liang Story), the scholar's hunt for fame and wealth is satirized most forcefully. The story describes a scholar, Tseng, who has just passed the examination for the highest degree, *chin-shih*. He is overjoyed at this great success and takes a trip to the suburbs with friends. Someone happens to suggest that there is a fortune-teller in a nearby temple. So the group goes to see the fortune-teller. The fortune-teller observes Tseng's joy and wants to please him. He therefore announces that Tseng is going to be a prime minister for twenty years. Overwhelmed by this prediction, Tseng later has a fantastic dream. The whole story is mainly a description of this dream. In the dream, Tseng becomes the prime minister and has all power and wealth at his disposal. First, he grants favors to a friend who once helped him with money; then he revenges an acquaintance who was not nice to him. From then on P'u Sung-ling describes how Tseng abuses his power to the extreme of killing innocents, robbing other people of their properties, taking in young and beautiful girls by force, and so forth. In a word, he uses Tseng's dream to expose the darkness and corruption in the inner soul of a scholar. He reminds the readers of the basic question: What is the examination system for? Is it only for the purpose of seeking power and wealth? If it is so, then the end is very clear: The end of the corruption of power is total self-destruction.

Besides analyzing the scholar's inner soul, P'u Sung-ling also wrote about the state of mind of scholars from their entering the examination hall until leaving; from their handing in their papers until preparing to sit again. In the story of **"Wang Tzu-an"** (A Scholar Named Wang Tzu-an), P'u gives us a vivid picture of the psychology of scholars in the process of examination. Due to tension, exhaustion, humiliation, and anxiety, the *hsiu-ts'ai* candidate Wang Tzu-an falls, after the examination, into a delirium in which he sees himself a successful *chin-shih* degree holder and a *han-lin* academician. Although he eventually wakes up to the suffering world, he thinks he has been tricked by the spirit of a fox. But such a traumatic ordeal is quite understandable to P'u Sung-ling, a longtime victim of the examination system. Commenting on the story, P'u asserts the insanity of the examination process, and describes the process and a candidate's state of mind as affected by it in terms of seven analogies. At the time of entering the examination enclosure, the candidate is like a beggar; he is like a felon when his name is called and checked by an examiner; he feels like a bee at the end of autumn when he is in his examination cell, and like a moulting bird leaving its cage when he comes out of the examination enclosure; he is like a chained monkey when he is restlessly waiting for the result of the examination; he feels just like a poisoned fly—dropping dead—when he is informed of his failure at the examination; and finally he comes to be like a pigeon whose eggs have been broken and which can only rebuild its nest anew, after a period of anguish, dispiritedness, and complete hostility towards the examination.

It is interesting to note that Wang Tzu-an's delirium readily finds an echo in the nineteenth century rebel leader Hung Hsiu-ch'üan (1814-1864). After failing four times at a *hsiu-ts'ai* examination, Hung Hsiu-ch'üan fell into a delirium in which he finally found liberation from the cruel experiences of the examinations by proclaming himself the son of (the Christian) God and launching into a total denunciation of the evils of Confucius, the man whose teachings were the subject matter of the examinations in traditional China. It is clear that the traumatic, pathetic experiences of Wang Tzu-an under P'u Sung-ling's pen were a common and real ordeal for all candidates of the imperial examinations. P'u's picture of the scholars' humiliation and degradation is the sharpest and most penetrating criticism of the evils of the examination system and of its effects on the character and personality of the candidate-scholars who were the elite, and future leaders, of traditional Chinese society.

V

The last category of stories in the *Liao-chai* are those that reflect the racial hatred of the Chinese people for their Manchu rulers. Here we should first point out that P'u Sung-ling was not a Ming loyalist of the caliber of the great thinkers of his time, like Ku Yen-wu (1613-1682) and Huang Tsung-hsi (1610-1695). He was not even close to it. In his collection of works, we find many distasteful "Pretended Memorials" that a Ming loyalist would never write. Nevertheless, as a writer he shared the general anti-Manchu emotion of his day. The fact that a considerable number of the stories in the *Liao-chai* were adopted by P'u from folk-tales makes him more or less a spokesman of his day. It is naturally for this reason that the anti-Manchu emotions exist in the *Liao-chai*. Thus one may reasonably assume that P'u Sung-ling's anti-Manchu feeling is more a reflection of the flavor of his age than a deliberate, sophisticated, well-engineered effort.

Generally speaking, these anti-Manchu feelings are expressed by P'u in a subtle and indirect style. For example, in the famous story of **"Lo-ch'a hai-shih"** (The Rakshasas and the Sea Market), he imagined an appallingly ugly race and named its country the Rakshasa—a Buddhist term meaning both *barbarians* and man-devouring demons. The hero of this story is a young Chinese travelling merchant whom all the people of the Rakshasa view as the most extraordinary-looking man they have ever seen. The author implies that the Rakshasas represent the Manchus, for he describes the dresses of Rakshasa women in terms of the Manchu style, which was different from that of the Han Chinese. Moreover, in the story, the author has the young Chinese put on a false ugly face everytime he goes to the Rakshasa court, where his disguise wins him tremendous praise. This reflects the fact that the Manchus wore their hair differently from the Han Chinese, and when they came to China they demanded that all Chinese shave and braid their hair the way the Manchus did. This was a big, bitter issue of the day and the Chinese, although revolted at seeing men with

braided hair and Manchu clothes, were forced to accept this custom after bloody struggles. So it is also possible that the author expressed his disgusted feeling by describing how ugly those Rakshasas were without mentioning their hair-style, because that would be too obvious and too dangerous. At the end of the story, the author comments rather explicitly:

> Men must put on false, ugly faces to please their superiors—such is the hypocritical way of the world. The foul and hideous are prized the world over. Something of which you feel a little ashamed may win praise, while something you feel exceedingly ashamed of may win much higher praise. But any man who dares to reveal his true self in public is almost certain to shock the multitude and make them shun him.

A part of these comments and criticisms is evidently directed to the Ming officials who served the new alien Manchu court by putting on new masks to spiritually and physically please the new master.

Along the same line of approach, in the story of **"Yeh-ch'a kuo"** (The Land of Yakshas), the author seems to use the ugly Yakshas (man-devouring demons) to express his disgust of the Manchus. For not only does his description of the female Yaksha styles correspond to that of the Manchus, but he also repeatedly mentions the custom of wearing a bead necklace when the Yakshas greeted their king. This is exactly the custom of the Manchu court: the high-ranking officials (grade five and above) in the Manchu court had to wear a bead necklace.

If the above two tales are too subtle to represent the author's anti-Manchu feelings, other stories are more explicit. Using ghost stories as a form of narration, the author reveals the terror of the Manchu massacres. In the story of **"Kung-sun Chiu-niang"** (The Lady Ghost Kung-sun Chiu-niang), the author plainly states the fact at the very beginning.

> In the case of Yü Ch'i (Revolt) [1661], most of the people who were involved with this case and got killed were from the two districts of Ch'i-hsia and Lai-yang. There were so many people killed—several hundreds a day—in the field of military training that the field was all soaked up by blood and the white bones of corpses were piled up to the sky.

Again, at the very beginning of another story, **"Yeh-kou"** (The Wild Dog), the author repeats: "In the case of Yü Ch'i (Revolt), there was a frightful mass slaughter." In the story of **"Kuei-li"** (The Ghost Clerks), P'u Sung-ling mentions the massacre of Chi-nan (Capital of Shantung) in plain language: "Shortly after the northern army [the Manchus] came, there was a massacre in Chi-nan and corpses were counted up to a million."

Another story in the *Liao-chai* directly exposes how the Manchu soldiers debauched women and girls. It is the story of **"Chang-shih fu"** (The Wife of a Man from the Chang Family), which begins with the following statement:

> In the year of *Chia-yin* [1674], the rebellion of the Three Feudatories took place. The southern expeditionary armies reached Yen-Chou [in southern Shantung]. The soldiers looted the area and debauched the women folks.

Besides exposing the terror of war and disorder, the author reveals the universal feelings of disgust toward those who ranked high but betrayed their loyalties. Using the notorious Ch'in Kuei (1090-1155) as a symbol (the Southern Sung prime minister who was traditionally regarded as a symbol of a Chinese traitor, and who was responsible for executing the national hero Yüeh Fei in 1141), P'u Sung-ling applied the Buddhist theory of karma to the story of **"Ch'in Kuei"** to illustrate the punishment of those who betrayed their loyalties. In the story, Ch'in Kuei is reincarnated as a pig and is butchered. But even as a pig, the meat of Ch'in Kuei is so rotten that nobody wants to eat it.

In the story of **"San-ch'ao Yüan-lao"** (The Elder Statesman of Three Reigns), P'u Sung-ling satirized Hung Ch'eng-ch'ou (1593-1665) who served as an elder statesman in both the Ming and the Ch'ing dynasties. He did not directly blame Hung, who surrendered to the Manchus when defeated, but made up a story based on the ironic event that the last Ming emperor Ch'ung-chen (1628-1644) received a false report of Hung's death in the battle and decreed a temple to be built in Peking in honor of Hung. In the story, a former student goes to see Hung, who has just reached Nanking after his victorious southern expedition for the Manchus. The former student tells Hung that he has a paper in hand and wishes Hung to see it. Hung refuses, with the excuse that he cannot see well. Then the student insists on reading it aloud, and does. The paper is the eulogy that Emperor Ch'ung-chen of the Ming wrote in honor of Hung upon hearing the false report of Hung's death.

In another story, **"She Chiang-chün"** (General She), the same theme of loyalty is repeated. General She is a military officer under the command of Tsu Shu-shun, who is very kind to She and promotes him several times until he becomes a Brigade General. Later on, when She feels that Tsu is fighting a losing war, he rebels against Tsu and captures him in order to surrender to the new regime. Bothered by his conscience, one night General She dreams that he has gone to Hell. Hades is so furious over She's treachery that he orders the ghosts to pour boiling oil over She's feet. When General She awakes, he feels a fiery burning pain over his feet. His health grows worse and worse, and he

finally dies. In his dying bed, his last words are: "It is indeed very treacherous of me to betray my loyalty!"

In contrast to his deploring disloyalty in these stories, P'u has high praise for the loyal hero General Huang Te-kung (d. 1645), of the Hung-kuang reign (1645) of the Southern Ming, in the story **"Huang Chiang-chün."** Huang is painted as a brave man, who fights the robbers with his bare hands and wins, while his travelling companions—two *chü-jen* degree holders—kneel down in front of the robbers and present their money to them.

When one considers all of these stories—fables, tales depicting the terror of massacres, stories satirizing the disloyal high-ranking official or praising loyalty, it is clear that anti-Manchu feelings do exist in the *Liao-chai*. The fact that some stories are very subtle and some are very explicit reflects their different time background, for P'u Sung-ling wrote these short stories over a span of twenty years. During this long period, the new regime's policy alternated between high pressure and appeasement. It is understandable that P'u Sung-ling was sometimes especially cautious and at other times more relaxed. Moreover, this collection was circulated in manuscript form for many decades. The first printed edition, which was also the most current edition until the 1950's, was published in 1766. In this edition, most of the anti-Manchu wordings were modified and some explicit stories were missing. These omissions and changes for the sake of political considerations can be seen only by a thorough comparison of the 1766 popular printed edition and the various existing hand-copied manuscripts of the *Liao-chai*, one of which is the recently discovered incomplete original manuscript of P'u Sung-ling. Our conclusions are based on such research.

VI

To conclude our study of P'u Sung-ling's short stories, it is important to point out what they mean to our study of ideas. As pointed out earlier, in his preface to the collection of *Liao-chai chih-i*, P'u Sung-ling made it very plain that he wrote the book to vent his feelings of distress and frustration. To the modern reader, this statement is nothing new; it merely conforms to the established modern concept that literature describes human experience. But to a student of Chinese intellectual history, the statement is highly significant. P'u's preface was written in 1679, at a time when literature was still viewed as "vehicle of the Way." To announce to the world that his writing is "venting his excited feelings" is rather unusual. It represents not only a deep sense of pessimistic protest, but also a spirit that was searching for a new meaning in life. Only when we keep this basic sentiment in mind can we obtain a better understanding of P'u Sung-ling and his work.

To understand P'u Sung-ling's thought, it is necessary to discern the intellectual influences and ethical values which lie behind his writing. In this regard, we are very fortunate, because in P'u Sung-ling's own preface to the collection of *Liao-chai chih-i*, he candidly admits the influences on his writing:

"Clad in wisteria, girdled with ivy," thus sang San-lü [Ch'ü Yüan, ca. 343-277 B.C.] in his *On Encountering Sorrow*; of ox-headed devils and serpent Gods, he of the long nails [Li Ho, a T'ang poet, 791-817, noted for his long nails] never wearied to tell. Each interprets in his own way the music of heaven; and whether it be discord or not, depends upon antecedent causes. As for me, [following Hsi K'ang, 223-262] I cannot, with my poor autumn fire-fly's light, match myself against the hobgoblins of the age. I am but the dust in the sunbeam, a fit laughingstock for devils. For my talents are not those of Kan Pao [fl. 323 A.D., author of the famous *Sou-shen chi* (Records of the Supernatural)] who was fond of exploring the supernatural; I am rather akin to the temperament of Huang-chou [Su Tung-p'o, the famous Sung statesman, poet, and essayist, 1036-1101] who loved to hear people talk about ghosts. Having heard what people say, I would put it in writing and subsequently dress it up in the form of a story. Thus in the lapse of time my friends from all quarters have supplied me with quantities of material, which, from my habit of collecting, has grown into a vast pile.

Human beings, I would point out, are not beyond the pale of fixed laws, and yet there are more unbelievable phenomena in their midst than in the country of those who crop their hair [southern savages of early ages]; and even before our very own eyes, many tales are to be found therein stranger than that of the nation of Flying Heads [a fabulous race mentioned in *Yu-yang tsa-tsu* (Yu-yang Miscellany) by Tuan Ch'eng-shih (d. 863 A.D.)]. [As the poet Wang Po (648-675) rightly says,] "Irrepressible bursts and refreshing ease," I was indeed but wild! "Forever indulging in farreaching thought" [as did Li Po (701-762)], I did not try to hide my foolishness. Were men like these to open my book, I should be a laughingstock to them indeed. However, although the stories heard at the crossroads might, like the story about [Confucius burying his mother at] the Wu-fu Crossroads [in modern Shantung], be nonsense, yet they might make sense if one views them through the Buddhist theory of the three states of human existence [—the present, the past, and the future]. Furthermore, [as Confucius once cautioned us,] never set aside words because of the man who utters them.

When the bow [a small towel announcing the birth of a boy] was hung at my father's door, he dreamed that a sickly-looking [Buddha], Ch'ü-t'an [Gautama], but half-covered by his stole, entered the chamber. On one of his breasts was a piece of plaster like a coin; and my father, waking from sleep, found that I, just born, had a similar black patch on my body. As a child I was thin and constantly ailing, and

unable to hold my own in the battle of life. Our home was chilly and desolate as a monastery; and working there for my livelihood with my pen, I was as poor as a priest with his alms-bowl. Often I put my hand to my head and exclaimed, "Surely he who sat with his face to the wall [referring to the Buddhist patriarch Bodhidharma who came as a missionary to China in the late fifth century] was myself in a previous incarnation," and thus I referred my non-success in this life to the influence of a destiny surviving from the last.

I have been tossed hither and thither in the direction of the ruling wind, like a flower falling in filthy places; but the [Buddhist] six paths of transmigrations [i.e., the paths of heaven, men, demons, hell (tortured sinners), hungry devils, and brute beasts] are inscrutable indeed, and I have no right to complain. As it is, midnight finds me with an expiring lamp, while the wind whistles mournfully without; and over my cheerless table I piece together my tales, vainly hoping to produce a sequel to the *Yu-ming lu* (The Infernal Regions) [written by Liu I-ch'ing (A.D. 403-444)]. With a bumper I stimulate my pen, yet I only succeed thereby in "venting my excited feelings," [as expressed by the philosopher Han Fei (ca. 281-233 B.C.) in his "Ku-fen" (Solitary Indignation)]. If I am obliged to vent my feelings in this way alone, it is sad enough. Alas! I am but the bird that, dreading the winter frost, finds no shelter in the tree; the autumn insect that chirps to the moon, and hugs the door for warmth. For where are they who know me? They are [as Tu Fu (712-770) once said in a poem to Li Po] "in the bosky grove and at the dark frontier pass"—wrapped in an impenetrable gloom!

The melancholy and emotional tone of the Preface reveals the inner soul of a lonely man who sees himself as one of the great writers in history who were unsuccessful in life, but achieved immortality after death. Four significant points are worthy of notice.

First, it seems that P'u Sung-ling identified himself as a spiritual brother among the great poets and essayists in Chinese history; Ch'ü Yüan, Li Ho, Su Tung-p'o, Wang Po, Tu Fu, and Li Po are the great poets he cherished. It is especially notable that the Preface begins with a quotation from the ancient Ch'u poet and statesman Ch'ü Yüan, who drowned himself in the Mi-lo River after having been unjustly dismissed from favor of the Ch'u Court, and ends by identifying the *Liao-chai chih-i* with the chapter "Ku-fen" (Solitary Indignation) of the *Han Fei Tzu* by Han Fei who, after rising to distinction, was unjustly thrown into prison in 233 B.C. All of these tell of P'u Sung-ling's strong feeling of being deserted and unappreciated and, above all, his sorrows and frustrations.

Second, it is interesting to note that while P'u Sung-ling admits that his tales are "wild" and "foolish," he reminds his reader: "Never set aside words because of the man who utters them," for no matter how absurd they seem, we might still learn something from them. It is obvious that P'u Sung-ling wants his reader to learn something from his tales.

The third notable aspect of the Preface is P'u Sung-ling's sense of predestination. He refers his "non-success" in his life to "the influence of a destiny surviving from the last." It seems that he really believes this when he tells about the possibility of his previous incarnation as a Buddhist monk. P'u Sung-ling's belief in a previous state of existence reveals the tremendous religious—mainly Buddhist and Taoist—influence on his life. This explains the many superstitious fears, customs, and beliefs that fill up the pages of his *Liao-chai chih-i.* P'u Sung-ling was living in a superstitious rural society in seventeenth-century China. No matter that his ideas were in many ways ahead of his time, he was still the child of his age, conditioned by the social, political, and cultural environment of that age. He wrote on a variety of subjects, not because he consciously attempted to serve his people and society, as portrayed by an eminent Western scholar, but because he felt the urge to express his ideas and feelings in writing. It is especially significant that, as already pointed out, he wrote in classical as well as vernacular language and also in every style and form: poems, essays, short stories, popular dramas, drum-songs, narrative folksongs, popular didactic works, and so on. He wrote in classical language because that was the established written language of his day; scholars seeking literary success wrote either classical essays (mostly for imperial examinations) and traditional poems, or devoted themselves to learning the interpretations of the Confucian Classics. Yet the fact that he wrote not only classical essays and poems, but also classical stories shows that he had already found the orthodox literature—essays and poetry—no longer the only effective, useful vehicle of literary expression. Furthermore, he also wrote various pieces in the vernacular because it was the spoken language of the day, and he desired his works to be widely read. That he attempted to use all possible literary media to express himself shows not only his original mind but also the new spirit of his age. The rising demand for popular literature among the people demonstrated its strength in the styles of P'u Sung-ling's writings. Without realizing its true historical significance, P'u wrote popular literature of every sort, going wherever his fancies led him.

The last but not the least notable impression one gathers from reading P'u Sung-ling's preface to the *Liao-chai chih-i* is its strong personal note of irony and disillusionment. This glum view of life is in sharp contrast to the generally lively and colorful outlook of the world of the *Liao-chai chih-i.* The *Liao-chai* stories, with all their popularity, had been generally viewed by their traditional readers as a form of entertainment and aesthetic enjoyment. The famous early Ch'ing

scholar, writer, and critic Wang Shih-chen (1631-1711) exhibits the contemporaneous and traditional view of the *Liao-chai chih-i.* In a poem commenting on the book, he humorously referred to P'u's stories as "those that are told light-heartedly should be received with the same light spirit." Responding to this comment, P'u Sung-ling himself admitted: "When the book *Liao-chai* was completed, people who read it have indeed felt it amusing" [Lu Ta-huang, ed., "P'u Liu-ch'üan hsien-sheng nien-p'u," in *P'u Sung-ling chi,* Vol. 2, p. 1778; both Wang Shih-chen's poem and P'u Sung-ling's reply are recorded under the year 1689 in this *nien-p'u*]. But P'u Sung-ling did not write the book merely for the sake of amusement. In a poem dated 1671, the year he went home from the South, ending his brief connection with the government as a secretary to Sun Hui (1632-1686), the district magistrate of Pao Ying and of Kao-yu (in modern Kiangsu), he described his book as his only hope for fame and success in life after all hopes of an official career were gone [P'u Sung-ling, *P'u Sung-ling shih-chi, chüan* 1 in *P'u Sung-ling chi,* Vol. 1, p. 483].

As we pointed out earlier, the greater part of the *Liao-chai chih-i* took form in the gloomiest period of P'u Sung-ling's life. Thus P'u wrote the stories to vent his excited feelings, and to compensate, by expressing profound ideas through popular literary means, for his sad failure in the examinations and his official career. Both of these motives were clearly revealed in his Preface. But to contemporary and later traditional scholars and readers, both intentions seem to have been lost. Take the previously-mentioned views of Wang Shih-chen and Chi Yün. Both scholars were fascinated by the literary power and imagination of P'u Sung-ling's *Liao-chai chih-i* as a piece of entertainment, but they did not consider it an expression of deep-grounded ideas and personal feelings. To the general reader, the *Liao-chai chih-i* was only a collection of fantastic, amusing tales, although readers were strongly influenced subconsciously by the ideas behind the stories. P'u Sung-ling's reputation as a truly great writer in Chinese history was, in general, not recognized until modern times—particularly recent decades. It is his ideas and thought, more than anything else, that have won him the respect and sympathy of modern readers.

In short, P'u Sung-ling's ideas and thought, and his means of expressing them as fiction, generally transcended his time and eluded most readers of the traditional period. Electrified by his fantastic tales, his readers gradually and subconsciously accepted his vivid and penetrating analysis of the comedies and tragedies of the human condition during a great dynastic transition; his revealing description of the intolerable tensions between the intellectuals and the government and the devastating consequences of these tensions; his views and criticisms of his time and his society; and his ideals of life and government. P'u Sung-ling's traditional readers thus unconsciously appreciated his work without recognizing its true literary merit.

We have seen P'u Sung-ling as an analyst of his life and his inner ego, as a teller of unusual tales, as an observer of human nature and human society, as a recorder of the local and national memories of the Ming-Ch'ing dynastic transition, and as a molder of the images of his age and the Chinese culture. Through his short stories, he communicates his sense of his country's culture and history; he allows his readers to see and share his perceptions of the inner orders and structures of the individual, the society, and the times. Some scholar may raise the question of the originality of some of P'u Sung-ling's stories: what was his own creation and what was only his re-creation based on old stories? But this misses a point of critical importance in understanding the spirit and methodology of traditional Chinese intellectual and literary pursuits. Re-creation has always been a form—in fact, the most prevailing form—of creation. This has been a unique character of Chinese thinking and intellectual endeavor, a tradition that has gone all the way back to Confucius (551-479 B.C.) and is well attested to by the fact that the most original Chinese philosophical ideas have been made in the form of commentaries on the Classics. Thus, through his short stories, P'u Sung-ling revealed not only the style and vision of his literary imagination, but also the creative process of Chinese intellectual consciousness, a process that has actually remained unchanged in the contemporary Chinese world of ideas and intellectual exercise.

Lin Lien-hsiang (essay date 1983)

SOURCE: "The Examination Syndrome in *Liao-chai-chih-yi*," in *Tamkang Review,* Vol. XIII, No. 4, Summer, 1983, pp. 367-96.

[*The following excerpt is taken from a biographical and critical essay relating P'u's stories about civil-service examinations to his own lifelong inability to pass the examination himself. The excerpted portion of the essay discusses examination stories that feature corrupt or incompetent administrators and those that feature retribution on the part of unsuccessful test-takers.*]

Sung-ling might have started collecting his strange stories just as a hobby or a time-killer to relax himself from teaching and preparation for all the examinations he took, yet in due course of time, while writing down the short stories he heard from his servants, friends, and neighbors, he came to realize the possibilities of employing them to criticize the society of his day and even give vent to his pent-up feelings. In a tyrannical society where realistic social criticism might endanger his own life,[13] the form of fiction, especially strange stories about supernatural beings, fox spirits, and ghosts, would make an ideal vehicle for his criticism. By the time he wrote "The Author's Account of Himself" for his *Strange Stories* in 1679, he openly declared:

> With a bumper I stimulate my pen, yet I only succeed thereby in 'venting my excited feelings,' and as I thus commit my thoughts to writing, truly I am an object worthy of commiseration. Alas! I am but the bird, that dreading the winter frost, finds no shelter in the tree; the autumn insect that chirps to the moon, and hugs the door for warmth. For where are they who know me? They are 'in the bosky grove, and at the frontier pass'—wrapped in an impenetrable gloom!

When he wrote "The Author's Account of Himself," he was actually at the lowest ebb in his life. At the end of the self-account he even expressed a naked self-pity and lamented his lack of *chih yin,* friends who knew him very well and thus were willing to help him with his quest for advancements, especially such influential friends as were able to help him succeed in the examination and win an official appointment. In his opinion his scholarship and writing far exceeded the achievements of those who had defeated him in the examinations.

I

It was only natural that Sung-ling would ascribe his failure to the unfair or even incompetent examiners. And there in his short stories we do find some merciless exposure of the incompetence of the examiners. In the story of **"Ssu-wen-lang"** ("Secretary to the God of Literature")[14] he presents a blind monk who was able to smell a burning essay and pass his judgement on it. To this monk, there came three examinees who after their examination asked him to smell their essays and tell them if they could pass the examination. He passed favorable judgements on those of Examinee Sung and Examinee Wang who were quite modest and friendly to each other, but commented unfavorably on that of Examinee Yu-hang who was behaving quite arrogantly. When the results of the examination were published, they were surprised to find that Sung and Wang were not among the successful but Yu-hang was, just contrary to the monk's prediction. Examinee Yu-hang immediately went to chide the Buddhist monk, who quietly replied that he had passed his judgements purely on the basis of the merits of the essays and that he had no knowledge of their writers' individual fortunes. He meant that Yu-hang had succeeded just because he was lucky. He further commented on the examiners: "I am merely eye-blind, but the examiners are at once eye-blind and nose-blind." The monk, to prove the validity of his judgement, volunteered to find out who his teacher was if he could bring his teacher's essay and burn it for him. Yu-hang did accordingly, and to his great dismay the monk called him to stop burning it further because it was getting so unbearable for him to smell such a poor essay. The monk implied the teacher's essay was even worse than the student's. Sung-ling implied that only such skunkish essays as Examinee Yu-hang's and also his teacher's were acceptable to the examiners. If one wants to succeed, one should follow the poor style of Yu-hang and his teacher. Should one uphold one's own style, one would be doomed.

Therefore, in the story of **"Chia Fung-chih,"**[15] Sung-ling presents a scholar already holding the status of *sheng-yüan* called Chia Fung-chih. Chia was well known for his talent in literature, and yet he had been unsuccessful in the provincial examination. One day he came across a man of good manners and found him to be an expert in writing examination essays. Chia invited the scholar, who called himself Lang, to come to his home to comment on his own essays. On perusing Chia's examination essays, Lang commented: "They might be good enough to win you the top place in an ordinary school test, but never good enough to win you the last place in the formal civil-service examination." "How come?" asked Chia. "Do you think you need my explanation? It's always more difficult for you to do a thing with your head and heels raised than for you to do a thing with your head and back bent forward." Lang then cited some essays as the target to emulate. Chia found them to be the ones that he despised most and complained: "A gentleman writes to be immortal. Even if I could gain the premiership by such nasty essays, I would still think it very mean of me to write them." Lang left him with a comment that he was too young to accept his suggestion. In the next fall he took the provincial examination again without any success. Then he remembered what Lang had said and forced himself to study the recommended nasty essays carefully. Three years flew and it was again time to get ready for the provincial examination. When Lang showed up again, Chia made haste to ask him to make comments again on his essays. Again his comments were not favorable. Chia was very much depressed and went ahead to put together all the poor sentences he could remember from his study of the nasty essays. And he was quite dismayed to acquire high praises from Lang for this essay. Lang wanted him to recite this essay and told him to write such a one in the coming examination. Lang even made him take off his shirt and write a magic spell on his back to make sure that Chia would not forget the essay. In the examination, he could remember nothing but that essay. So he wrote down the nasty essay with a great regret. Nevertheless, when the results were published, he was immensely disturbed to find his name among the successful candidates. He felt so much ashamed of himself that he decided to leave his family for good and pursue the life of a Taoist monk. Hearing of his decision, Lang volunteered to take him to a Taoist fairyland. It was very obvious from the story that Sung-ling wanted to expose the incompetence of the examiners and also their lack of ability to appreciate really good writing. In his eyes, the society of his day was upsidedown and the good was driven away by the bad. As a matter of fact, he wrote a story of an up-side-down country called *Lo-ch'a*.[16]

Lo-ch'a was a country where government officials were selected not according to their scholarship but according to their facial "beauty"; the more beautiful faces people had the higher positions they were offered. The true intention of this funny idea was to sneer at the examiners' inabilities to choose the right persons for the government to fill in the right posts. The prime minister of the country, whose face was supposed to be the the most beautiful, was indeed special: "His ears drooped forward in flaps; he had three nostrils, and his eye-lashes were just like bamboo screens hanging in front of his eyes."[17] To make the satire sharper, Sung-ling turned the situation upside down twice. First he made us doubt the wisdom of the examiners and then he made us doubt the value of comely faces, by calling a hideous face beautiful and according it with high honors. The double twist makes us stop and think.

As P'u Sung-ling suffered again and again from defeats at the examinations, for which he thought the examiners should assume full responsibilities, he hit upon an idea to improve the situation: screening of the examiners themselves. To get the right people to play the part of examiners, the government should not just appoint them but must hold examinations to select the fully qualified examiners. In the first story of his **Strange Stories, "K'ao ch'eng-huang"** ("Examination for the Post of the Local Guardian God,")[18] he began to hint that even the post of a local guardian god required an examination to find the right man to fill it, let alone the post of an examiner. And then in Volume II, we find a story entitled **"Yü-ch'ü-ê"** ("Examinee Yü Ch'ü-ê.")[19] As the story goes, an examinee called T'ao Sheng-yü went up to the provincial capital to take the provincial examination. Some time before it took place, he found lodging in the suburb and planned to make the final dash for the examination. One day when he went out for a walk, he came across a man looking like an examinee still with his luggage on his back. As he found him a man of good manners, Tao invited him to stay with him. The man was called Yü Ch'ü-ê, who carried no books with him except an ink-stick, an ink-slab, and a writing brush. He said he did not like to study. Yet one day he came to borrow books from T'ao and shut himself up inside the room copying from the books in great haste. With his curiosity aroused, T'ao peeped into the room and found Yü burned the essays that he had copied and swallowed the ashes. Later T'ao asked him what magic he was rendering to himself. Yü replied that once he swallowed the ashes he would never forget the essays. Quite amused by this magic, T'ao asked Yü if he could teach him that magic so that he might memorize all those essays for himself. Yü seemed to have some difficulty in complying with his request. When he was pressed very hard, he finally told T'ao that he was not a man but a ghost. So what Yü could do as a ghost could not be taught to T'ao as a man. Yü also told T'ao that he was preparing himself for an examination to be held in the underworld for the posts of examiners, because most of the officials had neglected their studies for years and would not make good examiners. That was why the underworld emperor wanted to hold a special examination to choose the right persons to play the part of the examiner. One day Yü came back downcast and told T'ao that as the god of literature was going to be transferred to become king of a distant land the examination was canceled. The examiners' posts would be taken over by those drifting hungry ghosts like the blind musician Shih K'uang and the money lover Ho Ch'iao who had been detained in the darkness for quite a few hundred years and thus were no longer used to the daylight and could not read the examination essays. Here we notice Sung-ling pointed out the blindness and corruption of the examiners by comparing them to "those drifting hungry blind ghosts." From this we could imagine how bitterly Sung-ling hated the incompetent and corrupt examiners. The story was about the underworld, but through a ghost story P'u Sung-ling evidently wanted to say: we can find the same situation here in the human world, but we do not have the examination to choose the right men to become examiners. In other words, he presented his idea through a ghost story. Following the tradition of Wei and Chin ghost stories, his ghost stories present much similarity and intercommunication between the world of men and that of ghosts.

As his experience in taking examinations and his familiarity with the inside world of the examiners grew, he came to find that his *Kung-ming* career was not only marred by those incompetent and corrupt examiners but also by some competent but lazy and irresponsible examiners, for these negligent examiners found their job of grading the examination essays boring and so let their assistants or secretaries do their job. They never cared if their secretaries would choose the right candidates for the government; they cared only for their own ease and comfort. Therefore, in the story of **"Ho-hsien"** (**"Immortal Ho,"**)[20] he lashed out against those lazy irresponsible examiners. There was a young scholar named Wang Jui-t'ing in Ch'ang-shan, who could act as a medium to a spirit calling himself Ho Hsien, a disciple of Lü Tung-pin's, who sometimes said he used to be Lü Tung-pin's stork. This Ho Hsien was very much fond of discussing essay and poetry writing with the local scholars. He could also advise them on medicine and examination-essay writing. *A Han-lin* scholar Li Chih-chun as well as a number of local scholars often turned to him for advice and for fortune telling. In his fortune telling he reasoned very logically, free from mystic guessing. One day Ho Hsien was asked to comment on the examination essays that some of the local scholars had just written in the provincial examination which was held shortly before and the results of which were yet to be published. One of the scholars present at the gathering presented the essay of a Li Pien whose academic performance had been excellent and thus whose grades they wished to know as soon as possible. After a while, through the medium, Ho Hsien passed his judgement: "Grade one." But in another while Ho Hsien came back to say: "The judgement just made a little while ago was entirely based on the merits of the essay itself, while it is really a pity to say that Li's present fortune is no good and that the merits of the essay do not match his fortune. This is quite unusual; I suspect the chief examiner does not grade the essays but lets his secretaries handle the job. Let me go and have a look." In a while Ho Hsien came back to say: "When I visited the chief examiner's office, I found him fully occupied with other miscellaneous jobs and the job of grading the examination papers was being handled by a few assistants of his, who in their previous existence were all drifting hungry ghosts for eight hundred years in the total darkness and thus became unaccustomed to daylight just like primitive cavesmen fresh from their long years of imprisonment inside a dark cave. So Li's case looks hopeless." The scholars present at the gathering were quite worried and asked for remedial measures. Ho's answer was: "The remedial measure is always there for you to take; everybody knows what to do." He of course implied: the hungry ghosts need feeding, i.e., you've got to bribe those assistants now grading your essays if you want to pass the examination. When Li Pien heard of the story, he was quite worried and presented his examination essay to *han-lin* scholar Sung Tsu-wei for comments. His comments were quite favorable; he assured him of success. And yet when the results were published, Li's essays were graded grade four: he flunked. Sung was surprised at hearing the results and had a second perusal of the essays and commented with a deep regret: "Mr. Chu, the chief examiner, is a very good scholar; he should not have made such a mistake; the mistake must have been made by his secretaries who even do not know how to punctuate an article!"

According to Chang Chin-chiao's exhaustive study in his *P'u Sung-ling Nien-piao (P'u Sung-ling's Chronicle),* this was a true story. Here in this story we notice that P'u Sung-ling was repeating the same epithet of "hungry ghosts detained in darkness for a few hundred years and thus unaccustomed to daylight" in his description of those imcompetent assistants who helped the chief examiner with grading examination essays. P'u Sung-ling really hated such heartless people that treated the examinees in such a thoughtless manner. No matter how much you might hate the blind examiners, the corrupt examiners, the lazy, irresponsible examiners, and the greedy assistants of the examiners, you could never improve the situation, you could just feel powerless and helpless. It was not merely a matter of the examiners, but a matter of a social system that authorized them with that fatal power to play with the poor lives of the Chinese scholars. Yes, it was the whole social system, the examination-oriented social system or the *kung-ming*-oriented social system that trapped all the Chinese scholars like a hunter did his game. Who was then the hunter? It was Chu Yüan-chang the founding emperor of Ming dynasty (1368-1661 A.D.), with the help of Liu Chi who had designed this examination system to screen candidates for his government posts. Chu Yüan-chang excitedly exclaimed: "Now I'm sure all the Chinese scholars will be trapped in my net!"[21] No wonder that the first emperor of the Ming dynasty got so excited, for his was a net the proud Chinese intellectuals all jumped into of their own will. P'u Sung-ling was among those who flew into the net like a blind sparrow. After he got caught he could not escape. When he realized there was no way out but to stay quiet there in the net, he naturally developed resignation and even a fatalist philosophy of life. He took to the Buddhist conception of retribution: one's destiny in this life has been decided by one's last life.

As he indicated in the account of himself, in his last life he was a Buddhist monk and so in this life he was supposed to live a poor, lonely life like a Buddhist monk. Sung-ling's dilemma was that in spite of his full awareness of his fate, as he declared in his preface to the book, he could not say die with good grace. The deep-rooted *kung-ming* orientation of his character was too much strong for him to change or even cut off. As a genuine writer, he had a good knowledge of himself and wrote a pathetic story to satirize himself, entitled **"Ssu-chiu"** (**"Ssu-chiu, an Unusual Girl"**)[22].

Yü Shen, a young scholar from an old family in Shun-t'ien, was now living in the provincial capital preparing himself for the provincial examination. He noticed a comely boy living opposite his house and took great interest in him. Later on he managed to have a talk with him and got quite attracted. The comely boy happened to carry the same surname as his and called himself Yü Shih-ch'en. Before long they agreed to become sworn brothers and Yü Shih-ch'en dropped the middle character from his three-character name to make his name sound like that of a brother of Yü Shen's. Yü Shih-ch'en, now calling himself Yü Ch'en, invited Yü Shen to visit his house across the street, which was very tidy and clean, where he introduced Shen to his younger sister Ssu-chiu, quite a charming girl about the age of thirteen. In his talk with Ch'en, Shen found him to be a bright boy with a very strong memory. Shen sometimes let him write examination essays and found his essays very well written. When Shen asked him why he had not taken the *t'ung-shih* and pursued a *king-ming* career, he replied that he did not have that good fortune for such a career and so

would have to worry so much about one's career that life would become unbearable. That was why he did not like it. Time flew and very soon it was time to take the provincial examination, which was held every three years. Ch'en was extremely disappointed to learn Shen was again flunked. He did not believe that an examination should be so difficult and began to realize a strong urge to try it himself. With the help of Shen's persuasion, the urge eventually overran his resistance. "At first I did not like it only because I hate to be disturbed by concern over my success. Now that I see your repeated failure, I cannot help feeling a strong urge for it. Let me have a try!"[23] Ch'en walked right into the trap of his own will in spite of his awareness that it was a trap, a trap of no return. Just like Sung-ling himself, Ch'en was successful in the *t'ung-shin;* he passed all the three tests with the highest honors. Famous did he become overnight; everybody knew him to be a very promising young scholar. In the preliminary test next year Ch'en again won the highest honors. It seemed as if success at the provincial examination were right in his grasp. Shen and Ch'en happily participated in the provincial examination the next year and were regarded as the most promising, especially Ch'en whose examination essays were then being copied by so many examinees for future imitation. Both of them felt hopeful but when the results came out they were not among the successful candidates. Ch'en could not believe his eyes, but it was true that his name was not on the list. He now remembered all the days and nights he had spent on preparation for the examination and all the admiration and praises that he had aquired and all the dreams of a glorious day, and at this moment he had to face his failure and taste its bitterness! It was too much for him to bear all this—he collapsed right there when Shen, who had had much experience with failure, wanted to cheer him up. Shen sent for his sister Ssu-chiu, who arrived in time to hear his last word asking her to put his body into a coffin and close it right after his death, not letting other people see his body. Shen was greatly distressed to find his sworn brother dying and yet when he heard Ch'en's admonition to his sister he became very curious and, taking advantage of Ssu-chiu's short absense, opened the coffin lid and had a look at his friend's body and lo! What he found there inside the coffin was not a human body but the body of a big bookworm. Ch'en had been a bookworm assuming a human form and after his death he returned to his original form. What does P'u Sung-ling want to say by this story? At the end of the story there is a moralizing remark:[24]

> The historian of strange events comments: It is very long since Master Kuan-ch'eng (Master Tube-Castle = Master Writing Brush) was supposed not to eat meat. Since you have a very good understanding of a *kung-ming* career from the very beginning, why have you not managed to keep clear from it? You should have known that the blind examiners do not evaluate your examination essays but your fortune.

Now you die just because your whole-hearted strike has missed the mark. How piteous you are, you silly devoted bookworm! Alas, one would rather remain indolent than attempt a high flight!

"The historian of strange events" obviously refers to the author of the book, P'u Sung-ling himself, and "Master Writing Brush" of course also refers to himself. Then "It is very long since Master Writing Brush was supposed not to eat meat" refers to his own story of his pre-existence as a Buddhist monk who is supposed not to eat meat. "Meat" can be construed to mean *kung-ming*. So a man like him, with the personal background of a Buddhist monk, was supposed not to have anything to do with *kung-ming* from the very beginning. He should have managed to keep far away from it and yet he didn't! Sung-ling now took himself to task. He was comparing himself to a bookworm. By this self-derogation, he implied: Because of his inability to maneuver among the examiners, i.e., to flatter them and even to bribe them, he had to remain unsuccessful. The self-derogation was actually a very fierce accusation against the examiners. The bookworm's death represents the utter exhaustion of an examinee after long years of hard work and also his desire for an immediate death and total disappearance of himself from this world. We could very well imagine that the story was written shortly after his failure in one of the ten or eleven provincial examinations that Sung-ling took. This pathetic story was in a sense Sung-ling's self-mockery, self-pity, or self-elegy. He wanted to give it up, he wanted to say good-bye to his *kung-ming* career, for a bookworm like him should not have tried it at all. Sung-ling was fully aware of the examination complex that he himself was developing. As a matter of fact, he used "seven likes"[25] to illustrate the psychological process of an examinee: First he looks like a beggar when he first enters the examination hall, barefooted and with a basket in his hand; second, he looks like a prisoner as soon as the government officials start calling the roll; third, he looks like a lonesome autumn bee worrying about the advance of the year when he enters the assigned examination room; fourth, he looks like a sick bird just released from its cage when he comes out from his examination room exhausted and tranced; fifth, he looks like a monkey chained to a post, worried and uneasy, while he is waiting for the outcome of the examination; sixth, he looks like an impoisoned fly, immobile and unfeeling, when he cannot find his name in the roll of honors, and then he begins to roar up, throwing all his stationary, books, etc., into the waste basket, cursing the blind examiners, and swearing never to take the examination again, until his fury subsides; seventh, he looks like a pigeon just breaking through the eggshell, beginning anew to prepare himself for the next examination. It was an unescapable cycle to the Chinese scholar of the day, unless he could break through it and edge into officialdom.

II

Side by side with Sung-ling's fatalistic views are his retributive ideas and sometimes Taoist escapist concepts. These constitute the three basic key notes of his fiction. That is why Hu Shih calls him a great writer but a poor thinker.[26] Just like the common people of his day he believed in fate, retribution, and Taoist escape in case of necessity.

Innumerable Chinese folk tales could be found on the topic of retribution. P'u Sung-ling's **Strange Stories** is no exception to this. Among the many stories on the topic of retribution, there are some related with young scholars' examination careers. In the story of **"Yeh-sheng"** (**"Studnet Yeh"**[27]), Yeh was a very brilliant scholar, well known in his native town and yet he had been a failure in his examination career. There came to his town a new magistrate called Ting Ch'eng-ho, who paid great respect to good scholars. Very soon Ting was greatly attracted to Yeh's writing. One day he invited Yeh to visit his office for a talk, after which he respected Yeh the more and asked him to come and study at his office at night, using the official lamps. Besides, he also sent money and food to his family very frequently. Yeh, because of gaining such an appreciative friend in the person of the town magistrate, worked even harder than before. In the preliminary test to the provincial examination Yeh won the highest honors and bathed in the shower of congratulations from his friends. When he took the next provincial examination, he did his best and left the examination hall with a heart swelled with hope. He showed Ting a copy of his examination essays. Having perused the essays, Ting praised him highly for his talent in writing and expressed strong confidence in his success. In spite of Ting's favorable comments, however, he flunked again. He came across blind examiners, examiners who did not evaluate the examinee's essays but his fortune. Ting wanted to cheer him up but in vain; Yeh went home and fell ill. The illness got worse every day regardless of the tending of his family and Ting. An evil thing is often followed by another: Ting was fired from his post because he failed to get along well with his superior officials. As Ting was getting ready to leave the town for his home, he sent for Yeh, for he wanted Yeh to come along with him, but Yeh was too ill to accept the invitation. Hearing of Yeh's illness, Ting put off his departure to wait for Yeh's recovery. A few days later, Ting's servant reported Yeh's arrival and request to leave with him immediately. Back at his home, Ting had a son sixteen years old who knew nothing about essay writing. He trusted his son in the hand of Yeh for his education. To reciprocate Ting's respect for him, Yeh made every effort in his teaching and managed to turn Ting's son into a good scholar in a short time. Ting's son passed the primary *t'ung-shih* and then the provincial examination successively without any failure. Thankful to Yeh's teaching of his son,

Ting also thought of Yeh's own examination career and reminded him of this. Yeh replied: "Everybody has his own fortune. I've just managed to prove, through your son's fortune, that my failure was not due to my lack of ability but due to my lack of good fortune. Besides, I have nothing to regret now that I have had such an appreciative friend as you. What else can I expect from life?"[28] However, when Ting's son was going to travel to the capital for the palace examination, Ting told his son to take Yeh along and purchased a studentship in the Imperial College for Yeh. Through this arrangement Yeh was qualified to take the special secondary examination equivalent to the provincial examination in the capital. Ting's son passed the palace examination and was assigned to a governmental post. And then Yeh also passed the secondary examination and gained his long-delayed honorable title of *chü-jen*. Ting then suggested now that he had acquired the long-sought honor he should go home and let his family share it, to which Yeh agreed and left for home. Approaching his home from afar, Yeh saw his wife come out from his home dressed in a miserable manner and the surroundings of his home also looked quite desolate. When she found him, she looked immensely frightened. Yeh asked why she treated him like a stranger after only a few year's absence. She replied in a fearful voice: "Please do not frighten us in this manner. You died a few years ago. We have not been able to bury you because we have been extremely poor. Now that our oldest son has grown up, we are now planning to find a piece of land to bury you!" Yeh was surprised to be treated like a ghost. He walked right into his own house and found a coffin still standing there and then the next moment he fell onto the ground and disappeared, leaving his clothes behind. When his son came back from his school, he found a horse-drawn carrige with a servant in front of his house. He rushed into his house to ask his mother what all this was about; she told him what had just happened. Later on they learned all about Yeh's life in the past few years and his recent achievement in the long-sought honor. The story has a double motif of retribution and posthumous quest for *kung-ming*.

Here is another story on the topic of retribution, **"Ch'u-sheng"** (**"Student Ch'u"**[29]). Ch'u was a ghost permitted to stay in this world while waiting for his turn of transmigration. As he used to be a very good scholar, he continued to work hard even during this short stay in this world. And during this short stay he came across a very good teacher Lu, very much appreciative of his talent who thus treated him as if he were his own child, and a very kind friend Ch'en who volunterred to help him with his tuition even by stealing from his father. To repay what he owed the friend, he went to take the provincial examination for Ch'en in Ch'en's person, while his friend ghost Liu, on his request, took Ch'en's spirit out visiting scenic spots and amusing places, and he succeeded in the examination. And then

to reciprocate Lu's kind treatment, Ch'u asked his cousin who was then in charge of the job of transmigration in the netherworld to assign him to be reborn as a son to Lu.

As we observed in the afore-mentioned two stories on the topic of retribution, reciprocation, the other side of retribution, seemed to get more emphasis by P'u Sung-ling in his construction of the story-plots. Compared with the first story, where reciprocation takes the form of fully devoted teaching of the friend's son, the second story provides two special ways of reciprocation: one is to take the difficult examination in the person of the friend and the other to be reborn as a son to the teacher. The ways of reciprocation are different mainly because the reciprocators realize their benefactors' individual needs, needs usually very important to the benefactors and yet very difficult to meet in normal ways. The reciprocators will then take drastic measures, very often in supernatural ways, to meet their needs: to give the benefactor's son very effective tutoring and convert him into a very successful candidate in the examinations, to take an important examination in the place of the benefactor lacking in confidence, and to be reborn a son to the benefactor, whose other children are not talented, and win him honors in the future.

The third story we want to cite here is **"Lei-ts'ao"** (**"A God of Thunder"**[30]). Yao Yun-ho and Hsia Ping-tsu were close friends, growing up and studying together. Hsia was particularly intelligent and became a well-known scholar even when he was ten. Very naturally Yao assumed a very respectable attitude towards Hsia and learned quite a lot from him. No matter how hard they might work, they remained a failure in the provincial examination. Hsia, physically rather weak, died during an epidemic one summer. As a good friend, Yao gladly took care of Hsia's family and eventually found it impossible for him to continue his study because of the financial burden. He was obliged to give up his studies and then engaged himself in business. In a short period of time Yao became fairly well-to-do but always thought it a pity that he had to give up his examination career. One day on his way back home from a business trip to Nanking, he took a rest at a restaurant, where he found a tall, sturdy man sitting in a corner with a downcast look. Out of compassion he asked him if he had taken his meal. Yao got no answer from him; nevertheless, Yao pushed his plate of food to him and asked him to help himself to the food. Yao was then amazed to find him eating it very voraciously with his fingers. Yao ordered the second, third, and fourth servings for him until he said he had enough. Yao never expected this man to be a god of thunder, let alone have reciprocation from him, but he made friends with a god of thunder and would get his reciprocation very soon—he was saved by him from drowning in a stormy river. Besides, the god of thunder took him on a trip in space, where he plucked a star and pocketed it as a souvenir. He was also given an opportunity to watch a group of gods of thunder sprinkling rain-water and actually helped with the sprinkling. When it was time for the god of thunder to say goodbye to him, for his sentence of three years to roam in the human world had now come to the end, he let Yao hold the end of a rope and slide over the edge of the cloud down to the earth. The small star that Yao pocketed home began flying like a firefly one night in the presence of Yao and his wife and as they were watching agape it flew into his wife's mouth and went into her body. That night Hsia appeared in Yao's dream saying that small star was he and to repay what he and his family had received from Yao he wanted to be reborn as his son. Yao's wife got pregnant soon and delivered a cute babyboy in due course of time. They named it Hsin-er ("Starlet") in memory of the star. Hsin-er grew up to be a very intelligent boy and achieved the high honor of *chin-shih* at the age of sixteen. Again the reciprocator repays the benefactor what the latter needs most: Yao was thirty and yet without a child. Hsia did not only repay what Yao needed most but also in the best way one could expect. The story here has the same basic plot structure of retribution stories except that it contains a sub-plot of the god of thunder which plays a double function of an independent retribution story for itself and a catalyst to set in motion Hsia's reciprocation. Just because of the subplot the story becomes more ethereally romantic and beautiful. Psychologically these retribution stories echo not only Sung-ling's lonesomeness and yearning to have an appreciative friend but that of all luckless Chinese scholars. In the old tradition of Chinese creeds, a scholar could die to reciprocate an appreciative friend while a woman accepts a man who is very much fond of her. If one could die to reciprocate, what else one could not do?

Another interesting retribution story is **"Hsü-huang-liang" ("The Millet Dream Continued)."**[31] As the title suggests, Sung-ling intends the story to be a continuation of the famous "Huang-liang-meng" ("A Millet Dream," by Shen Chi-chi [c. 750-800]) which is also known as "Chen-chung chi" ("Travel Inside a Pillow"). As is well known, "Huang-liang-meng" is the story of a young scholar, luckless in his examination career, who came across an old Taoist, to whom he complained about himself still leading a farming life while the dream of his childhood was to pass the examinations, get into the lift of official promotion, and acquire the highest position of premiership, to enjoy all the luxuries and honors of the world. While talking, the young scholar felt like lying down for a good sleep. The old Taoist, taking out from his old bag a bluish ceramic pillow with a hole in both ends, presented it to the young scholar: "Lie down on this pillow of mine, young fellow, and you'll achieve whatever you want to."[32] Accepting the pillow and lying down upon it, he

dreamed of himself entering the pillow from the hole in one of the ends and went back to his own home, marrying a charming lady from the big old Ts'ui family, passing the examinations, acquiring the coveted status of *chin-shih,* stepping into the lift of official promotion, and rising to the position of premiership. He suffered from only one setback caused by a jealous colleague's false accusation of his treason together with some generals guarding the national borders, otherwise his life was all very smooth sailing until his death and awakening from the dream. When he woke up, he found the millet that the landlord had started cooking before he fell asleep was still being cooked. The end of the story is quite didactic: life is a dream after all no matter how glorious it might be. Sung-ling's millet dream is markedly different. First, the hero was not a farming scholar luckless in the examinations but a lucky scholar having just passed the palace examination and having acquired the status of *chin-shih* and dreaming of climbing to the top of the ladder of success as soon as possible. Second, Sung-ling's millet dream covered two lives while Shen Chi-chi's covered only one life. The former was actually an independet retribution story of doing evils this life and harvesting the fruit of the evils in the next life. In his story Sung-ling emphasizes the retribution of doing evils, while Shen Chi-chi writes on the theme of life-is-dream. It was very likely that Sung-ling wrote such a story to frighten those wicked government officials. As the story goes, Tseng Hsiao-lien went to the suburbs with the new *chin-shihs* for a walk one day and heard of a very experienced fortune-teller living in the Buddhist temple there. Some suggested that they go and have their fortune told and the suggestion got unanimous agreement. As soon as they saw the fortune teller, Tseng asked if he had that good fortune to become a premier. To flatter him, the fortune teller replied: "Yes, of course. You'd enjoy at least twenty years of peaceful premiership."[33] At the reply Tseng got very much intoxicated and right there started talking about how he was going to assign different posts to all his close friends and relatives. Soon there was a rainshower preventing them from leaving the temple and while they were waiting there for the sky to clear up, Tseng fell asleep and began to dream. In his dream he received two messengers from the Emperor who asked him to proceed to the palace immediately. At the palace he was made the premier to help the Emperor work out national policies and supervise the officialdom. The first thing he did was to acquire posts for all his close friends and relatives and fire those from their posts who had offended him in the past. No luxury he left unenjoyed and no cash gift he left unaccepted. In a matter of a few years Tseng got very wealthy and his luxuries of life almost comparable to those of the Emperor himself. Then the famous censor Pao as well as other censors began to report what he had been doing to the Emerpor, which eventually led to his discharge from his post and punishment to military service near the western borders.

Retribution to all his evil doings began to befall him, with his downfall. On his way to the western borders, he was killed by people who had been maltreated by him and his soul was led to the big wheel in the underworld for transmigration. Then he found himself reborn a daughter in a beggar's family. As he grew up quite charming he was purchased to be a concubine to a scholar who had a very jealous wife. Under this jealous wife he had to live a very miserable life. One night when this scholar was with him, two thieves broke in and killed the scholar. The wife accused him of murdering the husband at the magistrate's office and he was sentenced to death immediately. On his way to the execution ground he bitterly felt the lack of righteousness in the world for he had to be killed because of the crime he had not committed. Just at this painful moment his friends woke him up for the sky had cleared up and they had to leave. Sung-ling seemed to warn the examiners not to do too many evil things since they were all subject to retribution.

In **"San-sheng" ("Three Lives")**,[34] we have another very interesting story of retribution and counter-retribution over three lives. In the first life a scholar called Hsing Yu-tang took an examination and flunked. He felt the examiner was unfair and so accused him of unfair treatment to the king of the underworld after his death. The underworld king summoned the examiner to his court to answer the accusation. The examiner said he was then acting as the chief examiner and he decided his cases mostly according to the recommendations made by the lower examiners. The king retorted: "Since you are in charge of the job, you cannot dodge the blame. For your negligence you should be lashed."[35] Thousands of ghosts who had been maltreated by him in the previous life were watching the proceeding of the interrogation there. When they heard of this sentence, they protested all in a voice to the light punishment. They all requested a much heavier punishment, say, cutting out of the examiner's heart. The king could not help complying with their request and ordered the punishment. After the punishment the examiner was sent to the great wheel of transmigration and was reborn a boy in an ordinary family. One day a band of bandits stormed his village and imprisoned him and many other villagers. Soon the official troops came and crushed the bandits. Some bandits and villagers were arrested as they were staying together. The villagers were interrogated one after another and set free but when it was the boy's turn to be interrogated he found the interrogator, the commander of the troop, was nobody but the luckless scholar who accused him at the underworld king's court. He was summarily beheaded without any interrogation. So now it was his turn to go and accuse the former examinee before the court of the netherworld king. This time, as the examiner had beaten the examinee's parents before, the king said now they were even with each other. Then both of them were sentenced to be reborn as two dogs in the

third life, where they fought against each other to death. It was a very fierce dog-eat-dog battle literally. Now they had no reason to charge each other, but in order to keep peace between them the underworld king ordered the examinee to be reborn a boy and the examiner's future son-in-law. And yet it was not until the examinee succeeded in the provincial examination that relationship between them became really harmonious. We might laugh it off as Sung-ling's imagination, and yet we do realize how much embittered anger the luckless examinees harbored against the examiners, particularly those blind ones, those who did not evaluate the examinees' essays but their fates and their gifts. Sung-ling was among those luckless examinees whose examination essays had not been properly evaluated. He had good reason to punish such examiners in his retribution stories.

Notes

[13] Throughout P'u's life there were five purges of scholar-writers on a very big scale (cf. Chang Chin-chiao, op. cit., p. 2).

[14] Liu Chieh-ping, ed. and rev., *Tseng-t'u pu-chiao tan-ke liao-chai-chih-yi* (Taipei: Taiwan Student Book, 1978), Vol. 12.

[15] Ibid., Vol. 10.

[16] Ibid., Vol. 6.

[17] Trans. Herbert A. Giles.

[18] Liu Chieh-ping, ibid., Vol. 1.

[19] Ibid., Vol. 11.

[20] Ibid., Vol. 15.

[21] [This reference is rendered in untranslated Chinese in the original source.]

[22] Liu Chieh-ping, ibid., Vol. 10, p. 22.

[23] Ibid., p. 23.

[24] Ibid., p. 29.

[25] Ibid., "Wang Tzu-an", Vol. 16, p. 24.

[26] Hu Shih, *Hu-shih-wen-tsuen* (Collection of Hu Shih's Writings), Col. IV, Vol. 3, p. 375.

[27] Liu Chieh-ping, ibid., Vol. 1, p. 25.

[28] Ibid., p. 26.

[29] Ibid., Vol. 11, p. 59.

⁰ Ibid., Vol. 6, p. 30.

³¹ Ibid., Vol. 5, p. 5.

³² Wang Pi-chiang, compld., "Chen-chung Chi," *T'ang-jen-hsiao-shuo* (T'ang Fiction) (Taipei: Ho Lo, 1974), p. 37.

³³ Liu Chieh-ping, ibid., Vol. 5, p. 5.

³⁴ Ibid., Vol. 10, p. 7.

³⁵ Ibid.

Fatima Wu (essay date 1986)

SOURCE: "Foxes in Chinese Supernatural Tales (Part I)," in *Tamkang Review,* Vol. XVII, No. 2, Winter, 1986, pp. 121-54.

[*In the following excerpt, Wu examines P'u's innovative use of the images, symbols, themes, and motifs of the traditional Chinese fox tale.*]

Fox Spirits in P'u Sung-ling's **Liao-chai chih-yi**

It can be said that P'u wrote the most fox tales up to his time in his one collection of **Liao-chai chih-yi.** There are almost seventy-one fox tales in his book. P'u's fox spirits can be put into two categories: the good and the bad. There are also vengeful foxes that are used to emphasize a satiric viewpoint, such as in the tale named **"Yi yüan kuan"** and **"Tao-hu."** The fox spirit in the first story dares speak the truth in contrast to others who are timid and quiet. The fox in **"Tao-hu"** is used to satirize the impotence of the government officials at that time.

The fox spirit from the tale **"Ch'ou hu"** is an ambivalent character. She is both good and bad. She is good to Mu when he agrees to love her. Whenever she comes, she gives presents of gold and silk to the entire household. Yet when Mu gets tired of her and plans to get rid of her, she takes full revenge on him. She hurts him physically with a cat; she ruins his home, and snatches all his property, causing him to be as poor as he once was.

"Hu ch'êng yin" has another "bad" character. In the tale, there is a typical cunning and dangerous fox spirit. It damages the new landlord's clothes and puts dirt in his food. Moreover, it secretly places aphrodisiacs in the mistress' food when the master is away. The mistress has to run to her guest, who insults and refuses her. She almost dies of shame afterwards. Yet the reader must not be distracted just by the fox's bad behavior; he must also be aware of why the fox is acting that way toward the humans. The two fox spirits

mentioned above are actually doing the man a favor by teaching him a lesson: that he should value genuine love over monetary gains and mere physical pleasure. By using a fox which is lewd in character to punish a lewd human-being, P'u shows his skillful hand in writing satire. Can there be a worse man when even the lewd fox thinks him lascivious? These in-between fox characters are important characters for P'u, for they help him to illustrate his view of life and comment on the moral character of men. In a sense, these foxes are good foxes to P'u, for they know what is right and wrong, while the mortals in the tales do not. These fox spirits act as P'u's didactic agents to punish the bad and the immoral.

P'u's bad fox characters are very traditional, so much so that they are simply repetitions of their predecessors. Examples of these negative fox characters from *Liao-chai* are in: **"Chia êrh," "Tung shêng," "Hu Ss -chieh," "Hsia nü," "Chi shêng,"** and finally, **"Nung-jên,"** and **"Chiao Mi."** These bad fox spirits usually bewitch and possess their victims, ruining their health and causing their families' concern. In most of these tales, the fox spirits are exorcised by a Taoist priest or a helper who drives away or kills the spirit. Many of these bad spirits die of lasciviousness. In **"Chia êrh,"** the young boy kills the fox because he bewitches his mother and forces her into an illicit relationship. The fox in **"Nung-jên"** also has his eyes on a young girl. The unluckiest fox is the one in **"Hsia nü."** He does not have a chance to do anything yet before he is killed. The female foxes in **"Tung shêng"** and **"Hu Ss -chieh"** catch their victims. In **"Tung shêng,"** though the fox lady is successful in assimilating the vital spirit from the scholar and causing his death at the end, this death is avenged by another man. This second man takes the place of the exorcist in destroying the fox lady.

"Hu Ss -chieh" is an unusual story in that in the same story, there are simultaneously good and bad fox ladies. First there is Miss Hu the Fourth, a good fox, but her older sister, Miss Wu the Third, plans to kill the scholar after they have met. Although Miss Hu the Fourth truly loves the man and saves him from her vicious sister, she is astonished to find that he is again bewitched by another fox. Both sisters at this time join forces to save him from the third spirit. P'u is having a lot of fun here, confusing the reader with both good and bad foxes interacting with one man. This is one of the ways in which P'u makes his stories interesting, filling them with excitement and suspense. A similar story to the above can be found in **"Chou San."** In this story, a man's house is pestered by a fox spirit. The master of the house asks another fox to perform the exorcism. The second fox refuses because he thinks that there is another fox who is better qualified for the job. He recommends a third fox, who after the exorcism, stays at the master's house for good. Both **"Hu Ss -chieh"** and **"Chou San"** indicate that there are different ranks among the fox spirits. As I have discussed earlier, there are fox fairies and fox spirits. The former have devoted more years to their Taoist training and hence are more powerful than the latter, who are just beginning theirs. The difference in rank in the fox spirits allows P'u to create stories which sometimes act as a reflection of the human world, which has both positive and negative characteristics.

P'u's fox tales are different from the collection in *T'ai-p'ing kuang-chi* [977-981] in that almost eighty percent of P'u's fox tales have good fox characters. In *T'ai-p'ing kuang-chi,* only less than one-fourth of the tales carry good fox images. It is in the writing of good fox characters that P'u is best. His good fox characters include: 1) scholars or educated and refined individuals who help men in their studies, 2) drinking foxes who develop with men a relationship of trust and love, 3) female or male fox spirits who assist men in various matters, for example, to achieve a fortune and to drive away a shrewish wife, and, 4) single women who become involved with men, help men in their career, and start a family with them.

Since the time of *So shên chi,* fox scholars have been popular characters in tales. P'u picks up this tradition but adds his own imagination to create new fox stories. The story **"Hu-shih"** is a good example. Mr. Hu, who is a fox spirit, turns himself into an educated man and works as a tutor in a prominent man's house. Even though the family later finds out the tutor's identity, they still respect him because of his good will and literary talent. At the end, he is even accepted as a family member when the master agrees to marry his son to Mr. Hu's sister. Another story, **"Lêng shêng,"** has a talented fox spirit. We do not know whether this fox is female or male; we do not even get to see its face. Yet we know it is very talented scholastically because the fox has transformed the young retarded student, Lêng, into a quick and intelligent scholar. Before Lêng meets the fox, he could not familiarize himself with any one of the great books, even at over the age of twenty. Only days after they have been together, Mr. Lêng's personality is totally changed. He loves to laugh no matter where he is, and he can finish a good essay in one sitting. At the end, he is remembered by the books he has written. **"Kuo shêng"** also has an intelligent and witty fox. In this tale, we do not see the fox's face either, yet we see its pen strokes. Kuo, the man of the house, is very upset by his essays because they have been ruined by a fox who blots and covers part of them with ink. Slowly, his friends realize that the fox was trying to correct his essays by cutting the bad parts out. Since then, Kuo follows the fox's instructions and manages to pass his examinations. Again, we see a scholarly fox guiding a man's studies without any intention of hurting him or receiving any rewards from him. Educated, talented, and witty foxes also appear in **"Hu hsieh," "Hu Ssu-hsiang-kung," "Hu lien,"** and **"Yi yüan kuan."**

Fox spirits tend to adore drinking. Through the medium of wine, fox spirits become good friends with humans. In a story called **"Chiu yu,"** a male fox spirit carries on a relationship with his drinking friend, who is mortal. Instead of hurting him, the spirit uses his power of prediction to make his friend rich. **"Hu Ssu-hsiang-kung"** and **"Hu hsieh"** are tales of male and female fox spirits who drink and write poems with their human companions. The fox spirit in **"Chi shêng"** also loves to steal wine and food from the master's house. The protagonist in **"Ch'in shêng"** dies because he has drunk some poisonous wine. A fox spirit comes by and heals him, saying that she has just rescued her husband who has died of the same cause. The scholar in **"Hê-chien shêng"** loves to drink, and so does the fox spirit that lives in the dry weeds in his fields. In the form of an old man, the fox goes out every night to his friends' drinking parties. The fox spirit in **"Chin-ling Yi"** steals wine from a brewer. When he is caught, he has to take the brewer on an amorous adventure in order to save himself. Here is another example in which a fox spirit gets into trouble because of his affinity for wine.

The third category of good fox spirits in the *Liao-chai,* male or female spirits which assist humans in various situations, excludes a love relationship between the spirit and the human. The assistance rendered by the spirits in most cases is voluntary, and they are not rewarded. The spirits help humans for the following reasons: a) they are repaying what the man has done for them in the past, b) they do it totally out of sympathy and compassion, or the feeling of indignation at the situation, and lastly, c) the spirits are involved in a very trusting and close friendship with the humans. **"Chiao-na"** is a moving story of friendship. Scholar Kung is in love with Chiao-na at first sight, yet he does not pursue her when he knows that she is not available. The feeling Kung has for her enables him to fight the monster. In return, Chiao-na for the second time cures him and saves his life. The two lead a relationship between a man and a woman rare in classical tales. It is a friendship based on trust, love, and the will to sacrifice oneself.

The story **"Hêng-niang"** involves a deep and trusting relationship between two women, a fox spirit and a housewife. The spirit, in the course of helping the mistress to gain back her husband's heart from another concubine, has become a good friend of the concubine. Their relationship is described by the spirit as *"ch'ing jo yi t'i,"* which literally means "two in one." Because of the trust that exists between the two of them, the spirit even discloses to her good friend that she is actually a fox. Another story of friendship is **"Ma Chieh-fu."** The fox spirit, a sworn brother to the protagonist, out of compassion and love for him raises his nephew, takes care of his father, and helps him, as much as he can, to counteract his shrewish wife. Moreover, the spirit respects him when he chooses not to condemn his wife. Though possessing supernatural power, the spirit does not take the liberty to get rid of this vicious woman himself. This shows that he cares for and loves Ma, who is a kind but cowardly man. This spirit, like the other spirits mentioned earlier, receives no reward for what he has done for his friend.

Another moving fox tale comes at the end of the *Liao-chai* collection. In **"Liu Liang-ts'ai,"** since the spirit has made a lasting relationship with Liu's father, he decides to be reborn as Liu's heir. His reason for doing that is because Liu has never rejected or despised him though he knows that he is a fox. The trust and respect which Liu has bestowed on the spirit move him. In return for the favor, the fox is born as the only heir for his friend.

One can see that these fox spirits are human in their actions, thoughts, and beliefs. They value friendship, trust and love. They show their gratitude with whatever they can do: healing the human of sickness, saving a man from death, helping a man out of poverty, teaching a man a lesson in life, warning him of imminent danger, or helping him to have an heir. Other fox spirits in **"Lêng shêng," "Chou San," "Kuo shêng," "Ssu-hsün," "Ch'in shêng,"** and **"Nien yang"** help men simply out of good will, compassion, indignation, or just plain enthusiasm.

By presenting foxes with human qualities, P'u has created in his tales an inseparable link between fox and man. This is something the authors in the past have failed to do. P'u has the ability and power to make the reader forget the identity of the animal. He does so totally by his narrative art. His descriptions, settings and dialogue are vivid and natural, given the limitations of classical Chinese. His fox spirits live, feel, laugh, and cry like men. As a result, they lose their animal identity and merge with that of the humans. Lu Hsün has said in his book, *A Brief History of Chinese Fiction:*

> **The Strange Tales of Liao-chai,** however, contain such detailed and realistic descriptions that even flower spirits and fox fairies appear human and approachable. . . .

The reader is so absorbed by such characters as Chiao-na and the aunt from **"Wang Ch'êng"** that he can follow the story without remembering that both characters are not human but foxes. This is exactly the illusion that P'u tries to create in his tales.

P'u's Female Fox Spirits

Though P'u writes about both male and female fox spirits in his *Liao-chai,* he puts much more emphasis on the female ones. Female spirit tales take up about eighty percent of his fox tales. For this reason, I would like to devote the last part of this section to a discussion of this topic.

Female fox spirits, from the early *So shên chi* to the *Jên-shih chuan* in the Tang Dynasty, slowly acquire a new image. They begin to shake off their negative and bestial qualities. From the dangerous, lewd, selfish, greedy, and cunning animals in the ancient tales, they slowly become kind, self-sacrificing, faithful, sincere, and caring individuals in the later ones. *Jên-shih chuan* is a very good example. She is the image of perfect womanhood. Very likely, *Jên-shih chuan* was one of the tales P'u had in mind when he began his own writing on female fox spirits.

As was stated earlier, many of P'u's foxes are human in that they possess human traits and respect human values. These human factors in P'u's foxes are revealed intricately through social injustice and human relations. We see scenes of touching friendship in **"Chiao-na"** and **"Chiu yu."** Kung and Chiao-na can be said to be the most truthful friends because they respect and love each other, yet they are not involved sexually. Chiao-na, the female fox here, has shaken off the traditional lewd image of female foxes. Also many of P'u's foxes have a sense of human dignity. In **"Hsin Shih-ssu-niang"** the female fox protagonist is portrayed as a quiet, submitting but dignified woman. She is not promiscuous, for she refuses the man's advances and even his marriage proposal. She only yields to his request when he is backed up by a powerful aunt. At this point, though she has no choice, she insists on a decent marriage. It is obvious that the character of the fox in this tale, Lady Hsin, is a proud and dignified person. Even though she is forced to marry a man of low moral character, she has kept her values. She is a good wife in that she shows concern for and obeys her husband. It is also the fox spirit who saves him from jail. She is intelligent enough to know that her husband is not the man for her, yet she is considerate enough to find him a mate before she leaves. This story shows the fox's concern, care and submission even for a man whom she does not love but is only bound to by a marriage oath. Though it is an unwanted relationship, the fox never tries to use her supernatural power to control or to desert him. She is willing to submit, as best she can, to do what is required of her.

The **"Hsin Shih-ssu-niang"** tale leads our discussion to a fox spirit's reaction against various kinds of treatment from human society. P'u's fox spirits possess love and trust for their mortal friends, yet they also manifest hatred and mistrust when mistreated. The fox in **"Chou hu"** has much more human dignity than her human lover. Although she is ugly and swarthy, she is generous to the men she loves. She gives them gold in return for their love. Everything she does is very straightforward and fair. When deserted by her men, she regards it as fair to retrieve her gold. Her clean-cut way in dealing with a love relationship, though it may seem commercial or unsincere, is far better than the man's attempt to hurt her while he is claiming love for her. In this story, P'u is emphasizing his point by using a fox spirit: the spirit, which is traditionally regarded as lewd, cunning, and dangerous, has changed places with man, who is usually thought of as distinguished from beasts because of his conscience and dignity.

Another story that exemplifies a similar idea is **"Wu hsiao-lien."** Shih, an educated man, at his worst stage in life, in sickness and poverty, is rescued by a woman who cures him and supports him financially. When he becomes well and has found himself an official post, he deserts his benefactor and marries another woman. Although eventually the fox lady comes and joins him at his house without causing any trouble with the concubine he has acquired, she does not have his love or respect. Instead, he wants to kill her when he finds out that she is really a fox spirit. Again, this is P'u's satire on the humanity of the animal versus the inhumanity of man. Shih, an educated and renowned court official, is heartless and ungrateful to the companion who has saved his life. But the fox lady is obedient, faithful, reliant and generous to him. She stays with him and helps him in his career until her life is threatened. Unlike the ugly fox, who demands all her belongings when she leaves, she only asks for her medicine back. She does not cause any trouble to anybody or to anything in the house. The story of **"Wu hsiao-lien"** suggests a moral degradation among the official class. The fox is a symbol of the good wife that is upheld in Chinese society.

P'u's female fox spirits are not just dignified, loving, and financially generous but are also magnanimous. Jealousy is a common theme in P'u's tales in **Liao-chai,** as it was a common practice for man to have more than one mate in old China. When a woman was sterile, the husband had a justified excuse in acquiring a concubine for the purpose of family heir. When more than one woman served the same man in the house, the situation sometimes was uncomfortable. Jealousy plays a big role in many of P'u's stories, which disclose his view on the subject. P'u thinks it is the man's fault if he is unable to insure his family's prosperity. But it is the woman's, especially the wife's, task to organize and pacify the concubines by being generous and kind to them. The fox in **"Wu hsiao-lien"** is a perfect model of a wife who loves and respects the concubine Wang. The latter, touched by her kindness, becomes very close to her. Very soon, they live just like sisters in harmony. It is only the man who causes a rift between the two by loving one and detesting the other.

In **"Ch'ing-mei"** the fox spirit arranges a wedding between her husband and her former mistress, not even for the purpose of reproduction. In **"Ch'ang-ê"** the fox spirit, after having a relationship with her man, even gives him money to marry a mortal woman. At the end of the story, the two women stay happily with the same husband. Some of P'u's mortal women, when compared with the fox spirits, are much more selfish and dangerous. A good example is **"Ma Chieh-fu,"** mentioned earlier. Ma's wife has no children. Though her husband acquires a concubine for the reason of propagation, he never dares talk to the concubine in the wife's presence. When the concubine becomes pregnant, the wife beats her on a pretext and causes her to have a miscarriage. At the end, P'u gives her a miserable end, showing his disapproval of her behavior. The jealous wife in **"Shao nü"** is again a senior wife who tortures two concubines to death until she is moved by the kindness of the third one.

Many of P'u's fox spirits possess the virtues which are found in a mortal woman. These inhuman beings turn into human beings in P'u's hands. They become traditional virtuous Chinese women with flesh and blood, with feelings and emotions. **"Ya-t'ou"** is a perfect model of a chaste and virtuous wife. Coming from a brothel, Ya-t'ou is different from her fox sister in that she is not promiscuous even by trade. Once she devotes herself to Wang, she swears fidelity to him. Despite physical torture inflicted by her fox mother, Ya-t'ou remains faithful. She suffers under her mother's hands for years until her son grows up to be a young man and rescues her from agony. Yet she does not want her mother to be hurt. She is heartbroken when she finds out that her half-human son has killed both her mother and sister. Ya-t'ou is a woman who dares to love and is willing to die for her daring. She is defeated only by her own kindness towards her family. She is very human, as she values chastity and family ties and is willing to sacrifice herself for both.

P'u Sung-ling's Use of Fox as Symbol

When P'u writes about foxes, he is actually writing about human beings. The human world involves many limitations: social injustice, moral obligations, lack of freedom, illness and mortality. Men also need good friends, true love, an amiable family, a prosperous career and wealth. Because of various reasons, many of these needs and limitations will never be satisfied or overcome by certain individuals except in fantasy or dreams. For example, a man who is impotent by birth would in those days never be able to overcome the deformity and live like a normal man. In P'u's **"Ch'iao-niang,"** the elderly ghost cures the young man Fu of his impotence, while the fox spirit teaches him his first lesson in sex. Another similar example can be found in the story of **"Lêng shêng."** The scholar is born retarded. In his life he would never be expected to have a scholastic career until a fox spirit comes to him one day and cures him of his retardation. **"Hsiao Ts'ui"** is almost the same story, in which the fox spirit is able to cure her companion Wang of his imbecility. Physical deformity imposes a limit in a person's life in different forms. In **"Ch'iao-niang,"** Fu's impotence deprives him of sexual pleasure in life, while Scholar Lêng and Wang are kept from having a career. By putting in his fox characters, P'u instills hope into the human world. In P'u's gothic world, miracles do happen to the hopeless.

By using foxes with supernatural powers, P'u's tales help to relieve the pain of death. In **"Ch'in shêng,"** the scholar is poisoned by his own wine and dies at his prime. While the wife is mourning for him, a fox spirit comes by and raises him from death.

P'u's fox spirits also help man to satisfy his secret desire for love. A stable but monotonous family life sometimes causes one to daydream and fantasize. **"Shuang teng"** is such a story. Wei, an ordinary young man who has no purpose in life except living and working for his in-laws, meets a fox spirit one evening when he is alone upstairs in a winery. For half a year, he has nothing but fun and sex with her, until one evening, the spirit comes to say good-bye and disappears in the dark. The spirit could be interpreted today as a figment of Wei's imagination and as a relief from everyday monotony, although P'u may not have intended such a psychological interpretation. Wei, a young man in his twenties, is already settled down for life. His lack of excitement and freedom in love helps build this fantasy tale. **"Fên-chou hu"** is another tale which can be interpreted as an elderly man's secret wish to have an extramarital affair. Ch'u is a state official. Because of his social standing, his secret desire to have a relationship cannot be fulfilled easily. The fox spirit appears in his house right in his room. Moreover, she is not just the casual type but cares for and loves the man. Her sincerity in this affair shows itself when he asks her to go home with him. Although it is forbidden for a fox to cross a river, she tries her best to obtain permission from the river god, who allows her to cross the river and stay with the official for ten more days. These two tales, on the surface, are simple short stories. Yet they are symbolic of a man's aspiration in a free and true love relationship. It is free because it is outside wedlock and free of obligation. It is true because the man and the fox usually get together for no reason at all but love. Often the fox spirit asks nothing from the man, and when their love calms down eventually, usually the spirit will disappear, leaving no obligations for the man, but only beautiful memories.

The fox spirit world for P'u also represents the ethical world to which he aspires. By using these spirits, P'u is able to create his idea of a Utopia in front of our eyes. He uses foxes to redress social injustice and family disputes; to remind and warn man of his moral obligation; and to reflect corruption in the governmental and examination systems. Many scholars claim that

P'u's tales are very didactic, that he emphasizes especially the Buddhist idea of cause and effect, in which the good will be rewarded while the bad will be punished for their deeds. P'u, in order to give the weak and oppressed emotional and poetic justice, takes the reader into a world of the supernatural, in which the weak are protected by a certain magical power. Not only are they able to escape oppression, but they are also given a chance to redress the injustice done to them.

The story of **"Chiu-shan wang"** tells us of the fate of the Li family when the master of the house decides to burn his tenant and his family to death. His tenant, an old fox spirit, offers a hundred pieces of gold to rent a deserted part of Li's residence. The fox family then invite Mr. Li over for dinner, during which he is offered very good food. Thinking it strange that his tenant has changed the deserted house into a fine mansion in such a short time, he decides that his new tenants must be foxes. In secret, he buys some sulphur and niter and one day sets fire on the whole household. Up to this point, P'u shows us the injustice Li has done to the foxes. Li, who has received a good rent from the foxes, has never been bothered by his tenants. Rather, his deserted house becomes very well decorated and taken care of. Moreover, the old fox spirit is friendly and respectful towards Li. Li is presented here as an obnoxious, cruel and greedy person. After the conflagration, the fox says to him,

> "There has not been any rejection or complaint between us. I have paid a hundred pieces of gold for your deserted land, no small amount. How can you then bear to kill us all? There is slim chance that I would not avenge this most obnoxious feud."

The old fox's revenge against him takes advantage of Li's greediness. As a fox, he is able to transform himself into a respectable fortune-teller who appears to Li a year later. By telling Li that he is destined to be king, and by assembling followers for him, the fox turns Li into a rebel leader. Li's end comes when the emperor's army is surrounding his fortress and the fortune-teller has disappeared. Li is captured and executed together with his whole family. At the end, P'u makes his comments in the guise of the Historian of the Strange. He says that Li's end serves him right, for his cruelty is seen when he murders the foxes. If Li had been a good man, the fox would never have been able to trap him. The fox's vengeance would not have been possible if the fox had not been a supernatural character. A mortal tenant would have died after the fire. Neither would he be able to change himself into another man in order to win Li's confidence or be able to recruit soldiers and win battles for Li. The fox spirit here is presented as a respectable, polite, and educated individual in the beginning. But at the end, in order to avenge himself, he has turned into a cunning and cruel old man.

The fox lady in **"Wu hsiao-lien"** is also able to avenge herself on her husband Shih only because she is a supernatural creature. She demands her medicine back. The result leads to Shih's death. If she were a mortal woman, she would have been deserted, insulted, cheated or even hurt by him. P'u makes use of his fox spirits as his didactic tools in teaching these human malefactors a lesson. By the end of his tales, the author is able to reinstall social justice.

Such tales as the **"Chou hu,"** **"Wu hsiao-lien,"** **"Chiu-shan wang,"** carry at least two messages from P'u Sung-ling. First, they are moral satires in which man, who is at the top of the scale in the animal world, is compared to the foxes, a rather low animal. The irony is that man (like the protagonists Mu, Shih and Li in the above three tales), who is educated and intelligent, does not act as he should. Yet the foxes, though they are bestial, act with human dignity and love. Shih, a man with a military degree and a government post, should be a man of understanding and discretion. He should be able to tell what is wrong and what is right. His unwillingness and inability to recognize the fox spirit's virtues and to accept her put him morally below the animal.

In **"Chou hu,"** Mu's fault lies in his greediness, ingratitude and cruelty. Compared with him, the fox lady is more generous, kind, fair and frank. P'u comments in the voice of the Historian of the Strange that even though she is a fox, for all she has done for Mu, she does not deserve such treatment. The moral character of the fox is elevated above the male protagonist in the tale. In **"Chiu-shan wang,"** Li kills the old fox and his family just because they are animal spirits. He fails to see them as polite, respectable and generous individuals.

The second message of these tales lies in P'u's intention to present to the reader his ideal world—an ethical world in which love, generosity, and kindness are highly valued. In his Utopia, human or unhuman beings with the above moral qualities will win over the immoral. P'u is disappointed by mankind and its vices and so creates a supernatural world in which improbable characters and events can correct these wrongs.

The Function of the Female in P'u's Fox Spirits

When one looks at the fox tales in *T'ai-p'ing kuan-chi*, it is not difficult to find that most Chinese traditional fox spirits are female. Many more than half of the fox characters in the tales are female. Female fox spirits are especially common when the tale is concerned with a man-and-woman relationship. When the woman is the seducer, she is always a fox spirit. This is such a traditional pattern that it has now become a modern cliche, which the Chinese still use in their daily speech. The modern expression *hu-li-ching,* "fox spirit," refers

to a "bad" woman who seduces a man sexually and tricks him into giving her whatever she desires. In modern language, the term is never used to refer to the male sex.

As in the past, some of P'u's less interesting female foxes do carry their traditional lewd image, such as the two foxes in **"Fu hu."** Both men in the two tales come across sexually demanding fox spirits. The man in the first tale becomes sick and weak as a result. One day a doctor gives him a kind of aphrodisiac which makes him so potent that he conquers the fox in bed and takes its life. The man in the second tale is born so sexually strong that when the fox spirit goes to him, his strength is enough to scare her away.

Descriptions of the sexual relationship between fox and man appear in many of P'u's fox tales. They indeed form a pattern of an initiation process, by which the male and female protagonists are attracted to each other and fall in love. In P'u's best fox tales, this apparently loose relationship later develops into a relationship of true love, devotion and sincerity. The female fox spirit's lewd image at the beginning of the tale, when she comes on her own accord to seduce the man she loves, can be explained as a female's expression of her need for free love in a morally restricted Confucian society. In such an environment, the human female does not have the right to choose her own lover, or the freedom to go out of her house to visit him. The Chinese tradition requires the young woman to follow the order of her parents, who decide her marriage and her life:

> With Confucianism, two barriers are erected to insure the cohesion of the feudal social order: the first is the door to the bedchamber, the second is writing and knowledge in general. A woman cannot cross them both at once.

In ancient Chinese society, only the males are free to visit friends, roam the streets, and join different social activities. P'u bestows supernatural power on the female foxes, so that they are able to express their love and hate without obstruction.

As I have mentioned earlier in the story of **"Wu hsiao-lien"** and **"Hsin Shih-ssu-niang,"** the female protagonists in these tales are able to avenge themselves on men because they are foxes possessing supernatural power. This is probably the only way that P'u can give emotional and poetic justice to the social imbalance that he sees in the world around him: that females are often oppressed by males, or sometimes by a more powerful female agent, such as the old aunt in **"Hsin Shih-ssu-niang."** The old aunt in the tale represents the powerful, prominent and vicious forces against which the weak, the poor and the powerless have to fight in society.

P'u's foxes, then, are mostly female for the following reasons:

1) Foxes are traditionally regarded as a lewd animal. Therefore, female foxes are ideal characters in a free love relationship.

2) These female foxes are used as symbols for mortal women who, in a sexist society, are oppressed and controlled by men and other superiors.

3) The female foxes with supernatural powers give vent to social injustice. With their superhuman power, they are able to correct the wrongs done to them.

4) By using female foxes in place of mortal females in his tales, P'u elevates the animal spirits to a higher level of existence. At the same time, since these animals are virtuous, they give an exaggerated effect. P'u is saying that even among mortals such virtuous women cannot be found. But for him, such virtuous women are essential in building an ethical world.

His tales of good female fox spirits are numerous. Among these are **"Ch'ing-mei," "Ya-t'ou," "Chiao-na," "Lien-hsiang," "Ch'iao-niang," "Hung-yü," "Hsin Shih-ssu-niang," "Fêng San-niang," "Hsiao-Ts'ui," "Fêng hsien," "Ch'ang-ê,"** and **"Wu hsiao-lien."** Most of these tales consist of a female fox spirit who falls in love with a mortal, helps him in various ways, and finally establishes a stable and longlasting relationship with him. The ending of these tales, in which the fox spirit is allowed to stay with her husband or lover, is the almost unique contribution of P'u Sung-ling. The fox tale section in *T'ai-p'ing kuang-chi* has only one tale, "Chi Chên," in which the female fox is allowed to marry a man and stay with him until she dies of a natural cause. All female spirits in other tales are either killed, driven away or leave on their own accord at the end. P'u's fox tales are different in that he unites man and animal not only on a love basis but also on an ethical one. Moral virtues and everlasting love are enough for P'u to break through the man-animal barrier. This barrier is dissolved in a very subtle way. P'u's fox spirits are so humanized that they not only look human but also act, think, and speak like mortals. The fox spirit's double identity, fox and mortal, overlap and mix to form a model character for P'u.

To end this essay, I would like to discuss two tales: **"Ch'ing-mei"** and **"Ya-t'ou."** I choose these two because they have much in common and both pertain to the points I have explicated above on P'u's good female fox spirits. 1) Both Ch'ing-mei and Ya-t'ou are fox spirits. Ya-t'ou is from a family of foxes, and Ch'ing-mei is the child of a fox and a mortal. 2) They both fall in love with a mortal man, who is rejected by the fox's family members. 3) Both fox spirits fight for freedom in love, acting against their own families. 4)

Both foxes, after much suffering and patience, are able to reunite with their loved ones and to enjoy the fruit of their struggle at the end. 5) Both foxes give birth to children. 6) Both spirits are virtuous, intelligent, sincere and loving individuals. 7) Neither of them has much if any supernatural power. Ch'ing-mei has none whatsoever. 8) In both tales, two generations of foxes show contrast between one another.

In **"Ya-t'ou,"** P'u places the female protagonist in the environment of a brothel in order to emphasize her background. Ya-t'ou is both fox and prostitute. Her mother and sister are typically greedy and lewd women. But out of this moral pollution, Ya-t'ou emerges as a perfect daughter, wife and mother. She is obedient to her mother. She loves and forgives her family, even though they have tortured her physically and separated her from her husband and son. She is a good wife because she is chaste. After she has spent her first night and has fallen in love with Wang, she will not take another man. She would rather suffer beating from her mother. After the elopement, it is also Ya-t'ou who works hard to support the family. As a mother, she is concerned about her son, who is impulsive and brutal. She uses tears to teach him love and forgiveness. Ya-t'ou is a spirit which possesses superhuman power, yet she does not use it unless she has to do so. In only two instances does she display her magical power. First, she speeds up the elopement by tying a talisman on the servant and on the donkey's rear. Secondly, she takes off the "evil tendons" from her son's hands and feet. But she does not use any magic to help herself while she is imprisoned by her mother for eighteen years. Nor does she use it to acquire money in order to help her husband when they first start life in a strange city. The two magical deeds she has performed could be left out without changing the tale substantially. This tale would then be just an ordinary tale without any supernatural elements. With the fox, the story becomes partly a fantasy and a fairy tale.

P'u emphasizes Ya-t'ou's moral character by contrasting her with her fox mother and sister. The fox mother in the tale has the image of a greedy and cruel parent. She forces her daughters to sell their bodies to the customers who come to the brothel. When her wish is ignored, she does all that she can to inflict pain and suffering on them. She does not value true love or family ties. Although Ya-t'ou's older sister, Ni-tz , is a minor character in the tale, she does not leave the reader with a good impression. She comes to fetch Ya-t'ou home after the elopement without trying to understand her younger sister. When Ya-t'ou is suffering at home, she does not even try to help her. Ni-tz , like her mother, does not have love and concern for her own family members. Ya-t'ou is exactly the opposite of her mother and her older sister.

"Ch'ing-mei" is another of P'u's good fox tales. She

is half human and half fox, born of a mortal father and fox spirit mother. Again P'u is ingenious in bringing out Ch'ing-mei's moral character by putting her in a low social stratum. Ch'ing-mei first starts out as an innocent child caught in her parents' dispute. Her father Ch'ing, impatient to have a male heir, marries Madam Wang, while Ch'ing-mei's mother, angry at being jilted by her husband, leaves the infant Ch'ing-mei to her own fate and disappears. When the father dies, Ch'ing-mei lives with her uncle, who is a heartless man. He sells her as a maid into another Wang family, in which she serves the master's daughter. Ch'ing-mei turns from a happy child with a family into an orphan and a maid in a stranger's house. With such a complicated and discouraging background, Ch'ing-mei could have been just an ordinary maid with no education, no money and no social status. She could have spent her life serving in the Wang family and marrying a fellow servant. Yet, because of her merits, she turns into the wife of a prominent court official, enjoying a happy family and prosperous life. Although she is a maid who must obey orders, Ch'ing-mei is portrayed as a strong character who recognizes what she wants and decides her own actions. Once she discovers that the poor scholar Chang is a kind, hard-working and filial man, Ch'ing-mei decides to match him with her mistress. She is not selfish, because she thinks of her mistress first when she sees a good man. Later, when her plan to unite the two fails, Ch'ing-mei volunteers herself to be the bride. She is confident that she has made the right decision. No matter what happens, she will not be swayed. When she tells her mistress of her decision to marry Chang, her mistress says:

"You foolish maid, can you act on your own?"

"If nothing avails, I'm ready to die!"

Although she successfully marries herself to Chang, she has nonetheless plunged into another difficult situation. Chang's family is extremely poor. His father is very sick and needs to be taken care of constantly. Chang himself needs time to study for the examination. Once Ch'ing-mei joins the Changs, she takes up the responsibility to serve her in-laws. At the same time, she embroiders to make a living, allowing her husband to have the time and money to go on with his studies. Here our heroine is portrayed as a diligent, self-sacrificing (for she eats rice bran herself and gives the rice to her in-laws) and filial daughter-in-law.

Ch'ing-mei remains a humble and kind person after she has become a government official's wife. Her magnanimity is manifested in her treatment of her former mistress when the latter is in great distress. Although now A-hsi is no longer her mistress, Ch'ing-mei still respects and loves her. When she knows that A-hsi is homeless, she insists on bringing her to her house. Far from being jealous, Ch'ing-mei is the one who arranges A-hsi to marry her husband. We are told in the tale that, for the rest of her life, she serves and respects A-hsi as she did before, even though she is the senior wife in the family. Ch'ing-mei is a person who values friendship, love and righteousness.

Ch'ing-mei serves as a strong contrast to her mother, the fox lady. Although in the tale, the daughter is said to resemble her mother physically, they have completely different characters. Ch'ing-mei's mother is promiscuous. She hangs on a man's belt and follows him home. But when she finds that he is fickle, she leaves the man and her own child without a second thought. This fox spirit gives us the impression of a lewd, selfish and cruel woman. Yet Ch'ing-mei, the fox's daughter, is humane and kind. When she reunites with her former mistress A-hsi, she takes up the responsibility to marry A-hsi to her husband. This is the crucial difference between the mother and daughter. The mother fox, enraged with jealousy, breaks up the family and ruins her daughter, while her child Ch'ing-mei harbors no jealous feelings at all but only love and understanding for the new couple. Rather than breaking up her relationship with her husband, Ch'ing-mei unites the couple and herself into one family, which prospers with wealth and children. For all this, Ch'ing-mei turns from a fox's daughter into a perfect model of a mortal woman. The reader should also notice that Ch'ing-mei has absolutely no superhuman power at all. At the beginning, she is not even able to save herself from being sold as a maid. In her early married life, she has to work even harder than a maid for a living. Ch'ing-mei has elevated herself from her animal status (as a fox), and her social status (as a maid) to an intelligent, sincere and virtuous woman in P'u's world.

One can say that many of P'u Sung-ling's fox tales are didactic tales. Everytime he tells a tale, he has in the back of his mind an ethical framework from which he never strays. In all of his tales, there exists a strong tendency to elucidate cause and effect. If a fox spirit is good, P'u never fails to reward it. If a man is bad, at the end, he will surely get his due. This has become a literary formula which underlies the whole collection of *Liao-chai.* As C. T. Hsia has said about the colloquial tales, the cause and effect formula limits the realism in the tales. Not only is the reader able to predict the ending while he is still reading the story, but the author has also limited his imagination and his art if he has to follow a certain pattern. The good foxes in P'u's stories all are rewarded with more or less the same thing: a successful and loving husband, with a prosperous family and children. Apparently, these are the only things that a woman would want in that social environment. Ch'ing-mei, Ya-t'ou, and Ch'iao-niang are examples. Since our author insists on staying inside his own ethical fence, he is not able to write such stories as *Jên-shih chuan* of the Tang Dynasty. Shên Chi-chi wrote the story because he thought that Miss Jên was a rare female who was understanding and righteous. He felt sorry for her and so wanted to record her life. This is different from P'u's purpose of expounding morals with his imagination.

Judith T. Zeitlin (essay date 1993)

SOURCE: "Obsession," in *Historian of the Strange: Pu Songling and the Chinese Classical Tale,* Stanford University Press, 1993, pp. 61-97.

[*In the following excerpt from her book-length study of P'u's life and works, Zeitlin examines some of Pu's stories within the context of the Chinese cultural construct of obsession. During the sixteenth and seventeenth centuries, the development of an obscure or unusual addiction, compulsion, mania, or craving became a fashionable pursuit of the intelligentsia and occasioned many works of literature and art.*]

> Without an obsession, no one is exceptional.
> —Yuan Hongdao, *A History of Flower Arranging*

According to one of the apocryphal anecdotes that later sprang up around *Liaozhai* and its author, Pu Songling never passed the higher examinations because "his love of the strange had developed into an obsession."[1] As a result, when he entered the examination hall, foxspirits and ghosts jealously crowded around to prevent him from writing about anything but them. This colorful legend continues the transformation of the author into a character in his tales that we glimpsed in the previous chapter. But it also contains an important insight: the nearly five hundred tales in the *Liaozhai* collection grew out of the author's lifelong obsession with the strange. We have seen that in his preface Pu Songling represented his fascination with the strange as an uncontrollable passion and linked his recording of strange stories with the paradigm of obsessive collecting, in which "things accrue to those who love them." Within the stories themselves, the notion of obsession and collecting is likewise a prominent theme, one translated with great art into fiction.

The Chinese Concept of Obsession

The concept of obsession, or *pi,* is an important Chinese cultural construct that after a long development reached its height during the late Ming and early Qing dynasties. A seventeenth-century dictionary, *A Complete Mastery of Correct Characters (Zhengzi tong),* offers the essential Ming definition of the term: "Pi is a pathological fondness for something" (*pi, shihao zhi bing*).[2] This pathological component of pi is significant: indeed a synonym for pi is sometimes "illness" or "mania" (*bing*). The medical usage of pi can be traced back to *The Classic Materia Medica (Bencao jing)* of the second century, where according to Paul Unschuld, the term *pi shi* or "indigestion" already figures as "one of the most important kinds of serious illnesses."[3] An influential early seventh-century medical book, *The Etiology and Symptomatology of All Diseases (Zhubing yuanhou lun)* offers the most detailed description of this syndrome: "If digestion stops, then the stomach will not work. When one then drinks fluid, it will be stopped from trickling and will not disperse. If this fluid then comes into contact with cold *qi* [energy], it will accumulate and form a pi. A pi is what inclines to one side between the two ribs and sometimes hurts."[4] According to a mid-eighth-century medical book, the *Secret Prescriptions of the Outer Tower (Waitai biyao),* a pi could even become as hard as stone and eventually develop into an abscess.[5]

From this sense of pathological blockage most likely evolved the extended meaning of obsession or addiction—something that sticks in the gut and cannot be evacuated, hence becoming habitual. When written in its alternative form with the "person" radical, rather than the "illness" radical, however, the primary meaning of *pi* becomes "leaning to one side," or "off-center."[6] An attempt to relate the meanings of both graphs (which share a phonetic element) becomes apparent in the etymology in *The Etiology and Symptomatology of All Diseases:* "A pi is what inclines [*pianpi*] between the two ribs and sometimes hurts." From this sense of one-sidedness or partiality, pi also comes to denote the individual proclivities inherent in all human nature, as in the compound *pixing* (personal taste), written with either radical. This paradoxical view of obsession as at once pathological and normative helps account for the peculiar range of behavior associated with it and for the contradictory interpretations assigned to it.

The concept of pi is not merely a matter of terminology, however: once the symptoms have been codified, this particular term need not be used for the condition to be instantly recognizable.

> The concept of pi is associated with a cluster of words, notably *shi* (a taste for) and *hao* (a fondness for). These characters are further combined to form almost synonymous compounds, such as *pihao, pishi,* and *shihao.* One caveat: I am not employing "obsession" in the technical psychiatric sense, which stresses negative and involuntary aspects. Compare the definition of obsession in Campbell, *Psychiatric Dictionary,* p. 492: "An idea, emotion, or impulse that repetitively and insistently forces itself into consciousness, even though it may be unwelcome."

Nonetheless, the term is charged with a strong emotional quality and has a wide range of implicit meanings; this was particularly true during the sixteenth and seventeenth centuries when the concept of obsession had deeply penetrated all aspects of literati life. As an indication of its range of meaning, "pi" has been translated into English as addiction, compulsion, passion, mania, fondness for, weakness for, love of, fanatical devotion, craving, idiosyncracy, fetishism, and even hobby. On this level, the idea of obsession is most apparent in the pronouncements of Yuan Hongdao (1568-1610), one of the great literary and intellectual figures of his time. As he wrote in his *History of Flower Arranging* in 1599:

> If someone has something he is really obsessed about, he will be deeply immersed, intoxicated with it. He will consecrate his life and even his death to it. What time would he have for the affairs of money-grubbers and traders in official titles?

> When someone in antiquity who was gripped by an obsession for flowers heard tell of a rare blossom, even if it were in a deep valley or in steep mountains, he would not be afraid of stumbling and would go to it. Even in the freezing cold and the blazing heat, even if his skin were cracked and peeling or caked with mud and sweat, he would be oblivious.

> When a flower was about to bloom, he would move his pillow and mat and sleep alongside it to observe how the flower would go from budding to blooming to fading. Only after it lay withered on the ground would he take his leave. . . . This is what is called a *genuine* love of flowers; this is what is called *genuine* connoisseurship.

> But as for *my* growing flowers, merely to break up the pain of idleness and solitude—I am incapable of genuinely loving them. Only someone already dwelling at the mouth of Peach Blossom Spring could genuinely love them—how could he still be an official in this dust-stained world![7]

Rather than condemning the flower-lover as frivolous or ridiculous, or lamenting the misdirection of his energies and passion, Yuan raises an obsession with flowers to unprecedented heights, praising it as an ideal of unswerving commitment and genuine integrity incompatible with worldly success and conspicuous consumption. This idealization arises in part from his disgust at the shallow vogue for obsession in his day. For Yuan, true obsession is always a marginal activity, an act of alienation and withdrawal from conventional society. His polemic aimed at wresting obsession from the inauthentic vulgar mainstream; ironically it may have merely reinforced obsession's fashionability.

Yuan's description also implies some of the general principles of obsession. First, obsession describes a habitual fixation on a certain object or activity, rather than on a particular person, and it is particularly associated with collecting and connoisseurship. Second, it must be excessive and single-minded. Third, it is a deliberately unconventional and eccentric pose.

A Brief History of Obsession

The identification of behavior as obsessive and the attitudes toward that behavior evolved over time. Obsession first began to crystallize as a distinct concept in anecdotes about the free and unrestrained eccentrics included in the fifth-century anthology *New Tales of the World (Shishuo xinyu)* with corresponding overtones of eremitism and nonconformity. The spectrum of obsessions in *New Tales of the World* ranges wildly, from a fondness for funeral dirges and donkey brays to a passion for ox fights and the *Zuo Commentary.* One anecdote in the anthology even recounts an informal competition between a lover of money and a lover of wooden clogs. The lover of clogs proves himself the superior, not because of the object of his obsession, but because of his utter self-absorption in his clogs even when observers pay him a visit.[8]

It was not until the late Tang, however, that obsession was mated with connoisseurship and collecting and people began to leave written records of their obsessions. Of particular interest is a moving passage by the great ninth-century art historian Zhang Yanyuan, which lays out the basic paradigms of the fanatical connoisseur's spirit: these paradigms will be re-enacted over and over in subsequent ages.

> Ever since my youth I've been a collector of rare things. . . . When there was a chance of getting something, I'd even sell my old clothes and ration simple foods. My wife, children, and servants nag and tease me, sometimes saying, "What's the point of doing such a useless thing all day long?" At which I sigh and say "If one doesn't do such useless things, then how can one take pleasure in this mortal life?" Thus my passion grows ever deeper, approaching an obsession. . . .

> Only in calligraphy and painting have I not yet forgotten emotion. Intoxicated by them I forget all speech; enraptured I gaze at and examine them. . . . Does this not seem wiser, after all, than all that burning ambition and ceaseless toil when fame and profit war within one's breast?[9]

This autobiographical sketch begins by enumerating the symptoms of obsession—the utter absorption and diligence, the willingness to endure physical privation, the transcendent joy. Zhang hints at the notion of obsession as a form of individual self-expression, but his statement also becomes a defense, an apology for a private obsession, that justifies the rejection of public life. Zhang introduces the notion of obsession as compensation for worldly failure at the same time as he criticizes the fame, profit, and vain ambition underlying success. He formulates the idea that an obsession should be *useless*—something that does not contribute to official success or material wealth. In this way, obsession is linked with the tradition of the recluse in Chinese culture and the worthy gentleman who does not achieve success but instead disdains competition for power and prestige as an inferior mode of life.

Zhang's statement foreshadows the flourishing of art connoisseurship during the Song dynasty. Not only ancient masterpieces of painting and calligraphy but all sorts of antiques—bronzes, carved jades, stone engravings, and ceramics—as well as things from nature, such as rocks, flowers, and plants, became objects of collecting. With the onset of printing, the compiling of handbooks and catalogues devoted to a particular type of object came into fashion. New paradigms of eccentric collectors emerged, firmly tying the pursuit of obsession to Song literati culture. This mania for collecting culminated in one of the most notorious episodes in Chinese history, "the levy on flowers and rocks" (*huashi gang*), the mass appropriations for the collection of Huizong (r. 1100-1125), the last Northern Song emperor and an aesthete whose decadence would be blamed for the loss of the north to the Jin barbarians.

As the craze for art collecting and connoisseurship became closely associated with the notion of obsession in Song culture, an uneasiness arose that an overattachment to objects courts disaster. Zhang Yanyuan's discovery of the joys of collecting could not be replicated unequivocally by the more self-conscious Song connoisseurs. Framed by the destruction of the Five Dynasties in the mid-tenth century and the devastation of the Northern Song in the early twelfth century, three famous essays debate the dangers of obsession. These essays should be read sequentially because the later ones seem in part a response to the previous ones.

The need to justify obsessive collecting despite its potential for harm is first raised in the eleventh century in Ouyang Xiu's preface to his catalogue of epigraphy. His solution is to posit a hierarchy of value based on the kind of objects collected. He distinguishes ordinary treasures—pearls, gold, and furs—which incite conventional greed, from relics of the past, whose collection does not entail great physical risk and which supplement our understanding of history. With ordinary treasures, what counts is the power to get them; with relics of the past, what counts is the collector's taste and his whole-hearted love of them. But even compiling a catalogue does not quite set to rest Ouyang Xiu's anxieties about the future of his collection. He consoles himself in a fabricated dialogue:

> Someone mocked me saying: "If a collection is large, then it will be hard to keep intact. After being assembled for a long time, it is bound to be scattered. Why are you bothering to be so painstaking?"

> I replied: "It's enough that I am collecting what I love and that I will enjoy growing old among them."[10]

Ouyang Xiu's fears about the dispersal of his collection must have been prompted in part by the destruction of the great Tang estates a century or two earlier, a subject he addressed in an essay called "The Ling Stream Rocks" ("Lingxi shi ji").[11] Another connoisseur, Ye Mengde (1077-1148), reported that "Ouyang Xiu used to laugh at Li Deyu's [787-848] remark that neither his sons nor grandsons would ever give away one tree or one plant of his Pingyuan estate,"[12] for as everyone knew, the estate had been utterly destroyed.

In the next generation, Su Shi adopts another strategy to mitigate the dangers of collecting, one implicit in Ouyang Xiu's defense that what is important is the act of loving what one collects rather than the collection itself. Su Shi, too, posits a hierarchy of value, but not of the sorts of *collections* but of the sorts of *collectors*:

> A gentleman may temporarily "lodge" his interest in things, but he must not "detain" his interest in things. For if he lodges his interest in things, then even trivial objects will suffice to give him joy and even "things of unearthly beauty" will not suffice to induce mania in him. If he detains his interest in things, then even trivial objects will suffice to induce mania in him, and even things of unearthly beauty will not suffice to give him joy.[13]

Su Shi draws a subtle distinction between "lodging" (*yu*) one's interest temporarily in things and "detaining" (*liu*) one's interest permanently in them. In his scheme, lodging implies viewing objects as vessels through which one fulfills oneself rather than as things that one values for their own sake. This maximizes the benign pleasures of loving things and prevents even "things of unearthly beauty" (*youwu*) from causing injury.[14] Detaining, on the other hand, implies a pathological attachment to actual things as *things*. Su Shi employs the clearly pejorative term "mania" (*bing*) rather than the more ambiguous "pi" to emphasize the harmful nature of the passions detaining engenders. He concludes that only the detaining kind of collecting brings personal and national catastrophe.

Ouyang Xiu's and Su Shi's clever arguments, however, are challenged by the poet Li Qingzhao (1081?-1149) in her autobiographical postface to the epigraphy catalogue of her husband, the antiquarian Zhao Mingcheng (1081-1129). Having survived the death of her husband, the destruction of their book collection, and the violent fall of the Northern Song dynasty, she speaks of experiencing the very disasters that Ouyang Xiu and Su Shi had most feared and warned against. She begins by echoing Ouyang Xiu's claims that epigraphy collections serve the lofty aims of redressing historiographic errors. But suddenly her tone shifts, and she attacks his privileging of scholarly collections over all others: "Alas! in the disasters that befell Wang Bo and Yuan Zai, what distinction was there between [collecting] books and paintings and [collecting] pepper?[15] Both He Qiao and Du Yu had a mania—what difference was there between an obsession with money and an obsession with the *Zuo Commentary?*[16] The reputations of such men may differ, but their delusion was one and the same."[17]

Li Qingzhao also rejects Su Shi's argument that the collector's self-control can prevent his passion from becoming pathological and thereby ward off disaster. In recounting the saga of the progressive worsening of her husband's obsession, she shows that Su Shi's distinction between "lodging" and "detaining" hangs by a thread. As Stephen Owen has pointed out, the book collecting that begins as a casual and joint pleasure for the young couple disintegrates into a nightmare of anxiety.[18] Ouyang Xiu had argued in an autobiographical essay that being encumbered by the things of office made him distressed and worried, but that being encumbered by his scholarly possessions made him detached and freed him from vexation.[19] The image of the lone woman Li Qingzhao stranded during the Jin invasion with fifteen boatloads of books that her dying husband had ordered her to protect renders the detachment posited by Ouyang Xiu and Su Shi utterly absurd.

The Late Ming Craze for Obsession

By the sixteenth century, however, most scruples or fears about the perils of obsession seem to have vanished. What is truly new in the explosion of writings in this period is the glorification of obsession, particularly in its most exaggerated form. Obsession becomes an important component of late Ming culture, in which it is linked with the new virtues of Sentiment (*qing*), Madness (*kuang*), Folly (*chi*), and Lunacy (*dian*). No longer do obsessives feel obliged to defend or apologize for their position. Although someone like the scholar-official Xie Zhaozhe (1567-1624) might caution his contemporaries that any preference, if sufficiently one-sided and extreme, should be considered "a form of illness,"[20] most of them were only too willing to contract such a pleasurable virus. Obsession had become a sine qua non, something the gentleman could not afford to do without.

As the preface to the sixteenth-century *Brief History of Obsession and Lunacy (Pidian xiaoshi)* puts it: "Everyone has a predilection; this gets called obsession. The signs of obsession resemble folly and madness. . . . The gentleman worries only about having no obsession."[21] Declares Yuan Hongdao: "I have observed that in this world, all those whose words are insipid and whose appearance is detestable are men without obsessions."[22] Zhang Dai (1599-1684?), a Ming loyalist, concurs: "One cannot befriend a man without obsessions, for he lacks deep emotion; nor can one befriend a man without faults, for he lacks integrity."[23] A seventeenth-century aphorism by Zhang Chao (fl. 1676-1700) clinches the indispensability of obsession on aesthetic grounds: "Flowers must have butterflies, mountains must have streams, rocks must have moss, water must have seaweed, old trees must have creepers, and people must have obsessions."[24]

The eleventh-century intellectuals had already argued that obsessions were valuable as an outlet for personal fulfillment; in the sixteenth century, obsession as a vehicle for self-expression becomes the dominant mode. The traditional Chinese understanding of the function of poetry, that it "speaks of what is intently on the mind," had long spread to the other arts, such as painting, music, and calligraphy; now this notion was extended to cover virtually any activity, no matter how preposterous. Moreover, this self-expression was no longer involuntary: it had become obligatory. Most important, the virtue of an obsession lay not in the object of devotion, not even in the act of devotion, but in self-realization. As Yuan Hongdao observes:

> The chrysanthemums of Tao Yuanming, the plum blossoms of Lin Bu, the rocks of Mi Fu—people all swap stories about these men's obsessions as delightful topics of conversation and then blithely take up something as an obsession in order to amuse themselves. Alas! they are mistaken. It wasn't that Tao loved chrysanthemums, Lin loved plum blossoms, or Mi loved rocks; rather, in each case, it was the self loving the self.[25]

In this most radical equation, the boundary between subject and object has utterly dissolved. Obsession is no longer understood as a form of alterity, but as a self-reflexive act: it is not the self loving the *other,* but the self loving the *self.*

But the idealization of obsession in the sixteenth century also arose from a new evaluation of love: the fanatical attachment of a person to a particular object was interpreted as a manifestation of "that idealistic, single-minded love,"[26] "that headlong, romantic passion,"[27] known as qing. Once the relationship between someone and the object of his obsession was conceptualized as qing, it was not a difficult leap to declare that the object itself could be moved by its lover's devotion and reciprocate his feelings. Since, for the most part, the objects of obsessions were not human, this meant anthropomorphizing the object, adopting the view that animate and inanimate things alike, are capable of sentiment. As we will see, this is one of the most important developments in the theory of obsession for *Liaozhai.*

Such a position was facilitated both by the traditional Chinese animistic view of the universe and by the broader implications of qing during this period as a universal force and even as life itself.[28] For example, the main project of the seventeenth-century compendium of fact and fiction called *A Classified History of Love* is to document the power of qing over every part of the universe—from wind and lightning to rocks and trees, from animals and birds to ghosts and spirits: "The myriad things are born of qing and die of qing," comments the Historian of Qing.[29] In this scheme, the human race becomes merely one more category subject to the forces of qing.

In earlier times, an important, though not mandatory, criterion for recording an obsession was that it be strange, peculiar, incomprehensible. As a preface to *A Brief History of Obsession and Lunacy* explains: "Nowadays, no one is able to fathom the appeal that watching ox fights or hearing donkey brays held for [those in the past] who were fond of such things. That is why they are all pi."[30] A particularly idiosyncratic obsession could win someone fame in the annals of unofficial history, such as Liu Yong of the Southern Dynasties who enjoyed eating human fingernail parings or Quan Changru of the Tang who liked to eat human scabs because he said they tasted like dried fish flakes.[31] But as the fad for obsession grew during the Ming, another change began to take place: the objects of obsessions became increasingly standardized as indexes of certain virtues and personalities. By the sixteenth century, obsessions have grown noticeably less variant. Although some unusual obsessions are mentioned, such as a penchant for football or for operas about ghosts, and particularly disgusting eating habits are still listed with relish,[32] most writings now concern highly conventionalized obsessions. The most frequent are books, painting, epigraphy, calligraphy, or rocks; a particular musical instrument, plant, animal, or game; tea or wine; cleanliness; and homosexuality.[33] But even within these, the actual choices—which flower, which game—have become circumscribed and stereotyped.

By the seventeenth century, a rich tradition of lore and a corpus of specialized manuals or catalogues for the connoisseur had accumulated around virtually every standard obsession. Pu Songling appears to have incorporated research from such manuals on a number of the objects that form the focus of his obsessional tales. *Liaozhai* commentators frequently cite specialized handbooks both to explain and to praise the accuracy of Pu Songling's connoisseurship. Allan Barr has demonstrated that Pu partially derived the cricket lore introduced into the famous tale **"The Cricket"** (**"Cuzhi"**; 4.484-90) from a late Ming guide to Beijing, *A Brief Guide to Sights in the Capital* (*Dijing jingwu lüe*), which Pu abridged and wrote a new preface for.[34] According to Barr, he made use of "a number of technical details from the guidebook—the different varieties of cricket, the insect's diet" and even "borrowed some phrases wholesale" from it.[35]

The stylistic influence of catalogues and manuals is particularly evident in the unusual opening of the tale **"A Strangeness of Pigeons"** (**"Ge yi"**; 6.939-43), which abandons the biographical or autobiographical formats typical of *Liaozhai* and most classical fiction. The opening of the story is virtually indistinguishable from a catalogue: it lists the different varieties of pigeons and their locales and provides advice on their care: "The classification of pigeons is extremely complicated. Among the rarest varieties are the Earth Star of Shanxi, the Delicate Stork of Shandong, the Butterfly Wings of Guizhou, the Acrobat of Henan, and the Pointed Tips of Zhejiang. In addition, there are types like Boot Head, Polka-Dot, Big White, Married Sparrow, Spotted-Dog Eyes, and innumerable other sorts that only connoisseurs can distinguish."[36] Pu Songling explicitly acknowledges his debt to such a catalogue when he informs us that the wealthy pigeon fancier of his story strove to amass an exhaustive collection "according to the handbook" (6.839).[37] In fact, Pu Songling himself compiled two catalogues on other subjects: a rock catalogue and a flower handbook in his own hand are still extant.[38]

Narratives recounting personal experiences with the subject of a manual or a catalogue were sometimes included in such books. Such accounts may be among the most important inspirations for Pu Songling's connoisseurship tales. For instance, Ye Mengde, a Song dynasty lover of rocks, in a colophon to a famous record of a Tang estate, relates how acquiring a wonderful rock miraculously cured him of sickness.[39] The therapeutic properties of obsession are carried even further in **"White Autumn Silk"** (**"Bai Qiulian"**; 11.1482-88), a *Liaozhai* tale about a poetry-obsessed carp-maiden, whose lover's recitation of her favorite Tang poems not only cures her of illness but even revives her from the dead. Yuan Hongdao's portrait of the ideal flower-lover in his handbook on flower arranging anticipates to a remarkable degree the peony fanatic in the tale **"Ge Jin"** (10.1436-44), who anxiously begins watching for peony shoots in the dead of winter and writes a hundred-line poem called "Longing for Peonies" ("Huai mudan") as he goes into debt waiting for the peonies to bloom.

As objects became associated with certain qualities and historical figures, the choice of obsession became dictated by those qualities and figures. By loving a particular object, the devotee was striving to claim allegiance to that quality or to emulate that figure. This idea can be glimpsed already in the twelfth-century preface to Du Wan's famous *Rock Catalogue of Cloudy Forest* (*Yunlin shipu*): "The Sage Confucius always said, 'The benevolent man finds joy in mountains.' The love of rocks implies 'finding joy in mountains,' for the stillness and longevity that Confucius mentioned can also be found in rocks."[40]

Thus an individual might favor rocks if he prized the moral virtues associated with rocks—benevolence, stillness, longevity, loyalty—or if he wanted to imitate the famous Song rock-lover known as Mi Fu or Mi the Lunatic (Mi Dian). Someone else, on the other hand, might feel drawn to chrysanthemums because of their association with purity and aloofness and with the recluse-poet Tao Yuanming. Although in theory the spontaneous impulse of a particular nature, in practice an obsession had become a studied act of self-cultivation. Once an object had become a fixed emblem of certain virtues, it was again an easy leap to attribute these virtues to the object itself. This again led to the anthropomorphizing of the obsessional object: the object not only symbolizes a particular virtue but also possesses that virtue and behaves accordingly.

The personification of objects is an ancient poetic trope. In the sixth-century anthology *New Songs from a Jade Terrace* (*Yutai xinyong*), for example, the attribution of sentiment and sentience to objects is a common device. Both natural objects, such as vegetation, and manufactured objects, such as mirrors, are portrayed as sharing or echoing the emotions of human beings. A typical couplet describes the grass growing over palace steps: "Fading to emerald as though it knew the season, / Holding in fragrance as though it had emotion."[41] This technique is later formulated in Chinese poetics as the overlapping of scene (*jing*) and emotion (*qing*): emotion is both aroused by the scene and located within it.[42] But this sort of personification differs from the personification of objects through obsession. In *New Songs from the Jade Terrace,* objects are like mirrors—they reflect the narcissistic emotions of the human world. Such objects have no separate identity or independent emotions; rather, they allegorically represent the speaker—for example, the discarded fan that symbolizes Lady Ban Jieyu's neglect by the emperor.[43]

In Yuan Hongdao's *History of Flower Arranging,* however, flowers, like human beings, experience different moods; for example, he advises fellow connoisseurs how to tell when flowers are happy or sad, drowsy or angry, so as to water them accordingly.[44] Here flowers are presented as feeling emotions of their own accord; they do not merely mirror or reinforce the emotions of a human being. Once things are seen as possessing independent emotions, they can be thought capable of responding to a specific person. Thus developed the idea that objects could find true friends or soul mates in those who love them. Zhang Chao distilled this idea into another aphorism: "If one has a single true friend in this world, one can be free of regrets. This is true not only for people, but also for things. For instance, the chrysanthemum found a true friend in Tao Yuanming . . . the flowering plum found a true friend in Lin Bu . . . and the rock found a true friend in Mi the Lunatic."[45]

The Ethereal Rock

It is this last offshoot of obsession that becomes the central theme of Pu Songling's brilliant tale **"The Ethereal Rock"** (**"Shi Qingxu"**; II.1575-79), which narrates the friendship between a fanatical rock collector called Xing Yunfei and the rock named in the story's title.[46] One day, Xing finds a rock entangled in his fishing net. It is a fantastic rock, shaped like a miniature mountain with peaks and crannies, and it has unusual powers—whenever it is going to rain, the rock puffs tiny clouds, just like a real mountain. When word of the rock gets around, a rich local bully brazenly orders his servant to walk off with it, but it slips through the servant's fingers and falls into a river. The bully offers a substantial reward but to no avail. The rock is not recovered until the desolate Xing happens to walk by the spot and sees it lying in a suddenly transparent spot in the river. Xing keeps his recovery of the rock a secret, but one day he is visited by a mysterious old man who demands the return of "his" rock. As proof for his claim, the old man names the number of the rock's crannies (92) and reveals that in the largest crevice is carved the miniature inscription OFFERED IN WORSHIP, ETHEREAL, THE CELESTIAL ROCK. Xing is finally granted ownership of the rock on the condition that he forfeit three years of his life. The old man then pinches together three of the crannies on the rock and tells Xing that the number of crannies (89) is now equal to the number of years he is fated to live. After more trials and tribulations—the rock is stolen by burglars, a corrupt official who wants the rock throws Xing into jail Xing, as foretold, dies at the age of eighty-nine and is buried, according to his last wishes, with his rock. But half a year later, grave robbers steal the rock. Xing's ghost hounds the men into giving up the rock, but once again an unscrupulous official confiscates the rock and orders a clerk to place it in his treasury. The rock twists out of his hands and smashes itself into a hundred pieces. Xing's son buries the pieces in his father's grave once and for all.

Pu Songling's comment, as Historian of the Strange, begins by raising the old fears of dangerous obsessions with beautiful things (*youwu*), but soon yields to the admiration of sentiment popularized during the late Ming:

> Unearthly beauty in a thing makes it the site of calamity. In this man's desire to sacrifice his life for the rock, wasn't his folly extreme! But in the end, man and rock were together in death, so who can say the rock was "unfeeling"? There's an old saying, "A knight will die for a true friend."[47] This is no lie. If it is true even for a rock, can it be any less true for men?

The Historian of the Strange's rhetoric underscores the irony that a technically "unfeeling" rock (the phrase *wu qing* is a play on "inanimate") displays more true feeling than most human beings, who are by definition animate and hence should "have feeling" (*you qing*).

Sentiment is not a static force in the narrative: the friendship between the hero and his rock grows and deepens, culminating in mutual self-sacrifice. The rock is an active participant in the tale. "Treasures should belong to those who love them," the proverbial saying about obsessive collectors reiterated by the divine old man in the tale, is interpreted in a new light: the object itself chooses and responds to the one who loves him. The rock flung himself into the rock-lover's fishing net and entangled himself in the world of passions; the rock's desire precipitated his premature entry into the world, like the rock that becomes the human Bao Yu in *The Story of the Stone*. As the old man informs Xing, the rock surfaced three years ahead of schedule, for "he was in a hurry to display himself." And once in Xing's possession, the rock beautifies himself for his lover: the clouds that he miraculously puffs up cease when he is in anyone else's custody. Even after the rock has once more been cruelly extorted from Xing, he comes in a dream to console Xing and arranges their final reunion. Thus this tale subtly inverts the roles of object and collector: Xing becomes the object of the rock's obsession.

The philosopher Li Zhi, one of the most powerful influences behind the iconoclastic trend in late Ming thought, had explored a similar idea in a brilliant polemic called "Essay on a Scroll Painting of Square Bamboo" ("Fangzhu tujuan wen").[48] It is a radical reinterpretation of a well-known anecdote from the fifth-century *New Tales of the World*. This classified anthology detailing the wit and exploits of the Wei-Jin eccentrics enjoyed particular popularity during the sixteenth and seventeenth centuries, judging from the numerous editions and sequels to it published during this time, and it became a veritable bible for Ming and Qing fanciers of obsession.[49] The anecdote that Li Zhi drew upon concerns the love of bamboos: "Wang Hui-chih [Wang Huizhi; d. 388] was once temporarily lodging in another man's vacant house, and ordered bamboos planted. Someone asked, 'Since you're only living here temporarily, why bother?' Wang whistled and chanted poems a good while; then abruptly pointing to the bamboos, replied, 'How could I live a single day without "these gentlemen" [*ci jun*]?'"[50]

In Li Zhi's misanthropic view, Wang Huizhi preferred the companionship of "these gentlemen" to the society of humans, and the bamboos themselves recognized a kindred spirit in a man of Wang's uncommon temperament:

> The one who in the past loved bamboos [Wang Huizhi] called them "gentlemen" out of love. He

didn't call them gentlemen because he meant they resembled refined gentlemen; rather he was depressed and had no one to converse with—he felt that "The only ones I can associate with are the bamboos."[51] For this reason he befriended them and gave them that designation. . . . Someone said, "Wang considered bamboos as 'these gentlemen,' so the bamboos must have considered Wang as 'that gentleman.'" . . . But it wasn't the case that Wang loved bamboos—rather the bamboos loved Wang of their own accord. For when a man of Wang's mettle gazed at mountains, rivers, stones, and earth, all would have naturally grown beautiful, these gentlemen not least of all.

> All things between heaven and earth have a spirit; especially these hollow gentlemen that rise straight up—could they alone be unspirited?[52] As the saying goes, "For a true friend, a knight exerts himself; for an admirer, a lady makes herself beautiful." So too these gentlemen. As soon as they encountered Wang, their distinct virtue and extraordinary energy [*qì*] would have naturally grown exhilarated; their lifelong principle of standing fast amid ice and frost would have blown away into the fluty love songs of phoenixes;[53] all must have been out of a desire to make themselves beautiful for the one who admired them. For how could they stand there so solitary, moaning in the wind for years on end, forever harboring the regret that they had no true friend?

In Li Zhi's polemic against the shallowness of the late Ming fashion for obsession, he reverses the hierarchy of object and obsessive and anthropomorphizes the bamboos by imputing to them human will and desire. He argues that every object has a *shen*, a spirit—an animate force within it—and extrapolates from this animistic view, perhaps tongue-in-cheek, that for a meaningful existence, an object, like a person, needs a true friend to love and understand him. Li cleverly imagines the scene of the bamboos' attempted seduction of Wang Huizhi through an elaborate series of puns that play on bamboo's conventional associations with integrity and steadfastness, but his anthropomorphizing of bamboo was clearly a rhetorical pose, a conceit.[54]

In **"The Ethereal Rock,"** Pu Songling takes the ideas of Li Zhi's essay further. Carefully, with all the techniques of a novelist, he gives the intense love between an inanimate object and a man a coherent narrative shape and in so doing realizes this rhetorical stance literally. But for an inanimate rock to be fully human, it must die. The most shocking moment in the tale is when the rock smashes himself into smithereens: the valuable has been made worthless; the permanent has been destroyed. The rock is able to know love, but at the price of suffering and mortality. His obsession with Xing culminates in self-sacrifice: to demonstrate his loyalty and remain with his true friend, the rock must in the end, like a knight-errant or a virtuous widow, sabotage his own beauty and commit suicide. Only in destruction is the rock safe and buried permanently with his beloved. As in Daoist parables of crooked trees that survive because they are useless, the rock, that "thing of unearthly beauty," can only be left in peace once his material value is gone.

It is no accident that Pu Songling chose an obsession with a rock to illustrate the theme of perfect friendship: the rock was conventionally valued as a symbol of loyalty and constancy. The phrase "a rock friend" (*shi you*), for instance, signified a faithful friend and was a common poetic designation for a rock.[55] The expression "a friendship of stone" (*shi jiao*) likewise describes a friendship as strong and permanent as stone; Pu Songling himself employed this phrase in a little homily on friendship.[56] Again, as I noted earlier, it was not uncommon to locate the qualities symbolized by an object in the object's innate nature. For instance, *A Classified History of Love* argues that since love is "as strong as stone or metal," it can actually transform itself into stone or metal.[57] In **"The Ethereal Rock,"** Pu Songling brilliantly gives these figurative expressions a concrete and literal form.[58]

By Ming times the rock had become a cult object. John Hay's study of the rock in Chinese art, *Kernels of Energy, Bones of Earth,* has revealed the extent to which the rock had assumed the stature of a cultural icon in late Imperial China. Rocks, like stories, were prized for being singular, bizarre, odd. A rock was no ordinary object; it was an objet d'art, valued not for the ingenuity and artifice of human skill but for its exquisite naturalness. An obsession with unpolished and uncarved rocks was considered refined; compared to it, a passion for jade and precious stones was merely vulgar. (During the late Ming jades were even carved to look like rough stones.[59]) Rocks were supposed to be prized only by real connoisseurs, but as Pu Songling makes clear, in a market where rocks commanded a high price, the powerful and wealthy extorted rocks for status and the ignorant chased after rocks for profit. Like Li Zhi's bamboos, who are said to detest their phony modern admirers, Pu Songling's rock could not possibly reciprocate the false love of the other collectors in the tale. It is the hero's pure and unwavering obsession amid this atmosphere of corruption that earns the rock's devotion.

The most obvious inspiration behind Pu Songling's rock-loving hero is the Song painter and calligrapher Mi Fu, whose obsession with rocks had become proverbial. Mi Fu's flamboyant brand of connoisseurship had enshrined him as the paragon of obsession and eccentricity. The numerous collections of anecdotes about Mi Fu published during the Ming attest to his great appeal.[60] The heady mixture of lunacy and sincere passion attributed to Mi Fu accorded well with the sensibility of the late Ming and can be detected in a number of Pu Songling's heroes. Xing's fanatical devotion in **"The Ethereal Rock"** had a precedent in the most celebrated anecdote about Mi Fu, which even figured in his official biography in the *Song History:* Mi Fu was said to have donned official garb to make obeisance to a favored rock in his collection and to have respectfully addressed it as "Older Brother Rock" (*shi xiong*) or, in a variant, as "Elder Rock" (*shi zhang*).[61]

We can be certain of Pu Songling's familiarity with at least this anecdote. Not only did stories about Mi Fu enjoy wide circulation during the seventeenth century, but a reworking of this anecdote appears in a poem by Pu Songling entitled **"Elder Rock."** The rock described in this poem is thought to be still standing today on the former site of the Stone Recluse Garden (Shiyin yuan), which belonged to Pu Songling's friend and employer, Bi Jiyou.[62]

> Elder Rock's inlaid sword juts up high, so high;
> He wears a turban, tablier, and sandals of straw.[63]
> Where dragon veins coil on bone, stands a mountain spirit,
> Still in a cloak of wood-lotus, in a belt of bryony.[64]
> Gong Gong hit the pillar of Heaven, and it came crashing down;
> Where one shard struck, a fold in the eastern mountains rose.[65]
> Uneven peaks like hair knots, dozens of feet tall,
> Brushed by white clouds moving through the sky.
> I ready my cap and robe and bow reverently:
> Brisk air fills my bosom, healing my grave malady.[66]

Pu Songling's poem may be read as the literary equivalent of the illustrations of Mi Fu bowing to his rock so popular in seventeenth-century art,[67] but with one important difference—it is the poet ("I") who bows to the rock in imitation of Mi Fu and finds therapeutic relief; Mi Fu himself is not depicted, as he often is in comparable poems by other writers.[68] In Pu Songling's version, the mythological description of the rock as a miniature mountain dominates the poem; the Mi Fu poet-figure has receded into the background and makes only an almost routine appearance in the closing couplet.

Compared with the description of the rock in this poem, the description of the rock in the tale is startlingly restrained and sparse. Gone are the ornate language and standard allusions of the poem: in their place is simply a brief but vivid description given when the rock first comes into view: it "was a rock barely a foot high. All four sides were intricately hollowed, with layered peaks jutting up." Further details of the rock's unearthly physical beauty—the number of crannies, the minuscule inscription bearing its name, the clouds it emits—are filled in only gradually as needed within the framework of the plot, but there are never enough details to dispel the rock's aura of mystery. The real image of the rock is left to the reader's imagination, to be inferred from the endless struggles to possess it.

Moreover, **"The Ethereal Rock"** does not retell any of the well-known Mi Fu anecdotes; instead it creates a new cluster of anecdotes within the heightened atmosphere of seventeenth-century obsessional culture. Pu Songling's hero does not simply imitate Mi Fu—he surpasses him, surrendering three years of his life and then risking what remains all for the rock, who in turn eclipses any previously recorded rock in history. As Feng Zhenluan exclaims: "Mi Fu bowed to a rock, but I imagine he didn't have a rock of this caliber. Niu Sengru was called a rock connoisseur, but I'll bet he never set eyes on such a rock" (*Liaozhai* 11.1575).[69] And Xing's rock is not only worshipped; invested with both demonic powers (*mojie*) and a deep humanity, he is able to respond to a true connoisseur's love as Elder Rock never could.

In addition to **"Elder Rock,"** Pu Songling wrote two other poems expressly on rocks and, as already mentioned, compiled a brief catalogue on rocks.[70] He brilliantly incorporated the knowledge of rock lore so evident in his poems and catalogue into his tale. The rock's miraculous feat of emitting clouds, for instance, may be imaginative invention, but it plays on the traditional associations of rocks, mountains, and clouds.[71] The rock's ability to predict the weather also has a quasi-historical basis in a description of a famed mountain-shaped inkstone said to have belonged to Mi Fu: "When it is going to rain, the 'dragon pool' [in a cranny of the rock] becomes wet."[72] Giving rocks personal names likewise had a foundation in historical and contemporary practice. As a poem written on a beautiful early seventeenth-century painting of a rock proclaims: "Rocks, too, have names and sobriquets, / This rock is called Mysterious Cloud."[73] (Surely it is no coincidence that the name Pu Songling gave his rock-lover, Xing Yunfei or Moving Clouds in Flight, sounds like the name of a rock.[74]) Lastly, the history of rock collecting is notorious for epic battles between connoisseurs. These battles are scaled down in **"The Ethereal Rock"**; to underscore the purity of the hero's obsession, his human competitors for the rock are not true connoisseurs, and the rock is resold cheaply in the common market.

Liaozhai contains a number of wonderful tales about obsessions with flowers and musical instruments. What distinguishes **"The Ethereal Rock"** from these other obsessional tales is not the anthropomorphism of the object, for the heroes in *Liaozhai* frequently fall in love with the human incarnations of their obsessions.

The sustained imputation of human-like behavior to the non-human (objects, plants, animals, ghosts) is a staple of the strange tale, but the ground covered by such anthropomorphism is quite broad. At one extreme, things retain their own form but are motivated by human ethics and desires; at the other extreme, things take on human form, often so convincingly that they are mistaken for people until the denouement of the tale. In the first case, there is no physical metamorphosis, and only the spirit of a thing is anthropomorphized; in the second case, metamorphosis is essential, and both spirit and form are anthropomorphized. Within any given instance of anthropomorphism, however, the ratio of thing to human is variable. Thus, although the objects of many different obsessions are anthropomorphized in *Liaozhai,* whether they seem more human or more thing-like varies enormously.

In the *Liaozhai* tales of flower obsession, the flowers primarily assume human female form in the story, although telltale clues to their floral nature are liberally provided. Part of the charm of a story about a peony-spirit like **"Ge Jin"** or a chrysanthemum-spirit like **"Yellow Pride"** (**"Huang Ying"**; 11.1446-52) is that the revelation the heroines are flowers rather than human beings is deferred; the tale becomes a riddle of identity, one that contemporary readers would have found enjoyable and not too difficult to unravel.[75] Pu Songling adopted a second approach in two tales of obsession with musical instruments, **"Huan Niang"** (7.985-90) and **"The Sting"** (**"Zu zha"**; 8.1029-34). Although the zither is the pivot of both plots, it is not anthropomorphized at all; it undergoes no metamorphosis and is given no distinct personality. It remains throughout a precious but passive object of desire.

"The Ethereal Rock" is unique in *Liaozhai* because the rock acquires a personality, an identity, a human presence, even though it remains an inanimate object. Only veiled in dream does the rock appear as a man

> As Mi Fu's addressing his rock as "Older Brother" affirms, rocks were gendered as male in the Chinese imagination, just as flowers were gendered as female.

and speak directly, introducing himself as Shi Qingxu. Ordinarily when a rock is given a name in a catalogue or in an inscription, the character *shi* or rock follows rather than precedes the name. This is why the miniature inscription carved on the rock in the story reads: "Ethereal, the Celestial Rock" ("Qingxu, tianshi"). This order, however, is reversed in the rock's self-introduction and in the story's title. Placed first rather than last, the character *shi* assumes the Chinese position of a surname. The deliberate inversion of the rock's name, then, suggests a subtle anthropomorphization. The delicate balance between the outward form of a rock and the inner soul of a man is thus encoded in this new name: "Shi" is in fact a common surname; "Qingxu" (pure and ethereal), the rock's given name, evokes his extraordinary quality of qì, for which rocks, as "kernels of energy," were prized.[76] Such a balance seems to have also been achieved in certain late Ming paintings of rocks, which, as John Hay suggests, may have been "portraying personalities as embodied in structural forms and textures."[77]

Pu Songling's rock may be fictional, but beginning in Song times numerous artists had portrayed their favorite rocks and imbued them with their own fantasies. An extraordinary handscroll painting from the early seventeenth century gives us additional insight into **"The Ethereal Rock"** and the cultural milieu out of which it emerged.[78] The rock in question belonged to Mi Wanzhong (1570-1628), a well-known official who adopted the sobriquet "Friend to Rocks" (You shi) and claimed descent from none other than Mi Fu himself. Contemporaries said of Mi Wanzhong that he possessed Mi Fu's obsession but not his lunacy.[79] Although Mi Wanzhong was a famous calligrapher and painter specializing in rock paintings, the handscroll was the work of his friend Wu Bin (fl. 1591-1626), a professional landscape painter and fellow rocklover.[80] At first glance, the painting seems to belong to the "still life" genre: the rock is methodically painted, and Mi Wanzhong's descriptions are factual and meticulous, documenting the size, shape, gesture, and texture of each of its peaks. But when we gaze at the painting longer, it becomes anything but still or photographic in feel; the rock is fantastic, bizarre, unearthly, with long stalagmite-like peaks, separated by mysterious spaces. It almost seems to be moving, writhing as though on fire or blown by wind; yet it still somehow retains the solidity of stone.[81]

Most unusually, the handscroll consists of ten life-size portraits of the rock, each painted from a different angle. Such attention lavished on a single rock reminds one of an infatuated lover reveling in his mistress's every pose, every shift of expression. Many wonderful albums devoted to rock paintings and illustrated rock catalogues were produced during the seventeenth century; unillustrated catalogues, like Pu Songling's, were even more common.[82] The aim of a rock catalogue or album is ordinarily to record a number of exceptional examples. What we find in Wu Bin's handscroll is in essence still a rock catalogue of sorts, but one uniquely devoted to a single example, one that catalogues a single rock as though it were multiple rocks.

This compulsive repetition of the same object characterizes both Wu Bin's painting and Pu Songling's tale. One of the most striking features of **"The Ethereal Rock"** is that the same plot with minor variations is repeated over and over: Xing, the rock-lover, finds the rock, and someone wrests it away from him, but each time the stone contrives to return to him. This pattern of loss and recovery occurs five

times, but the repetition does not become monotonous, for with each cycle, the man's display of grief at losing the rock becomes more violent; each time, his joy at regaining it becomes more profound. After each loss, the man goes to greater lengths to redeem the rock—he gives up three years of his life, mortgages his house and land, and tries repeatedly to hang himself. Even death does not break the cycle; Xing comes back as a vengeful ghost to demand the rock's return. The repetitive, cyclical nature of the story inscribes the compulsive structure of obsession: desire, possession, loss; desire, possession, loss. This repetitiveness is truly excessive, for it continues far beyond our expectations, just as Wu Bin's picture surprises the spectator with its excessive variations on the same object.

In a final, very personal inscription on the handscroll, Mi Wanzhong identifies himself as a rock-lover from birth, tracing his passion for rocks and his coming to consciousness to the same primal moment. He spent thirty years collecting rocks and won fame as a connoisseur, but this one rock, the subject of the handscroll, was the rock he had been preparing himself for and seeking all his life. So amazing was this new rock, he tell us, that upon its arrival all the rocks in his sizable collection withdrew in deference as if acknowledging their inferiority and defeat. Thus this rock is not merely the crowning jewel of his collection: it utterly effaces his collection. It *alone* is his collection.

This is perhaps the greatest parallel between Wu Bin's painting and Pu Songling's tale. In the opening to **"The Ethereal Rock,"** the rock connoisseur Xing is introduced as someone who would spare no expense to add to his collection. And yet from the moment that he fishes up the ethereal rock (who comes of his own accord, just as we are told Mi Wanzhong's rock "crossed the river" to him),[83] no other rock is ever mentioned again. Xing's rock collection no longer exists for him once he gives himself up to this rock. His collection simply disappears from the text, just as Mi Wanzhong's painstaking assemblage of rocks is displaced from the scene. Xing, like Mi Wanzhong, becomes uniquely obsessed with a single rock. Both Pu Songling and the painter Wu Bin seem to have captured the identical truth about obsession when idealized to its furthest extent.[84]

The late Ming sensibility that shaped both Pu Songling's and Wu Bin's representations of obsession was powerful enough to transform medical discourse. By the late sixteenth century, "pi" no longer retains much force as a medical term; this sense has been almost completely eclipsed by the extended meaning of "obsession" or "addiction."[85] In his encyclopedic *Classified Materia Medica*, Li Shizhen addresses obsession in a single entry on a drug called a *pishi,* or pi stone:

"There are people who concentrate on something until it becomes an obsession [pi]. When this develops into an illness, knots in their bowels will solidify and form a stone."[86] Li's medical understanding of pi springs from the extended notion of obsession and presumes a psychological rather than somatic etiology: single-minded concentration on something obstructs the digestion, and this obstruction may harden into stone. In this very interesting move, Li reconciles the old medical definition of pi with the now-predominant cultural understanding of it.

Li Shizhen's main interest lies in the problem of how obstructions within the body can turn to stone. He cites other known examples of petrifaction, including meteors, kidney stones, fossils, and Buddhist relics. This is so in each case, he explains, because "vital energy" (*jingqi*) has solidified.[87] But this traditional theory is too vague to satisfy him. To account for the petrifaction of human flesh, he draws on the Ming theory of the overwhelming power of single-minded passion.[88] As evidence, he cites an amazing story about a Persian who broke into an ancient tomb. "The Persian saw that all the skin and muscles [of the corpse] had disintegrated; all that remained was a heart hard as stone. He sawed it down the middle and found a landscape inside resembling a painting. On one side was a girl leaning out over a railing and gazing fixedly in the distance. In fact, this girl must have had an obsessive love of landscape for her to be recomposed in this fashion."[89] The picture formed inside the petrified heart records her fatal history. The girl's obsession with the landscape has literally etched itself into her heart, the seat of consciousness, figuring herself into this stone landscape. In fact, certain rocks, like marble, were indeed prized for the painting-like landscapes that could be glimpsed in them, natural pictures that John Hay has called "mountainscapes in marble."[90] In transmuting to stone, this heart has outlasted the organic process of decay, recording for posterity the obsession responsible for the metamorphosis.

Li Shizhen's entry concludes with a final prescription that follows the principle of curing like with like: a dissolved pi stone taken orally will cure a "blocked gullet" (*yege*), a condition whose symptoms include the inability to ingest food, vomiting, and constipation. Such a stone would be obtained, his final case suggests, among the cremated ashes of someone who had died from knots in the bowels.[91] A stone thus becomes at once the perfect symbol of obsession, the somatic result of obsession, and the cure for obsession. We have come full circle to Pu Songling's **"Ethereal Rock"** in which only the destruction of the rock can dissolve the rock-lover's obsession and bring peace.

Addiction and Satire

Although the rock-lover in **"The Ethereal Rock"** is disparaged by the Historian of the Strange for being "foolish" in his devotion, this is clearly not intended as a real rebuke. The admiring tone adopted in the final comment accords with the late Ming glorification of folly and sentiment that trumpeted the excesses of obsession as the highest form of self-expression.

In a number of other tales, however, Pu Songling parts company with the late Ming cult of feeling to expose the dark underside of obsession. In these tales of addiction, obsession is stripped of its glamor to reveal its potential to inflict human misery. *Liaozhai* paints devastating portraits of addictions to gambling, sex, alcohol, geomancy, and chess that are emphatically not idealized or applauded. These more conventional moral tales, on the whole, emphasize the consequences of immoderate indulgence and the loss of self-control. For instance, in **"The Gambling Charm"** (**"Du fu"**; 3.419-21), a chronic gambler loses his house and land in a game and, even after winning them back with the aid of a Daoist amulet, cannot bring himself to quit. Only after the amulet suddenly vanishes into thin air does he come to his senses and withdraw from the game. In case the point has not been driven home clearly enough, the Historian of the Strange appends a lengthy sermon to the story lamenting the evils of gambling, which begins: "Of all things on earth that destroy households, nothing is swifter than gambling; of all things on earth that wreck virtue, nothing is worse than gambling" (3.420). But even in the case of gambling, a subject that he evidently felt very strongly about, Pu Songling cannot resist including another tale, "Ren Xiu" (11.1473-75), in which a gambling addict's fatal weakness for dice ironically provides the very means through which ghosts restore his stolen family fortune.

In *Five-fold Miscellany* (*Wu za zu*), Xie Zhaozhe lists famous figures of the past whose deaths were caused by uncontrollable addictions, and dryly observes that "although life and death are both important, that which someone loves can be more important to him than life itself."[92] Pu Songling vividly translates this notion into fiction when his addicts not only forfeit their lives in this world for what they crave but also do the same again in the next. Even death cannot break the title character in **"The Chess Ghost"** (**"Qi gui"**; 4.532-34) or **"The Alcoholic"** (**"Jiu kuang"**; 4.583-88) of their addictions. Forgetting that he is dead, the alcoholic gets drunk as usual and kicks up a ruckus in hell until he is finally fished out of a foul, knife-infested stream. This explains the ferocious hangover that he faces upon waking the next morning back among the living, but it still does not cure him of his alcoholism, and he is soon marched back to hell for good.

In the more moving story, **"The Chess Ghost,"** a young scholar's uncontrollable passion for chess leads to his father's death; he himself is taken off to the purgatory of hungry ghosts as punishment. On his way to redeem himself by drafting an official inscription for the underworld authorities, he happens to pass by living men playing a chess game in the open air. He joins the game and, glued to the spot, loses every match until the deadline has passed and he has forfeited any further chance for rebirth. Comments the Historian of the Strange: "When he glimpsed a chessboard, he cared no more about death; once he was dead, he glimpsed a chessboard and cared no more about life. Isn't it the case that his desire to play was greater than his desire to live? But to be as obsessed as this and *still* be unable to score even one great move!" (4.533)

It is difficult to determine what saddens the Historian of the Strange more—the chess ghost's dooming himself to damnation for eternity or his inferior skills at the game. It goes against the grain of the late Ming idealization of obsession for a man to fail so miserably at what he sincerely loves; in fact, foolishness and talent should go hand in hand. In **"A Bao"** (2.233-39), the Historian of the Strange defends foolishness on precisely those grounds: "If one's nature is 'foolish,' then one's resolve will be firm: thus those who are foolish in their love of books are sure to excel in composition, and those who are foolishly devoted to the arts are bound to have excellent technique, whereas those people who make no progress and achieve nothing are always those who claim that they are not foolish" (2.239).[93]

Although the privileging of foolishness and single-mindedness enabled obsession to be idealized as a vehicle for self-expression in the first place, such excessive behavior also becomes an irresistible target for social satire. The comic possibilities of the subject are already discernible in Mi Fu's official biography in the *Song History,* where the anecdote about him bowing to the rock is reported as a current joke.[94] In fact, this anecdote also circulated with an additional punchline that completely undercut its seriousness. Someone is said to have asked Mi Fu whether he had really bowed to a rock, to which he slowly replied: "How could I have bowed to a rock?—I merely saluted it."

Both modes of treating obsession—glorification and satire—coexist in the writings of certain authors and even in certain books during the late Ming. Feng Menglong preaches the gospel of obsession and folly in his commentary to *A Classified History of Love,* but makes these same traits the butt of jokes in his *Survey of Talk New and Old (Gujin tan'gai).* The prefaces to *A Brief History of Obsession and Lunacy* advance solemn claims for the moral virtues of obsession, but most of the anecdotes in the book are quite funny and are clearly constructed as jokes; the comments also tend to maximize the humor by coining ludicrous epithets or pairing incompatible cravings. In **Liaozhai,** too, although certain stories treat obsession extremely seriously, it is also lampooned, even sometimes within the same story. The

hero of the tale **"Huang Jiulang"** (3.316-23), for example, has a fixed penchant for homosexuality ("the obsession with rent sleeves").[95] His love affair with a fox-boy is narrated fairly sympathetically since he manifests all the symptoms of the sincere love-fanatic and refuses to give up the boy even at the cost of his own life. But the story starts to slip into comedy when as a reward for his devotion he is "converted" to heterosexuality in his next incarnation. At the end of the story, in another, more abrupt change of tone, the Historian of the Strange indulges himself in an amazingly arcane and rather hostile parody in parallel prose on homosexual practices. The piece's scholastic, punning wit hinges on the contrast between its erudite style and obscene content.

In **"A Strangeness of Pigeons,"** the wealthy pigeon fancier Zhang Youliang, who boasts of the finest pigeon collection in Shandong, pampers his birds with all the attentiveness of a mother caring for her baby. Because of his exquisite devotion, he is honored with a visit from the pigeon god, who presents him with a pair of snow-white pigeons. These and their offspring become the gems of his collection. Sometime later, a friend of his father's, a high official, inquires about his pigeons. Assuming that the official is a fellow connoisseur and hoping to get into his good graces, Zhang sends him, after much agonizing, a pair of the snow-white pigeons. Later he meets the official, but to his chagrin the official says not a word about the pigeons.

> Unable to contain himself, Zhang blurted out: "And how were the pigeons?"
>
> "Nice and plump," replied the official.
>
> "You don't mean you *cooked* them?" asked Zhang, alarmed.
>
> "Why, yes."
>
> "But those were no ordinary pigeons . . . !" cried Zhang in shock. The official reflected for a moment. "Well, they didn't *taste* especially out of the ordinary." (6.841)

The joke is beautifully constructed with comic pauses and a slow buildup to the punchline as the pigeon fancier realizes that his worst fears have come true. The story ends sadly when the remaining snow-white pigeons desert Zhang for betraying them; in remorse, he gives away the rest of his collection. Once again, an obsession ends with dispersal and loss. The Historian of the Strange reprimands Zhang for trying to curry favor with an official but defends his passion: "We can see that gods and spirits are angered by greed but not by foolishness" (6.842).

Two short anecdotes appended to the comment are closer to jokes than to stories; they are essentially variations on the joke told in "A Strangeness of Pigeons." In the second anecdote, a monk, a fanatical tea connoisseur, entertains a high official with his second-best grade of tea. Since the official does not react, the monk, conscience-stricken, assumes he must be a true connoisseur and immediately offers him his best grade of tea. When a response is still not forthcoming, the monk breathlessly asks him what he thought of the tea. "It was hot," is the answer. These secondary items reinforce a comic rather than tragic reading of the main tale. As a final authorial comment explicitly points out: "These two anecdotes are funny in the same way as Master Zhang presenting his pigeons" (6.843).

A version of the pigeon joke in *A Brief History of Obsession and Lunacy* concerns the famous calligrapher Wang Xizhi, who was said to love geese because their sinuous necks inspired the curves of his brush strokes.[96] Knowing of his passion, a friend invites Wang to view a remarkable goose raised by his old nurse in the countryside. Upon hearing that the famous calligrapher is coming to visit, however, the old lady slaughters the goose and cooks it in order to have some delicacy to serve him. A joke about a beloved animal being eaten appears as early as *New Tales of the World* of the fifth century in which the grand marshal Wang Yan maliciously slaughters and consumes the Prince of Pengcheng's favorite ox.[97] It is not hard to understand why this kind of joke was common: it makes fun of both parties at once.

The satire in **"A Strangeness of Pigeons"** is double-edged but unmistakable: the aficionado is lampooned for his overfastidiousness and consequent misreading of other people, and the unappreciative philistine is ridiculed for his boorishness. When the targets of satire are less obvious, however, the tales become correspondingly more ambiguous. In the tales **"Yellow Pride"** (**"Huang Ying"**) and **"The Bookworm"** (**"Shu chi"**; 11.1453-58), the spirits of the objects themselves seem to take pleasure in debunking their stereotyped associations, to the shock and alarm of their devotees.

In **"Yellow Pride,"** Ma, a poor and austere chrysanthemum connoisseur, unknowingly befriends brother and sister chrysanthemum-spirits, who are the descendents of that most famous lover of chrysanthemums, the recluse-poet Tao Yuanming. (Chrysanthemums had become so identified with this poet by the Ming that in one anecdote a scholar hosting a chrysanthemum-viewing party in his garden cautioned his tipsy guests to take care lest they step on "Tao Yuanming."[98]) To Ma's horror, the brother and sister do not share his eremitic tastes and set up a profitable chrysanthemum business, trading on their phenomenal horticultural skills. After Ma marries the sister, Yellow Pride, he valiantly tries to hold onto his poverty and spiritual purity in the face of his bride's commercial wealth, but after some ludi-

crous maneuvering, is forced to live in the comfortable style she prefers.

Most important, Ma's obsession with chrysanthemums is not the fashionable pseudo-connoisseurship that Yuan Hongdao and Li Zhi attacked. Ma faithfully adheres to all the rules of idealized obsession, and the chrysanthemums duly love him back. But these rules are themselves called into question and mocked in this story. As befits the true connoisseur, Ma is steadfast in refusing to profit from the buying and selling of the things that he loves. He clearly prides himself on being a pure-minded recluse, a latter-day Tao Yuanming. But Ma's obdurate poverty and eremitism in the face of his improved financial circumstances are ridiculed as priggishness and affectation, most notably by his wife, the chrysanthemum-spirit, the very one who ought to understand these virtues best.

The paradoxically materialist behavior of the chrysanthemum-spirits becomes even more striking when we consider that in his poetry Pu Songling professed to be a chrysanthemum-lover in much the same conventional terms as his protagonist Ma. The first couplet of his poem **"Admiring Chrysanthemums in Sun Shengzuo's Studio, the Tenth Month"** (**"Shiyue Sun Shengzuo zhaizhong shang ju"**) reads: "My old love of chrysanthemums has become an obsession, / To seek a lovely variety I'd travel a thousand miles."[99] The couplet closely echoes the opening description of Ma in **"Yellow Pride"**: "Whenever he heard of a lovely variety, he would travel a thousand miles to buy it" (11.1446). Although the language is extremely conventional in both cases, Pu Songling does not employ this exact wording in any other poem on flowers or in any of his other obsessional tales in *Liaozhai*. In a consecutive poem entitled **"Drinking at Night and Composing Another Verse"** (**"Ye yin zaifu"**), Pu Songling likewise praises chrysanthemums in a model couplet that he could easily have attributed to Ma: "Literary groups delight in pouring the Sage's wine; / Worldly faces are shamed before the recluse flowers."[100] In light of these poems, Pu Songling's flouting of the chrysanthemum stereotype in "Yellow Pride" may come close to a mild form of self-satire.

In *Liaozhai,* although vulgarity is derided, poverty is decidedly not glamorized.[101] Pu Songling, as the son of a scholar turned merchant, tends to be concerned with the material well-being of his heroes. More often than not, the intrusion of the strange into the world of the hero vastly improves his finances: the satisfaction of one desire (love) leads to the satisfaction of other desires (fortune and career).[102] Business dealings are described in surprising detail, and the most lovely heroines often prove to be the most hardheaded businesswomen. Despite Ma's resistance, this pattern basically prevails in **"Yellow Pride."**

On the other hand, it is hard to avoid the impression that the commercialization of seventeenth-century society is also being mocked here or at least milked for its comic possibilities. The implication is that if Tao Yuanming himself somehow came back to earth in this late day and age, he too would turn his back on poetry and earn a fortune raising chrysanthemums instead. Underlying this fable of the industrious chrysanthemums is a subtext: the opening of that most famous of Tao Yuanming's poems, "Drinking Wine," no. 4 ("Yin jiu"):

> I built my cottage in the realm of men,
> And yet there is no noise [*xuan*] of horse and cart.
> You ask me, "How can this be so?"
> "When the mind is distant the place is naturally remote."
> I pick chrysanthemums beneath the eastern hedge.[103]

When Ma first learns of his friend Tao's proposal to sell chrysanthemums, he specifically alludes to this poem to dissuade him: "If you follow this plan, you will be converting your *eastern hedge* into a bazaar and profaning your chrysanthemums" (11.1447). Although Tao defends himself that it is not vulgar to make an honest living selling flowers, sure enough, before long the quiet refuge in the poem has been turned into a marketplace: "Crowds gathered outside T'ao's [Tao's] house, and the place was as noisy [*xuan*] and busy as the market. . . . [Ma] saw that the street was filled with people and carts loaded with chrysanthemums" (11.1447).[104] With the profits from the chrysanthemum business, Tao Yuanming's thatched cottage is torn down, and a palatial residence is built in its place. The Historian of the Strange carefully refrains from commenting on any of the controversial points in the story and merely praises the one obvious similarity between Tao the chrysanthemum and Tao Yuanming—insouciant drunkenness: "To die of drunkenness after spending a carefree life, though deplored by the world, need not be an unhappy ending" (11.1452).[105] He deliberately seems to leave open to the reader's interpretation the extent and scope of the tale's satire.

An underlying strain of self-satire is also discernible in the portrait of the impecunious scholar in **"The Bookworm."** Pu Songling seems to harbor a secret sympathy and affection for his bookish hero, Lang. In his naiveté and stubbornness, Lang carries to absurdity the philosopher Li Zhi's call to preserve one's "childlike heart" (*tongzi xin*), the supposed wellspring of spontaneity, authenticity, and literary creation.[106] Lang loves the books in his ancestral library with an almost-blind devotion, refusing to part with even a single volume despite his poverty. He is no true connoisseur or scholar, however, for no one book appears more or less valuable to him than any other. Although he spends

every waking moment studying, he does not know how to read between the lines or interpret what he reads; he takes everything literally and consequently never passes the exams.

Just as Tao Yuanming's poetry underlies the chrysanthemum story, so too in this tale there is a subtext: the "Exhortation to Study" ("Quanxue pian"), a pedantic poem "extolling the glory of scholarship" composed by the Northern Song emperor Zhenzong (r. 997-1022), which enjoyed particularly wide currency in the cheap popular primers of the sixteenth and seventeenth centuries.[107] This poem, which Lang's father had hung in an honored position by his desk, is a blueprint for the plot: the bookworm believes it will come true exactly as written, and as so often in *Liaozhai*, it miraculously does. The poem's most important line for the story is: "Regret not that you have no fine maid; / In books are girls with cheeks smooth as jade [*yan ruyu*]."[108] Sure enough, one day he happens to open volume eight of the *Han History*; there between the pages is a paper-cut of a beautiful woman. Beneath his ardent gaze, she comes to life and introduces herself as Miss Jadesmooth Cheek (Yan Ruyu), explaining dryly that she has been moved by his devotion: "I'm afraid there will never again be anyone like you who so profoundly believes the ancients" (11.1454). The bookworm is a fool because he cannot distinguish figurative and literal levels of meaning. Because he so profoundly believes obvious lies to be the truth, they come true after all. But in their coming true, he paradoxically learns that they were lies.

Although the bookworm is admired in the story for his sentimentality, naiveté, and childlike heart, all cardinal virtues in the late Ming cult of feeling, he is also ridiculed mercilessly for taking them to excess. Lang's total immersion in books has kept him so ignorant that even at the age of thirty-three he is completely unaware of the facts of life. Ironically, it is the spirit of the book, Jadesmooth Cheek herself, who forces him to stop reading and introduces him to the pleasures of gaming, music, and the bedroom arts, because as she tells him, "the reason you're not successful is simply because you're always studying" (II.1454). She even urges him to get rid of his library before it is too late; he refuses in horror: "But this is your native land, and my entire life! How can you suggest such a thing!" (II.1456) In fact, the book-spirit turns out to be the catalyst for the library's destruction, which paradoxically instigates Lang's worldly success. Under the pretext of searching for the beautiful demon, the district magistrate torches Lang's library, repeating, as the Historian of the Strange suggests, the trauma of the First Qin Emperor's burning of the books. Once again, obsession results in the destruction of the loved object and the dispersal of a collection. We are back to the poet Li Qingzhao contemplating the destruction of her husband's library.

But Lang's very different response to this catastrophe forces us to recognize that the world and official success are also being mocked. When Lang's library goes up in smoke, so does his foolishness. His passion for books is transformed into a passion for revenge. His career takes off only after he turns his back on reading and scholarship and forsakes the cardinal rule of the "Exhortation to Study"—"My boy, to achieve life's reward / just face the window and study hard." As soon as he realizes that the words of the ancients are lies, he swiftly passes the *jinshi* exam, becomes governor of his enemy's native province, and wreaks his revenge.

Notes

EPIGRAPH: *Yuan Hongdao ji,* p. 826.

[1] Wang Qishu, *Shuicao qingxia lu,* quoted in Wang Xiao-chuan, *Yuan Ming Qing sandai jinhui xiaoshuo,* p. 314. A portion of this chapter, with a somewhat different emphasis, appeared in my article "The Petrified Heart: Obsession in Chinese Literature, Medicine, and Art" in *Late Imperial China.*

[2] Zhang Zilie, *Zhengzi tong, wuji* 24a. This dictionary was based on Mei Yingzuo's (1570-1615) *Lexicon (Zihui),* printings of which were still extensive ca. 1691. *DMB* (pp. 1061-62) calls *Zhengzi tong* "the most successful of a large number of vulgate versions of the *Tzu-hui* [*Zihui*] which circulated widely in late Ming and early Qing times and which dominated both popular and professional Chinese lexicography until the *K'ang-hsi tzu* [Kangxi dictionary] became available." The *Kangxi Dictionary* cites *Zhengzi tong*'s definition of pi. I am indebted to Mi-chu Wiens for calling my attention to the importance of Mei Yingzuo's work.

[3] Unschuld, *Medicine in China: Pharmaceutics,* p. 20.

[4] Chao Yuanfang, *Zhubing yuanhou lun* 20.113. This section introduces eleven varieties of pi diseases, including *pijie* (pi nodules), *yinpi* (fluid-induced pi), *hanpi* (cold-induced pi), and *jiupi* (chronic pi). On Chao Yuanfang, see *Zhongyi dacidian,* p. 233.

[5] Wang Tao, *Waitai biyao* 12.329. See the entry "Pi ying ru shi fu man." This book synthesizes many pre-Tang works, including *Zhubing yuanhou lun,* whose discussion of pi is quoted verbatim at 12.321. For further information on this book, see *Zhongyi dacidian,* p. 53.

[6] *Pi* written with the "person" radical has a long history in its own right extending back to the *Odes (Mao shi,* no. 254) and the *Jiu zhang* in *Chu ci.*

[7] "No. 10: Connoisseurship" ("Shi: haoshi"), *Pingshi,* p. 846. "Peach Blossom Spring" alludes to a hidden utopian community in Tao Yuanming's famous account. For a complete French translation and discussion of *Pingshi,* see Vandermeesch, "L'arrangement de fleurs en Chine." Vandermeesch defines pi (written with the "person" radical) as "designating at once that which is distant and vague and that which diverges from the normal path."

[8] *Shishuo xinyu* 4.15, p. 199; trans. Mather, *New Tales of the World,* p. 185. *New Tales* has no specially designated category for obsession. The term "pi" occurs only once in Liu Xiaobiao's early sixth-century commentary to the work and even *shi* (a taste for) occurs only rarely. The characters most commonly used to describe fondness or attachment are *hao* (to be fond of) and, less often, *ai* (to like, to love); *bing jiu* (to be addicted to liquor) is employed once.

[9] Zhang Yanyuan, *Records of Famous Paintings Through the Ages (Lidai minghua ji),* in Yu Jian-hua, ed., *Zhongguo hualun leibian* 2: 1225-26. Trans. Bush and Shih, *Early Chinese Texts on Painting,* pp. 73-74 (modified).

[10] "Jigu lu mu xu," in *Ouyang Wenzhonggong quanji* 41. 7a-b.

[11] *Ouyang Wenzhonggong quanji* 40.1. For a translation of this essay, see Egan, *Literary Works of Ouyang Hsiu,* pp. 217-18.

[12] Ye Mengde, "Pingquan caomu ji ba"; trans. Hay, *Kernels of Energy,* p. 34.

[13] Su Shi, "On the Hall of Precious Paintings" ("Bao-huitang ji") in Yu Jianhua, *Zhongguo hualun leibian* I: 48. I have modified Bush and Shih's translation in *Early Chinese Texts on Painting,* p. 233. Su Shi probably borrowed his concept of "lodging" from Ouyang Xiu's autobiographical essay, "The Old Drunkard's Pavilion" ("Zuiweng ting ji,") (*Ouyang Wenzhonggong quanji* 39.9-10; trans. Egan, *Literary Works of Ouyang Hsiu,* p. 216): "The Old Drunkard's real interest is not the wine but the mountains and streams. Having captured the joys of the mountains and streams in his heart, he lodges them in wine."

[14] The locus classicus of the phrase *youwu* is *Zuo zhuan* Zhao 29 in which it refers to beautiful women: "Where there are beautiful creatures [*youwu*], they are capable of perverting men. Unless virtue and righteousness prevail there will surely by disaster" (trans. Dudbridge, *Tale of Li Wa,* p. 69).

[15] Both men were powerful Tang chief ministers who were disgraced and executed. According to the editor of *Li Qingzhao ji,* Wang Bo must be an error for Want Ya (ca. 760-835), who was renowned as a connoisseur

of books and paintings. His collection was destroyed after his fall from power. Yuan Zai, who accumulated great wealth during his tenure in office, was executed in 777. An official raid on his home unearthed a cache of 800 piculs of pepper.

[16] In a famous anecdote in the sixth-century commentary to *Shishuo xinyu* 20: 4, the scholar and general Du Yu tells the emperor that He Qiao has "an obsession with money"; he himself has "an obsession with the *Zuo Commentary*" (p. 381). Mather (*New Tales of the World,* p. 359) translates pi as "a weakness for."

[17] "Postface to *Records on Stone and Bronze*" ("*Jinshi lu* houxu"), in *Li Qingzhao ji,* pp. 176-77.

[18] For a partial translation and close reading of the postface, see Owen, *Remembrances,* pp. 80-98.

[19] Ouyang Xiu, "Biography of the Retired Scholar of Six Ones" ("Liuyi jushi zhuan"), in *Ouyang Wenzhonggong quanji* 44. 7a-b. For a translation, see Egan, *Literary Works of Ouyang Hsiu,* pp. 217-18.

[20] Xie Zhaozhe, *Wu za zu* 7.299. In an adjacent passage (7.296), Xie observes that human tastes and preferences have always differed and then erects a hierarchy of preferences drawing on historical examples. In the highest group he includes such benign passions as a fondness for roaming in scenic spots and for books one has never heard of before. This kind of thing, says Xie, "comes from natural disposition and doesn't warrant being considered an illness." His second group includes more problematic activities: a fondness for ox fights, braying like a donkey, and a love of rocks. "These," in Xie's words, "already verge on obsession, but are not yet harmful." Moving down the ladder, Xie covers weirder passions in his third category, such as a fetish for cleanliness, for taboo characters, and for ghosts. Here Xie allows himself a practical quibble: "These present obstacles for getting along in the world." But he draws the line at his final category, eating filth and a taste for foot-bindings: "This is too much!"

[21] Tang Binyin (1568-ca. 1628; *jinshi* 1595), "A Short Preamble to *History of Obsession*" ("*Pishi* xiaoyin"), in Hua Shu, *Pidian xiaoshi.* On Hua's publications, see Wang Zhongmin, *Zhongguo shanbenshu tiyao,* pp. 421, 425-26. Tang Binyin must have been a friend of Hua Shu's because we find a preface to Hua Shu's collected works ("Hua Wenxiu *Qingshuige ji* xu") in Tang Binyin's *Shui'an gao, juan* 5. Hua Shu reused part of Yuan Hongdao's famous essay on connoisseurship from *Pingshi* as Yuan Hongdao's preface to *Pidian xiaoshi.* I see no reason to doubt the attribution to Tang Binyin, although the preface to *Pishi* is not found in his *Shui'an gao;* it is possible that for this preamble, too, Hua Shu recycled some already existing essay of Tang Binyin's.

[22] *Yuan Hongdao ji,* p. 846.

[23] Zhang Dai, "The Obsessions of Qi Zhixiang" ("Qi Zhixiang pi"), in *Tao'an mengyi,* p. 39. Zhang was so taken with this aphorism that he repeated it in another piece, "The Biographies of Five Extraordinary Men" ("Wu yiren"), in *Langhuan wenji, juan* 4.

[24] Zhang Chao, *Invisible Dream Shadows* (*Youmeng ying*) 164.6. After this work had been completed, Yagi Akiyoshi's article "Fools in *Liaozhai zhiyi*" ("*Ryosai shii* no 'chi' ni tsuite") was brought to my attention. Yagi draws upon a number of the same sources to explore the close relationship between folly and obsession in Ming-Qing thought and the influence of this relationship on Pu Songling and *Liaozhai;* see esp. pp. 91-96.

[25] Each of these famous connoisseurs was proverbial for his obsession. Yuan Hongdao's comment appears after the entry on obsessions with rocks ("shi pi") in Hua Shu's *Pidian xiaoshi.* Feng Menglong included an abridged version of Yuan's comment in his *Gujin tan'gai* 9.426. To avoid redundancy in English, I have followed Feng's abridgment in the last line of my translation.

[26] Barr, "Pu Songling and *Liaozhai*," p. 217.

[27] Hanan, *Chinese Vernacular Story,* p. 79.

[28] The development of this new conception of qing is still inadequately understood, but is generally ascribed to the influence of Wang Yangming's (1472-1529) thought. The best discussion of the Ming philosophical influence underlying qing in literature is W. Y. Li, *Enchantment and Disenchantment.*

[29] *Qingshi leilüe* 23. 17a. The comment is probably by Feng Menglong, who is thought to have published *Qingshi leilüe* under the pseudonym Zhanzhan waishi. For a discussion of the authorship and contents of this book, see Hanan, *Chinese Vernacular Story,* pp. 95-97; and Mowry, *Chinese Love Stories.* Barr ("Pu Songling and *Liaozhai*," pp. 216-17) points out that the pseudonym Historian of Love parallels Pu Songling's Historian of the Strange and demonstrates that Pu was familiar with *Qingshi.* The resemblance between Pu's commentary and Feng's commentary goes even further; they sometimes express similar opinions, sometimes in similar language.

[30] Tang Binyin, "*Pishi* xiaoyin," in Hua Shu, *Pidian xiaoshi.*

[31] Gu Wenjian, *Fuxuan zalu,* under the entry "personal taste" ("xingshi") in *Shuo fu* 2.1319-20. The close connection between *shi* (a taste for), one of the main graphs associated with obsession, and food is indicated by the

presence of the "mouth" radical. The Tang-Song encyclopedia *Bai-Kong liutie* places its entry on obsession
in the food section under the heading "predilections"
("shihao") and primarily lists bizarre eating habits. The
Song encyclopedia *Taiping yulan* also uses the heading "shihao," but it subsumes non-food-related obsessions in this category as well.

[32] For two such lists, see Xie Zhaozhe, *Wu za zu* 7.296;
and Feng Menglong, *Gujin tan'gai* 9.8b-10a. The interest in eating habits of a bizarre nature is manifested
in two short *Liaozhai* anecdotes, "A Passion for Snakes"
("She pi"; 1.130) and "Nibbling Rocks" ("He shi";
2.137). The frequency of obsessions in Chinese writing with eating filth on the one hand and cleanliness
on the other seems to indicate some affinity with the
obsessive-compulsive syndromes familiar from psychoanalytic literature, and it would be interesting to
ponder the connection with obsessive collecting.

[33] Homosexuality presents a special case in that it involves human beings rather than things, but even here
I believe the emphasis is on a category of people or a
mode of behavior rather than on a particular person.
Although obsession with sex in general or with one's
own wife does occasionally crop up in the literature,
an obsession with a particular person, regardless of
gender, is generally not interpreted as obsession but as
qing. See, e.g., *Hairpins Beneath a Man's Cap* (*Bian
er chai*), a 1517 collection of sentimental stories of
male love, and the "Qingwai" (gay love) section of
Qingshi leilüe. At the same time, only exclusive homosexuality qualifies as an idiosyncrasy or obsession;
casual or occasional homosexual liaisons do not. See
Zhang Dai's account (*Tao'an mengyi*, p. 39) of a friend
said to have an obsession with homosexuality because
he abandoned his wife to run off with a male lover
during the fall of the Ming.

[34] Pu Songling's preface to this work appears in *PSLJ*
I:53.

[35] Barr, "Pu Songling and *Liaozhai*," pp. 278-79. Yuan
Hongdao's essay "Raising Crickets" ("Xu cuzhi," in
Yuan Hongdao ji, pp.728-29) cites Jia Qiuhuo's *Cricket Manual* (*Cuzhi jing*) as an authority on different
species of crickets and methods for raising them. For
a translation of Yuan's essay, see Chaves, *Pilgrims of
the Clouds*, pp. 83-88.

[36] For a few of the pigeon varieties, I have followed G.
Yang and Yang Xianyi's translations in *Selected Tales
of Liaozhai*, p. 96.

[37] It is possible that Pu Songling had consulted some
version of Zhang Wanzhong's *Pigeon Handbook* (*Gejing*). Pu's story displays some similarities in wording
and content with this manual. The story's list of pigeon varieties by region closely parallels a section of

the handbook that classifies pigeons by region of origin. The order of places in the story follows that in the
handbook, and under each region it names at least one
of the varieties named in the handbook. Another obvious similarity concerns the treatment of sick pigeons.
In the story, we are told, "If a pigeon took cold," the
pigeon fancier would "treat it with the finest variety of
sweet grass [*Glycyrrhiza glabra*]"; "if a pigeon became overheated, he would offer it grains of salt" [*leng
ze liao yi fencao, re ze tou yi yan ke*] (6.839). Under
the heading "Cures" ("Liaozhi"), the handbook reads:
"If a pigeon becomes overheated, treat it with salt; if
it takes cold, treat it with sweet grass" [*re, liao yi yan;
leng, liao yi gancao*] (50.5a). On the other hand, there
are a number of places in which the story and the
manual do not overlap, such as the etymologies given
for the Nightwanderer ("yeyou") pigeon and the treatment of other diseases.

Pu Songling's familiarity with this manual also seems
likely because the author of the manual, Zhang Wanzhong, styled Kouzhi, came from Zouping, one of the
counties in Pu Songling's native Ji'nan prefecture.
Zhang Wanzhong, son of the well-known official Zhang
Yandeng, was a late Ming senior licentiate who distinguished himself for his heroism during the fall of the
Ming. See the *Zouping xianzhi* (1696 ed.) 5.8b and
(1837 ed.) 15.47b-49a.

The wealthy pigeon fancier of Pu's story, Zhang Youliang, is also surnamed Zhang and comes from Zouping. In fact, both the story's pigeon-fancier and the
compiler of the pigeon handbook were members of the
wealthiest and most prominent gentry family in Zouping, and both had renowned gardens. See Cheng Jinzheng's private gazetteer-memoir, *Zouping xian jingwu zhi*, section on "famous gardens" ("ming yuan"),
3.11a, 3.15a. It is possible that Pu Songling intended
to call his pigeon-fancying protagonist after the author
of the pigeon manual, but mistook or misremembered
his name.

Curiously, Zhang Youliang, whose name appears on
no gazetteer list of degree holders, was well known for
his obsession not with pigeons but with *rocks*. Zhu
Jiuding of Qiantang's preface to his rock catalogue,
the *Ti'an shipu* (like the *Gejing*, printed in the *Tanji
congshu* [*juan* 44]), recounts that his friend and fellow
rock-lover Zhang Youliang of Zouping had once had a
rock that he admired dragged from the mountains to
his garden by a team of 300 oxen. The identical anecdote is recounted in both Wang Zhuo's *Jin shishuo*
(8.107) and Cheng Jinzheng's *Zouping xian jingwu zhi*.

Finally, Pu Songling's friend Gao Heng may have
known Zhang Youliang because he composed a poem
entitled "Zhang Youliang's Ancient Sword" ("Zhang
Youliang gujian pian"). See Lu Jianzeng, *Guochao
Shanzuo shichao* 6.12b-13a.

Pu Songling's story satirizes the pigeon collector for trying to curry favor with a friend of his father, a high official. It is possible that in addition to a general satire against obsessive collecting, spoiled rich sons of officials, and brownnosing, Pu Songling is also directing some sort of topical satire against the wealthy and powerful Zhangs of Zouping.

[38] For the rock catalogue and the flower handbook, see *Liaozhai yiwen jizhu,* pp. 151-58 and 107-23, respectively.

[39] Ye Mengde, "*Pingquan caomu ji* ba." We know that Pu Songling was familiar with the *Pingquan caomu ji,* because in 1707 he wrote a poem called "Reading the *Record of the Pingquan Estate*" ("Du *Pingquan ji*"), *PSLJ* 1.613.

[40] Kong Chuan, "*Yunlin shipu* xu." The allusion is to *Analects* 6.23: "The wise find joy in water; the benevolent find joy in mountains. The wise are active; the benevolent are still. The wise are joyful; the benevolent are long-lived" (trans. D. C. Lau, p. 84).

[41] *Yutai xinyong (Gyokudai shin'ei),* p. 705.

[42] A simplified formulation of an important point in Chinese poetics. See Siu-kit Wong, "Ch'ing and Ching in the Critical Writings of Wang Fuchih."

[43] "Lament" ("Yuan shi"), attributed to Ban Jieyu, *Yutai xinyong,* p. 78. For a translation, see Watson, *Chinese Lyricism,* pp. 94-95.

[44] "No. 8: On Watering" ("Ba: ximu"), *Pingshi,* p. 824.

[45] Zhang Chao, *Youmeng ying,* 4b-5a. Zhang's full list is quite long and encompasses many of the best-known paragons of obsession.

[46] For the original text, see *Liaozhai* 11.1575-79. For my translation, see the Appendix. Giles's translation (*Strange Stories,* pp. 181-91) calls the hero a "mineralogist" and his rocks "specimens," but these terms are misguided; the hero's love for rocks is emotional and aesthetic and not in the spirit of Victorian science and its impartial interest in collecting "specimens." It is extremely interesting, however, that Giles, writing for a turn-of-the-century English audience, tried to make sense of the Chinese obsession with rocks in terms of a *scientific* passion.

[47] Originally said of Yu Rang, an assassin-retainer who commits suicide (Sima Qian, *Shiji* 86.2519).

[48] Li Zhi, *Fen shu,* pp. 130-31.

[49] Lu Xun (*Zhongguo xiaoshuo shilüe,* pp. 52-53) notes the revival of interest in *New Tales of the World* dur-ing the late Ming and early Qing. During this period, which was also the heyday of obsession, the predilections of the *New Tales* eccentrics were reinterpreted in light of the late Ming notion of obsession. Although as I have already mentioned, no category in *New Tales* was specifically devoted to obsession, the chapter heading "Blind Infatuations" ("Huo ni"), which recounted men's infatuations with women, was converted into a rubric for obsession in a number of the sixteenth- and seventeenth-century updates. For example, the "Blind Infatuations" chapter in He Liangjun's *Shishuo xinyu bu,* which was published with great success in 1556, constructs a history of famous obsessions up to the Ming. The entries under the heading "Blind Infatuations" in Wang Zhuo's *Jin shishuo* (preface dated 1683) have nothing to do with romantic love; all are examples of obsessions. A disproportionate number of the entries in Hua Shu's *Pidian xiaoshi* retell or simply reprint anecdotes from *New Tales.* The chapter on obsession in Feng Menglong's *Gujin tan'gai* also includes many anecdotes from *New Tales.*

According to his friend and biographer Yuan Zhongdao, Li Zhi himself had "an obsession with cleanliness" ("Li Wenling zhuan" in *Fen shu,* p. 3). Li Zhi was profoundly interested in drawing connections between the *New Tales* eccentrics and nonconformists of his own time (see Billeter, *Li Zhi,* pp. 232-33). In 1588 Li Zhi published his *Chutan ji,* which was based on his readings of *New Tales* and *Jiaoshi leilin,* a sequel to *New Tales* that his friend, the bibliophile and scholar Jiao Hong (1541-1620), had published the year before. In recognition of Li Zhi's association with the *New Tales* eccentrics in the eyes of the reading public, a late Wanli edition of He Liangjun's *Shishuo xinyu bu* was brought out with a commentary by Li Zhi. According to Wang Zhongmin (*Zhongguo shanbenshu tiyao,* p. 391), this commentary was based on Li Zhi's annotations to his personal copy of *New Tales,* the rough draft for his *Chutan ji.*

[50] *Shishuo xinyu* 23: 46; trans. Mather, *New Tales of the World,* p. 388.

[51] See Billeter, *Li Zhi,* on the acutely felt lack of a true friend as a major theme in Li Zhi's work.

[52] *Bu shen*—a pun, for the meaning of *shen* as a noun and as an adjective differ. As a noun, *shen* means "spirit"; as an adjective, it is closer to "extraordinary," "amazing," "divine."

[53] A reworking of the title and a line in the *Book of Documents* (*Shang shu*) concerning the flute songs of Shao.

[54] Here, in the cleverest and most playful writing in the piece, Li Zhi creates a virtual pastiche of phrases and

puns (such as *jie,* which means both "integrity" and "a segment of bamboo") from the considerable corpus of inscriptions written on paintings of bamboo. The most famous is probably Su Shi's colophon on Wen Tong's painting "Bent Bamboos," which included the following poem:

> The ink gentlemen [bamboos] on the wall
>   cannot speak,
> But just seeing them can dissipate one's
>   myriad griefs;
> And further, as for my friend's resembling
>   these gentlemen,
> The severity of his simple virtue defies the
>   frosty autumn.
>
> (Trans. Bush and Shih, *Early Chinese Texts
>   on Painting,* p. 35)

The piece that Li Zhi's description resembles most closely is Ke Qian's (1251-1319) preface to Li Kan's *Manual of Bamboos* (*Zhu pu;* 1319):

> How fortunate is it that in recent times the family of bamboo met up with Master Li K'an [Li Kan]. . . . Because Li absorbs the purest air in the world, his mind is clear and open, and his spirit is brilliant, both of which are congenial to the manner and disposition of the "Gentlemen." . . . What neither description nor painting can encompass are the virtues for which bamboo stands. Bamboo stems are hollow. . . . The nature of bamboo is to be straight. . . . Bamboo's joints are clear-cut. (Trans. Bush and Shih, *Early Chinese Texts on Painting,* pp. 274-75)

[55] In a short rock catalogue entitled *Encomia for Rock Friends* (*Shiyou zan,* in *Zhaodai congshu, ce* 77), Wang Zhuo compares himself unfavorably to the rocks whose histories he records. The allegorical associations of this phrase are apparent in Zhu Xi's (1130-1200) colophon on a scroll of rocks and bamboos painted by Su Shi: "As for Old Tung-p'o [Su Shi], he possessed lofty and enduring qualities and a firm and immovable nature. One might say that he resembled these 'bamboo gentlemen' and 'rock friends' (trans. Bush, *Chinese Literati on Painting,* p. 103).

[56] "When he is alive, I uphold him in times of crisis; when he is no longer alive, I support his children and grandchildren: this is how to conduct 'a friendship of stone'" ("The Principles of Human Behavior" ["Weiren yaoze"], *PSLJ* 1: 291). It is significant that Pu Songling uses this phrase here in the context of personal friendship rather than in the context of Ming loyalism.

Barr ("Pu Songling and *Liaozhai*," pp. 121-23) has sensibly placed Pu Songling, who was only four years old at the time of the Qing conquest, in a broad "middle" category of early Qing intellectuals who recognized the legitimacy of the new dynasty but did not flinch from expressing sympathy toward Ming loyalists and toward the suffering of the people during the takeover.

Hay (*Kernels of Energy,* pp. 92-96) discusses an album of rocks painted by Ni Yuanlu (1594-1644) entitled "A Friendship of Stone" ("Shijiao tu"), which he translates as "Rock Bound." The painter was a Ming statesman and loyalist martyr who hung himself in 1644. Given this background, it is not difficult to interpret these paintings as allegorical allusions to the painter's loyalty to the fallen Ming dynasty; rocks in the mid-seventeenth century could certainly connote Ming loyalism. Thus an early Qing collection of vernacular short stories with a strong loyalist theme is entitled *The Sobering Stone* (*Zuixing shi*). It is likely that the presence of the rock in the title was intended to call attention to the collection's loyalist bent (see Hanan, "The Fiction of Moral Duty," p. 204).

Despite the strong association of rocks with Ming loyalist sentiments in some works of the mid-seventeenth century, however, we have no evidence to interpret "The Ethereal Rock" as topical allegory or as an expression of Ming sympathies. No hints or clues favoring such an interpretation can be found within the tale or in the Historian of the Strange's commentary. The same is true of other *Liaozhai* tales about flowers or dreams, which are devoid of the loyalist symbolism assigned them in the writings of Ming loyalists such as Gui Zhuang or Dong Yue. What becomes most apparent is the multivalence and flexibility of cultural symbols during this period.

[57] *Qingshi leilüe,* comment following the chapter entitled "Qinghua" ("Metamorphosis through love"), *juan* 11.

[58] Karl Kao (*IC,* p. 129) points out that *Liaozhai* contains what he calls "narrativized instances of figures." W. Y. Li ("Rhetoric of Fantasy," pp. 50-52) discusses "the literalization of metaphor" in *Liaozhai* as a way of naturalizing other worlds. For a more detailed discussion of the literalization of figurative language, see Chapter 5 and the Conclusion to this book.

[59] See Wu Hung, "Tradition and Innovation," which discusses the literati vogue during the Ming for uncarved jade to capture the spiritual and visual "naturalness" of rock and to distinguish its owner from vulgar folk who could appreciate only "artificial" beauty.

[60] Although there were other famous rock connoisseurs in Chinese history such as Niu Sengru of the Tang and the ubiquitous Su Shi, Mi Fu seems to have eclipsed them all. In the writings on obsession, it is Mi Fu's name that is invariably coupled with rocks, and in that

role he is heavily featured in Feng Menglong's *Gujin tan'gai* and in the Ming sequels to *New Tales of the World*. For a discussion of different Ming editions of Mi Fu anecdotes, see van Gulik, *Mi Fu on Inkstones,* pp. 3-4.

[61] *Song shi* 444.13124. In his preface to a collection of stories entitled *Rocks That Nod Their Heads* (*Shi dian tou,* p. 329), Feng Menglong provides a cosmological rationale for Mi Fu's apellation of his rock: "Now when Heaven gives birth to the myriad things, though their endowments of material may differ, they are alike in receiving qì [energy]. When qì congeals, it becomes a rock; when it melts it becomes a spring; when qì is limpid, it becomes a human being; when it is turbid, it becomes an animal. It is simply that men and rocks are brothers." Feng then argues that rocks, too, have intelligence and reaches this rhetorical climax: "As for calling a rock 'my elder'—why shouldn't a rock be the equal of a human being?" Pu Songling's Historian of the Strange takes this position one step further: the rock shows himself not merely the equal but the superior of most men.

[62] I am grateful to Professor Ma Ruifang of Shandong University for taking me to see this rock in June 1987.

[63] There is a lacuna in the text in this line and the fifth character is missing. Pu Songling is making a play on words between clothes and the names of plants here.

[64] A variation on a line from "The Mountain Spirit" in *Songs of the South*. This line must have been one of Pu Songling's favorites; he also included it in the opening of his powerful preface to *Liaozhai*.

[65] According to ancient legend, Gong Gong knocked down the sky by bumping into the pillar of Heaven; the Goddess Nü Wa eventually repaired the damage with rocks.

[66] *PSLJ* 1: 620.

[67] For illustrations of Mi Fu bowing to his rock, see Hay, *Kernels of Energy*.

[68] Contrast with Yuan Hongdao's poem "Shizong," no. 1: "The rock is one Mi Fu pulled from his sleeve" (*Yuan Hongdao ji*, p. 1460).

[69] Niu Sengru, a Tang statesman and author of a book of strange tales, was one of the earliest famed rock collectors.

[70] The two poems are "Inscribed on a Stone" ("Tishi"), *PSLJ* 1: 620; and "Stone Recluse Garden" ("Shiyin yuan"), *PSLJ* 1: 619.

[71] According to Stein (*World in Miniature*, p. 37), the *Yunlin shipu* describes a stone shaped like a miniature mountain that could be made to emit smoke that looked like clouds: "There are high peaks and holes that communicate through twists and turns. At the bottom is a communication hole in which one may set up a two-story incense burner. [If one lights it,] it is as though clouds were buffeting each other among the summits." Stein traces the Chinese interest in stones as miniature mountains back to the mountain-shaped incense burners of the Han.

[72] Trans. Hay, *Kernels of Energy*, p. 83. For a woodblock print of this ink stone with the inscriptions—it resembles the map of a mountain in a local gazetteer—see Tao Zongyi's (1316-1403) *Chuogeng lu* and Hay, *Kernels of Energy*, p. 81.

[73] From an inscription on an album leaf by Li Liufang (1575-1629); the last leaf is signed by the artist and is dated 1625. Reproduced in Sotheby's *Catalogue of Fine Chinese Paintings* (New York, Dec. 6, 1989), p. 43. According to Schaefer (*Tu Wan's Stone Catalogue,* p. 8), the last Northern Song emperor, Huizong, "that notorious petromaniac," went so far as to "formally enfeoff a prodigious stone as 'marklord of P'an-ku,'" Pangu (P'an-ku) being "a primordial cosmogonic deity, fashioner of the earth and its rocky bones."

[74] Taking the surname Xing as a pun for the verb *xing* "to move."

[75] On Pu Songling's flower obsession stories, see W. Y. Li, *Enchantment and Disenchantment*.

[76] This often-repeated definition of rocks appeared as early as a Jin dynasty work *A Discussion of the Pattern of Things (Wuli lun)*. See Hay, *Kernels of Energy*, p. 128 n72.

[77] Hay, *Kernels of Energy*, p. 97.

[78] This handscroll is reproduced in Sotheby's *Catalogue of Fine Chinese Paintings* (New York, Dec. 6, 1989), pp. 38-39. I am indebted to Nancy Berliner for lending me additional photographs of the paintings and inscriptions.

[79] *Zhongguo meishujia renming cidian*, p. 242.

[80] Based on Mi Wanzhong's final inscription, dated 1510 (photograph of the handscroll).

[81] An inscription on the painting by the influential painter and art theorist Dong Qichang (1555-1636) emphasizes this point.

[82] A particularly interesting catalogue is Lin Youlin's 1603 *Suyuan shipu*, which features woodblock prints of famous rocks created from the artist's imagination.

Unillustrated rock catalogues are well represented in collectanea such as *Shuofu, Tanji congshu, Zhaodai congshu, Meishu congshu,* and *Yushi guqi pulu.*

83 Mi Wanzhong's final inscription (photograph of the handscroll).

84 The Ming and Qing ideology of collecting, taken to such extremes in Pu Songling's tale and Wu Bin's handscroll, forestalls or diffuses the postmodernist critiques leveled against collecting by contemporary Western critics such as Susan Stewart in *On Longing.* In the Chinese idealization of obsession, the relationship between collectors and the objects of their collection is not arbitrary, because objects have become imbued with cultural significance, especially moral virtues. Nor is the relationship one-sided, because objects are said to need collectors as much as collectors need objects. Thus the conceit that the object itself deliberately "finds" the proper collector. Finally it is not luck or even connoisseurship that enables the collector to locate a rare object, but a moral causality. The sufficiently devoted collector comes to possess an object because he merits it.

85 In contrast to earlier medical books that treated pi as a category of digestive illness, pi is no longer a serious disease category in any standard nosological list that reflects contemporary sixteenth- or seventeenth-century practice, including Li Shizhen's encyclopedic *Classified Materia Medica* (see *juan* 3-4). When the term "pi" does crop up in sixteenth- and seventeenth-century medical literature, it is simply as a verb for tobacco or alcohol addiction. I am indebted to Charlotte Furth for alerting me to the eclipse of pi as a disease category. Of course, Ming dictionaries like *Zhengzi tong* still list the earlier medical meanings of pi in their definitions.

86 Li Shizhen, *Bencao gangmu* 52.96.

87 Ibid.

88 For a fuller discussion of this point and a more detailed reading of Li Shizhen's entry, see my article "The Petrified Heart."

89 Li Shizhen, *Bencao gangmu* 52.96-97.

90 Hay, *Kernels of Energy,* p. 84.

91 Li Shizhen, *Bencao gangmu* 52.96.

92 Xie Zhaozhe, *Wu za zu* 7.300.

93 Trans. Barr, "Pu Songling and *Liaozhai,*" p. 223.

94 *Song shi* 444.13124.

95 A widely used allusion that refers to an anecdote in "The Biography of Dong Xian" ("Dong Xian zhuan") in Ban Gu, *Han shu* 13.3733. The emperor, wishing to get out of bed, chose to tear off the sleeve of his robe rather than awaken his favorite male lover.

96 Qian Xuan's (ca. 1235-after 1301) beautiful handscroll in the Metropolitan Museum depicts Wang Xizhi in a waterside pavilion watching geese (see Cahill, *Hills Beyond a River,* p. 353, color pl. 35).

97 *Shishuo xinyu* 30: 11; trans. Mather, *New Tales of the World,* p. 464. Pu Songling mentions this anecdote in an essay written in 1670 on behalf of Sun Hui, "Inscription on a Stela at the Pond for Releasing Life" ("Fangsheng chi bei ji"), *PSLJ* 1: 39.

98 *Peiwen yunfu* 3: 3456, under the entry "potted chrysanthemums" ("penju"); cited in Vandermeersch, "L'arrangement de fleurs," p. 83.

99 *PSLJ* 1:641.

100 Ibid.

101 Like most lower-degree holders, Pu Songling prided himself on his sensitivity to "vulgarity." This is particularly evident in his list of "unbearable things" ("bu ke nai shi") appended to a tale about a vulgar scholar who selects money over calligraphy when put to the test by two beautiful foxmaidens. See "A Licentiate of Yishui" ("Yishui xiucai"; 7.906).

102 In this, Pu Songling may be following the conventions of the drama. As Swatek has asserted in "Feng Menglong's *Romantic Dream*": "One of the paradigms of chuanqi drama is that the pursuit of love and the pursuit of fame are connected" (p. 232); and "in *Mudan ting,* the fulfillment of sexual desire is the precondition for all other resolutions" (p. 214). *Liaozhai*'s interest in the mechanics of the hero's financial success, however, resembles as well the concerns of many vernacular stories that unfold in a mercantile milieu.

103 Tao Qian, *Tao Yuanming ji,* p. 89.

104 Trans. H. C. Chang, *Tales of the Supernatural,* p. 142.

105 Ibid., p. 147.

106 Barr ("Pu Songling and *Liaozhai,*" pp. 217-26) discusses the influence of Li Zhi's "Tongxin shuo" on *Liaozhai*'s naive heroes and draws an explicit parallel to "The Bookworm."

107 "Exhortation to Study" (the locus classicus is a chapter title in *Xunzi*) was a favorite theme, especially during the Song. Wai-kam Ho ("Late Ming Literati," p. 26)

notes the reasons for the popularity of cheap didactic primers in sixteenth- and seventeenth-century publishing: "The main purpose of course for children was to extol the glory of scholarship, to impress young minds with the power of wealth, even the 'face of jadelike beauty' that one could expect to find in books, or to rhapsodize about the joy of studying in poems such as 'Sishi dushu le' [The pleasures of studying in the four seasons]."

[108] Liu Mengmei, the romantic hero of *The Peony Pavilion,* complains in his self-introduction about the false promises of "Exhortation to Study": "In books lie fame and fortune, they say, / Then tell me, where are the jadesmooth cheeks / the rooms of yellow gold?" (trans. Birch, *Peony Pavilion,* p. 3)

FURTHER READING

Barr, Allan. "The Textual Transmission of *Liaozhai zhiyi."* *Harvard Journal of Asiatic Studies* 44, No. 2 (December 1984): 515-62.

> Surveys the *Liao-chai's* textual history in an attempt to place P'u's stories in chronological order.

———. "A Comparative Study of Early and Late Tales in *Liaozhai zhiyi."* *Harvard Journal of Asiatic Studies* 45, No. 1 (1985): 157-202.

> Compares the first and last volumes of the collection and considers some differences between subject, theme, plot, and characterization that demonstrate P'u's development.

———. "Disarming Intruders: Alien Women in *Liaozhai zhiyi"* *Harvard Journal of Asiatic Studies* 49, No. 2 (December 1989): 501-17.

> Discusses the many types of ghost women in P'u's *Strange Stories.*

Chun-shu Chang and Hsüeh-lun Chang. "The World of P'u Sung-ling's 'Liao-chai chih-I': Literature and the Intelligentsia During the Ming-Ch'ing Dynastic Transition." *Journal of the Institute of Chinese Studies of the Chinese University of Hong Kong* 6, No. 2 (1973): 401-21.

> The critics examine unresolved tensions between Confucianism and Taoism, individualism and conformism, and fatalism and justice in *Strange Stories.*

Prušek, Jaroslav. "Two Documents Relating to the Life of P'u Sung-ling" and "*Liao-chai-chih-I* by P'u Sung-ling: An Inquiry into the Circumstances Under Which the Collection Arose." In *Chinese History and Literature,* pp. 84-91; 92-108. Dordrecht, Holland: D. Reidel Publishing Co., 1970.

> Translations of P'u's biography of his wife and of the inscription that appeared on P'u's tomb; examination of new information concerning P'u's life. Prušek contends that the biographical material necessarily alters one's understanding of *Strange Stories.*

Tsung Shu. "An Outstanding Collection of Tales." *Chinese Literature,* No. 10 (October 1962): 89-94.

> Discusses the importance of P'u's essentially optimistic, romantic outlook as a key to understanding the popularity of *Strange Stories.*

Yu, Anthony C. "'Rest, Rest, Perturbed Spirit!' Ghosts in Traditional Chinese Prose Fiction." *Harvard Journal of Asiatic Studies* 47, No. 2 (December 1987): 397-434.

> Places P'u's tales within the genre of traditional Chinese ghost fiction.

Zeitlin, Judith T. *Historian of the Strange: Pu Songling and the Chinese Classical Tale.* Palo Alto, Cal.: Stanford University Press, 1993, 332 p.

> Comprehensive overview of P'u's stories, which includes several translations and an extensive bibliography containing Chinese, Japanese, and Western sources.

Additional coverage of P'u Sung-ling's life and career is contained in the following sources published by The Gale Group: *Literature Criticism from 1400-1800,* Vol. 3, and *Short Story Criticism,* Vol. 31.

Horace Walpole

1717-1797

English novelist, biographer, memoirist, historian, essayist, and letter writer.

For additional information on Walpole's life and works, see *LC,* Volume 2.

INTRODUCTION

One of the most flamboyant personalities in eighteenth-century English letters, Walpole is often considered the outstanding chronicler and correspondent of his era. His *Letters,* which date from 1732 to 1797 and number in the thousands, are noted for their remarkable content as well as their distinctive style. In addition to this achievement, Walpole is widely recognized as one of England's first art historians, an influential revivalist of Gothic architecture, and the author of *The Castle of Otranto,* a work that introduced supernaturalism and mystery into the romance and is regarded as the first Gothic novel.

Biographical Information

Walpole was born into a family of old Norfolk stock which could be traced back to the last king of Britons. Horace's immediate family came into wealth during his father's political career; Sir Robert Walpole, who held many influential posts, including secretary of war and treasurer of the navy, served during the reign of George II as England's first prime minister and became the first Earl of Oxford.

From 1727 to 1734 Horace attended Eton. There he became close friends with Thomas Ashton, Richard West, and Thomas Gray. Referring to themselves as the Quadruple Alliance, the four schoolmates prided themselves on their intellectual precocity and delved into Latin classics as well as French and English literature, which they read, translated, and parodied. Along with Gray, Walpole entered Cambridge, but he did not take a degree; in 1739 he left school to travel in Europe with Gray as a companion. They toured for two years but eventually quarreled and returned to England separately. While on the Continent Walpole was elected to Parliament, and he served in that body intermittently until 1768.

In 1747, Walpole moved into a former coachman's cottage near Twickenham. He named this residence Strawberry Hill and began remodeling it in 1753, a project which grew in extravagance year by year. The original Strawberry Hill was a fairly modest dwelling; Walpole turned it into a late-medieval castle designed in the Gothic style. The architectural "committee" responsible for the castle's appearance consisted of Walpole and two of his friends, John Chute and Richard Bentley. Their primary goal was to create a structure that reflected the beauty of older English architecture, but that also captured a viewer's imagination. The result was a museum-like tribute to Gothic detail: the completed Strawberry Hill exhibited lavish examples of Gothic ornamentation, including stained-glass windows, balustrades, loggias, and hidden stairways. Walpole also established a private press at Strawberry Hill in 1757 which operated for thirty-two years and is still recognized for publishing one of the most impressive lists of titles of any private press in England, including Walpole's works and the poems of Thomas Gray.

In 1765 Walpole made the first of four extended trips to Paris, where he was received by members of the French upper class; especially noteworthy is his friendship with the socially prominent Madame du Deffand, who was twenty years his senior and with whom he corresponded until her death in 1780. While in Paris, Walpole was bedridden with a severe case of gout, to which he finally succumbed at age eighty.

Major Works

Critics generally consider Walpole's letters the masterwork for which he is most deservedly known to posterity. Many commentators support Lytton Strachey's appraisal that "the collected series of his letters forms by far the most important single correspondence in the language." The primary purpose of the letters was to entertain Walpole's readers; their secondary purpose was to inform. Therefore the letters are marked by a highly distinctive style—witty, colorful, and vividly descriptive—but they are not always factually accurate.

The only fictional work for which Walpole is widely known is his novel *The Castle of Otranto.* Although considered a seriously flawed work, *Otranto* is credited with introducing a number of important innovations that influenced the development of the Gothic novel, which enjoyed a great vogue during the late eighteenth and early nineteenth centuries. According to Walpole, *Otranto* was inspired by a dream in which he was in a castle and a gigantic armor-clad hand appeared to him at the top of a staircase. Walpole published the book anonymously under the pretense that it was an Italian manuscript written during the Last Crusade and translated by one "William Marshall." Some early reviewers were not convinced or amused by this claim: the novel was generally criticized as being preposterously unbelievable and insulting to its readers. However, the negative critical reception of *Otranto* did not prevent it from becoming extremely popular, which encouraged Walpole to reveal his authorship in the second edition. In his preface he defined the work as "an attempt to blend the two kinds of romance, the ancient and the modern." The former, he explained, relied on imagination and improbability, with the result frequently being grossly incredible; the latter attempted to copy nature, but often lacked imagination. He concluded that these elements must be adequately balanced in order to create a plausible yet interesting narrative. An admirer of legends of the Middle Ages, he incorporated their fairy-tale elements and chivalric code into a storyline which featured characters who were contemporary in speech and thought. His use of a Gothic castle and its array of machinery (including trap doors, vaults, dungeons, and rattling chains), his manipulation of the forces of nature to accentuate the sense of ominousness, and his characterizations introduce elements central to the Gothic genre.

Walpole's lesser-known fictional works include *The Mysterious Mother*, a drama in blank verse, and *Hieroglyphic Tales*. The theme of *The Mysterious Mother*—incest—was such that Walpole printed the work himself and distributed it only to selected friends. Although it has received relatively little critical comment, the drama has come to be recognized as an important forerunner of Gothic drama. In the *Hieroglyphic Tales,* an early example of automatic writing, Walpole completely defies fictional conventions of his day as well as prevailing moral taste to create works rife with incest, scatology, and unwitting cannibalism and populated by concubines, dead children, and such fantastic elements as giant hummingbirds and carts made of giant pistachio shells. The effect is one of delirium and surrealism with—some critics claim—a detectable undercurrent of Walpole's obsessions and psychological disturbances.

Critical Reception

Ambivalent assessments of Walpole and his works are conspicuously scarce. He seems to inspire the highest praise or the most acerbic criticism. A significant number of critics—most notably Thomas Babington Macauley—harshly attacked what they considered exaggeration or distortion in his correspondence, but twentieth-century critics, who have generally reevaluated Walpole's work, defend the significance of his letters as one of the most trustworthy and indispensable sources available for a thorough depiction of society, politics, and manners in eighteenth-century England. Responses to *The Castle of Otranto* have similarly varied.

General critical assessment maintains that, in spite of its important historical contributions, *Otranto*'s shortcomings are too serious to overlook. Many claim that the novel suffers from a convoluted and confusing plot, insufficient character development, and stilted dialogue, all of which discourage reader involvement. Nevertheless, these defects have not obscured *Otranto*'s influence. Both Clara Reeve and Ann Radcliffe, prominent Gothic novelists, as well as Walter Scott, acknowledged their indebtedness to Walpole's work, with Reeve calling her acclaimed novel *The Old English Baron* "the literary offspring of *The Castle of Otranto*" and Scott praising *Otranto* as "not only . . . the original and model of a peculiar species of composition, attempted and successfully executed by a man of great genius, but . . . one of the standard works of our lighter literature." All told, Walpole's works—primarily his *Letters* and *The Castle of Otranto*—are considered to be of primary importance to the history of English literature: his *Letters* as one of the most complete and entertaining records of eighteenth-century English society and *The Castle of Otranto* as the quintessential source of Gothic literary conventions.

PRINCIPAL WORKS

The Beauties: An Epistle to Mr. Eckardt, the Painter (poetry) 1746

Aedes Walpolianae; or, A Description of the Collection of Pictures at Houghton Hall in Norfolk, the Seat of the Right Honourable Sir Robert Walpole, Earl of Orford (catalog) 1747
A Letter to the Whigs, Occasioned by the "Letter to the Tories" (essay) 1747
A Letter from Xo Ho, a Chinese Philosopher at London, to His Friend Lien Chi at Peking (satire) 1757
A Catalogue of the Royal and Noble Authors of England, with Lists of Their Works 2 vols. (biography) 1758
A Dialogue between Two Great Ladies (satire) 1760
Anecdotes of Painting in England, with Some Account of the Principle Artists, and Incidental Notes on Other Arts 4 vols. (art history) 1762-71
The Opposition to the Late Minister Vindicated from the Aspersions of a Pamphlet Entitled "Considerations on the Present Dangerous Crisis" (essay) 1763
The Castle of Otranto: A Story (novel) 1765
Historic Doubts on the Life and Reign of King Richard the Third (essay) 1768
The Mysterious Mother: A Tragedy (drama) 1768
A Description of the Villa of Horace Walpole, Youngest Son of Sir Robert Walpole, Earl of Orford, at Strawberry-Hill, near Twickenham (catalog) 1774
Hieroglyphic Tales (short stories) 1785
Memoirs of the Last Ten Years of the Reign of George the Second 2 vols. (memoirs) 1822

CRITICISM

Horace Walpole (essay date 1765)

SOURCE: Preface to the Second Edition of *The Castle of Otranto,* by Horace Walpole, pp. 7-12. London: Oxford University Press, 1964.

[*In this preface, written in 1765, alpole explains his intentions in writing the book: "to blend the two kinds of romance, the ancient and the modern."*]

The favourable manner in which this little piece has been received by the public, calls upon the author to explain the grounds on which he composed it. But before he opens those motives, it is fit that he should ask pardon of his readers for having offered his work to them under the borrowed personage of a translator. As diffidence of his own abilities, and the novelty of the attempt, were his sole inducements to assume that disguise, he flatters himself he shall appear excusable. He resigned his performance to the impartial judgment of the public; determined to let it perish in obscurity, if disapproved; nor meaning to avow such a trifle, unless better judges should pronounce that he might own it without a blush.

It was an attempt to blend the two kinds of romance, the ancient and the modern. In the former all was imagination and improbability: in the latter, nature is always intended to be, and sometimes has been, copied with success. Invention has not been wanting; but the great resources of fancy have been dammed up, by a strict adherence to common life. But if in the latter species Nature has cramped imagination, she did but take her revenge, having been totally excluded from old romances. The actions, sentiments, conversations, of the heroes and heroines of ancient days were as unnatural as the machines employed to put them in motion.

The author of the following pages thought it possible to reconcile the two kinds. Desirous of leaving the powers of fancy at liberty to expatiate through the boundless realms of invention, and thence of creating more interesting situations, he wished to conduct the mortal agents in his drama according to the rules of probability; in short, to make them think, speak and act, as it might be supposed mere men and women would do in extraordinary positions. He had observed, that in all inspired writings, the personages under the dispensation of miracles, and witnesses to the most stupendous phenomena, never lose sight of their human character: whereas in the productions of romantic story, an improbable event never fails to be attended by an absurd dialogue. The actors seem to lose their senses the moment the laws of nature have lost their tone. As the public have applauded the attempt, the author must not say he was entirely unequal to the task he had undertaken: yet if the new route he has struck out shall have paved a road for men of brighter talents, he shall own with pleasure and modesty, that he was sensible the plan was capable of receiving greater embellishments than his imagination or conduct of the passions could bestow on it.

With regard to the deportment of the domestics, on which I have touched in the former preface, I will beg leave to add a few words. The simplicity of their behaviour, almost tending to excite smiles, which at first seem not consonant to the serious cast of the work, appeared to me not only not improper, but was marked designedly in that manner. My rule was nature. However grave, important, or even melancholy, the sensations of princes and heroes may be, they do not stamp the same affections on their domestics: at least the latter do not, or should not be made to express their passions in the same dignified tone. In my humble opinion, the contrast between the sublime of the one, and the *naïveté* of the other, sets the pathetic of the former in a stronger light. The very impatience which a reader feels, while delayed by the coarse pleasantries of vulgar actors from arriving at the knowledge of the important catastrophe he expects, perhaps heightens, certainly proves that he has been artfully interested in, the depending event. But I had higher authority than my own opinion for this conduct. That great master of nature, Shakespeare, was the model I copied. Let me ask if his tragedies of Hamlet and Julius Caesar would not lose a considerable share of the spirit and wonderful beauties, if the humour of the grave-diggers, the fooleries of Polonius, and the clumsy jests of the Roman citizens were omitted, or vested in heroics? Is not the eloquence of Antony, the nobler and affectedly unaffected oration of Brutus, artificially exalted by the rude bursts of nature from the mouths of their auditors? These touches remind one of the Grecian sculptor, who, to convey the idea of a Colossus within the dimensions of a seal, inserted a little boy measuring his thumb.

No, says Voltaire in his edition of Corneille, this mixture of buffoonery and solemnity is intolerable—Voltaire is a genius[1]—but not of Shakespeare's magnitude. Without recurring to disputable authority, I appeal from Voltaire to himself. I shall not avail myself of his former encomiums on our mighty poet; though the French critic has twice translated the same speech in Hamlet, some years ago in admiration, latterly in derision; and I am sorry to find that his judgment grows weaker, when it ought to be farther matured. But I shall make use of his own words, delivered on the general topic of the theatre, when he was neither thinking to recommend or decry Shakespeare's practice; consequently at a moment when Voltaire was impartial. In the preface to his Enfant prodigue, that exquisite piece of which I declare my admiration, and which, should I live twenty years longer, I trust I should never attempt to ridicule, he has these words, speaking of comedy, [but equally applicable to tragedy, if tragedy is, as surely it ought to be, a picture of human life; nor can I conceive why occasional pleasantry ought more to be banished from the tragic scene, than pathetic seriousness from the comic] *On y voit un melange de serieux et de plaisanterie, de comique et de touchant;* souvent même une seule avanture *produit tous ces contrastes.* Rien *n'est si commun qu'une maison dans laquelle* un pere gronde, une fille occupée de sa passion pleure; *le fils se moque des deux, et quelques parens prennent part differemment à la scene, &c. Nous n'inferons pas de là que toute comedie doive avoir des scenes de bouffonnerie et des scenes attendrissantes: il y a beaucoup de tres bonnes pieces où il ne regne que de la gayeté; d'autres toutes serieuses; d'autres melangées: d'autres où l'attendrissement va jusques aux larmes:* il ne faut donner l'exclusion à aucun genre: *et si l'on me demandoit, quel genre est le meilleur, je repondrois, celui qui est le mieux traité.* Surely if a comedy may be *toute serieuse,* tragedy may now and then, soberly, be indulged in a smile. Who shall proscribe it? Shall the critic, who in self-defence declares that *no kind* ought to be excluded from comedy, give laws to Shakespeare?

I am aware that the preface from whence I have quoted these passages does not stand in monsieur de Voltaire's name, but in that of his editor; yet who doubts that the editor and author were the same person? Or where is the editor, who has so happily possessed himself of his author's style and brilliant ease of argument? These passages were indubitably the genuine sentiments of that great writer. In his epistle to Maffei, prefixed to his Merope, he delivers almost the same opinion, though I doubt with a little irony. I will repeat his words, and then give my reason for quoting them. After translating a passage in Maffei's Merope, monsieur de Voltaire adds, *Tous ces traits sont naïfs: tout y est convenable à ceux que vous introduisez sur la scene,* et aux mœurs que vous leur donnez. *Ces familiarités naturelles eussent été, à ce que je crois, bien reçues dans Athenes; mais Paris et notre parterre veulent une autre espece de simplicité.* I doubt, I say, whether there is not a grain of sneer in this and other passages of that epistle; yet the force of truth is not damaged by being

tinged with ridicule. Maffei was to represent a Grecian story: surely the Athenians were as competent judges of Grecian manners, and of the propriety of introducing them, as the parterre of Paris. On the contrary, says Voltaire [and I cannot but admire his reasoning] there were but ten thousand citizens at Athens, and Paris has near eight hundred thousand inhabitants, among whom one may reckon thirty thousand judges of dramatic works.—Indeed!—But allowing so numerous a tribunal, I believe this is the only instance in which it was ever pretended that thirty thousand persons, living near two thousand years after the æra in question, were, upon the mere face of the poll, declared better judges than the Grecians themselves of what ought to be the manners of a tragedy written on a Grecian story.

I will not enter into a discussion of the *espece de simplicité,* which the *parterre* of Paris demands, nor of the shackles with which *the thirty thousand judges* have cramped their poetry, the chief merit of which, as I gather from repeated passages in The New Commentary on Corneille, consists in vaulting in spite of those fetters; a merit which, if true, would reduce poetry from the lofty effort of imagination, to a puerile and most contemptible labour—*difficiles nugæ* with a witness! I cannot help however mentioning a couplet, which to my English ears always sounded as the flattest and most trifling instance of circumstantial propriety; but which Voltaire, who has dealt so severely with nine parts in ten of Corneille's works, has singled out to defend in Racine;

De son appartement cette porte est prochaine,
Et cette autre conduit dans celui de la reine.

In English,

To Cæsar's *closet through this door you come,*
And t'other leads to the queen's drawing-
room.

Unhappy Shakespeare! hadst thou made Rosencrans inform his compeer Guildenstern of the ichnography of the palace of Copenhagen, instead of presenting us with a moral dialogue between the prince of Denmark and the grave-digger, the illuminated pit of Paris would have been instructed a *second time* to adore thy talents.

The result of all I have said is to shelter my own daring under the cannon of the brightest genius this country, at least, has produced. I might have pleaded, that having created a new species of romance, I was at liberty to lay down what rules I thought fit for the conduct of it: but I should be more proud of having imitated, however faintly, weakly, and at a distance, so masterly a pattern, than to enjoy the entire merit of invention, unless I could have marked my work with genius as well as with originality. Such as it is, the public have honoured it sufficiently, whatever rank their suffrages allot to it.

Notes

[1] The following remark is foreign to the present question, yet excusable in an Englishman, who is willing to think that the severe criticisms of so masterly a writer as Voltaire on our immortal countryman, may have been the effusions of wit and precipitation, rather than the result of judgment and attention. May not the critic's skill in the force and powers of our language have been as incorrect and incompetent as his knowledge of our history? Of the latter his own pen has dropped glaring evidence. In his preface to Thomas Corneille's Earl of Essex, monsieur de Voltaire allows that the truth of history has been grossly perverted in that piece. In excuse he pleads, that when Corneille wrote, the noblesse of France were much unread in English story; but now, says the commentator, that they study it, such misrepresentation would not be suffered————Yet forgetting that the period of ignorance is lapsed, and that it is not very necessary to instruct the knowing, he undertakes from the overflowing of his own reading to give the nobility of his own country a detail of queen Elizabeth's favourites—of whom, says he, Robert Dudley was the first, and the earl of Leicester the second.————Could one have believed that it could be necessary to inform monsieur de Voltaire himself, that Robert Dudley and the earl of Leicester were the same person?

Friedrich Melchior Grimm (essay date 1767

SOURCE: *Historical and Literary Memoirs and Anecdotes Selected from the Correspondence of Baron De Grimm . . . Between the Years 1753 and 1969,* and reprinted in *Horace Walpole: the Critical Heritage,* edited by Peter Sabor, Routledge and Kegan Paul, 1987.

[*In the following excerpt from his* Memoirs, *Grimm expresses a favorable opinion of* The Castle of Otranto.]

I alluded, on a former occasion, to a romance, in the old Gothic style, written by Mr. Horace Walpole, son to the celebrated English minister, and author of the letter from the King of Prussia to Rousseau, which was made by the latter the foundation of his quarrel with Mr. Hume. Mr. Walpole is the author of many other things besides the romance in question; his works must not be judged as those of a man of letters by profession, but as amusements of the leisure hours of a man of quality. A translation of his Gothic romance, which is entitled, **The Castle of Otranto,** has just been published.[1] It is a series of supernatural appearances, put together under the most interesting form imaginable. Let one be ever so much of a philosopher, that enormous helmet, that monstrous sword, the portrait which starts from its frame and walks away, the skeleton of the hermit praying in the oratory, the vaults, the subterranean passages, the moonshine,—all these things make the hair of the sage stand on end, as much as that of the child and his nurse; so much are the sources of the marvellous the same to all men. It is true that nothing very important results at last from all these wonders, but the aim of the author was to amuse, and he certainly cannot be reproached with having missed his aim. . . .

Notes

[1] *Le Château d'Otrante,* tr. Marc-Antoine Eidous, 1767. In his 'Short Notes' for March 1767, Walpole calls it a 'bad translation'. . . .

Walter Scott (essay date 1811)

SOURCE: Introduction to *The Castle of Otranto,* by Horace Walpole, reprinted in *Walpole: The Critical Heritage,* edited by Peter Sabor, Routledge & Kegan Paul, 1987.

[*In the following introduction to the 1811 edition of* The Castle of Otranto, *Scott cites Walpole's originality in initiating Gothic literature.*]

The **Castle of Otranto** is remarkable not only for the wild interest of the story, but as the first modern attempt to found a tale of amusing fiction upon the basis of the ancient romances of chivalry. The neglect and discredit of these venerable legends had commenced so early as the reign of Queen Elizabeth, when, as we learn from the criticism of the times, Spenser's fairy web was rather approved on account of the mystic and allegorical interpretation, than the plain and obvious meaning of his chivalrous pageant. The drama, which shortly afterwards rose into splendour, and versions from the innumerable novelists of Italy, supplied to the higher class the amusement which their fathers received from the legends of *Don Belianis* and the *Mirror of Knighthood;*[1] and the huge volumes which were once the pastime of nobles and princess, shorn of their ornaments, and shrunk into abridgements, were banished to the kitchen and nursery, or, at best, to the hall-window of the old-fashioned country manor-house. Under Charles II the prevailing taste for French literature dictated the introduction of those dullest of dull folios, the romances of Calprenede and Scuderi, works which hover between the ancient tale of chivalry and the modern novel. The alliance was so ill conceived, that they retained all the insufferable length and breadth of the prose volumes of chivalry, the same detailed account of reiterated and unvaried combats, the same unnatural and extravagant turn of incident, without the rich and sublime strokes of genius, and vigour of imagination, which often distinguished the early romance; while they exhibited all the sentimental languor and flat love-intrigue of the novel, without being enlivened by its variety of character, just traits of feeling, or acute views of life. Such an ill-imagined species of composition retained its ground longer than might have been expected, only because these romances were called works of entertainment, and there was nothing better to supply their room. Even in the days of the *Spectator, Clelia, Cleopatra,* and the *Grand Cyrus,* (as that precious folio is christened by its butcherly translator,)[2] were the favourite closet companions of the fair sex. But this unnatural taste began to give way early in the seventeenth century; and, about the middle of it, was entirely superseded by the works of Le Sage, Richardson, Fielding, and Smollett; so that even the very name of romance, now so venerable in the ear of antiquaries and book-collectors, was almost forgotten at the time the *Castle of Otranto* made its first appearance.

The peculiar situation of Horace Walpole, the ingenious author of this work, was such as gave him a decided predilection for what may be called the Gothic style, a term which he contributed not a little to rescue from the bad fame into which it had fallen, being currently used before his time to express whatever was in pointed and diametrical opposition to the rules of true taste. . . .

As, in his model of a Gothic modern mansion, our author had studiously endeavoured to fit to the purposes of modern convenience, or luxury, the rich, varied, and complicated tracery and carving of the ancient cathedral so, in the *Castle of Otranto,* it was his object to unite the marvellous turn of incident, and imposing tone of chivalry, exhibited in the ancient romance, with that accurate exhibition of human character, and contrast of feelings and passions, which is, or ought to be, delineated in the modern novel. But Mr Walpole, being uncertain of the reception which a work upon so new a plan might experience from the world, and not caring, perhaps, to encounter the ridicule which would have attended its failure, the *Castle of Otranto* was ushered into the world as a translation from the Italian. It does not seem that the authenticity of the narrative was suspected. Mr Gray writes to Mr Walpole, on 30th December, 1764: 'I have received the *Castle of Otranto,* and return you my thanks for it. It engages our attention here, (*i.e.* at Cambridge,) makes some of us cry a little; and all, in general, afraid to go to bed o'nights. We take it for a translation; and should believe it to be a true story, if it were not for St Nicholas.' The friends of the author were probably soon permitted to peep beneath the veil he had thought proper to assume; and, in the second edition, it was altogether withdrawn by a preface, in which the tendency and nature of the work are shortly commented upon and explained. From the following passage, translated from a letter by the author to Madame Deffand,[3] it would seem that he repented of having laid aside his incognito; and, sensitive to criticism, like most dilletante authors, was rather more hurt by the raillery of those who liked not his tale of chivalry, than gratified by the applause of his admirers. 'So they have translated my *Castle of Otranto,* probably in ridicule of the author.[4] So be it;—however, I beg you will let their raillery pass in silence. Let the critics have their own way; they give me no uneasiness. I have not written the book for the present age, which will endure nothing but *cold common sense.* I confess to you, my dear friend, (and you will think me madder than ever,) that this is the only one of my works with which I am myself pleased; I have given reins to my imagination till I became on fire with the visions and feelings which it excited. I have composed it in defiance of rules, of critics, and of philosophers; and it seems to me just so much the better for that very reason. I am even persuaded, that some time hereafter, when taste shall resume the place which philosophy now occupies, my poor *Castle* will find admirers: we have actually a few among us already, for I am just publishing the third edition.[5] I do not say this in order to mendicate your approbation.[a] I told you from the beginning you would not like the book,—your visions are all in a different style. I am not sorry that the translator has given the second preface; the first, however, accords best with the style of the fiction. I wished it to be believed ancient, and almost every body was imposed upon.' If the public applause, however, was sufficiently qualified by the voice of censure to alarm the feelings of the author, the continued demand for various editions of the *Castle of Otranto* showed how high the work really stood in popular estimation, and probably eventually reconciled Mr Walpole to the taste of his own age. This Romance has been justly considered not only as the original and model of a peculiar species of composition, but as one of the standard works of our lighter literature. A few remarks both on the book itself, and on the class to which it belongs, have been judged an apposite introduction to an edition of the *Castle of Otranto,* which the publishers have endeavoured to execute in a style of elegance corresponding to the estimation in which they hold the work, and the genius of the author.

It is doing injustice to Mr Walpole's memory to allege, that all which he aimed at in the *Castle of Otranto* was 'the art of exciting surprise and horror;' or, in other words, the appeal to that secret and reserved feeling of love for the marvellous and supernatural, which occupies a hidden corner in almost every one's bosom. Were this all which he had attempted, the means by which he sought to attain his purpose might, with justice, be termed both clumsy and puerile. But Mr Walpole's purpose was both more difficult of attainment, and more important when attained. It was his object to draw such a picture of domestic life and manners, during the feudal times, as might actually have existed, and to paint it chequered and agitated by the action of supernatural machinery, such as the superstition of the period received as matter of devout credulity. The natural parts of the narrative are so contrived, that they associate themselves with the marvellous occurrences; and, by the force of that association, render those *speciosa miracula*[6] striking and impressive, though our cooler reason admits their impossibility. Indeed to produce, in a well-cultivated mind, any portion of that surprise and fear which is founded on supernatural events, the frame and tenor of the whole story must be adjusted in perfect harmony with this main-spring of the interest. He who, in early youth, has happened to pass a solitary night in one of the few ancient mansions which the fashion of more modern times has left undespoiled of their original furniture, has probably experienced, that the gigantic and preposterous figures dimly visible in the defaced tapestry, the remote clang of the distant doors which divide him from living society, the deep darkness which involves the high and fretted roof of the apartment, the dimly-seen pictures of ancient knights, renowned for their valour, and perhaps for their crimes, the varied and indistinct sounds which disturb the silent desolation of a half-deserted mansion; and, to crown all, the feeling that carries us back to ages of feudal power and papal superstition, join together to excite a corresponding sensation of supernatural awe, if not of terror. It is in such situations, when superstition becomes contagious, that we listen with respect, and even with dread, to the legends which are our sport in the garish light of sun-shine, and amid the dissipating sights and sounds of every-day life. Now it seems to have been Walpole's object to attain, by the minute accuracy of a fable, sketched with singular attention to the costume of the period in which the scene was laid, that same association which might prepare his reader's mind for the reception of prodigies congenial to the creed and feelings of the actors. His feudal tyrant, his distressed damsel, his resigned, yet dignified, churchman,—the Castle itself, with its feudal arrangement of dungeons, trap-doors, oratories, and galleries, the incidents of the trial, the chivalrous procession, and the combat;—in short, the scene, the performers, and action, so far as it is natural, form the accompaniments of his spectres and his miracles, and have the same effect on the mind of the reader that the appearance and drapery of such a chamber as we have described may produce upon that of a temporary inmate. This was a task which required no little learning, no ordinary degree of fancy, no common portion of genius, to execute. The association of which we have spoken is of a nature peculiarly delicate, and subject to be broken and disarranged. It is, for instance, almost impossible to build such a modern Gothic structure as shall impress us with the feelings we have endeavoured to describe. It may be grand, or it may be gloomy; it may excite magnificent or melancholy ideas; but it must fail in bringing forth the sensation of supernatural awe, connected with halls that have echoed to the sounds of remote generations, and have been pressed by the footsteps of those who have long since passed

away. Yet Horace Walpole has attained in composition, what, as an architect, he must have felt beyond the power of his art. The remote and superstitious period in which his scene is laid, the art with which he has furnished forth its Gothic decorations, the sustained, and, in general, the dignified tone of feudal manners, prepare us gradually for the favourable reception of prodigies which, though they could not really have happened at any period, were consistent with the belief of all mankind at that in which the action is placed. It was, therefore, the author's object, not merely to excite surprise and terror, by the introduction of supernatural agency, but to wind up the feelings of his reader till they became for a moment identified with those of a ruder age, which

Held each strange tale devoutly true.[7]

The difficulty of attaining this nice accuracy of delineation may be best estimated by comparing the *Castle of Otranto* with the less successful efforts of later writers; where, amid all their attempts to assume the tone of antique chivalry, something occurs in every chapter so decidedly incongruous, as at once reminds us of an ill-sustained masquerade, in which ghosts, knights-errant, magicians, and damsels gent, are all equipped in hired dresses from the same warehouse in Tavistock-street.

There is a remarkable particular in which Mr Walpole's steps have been departed from by the most distinguished of his followers.

Romantic narrative is of two kinds,—that which, being in itself possible, may be matter of belief at any period; and that which, though held impossible by more enlightened ages, was yet consonant with the faith of earlier times. The subject of the *Castle of Otranto* is of the latter class. Mrs Radcliffe, a name not to be mentioned without the respect due to genius, has endeavoured to effect a compromise between those different styles of narrative, by referring her prodigies to an explanation, founded on natural causes, in the latter chapters of her romances. To this improvement upon the Gothic romance there are so many objections, that we own ourselves inclined to prefer, as more simple and impressive, the narrative of Walpole, which details supernatural incidents as they would have been readily believed and received in the eleventh or twelfth century. In the first place, the reader feels indignant at discovering he has been cheated into a sympathy with terrors which are finally explained as having proceeded from some very simple cause; and the interest of a second reading is entirely destroyed by his having been admitted behind the scenes at the conclusion of the first. Secondly, The precaution of relieving our spirits from the influence of supposed supernatural terror, seems as unnecessary in a work of professed fiction, as that of the prudent Bottom, who proposed that the human face of the representative of his lion should appear from under his masque, and acquaint the audience plainly that he was a man as other men, and nothing more than Snug the joiner.[8] Lastly, These substitutes for supernatural agency are frequently to the full as improbable as the machinery which they are introduced to explain away and to supplant. The reader, who is required to admit the belief of supernatural interference, understands precisely what is demanded of him; and, if he be a gentle reader, throws his mind into the attitude best adapted to humour the deceit which is presented for his entertainment, and grants, for the time of perusal, the premises on which the fable depends.[b] But if the author voluntarily binds himself to account for all the wondrous occurrences which he introduces, we are entitled to exact that the explanation shall be natural, easy, ingenious, and complete. Every reader of such works must remember instances in which the explanation of mysterious circumstances in the narrative has proved equally, nay, even more incredible, than if they had been accounted for by the agency of supernatural beings. For the most incredulous must allow, that the interference of such agency is more possible than that an effect resembling it should be produced by an inadequate cause. But it is unnecessary to enlarge further on a part of the subject, which we have only mentioned to exculpate our author from the charge of using machinery more clumsy than his tale from its nature required. The bold assertion of the actual existence of phantoms and apparitions seems to us to harmonise much more naturally with the manners of feudal times, and to produce a more powerful effect upon the reader's mind, than any attempt to reconcile the superstitious credulity of feudal ages with the philosophic scepticism of our own, by referring those prodigies to the operation of fulminating powder, combined mirrors, magic lanthorns, trapdoors, speaking trumpets, and such like apparatus of German phantasmagoria.

It cannot, however, be denied, that the character of the supernatural machinery in the **Castle of Otranto** is liable to objections. Its action and interference is rather too frequent, and presses too hard and constantly upon the same feelings in the reader's mind, to the hazard of diminishing the elasticity of the spring upon which it should operate. The fund of fearful sympathy which can be afforded by a modern reader to a tale of wonder, is much diminished by the present habits of life and mode of education. Our ancestors could wonder and thrill through all the mazes of an interminable metrical romance of fairy land, and of enchantment, the work perhaps of some

> Prevailing poet, whose undoubting mind
> Believed the magic wonders which he sung.[9]

But our habits and feelings and belief are different, and a transient, though vivid, impression is all that can be excited by a tale of wonder even in the most fanciful mind of the present day. By the too frequent recurrence of his prodigies, Mr Walpole ran, perhaps, his greatest risk of awakening *la raison froide,* that cold common sense, which he justly deemed the greatest enemy of the effect which he hoped to produce. It may be added also, that the supernatural occurrences of the **Castle of Otranto** are brought forward into too strong day-light, and marked by an over degree of distinctness and accuracy of outline. A mysterious obscurity seems congenial at least, if not essential, to our ideas of disembodied spirits, and the gigantic limbs of the ghost of Alphonso, as described by the terrified domestics, are somewhat too distinct and corporeal to produce the feelings which their appearance is intended to excite. This fault, however, if it be one, is more than compensated by the high merit of many of the marvellous incidents in the romance. The descent of the picture of Manfred's ancestor, although it borders on extravagance, is finely introduced, and interrupts an interesting dialogue with striking effect. We have heard it observed, that the animated figure should rather have been a statue than a picture. We greatly doubt the justice of the criticism. The advantage of the colouring induces us decidedly to prefer Mr Walpole's fiction to the proposed substitute. There are few who have not felt, at some period of their childhood, a sort of terror from the manner in which the eye of an ancient portrait appears to fix that of the spectator from every point of view. It is, perhaps, hypercritical to remark, (what, however, Walpole of all authors might have been expected to attend to,) that the time assigned to the action, being about the eleventh century, is rather too early for the introduction of a full-length portrait. The apparition of the skeleton hermit to the prince of Vicenza was long accounted a master-piece of the horrible; but of late the valley of Jehosophat could hardly supply the dry bones necessary for the exhibition of similar spectres, so that injudicious and repeated imitation has, in some degree, injured the effect of its original model. What is most striking in the **Castle of Otranto,** is the manner in which the various prodigious appearances, bearing each upon the other, and all upon the accomplishment of the ancient prophecy, denouncing the ruin of the house of Manfred, gradually prepare us for the grand catastrophe. The moon-light vision of Alphonso dilated to immense magnitude, the astonished group of spectators in the front, and the shattered ruins of the castle in the back-ground, is briefly and sublimely described. We know no passage of similar merit, unless it be the apparition of Fadzean in an ancient Scottish poem.[c]

That part of the romance which depends upon human feelings and agency, is conducted with the dramatic talent which afterwards was so conspicuous in the **Mysterious Mother.** The persons are indeed rather generic than individual, but this was in a degree necessary to a plan, calculated rather to exhibit a general view of society and manners during the times which the author's imagination loved to contemplate, than the more minute shades and discriminating points of particular characters. But the actors in the romance are strikingly drawn, with bold outlines becoming the age and nature of the story. Feudal tyranny was, perhaps, never better exemplified, than in the character of Manfred. He has the courage, the art, the duplicity, the ambition of a barbarous chieftain of the dark ages, yet with touches of remorse and natural feeling, which preserve some sympathy for him when his pride is quelled, and his race extinguished. The pious monk, and the patient Hippolita, are well contrasted with this selfish and tyrannical prince. Theodore is the juvenile hero of a romantic tale, and Matilda has more interesting sweetness than usually belongs to its heroine. As the character of Isabella is studiously kept down, in order to relieve that of the daughter of Manfred, few readers are pleased with the concluding insinuation, that she became at length the bride of Theodore. This is in some degree a departure from the rules of chivalry; and, however natural an occurrence in common life, rather injures the magic illusions of romance. In other respects, making allowance for the extraordinary incidents of a dark and tempestuous age, the story, so far as within the course of natural events, is happily detailed, its progress is uniform, its events interesting and well combined, and the conclusion grand, tragical, and affecting.

The style of the *Castle of Otranto* is pure and correct English of the earlier and more classical standard. Mr Walpole rejected, upon taste and principle, those heavy though powerful auxiliaries which Dr Johnson imported from the Latin language, and which have since proved to many a luckless wight, who has essayed to use them, as unmanageable as the gauntlets of Eryx,

> —————————et pondus et ipsa
> Huc illuc vinclorum immensa volumina
> versat.[10]

Neither does the purity of Mr Walpole's language, and the simplicity of his narrative, admit that luxuriant, florid, and high-varnished landscape painting with which Mrs Radcliffe often adorned, and not unfrequently incumbered, her kindred romances. Description, for its own sake, is scarcely once attempted in the *Castle of Otranto;* and if authors would consider how very much this restriction tends to realise narrative, they might be tempted to abridge at least the showy and wordy exuberance of a style fitter for poetry than prose. It is for the dialogue that Walpole reserves his strength; and it is remarkable how, while conducting his mortal agents with all the art of a modern dramatist, he adheres to the sustained tone of chivalry, which marks the period of the action. This is not attained by patching his narrative or dialogue with glossarial terms, or antique phraseology, but by taking care to exclude all that can awaken modern associations. In the one case,

his romance would have resembled a modern dress, preposterously decorated with antique ornaments; in its present shape, he has retained the form of the ancient armour, but not its rust and cobwebs. In illustration of what is above stated, we refer the reader to the first interview of Manfred with the prince of Vicenza, where the manners and language of chivalry are finely painted, as well as the perturbation of conscious guilt confusing itself in attempted exculpation, even before a mute accuser. The characters of the inferior domestics have been considered as not bearing a proportion sufficiently dignified to the rest of the story. But this is a point on which the author has pleaded his own cause fully in the original prefaces.

We have only to add, in conclusion to these desultory remarks, that if Horace Walpole, who led the way in this new species of literary composition, has been surpassed by some of his followers in diffuse brilliancy of description, and perhaps in the art of detaining the mind of the reader in a state of feverish and anxious suspence, through a protracted and complicated narrative, more will yet remain with him than the single merit of originality and invention. The applause due to chastity and precision of style, to a happy combination of supernatural agency with human interest, to a tone of feudal manners and language, sustained by characters strongly drawn and well discriminated, and to unity of action producing scenes alternately of interest and of grandeur;—the applause, in fine, which cannot be denied to him who can excite the passions of fear and of pity, must be awarded to the author of the *Castle of Otranto.*

Notes

[a] Madame Deffand had mentioned having read the *Castle of Otranto* twice over; but she did not add a word of approbation. She blamed the translator for giving the second preface, chiefly because she thought it might commit Walpole with Voltaire . . .

[b] There are instances to the contrary however. For example, that stern votary of severe truth, who cast aside *Gulliver's Travels* as containing a parcel of improbable fictions.

[c] This spectre, the ghost of a follower he had slain upon suspicion of treachery, appeared to no less a person than Wallace, the champion of Scotland, in the ancient castle of Gask-hall. [See the 'Life of Wallace' by Henry the Minstrel in G. Ellis, *Specimens of Ancient English Poetry,* 1803.]

[1] *Don Belianis de Grecia* (1547-9) by Jeronimo Fernandez; *The Mirror of Knighthood,* tr. of *Espeio de Caballerias,* by Diego Ortunez (1562), *et al.*

[2] *Clélié* (1654-60) and *Artamène, ou le Grand Cyrus* (1649-53) by Madeleine de Scudéri; *Cléopatre* (1647-

56) by Gauthier de Costes de la Calprenède. The 'butch-erly translator' of the *Grand Cyrus* (1653-5) is the pseudonymous 'F.G. gent.'

³ 13 March 1767.

⁴ See No. 21, n. 1 for Walpole's view of this translation.

⁵ It had already been published in 1766.

⁶ Apparent miracles.

⁷ Not identified.

⁸ *A Midsummer Night's Dream*, III, i.

⁹ William Collins, *Ode on the Popular Superstitions of the Highlands of Scotland* (1749), ll. 198-9.

¹⁰ 'Turns this way and that the thongs' huge and ponderous folds'; Virgil, *Aeneid*, v, 407-8.

John Dunlop (essay date 1816)

SOURCE: *The History of Fiction*, 2nd. ed., and reprinted in *Walpole: The Critical Heritage*, edited by Peter Sabor, Routledge & Kegan Paul, 1987.

[*In the following excerpt from* The History of Fiction *(1814, 1816), Dunlop declares* The Castle of Otranto *to be true to its Gothicism but a failure at meeting Walpole's intentions.*]

The production was ill received on its first appearance, and the extravagant commendations heaped on the imaginary author by the real one, appear abundantly absurd, now that the deception has been discovered.

The work is declared by Mr Walpole to be an attempt to blend the ancient romance and modern novel; but, if by the ancient romance be meant the tales of chivalry, the extravagance of the *Castle of Otranto* has no resemblance to their machinery. What analogy have skulls or skeletons—sliding pannels—damp vaults—trap-doors—and dismal apartments, to the tented fields of chivalry and its airy enchantments?

It has been much doubted, whether the *Castle of Otranto* was seriously or comically intended; if seriously, it is a most feeble attempt to excite awe or terror; an immense helmet is a wretched instrument for inspiring supernatural dread, and the machinery is so violent that it destroys the effect it was intended to raise. A sword which requires a hundred men to lift it—blood dropping from the nose of a statue—the hero imprisoned in a helmet, resemble not a first and serious attempt at a new species of composition, but look

as if devised in ridicule of preceding extravagance, as *Don Quixote* was written to expose the romances of chivalry, by an aggravated representation of their absurdities.

But, whether seriously intended or written in jest, the story of the *Castle of Otranto* contains all the elements of this species of composition. We have hollow groans, gothic windows that exclude the light, and trap-doors with flights of steps descending to dismal vaults. The deportment, too, of the domestics, the womanish terrors of waiting-maids, and the delay produced by their coarse pleasantries and circumlocutions, have been imitated in all similar productions. For this incongruity, Mr Walpole offers as an apology, that Shakspeare was the model he copied, who, in his deepest tragedies, has introduced the coarse humour of grave-diggers and clumsy jests of Roman citizens. He argues, that however important may be the duties, and however grave and melancholy the sensations, of heroes and princes, the same affections are not stamped on their domestics, at least they do not express their passions in the same dignified tone, and the contrast thus produced between the sublime of the one, and the *naiveté* of the other, sets the pathetic of the former in a stronger point of view.

William Hazlitt (essay date 1819)

SOURCE: *The Complete Works of William Hazlitt*, 1933. Reprinted in *Walpole: The Critical Heritage*, edited by Peter Sabor, Routledge & Kegan Paul, 1987.

[*In the following excerpt from his* Lectures on the Comic Writers, *delivered to the Surrey Institute in 1819, Hazlitt declares the ineffectiveness of Walpole's supernatural imagery.*]

The Castle of Otranto (which is supposed to have led the way to this style of writing) is, to my notion, dry, meagre, and without effect. It is done upon false principles of taste. The great hand and arm, which are thrust into the court-yard, and remain there all day long, are the pasteboard machinery of a pantomime; they shock the senses, and have no purchase upon the imagination. They are a matter-of-fact impossibility; a fixture, and no longer a phantom. *Quod sic mihi ostendis, incredulus odi.*¹ By realising the chimeras of ignorance and fear, begot upon shadows and dim likenesses, we take away the very grounds of credulity and superstition; and, as in other cases, by facing out the imposture, betray the secret to the contempt and laughter of the spectators.

Notes

¹ 'Whatever you thus show me openly leaves me in-

credulous and revolted'; Horace, *Art of Poetry,* l. 188.

Edith Birkhead (essay date 1921)

SOURCE: "The Beginnings of Gothic Romance" in *The Tale of Terror: A Study of the Gothic Romance,* Constable 4 Co., 1921.

[*In this excerpt, Birkhead enumerates the qualities of* The Castle of Otranto *that appealed to the popular taste of Walpole's contemporaries and briefly describes its legacy for later romances.*]

To Horace Walpole, whose **Castle of Otranto** was published on Christmas Eve, 1764, must be assigned the honour of having introduced the Gothic romance and of having made it fashionable. Diffident as to the success of so "wild" a story in an age devoted to good sense and reason, he sent forth his mediaeval tale disguised as a translation from the Italian of "Onuphrio Muralto," by William Marshall. It was only after it had been received with enthusiasm that he confessed the authorship. As he explained frankly in a letter to his friend Mason: "It is not everybody that may in this country play the fool with impunity."[1] That Walpole regarded his story merely as a fanciful, amusing trifle is clear from the letter he wrote to Miss Hannah More reproving her for putting so frantic a thing into the hands of a Bristol milkwoman who wrote poetry in her leisure hours.[2] **The Castle of Otranto** was but another manifestation of that admiration for the Gothic which had found expression fourteen years earlier in his miniature castle at Strawberry Hill, with its old armour and "lean windows fattened with rich saints."[3] The word "Gothic" in the early eighteenth century was used as a term of reproach. To Addison, Siena Cathedral was but a "barbarous" building, which might have been a miracle of architecture, had our forefathers "only been instructed in the right way."[4] Pope in his *Preface to Shakespeare* admits the strength and majesty of the Gothic, but deplores its irregularity. In *Letters on Chivalry and Romance,* published two years before **The Castle of Otranto,** Hurd pleads that Spenser's *Faerie Queene* should be read and criticised as a Gothic, not a classical, poem. He clearly recognises the right of the Gothic to be judged by laws of its own. When the nineteenth century is reached the epithet has lost all tinge of blame, and has become entirely one of praise. From the time when he began to build his castle, in 1750, Walpole's letters abound in references to the Gothic, and he confesses once: "In the heretical corner of my heart I adore the Gothic building."[5] At Strawberry Hill the hall and staircase were his special delight and they probably formed the background of that dream in which he saw a gigantic hand in armour on the staircase of an ancient castle. When Dr. Burney visited Walpole's home in 1786 he remarked on the striking recollections of **The Castle of Otranto,** brought to mind by "the deep shade in which some of his an-tique portraits were placed and the lone sort of look of the unusually shaped apartments in which they were hung."[6] We know how in idle moments Walpole loved to brood on the picturesque past, and we can imagine his falling asleep, after the arrival of a piece of armour for his collection, with his head full of plans for the adornment of his cherished castle. His story is but an expansion of this dilettante's nightmare. His interest in things mediaeval was not that of an antiquary, but rather that of an artist who loves things old because of their age and beauty. In a delightfully gay letter to his friend, George Montagu, referring flippantly to his appointment as Deputy Ranger of Rockingham Forest, he writes, after drawing a vivid picture of a "Robin Hood reformé"; "Visions, you know, have always been my pasture; and so far from growing old enough to quarrel with their emptiness, I almost think there is no wisdom comparable to that of exchanging what is called the realities of life for dreams. Old castles, old pictures, old histories and the babble of old people make one live back into centuries that cannot disappoint one. One holds fast and surely what is past. The dead have exhausted their power of deceiving—one can trust Catherine of Medicis now. In short, you have opened a new landscape to my fancy; and my lady Beaulieu will oblige me as much as you, if she puts the long bow into your hands. I don't know, but the idea may produce some other **Castle of Otranto.**"[7] So Walpole came near to anticipating the greenwood scenes of *Ivanhoe.* The decking and trappings of chivalry filled him with boyish delight, and he found in the glitter and colour of the middle ages a refuge from the prosaic dullness of the eighteenth century. A visit from "a Luxembourg, a Lusignan and a Montfort" awoke in his whimsical fancy a mental image of himself in the guise of a mediaeval baron: "I never felt myself so much in **The Castle of Otranto.** It sounded as if a company of noble crusaders were come to sojourn with me before they embarked for the Holy Land";[8] and when he heard of the marvellous adventures of a large wolf who had caused a panic in Lower Languedoc, he was reminded of the enchanted monster of old romance and declared that, had he known of the creature earlier, it should have appeared in **The Castle of Otranto.**[9] "I have taken to astronomy," he declares on another occasion, "now that the scale is enlarged enough to satisfy my taste, who love gigantic ideas—do not be afraid; I am not going to write a second part to **The Castle of Otranto,** nor another account of the Patagonians who inhabit the new Brobdingnag planet."[10] These unstudied utterances reveal, perhaps more clearly than Walpole's deliberate confessions about his book, the mood of irresponsible, light-hearted gaiety in which he started on his enterprise. If we may rely on Walpole's account of its composition, **The Castle of Otranto** was fashioned rapidly in a white heat of excitement, but the creation of the story probably cost him more effort than he would have us believe. The result, at least, lacks spontaneity. We never feel for a moment that we are living invisible amidst the characters, but we sit aloof like Puck, thinking: "Lord, what fools these mortals be!" His supernatural machinery is as undignified as the pantomime properties of Jack the Giant-killer. The huge body scattered piecemeal about the castle, the unwieldy sabre borne by a hundred men, the helmet "tempestuously agitated," and even the "skeleton in a hermit's cowl" are not only unalarming but mildly ridiculous. Yet to the readers of his day the story was captivating and entrancing. It satisfied a real craving for the romantic and marvellous. The first edition of five hundred copies was sold out in two months, and others followed rapidly. The story was dramatised by Robert Jephson and produced at Covent Garden Theatre under the title of *The Count of Narbonne,* with an epilogue by Malone. It was staged again later in Dublin, Kemble playing the title rôle. It was translated into French, German and Italian. In England its success was immediate, though several years elapsed before it was imitated. Gray, to whom the story was first attributed, wrote of it in March, 1765: "It engages our attention here (at Cambridge), makes some of us cry a little, and all in general afraid to go to bed o' nights." Mason praised it, and Walpole's letters refer repeatedly to the vogue it enjoyed. This widespread popularity is an indication of the eagerness with which readers of 1765 desired to escape from the present and to revel for a time in strange, bygone centuries. Although Walpole regarded the composition of his Gothic story as a whim, his love of the past was shared by others of his generation. Of this Macpherson's *Ossian* (1760-3), Hurd's *Letters on Chivalry and Romance* (1762), and Percy's *Reliques* (1765), are, each in its fashion, a sufficient proof. The half-century from 1760 to 1810 showed remarkably definite signs of a renewed interest in things written between 1100 and 1650, which had been neglected for a century or more. *The Castle of Otranto,* which was "an attempt to blend the marvellous of old story with the natural of modern novels" is an early symptom of this revulsion to the past; and it exercised a charm on Scott as well as on Mrs. Radcliffe and her school. *The Castle of Otranto* is significant, not because of its intrinsic merit, but because of its power in shaping the destiny of the novel.

The outline of the plot is worth recording for the sake of tracing ancestral likenesses when we reach the later romances. The only son of Manfred—the villain of the piece—is discovered on his wedding morning dashed to pieces beneath an enormous helmet. Determined that his line shall not become extinct, Manfred decides to divorce Hippolyta and marry Isabella, his son's bride. To escape from her pursuer, Isabella takes flight down a "subterranean passage," where she is succoured by a "peasant" Theodore, who bears a curious resemblance to a portrait of the "good Alfonso" in the gallery of the castle. The servants of the castle are alarmed at intervals by the sudden appearance of massive pieces of armour in different parts of the building. A clap of thunder, which shakes the castle to its foundations, heralds the culmination of the story. A hundred men bear in a huge sabre; and an apparition of the illustrious Alfonso—whose portrait in the gallery once walks straight out of its frame[11]—appears, "dilated to an immense magnitude,"[12] and demands that Manfred shall surrender Otranto to the rightful heir, Theodore, who has been duly identified by the mark of a "bloody arrow." Alfonso, thus pacified, ascends into heaven, where he is received into glory by St. Nicholas. As Matilda, who was beloved of Theodore, has incidentally been slain by her father, Theodore consoles himself with Isabella. Manfred and his wife meekly retire to neighbouring convents. With this anti-climax the story closes. To present the "dry bones" of a romantic story is often misleading, but the method is perhaps justifiable in the case of *The Castle of Otranto,* because Walpole himself scorned embellishments and declared in his grandiloquent fashion:

"If this air of the miraculous is excused, the reader will find nothing else unworthy of his persual. There is no bombast, no similes, flowers, digressions or unnecessary descriptions. Everything tends directly to the catastrophe."[13] But with all its faults *The Castle of Otranto* did not fall fruitless on the earth. The characters are mere puppets, yet we meet the same types again and again in later Gothic romances. Though Clara Reeve renounced such "obvious improbabilities" as a ghost in a hermit's cowl and a walking picture, she was an acknowledged disciple of Walpole, and, like him, made an "interesting peasant" the hero of her story, *The Old English Baron.* Jerome is the prototype of many a count disguised as father confessor, Bianca the pattern of many a chattering servant. The imprisoned wife reappears in countless romances, including Mrs. Radcliffe's *Sicilian Romance* (1790), and Mrs. Roche's *Children of the Abbey* (1798). The tyrannical father—no new creation, however—became so inevitable a figure in fiction that Jane Austen had to assure her readers that Mr. Morland "was not in the least addicted to locking up his daughters," and Miss Martha Buskbody, the mantua-maker of Gandercleugh, whom Jedediah Cleishbotham ingeniously called to his aid in writing the conclusion of *Old Mortality,* assured him, as the fruit of her experience in reading through the stock of three circulating libraries that, in a novel, young people may fall in love without the countenance of their parents, "because it is essential to the necessary intricacy of the story." But apart from his characters, who are so colourless that they hardly hold our attention, Walpole bequeathed to his successors a remarkable collection of useful "properties." The background of his story is a Gothic castle, singularly unenchanted it is true, but capable of being invested by Mrs. Radcliffe with mysterious grandeur. Otranto contains underground vaults, ill-fitting doors with rusty hinges, easily extinguished lamps and a trapdoor—objects trivial and insignificant in Walpole's hands, but fraught with terrible possibilities. Otranto would have fulfilled admirably the requirements of Barrett's Cherubina, who, when looking for lodgings demanded—to the indignation of a maidservant, who came to the door—old pictures, tapestry, a spectre and creaking hinges. Scott, writing in 1821, remarks: "The apparition of the skeleton-hermit to the prince of Vicenza was long accounted a masterpiece of the horrible; but of late the valley of Jehosaphat could hardly supply the dry bones necessary for the exhibition of similar spectres." But Cherubina, whose palate was jaded by a surfeit of the pungent horrors of Walpole's successors, would probably have found **The Castle of Otranto** an insipid romance and would have lamented that he did not make more effective use of his supernatural machinery. His story offered hints and suggestions to those whose greater gifts turned the materials he had marshalled to better account, and he is to be honoured rather for what he instigated others to perform than for what he actually accomplished himself. **The Castle of Otranto** was not intended as a serious contribution to literature, but will always survive in literary history as the ancestor of a thriving race of romances.

Notes

[1] April 17, 1765.

[2] Nov. 13, 1784.

[3] June 12, 1753.

[4] *Remarks on Italy.*

[5] Aug. 4, 1753.

[6] *Diary and Letters of Madame D'Arblay,* vol. ii. Appendix ii.: *A Visit to Strawberry Hill in 1786.*

[7] Jan. 5, 1766.

[8] July 15, 1783.

[9] March 26, 1765.

[10] Nov. 5, 1782.

[11] It has been pointed out (Scott, *Lives of the Novelists,* note) that in Lope de Vega's *Jerusalem* the picture of Noradine stalks from its panel and addresses Saladine.

[12] Cf. Wallace, *Blind Harry.*

[13] *Preface,* 1764.

Karl J. Holzknecht (essay date 1929)

SOURCE: "Horace Walpole as Dramatist," *The South Atlantic Quarterly,* XXVIII, No. 2, April, 1929, pp. 174-89.

[*In this essay, Holzknecht reevaluates Walpole's importance to the historical development of drama by examining the romantic elements of* The Castle of Otranto *alongside the unacted drama* The Mysterious Mother.]

The varied career of Horace Walpole is perhaps the greatest example English literature affords of what a man can do who is so fortunate as not to be obliged to have a definite aim in life. A dilettante primarily, he combined the rôles of politician, man of the world, literary amateur, art collector, spiteful gossip, archeologist, architect, and patron of art and letters. But dilettante virtuosity dominates everything the Earl of Orford attempted. Like Congreve, he affected even a contempt for authorship[1] as being incompatible with the high social state of a gentleman, and sure that he had once possessed some talents, he himself seems to have been most aware of his own trifling. "My pursuits," he wrote in his letters,

> have always been light and trifling and tended to nothing but my casual amusement; I will not say, without a little vain ambition of showing some parts; but never with industry sufficient to make me apply to anything solid. My studies, if they could be called so, and my productions, were alike desultory.[2]

> Pray, my dear child, don't compliment me any more upon my learning; there is nobody so superficial. Except a little history, a little poetry, a little painting, and some divinity, I know nothing. How should I? I, who have always lived in the big busy world; who lie abed all the morning, calling it morning as long as you please; who sup in company; who have played at pharaoh half my life, and now at loo till two or three in the morning; who have always loved pleasure; haunted auctions—in short, who don't know so much astronomy as would carry me to Knightsbridge, nor more physic than a physician, nor in short anything that is called science. If it were not that I lay up a little provision in summer, like the ant, I should be as ignorant as all the people I live with. How I have laughed when some of the magazines have called me the *learned gentleman.*[3]

To be sure, the gentleman doth protest too much; but because his achievements so throughly illustrated the truth of his statements, for too long we have passed Horace Walpole with the shrug due the literary snob and have not allowed him to meet his due in literature. We have recognized him as an admirable letter writer in an age of clever letter writers; we sometimes take him seriously as a critic; we certainly concede him an historic interest and mention him as the originator of one characteristic aspect of romantic literature, the gothic novel. But it is of Walpole the letter writer or romancer that we think when his name is mentioned. We forget the work which he wrought most seriously, his unacted drama, *The Mysterious Mother.* Lord Byron alone of his near contemporaries appreciated the power of the play. In the preface to *Marino Faliero, Doge of Venice,* he wrote:

> It is the fashion to underrate Horace Walpole; firstly, because he was a nobleman, and, secondly, because he was a gentleman; but, to say nothing of his incomparable **"Letters"**, and of the **"Castle of Otranto"**, he is the "Ultimus Romanorum", the author of the **"Mysterious Mother"**, a tragedy of the highest order, and not a puling love-play. He is the father of the first romance and of the last tragedy in our language, and surely worthy of a higher place than any living writer, be he who he may.[4]

This is extravagant praise, even from Byron, and it suggests a new aspect of the Eighteenth Century wit. *The Mysterious Mother* was Walpole's only excursion into the type of writing for which, as I hope to show, his talent was best adapted, and which most truly reveals his abilities as an author. It is upon Horace Walpole the dramatist that I wish to concentrate attention, though it shall not be the purpose of my paper, like Byron's preface, to hail him as a great romantic playwright. It will be my aim, by taking advantage of what seems to be a revival of interest in him,[5] merely to point out by allusion to the *The Castle of Otranto* and *The Mysterious Mother* that Walpole's talent was, as he himself recognized, a talent for drama,[6] and by allusion to some contemporary plays, to show that Walpole possessed certain qualities which the drama of the time needed. To do this, it will be necessary to re-examine very briefly the romanticism of Horace Walpole to see of what it chiefly consisted, to note the essentially dramatic structure of *The Castle of Otranto,* and then by a study of *The Mysterious Mother* to observe how those qualities which made *The Castle of Otranto* romantic are used in drama.

It is generally conceded that the fantastic architectural experiments at Strawberry Hill stand as a symbolic manifestation of the spirit which for so long a time had dominated the artistic and intellectual life of Horace Walpole.[7] That spirit was gothic. Walpole loved "to gaze on Gothic toys through Gothic glass." But to neither Walpole nor his contemporaries had gothic a definite meaning. It related merely to things old;[8] his pleasure in it was largely temperamental or fostered by his travel and education. He had no real knowledge to weave into an intelligent whole the bits of information about ancient monuments he picked up here and there or the impressions made upon his susceptible imagination by the sense of mystery and solemnity and agreeable fear that hang about the ruins of abbeys and churches. As Macaulay says:

He had a strange ingenuity peculiarly his own, an ingenuity which appeared in all that he did, in his building, in his gardening, in his upholstery, in the matter and in the manner of his writing. If we were to adopt the classification, not a very accurate classification, which Akenside has given of the pleasures of the imagination, we should say, that with the Sublime and the Beautiful Walpole had nothing to do, but that the third province, the Odd, was his peculiar domain.[9]

Bits of medieval decoration, such as stained glass, traceries, tombs and towers, spires and turrets, had a vivid attraction for him, and inspired him with picturesque speculations about monastic and heroic ages,[10] and he expressed his real if superficial admiration for them with the enthusiasm of an impressionable American tourist.[11] Hence his mansion at Strawberry Hill offended not from lack of enthusiasm, but from lack of science. Although the details of ceilings, screens, and niches, so dear to his heart, were all copied from existing examples, Walpole had adopted them without regard to the original purpose of the design. These were gothic bits that pleased him, that is all that mattered, and he arranged them to satisfy the romantic cast of his own imagination. "He would have turned an altar-slab into a hall-table, or made a cupboard of a piscina, with the greatest complacency if it only served his purpose."[12] Prince Arthur's tomb at Worcester furnished the design for the wall paper of his hall and staircase. The ceiling of his gallery borrowed its design from Henry VII's chapel in Westminster Abbey, one side of the room was designed after Archbishop Bourchier's tomb at Canterbury, the door to the apartment after the north door of St. Albans. The pattern for the piers of his garden gate he found on Bishop Luda's tomb in the choir of Ely Cathedral; and when he needed a chimney piece for the north bed chamber, he adopted the form of Bishop Dudley's tomb in Westminster Abbey. Walpole's gothic taste and sentiment were never clarified and were never a reasoned scientific appreciation.

With his pleasure in these old things and the desire to be thought learned in them, came also in Walpole the desire to patronize something. Fantastic as Strawberry Hill was, no one knew any more about such matters than Walpole. The building set a fashion, and the experiment is important because it awoke a taste for the middle age and led to a study and appreciation of its architecture, its manners, its art, and its literature.

Strawberry Hill is symbolic of everything pertaining to Walpole. Just as that villa was an odd blend of ecclesiastical and castellated Gothic applied to domestic uses because of the medieval predilections of Walpole, so his writing approached the absurd because of his eccentricity and extravagance. To his love for old things Walpole joined a taste for the strange, the horrible, or at least the fantastic. He had an extraordinary interest in persons like Richard III whom legend presented as monstrous of body or spirit, and he had the faculty of appreciating sombre ors frightening pictures, like those of Salvator Rosa. *The Castle of Otranto* is a product of this gothic fancy. It is begotten of Strawberry Hill, and the castle, more than any character, dominates the story.

It is not necessary to sketch the plot of this epoch-making book. Today we find it as impossible to take the romance seriously as it is to take Strawberry Hill seriously, and for much the same reason. It is an extravagant hodge-podge that would have deceived no one who knew the old romances into believing it written by an old Italian monk. Clara Reeve was right in declaring the machinery too violent. The sword that requires a hundred men to lift, the casque that by its own weight forces through a vaulted arch a passage big enough for a man to crawl through, the gauntlet upon the banister of the great staircase, the mailed foot in one apartment, a picture that walks from its frame, the skeleton ghost with a hermit's cowl and a hollow voice, the statue that bleeds at the nose, and above all "the form of Alfonso, dilated to an immense magnitude," ascending into heaven with a clap of thunder and being received by St. Nicholas—these things, surely, picturesque as they may be, "destroy the work of the imagination, and instead of attention, excite laughter."[13]

The Castle of Otranto sins for the same reason that Strawberry Hill sins—the medievalism is too thin. The book is not historical, the descriptions are incorrect and poor in detail, and the manners and sentiments and language are modern. The importance of the novel lies in its attempt to do something new—to make use of a gothic setting. And just as the architecture of Strawberry Hill led to an interest in gothic and a study of it, only to be laughed at when knowledge increased, so *The Castle of Otranto* set the fashion for medieval setting, which was gradually refined until it produced the novels of Scott.

But this much about the romance is significant to our study of Walpole as dramatist—it was built like a drama,[14] and it was easily turned by Jephson into a good play, *The Count of Narbonne*.[15] "The plan of *The Castle of Otranto* was regularly a drama," wrote Bishop Warburton with no little acumen in his notes to Pope's *Works*. "An intention," adds Walpole, "I do not pretend to have conceived; nor, indeed, can I venture to affirm that I had any intention at all but to amuse myself—no not even a plan, till some pages were written."[16] In spite of the contradiction involved, it would seem that Walpole recognized the truth of the bishop's criticism. In the preface to the first edition of the novel, attributing the work to an ancient Italian, he had written:

Every thing tends directly to the catastrophe. Never is the reader's attention relaxed. The rules of the drama are almost observed throughout the conduct of the piece. The characters are well-drawn, and still better maintained. Terror, the author's principal engine, prevents the story from ever languishing: and it is so often contrasted by pity, that the mind is kept up to a constant vicissitude of interesting passions. . . . It is a pity that he did not apply his talents to what they were evidently proper for, the theatre.

The Mysterious Mother, like the novel and like Strawberry Hill, was the outgrowth of Walpole's eccentricity of taste and fondness for medieval lore. But it is more serious in general conception. The drama, less than the other experiments, reveals his romanticism as a veneer. Like *The Castle of Otranto* and Strawberry Hill, it shows his interest in the unusual and the gothic, but because of the skill with which he employed them the play deserves more serious attention than the novel or the mansion. The theme of *The Mysterious Mother* must have appealed to Walpole because of its very oddity. Walpole tells us he derived the story from an anecdote he once heard concerning John Tillotson, Archbishop of Canterbury, 1691-94:

I had heard when very young, that a gentlewoman, under uncommon agonies of mind, had waited on Archbishop Tillotson, and besought his counsel. A damsel that had served her, had many years before, acquainted her that she was importuned by the gentlewoman's son to grant him a private meeting. The mother ordered the maiden to make the assignation, when she said she would discover herself, and reprimand him for his criminal passion; but, being hurried away by a much more criminal passion herself, she kept the assignation without discovering herself. The fruit of this horrid artifice was a daughter, whom the gentlewoman caused to be educated very privately in the country; but proving very lovely, and being accidentally met by her father-brother, who never had the slightest suspicion of the truth, he had fallen in love with, and actually married her. The wretched guilty mother learning what had happened, and distracted with the consequence of her crime, had now resorted to the archbishop to know in what manner she should act. The prelate charged her never to let her son and daughter know what had passed, as they were innocent of any criminal intention. For herself, he bade her almost despair.[17]

The drama, then, has an incest theme and follows in almost every detail the story outlined. The Count of Narbonne, sixteen years before the opening of the play, had been accidentally killed. On the night of his death, September 20, his son, Edmund, then a youth, had crept into the chamber of his mother's woman, Beatrice, who had previously acquainted the Countess with Edmund's passion and learned her determination to reprimand her son. As a consequence, Edmund has been banished the castle, his mother's anger unreasonably hot against him, while the Countess spends her days in prayer and penance for sins she will not even confess. As the play opens Edmund returns, falls in love with a young girl, Adeliza, a charge of the Countess, and marries her, not knowing that she is his own daughter. In the last scene the Countess discloses what has happened, and stabs herself. Adeliza faints, and Edmund goes off to the wars to find an honorable death.

Literature, of course, from the time of the Oedipus story to Walpole's own day, had furnished many examples of the incest theme,[18] and the Tillotson version itself has a decided literary flavor. It is very similar in detail to Novel XXX of Margaret of Navarre's *Heptameron*,[19] a tale which is almost precisely paralleled by Bandello,[20] and hence probably based upon some current tradition. The parallel with the *Heptameron* was pointed out to Walpole by his friend Chute, and Walpole expressed surprise at the circumstance.[21] The general matter of source need not concern us greatly. Walpole seems to have taken a fairly current story, and what he thought was a true one, but two circumstances seem to me to be of some interest: the theme had been revolving in his mind for some time, and the incest plot had been in use by the Elizabethan and Restoration playwrights. That such a theme had impressed itself upon Walpole several years before is certain from his memory of Tillotson's story as well as from another circumstance. On July 12, 1753, he had published as Number 28 of the *World*, an essay on the theme that love late in life is best, and in it he had cited the legend about Ninon de L'Enclos and the Chevalier de Villiers, a series of circumstances similar to those out of which he made *The Mysterious Mother*.[22] More important than this fact, however, which shows nothing more than that Walpole pondered his drama for a longer time than his novel, is the fact that he had early examples of the use of the theme in drama. Beaumont and Fletcher, Middleton, and Ford, to name only a few, had used it, and it was common on the Restoration stage.[23] Not all such plays had themes precisely similar to that of *The Mysterious Mother*, not all made the incest theme the main plot of the drama, but all introduced it as not unfit for the stage. Two tragedies, indeed, one of them acted, had dealt with the same story as Walpole's, the anonymous *Fatal Discovery, or Love in Ruins* (D. L., 1697-8), and Robert Gould's *Innocence Distress'd, or the Royal Penitents*, printed 1737,[24] both founded, doubtless, upon the *Heptameron* or Bandello. Walpole, therefore, had precedent for his use of the theme as drama, even among the Elizabethans, in whose manner he endeavored to unfold his play. This relationship to the Elizabethan manner there is danger of overstressing. There is nothing to show that Walpole's knowledge of the old drama was any less superficial than his knowledge of Gothic architecture.

He seems to have had some knowledge of the stage of the time. He cites Nature and Shakespeare's gravediggers, to be sure, to justify the foolishness of his bumpkins in *The Castle of Otranto*.[25] There are scenes and lines in the romance which seem to show that Walpole had read *Hamlet* recently. Of *The Mysterious Mother* the same might be said. The opening of the play suggests *Hamlet;* there are lines, words, and situations here and there which are likewise suggestive— notably the deep-toned "Forebear," as Benedict and Martin, the crafty monks, are plotting (Act IV, sc. 1). There are reminiscences of *Othello* and *Macbeth*, too; there is even a hint of *Romeo and Juliet*, but though comparison to Shakespeare is hinted at in the unused Prologue[26] the similarity may be said to be very general. He may have made use of Marlowe's *Faustus*, Webster's *Duchess of Malfi*, and Congreve's *Mourning Bride*. But his knowledge and use of the past was that of a clever, not a profound man. Whatever his inspiration, and it seems Elizabethan more than Eighteenth Century, Walpole's handling of his difficult subject is characterized by a fine restraint and dignity and a full appreciation of dramatic possibilities.

The Mysterious Mother is a mixture of classic and romantic notions. As with *The Castle of Otranto*, the purpose of the play is the classic one of producing pity and terror. The unities are also to be found in the piece:

> I have said that terror and pity naturally arose from the subject, and that the moral is just. These are the merits of the story, and not of the author. It is true, also, that the rules laid down by the critics, are strictly *inherent* in the piece—remark I do not say *observed;* for I had written above three acts before I had thought of, or set myself down to observe those rules; and consequently it is no vanity to say, that the three unities reign throughout the whole play. The *time* necessary is not above two or three hours longer than the representation, or at most does not require more than half the four and twenty hours granted to poets by those their masters. The unity of place is but once shifted, and that merely from the platform without the castle to the garden within it, so that a single wall is the whole infringement of the second law. And for the third unity of action, it is so entire that not the smallest episode intervenes. Every scene tends to bring on the catastrophe, and the story is never interrupted or diverted from its course. The return of Edmund, and his marriage, necessarily produce the denouement.
>
> If the critics are pleased with this conformity to their laws, I shall be glad they have that satisfaction. For my own part, I set little value on that merit which was accidental; it is at best but mechanic and of a subordinate kind, and more apt to produce improbable situations than to remove them.

On the romantic side *The Mysterious Mother* is the

expression of the gothic that was unexpressed in *The Castle of Otranto.* The action takes place in a "gothic" time—at the dawn of the Reformation. There is mention of Vaudois heretics and of the deaths of Henri III and IV, all of which is of a time sufficiently removed to be in harmony with the theme and general supernatural atmosphere.

The success of any treatment of so horrible a theme Walpole recognized would depend upon two things:

> to palliate the crime, and raise the character of the criminal. To attain the former end, I imagined the moment in which she has lost a beloved husband, when grief and disappointment and a conflict of passions might be supposed to have thrown her reason off its guard, and exposed her to the danger under which she fell. Strange as the moment may seem for vice to have seized on her, still it makes her less hateful than if she had coolly meditated so foul a crime. I have also endeavored to make her very fondness for her husband in some measure the cause of her guilt.[27]

Or, to let the Countess speak:

> Ye know how fondly my luxurious fancy
> Doated upon my lord. For eighteen months
> An embassy detain'd him from my bed.
> A harbinger announc'd his near return.
> Love dress'd his image to my longing
>   thoughts
> In all its warmest colours—but the morn,
> In which impatience grew almost to sickness,
> Presented him a bloody corse before me.
> I rav'd—the storm of disappointed passions
> Assail'd my reason, fever'd all my blood—
> Whether too warmly press'd or too officious
> To turn the torrent of my grief aside,
> A damsel, that attended me, disclos'd
> Thy suit, unhappy boy! . . .
> Guilt rush'd into my soul—my fancy saw thee
> Thy father's image— . . .
>   Yes, thou polluted son!
> Grief, disappointment, opportunity,
> Rais'd such a tumult in my madding blood,
> I took the damsel's place.

This passage reveals Walpole as a psychologist, and in spite of Mason's objections[28] is one of the keenest touches in the whole play. His method of raising the character of the Countess is less open to question:

> But as the guilt could not be lessened without destroying the subject itself, I thought that her immediate horror and consequent repentance were essential to her being suffered on the stage. Still more was necessary. The audience must be prejudiced in her favour, or an uniform sentiment of disgust would have been raised against her through the whole piece. For this reason I suppressed

the story till the last scene, and bestowed every ornament of sense, unbigotted piety, and interesting contrition on the character that was at last to raise universal indignation; in hopes that some degree of pity would linger in the breast of the audience, and that a whole life of virtue and penance might in some measure atone for a mom-ent, though a most odious moment, of depraved imagination.

It is here that the skill of the dramatic architect is seen. The plot of *The Mysterious Mother* is strong; the mystery is preserved till the end; everything tends to bring on the catastrophe, the revelation of the mystery in a scene which rises to remarkable heights. If he succeeds in making the play terrible instead of tragic, the case is little altered.

The characters of the play, too, deserve some commendation. No longer lifeless as those of *The Castle of Otranto,* those of the drama are well defined. The Countess is an imposing tragic figure; the porter, though a type, is a real creation; even Edmund is plausible, and Adeliza, the weakest of the lot, is less sentimentalized than might be expected.

The dialogue is rapid and has plenty of give and take, and even at times suggests a little the Elizabethan feeling, though there is no great poetry to add to a nervous, and often beautiful, blank verse. An example is Edmund's soliloquy after his first interview with his mother after his return:

> Why this *is* majesty. Sounds of such accent
> Ne'er struck mine ear till now. Commanding
>   sex!
> Strength, courage, all our boasted attributes,
> Want estimation; ev'n the preheminence
> We vaunt in wisdom, seems a borrow'd ray,
> When virtue deigns to speak with female
>   organs.
> Yes, O my mother, I *will* learn t'obey;
> I *will* believe, that, harsh as thy decrees,
> They wear the warrant of benign intention.
> Make but the blooming Adeliza mine,
> And bear, of me unquestion'd, Narbonne's
>   sceptre;
> Till Life's expiring lamp by intervals
> Throws but a fainter and fainter flash,
> And then relumes its wasted oil no more.

But it is the setting of romantic gloom that is the real feature of *The Mysterious Mother.* All of the gothic machinery of *The Castle of Otranto* is present; from the very opening of the play the shadow of impending tragedy hangs over the castle. The play has that totality of effect so much talked about by Poe. The castle is gloomy, to begin:

> What awfull silence! How these antique
>   towers

And vacant courts chill the suspended soul,
Till expectation wears the cast of fear;
And fear, half-ready to become devotion,
Mumbles a kind of mental orison,
It knows not wherefore. What a kind of being
Is circumstance!
I am a soldier, and were yonder battlements
Garnish'd with combatants, and cannon-
    mounted,
My daring breast would bound with exultation,
And glorious hopes enliven this drear scene.
Now dare not I scarce tread to my own
    bearing,
Lest echo borrow superstition's tongue,
And seem to answer me, like one departed.
I met a peasant, and enquir'd my way:
The carle, not rude of speech, but like the
    tenant
Of some night-haunted ruin, bore an aspect
Of horror, worn to habitude. He bade
God bless me; and pass'd on. I urg'd him
    farther:
Good master, cried he, go not to the castle;
There sorrow ever dwells, and moping misery.
I press'd him yet—None there, said he, are
    welcome,
But now and then a mass-priest, and the poor;
To whom the pious Countess deals her alms,
On covenant, that each revolving night
They beg of heav'n the health of her son's
    soul
And of her own: but often as returns
The twentieth of September, they are bound
Fast from the midnight watch to pray till
    morn.

There are numerous allusions to apparitions. Under the porch of an abbey nearby is said to sit the spectre of the late master of the castle, with eyes like burning stars. Lightning strikes the cross erected to the old count and destroys it. The porter who believes in dreams and who forecasts events from the croaking of ravens, whispers mystery. There are plottings of unscrupulous confessors, and whispers about the fate of the woman Beatrice, who has not been heard of since the event years before. Above all, there is the countess herself, a woman given to prayer and penance and despair for a sin she will not confess. Finally, there is the grim significance attached to a fatal date, September 20, a day celebrated in the castle on the damp marble slabs of the oratories.

If gothic is admitted to be in part horrible and terrifying, then **The Mysterious Mother** leaves nothing to be desired. But this much is notable: in the drama the gothic machinery is less violent than in the novel, and is managed with much more skill. "I am firmly convinced that a history may be written with all the incidents appearing as supernatural and which show themselves naturally," he writes, and the result is **The Mysterious Mother.** Fidelity to the manners of the time, which he had claimed for the **Otranto,** except as the terror and superstitious fears of the people advance his story, is all made secondary. Walpole's purpose in **The Mysterious Mother,** like Coleridge's in *The Ancient Mariner,* was to present the supernatural naturally. Only the obvious and inevitable concern with character approaches this purpose in the playwright's interest.

To conclude: although theatrically the real feature of the play is the romance of mystery, noticeable from the very first line, dramatically the feature of the play is its structure. It is beautifully built up line by line. **The Mysterious Mother** is the work of one who had no practical knowledge of the stage, to be sure, but who had an instinct for drama. True, the play is stationary, in spite of a racy dialogue, but this is true of most of the contemporary plays. Compared, however, with the only other noteworthy attempts at romantic drama of the time, Home's *Douglas* and Dodsley's *Cleone*, **The Mysterious Mother** has something they to a degree lacked—structure. *Cleone,* an *Othello* play, had the action Walpole's play lacked, as well as the conversation, for Dodsley had learned well in his Elizabethan school. *Douglas* had the advantage of theme and sinew, but **The Mysterious Mother** had architecture. Could these various elements have been blended into one play, we should perhaps not be speaking of the poor showing of the drama in the early romantic movement. As it is, Walpole's seems, all things considered, the most powerful, at least, of the gothic tragedies. Hannah More's *Percy,* Jephson's *Braganza,* and Cumberland's *Carmelites* are, after all, pale shadows.

Walpole's play was never acted; that he intended to have it try the stage at the beginning is certain, in spite of his later contradictions. He wrote a prologue and an epilogue for it, the latter "to be spoken by Mrs. Clive." But he bowed to the opinion that it was too terrible for the stage, and was exceedingly cautious about its printing. The first edition of fifty copies might also have been the last had not piratical book-sellers' announcements of it made two other editions, one with postscript, necessary. It has been reprinted, as far as I am able to discover, only twice, in Scott's collection of *British Drama,* 1811, and by Mr. Montague Summers, 1924. Hence, **The Mysterious Mother** is not so well known as **The Castle of Otranto.** But, while not a great play, it shows the author's talent for drama to be greater than that for fiction. It belongs, along with **The Castle of Otranto,** to the gothic tradition, and its only literary influence seems to be that it supplied Mrs. Radcliffe with some of the chapter headings of her romances.

Notes

[1] See especially his letter to Lady Ossory, Sept., 1770

(*Letters of Horace Walpole,* ed. Mrs. Paget Toynbee, VII, 404-5), and compare the letters to the Rev. H. Zouch, May 14, 1759 (IV, 263); to George Montague, Oct. 24, 1758 (IV, 210); to Mason, May 15, 1773 (VIII, 279).

2 To John Pinkerton, Aug. 19, 1789 (XIV, 192). Cf. to Hannah More, July 12, 1788 (XIV, 567).

3 To Horace Mann, Feb. 6, 1760 (IV, 354-5); compare the letters to Mason, May 15, 1773 (VIII, 279); to Cole, Apr. 25, 1775 (IX, 190); to the Countess of Upper Ossory, July 9, 1785 (XIII, 292); to Cole, Apr. 27, 1773 (VIII, 268); to the Countess of Ossory, Oct. 11, 1788 (XIV, 87). Another letter, dated June 1778, is printed in Disraeli, *Calamities and Quarrels of Authors,* 47.

4 Sir Walter Scott also praised it: "Essay on Drama," *The Miscellaneous Prose Works of Sir Walter Scott, Bart.,* Boston, 1829, VI, 281-2, and *Biographical Memoirs of Eminent Novelists and other Distinguished Persons,* Edinburgh, 1834, I, 311, 321. So did Nichols, *Literary Anecdotes of the Eighteenth Century,* London, 1814, VIII, 526.

5 Witness the recent limited edition of the *Castle of Otranto* and *The Mysterious Mother,* edited by Montague Summers, Constable, 1924; the new collection of his letters, *A Selection of the Letters of Horace Walpole,* edited by W. S. Lewis, Harpers', 1926; the biographical and critical studies of Gamaliel Bradford, *Bared Souls,* 1924; Paul Yvon, *La Vie d'un Dilettante Horace Walpole (1717-1797) Essai de Biographie Psychologigue et Litteraire,* Paris, 1924 and *Horace Walpole as Poet,* Paris, 1924; and Dorothy Margaret Stuart, *Horace Walpole,* (English men of Letters), 1927; as well as *The Journal of the Printing Office at Strawberry Hill,* Constable, 1923; and *Strawberry Hill Accounts,* Oxford, 1927, both edited by Paget Toynbee.

6 He confesses to it in a letter to Jephson, Feb. 1775 (Suppl. I, 248).

7 Yvon, *La Vie d'un Dilettante Horace Walpole . . . ,* Paris, 1924, 488.

8 On the word "gothic" see A. E. Longueil, "The word 'Gothic' in Eighteenth Century Criticism," *MLN,* XXXVIII, 453-60. The author makes the point here (p. 457) that to Walpole as to Hurd "gothic" equals "medieval," and that *Otranto* is a gothic story simply because it is medieval. In general principle this is true, but as a matter of fact, "gothic" to both meant anything old—anything earlier than the Restoration. When Hurd (*Letters on Chivalry and Romance,* III) sought for suggestive gothic examples, he went no further than the age of Elizabeth, to the jousts and tournies, "the

barbarous and Gothic chivalry," at Kenilworth.

9 *Critical and Historical Essays,* Cambridge Edition, II, 203.

10 See Letter to Cole, May 22, 1777 (X, 53).

11 *Letters,* III. 181.

12 Eastlake, *History of the Gothic Revival,* 47.

13 Clara Reeve, *The Old English Baron,* "Address to the Reader." The comment seems to have nettled Walpole somewhat. See the letter to Cole, Aug. 22, 1778 (X, 302). It is not difficult to account for the success of the book in Walpole's immediate circle. When Gray writes acknowledging receipt of his copy (December 30, 1764, just six days after the first private printing, *Letters of Gray,* ed. Tovey, III, 55) that it "makes some of us cry a little, and all in general afraid to go to bed o'nights," he is very possibly only trying to please his friend and is not to be taken seriously.

14 The division into five chapters, which suggest acts, offers some entertaining speculation. Each with the exception of the second, and here there is only a slight overlapping with the third chapter, accomplishes approximately what the corresponding act of a five-act drama would accomplish, and the chapters are further easily divided into scenes.

15 1779-80. Jephson accomplished his purpose by eliminating the miraculous casque entirely, generally toning down the supernatural element, and concentrating upon two characters.

16 Letter to Robert Jephson, Jan. 27, 1780 (XI, 112).

17 Postscript, Dublin edition, 1791.

18 See Montague Summers' edition of *The Castle of Otranto* and *The Mysterious Mother* for a long list of similar stories. I mention here only a few: the legend of St. Gregory (No. 81 of the *Gesta Romanorum,* see Wells, *Manual of the Writings in Middle English* for English versions); the Latin chronicle of St. Albinus, of which Cole sent Walpole a manuscript; the tale in Luther's *Colloquia Mensalia;* and the stories in Margaret of Navarre's *Heptameron* and Bandello's *Novelle.* Summers mentions several thoroughly authenticated instances. The whole subject of the incest theme has been treated by Otto Rank, *Das Inzest-Motiv in Dichtung und Sage,* Leipzig und Wien, 1912.

19 The *Heptameron* may have been the source of Tillotson's story, which is known to us only through Walpole. The two versions agree even to the detail of the

prelate's giving advice entirely out of accord with ecclesiastical law. The same may be said of Luther's story, told under the article "Auricular Confession."

[20] *Novelle,* Part II, No. 35.

[21] Letter to the Hon. H. S. Conway, June 16, 1768 (VII, 199). "Mr. Chute has found the subject of my tragedy which I thought happened in Tillotson's time, in the Queen of Navarre's Tales; and what is very remarkable, I had laid my plot at Narbonne and about the beginning of the Reformation, and it really did happen in Languedoc and in the time of Francis the First. Is not this singular?"

[22] The story, discredited by the most recent biographer of the famous French beauty, Émile Magne, (*Ninon de Lanclos,* Paris, 1925, pp. 71-2, note), runs as follows: About 1672 the young Chevalier de Villiers fell ardently in love with the still remarkable Ninon (aged according to some accounts sixty, to others, fifty-two). His father, the Chevalier de Gersay, wished to keep his parentage secret, and this Ninon had endeavored to do. The disastrous consequences came when the chevalier became more ardent, and Ninon, permitted to tell her son, wrote to him appointing a private meeting. He came eagerly, was horrified at her revelations, and unable to realize the relationship sufficiently to destroy his passion, fled into the garden and fell upon his sword. Compare the characters of Inesilla de Cantarilla, who is much like Ninon, and Don Valerio de Luna in Le Sage's *Gil Blas,* where the hero, like the Chevalier de Villiers, regrets that he has been unable to accomplish his purpose and stabs himself.

[23] Before the Restoration: Beaumont and Fletcher, *King and No King,* and *The Captain,* 1612; Arthur Wilson, *The Swizzer,* 1631; Middleton, *Women Beware Women,* c. 1612; Massinger, *The Unnatural Combat,* 1621; Ford, *'Tis Pity,* 1631; Tourneur, *Revenger's Tragedy,* 1607; Brome, *Love Sick Count,* 1658. After the Restoration: Dryden, *Spanish Fryar or the Double Discovery,* 1679-80, *Aureng-Zebe,* 1675, *Love Triumphant, or Nature will Prevail,* 1693, *Don Sebastian,* 1689; Dryden and Lee, *Oedipus,* 1679; Otway, *Orphan,* 1680; Lee, *Tragedy of Nero, Emperour of Rome,* 1674; Crowne, *Thyestes,* 1681, *City Politiques,* 1683; and Mrs. Behn, *Dutch Lover,* 1673. The last two are comic treatments.

[24] Genest, *Some Account of the English Stage from the Restoration in 1660 to 1830,* X, 185 ff., gives a sketch of their plots and characters.

[25] Preface to the second edition. "That great master of nature Shakespeare, was the model I copied."

[26]

> "From no French model breathes the muse to-
> night;

> The scene she draws is horrid, not polite.
> She dips her pen in terror. Will ye shrink?
> Shall foreign critics teach you how to think?
> Had Shakespeare's magic dignified the stage,
> If timid laws had school'd th' insipid age?"

[27] Postscript.

[28] "The canvass by this means render'd less shocking (by making the crime of the countess arise from mistake rather than prepense) would even still be too much so if the character of the Criminal was not so greatly rais'd as it is by the Author, nevertheless, *his* manner of palliating the Crime, by imagining her to commit it at the moment in which she had lost a beloved husband is *a strange one indeed.* by this Our *delicacy* is very reasonably shocked whatever becomes of our good nature; Our Common Feelings are more shocked than either because common Experience pronounces the fact unnatural & absolutely improbable."

Jess M. Stein (essay date 1934)

SOURCE: "Horace Walpole and Shakespeare" *Studies in Philology* XXXI, No. 1, January, 1934, pp. 51-68.

[*In the following essay, Stein examines Walpole's attitude toward Shakespeare—especially through his defense of Shakespeare against Voltaire. Stein concludes that, although Walpole regarded Shakespeare, highly he was not one of Walpole's literary influences.*]

Within the last twenty-five years, there has been a marked growth of interest in Horace Walpole and the Gothic movement, of which he was both the originator and the outstanding representative.[1] There have appeared a number of theories,[2] pointing to possible sources of the "goose-flesh" tendency, most of them trying to show that the Elizabethan influence was quite potent in the formation and development of Gothicism,[3] although some critics stray too far in their attempt to prove their theory.[4] They are in agreement that the Elizabethan influence, if there was any, was transmitted mainly through Shakespeare, towards whom there was a "steady rise of idolatry . . . throughout the late eighteenth century."[5] And yet, surprisingly little has been said about Walpole's critical attitude towards Shakespeare. This paper proposes to discuss the larger sphere of Walpole's relationship to Shakespeare, thus embracing the following three topics: (1) Walpole's attitude towards Shakespeare, (2) Walpole's attacks upon Voltaire, and (3) Shakespeare's literary influences upon Walpole's play and novel.

I. *Walpole's Attitude Towards Shakespeare.*

There has been too much learned controversy over the quality of Walpole's literary evaluations. Lord Macaulay, with his customary Victorian pomposity, scolded Walpole briskly. "His judgment of literature," he says, "of contemporary literature, especially, was altogether perverted by his aristocratical feelings. No writer surely was ever guilty of so much faults and absurd criticism."[6] The best counter-remark to this is Austin Dobson's simple statement that "his critical taste was good."[7] Paul Yvon, the French scholar, settles the matter for our purposes. He writes, "After all, on these poetical questions, Walpole had by no means so versatile or inconstant a taste as his reputation would lead us to suppose. Even if he had expressed opinions now and then contradictory, it might be pardonable. But his ideas are generally consistent and to the point . . . Walpole had a cultivated and refined taste."[8]

The matter which seems to have concerned Walpole most about Shakespeare was the traditional question of the justification of Shakespeare's disregard for the classical laws. He recognized Shakespeare's neglect of the "rules" and consequently busied himself in preparing defenses for him.

As early as 1760, five years before Dr. Samuel Johnson launched "the greatest individual defense of Shakespeare against this doctrine,"[9] Walpole, in a private letter, showed a definite opposition to the unities: "I should not expect a bard to write by the rules of Aristotle."[10] In 1765, he wrote to a friend, "You must remember, Sir, that whatever good sense we have, we are not yet in any light chained down to precepts and inviolable laws."[11] In 1775, the year before Voltaire's famous letter to the Academy, he cried out, "What French criticism can wound the ghosts of Hamlet or Banquo? Scorn rules, Sir, that cramp genius, and substitute delicacy to imagination in a barren language. Shall we not soar, because the French dare not rise from the ground?"[12] In his Postscript of 1781 to *The Mysterious Mother,* after pointing to a chance conformity to rules of classicism in his own play, he added: "For my own part, I set little value on that merit which was accidental; it is at best but mechanic and of a subordinate kind, and more apt to produce improbable situations than to remove them."[13] In the same year, he wrote, "He [Harris of Salisbury] dwells on Aristotle's old hacked rules for the drama, and the pedantry of a beginning, middle and end."[14] In short, his attitude towards the problem of the unities reveals a rapid shift from a justification of a bard's disregard for laws to a general denunciation of rules as outworn and obsolete.

Obviously, Walpole's reason for rejecting the unities was that natural genius was superior to a superficial conformity to rules. Having already denounced rules as chains to genius, he changed his method of Shakespearean defense into the traditional eulogy of Shakespeare as an original genius.[15] The change is from "the

earlier application of the term as a mere explanation of his triumph over the 'rules'" to "a paean of praise in terms of the intrinsic superiority of original genius itself." Late in 1764, Walpole explains that "one of the greatest geniuses that ever existed, Shakespeare, undoubtedly wanted taste. . . . Genius is original, invents, and taste selects, perhaps copies, with judgement [sic]."[16] He writes again in 1765: "All that Aristotle or his superior commentators, your authors [the French writers and critics] have taught us, has not yet subdued us to regularity: we still prefer the extravagant beauties of Shakespeare and Milton to the cold and well-disciplined merit of Addison, and even to the sober and correct march of Pope."[17] In 1768, Walpole writes to Mme. du Deffand that Shakespeare is "le plus beau génie qu'ait jamais enfanté la nature."[18] In his well-known letter to Robert Jephson (1775), he remarks that "if there is art in *Othello* and *Macbeth,* it seems to have been by chance; for Shakespeare certainly took no pains to adjust a plan."[19] This matter of original genius was concluded in 1778, thus, "We commentators do sometimes discover more than our author intended; but when nature speaks, it is prodigious how far the justness of her thoughts will vibrate. Shakespeare who wrote down what she dictated, must often have perceived more beauties than he was aware of at first, in committing her words to paper."[20]

On the point of tragi-comedy, Walpole was with the critics of the last years of the eighteenth century, in their defense of it by an "appeal to nature, real life, the original Johnsonian defense."[21] Discussing the "deportment of the domestics" in *The Castle of Otranto,* he says in the preface to the second edition, "The simplicity of their behavior, almost tending to excite smiles, which, at first, seems not consonant to the serious cast of the work, appeared to me not only not improper, but was marked designedly in that manner. My rule was nature. However grave, important, or even melancholy, the sensations of princes and heroes may be, they do not stamp the same affectations on their domestics: at least the latter do not, or should not be made to, express their passions in the same dignified tone."[22] Continuing, he makes a point, the importance of which has been neglected by historians of Shakespeare criticism. "In my humble opinion," he remarks, "the contrast between the sublime of the one and the naïveté of the other, sets the pathetic of the former in a stronger light. The very impatience which a reader feels, while delayed, by the coarse pleasantries of vulgar authors, from arriving at the knowledge of the important catastrophe he expects, perhaps heightens, certainly proves that he has been artfully interested in, the depending event. But, I had higher authority than my own opinion for this conduct. That great master of nature, *Shakespeare,* was the model I copied. Let me ask, if his tragedies of *Hamlet* and *Julius Caesar* would not lose a considerable share of their spirit and wonderful beauties, if the humour of the grave-diggers, the fooleries of Polonius, and the clumsy jests of the Roman citizens, were omitted, or vested in heroics? Is not the eloquence of Anthony, the nobler and affectedly-unaffected oration of Brutus, artificially exalted by the rude bursts of nature from the mouths of their auditors? These touches remind one of the Grecian sculptor, who, to convey the idea of a Colossus, within the dimensions of a seal inserted a little boy measuring his thumb."[23] Likewise, Walpole had commented on *Hamlet* in a letter to Jephson: "Yet who but Shakespeare could render mirth pathetic? His exquisite scene of the grave-diggers is an instance of that magic and creative power."[24] Walpole had struck something new in his treatment of Shakespeare's tragicomedy, justifying it, not defensively, but as a factor which adds to the beauty of the plays, "a most interesting shift," which Babcock assigns to the end of the century.[25]

Walpole made two attempts at historical criticism, both of them quite unreliable. In 1768 his ***Historic Doubts on the Life and Reign of Richard III*** contained a theory that *The Winter's Tale* represents a sequel to *Henry VIII*.[26] He also had the queer notion that "Shakespeare drew Hamlet from Claus Ostrogothus, or some such name."[27]

On the individual plays and characters in Shakespeare, Walpole said very little. After reading *First Part of Henry I,V,* he declares he "was ready to set fire to my own printing-house."[28] On the other hand, after seeing Garrick play *Cymbeline,* in the actor's altered form, he remarks, "It . . . appeared to me as long as if everybody in it went really to Italy in every act, and came back again. With a few pretty passages and a scene or two, it is so absurd and tiresome. . . . "[29] *Midsummer's Night's Dream* he condemns as "forty times more nonsensical than the worst translation of any Italian opera-books" and yet, with a typical Walpolian turn, he exclaims, "But such sense and such harmony are irresistible!"[30] Concerning *The Merchant of Venice,* he wrote, "With all my enthusiasm for Shakespeare, it is one of his plays that I like least. The story of the caskets is silly, and, except the character of Shylock, I see nothing beyond the attainment of a mortal."[31] In the Postscript (1781), to the ***Mysterious Mother,*** he said: "The finest picture ever drawn of a head distempered by misfortune is that of *King Lear.*"[32] While he never interested himself in the problem of Falstaff's cowardice, a matter which bothered his contemporaries, Walpole saw the more important side of Falstaff, that of the great humor in his character. He called Johnson's exclamation, "Inimitable, unimitated Falstaff!", a "fit of just enthusiasm."[33] In a letter written in 1776, he remarks about the untranslatability of Falstaff's character, when he had heard that a French version was being made. "What will they do with Falstaff?" he asks.[34] On another occasion, he writes, "Now I hold a perfect comedy to be the perfection of human composition, and believe firmly that fifty *Iliads*

or *Aeneids* could be written sooner than such a character as Falstaff's."[35]

Walpole's idolatry of Shakespeare was not the "idolatry ad astra," as Babcock calls it,[36] of most of the other Shakespeare critics of the late eighteenth century; although at times he waxed rhapsodic on the subject, he tempered his judgment with a recognition of some mediocrity. He did not, as Professor Nicol Smith said of the bulk of eighteenth-century critics, "lose [himself] in panegyric of Shakespeare."[37] His was a calm respect for Shakespeare's pre-eminence. In 1756, he wrote the following motto with which he desired to decorate Garrick's "temple to his master Shakespeare":

Quod spiro et placeo, si placeo, tuum est.

That I spirit have and nature,
That sense breathes in every feature,
That I please, if please I do,
Shakespear, all I owe to you.[38]

In another letter, he referred to Shakespeare as "one of the greatest geniuses that ever existed."[39] Writing to a friend during his quarrel with Voltaire, he speaks of Shakespeare's "merveilleuses beautés,"[40] and, again, he declares, "Moi, je me ferais brûler pour la primauté de Shakespeare."[41] In a discussion of the English drama, he remarks, "Ce sont nos auteurs tragiques que j'aime, c'est-à-dire Shakespeare qui est mille auteurs."[42] To Jephson, he once wrote about Shakespeare's "divine genius" which led him to exclaim, "Well, Sir, I give up Shakespeare's dramas; and yet prefer him to every man. Why? For his exquisite knowledge of the passions and nature; for his simplicity too, which he possesses too when most natural."[43] Walpole called Milton and Shakespeare "the only two mortals I am acquainted with who ventured beyond the visible diurnal sphere, and preserved their intellects."[44] And once, when someone had suggested a parallel to Shakespeare,[45] he cried out, "Oh, I have not words adequate to my contempt for those who can suppose such a possibility!"[46] On many occasions he referred to Shakespeare as "that first genius of the world,"[47] "that most sublime genius," "our first of Men,"[48] "superior to all mankind,"[49] "the first of writers,"[50] and so on.[51] And yet he was able to maintain a judicial equilibrium, and write: "They who think her[52] *Earl Godwin* will outgo Shakespeare might be in the right, if they specified in what way. I believe she may write worse than he sometimes did, though that is not easy."[53] The same idea was expressed a few years before, thus: "Our modern tragedies, hundreds of them do not contain a good line, nor are they a jot better, because Shakespeare, who was superior to all mankind, wrote some whole plays that are as bad as any of our present writers."[49] To this, one might add Walpole's critical remarks on *Cymbeline,* and *The Merchant of Venice,*[54] in which he points out that

Shakespeare (or the authors of the alterations?) was frequently mediocre.

In closing this portion of the paper, we may summarize by saying, as Yvon put it, "One man summed up the drama for Walpole," Shakespeare, but this was not "blind idolatry" or "the effect of national pride," for Walpole was "alive to his most glaring faults."[55]

II. *Walpole's Attacks upon Voltaire.*

It is unnecessary to review here the details of the correspondence which passed between Voltaire and Walpole after the latter had risen to Shakespeare's defense against the malicious strictures of the Frenchman. The mere historical outline will be found in a number of places, the best of which remains that which Lounsbury wrote thirty years ago.[56] The whole matter has been packed into a paragraph written by Walpole himself.[57] Throughout the correspondence, Walpole wrote to his friends that he did not want to quarrel with Voltaire. He wrote: "Je ne cherche pas querelle avec Voltaire,"[58] and, again, "Je n'ai jamais pensé entrer en lice avec lui."[59] And yet, he quarrelled. And the irony of it all is that he later wrote, "How very foolish are the squabbles of authors! They buzz and are troublesome for a day, and then repose for ever on some shelf in a college library, close by their antagonists, like Henry VI and Edward IV at Windsor."[60]

Walpole attacked Voltaire from a number of angles. In his attack upon him as a writer he did not draw any particular parallels between the ability of the Frenchman and Shakespeare, as many of the other English critics had done in their reactions;[61] he tried merely to belittle Voltaire's literary ability, but was often forced to admit some greatnesses in the writings of the "wicked wasp of Ferney." He called Voltaire's system in the *Dictionnaire Philosophique* "much more foolish and absurd than anything he has ever ridiculed."[62] The Marquise du Deffand once took him to task for saying, "Les vers de Voltaire sont à faire pitié."[63] Certain of his verses he termed "not only very bad, but very contemptible."[64] He referred to other lines as "intolerably stupid, and not above the level of officers in garrison."[65] In 1788 he wrote: "Voltaire ought to have pretended to die after *Alzire, Mahomet,* and *Semiramis,* and not have produced his wretched last pieces."[66] It is here that Walpole may seem inconsistent in his critical opinions, for in different letters he speaks of "great flashes of genius, single lines and starts of passion of the first fire" in *Tancred,*[67] of his infinite admiration for Voltaire,[68] "a charming copy of verses of Voltaire,"[69] of "that admirable chapter in Voltaire,"[70] of his lucidity,[71] and, in 1778, when he had heard of Voltaire's death, he wailed, "The meteor of the reading world is dead, Voltaire. That throne is quite vacant."[72]

The second major point upon which Walpole scored

Voltaire was his inability as an historian. While this attack had no direct bearing upon Voltaire's criticisms of Shakespeare, its purpose was, by showing Voltaire's ignorance of history, to lower his position in the intellectual world in which he reigned; by doing that, Walpole, had hoped to rob Voltaire of his authoritative tone in all other fields. Late in 1755, Walpole remarked about an historical romance by Voltaire "of the last war, in which is so outrageous a lying anecdote about old Marlborough, as would have convinced her,[73] that when poets write history they stick as little to truth in prose as in verse."[74] Five years later he wrote: "The first volume of Voltaire's *Peter the Great* is arrived. I weep over it! It is as languid as the campaign; he is grown old. He boasts of the materials communicated to him by the Czarina's orders—but, alas! he need not be so proud of them. They only serve to show how much worse he writes history with materials than without. . . . I had heard before that when he sent the work to Petersburgh for imperial approbation, it was returned with orders to increase the panegyric."[75] A short time afterwards he wrote, in denouncing Voltaire's constant inaccuracy: "As Voltaire has unpoisoned so many persons of former ages, methinks he ought to do as much for the present time, and assure posterity that there never was such a lamb as Catherine II, and that, so far from assassinating her own husband and Czar Ivan, she wept over every chicken that she had for dinner."[76] In the preface to the second edition of ***The Castle of Otranto*** (1765), Walpole noted how "incorrect and incompetent" Voltaire's knowledge of history was, by showing Voltaire's mistake of thinking Robert Dudley and the Earl of Leicester were two separate favorites of Elizabeth's, when they were the same person.[77] In 1789, on the other hand, he said of Voltaire's *Universal History,* which he considered his *chef-d'oeuvre,* "It is a marvelous mass of genius and sagacity, and quintessence of political wisdom as well as of history. . . . Whatever may be said of his incorrectness in some facts, his observations and inferences are always just and profound."[78] And yet, five years later, Walpole commented upon Voltaire's historical accuracy as being one of "N'est-ce pas mieux comme cela?" and accused him of "treating history like a wardrobe of ancient habits, that he would cut, and alter, and turn into what dresses he pleased."[79]

The third attack upon Voltaire concerned his critical capacity. In the preface to the second edition to ***The Castle of Otranto,*** Walpole seems to have been motivated by Voltaire's *Appel* (1761). He called the Frenchman's criticisms only "the effusions of wit and precipitation, rather than the result of judgment and attention. May not the critic's skill, in the force and powers of our language, have been as incorrect and incompetent as his knowledge of our history? of the latter, his own pen has dropped glaring evidence."[80]

He followed this up with a comparison of Voltaire to

Shakespeare, admitting that "Voltaire is a genius—but not of Shakespeare's magnitude." He then turned to Voltaire's objections to tragi-comedy, refuting his strictures with quotations from Voltaire himself.[81] In a letter written in the same year, he refers to "Voltaire's impertinent criticisms on our matchless poet."[82] On another occasion, he laughed at Voltaire's admiration of certain lines from Racine.[83] Again, he said Voltaire "is incapable of feeling that simplicity is the height of the sublime,[84] this comment coming probably as a reaction to Voltaire's letter to the French Academy (1776). And, to top it all, he ridiculed Voltaire's knowledge of the English language. "Voltaire's English," he wrote, "would be good English in any other foreigner; but a man who gave himself the air of criticising our—and, I will say, the world's—greatest author, ought to have been a better master of our language, though this letter and his commentary prove that he could neither write it nor read it accurately and intelligently."[85]

Walpole's fourth attack was on Voltaire as a man.[86] As early as 1765, he began calling Voltaire a "scoffer,"[87] and three years later, he asked, "Mais est-il possible qu'il s'avoue offensé de ce qu'on lui conteste le rang du premier génie?[88] In the middle of 1776, Voltaire's letter to d'Argental (July 19, 1776) appeared; Walpole turned upon him with an invigorated fury. He sent a copy of the "wasp's" letter to William Mason with the following brief note: "I have a mind to provoke you, and so I send you this silly torrent of ribaldry. May the spirit of Pope that dictated your Musaeus, animate you to punish this worst of dunces, a genius turned fool with envy!"[89] In the same year, probably thinking of Voltaire's letter to the Academy on August 25, he refers to Voltaire's "paltry scurrilous letter against Shakespeare."[90] And, to Mason again, he exclaims, "Poor old wretch! how an envy disgraces the brightest talents! . . . It hurts one when a real genius like Voltaire can feel more spite than admiration, though I am persuaded that his rancour is grounded in his conscious inferiority. I wish," he adds, "you would lash this old scorpion a little, and teach him awe of English poets."[91] In the same year he writes, "Out of envy to writers of his own nation, he cried up Shakespeare; and now is distracted at the just encomiums bestowed on that first genius of the world."[92] At another time, he denounces Voltaire because he had "out of envy taken pains to depreciate all the really great authors of his own country, and of this."[93] Elsewhere, he calls Voltaire the "god of Envy,"[94] and taunts him on his vanity.[95] He speaks of him as the "envious depreciator of Shakespeare,"[96] says he was "mean and dirty," and paints him as "one of those heroes who liked better to excite martyrs than to be one."[97]

Walpole met Voltaire on his own ground. He attacked him from four sides—as a writer, as an historian, as a critic, and as a man. Hitting sharply and accurately, "at

their heel, at their vulnerable part,"[98] as Walpole had said, the Englishman soon cornered his opponent. Voltaire could only squirm and reply weakly.[99]

III. *Shakespeare's Influence Upon Walpole.*

An examination of Walpole's **The Castle of Otranto** will hardly show much Shakespearean influence, although Railo continually insists upon its presence.[100] While some likeness must be admitted, it is wrong to force the comparison too far. Railo claims that his opinion is upheld by Sir Walter Raleigh,[101] and yet, on the page following that which he quotes as evidence of Raleigh's support, the following statement by Raleigh appears. "But romantic after the manner of Shakespeare the work is not. For nothing is more characteristic of the great masters of romance than the subtlety and guardedness of their use of the supernatural. The ghosts do not come uncalled for. Macbeth is startled when the witches speak to him, because what they have to tell him is familiar to his thoughts. The tricks and fantasies of supernaturalism are meaningless and powerless save in alliance with the mysterious powers of human nature, and, failing this, not all the realistic circumstance in the world can give them life or meaning."[102] When Railo tries to prove that Shakespeare's influence was central to Walpole's work on the basis of evidence drawn from minor devices, he misses the fact that, while these devices may contribute to the whole, they are not the real essence of the Gothic literary production. Constant terror is the central quality of Gothic writings; and Walpole did not get this effect from Shakespeare. Various minor devices may have come from Shakespeare, although one can more easily conceive of their coming from contact with medieval ruins.

The possibility of drawing a close parallel between Shakespeare and Walpole's Gothic drama, **The Mysterious Mother** (1768), is just as remote. The plot of the play seems to have come from ancient literature, most likely Sophocles' *Oedipus.* The incest-theme, which Railo tries to call Elizabethan,[103] was really of Greek origin. Yvon suggests that Walpole "probably had the subject of Oedipus in his mind."[104] And Walpole, in his Postscript, refers to *Oedipus,* in comparison to his own work.[105]

As to the general spirit of the play, the emphasis upon an unusual filial relationship, tending towards horror and repulsiveness, there seems to be no possible parallel source in Shakespeare, although one might track down scattered instances of likeness in the abundant works of Shakespeare. This would immediately rule out one of the central influences which one writer may have upon another.

The form of the play may be called Shakespearean, in that it has frequent verse effects, comparable to those of the Elizabethans. One finds "the power to concentrate much feeling in a phrase, the gift of compelling imagery upon which the imagination can feed, that rapid connection of ideas of which some of the Elizabethans were such great masters, . . . those unforgettably vivid sentences shot out swiftly to define a phase, like lightning showing up the murk."[106] For example:

> What awful silence! How these antique towers
> And vacant courts chill the suspended soul,
> Till expectation wears the cast of fear;
> And fear half-ready to become devotion,
> Mumbles a kind of mental orison,
> It knows not wherefore.[107]

Throughout the play are long passages showing intense emotional conditions, culminating in such a splendid set of lines as:

> Globe of the world,
> If thy frame split not with such crimes as these,
> It is immortal.[108]

The matter in the play is by no means centrally influenced by Shakespeare. Of the characters, little can be said. Though Edmund reminds one sometimes of Hamlet, Florian of the Bastard, Adeliza of Perdita, and Peter of any of the Shakespeare servants, it would be too much to claim that Shakespeare influenced Walpole in his selection of character-types.

There are, indeed, a number of passages in the play which remind one vaguely of Shakespearean passages or effects; but these parallels are in Walpole no closer than in almost any other writer of blank verse tragedy of the century and are hardly more pointed. For example, the following speech by Florian might be regarded as reminiscent of the Bastard in *Kind John:*

> —What precious mummery! Her son in exile,
> She wastes on monks and beggars her inheritance,
> For his son's health! I never knew a woman
> But loved our bodies or our souls too well.
> Each master-whim maintains its hour of empire,
> And obstinately faithfull [sic] to its dictates,
> With equal ardor, equal importunity,
> They teaze us to be damn'd or to be saved,
> I hate to love or pray too long.[109]

The following parallels might also be noted.

> Merey befall me!—now my dream is out,
> Last night the raven croak'd, and from the bars
> Of our lodge-fire flitted a messenger—
> I knew no good would follow—Bring you ill

> tidings,
> Sir gentlemen?[110]

This may be related to the scene in *Macbeth* where the old man tells Ross of the stormy night and its omens. Another passage resembles the "Alas, poor Yorick!" speech in *Hamlet:*

> Meantime in ruin laid
> My mouldring castles—Yes, ye moss-grown walls!
> Ye tow'rs defenceless!—I revisit ye
> Shame-stricken.—Where are all your trophies now?
> Your thronged courts, the revelry, the tumult,
> That spoke the grandeur of my house, the homage
> Of neighb'ring barons?[111]

The following lines remind one of a scene in *Hamlet:*

Benedict

> Dastard, tremble, if we fail
> What can we fear, when we have ruin'd them?
> *(A deep-toned voice is heard)* Forbear!

Benedict

> Ha! whence that sound?
> *(Voice again)* Forbear!

Benedict

> Again?
> Comes it from heav'n or hell?
> *(Voice again)* Forbear!

Martin

> Good angels
> Protect me!—Benedict, thy unholy purpose. . .
> .[113]

Such, then, briefly considered, is the influence of Shakespeare upon Walpole's two important original productions,—a marginal rather than a central influence.

An examination of the evidence shows, first, that Walpole insisted upon the native genius of Shakespeare as a literary workman, and therefore felt that conformity to rules should not be expected of him; he justified tragi-comedy in Shakespeare as a natural feature, intensifying the "spirit and wonderful beauties" of the tragedies. Walpole's worship of Shakespeare was an enthusiastic idolatry tempered by a judicial equilibrium. Second, Walpole's defense of Shakespeare against the strictures of Voltaire became mainly an attack on the latter as writer, historian, critic, and man; yet, in this reaction, he showed a respect for Voltaire, whom he regarded as "a genius turned fool with envy."

Finally, though he thought highly of Shakespeare, Walpole was not centrally influenced by him in his own writings. One finds traces of minor parallels which could not, however, be forced to support a theory of direct relationship. The influence was not as thorough as Railo makes it; it was mainly incidental and marginal.

Notes

[1] The most comprehensive bibliography for Walpole and the Gothic movement will be found in the appendix to Oswald Doughty's edition of *The Castle of Otranto* (London, 1929), 107 ff. The best collection of Walpole's letters is *The Letters of Horace Walpole,* ed. Mrs. Paget Toynbee (Oxford, 1903), 16 vols., and *Supplement,* ed. Dr. Paget Toynbee (Oxford, 1918), 3 vols. The latest edition of *The Castle of Otranto* is by Doughty (see above), and the only popularly available text of *The Mysterious Mother* will be found in Montague Summers' *The Castle of Otranto and The Mysterious Mother* (London, 1924). An excellent selection of Walpole's letters has been made by W. S. Lewis, *Letters of Horace Walpole: A Selection* (New York, 1926), 2 vols.

The most worthwhile secondary material on Walpole includes: Baker, Reed, Jones, *Biographica Dramatica* (London, 1812), 3 vols.; T. R. Lounsbury, *Shakespeare and Voltaire* (New York, 1902), pp. 258-281; Edith Birkhead, *The Tale of Terror* (London, 1921); W. P. Harbeson, *The Elizabethan Influence on the Tragedy of the Late Eighteenth and Early Nineteenth Centuries* (Philadelphia, 1921); Paul Yvon, *Horace Walpole as a Poet* (Paris, 1924); Paul Yvon, *La Vie d'un Dilettante: Horace Walpole* (Paris, 1924); A. Nicoll, *History of the Late Eighteenth Century Drama, 1750-1800* (Cambridge, 1927); Eino Railo, *The Haunted Castle* (London, 1927); Dorothy M. Stuart, *Horace Walpole* (New York, 1927); Kenneth Clark, *The Gothic Revival* (London, 1928); L. L. Hanawalt, *The Rise of the Gothic Drama, 1765-1800* (University of Michigan, thesis, 1929; in MS.); A. B. Mason, *Horace Walpole* (London, 1930); and S. Gwynn, *The Life of Horace Walpole* (London, 1932).

[2] See especially Railo, Clark, Birkhead, and Yvon.

[3] For the opposite view, see W. P. Harbeson, *op. cit.,* p. 85. Throughout his thesis, Harbeson contends that the influence of the Elizabethan writers upon those of the late eighteenth and early nineteenth centuries was almost nil. "At any rate," he concludes, "we come back to the original finding that there was practically no revival of Elizabethan feeling in the drama prior to the advent of the German influence and the French revoluation." Yet, he recognizes that of all the drama of the period, two plays, Dodsley's *Cleone* and Walpole's *Mysterious Mother,* "have strong suggestions of the Elizabethan drama." The Walpole play, says Harbeson on page 83, "is strangely suggestive of a knowledge of the stage in Shakespeare's time."

[4] The work I have in mind particularly is Eino Railo's *The Haunted Castle.* Railo has taken the idea of the Shakespearean influence upon the Gothic movement, and has pressed it with such emphasis that one almost suspects Shakespeare of having written the Gothic plays and novels. On page 15, he writes: "I must here point out that the object of these passages is rather to provide analogies and historical perspective than to make it appear that Shakespeare is the actual *source* [Railo's italics] of Walpole's inventions in each separate case." This said, he points to a number of separate cases to show that Shakespeare is the source. On page 36: "When we recollect that mysterious prophecies of the nature indicated are not infrequent in Shakespeare, we may assume that Walpole founded his on the models thus provided." On page 63: "To my mind the most obvious and influential source is Shakespeare, of whose machinery of the supernatural a brief summary may be given." See also pp. 32-3, 36 (second reference).

[5] R. W. Babcock, *Genesis of Shakespeare Idolatry, 1766-1799* (Chapel Hill, N.C., 1931), p. 11.

[6] Horace Walpole," *Essays* (New York, 1900), II, 194.

[7] *Dictionary of National Biography.*

[8] *Horace Walpole as a Poet,* p. 23.

[9] Babcock, *op. cit.,* p. 46.

[10] *Letters,* Toynbee, IV, 398. To Sir David Dalrymple (June 20, 1760), No. 694.

[11] *Ibid.,* VI, 200-1. To Élie de Beaumont (March 18, 1765), No. 1014.

[12] *Letters: Supp.,* Toynbee, I, 256. To Robert Jephson (Feb., 1775), No. 1608.

[13] *Mysterious Mother* (ed. Summers), p. 259. This Postscript was first published in 1781, in J. Dodsley's edition.

[14] *Letters,* Toynbee, XI, 439. To the Rev. William Mason (May 6, 1781), No. 2172.

[15] Babcock, *op. cit.,* pp. 123 ff.

[16] *Letters,* Toynbee, VI, 105. To Christopher Wren (Aug. 9, 1764), No. 972.

[17] See note 11.

[18] *Letters: Supp.,* Toynbee, I, 169-70. To Marquise du Deffand (July, 1768), No. 1221.

[19] *Ibid.,* I, 253. To Robert Jephson (Feb. 1775), No. 1608.

[20] *Ibid.,* III, 34. To Edward Jerningham (Feb. 13, 1778), No. 1837.

[21] Babcock, *op. cit.,* p. 75.

[22] Ed. Caroline Spurgeon (New York, n. d.), p. lvii.

[23] *Ibid.,* lvii-lviii.

[24] See note 19.

[25] Babcock, *op. cit.,* p. 76.

[26] *Historic Doubts* (1768), p. 114. See also Babcock, *op. cit.,* p. 33, for a list of critical remarks upon Walpole's theory made in the years immediately following the publication of the idea.

[27] *Letters,* Toynbee, IX, 330. To Rev. William Mason (Feb. 18, 1776), No. 1682.

[28] *Ibid.,* XIV, 22. To Countess of Upper Ossory (Sept. 15, 1787), No. 2621.

[29] *Ibid.,* V, 150-1. To George Montagu (Dec. 8, 1761), No. 793. See J. Genest, *Some Account of the English Stage from the Restoration in 1660 to 1830* (Bath, 1832), III, 635.

[30] *Letters,* Toynbee, III, 288. To Richard Bentley (Feb. 23, 1755), No. 419. Walpole may have been thinking of Garrick's alteration of it into an opera, *The Fairies.* See Genest, *op. cit.,* pp. 442, 452.

[31] *Ibid.,* XIV, 42. To Countess of Upper Ossory (Jan. 15, 1788), No. 2629. Five days before this letter, Macklin's memory failed him badly during the performance of this play. See Genest, *op. cit.,* p. 555.

[32] Summers, *ed. cit.,* p. 257.

[33] See note 28.

[34] *Letters,* Toynbee, IX, 344. To Rev. William Mason (April 8, 1776), No. 1688.

[35] *Ibid.,* IX, 446. To Countess of Upper Ossory (Dec. 3, 1776), No. 1736.

[36] *Op. cit.,* pp. 199 ff.

[37] Introduction to *Eighteenth Century Essays on Shakespeare* (Oxford, 1903), p. xii.

[38] *Letters,* Toynbee, IV, 2. To George Montagu (Oct. 14, 1756), No. 492.

[39] See note 16.

[40] *Letters: Supp.,* Toynbee, I, 170. To Marquise du Deffand (July 26-7, 1768), No. 1222.

[41] See note 18.

[42] *Letters, Supp.,* Toynbee, I, 219. To Marquise du Deffand (Aug. 1773), No. 1480.

[43] See note 19.

[44] *Letters,* Toynbee, XII, 172. To Rev. William Mason (1782), No. 2272.

[45] Mrs. Yearsley's *Earl Godwin,* a tragedy, which was first performed at Bath on Nov. 2, 1789.

[46] *Letters,* Toynbee, XIV, 229. To Hannah More (Nov. 4, 1789), No. 2717.

[47] *Ibid.,* IX, 444-5. To Sir Horace Mann (Dec. 1, 1776), No. 1735.

[48] *Ibid.,* X, 155-6. To Robert Jephson (Nov. 8, 1777), No. 1818.

[49] *Ibid.,* X, 329. To Sir Horace Mann (Oct. 8, 1778), No. 1895.

[50] *Ibid.,* X, 371. To Countess of Upper Ossory (Feb. 1, 1779), No. 1922.

[51] *Ibid.,* VIII, 107. To Sir Horace Mann (Nov. 18, 1771), No. 1381; VIII, 392. To Countess of Upper Ossory (Dec. 30, 1773), No. 1517; XIII, 426-7. To Countess of Upper Ossory (Dec. 12, 1786), No. 2600; XIV, 29. To Hannah More (Oct. 14, 1787), No. 2623. Also *Supp.,* I, 152. To Marquise du Deffand (March 13, 1767), No. 1164; I, 251. To Robert Jephson (Feb. 1775), No. 1608.

[52] See note 45.

[53] See note 46.

[54] See above, p. 56.

[55] Paul Yvon, *Horace Walpole as a Poet,* pp. 153·5.

[56] *Shakespeare and Voltaire* (see above). See also C. M. Haines, *Shakespeare in France* (London, 1925).

[57] *Letters,* Toynbee, I, l-li.

[58] *Letters: Supp.,* Toynbee, I, 152. To Marquise du Deffand (March 13, 1767), No. 1164.

[59] *Ibid.,* I, 171. To Marquise du Deffand (July 26-7, 1768), No. 1222.

[60] *Letters,* Toynbee, X, 302. To Rev. William Cole

(Aug. 22, 1778), No. 1885.

[61] Babcock, *op. cit.,* pp. 102-3.

[62] *Letters,* Toynbee, VI, 343. To Miss Anne Pitt (Nov. 4, 1765), No. 1067.

[63] *Letters: Supp.,* Toynbee, I, 227. To Marquise du Deffand (Oct. 1773), No. 1493.

[64] *Letters,* Toynbee, IX, 111. To Hon. Henry Seymour Conway (Dec. 26, 1774), No. 1584.

[65] *Ibid.,* IX, 132. To Hon. Henry Seymour Conway and Countess of Ailesbury (Jan. 15, 1775), No. 1596.

[66] *Ibid.,* XIV, 100. to Lady Craven (Dec. 11, 1788), No. 2657. See also: *Ibid.,* VII, 252. To Sir Horace Mann (Jan. 31, 1769), No. 1246; VII, 309. To John Chute (Aug. 30, 1769), No. 1272; XI, 55. To Countess of Upper Ossory (Nov. 15, 1779), No. 1992; XII, 274. To Rev. William Mason (June 25, 1782), No. 2323; XIII, 283. To John Pinkerton (June 26, 1785), No. 2534; XIV, 57. To Miss Hannah More (July 12, 1788). No. 2638.

[67] *Ibid.,* V, 32. To Rev. Henry Zouch (March 7, 1761), No. 737.

[68] See note 19.

[69] *Letters,* Toynbee, IX, 392. To Countess of Upper Ossory (July 17, 1776), No. 1712.

[70] *Ibid.,* XI, 248. To Countess of Upper Ossory (July 18, 1780), No. 2078. See also: XII, 303. To Rev. William Cole (July 23, 1782), No. 2337; XIV, 86. To Countess of Upper Ossory (Oct. 11, 1788), No. 2651.

[71] *Ibid.,* XIV, 235-6. To Countess of Upper Ossory (Nov. 8, 1789), No. 2718.

[72] *Ibid.,* X, 265. To Sir Horace Mann (June 16, 1778), No. 1868.

[73] "Lady Marlborough left five hundred pounds each to Glover and Mallet as payment for writing her husband's life, none of which was to be in verse."—Toynbee, note.

[74] *Ibid.,* III, 377-8. To Richard Bentley (Dec. 17, 1755), No. 458.

[75] *Ibid.,* V, 5-6. To George Montagu (Nov. 24, 1760), No. 723.

[76] *Ibid.,* VI, 108. To Sir Horace Mann (Aug. 13, 1764), No. 973.

[77] Ed. Spurgeon, lviii n.

[78] *Letters,* Toynbee, XIV, 235. To Countess of Upper Ossory (Nov. 8, 1789), No. 2718.

[79] *Letters,* Toynbee, XV, 334. To Countess of Upper Ossory (Dec. 8, 1794), No. 2954. See also: *Ibid.,* IV, 72. To the Earl of Strafford (July 5, 1757), No. 526; VI, 124. To the Earl of Hertford (Oct. 5, 1764), No. 984; VII, 369. To Sir Horace Mann (Feb. 27, 1770), No. 1295; VII, 377. To Sir Horace Mann (April 19, 1770), No. 1300; and, IX, 329. To Rev. William Mason (Feb. 18, 1776), No. 1682.

[80] Ed. Spurgeon, p. lix.

[81] *Ibid.,* pp. lix-lxiii.

[82] *Letters,* Toynbee, VI, 183. To Rev. Thomas Percy (Feb. 5, 1765), No. 1007.

[83] *Letters; Supp.,* Toynbee, I, 170-1. To Marquise du Deffand (July 26-7, 1768), No. 1222. See also *ibid.,* I, 172-3. To Marquise du Deffand (Aug. 1768), No. 1227; and Spurgeon, *ed. cit.,* lxii-lxiii.

[84] *Letters,* Toynbee, X, 155-6. To Robert Jephson (Nov. 8, 1777), No. 1818.

[85] *Ibid.,* XIII, 230. To Dr. Warton (Dec. 9, 1784), No. 2515.

[86] Babcock, *op. cit.,* pp. 105-8.

[87] *Letters,* Toynbee, VI, 358-9. To George Montagu (Nov. 21, 1765), No. 1073.

[88] *Letters: Supp.,* Toynbee, I, 169-70. To Marquise du Deffand (July 1768), No. 1221.

[89] *Letters,* Toynbee, IX, 436-7. To Rev. William Mason (July 1776), No. 1732.

[90] *Ibid.,* IX, 414. To Rev. William Mason (Sept. 17, 1776), No. 1722.

[91] *Ibid.,* IX, 419. To Rev. William Mason (Oct. 8, 1776), No. 1725.

[92] *Ibid.,* IX, 444-5. To Sir Horace Mann (Dec. 1, 1776), No. 1735.

[93] *Ibid.,* X, 2. To Countess of Upper Ossory (Jan. 7, 1777), No. 1744.

[94] *Ibid.,* X, 91. To Rev. William Mason (Aug. 4, 1777), No. 1783.

[95] *Ibid.,* X, 223. To Rev. William Mason (April 18, 1778), No. 1851.

[96] *Ibid.,* XII, 102. To Edmond Malone (Nov. 23, 1781),

No. 2237.

[97] *Ibid.,* XIV, 150. To Miss Mary Berry (July 9, 1789), No. 2685.

[98] *Ibid.,* VI, 397. To Hon. Henry Seymour Conway (Jan. 12, 1766), No. 1087.

[99] See Lounsbury, *op. cit.,* pp. 258-80.

[100] *Op cit.*

[101] *Ibid.,* p. 335 n.

[102] *The English Novel* (London, 1894), pp. 223-4.

[103] *Op. cit.,* pp. 267 ff.

[104] *Horace Walpole as a Poet,* p. 182.

[105] Postscript to the *Mysterious Mother* (ed. Summers), p. 253.

[106] Bonamy Dobrée, *Restoration Tragedy* (Oxford, 1929), p. 147.

[107] Summers, *ed. cit.* (I, 1), p. 155.

[108] *Ibid.* (V, 5), p. 245.

[109] *Ibid.* (I, 1), p. 156. Cf. *King John,* I, 1.

[110] *Ibid.* (I, 2), p. 158. Cf. *Macbeth,* II, 4.

[111] *Ibid.* (I, 5), p. 173. Cf. *Hamlet,* V, 1.

[112] *Ibid.* (IV, 1), pp. 214-5. Cf. *Hamlet,* I, 5.

Montague Summers (essay date 1938)

SOURCE: "Historical Gothic," in *The Gothic Quest: A History of the Gothic Novel,* Fortune Press, 1938.

[*In this excerpt, Summers describes the importance of Walpole's extravagant residence, Strawberry Hill, to understanding* The Castle of Otranto *and briefly surveys the critical reaction to the novel.*]

To **The Castle of Otranto** "we owe nothing less than a revolution in public taste, and its influence is strong even at the present day. It is hardly an exaggeration to say that to Walpole's romance is due the ghost story and the novel, containing so much of the supernatural and occult, than which no forms of literature are now [1923] more common and applauded. **The Castle of Otranto** is, in fine, a notable landmark in the history of English taste and English literature."[51] This is high praise, but I bate no jot of it, yet when I wrote more

than a decade ago I chose my words carefully to say enough but not too much. We must not, we may not, go beyond what I have said.

As I have already shown, the tendencies of taste which culminated in the Gothic Novel had origins wider and deeper than any one book, even **The Castle of Otranto,** could develop. The dominant elements in the terror novel of the 1790's, of which the most famous exemplar is *The Monk,* came from Germany; the historical romance, which we have just examined, accounts for much; the French influences of Baculard d'Arnaud and his "drames monacales" are of the first importance. It is an error, and a fundamental error, to treat **The Castle of Otranto** as the one and only source of the Gothic Novel.

On June 5th, 1747, Walpole wrote to Horace Mann, I "may retire to a little new farm that I have taken just out of Twickenham,"[52] which is the first mention of the famous Strawberry Hill. He first rented "this little rural *bijou*" from Mrs. Chenevix, taking over the remainder of her lease, and in 1748 he bought it by Act of Parliament, it being the property of three minors, named Mortimer. On January 10th, 1750, Walpole says to the same correspondent: "I am going to build a little Gothic castle at Strawberry Hill. If you can pick me up any fragments of old painted glass, arms, or anything, I shall be excessively obliged to you." In September, 1749, Walpole was begging the Duke of Bedford for some windows from the dilapidated Cheneys—"in half the windows are beautiful arms in painted glass. . . . They would be magnificent for Strawberry Castle." In fact his new Gothic castle gave him a new interest in life, for he had been vastly bored with most things he endured. Yet of Strawberry he never tired. In March, 1753, he proclaims that as Chiswick House "is a model of Grecian architecture, Strawberry Hill is to be so of Gothic." "My house is so monastic," he tells Mann, "that I have a little hall decked with long saints in lean arched windows and with taper columns, which we call the Paraclete, in memory of Eloise's cloister." "Under two gloomy arches, you come to the hall and staircase . . . the most particular and chief beauty of the castle. Imagine the walls covered with . . . Gothic fretwork: the lightest Gothic balustrade to the staircase, adorned with antelopes (our supporters) bearing shields; lean windows fattened with rich saints in painted glass, and a vestibule open with three arches on the landing-place . . . the castle, when finished, will have two-and-thirty windows enriched with painted glass." The living-room had "a bow-window commanding the prospect, and gloomed with limes that shade half each window, already darkened with painted glass in chiaroscuro, set in deep blue glass." In May, 1760, Walpole had "flounced again into building—a round tower, gallery, cloister, chapel, all starting up—" and three years later, "The chapel is quite finished, except the carpet. The sable mass of the altar gives it a very sober air; for, notwithstanding the solemnity of the painted windows, it had a gaudiness that was a little profane."

What wonder that Walpole loved to fit himself to his mock-mediæval world, that now he conceived himself as the 'sensechal' of his castle, and now again he was a friar of orders grey or a swart-cowled monk burying manuscripts under the gnarled oak in his garden-garth or behind some secret panel in his old-new wainscot.

At first he welcomed visitors to his retreat. In May, 1755, he "gave a great breakfast to the Bedford court," the sun shone, "and Strawberry was all gold, and all green. I am not apt to think people really like it, that is understand it." Walpole hated that Strawberry Hill should be laughed at, jeered (although politely and among friends), and regarded as one of the 'lions.' In June, 1755, he writes that Princess Emily was there: "Liked it?" "Oh no!" but peeped and pryed into every corner, even the very offices and servants' rooms. "In short, Strawberry-Hill is the puppet-show of the times."

"The Abbot of Strawberry," as he once signed himself, withdrew more and more to Strawberry and solitude.

The fact is that Strawberry Castle—"my child Strawberry"—was infinitely precious to him, it was his own creation, the summum of his own life, the actual and external embodiment of his own dreams. Here he had built his love of Gothic, as he understood it, his romantic passion for old castles and ruined abbeys, his dreams of a mediæval world. "Tread softly," says the poet, "Tread softly because you tread upon my dreams." Strawberry, as Walpole himself wrote, "was built to please myself in my own taste, and in some degree to realize my own visions." As he wrote to Madame Du Deffand: "de tous mes ouvrages, c'est l'unique où je me sois plu; j'ai laissé courir mon imagination; les visions et les passions m'échauffaient." *The Castle of Otranto* is Strawberry in literature. As the years went by he withdrew more and more into his retreat; the world of his dreams became more and more the real world for him, the only thing that counted. Night after night he would sit up reading into the small hours, not a little conscious of his own isolation, his mental and spiritual detachment, and at times not a little weary. In some such mood he began to put his dreams upon paper, his midsummer dreams. *The Castle of Otranto* was commenced in June, 1764, and finished on the following August 6th. It was published in an edition of five hundred copies on Christmas Eve of the same year, the most apposite of days, and in January, 1765, sending a copy to the Earl of Hertford, he is able proudly to boast, "the enclosed novel is much in vogue."

In a letter dated March 9th, addressed to the Reverend William Cole, he gives the famous account of his original inspiration. "Your partiality to me and Strawberry have, I hope, inclined you to excuse the wildness of the story. You will ever have found some traits to put you in mind of the place. When you read of the picture quitting its panel, did you not recollect the portrait of Lord Falkland, all in white, in my gallery? Shall I even confess to you, what was the origin of this romance? I waked one morning, in the beginning of last June, from a dream, of which all I could recover was, that I had thought myself in an ancient castle (a very natural dream for a head like mine filled with Gothic story), and that on the uppermost banister of a great staircase I saw a gigantic hand in armour. In the evening I sat down, and began to write, without knowing in the least what I intended to say or relate. The work grew on my hands and I grew so fond of it that one evening, I wrote from the time I had drunk my tea, about six o'clock, till half an hour after one in the morning, when my hand and fingers were so weary, that I could not hold the pen tso finish my sentence, but left Matilda and Isabella talking in the middle of a paragraph. In short, I was so engrossed with my Tale, which I completed in less than two months."

People, even the best people, had laughed at Strawberry Hill, and Walpole, fearing ridicule, published *The Castle of Otranto* as a "Story Translated by William Marshal, Gent. From the Original Italian of Onuphrio Muralto, Canon of the Church of St. Nicholas at Otranto." An elaborate translator's preface relates how "The following work was found in the library of an ancient Catholic family in the north of England. It was printed at Naples, in the black letter, in the year 1529 . . . the style is the purest Italian."[53]

On March 26th, 1765, Walpole, writing to the Earl of Hertford, mentions with some pride *The Castle of Otranto,* "the success of which has, at last, brought me to own it," although he was (he confesses) for a long while terribly afraid of being bantered, "but it met with too much honour, for at first it was universally believed to be Mr. Gray's."

The second edition appeared on April 11th, 1765, an issue of five hundred copies. In the Preface, Walpole entirely discards the mask; he explains his reasons for pretending the book was a translation, and incontinently dismisses William Marshal and Canon Onuphrio Muralto. *The Monthly Review* was obviously at a loss how to treat the new romance, and whilst praising the performance as written with no common pen, allowing that the language was accurate and elegant, and proclaiming that the adventures provided considerable entertainment, the critic, forgetful of the Scriptures, objected that the moral "visiting the sins of the fathers upon the children" was useless and very insupportable.

The Critical Review was extremely unfriendly and cantankerous: "The publication of any work at this time, in England composed of such rotten materials, is a phenomenon we cannot account for," whilst the supernatural machinery is ridiculed in most clumsy fashion. None the less, the enthusiasm which greeted *The Cas-*

tle of Otranto permeated all ranks of society and did not wane.

In 1767 the romance was translated into French by M. E., Marc-Antoine Eidous, but the dialogue had been abbreviated, and the Amsterdam edition of 1777, *Le Château d'Otrante,* translated from the second English edition of 1765, is far better done and more exact. In 1791 was printed at Parma Bodoni's fine edition, whilst in 1795 Sivrac issued his well-known Italian version, *Il Castello di Otranto,* with seven illustrations which, beautifully coloured, were used in Jeffery's fine edition of 1796.[54]

In his first Preface, 1765, the anonymous Walpole says: "The scene is undoubtedly laid in some real castle." There needs no detailed comparison between Otranto and Strawberry Hill, suffice to say that in a hundred touches the galleries, the staircases, even the very rooms, are particularized.[55] Thus in Walpole's letters there are several references to the Blue Room at Strawberry. On January 7th, 1772, he writes to the Hon. Henry Conway how an explosion injured the Castle but providentially the windows in the "gallery, and blue room, and green closet, &c.," escaped. In the romance, Chapter V, Bianca was going to the Lady Isabella's chamber—"she lies in the watchet-coloured chamber, on the right hand, one pair of stairs."

The Castle of Otranto is none other than Strawberry Hill, which, indeed, Walpole explicitly acknowledged when he said that Strawberry was "a very proper habitation of, as it was the scene that inspired, the author of the Castle of Otranto."

Yet Amédé Pichot wrote of Strawberry Hill as "ce château, modèle du gout et d'élégance, serait plutôt une miniature gothique. C'est encore plus la *villa* du grand seigneur homme du monde, que le manoir du baron féodal."[56]

In November, 1786, when Lady Craven sent Walpole a delightful drawing of the Castle of Otranto, made on the spot, he told her: "I did not even know that there was a castle of Otranto. When the story was finished, I looked into the map of the kingdom of Naples for a well-sounding name, and that of Otranto was very sonorous." At the same time it seems difficult to suppose that Walpole had never heard of Otranto and its castle. Perhaps during his stay in Italy he had even seen some pictures of it, and he may have retained the name and the views quite subconsciously. In his Translator's Preface to the first edition he vaguely plans the incidents as having happened "between 1095, the æra of the first crusade, and 1243, the date of the last, or not long afterwards." *"Manfred,* Prince of *Otranto,"* may even have a historical counterpart in Manfred or Manfroi,[57] a natural son of the Emperor Frederick II. Manfred, who was born in 1233 and killed in battle

1266, usurped the throne of Sicily in 1258, spreading a report that Conrad II, a mere child, was dead. He also bore the title Prince of Otranto. In the romance Manfred has seized the possessions of Frederic of Vincenza, who is supposed to have perished in Palestine, but who reappears upon the scene. The historical Manfred unlawfully acquired the heritage of Frederick II, who common rumour had it did not die in 1250, as was supposed. In 1259 a certain hermit, who much resembled the late Emperor, raised a revolt against Manfred in the South of Italy, and many hostile barons espoused his cause.

It were equally easy and equally futile to suggest sources for various incidents in the story. To write that Sidney's *Arcadia* is the original of "a part of the supernatural element" is quite absurd.[58] Walpole was, moreover, very much in earnest in his narrative, and, grotesque as the vast size of the enchanted casque, of the gigantic greaved leg, and the great hand in armour may appear, it is ridiculous to suppose that Walpole had these phantoms of unwieldy horror from *Les Quatre Facardins.*[59] Actually, of course, all this is from the romances of chivalry, *Primaleon, Palmerin of England, Felixmarte of Hyrcania,* and *Tirante the White.*

To give any analysis of the plot of *The Castle of Otranto* were superfluous.

"Horace Walpole wrote a goblin tale which has thrilled through many a bosom," says Scott in the Dedicatory Epistle to *Ivanhoe,* and however awkward to modern taste may seem the handling of certain incidents, however naïve the development of the narrative in certain particulars, there can be no doubt that Walpole has achieved a great and most remarkable work. As I have said elsewhere, *The Castle of Otranto* is "a notable landmark in the history of English taste and English literature."

In his notes to Pope's *Imitations of Horace,* Warburton remarked that *The Castle of Otranto* was "a Master piece, in the Fable," at any rate. "The scene is laid in *Gothic Chivalry* where a beautiful imagination, supported by strength of judgement, has enabled the author to go beyond his subject, and to effect the full purpose of the *Ancient Tragedy,* that is, *to purge the passions by pity and terror,* in colouring as great and harmonious as in any of the best dramatic Writers."

This is no light praise, at least. Scott, also, concludes his admirable Essay upon Walpole with the following: "The applause due to chastity and precision of style—to a happy combination of supernatural agency with human interest—to a tone of feudal manners and language, sustained by characters strongly drawn and well discriminated—and to unity of action, producing scenes alternately of interest and of grandeur—the applause, in fine, which cannot be denied to him who can excite the passions of fear and of pity, must be awarded to the author of *The Castle of Otranto.*"

Bishop Warburton, again, in his additional notes to Pope's *Works,* pregnantly observed that "the plan of *The Castle of Otranto* was regularly a drama," and Robert Jephson, an applauded dramatist of the day, in the autumn of 1779, fitted Walpole's Romance for the stage. He duly submitted his adaptation to the author, and so far engaged Walpole's interest, and even enthusiasm, that when *The Count of Narbonne* went into rehearsal at Covent Garden the exquisite recluse was actually attracted from Strawberry Hill to attend and advise. Produced on Saturday, November 17th, 1781, the new tragedy proved a veritable triumph. The play kept the stage for some forty years, and it certainly is not without merit. Kemble and Mrs. Siddons were more than once seen in the principal rôles, which they acted with great power and effect.

The Castle of Otranto, "a grand romantic extravaganza" given at the Haymarket, on Monday, April 24th, 1848, by way of an Easter novelty, to us seems a vapid burletta without fun or consequence, but it was greeted with applause, which one supposes must have been due to the acting of Keeley, Priscilla Horton, and Mrs. W. Clifford. At any rate it is interesting to note that as late as the middle of the last century a burlesque founded upon *The Castle of Otranto* was received with general favour, and this goes far to show how popular the romance still remained with the larger public, for to those who were not well acquainted with Walpole's original such a travesty must have been utterly pointless and a bore.[60]

It is surprising that a decade and more passed before the influence of *The Castle of Otranto* made itself really felt in literature.[61] It is, of course, possible to trace some resemblances in *The Hermit,* by Lady Atkyns, 2 vols., 1769; in *The Prince of Salerno,* 1770; and in William Hutchinson's *The Hermitage,* 1772; but these are nugatory and superficial. The famous *Sir Bertrand,* 1773, is merely A Fragment.

In 1797, T. J. Matthias could jeer the virtuoso Walpole, who "mus'd o'er Gothick toys through Gothick glass," and in a gloss could declare that "his Otranto Ghosts have propagated their species with unequalled fecundity. The spawn is in every novel shop."[62]

Notes

[51] *The Castle of Otranto,* edited, with an Introduction and Notes, by Montague Summers, 1924, Introduction, p. lvii.

[52] *The Letters of Horace Walpole . . . edited . . . by* Mrs. Paget Toynbee. Sixteen Volumes, Oxford, 1903-5. Vol. II, p. 278. All my references are to this edition, but I have dispensed with notes, as the passages in question can be immediately turned up from the dates and Mrs. Toynbee's indexes in Vol. XVI, whilst continual reference numbers could only serve to chafe the reader.

[53] It is just possible that Walpole remembered a Croxall publication, *The Secret History of Pythagoras,* Part I. "Translated from the original copy lately found at Otranto in Italy. By J. W. M. D.," 1721. There was a reprint of this in 1751.

[54] There have, of course, been a very great many reprints of *The Castle of Otranto.* "Constable's Edition of *The Castle of Otranto* and *The Mysterious Mother,*" was edited by Montague Summers, 1924,

[55] *A Description of the Villa of Mr. Horace Walpole,* 1784, Preface, p. iii. Walpole speaks of Miss Hickes desiring "to see The Castle of Otranto"; in other words, visiting him at Strawberry Hill.

[56] Amédé Pichot, *Voyage historique et litéraire en Angleterre et en Écosse,* Paris, 3 tomes, 1825; Tome I, p. 214.

[57] Dante, *Purgatorio,* III, pp. 121-4.

[58] Mehrotra, *Horace Walpole and the English Novel,* 1934, pp. 15-16.

[59] A casual surmise of Mrs. Barbauld, 1810, echoed without acknowledgement as his own bright suggestion by Mr. Mehrotra, 1934.

[60] For a fuller account of Jephson and his tragedy, and the burletta of 1848, see the Introduction to my edition of *The Castle of Otranto.*

[61] In French: *Le Château d'Otrante,* trad. sur la 2ᵉ édition, by Marc-Antoine Eidous, Paris, 12mo, 1767, and 12mo, 1774; as *Isabelle et Théodore,* an anonymous version, Paris, 1797, 2 vols., 12mo, and 2 vols., 18mo; *Le Château d'Otrante,* Paris, 1798.

[62] *The Pursuits of Literature,* the Sixth Edition, 1798, p. 343.

Devendra P. Varma (essay date 1957)

SOURCE: "The First Gothic Tale: Its Potentialities," in *The Gothic Flame,* Russell & Russell, 1957.

[*In the following excerpt from* The Gothic Flame *(1957), Varma conjectures about the impetuses to Walpole's composing* The Castle of Otranto *and discusses its strong and lasting influence on the Gothic and other genres.*]

The *Schauer-romantik,* or "horror-romanticism", of the eighteenth century may be said to have originated one midsummer night, when Horace Walpole, sleeping beneath his stucco pinnacles at Strawberry Hill, dreamt he saw a giant hand in armour on the balustrade of the staircase. In this dream was born the first Gothic story, **The Castle of Otranto:** a bold and amazingly successful experiment in an absolutely untried medium. This immensely popular wild tale stands as a landmark in literary development and literary fashion. Although it has been alleged that this work is crude in attempt, incongruous and grotesque in its use of the supernatural, unrefined, distorted, and inartistic as a story form, yet it is not to be denied that this tale had far-reaching potentialities that were consciously developed by authors of succeeding generations. It is the parent of all goblin tales, the prelude to a long line of novels as unending as the spectral show of Banquo's progeny. It anticipates the genteel shudderings of Clara Reeve and Ann Radcliffe, and sets the scene for the crazy phantasmagoria of *Vathek* and the prurient nightmares of 'Monk' Lewis, while its properties were to receive artistic touches of genius at the hands of Scott and Byron, Coleridge and Poe.

Otranto opened the floodgates for a whole torrent of horror-novels. Since Walpole's time, for a stretch of about forty years, readers "supped full with horrors", but none of those compositions had a livelier play of fancy than **The Castle of Otranto.** "It is the sportive effusion of a man of genius, who throws the reins loose upon the neck of his imagination. The large limbs of the gigantic figure which inhabits the castle, and which are visible at intervals; the plumes of the helmet, which rise and wave with ominous meaning; and the various enchantments of the palace, are imagined with the richness and wildness of poetic fancy," we read in Mrs. Barbauld.

Walpole's Gothic story, like Bishop Percy's *Reliques of Ancient English Poetry* (1765), was at once a symptom and a cause of that change in sensibility which has been styled by Watts-Dunton "The Renascence of Wonder". Indeed, as W. P. Ker says in his essay on Horace Walpole, Walpole "in so many things touches . . . slightly on a region that was to be explored and exploited after him by a great host of followers". Walpole records in a letter to Richard West one of the first vivid appreciations in English of romantic and savage landscape; an experience on his journey to Italy with Gray, of "precipices, mountains, torrents, wolves, rumblings, Salvator Rosa":

> But the road, West, the road! winding round a prodigious mountain, and surrounded with others, all shagged with hanging woods, obscured with pines, or lost in clouds! Below, a torrent breaking through cliffs, and tumbling through fragments of rocks! Sheets of cascades forcing their silver speed down channelled precipices, and hasting into the roughened river at the bottom! Now and then an old foot-bridge, with a broken rail, a leaning cross, a cottage, or the ruin of an hermitage!

Horace Walpole stands as one of the most interesting literary figures of the eighteenth century. By training, literary tastes, and antiquarian propensities, he was the one man in England most likely to foster Gothic romance. A monumental edition of his letters has been published revealing the various facets of his personality and recording anecdotes of a long life of eighty years. These vivid, detailed, and quotable memoirs and letters, chronicle the social and political history of his age, and behind them lurks an elaborate panorama of his own experiences. Biographers have brought to light incidents of his school and college days, his relation to his father and to politics, his travels and books, his Whiggism and virtuoso tastes, his 'castle' at Strawberry Hill and its famous printing press, his detestation of war, whist, and Italian opera, his love of gossip and scandal, his intimate acquaintance with so many famous people. The personality of this writer has now emerged from the clouds of critical disapproval which hung round him during the nineteenth century. Macaulay's famous essay in the *Edinburgh Review* for October 1833, was a brilliant distortion of Walpole's mind, but it was accepted by an unsympathetic age. Walpole's serious achievement was dismissed as insignificant and his character much maligned. The twentieth century looks upon him with a more friendly eye, although traces of old prejudice linger on. But through the efforts of reasonable critics, the age has now tried to give full value to the extent and variety of Walpole's achievement.

His sensitive and dreaming mind absorbed the growing romantic influences of the early eighteenth century. His delicate and sensitive imagination shaped them into visions of a lost medieval world. His love of the Gothic, of old castles and abbeys, his romantic dreams of a pseudo-medieval world, inspired the creation of his 'castle' at Strawberry Hill, which reflected the curious, nightmarish nature of the romantic imaginings hidden in his unconscious mind: and how extraordinarily powerful was his imagination! At times, in his retirement, he imagined his castle a monastery and himself a monk!

The year 1764 reveals to us a Walpole disillusioned and exhausted by political and personal tension. We imagine him worried and depressed, wandering about his little mock castle of brick and wood and plaster. His secret hopes of political preferment were dying at last, and he began to stay away from the House of Commons. He had seen politics at close quarters as a sport for fools and knaves. Additions to Strawberry had ceased for some time and he was bored. The outer world was slow to perceive his finer qualities. He found those on whom he lavished his affections comparatively heedless or openly indifferent, and he was hurt and sad. Already Montagu failed to respond with sufficient ardour to his warmth of affection. Conway was to disappoint him bitterly and long afterwards Mann also was to wound him by what he deemed neglect. Thus many circumstances in the earlier months of 1764 drove Walpole into sombre retreat at Strawberry, and there he experienced, as never before, his increasing disgust with reality. This mental and spiritual detachment and physical isolation liberated his romantic imagination. Gradually the repressed dream world of his youth was re-created about him, enriched by the antiquarianism of his later years. Oswald Doughty describes him thus: "the tall, thin, unhealthy, pale eighteenth-century gentleman with eyes strangely bright, sitting alone in his brick and cement castle, wielding his goose-quill so persistently, was to himself one of that rough, rude world of chivalry and piety, the middle ages".

Professor Dobrée has called Walpole "an uneasy romantic" who, like Hamlet, felt that the time was out of joint. Failure in politics, his father's downfall, the influence of Gray and Cole, his own natural impulses—all made him shrink from the Downing Street world, and as Oswald Doughty in his (above quoted) admirable essay on Walpole expresses it, he was "a spiritual exile in his native land". He longed to escape from "the haven of bright, calm, and serene civilization"—its politics, wars and follies, its drabness and dullness to the superior and mystic realm of the Middle Ages. He observed the hard, coruscating brilliance of eighteenth-century society with the detachment of a visionary dreamer, and all the while became more engrossed in his medieval interests. Paul Yvon, in *Horace Walpole as a Poet* (1924), says, "How often did he tell Madame du Deffand, that in order to forget the unpleasant realities of life, he not seldom took refuge in visions, the outcome of which were **The Castle of Otranto** and **The Hieroglyphic Tales**". Not completely stifled by his man-of-the-world character, his love of solitude is constantly hinted at in his letters, and it was his true artistic nature that elaborated his fantasies. Gray wrote to him from Cambridge: "You are in a confusion of wine and roaring, and bawdy, and tobacco. . . . I imagine however you rather choose to converse with the living dead, that adorn the walls of your apartments . . . and prefer a picture of still-life to the realities of a noisy one." And Walpole remained, to the last, an inveterate dreamer of dreams.

The Castle of Otranto is an expression of Walpole's repressed, romantic, visionary nature. From a thousand circumstances of his environment, from antiquarian interests and the abundant impressions of the past which they invoked, from Gothic castles and abbeys, from pictures by Claude, Poussin, and Salvator Rosa, from landscape gardens modelled upon their works, and from the poetry of Shakespeare and Spenser and Milton, he fashioned dreams of a world in which the beauty of antiquity, of wonder and terror and awe were supreme.

These influences were bodied forth in dreams, and Otranto rose in gloom and terror upon the slender foundations of Strawberry. The winding wooden staircase, "the most particular and chief beauty of the castle" took a grim, bare, and enormous shape. Elegant bedrooms transformed themselves into forbidding chambers, hung with tapestry and carpeted with matting or rushes of more ancient days. The walls of Strawberry decorated with antelopes holding shields became the echoing cloister of an ancient castle. And even earlier impressions, the subconscious memories of Cambridge, helped to form his dream castle. The structure of Trinity Great Court, another Gothic building, was lying dormant in Walpole's mind. Walpole had visited Cambridge in 1763, and when five years afterwards he went there again, on entering one of the colleges, "he suddenly found himself in the courtyard of Otranto", as he expresses his impression in a letter to Madame du Deffand. This College, which was later identified with Trinity, supplied Otranto with a courtyard, great Hall and other features which were absent in Strawberry Hill.

From dreaming at Strawberry, through a long summer moonlight, of knights in armour, clanking swords, and menacing portents, Walpole awoke with a head filled with materials for a Gothic tale. His letter to Cole, in which he narrates the details of his dream, has often been quoted. He dreamt of "the gigantic hand in armour" on "the uppermost banister of a great staircase"—"a very natural dream for a head like mine filled with Gothic story"—and he experienced an immediate reaction in his impulse towards romance writing. "The scene is undoubtedly laid in some real castle" he says in his preface to the first edition, and the staircase at Strawberry Hill which was "the most particular and chief beauty of the castle", as he had mentioned earlier in 1753, was indelibly associated with his romance. The fact is well illustrated by his letter to Countess of Upper Ossory, when he made a triumphant purchase in Paris of the complete armour of Francis the First. "The armour", he writes in December 1771, seven years after the publication of **Otranto,** "is actually here, and in its niche, which I have had made for it on the staircase; and a very little stretch of imagination will give it all the visionary dignity of the gigantic hand in armour that I dreamt of seeing on the balustrade of the staircase of Otranto. If this is not realising one's dreams, I don't know what is."

Mario Praz, in *The Times Literary Supplement* of 13 August 1925, says of him, "In Horace Walpole the romantic impulses of the eighteenth century converge to a fine point". He embodies in himself the particular antiquarian phases of early English romanticism. He, indeed, largely initiated all three sides of it: the collection of things having old world associations, the revival of Gothic architecture, and the taste for the chivalric tales of long ago. The one followed naturally out of the other. The enthusiasm for old collected things deepened into an appreciation of Gothic architecture which later gave impetus to the creation of the first Gothic novel.

Walpole did not love Gothic for its virile or aspiring qualities, but for its suggestiveness to a truant fantasy. What appealed to him in Gothic art and in romance generally was its quaintness. As Lytton Strachey states: "He liked Gothic architecture, not because he thought it beautiful but because he found it queer." For Walpole, at least in the beginning, to Gothicize was a game. The Gothic was, to begin with, a decorative motif as is evident from his letter to Mann, 27 April 1753:

> I thank you a thousand times for thinking of procuring me some Gothic remains from Rome; but I believe there is no such thing there; I scarce remember any morsel in the true taste of it in Italy. Indeed, my dear Sir, kind as you are about it, I perceive you have no idea what Gothic is; you have lived too long amidst true taste, to understand venerable barbarism. You say you suppose my garden to be Gothic too. That can't be; Gothic is merely architecture; and as one has a satisfaction in imprinting the gloomth of abbeys and cathedrals on one's house, so one's garden, on the contrary, is to be nothing but *riant,* and the gaiety of nature.

But this should not lead us to suppose that he was at bottom a dilettante, as it has been suggested in certain quarters. A man who took great pains over his prodigious and prolific literary output like the ***Anecdotes of Painting in England, Historic Doubts on the reign of Richard III, Description of Strawberry, History of Tastes in Gardens,*** the essays in *The World,* the amazing number of short satirical pieces, and over the monumental ***Letters,*** was no dilettante. His printing press, which worked for some forty years, certainly did something to improve typography and it involved considerable personal labour on his part. For it, Walpole did a fair amount of editing, including the first edition of the delightful *Memoirs of Lord Herbert of Cherbury.* Then there was his astonishing collection of things of no intrinsic or artistic worth, but of great associative interest.

Walpole took pains to pretend that his work was not work but a pastime, for he feared being thought erudite. He was abnormally self-conscious but he was not trivial. Professor Ker pointed out that "Horace Walpole was a man of taste and sensibility, interested in all trifles if only they had anything of singularity, tolerant of everything except what was commonplace". Cole once wrote that it was a misfortune to have so much sensibility in one's nature as Walpole was en-

dued with. It is true that Walpole's mind was easily pleased by oddities rather than by things of more solid worth; and accordingly his Gothic castles which he himself constructed, whether of Otranto or at Strawberry, were more remarkable for their queerness than for their beauty. Macaulay as well wrote: " . . . with the Sublime and the Beautiful Walpole had nothing to do, but the third province, the Odd, was his peculiar domain."

Strawberry Hill started as a toy—straight out of Mr. Chevenix's toy-shop, as he declared; and then early in 1750 he tells Mann: "I am going to build a little Gothic structure at Strawberry Hill." A new chapter in the life of Walpole now begins. It all started as a fanciful game: but it soon became serious. From now onwards, for full fourteen years, before he wrote the first Gothic novel, Walpole was deep in architectural activities, full of enthusiasm about his miniature castle: decorating a grotesque house with pie-crust battlements; procuring rare engravings and antique chimney-boards; matching odd gauntlets; and laying out a maze of walks within five acres of ground. The villa at Strawberry Hill "gradually swelled into a feudal castle, by the addition of turrets, towers, galleries . . . garnished with appropriate furniture of scutcheons, armorial bearings, shields, tilting-lances, and all the panoply of chivalry". *The Edinburgh Review* writes: "The motto which he prefixed to his *'Catalogue of Royal and Noble Authors',* might have been inscribed with perfect propriety over the door of every room in his house, and on the title page of every one of his books. *'Dove diavolo, Messer Ludovico, avete pigliate tante coglionerie?'* In his villa every apartment is a museum, every piece of furniture is a curiosity; there is something strange in the form of the shovel; there is a long story belonging to the bell-rope. We wander among a profusion of rarities, of trifling intrinsic value, but so quaint in fashion, or connected with such remarkable names and events, that they may well detain our attention for a moment. A moment is enough. Some new relic, some new curio, some new carved work, some new enamel, is forthcoming in an instant. One cabinet of trinkets is no sooner closed than another is opened. It is the same with Walpole's writings. It is not in their utility, it is not in their beauty, that their attraction lies. . . . Walpole is constantly showing us things—not of great value indeed—yet things which we are pleased to see, and which we can see nowhere else. They are baubles; but they are made curiosities either by his grotesque workmanship, or by some association belonging to them."

Walpole had a purse long enough to give visible and tangible expression—in prints, in gates, in Gothic temples, in bowers, in old manuscripts, in a thousand gimcracks, to the smouldering and inarticulate passion for the darkness of the Past. William Lyon Phelps judges that, "As a collector of curiosities he was probably influenced more by a love of old world associations than any sound appreciation of artistic design". The deckings and trappings of the chivalric age infused into him a boyish delight, while the glitter and colour of the Middle Ages offered unto him an escape from the prosaic dullness of his own times. Oliver Elton thinks that "his house and Museum, along with his letters, may be regarded as his chief work of art and as the mirror of his mind and taste". The romantic ideals of his literary mind were realized in actual life at Strawberry. His letters to Montagu during the period of architectural activities reveal a mind full of buried manuscripts and valuable documents concealed behind Gothic panelling.

His interest in things medieval may not have been that of an antiquary, but it was surely that of an artist who loves things old because of their age and beauty. Virginia Woolf in an article stated that "Walpole had imagination, taste, style, in addition to a passion for the romantic past". On the contrary Professor Saintsbury holds: "Of real poetry, real romance, and real passion of any kind, he had no share, no inkling even". We beg leave not to agree with this remark. "I have got an immense cargo of painted glass from Flanders," Walpole wrote in 1750, "indeed several of the pieces are Flemish arms, but I call them the achievements of the old Count of Strawberry."

Visiting Stratford, he is disgusted with the "wretched old town", which he expected "for Shakespeare's sake to find smug and pretty, and *antique, not old*". This extract illustrates the quality of Walpole's medievalism; things smug and pretty and *antique, not old,* were what he loved; things approaching the imaginative reconstruction of the past were never foreign to his thought. As Scott said: "A Horace Walpole, or a Thomas Warton, is not a mere collector of dry and minute facts, which the general historian passes over with disdain. He brings with him the torch of genius, to illuminate the ruins through which he loves to wander." Indeed, the ointment is rare and rich, of a subtle and delicious perfume. The aroma of a wonderful age comes wafting out from the hundred pages of *The Castle of Otranto,* and enchants our senses: who else could have written the first Gothic novel but this amiable virtuoso, who dreamed of ghosts, went about collecting armour and tombstones in a Gothic castle, and read Dr. Dee on spirits?

Although *The Monthly Review,* commenting upon *The Castle of Otranto,* said, "To present an analysis of the story would merely introduce the reader to 'a company of skeletons', but to refer him to the book would be to recommend him an assemblage of beautiful pictures", it is worth while to recount the major incidents of the story.

Manfred, the usurping prince of Otranto, haunted by a mysterious prophecy, hastens to secure Isabella, the only daughter of the real heir of Otranto, as bride for his only son Conrad. On the very eve of marriage, Conrad is crushed to death by the mysterious fall of an enormous helmet shaded with black plumes. Theodore, a peasant boy, who discovers that the miraculous helmet is identical with the one now missing from the black marble statue of Alfonso the Good, is imprisoned as a sorcerer under the helmet itself. Frantic with rage and fear, Manfred declares his intention of himself marrying Isabella, on which some prodigies appear: the sable plumes of the helmet wave backward and forward in a tempestuous manner; the portrait of his grandfather utters a deep sigh, quits its panel, descends on the floor and vanishes into a chamber.

Isabella meanwhile escapes through a subterraneous passage to the church of St. Nicholas. On her way she encounters Theodore who has been accidentally released, and sympathy very soon ripens into love. As Manfred, in his hot pursuit of Isabella, enters the vaults of the castle, the affrighted servants bring news of a ghost or giant whose foot was seen in the upper chamber. Nevertheless, Manfred pursues his designs, and orders Father Jerome to deliver Isabella from the sanctuary. He also orders Theodore to be beheaded, but the execution is set aside as Father Jerome, by means of a birth-mark, discovers in Theodore his long-lost child.

Frederic, Marquis of Vicenza, father of Isabella and the real claimant of Otranto, arrives, and his arrival is followed by further prodigies: a brazen trumpet miraculously salutes him at the gate of the castle; the plumes of the enchanted helmet nod vigorously. He is accompanied by a hundred knights who bear an enormous sword which, bursting from their hands, falls on the ground opposite the helmet and remains immovable. Manfred tries to quell animosities by a matrimonial alliance by which each is to marry the daughter of the other. Frederic agrees. On the mere proposal three drops of blood fall from the nose of Alfonso's statue. The apparition of the holy hermit of Joppa discloses to Frederic "the fleshless jaws and empty sockets of a skeleton wrapt in a hermit's cowl" and adjures him to forget Matilda. The story ends with the tragic death, by mistake, of Matilda at the hands of her father.
As she expires, a clap of thunder shakes the castle to its foundations, and the form of Alfonso, dilated to an immense magnitude, appears in the centre of the ruins, exclaiming "Behold in Theodore the true heir of Alfonso!"

Besides the atmosphere and background of chivalry and enchantment typical of "old romances", there are three other literary forms shedding influences on *The Castle of Otranto:* the heroic romance, the fairy-story, and the tale of Oriental Magic; and these blend and fuse with three other elements from contemporary prose fiction: excessive sensibility, exemplary piety, and an explicit moral. Walpole's historical and antiquarian knowledge is well illustrated in his collection of books at Strawberry Hill. Over two hundred of the volumes were works on ancient chivalry and historical themes. These were sufficient to bestow a consistent atmosphere of chivalry on his romance, by means of stories of knights in armour and crusades, through descriptions of feudal tyrants and dungeons, and by recorded incidents of challenge and chivalric procession. Details, such as a lady arming her knight, his vow of eternal fealty to her, and knightly oaths as "by my halidame" (cf. *Longsword*), though this is oddly put into the mouth of a chattering domestic, does create an old-world chivalric atmosphere. We note the influence of heroic romance and drama in the struggle of generosity between the "sentimental, self-sacrificing heroines" and in the melting forgiveness of the pious hero for the barbarous treatment of the tyrant—the supernatural magnanimity of the heroic prince type (cf. for example Dryden's *Aurengzebe*). The temporary emergence of the "tender-hearted villain" in the scene where Manfred is 'touched' and weeps, seems to be influenced by *Longsword.*

The supernatural element in the book is probably its greatest innovation, and is a curious blend of fairy-tale and magic, with one genuine spectre episode, the appearance of the skeleton hermit in the oratory, of which Scott said that it "was long accounted a masterpiece of the horrible". The appearance of this spectre as an instrument of fate, with its sepulchral warning, influenced the later Romanticism of Horror. But no one apparently ever attempted to imitate the much more elaborate but fantastic creation of the dismembered giant distributing himself piecemeal about the castle and at last shaking it to its foundations. This is quite different from the conventional ghosts, spirits, and spectres that stalk rampant through the pages of the later Gothic novels. In *The Castle of Otranto,* curiously, the word 'ghost' does not occur, but instead we find occasional references to 'sorcerer', 'talisman', and 'enchantment'. Certain episodes, too, such as the apparition of the giant seen by Bianca, when she was rubbing her ring, definitely suggest the fairytales of the East that Walpole was so fond of reading. The episode reminds us of the appearance of the genii in *Aladdin and the Wonderful Lamp,* one of the stories in *Arabian Nights Entertainments.*

Walpole raised the apparition of Alfonso to gigantic proportions. In this particular device Walpole seems to have imitated Eastern tales, in which enormous size not only suggests embodiment of power, but also strikes and evokes a feeling of terror. Various forms of Oriental fiction had become popular in England during the first twenty years of the eighteenth century. Most of these works reached England through France. Antoine Galland's French version of the *Arabian Nights Entertainment* was translated into English between 1708 and 1715. In the following few years Turkish, Persian,

Arabic, Chinese, and Mogul tales were translated from the French of François Pétis de la Croix, Jean Terrason, Jean Paul Bignom, and Simon Gueullette. It is likely that these may have attracted Johnson to seek in Abyssinia the scene of *Rasselas,* and they give clues to the extravagant incidents and luxuriant descriptions in Beckford's *Vathek* (1786), "the most famous Oriental tale in the English language".

There had also been during the period a growing interest in voyage, travel, and discovery, and a heightening of curiosity concerning the mystic charms of the East. Also, the opening of the first Gothic novel: "Manfred, Prince of Otranto, had one son and one daughter . . ." reads almost like a fairy-tale, with its irrational parent, one lovely and one unlovely child. The tragic ending, however, is typical neither of fairy-stories nor of later Gothic romances, which ring incessant changes on the conventional fairy-tale endings like: "And they were married and lived happily ever after."

There is a definite resemblance between the supernatural machinery of *The Castle of Otranto* and that treated in Dr. Dee's book on imps and spirits. We get here a profusion of gigantic dismembered limbs, such as the "mighty arm and hand", the arm "with a broad-axe", "a right hand (and no body appearing), the hand being very big", "a great huge man, with a great sword in his hand", "a head cut off from a body", and, more than once, a figure ascending heavenward, like Alfonso the Good at the climax of *The Castle of Otranto.* Taken all together, these suggestions of resemblances are too numerous and too striking to be overlooked as even a minor influence that went to the making of Walpole's Gothic story. Nor did these stray suggestions exist only in Dr. Dee's book. Ideas of this kind may be traced in the folk-lore of different nations ever since the fairy-tale of *Jack and the Bean Stalk.*

One of Madame D'Aulnoy's fairy-tales, *The White Cat,* mentioned by Walpole, has examples of dissected beings, and in it the prince is served by *bodiless hands,* in the palace of the white cat. Also, Becquer's legend of *The Devil's Cross* records an extraordinary story of dismembered armour that at the touch of a ray of light could always gather itself together, no matter how hewed and separated, and continue the devilish raids. Also there is a reference to a gigantic hand grasping a gigantic key on the keystone of the Alhambra's portal. W. B. Yeats's collection of old *Irish Fairy and Folk Tales* includes the story of *A Queen's Country Witch* who takes the form of a man's legs walking without head or body. So, besides Dee's work, other literary models may have played their part in the formation of the first Gothic tale. Pope's description of the Paraclete in *Eloisa to Abelard,* and Swift's Brobdingnag in *Gulliver's Travels,* had appealed to Walpole, and they did leave some impress on *The Castle of Otranto.* And so the readers who eagerly explored Walpole's Gothic castle had previously enjoyed the thrill of chimney-corner legends by a winter fireside.

There is a tale by Count Anthony Hamilton, *The Four Facardins* (1646), with which Walpole was perhaps quite familiar. The 'giant' and 'his leg' and 'armour' occur there. Facardin of Mount Atlas, during the course of his adventures, has a fight with 'an enormous giant' who had a very long nail on the toe of his right foot. Facardin is injured by this nail, and being infuriated lops off the right leg of the giant. The fall of the giant "was like that of a tower and the earth trembled as he touched it". Facardin, to his great surprise, finds that the giant has disappeared and carried his leg away with him! While Walpole enlarged the suggestion of his dream of "a big hand in armour" in **The Castle of Otranto,** he might have had the subconscious memories of Hamilton's supernatural as well. There is a great similarity in the handling of the material by Walpole and Hamilton in their characteristic naive simplicity in the use of the supernatural where atmosphere or suggestion does not play any part. The crude machinery of their tales belongs to an ideal world of fancy and fairy-tale, where there is neither probability nor a necessary correspondence between effect and cause.

Walpole looked to ancient romances as well for inspiration. He knew the *Arcadia* of Sidney, and had a tender regard for the works of Scudéry and the Heroic school. These may have partly been the source of the supernatural in **The Castle of Otranto.** In the *Arcadia* the oracle predicts strange events; the plot of **Otranto,** too, veers round a similar mysterious prophecy. In *Arcadia,* as the story slowly unfolds itself, we find the predictions of the oracle unrelentingly fulfilled, although King Basilius endeavours to prevent their materialization. Manfred too, in **The Castle of Otranto,** fruitlessly attempts to ward off the realization of the prophecy.

These minor points go to establish that Walpole cannot be said to have invented anything absolutely new as far as mere machinery goes. His originality lay in combining such machinery with historical romance, and in assigning to his unearthly beings a definite role in enforcing retributive justice—just such a part as common belief assigned to departed spirits. The old properties of folk-lore and fairy-tales were ill-balanced and ill-conceived. Walpole welds these ingredients together with the fire of his innovating genius.

In the Preface to the second edition, the title of which was merely **The Castle of Otranto, a Gothic story,** the still generally unknown author explained his purpose in writing it by the oft-quoted statement that "it was an attempt to blend two kinds of romance, the ancient and the modern", a remark sufficiently illuminated in a letter to Dr. Warton. The book reveals these dual characteristics. The 'modern' element is evident in the method of characterization and dialogue. The characters happen to be mostly stock-figures, while the domestics of the story stand as contrast to the figures of high life. The minor characters, and specially the loquacious maid, Bianca, have their clay from Shakespeare, as Walpole said. Referring in his preface to the second edition of these domestic minor figures, he writes: "That great master of nature Shakespeare was the model I copied." Then follows a spirited defence of the Shakespearean trick of relieving tragic scenes with flashes of farce. The actions of the actors are within bounds of reason, and here "the natural of modern novel" comes to an end. The union of real life with the wonders of romance was a reconciliation between nature and imagination, giving a new lease of life to Romance in England. The type made strides towards development and consequently entered the borders of fine art.

Walpole's manifesto in this second preface that his object in this tale was to make the supernatural appear natural, by the portrayal of characters placed in unusual circumstances, was identical with the aim which Coleridge set before himself in the *Lyrical Ballads* some thirty-five years after. Walter Scott, remarking upon "the wild interest of the story", pointed out that it was "the first modern attempt to found a tale of amusing fiction upon the basis of the ancient romances of chivalry". He goes on to say: "As, in his model of a Gothic modern mansion, our author had studiously endeavoured to fit to the purposes of modern convenience or luxury, the rich, varied, and complicated tracery and carving of the ancient cathedral, so, in **The Castle of Otranto,** it was his object to unite the marvellous turn of incident, and imposing tone of chivalry, exhibited in the ancient romance, with that accurate exhibition of human character, and contrast of feelings and passions, which is or ought to be, delineated in the modern novel."

It has been alleged that Walpole could not fully achieve his aim of blending ancient romance and the contemporary novel; that the characters in **The Castle of Otranto** speak the language of eighteenth-century fiction and exhibit corresponding emotions. Although Walpole could not bestow upon his heroine those delicate shades of character which we get in Richardson and Fielding, Matilda and Isabella talk and behave, amid a welter of phantoms and supernatural portents, as Clarissa Harlowe or Sophia Western could have done. "Certainly the blending of supernatural events and Gothic savagery with the *beaux sentiments* of his own day was the least successful feature of Walpole's novel," says R. W. Ketton-Cremer; but Walpole employed the old supernatural agencies of Scudéry and La Calprenède as the background to the adventures of personages modelled as closely upon ordinary life as the personages of *Tom Jones*. According to Austin Dobson "the actions, sentiments, conversation, of the heroes and heroines of ancient days were as unnatural as the machines employed to put them in motion".

Walpole did model his characters on a contemporary pattern, but borrowed from the old romances some fancy and imagination and art of invention which, in the literal reproduction of life, he found neglected and forgotten.

It has been assumed in some quarters that Walpole's story was a literary 'joke'. This appears to be a wild surmise, and this conjecture has no sound foundation. Walpole meant it as seriously as he ever meant anything, and was quite sincere about it. He told Élie de Beaumont that when he published his "little story" it was because he "was so diffident of its merit" that he gave it as a translation from an Italian manuscript. Walpole seriously repeated and amplified in this letter what he had already conveyed to Dr. Warton: "To tell you the truth, it was not so much my intention to recall the exploded marvels of ancient romance as to blend the wonderful of old stories with the natural of modern novels." The latter kind of writing, Walpole added, Richardson had made 'insupportable' to him: "I thought the *nodus* was become *dignus vindice,* and that a god, or at least a ghost, was absolutely necessary to frighten us out of too much sense." In another letter, written a few days later to the Earl of Hertford, he says, the success of the romance has at least brought him to own it, though the wildness of it made him terribly afraid.

Probably this conception of a literary joke arose out of some casual statements made in the past. Scott has called it "one of the standard works of our lighter literature". Miss Dorothy M. Stuart remarked that "Otranto . . . was a pastime, the sequel to a Gothic dream, the *tour de force* of a brilliant amateur". Walpole himself had ridiculed the ghosts and omens of Clarendon's stories in his *Catalogue of Royal and Noble Authors* and his dictum was "there is no medium between believing and laughing at them". These need not, however, lead us to assume that this romance was necessarily a literary joke.

Horace Walpole, in his letters to the Rev. William Mason, the Rev. William Cole, and Robert Jephson, frequently discussed the revival of the Gothic romance as initiated by himself and carried on by Clara Reeve. He felt that during the 'eighties the reaction against neoclassicism had gone too far from reason and common sense. In the 'sixties people needed to be impressed with the charms of the fanciful. While writing to Miss Hannah More, he ventured to tell the truth: "It was fit for nothing but the age in which it was written; . . . that required only to be amused . . . and rather wanted to be brought back to imagination, than to be led astray by it." Besides, it was of all his writings, the one Walpole himself most liked. "I confess, my dear," he wrote to Madame du Deffand, "that of all my works this is the only one I enjoyed writing." And the subsequent rendering may follow thus: " . . . I have given reins to my imagination till I became on fire with the visions and feelings which it excited. I have composed it in defiance of rules, of critics, and of philosophers; and it seems to me just so much the better for that very reason. I am even persuaded, that sometime hereafter, when taste shall resume the place which philosophy now occupies, my poor Castle will find admirers!"

Walpole was a genius of no ordinary kind. C. S. Fearnside, in his introduction to *Classic Tales,* says: "*The Castle of Otranto* deserves the praise of being the outcome of a vision of a world beyond and above that in which the author himself moved and which he described in his letters with a vivacity that would never be expected by those who knew him solely in his 'Gothic Story'." Even though it has been abused, criticized, praised, and even laughed at, "*The Castle of Otranto,* despite its tinselled gloss, is historically important because of its influence". A. T. Hazen of Yale says that "In the total number of editions the book has displayed a rather astonishing vitality". It is not a great work—Walpole was not a poet, not a creator, but it was, indeed, a fruitful work. It would be, therefore, worth while to look into the potentialities of this first Gothic tale.

There is hardly a feature of Gothic romance that was not employed by Walpole in *The Castle of Otranto.* Walpole bequeathed to his successors a remarkable collection of useful 'properties', and his 'machinery' and 'motifs' quickly accumulated as conventions of the Gothic school. *The Castle of Otranto* possessed potentialities in three directions, of which the ingenious innovator was Horace Walpole: the Gothic machinery, the atmosphere of gloom and terror, and stock romantic characters. Countless Gothic novels have in their titles 'castle', 'abbey', 'priory', 'convent' or 'church'. A glance at *A Gothic Bibliography* by Montague Summers would satisfy anyone. The buildings seem to acquire a personality and an empery of their own, ever since the Gothic tale of *Otranto.* The shilling shockers of the Gothic school that flooded the market during the nineteenth century exploited many of the devices employed in the first Gothic tale. Walpole had called his novel *The Castle of Otranto: a Gothic Story.* The shockers imitated Walpole's method of using a secondary title. Eventually the crude materials in the novel were transformed to finer qualities in romantic poetry. What in Walpole's compact book are merely hints were expanded in the later novels to a greater breadth and variety.

The background of Walpole's story is a Gothic castle, singularly unenchanted, but capable of being invested with mysterious grandeur as later in the novels of Ann Radcliffe. The Castle has been called the true hero of the book, the hub around which all action gravitates. The remote castle, with its antique courts and ruined turrets, deserted and haunted chambers where hang age-old tapestries; its grated windows that exclude the light; its dark, eerie galleries amid whose mouldering gloom is heard the rustle of an unseen robe, a sigh, a hurried footfall where no mortal step should tread; its dark, machicolated and sullen towers set high upon some precipice of the Apennines frowning upon the valleys below—it is the Castle itself which is the focal point of Walpole's romance. The haunted castle forms the stage-setting; while its accessory properties powerfully seize the imagination. If we eliminate it, the whole fabric of the romance would be bereft of its foundation and its predominant atmosphere would fade away.

The Castle brought in its train other architectural associations evoking an atmosphere of Gothic gloom. The bewildering vaults and secret panels, the subterranean passages, the broken winding spiral staircases, the trap-door creaking on rusty hinges, the decayed apartments and mouldering floors—objects trivial and insignificant in Walpole's hands, were fraught with terrible possibilities. The convent and the cavern, and the deepest dungeon of the darkest tower, all were the accessories of this Gothic castle of romance, and are hinted in the story of Otranto. "Horace Walpole's experiments in Gothic architecture and the machinery of medieval romance are easily ridiculed", says W. P. Ker, "but the meaning of these diversions can hardly be mistaken: the quickness of his nature required more vivid fancies, more exciting pictures for the mind, than were commonly provided by contemporary taste."

Walpole successfully creates an atmosphere of mystery, gloom, and terror, through his specialized settings, machinery, character-types, theme, plot, or technique. They are so selected and combined as to throw out dark suggestions and intensify the mystery. A heavy pall hangs over the Gothic scene, and "the gloomth of abbeys and cathedrals" spreads over the atmosphere. The tolling of the midnight bell, and the clank of chains break the silence of the night. Walpole's "subterranean passage" connecting the castle with the church of St. Nicholas, became very popular with the later romance writers of the Gothic school. The palpitating heroine Isabella escapes through these very awfully silent subterranean regions. Her flight is an episode of eerie atmosphere:

> The lower part of the castle was hollowed into several intricate cloisters. . . . An awful silence reigned throughout those subterraneous regions; except now and then, some blasts of wind, that shook the doors she had passed, and which grating on the rusty hinges, were re-echoed through that long labyrinth of darkness. Every murmur struck her with new terror. . . . In one of those moments she thought she heard a sigh. She shuddered and recoiled a few paces. In a moment she thought she heard the step of some person. Her blood curdled. . . . Every suggestion that horror could inspire rushed into her mind.

A sudden gust of wind extinguishes her lamp, leaving her in total darkness, and then a "clouded ray of moonshine" comes to her aid. "Words cannot paint the horror of the princess's situation." The succeeding generation of authors attempted to paint the horror of just such situations after Walpole wrote that most fruitful and creative description. That paragraph, well adapted to heighten curiosity, bristles with appropriate atmospheric conditions. The blasts of wind, which at the critical moment extinguished Isabella's lamp, were for more than half a century to be heard whistling through the pages of Clara Reeve, Mrs. Radcliffe, 'Monk' Lewis, Scott, and others. And there is the pale gleam of the moon as

> gliding softly between the aisles, and guided by an imperfect gleam of moonshine that shone faintly, Manfred steals forward.

In later Gothic novels, at the very moment when the tyrant is engaged in blackest night on some deed of darkness, the same moon emerges from behind a patch of cloud, revealing a ghastly scene that alarms him and prevents the crime from being committed. It shines through the Gothic windows of ruined abbeys, dim and mysterious, illuminating to the tyrant's view the glassy eyes of his dead heir, a witness to the violent and tragic end of his line. The moon is intended to awaken a nocturnal atmosphere fraught with mystery and tinged with fantasy, fear, and sadness. It lends an indistinct and weird shape to each feature. As Eino Railo observes, in *The Haunted Castle* (1927), the moon "is a theatrical searchlight cast from the wings at suitable moments to reveal to the terror-stricken audience visions and scenes of fear".

The wind that caused the doors to creak on their rusty hinges, the draught that wandered through the subterranean passages, had a special duty assigned to it by Walpole. It sweeps fast through the vaults in sudden gusts, to extinguish the fluttering candle flame borne by the persecuted heroine just at the time when her flight is at its climax, launching her into awful, pitch-black darkness. In later novels, when it whines in the night outside the despairing and trembling maiden's window, the loquacious chamber-maid takes it for a sighing ghost. The lamp of Isabella in the later works, develops the virtue of "burning blue" to warn its possessor of an approaching ghost, or reveals the emaciated 'unknown' locked in the dank dungeon; its one defect being that it has to go out when most needed by an intrepid explorer or palpitating heroine. Lightning is the mighty ally of wind and storm; at a critical moment there comes a sudden burst of thunder shaking the foundations of the haunted castle, hinting at the existence of avenging eternal powers. Thunder and lightning recur again in the later work of the Schauer-Romantiks.

While enumerating Walpole's innovation of Gothic

machinery, one cannot afford to omit "the Ancestral Portrait" and "the time-yellowed scroll". The mysterious manuscript is usually discovered in some secret drawer or dusty corridor of the deserted wing and contains the detailed confession of some foul murder committed in the past, or perhaps uselessly warns the inquisitive heroine or hero to "look no further". In later works, these scrolls are tied with faded ribbon, and around them hovers a breath of past happiness or of sorrows now ended. Walpole endowed "the ancestral portrait" with life, and the power of stepping down from its frame. In the hands of Mrs. Radcliffe it turns into a miniature invested with tender memories, and in the later Gothic novels there is displayed on every castle wall the feature of some glorious ancestor. Finally it was to prove effectual in transmitting a sombre impression of that mysterious Melmoth the Wanderer, where this property is endowed with a demonic power, awakening an indefinite suspicion of some hidden dreadful crime, as the portrait instils a magnetic terror with its mysterious blazing eyes.

Besides these Gothic settings, Walpole had anticipated the character-types. The gloomy tyrant or Byronic hero is foreshadowed in Walpole's Manfred, imitated in Radcliffe's Montoni. Walpole gave the first sketch of the dark, handsome, melancholy, passionate, and mysterious hero of Byronic poems. Bianca describes to her mistress her ideal love "with large black eyes, a smooth white forehead and manly curling locks like jet". Theodore, at the end of the story, carried with him "a melancholy that had taken possession of his soul". Here is the progenitor of melancholy Lara, or the wild Corsair, or the handsome Giaour. The Gothic heroine or damsel in distress had always been a beautiful shadow, ever since Walpole pictured Isabella. Her beauties and virtues attain perfection in later works as the realism in her character tends to melt away.

With Theodore the noble peasant hero with his birthmark, the theme of the long-lost relative emerges. The chief characters of Walpole's romance, the usurping tyrant, the persecuted heroine, the "noble peasant" hero, the hermit, the monk, and the comic element supplied by garrulous, ghost-scared domestic servants—all became stock properties of later Gothic novels; as did the general plan of Walpole's plot: the restoration to hereditary rights of an unknown and defrauded heir by means of supernatural agents acting on behalf of divine justice. Jerome is the prototype of many a count disguised as father confessor, Bianca the model of many a chattering servant. The imprisoned wife reappears in countless romances, including Mrs. Radcliffe's *Sicilian Romance* (1790), and Mrs. Roche's *Children of the Abbey* (1798). Along with all this, Walpole's importation of "old romance" material bequeathed to the later novels the pirates, prophecies, dreams, and birthmarks, which recur again and again.

In order that the passions and characters could develop new dimensions, Walpole placed the setting of his tale in Italy, and horror-romanticism long retained this love for a southern setting. This longing for the South, for an alien and distant setting, is typical of the romantic attitude, and reflects the effort of the Gothic mind to break away from the fetters of homely experience. The southern setting made possible truly romantic effects; it was associated with monasteries and mysterious monastic life, and there the reign of the Inquisition was no very distant matter, and could supply a series of pleasing and torturing visions to Protestant readers. *The Castle of Otranto* is in Italy, whither also Mrs. Radcliffe places her *Udolpho* and *The Italian* and her *Sicilian Romance*. The action of *The Romance of the Forest* takes place in France, and that of *The Monk* in Spain. St. Leon is a Frenchman, Schemoli an Italian.

Thus the hints vaguely thrown out by Walpole, his stray suggestions and use of crude Gothic properties— castle, picture, vaults, galleries, subterranean passages, monasteries, convents, statues, ruins, music, moon, and wind—everything was developed by later novelists and made to yield maximum results.

The defects of the machinery are glaring to a modern eye, but they matter as little as the fallen tree-trunks, the strewn rocky pebbles or the snowdrifts which retard for a while, but do not stem, the Alpine torrent in its tumultuous course down the mountain-side. Austin Dobson, in his memoirs of Horace Walpole, says: "A generation like the present for whom fiction has unravelled so many intricate combinations . . . no longer feels its soul harrowed up in the same way as did his hushed and awe-struck readers of the days of the third George. . . . We doubt if that many-plumed and monstrous helmet, which crashes through stone walls and cellars, could now give a single shiver." To Miss Birkhead "His (Walpole's) supernatural machinery is as undignified as the pantomime properties of Jack the Giant Killer. The huge body scattered piecemeal about the castle, the unwieldy sabre, borne by a hundred men, the helmet 'tempestuously agitated', and even the 'skeleton in hermit's cowl' are not alarming but mildly ridiculous." It is true that the supernatural machinery, its actions and interference, is rather too frequent and palls constantly on the reader's mind; while supernatural occurrences are brought forward sometimes in strong daylight. But Walpole's task was stupendous; his object was to wind up the feelings of his reader till they became for a moment identified with those of a ruder age, and to harmonize the phantoms and apparitions with the manners of feudal times. This was a task which required no little learning, no ordinary degree of fancy, and no common portion of genius to execute. And he very nearly succeeded!

The potentialities of the book can never be questioned. When we look at the careless profusion of cyclamen petals, we are amazed that such a rich exotic sprinkle of colours should have sprung from a mere grain of seed. And so it was with the productive seed *The Castle of Otranto* that gave rise to an immortal school in fiction.

Considering what Walpole contributed to the novel as an art-form, it would be worth while examining his technique, and analysing his art of characterization, atmosphere and description, his method of plot construction, and use of dialogue, suspense, and climax.

Fiction in the first three-quarters of the eighteenth century had concentrated on reason, common sense, and satirical wit. The birth of *The Castle of Otranto* satisfied the requirements of the new age which was groping after new sources of pleasure. There was from now onwards a longing for imagination, mystery, and gloom. From a stress on photographic representation of life, there was an increased interest in action and adventure. Walpole furnished writers with the materials to work on. Under his influence, the attraction towards chivalry paved the way for historical tales. But Walpole's goblin tale also gratified the love of mystery by its castle, its technique of suspense, and its element of terror. It diffused a new spirit, and became a fingerpost to mark the art of fiction undergoing a romantic revival. The novel was to make great strides towards maturity. The theory of truthful characterization was constantly emphasized during the eighteenth century, but Walpole injected variety into the plot and setting of the story by bringing in medieval marvels. From now onwards fiction would gradually tend to favour the romantic rather than the realistic type.

In more than one way *The Castle of Otranto* was a challenge to the methods and subject-matter of contemporary novelists. It substituted invention for observation, a picture of the past for that of the present, the supernatural and the marvellous for ordinary everyday experiences. The conception was original, and the attempt was abundantly rich in results. *Otranto* was a revolt against the moral lessons, sentiment, domestic familiarities, and boisterous rowdyism of middle-class fiction. Walpole's crude manifesto of the novel of the future hints at the confession of poetic faith put forward forty years later in *Lyrical Ballads*. Transferred to the realm of poetry and generalized into philosophy, these were the respective spheres of Wordsworth and Coleridge. We miss in *Otranto* the delicate representation of the follies and foibles of eighteenth-century life, as well as that healthy animalism that characterized the school of Fielding; we are now bordering on regions of romance, of secluded cottages and Rousseauistic sentiment, of hills and barren moors.

Walpole endows his characters with distinct individuality, in tune with the age and nature of the story. Manfred is presented as an embodiment of feudal tyr-

anny, whose courage, art, and duplicity are true ingredients of the barbarous chieftain of dark ages. He can excite fear and pity when his pride is quelled and his race extinguished. The touches of remorse and natural feeling in his character make him human and draw our sympathies. As a contrast to this selfish and tyrannical prince stand the pious monk and the patient Hippolita. Theodore is the juvenile hero, who seems to have walked out of the pages of old fairytales, and Matilda has all the necessary interesting sweetness to match him as the heroine. Walpole deliberately keeps the character of Isabella subdued, in order to relieve that of Manfred's daughter. But the magic spell of romance is broken when Isabella becomes the bride of Theodore.

The Critical Review, making allowances for the "monstrosities of this story", said that "the characters are well marked, and the narrative kept up with surprising spirit and propriety". The *Monthly Review* praised Walpole's language as "accurate and elegant" and the characters as "highly finished". It concluded: "The disquisition into human manners, passions, and pursuits, indicate the keenest penetration and the most perfect knowledge of mankind." It was "a work of genius evincing great dramatic powers".

Indeed, *The Castle of Otranto* is a deftly constructed piece of work preserving all the dramatic unities, moving straight towards the climax, and emphasizing the structural technique to excite the reader's curiosity. The five chapters of the story resemble five acts of a tragedy, and the complications of the plot are resolved only in the end. The various portents succeed one another in a most striking manner and gradually prepare us for the grand catastrophe. They bear each upon the other towards the accomplishment of the ancient prophecy, announcing the ruin of the house of Manfred. Despite the extraordinary incidents of a dark and barbarous age, the story within the compass of natural events is happily detailed; its progress is uniform, its events interesting and well combined, and the conclusion grand, tragical, and affecting. Warburton, writing in his notes to Pope's *Imitations of Horace* said: ". . . We have been lately entertained with what I venture to call, a Masterpiece, in the Fable; . . . The piece I mean, is, *The Castle of Otranto* . . . where a beautiful imagination, supported by strength of judgment, has enabled the author to go beyond his subject, and effect the full purpose of the Ancient Tragedy; that is, to purge the passions by pity and terror, in colouring as great and harmonious as in any of the best dramatic writers."

While this dramatic conception was, in the hands of Walpole, an innovation in technique, the desire to arouse curiosity and suspense was another new feature of this novel. The basic principle of construction in *The Castle of Otranto* is 'suspense', and Walpole creates suspense even in minor incidents and scenes, and employs various tricks to excite curiosity and heighten the tension of nerves:

"What noise is that?"

"It is the wind", said Matilda, "whistling through the battlements in the tower above. You have heard it a thousand times."

Matilda and Theodore are both startled by "a deep and hollow groan". "They listened; but perceived no further noise: they both concluded it the effect of pent-up vapours." This very technique was to become a fine art in the hands of Mrs. Radcliffe. Half-finished sentences are another device used by Walpole. When Frederic seeks the holy hermit in the Holy Land, he finds him dying; but the actual death does not take place till the hermit has excited curiosity by the revelation of half a secret.

Written with a vigour, violent and abrupt in methods of treatment, the story moves briskly, with dialogue and action; and it is for the dialogue that Walpole reserves his strength. He mentions in his preface to the first edition of the novel: "There is no bombast, no similes, flowers, digressions, or unnecessary descriptions. Everything tends directly to the catastrophe." The dramatic power of the story holds our attention from the opening sentences. Even the prejudiced Macaulay said: "The story . . . never flags for a single moment. . . . There are no digressions, or unseasonable descriptions, or long speeches. Every sentence carries the action forward. . . . The excitement is constantly renewed. . . . No reader probably ever thought the book dull." He goes on to add: "He keeps the mind of the reader constantly attentive, and constantly entertained. He had strange ingenuity peculiarly his own." The language is simple, nervous, and appropriate to the several characters. George Hardinge, writing to John Nichols on 22 June 1813, said "*The Castle of Otranto* is a model of its kind; and there is a wonderful grace in the language, which is neither too familiar nor too elevated. It seems inseparable from the characters, the scenery, and the incidents."

Although there are none of the luxuriant, florid, and highly varnished landscape paintings with which Mrs. Radcliffe often adorned her romances, yet there are in *Otranto* certain astonishing pictorial effects that were exclusive to Walpole. One brief and sublime description is of the moonlight vision of Alfonso dilated to immense magnitude, with the astonished group of spectators in the front, and behind them shattered ruins of the castle. Miss Dorothy Scarborough has asserted that "the genealogical founder of the family of Gothic ghosts is the giant apparition in *The Castle of Otranto*". Walpole's canvas resembles the manner of El Greco where in a sombre, arid landscape, hung with thunderclouds, emaciated figures flicker with unearthly emotion while a streak of pallid lightning adds a mys-

terious terror to the scene.

Walpole reflects the passions and the sins and miseries of human souls in the magic glass of *Otranto*, and sets out to offer a combination of the supernatural agency with human interest. He makes use of the supernatural not merely as an instrument of terror, but also as a means to create a medieval atmosphere. The novel is set in Italy, at some vague period between 1095 and 1243 during the period of the crusades. Walpole used the Castle of Otranto as Victor Hugo used Notre Dame. Giving a medieval flavour to the whole, it was more than a setting for his story. Walpole attempted to paint a picture of domestic life and manners such as might actually have existed during feudal times, and by bringing in the supernatural machinery he hinted at the superstitions of the olden times. Therefore the natural parts of the narrative are blended with marvellous occurrences. Surprise and fear founded on supernatural events are harmoniously adjusted to the main spring of interest in the central plot. The bold assertion of the actual existence of phantoms and apparitions seems to harmonize naturally with manners of the Middle Ages, and casts a powerful spell upon the reader's mind.

The desire to be true to medieval costume contributes in part to the atmosphere of the period which Walpole very successfully creates in the description of Lord Frederic, his Knights, and their train entering the castle. This picture evokes a realistic impression of those olden times: the bell tolls at the postern gate; the brazen trumpet sounds when the Cavalcade arrives at the castle; a herald conveys to Manfred the wishes of his lord, and in failure of compliance delivers his master's challenge to a single combat by throwing down his warder; there are references to the laws of arms, of hospitality, and chivalry; Matilda waits on her mother on the ramparts of the castle in the cool of the evening. All these and other details are a true reflection of bygone ages.

One need not be surprised when the Surrealists claim *The Castle of Otranto* as an example of their school, for it is a claim they can justifiably make. Professor Dobrée has pointed out that "Horace Walpole was a sensitive, and perhaps the first surrealist, writer". It is a pity that the bibliophile genius of Montague Summers, a keen admirer and collector of Gothic novels, failed to perceive the surrealistic element in the first Gothic tale. In the beautifully written last chapter of his monumental work, *The Gothic Quest,* he remarks: "The connexion which the Surrealists are anxious to trace between their own paths and principles and the ideals and inspiration of the Gothic novelists . . . to me appears to have no existence. . . . Such arguments as are adduced . . . seem to be based upon misapprehensions . . . are far-fetched and fantastical." But when we consider the romantic principles of surrealist art, as evident in *The Castle of Otranto,* the part played by 'unconscious' and 'automatic writing in this goblin tale, and the methods employed by Walpole, the claim of the surrealists is finally established. It is interesting and fruitful therefore to compare the effect of this novel with some of the paintings of the Surrealistic School, and attempt an analysis of the impulses that led Walpole to such a fantastic creation.

Let us first determine what exactly is implied by Surrealism, what are its methods and aims, and where lie hidden the qualities, values and inspiration of this "conscious and deliberate artistic principle". Herbett Read has defined Surrealism as "a reaffirmation of the romantic principle—a process like that of life, of creation, of liberation". To use a grandiloquent phrase to describe the general aim of Surrealism, we may call it "The Renascence of Wonder". A surrealist painter "turns all his perceptive faculties inwards, to the realm of his subjective fancies, his day dreams, his pre-conscious images. He replaces observation by intuition, analysis by synthesis, reality by super-reality." The dream and the reality resolve therefore into a reality absolute, a surreality. Arnold Hauser describes it thus: "The dream becomes the paradigm of the whole-world picture, in which reality and unreality, logic and fantasy, banality and sublimation of existence, form an indissoluble and inexplicable unity."

The 'surréaliste' finds his best inspiration in "psychic automatism" and in "the mystery of the subconscious". The first of these is directed towards expressing the true processes of thought, and the latter translates objects into strange, horrible, or sentimental forms. So the main doctrine of this school expresses a belief in the higher reality of certain forms of association: in the omnipotence of dreams, and in the detached play of thought. It believes that these hidden springs of the 'unconscious' can be tapped if imagination is given free rein, and if thought is allowed to be automatic; and a new truth, and a new art, will arise from the chaos of the 'unconscious' and the irrational. And thereby, plunging into the unconscious, what Breton calls "a vertiginous descent into ourselves" into the whole force of the mental personality, the Surrealists take over the psycho-analytical method of free-association, that is, the automatic development of ideas and their reproduction without any rational, moral, or aesthetic censorship. The repressed content of the 'unconscious' mingles freely with the more conscious images and a new art form results.

There was a constant conflict between the 'personality' and 'character' of Walpole, and if we begin to psychoanalyse Walpole's personality we may suspect that he had suppressed his impulses in the process of building up character. But his repressed self broke loose that fateful night in 1764 when he had a dream that gave birth to **The Castle of Otranto.** The part played by 'unconscious' and the "automatism of creative activi-

ty," which André Breton has always made the criterion of a surrealist attitude in art, is apparent in the formation of the first Gothic novel. The story sprang from a dream. The writing was guided by impulse into which the subconscious partly intruded. "The production of such a work (**The Castle of Otranto**) . . . approaches, indeed, nothing less than the surrealist method . . . highly significant in their cumulative effect, must be put to the credit of *dreams* and of the employment of *automatic writing.*"

We have already noted that the Castle is a picture of Trinity College, Cambridge. Walpole had paid a visit to Cambridge in 1763 (a year before he wrote **The Castle of Otranto**) and saw Trinity, St. John's, and Queen's. He had probably forgotten how closely this short visit preceded the writing of his romance. Walpole probably found his courtyard at Trinity College, since Trinity's main court was the only one to possess towers and gates, as well as chapel and hall. "Otranto's hall corresponds more closely to a Cambridge hall than to any room at Strawberry."

So during those hours of feverish creation Walpole unconsciously utilized a number of experiences, incidents, and impressions, buried in his unconscious memory. Pacing the silent and deserted chambers at Strawberry, and walking along its lonely galleries in summer dusks or winter eves with a candle in hand, he probably yielded to strange imaginings; ghosts, "magic shapes and visions airy", haunted him, and the eyes in the portrait of Lord Falkland cast a curious spell. The waking thoughts merged into dream visions and became a collection of sensory images and visual scenes. **The Castle of Otranto** has been called by Doughty "a vision or dream projected into real life"—really, it was an expression of Walpole's hidden dreams.

In 1721 was published *The Secret History of Pythagoras.* Part II. Translated from the original copy lately found at Otranto in Italy. By J. W. M. D. Its second edition came out in 1751. Walpole stated that "it was not till the story was finished that he looked up in the map of the kingdom of Naples for a well-sounding name and that Otranto was sonorous". But there is a remarkable similarity between the manuscript device and the title of Walpole's tale, and it may be possible that Walpole had read the work. Miss Alice M. Killen, in her dissertation on *Le Roman Terrifiant ou Roman Noir* (1915), page 15, note ii, has pointed out the similarity between the Manfred of history and the Manfred of the first Gothic novel. The points of resemblance have been adroitly summarized in the admirable edition of the work by Oswald Doughty. It appears therefore that Walpole's past studies and scholarly interests had worked their way through the 'unconscious'.

As regards the "automatism of creative activity", a point so much emphasized by the Surrealists, one finds that

Walpole had plunged into the writing of his novel without premeditation; it is a sample of "unpremeditated art"; and he was always rather proud of the artless manner in which he had gone about his composition. In his letter to Cole on 9 March 1765 he mentions: "I began to write without knowing in the least what I intended to say or relate." One summer morn found him moved by the memory of a vivid dream; during the day its influence was strong upon him, and with the deepening hours of twilight he took up his quill and started scribbling. Solitary in his castle, he sat night after night, scribbling and sipping coffee, wandering farther and farther into a fantastic and visionary world, escaping from the bitterness of grim realities. The summer nights one after another mingled with the dawn and Walpole, utterly fatigued and exhausted, sometimes with the last sentence incomplete, broke away and flung himself upon his bed. On the eighth night he laid down his quill. Now, if this was not "automatic writing" what else could it be?

It has always been the function of art to stretch the mind beyond the limits of understanding. Herbert Read says in *The Meaning of Art* that "distance beyond may be spiritual, or transcendental, or perhaps, merely fantastical". *The Castle of Otranto* belongs to the third category. Art in its wider sense is an extension of the personality; while a personality without contradictions is incapable of creating a work of art. "The contradictions of the personality are resolved in the work of art," says Herbert Read, "that is one of the first principles of Surrealism." It is needless to point out here the inherent contradictions in the personality of Walpole. These have been admirably indicated by Lytton Strachey and Virginia Woolf.

Walpole's own method employed in his Gothic story is truly surrealistic. His manner of 'telescoping' different ages, settings, and characters, his strong manipulation of "the sense of contrast", his use of dialogue and style, his story as it unfolds swiftly giving a nightmarish sensation: all these are methods of surrealism in particular. The scenes change with a dramatic swiftness, the incidents evoke a nightmarish sensation, and the whole story has a very dream-like insequence. The tale had its origin in the fantasy of an exhausted and repressed brain, and we do not fail to find the "unearthly impulse" of the original dream lingering in the narrative. The atmosphere of *The Castle of Otranto* is stamped by unreason and exaggeration of its events, and one does not fail to observe the nightmare juxtaposition of unrelated objects. The story sums up all the fantastic possibilities inherent in 'Surrealism': the fatal descent of the vast and *gigantic* black plumed helmet on the *little* prince has, besides its sensation of contrast, a sinister significance; the portrait that walks sighing from the frame and vanishes into an upper chamber; the statue that bleeds; a skeleton wrapped in hermit's cowl; the gigantic armour-clad foot in the gallery and the gigantic hand on the banister; the immense Brobdingnagian sword carried by one hundred gentlemen with difficulty; the nodding and waving plumes of the giant helmet; the narrative unfolding a tale of unexpected paternities and dreadful injustices; and, finally, Alfonso's enormous spectre bursting the Castle of Otranto asunder. It is all absurd and nonsensical and oddly exciting to read; it evokes the same sensations as might the paintings of a Picasso, a Chirico, or a Chagall. It might also be likened to one of the early Flemish paintings depicting the burial of Christ, wherein the anguished grimaces of the emaciated creatures, their stiff, ungainly gestures seem to add a greater horror and poignancy to the scene.

The first 'surrealistic' method that we observe in Walpole's technique is the method of 'telescoping'. He attempts to 'telescope' age and characters. He wrote in the preface to the second edition of *The Castle of Otranto* that his aim was "to blend two kinds of romance, the ancient and the modern". It is a telescoping of "the imagination and improbability" of the former with "the rules of probability" in the latter. He said that he wanted to make his characters think, speak, and act as they would do in extraordinary circumstances. He introduced the supernatural in contrast to the natural, represented real personages in unusual, unreal circumstances, and tried to picture realistically human nature and its reactions in different settings and environments. This is the grotesque method of which Chagall is a master.

The contemporary figures are placed in medieval settings. As the heroine or the hero move about the medieval scene, the castles and moats, vaults, turrets and galleries appear strange and awful to them. Walpole's Isabella is no more born to the medieval scene than are Pamela or Evelina. Uprooted from her proper society with contemporary emotional and intellectual pattern intact, thrust into a barbarous and primitive age, subjected to the various menaces of the Dark Ages, she serves as a projection of the nervous system of her own time, as a sensitive barometer of emotional reaction to horrors, and clearly, as transmitter of the thrills of their exposure. The effect thus is of a thing taken away from its own particular setting, an impression of "the grotesque" that justifies comparison with the paintings of Chirico.

The surrealist painters base their colours on the principle of contrast. The same sinister tones and overtones, a display of light and shade, effects of sound and silence, we find in *The Castle of Otranto.* There are contrasting situations and incidents displaying pitch-black darkness on the one hand, intermitted by thunder and lightning; gloomy recesses and dark dungeons contrastingly presented to a gleam of moonshine or the ray of a flickering lamp. There are, besides the sublimity of description and moonlit effects, contrast presented in the theme itself: the emotion of 'fear' balanced against that of 'love'.

The third method in 'Surrealism' is a queer combination of the 'trivial' and the 'mighty', a mixture of the 'big' and 'small'. The 'gigantic' helmet descending on a 'little' prince, the gigantic hand in armour and the giant's foot, the spectre of the dilated Alfonso cracking the walls of the castle, a large portrait inspiring observers with fear, are some of the tricks used by Walpole. The statue bleeds, and the figure in the portrait walks away, and Walpole masters both the active and inactive agents of terror: the villain and the castle.

The Castle of Otranto is particularly surrealist in its dialogue, and the juxtaposition of the language and sentiments, of the *beau monde* with Gothic violence. Commenting on Walpole's strange combination of words and far-fetched allusions Macaulay said: "He coins new words, distorts the sense of old words, and twists sentences into forms which make grammarians stare. . . . His wit was, in its essential properties, of the same kind with that of Cowley and Donne. Like this, it consisted in an exquisite perception of points of analogy, and points of contrast too subtle for common observation. Like them, Walpole perpetually startles us by the ease with which he yokes together ideas between which there would seem at first sight to be no connection."

Few writers can have fluctuated more in critical extreme than the author of the first Gothic novel. Wilmarth Lewis finds that "time and patience are required to understand Horace Walpole". To his own times, which knew nothing of his letter-writing, he was a brilliant historian and essayist. Byron, during the nineteenth century, stated that Walpole was a greater writer than any man living "be he who he may". To Croker and Lord Liverpool, he was the most evil man that had ever lived, for Walpole had poisoned history at its source. Carlyle saw him as a light shining in darkness; to Macaulay he was *pâté de foie gras* produced by an effete society. The latter pictured Walpole as a gossipy little dilettante, cold-blooded and sneering, whose mind was "a bundle of whims and affectations", and whose features "were covered by mask within mask". He went so far as to remark that the works of Walpole were "literary luxuries", a product of "an unhealthy and disorganised mind". To Macaulay, Walpole's works are "destitute of every charm", which only can amuse without exciting. "He never convinces the reason, nor fills the imagination, nor touches the heart." Isaac D'Israeli in 1812 saw in Walpole "fancy and ingenuity", and a "recourse to the *marvellous* in imagination". He continues to say that "*The Castle of Otranto* and *The Mysterious Mother* are the productions of ingenuity rather than genius; and display the miracles of Art rather than the spontaneous creations of Na-

ture". To Hazlitt, as far back as 1819, *The Castle of Otranto* appeared "dry, meagre, and without effect . . . done upon the false principles of taste", shocking the senses and "having no purchase upon the imagination".

The twin currents of ridicule and eulogy continue to flow down to the twentieth century. To C. S. Fearnside "Walpole lacks imagination; his characters are wooden in motive and in action". To Oswald Doughty "aesthetically *The Castle of Otranto* is a failure. . . . His (Walpole's) imagination was not sufficiently clear and intense for artistic creation. . . . Walpole tried but failed to re-create the enchanted castle of his subconscious dream world." To Alice M. Killen "he (Walpole) has carried his wonders too far, until they are almost ridiculous". Walpole had, according to Miss Killen, no mastery over the half-shades that heighten the mysterious and the unknown; rather he leads his readers rapidly from horror to horror, wonder to wonder, and does not prepare them, by thrills cunningly regulated, to receive the finishing stroke of superstitious terror. But "it is a strange sort of niggardliness", says the *Gentleman's Magazine,* "which denies the praise of genius to *The Castle of Otranto.* It exhibits picturesque fancy, invention and even . . . pathos." Mrs. Elizabeth Carter thought it "a great pity that Horace Walpole ever wrote anything but *The Castle of Otranto*". And it is enough that in our own century we have had the praises of George Saintsbury, Lytton Strachey, and Bonamy Dobrée.

Although "Horace Walpole has been the object of hatred, adulation, condescension, and respect," there is no doubting the statement made in the Dedicatory Epistle to *Ivanhoe* by Sir Walter Scott that "Horace Walpole wrote a goblin tale which has thrilled through many a bosom". As Stephen Gwynn remarked: "The book is a literary curiosity"; and as Melville observed: "With *The Castle of Otranto,* Walpole struck an unexplored vein of romance." It is "literally an epoch-making book", said Montague Summers, "in fine, a notable landmark in the history of English taste and English literature".

Yet, does he require the patronage of these eulogies? He needs "no more such laurels" but "shall be quite content with a sprig of rosemary thrown after him". In 1773 he wrote to Madame du Deffand: "My dreams will never again give me a castle of Otranto. It is a sad thing to exchange dreams for accounts." And will it not be too harsh to bring his 'dreams' to 'accounts', and weigh his "midsummer fantasy" on "the balance of criticism"? But there is no doubting one fact: that the tale had vast potentialities; the seed sown by Walpole did flower and bear fruit, and then ran to seed again. *The Castle of Otranto* continues till today a towering achievement of art and beauty exciting curiosity and admiration.

Eino Railo (essay date 1964)

SOURCE: "*The Castle of Otranto*—Horace Walpole, His Life and Pursuits—Strawberry Hill—*The Mysterious Mother*," in *The Haunted Castle: A Study of the Elements of English Romanticism,* Routledge and Kegan Paul, 1927. Reprint: Humanities Press, 1964.

[*In the following excerpt from* The Haunted Castle: A Study of the Elements of English Romanticism *(1964), Railo discusses the importance of castle imagery—and specifically Strawberry Hill—to* The Castle of Otranto.]

I

The student of English literature is fairly certain at one time or another, as he arrives at the dawning romanticism of the latter half of the eighteenth century, to come across a small and unassuming booklet entitled *The Castle of Otranto,* with the subtitle *A Gothic Story.* The book consists of some hundred and fifty pages and has as frontispiece a fine steel engraving of an elderly man with a wide-awake expression dressed in eighteenth-century costume; underneath is the magnificent name: HORACE WALPOLE, EARL OF ORFORD. Acquaintance with the book in question, which appeared in 1764, is apt to awaken a varied series of visions of romantic authors and of the materials and history of romanticism, for scarcely a handbook of English literature exists in which some kind of mention is not made of it and of its noble author.[1]

Horace Walpole, born in 1717, was the third son of Robert Walpole, the all-powerful minister of George II. After the usual education at Eton and Cambridge, he was despatched on the Grand Tour to France and Italy, in the company of an Eton schoolmate of like age, the poet Thomas Gray. Their travels lasted two years, after which the friends fell out[2] and returned to England. Walpole was now entrusted with certain lucrative posts and for twenty-six years continued a Member of Parliament. At no time had he any particular reputation in political circles, and when his father's career closed in 1742, his private interests began gradually to gain the upper hand. In 1747 he purchased the property called Strawberry Hill, on the Thames, near Windsor, and there he spent the remainder of his life, wholly absorbed in antiquarian, artistic and literary interests. He inherited the title of Earl of Orford in 1791 and in 1797 he died.

We may regard Walpole as a typical upper-class dilettante who, living in comfortable circumstances and lacking a definite aim in life, is tempted to devote his time to congenial minor occupations. Feeling himself attracted by the past, by the "Gothic Era,"[3] he commenced to study the period with all the spasmodic enthusiasm of the amateur. The antiquarian spirit has ever been strong in England, and in the middle of the eighteenth century, when the bonds of classicism were beginning to break and attention was concentrating upon those things which seemed to bear the ennobling and inspiring marks of time, it broke out in a laborious studying, describing and collecting of old coins, buildings and ruins, ancient poetry, etc. While better-equipped men were patiently creating a scientific basis for such study, devoted and enthusiastic laymen of the type of Walpole appeared; men of a class whose ludicrous side has been perpetuated by Scott in the person of Mr. Oldbuck, who provided the model for Dickens' immortal chairman of the Pickwick Club. To be sure, the satire hardly applies to Walpole, who was in his way a learned man, and whose keen intelligence and refined, even if sometimes mistaken, feeling for art awaken respect; nevertheless, the "Gothic" rubbish collected at his country-house recalls irresistibly certain of the best and most stupendous finds of Messrs. Oldbuck and Pickwick.[4]

The memory of Walpole as a collector of antiquities has been preserved chiefly through his whim of transforming Strawberry Hill into a kind of Gothic castle. The elements and basic outlines of Gothic architecture had not at that time been fully investigated, and the necessity for a thorough reconstruction on the basis of style remaining unperceived, the methods adopted were simple enough. In the measure permitted by the previous structure of Strawberry Hill and the disposition of its rooms, a round tower was added here, a chapel thrown out there, stained glass placed in the windows, old armour and weapons distributed in suitable spots, a mantelpiece made out of an altar, and so on, the result being fondly imagined to constitute a Gothic castle. Thus twenty years were occupied in these reconstructions and the collection of material, during which time Strawberry Hill acquired fame and became a resort for hosts of the curious. The proprietor and creator of the establishment was apparently well satisfied with the result, for he published an illustrated account of the place.[5]

Though Walpole had thus revealed his imperfect acquaintance with the Gothic style, Strawberry Hill helped considerably in bringing about renewed knowledge and appreciation of the period. It is permissible for us to smile at Walpole's building, but it has its own special significance as an expression of the conception which, despite the many well-preserved real medieval relics in England, Walpole and the majority of his contemporaries had formed for themselves of that almost legendary building, "the haunted castle," the notion of which he attempted to delineate in his new romanticism. The knowledge that this famous stage-setting of the "terror-romanticists" actually existed in two separate versions before its introduction into literature is not without interest.

This is not to be taken as implying that Walpole's

Gothic building activities at Strawberry Hill were the sole generators of his desire to experiment with the Gothic spirit in literature. The attention of those days was in general, and in a manner expressly calculated to inspire authors, directed towards the Gothic. Edmund Burke had, in 1756, published his study of our ideas of the sublime and beautiful, thereby formulating the theory which the whole school of terror followed in practice. And in 1762, two years before the appearance of *The Castle of Otranto,* Bishop Hurd (1720-1808) had published those *Letters on Chivalry and Romance,* which furnished powerful support to the brothers Warton in their delight and interest in antiquities. Hurd appears as an enthusiastic advocate of the "Gothic Era," propounding the question whether Gothic romance might not contain something peculiarly suited to the views of a genius and to the ends of poetry, and whether the philosophically inclined people of his own day had not gone too far in making of it a perpetual source of ridicule and contempt. He avers that if Homer had known it, he would have preferred it to the manners of his own times, as he would have found in it more "gallantry" and "superior solemnity of superstitions." The influence of such views and of Hurd's book in drawing attention to Gothicism cannot be overestimated. Among those in whom a desire was born to attempt practical results in this field was Walpole. His knowledge of medieval conditions was, however, fragmentary and inexact. He had his own conception of its architecture, but he knew nothing of its literature, with the exception, perhaps, of a few popular ballads. When speaking of Gothicism in the prologues and epilogues to the *Castle of Otranto* and to his play *The Mysterious Mother,* he instinctively appeals to Shakespeare who was, as we shall see later, an important guide for the author in matters and conceptions connected with Gothicism.

Walpole was a busy letter-writer, his correspondents including the poet Gray and Madame du Deffand, whom he had met in Paris in 1765. As a composer of lively and witty letters he was among the foremost writers of his day. Of the rest of his productions I have mentioned only his play *The Mysterious Mother,* written in 1768, that being the only work except *The Castle of Otranto,* which falls within the sphere of this study.[6]

3

During his constant endeavours to provide his "Gothic" castle with relics of medieval days, the idea seems to have occurred to Walpole that it might be worth while trying to affix and to present to others, in the form of fiction, some of the Gothic fancies with which his own brain was teeming. As to the manner in which this idea was realized, he himself has left us, in a letter to a friend, the following original account: "Shall I even confess to you, what was the origin of this romance? I waked one morning in the beginning of last June from a dream, of which all I could recover was, that I had thought myself in an ancient castle (a very natural dream for a head filled, like mine, with Gothic story) and that, on the uppermost banister of a great staircase, I saw a gigantic hand in armor. In the evening I sat down and began to write, without knowing in the least what I intended to say or relate. The work grew on my hands, and I grew fond of it. Add, that I was very glad to think of anything rather than politics. In short, I was so engrossed with my tale, which I completed in less than two months, that one evening I wrote from the time I had drank my tea, about six o'clock, till half an hour after one in the morning, when my hands and fingers were so weary, that I could not hold the pen to finish the sentence, but left Matilda and Isabella talking in the middle of a paragraph."[8]

We observe the author's satisfaction with his work and that he was no longer afraid to disclose himself as its writer. In this he was affected by the reception accorded to the book, as until he was assured of its success he had attempted to hide his paternity. The first edition of *The Castle of Otranto,* printed at his own printing-press at Strawberry Hill, had been given out as a translation by "W. Marshall, Gent.," from the Italian manuscript of a certain "Onuphrio Muralto." To mislead the public Walpole had written in his preface: "The following work was found in the library of an ancient Catholic family in the north of England. It was printed at Naples, in the black letter, in the year 1529. How much sooner it was written does not appear. The principal incidents are such as were believed in the darkest ages of christianity; but the language and conduct have nothing that savours of barbarism. The style is the purest Italian. If the story was written near the time when it is supposed to have happened, it must have been 1095, the era of the first crusade, and 1243, the date of the last, or not long afterwards." . . . The author had obviously been afraid that the strangeness of his book might well, at a time when his father's enemy, Doctor Johnson, and the school of taste represented by him still wielded an unshaken and formidable power over the reading public, expose him to ridicule, and had therefore deemed it prudent to hide for the time being behind a pseudonym and the artifice of a literary hoax. But critics and the public are not so easily misled. Was not the book printed at Strawberry Hill, whose owner's Gothic interests were widely known? Even the name "Onuphrio Muralto" carried a faint oral suggestion of "Horace Walpole." The preface, too, contained unmistakable hints that the author had had some actual castle in his mind, which could be none other than Strawberry Hill. Therefore, when the book was favourably received, Walpole emerged from his hiding-place, in the next edition defending his tactics by explaining that he had mistrusted his own abilities and the novelty of the attempt. He had "resigned his performance to the impartial judgment of the public, determined to let it perish in obscurity, if disapproved; nor meaning to avow such a trifle, unless better judges should pronounce that he might own it without a blush."[9]

4

The stage-setting with which before long the student of horror-romanticism is inevitably confronted is a species of old "Gothic" castle, the scene of innumerable horrors, capable of touching the imagination each time we see it, as when the curtain rises on ramparts and towers bathed in the spectral moonlight of *Hamlet.* The reader quickly observes that this "haunted castle" plays an exceedingly important part in these romances; so important, indeed, that were it eliminated the whole fabric of romance would be bereft of its foundation and would lose its predominant atmosphere. The entire stock-in-trade of horror-romanticism in its oldest and purest form consists, as will be shown in the following pages, chiefly of the properties and staff of this haunted castle, and, as we proceed farther in time, of motives based in the first instance upon these, so that to my mind acquaintance with the materials of horror-romanticism is best begun with this central stage and its appurtenances. Let us start, therefore, with a visit to the ancient vaults of Otranto Castle.[10]

Of the castle's outward appearance no actual description is given, nor does the rapidity of the narrator's style permit him to linger over a calm and detailed picture of his setting. Nevertheless, the reader's imagination is soon aware of a concentration on the limited sphere of what seems to be a medieval castle. We are taken into the castle-yard and the chapel, where a marriage is taking place, and into various rooms, of which one contains the collection of ancestral portraits indispensable to such an edifice. The underground portion is full of bewildering vaulted passages, one of which leads through a secret door to a cave beyond the castle confines, another to the church of St. Nicholas. An awesome silence reigns in these subterranean vaults, a silence broken only by the creak of rusty hinges as a breath of air somewhere sets an old door moving. In their gloomy shade the maiden, flying from the lord of the castle, can at first hardly make out the faintly gleaming object in some hiding-place, and then only with difficulty does she perceive it to be the key to the complicated lock of a secret trap-door. The banqueting-hall is fitted with galleries whence the young heroine can, unseen, regard her lover and where she can fall into the inevitable swoon when the tyrant sentences him to death or lifelong confinement in the deepest dungeon of the darkest tower. Over the gate hangs a brazen horn which one cannot fail to notice, especially as the reason for its being there is hard to understand.

With some few such strokes Walpole conjures up his castle before the reader, avoiding overmuch detail, but continually stimulating the imagination. It must be

admitted, too, that he has succeeded, for some hint of strangeness and austere majesty is undoubtedly left in the mind.[11] A good example of what his fantasy of a Gothic castle betokened to him in importance and atmosphere is provided by the opening lines of *The Mysterious Mother,* into which he has effectively condensed the whole of Gothic horror:

> What awful silence! How these antique towers
> And vacant courts chill the suspended soul,
> Till expectation wears the cast of fear;
> And fear, half-ready to become devotion,
> Mumbles a kind of mental orison,
> It knows not wherefore.

Notes

[1] A portrait of Walpole accompanies the 1907 edition (Chatto & Windus) which I have used. He was refined to the point of effeminacy. "He always entered a room in a style of affected delicacy, *chapeau bras* between his hands, knees bent and feet on tiptoe. He usually dressed in lavender, with partridge silk stockings and gold buckles, and with lace ruffles and frill." R. Garnett and E. Gosse: *English Literature,* III, p. 367 (1903). A fine edition de luxe (containing also *The Mysterious Mother*), with a preface by Montague Summers, was issued by Constable in 1924 (*vide* article by E. Gosse in *The Sunday Times,* Nov. 2). The above description of Walpole hails originally from Letitia Matilda Hawkins's *Anecdotes, Biographical Sketches, and Memoirs,* where pp. 87-117 and 307-312 are devoted to Walpole. The father of this author, Sir John Hawkins, was a friend and neighbour of Walpole and wrote the biography of Doctor Johnson which was so severely handled by Boswell. She gives the further information regarding Walpole's personal appearance: "His figure was . . . not merely tall, but more properly long, and slender to excess; his complexion, and particularly his hands, of a most unhealthy paleness." Quoted from De Quincey's article *Anecdotage.*

[2] The cause of the quarrel was Walpole's inability to refrain from boasting of his position as the son of the omnipotent minister. In any case they were not well-matched travelling companions; Walpole danced and amused himself, while Gray studied Art and Music. Later they were reconciled and Walpole acknowledged himself to have been at fault. E. Gosse: *Gray,* pp. 43-44.

[3] "Gothic, a term of reproach, synonymous with barbarous, lawless and tawdry." W. L. Phelps: *The Beginnings of the English Romantic Movement,* p. 15 (1893).

[4] Scott makes good-natured fun of this description in *The Antiquary.* Mr. Oldbuck's find, a stone with what he takes to be an important ancient inscription, appears in much the same way as that of "Bil Stumps His Mark" in *Pickwick Papers.*

[5] *A Description of the Villa of Mr. Horace Walpole at Strawberry Hill,* 1768. I have not had the opportunity of reading this work. Descriptions of Walpole's villa are included in all works written about him, amongst which I would mention Austin Dobson: *Eighteenth Century Vignettes* (undated), "A Day at Strawberry Hill," pp. 206-217, 2nd ed. A picture of Strawberry Hill is given by Garnett and Gosse. The most exhaustive source is Paul Yvon's book *La Vie d'un Dilettante,* Book IV, pp. 487-646; "Walpole 'gothicisant'"; p. 551: *"Strawberry Hill et le Château d'Otranto, le roman de Walpole, sont donc, selon la volanté de leur créateur, indissolublement liés."*

[6] "Gray and Horace Walpole exceeded all their English contemporaries in the composition of charmingly picturesque familiar letters." (Garnett and Gosse, *op. cit.,* III, p. 363.) Information regarding Walpole: the work by Dobson mentioned in the preceding note; Sir Walter Scott: *The Lives of the Novelists* (1821), originally published as an introduction to Ballantyne's edition of *The Castle of Otranto* (1811) and included with the latter in *Ballantyne's Novelists' Library,* Part V; my own copy is from the *Everyman's Library* Series, London, pp. 188-203; Henry A. Beers: *A History of English Romanticism in the Eighteenth Century,* pp. 229-243 and 249-255 (1906); Oliver Elton: *A Survey of English Literature, 1780-1830,* I, p. 203; Wilbur L. Cross: *Development of the English Novel,* pp. 101-103 (1911); Fr. Hovey Stoddard: *The Evolution of the English Novel,* p. 95 (1913); Helene Richter: *Geschichte der Englischen Romantik,* I, pp. 172-191 (1911); Austin Dobson: *Eighteenth Century Studies,* pp. 166-177; *Dictionary of English Biography;* Macaulay: *Critical and Historical Essays,* in which is a murderous criticism of Walpole as a politician and an author; *Chamber's Cyclopedia of English Literature* (1901); Henrik Schück: *Allmän litteraturhistoria,* V, pp. 372-376; P. v. Tieghem: *Le mouvement romantique,* 2nd ed., Paris (1923).

The most noteworthy and exhaustive sources of information regarding Walpole are Paul Yvon's *La Vie d'un Dilettante; Horace Walpole,* 1717-1797; *Essai de Biographie psychologique et littéraire* (XV + 872 pages, large 8vo); and his *Horace Walpole as a Poet* (XV + 217) (1924), both of which I have utilized. The passage relating to Hurd has been compiled from the textbooks mentioned and the preface written by Montague Summers. Schück declares Walpole to have been ignorant of medievalism. . . .

[8] March 9th, 1765, to William Cole. Quoted also by Beers, p. 236.

[9] Walpole founded his printing-press, *Officina arbuteana,* as he called it, at Strawberry Hill, in the summer of 1757; its first publication was Gray's *Odes.* He had been so severely criticized for his earlier literary production that he had become timid. *The Castle of Otranto*

was at first ascribed to Gray, which made Walpole remark that people msut be fools indeed to think such a trifle worthy of a genius like Gray. Gosse: *Gray,* p. 169. Doctor Johnson admitted that "Horry Walpole . . . got together a great many curious little things, and told them in an elegant manner." By this the Doctor did not however intend *The Castle of Otranto,* which it is hardly likely that he had read, as Boswell is silent on the matter. Walpole did not belong to the admirers of the "Great Bear," or even to his circle of acquaintance, for the Doctor had made acquaintance difficult by his Parliamentary Reports in *The Gentleman's Magazine,* in which he invariably made out a poor case for Sir Robert Walpole. Moreover, Walpole was a Whig, and thus in the Doctor's eyes a "dog" and a "rascal." The only question on which Walpole and Johnson were of the same opinion was in regard to Ossian. Phelps, *op. cit.,* p. 110.

[10] Both Beers, p. 253, and Dibelius: *Englische Romankunst,* I, pp. 290-293, 2nd ed. (1922), and other investigators of terror-romanticism take into account the central position of the Haunted Castle, but they have not arrived at the synthesis of the material, at its decisive significance, to which my own studies have led. Yvon, *op. cit.,* p. 490: "Comment cet Anglais du milieu du XVIII siècle (Walpole), grand seigneur, homme en place et homme à la mode, s'était-il ainsi épris du charme du passé? Pour le comprendre, il suffit de garder sans cesse, présente à l'esprit, l'image du petit château gothique de Strawberry Hill à travers toutes ses transformations, et de rappeler que ce château est moins une tentative de reconstitution archéologique, que l'expression d'un état d'âme."

[11] The account given in the paragraph can be compared with pp. 18, 19, 21, 62 and 72 of *The Castle of Otranto.*

Frederick R. Karl (essay date 1974)

SOURCE: "Gothic, Gothicism, and Gothicists," in *The Adversary Literature: The English Novel in the Eighteenth Century—A Study in Genre,* Farrar, Straus and Giroux, 1974.

[*In this essay, Karl discusses elements of different genres found in* The Castle of Otranto.]

So much of ***The Castle of Otranto*** seems nonsensical today that it is hard to believe it was taken seriously and still should be. Walpole, in his way, was a genius of the large and the outlandish, and we can say that with him a subgenre came into being. Although we must be careful not to make him the sole founder of Gothic,[3] we can agree with Varma that Walpole brought together the various elements that we now identify as typical: "the Gothic machinery, the atmosphere of gloom and terror, and stock romantic characters." (*The Gothic Flame,* p. 57)

Even more, Walpole had the supremely romantic turn of mind which demanded that the supernatural appear natural. In his preface to the first edition, he speaks of belief as relative to an age; so that "belief in every kind of prodigy was so established in those dark ages [ca. twelfth century] that an author would not be faithful to the manners of the times who would omit all mention of them." Walpole asks the reader to excuse "the air of the miraculous" and "allow the possibility of the facts." Thus, Walpole is very careful to turn the unusual into realistic detail. Through it all, he speaks of himself as no more than a translator of a manuscript found in the library of "an ancient Catholic family in the north of England," written at some undetermined time and printed at Naples in 1529. In this way, too, Walpole preserves realistic appearances, placing this bizarre undertaking within the mainstream of the eighteenth-century novel as an edited manuscript, a true history, a journal or series of letters, all authentic. We should stress this point lest Walpole's novel appear too much of an aberration in the eighteenth century. On the contrary, it is closer to the center than we are often led to suppose.

Walpole also associates his work with the drama, and we recall the revival of interest in Elizabethan drama. In his preface to the second edition, Walpole defends his method as a combination of low-comedy scenes and high tragedy based on no less authority than Shakespeare's own practice in *Hamlet* and *Julius Caesar.* And Sir Walter Scott, in his introduction to a later edition, speaks of Walpole's structuring as suitable to the modern novel, although we recognize his remarks as appropriate to the drama: "It was," Scott wrote, "his object to unite the marvellous turn of incident, and imposing tone of chivalry, exhibited in the ancient romance, with that accurate exhibition of human character, and contrast of feelings and passions, which is, or ought to be, delineated in the modern novel."

Walpole's Gothic is, really, close to a special type of drama, what developed contemporaneously in Mozartian opera buffa and in later Italian opera. The contrasts of low comedy and high tragedy are the stock-in-trade of the operatic composer; and the machinery of Gothic that Walpole employed allowed necessary modulation from low to high to low. In fact, one of the oldest devices of both the early novel and of opera is the low-born young man—here Theodore—who turns out to be well-born, indeed princely. This is part of opera's "fabulous" heritage, and, curiously, one of the stock devices of the realistic novel—consider Tom Jones, Humphry Clinker, et al. Thus, within the protagonist himself, we find this characteristic movement between high and low.

The point warrants further exploration. Although the Gothic novel would appear by its trappings and major interests to be completely outside the realistic social frame of reference, there is, in fact, considerable overlap. And that overlap occurs in its modulation of movements from low to high and back again to low, or a comparable sequence, as embodied in a major character. The device is not, of course, new—it is part of the romance and fairy tale. But when it appears in the eighteenth-century novel, it becomes something else, the representative of an idea not yet ready for acceptance, but nevertheless ready for testing.

The ancient romance does become wedded to the modern novel in certain social assumptions. Theodore, for example, makes his mark is a "virtuous" young man while his social role is low; and though he turns out to be an aristocrat, the testing out of social roles indicates that innate virtue is as significant as birth. This is surely the conclusion of Fielding and Smollett, with Tom and Humphry, respectively, although as novelists they failed to resolve the social idea fully. Walpole is in this tradition, although his novel is not realistic; and it is precisely in this tradition that we find a good deal of Italian opera, as an amalgam of ancient romance and modern social ideas.

It is necessary to see Walpole, then, in the line of the eighteenth-century novel before proceeding to his deviations from it. In both his resemblance to the novel and his departures from it, he was moving toward alternate assumptions about man and his milieu, away from a settled, rational view toward other aspects of the human being which the romantics were to explore.[4] Likewise, the Methodist movement parallels the literary development of emotionalism, and the belief in redemption through faith finds its counterpart in certain Gothic trappings that Walpole helped to make famous.

First of these is the Gothic castle, whose atmosphere thins the line between supernatural and natural. The castle, if we wish to extend the analogy, provides a kind of religious experience based on awe, fear, and transcedence. Second are the climatic conditions, of storm, wind blasts, moonlight—all of which act as suitable background for the awesome castle. The climate creates sound for the castle's visual effects; we have here, really, the stage sets for Italian opera. Third in this swirl of events and effects is the melancholy young man who seems to carry a weight on his heart and shoulders—the Byronic hero of later years. He is, of course, perfectly suitable for the melancholy castle and weather, and his apotheosis as a figure of morbid gloom is Emily Brontë's Heathcliff. Once again, as in opera, the three elements of castle, weather, and moody, sullen protagonist are completely wedded, virtually indistinguishable, so that character, scene, and sound seem part of one single development. Such an achievement on a meaningful scale was, evidently, beyond Walpole's powers as a novelist, but it was clearly the aim of Gothic, as Scott's comments on the uniting of elements would appear to indicate.

If we view **The Castle of Otranto** as a vision of certain elements rather than as a novel in any traditional sense, we can gauge Walpole's achievement more effectively. As a novel, it is nonsense; as a vision (dream, nightmare, prophecy), it gains significance. Primarily, it is an observation of a life teeming with emotional crises denied in the contemporary literature of the period. It is a vision of omens, curses, extravagant stage sets (the helmet which crushes, the sword of monstrous size); a lustful, domineering father (Walpole's own was Fielding's model for Jonathan Wild) who goes well beyond the Harlowes; a devout, compliant, priest-ridden wife; a vision of doom, blood, terrified servants, apparitions, vengeance, and sadism. The novel suggests an imaginary, dreamlike state, one of ecstasy, in which the author stands "outside" normality and surveys the terrain of his own fantasies.[5]

There is, in this vision, something of the Sadean view of man. Manfred is the resident tyrant who uses his strong will to dominate men and his sexual power to overwhelm his weakling son, Conrad. (Cf. Heathcliff and *his* weakling son, whom he drives into an arranged, unconsummated marriage.) As a tyrant, Manfred is a man of violent extremes, a man who assumes that whatever he is, nature is also, a man whose libido is so strong it must manifest itself in every situation. The cruelty of such a man is obvious if anyone attempts to interfere with his plans, needs, or lusts.

It is more than coincidence that Walpole's father figure, Manfred, should so closely resemble Fielding's interpretation of Sir Robert Walpole in *his* portrait of Jonathan Wild as a man of uncontrollable hands. Or that the son, Conrad, should be portrayed as a weakling, crushed under a helmet, while another, Theodore, eventually usurps the young man's role and marries his intended, Isabella. The vision is a fantasy of family life carried to its extravagant extremes, a medievalism that has little relationship to eighteenth-century reality but considerable connection to a view of family life by one who sits outside normality and can turn his personal vision into opera.

When Clara Reeve, Mrs. Radcliffe, and others rejected, in part at least, the extravagance of Walpole's tale and tried in their own work to be more realistic, they missed an essential factor: Walpole's entire scheme rested on the very aspect they rejected, on a vision or fantasy of his inner life posing as a medieval document. Summers quotes from a letter Walpole wrote to George Montagu: "Visions, you know, have always been my pasture; and so far from growing old enough to quarrel with their emptiness, I almost think there is no wisdom comparable to exchanging what is called

the realities of life for dreams." (*The Gothic Quest*, p. 409). We also recall that Walpole claimed that **The Castle of Otranto** began with a dream. Writing to the Reverend William Cole, on February 28, 1765, he said: "Shall I even confess to you what was the origin of this romance? I waked one morning, in the beginning of last June, from a dream, of which all I could recover was, that I had thought myself in an ancient castle (a very natural dream for a head like mine filled with Gothic story) and that on the uppermost banister of a great staircase I saw a gigantic hand in armour. In the evening, I sat down, and began to write . . ."[6]

If we accept Walpole's romance as fantasy, then we are no longer troubled by extravagance and not worried about its purely novelistic qualities. While utilizing typical eighteenth-century devices also found in the realistic novel—the blending of social types, the use of the unknown young man who turns out to be well-born, the testing out of social roles, et al.—Walpole made his mark by his departure from the realistic novel then establishing itself. And he did so by moving from fiction based on a social vision to a fiction founded on a private vision, which is impervious to the usual criticism employed with novels. A fantasy life, and all its accounterments, is always true in its own terms, valid at every stage of its development; precisely as a schizophrenic's version of reality is *the* version, held on to tenaciously as *the* truth.

Thus, that strong, overwhelming father figure, Manfred, arranging everyone's destiny and then being brought down, indeed being unmanned by his signing his abdication from the principality, has significant psychological overtones. For when Manfred is forced from power, is made to take on "the habit of religion," the new prince is Theodore, a young man who has overthrown the father and gained power. The play of events suggests Freud's short essay "Family Romances" (1909), in which the child fantasizes about his background, sees himself as secretly allied to the aristocracy (born to a prince, etc.), and, through his dreams, hopes to replace his actual parents with others of different quality. Such a replacement, or an Oedipal variation thereon, occurs in Walpole's tale, all under the guise of a medieval document discovered by the teller. Even here, in the documentation, as in the substance of the tale itself, we have the elements of a fantasy life attempting to manipulate reality in order to further its own needs, in order to reinforce and implement its own vision: of a strong father brought down, despite a weakling son himself incapable of doing the deed.

Notes

[3] Montague Summers reminds us that the "tendencies of taste which culminated in the Gothic novel had or-

igins wider and deeper than any one book, even *The Castle of Otranto,* could develop. The dominant elements in the terror novel of the 1790's, of which the most famous exemplar is *The Monk,* came from Germany; the historical romance, which we have just examined, accounts for much; the French influence of Baculard d'Arnaud and his 'drames monacles' [monastic] are of the first importance." (*The Gothic Quest,* p. 180) See also my comments on the "atmospherics" of Gothic, pp. 236-7.

[4] It was this development that Clara Reeve had in mind in her preface to *The Old English Baron* (1780; originally published in 1777 as *The Champion of Virtue, a Gothic Tale* and dedicated to Richardson's daughter). A disciple of Richardson's novel of sensibility, she was worried about the excess of feeling in Walpole's novel: " . . . the machinery is so violent that it destroys the effect it is intended to excite. Had the story been kept within the utmost *verge* of probability the effect had been preserved, without losing the least circumstance that excites or detains the attention." She then speaks of the "limits of credibility," citing, for example, the sword and helmet as destroying the imagination because of their monstrosity. "I was both surprised and vexed to find the enchantment dissolved, which I wished might continue to the end of the book . . ." She gives her own plan, which is to combine Richardsonian sensibility with Gothic trappings which will never become excessive:

"In the course of my observations upon this singular book, it seemed to me that it was possible to compose a work upon the same plan, wherein these defects might be avoided; and the *keeping* [harmony among parts], as in *painting,* might be preserved."

In this way, she hoped to achieve her end of exciting the attention and directing it to some useful end; that is, to entertain and to instruct. However, as a counter to her realism, Varma observes, Miss Reeve makes extensive use of dream material. Dreams, as we shall see, became common in Gothic novels and often served to provide the fantasy side to novels that purported to be realistic. Further, the utilization of dream material helped the novelist explore the unknown, dark, fearful, subterranean, or "psychological" side of human behavior, all of which characterized the Gothic aspect of Gothicism.

[5] William Beckford's *Vathek* (written in 1782 in French, published, in English, 1786) fits loosely into this literature of vision and fantasy. Although *Vathek* in a few of its aspects recalls Johnson's *Rasselas,* it is, actually, a very different sort of thing—operatic in its way, certainly theatrical, a musical extravaganza directed by Busby Berkeley or Tom O'Horgan.

Beckford's Vathek is, to some extent, a thousand-and-one-nights version of Walpole's Manfred. Although Beckford appears to be satirizing Vathek's lust for pow-

er and his sensuality, the reader senses, behind the satire, a distinct feel for the exaggerated event, a sympathetic indulgence in sadistic acts and savage murder—the feeding of fifty innocent young men to the Giaour, for example. While such acts are purportedly part of the satirical exaggeration, they are described lovingly as elements of the author's own sexual fantasies.

Ostensibly, the tale is a moral one, pointing up the abuses of power; but the filigree work of the narrative focuses, instead, on the pleasures derived from such abuses. Never distant from sight or mind are the capricious tastes, the sexual content of the rich descriptions, the indifference to human life.

If we pull together the pieces, *Vathek* is a homoerotic fantasy, comparable in this respect to many aspects of *The Castle of Otranto.* Its chief victims are young men, its man of power (Vathek) is mother-ridden, its splendors are extravaganzas of design and indulgence.

[6] Quoted by Summers in his introduction to *The Castle of Otranto,* 1924, pp. xxvi-vii.

Bibliography

Summers, Montague, *The Gothic Quest: A History of the Gothic Novel,* 1938, 1964.

Varma, Devendra, *The Gothic Flame,* 1957, 1966.

Leigh A. Ehlers (essay date 1979)

SOURCE: "The Gothic World as Stage: Providence and Character in *The Castle of Otranto,*" *Wascana Review* 14, No. 2, Fall, 1979, pp. 17-30.

[*In the following essay, Ehlers analyzes the theatrical elements of* The Castle of Otranto.]

Perhaps no eighteenth-century writer has elicited more conflicting responses than has Horace Walpole. Known today primarily for his voluminous collection of letters, Walpole is also familiar to every beginning student of literature as the author of that notorious, entertaining piece of Gothic fiction, **The Castle of Otranto.** While **Otranto** is, and was in its own day, widely read, the question remains whether it has been well read. Walpole's self-proclaimed purpose is "to blend the two kinds of romance, the ancient and the modern. In the former all was imagination and improbability: in the latter, nature is always intended to be, and sometimes has been, copied with success."[1] But the critical reception of his Gothic romance was at best contradictory; while the book was popular with the reading public and went through six editions between 1764 and 1791, one reviewer sneered at its "rotten materials," particularly the giant helmet and sighing portrait.[2] Modern critics are no less divided in their responses. Robert Kiely considers it a "slight work" betraying an "apparent lack of seriousness" and "total confusion."[3] In contrast, Martin Kallich finds *Otranto* to be a coherent narrative with "a strict unity of action."[4] Evidently the twentieth century is as much bemused by this Gothic romance as was the eighteenth.

This critical debate arises from the relation of the supernatural, that most outstanding manifestation of disorder, to the overall order or narrative structure of the romance. To comprehend the true "unity of action" behind *Otranto,* we must first recognize that it clearly draws on the stage as an appropriate analogy for its own narrative order. Walpole's interest in the stage is, of course, apparent in both his dramatization of incest in *The Mysterious Mother* (1768, unstaged) and his approval of the successful stage adaptation of *Otranto* as *The Count of Narbonne* (1781, by Robert Jephson).[5] While Kallich notes that *Otranto* is much like a melodramatic play, with a five-act division, stock characters and a catharsis of pity and terror, the implications of this stage analogy are more central to the romance's narrative unity than has been acknowledged heretofore. Just as the five-act structure subsumes disorder (the supernatural) into an overall movement toward order (the happy ending) the religious context of *Otranto* is that of a providential manipulation of disorder into order. Walpole, in fact, has a serious purpose in allowing the seeming disorder of the supernatural to rule his fictive world. The ghosts, giant helmet, portraits and apparitions are agents of providence and as such introduce chaos into the princedom in order to expose the villain Manfred and to reveal the true heir Theodore. In a sense the supernatural is the means to a theatrical-religious poetic justice that affirms the power of Heaven to intervene in the affairs of man. Much earlier in the century Thomas Rymer made explicit the parallel between God's justice and the poetical justice of the playwright.[6] Following this pattern, Walpole creates in prose a Gothic *theatrum mundi* in which the hand of God operates in and through the supernatural and the human responses to such ghosts. Though one should not ignore the amusing aspects of *Otranto*— the preface to the first edition calls it "a matter of entertainment" (p.4)—something of Walpole's didactic purpose is evident in the prefatory poem that requires its reader to "guard the marvels I relate/Of fell ambition scourg'd by fate,/From reason's peevish blame" (p.13).

The religious and theatrical contexts affect both narrative structure and characterization in *Otranto.* To establish a fictive world governed by a Christian providence, Walpole relies on a religiously oriented pattern of events. The initial vision of earthly order, a stable society headed by the prince Manfred, is replaced by instability as the supernatural agents of providence bring about the villain's downfall and the restoration of order in the accession of the true heir to the throne. This tripartite structure of prose romance reflects, for an eighteenth-century critic like John Dennis, man's position within a Christian universe: "as soon as [Man] . . . fell from his Primitive State, by transgressing Order, Weakness and Misery was the immediate Consequence of that universal Disorder that immediately follow'd his Conceptions, in his Passions and Actions. The great Design of Arts is to restore the Decays that happen'd to human Nature by the Fall, by restoring Order."[7] The result is a fiction shaped, as Martin C. Battestin remarks, by "fortunate contingencies and surprising turns" under the direction of "a personal and particular Providence," and with, as Aubrey Williams notes, the ultimate purpose that "virtuous characters can be *tested* and then rewarded and so that the evil can be *proved* and punished."[8] In *Otranto* the overall "providential" pattern emerges from three central conflicts: villain vs. hero, villain vs. heroine, villain vs. priest. The fortunes of the principal virtuous characters, Theodore, Isabella and Jerome, embody different human concerns, politics, society and religion, that fall under the ultimate guidance of heaven and that are manipulated toward the rather "stagy" denouement restoring truth and justice to the world.

Similarly religious and theatrical are the characterizations. While the good people are stock characters identified by their sentimental speeches, the villain Manfred is developed by his struggles against the supernatural and particularly by a series of allusions to Shakespearean plays. The result of Manfred's role-playing is the exposure of his evil and finally his confession of his crimes and inner torments. *Otranto* unites both the religious and the theatrical and thus demonstrates the power of divine intervention into the affairs of prince and state.

i

Otranto opens with a shock. The young Conrad, heir apparent to the princedom, is killed on his wedding day by the falling of the giant helmet. This "accident" not only deprives Manfred of his only son but also immediately brings him into conflict with the hero Theodore, the "peasant" who provokes the prince's anger by commenting on the similarity between the helmet and the statue of the good prince Alfonso. This conflict between villain and hero is at the heart of the political manifestation of the providential pattern. Centering on problems of dynasty and true identity, this political conflict involves the overthrow of an establishment founded on murder and usurpation and the restoration of the true family line. The outline of this political upheaval is summarized by the ancient prophecy predicting *"that the castle and lordship of Otranto should pass from the present family, whenever the real owner should be grown too large to inhabit it"* (pp. 15-16). In the end Manfred becomes his true self, a deposed tyrant accorded only the courtesy title of "your *lordship"* (p.109), and Theodore, no longer the peasant, becomes the "real owner" of Otranto.

Although Manfred struggles against loss of power,

providence thwarts his attempts to re-establish his dynasty. Despite his wife Hippolita's warning that "the hand of Providence is stretched out" against them (p.87), Manfred plots an intermarriage between his and Frederic's family, which has the closer claim to the throne. But when Manfred proposes marriage to Isabella, the giant helmet emits "a hollow and rustling sound" (p.23). Isabella's warning that "heaven itself declares against your impious intentions" provokes Manfred's defiance: "Heaven nor hell shall impede my designs" (p.23). Reinforcing the prince's dynastic concern is the obvious allusion to Henry VIII's arguments for his divorce from Catherine of Aragon, who like Hippolita failed to provide a living male heir: "Hippolita is related to me in the fourth degree. . . . To this state of unlawful wedlock I impute the visitation that has fallen on me in the death of Conrad!" (p.49). The villain's sophistry obscures the real purpose of the "visitation," and only after the death of Matilda and irrevocable destruction of his dynastic line does Manfred admit his and his grandfather's guilt: "May this bloody record be a warning to future tyrants. . . . Alfonso died by poison. A fictitious will declared Ricardo his heir. His crimes pursued him—yet he lost no Conrad, no Matilda! I pay the price of usurpation for all!" (p.109). Thus "the will of heaven" (p.109) has destroyed the prince's political power, shattering his castle's walls as well, and forced the usurper into exile and atonement for the remainder of his life.

While engaged in bringing down the usurper, providence arranges a series of dramatic manipulations which reveal Theodore as the true prince of Otranto. In the guise of a peasant, Theodore "happens" to wander into the castle and to arouse Manfred's anger. When the villain subjects the hero to imprisonment within the giant helmet, that very confinement providentially works to Theodore's advantage. Describing his discovery of the entrance to the underground passage, Theodore states, "Providence, that delivered me from the helmet, was able to direct me to the spring of a lock" (pp. 29-30) by means of a timely "ray of moonshine" (p.27). Theodore demonstrates his nobility by his "courteous" and "generous" (p.27) behavior to the princess Isabella, whom he helps to escape into the passage. When Manfred condemns him to death, the hero displays both courage and "undaunted . . . resignation" (p.53) as well as the birthmark by which Jerome recognizes the youth as his long-lost son. Finally, providence offers dramatic proof of Theodore's true identity when the vision of Alfonso appears in the castle ruins and declares, "Behold in Theodore, the true heir of Alfonso!" (p.108). The import of these discoveries of identity is not, as Kiely argues, that Walpole reveals lack of artistry in relying on an "overused stock device."[9] Rather, the repeated instances of identity reversals affirm providence's power to turn the seeming confusion of mistaken identities into political and dynastic order and to reward the hero's courage and virtue while punishing the villain's defiance and crimes.

Paralleling the political conflict between Manfred and Theodore is the sexual tension between Manfred and Isabella, which is part of a larger context of social disorder. The opening scene briefly establishes a stable social hierarchy including all ranks—peasants, servants, aristocrats and the family of Manfred. Soon, however, the reluctant bride is saved, in the providential "nick of time," by Conrad's sudden death, throwing society into a disorder that lasts until providence makes possible Isabella's true marriage. The transition between the two weddings is marked by social chaos throughout the population. The crowd of spectators at the first wedding quickly becomes a mob after Conrad's death; the servants Diego and Jaques are thoroughly frightened and provoke Manfred's wrath by their hesitations and superstitious chatterings. Manfred himself seeks to dissolve his own family by disowning his daughter and divorcing his wife, but Jerome suddenly gains a family in his son Theodore. Such pervasive social disorder is resolved only when providence has punished Manfred and frees Isabella to marry her true love.

At the heart of that social disorder is Manfred's rampant sexuality, which because of its incestuous overtones presents a most damaging challenge to family and society. At the outset Manfred is the respectable paterfamilias, and his sexuality is contained within the proper family unit and sanctioned by the church. Once his son is dead, Manfred despairs of another heir from Hippolita because of her "sterility" (p.15), and his awakened lust turns to the young and beautiful Isabella, from whom he expects "a numerous offspring" (p.23). Outraged, Isabella resists an incestuous and immoral union with her "father in law! the father of Conrad! the husband of the virtuous and tender Hippolita!" (p.23). Likewise, Jerome later warns the prince "not to pursue the incestuous design on thy contracted daughter" (p.48). Ironically, the union that Manfred wishes to dissolve is almost as incestuous as the projected union with Isabella, for the prince and Hippolita are close cousins, married under a special dispensation. Having once defied social taboos to marry Hippolita, Manfred now disregards the sanctity of the marriage bond and pursues Isabella so lustfully that she fears rape in the basement of his castle, "a place where her cries were not likely to draw any body to her assistance" (p.25).

In the end the prince's forbidden lust providentially causes his downfall. Angered by his intended's coolness and "flushed by wine and love" (p.103), Manfred jealously mistakes the lady with Theodore in the chapel for Isabella and assaults her in a sexual manner by "plunging . . . [his dagger] over her shoulder into the bosom . . ." (p.104). The death of Matilda punishes

Manfred for his incestuous sexuality and the attempt to break the marriage bond; in effect, providence has turned the villain's own weakness against himself. The ancient prophecy from St. Nicholas has predicted prosperity for Manfred's family "as long as issue-male from Ricardo's loins should remain to enjoy it" (p.109). Once Manfred's sexuality breaks out of the legal bounds, his lust works to his ultimate downfall and exile to a sterile life in a monastery.

In addition to the political and sexual conflicts, the villain struggles with a third opponent, Father Jerome, the spokesman for the church. As an agent of providence, Jerome is instrumental in defeating the villain's challenge against church authority. Realizing that to allow a divorce and nullification of a special dispensation would undermine the church's spiritual and moral influence in the princedom, Jerome bluntly reprimands the prince's "adulterous intention" (p.48). Manfred, however, extends his challenge from mere requests for a divorce to an actual invasion of the monastery church. Here the villain attempts to separate Hippolita from her confessor and provokes Jerome's denunciation: "The church despises thy menaces. . . . Dare to proceed in thy curst purpose of a divorce, until her sentence be known, and here I lance [sic] her anathema at thy head" (p.93). The seriousness of Manfred's threat to ecclesiastical authority is indicated by his later plot to "advance his suit at the court of Rome" by bribery (p.96). The corruption that began in the castle has moved to the neighboring church and verges on becoming universal.

Heaven defends the earthly church by the various supernatural interventions, which Jerome underscores by overtly religious commentary. Repeatedly the father provides a providential interpretation of events. In Jerome's hands the death of Conrad becomes an example of the *ubi sunt* theme: "Heaven mocks the short-sighted views of man. But yester-morn, whose house was so great, so flourishing as Manfred's?—Where is young Conrad now?" (p.48). The death of Matilda elicits Jerome's most providential denunciation: "Now, tyrant! behold the completion of woe fulfilled on thy impious and devoted head! The blood of Alfonso cried to heaven for vengeance: and heaven has permitted its altar to be polluted by assassination, that thou mightest shed thy own blood at the foot of that prince's sepulchre!" (p.105). The Biblical echo (Abel's blood crying to the Lord) reinforces and epitomizes the clearly religious nature of Jerome's position of spokesman for an "offended heaven" that moves to punish murder and usurpation (p.109).

The final paragraph of the romance ties together the political, social and religious manifestations of the providential pattern. Theodore, Isabella and Jerome are united in a single act of poetic justice, while Manfred is cast out. The virtuous characters are rewarded by marriage and parenthood, but the villain is punished by exile from his wife and loss of children. Thus the romance has moved toward a strict fulfillment of the basic principle, "a tyrant's race must be swept from the earth to the third and fourth generation" (pp. 90-91). Murder and usurpation merit severe punishment, while faith and virtue merit reward. Both dispositions are achieved simultaneously by the providential appearance of Alfonso's apparition.

If this providential pattern is, as I have attempted to demonstrate, the informing structure of *Otranto,* the question remains why certain critics have failed to note any didactic point in the romance. Both modern and eighteenth-century responses often see *Otranto* as a frivolous or even dangerous work. Kiely charges Walpole with "ambiguity of . . . moral and aesthetic position" (*Romantic Novel,* p.37), while Stanley J. Solomon concludes that the romance lacks "apparent didactic point."[10] More to the heart of the issue is *The Monthly Review*'s complaint that *Otranto* presents "not only a very useless, but a very insupportable moral" in its "unchristian doctrine of visiting the sins of the fathers upon the children."[11] The crucial factor in such distaste for the providential denouement is the fate of Matilda, the seemingly innocent "fourth generation" of the tyrant's (Ricardo's) family. Even Theodore is somewhat dissatisfied with the outcome, for despite marriage to Isabella, he remains in a permanent state of semi-mourning, knowing "no happiness but in the society of one with whom he could forever indulge the melancholy that had taken possession of his soul" (p.110). Matilda's death may seem an unnecessarily harsh punishment for helping Theodore escape and for seeing him despite her vow to the contrary. However, this defiance of her father, albeit a tyrant-father, is after all a sin of disobedience, with all the attendant Edenic overtones. Like Matilda's disobedience, the usurpation of Ricardo and hence that of Manfred also constitutes a defiance of the father-prince Alfonso, the divinely designated ruler.

The fact that *Otranto* ends on a note of sorrow mixed with joy does not undermine Walpole's didactic point. The death of Matilda underscores the essentially fallen nature of man and his world. Theodore's melancholy responds to the inevitability of suffering in this world, but his marriage and restoration to the throne affirm the power of providence to dispose human lives for the overall good and to restore eventually the faithful to full happiness in heaven. Thus in contrast to the "perfectly" happy ending of Clara Reeve's *The Old English Baron,* another extremely didactic Gothic romance, Walpole's ending prepares his reader for providential dispositions resulting in sorrows amid the joy, a condition more closely approximating the reader's everyday experience. In effect, Walpole warns us not to expect perfect restoration until we enter heaven. No conclusion could seem more properly didactic or Christian.

ii

Walpole's characterizations have been misunderstood by critics who attempt to impose on his romance standards of the modern psychological novel. For instance, Solomon faults **Otranto** for having "no organizing intelligence . . . neither a narrative personality nor a character's mind."[12] Walpole's interest is not in the hidden depths of the human psyche but rather in the responses of his characters to the providential interventions in their lives. In his first preface Walpole requests his reader to accept "this *air* of the *miraculous*" and to note that the characters exist exclusively within that providential context: "Allow the possibility of the facts, and all the actors comport themselves as persons would do in their situation" (p.4). The word "actors" is highly significant. The characters in **Otranto** are conceived and presented rather theatrically, as participants in a Gothic drama revealing the means by which providence resolves chaos into order.

To reinforce the general theatrical context, Walpole draws certain characters and lines from Shakespeare, as one might expect from his defense of Shakespearean tragicomedy in his second preface. Kiely argues that the evidence of this "adoption of character-types and episodes from Shakespeare" and the attempt to show a character's "emotional agitation by means of theatrical gesture and movement"[13] is proof of Walpole's artistic ineptitude. To the contrary, such theatricality is deliberate and well suited to the dramatized demonstration of providence. Most of the characters are stock types, especially associated with Shakespeare—the "humorous" servants, the talkative nurse, the doomed lovers, the ghosts, among others. As E.L. Burney notes, "the spirit of Shakespeare haunts the courtyard, the halls, galleries, battlements and dungeons of the Castle of Otranto."[14] Within that setting (a stage set, if you will), characters like Isabella, Hippolita and Theodore reveal themselves in actions and brief, often sentimental speeches. For example, Hippolita not only demonstrates her unswerving loyalty to her husband by repeated "marks of tenderness and duty" (p.35), but she also delivers a speech indicative of her type as the submissive wife. She reminds the young princesses "it is not ours to make election for ourselves; heaven, our fathers, and our husbands, must decide for us" (p.88). Modern readers quite frequently are impatient with such stock theatrical figures (if not with such "male chauvinistic" paternalism) as they also are with the sentimental characters like Matilda, who broods over her love while "leaning pensively on her arm" (p.84). Walpole, however, demands that we see characters as actors on a providential stage, as role players representing all the conceivable responses (albeit outwardly presented) to the evidence of divine intervention in their lives. Character, then, is a kind of structural cor-

relative; a Theodore or Manfred simply does not exist apart from the providential pattern of the romance at large.

Given that the providential pattern ultimately controls characterization, we can see why Walpole focuses the greatest detail on his villain while the good characters like Theodore remain sketchy. Providence's first concern is to expose and defeat evil, in this case Manfred's defiance of the divine anointment of Alfonso. Because Manfred *is* that disorder preventing the harmonious establishment of God-prince-people, providence puts into motion a long series of events leading to his deposition. This initial recognition of evil requires a greater amount of detail for his characterization than for any other principal.

The details of Manfred's exposure function in a suitably theatrical and providential context. The various allusions to Shakespearean plays, more than mere attempts for "atmosphere," undermine Manfred's authority and emphasize his unstable vacillation between reason and passion resulting in eventual madness and self-defeat. Taking on progressively evil roles from Shakespearean plays, the villain reveals, rather than masks, his past and present crimes. This is not to say that Manfred is the only Shakespearean role-player. Certainly we might recognize in Bianca the nurse to Matilda's Juliet or in the garrulous servants Diego and Jaques any number of gravediggers, rude mechanics and jesters. These Shakespearean "low" characters are, as Walpole notes, a counterpoint to the tribulations of the aristocrats so that "the contrast between the sublime of one, and the *naïveté* of the other, sets the pathetic of the former in a stronger light" (p. 8). Hence the Shakespearean allusions highlight the conflict within the nobility and especially focus attention on Manfred, the central power of the aristocracy.

We first see Manfred as the prince of Otranto desperately attempting to control the disorder in his realm. His proposal of marriage to Isabella is interrupted by the ghost of Ricardo, who steps out of his portrait and descends "on the floor with a grave and melancholy air" (p.24). Manfred, of course, echoes Hamlet in saying "Speak, infernal spectre!" and again "Lead on! . . . I will follow thee to the gulph of perdition" (p.24). Although Manfred's obvious courage may lend him a kind of heroic stature, the hints about his guilt establish him as the flawed, self-tormented prince. His interrupted description of himself as Ricardo's "wretched descendant, who too dearly pays for—" (p.24) indicates a desire to conceal his guilt despite the ghostly visitation, and his renewed pursuit of Isabella indicates his desperation to retain his political power.

The somewhat heroic overtones of Manfred's courageous dealings with the ghosts give way to a stronger impression of his evil tyranny over his estate and family. If, as seems abundantly clear, Matilda and Theodore are Juliet and Romeo, the star-crossed lovers sharing stolen interviews, Manfred then becomes the tyrant-father bent on separating the lovers. Thus, Matilda ends her first meeting with Theodore in her father's name: "Dost thou come hither to pry into the secrets of Manfred? Adieu. I have been mistaken in thee" (p.42). Again Manfred's villainy comes between the lovers when Matilda and her family is answered "supernaturally" by "a deep and hollow groan" (p.70), which is, of course, providentially designed to separate the lovers. As Jerome later states, it is heaven's will that "the blood of Alfonso will never mix with that of Manfred" (p.93). Hence the father's tyranny in dividing the lovers actually furthers the designs of providence by preventing an intermarriage and reconciliation between the rival families claiming the throne.

Far more villainous is Manfred's next Shakespearean role—that of the murderer plagued by his victim's ghost. The prince reveals a guilty conscience to the assembled cast in what we might term the "Banquo scene":

> Ha! what are thou, thou dreadful spectre! Is my hour come?—My dearest, gracious lord, cried Hippolita, clasping him in her arms, what is it you see? Why do you fix your eye-balls thus?—What! cried Manfred breathless—dost thou see nothing, Hippolita? Is this ghastly phantom sent to me alone—to me, who did not—For mercy's sweetest self, my lord, said Hippolita, resume your soul, command your reason. There is none here but we your friends.—What, is not that Alfonso? cried Manfred: dost thou not see him? Can it be my brain's delirium?—This! my lord, said Hippolita: this is Theodore, the youth who has been so unfortunate—Theodore! said Manfred mournfully, and striking his forehead—Theodore, or a phantom, he has unhinged the soul of Manfred. (p.80).

In this highly theatrical scene, complete with dialogue and stage gestures, Manfred like Macbeth outwardly reveals "his most secret sensations" (p.82), his obsession with murder and usurpation. Significantly, this revelation is exceedingly public, before the entire royal family and noble visitors so that no question of the villain's guilty past remains.

While exposing Manfred as a murderer's descendant, providence also manipulates the villain into situations driving him toward madness and self-defeat. Manfred's downfall stems from his chief weakness, his tendency to allow "passion" to "obscure his reason" (p.30). Repeatedly providence places the prince in situations that paralyze his reason and leave him at the mercy of uncontrollable passions. The giant helmet, for example, stuns Manfred and takes "away the prince's speech" (p.17). Again, when trying to

hide from Frederic the fact of Isabella's flight, the villain is so disconcerted by Jerome's sudden intrusion that he utters "nothing but incoherent sentences" (p.67). In the end, Manfred is totally mad, and once more a Shakespearean allusion underscores his evil. Offended by Frederic and Isabella, Manfred loses all rational control over "a frame of mind capable of the most fatal excesses" (p.103), and mistakenly stabs Matilda. The parallel to Hamlet's stabbing Polonius hidden behind the arras seems clear. Manfred's madness is like the "imperfect gleam of moonshine" (p.104), which deludes him into destroying his daughter and his power, a self-destruction visually suggested by the collapse of the castle itself. This his last Shakespearean role as the deluded, self-defeating, murderous Hamlet completes Manfred's progression from heroic courage to exposed villainy and also emphasizes the means by which providence has manipulated him into achieving his own downfall. Manfred has indeed been, as Shakespeare says, "hoist with his own petar."

The poetic justice of the conclusion brings both characterization and narrative structure into a clear, final relationship. Within the theatrical context of five acts and "Shakespearean" actors, *Otranto* embodies a providential pattern and character response to divine intervention culminating in a restoration of justice in the world of men. Even the seeming disorder of the Gothic machinery—ghosts, skeletons, apparitions, hidden passages, dungeons, bleeding statues—is ultimately subsumed by the providential order, just as the physical presence of the proscenium arch contains the action of a play. *Otranto,* in fact, functions as a kind of Gothic *theatrum mundi,* a staging of the providential means by which the prevailing disorder and confusion in human affairs is resolved into a final order and justice.

Notes

[1] "Preface to Second Edition," *The Castle of Otranto,* ed. W.S. Lewis (London: Oxford Univ. Press, 1969), p.7. All subsequent references to *Otranto* are to this edition.

[2] *Critical Review,* 19 (1765), 51.

[3] Kiely, *The Romantic Novel in England* (Cambridge: Harvard Univ. Press, 1972), pp. 33, 36.

[4] Kallich, *Horace Walpole* (New York: Twayne, 1971), p. 94.

[5] Bertrand Evans, *Gothic Drama from Walpole to Shelley* (Berkeley: Univ. of California Press, 1947), pp. 34, 50. Jephson's adaptation omitted, as unstageable with eighteenth-century methods of production, the more startling instances of the supernatural—the

giant helmet, bleeding portraits, Alfonso's apparition—and stressed instead the guilty agonies of Manfred.

[6] Rymer argues for the necessity of "Poetical Justice" in literature: "a *Poet* must of necessity see *justice* exactly administered, if he intended to please. For . . . if the World scarce be satisfi'd with God Almighty . . . a Poet (in these matters) shall never be pardon'd. . . . " *See The Critical Works of Thomas Rymer,* ed. Curt. A. Zimansky (New Haven: Yale Univ. Press, 1956), pp. 22-23.

[7] Dennis, *The Grounds of Criticism in Poetry (1704),* in *Critical Works,* ed. E.N. Hooker (Baltimore: Johns Hopkins Press, 1939-43), I, 335-36.

[8] Batttestin, *The Providence of Wit: Aspects of Form in Augustan Literature and the Arts* (Oxford: Clarendon Press, 1974), p. 151. Williams, "Interpositions of Providence and the Design of Fielding's Novels," *SAQ,* 70 (1971), 284.

[9] *Romantic Novel,* p. 39.

[10] Solomon, "Subverting Propriety as a Pattern of Irony in Three Eighteenth-Century Novels: *The Castle of Otranto, Vathek,* and *Fanny Hill,*" *Erasmus Review,* 1 (1971), 109.

[11] *Monthly Review; or Literary Journal,* 32 (1765), 99.

[12] Solomon, p. 109.

[13] *Romantic Novel,* p. 34.

[14] Burney, "Shakespeare in Otranto," *Manchester Review,* 12 (1972), 62. Burney also notes an allusion to *Julius Caesar* and the Shakespearean style of "rustic prose" for the servants and "irregular iambic rhythm" for the aristocrats (p.62). Allusions to *Cymbeline, Romeo and Juliet, Macbeth* and *Hamlet* have also been identified by Lewis in his preface to the Oxford edition of *Otranto,* p.xiv.

Gilbert Phelps (essay date 1979)

SOURCE: "*The Castle of Otranto:* A Gothic Story, in *A Reader's Guide to Fifty British Novels, 1600 - 1900,* Heinemann, 1979.

[*In the following excerpt, Phelps considers the historical importance of* The Castle of Otranto.]

Summary

The events which the story narrates are supposed to have occurred sometime in the twelfth or the thirteenth century, and although there is a real Otranto (on the Strait of Otranto, in southern Italy) the location is essentially dreamlike, while the names of Manfred, the Prince of Otranto in the story, and of Conrad, his ailing son, sound more German than Italian.

The story opens as Manfred is making hasty preparations for the marriage of Conrad to Isabella, daughter of the Marquis of Vicenza, whom he has secured in the castle with the connivance of her guardians and during the absence of her father. Manfred's servants attribute the haste to his dread of an old prophecy which declares *'That the castle and lordship of Otranto should pass from the present family, whenever the real owner should be grown too large to inhabit it.'*

Before the wedding can be solemnized, Conrad is crushed to death by a giant helmet which suddenly crashes into the courtyard. Afraid of being left without a male heir, Manfred determines to divorce his devoted wife, Hippolita, and to marry Isabella himself. Horrified by the proposal, Isabella escapes through an underground passage to the nearby church of St Nicholas and the protection of Father Jerome. She is aided in her escape by a handsome young peasant named Theodore, who bears a striking resemblance to the portrait of Alonso, the original Prince of Otranto (poisoned by Manfred's grandfather so that he could usurp the principality).

Theodore, already under suspicion of playing some part, through sorcery, in the death of Conrad, and now also suspected of helping Isabella, is imprisoned but secretly released by Manfred's daughter Matilda, with whom Theodore falls in love.

All kinds of complications follow, including the arrival of Isabella's father to demand the restoration of his daughter and to challenge Manfred to a duel; the flight of Isabella to a nearby cave, where she is protected by Theodore, who wounds her father when he mistakes him for one of Manfred's retainers; and a treaty between Isabella's father, who has recovered from his wounds, and Manfred whereby the former gives his consent to the match between Isabella and Manfred. Attending these complications are a number of mysterious and supernatural manifestations, all full of dire warning to Manfred.

Eventually Manfred, believing that Isabella and Theodore are in love, and hearing that Theodore and a lady are praying together before the tomb of Alonso, hurries to the church himself, and stabs the lady—only to discover that he has killed his own daughter, Matilda. The supernatural forces that have been at work in the background now bring matters to a climax. The ghost of Alonso, a gigantic figure (the owner of the helmet and of an equally outsize sword) has, in accordance with the prophecy, grown too big for the edifice and begins to break it asunder. Terror at last drives Manfred to admit that he is a usurper. Theodore turns out to be the son of Father Jerome and also the rightful heir to Alonso. Manfred and his wife Hippolita retire to houses of religion, while Theodore is established as prince of Otranto and, although still sorrowing for Matilda, marries her best friend Isabella 'persuaded he could know no happiness but in the society of one with whom he could forever indulge the melancholy that had taken possession of his soul.'

Critical commentary

It will be seen from the summary that supernatural elements play as important a part in *The Castle of Otranto* as the mediaeval trappings, and contemporary readers were duly terrified. Gray, for example, wrote that he and his Cambridge friends were 'afraid to go to bed o'nights'. Besides the mysterious appearance of the giant helmet and sword accompanied by 'a hollow and rustling sound', there are a huge armoured hand on a bannister (as in Walpole's dream), a skeleton in a monk's habit, drops of blood that fall from the nose of Alonso's statue, and a portrait of Manfred's grandfather, the original usurper, that suddenly comes to life. This last device—which has, of course, grown stale over the years by constant repetition—was long regarded as particularly horrifying—especially as the portrait, with 'an audible sigh', steps down from the frame, causing Manfred to exclaim (with echoes of Hamlet when confronted by his father's ghost):

> 'Do I dream? . . . or are the devils themselves in league against me? Speak, infernal spectre! Or, if thou art my grandsire, why dost thou too conspire against thy wretched descendant?'

Then, as the vision gestures him to follow:

> 'Lead on!' cried Manfred; 'I will follow thee to the gulph of perdition!' The spectre marched sedately, but dejected, to the end of the gallery, and turned into a chamber on the right hand . . .

That gives something of the flavour of the novel, which was an important harbinger of certain aspects of the Romantic Revival, in which fondness for supernatural terrors was to some extent symptomatic of the desire to break out of the imaginative and emotional restraints imposed by the realism of Defoe, Richardson, Fielding and Smollett.

The contribution of *The Castle of Otranto* to the future of the English novel was twofold. First, it initiated the Gothic novel, which soon began to be called also 'the novel of terror', and which had a long progeny. There were a number of genuinely original works of fiction inspired by it, among them Mrs Ann Radcliffe's

The Mysteries of Udolpho (1794), and Matthew Gregory Lewis's *The Monk* (1796)—which was so popular that its author was nicknamed 'Monk' Lewis. Later, famous writers of tales of horror and the supernatural who were indirectly influenced by Walpole's example included Charles Maturin, author of *Melmoth the Wanderer* (1820), Sheridan Le Fanu in *Uncle Silas* (1864) and the early nineteenth-century American, Edgar Allen Poe, as well as numerous later writers in the same genre—not to mention the makers of horror movies in our own times.

Second, the fact that Walpole had turned to the historical past, no matter how amateurishly, was of considerable importance in itself. At the height of the Augustan period, the past (except for that of classical Greece and Rome) was regarded as something dark and barbaric with little to teach a society which, to the Augustans, marked the highest possible point of cultural development—even Shakespeare was considered an 'untutored genius', several of whose plays had been 'civilized' by being put into heroic couplets.

The Castle of Otranto helped to shake a cultural confidence that showed signs of degenerating into complacency, and to point the way to that fruitful rediscovery of the past and of a sense of history, which was one of the most striking outcomes of the Romantic Revival. It was not surprising, therefore, that Sir Walter Scott should, in 1811, have praised *The Castle of Otranto* as 'remarkable not only for the wild interest of the story, but as the first modern attempt to found a tale of amusing fiction upon the basis of the ancient romances of chivalry.'

When *The Castle of Otranto* was reissued in 1964, to mark the two hundredth anniversary of its first publication, it was its hundred and fifteenth appearance at least—with many more editions still unaccounted for. It was obviously, in its day, very popular indeed. It still arouses sufficient interest to make the reader want to know how it works out, especially as, in marked contrast to most eighteenth-century novels, it is only about a hundred pages long. But its importance today is that it was a kind of bridging novel, published within the Age of Reason but inaugurating a number of developments usually associated with the period that followed it. As such, no account of the growth of the English novel would be complete without some examination of it.

Judith Wilt (essay date 1980)

SOURCE: "Gothic Fathers: *The Castle of Otranto, The Italian, The Monk, Melmoth the Wanderer*," in *Ghosts of the Gothic: Austen, Eliot, & Lawrence*, Princeton University Press, 1980.

[*In the following excerpt from her* Ghosts of the Gothic: Austen, Eliot, & Lawrence *(1980), Wilt examines the religious import of Walpole's Gothic tale.*]

Horace Walpole's **The Castle of Otranto** (1765) is a rather gormless tale for which Walpole claimed little, and even the claim he did make—"Terror, the author's principal engine, prevents the story from ever languishing"[1]—is not entirely true. Its merits are not in character, plot, or prose, nor as he had thought, in the dramatic structure, but in half a dozen memorable tableaux,[2] frozen moments of action, which are almost certainly lifted from Walpole's dreams, and maybe yours and mine too.

The narrative proper begins, like a primer in Gothic plot, with the father: "Manfred, Prince of Otranto, had one son and one daughter." A page later, on young Conrad's wedding day, the cry "Oh! the helmet! the helmet!" brings the family to the courtyard, where "—but what a sight for a father's eyes!—he beheld his child dashed to pieces, and almost buried under an enormous helmet, an hundred times more large than any casque ever made for human being, and shaded with a proportionable quantity of black feathers." Manfred's stupefied gazing at this portent establishes the first tableau; and the second comes pat a few pages later as, trying to become his own son, Manfred offers himself to the bereft bride, Isabella: "Heaven nor hell shall impede my designs, said Manfred, advancing again to seize the princess. At that instant the portrait of his grandfather . . . quit its panel and [descended] on the floor with a grave and melancholy air" (p. 24). The third tableau, Isabella escaping through the lower vaults of the castle, became the subject of numerous sketches and paintings in the late eighteenth century, for as Walpole says only too truly of his own prose: "Words cannot paint the horror of the princess' situation" (p. 27).

Wanting no daughter, "raving" for more sons, and intending to put away his infertile wife and beget more sons upon Isabella, Manfred meets his match, another father, in the priest Jerome. "I am sovereign here, and will allow no meddling priest to interfere," he says (p. 47), but Jerome refuses to hand over the bride: "she is where orphans and virgins are safest from the wiles and snares of this world, and nothing but a parent's authority shall take her thence." "I am her parent, and demand her," returns Manfred, leaving himself open to Jerome's unanswerable riposte: "By me are thou warned not to pursue the incestuous design on thy contracted daughter" (pp. 49-50). The property of Otranto at stake, Manfred and the real father of Isabella compromise, each to his own best advantage: each will marry the other's daughter, each hopes that his own daughter will bear no sons to his enemy and thus secure the property to him. "Thou art no lawful prince," thunders the substitute father Jerome. "It is done," responds the separated Manfred, and "as he spoke these words three

drops of blood fell from the nose of Alfonso's statue" (p. 98).

This serio-comic tableau marks the third ponderous intervention of Alfonso the Good, the true prince, foully done to death by Manfred's grandfather for the lordship of Otranto, but not before he had secretly married and begotten a daughter, who married the Count of Falconara, who fathered the true heir Theodore and then became Father Jerome after Theodore's disappearance. This young "lost heir" appears at Otranto in time to be fallen in love with by both of the girlchildren, Matilda and Isabella, who are coveted as property by the middle-aged fathers. Thus in this first of the classic Gothic tales the male ingenue has almost no active role, not even as an object of persecution. He is simply the convenient receptacle of the least interesting, most conventional sentiments; he loses his own beloved, marries her friend as an afterthought, and after an odyssey as sentimentally banal as Charles II's, he is only a spectator at his own restoration, which provides the last spectacular tableau of the tale:

> The moment Theodore appeared, the walls of the castle behind Manfred were thrown down by a mighty force, and the form of Alfonso, dilated to an immense magnitude, appeared in the centre of the ruins. "Behold in Theodore the true heir of Alfonso!" said the vision; and having pronounced those words, accompanied by a clap of thunder, it ascended solemnly towards heaven, where the clouds parting asunder, the face of St. Nicholas was seen; and receiving Alfonso's shade, they were soon swept from mortal eyes in a blaze of glory. (p. 113)

One feels impelled to start a round of applause, though Walpole's priest-narrator informs us instead that the beholders fell on their faces, "acknowledging the divine will."

This narrator, it is important to note, is the first of the holy fathers in the tale, and he may indeed have devious clerkly motives in telling the story. In a reflex absolutely central to English Gothic, Walpole affects to find the manuscript of this story "in the library of an ancient Catholic family in the north of England"—that is, to the comfortable home-counties' Anglican mind, at the edge of the civilized world, where the minions of the great old religion might still dwell. Now, to the enlightened eighteenth-century mind of course, says Walpole in his "translators preface," marvelous visitations, dreams and portents, priestly tyranny, have been "exploded . . . even from romances." Two hundred and fifty years ago it was different, and "an author would not be faithful to the *manners* of the times" to omit them (p. 4).

On the other hand, Walpole offers a singular explanation for the telling of the story. Carefully deducing from stylistic evidence that the manuscript he has found dates from early sixteenth-century Italy, he theorizes:

> Letters were then in their flourishing state . . . and contributed to dispel the empire of superstition, at that time so forcibly attacked by the reformers. It is not unlikely that an artful priest might endeavor to turn their own arms on the innovators; and might avail himself of his abilities as an author to confirm the populace in their ancient errors and superstitions.

"Such a work as the following," Walpole adds solemnly, "would enslave a hundred vulgar minds beyond half the books of controversy that have been written from the days of Luther to the present hour" (pp. 3-4).

Thus in Walpole's crucial narrative conceit, the Gothic arises in "the days of Luther" as a tool of the Catholic Counter-Reformation, the priests of the old dispensation striking from beyond the grave at the new. In the 1760s, as an embattled Catholic Church suppresses the Jesuit Order under pressure from the "rational" despots of the continent, Walpole's "modern" romance restores the Jesuits to the English reader's mind.

Pursuing his scheme for material power, Isabella's father approaches a figure that, "turning slowly round, discovered to him the fleshless jaws and empty sockets of a skeleton, wrapt in a hermit's cowl" (p. 107). In a "conflict of penitence and passion" he is recalled to his errand, which is to work the dead Jesuit's will upon the house of Manfred according to the story's governing moral. "Yet I could wish," says the "translator" airily of that other living/dead priest, the writer of the manuscript, that "he had grounded his plan on a more useful moral than this: that the sins of the fathers are visited on their children to the third and fourth generation. I doubt whether in his time, any more than at present, ambition curbed its appetite of dominion from the dread of so remote a punishment" (p. 5). The secret sin that works itself poisonously out into the open, destroying at a distance of years or even generations, is a staple of Gothic plot; it is prime evidence for a theological universe, one in which any human act, occasionally a selfless one like Christ's sacrifice but more often a selfish one, may call to itself a power that will magnify the act far beyond the human scale. Time and distance supply some of the magnification; the Gothic portrays exactly that special dread which arises from the anticipation of remote, therefore magnified, punishment.

In terms of narrative, however, immediate punishment is what the Gothic delivers; from the death that opens *The Castle of Otranto* to the death that opens the novel *Jaws,* punishment comes first—not, certainly, before the sin, but before the revelation of the sin. In the Gothic, then, a world that first seems rational and calm is shattered by an irrational or random punishment,

which is then rerationalized by the revelation of the generating, the original sin. And punishment in the Gothic, we will note, is most often for the young, while sin, the ambition for dominion, is the province of the old. This is one hidden reason why Manfred is "mad for sons"—not only will a son secure the domain but a son will receive the promised doom. The son must die so that the old man may live.

Or, in the last resort, the daughter must die. Manfred and Matilda are a curious pair. As Walpole rather casually creates her, Manfred's daughter is as mysterious an object of hatred to Manfred as Isabella is an object of lust. In the "conduct of the passions . . . according to probability" that Walpole feels is the central interest of his "new" kind of romance, these two passions are clearly linked. "I do not want a daughter" rages Manfred to his daughter; "I will be her parent" he insists of Isabella, his son's contracted wife. In the last pages of the book the two women and the two passions link together in a kind of murder/rape: hated by Isabella and haplessly loved by Matilda, Manfred in a fury plunges his dagger into the object of his lust and finds that he has killed the object of his hatred, his daughter. Attempting to shed "Alfonso's blood," he had "shed his own." Alfonso's revenge is complete, and his monk-substitutes are triumphant. Matilda forgives Manfred and thus locks him forever into guilt; he takes the cowl and goes into eternal penitence; woman and priest meet victorious beyond the grave, clouds parting asunder. Isabella and Theodore survive, like Shakespeare's Edgar, never to see so much nor live so intensely again.[3] Manfred and Frederick, two mighty old ones, are defeated by the still older ones, priests of the old empire of superstition. Like Marlowe's Faustus, Manfred believed hell was a fable and learns his mistake: hell is a truth, and it is wherever the sinner is. The artful priest, whom Walpole's "translator" suggests cynically contrived the whole story, has had his sadistic will with the Gothic antihero, the separated one, the "man of sorrows" as Manfred calls himself in echo of that ambiguous model Separated Son. Manfred is also the skeptic, who "doubts whether Heaven notifies its will through friars" (p. 65). Here we locate the real and empathetic terror of the Gothic antihero: in the midst of his power he doubts. Heretic and would-be atheist, he yet wonders whether in fact there is not, somewhere, if not in friars, the face, the portent, the pattern of events in which he should be reading the writing of heaven. No simple savage, Manfred is usually, in the easy eighteenth-century formula Walpole uses, humane and virtuous "when his passions did not obscure his reason" (p. 31). He bears the guilty burden of the tale and shares in the secret sin, but in the midst of his obsession that his house not fall, his mortality not end, he is at least partly drawn to propagate sons on Isabella because she is distantly of Alfonso's blood. So a son of theirs might both preserve his house and restore Alfonso's: a reasonable compromise, it would seem, in any universe but the Gothic, where the powers of evil and good, "dilated to an immense magnitude," pursue their own passionate symmetries, powers made even more dreadful in their abstract emptiness by an eerie familiarity. "This can be no evil spirit," says Matilda in the most Gothic moment of all, "it is undoubtedly one of the family" (p. 41).

Notes

[1] Horace Walpole, *The Castle of Otranto,* reprinted with *The Mysteries of Udolpho* and *Northanger Abbey* (New York: Holt, Rinehart and Winston, Inc., 1963), p. 4. Walpole published this preface in his own personna in the second edition; the first edition, published several months earlier, contained only the "translator's preface" in his assumed personna. Subsequent references are to this edition and will be cited by page number in the text.

[2] Gothic melodrama really does derive from *The Castle of Otranto* in this respect; most of the important Gothic romances were immediately dramatized in their entirety or contributed familiar "bits" to the wildly successful plays of this genre. A wounderfully entertaining picture of the process is Montague Summers' account of Matthew Gregory Lewis's career as a playwright; he quotes Lewis's candid admission of what "business" was borrowed from *Otranto* and what from *The Mysteries of Udolpho* or other novels for his most successful play, *The Castle Spectre.*

[3] It is interesting to note that the century that produced Tate's "happily-ever-after" *Lear* and Johnson's strictures on the lamentably "mixed" and "painful" Shakespeare also responded powerfully to the dark and formally rough Shakespeare as administered through the Gothic novel. Quotations from *Macbeth, Lear, Titus Andronicus,* and *Richard III* abound as headnotes in Mrs. Radcliffe's and Monk Lewis's works, for instance, and in his second preface to *The Castle of Otranto* Walpole claimed Shakespeare for his model above all in that mixture of "buffoonery and solemnity" (p. 11) which is a peculiar hallmark of the Gothic imagination and which Barm Stoker's *Dracula,* in a passage I want to advert to later, formalizes as a kind of dance between King Death and King Laugh.

Frederick S. Frank (essay date 1986)

SOURCE: "Proto-Gothicism: The Infernal Iconography of Walpole's *Castle of Otranto, Orbis Litter grum,* 41, 1986, pp. 199-212.

[*In the essay that follows, Frank explores the iconography of* The Castle of Otranto *as a fully developed*

Gothic inversion of positive value systems.]

The amazing preeminence of the Gothic novel from the death of Smollett in 1771 to the publication of Sir Walter Scott's *Waverley* in 1814 saw the ascendancy of many varieties of horror and the proliferation of many types of terror. Historians of the Gothic are still debating how many Gothics were written during these four frantic decades and they continue to make deeper inquiries about why the Gothic dominated English literature between Smollett's death and Scott's first successful novel.[1] Whatever the answers to these questions of quantity, intention, and literary influence might be, the fact is undeniable that the scores of Gothic titles which flooded the literary market-place during the period could all claim one common point of origin: Horace Walpole's *The Castle of Otranto,* Gothicism's primal "long labyrinth of darkness."[2] All critical considerations of what the Gothic communicates and how the genre does so must commence with an acknowledgement of Walpole's ingenious prototype.

Written in defiance of neoclassic forms and norms, Walpole's *Castle of Otranto* remains a well-defined technical prototype for all later literature of horror and terror. Every necessary piece of supernatural apparatus for sustaining the ambience of irrational horror was installed by Walpole within the first haunted castle. In short, the infernal iconography of Gothic fiction requires no additional development beyond Walpole's prototype. In the estimate of one of his earliest twentieth-century defenders, Edith Birkhead, Walpole "bequeathed to his successors a remarkable collection of useful 'properties.'"[3] In his monumental history of the Gothic movement, Maurice Lévy maintains that it is Walpole's properties which endow all later Gothic fiction with its profounder symbolic qualities. For Lévy, it was Walpole who defined the iconographic necessities of the Gothic novel and created a model for his Gothic successors. Furthermore, Walpole's proto-Gothic achievement involved an artistic awareness of the systematic symbolism or iconography of horror, terror, and the malign supernatural. Writes Lévy:

On peut dire que le *Château d'Otrante* est le premier *conte fantastique* anglais, prêcisêment dans le mesure ou il y a irruption du surnatural dans un monde par ailleurs en conformité avec la réalité familiére. L'originalité de Walpole fut not pas tant d'escrire une oeuvre qui teindrait, à part égale, du "romance" et du "novel", que de viser à confronter le lecteur avec l'irrationnel du premier par le truchement des éléments familiers du second.[4]

Within the context of Lévy's approach to Walpole's achievement, the term iconography can be used to refer to the study of those symbols and images signifying the displacement of reason or collapse of value systems in *The Castle of Otranto.* As a general term, iconography means any set of symbols, images, and spatial motifs which give form to the work and thematic substance to the work's intentions. According to the art historian, Erwin Panofsky, in his essay, "Iconography and Iconology: An Introduction to the Study of Renaissance Art," the iconologist or student of literary icons makes "a description and classification of images much as ethnography is a description and classification of human races."[5] Panofsky's general definition has been specifically applied to questions of iconography in the first Gothic novel by Theodore Ziolkowski. Ziolkowski concentrates on the particular icon of the mobile or animate portrait of a former master of the castle whose spirit has reimbued the object of art in order to demand retribution for the crime of usurpation. In "Image as Motif: The Haunted Portrait," Ziolkowski traces the activities of this particular supernatural object and argues that the walking picture is best understood iconographically as a deliberate repudiation of natural law, "an incipient reaction against the Enlightenment."[6]

It can further be demonstrated by a broader iconographic analysis of the contraptions found within the primordial Gothic castle that the proto-Gothicism of the novel furnishes a symbolic glossary for evoking dread, for arousing pleasure in the irrational and for establishing an iconography of an unholy and malignant cosmos governed only by absurd forces. On the psychological level as well, Walpole's infernal iconography reflects the subconscious fears and desires of an age grown too dependent on reason. Walpole himself had announced his intention of challenging the rational complacency of his age when he observed in the Preface to the second edition of the novel that "the great resources of fancy have been damned up by a strict adherence to the common life."[7] The castle's hardware of horror points to a metamorphic or constantly shifting iconography symbolizing a fallen and unstable universe where traditional religious values and moral imperatives no longer operate. For much of the novel, the malevolent supernatural seems about to take control. Virtue is helpless, religious faith is useless, chivalry is ludicrous, and depravity is relentless while the triumph of moral evil seems an omnipresent possibility.

The iconography developed by Walpole reenforces the themes of cosmic skepticism and a darkly ambiguous universe. We are conveyed to a seemingly strong but actually weak piece of architecture saturated with the phantasmic segments of a huge and apparently growing body of the castle's wronged former master. Both a prop and a proposition, the gigantic frame of Alfonso the Good is the Gothic novel's first ghost of the past, a genealogical icon scheduled to make many reappearances in the pages of the Gothic novel. Each of Walpole's Gothic props should be interpreted symbolically as an icon of dread, uncanny power, awe, and terminal unreason capable of destroying faith in a stable and controllable universe. Darkness devours light, passions threaten to displace reason, and the various Gothic symbols of ancient power strategically located throughout the castle inspire demonic fear rather than pious wonder or consolation in the characters who confront them. Enclosed by this Gothic world, all of the characters, good and bad, are victims of an unremitting ontological malaise. Commencing with the heroine, Isabella's, flight through "vaults totally dark,"[8] the pattern of action entails a "radical confrontation, a process of emerging cognition forced upon those whose values have not prepared them for what has just come to meet them."[9] Plagued by universal instability, the characters seek desperately and usually without any success for a way out of the castle. Iconographically, they hope for some form of salvation by reason or delivery from their own savage passions. Once the sanctified emblem of the grail quest as well as a place of refuge and a security, the castle now becomes a place of danger. Many modern critics of the Gothic interpret the haunted castle as a type of hell where "Nobody is entirely safe; nothing is secure."[10] Symbols of reason, security, and faith have undergone a "process of secularization"[11] whereby an iconography deriving originally from conventional systems of belief is divested of its salvational and redemptive significance and becomes instead a perverse opposite or even a hollow parody of itself. A Gothified icon such as the mighty castle retains its initial potency but foregoes the enchantment of religious assurance and assumes a disenchanted or nihilistic status.

In the figurative sense, the act of entering the haunted castle is an irrational crossover symbolizing loss of reason and separation from faith. To be entrapped within the castle is to be returned to the interior of the Platonic cave wherein the shadows cast on the mind's wall supplant the higher realities of a defunct religious ideal. The interior icons transmute God into Satan, heroic quest into perverse pilgrimage, hero into mad villain, votary into victim. The free space of pastoral landscape gives way to the hysterical restrictions of Gothic containment. The castle appears solid and indestructible but is actually doomed to annihilation by internal forces; the castle as a traditional icon of spiritual order and moral safety now represents disorder and the disintegration of hope in an environment which has a will and a spirit of its own and behaves independently of any human control. While not a deserted ruin at the outset of the story, the very ownership of the Castle of Otranto—and by extension, its structural worthiness—is in doubt from the beginning. It functions as an arena of struggle between natural and supernatural wills. All things that should be stationary move mysteriously. All natural causation is neutralized by the supernatural, occult forces imbuing the turrets, walls, and most especially the subterranean segments of the castle with an alien vitality. These icons project the moral darkness, philosophic confusion, and spiritual void felt by maiden and villain alike.

On a still profounder level, the icons found throughout Walpole's dreamworld suggest an impending apocalypse. Such animated icons as the sanguinary statue of Alfonso the Good, former master of the castle, or the peripatetic portrait of Ricardo, usurper of power and progenitor of the absurd curse which hangs over Manfred, may be viewed as symbolic expressions of the displacement of reason. Such icons can titillate as well as terrify by their magical animation but, as will be the case in much later Gothic fiction, diversion of the reader is never their sole aim or end. The volatile icons of *The Castle of Otranto* engage the imagination by revealing a paradoxically ambiguous world in which evil may be stronger than good and disorder far more likely than order. Manfred's ancestral home, like other places of former security and family unity such as the mansion, abbey, or manor house, is forbidding, unsafe, and about to be transformed into a ruin by mysterious forces acting from inside. In this sense, Walpole's novel offers the plan for the violent plotting of many Gothics to follow in which social institutions and authority-figures are twisted, barbaric, and dehumanized. Once-revered figures of respectability such as parents and clergymen suddenly become despotic, violent, or in the case of *Otranto*'s saintly but bungling priest, Father Jerome, simply inept. Reaching a climax in the imploding walls of the castle—a scene which should be read as symbolizing the shattering of the decayed remnants of an empty ideology—the iconography of *The Castle of Otranto* clearly presents an irrational picture of both self and society.

Secularized and disenchanted by Walpole's art, the icons of faith, justice, reason, and hope undergo malign inversions. The process of "disenchantment" whereby a symbol traditionally associated with sacred values is rendered in sinister fashion is an indication of Walpole's recognition of a universe entirely contradictory to the confident postulates of the deists: "Morally the Gothic romance marked a shift from faith in a simple dualism to a fascination with the more complex interrelatedness of good and evil. Politically it embodied the new sense of freedom that characterized the revolutionary age. Psychologically it signalled a turn from the portrayal of manners in an integrated society to the analysis of lonely, guilt-ridden outsiders."[12]

If Walpole's Gothic vision presents a dissolution of all norms—ontological, epistemological, and aesthetic—his characters, too, reflect the new metaphysical anxiety, for their primary function is to lose their way, with their disorientation or "disenchantment" constantly imaged by their entrapment within the subterranean maze. Iconographically, the ordeal of underground confinement together with the gropings of the hero-villain and heroine deep within the "hell" of the castle suggest metaphysical consternation and spiritual claus-

trophobia for both of these "lonely, guilt-ridden outsiders." The primal maze of dark corridors underlying the Castle of Otranto refers us iconographically to the "amazement" of the characters, their flight and pursuit reflecting a disruption of belief in traditional systems of order. Directly beneath the heavenly and earthly portions of the castle complex lies the new iconographic hell, shortly to become the Gothic's novel's most recurrent symbolic fixture:

> The lower part of the castle was hollowed into several intricate cloisters; and it was not easy for one under so much anxiety to find the door that opened into the cavern. An awful silence reigned throughout those subterraneous regions, except now and then some blasts of wind that shook the doors she had passed, and which grating on the rusty hinges were re-echoed through that long labyrinth of darkness.[13]

Here we have the fundamental imagery of Gothic crisis, a hysterical subterranean wayfarer depicted in the act of anxious flight through a gloomy atmosphere that Milton might have described as "darkness visible."[14] Now furnished with its own iconic version of hell, the Gothic novel could then begin to extend its motif of the descent or vertical quest. Walpole's proto-Gothicism made available through the castle and its horrific contents a symbolic vocabulary whose awesome mystery could effectively dissolve traditional moral categories while at the same time elevate the imagination to a peak of pleasure arising out of its contact with the ineffably gruesome. Walpole sought to astonish, amaze, and eventually to obliterate the security of the reader by involving him beyond recall in a series of supernatural events that might almost constitute a quasi-religious experience. Gothic iconography might be made the means of conveying the power of a Gothic aesthetic to produce pleasure in spectacles of chaos, pain, absurdity, death, spectral encroachment, and other varieties of horror. From its birth, Gothic symbolism concentrated on the depiction of an intense series of phantasmagoric confrontations with a perverse otherness which allowed no chance for rational reflection or recovery of common sense. Beginning with the arrival of the huge airborne helmet on the opening page of the novel, the outrageous supernatural occurrences thrust themselves into the foreground and demand an immediate response from the characters. The moments of high Gothic experience as Walpole conceived of them were iconographic applications of a psychological law of fear first stated by Edmund Burke, a type of Gothic pleasure principle uniting the horrible with the sublime and beautiful. Burke's law of Gothic emotion, a law set in operation throughout the novel, states that "the mind is so entirely filled with its object that it cannot entertain any other, nor by consequence reason on that object which employs it."[15]

Some of the exact objects and the artistic objectives of the new Gothic terror were considered in detail in the two informative prefaces which Walpole prepared for the first and second editions of **The Castle of Otranto.** Each of these statements on the art of Gothic fiction proposes important criteria for the construction of catastrophic narrative. In an expertly chosen metaphor, Walpole labels terror as "the author's principal engine [which] prevents the story from ever languishing."[16] His notion of Gothic terror was heavily formulaic and mechanical; like the symmetrical constructs of the deists, the engine of the Gothicists was to be a grand and complex machine operating by its own fixed and inexorable laws. Once activated by the forces of the unconscious, the engine's dark flow of Gothic energy would generate the emotional voltage required to electrify both characters and readers.

Walpole further maintained that the inmates of the haunted castle could be expected to occupy various "extraordinary positions [like] personages under the dispensation of miracles, and witnesses to the most stupendous phenomena."[17] Shrewdly, Walpole did not specify his phrase "extraordinary positions" just as he did not qualify exactly what he meant by "interesting passions" but the narrative makes it clear that a typical "extraordinary position" for a Gothic victim or victimizer might be either physical or psychological, a lethal predicament of body or mind or a combination of both. When Alfonso's immense helmet descends like a lunar module to crush the sickly Conrad on the novel's opening page, this initial spectacular event precipitates an "extraordinary position" of body for the unfortunate Conrad and an equally "extraordinary position" of mind for the astounded Manfred. The falling helmet is a first Gothic icon for the artist's imaginative perception of a cosmic disharmony which could not be redressed. In the absence of a righteous and reasonable God, the prime mover of the Gothic universe is an enormous but empty headpiece. From the outset, the iconography becomes a perverse negation of Newtonian law and Shaftesburyian benevolence. Manfred's reaction to the absurd death of his son illustrates the "process of secularization" whereby a deific icon—the god's head—is transformed into an anti-deific icon—a headless void in armor—while maintaining and even increasing all of its former deific force. The fall of the gigantic helmet is not the rightous vengeance of God but the absurd revenge of the void, a perfect infernal icon of a once mighty but now absent divine head. Manfred takes "the miracle of the helmet"[18] to be a portent of savage and meaningless power. But rather than contemplating the religious meaning behind the event, Manfred is immediately obsessed with the object itself. Like other icons of void and nothingness which follow the falling helmet, the object itself is secularized into subject and becomes a godlike, godless assertion of colossal emptiness. Instead of being awed by the arrival of the Brobdingnagian helmet. Manfred can only contemplate the object itself. Subjectively filling his mind's eye, the object becomes a numinous manifestation of the metaphysical absurdity of the universe.

> He beheld his child dashed to pieces, and almost buried under an enormous helmet, an hundred times more large than any casque ever made for human being, and shaded with a proportionable quantity of black feathers. The horror of the spectacle, the ignorance of all around how this misfortune happened, and above all, the tremendous phaenomenon before him, took away the prince's speech. Yet his silence lasted longer than even grief could occasion. He fixed his eyes on what he wished in vain to believe a vision; and seemed less attentive to his loss, than buried in meditation on the stup-endous object that had occasioned it. He touched, he examined the fatal casque; nor could even the bleeding mangled remains of the young prince divert the eyes of Manfred from the portent before him.[19]

The other supernatural events and situations of the novel inspire a similar astonishment in the characters. The architectural dilemmas, cadaverous surprises, converging gigantism, and the eventual crash of the castle walls are all suggestive of the breakdown of rational order. Under these conditions, the anxieties of the characters express their metaphysical exasperation. All previous assumptions about a rationally directive universe must be false since the universe is under the jurisdiction of dark and demonic forces present everywhere throughout the castle. The iconography of early Gothicism, then, raises desperate questions about the supposed rational symmetry of the universe. The inhabitants of the castle seem doomed and imprisoned by their own obsolete ideals, walled in by their fates as well as by the fiendish building itself. As belief gives way to doubt the castle gives way to collapse since it contains, like the social and religious systems it represents, the seeds of its own destruction. Manfred and Isabella, the two prisoners of the contracting and unstable Gothic world, find themselves in the "extraordinary position" of being caught between two alien value systems; the empirically beautiful outlook of the deists now transformed into a hellish engine of terror; and the once-unquestioned and fixed body of traditional religious truth now symbolized by the mock medievalism, perverted chivalry, and organic misbehavior of the castle's totally mobile icons.

If we take the sentient castle itself to be the major icon of dark mutability and profound disenchantment, it is quite simple to draw an isomorphic analogy between haunted castle and haunted self. The individual icons of a once stable world contained within the castle all seem to be motivated by a perplex of forces operating outside the confines of reason. The rational abilities of the characters to deal with the bizarre conditions of the castle interior are repeatedly frustrated and finally rendered impotent by a series of supernaturally shocking and inexplicable events presented as iconographic manifestations of tormenting uncertainty. After the great helmet buries Conrad, all rational defense deserts Manfred, who, as Walpole was careful to inform the reader, is a figure somewhat like the protagonist of tragedy, a man of potential nobility and whose temperament "was naturally humane. . . . his virtues were always ready to operate, when his passion did not obscure his reason."[20] Confronted by the huge helmet, the bleeding statue, the walking portrait, the protuberance of a mighty foot from the castle walls, the grasping of a mighty hand in armor after an equally titanic sword and the other malign movements of the castle's icons, Manfred is driven to dreadful deeds in the all-consuming darkness. His light of reason is extinguished, its place taken by the basest of passions which drive him to the cryptic murder of his own daughter, Matilda, following the abrupt "transition of his soul . . . to exquisite villainy."[21] If not quite tragic, the fall of the Gothic hero is nevertheless the consequence of his loss of faith in the efficacy of reason. His solipsistic struggle isolates him for he cannot overcome irrational forces residing in the cosmos and in the mind. The sinister and shifting icons define his equivocal relationship with God, self, and universe, a condition of almost existential dread for the Gothic hero. Torn by metaphysical anxiety over the cause, nature, and end of existence, Manfred is the first in a long line of Gothic heroes to attempt to alleviate this unbearable state of consciousness by committing himself to evil. Faced with the realization of an absurd cosmos, he becomes the agent of terror, madness, death, and disorder in a desperate attempt to confer some identity upon himself. In a recent essay on the nature of Gothic heroism, Syndy McMillen Conger argues that what is seen in the curious career of Manfred and his Gothic descendants is a type of tragic anguish manifesting itself in the actions of the Gothic hero not as suffering but as hatred and defiant evil. "Uncertainty has transformed itself into the heretical fear that unknown, irrational, even malevolent forces may control the world, a terror which becomes, when it takes the shape of belief, primitive superstition. Manfred's 'Do I dream . . . or are the devils themselves in league against me?'—this is a Manichean cry of doubt echoed by Gothic villains and victims from Ambrosio and Raymond in Lewis's The Monk and the younger Melmoth in Maturin's Melmoth the Wanderer to the characters of Mary Shelley, Hoffmann, Poe, Hawthorne, Twain, and Henry James."[22] An iconography of religious doubt and supernatu-

ral dread is fundamental to a context of terror and horror which deprives the soul of its heavenly aspirations and denies to the mind its deistic assumptions about the universality of reason and natural law. By substituting a Gothic nightmare for a rationalist's dream of bliss, Walpole evolved a terrifying new hypothesis in The Castle of Otranto: what if all traditional norms of reality, psychic, social, and spiritual, turned out to be illusory and self-deceiving? Such a tormented scepticism is the philosophic basis for terror and horror in all later Gothic fiction.

The shocked awareness of a disharmonious universe is one of the key themes of dark or negative romanticism.[23] Walpole's iconographic management of the theme is witnessed most vividly in what might be called a reverse conversion episode during which an insider or believer is compelled to abandon his faith in religious mystery and reason to accept its opposite, Gothic mystery and unreason. The character's conversion to doubt and madness is effected through the icon of the grinning skull. In a scene in Chapter Five, the novel's most chivalrous personage and the defender of morality and justice, Frederic, the Marquis of Vicenza, encounters a hooded monk kneeling before the altar in Hippolita's private chapel. Iconographically, the scene illustrates the instantaneous destruction of Frederic's rational values as holy father is suddenly transmogrified into skeletal phantom. Frederic's encounter later becomes a familiar moment of supernatural sensation in Gothic novels,—the ghastly rotation or terrible turn. "The marquis, expecting the holy person to come forth, and meaning to excuse his uncivil interruption, said, 'Reverend father, I sought the lady Hippolita.—Hippolita! replied a hollow voice: camest thou to this castle to seek Hippolita?'—And then the figure, turning slowly round, discovered to Frederic the fleshless jaws and empty sockets of a skeleton, wrapt in a hermit's cowl."[24] A hollow helmet and a death's head in monastic garb,—are these revelations not to be taken as complementary icons of the ideals of chivalry and religion now secularized and transformed into images of cosmic dread and doubt? As was the case with Manfred's startled encounter with the fallen helmet, Frederic's confrontation is also with an icon of appalling nothingness whose most horrifying aspect is its hollowness which gruesomely mocks the anticipated religious ideal.

When Frederic looks directly into the hollow sockets of the death's head, he is forced to accept the cynical substantiality of the agent of God now become Gothic literature's first of many animated skeletons.[25] Frederic's communion with dread has begun just as Manfred's perverse conversion to the absurd hollowness of existence is consummated by the fall of the house of Otranto. Iconographically, the climax can be seen not as a restoration of order but as a victory for the irrational, perhaps the most effective type of Gothic ending because it leaves unreasonable and disintegrative forces in control of the world.

> A clap of thunder, at that instant, shook the castle to its foundations; the earth rocked, and the clank of more than mortal armour was heard behind . . . The moment Theodore appeared, the walls of the castle behind Manfred were thrown down with a mighty force, and the form of Alfonso, dilated to an immense magnitude, appeared in the centre of the ruins.[26]

The monstrous figure exploding from the ruins of Otranto may indeed be the great form of Alfonso reclaiming its lost legacy of power, but on a deeper iconographic level what we are also witnessing in the anti-rational *dénouement* is Walpole's iconic inversion of the conventional *deux ex machina* of classic drama. The giant that bursts through the walls of the castle is a *diabolus ex machina,* or an all-destroying icon of infernal power born of the skeptical Gothic imagination. In its insistence upon unmitigated chaos, **The Castle of Otranto** would establish itself as the iconographic prototype for a new and subversive literary genre which would in time lay the foundations for the anti-visions of the dark Romantics. One of these Romantics, Sir Walter Scott, saluted Walpole's foresight in his own preface to **The Castle of Otranto** (1811) by remarking of Walpole and his Gothic prototype that "He brings with him the torch of genius, to illuminate the ruins through which he loves to wander."[27]

Notes

[1] Until quite recently, literary criticism has remained indifferent or even hostile to the history of the Gothic genre. Since the 1950's, however, the situation in Gothic criticism has reversed. For full-length histories of the Gothic novel which place *The Castle of Otranto* at the head of the tradition, see: Eino Railo, *The Haunted Castle: A Study of the Elements of English Romanticism.* (London: Routledge & Kegan Paul, 1927; Rpt. New York: Humanities Press, 1964); Montague Summers, *The Gothic Quest: A History of the Gothic Novel.* (London: Fortune Press, 1938; Rpt. New York: Russell & Russell, 1964); Devendra P. Varma, *The Gothic Flame: Being a History of the Gothic Novel in England.* (London: A. Barker, 1957; Rpt. New York: Russell & Russell, 1966); Coral Ann Howells, *Love, Mystery, and Misery: Feeling in Gothic Fiction.* (London: Athlone Press, 1979; Atlantic Highlands, NJ: Humanities Press, 1979); Elizabeth MacAndrew, *The Gothic Tradition in Fiction.* (New York; Columbia University Press, 1979); David Punter, *The Literature of Terror: A History of Gothic Fiction from 1765 to the Present Day.* (Lon-

don and New York: Longman, 1980); Brendan Hennessy, "The Gothic Novel," in *British Writers,* ed. Ian Scott-Kilvert. (New York: Charles Scribner's Sons, 1980), III, pp. 324-346; Frederick S. Frank, "The Gothic Romance, 1762-1820," in *Horror Literature: A Core Collection and Reference Guide,* ed. Marshall B. Tymn. (New York: R. R. Bowker, 1981), pp. 3-175; Patrick Day, *In the Circles of Fear and Desire: A Study in Gothic Fantasy.* (Chicago: University of Chicago Press, 1985).

[2] Horace Walpole, *The Castle of Otranto: A Gothic Story* in *Three Gothic Novels,* ed. E. F. Bleiler. (New York: Dover Publications, 1966), p. 36. Hereafter cited as Walpole, *Otranto.* In the Twentieth Century, hundreds of critics have attempted to wend their way through "the long labyrinth of darkness" to discover the sources of Gothic energy and iconography in Walpole's first Gothic novel. For a bibliographical overview, together with a thorough coverage of published scholarship on *The Castle of Otranto,* see: Dan J. McNutt, *The Eighteenth-Century Gothic Novel: An Annotated Bibliography of Criticism and Selected Text.* (New York: Garland Publishing, 1975); Frederick S. Frank, "The Gothic Novel: A Checklist of Modern Criticism," *Bulletin of Bibliography,* 30 (1973): 45-54; Frederick S. Frank, "The Gothic Novel: A Second Bibliography of Criticism," *Bulletin of Bibliography,* 35 (1978): 1-14, 52; Frederick S. Frank, *Guide to the Gothic: An Annotated Bibliography of Criticism.* (Metuchen, New Jersey and London: Scarecrow Press, 1984).

[3] Edith Birkhead, *The Tale of Terror: A Study of the Gothic Romance.* (London: Constable, 1921; Rpt. New York: Russell & Russell, 1963), p. 22. For a counter argument that Gothic properties are subordinate in importance to Gothic atmosphere, see: James M. Keech, "The Survival of the Gothic Response," *Studies in the Novel,* 6 (1974): 130-144.

[4] Maurice Lévy, "Le Rêve gothique d'Horace Walpole," in *Le Roman "gothique" anglais* (Toulouse, France: Association des Publications de la Faculté des Lettres et Sciences Humaines de Toulouse, 1968), p. 112.

[5] Erwin Panofsky, "Iconography and Iconology: An Introduction to the Study of Renaissance Art," in *Meaning in the Visual Arts.* (Garden City, NY: Doubleday-Anchor, 1955), p. 31.

[6] Theodore Ziolkowski, *Disenchanted Images: A Literary Iconology.* (Princeton, NJ: Princeton University Press, 1977), p. 84. On the specific matter of infernal iconography in early Gothic fiction, G. R. Thompson comments: "One may argue that the Gothic castle, in addition to its other metaphoric values, constitutes, with its narrow passageways and interior chambers,

ornamented with burning swords in the vestibules, an iconography of the female body threatened with assault." See: G. R. Thompson, "Gothic Fiction of the Romantic Age," in *Romantic Gothic Tales, 1790-1840.* (New York: Harper & Row, 1979), p. 5.

[7] Walpole, Preface to the Second Edition of *Otranto,* p. 21.

[8] Walpole, *Otranto,* p. 38.

[9] Frederick Garber, "Meaning and Mode in Gothic Fiction," in *Racism in the Eighteenth Century.* (Cleveland, OH: Case Western Reserve University Press, 1973), pp. 155-169. Among many recent books, essays, and monographs on Gothic fiction, several studies concentrate on the anti-religious quality of Gothic symbolism and its iconography of cosmic doubt. See: Joel Porte, "In the Hands of an Angry God: Religious Terror in Gothic Fiction," in *The Gothic Imagination: Essays in Dark Romanticism,* ed. G. R. Thompson. (Pullman, Washington: Washington State University Press, 1974), pp. 42-64; Leigh Ann Ehlers, "From Polarity to Perspective: The Development of Structure and Character in Gothic Fiction," *Dissertation Abstracts International,* 39 (1978): 294-A; Leigh A. Ehlers, "The Gothic World as Stage: Providence and Character in *The Castle of Otranto."* *Wascana Review,* 14, ii (1980): 17-30.

[10] Ann B. Tracy, Introduction to *The Gothic Novel 1790-1830: Plot Summaries and Index to Motifs.* (Lexington, Kentucky: Kentucky UP), pp. 1-11. Tracy notes "the oddly hopeless tone one perceives in the Gothic world; man has a soul to lose, but no expectation of mercy or possible atonement. The search for one's origins, identity, and family connections in Gothic fiction may be seen as an attempt to impose order upon a chaotic environment." (p. 10).

[11] Ziolkowski, *Disenchanted Images,* p. 15.

[12] Ziolkowski, *Disenchanted Images,* p. 84.

[13] Walpole, *Otranto,* pp. 35-36.

[14] John Milton, *Paradise Lost, Book One,* line 63.

[15] Edmund Burke, *A Philosophical Enquiry into the Origin of Our Ideas of the Sublime and Beautiful* in *Eighteenth Century Poetry and Prose,* eds. Louis I. Bredvold, Alan D. McKillop, and Louis Whitney. (New York: Ronald Press, 1956), p. 565.

[16] Walpole, Preface to the First Edition of *Otranto,* p. 18.

[17] Walpole, Preface to the Second Edition of *Otranto,* p. 21.

[18] Walpole, *Otranto,* p. 29.

[19] Walpole, *Otranto,* pp. 28-29.

[20] Walpole, *Otranto,* p. 40.

[21] Walpole, *Otranto,* p. 44.

[22] Syndy McMillen Conger, "Faith and Doubt in *The Castle of Otranto,"* *Gothic: The Review of Supernatural Horror Fiction,* 1 (1979): 51-59.

[23] The term, "negative romanticism," was originally applied by Morse Peckham to denote the breakdown or fragmentation of vision in Enlightenment beliefs as the Eighteenth Century drew to a close. Any harmonious relationship between the order of the mind and the order of nature was becoming almost impossible to maintain. See: Morse Peckham, "Toward a Theory of Romanticism," *Studies in Romanticism,* 1 (1961): 1-8. "Dark romanticism" is one extreme form of fragmented vision and particularly relevant to the Gothic phenomenon. Positive romanticism "usually evokes an ideal world, infused with internal energy and dynamically evolving toward a yet higher state, in which the single, separate self seeks unity with nature, itself symbolic of the aesthetic harmony of the cosmos." But "negative" or Gothic romanticism negates such transcendence and unity and deals instead "with the tormented condition of a creature suspended between the extremes of faith and skepticism, beatitude and horror, being and nothingness, love and hate—and anguished by an indefinable guilt for some crime it cannot remember having committed." For further discussions of the Gothic as a manifestation of "negative romanticism," see: G. R. Thompson, ed. *The Gothic Imagination: Essays in Dark Romanticism.* (Pullman, WA: Washington State University Press, 1974).

[24] Walpole, *Otranto,* p. 99.

[25] In later Gothic fiction, the meeting of the hero or villain with an animated skeleton is a horrific commonplace. See, for example, the anonymous Gothic, *The Animated Skeleton.* (London: Minerva-Press for William Lane, 1798) and Isabella Kelly's monastic shocker, *The Abbey of St. Asaph.* (London: Minerva-Press for William Lane, 1795).

[26] Walpole, *Otranto,* p. 104.

[27] Sir Walter Scott, Introduction to the 1811 Edinburgh Edition of *Otranto* in *Three Gothic Novels,* ed. E. F. Bleiler, p. 6.

Ian P. Watt (essay date 1986)

SOURCE: "Time and Family in the Gothic Novel:

The Castle of Otranto." *Eighteenth Century Life*, Vol X, n.s. 3, October, 1986, pp. 159-71.

[*In this essay, Watt contends that the elements of the "imaginative matrices" of* The Castle of Otranto *that particularly structure the Gothic tradition are Walpole's treatment of time and the family.*]

Long ago Matthew Arnold, confronting what Darwin had recently demonstrated to be our common ancestor—"a hairy quadruped furnished with a tail and pointed ears, probably arboreal in his habits"—was moved to wonder how "this good fellow" could ever have "carried in his nature, also, a necessity for Greek."[1] It was even longer ago that an unpromising stripling named Conrad was dashed to pieces by some archaic military hardware in the courtyard of the Castle of Otranto; and even today we still hardly know how it was that this "enormous helmet, a hundred times more large than any casque ever made for human being, and shaded with a proportionable quantity of black feathers"[2] also carried in its nature an evolutionary necessity for Emily Brontë's Heathcliff and Faulkner's Thomas Sutpen.

Two aspects of that necessity are the subject of the present enquiry. What gave **The Castle of Otranto**—at first sight the most sensationally unpretentious novelette that can well be imagined—its power to bring into being a whole new fictional mode that has been characteristic of the last two centuries? What was the essential imaginative matrix which struck off, not only the nine hundred odd works that are listed—however dubiously—in Montague Summers' *A Gothic Bibliography* (1941), but also many later novels that are often placed in the Gothic tradition? I will suggest that two elements in that matrix, the function of time and the treatment of the family, provide a set of particular characteristics in the very miscellaneous literary phenomena to which the label "Gothic" is currently applied.

The very word "Gothic" suggests that the genre has got something to do with time. It is hardly too much to say that etymologically the term "Gothic Novel" is an oxymoron for "Old New." When Horace Walpole subtitled **The Castle of Otranto** "A Gothic Story" in the second edition, to him the term "Gothic," as he had already made clear in the original Preface, meant "the darkest ages of Christianity," or, more generally, merely "very old." "Novel," on the other hand, originally meant the "new"; and such were the contemporary subjects of what, in 1764, were beginning to be called novels. Walpole himself was aware that the essential originality of **The Castle of Otranto** depended on this temporal dichotomy of past and present:

> It was an attempt to blend the two kinds of romance, the ancient and the modern. In the former all was

imagination and improbability: in the latter, nature is always intended to be, and sometimes has been, copied with success.[3]

(p. 7)

A closer scrutiny reveals that the relation of ancient and present time in Walpole's narrative is somewhat more specific and complex in nature; obviously all the events take place in Gothic times, but that past itself has considerable depth, and the psychological present in which the characters live is only the immediate surface on which the power of a long anterior past is manifested.

The distant pastness of the whole tale is insisted on in Walpole's title-page and Preface. The original Italian version, he asserts, was printed in black letter—what we now call Gothic type—in 1529; but internal evidence points to a much earlier date of composition; and the actual period of the action, we are told, must go further back still, to some time between 1095 and 1243, the dates of the first and last crusades, "or not long afterwards." This defines what we may call the period both of the narrative present of the story and of its anterior past.

The events of the plot, in what the reader experiences as the narrative present, take only three days. The action begins on Conrad's fifteenth birthday, which is supposed to be the day of his wedding to Isabella—a wedding which will strengthen the position of his father, Manfred, Prince of Otranto; but it is in fact the day of Conrad's death. From the opening of the temporal sequence is a progression whose intervals are related to calendar time by signals in the narrative—sunset, moonshine, dawn, etc.

The plot, in five chapters like the acts of a tragedy, is equally linear, logical, and concentrated. In the first chapter, Conrad is crushed by the gigantic helmet. Then a handsome young peasant announces that this helmet is "exactly like that on the figure in black marble of Alfonso the Good . . . in the church of St. Nicholas" (p. 18). Almost immediately that particular helmet is reported missing: an ominous coincidence. Meanwhile, Manfred resolves that he must cast aside his wife, Hippolita, and marry Conrad's intended, Isabella. Horrified, Isabella attempts to escape and in her flight through a subterranean passage sees a ghostlike figure who turns out to be the handsome peasant, called Theodore. He tries to help her but in the process is discovered by Manfred, who is on the point of sentencing Theodore to death when the news comes that an armed giant—or at least an awfully big leg and foot—has been seen lying in the long gallery.

The remaining chapters work out these puzzles. The

next day Father Jerome, a priest at the convent near the church of St. Nicholas, announces that Isabella has taken sanctuary there. Theodore is once again on the point of being executed when a birthmark on his neck luckily reveals that he is really Father Jerome's son. Then a great procession arrives, with a gigantic sword that is carried by a hundred knights. (This echo of the "hundred times" larger scale of the helmet illustrates Walpole's rough and ready use of numbers to indicate the supernatural dimension of his narrative.) The leader of the knights, who remains masked, eventually proves to be Isabella's father, the Marquis of Vicenza. He found the sword in the Holy Land; and on its blade is written

> Wher'er a casque that suits this sword is
>   found,
> With perils is thy daughter compass'd round:
> Alfonso's blood alone can save the maid,
> And quiet a long-restless prince's shade.
>
>   (p. 79)

We surmise that the matching accessory which "suits this sword" must be the huge casque that landed on Conrad. As to "who alone can save the maid" (presumably Isabella), it must surely be Theodore, who must therefore be of Alfonso's noble blood. As for "quieting" the "long-restless prince's shade" we are given many clues as to what person may own the "shade." The first and most obvious comes very early: "ancient prophecy which was said to have pronounced, 'That the castle and lordship of Otranto should pass from the present family, whenever the real owner should be grown too large to inhabit it.'" (pp. 15-16). Manfred has shown no sign of abnormal growth; and so he cannot be "the real owner," and eventually proves to be the grandson of Richard, Alfonso's false chamberlain, who long ago poisoned his master and made himself the owner of Otranto by a forged will. We must, then, wait until someone's shade gets big enough to wear the helmet; that shade, of course, proves to be Alfonso's own. He is literally a shade—a ghost—and when he throws the castle down according to the prophecy, Manfred is frightened into abdicating, and Alfonso's grandson, Theodore, is restored to the rule of his rightful principality.

The essence of *The Castle of Otranto,* then, is the progressive revelation of the secrets of the two family pasts; but its interest for the reader depends not on this in itself—the disclosure of the rather murky genealogies of the descendants of Alfonso and Richard—but on the excitement generated by how the ghostly survivors of the anterior past operate on in the affairs of the fictional present, which wholly preoccupies them. Past and present are, it seems, locked together; the living characters are the captives of the past, while the char-

acters of the past—notably Alfonso—live on as spirits only to be their vigilant captors. The anterior past has all the power. Whenever the present generation attempts to avoid its fate, as when Manfred attempts to marry off his son, its effort is wholly ineffectual. The only imperative causality in the life of the present, apparently, is to complete what was done long ago; only when the helmet, sword, armor, and the giant hands and feet are finally reconstituted can Theodore succeed to Otranto, and the perturbed spirit of his ancestor leave its sublunary caves and rises in apotheosis through the clouds to be received into the arms of his patron St. Nicholas.

The history of the word "gothic" supplies one basic clue to the meaning of the power and the appeal of the past. The *Oxford English Dictionary* informs us that in the sense of medieval, "gothic" was early used with the pejorative connotation expressed by Dryden: "all that has something of the Ancient gust is called a barbarous or Gothique manner"[4] (1695). Such reprobation continued well into the eighteenth century, partly because no reasonably precise architectural or chronological meaning was as yet attached to "gothic."[5]

But long before there was any genuine understanding of what we call Gothic architecture, there arose the fashion for imitations of Gothic buildings and ruins. Walpole's own house, Strawberry Hill (begun 1749) was the most celebrated of many early examples; and literature, in Richard Hurd's *Letters on Chivalry and Romance* (1762), for example, reflected a parallel counter-movement to the previous prejudice against the barbarism of the gothic. "Gothic," in Walpole's day was exchanging the disgrace of being old-fashioned for the distinction of being antique.

The Augustan nostalgia for its antithesis was itself dependent on the new sense that the present was radically separate from the past. This historical awareness began in the Renaissance, which looked back at the classical world through the darkness of the Gothic period; but both the increasing body of historical knowledge (to which Walpole himself made many contributions), and the conscious Augustan effort to follow Roman models, developed historical consciousness much further. Anachronism in Renaissance painting or drama seems unconscious; in Walpole it is a conscious fashion which also reflects his spiritual and aesthetic needs.

The new need for conscious anachronism brings us to the psychological basis of the tension in Gothic between past and present—the individual's awareness of the quotidian dullness of the present and the consequent longing for something totally different. This contrast was to lead the rich, and later their humbler imitators,[6] to cover the land with castles and mansions, suburban villas, and country cottages—all in the Gothic manner—and the same contrast was to become a great theme of the Romantic poets. But the spiritual appeal of the Gothic past is already explicit in Walpole. Thus he writes in a letter to George Montagu (5 January 1766):

> Visions, you know, have always been my pasture, and so far from growing old enough to quarrel with their emptiness, I almost think there is no wisdom comparable to that of exchanging what is called the realities of life for dreams. Old castles, old pictures, old histories, and the babble of old people make one live back into centuries that cannot disappoint one.

(Corr., 10:192)

In earlier ages there had been nothing picturesque about wearing swords or going into gloomy dungeons;[7] their appeal to the imagination depended on a social order based on life insurance rather than carrying swords; on *habeas corpus,* the rule of law and the beginnings of an organized police force. As Thomas Blackwell put it in his contrast between Homeric times and his own: "The marvellous and wonderful is the nerve of the epic strain: but what marvellous things happen in a well-ordered state? We can hardly be surprised."[8] Or Walpole, speaking of the modern novel: "the great resources of fancy have been dammed up, by a strict adherence to common life" (p. 7).

Escaping the milieu of the common life, Walpole's title proclaimed as the chief protagonist in his novel what was to become the most characteristic symbolic element in Gothic fiction generally, the castle. The "dramatised decay" of the ruin, as Kenneth Clark terms it (p. 30) inspired fascination and awe, and the later part of the century saw ruins become a major preoccupation of art, architecture, and landscape. And in the Gothic novel, the castle becomes connected with the family because it is essentially the material survivor of a powerful lineage, a symbol of the continuing life of its founder. Only, therefore, when Otranto's living heir, Theodore, is safely in the courtyard can "the walls of the castle" be "thrown down by a mighty force," and the form of its founder, Alfonso, "dilated to an immense magnitude," appear "in the centre of the ruins" (p. 108). Within the walls the most common material objects are likenesses—either portraits or sculptures—which, like ancient documents attest the continuing presence of the dead. The portrait of Alfonso, his statue, even the helmet, armor, and sword—all assert his paternal power. So do the ancient prophecy and the riddling quatrain.

From likenesses of the dead to the world of the supernatural is no great leap for Walpole's liberated "resources of the fancy"—as Alfonso presumably discovers when he steps down out of his picture frame.

Walpole was at some pains to excuse the element of superstition in his story on the grounds that it was typical of the times depicted, and that he had in any case much restricted its operation, as compared to earlier writers of romance, where "the actors seem to lose their senses the moment the laws of nature lose their tone." So in general his motive for seeking the greater imaginative freedom of the supernatural must be seen as yet another aspect of how Gothic was a reaction to the intellectual temper of the century. Walpole liked *The Castle of Otranto* most among his works, he wrote to Madame du Deffand, because there alone he had given "reign to . . . imagination. . . . I am even persuaded that in the Future, when taste will be restored to the place now occupied by philosophy, my poor *Castle* will find admirers."[9] His own time, alas, wanted "only cold reason," which had established a rigid distinction between the natural and the supernatural after Newton had cast light on nature's laws, and definitively depersonalized and demythologized the physical world.

The systematizing of this division between the natural and the supernatural orders inevitably affected general attitudes to the past and to the unseen world. By the time of Pope the supernatural had become to the enlightened a dubious and rather fanciful rival order, like the sylphs in *The Rape of the Lock;* and by the middle of the century such beliefs were becoming a sign of religious archaism, as in John Wesley and Parson Adams. To give the occult power of the past a real existence in fiction it was now necessary to set the narrative back in time into the Gothic past, to the times before the Reformation when Roman Catholic superstition held sway, and to the countries—most notably Italy—where it was still rampant.

To an Enlightenment sceptic like Walpole, of course, religious superstition was equally repulsive to political liberty and scientific reason; but it remained congenial to the aesthetic imagination. Hence Walpole compromised with his times both by setting the events back in times and places where credulity was universal, and by presenting his supernatural interventions in a selective way.

Walpole's supernature is entirely populated with beings who, for all their monstrous size and power, are essentially historical beings with rational human aims. This is typical of the Gothic novel in general; supernature is both secularized and individualized. Alfonso the Good, or whichever of his unseen adjutants is currently on duty to ruffle the helmet's plumes at the appropriate time, seems to be wholly concerned with bringing about a more satisfactory state of affairs in the secular world of his genealogical descendants; and when this rectifying mission has been accomplished, he can be trusted to hand Otranto back to the custody of Newtonian physics.

There are other orders of experience besides the supernatural which exist outside time as it is viewed by natural science: there is the sacred time of myth and ritual and the mystics; and—much more important for the Gothic tradition—there are the special kinds of time in which dreams and the unconscious have their being; and both are peculiarly open to the irruptions of the forces of the past.

In dreams, time is intensely real in the sense that we are immersed in a series of scenes which follow each other with hallucinatory vividness: it is very much a question of now, and now, and now. The connection of these scenes is not causal; the fragments are real, but they have their own kind of temporal order which is unconscious or imaginative, rather than consecutive in any logical way. The specific time-setting of the dream is typically unlocalized or shifting; but when we recall the dream later we often realize that we have revisited various scenes of our long-past life, though not in their chronological order. What initially provokes the dream, though, is normally some present occasion; and this provides a basic structural analogy to the symbiosis of past and present in Gothic.

The closeness of the two kinds of mental representation—dreams and Gothic fiction—is reflected in two well-known facts. First, dreams, particularly nightmares, are common in Gothic novels; many of the best are like nightmares—*Frankenstein* or "The Fall of the House of Usher." Second, many Gothic novels apparently began as actual dreams. In her Preface, Mary Shelley, for instance, says *Frankenstein* did, and so does Walpole in a letter to William Cole (9 March 1765):

Shall I even confess to you what was the origin of this romance? I waked one morning in the beginning of last June from a dream, of which all I could recover was, that I had thought myself in an ancient castle (a very natural dream for a head filled like mine with Gothic story) and that on the uppermost bannister of a great staircase I saw a gigantic hand in armour. In the evening I sat down and began to write, without knowing in the least what I intended to say or relate. The work grew on my hands, and I grew fond of it—add that I was very glad to think of anything rather than politics . . .

(*Corr.,* 1: 88)

We can be fairly confident, I think, that Walpole's dream was a transposition of sights familiar to him partly from Strawberry Hill and particularly, as he wrote, from the great court of Trinity College, Cambridge.[10] We can also see how the symbolic meanings of these images reflect the unconscious life.

The unconscious shares with Gothic the characteristic that anything (we are credibly informed) can happen there, and that its psychological spectrum reflects the extremes of what we seek and what we fear much more dramatically than is common either in the novel or in real life. There is a further parallel: both dreams and the unconscious share with Gothic fiction the tendency to deal with present problems through a special reliving of the past. As Auden puts it in his elegy for Sigmund Freud, "He wasn't clever at all: he merely told/ the unhappy Present to recite the Past."

This particular aspect of Gothic—the unhappy present reciting the past—is clearest, I suppose, in the later Gothic tradition, in Dickens, with Miss Havisham immobilised in the posture of frustration, or in Ibsen's *Ghosts* and *John Gabriel Borkman,* where the past has irrevocably foreclosed the possibilities of the present. In all these, once again we have a double past; for the crucial events of the past, whether betrayal, theft, murder, rape, or incest, were themselves the residue of an infinitely earlier past, which lived on in the archaic violence of the unconscious.

The unconscious, as we have all learned, is very like a Gothic castle: not the clean, well-lighted and cellarless place of the modern single-family residence, but a many-tiered vertical maze—and a dark and dirty one at that. Its many levels connect only through narrow, turning staircases and concealed trapdoors; and its towers, vaults, caverns, and dungeons are both the natural scene of death and terror and rape, and established symbols for our unconscious drives. Their sexual symbolism is now an open book to a normally contaminated mind; but it may be worth suggesting how the facts that, as Freud put it, "We are not masters in our own house," and that there are rooms in it that we may never really see, both supply an enduring psychological basis for the appeal of the Gothic genre, and help explain its frequent concentration on family relationships.

Melodrama and Gothic are not always clearly distinct genres, but the reader's responses to their characters usually differ. In melodrama, we hiss at the villain. In Gothic our attitude is more complex; the villain nearly always excites some degree of identification, whether he is predominately evil, like Mrs. Radcliffe's Montoni in *The Mysteries of Udolpho,* or predominately sympathetic, like Ambrosio in *The Monk,*[11] Melmoth, or Heathcliff. Most typically the reader has a divided sympathy, and this ambivalence seems to follow the division between the id and the superego.

Here, too, Walpole is a precursor. His hero, Manfred, is on one hand a cruel and tyrannical usurper whose mind often turns, in Walpole's phrase, "to exquisite villainy"; yet on the other hand, something in us finds much to admire and to envy in his cunning and self-confident resolution to pursue his aims; Walpole's own unconscious sympathy is made clear very early when he gives Manfred so firm a command of irony at the expense of superstition and sentimental pretence. Like Walpole, we know we ought to condemn Manfred, but we find we cannot; he appeals to a division in us between the conscious and the unconscious, between the public and the private, between the day and night side of the personality. These tensions provide a complexity which does something to atone for the thin psychological characterization of *The Castle of Otranto,* and is also typical of Gothic fiction. When there is character development in the Gothic, as in *The Monk,* it is a morally emblematic series of accelerating villainies rather than a psychologically cumulative process; more typically, the Gothic character is sustained by a labile balance between the past and the present, between the unrestrained impulses of the id and the controls of reason and normality.

Perhaps it is this unconscious irresolution that explains one puzzle about so many Gothic novels. At times Manfred and Montoni seem so potently and enviably demonic that we see no reason whatever that their victims, or their whole social order, should survive at all. Yet we also find these Gothic supermen having occasional spasms of normality—moral qualms, moments of kindness, ordinary muddled human sympathy. Their destructive power is apparently not limitless, and oddly defeats our expectation. This contradiction becomes more apparent in the nineteenth century, when the Gothic theme becomes psychologically internalized in such characters as Ahab and Heathcliff: they seem much more terrifying persons than their actions turn out to be.

It may be that the essential explanation of why Gothic villains never realized their full destructive potential is in the Freudian view of the relation between parents and children. Perhaps Manfred, for instance, alternates between the demonic and the normal because Walpole was torn between deep admiration for his father, and an equally deep fear of his father's power. Of course Horace Walpole knew that he was no more likely to continue the family's greatness than was Conrad; and so the dread giant hand on the bannister belonged to the paternal authority that was both desired and hated. But it also had its limits—Sir Robert was now dead.[12]

In any case it is surely within the nucleus of the family that the basic conflicts of the Gothic take place; and for at least three reasons. First, that the most universal of man's social and moral regulations all concern the interplay of power, property, marriage, and sex within the family; second, that these regulations, and the forces which oppose them, are internalised in the uncon-

scious; and last, that these conflicts directly and continuously affect the relationships of the past and the present in the individual's experience. Here again Walpole anticipated later developments; the moral of his work, he wrote in the Preface to the first edition, was "that *the sins of fathers are visited on their children to the third and fourth generation*" (p. 5).

The psychological contradictions concerning character and the family, it should perhaps be added, work both ways: Freudian theory can itself be seen as a Gothic myth. It presents the individual, much as Gothic does, as essentially imprisoned by the tyranny of an omnipotent but unseen past. The oedipal situation, or more generally, the terrible authority of the parents in the unconscious, is the Freudian equivalent of the supernatural or demonic power of the Gothic protagonist. The parallel is strengthened by the prevalence of paternal incest in Gothic fiction (of which Manfred's passion for Isabella, the girl who was to have been his daughter-in-law, is an example).[13] There is a further parallel in that tradition of Gothic which goes from *The Castle of Otranto* to "The Fall of the House of Usher" and *The House of the Seven Gables,* where the supreme power is the patriarchal authority of the long-dead lineal ancestor, who is still the real, though invisible, master of the house and its occupants.

More generally, we can conclude that although a sense of the mysterious and immobilising power of the past is one of the characteristic features both of psychoanalysis and Gothic fiction, that power is normally humanised as far as our quotidian experience is concerned. In this respect it seems that characterization in the Gothic novel has a somewhat similar function to that allotted the individual ego in psychoanalytic theory: to mediate between the conflicting demands of two sides of the unconscious, the superego and the id.[14]

So much for the psychology of the Gothic. I have obviously not been attempting a complete account either of *The Castle of Otranto* or of its genre. Such an account would have to concede that it is often forced, sometimes dull, and stylistically Walpole's worst piece of prose writing—with hardly a suggestion of the brilliance and understanding of the letters or the memoirs, for instance. *The Castle of Otranto,* in fact, very largely lacks the courage of its Gothic convictions; and yet its basic structure contains enough of the essential features of the later Gothic tradition both to explain its historical importance in establishing the new form, and to help us understand some of its characteristic elements.

Walpole himself shared much of the optimism of the Enlightenment; in his Gothic tale, therefore, the past is fairly benign: Manfred repents, and Theodore is returned to his rightful place. For the most part Mrs. Radcliffe followed this comfortable ideological perspective. After the end of the eighteenth century, however, the Gothic tradition took a darker turn. Gothic was still the world of the ancient romance, in the sense that it was a kind of fiction in which all the most violent and destructive extremes of human possibility could be realised, as opposed to the novel, which habitually confines its characters and events within the more normal quotidian spectrum of action and motive. But whereas Walpole had allowed the more affirmative forces of justice and virtue to vanquish evil, Monk Lewis and Charles Maturin and later Gothic writers operated more and more within the darker shades of the moral spectrum; the past is evil and tends to triumph; the fate of both the Monk and of Melmoth is eternal damnation.

Whether the balance of power in the world of the Gothic novel is held by good or evil, however, it is typically—though not always—a world where, in a variety of forms, the redoubtable past haunts the impotent present; it is the past which holds the key.

The Gothic tradition in its specialised historical sense is usually agreed to end with *Melmoth the Wanderer* in 1820: more precisely, perhaps, we might say that one branch of it continues in an increasingly sub-literary and specialised tradition about vampires and werewolves, while the other branch continues to deepen the main moral perspectives of Gothic in works which in other respects come closer to the main tradition of the novel.

The immediate setting in an historical past, and the use of the supernatural, became rarer in this later and looser version of the Gothic; and at the same time it incorporates many of the interests and techniques of the main fictional tradition. With the Brontës,[15] for instance, it assimilates the fuller psychological characterization and the denser presentation of the environment of the Victorian novel in general.

On this issue the roles of time and the family offer an interesting contrast in two acknowledged classics of the Gothic in its wider sense. In *Wuthering Heights,* for instance, the most memorable part of the narrative—from chapters 3 to 17—deals with events of a generation ago (between 1771, the arrival of Heathcliff at Wuthering Heights, to the deaths of Catherine and Hindley Earnshaw in 1784); Lockwood learns them after his calls at Wuthering Heights in 1801. To that extent the story enacts a double plunge backwards into time: to the days of Cathy's marriage, and then further back to her childhood with Heathcliff; and this backward movement itself takes us even further back symbolically to an unconscious world of eternal primitive possession. On the other hand the optimistic conclusion of the novel—Heathcliff's death and the marriage

of Catherine and Hareton—occurs in the present tense of the novel, in 1802 and 1803. This contrast suggests an inherent contradiction in the book. One way of looking at it would be as a working out of the dual role of the Gothic hero: the dark powers of the id have their way for a time, but they succumb to the attrition of moral and social norms in the end. As Thomas Moser has argued,[16] the later parts of the book really amount to a final denial of Emily Brontë's initial psychological premises: the bad, exciting past is not omnipotent; the demonic Heathcliff, of all people, goes soft; Cathy and Wuthering Heights cease to be haunted by him; and the Gothic world fades into the dull domestic Victorian one almost without a protest.

On the other hand Hawthorne's *The House of the Seven Gables,* (1851), is much closer to the **Otranto** pattern. There is—first of all—the Gothic present embodied in the colonial house itself which has survived into the eighteen-fifties. The movement back in time reveals the secrets of two anterior pasts: that of one generation back, when Clifford Pyncheon was sentenced to prison, thirty years before, for the alleged murder of his uncle, Jaffrey Pyncheon; and that of about two centuries before, when Colonel Pyncheon had originally seized the land from Matthew Maule, and has him executed as a wizard. In the narrative present, Judge Pyncheon, sitting beneath the portrait of the founder of his lineage, Colonel Pyncheon, dies choked with blood according to Maule's curse, the same fate that had befallen the original Colonel Pyncheon and his descendant, Jaffrey Pyncheon. The past is beginning to be expiated, and the present must now be reconstituted. The old deed to the Indian lands is discovered by the lodger, Mr. Holgrave, who turns out to be a descendant of Matthew Maule, and of his son, Thomas, who had built the house; and time can start going forward once again, instead of back, when Holgrave, now called Maule, gives his family name to Phoebe, the only representative of the Pyncheon lineage who has a future.

In the twentieth century, certainly, there has been no inclination to underestimate the extent to which we are haunted by the past and the family; and so the Gothic theme has surfaced in many new, concealed, or unexpected forms. In Faulkner's *Absalom, Absalom!,* for instance, the central pattern is very clear; the two generations which haunt Sutpen's Hundred are traced back to the intractable brutalities and the mysterious inheritance of Thomas Sutpen: the densely layered family history of the Sutpens, cannot, any more than the past of the South, be altered; Quentin Compson, and other defeated survivors of history, can only attempt to understand its multifarious power. One could also argue that the tradition continues in the literature of the mindless molecular now, and even that, the present times being what they are, contemporary fiction in general is rapidly becoming more and more indistinguishable from the Gothic novel—in Thomas Pynchon, Joyce Carol Oates, or Kurt Vonnegut, for example.

In general, we can be reasonably certain that, unlike the Gothic language, the Gothic novel is unlikely to disappear. As long as we are ambivalent about our incomparable modernity; as long as our political sky gets blacker daily with chickens coming home to roost; as long as children have parents, and so do parents; as long as we continue to experience boredom, night, sleep, and fear; as long as we fail to experience freedom and happiness; the past, alas! will continue to haunt us, and see to it that we spend much of our lives on Gothic time.

Notes

[1] "Literature and Science," *Philistinism in England and America,* ed. R. H. Super (Ann Arbor: Univ. of Michigan, 1974), p. 64. The Darwin citation is from *The Descent of Man,* Part III, ch. 21, p. 7.

[2] Horace Walpole, *The Castle of Otranto: A Gothic Story,* ed. W. S. Lewis (London: Oxford Univ., 1964), p. 17. Later quotations are from this edn.

[3] Walpole said much the same thing in a 16 March 1765 letter to Joseph Warton, where he wrote that he wished to "blend the marvellous of old story with the natural of modern novels" (W. S. Lewis, ed., *The Yale Edition of Horace Walpole's Correspondence* (New Haven: Yale Univ., 1937-83), 40:377. Subsequently cited as *Corr.*

[4] s.v. Gothic, 4.

[5] Renaissance usage, as in Giorgio Vasari (1551), merely connected the term with the *maniera tedesca* of the Goths who had sacked Rome and destroyed the classical orders of architecture. Our less derogatory and more historical classification awaited François Blondel the Younger, who in 1771 established the distinction between *architecture gothique ancienne—* the 6th to the 11th c. (the word "romanesque" wasn't to appear until 1819)—and the *architecture gothique moderne,* from the 12th c. to 1515, the accession of François Premier. In 18th-c. England, although many of his contemporaries made a vague equation between "Gothic" buildings and the Saxon period, Walpole in general equated "Gothic" with the pointed arch and perpendicular ornamentation (Kenneth Clark, *The Gothic Revival* [N.Y.: Holt, 1962], pp. 46-65), although the issue is not raised in *The Castle of Otranto.*

[6] As Ernest Fischer puts it, "The bourgeois wanted to disguise his capital in fancy dress" (*The Necessity of Art* [Harmondsworth, Middlesex: Penguin, 1971], p. 208).

[7] Walpole was delighted with a dungeon at Hurstmonceaux, an elaborate 15th-c. castellated mansion, because it "gives one a delightful idea of living in the days of soccage and under such goodly tenures" (*Corr.,* 35:138, to Bentley, 5 Aug. 1752).

[8] *Enquiry into the Life and Writings of Homer* (London, 1735), p. 26.

[9] Letter dated 13 March 1767 (*Corr.,* 3:260), trans. from the French by the author.

[10] As Warren H. Smith showed in a letter to the ed., *Times Literary Supplement* (23 May 1936), p. 440.

[11] In *The Monk* the literal haunting of the narrative present by an anterior past mainly occurs in the subplots (the legend of the bleeding nun, e.g.). As far as the protagonist is concerned, it is his own atavistic passions that are gradually revealed, to the astonishment of his admirers (including himself), and that lead to rape, murder, and his own damnation.

[12] The relationship of the Gothic novel to the archetypal and primordial structures of psychological development have been illuminatingly explored, in Leslie Fiedler's *Love and Death in the Americal Novel* (Cleveland: Meridian, 1962), for instance, and Frederick Crews' *The Sins of the Fathers* (N.Y.: Oxford Univ., 1966); while more recently, Maurice Lévy, in his *Le Roman Gothique Anglais 1764-1824* (Toulouse: Faculté des Lettres et Sciences Humaines, 1968), has investigated those aspects of the Gothic novel which appealed to the French surrealists, notably to André Breton and Paul Eluard. See also *The Female Gothic,* ed. Juliann E. Fleenor (Montreal: Eden, 1983).

[13] Walpole's play, *The Mysterious Mother,* contains a double incest: the mother sleeps with her son, and later kills herself when he marries their joint offspring. The Freudian aspect of *The Castle of Otranto* is treated in Martin Kallich's *Horace Walpole* (N.Y.: Twayne, 1971), pp. 101-4.

[14] The implications of this for characterization have been well demonstrated in Francis Russel Hart's essay "The Experience of Character in the English Gothic Novel." Hart argues that we must not make the common assumption that the Gothic protagonists are merely flat emblematic portrayals of the demonic in the non-representational world of the romance; they are that, and they are also human beings; and so the central mystery in Gothic novels is one where "autonomous natural existences—characters—come to assume demonic roles" and this is the "terrifying truth in an enlightenment context . . . that the demonic is

no myth, no superstition, but a reality in human character or relationship, a novelistic reality" (*Experience in the Novel: Selected Papers from the English Institute,* ed. Roy Harvey Pearce [N.Y.: Columbia Univ., 1968] p. 99).

[15] See especially Robert B. Heilman, "Charlotte Brontë's 'New Gothic'", in *From Jane Austen to Joseph Conrad,* ed. Robert C. Rathburn and Martin Steinmann, Jr. (Minneapolis: Univ. of Minnesota, 1958), pp. 118-32.

[16] "'What is the Matter with Emily Jane?' Conflicting Impulses in *Wuthering Heights,*" *Nineteenth-Century Fiction* 17 (1962): 1-19.

Carol M. Dole (essay date 1988)

SOURCE: "Three Tyrants *in The Castle of Otranto,*" *English Language Notes,* Vol. XXVI, No. 1, September, 1988, pp. 26-35.

[*In the following essay, Dole suggests that Walpole borrowed a number of Shakespearean characters, themes, and motifs in writing* The Castle of Otranto *in response to current political events.*]

Horace Walpole's well-known account of the genesis of *The Castle of Otranto* indicates that he wrote the first Gothic romance in an effort to distract himself from disturbing political events:

> I waked one morning in the beginning of last June from a dream, of which all I could recover was, that I had thought myself in an ancient castle (a very natural dream for a head filled like mine with Gothic story) and that on the uppermost bannister of a great staircase I saw a gigantic hand in armour. In the evening I sat down and began to write, without knowing in the least what I intended to say or relate. The work grew on my hands, and I grew fond of it— add that I was very glad to think of anything rather than politics—In short I was . . . engrossed with my tale, which I completed in less than two months.[1]

A member of Parliament for twenty-seven years, Walpole was often deeply involved in political intrigue, usually to promote the causes of friends such as his cousin Henry Conway, to whom he was deeply devoted. When Walpole began his novel in June 1764, he was obsessed with a controversy surrounding Conway. The previous year John Wilkes, a member of the House of Commons, had published an article attacking George III. Wilkes was arrested on a General Warrant, a warrant not unlike the notorious French *lettres de cachet.* At Walpole's instigation, Conway, a member of Parliament as well as an army officer, voted against the General Warrants and related issues. As a consequence, he was dismissed in April 1764 from his positions as

regimental commander and Groom of the King's Bedchamber. Walpole, enraged at these tyrannous actions against his cousin and others who spoke their minds, wrote a pamphlet on the subject in June, and throughout the summer tried to organize active opposition.[2] As his *Memoirs* attest, tyranny was Walpole's *bête noire.* In his bedroom he hung a copy of the warrant for the execution of Charles I, which he inscribed "Major Charta."[3] Walpole did not oppose monarchy, but he detested a monarch who overstepped his powers—as George III had just done.[4] Therefore tyrants were very much on Walpole's mind in June 1764 when he conceived *The Castle of Otranto.*

It is hardly surprising that tyranny, imaged as a giant armored hand, should be one of the elements of Walpole's feverish dream and, in the person of the tyrant Manfred, of Walpole's Gothic romance. But Walpole could hardly model his fictional tyrant openly on his own monarch.[5] I will argue that in creating the powerful, passion-ridden Manfred, a monstrous personification of his vision of his own monarch at this period, Walpole drew on two other tyrants, one fictional and one historical: Leontes and Henry VIII.

Walpole's second preface to the novel, written in 1765 after the popularity of the first edition had convinced him to reveal his authorship, attests that he copied "that great master of nature, Shakespeare," especially in creating the comic foibles of the domestics of Otranto. Walpole repeatedly invokes England's "brightest genius" as his model:

> I might have pleaded, that having created a new species of romance, I was at liberty to lay down what rules I thought fit for the conduct of it: but I should be more proud of having imitated, however faintly, weakly, and at a distance, so masterly a pattern, than to enjoy the entire merit of invention.[6]

Taking this cue, critics have pointed to Walpole's borrowing of scenes and motifs from a number of Shakespearean plays.[7] It is possible to make too much of Walpole's use of the supernatural, which probably had more to do with his desire to recreate the Middle Ages than it did with his admiration of the Bard, but the plot parallels between *Otranto* and one of the late plays are too numerous to be coincidental.[8] *The Winter's Tale,* like *Otranto* a romance set in Italy in the distant past, chronicles the consequences of the tyrannical acts of a monarch very like Manfred.

But *The Winter's Tale,* one immediately objects, seems not at all like *Otranto,* for its effect is that of the wondrous, not the terrible. The magical mood of the later acts of Shakespeare's play, however, is very different from that of the first half of his tale "Of sprites and goblins,"[9] which is replete with the "pity" and "terror" that Walpole, in his first preface, attributes to his own story (p. 4). When *The Castle of Otranto* closes, Manfred is in the same state in which we see Leontes just before the action shifts to Bohemia: horrified, repentant, and alone.

The striking plot parallels testify to Walpole's debt to the play.[10] Each work centers on a ruler and his wife—in Shakespeare, Leontes and Hermione, King and Queen of Sicilia; in Walpole, Manfred and Hippolita, Prince and Princess of Otranto. Each couple has a daughter and a son; the mother loves both children but the father loves only the son. Leontes has evident cause to love his charming little boy, Mamillius, "a gallant child" who "makes old hearts fresh" (I.i.36-37). He hates his newborn daughter, later named Perdita, for an even stronger reason: he believes her to be the child of his friend Polixenes. Manfred's similar feelings are unmotivated: he dotes on his son Conrad, "a homely youth, sickly, and of no promising disposition" (p. 15), while showing no affection for his beautiful and virtuous daughter, Matilda. In each tale, the son dies unexpectedly at a moment of crisis—Mamillius, as his mother is undergoing trial for adultery; Conrad, moments before his marriage to a woman Manfred has chosen to strengthen his claim to Otranto.

For each ruler, the loss of the son means the loss of an heir. Since Hippolita is too old to bear children and since Hermione dies (ostensibly) when she learns of her son's death, each father is left with no issue other than one daughter. Yet each father, under a misapprehension, violently disposes of his daughter: Leontes orders his to be abandoned because he believes her to be another man's child, and Manfred kills his in a fit of jealousy, mistaking her for Isabella, his son's betrothed and the object of his own passion. Neither man can remarry to obtain a new heir; Manfred cannot get rid of his wife, and Leontes cannot get rid of his wife's memory.

Loving and dutiful, the two rejected wives are similar in character. Leontes' daughter, Perdita, and Manfred's foster daughter, Isabella, are similar not only in personality but in situation. Both are lost from infancy but at last restored to fathers they do not recognize. Both are faced with the incestuous attentions of a parental figure: for Perdita this is no more than Leontes' remark to Florizel that "I'd beg your precious mistress" (V.i.222), but for Isabella it is a desperate flight from the passions of Manfred, who has raised her and who claims, when it serves him, "I am her parent" (p. 47). And both are virtuous young women in love with a prince disguised as a peasant.

In working out these similar plots, Walpole and Shakespeare select the same motifs from romance tradition. One is the token by which a lost child might be known. In *The Castle of Otranto,* Theodore, lost to his father since age five when he was taken by pirates from Sicily—the setting also of *The Winter's Tale*—is identified as Jerome's son by his birthmark and by the writings his mother bound to him. Likewise, in *The Winter's Tale,* Perdita is identified by her mother's jewel and the letters of Antigonus. A second motif is that of innate aristocracy. Just as the supposed shepherdess Perdita seems to Polixenes "something greater than herself" (IV.iv.158), the disguised Theodore strikes Manfred as animated by sentiments unusual for a "peasant within the sight of death" (p. 52). A third motif is that of art come to life. In *The Winter's Tale,* the statue of Hermione turns out to be the living woman; in *Otranto,* a statue bleeds, and a portrait descends from its frame and walks away.

The two troubled kingdoms are restored to right order in the same way: through the miraculous. Supernatural portents reveal Theodore to be the legitimate ruler of Otranto; and the seemingly miraculous animation of the "statue" of Hermione (who has been hidden for the sixteen years she was believed dead) and the unlikely return of the long-lost Perdita restore harmony to Sicilia.

The most compelling parallel between these two works is the resemblance of Manfred to Leontes. As Shakespeare's play opens, Leontes appears to be a devoted husband, father, and friend. The reactions of his courtiers to the sudden on-set of his jealous tyranny suggest that they are accustomed to a rational, moderate king. His abrupt transformation is the result of an action which he himself has urged: Hermione's successful plea to her husband's friend Polixenes that he prolong his visit. Leontes' jealousy is as extreme as it is quick. When his secret attempt to murder Polixenes fails, he denounces and imprisons the queen, in spite of her advanced pregnancy, refusing to listen to her or to anyone else. Yet his people still seek to excuse their king as the victim of passion, madness, or deception rather than judge him a tyrant. After bringing him his newborn daughter, whom he rejects in spite of her obvious resemblance to him, Paulina moves a step closer to the dreadful epithet: "I'll not call you tyrant; / But this most cruel usage of your queen . . . something savors / Of tyranny" (II.iii.115-19). In spite of the warning, Leontes sends the baby to be burnt or abandoned. But he remains conscious of the accusation, for he opens his wife's trial by saying, "Let us be cleared / Of being tyrannous, since we so openly / Proceed injustice" (III.ii.4-6). Nonetheless, the queen speaks of his tyranny and calls on Apollo to judge her. Although he himself had sent for the oracle to judge the case, Leontes rejects it when it pronounces him a "jealous tyrant" (III.ii.132). His blasphemy is answered with the immediate announcement of his son's death.

The characterization of Leontes, then, mingles hatred of tyranny with a fundamental faith in monarchy—both elements of Walpole's attitude toward his own king. Walpole, though a Whig who "approve[d] the name of King" only "when it exclude[d] the essence,"[11] was nonetheless committed to the Hanoverian line that his father (Sir Robert Walpole) had served and the people had chosen, and was, as an antiquary, keenly interested in courts and castles. Leontes provided a model for both the attractive and the dangerous faces of kingship, with the latter predominant—an emphasis particularly suitable to Walpole's anger at George III in 1764.

Walpole's mixed attitude toward monarchy, along with his adoption of the Janus-like Leontes as a model for his own fictional tyrant, helps explain the oddity of characterization that critics, most recently Elizabeth Napier, have remarked in Manfred.[12] The novel waffles on whether Manfred is a tyrannous villain or a just ruler gone wrong. The descriptions of Manfred's "severe temper" in the opening pages seem to brand him a tyrant even before we witness his many wrongdoings (p. 15): his cruelty to his wife, his pursuit of Isabella, his unjust condemnation of Theodore, and finally the murder of his own daughter. Yet Manfred's family and retinue, like Leontes', are slow to admit his tyranny; they attribute his excesses to his disordering by grief. The narrator too tries to excuse him:

> Manfred was not one of those savage tyrants who wanton in cruelty unprovoked. The circumstances of his fortune had given an asperity to his temper, which was naturally humane; and his virtues were always ready to operate, when his passions did not obscure his reason. (p. 30)

But finally Theodore pronounces him a tyrant, and in later chapters Manfred is referred to as "the Tyrant" in exposition as well as in dialogue. A clumsy narrative device at the end of Chapter I frees Walpole to paint Manfred as thoroughly villainous in the rest of the novel:

> Ashamed too of his inhuman treatment of a princess, who returned every injury with new marks of tenderness and duty, he felt returning love forcing itself into his eyes—but not less ashamed of feeling remorse towards one, against whom he was inwardly meditating a yet more bitter outrage, he curbed the yearnings of his heart, and did not dare to lean even towards pity. The next transition of his soul was to exquisite villainy. (p. 35)

The metamorphosis from despot to hyperbolic villain gives Walpole the opportunity to indulge in a fantasy of revenge against his own tyrannous king. That fantasy too borrows its shape from *The Winter's Tale.* Both Leontes and Manfred are punished when they refuse to heed the criticism of others (as had George III) or even to respect supernatural portents. Just as Leontes insists the oracle is false, Manfred defies gigantic ghosts and walking portraits, vowing, "Heaven nor hell shall impede my designs" (p. 23). After both

tyrants ignore enigmatic prophecies regarding the succession to their dominions, supernatural agents finally force them to acknowledge their wrongs. Each ruler finally commits himself to a long period of celibate repentance: Leontes mourns at the chapel containing his wife's purported tomb every day for sixteen years, and Manfred enters the convent.

The extraordinary number of similarities between *The Winter's Tale* and *Otranto* testifies that Walpole turned to Shakespeare for a model when fashioning his dream, and his obsession with a king's tyranny, into a novel. Whether Walpole's use of *The Winter's Tale* was deliberate, or unconscious—as would befit a romance bred of a dream—is less certain. After all, why would Walpole deliberately adopt a fictional despot as the model for his exaggerated portrait of George III, when there were so many English kings he regarded as reprehensible tyrants?

One answer is that Walpole regarded Leontes not as an imaginary character but as a portrait of an English king. A lengthy digression in *Historic Doubts on the Life and Reign of King Richard the Third* (1768), a study in which Walpole tries to exonerate Richard III, claims that *The Winter's Tale* is in reality a veiled historical play, "which was certainly intended (in compliment to Queen Elizabeth) as an indirect apology for her mother Anne Boleyn." Walpole goes on to compare Leontes to Henry VIII, Hermione to Anne Boleyn, and Mamillius to Anne's "still-born son," concluding that *The Winter's Tale* "was therefore in reality a second part of Henry the Eighth."[13]

No great leap is needed to move from the similarity between Henry's story and Leontes' to the similarity between Henry's story and Manfred's. "The unreasonable jealousy of Leontes," Walpole claims, "and his violent conduct in consequence, form a true portrait of Henry the Eighth, who generally made the law the engine of his boisterous passions."[14] He alludes, of course, to Henry's possibly unfounded accusation that Anne Boleyn was an adulteress and traitor, for which she was condemned to death—circumstances very like those of Leontes and Hermione. But in fact Henry VIII is more generally remembered for the momentous decision he shares with Manfred: to divorce his first wife for a younger woman who could provide him with a male heir. Henry's dilemma closely paralleled that of Manfred after his son's death: no male heir, one daughter, and a barren wife. Both husbands seized on the same solution, a divorce based on the claim that the first marriage was null because it was a form of incest. Both men argued that the death of the children had proved God's judgment on the marriage. Both presented their suits to the Church (represented in *Otranto* by Father Jerome), and both were told to wait, only to have their petitions denied in the end. Walpole's characterization of Manfred as a tyrant subject to unruly passions matches his description of Henry VIII as "a tyrant" ruled by "boisterous passions." And like Manfred, Henry was a murderer, "that butchering Husband our Henry 8th."[15]

There are also intriguing parallels between Henry's family and Manfred's. Edward, Henry's only son and heir, was, like Manfred's son Conrad, a sickly youth who died at the age of fifteen. Henry's daughter Elizabeth has a counterpart in Isabella (Manfred's foster daughter), whose name is a variant of hers. It is Isabella who, having married Theodore, eventually inherits Manfred's dominion, just as Elizabeth, though last in the line of succession, was the only one of Henry's children to get a firm hold on the throne.

The usurpation theme of Walpole's novel, which is related neither to Leontes nor to George III, has its source in Henry's story. Manfred's villainies stem principally from his attempt to retain the principality that his grandfather had usurped. Henry VIII, who united the long-feuding houses of Lancaster and York, would seem to have a legitimate claim to *his* title. Not so, in Walpole's view. Walpole defended the claim of Richard III, who lost the throne to Henry's father. Of Henry VII and Henry VIII Walpole remarks, "The former, all the world agrees now, had no title: the latter had none from his father and a very defective one from his mother."[16] Thus Walpole regarded Henry VIII as a usurper as well as a tyrant, just like Manfred.

The association of Manfred with Leontes and Henry VIII is valuable in suggesting reasons for some of the oddities of characterization in Walpole's novel, and intriguing in adding another ingredient to the strange brew of motifs that was to define the Gothic novel tradition. More importantly, the recognition of Manfred's similarity to three tyrants—Leontes, Henry VIII, and George III—alerts us that tyranny is a central concern of *The Castle of Otranto.* The preface to the first edition identifies the moral of the book differently: "the sins of fathers are visited on their children to the third and fourth generation" (p. 5). But this ostensible moral is a red herring, as the preface itself hints. Speaking from the safe vantage of "William Marshal, Gent.," purported translator of a rediscovered Italian manuscript, Walpole doubts whether in Manfred's time, "any more than at present, ambition curbed its appetite of dominion from the dread of so remote a punishment" (p. 5). This veiled thrust at George III suggests that *The Castle of Otranto* may not be the innocent fantasy Walpole always claimed it to be.[17] With his love of covert political maneuvering, the man who could interpret *The Winter's Tale* as a Tudor *roman à clef* was certainly capable of concealing a political tract in a Gothic romance. But whether the novel originated in shrewd plotting or fevered fantasy, the association of Manfred with historical tyrants, and with a fictional tyrant Walpole believed to be the portrait of a historical tyrant, argues that the true moral of the novel is found in Manfred's tormented cry in the concluding pages of the book (p. 109): "List, sirs, and may this bloody record be a warning to future tyrants!"

Notes

[1] *Horace Walpole's Correspondence,* ed. W. S. Lewis, 48 vols. (New Haven, 1937-1983), I, 88.

[2] See R. W. Ketton-Cremer, *Horace Walpole: A Biography* (Ithaca, 1966), 198-203. Walpole's own account of the Wilkes affair appears in his *Memoirs of the Reign of King George the Third,* ed. G. F. Russell Barker, 4 vols. (New York, 1894), I, 319-330; II, 1-9.

[3] *Correspondence,* IX, 197-198.

[4] Although the Wilkes incident brought Walpole's anxieties about royal prerogative to a pitch, his concern about the concentration of power at Court had begun in the time of George II and intensified throughout the reign of his successor (*Memoirs of King George II,* ed. John Brooke, 3 vols. [New Haven, 1985], II, 3). All the measures of George III, Walpole judged, "tended to the sole object of acting by his own will" (*Memoirs of George III,* IV, 84; see also *Correspondence,* XXXI, 285).

[5] Lacking sufficient support among the Opposition, Walpole feared to attack George III openly in spite of his rage at the king's treatment of Conway. His memoirs, which he designed to be published only a quarter-century after his death, record this fear: "I had seen the fate of Wilkes, abandoned by all he had served; and had no mind to accompany him in his exile" (*Memoirs of George III,* II, 3). Upon Conway's dismissal, Walpole's tactics were characteristically indirect: he secluded himself to conceal his "rage" and vowed revenge, choosing the pen as his weapon (*Memoirs of George III,* I, 325; II, 3). The pen too he wielded indirectly. His pamphlet, "A Counter Address to the Public on the Late Dismission of a General Officer," is an attack not on the king but on his advisors and on the author of a previous pamphlet. If his novel, written within days of the pamphlet, was also directed at George III, it would be similarly indirect.

[6] *The Castle of Otranto,* ed. W. S. Lewis (New York, 1964), 12. Parenthetical citations of the novel and its prefaces are to this edition.

[7] In his introduction to the novel (p. xiv), Lewis cites several "conspicuous" borrowings from *Macbeth, Hamlet, Cymbeline,* and *Romeo and Juliet.* Eino Railo, in *The Haunted Castle: A Study of the Elements of English Romanticism* (New York, 1927), and Devendra Varma, in *The Gothic Flame* (London, 1957), provide

numerous Shakespearean analogues to Walpole's novel, many involving use of the supernatural. Both Walter Raleigh (*The English Novel* [London, 1894]) and Jess Stein ("Horace Walpole and Shakespeare," *Studies in Philology,* 31 [1934], 51-68) find parallels but object that there are fundamental differences in the effect of the supernatural in Walpole and in Shakespeare.

[8] Railo notes the plot similarities briefly (pp. 35-36).

[9] *The Winter's Tale,* II.i.26, in Shakespeare's *Complete Works,* ed. Alfred Harbage (New York, 1977).

[10] Although Walpole mentions *The Winter's Tale* less frequently than he does some of Shakespeare's other plays, his letters suggest that he knew it in considerable detail (*Correspondence,* XXIX, 11-12; XLI, 291). He may well have seen it performed in 1741 or 1742, the only times during his life prior to the publication of *Otranto* that Shakespeare's version was performed, for he was in London during that period and very interested in the theater. During the 1750s and 60s only substantially altered versions of the play were staged, notably David Garrick's *Florizel and Perdita*—which Walpole owned in its 1762 edition. Although Garrick's play may have renewed Walpole's interest in Shakespeare's, Walpole is unlikely to have been influenced by Garrick's version, given his aversion to Garrick's alterations of Shakespeare's plays. See *Correspondence,* I, 248; and W. S. Lewis, "Edmond Malone, Horace Walpole, and Shakespeare," in *Evidence in Literary Scholarship: Essays in Memory of James Marshall Osborn,* ed. Rene Wellek and Alvaro Ribeiro (Oxford, 1979), 355-360.

[11] *Memoirs of George II,* II, 3.

[12] Napier, in *The Failure of Gothic* (New York, 1987), 94, attributes the mixed characterization of Manfred to Walpole's "willingness to violate character to move the storyline ahead."

[13] *Historic Doubts on the Life and Reign of King Richard the Third* (London, 1768), 114-116. Walpole is mistaken, of course, about the compliment to Queen Elizabeth. Modern scholars date the play at 1610-11, several years after James I took the throne. Walpole would not have known the date of composition, especially since this particular play was first published in the 1623 folio.

[14] *Historic Doubts,* 115.

[15] *Reminiscences Written by Mr. Horace Walpole in 1788,* ed. Paget Toynbee (Oxford, 1924), 24.

[16] *Historic Doubts,* 100.

[17] Walpole consistently spoke of his romance as an amusing trifle. See *Correspondence,* XV, 105; XXXI, 221.

FURTHER READING

Bibliography

Hazen, Allen T. *A Bibliography of Horace Walpole.* New Haven: Yale University Press, 1948, 189 p.

   The most complete bibliography of Walpole's writings.

Sabor, Peter. *Horace Walpole: A Reference Guide.* Boston: G. K. Hall, 1984, 270 p.

   Complete annotated bibliography of Walpole criticism through 1983.

Spector, Robert Donald. "The Beginnings: Horace Walpole and Clara Reeve." In *The English Gothic: A Bibliographic Guide to Writers from Horace Walpole to Mary Shelley,* pp. 83-110. Westport, Conn.: Greenwood Press, 1984.

   Surveys and describes the history of critical literature written on Walpole.

Biography

Dobson, Austin. *Horace Walpole: A Memoir.* 4th ed. Revised and enlarged by Paget Toynbee. London: Humphrey Milford, 1927, 395 p.

   First reliable biography of Walpole, originally published in 1890. Dobson relies extensively on quotations from the *Memoirs* and *Letters* and includes a history of Walpole criticism.

Kallich, Martin. *Horace Walpole.* New York: Twayne Publishers, 1971, 147 p.

   Critical biography of Walpole, with an extensive discussion of his works.

Lewis, Wilmarth Sheldon. *Horace Walpole.* New York: Pantheon Books, 1960, 215 p.

   Series of biographical lectures on Walpole's social and political lives, and his works.

Smith, Warren Hunting, ed. *Horace Walpole: Writer, Politician, and Connoisseur.* New Haven: Yale University Press, 1967, 358 p.

   Contains nineteen primarily biographical essays in three sections: "Walpole as Politician and Political Commentator," "Walpole as Connoisseur and Antiquarian," and "Walpole as a Literary Figure."

Stuart, Dorothy Margaret. *Horace Walpole.* New York: Macmillan, 1927, 229 p.

   Biography of Walpole for the general reader. Stuart discusses several of Walpole's minor writings that are rarely discussed by other critics.

Yvon, Paul. *La vie d'un dilettante: Horace Walpole (1717-*

1797); essai de biographie psychologique et letteraire.
Paris: Les presses universitaires de France, 1924, 872 p.
  The most thorough critical biography of Walpole to
  date.

Criticism

Bradford, Gamaliel. "The Letters of Horace Walpole." In
Biography and the Human Heart, pp. 213-360. Boston:
Houghton Mifflin, 1932.
  Summary of Walpole's era, his opinions, and his
  enthusiasms as revealed in his letters.

Brandenburg, Alice Stayert. "The Theme of *The Mysterious
Mother.*" *Modern Language Quarterly* 10 (December
1949): 464-74.
  Discusses incest as the tragic theme of *The Mysterious
  Mother.*

Christie, Ian. "Walpole: The Gossip as Historian." *History
Today* IV, No. 5 (May 1954): 291-300.
  Discusses the importance of Walpole's letters as a
  history of his era.

Collins, Norman. "The Major Minor Novelists." In *The
Facts of Fiction,* pp. 82-103. New York: Dutton, 1933.
  Notes that *The Castle of Otranto* was significant to
  the development of the novel form in that Walpole
  changed "the story from a mere string of events into
  a cat's cradle of ingenious complexity" and laid "out
  a plot like a pattern . . . not merely uncoil[ing] it like
  a rope."

Cooke, Arthur L. "Some Side Lights on the Theory of the
Gothic Romance." *Modern Language Quarterly* XII, No.
4 (December 1951): 429-36.
  Supplements traditional critical theories of the Gothic
  with neglected "side lights," including Walpole's
  appeal to Aristotelian principles of tragedy.

Dobrée, Bonamy. "Horace Walpole." In *Restoration and
Eighteenth-Century Literature: Essays in Honor of Alan
Dugald McKillop,* edited by Carroll Camden, pp. 185-
200. Chicago: University of Chicago Press, 1963.
  Discusses Walpole as a transitional figure between
  the Age of Reason and the Romantic age. To Dobrée,
  Walpole was a reluctant Romantic, whose life was
  based on a tense dichotomy between his need to satisfy
  his impulses and his desires and his need to conform
  to social conventions.

Evans, Bertrand. *Gothic Drama from Walpole to Shelley.*
Berkeley and Los Angeles: University of California Press,
1947, 257 p.
  Explores the role of the Gothic novel under British
  Romanticism, paying special attention to the motifs
  that Walpole initiated.

Haggerty, George E. "Literature and Homosexuality in the

Late Eighteenth Century: Walpole, Beckford, and Lewis."
Studies in the Novel XVIII, No. 4 (Winter 1986): 341-52.
  Explores the recurring themes that appear in the
  writings of Walpole, Beckford, and Lewis as arising
  from their attitude toward their homosexuality.

Harfst, Betsy Perteit. *Horace Walpole and the Unconscious:
An Experiment in Freudian Analysis.* New York: Arno Press,
1980, 264 p.
  Analyzes Walpole's works as expressions of his
  repressed unconscious.

Haring-Smith, Tori. "The Gothic Novel: A Tale of Terrors
Tamed." *Wissenschaftliche Zeitschrift der Wilhelm-Pieck-
Universität Rostock* XXXI, No. 8 (1982): 49-55.
  Claims that "the Gothic novelist conveyed a comforting
  message by presenting a catalogue of contemporary
  fears and showing them overcome"; Haring-Smith
  discusses *The Castle of Otranto, The Mysteries of
  Udolpho, The Monk, The Italian,* and *The Old English
  Baron.*

Havens, Munson Aldrich. *Horace Walpole and the
Strawberry Hill Press, 1757-1789.* Canton, Penn.: Kirgate
Press, 1901, 86 p.
  History of Walpole's private press.

Honour, Hugh. *Horace Walpole.* London: Longmans, Green,
and Co., 1957, 44 p.
  Brief introduction to Walpole's works. Honour harshly
  appraises *The Castle of Otranto.*

Ker, W. P. "Horace Walpole." In *English Prose: Selections,*
edited by Henry Craik, pp. 233-37. London: Macmillan,
1911.
  Brief appraisal of the principle aspects of Walpole's
  prose style.

McWhir, Anne. "The Gothic Transgression of Disbelief:
Walpole, Radcliffe and Lewis." In *Gothic Fictions:
Prohibition/Transgression,* edited by Kenneth W. Graham,
pp. 29-47. New York: AMS Press, 1989.
  Contends that the "separation of belief from fact is
  reflected in the Gothic novel, where the realm of
  superstition . . . becomes a vast image for the darkness
  and mystery of inner experience."

Mehrotra, K. K. *Horace Walpole and the English Novel.*
Oxford: Basil Blackwell, 1934, 197 p.
  Chronicles the arc of *The Castle of Otranto*'s creative
  influence, especially from 1764 to 1797.

Merritt, Edward Percival. *Horace Walpole: Printer.* Boston:
Riverside Press, 1907, 67 p.
  History of Walpole's private press and of private presses
  in England.

Punter, David. "Horace Walpole." In *The Literature of
Terror: A History of Gothic Fictions from 1765 to the*

Present Day, pp. 49-53. London: Longman, 1980.
History of the Gothic novel that considers Walpole and Tobias Smollett the originators of the form.

Riely, John. "*The Castle of Otranto* Revisited." *The Yale University Library Gazette* LIII, No. 1 (July 1978): 1-17.
Considers the circumstances under which Walpole wrote *The Castle of Otranto* and explores the public's reaction to the novel.

Rose, Edward J. "'The Queenly Personality': Walpole, Melville and Mother." *Literature and Psychology* XV, No. 4 (Fall 1965): 216-25.
Contrasts Walpole's novel *The Mysterious Mother* with Herman Melville's *Pierre,* focusing on the waysthat each author portrayed sexuality, guilt, and the enduring influence of the past on the present.

Solomon, Stanley J. "Subverting Propriety as a Pattern of Irony in Three Eighteenth-Century Novels: *The Castle of Otranto, Vathek,* and *Fanny Hill.*" *Erasmus Review* I, No. 2 (November 1971): 107-16.
Considers that novels by Walpole, William Beckford, and John Cleland controverted literary propriety through irony and rejection of didacticism.

Steeves, Harrison R. "The Gothic Romance: Walpole, Ann Radcliffe, Lewis." In *Before Jane Austen: The Shaping of the English Novel in the Eighteenth Century,* pp. 243-71. New York: Holt, Rinehart, and Winston, 1965.
Finds *The Castle of Otranto* impossible to take seriously as anything but a literary landmark.

Summers, Montague. "Historical Gothic." In *The Gothic Quest: A History of the Gothic Novel,* pp. 153-201. London: Fortune Press, 1938.
Credits *Otranto* twith inspiring a revolution in public taste. An excerpt from *The Gothic Quest* appears in the entry above

Woolf, Virginia. "Horace Walpole." *The Times Literary Supplement* (July 1919): 411.
Character study and analysis of Walpole's prose style.

Yvon, Paul. *The Poetical Ideals of a Gentleman Author in the XVIIIth Century: Horace Walpole as a Poet.* Paris: Les presses universitaires de France, 1924, 217 p.
Examines Walpole's theories of poetry, his poetic works, and his drama, and compares his poetry to the works of other poets of his era.

Literature Criticism from 1400 to 1800

Cumulative Indexes

How to Use This Index

The main references

Calvino, Italo
1923–1985 .... **CLC 5, 8, 11, 22, 33, 39,**
73; SSC 3

list all author entries in the following Gale Literary Criticism series:

BLC = *Black Literature Criticism*
CLC = *Contemporary Literary Criticism*
CLR = *Children's Literature Review*
CMLC = *Classical and Medieval Literature Criticism*
DA = *DISCovering Authors*
DAB = *DISCovering Authors: British*
DAC = *DISCovering Authors: Canadian*
DAM = *DISCovering Authors: Modules*
      DRAM: *Dramatists Module;* *MST*: *Most-Studied Authors Module;*
      MULT: *Multicultural Authors Module;* *NOV*: *Novelists Module;*
      POET: *Poets Module;* *POP*: *Popular Fiction and Genre Authors Module*
DC = *Drama Criticism*
HLC = *Hispanic Literature Criticism*
LC = *Literature Criticism from 1400 to 1800*
NCLC = *Nineteenth-Century Literature Criticism*
PC = *Poetry Criticism*
SSC = *Short Story Criticism*
TCLC = *Twentieth-Century Literary Criticism*
WLC = *World Literature Criticism, 1500 to the Present*

The cross-references

See also CANR 23; CA 85-88;
   obituary CA116

list all author entries in the following Gale biographical and literary sources:

AAYA = *Authors & Artists for Young Adults*
AITN = *Authors in the News*
BEST = *Bestsellers*
BW = *Black Writers*
CA = *Contemporary Authors*
CAAS = *Contemporary Authors Autobiography Series*
CABS = *Contemporary Authors Bibliographical Series*
CANR = *Contemporary Authors New Revision Series*
CAP = *Contemporary Authors Permanent Series*
CDALB = *Concise Dictionary of American Literary Biography*
CDBLB = *Concise Dictionary of British Literary Biography*
DLB = *Dictionary of Literary Biography*
DLBD = *Dictionary of Literary Biography Documentary Series*
DLBY = *Dictionary of Literary Biography Yearbook*
HW = *Hispanic Writers*
JRDA = *Junior DISCovering Authors*
MAICYA = *Major Authors and Illustrators for Children and Young Adults*
MTCW = *Major 20th-Century Writers*
NNAL = *Native North American Literature*
SAAS = *Something about the Author Autobiography Series*
SATA = *Something about the Author*
YABC = *Yesterday's Authors of Books for Children*

Literary Criticism Series
Cumulative Author Index

27; WLC
See also AAYA 20; CDALB 1865-1917; CLR
1, 38; DLB 1, 42, 79; DLBD 14; JRDA;
MAICYA; SATA 100; YABC 1

Aldanov, M. A.
See Aldanov, Mark (Alexandrovich)

Aldanov, Mark (Alexandrovich) 1886(?)-1957
TCLC 23
See also CA 118

Aldington, Richard 1892-1962 .... **CLC 49**
See also CA 85-88; CANR 45; DLB 20, 36, 100,
149

Aldiss, Brian W(ilson) 1925- . **CLC 5, 14, 40;**
DAM NOV
See also CA 5-8R; CAAS 2; CANR 5, 28, 64;
DLB 14; MTCW 1, 2; SATA 34

Alegria, Claribel 1924-**CLC 75; DAM MULT**
See also CA 131; CAAS 15; CANR 66; DLB
145; HW; MTCW 1

Alegria, Fernando 1918-................... **CLC 57**
See also CA 9-12R; CANR 5, 32, 72; HW

Aleichem, Sholom .... **TCLC 1, 35; SSC 33**
See also Rabinovitch, Sholem

Aleixandre, Vicente 1898-1984 ... **CLC 9, 36;**
DAM POET; PC 15
See also CA 85-88; 114; CANR 26; DLB 108;
HW; MTCW 1, 2

Alepoudelis, Odysseus
See Elytis, Odysseus

Aleshkovsky, Joseph 1929-
See Aleshkovsky, Yuz
See also CA 121; 128

Aleshkovsky, Yuz .... **CLC 44**
See also Aleshkovsky, Joseph

Alexander, Lloyd (Chudley) 1924- .. **CLC 35**
See also AAYA 1, 27; CA 1-4R; CANR 1, 24,
38, 55; CLR 1, 5, 48; DLB 52; JRDA;
MAICYA; MTCW 1; SAAS 19; SATA 3, 49,
81

Alexander, Samuel 1859-1938 .... **TCLC 77**

Alexie, Sherman (Joseph, Jr.) 1966- **CLC 96;**
DAM MULT
See also CA 138; CANR 65; DLB 175, 206;
MTCW 1; NNAL

Alfau, Felipe 1902- .... **CLC 66**
See also CA 137

Alger, Horatio, Jr. 1832-1899 .... **NCLC 8**
See also DLB 42; SATA 16

Algren, Nelson 1909-1981**CLC 4, 10, 33; SSC**
33
See also CA 13-16R; 103; CANR 20, 61;
CDALB 1941-1968; DLB 9; DLBY 81, 82;
MTCW 1, 2

Ali, Ahmed 1910- .... **CLC 69**
See also CA 25-28R; CANR 15, 34

Alighieri, Dante
See Dante

Allan, John B.
See Westlake, Donald E(dwin)

Allan, Sidney
See Hartmann, Sadakichi

Allan, Sydney
See Hartmann, Sadakichi

Allen, Edward 1948- .... **CLC 59**

Allen, Fred 1894-1956 .... **TCLC 87**

Allen, Paula Gunn 1939- .... **CLC 84; DAM**
MULT
See also CA 112; 143; CANR 63; DLB 175;
MTCW 1; NNAL

Allen, Roland
See Ayckbourn, Alan

Allen, Sarah A.
See Hopkins, Pauline Elizabeth

Allen, Sidney H.
See Hartmann, Sadakichi

Allen, Woody 1935- **CLC 16, 52; DAM POP**
See also AAYA 10; CA 33-36R; CANR 27, 38,
63; DLB 44; MTCW 1

Allende, Isabel 1942- . **CLC 39, 57, 97; DAM**
MULT, NOV; HLC; WLCS
See also AAYA 18; CA 125; 130; CANR 51,
74; DLB 145; HW; INT 130; MTCW 1, 2

Alleyn, Ellen
See Rossetti, Christina (Georgina)

Allingham, Margery (Louise) 1904-1966**CLC**
19
See also CA 5-8R; 25-28R; CANR 4, 58; DLB
77; MTCW 1, 2

Allingham, William 1824-1889 ...... **NCLC 25**
See also DLB 35

Allison, Dorothy E. 1949- .... **CLC 78**
See also CA 140; CANR 66; MTCW 1

Allston, Washington 1779-1843 .... **NCLC 2**
See also DLB 1

Almedingen, E. M. .... **CLC 12**
See also Almedingen, Martha Edith von
See also SATA 3

Almedingen, Martha Edith von 1898-1971
See Almedingen, E. M.
See also CA 1-4R; CANR 1

Almodovar, Pedro 1949(?)- .... **CLC 114**
See also CA 133; CANR 72

Almqvist, Carl Jonas Love 1793-1866 **N C L C**
42

Alonso, Damaso 1898-1990 .... **CLC 14**
See also CA 110; 131; 130; CANR 72; DLB
108; HW

Alov
See Gogol, Nikolai (Vasilyevich)

Alta 1942- .... **CLC 19**
See also CA 57-60

Alter, Robert B(ernard) 1935- .... **CLC 34**
See also CA 49-52; CANR 1, 47

Alther, Lisa 1944- .... **CLC 7, 41**
See also CA 65-68; CAAS 30; CANR 12, 30,
51; MTCW 1

Althusser, L.
See Althusser, Louis

Althusser, Louis 1918-1990 .... **CLC 106**
See also CA 131; 132

Altman, Robert 1925- .... **CLC 16, 116**
See also CA 73-76; CANR 43

Alvarez, A(lfred) 1929- .... **CLC 5, 13**
See also CA 1-4R; CANR 3, 33, 63; DLB 14,
40

Alvarez, Alejandro Rodriguez 1903-1965
See Casona, Alejandro
See also CA 131; 93-96; HW

Alvarez, Julia 1950- .... **CLC 93**
See also AAYA 25; CA 147; CANR 69; MTCW
1

Alvaro, Corrado 1896-1956 .... **TCLC 60**
See also CA 163

Amado, Jorge 1912- **CLC 13, 40, 106; DAM.**
MULT, NOV; HLC
See also CA 77-80; CANR 35, 74; DLB 113;
MTCW 1, 2

Ambler, Eric 1909-1998 .... **CLC 4, 6, 9**
See also CA 9-12R; 171; CANR 7, 38, 74; DLB
77; MTCW 1, 2

Amichai, Yehuda 1924- ... **CLC 9, 22, 57, 116**
See also CA 85-88; CANR 46, 60; MTCW 1

Amichai, Yehudah
See Amichai, Yehuda

Amiel, Henri Frederic 1821-1881 .... **NCLC 4**

Amis, Kingsley (William) 1922-1995**CLC 1, 2,**

3, 5, 8, 13, 40, 44; DA; DAB; DAC; DAM
MST, NOV
See also AITN 2; CA 9-12R; 150; CANR 8, 28,
54; CDBLB 1945-1960; DLB 15, 27, 100,
139; DLBY 96; INT CANR-8; MTCW 1, 2

Amis, Martin (Louis) 1949-**CLC 4, 9, 38, 62,**
101
See also BEST 90:3; CA 65-68; CANR 8, 27,
54, 73; DLB 14, 194; INT CANR-27; MTCW
1

Ammons, A(rchie) R(andolph) 1926-**CLC 2, 3,**
5, 8, 9, 25, 57, 108; DAM POET; PC 16
See also AITN 1; CA 9-12R; CANR 6, 36, 51,
73; DLB 5, 165; MTCW 1, 2

Amo, Tauraatua i
See Adams, Henry (Brooks)

Amory, Thomas 1691(?)-1788 .... **LC 48**

Anand, Mulk Raj 1905- .. **CLC 23, 93; DAM**
NOV
See also CA 65-68; CANR 32, 64; MTCW 1, 2

Anatol
See Schnitzler, Arthur

Anaximander c. 610B.C.-c. 546B.C.**CMLC 22**

Anaya, Rudolfo A(lfonso) 1937- ..... **CLC 23;**
DAM MULT, NOV; HLC
See also AAYA 20; CA 45-48; CAAS 4; CANR
1, 32, 51; DLB 82, 206; HW 1; MTCW 1, 2

Andersen, Hans Christian 1805-1875**NCLC 7;**
DA; DAB; DAC; DAM MST, POP; SSC
6; WLC
See also CLR 6; MAICYA; SATA 100; YABC
1

Anderson, C. Farley
See Mencken, H(enry) L(ouis); Nathan, George
Jean

Anderson, Jessica (Margaret) Queale 1916-
CLC 37
See also CA 9-12R; CANR 4, 62

Anderson, Jon (Victor) 1940-..**CLC 9; DAM**
POET
See also CA 25-28R; CANR 20

Anderson, Lindsay (Gordon) 1923-1994**C L C**
20
See also CA 125; 128; 146; CANR 77

Anderson, Maxwell 1888-1959**TCLC 2; DAM**
DRAM
See also CA 105; 152; DLB 7

Anderson, Poul (William) 1926- ...... **CLC 15**
See also AAYA 5; CA 1-4R; CAAS 2; CANR
2, 15, 34, 64; DLB 8; INT CANR-15; MTCW
1, 2; SATA 90; SATA-Brief 39

Anderson, Robert (Woodruff) 1917-**CLC 23;**
DAM DRAM
See also AITN 1; CA 21-24R; CANR 32; DLB
7

Anderson, Sherwood 1876-1941 **TCLC 1, 10,**
24; DA; DAB; DAC; DAM MST, NOV;
SSC 1; WLC
See also CA 104; 121; CANR 61; CDALB
1917-1929; DLB 4, 9, 86; DLBD 1; MTCW
1, 2

Andier, Pierre
See Desnos, Robert

Andouard
See Giraudoux, (Hippolyte) Jean

Andrade, Carlos Drummond de .... **CLC 18**
See also Drummond de Andrade, Carlos

Andrade, Mario de 1893-1945 .... **TCLC 43**

Andreae, Johann V(alentin) 1586-1654**LC 32**
See also DLB 164

Andreas-Salome, Lou 1861-1937 ... **TCLC 56**
See also DLB 66

Andress, Lesley

Banks, Iain M(enzies) 1954- .... **CLC 34**
See also CA 123; 128; CANR 61; DLB 194;
INT 128
Banks, Lynne Reid .... **CLC 23**
See also Reid Banks, Lynne
See also AAYA 6
Banks, Russell 1940- .... **CLC 37, 72**
See also CA 65-68; CAAS 15; CANR 19, 52,
73; DLB 130
Banville, John 1945- .... **CLC 46, 118**
See also CA 117; 128; DLB 14; INT 128
Banville, Theodore (Faullain) de 1832-1891
NCLC 9
Baraka, Amiri 1934-**CLC 1, 2, 3, 5, 10, 14, 33,
115; BLC 1; DA; DAC; DAM MST, MULT,
POET, POP; DC 6; PC 4; WLCS**
See also Jones, LeRoi
See also BW 2; CA 21-24R; CABS 3; CANR
27, 38, 61; CDALB 1941-1968; DLB 5, 7,
16, 38; DLBD 8; MTCW 1, 2
Barbauld, Anna Laetitia 1743-1825**NCLC 50**
See also DLB 107, 109, 142, 158
Barbellion, W. N. P. .... **TCLC 24**
See also Cummings, Bruce F(rederick)
Barbera, Jack (Vincent) 1945- .... **CLC 44**
See also CA 110; CANR 45
Barbey d'Aurevilly, Jules Amedee 1808-1889
NCLC 1; SSC 17
See also DLB 119
Barbour, John c. 1316-1395 .... **CMLC 33**
See also DLB 146
Barbusse, Henri 1873-1935 .... **TCLC 5**
See also CA 105; 154; DLB 65
Barclay, Bill
See Moorcock, Michael (John)
Barclay, William Ewert
See Moorcock, Michael (John)
Barea, Arturo 1897-1957 .... **TCLC 14**
See also CA 111
Barfoot, Joan 1946- .... **CLC 18**
See also CA 105
Baring, Maurice 1874-1945 .... **TCLC 8**
See also CA 105; 168; DLB 34
Baring-Gould, Sabine 1834-1924 .. **TCLC 88**
See also DLB 156, 190
Barker, Clive 1952- .... **CLC 52; DAM POP**
See also AAYA 10; BEST 90:3; CA 121; 129;
CANR 71; INT 129; MTCW 1, 2
Barker, George Granville 1913-1991 **CLC 8,
48; DAM POET**
See also CA 9-12R; 135; CANR 7, 38; DLB
20; MTCW 1
Barker, Harley Granville
See Granville-Barker, Harley
See also DLB 10
Barker, Howard 1946- .... **CLC 37**
See also CA 102; DLB 13
Barker, Jane 1652-1732 .... **LC 42**
Barker, Pat(ricia) 1943- .... **CLC 32, 94**
See also CA 117; 122; CANR 50; INT 122
Barlach, Ernst 1870-1938 .... **TCLC 84**
See also DLB 56, 118
Barlow, Joel 1754-1812 .... **NCLC 23**
See also DLB 37
Barnard, Mary (Ethel) 1909- .... **CLC 48**
See also CA 21-22; CAP 2
Barnes, Djuna 1892-1982**CLC 3, 4, 8, 11, 29;
SSC 3**
See also CA 9-12R; 107; CANR 16, 55; DLB
4, 9, 45; MTCW 1, 2
Barnes, Julian (Patrick) 1946-**CLC 42; DAB**
See also CA 102; CANR 19, 54; DLB 194;
DLBY 93; MTCW 1

Barnes, Peter 1931- .... **CLC 5, 56**
See also CA 65-68; CAAS 12; CANR 33, 34,
64; DLB 13; MTCW 1
Barnes, William 1801-1886 ....**NCLC 75**
See also DLB 32
Baroja (y Nessi), Pio 1872-1956**TCLC 8; HLC**
See also CA 104
Baron, David
See Pinter, Harold
Baron Corvo
See Rolfe, Frederick (William Serafino Austin
Lewis Mary)
Barondess, Sue K(aufman) 1926-1977 **CLC 8**
See also Kaufman, Sue
See also CA 1-4R; 69-72; CANR 1
Baron de Teive
See Pessoa, Fernando (Antonio Nogueira)
Baroness Von S.
See Zangwill, Israel
Barres, (Auguste-) Maurice 1862-1923**T C L C
47**
See also CA 164; DLB 123
Barreto, Afonso Henrique de Lima
See Lima Barreto, Afonso Henrique de
Barrett, (Roger) Syd 1946- ....**CLC 35**
Barrett, William (Christopher) 1913-1992
CLC 27
See also CA 13-16R; 139; CANR 11, 67; INT
CANR-11
Barrie, J(ames) M(atthew) 1860-1937 **T C L C
2; DAB; DAM DRAM**
See also CA 104; 136; CANR 77; CDBLB
1890-1914; CLR 16; DLB 10, 141, 156;
MAICYA; MTCW 1; SATA 100; YABC 1
Barrington, Michael
See Moorcock, Michael (John)
Barrol, Grady
See Bograd, Larry
Barry, Mike
See Malzberg, Barry N(athaniel)
Barry, Philip 1896-1949 .... **TCLC 11**
See also CA 109; DLB 7
Bart, Andre Schwarz
See Schwarz-Bart, Andre
Barth, John (Simmons) 1930-**CLC 1, 2, 3, 5, 7,
9, 10, 14, 27, 51, 89; DAM NOV; SSC 10**
See also AITN 1, 2; CA 1-4R; CABS 1; CANR
5, 23, 49, 64; DLB 2; MTCW 1
Barthelme, Donald 1931-1989**CLC 1, 2, 3, 5, 6,
8, 13, 23, 46, 59, 115; DAM NOV; SSC 2**
See also CA 21-24R; 129; CANR 20, 58; DLB
2; DLBY 80, 89; MTCW 1; SATA 7; SATA-
Obit 62
Barthelme, Frederick 1943- ......**CLC 36, 117**
See also CA 114; 122; CANR 77; DLBY 85;
INT 122
Barthes, Roland (Gerard) 1915-1980**CLC 24,
83**
See also CA 130; 97-100; CANR 66; MTCW
1, 2
Barzun, Jacques (Martin) 1907- ....**CLC 51**
See also CA 61-64; CANR 22
Bashevis, Isaac
See Singer, Isaac Bashevis
Bashkirtseff, Marie 1859-1884 ......**NCLC 27**
Basho
See Matsuo Basho
Bass, Kingsley B., Jr.
See Bullins, Ed
Bass, Rick 1958- ....**CLC 79**
See also CA 126; CANR 53
Bassani, Giorgio 1916- ....**CLC 9**
See also CA 65-68; CANR 33; DLB 128, 177

MTCW 1
Bastos, Augusto (Antonio) Roa
See Roa Bastos, Augusto (Antonio)
Bataille, Georges 1897-1962 ....**CLC 29**
See also CA 101; 89-92
Bates, H(erbert) E(rnest) 1905-1974**CLC 46;
DAB; DAM POP; SSC 10**
See also CA 93-96; 45-48; CANR 34; DLB 162,
191; MTCW 1, 2
Bauchart
See Camus, Albert
Baudelaire, Charles 1821-1867 **NCLC 6, 29,
55; DA; DAB; DAC; DAM MST, POET;
PC 1; SSC 18; WLC**
Baudrillard, Jean 1929- ....**CLC 60**
Baum, L(yman) Frank 1856-1919 ... **TCLC 7**
See also CA 108; 133; CLR 15; DLB 22; JRDA;
MAICYA; MTCW 1, 2; SATA 18, 100
Baum, Louis F.
See Baum, L(yman) Frank
Baumbach, Jonathan 1933- .... **CLC 6, 23**
See also CA 13-16R; CAAS 5; CANR 12, 66;
DLBY 80; INT CANR-12; MTCW 1
Bausch, Richard (Carl) 1945- ....**CLC 51**
See also CA 101; CAAS 14; CANR 43, 61; DLB
130
Baxter, Charles (Morley) 1947- **CLC 45, 78;
DAM POP**
See also CA 57-60; CANR 40, 64; DLB 130
Baxter, George Owen
See Faust, Frederick (Schiller)
Baxter, James K(eir) 1926-1972 ....**CLC 14**
See also CA 77-80
Baxter, John
See Hunt, E(verette) Howard, (Jr.)
Bayer, Sylvia
See Glassco, John
Baynton, Barbara 1857-1929 ....**TCLC 57**
Beagle, Peter S(oyer) 1939- .... **CLC 7, 104**
See also CA 9-12R; CANR 4, 51, 73; DLBY
80; INT CANR-4; MTCW 1; SATA 60
Bean, Normal
See Burroughs, Edgar Rice
Beard, Charles A(ustin) 1874-1948 **TCLC 15**
See also CA 115; DLB 17; SATA 18
Beardsley, Aubrey 1872-1898 ....**NCLC 6**
Beattie, Ann 1947-**CLC 8, 13, 18, 40, 63; DAM
NOV; POP; SSC 11**
See also BEST 90:2; CA 81-84; CANR 53, 73;
DLBY 82; MTCW 1, 2
Beattie, James 1735-1803 ....**NCLC 25**
See also DLB 109
Beauchamp, Kathleen Mansfield 1888-1923
See Mansfield, Katherine
See also CA 104; 134; DA; DAC; DAM MST
Beaumarchais, Pierre-Augustin Caron de 1732-
1799 .... **DC 4**
See also DAM DRAM
Beaumont, Francis 1584(?)-1616**LC 33; DC 6**
See also CDBLB Before 1660; DLB 58, 121
**Beauvoir, Simone (Lucie Ernestine Marie
Bertrand) de** 1908-1986 **CLC 1, 2, 4, 8,
14, 31, 44, 50, 71; DA; DAB; DAC; DAM
MST, NOV; WLC**
See also CA 9-12R; 118; CANR 28, 61; DLB
72; DLBY 86; MTCW 1, 2
Becker, Carl (Lotus) 1873-1945 ..... **TCLC 63**
See also CA 157; DLB 17
Becker, Jurek 1937-1997 .... **CLC 7, 19**
See also CA 85-88; 157; CANR 60; DLB 75
Becker, Walter 1950- ....**CLC 26**
Beckett, Samuel (Barclay) 1906-1989 **CLC 1,
2, 3, 4, 6, 9, 10, 11, 14, 18, 29, 57, 59, 83**

See also CA 104
Blom, Jan
See Breytenbach, Breyten
Bloom, Harold 1930- .... **CLC 24, 103**
See also CA 13-16R; CANR 39, 75; DLB 67;
MTCW 1
Bloomfield, Aurelius
See Bourne, Randolph S(illiman)
Blount, Roy (Alton), Jr. 1941- .... **CLC 38**
See also CA 53-56; CANR 10, 28, 61; INT
CANR-28; MTCW 1, 2
Bloy, Leon 1846-1917 .... **TCLC 22**
See also CA 121; DLB 123
Blume, Judy (Sussman) 1938- ... **CLC 12, 30;**
DAM NOV, POP
See also AAYA 3, 26; CA 29-32R; CANR 13,
37, 66; CLR 2, 15; DLB 52; JRDA;
MAICYA; MTCW 1, 2; SATA 2, 31, 79
Blunden, Edmund (Charles) 1896-1974 **C L C**
2, 56
See also CA 17-18; 45-48; CANR 54; CAP 2;
DLB 20, 100, 155; MTCW 1
Bly, Robert (Elwood) 1926-**CLC 1, 2, 5, 10, 15,**
38; DAM POET
See also CA 5-8R; CANR 41, 73; DLB 5;
MTCW 1, 2
Boas, Franz 1858-1942 .... **TCLC 56**
See also CA 115
Bobette
See Simenon, Georges (Jacques Christian)
Boccaccio, Giovanni 1313-1375 .. **CMLC 13;**
SSC 10
Bochco, Steven 1943- .... **CLC 35**
See also AAYA 11; CA 124; 138
Bodel, Jean 1167(?)-1210 .... **CMLC 28**
Bodenheim, Maxwell 1892-1954 .... **TCLC 44**
See also CA 110; DLB 9, 45
Bodker, Cecil 1927- .... **CLC 21**
See also CA 73-76; CANR 13, 44; CLR 23;
MAICYA; SATA 14
Boell, Heinrich (Theodor) 1917-1985 **CLC 2,**
3, 6, 9, 11, 15, 27, 32, 72; DA; DAB; DAC;
DAM MST, NOV; SSC 23; WLC
See also CA 21-24R; 116; CANR 24; DLB 69;
DLBY 85; MTCW 1, 2
Boerne, Alfred
See Doeblin, Alfred
Boethius 480(?)-524(?) .... **CMLC 15**
See also DLB 115
Bogan, Louise 1897-1970 . **CLC 4, 39, 46, 93;**
DAM POET; PC 12
See also CA 73-76; 25-28R; CANR 33; DLB
45, 169; MTCW 1, 2
Bogarde, Dirk .... **CLC 19**
See also Van Den Bogarde, Derek Jules Gaspard
Ulric Niven
See also DLB 14
Bogosian, Eric 1953- .... **CLC 45**
See also CA 138
Bograd, Larry 1953- .... **CLC 35**
See also CA 93-96; CANR 57; SAAS 21; SATA
33, 89
Boiardo, Matteo Maria 1441-1494 .... **LC 6**
Boileau-Despreaux, Nicolas 1636-1711 **LC 3**
Bojer, Johan 1872-1959 .... **TCLC 64**
Boland, Eavan (Aisling) 1944- .. **CLC 40, 67,**
113; DAM POET
See also CA 143; CANR 61; DLB 40
Boll, Heinrich
See Boell, Heinrich (Theodor)
Bolt, Lee
See Faust, Frederick (Schiller)
Bolt, Robert (Oxton) 1924-1995 ..... **CLC 14;**

DAM DRAM
See also CA 17-20R; 147; CANR 35, 67; DLB
13; MTCW 1
Bombet, Louis-Alexandre-Cesar
See Stendhal
Bomkauf
See Kaufman, Bob (Garnell)
Bonaventura .... **NCLC 35**
See also DLB 90
Bond, Edward 1934- **CLC 4, 6, 13, 23; DAM**
DRAM
See also CA 25-28R; CANR 38, 67; DLB 13;
MTCW 1
Bonham, Frank 1914-1989 .... **CLC 12**
See also AAYA 1; CA 9-12R; CANR 4, 36;
JRDA; MAICYA; SAAS 3; SATA 1, 49;
SATA-Obit 62
Bonnefoy, Yves 1923- .. **CLC 9, 15, 58; DAM**
MST, POET
See also CA 85-88; CANR 33, 75; MTCW 1, 2
Bontemps, Arna(ud Wendell) 1902-1973**C L C**
1, 18; BLC 1; DAM MULT, NOV, POET
See also BW 1; CA 1-4R; 41-44R; CANR 4,
35; CLR 6; DLB 48, 51; JRDA; MAICYA;
MTCW 1, 2; SATA 2, 44; SATA-Obit 24
Booth, Martin 1944- .... **CLC 13**
See also CA 93-96; CAAS 2
Booth, Philip 1925- .... **CLC 23**
See also CA 5-8R; CANR 5; DLBY 82
Booth, Wayne C(layson) 1921- .... **CLC 24**
See also CA 1-4R; CAAS 5; CANR 3, 43; DLB
67
Borchert, Wolfgang 1921-1947 .... **TCLC 5**
See also CA 104; DLB 69, 124
Borel, Petrus 1809-1859 .... **NCLC 41**
Borges, Jorge Luis 1899-1986**CLC 1, 2, 3, 4, 6,**
8, 9, 10, 13, 19, 44, 48, 83; DA; DAB; DAC;
DAM MST, MULT; HLC; PC 22; SSC 4;
WLC
See also AAYA 26; CA 21-24R; CANR 19, 33,
75; DLB 113; DLBY 86; HW; MTCW 1, 2
Borowski, Tadeusz 1922-1951 .... **TCLC 9**
See also CA 106; 154
Borrow, George (Henry) 1803-1881 **NCLC 9**
See also DLB 21, 55, 166
Bosman, Herman Charles 1905-1951 . **T C L C**
49
See also Malan, Herman
See also CA 160
Bosschere, Jean de 1878(?)-1953 ... **TCLC 19**
See also CA 115
Boswell, James 1740-1795 . **LC 4; DA; DAB;**
DAC; DAM MST; WLC
See also CDBLB 1660-1789; DLB 104, 142
Bottoms, David 1949- .... **CLC 53**
See also CA 105; CANR 22; DLB 120; DLBY
83
Boucicault, Dion 1820-1890 .... **NCLC 41**
Boucolon, Maryse 1937(?)-
See Conde, Maryse
See also CA 110; CANR 30, 53, 76
Bourget, Paul (Charles Joseph) 1852-1935
TCLC 12
See also CA 107; DLB 123
Bourjaily, Vance (Nye) 1922- .... **CLC 8, 62**
See also CA 1-4R; CAAS 1; CANR 2, 72; DLB
2, 143
Bourne, Randolph S(illiman) 1886-1918
TCLC 16
See also CA 117; 155; DLB 63
Bova, Ben(jamin William) 1932- ...... **CLC 45**
See also AAYA 16; CA 5-8R; CAAS 18; CANR
11, 56; CLR 3; DLBY 81; INT CANR-11;

MAICYA; MTCW 1; SATA 6, 68
Bowen, Elizabeth (Dorothea Cole) 1899-1973
CLC 1, 3, 6, 11, 15, 22, 118; DAM NOV;
SSC 3, 28
See also CA 17-18; 41-44R; CANR 35; CAP 2;
CDBLB 1945-1960; DLB 15, 162; MTCW
1, 2
Bowering, George 1935- .... **CLC 15, 47**
See also CA 21-24R; CAAS 16; CANR 10; DLB
53
Bowering, Marilyn R(uthe) 1949- ... **CLC 32**
See also CA 101; CANR 49
Bowers, Edgar 1924-.......................... **CLC 9**
See also CA 5-8R; CANR 24; DLB 5
Bowie, David .... **CLC 17**
See also Jones, David Robert
Bowles, Jane (Sydney) 1917-1973 **CLC 3, 68**
See also CA 19-20; 41-44R; CAP 2
Bowles, Paul (Frederick) 1910-**CLC 1, 2, 19,**
53; SSC 3
See also CA 1-4R; CAAS 1; CANR 1, 19, 50,
75; DLB 5, 6; MTCW 1, 2
Box, Edgar
See Vidal, Gore
Boyd, Nancy
See Millay, Edna St. Vincent
Boyd, William 1952-.............. **CLC 28, 53, 70**
See also CA 114; 120; CANR 51, 71
Boyle, Kay 1902-1992**CLC 1, 5, 19, 58; SSC 5**
See also CA 13-16R; 140; CAAS 1; CANR 29,
61; DLB 4, 9, 48, 86; DLBY 93; MTCW 1,
2
Boyle, Mark
See Kienzle, William X(avier)
Boyle, Patrick 1905-1982 .... **CLC 19**
See also CA 127
Boyle, T. C. 1948-
See Boyle, T(homas) Coraghessan
Boyle, T(homas) Coraghessan 1948-**CLC 36,**
55, 90; DAM POP; SSC 16
See also BEST 90:4; CA 120; CANR 44, 76;
DLBY 86
Boz
See Dickens, Charles (John Huffam)
Brackenridge, Hugh Henry 1748-1816**N C L C**
7
See also DLB 11, 37
Bradbury, Edward P.
See Moorcock, Michael (John)
Bradbury, Malcolm (Stanley) 1932-**CLC 32,**
61; DAM NOV
See also CA 1-4R; CANR 1, 33; DLB 14, 207;
MTCW 1, 2
Bradbury, Ray (Douglas) 1920-**CLC 1, 3, 10,**
15, 42, 98; DA; DAB; DAC; DAM MST,
NOV, POP; SSC 29; WLC
See also AAYA 15; AITN 1, 2; CA 1-4R; CANR
2, 30, 75; CDALB 1968-1988; DLB 2, 8;
MTCW 1, 2; SATA 11, 64
Bradford, Gamaliel 1863-1932 ...... **TCLC 36**
See also CA 160; DLB 17
Bradley, David (Henry), Jr. 1950- .. **CLC 23,**
118; BLC 1; DAM MULT
See also BW 1; CA 104; CANR 26; DLB 33
Bradley, John Ed(mund, Jr.) 1958- . **CLC 55**
See also CA 139
Bradley, Marion Zimmer 1930-**CLC 30; DAM**
POP
See also AAYA 9; CA 57-60; CAAS 10; CANR
7, 31, 51, 75; DLB 8; MTCW 1, 2; SATA 90
Bradstreet, Anne 1612(?)-1672**LC 4, 30; DA;**
DAC; DAM MST, POET; PC 10
See also CDALB 1640-1865; DLB 24

See also CA 9-12R; 33-36R; CANR 63; DLB 9, 206; SATA 8

Clark Bekederemo, J(ohnson) P(epper)
See Clark, John Pepper

Clarke, Arthur C(harles) 1917-**CLC 1, 4, 13, 18, 35; DAM POP; SSC 3**
See also AAYA 4; CA 1-4R; CANR 2, 28, 55, 74; JRDA; MAICYA; MTCW 1, 2; SATA 13, 70

Clarke, Austin 1896-1974 ....**CLC 6, 9; DAM POET**
See also CA 29-32; 49-52; CAP 2; DLB 10, 20

Clarke, Austin C(hesterfield) 1934-**CLC 8, 53; BLC 1; DAC; DAM MULT**
See also BW 1; CA 25-28R; CAAS 16; CANR 14, 32, 68; DLB 53, 125

Clarke, Gillian 1937- .... **CLC 61**
See also CA 106; DLB 40

Clarke, Marcus (Andrew Hislop) 1846-1881 **NCLC 19**

Clarke, Shirley 1925- .... **CLC 16**

Clash, The
See Headon, (Nicky) Topper; Jones, Mick; Simonon, Paul; Strummer, Joe

Claudel, Paul (Louis Charles Marie) 1868-1955 **TCLC 2, 10**
See also CA 104; 165; DLB 192

Claudius, Matthias 1740-1815 ....**NCLC 75**
See also DLB 97

Clavell, James (duMaresq) 1925-1994**CLC 6, 25, 87; DAM NOV, POP**
See also CA 25-28R; 146; CANR 26, 48; MTCW 1, 2

Cleaver, (Leroy) Eldridge 1935-1998**CLC 30, 119; BLC 1; DAM MULT**
See also BW 1; CA 21-24R; 167; CANR 16, 75

Cleese, John (Marwood) 1939- .... **CLC 21**
See also Monty Python
See also CA 112; 116; CANR 35; MTCW 1

Cleishbotham, Jebediah
See Scott, Walter

Cleland, John 1710-1789 .... **LC 2, 48**
See also DLB 39

Clemens, Samuel Langhorne 1835-1910
See Twain, Mark
See also CA 104; 135; CDALB 1865-1917; DA; DAB; DAC; DAM MST, NOV; DLB 11, 12, 23, 64, 74, 186, 189; JRDA; MAICYA; SATA 100; YABC 2

Cleophil
See Congreve, William

Clerihew, E.
See Bentley, E(dmund) C(lerihew)

Clerk, N. W.
See Lewis, C(live) S(taples)

Cliff, Jimmy .... **CLC 21**
See also Chambers, James

Clifton, (Thelma) Lucille 1936- **CLC 19, 66; BLC 1; DAM MULT, POET; PC 17**
See also BW 2; CA 49-52; CANR 2, 24, 42, 76; CLR 5; DLB 5, 41; MAICYA; MTCW 1; SATA 20, 69

Clinton, Dirk
See Silverberg, Robert

Clough, Arthur Hugh 1819-1861 ...**NCLC 27**
See also DLB 32

Clutha, Janet Paterson Frame 1924-
See Frame, Janet
See also CA 1-4R; CANR 2, 36, 76; MTCW 1, 2

Clyne, Terence
See Blatty, William Peter

Cobalt, Martin

See Mayne, William (James Carter)

Cobb, Irvin S. 1876-1944 .... **TCLC 77**
See also DLB 11, 25, 86

Cobbett, William 1763-1835 ....**NCLC 49**
See also DLB 43, 107, 158

Coburn, D(onald) L(ee) 1938- ....**CLC 10**
See also CA 89-92

Cocteau, Jean (Maurice Eugene Clement) 1889-1963**CLC 1, 8, 15, 16, 43; DA; DAB; DAC; DAM DRAM, MST, NOV; WLC**
See also CA 25-28; CANR 40; CAP 2; DLB 65; MTCW 1, 2

Codrescu, Andrei 1946-**CLC 46; DAM POET**
See also CA 33-36R; CAAS 19; CANR 13, 34, 53, 76

Coe, Max
See Bourne, Randolph S(illiman)

Coe, Tucker
See Westlake, Donald E(dwin)

Coen, Ethan 1958- .... **CLC 108**
See also CA 126

Coen, Joel 1955- .... **CLC 108**
See also CA 126

The Coen Brothers
See Coen, Ethan; Coen, Joel

Coetzee, J(ohn) M(ichael) 1940- **CLC 23, 33, 66, 117; DAM NOV**
See also CA 77-80; CANR 41, 54, 74; MTCW 1, 2

Coffey, Brian
See Koontz, Dean R(ay)

Cohan, George M(ichael) 1878-1942**TCLC 60**
See also CA 157

Cohen, Arthur A(llen) 1928-1986 **CLC 7, 31**
See also CA 1-4R; 120; CANR 1, 17, 42; DLB 28

Cohen, Leonard (Norman) 1934- **CLC 3, 38; DAC; DAM MST**
See also CA 21-24R; CANR 14, 69; DLB 53; MTCW 1

Cohen, Matt 1942- ....**CLC 19; DAC**
See also CA 61-64; CAAS 18; CANR 40; DLB 53

Cohen-Solal, Annie 19(?)- ....**CLC 50**

Colegate, Isabel 1931- ....**CLC 36**
See also CA 17-20R; CANR 8, 22, 74; DLB 14; INT CANR-22; MTCW 1

Coleman, Emmett
See Reed, Ishmael

Coleridge, M. E.
See Coleridge, Mary E(lizabeth)

Coleridge, Mary E(lizabeth) 1861-1907**TCLC 73**
See also CA 116; 166; DLB 19, 98

Coleridge, Samuel Taylor 1772-1834**NCLC 9, 54; DA; DAB; DAC; DAM MST, POET; PC 11; WLC**
See also CDBLB 1789-1832; DLB 93, 107

Coleridge, Sara 1802-1852 ....**NCLC 31**
See also DLB 199

Coles, Don 1928- ....**CLC 46**
See also CA 115; CANR 38

Coles, Robert (Martin) 1929- .... **CLC 108**
See also CA 45-48; CANR 3, 32, 66, 70; INT CANR-32; SATA 23

Colette, (Sidonie-Gabrielle) 1873-1954**TCLC 1, 5, 16; DAM NOV; SSC 10**
See also CA 104; 131; DLB 65; MTCW 1

Collett, (Jacobine) Camilla (Wergeland) 1813-1895 ....**NCLC 22**

Collier, Christopher 1930-................**CLC 30**
See also AAYA 13; CA 33-36R; CANR 13, 33; JRDA; MAICYA; SATA 16, 70

Collier, James L(incoln) 1928-**CLC 30; DAM POP**
See also AAYA 13; CA 9-12R; CANR 4, 33, 60; CLR 3; JRDA; MAICYA; SAAS 21; SATA 8, 70

Collier, Jeremy 1650-1726 .... **LC 6**

Collier, John 1901-1980 ....**SSC 19**
See also CA 65-68; 97-100; CANR 10; DLB 77

Collingwood, R(obin) G(eorge) 1889(?)-1943 **TCLC 67**
See also CA 117; 155

Collins, Hunt
See Hunter, Evan

Collins, Linda 1931- .... **CLC 44**
See also CA 125

Collins, (William) Wilkie 1824-1889**NCLC 1. 18**
See also CDBLB 1832-1890; DLB 18, 70, 159

Collins, William 1721-1759 . **LC 4, 40; DAM POET**
See also DLB 109

Collodi, Carlo 1826-1890 ....**NCLC 54**
See also Lorenzini, Carlo
See also CLR 5

Colman, George 1732-1794
See Glassco, John

Colt, Winchester Remington
See Hubbard, L(afayette) Ron(ald)

Colter, Cyrus 1910- .... **CLC 58**
See also BW 1; CA 65-68; CANR 10, 66; DLB 33

Colton, James
See Hansen, Joseph

Colum, Padraic 1881-1972 .... **CLC 28**
See also CA 73-76; 33-36R; CANR 35; CLR 36; MAICYA; MTCW 1; SATA 15

Colvin, James
See Moorcock, Michael (John)

Colwin, Laurie (E.) 1944-1992**CLC 5, 13, 23, 84**
See also CA 89-92; 139; CANR 20, 46; DLBY 80; MTCW 1

Comfort, Alex(ander) 1920-**CLC 7; DAM POP**
See also CA 1-4R; CANR 1, 45; MTCW 1

Comfort, Montgomery
See Campbell, (John) Ramsey

Compton-Burnett, I(vy) 1884(?)-1969**CLC 1, 3, 10, 15, 34; DAM NOV**
See also CA 1-4R; 25-28R; CANR 4; DLB 36; MTCW 1

Comstock, Anthony 1844-1915 ......**TCLC 13**
See also CA 110; 169

Comte, Auguste 1798-1857 ....**NCLC 54**

Conan Doyle, Arthur
See Doyle, Arthur Conan

Conde, Maryse 1937- .... **CLC 52, 92; BLCS; DAM MULT**
See also Boucolon, Maryse
See also BW 2; MTCW 1

Condillac, Etienne Bonnot de 1714-1780 **LC 26**

Condon, Richard (Thomas) 1915-1996**CLC 4, 6, 8, 10, 45, 100; DAM NOV**
See also BEST 90:3; CA 1-4R; 151; CAAS 1; CANR 2, 23; INT CANR-23; MTCW 1, 2

Confucius 551B.C.-479B.C. .. **CMLC 19; DA; DAB; DAC; DAM MST; WLCS**

Congreve, William 1670-1729 **LC 5, 21; DA; DAB; DAC; DAM DRAM, MST, POET; DC 2; WLC**
See also CDBLB 1660-1789; DLB 39, 84

Connell, Evan S(helby), Jr. 1924-**CLC 4, 6, 45;**

Dersonnes, Jacques
See Simenon, Georges (Jacques Christian)
Desai, Anita 1937-**CLC 19, 37, 97; DAB; DAM NOV**
See also CA 81-84; CANR 33, 53; MTCW 1; SATA 63
Desai, Kiran 1971- .... **CLC 119**
See also CA 171
de Saint-Luc, Jean
See Glassco, John
de Saint Roman, Arnaud
See Aragon, Louis
Descartes, Rene 1596-1650 .... **LC 20, 35**
De Sica, Vittorio 1901(?)-1974 .... **CLC 20**
See also CA 117
Desnos, Robert 1900-1945 .... **TCLC 22**
See also CA 121; 151
Destouches, Louis-Ferdinand 1894-1961**C L C 9, 15**
See also Celine, Louis-Ferdinand
See also CA 85-88; CANR 28; MTCW 1
de Tolignac, Gaston
See Griffith, D(avid Lewelyn) W(ark)
Deutsch, Babette 1895-1982 .... **CLC 18**
See also CA 1-4R; 108; CANR 4; DLB 45; SATA 1; SATA-Obit 33
Devenant, William 1606-1649 .... **LC 13**
Devkota, Laxmiprasad 1909-1959 . **TCLC 23**
See also CA 123
De Voto, Bernard (Augustine) 1897-1955 **TCLC 29**
See also CA 113; 160; DLB 9
De Vries, Peter 1910-1993 **CLC 1, 2, 3, 7, 10, 28, 46; DAM NOV**
See also CA 17-20R; 142; CANR 41; DLB 6; DLBY 82; MTCW 1
Dexter, John
See Bradley, Marion Zimmer
Dexter, Martin
See Faust, Frederick (Schiller)
Dexter, Pete 1943- ... **CLC 34, 55; DAM POP**
See also BEST 89:2; CA 127; 131; INT 131; MTCW 1
Diamano, Silmang
See Senghor, Leopold Sedar
Diamond, Neil 1941- .... **CLC 30**
See also CA 108
Diaz del Castillo, Bernal 1496-1584 ... **LC 31**
di Bassetto, Corno
See Shaw, George Bernard
Dick, Philip K(indred) 1928-1982**CLC 10, 30, 72; DAM NOV, POP**
See also AAYA 24; CA 49-52; 106; CANR 2, 16; DLB 8; MTCW 1
Dickens, Charles (John Huffam) 1812-1870 **NCLC 3, 8, 18, 26, 37, 50; DA; DAB; DAC; DAM MST, NOV; SSC 17; WLC**
See also AAYA 23; CDBLB 1832-1890; DLB 21, 55, 70, 159, 166; JRDA; MAICYA; SATA 15
Dickey, James (Lafayette) 1923-1997 **CLC 1, 2, 4, 7, 10, 15, 47, 109; DAM NOV, POET, POP**
See also AITN 1, 2; CA 9-12R; 156; CABS 2; CANR 10, 48, 61; CDALB 1968-1988; DLB 5, 193; DLBD 7; DLBY 82, 93, 96, 97; INT CANR-10; MTCW 1
Dickey, William 1928-1994 .... **CLC 3, 28**
See also CA 9-12R; 145; CANR 24; DLB 5
Dickinson, Charles 1951- .... **CLC 49**
See also CA 128
Dickinson, Emily (Elizabeth) 1830-1886 **NCLC 21; DA; DAB; DAC; DAM MST, POET; PC 1; WLC**
See also AAYA 22; CDALB 1865-1917; DLB 1; SATA 29
Dickinson, Peter (Malcolm) 1927-**CLC 12, 35**
See also AAYA 9; CA 41-44R; CANR 31, 58; CLR 29; DLB 87, 161; JRDA; MAICYA; SATA 5, 62, 95
Dickson, Carr
See Carr, John Dickson
Dickson, Carter
See Carr, John Dickson
Diderot, Denis 1713-1784 .... **LC 26**
Didion, Joan 1934-**CLC 1, 3, 8, 14, 32; DAM NOV**
See also AITN 1; CA 5-8R; CANR 14, 52, 76; CDALB 1968-1988; DLB 2, 173, 185; DLBY 81, 86; MTCW 1
Dietrich, Robert
See Hunt, E(verette) Howard, (Jr.)
Difusa, Pati
See Almodovar, Pedro
Dillard, Annie 1945-...**CLC 9, 60, 115; DAM NOV**
See also AAYA 6; CA 49-52; CANR 3, 43, 62; DLBY 80; MTCW 1; SATA 10
Dillard, R(ichard) H(enry) W(ilde) 1937- **CLC 5**
See also CA 21-24R; CAAS 7; CANR 10; DLB 5
Dillon, Eilis 1920-1994 .... **CLC 17**
See also CA 9-12R; 147; CAAS 3; CANR 4, 38; CLR 26; MAICYA; SATA 2, 74; SATA-Essay 105; SATA-Obit 83
Dimont, Penelope
See Mortimer, Penelope (Ruth)
Dinesen, Isak .... **CLC 10, 29, 95; SSC 7**
See also Blixen, Karen (Christentze Dinesen)
Ding Ling ....**CLC 68**
See also Chiang, Pin-chin
Diphusa, Patty
See Almodovar, Pedro
Disch, Thomas M(ichael) 1940- ... **CLC 7, 36**
See also AAYA 17; CA 21-24R; CAAS 4; CANR 17, 36, 54; CLR 18; DLB 8; MAICYA; MTCW 1; SAAS 15; SATA 92
Disch, Tom
See Disch, Thomas M(ichael)
d'Isly, Georges
See Simenon, Georges (Jacques Christian)
Disraeli, Benjamin 1804-1881 ....**NCLC 2, 39**
See also DLB 21, 55
Ditcum, Steve
See Crumb, R(obert)
Dixon, Paige
See Corcoran, Barbara
Dixon, Stephen 1936- .... **CLC 52; SSC 16**
See also CA 89-92; CANR 17, 40, 54; DLB 130
Doak, Annie
See Dillard, Annie
Dobell, Sydney Thompson 1824-1874 **N C L C 43**
See also DLB 32
Doblin, Alfred .... **TCLC 13**
See also Doeblin, Alfred
Dobrolyubov, Nikolai Alexandrovich 1836-1861 **NCLC 5**
Dobson, Austin 1840-1921 .... **TCLC 79**
See also DLB 35; 144
Dobyns, Stephen 1941-.......................**CLC 37**
See also CA 45-48; CANR 2, 18
Doctorow, E(dgar) L(aurence) 1931- **CLC 6, 11, 15, 18, 37, 44, 65, 113; DAM NOV, POP**
See also AAYA 22; AITN 2; BEST 89:3; CA
45-48; CANR 2, 33, 51, 76; CDALB 1968-1988; DLB 2, 28, 173; DLBY 80; MTCW 1
Dodgson, Charles Lutwidge 1832-1898
See Carroll, Lewis
See also CLR 2; DA; DAB; DAC; DAM MST, NOV, POET; MAICYA; SATA 100; YABC 2
Dodson, Owen (Vincent) 1914-1983 **CLC 79; BLC 1; DAM MULT**
See also BW 1; CA 65-68; 110; CANR 24; DLB 76
Doeblin, Alfred 1878-1957 .... **TCLC 13**
See also Doblin, Alfred
See also CA 110; 141; DLB 66
Doerr, Harriet 1910- .... **CLC 34**
See also CA 117; 122; CANR 47; INT 122
Domecq, H(onorio) Bustos
See Bioy Casares, Adolfo; Borges, Jorge Luis
Domini, Rey
See Lorde, Audre (Geraldine)
Dominique
See Proust, (Valentin-Louis-George-Eugene-) Marcel
Don, A
See Stephen, SirLeslie
Donaldson, Stephen R. 1947- **CLC 46; DAM POP**
See also CA 89-92; CANR 13, 55; INT CANR-13
Donleavy, J(ames) P(atrick) 1926-**CLC 1, 4, 6, 10, 45**
See also AITN 2; CA 9-12R; CANR 24, 49, 62; DLB 6, 173; INT CANR-24; MTCW 1
Donne, John 1572-1631**LC 10, 24; DA; DAB; DAC; DAM MST, POET; PC 1; WLC**
See also CDBLB Before 1660; DLB 121, 151
Donnell, David 1939(?)- .... **CLC 34**
Donoghue, P. S.
See Hunt, E(verette) Howard, (Jr.)
Donoso (Yanez), Jose 1924-1996**CLC 4, 8, 11, 32, 99; DAM MULT; HLC**
See also CA 81-84; 155; CANR 32, 73; DLB 113; HW; MTCW 1
Donovan, John 1928-1992 .... **CLC 35**
See also AAYA 20; CA 97-100; 137; CLR 3; MAICYA; SATA 72; SATA-Brief 29
Don Roberto
See Cunninghame Graham, R(obert) B(ontine)
Doolittle, Hilda 1886-1961**CLC 3, 8, 14, 31, 34, 73; DA; DAC; DAM MST, POET; PC 5; WLC**
See also H. D.
See also CA 97-100; CANR 35; DLB 4, 45; MTCW 1
Dorfman, Ariel 1942- ...... **CLC 48, 77; DAM MULT; HLC**
See also CA 124; 130; CANR 67, 70; HW; INT 130
Dorn, Edward (Merton) 1929-... **CLC 10, 18**
See also CA 93-96; CANR 42; DLB 5; INT 93-96
Dorris, Michael (Anthony) 1945-1997 ..**C L C 109; DAM MULT, NOV**
See also AAYA 20; BEST 90:1; CA 102; 157; CANR 19, 46, 75; DLB 175; NNAL; SATA 75; SATA-Obit 94
Dorris, Michael A.
See Dorris, Michael (Anthony)
Dorsan, Luc
See Simenon, Georges (Jacques Christian)
Dorsange, Jean
See Simenon, Georges (Jacques Christian)
Dos Passos, John (Roderigo) 1896-1970 **C L C 1, 4, 8, 11, 15, 25, 34, 82; DA; DAB; DAC;**

DAM MST, NOV; WLC
See also CA 1-4R; 29-32R; CANR 3; CDALB 1929-1941; DLB 4, 9; DLBD 1, 15; DLBY 96; MTCW 1

Dossage, Jean
See Simenon, Georges (Jacques Christian)

Dostoevsky, Fedor Mikhailovich 1821-1881 **NCLC 2, 7, 21, 33, 43; DA; DAB; DAC; DAM MST, NOV; SSC 2, 33; WLC**

Doughty, Charles M(ontagu) 1843-1926 **TCLC 27**
See also CA 115; DLB 19, 57, 174

Douglas, Ellen .... **CLC 73**
See also Haxton, Josephine Ayres; Williamson, Ellen Douglas

Douglas, Gavin 1475(?)-1522 .... **LC 20**
See also DLB 132

Douglas, George
See Brown, George Douglas

Douglas, Keith (Castellain) 1920-1944 **T C L C 40**
See also CA 160; DLB 27

Douglas, Leonard
See Bradbury, Ray (Douglas)

Douglas, Michael
See Crichton, (John) Michael

Douglas, (George) Norman 1868-1952 **T C L C 68**
See also CA 119; 157; DLB 34, 195

Douglas, William
See Brown, George Douglas

Douglass, Frederick 1817(?)-1895 **NCLC 7, 55; BLC 1; DA; DAC; DAM MST, MULT; WLC**
See also CDALB 1640-1865; DLB 1, 43, 50, 79; SATA 29

Dourado, (Waldomiro Freitas) Autran 1926- **CLC 23, 60**
See also CA 25-28R; CANR 34; DLB 145

Dourado, Waldomiro Autran
See Dourado, (Waldomiro Freitas) Autran

Dove, Rita (Frances) 1952-**CLC 50, 81; BLCS; DAM MULT, POET; PC 6**
See also BW 2; CA 109; CAAS 19; CANR 27, 42, 68, 76; DLB 120

Doveglion
See Villa, Jose Garcia

Dowell, Coleman 1925-1985 .... **CLC 60**
See also CA 25-28R; 117; CANR 10; DLB 130

Dowson, Ernest (Christopher) 1867-1900 **TCLC 4**
See also CA 105; 150; DLB 19, 135

Doyle, A. Conan
See Doyle, Arthur Conan

Doyle, Arthur Conan 1859-1930**TCLC 7; DA; DAB; DAC; DAM MST, NOV; SSC 12; WLC**
See also AAYA 14; CA 104; 122; CDBLB 1890-1914; DLB 18, 70, 156, 178; MTCW 1; SATA 24

Doyle, Conan
See Doyle, Arthur Conan

Doyle, John
See Graves, Robert (von Ranke)

Doyle, Roddy 1958(?)-...................... **CLC 81**
See also AAYA 14; CA 143; CANR 73; DLB 194

Doyle, Sir A. Conan
See Doyle, Arthur Conan

Doyle, Sir Arthur Conan
See Doyle, Arthur Conan

Dr. A
See Asimov, Isaac; Silverstein, Alvin

Drabble, Margaret 1939-**CLC 2, 3, 5, 8, 10, 22, 53; DAB; DAC; DAM MST, NOV, POP**
See also CA 13-16R; CANR 18, 35, 63; CDBLB 1960 to Present; DLB 14, 155; MTCW 1; SATA 48

Drapier, M. B.
See Swift, Jonathan

Drayham, James
See Mencken, H(enry) L(ouis)

Drayton, Michael 1563-1631 ......**LC 8; DAM POET**
See also DLB 121

Dreadstone, Carl
See Campbell, (John) Ramsey

Dreiser, Theodore (Herman Albert) 1871-1945 **TCLC 10, 18, 35, 83; DA; DAC; DAM MST, NOV; SSC 30; WLC**
See also CA 106; 132; CDALB 1865-1917; DLB 9, 12, 102, 137; DLBD 1; MTCW 1

Drexler, Rosalyn 1926-..................... **CLC 2, 6**
See also CA 81-84; CANR 68

Dreyer, Carl Theodor 1889-1968 ......**CLC 16**
See also CA 116

Drieu la Rochelle, Pierre(-Eugene) 1893-1945 **TCLC 21**
See also CA 117; DLB 72

Drinkwater, John 1882-1937 .... **TCLC 57**
See also CA 109; 149; DLB 10, 19, 149

Drop Shot
See Cable, George Washington

Droste-Hulshoff, Annette Freiin von 1797-1848 **NCLC 3**
See also DLB 133

Drummond, Walter
See Silverberg, Robert

Drummond, William Henry 1854-1907 **T C L C 25**
See also CA 160; DLB 92

Drummond de Andrade, Carlos 1902-1987 **CLC 18**
See also Andrade, Carlos Drummond de
See also CA 132; 123

Drury, Allen (Stuart) 1918-1998 ....**CLC 37**
See also CA 57-60; 170; CANR 18, 52; INT CANR-18

Dryden, John 1631-1700**LC 3, 21; DA; DAB; DAC; DAM DRAM, MST, POET; DC 3; PC 25; WLC**
See also CDBLB 1660-1789; DLB 80, 101, 131

Duberman, Martin (Bauml) 1930-......**CLC 8**
See also CA 1-4R; CANR 2, 63

Dubie, Norman (Evans) 1945-...........**CLC 36**
See also CA 69-72; CANR 12; DLB 120

Du Bois, W(illiam) E(dward) B(urghardt) 1868-1963 ..**CLC 1, 2, 13, 64, 96; BLC 1; DA; DAC; DAM MST, MULT, NOV; WLC**
See also BW 1; CA 85-88; CANR 34; CDALB 1865-1917; DLB 47, 50, 91; MTCW 1; SATA 42

Dubus, Andre 1936- **CLC 13, 36, 97; SSC 15**
See also CA 21-24R; CANR 17; DLB 130; INT CANR-17

Duca Minimo
See D'Annunzio, Gabriele

Ducharme, Rejean 1941- ....**CLC 74**
See also CA 165; DLB 60

Duclos, Charles Pinot 1704-1772 ....**LC 1**

Dudek, Louis 1918- ....**CLC 11, 19**
See also CA 45-48; CAAS 14; CANR 1; DLB 88

Duerrenmatt, Friedrich 1921-1990 **CLC 1, 4, 8, 11, 15, 43, 102; DAM DRAM**
See also CA 17-20R; CANR 33; DLB 69, 124;

MTCW 1

Duffy, Bruce 1953(?)- .... **CLC 50**
See also CA 172

Duffy, Maureen 1933- .... **CLC 37**
See also CA 25-28R; CANR 33, 68; DLB 14; MTCW 1

Dugan, Alan 1923- .... **CLC 2, 6**
See also CA 81-84; DLB 5

du Gard, Roger Martin
See Martin du Gard, Roger

Duhamel, Georges 1884-1966 .... **CLC 8**
See also CA 81-84; 25-28R; CANR 35; DLB 65; MTCW 1

Dujardin, Edouard (Emile Louis) 1861-1949 **TCLC 13**
See also CA 109; DLB 123

Dulles, John Foster 1888-1959 .... **TCLC 72**
See also CA 115; 149

Dumas, Alexandre (pere)
See Dumas, Alexandre (Davy de la Pailleterie)

Dumas, Alexandre (Davy de la Pailleterie) 1802-1870 ..**NCLC 11; DA; DAB; DAC; DAM MST, NOV; WLC**
See also DLB 119, 192; SATA 18

Dumas, Alexandre (fils) 1824-1895**NCLC 71; DC 1**
See also AAYA 22; DLB 192

Dumas, Claudine
See Malzberg, Barry N(athaniel)

Dumas, Henry L. 1934-1968 .... **CLC 6, 62**
See also BW 1; CA 85-88; DLB 41

du Maurier, Daphne 1907-1989**CLC 6, 11, 59; DAB; DAC; DAM MST, POP; SSC 18**
See also CA 5-8R; 128; CANR 6, 55; DLB 191; MTCW 1; SATA 27; SATA-Obit 60

Dunbar, Paul Laurence 1872-1906 . **TCLC 2, 12; BLC 1; DA; DAC; DAM MST, MULT, POET; PC 5; SSC 8; WLC**
See also BW 1; CA 104; 124; CDALB 1865-1917; DLB 50, 54, 78; SATA 34

Dunbar, William 1460(?)-1530(?) .... **LC 20**
See also DLB 132, 146

Duncan, Dora Angela
See Duncan, Isadora

Duncan, Isadora 1877(?)-1927 .... **TCLC 68**
See also CA 118; 149

Duncan, Lois 1934- ....**CLC 26**
See also AAYA 4; CA 1-4R; CANR 2, 23, 36; CLR 29; JRDA; MAICYA; SAAS 2; SATA 1, 36, 75

Duncan, Robert (Edward) 1919-1988 **CLC 1, 2, 4, 7, 15, 41, 55; DAM POET; PC 2**
See also CA 9-12R; 124; CANR 28, 62; DLB 5, 16, 193; MTCW 1

Duncan, Sara Jeannette 1861-1922 **TCLC 60**
See also CA 157; DLB 92

Dunlap, William 1766-1839 .... **NCLC 2**
See also DLB 30, 37, 59

Dunn, Douglas (Eaglesham) 1942-**CLC 6, 40**
See also CA 45-48; CANR 2, 33; DLB 40; MTCW 1

Dunn, Katherine (Karen) 1945-........**CLC 71**
See also CA 33-36R; CANR 72

Dunn, Stephen 1939-........................**CLC 36**
See also CA 33-36R; CANR 12, 48, 53; DLB 105

Dunne, Finley Peter 1867-1936 ......**TCLC 28**
See also CA 108; DLB 11, 23

Dunne, John Gregory 1932- ....**CLC 28**
See also CA 25-28R; CANR 14, 50; DLBY 80

Dunsany, Edward John Moreton Drax Plunkett 1878-1957
See Dunsany, Lord

See also CA 104; 148; DLB 10

Dunsany, Lord .... **TCLC 2, 59**
See also Dunsany, Edward John Moreton Drax
Plunkett
See also DLB 77, 153, 156

du Perry, Jean
See Simenon, Georges (Jacques Christian)

Durang, Christopher (Ferdinand) 1949-**C L C 27, 38**
See also CA 105; CANR 50, 76

Duras, Marguerite 1914-1996**CLC 3, 6, 11, 20, 34, 40, 68, 100**
See also CA 25-28R; 151; CANR 50; DLB 83;
MTCW 1

Durban, (Rosa) Pam 1947- .... **CLC 39**
See also CA 123

Durcan, Paul 1944-**CLC 43, 70; DAM POET**
See also CA 134

Durkheim, Emile 1858-1917 .... **TCLC 55**

Durrell, Lawrence (George) 1912-1990 **C L C 1, 4, 6, 8, 13, 27, 41; DAM NOV**
See also CA 9-12R; 132; CANR 40, 77; CDBLB
1945-1960; DLB 15, 27, 204; DLBY 90;
MTCW 1

Durrenmatt, Friedrich
See Duerrenmatt, Friedrich

Dutt, Toru 1856-1877 .... **NCLC 29**

Dwight, Timothy 1752-1817 .... **NCLC 13**
See also DLB 37

Dworkin, Andrea 1946- .... **CLC 43**
See also CA 77-80; CAAS 21; CANR 16, 39,
76; INT CANR-16; MTCW 1

Dwyer, Deanna
See Koontz, Dean R(ay)

Dwyer, K. R.
See Koontz, Dean R(ay)

Dwyer, Thomas A. 1923- .... **CLC 114**
See also CA 115

Dye, Richard
See De Voto, Bernard (Augustine)

Dylan, Bob 1941- .... **CLC 3, 4, 6, 12, 77**
See also CA 41-44R; DLB 16

Eagleton, Terence (Francis) 1943-
See Eagleton, Terry
See also CA 57-60; CANR 7, 23, 68; MTCW 1

Eagleton, Terry .... **CLC 63**
See also Eagleton, Terence (Francis)

Early, Jack
See Scoppettone, Sandra

East, Michael
See West, Morris L(anglo)

Eastaway, Edward
See Thomas, (Philip) Edward

Eastlake, William (Derry) 1917-1997 .**CLC 8**
See also CA 5-8R; 158; CAAS 1; CANR 5, 63;
DLB 6, 206; INT CANR-5

Eastman, Charles A(lexander) 1858-1939
TCLC 55; DAM MULT
See also DLB 175; NNAL; YABC 1

Eberhart, Richard (Ghormley) 1904-**CLC 3, 11, 19, 56; DAM POET**
See also CA 1-4R; CANR 2; CDALB 1941-
1968; DLB 48; MTCW 1

Eberstadt, Fernanda 1960-............... **CLC 39**
See also CA 136; CANR 69

Echegaray (y Eizaguirre), Jose (Maria Waldo)
1832-1916 .... **TCLC 4**
See also CA 104; CANR 32; HW; MTCW 1

Echeverria, (Jose) Esteban (Antonino) 1805-
1851 .... **NCLC 18**

Echo
See Proust, (Valentin-Louis-George-Eugene-)
Marcel

Eckert, Allan W. 1931- .... **CLC 17**
See also AAYA 18; CA 13-16R; CANR 14, 45;
INT CANR-14; SAAS 21; SATA 29, 91;
SATA-Brief 27

Eckhart, Meister 1260(?)-1328(?) ... **CMLC 9**
See also DLB 115

Eckmar, F. R.
See de Hartog, Jan

Eco, Umberto 1932-**CLC 28, 60; DAM NOV, POP**
See also BEST 90:1; CA 77-80; CANR 12, 33,
55; DLB 196; MTCW 1

Eddison, E(ric) R(ucker) 1882-1945**TCLC 15**
See also CA 109; 156

Eddy, Mary (Morse) Baker 1821-1910**T C L C 71**
See also CA 113

Edel, (Joseph) Leon 1907-1997 .. **CLC 29, 34**
See also CA 1-4R; 161; CANR 1, 22; DLB 103;
INT CANR-22

Eden, Emily 1797-1869 .... **NCLC 10**

Edgar, David 1948-... **CLC 42; DAM DRAM**
See also CA 57-60; CANR 12, 61; DLB 13;
MTCW 1

Edgerton, Clyde (Carlyle) 1944- ...... **CLC 39**
See also AAYA 17; CA 118; 134; CANR 64;
INT 134

Edgeworth, Maria 1768-1849 ....**NCLC 1, 51**
See also DLB 116, 159, 163; SATA 21

Edmonds, Paul
See Kuttner, Henry

Edmonds, Walter D(umaux) 1903-1998 **C L C 35**
See also CA 5-8R; CANR 2; DLB 9; MAICYA;
SAAS 4; SATA 1, 27; SATA-Obit 99

Edmondson, Wallace
See Ellison, Harlan (Jay)

Edson, Russell .... **CLC 13**
See also CA 33-36R

Edwards, Bronwen Elizabeth
See Rose, Wendy

Edwards, G(erald) B(asil) 1899-1976**CLC 25**
See also CA 110

Edwards, Gus 1939- .... **CLC 43**
See also CA 108; INT 108

Edwards, Jonathan 1703-1758 .... **LC 7; DA; DAC; DAM MST**
See also DLB 24

Efron, Marina Ivanovna Tsvetaeva
See Tsvetaeva (Efron), Marina (Ivanovna)

Ehle, John (Marsden, Jr.) 1925- .... **CLC 27**
See also CA 9-12R

Ehrenbourg, Ilya (Grigoryevich)
See Ehrenburg, Ilya (Grigoryevich)

Ehrenburg, Ilya (Grigoryevich) 1891-1967
CLC 18, 34, 62
See also CA 102; 25-28R

Ehrenburg, Ilyo (Grigoryevich)
See Ehrenburg, Ilya (Grigoryevich)

Ehrenreich, Barbara 1941- .... **CLC 110**
See also BEST 90:4; CA 73-76; CANR 16, 37,
62; MTCW 1

Eich, Guenter 1907-1972 .... **CLC 15**
See also CA 111; 93-96; DLB 69, 124

Eichendorff, Joseph Freiherr von 1788-1857
NCLC 8
See also DLB 90

Eigner, Larry .... **CLC 9**
See also Eigner, Laurence (Joel)
See also CAAS 23; DLB 5

Eigner, Laurence (Joel) 1927-1996
See Eigner, Larry
See also CA 9-12R; 151; CANR 6; DLB 193

Einstein, Albert 1879-1955 .... **TCLC 65**
See also CA 121; 133; MTCW 1

Eiseley, Loren Corey 1907-1977 ....**CLC 7**
See also AAYA 5; CA 1-4R; 73-76; CANR 6;
DLBD 17

Eisenstadt, Jill 1963- .... **CLC 50**
See also CA 140

Eisenstein, Sergei (Mikhailovich) 1898-1948
TCLC 57
See also CA 114; 149

Eisner, Simon
See Kornbluth, C(yril) M.

Ekeloef, (Bengt) Gunnar 1907-1968 **CLC 27; DAM POET; PC 23**
See also CA 123; 25-28R

Ekelof, (Bengt) Gunnar
See Ekeloef, (Bengt) Gunnar

Ekelund, Vilhelm 1880-1949 .... **TCLC 75**

Ekwensi, C. O. D.
See Ekwensi, Cyprian (Odiatu Duaka)

Ekwensi, Cyprian (Odiatu Duaka) 1921-**CL C 4; BLC 1; DAM MULT**
See also BW 2; CA 29-32R; CANR 18, 42, 74;
DLB 117; MTCW 1; SATA 66

Elaine .... **TCLC 18**
See also Leverson, Ada

El Crummo
See Crumb, R(obert)

Elder, Lonne III 1931-1996 .... **DC 8**
See also BLC 1; BW 1; CA 81-84; 152; CANR
25; DAM MULT; DLB 7, 38, 44

Elia
See Lamb, Charles

Eliade, Mircea 1907-1986 .... **CLC 19**
See also CA 65-68; 119; CANR 30, 62; MTCW
1

Eliot, A. D.
See Jewett, (Theodora) Sarah Orne

Eliot, Alice
See Jewett, (Theodora) Sarah Orne

Eliot, Dan
See Silverberg, Robert

Eliot, George 1819-1880 **NCLC 4, 13, 23, 41, 49; DA; DAB; DAC; DAM MST, NOV; PC 20; WLC**
See also CDBLB 1832-1890; DLB 21, 35, 55

Eliot, John 1604-1690 .... **LC 5**
See also DLB 24

Eliot, T(homas) S(tearns) 1888-1965**CLC 1, 2, 3, 6, 9, 10, 13, 15, 24, 34, 41, 55, 57, 113; DA; DAB; DAC; DAM DRAM, MST, POET; PC 5; WLC**
See also CA 5-8R; 25-28R; CANR 41; CDALB
1929-1941; DLB 7, 10, 45, 63; DLBY 88;
MTCW 1

Elizabeth 1866-1941 .... **TCLC 41**

Elkin, Stanley L(awrence) 1930-1995 **CLC 4, 6, 9, 14, 27, 51, 91; DAM NOV, POP; SSC 12**
See also CA 9-12R; 148; CANR 8, 46; DLB 2,
28; DLBY 80; INT CANR-8; MTCW 1

Elledge, Scott .... **CLC 34**

Elliot, Don
See Silverberg, Robert

Elliott, Don
See Silverberg, Robert

Elliott, George P(aul) 1918-1980 ....**CLC 2**
See also CA 1-4R; 97-100; CANR 2

Elliott, Janice 1931- .... **CLC 47**
See also CA 13-16R; CANR 8, 29; DLB 14

Elliott, Sumner Locke 1917-1991 .... **CLC 38**
See also CA 5-8R; 134; CANR 2, 21

Elliott, William

Author Index

See also CA 69-72; 109; CANR 23; DLB 130;
DLBY 83

Farah, Nuruddin 1945-**CLC 53; BLC 2; DAM
MULT**
See also BW 2; CA 106; DLB 125

Fargue, Leon-Paul 1876(?)-1947 ... **TCLC 11**
See also CA 109

Farigoule, Louis
See Romains, Jules

Farina, Richard 1936(?)-1966 .... **CLC 9**
See also CA 81-84; 25-28R

Farley, Walter (Lorimer) 1915-1989 **CLC 17**
See also CA 17-20R; CANR 8, 29; DLB 22;
JRDA; MAICYA; SATA 2, 43

Farmer, Philip Jose 1918- .... **CLC 1, 19**
See also CA 1-4R; CANR 4, 35; DLB 8; MTCW
1; SATA 93

Farquhar, George 1677-1707 ... **LC 21; DAM
DRAM**
See also DLB 84

Farrell, J(ames) G(ordon) 1935-1979 **CLC 6**
See also CA 73-76; 89-92; CANR 36; DLB 14;
MTCW 1

Farrell, James T(homas) 1904-1979**CLC 1, 4,
8, 11, 66; SSC 28**
See also CA 5-8R; 89-92; CANR 9, 61; DLB 4,
9, 86; DLBD 2; MTCW 1

Farren, Richard J.
See Betjeman, John

Farren, Richard M.
See Betjeman, John

Fassbinder, Rainer Werner 1946-1982**CLC 20**
See also CA 93-96; 106; CANR 31

Fast, Howard (Melvin) 1914- **CLC 23; DAM
NOV**
See also AAYA 16; CA 1-4R; CAAS 18; CANR
1, 33, 54, 75; DLB 9; INT CANR-33; SATA
7

Faulcon, Robert
See Holdstock, Robert P.

Faulkner, William (Cuthbert) 1897-1962**CLC
1, 3, 6, 8, 9, 11, 14, 18, 28, 52, 68; DA; DAB;
DAC; DAM MST, NOV; SSC 1; WLC**
See also AAYA 7; CA 81-84; CANR 33;
CDALB 1929-1941; DLB 9, 11, 44, 102;
DLBD 2; DLBY 86, 97; MTCW 1

Fauset, Jessie Redmon 1884(?)-1961**CLC 19,
54; BLC 2; DAM MULT**
See also BW 1; CA 109; DLB 51

Faust, Frederick (Schiller) 1892-1944(?)
TCLC 49; DAM POP
See also CA 108; 152

Faust, Irvin 1924- .... **CLC 8**
See also CA 33-36R; CANR 28, 67; DLB 2,
28; DLBY 80

Fawkes, Guy
See Benchley, Robert (Charles)

Fearing, Kenneth (Flexner) 1902-1961 . **C L C
51**
See also CA 93-96; CANR 59; DLB 9

Fecamps, Elise
See Creasey, John

Federman, Raymond 1928- .... **CLC 6, 47**
See also CA 17-20R; CAAS 8; CANR 10, 43;
DLBY 80

Federspiel, J(uerg) F. 1931- .... **CLC 42**
See also CA 146

Feiffer, Jules (Ralph) 1929- ..... **CLC 2, 8, 64;
DAM DRAM**
See also AAYA 3; CA 17-20R; CANR 30, 59;
DLB 7, 44; INT CANR-30; MTCW 1; SATA
8, 61

Feige, Hermann Albert Otto Maximilian

See Traven, B.

Feinberg, David B. 1956-1994 .... **CLC 59**
See also CA 135; 147

Feinstein, Elaine 1930- .... **CLC 36**
See also CA 69-72; CAAS 1; CANR 31, 68;
DLB 14, 40; MTCW 1

Feldman, Irving (Mordecai) 1928- ..... **CLC 7**
See also CA 1-4R; CANR 1; DLB 169

Felix-Tchicaya, Gerald
See Tchicaya, Gerald Felix

Fellini, Federico 1920-1993 .... **CLC 16, 85**
See also CA 65-68; 143; CANR 33

Felsen, Henry Gregor 1916- .... **CLC 17**
See also CA 1-4R; CANR 1; SAAS 2; SATA 1

Fenno, Jack
See Calisher, Hortense

Fenollosa, Ernest (Francisco) 1853-1908
TCLC 91

Fenton, James Martin 1949- .... **CLC 32**
See also CA 102; DLB 40

Ferber, Edna 1887-1968 .... **CLC 18, 93**
See also AITN 1; CA 5-8R; 25-28R; CANR 68;
DLB 9, 28, 86; MTCW 1; SATA 7

Ferguson, Helen
See Kavan, Anna

Ferguson, Samuel 1810-1886 .... **NCLC 33**
See also DLB 32

Fergusson, Robert 1750-1774 .... **LC 29**
See also DLB 109

Ferling, Lawrence
See Ferlinghetti, Lawrence (Monsanto)

Ferlinghetti, Lawrence (Monsanto) 1919(?)-
CLC 2, 6, 10, 27, 111; DAM POET; PC 1
See also CA 5-8R; CANR 3, 41, 73; CDALB
1941-1968; DLB 5, 16; MTCW 1

Fernandez, Vicente Garcia Huidobro
See Huidobro Fernandez, Vicente Garcia

Ferrer, Gabriel (Francisco Victor) Miro
See Miro (Ferrer), Gabriel (Francisco Victor)

Ferrier, Susan (Edmonstone) 1782-1854
NCLC 8
See also DLB 116

Ferrigno, Robert 1948(?)- .... **CLC 65**
See also CA 140

Ferron, Jacques 1921-1985 ....**CLC 94; DAC**
See also CA 117; 129; DLB 60

Feuchtwanger, Lion 1884-1958 .... **TCLC 3**
See also CA 104; DLB 66

Feuillet, Octave 1821-1890 .... **NCLC 45**
See also DLB 192

Feydeau, Georges (Leon Jules Marie) 1862-
1921 .... **TCLC 22; DAM DRAM**
See also CA 113; 152; DLB 192

Fichte, Johann Gottlieb 1762-1814**NCLC 62**
See also DLB 90

Ficino, Marsilio 1433-1499 .... **LC 12**

Fiedeler, Hans
See Doeblin, Alfred

Fiedler, Leslie A(aron) 1917- . **CLC 4, 13, 24**
See also CA 9-12R; CANR 7, 63; DLB 28, 67;
MTCW 1

Field, Andrew 1938- .... **CLC 44**
See also CA 97-100; CANR 25

Field, Eugene 1850-1895 .... **NCLC 3**
See also DLB 23, 42, 140; DLBD 13; MAICYA;
SATA 16

Field, Gans T.
See Wellman, Manly Wade

Field, Michael 1915-1971 .... **TCLC 43**
See also CA 29-32R

Field, Peter
See Hobson, Laura Z(ametkin)

Fielding, Henry 1707-1754 ..... **LC 1, 46; DA;**

**DAB; DAC; DAM DRAM, MST, NOV;
WLC**
See also CDBLB 1660-1789; DLB 39, 84, 101

Fielding, Sarah 1710-1768 .... **LC 1, 44**
See also DLB 39

Fields, W. C. 1880-1946 .... **TCLC 80**
See also DLB 44

Fierstein, Harvey (Forbes) 1954- .... **CLC 33;
DAM DRAM, POP**
See also CA 123; 129

Figes, Eva 1932- .... **CLC 31**
See also CA 53-56; CANR 4, 44; DLB 14

Finch, Anne 1661-1720 .... **LC 3; PC 21**
See also DLB 95

Finch, Robert (Duer Claydon) 1900- **CLC 18**
See also CA 57-60; CANR 9, 24, 49; DLB 88

Findley, Timothy 1930- . **CLC 27, 102; DAC;
DAM MST**
See also CA 25-28R; CANR 12, 42, 69; DLB
53

Fink, William
See Mencken, H(enry) L(ouis)

Firbank, Louis 1942-
See Reed, Lou
See also CA 117

Firbank, (Arthur Annesley) Ronald 1886-1926
TCLC 1
See also CA 104; DLB 36

Fisher, Dorothy (Frances) Canfield 1879-1958
TCLC 87
See also CA 114; 136; DLB 9, 102; MAICYA;
YABC 1

Fisher, M(ary) F(rances) K(ennedy) 1908-1992
CLC 76, 87
See also CA 77-80; 138; CANR 44

Fisher, Roy 1930- .... **CLC 25**
See also CA 81-84; CAAS 10; CANR 16; DLB
40

Fisher, Rudolph 1897-1934**TCLC 11; BLC 2;
DAM MULT; SSC 25**
See also BW 1; CA 107; 124; DLB 51, 102

Fisher, Vardis (Alvero) 1895-1968 ...... **CLC 7**
See also CA 5-8R; 25-28R; CANR 68; DLB 9,
206

Fiske, Tarleton
See Bloch, Robert (Albert)

Fitch, Clarke
See Sinclair, Upton (Beall)

Fitch, John IV
See Cormier, Robert (Edmund)

Fitzgerald, Captain Hugh
See Baum, L(yman) Frank

FitzGerald, Edward 1809-1883 .... **NCLC 9**
See also DLB 32

Fitzgerald, F(rancis) Scott (Key) 1896-1940
**TCLC 1, 6, 14, 28, 55; DA; DAB; DAC;
DAM MST, NOV; SSC 6, 31; WLC**
See also AAYA 24; AITN 1; CA 110; 123;
CDALB 1917-1929; DLB 4, 9, 86; DLBD 1,
15, 16; DLBY 81, 96; MTCW 1

Fitzgerald, Penelope 1916- ... **CLC 19, 51, 61**
See also CA 85-88; CAAS 10; CANR 56; DLB
14, 194

Fitzgerald, Robert (Stuart) 1910-1985**CLC 39**
See also CA 1-4R; 114; CANR 1; DLBY 80

FitzGerald, Robert D(avid) 1902-1987**CLC 19**
See also CA 17-20R

Fitzgerald, Zelda (Sayre) 1900-1948**TCLC 52**
See also CA 117; 126; DLBY 84

Flanagan, Thomas (James Bonner) 1923-
CLC 25, 52
See also CA 108; CANR 55; DLBY 80; INT
108; MTCW 1

DRAM, NOV, POP
See also CA 69-72; CANR 3, 31; INT CANR-31; MTCW 1

French, Paul
See Asimov, Isaac

Freneau, Philip Morin 1752-1832 ... **NCLC 1**
See also DLB 37, 43

Freud, Sigmund 1856-1939 .... **TCLC 52**
See also CA 115; 133; CANR 69; MTCW 1

Friedan, Betty (Naomi) 1921- .... **CLC 74**
See also CA 65-68; CANR 18, 45, 74; MTCW 1

Friedlander, Saul 1932- .... **CLC 90**
See also CA 117; 130; CANR 72

Friedman, B(ernard) H(arper) 1926- .**CLC 7**
See also CA 1-4R; CANR 3, 48

Friedman, Bruce Jay 1930- ...... **CLC 3, 5, 56**
See also CA 9-12R; CANR 25, 52; DLB 2, 28; INT CANR-25

Friel, Brian 1929- . **CLC 5, 42, 59, 115; DC 8**
See also CA 21-24R; CANR 33, 69; DLB 13; MTCW 1

Friis-Baastad, Babbis Ellinor 1921-1970**C L C 12**
See also CA 17-20R; 134; SATA 7

Frisch, Max (Rudolf) 1911-1991**CLC 3, 9, 14, 18, 32, 44; DAM DRAM, NOV**
See also CA 85-88; 134; CANR 32, 74; DLB 69, 124; MTCW 1

Fromentin, Eugene (Samuel Auguste) 1820-1876 .... **NCLC 10**
See also DLB 123

Frost, Frederick
See Faust, Frederick (Schiller)

Frost, Robert (Lee) 1874-1963**CLC 1, 3, 4, 9, 10, 13, 15, 26, 34, 44; DA; DAB; DAC; DAM MST, POET; PC 1; WLC**
See also AAYA 21; CA 89-92; CANR 33; CDALB 1917-1929; DLB 54; DLBD 7; MTCW 1; SATA 14

Froude, James Anthony 1818-1894 **NCLC 43**
See also DLB 18, 57, 144

Froy, Herald
See Waterhouse, Keith (Spencer)

Fry, Christopher 1907- **CLC 2, 10, 14; DAM DRAM**
See also CA 17-20R; CAAS 23; CANR 9, 30, 74; DLB 13; MTCW 1; SATA 66

Frye, (Herman) Northrop 1912-1991**CLC 24, 70**
See also CA 5-8R; 133; CANR 8, 37; DLB 67, 68; MTCW 1

Fuchs, Daniel 1909-1993 .... **CLC 8, 22**
See also CA 81-84; 142; CAAS 5; CANR 40; DLB 9, 26, 28; DLBY 93

Fuchs, Daniel 1934- .... **CLC 34**
See also CA 37-40R; CANR 14, 48

Fuentes, Carlos 1928-**CLC 3, 8, 10, 13, 22, 41, 60, 113; DA; DAB; DAC; DAM MST, MULT, NOV; HLC; SSC 24; WLC**
See also AAYA 4; AITN 2; CA 69-72; CANR 10, 32, 68; DLB 113; HW; MTCW 1

Fuentes, Gregorio Lopez y
See Lopez y Fuentes, Gregorio

Fugard, (Harold) Athol 1932-**CLC 5, 9, 14, 25, 40, 80; DAM DRAM; DC 3**
See also AAYA 17; CA 85-88; CANR 32, 54; MTCW 1

Fugard, Sheila 1932- .... **CLC 48**
See also CA 125

Fuller, Charles (H., Jr.) 1939-**CLC 25; BLC 2; DAM DRAM, MULT; DC 1**
See also BW 2; CA 108; 112; DLB 38; INT 112;

MTCW 1

Fuller, John (Leopold) 1937- .... **CLC 62**
See also CA 21-24R; CANR 9, 44; DLB 40

Fuller, Margaret .... **NCLC 5, 50**
See also Ossoli, Sarah Margaret (Fuller marchesa d')

Fuller, Roy (Broadbent) 1912-1991**CLC 4, 28**
See also CA 5-8R; 135; CAAS 10; CANR 53; DLB 15, 20; SATA 87

Fulton, Alice 1952- .... **CLC 52**
See also CA 116; CANR 57; DLB 193

Furphy, Joseph 1843-1912 .... **TCLC 25**
See also CA 163

Fussell, Paul 1924- .... **CLC 74**
See also BEST 90:1; CA 17-20R; CANR 8, 21, 35, 69; INT CANR-21; MTCW 1

Futabatei, Shimei 1864-1909 .... **TCLC 44**
See also CA 162; DLB 180

Futrelle, Jacques 1875-1912 .... **TCLC 19**
See also CA 113; 155

Gaboriau, Emile 1835-1873 .... **NCLC 14**

Gadda, Carlo Emilio 1893-1973 .... **CLC 11**
See also CA 89-92; DLB 177

Gaddis, William 1922-1998**CLC 1, 3, 6, 8, 10, 19, 43, 86**
See also CA 17-20R; 172; CANR 21, 48; DLB 2; MTCW 1

Gage, Walter
See Inge, William (Motter)

Gaines, Ernest J(ames) 1933- **CLC 3, 11, 18, 86; BLC 2; DAM MULT**
See also AAYA 18; AITN 1; BW 2; CA 9-12R; CANR 6, 24, 42, 75; CDALB 1968-1988; DLB 2, 33, 152; DLBY 80; MTCW 1; SATA 86

Gaitskill, Mary 1954- .... **CLC 69**
See also CA 128; CANR 61

Galdos, Benito Perez
See Perez Galdos, Benito

Gale, Zona 1874-1938**TCLC 7; DAM DRAM**
See also CA 105; 153; DLB 9, 78

Galeano, Eduardo (Hughes) 1940- ... **CLC 72**
See also CA 29-32R; CANR 13, 32; HW

Galiano, Juan Valera y Alcala
See Valera y Alcala-Galiano, Juan

Galilei, Galileo 1546-1642 .... **LC 45**

Gallagher, Tess 1943- ...... **CLC 18, 63; DAM POET; PC 9**
See also CA 106; DLB 120

Gallant, Mavis 1922- ... **CLC 7, 18, 38; DAC; DAM MST; SSC 5**
See also CA 69-72; CANR 29, 69; DLB 53; MTCW 1

Gallant, Roy A(rthur) 1924- .... **CLC 17**
See also CA 5-8R; CANR 4, 29, 54; CLR 30; MAICYA; SATA 4, 68

Gallico, Paul (William) 1897-1976 ..... **CLC 2**
See also AITN 1; CA 5-8R; 69-72; CANR 23; DLB 9, 171; MAICYA; SATA 13

Gallo, Max Louis 1932- .... **CLC 95**
See also CA 85-88

Gallois, Lucien
See Desnos, Robert

Gallup, Ralph
See Whitemore, Hugh (John)

Galsworthy, John 1867-1933**TCLC 1, 45; DA; DAB; DAC; DAM DRAM, MST, NOV; SSC 22; WLC**
See also CA 104; 141; CANR 75; CDBLB 1890-1914; DLB 10, 34, 98, 162; DLBD 16

Galt, John 1779-1839 .... **NCLC 1**
See also DLB 99, 116, 159

Galvin, James 1951- .... **CLC 38**

See also CA 108; CANR 26

Gamboa, Federico 1864-1939 .... **TCLC 36**
See also CA 167

Gandhi, M. K.
See Gandhi, Mohandas Karamchand

Gandhi, Mahatma
See Gandhi, Mohandas Karamchand

Gandhi, Mohandas Karamchand 1869-1948 **TCLC 59; DAM MULT**
See also CA 121; 132; MTCW 1

Gann, Ernest Kellogg 1910-1991 ..... **CLC 23**
See also AITN 1; CA 1-4R; 136; CANR 1

Garcia, Cristina 1958- .... **CLC 76**
See also CA 141; CANR 73

Garcia Lorca, Federico 1898-1936**TCLC 1, 7, 49; DA; DAB; DAC; DAM DRAM, MST, MULT, POET; DC 2; HLC; PC 3; WLC**
See also CA 104; 131; DLB 108; HW; MTCW 1

Garcia Marquez, Gabriel (Jose) 1928-**CLC 2, 3, 8, 10, 15, 27, 47, 55, 68; DA; DAB; DAC; DAM MST, MULT, NOV, POP; HLC; SSC 8; WLC**
See also AAYA 3; BEST 89:1, 90:4; CA 33-36R; CANR 10, 28, 50, 75; DLB 113; HW; MTCW 1

Gard, Janice
See Latham, Jean Lee

Gard, Roger Martin du
See Martin du Gard, Roger

Gardam, Jane 1928- .... **CLC 43**
See also CA 49-52; CANR 2, 18, 33, 54; CLR 12; DLB 14, 161; MAICYA; MTCW 1; SAAS 9; SATA 39, 76; SATA-Brief 28

Gardner, Herb(ert) 1934- .... **CLC 44**
See also CA 149

Gardner, John (Champlin), Jr. 1933-1982 **CLC 2, 3, 5, 7, 8, 10, 18, 28, 34; DAM NOV, POP; SSC 7**
See also AITN 1; CA 65-68; 107; CANR 33, 73; DLB 2; DLBY 82; MTCW 1; SATA 40; SATA-Obit 31

Gardner, John (Edmund) 1926-**CLC 30; DAM POP**
See also CA 103; CANR 15, 69; MTCW 1

Gardner, Miriam
See Bradley, Marion Zimmer

Gardner, Noel
See Kuttner, Henry

Gardons, S. S.
See Snodgrass, W(illiam) D(e Witt)

Garfield, Leon 1921-1996 .... **CLC 12**
See also AAYA 8; CA 17-20R; 152; CANR 38, 41; CLR 21; DLB 161; JRDA; MAICYA; SATA 1, 32, 76; SATA-Obit 90

Garland, (Hannibal) Hamlin 1860-1940 **TCLC 3; SSC 18**
See also CA 104; DLB 12, 71, 78, 186

Garneau, (Hector de) Saint-Denys 1912-1943 **TCLC 13**
See also CA 111; DLB 88

Garner, Alan 1934-**CLC 17; DAB; DAM POP**
See also AAYA 18; CA 73-76; CANR 15, 64; CLR 20; DLB 161; MAICYA; MTCW 1; SATA 18, 69

Garner, Hugh 1913-1979 .... **CLC 13**
See also CA 69-72; CANR 31; DLB 68

Garnett, David 1892-1981 .... **CLC 3**
See also CA 5-8R; 103; CANR 17; DLB 34

Garos, Stephanie
See Katz, Steve

Garrett, George (Palmer) 1929-**CLC 3, 11, 51; SSC 30**

See also CA 1-4R; CAAS 5; CANR 1, 42, 67; DLB 2, 5, 130, 152; DLBY 83

Garrick, David 1717-1779 ....**LC 15; DAM DRAM**
See also DLB 84

Garrigue, Jean 1914-1972 .... **CLC 2, 8**
See also CA 5-8R; 37-40R; CANR 20

Garrison, Frederick
See Sinclair, Upton (Beall)

Garth, Will
See Hamilton, Edmond; Kuttner, Henry

Garvey, Marcus (Moziah, Jr.) 1887-1940
TCLC 41; BLC 2; DAM MULT
See also BW 1; CA 120; 124

Gary, Romain .... **CLC 25**
See also Kacew, Romain
See also DLB 83

Gascar, Pierre .... **CLC 11**
See also Fournier, Pierre

Gascoyne, David (Emery) 1916- ...... **CLC 45**
See also CA 65-68; CANR 10, 28, 54; DLB 20; MTCW 1

Gaskell, Elizabeth Cleghorn 1810-1865**NCLC 70; DAB; DAM MST; SSC 25**
See also CDBLB 1832-1890; DLB 21, 144, 159

Gass, William H(oward) 1924-**CLC 1, 2, 8, 11, 15, 39; SSC 12**
See also CA 17-20R; CANR 30, 71; DLB 2; MTCW 1

Gasset, Jose Ortega y
See Ortega y Gasset, Jose

Gates, Henry Louis, Jr. 1950-**CLC 65; BLCS; DAM MULT**
See also BW 2; CA 109; CANR 25, 53, 75; DLB 67

Gautier, Theophile 1811-1872 .. **NCLC 1, 59; DAM POET; PC 18; SSC 20**
See also DLB 119

Gawsworth, John
See Bates, H(erbert) E(rnest)

Gay, John 1685-1732 ... **LC 49; DAM DRAM**
See also DLB 84, 95

Gay, Oliver
See Gogarty, Oliver St. John

Gaye, Marvin (Penze) 1939-1984 .... **CLC 26**
See also CA 112

Gebler, Carlo (Ernest) 1954- .... **CLC 39**
See also CA 119; 133

Gee, Maggie (Mary) 1948- .... **CLC 57**
See also CA 130; DLB 207

Gee, Maurice (Gough) 1931-............ **CLC 29**
See also CA 97-100; CANR 67; CLR 56; SATA 46, 101

Gelbart, Larry (Simon) 1923- .... **CLC 21, 61**
See also CA 73-76; CANR 45

Gelber, Jack 1932- .... **CLC 1, 6, 14, 79**
See also CA 1-4R; CANR 2; DLB 7

Gellhorn, Martha (Ellis) 1908-1998 **CLC 14, 60**
See also CA 77-80; 164; CANR 44; DLBY 82

Genet, Jean 1910-1986**CLC 1, 2, 5, 10, 14, 44, 46; DAM DRAM**
See also CA 13-16R; CANR 18; DLB 72; DLBY 86; MTCW 1

Gent, Peter 1942- .... **CLC 29**
See also AITN 1; CA 89-92; DLBY 82

Gentlewoman in New England, A
See Bradstreet, Anne

Gentlewoman in Those Parts, A
See Bradstreet, Anne

George, Jean Craighead 1919- .... **CLC 35**
See also AAYA 8; CA 5-8R; CANR 25; CLR 1; DLB 52; JRDA; MAICYA; SATA 2, 68

George, Stefan (Anton) 1868-1933**TCLC 2, 14**
See also CA 104

Georges, Georges Martin
See Simenon, Georges (Jacques Christian)

Gerhardi, William Alexander
See Gerhardie, William Alexander

Gerhardie, William Alexander 1895-1977
CLC 5
See also CA 25-28R; 73-76; CANR 18; DLB 36

Gerstler, Amy 1956- .... **CLC 70**
See also CA 146

Gertler, T. .... **CLC 34**
See also CA 116; 121; INT 121

Ghalib ....**NCLC 39**
See also Ghalib, Hsadullah Khan

Ghalib, Hsadullah Khan 1797-1869
See Ghalib
See also DAM POET

Ghelderode, Michel de 1898-1962**CLC 6, 11; DAM DRAM**
See also CA 85-88; CANR 40, 77

Ghiselin, Brewster 1903- .... **CLC 23**
See also CA 13-16R; CAAS 10; CANR 13

Ghose, Aurabinda 1872-1950 .... **TCLC 63**
See also CA 163

Ghose, Zulfikar 1935- .... **CLC 42**
See also CA 65-68; CANR 67

Ghosh, Amitav 1956-.......................... **CLC 44**
See also CA 147

Giacosa, Giuseppe 1847-1906 .... **TCLC 7**
See also CA 104

Gibb, Lee
See Waterhouse, Keith (Spencer)

Gibbon, Lewis Grassic .... **TCLC 4**
See also Mitchell, James Leslie

Gibbons, Kaye 1960-**CLC 50, 88; DAM POP**
See also CA 151; CANR 75

Gibran, Kahlil 1883-1931 . **TCLC 1, 9; DAM POET, POP; PC 9**
See also CA 104; 150

Gibran, Khalil
See Gibran, Kahlil

Gibson, William 1914- .. **CLC 23; DA; DAB; DAC; DAM DRAM, MST**
See also CA 9-12R; CANR 9, 42, 75; DLB 7; SATA 66

Gibson, William (Ford) 1948- ... **CLC 39, 63; DAM POP**
See also AAYA 12; CA 126; 133; CANR 52

Gide, Andre (Paul Guillaume) 1869-1951
TCLC 5, 12, 36; DA; DAB; DAC; DAM MST, NOV; SSC 13; WLC
See also CA 104; 124; DLB 65; MTCW 1

Gifford, Barry (Colby) 1946- .... **CLC 34**
See also CA 65-68; CANR 9, 30, 40

Gilbert, Frank
See De Voto, Bernard (Augustine)

Gilbert, W(illiam) S(chwenck) 1836-1911
TCLC 3; DAM DRAM, POET
See also CA 104; 173; SATA 36

Gilbreth, Frank B., Jr. 1911-............. **CLC 17**
See also CA 9-12R; SATA 2

Gilchrist, Ellen 1935-**CLC 34, 48; DAM POP; SSC 14**
See also CA 113; 116; CANR 41, 61; DLB 130; MTCW 1

Giles, Molly 1942- .... **CLC 39**
See also CA 126

Gill, Eric 1882-1940 .... **TCLC 85**

Gill, Patrick
See Creasey, John

Gilliam, Terry (Vance) 1940- ....**CLC 21**
See also Monty Python
See also AAYA 19; CA 108; 113; CANR 35; INT 113

Gillian, Jerry
See Gilliam, Terry (Vance)

Gilliatt, Penelope (Ann Douglass) 1932-1993
CLC 2, 10, 13, 53
See also AITN 2; CA 13-16R; 141; CANR 49; DLB 14

Gilman, Charlotte (Anna) Perkins (Stetson) 1860-1935 .... **TCLC 9, 37; SSC 13**
See also CA 106; 150

Gilmour, David 1949-........................**CLC 35**
See also CA 138, 147

Gilpin, William 1724-1804 .... **NCLC 30**

Gilray, J. D.
See Mencken, H(enry) L(ouis)

Gilroy, Frank D(aniel) 1925- ....**CLC 2**
See also CA 81-84; CANR 32, 64; DLB 7

Gilstrap, John 1957(?)- .... **CLC 99**
See also CA 160

Ginsberg, Allen 1926-1997**CLC 1, 2, 3, 4, 6, 13, 36, 69, 109; DA; DAB; DAC; DAM MST, POET; PC 4; WLC**
See also AITN 1; CA 1-4R; 157; CANR 2, 41, 63; CDALB 1941-1968; DLB 5, 16, 169; MTCW 1

Ginzburg, Natalia 1916-1991**CLC 5, 11, 54, 70**
See also CA 85-88; 135; CANR 33; DLB 177; MTCW 1

Giono, Jean 1895-1970 .... **CLC 4, 11**
See also CA 45-48; 29-32R; CANR 2, 35; DLB 72; MTCW 1

Giovanni, Nikki 1943- **CLC 2, 4, 19, 64, 117; BLC 2; DA; DAB; DAC; DAM MST, MULT, POET; PC 19; WLCS**
See also AAYA 22; AITN 1; BW 2; CA 29-32R; CAAS 6; CANR 18, 41, 60; CLR 6; DLB 5, 41; INT CANR-18; MAICYA; MTCW 1; SATA 24

Giovene, Andrea 1904- .... **CLC 7**
See also CA 85-88

Gippius, Zinaida (Nikolayevna) 1869-1945
See Hippius, Zinaida
See also CA 106

Giraudoux, (Hippolyte) Jean 1882-1944
TCLC 2, 7; DAM DRAM
See also CA 104; DLB 65

Gironella, Jose Maria 1917-..............**CLC 11**
See also CA 101

Gissing, George (Robert) 1857-1903**TCLC 3, 24, 47**
See also CA 105; 167; DLB 18, 135, 184

Giurlani, Aldo
See Palazzeschi, Aldo

Gladkov, Fyodor (Vasilyevich) 1883-1958
TCLC 27
See also CA 170

Glanville, Brian (Lester) 1931- ....**CLC 6**
See also CA 5-8R; CAAS 9; CANR 3, 70; DLB 15, 139; SATA 42

Glasgow, Ellen (Anderson Gholson) 1873-1945
TCLC 2, 7
See also CA 104; 164; DLB 9, 12

Glaspell, Susan 1882(?)-1948**TCLC 55; DC 10**
See also CA 110; 154; DLB 7, 9, 78; YABC 2

Glassco, John 1909-1981 .... **CLC 9**
See also CA 13-16R; 102; CANR 15; DLB 68

Glasscock, Amnesia
See Steinbeck, John (Ernst)

Glasser, Ronald J. 1940(?)- ....**CLC 37**

Glassman, Joyce
See Johnson, Joyce

Grau, Shirley Ann 1929- ..**CLC 4, 9; SSC 15**
See also CA 89-92; CANR 22, 69; DLB 2; INT
CANR-22; MTCW 1
Gravel, Fern
See Hall, James Norman
Graver, Elizabeth 1964- .... **CLC 70**
See also CA 135; CANR 71
Graves, Richard Perceval 1945- ...... **CLC 44**
See also CA 65-68; CANR 9, 26, 51
Graves, Robert (von Ranke) 1895-1985 **C L C
1, 2, 6, 11, 39, 44, 45; DAB; DAC; DAM
MST, POET; PC 6**
See also CA 5-8R; 117; CANR 5, 36; CDBLB
1914-1945; DLB 20, 100, 191; DLBD 18;
DLBY 85; MTCW 1; SATA 45
Graves, Valerie
See Bradley, Marion Zimmer
Gray, Alasdair (James) 1934- .... **CLC 41**
See also CA 126; CANR 47, 69; DLB 194; INT
126; MTCW 1
Gray, Amlin 1946- .... **CLC 29**
See also CA 138
Gray, Francine du Plessix 1930- ..... **CLC 22;
DAM NOV**
See also BEST 90:3; CA 61-64; CAAS 2;
CANR 11, 33, 75; INT CANR-11; MTCW 1
Gray, John (Henry) 1866-1934 ...... **TCLC 19**
See also CA 119; 162
Gray, Simon (James Holliday) 1936- **CLC 9,
14, 36**
See also AITN 1; CA 21-24R; CAAS 3; CANR
32, 69; DLB 13; MTCW 1
Gray, Spalding 1941-**CLC 49,112; DAM POP;
DC 7**
See also CA 128; CANR 74
Gray, Thomas 1716-1771**LC 4, 40; DA; DAB;
DAC; DAM MST; PC 2; WLC**
See also CDBLB 1660-1789; DLB 109
Grayson, David
See Baker, Ray Stannard
Grayson, Richard (A.) 1951- .... **CLC 38**
See also CA 85-88; CANR 14, 31, 57
Greeley, Andrew M(oran) 1928- ..... **CLC 28;
DAM POP**
See also CA 5-8R; CAAS 7; CANR 7, 43, 69;
MTCW 1
Green, Anna Katharine 1846-1935 **TCLC 63**
See also CA 112; 159; DLB 202
Green, Brian
See Card, Orson Scott
Green, Hannah
See Greenberg, Joanne (Goldenberg)
Green, Hannah 1927(?)-1996 ....**CLC 3**
See also CA 73-76; CANR 59
Green, Henry 1905-1973 .... **CLC 2, 13, 97**
See also Yorke, Henry Vincent
See also DLB 15
Green, Julian (Hartridge) 1900-1998
See Green, Julien
See also CA 21-24R; 169; CANR 33; DLB 4,
72; MTCW 1
Green, Julien .... **CLC 3, 11, 77**
See also Green, Julian (Hartridge)
Green, Paul (Eliot) 1894-1981**CLC 25; DAM
DRAM**
See also AITN 1; CA 5-8R; 103; CANR 3; DLB
7, 9; DLBY 81
Greenberg, Ivan 1908-1973
See Rahv, Philip
See also CA 85-88
Greenberg, Joanne (Goldenberg) 1932-**C L C
7, 30**
See also AAYA 12; CA 5-8R; CANR 14, 32

69; SATA 25
Greenberg, Richard 1959(?)- .... **CLC 57**
See also CA 138
Greene, Bette 1934- .... **CLC 30**
See also AAYA 7; CA 53-56; CANR 4; CLR 2;
JRDA; MAICYA; SAAS 16; SATA 8, 102
Greene, Gael ....**CLC 8**
See also CA 13-16R; CANR 10
Greene, Graham (Henry) 1904-1991**CLC 1, 3,
6, 9, 14, 18, 27, 37, 70, 72; DA; DAB; DAC;
DAM MST, NOV; SSC 29; WLC**
See also AITN 2; CA 13-16R; 133; CANR 35,
61; CDBLB 1945-1960; DLB 13, 15, 77,
100, 162, 201, 204; DLBY 91; MTCW 1;
SATA 20
Greene, Robert 1558-1592 .... **LC 41**
See also DLB 62, 167
Greer, Richard
See Silverberg, Robert
Gregor, Arthur 1923- ....**CLC 9**
See also CA 25-28R; CAAS 10; CANR 11;
SATA 36
Gregor, Lee
See Pohl, Frederik
Gregory, Isabella Augusta (Persse) 1852-1932
TCLC 1
See also CA 104; DLB 10
Gregory, J. Dennis
See Williams, John A(lfred)
Grendon, Stephen
See Derleth, August (William)
Grenville, Kate 1950- .... **CLC 61**
See also CA 118; CANR 53
Grenville, Pelham
See Wodehouse, P(elham) G(renville)
Greve, Felix Paul (Berthold Friedrich) 1879-
1948
See Grove, Frederick Philip
See also CA 104; 141; DAC; DAM MST
Grey, Zane 1872-1939 .. **TCLC 6; DAM POP**
See also CA 104; 132; DLB 9; MTCW 1
Grieg, (Johan) Nordahl (Brun) 1902-1943
TCLC 10
See also CA 107
Grieve, C(hristopher) M(urray) 1892-1978
CLC 11, 19; DAM POET
See also MacDiarmid, Hugh; Pteleon
See also CA 5-8R; 85-88; CANR 33; MTCW 1
Griffin, Gerald 1803-1840 .... **NCLC 7**
See also DLB 159
Griffin, John Howard 1920-1980 .... **CLC 68**
See also AITN 1; CA 1-4R; 101; CANR 2
Griffin, Peter 1942- .... **CLC 39**
See also CA 136
Griffith, D(avid Lewelyn) W(ark) 1875(?)-1948
TCLC 68
See also CA 119; 150
Griffith, Lawrence
See Griffith, D(avid Lewelyn) W(ark)
Griffiths, Trevor 1935- .... **CLC 13, 52**
See also CA 97-100; CANR 45; DLB 13
Griggs, Sutton Elbert 1872-1930(?)**TCLC 77**
See also CA 123; DLB 50
Grigson, Geoffrey (Edward Harvey) 1905-1985
CLC 7, 39
See also CA 25-28R; 118; CANR 20, 33; DLB
27; MTCW 1
Grillparzer, Franz 1791-1872 .... **NCLC 1**
See also DLB 133
Grimble, Reverend Charles James
See Eliot, T(homas) S(tearns)
Grimke, Charlotte L(ottie) Forten 1837(?)-1914
See Forten, Charlotte L.

See also BW 1; CA 117; 124; DAM MULT,
POET
Grimm, Jacob Ludwig Karl 1785-1863**NCLC
3**
See also DLB 90; MAICYA; SATA 22
Grimm, Wilhelm Karl 1786-1859 ....**NCLC 3**
See also DLB 90; MAICYA; SATA 22
Grimmelshausen, Johann Jakob Christoffel von
1621-1676 .... **LC 6**
See also DLB 168
Grindel, Eugene 1895-1952
See Eluard, Paul
See also CA 104
Grisham, John 1955- .....**CLC 84; DAM POP**
See also AAYA 14; CA 138; CANR 47, 69
Grossman, David 1954- .... **CLC 67**
See also CA 138
Grossman, Vasily (Semenovich) 1905-1964
CLC 41
See also CA 124; 130; MTCW 1
Grove, Frederick Philip .... **TCLC 4**
See also Greve, Felix Paul (Berthold Friedrich)
See also DLB 92
Grubb
See Crumb, R(obert)
Grumbach, Doris (Isaac) 1918-**CLC 13, 22, 64**
See also CA 5-8R; CAAS 2; CANR 9, 42, 70;
INT CANR-9
Grundtvig, Nicolai Frederik Severin 1783-1872
NCLC 1
Grunge
See Crumb, R(obert)
Grunwald, Lisa 1959- .... **CLC 44**
See also CA 120
Guare, John 1938- . **CLC 8, 14, 29, 67; DAM
DRAM**
See also CA 73-76; CANR 21, 69; DLB 7;
MTCW 1
Gudjonsson, Halldor Kiljan 1902-1998
See Laxness, Halldor
See also CA 103; 164
Guenter, Erich
See Eich, Guenter
Guest, Barbara 1920- .... **CLC 34**
See also CA 25-28R; CANR 11, 44; DLB 5,
193
Guest, Judith (Ann) 1936- **CLC 8, 30; DAM
NOV, POP**
See also AAYA 7; CA 77-80; CANR 15, 75;
INT CANR-15; MTCW 1
Guevara, Che .... **CLC 87; HLC**
See also Guevara (Serna), Ernesto
Guevara (Serna), Ernesto 1928-1967
See Guevara, Che
See also CA 127; 111; CANR 56; DAM MULT;
HW
Guicciardini, Francesco 1483-1540 .... **LC 49**
Guild, Nicholas M. 1944- .... **CLC 33**
See also CA 93-96
Guillemin, Jacques
See Sartre, Jean-Paul
Guillen, Jorge 1893-1984 .... **CLC 11; DAM
MULT, POET**
See also CA 89-92; 112; DLB 108; HW
Guillen, Nicolas (Cristobal) 1902-1989 .**C L C
48, 79; BLC 2; DAM MST, MULT, POET;
HLC; PC 23**
See also BW 2; CA 116; 125; 129; HW
Guillevic, (Eugene) 1907- .... **CLC 33**
See also CA 93-96
Guillois
See Desnos, Robert
Guillois, Valentin

See Desnos, Robert

Guiney, Louise Imogen 1861-1920 **TCLC 41**
See also CA 160; DLB 54

Guiraldes, Ricardo (Guillermo) 1886-1927
TCLC 39
See also CA 131; HW; MTCW 1

Gumilev, Nikolai (Stepanovich) 1886-1921
TCLC 60
See also CA 165

Gunesekera, Romesh 1954- .... **CLC 91**
See also CA 159

Gunn, Bill .... **CLC 5**
See also Gunn, William Harrison
See also DLB 38

Gunn, Thom(son William) 1929-**CLC 3, 6, 18,
32, 81; DAM POET**
See also CA 17-20R; CANR 9, 33; CDBLB
1960 to Present; DLB 27; INT CANR-33;
MTCW 1

Gunn, William Harrison 1934(?)-1989
See Gunn, Bill
See also AITN 1; BW 1; CA 13-16R; 128;
CANR 12, 25, 76

Gunnars, Kristjana 1948-................. **CLC 69**
See also CA 113; DLB 60

Gurdjieff, G(eorgei) I(vanovich) 1877(?)-1949
TCLC 71
See also CA 157

Gurganus, Allan 1947-.. **CLC 70; DAM POP**
See also BEST 90:1; CA 135

Gurney, A(lbert) R(amsdell), Jr. 1930- . **C L C
32, 50, 54; DAM DRAM**
See also CA 77-80; CANR 32, 64

Gurney, Ivor (Bertie) 1890-1937 ... **TCLC 33**
See also CA 167

Gurney, Peter
See Gurney, A(lbert) R(amsdell), Jr.

Guro, Elena 1877-1913 .... **TCLC 56**

Gustafson, James M(oody) 1925- .. **CLC 100**
See also CA 25-28R; CANR 37

Gustafson, Ralph (Barker) 1909- .... **CLC 36**
See also CA 21-24R; CANR 8, 45; DLB 88

Gut, Gom
See Simenon, Georges (Jacques Christian)

Guterson, David 1956- .... **CLC 91**
See also CA 132; CANR 73

Guthrie, A(lfred) B(ertram), Jr. 1901-1991
CLC 23
See also CA 57-60; 134; CANR 24; DLB 6;
SATA 62; SATA-Obit 67

Guthrie, Isobel
See Grieve, C(hristopher) M(urray)

Guthrie, Woodrow Wilson 1912-1967
See Guthrie, Woody
See also CA 113; 93-96

Guthrie, Woody .... **CLC 35**
See also Guthrie, Woodrow Wilson

Guy, Rosa (Cuthbert) 1928- .... **CLC 26**
See also AAYA 4; BW 2; CA 17-20R; CANR
14, 34; CLR 13; DLB 33; JRDA; MAICYA;
SATA 14, 62

Gwendolyn
See Bennett, (Enoch) Arnold

H. D. .... **CLC 3, 8, 14, 31, 34, 73; PC 5**
See also Doolittle, Hilda

H. de V.
See Buchan, John

Haavikko, Paavo Juhani 1931- .. **CLC 18, 34**
See also CA 106

Habbema, Koos
See Heijermans, Herman

Habermas, Juergen 1929-................ **CLC 104**
See also CA 109

Habermas, Jurgen
See Habermas, Juergen

Hacker, Marilyn 1942-.**CLC 5, 9, 23, 72, 91;
DAM POET**
See also CA 77-80; CANR 68; DLB 120

Haeckel, Ernst Heinrich (Philipp August) 1834-
1919 .... **TCLC 83**
See also CA 157

Haggard, H(enry) Rider 1856-1925**TCLC 11**
See also CA 108; 148; DLB 70, 156, 174, 178;
SATA 16

Hagiosy, L.
See Larbaud, Valery (Nicolas)

Hagiwara Sakutaro 1886-1942**TCLC 60; PC
18**

Haig, Fenil
See Ford, Ford Madox

Haig-Brown, Roderick (Langmere) 1908-1976
CLC 21
See also CA 5-8R; 69-72; CANR 4, 38; CLR
31; DLB 88; MAICYA; SATA 12

Hailey, Arthur 1920-**CLC 5; DAM NOV, POP**
See also AITN 2; BEST 90:3; CA 1-4R; CANR
2, 36, 75; DLB 88; DLBY 82; MTCW 1

Hailey, Elizabeth Forsythe 1938- ..... **CLC 40**
See also CA 93-96; CAAS 1; CANR 15, 48;
INT CANR-15

Haines, John (Meade) 1924-.............. **CLC 58**
See also CA 17-20R; CANR 13, 34; DLB 5

Hakluyt, Richard 1552-1616 .... **LC 31**

Haldeman, Joe (William) 1943- .... **CLC 61**
See also CA 53-56; CAAS 25; CANR 6, 70,
72; DLB 8; INT CANR-6

Hale, Sarah Josepha (Buell) 1788-1879**NCLC
75**
See also DLB 1, 42, 73

Haley, Alex(ander Murray Palmer) 1921-1992
**CLC 8, 12, 76; BLC 2; DA; DAB; DAC;
DAM MST, MULT, POP**
See also AAYA 26; BW 2; CA 77-80; 136;
CANR 61; DLB 38; MTCW 1

Haliburton, Thomas Chandler 1796-1865
NCLC 15
See also DLB 11, 99

Hall, Donald (Andrew, Jr.) 1928- **CLC 1, 13,
37, 59; DAM POET**
See also CA 5-8R; CAAS 7; CANR 2, 44, 64;
DLB 5; SATA 23, 97

Hall, Frederic Sauser
See Sauser-Hall, Frederic

Hall, James
See Kuttner, Henry

Hall, James Norman 1887-1951 ..... **TCLC 23**
See also CA 123; 173; SATA 21

Hall, Radclyffe
See Hall, (Marguerite) Radclyffe

Hall, (Marguerite) Radclyffe 1886-1943
TCLC 12
See also CA 110; 150; DLB 191

Hall, Rodney 1935-............................ **CLC 51**
See also CA 109; CANR 69

Halleck, Fitz-Greene 1790-1867 .... **NCLC 47**
See also DLB 3

Halliday, Michael
See Creasey, John

Halpern, Daniel 1945-........................ **CLC 14**
See also CA 33-36R

Hamburger, Michael (Peter Leopold) 1924-
CLC 5, 14
See also CA 5-8R; CAAS 4; CANR 2, 47; DLB
27

Hamill, Pete 1935- .... **CLC 10**
See also CA 25-28R; CANR 18, 71

Hamilton, Alexander 1755(?)-1804 **NCLC 49**
See also DLB 37

Hamilton, Clive
See Lewis, C(live) S(taples)

Hamilton, Edmond 1904-1977 .... **CLC 1**
See also CA 1-4R; CANR 3; DLB 8

Hamilton, Eugene (Jacob) Lee
See Lee-Hamilton, Eugene (Jacob)

Hamilton, Franklin
See Silverberg, Robert

Hamilton, Gail
See Corcoran, Barbara

Hamilton, Mollie
See Kaye, M(ary) M(argaret)

Hamilton, (Anthony Walter) Patrick 1904-1962
CLC 51
See also CA 113; DLB 191

Hamilton, Virginia 1936-........ **CLC 26; DAM
MULT**
See also AAYA 2, 21; BW 2; CA 25-28R;
CANR 20, 37, 73; CLR 1, 11, 40; DLB 33,
52; INT CANR-20; JRDA; MAICYA;
MTCW 1; SATA 4, 56, 79

Hammett, (Samuel) Dashiell 1894-1961 **C L C
3, 5, 10, 19, 47; SSC 17**
See also AITN 1; CA 81-84; CANR 42; CDALB
1929-1941; DLBD 6; DLBY 96; MTCW 1

Hammon, Jupiter 1711(?)-1800(?) . **NCLC 5;
BLC 2; DAM MULT, POET; PC 16**
See also DLB 31, 50

Hammond, Keith
See Kuttner, Henry

Hamner, Earl (Henry), Jr. 1923- ..... **CLC 12**
See also AITN 2; CA 73-76; DLB 6

Hampton, Christopher (James) 1946- **CLC 4**
See also CA 25-28R; DLB 13; MTCW 1

Hamsun, Knut .... **TCLC 2, 14, 49**
See also Pedersen, Knut

Handke, Peter 1942-**CLC 5, 8, 10, 15, 38; DAM
DRAM, NOV**
See also CA 77-80; CANR 33, 75; DLB 85, 124;
MTCW 1

Hanley, James 1901-1985 ..... **CLC 3, 5, 8, 13**
See also CA 73-76; 117; CANR 36; DLB 191;
MTCW 1

Hannah, Barry 1942-............. **CLC 23, 38, 90**
See also CA 108; 110; CANR 43, 68; DLB 6;
INT 110; MTCW 1

Hannon, Ezra
See Hunter, Evan

Hansberry, Lorraine (Vivian) 1930-1965**CLC
17, 62; BLC 2; DA; DAB; DAC; DAM
DRAM, MST, MULT; DC 2**
See also AAYA 25; BW 1; CA 109; 25-28R;
CABS 3; CANR 58; CDALB 1941-1968;
DLB 7, 38; MTCW 1

Hansen, Joseph 1923- .... **CLC 38**
See also CA 29-32R; CAAS 17; CANR 16, 44,
66; INT CANR-16

Hansen, Martin A(lfred) 1909-1955**TCLC 32**
See also CA 167

Hanson, Kenneth O(stlin) 1922- ...... **CLC 13**
See also CA 53-56; CANR 7

Hardwick, Elizabeth (Bruce) 1916- **CLC 13;
DAM NOV**
See also CA 5-8R; CANR 3, 32, 70; DLB 6;
MTCW 1

Hardy, Thomas 1840-1928**TCLC 4, 10, 18, 32,
48, 53, 72; DA; DAB; DAC; DAM MST,
NOV, POET; PC 8; SSC 2; WLC**
See also CA 104; 123; CDBLB 1890-1914;
DLB 18, 19, 135; MTCW 1

Hare, David 1947- .... **CLC 29, 58**

See also CA 97-100; CANR 39; DLB 13; MTCW 1

Harewood, John
See Van Druten, John (William)

Harford, Henry
See Hudson, W(illiam) H(enry)

Hargrave, Leonie
See Disch, Thomas M(ichael)

Harjo, Joy 1951- .... **CLC 83; DAM MULT**
See also CA 114; CANR 35, 67; DLB 120, 175; NNAL

Harlan, Louis R(udolph) 1922-........ **CLC 34**
See also CA 21-24R; CANR 25, 55

Harling, Robert 1951(?)- .... **CLC 53**
See also CA 147

Harmon, William (Ruth) 1938-........ **CLC 38**
See also CA 33-36R; CANR 14, 32, 35; SATA 65

Harper, F. E. W.
See Harper, Frances Ellen Watkins

Harper, Frances E. W.
See Harper, Frances Ellen Watkins

Harper, Frances E. Watkins
See Harper, Frances Ellen Watkins

Harper, Frances Ellen
See Harper, Frances Ellen Watkins

Harper, Frances Ellen Watkins 1825-1911
TCLC 14; BLC 2; DAM MULT, POET; PC 21
See also BW 1; CA 111; 125; DLB 50

Harper, Michael S(teven) 1938-... **CLC 7, 22**
See also BW 1; CA 33-36R; CANR 24; DLB 41

Harper, Mrs. F. E. W.
See Harper, Frances Ellen Watkins

Harris, Christie (Lucy) Irwin 1907- **CLC 12**
See also CA 5-8R; CANR 6; CLR 47; DLB 88; JRDA; MAICYA; SAAS 10; SATA 6, 74

Harris, Frank 1856-1931 .... **TCLC 24**
See also CA 109; 150; DLB 156, 197

Harris, George Washington 1814-1869 **NCLC 23**
See also DLB 3, 11

Harris, Joel Chandler 1848-1908 ... **TCLC 2; SSC 19**
See also CA 104; 137; CLR 49; DLB 11, 23, 42, 78, 91; MAICYA; SATA 100; YABC 1

Harris, John (Wyndham Parkes Lucas) Beynon 1903-1969
See Wyndham, John
See also CA 102; 89-92

Harris, MacDonald .... **CLC 9**
See also Heiney, Donald (William)

Harris, Mark 1922- .... **CLC 19**
See also CA 5-8R; CAAS 3; CANR 2, 55; DLB 2; DLBY 80

Harris, (Theodore) Wilson 1921-..... **CLC 25**
See also BW 2; CA 65-68; CAAS 16; CANR 11, 27, 69; DLB 117; MTCW 1

Harrison, Elizabeth Cavanna 1909-
See Cavanna, Betty
See also CA 9-12R; CANR 6, 27

Harrison, Harry (Max) 1925- .... **CLC 42**
See also CA 1-4R; CANR 5, 21; DLB 8; SATA 4

Harrison, James (Thomas) 1937- **CLC 6, 14, 33, 66; SSC 19**
See also CA 13-16R; CANR 8, 51; DLBY 82; INT CANR-8

Harrison, Jim
See Harrison, James (Thomas)

Harrison, Kathryn 1961-.................. **CLC 70**
See also CA 144; CANR 68

Harrison, Tony 1937- .... **CLC 43**
See also CA 65-68; CANR 44; DLB 40; MTCW 1

Harriss, Will(ard Irvin) 1922- .... **CLC 34**
See also CA 111

Harson, Sley
See Ellison, Harlan (Jay)

Hart, Ellis
See Ellison, Harlan (Jay)

Hart, Josephine 1942(?)- **CLC 70; DAM POP**
See also CA 138; CANR 70

Hart, Moss 1904-1961 **CLC 66; DAM DRAM**
See also CA 109; 89-92; DLB 7

Harte, (Francis) Bret(t) 1836(?)-1902 **TCLC 1, 25; DA; DAC; DAM MST; SSC 8; WLC**
See also CA 104; 140; CDALB 1865-1917; DLB 12, 64, 74, 79, 186; SATA 26

Hartley, L(eslie) P(oles) 1895-1972 **CLC 2, 22**
See also CA 45-48; 37-40R; CANR 33; DLB 15, 139; MTCW 1

Hartman, Geoffrey H. 1929- .... **CLC 27**
See also CA 117; 125; DLB 67

Hartmann, Sadakichi 1867-1944 ... **TCLC 73**
See also CA 157; DLB 54

Hartmann von Aue c. 1160-c. 1205 **CMLC 15**
See also DLB 138

Hartmann von Aue 1170-1210 ...... **CMLC 15**

Haruf, Kent 1943- .... **CLC 34**
See also CA 149

Harwood, Ronald 1934-......... **CLC 32; DAM DRAM, MST**
See also CA 1-4R; CANR 4, 55; DLB 13

Hasegawa Tatsunosuke
See Futabatei, Shimei

Hasek, Jaroslav (Matej Frantisek) 1883-1923 **TCLC 4**
See also CA 104; 129; MTCW 1

Hass, Robert 1941-... **CLC 18, 39, 99; PC 16**
See also CA 111; CANR 30, 50, 71; DLB 105, 206; SATA 94

Hastings, Hudson
See Kuttner, Henry

Hastings, Selina .... **CLC 44**

Hathorne, John 1641-1717 .... **LC 38**

Hatteras, Amelia
See Mencken, H(enry) L(ouis)

Hatteras, Owen .... **TCLC 18**
See also Mencken, H(enry) L(ouis); Nathan, George Jean

Hauptmann, Gerhart (Johann Robert) 1862-1946 .... **TCLC 4; DAM DRAM**
See also CA 104; 153; DLB 66, 118

Havel, Vaclav 1936-... **CLC 25, 58, 65; DAM DRAM; DC 6**
See also CA 104; CANR 36, 63; MTCW 1

Haviaras, Stratis .... **CLC 33**
See also Chaviaras, Strates

Hawes, Stephen 1475(?)-1523(?) .... **LC 17**
See also DLB 132

Hawkes, John (Clendennin Burne, Jr.) 1925-1998 .. **CLC 1, 2, 3, 4, 7, 9, 14, 15, 27, 49**
See also CA 1-4R; 167; CANR 2, 47, 64; DLB 2, 7; DLBY 80; MTCW 1

Hawking, S. W.
See Hawking, Stephen W(illiam)

Hawking, Stephen W(illiam) 1942- **CLC 63, 105**
See also AAYA 13; BEST 89:1; CA 126; 129; CANR 48

Hawkins, Anthony Hope
See Hope, Anthony

Hawthorne, Julian 1846-1934 .... **TCLC 25**
See also CA 165

Hawthorne, Nathaniel 1804-1864 **NCLC 39; DA; DAB; DAC; DAM MST, NOV; SSC 3, 29; WLC**
See also AAYA 18; CDALB 1640-1865; DLB 1, 74; YABC 2

Haxton, Josephine Ayres 1921-
See Douglas, Ellen
See also CA 115; CANR 41

Hayaseca y Eizaguirre, Jorge
See Echegaray (y Eizaguirre), Jose (Maria Waldo)

Hayashi, Fumiko 1904-1951 .... **TCLC 27**
See also CA 161; DLB 180

Haycraft, Anna
See Ellis, Alice Thomas
See also CA 122

Hayden, Robert E(arl) 1913-1980 **CLC 5, 9, 14, 37; BLC 2; DA; DAC; DAM MST, MULT, POET; PC 6**
See also BW 1; CA 69-72; 97-100; CABS 2; CANR 24, 75; CDALB 1941-1968; DLB 5, 76; MTCW 1; SATA 19; SATA-Obit 26

Hayford, J(oseph) E(phraim) Casely
See Casely-Hayford, J(oseph) E(phraim)

Hayman, Ronald 1932- .... **CLC 44**
See also CA 25-28R; CANR 18, 50; DLB 155

Haywood, Eliza (Fowler) 1693(?)-1756 **LC 1, 44**
See also DLB 39

Hazlitt, William 1778-1830 .... **NCLC 29**
See also DLB 110, 158

Hazzard, Shirley 1931- .... **CLC 18**
See also CA 9-12R; CANR 4, 70; DLBY 82; MTCW 1

Head, Bessie 1937-1986 **CLC 25, 67; BLC 2; DAM MULT**
See also BW 2; CA 29-32R; 119; CANR 25; DLB 117; MTCW 1

Headon, (Nicky) Topper 1956(?)- ..... **CLC 30**

Heaney, Seamus (Justin) 1939- **CLC 5, 7, 14, 25, 37, 74, 91; DAB; DAM POET; PC 18; WLCS**
See also CA 85-88; CANR 25, 48, 75; CDBLB 1960 to Present; DLB 40; DLBY 95; MTCW 1

Hearn, (Patricio) Lafcadio (Tessima Carlos) 1850-1904 .... **TCLC 9**
See also CA 105; 166; DLB 12, 78, 189

Hearne, Vicki 1946-........................... **CLC 56**
See also CA 139

Hearon, Shelby 1931- .... **CLC 63**
See also AITN 2; CA 25-28R; CANR 18, 48

Heat-Moon, William Least .... **CLC 29**
See also Trogdon, William (Lewis)
See also AAYA 9

Hebbel, Friedrich 1813-1863 **NCLC 43; DAM DRAM**
See also DLB 129

Hebert, Anne 1916- **CLC 4, 13, 29; DAC; DAM MST, POET**
See also CA 85-88; CANR 69; DLB 68; MTCW 1

Hecht, Anthony (Evan) 1923- **CLC 8, 13, 19; DAM POET**
See also CA 9-12R; CANR 6; DLB 5, 169

Hecht, Ben 1894-1964 .... **CLC 8**
See also CA 85-88; DLB 7, 9, 25, 26, 28, 86

Hedayat, Sadeq 1903-1951 .... **TCLC 21**
See also CA 120

Hegel, Georg Wilhelm Friedrich 1770-1831 **NCLC 46**
See also DLB 90

Heidegger, Martin 1889-1976 .... **CLC 24**

57; DLB 5

Ihimaera, Witi 1944- .... **CLC 46**
  See also CA 77-80

Ilf, Ilya .... **TCLC 21**
  See also Fainzilberg, Ilya Arnoldovich

Illyes, Gyula 1902-1983 .... **PC 16**
  See also CA 114; 109

Immermann, Karl (Lebrecht) 1796-1840
  NCLC 4, 49
  See also DLB 133

Ince, Thomas H. 1882-1924 .... **TCLC 89**

Inchbald, Elizabeth 1753-1821 ...... **NCLC 62**
  See also DLB 39, 89

Inclan, Ramon (Maria) del Valle
  See Valle-Inclan, Ramon (Maria) del

Infante, G(uillermo) Cabrera
  See Cabrera Infante, G(uillermo)

Ingalls, Rachel (Holmes) 1940- .... **CLC 42**
  See also CA 123; 127

Ingamells, Reginald Charles
  See Ingamells, Rex

Ingamells, Rex 1913-1955 .... **TCLC 35**
  See also CA 167

Inge, William (Motter) 1913-1973 **CLC 1, 8, 19; DAM DRAM**
  See also CA 9-12R; CDALB 1941-1968; DLB 7; MTCW 1

Ingelow, Jean 1820-1897 .... **NCLC 39**
  See also DLB 35, 163; SATA 33

Ingram, Willis J.
  See Harris, Mark

Innaurato, Albert (F.) 1948(?)- .. **CLC 21, 60**
  See also CA 115; 122; INT 122

Innes, Michael
  See Stewart, J(ohn) I(nnes) M(ackintosh)

Innis, Harold Adams 1894-1952 .... **TCLC 77**
  See also DLB 88

Ionesco, Eugene 1909-1994**CLC 1, 4, 6, 9, 11, 15, 41, 86; DA; DAB; DAC; DAM DRAM, MST; WLC**
  See also CA 9-12R; 144; CANR 55; MTCW 1; SATA 7; SATA-Obit 79

Iqbal, Muhammad 1873-1938 .... **TCLC 28**

Ireland, Patrick
  See O'Doherty, Brian

Iron, Ralph
  See Schreiner, Olive (Emilie Albertina)

Irving, John (Winslow) 1942-**CLC 13, 23, 38, 112; DAM NOV, POP**
  See also AAYA 8; BEST 89:3; CA 25-28R; CANR 28, 73; DLB 6; DLBY 82; MTCW 1

Irving, Washington 1783-1859 . **NCLC 2, 19; DA; DAB; DAC; DAM MST; SSC 2; WLC**
  See also CDALB 1640-1865; DLB 3, 11, 30, 59, 73, 74, 186; YABC 2

Irwin, P. K.
  See Page, P(atricia) K(athleen)

Isaacs, Jorge Ricardo 1837-1895 ... **NCLC 70**

Isaacs, Susan 1943- .... **CLC 32; DAM POP**
  See also BEST 89:1; CA 89-92; CANR 20, 41, 65; INT CANR-20; MTCW 1

Isherwood, Christopher (William Bradshaw) 1904-1986 ... **CLC 1, 9, 11, 14, 44; DAM DRAM, NOV**
  See also CA 13-16R; 117; CANR 35; DLB 15, 195; DLBY 86; MTCW 1

Ishiguro, Kazuo 1954-..**CLC 27, 56, 59, 110; DAM NOV**
  See also BEST 90:2; CA 120; CANR 49; DLB 194; MTCW 1

Ishikawa, Hakuhin
  See Ishikawa, Takuboku

Ishikawa, Takuboku 1886(?)-1912 **TCLC 15;**

DAM POET; PC 10
  See also CA 113; 153

Iskander, Fazil 1929- .... **CLC 47**
  See also CA 102

Isler, Alan (David) 1934- .... **CLC 91**
  See also CA 156

Ivan IV 1530-1584 .... **LC 17**

Ivanov, Vyacheslav Ivanovich 1866-1949
  TCLC 33
  See also CA 122

Ivask, Ivar Vidrik 1927-1992 .... **CLC 14**
  See also CA 37-40R; 139; CANR 24

Ives, Morgan
  See Bradley, Marion Zimmer

Izumi Shikibu c. 973-c. 1034 .... **CMLC 33**

J. R. S.
  See Gogarty, Oliver St. John

Jabran, Kahlil
  See Gibran, Kahlil

Jabran, Khalil
  See Gibran, Kahlil

Jackson, Daniel
  See Wingrove, David (John)

Jackson, Jesse 1908-1983 .... **CLC 12**
  See also BW 1; CA 25-28R; 109; CANR 27; CLR 28; MAICYA; SATA 2, 29; SATA-Obit 48

Jackson, Laura (Riding) 1901-1991
  See Riding, Laura
  See also CA 65-68; 135; CANR 28; DLB 48

Jackson, Sam
  See Trumbo, Dalton

Jackson, Sara
  See Wingrove, David (John)

Jackson, Shirley 1919-1965 . **CLC 11, 60, 87; DA; DAC; DAM MST; SSC 9; WLC**
  See also AAYA 9; CA 1-4R; 25-28R; CANR 4, 52; CDALB 1941-1968; DLB 6; SATA 2

Jacob, (Cyprien-)Max 1876-1944 .... **TCLC 6**
  See also CA 104

Jacobs, Harriet A(nn) 1813(?)-1897**NCLC 67**

Jacobs, Jim 1942- .... **CLC 12**
  See also CA 97-100; INT 97-100

Jacobs, W(illiam) W(ymark) 1863-1943
  TCLC 22
  See also CA 121; 167; DLB 135

Jacobsen, Jens Peter 1847-1885 .... **NCLC 34**

Jacobsen, Josephine 1908- .... **CLC 48, 102**
  See also CA 33-36R; CAAS 18; CANR 23, 48

Jacobson, Dan 1929- .... **CLC 4, 14**
  See also CA 1-4R; CANR 2, 25, 66; DLB 14, 207; MTCW 1

Jacqueline
  See Carpentier (y Valmont), Alejo

Jagger, Mick 1944- .... **CLC 17**

Jahiz, al- c. 780-c. 869 .... **CMLC 25**

Jakes, John (William) 1932-..**CLC 29; DAM NOV, POP**
  See also BEST 89:4; CA 57-60; CANR 10, 43, 66; DLBY 83; INT CANR-10; MTCW 1; SATA 62

James, Andrew
  See Kirkup, James

James, C(yril) L(ionel) R(obert) 1901-1989
  CLC 33; BLCS
  See also BW 2; CA 117; 125; 128; CANR 62; DLB 125; MTCW 1

James, Daniel (Lewis) 1911-1988
  See Santiago, Danny
  See also CA 125

James, Dynely
  See Mayne, William (James Carter)

James, Henry Sr. 1811-1882 .... **NCLC 53**

James, Henry 1843-1916 **TCLC 2, 11, 24, 40, 47, 64; DA; DAB; DAC; DAM MST, NOV; SSC 8, 32; WLC**
  See also CA 104; 132; CDALB 1865-1917; DLB 12, 71, 74, 189; DLBD 13; MTCW 1

James, M. R.
  See James, Montague (Rhodes)
  See also DLB 156

James, Montague (Rhodes) 1862-1936**TCLC 6; SSC 16**
  See also CA 104; DLB 201

James, P. D. 1920- .... **CLC 18, 46**
  See also White, Phyllis Dorothy James
  See also BEST 90:2; CDBLB 1960 to Present; DLB 87; DLBD 17

James, Philip
  See Moorcock, Michael (John)

James, William 1842-1910 .... **TCLC 15, 32**
  See also CA 109

James I 1394-1437 .... **LC 20**

Jameson, Anna 1794-1860 .... **NCLC 43**
  See also DLB 99, 166

Jami, Nur al-Din 'Abd al-Rahman 1414-1492
  LC 9

Jammes, Francis 1868-1938 .... **TCLC 75**

Jandl, Ernst 1925- .... **CLC 34**

Janowitz, Tama 1957- ...... **CLC 43; DAM POP**
  See also CA 106; CANR 52

Japrisot, Sebastien 1931- .... **CLC 90**

Jarrell, Randall 1914-1965**CLC 1, 2, 6, 9, 13, 49; DAM POET**
  See also CA 5-8R; 25-28R; CABS 2; CANR 6, 34; CDALB 1941-1968; CLR 6; DLB 48, 52; MAICYA; MTCW 1; SATA 7

Jarry, Alfred 1873-1907 . **TCLC 2, 14; DAM DRAM; SSC 20**
  See also CA 104; 153; DLB 192

Jarvis, E. K.
  See Bloch, Robert (Albert); Ellison, Harlan (Jay); Silverberg, Robert

Jeake, Samuel, Jr.
  See Aiken, Conrad (Potter)

Jean Paul 1763-1825 .... **NCLC 7**

Jefferies, (John) Richard 1848-1887**NCLC 47**
  See also DLB 98, 141; SATA 16

Jeffers, (John) Robinson 1887-1962**CLC 2, 3, 11, 15, 54; DA; DAC; DAM MST, POET; PC 17; WLC**
  See also CA 85-88; CANR 35; CDALB 1917-1929; DLB 45; MTCW 1

Jefferson, Janet
  See Mencken, H(enry) L(ouis)

Jefferson, Thomas 1743-1826 .... **NCLC 11**
  See also CDALB 1640-1865; DLB 31

Jeffrey, Francis 1773-1850 .... **NCLC 33**
  See also DLB 107

Jelakowitch, Ivan
  See Heijermans, Herman

Jellicoe, (Patricia) Ann 1927- .... **CLC 27**
  See also CA 85-88; DLB 13

Jen, Gish .... **CLC 70**
  See also Jen, Lillian

Jen, Lillian 1956(?)-
  See Jen, Gish
  See also CA 135

Jenkins, (John) Robin 1912- .... **CLC 52**
  See also CA 1-4R; CANR 1; DLB 14

Jennings, Elizabeth (Joan) 1926- **CLC 5, 14**
  See also CA 61-64; CAAS 5; CANR 8, 39, 66; DLB 27; MTCW 1; SATA 66

Jennings, Waylon 1937- .... **CLC 21**

Jensen, Johannes V. 1873-1950 ...... **TCLC 41**
  See also CA 170

See also CA 150

Kessler, Jascha (Frederick) 1929-.......**CLC 4**
See also CA 17-20R; CANR 8, 48

Kettelkamp, Larry (Dale) 1933- ......**CLC 12**
See also CA 29-32R; CANR 16; SAAS 3; SATA 2

Key, Ellen 1849-1926 ....**TCLC 65**

Keyber, Conny
See Fielding, Henry

Keyes, Daniel 1927-**CLC 80; DA; DAC; DAM MST, NOV**
See also AAYA 23; CA 17-20R; CANR 10, 26, 54, 74; SATA 37

Keynes, John Maynard 1883-1946 **TCLC 64**
See also CA 114; 162, 163; DLBD 10

Khanshendel, Chiron
See Rose, Wendy

Khayyam, Omar 1048-1131 **CMLC 11; DAM POET; PC 8**

Kherdian, David 1931- ....**CLC 6, 9**
See also CA 21-24R; CAAS 2; CANR 39; CLR 24; JRDA; MAICYA; SATA 16, 74

Khlebnikov, Velimir ....**TCLC 20**
See also Khlebnikov, Viktor Vladimirovich

Khlebnikov, Viktor Vladimirovich 1885-1922
See Khlebnikov, Velimir
See also CA 117

Khodasevich, Vladislav (Felitsianovich) 1886-1939 ....**TCLC 15**
See also CA 115

Kielland, Alexander Lange 1849-1906 **TCLC 5**
See also CA 104

Kiely, Benedict 1919- ....**CLC 23, 43**
See also CA 1-4R; CANR 2; DLB 15

Kienzle, William X(avier) 1928- .....**CLC 25; DAM POP**
See also CA 93-96; CAAS 1; CANR 9, 31, 59; INT CANR-31; MTCW 1

Kierkegaard, Soren 1813-1855 ......**NCLC 34**

Killens, John Oliver 1916-1987 ....**CLC 10**
See also BW 2; CA 77-80; 123; CAAS 2; CANR 26; DLB 33

Killigrew, Anne 1660-1685 ....**LC 4**
See also DLB 131

Kim
See Simenon, Georges (Jacques Christian)

Kincaid, Jamaica 1949- **CLC 43, 68; BLC 2; DAM MULT, NOV**
See also AAYA 13; BW 2; CA 125; CANR 47, 59; DLB 157

King, Francis (Henry) 1923-**CLC 8, 53; DAM NOV**
See also CA 1-4R; CANR 1, 33; DLB 15, 139; MTCW 1

King, Kennedy
See Brown, George Douglas

King, Martin Luther, Jr. 1929-1968 **CLC 83; BLC 2; DA; DAB; DAC; DAM MST, MULT; WLCS**
See also BW 2; CA 25-28; CANR 27, 44; CAP 2; MTCW 1; SATA 14

King, Stephen (Edwin) 1947-**CLC 12, 26, 37, 61, 113; DAM NOV, POP; SSC 17**
See also AAYA 1, 17; BEST 90:1; CA 61-64; CANR 1, 30, 52, 76; DLB 143; DLBY 80; JRDA; MTCW 1; SATA 9, 55

King, Steve
See King, Stephen (Edwin)

King, Thomas 1943- ....**CLC 89; DAC; DAM MULT**
See also CA 144; DLB 175; NNAL; SATA 96

Kingman, Lee.....................................**CLC 17**

See also Natti, (Mary) Lee
See also SAAS 3; SATA 1, 67

Kingsley, Charles 1819-1875 ....**NCLC 35**
See also DLB 21, 32, 163, 190; YABC 2

Kingsley, Sidney 1906-1995 ....**CLC 44**
See also CA 85-88; 147; DLB 7

Kingsolver, Barbara 1955-**CLC 55, 81; DAM POP**
See also AAYA 15; CA 129; 134; CANR 60; DLB 206; INT 134

Kingston, Maxine (Ting Ting) Hong 1940-**CLC 12, 19, 58; DAM MULT, NOV; WLCS**
See also AAYA 8; CA 69-72; CANR 13, 38, 74; DLB 173; DLBY 80; INT CANR-13; MTCW 1; SATA 53

Kinnell, Galway 1927- **CLC 1, 2, 3, 5, 13, 29**
See also CA 9-12R; CANR 10, 34, 66; DLB 5; DLBY 87; INT CANR-34; MTCW 1

Kinsella, Thomas 1928- ....**CLC 4, 19**
See also CA 17-20R; CANR 15; DLB 27; MTCW 1

Kinsella, W(illiam) P(atrick) 1935- **CLC 27, 43; DAC; DAM NOV, POP**
See also AAYA 7; CA 97-100; CAAS 7; CANR 21, 35, 66, 75; INT CANR-21; MTCW 1

Kinsey, Alfred C(harles) 1894-1956 **TCLC 91**
See also CA 115; 170

Kipling, (Joseph) Rudyard 1865-1936 **T C L C 8, 17; DA; DAB; DAC; DAM MST, POET; PC 3; SSC 5; WLC**
See also CA 105; 120; CANR 33; CDBLB 1890-1914; DLB 19, 34, 141, 156; MAICYA; MTCW 1; SATA 100; YABC 2

Kirkup, James 1918- ....**CLC 1**
See also CA 1-4R; CAAS 4; CANR 2; DLB 27; SATA 12

Kirkwood, James 1930(?)-1989 ....**CLC 9**
See also AITN 2; CA 1-4R; 128; CANR 6, 40

Kirshner, Sidney
See Kingsley, Sidney

Kis, Danilo 1935-1989 ....**CLC 57**
See also CA 109; 118; 129; CANR 61; DLB 181; MTCW 1

Kivi, Aleksis 1834-1872 ....**NCLC 30**

Kizer, Carolyn (Ashley) 1925-**CLC 15, 39, 80; DAM POET**
See also CA 65-68; CAAS 5; CANR 24, 70; DLB 5, 169

Klabund 1890-1928 ....**TCLC 44**
See also CA 162; DLB 66

Klappert, Peter 1942- ....**CLC 57**
See also CA 33-36R; DLB 5

Klein, A(braham) M(oses) 1909-1972 **CLC 19; DAB; DAC; DAM MST**
See also CA 101; 37-40R; DLB 68

Klein, Norma 1938-1989 ....**CLC 30**
See also AAYA 2; CA 41-44R; 128; CANR 15, 37; CLR 2, 19; INT CANR-15; JRDA; MAICYA; SAAS 1; SATA 7, 57

Klein, T(heodore) E(ibon) D(onald) 1947-**CLC 34**
See also CA 119; CANR 44, 75

Kleist, Heinrich von 1777-1811 **NCLC 2, 37; DAM DRAM; SSC 22**
See also DLB 90

Klima, Ivan 1931- ....**CLC 56; DAM NOV**
See also CA 25-28R; CANR 17, 50

Klimentov, Andrei Platonovich 1899-1951
See Platonov, Andrei
See also CA 108

Klinger, Friedrich Maximilian von 1752-1831 **NCLC 1**

See also DLB 94

Klingsor the Magician
See Hartmann, Sadakichi

Klopstock, Friedrich Gottlieb 1724-1803 **NCLC 11**
See also DLB 97

Knapp, Caroline 1959- ....**CLC 99**
See also CA 154

Knebel, Fletcher 1911-1993 ....**CLC 14**
See also AITN 1; CA 1-4R; 140; CAAS 3; CANR 1, 36; SATA 36; SATA-Obit 75

Knickerbocker, Diedrich
See Irving, Washington

Knight, Etheridge 1931-1991 **CLC 40; BLC 2; DAM POET; PC 14**
See also BW 1; CA 21-24R; 133; CANR 23; DLB 41

Knight, Sarah Kemble 1666-1727 ....**LC 7**
See also DLB 24, 200

Knister, Raymond 1899-1932 ....**TCLC 56**
See also DLB 68

Knowles, John 1926- ..**CLC 1, 4, 10, 26; DA; DAC; DAM MST, NOV**
See also AAYA 10; CA 17-20R; CANR 40, 74, 76; CDALB 1968-1988; DLB 6; MTCW 1; SATA 8, 89

Knox, Calvin M.
See Silverberg, Robert

Knox, John c. 1505-1572 ....**LC 37**
See also DLB 132

Knye, Cassandra
See Disch, Thomas M(ichael)

Koch, C(hristopher) J(ohn) 1932- ... **CLC 42**
See also CA 127

Koch, Christopher
See Koch, C(hristopher) J(ohn)

Koch, Kenneth 1925- .... **CLC 5, 8, 44; DAM POET**
See also CA 1-4R; CANR 6, 36, 57; DLB 5; INT CANR-36; SATA 65

Kochanowski, Jan 1530-1584 ....**LC 10**

Kock, Charles Paul de 1794-1871 ..**NCLC 16**

Koda Shigeyuki 1867-1947
See Rohan, Koda
See also CA 121

Koestler, Arthur 1905-1983 **CLC 1, 3, 6, 8, 15, 33**
See also CA 1-4R; 109; CANR 1, 33; CDBLB 1945-1960; DLBY 83; MTCW 1

Kogawa, Joy Nozomi 1935-.. **CLC 78; DAC; DAM MST, MULT**
See also CA 101; CANR 19, 62; SATA 99

Kohout, Pavel 1928- ....**CLC 13**
See also CA 45-48; CANR 3

Koizumi, Yakumo
See Hearn, (Patricio) Lafcadio (Tessima Carlos)

Kolmar, Gertrud 1894-1943 ....**TCLC 40**
See also CA 167

Komunyakaa, Yusef 1947-**CLC 86, 94; BLCS**
See also CA 147; DLB 120

Konrad, George
See Konrad, Gyoergy

Konrad, Gyoergy 1933- .... **CLC 4, 10, 73**
See also CA 85-88

Konwicki, Tadeusz 1926- **CLC 8, 28, 54, 117**
See also CA 101; CAAS 9; CANR 39, 59; MTCW 1

Koontz, Dean R(ay) 1945- .....**CLC 78; DAM NOV, POP**
See also AAYA 9; BEST 89:3, 90:2; CA 108; CANR 19, 36, 52; MTCW 1; SATA 92

Kopernik, Mikolaj
See Copernicus, Nicolaus

Kopit, Arthur (Lee) 1937-**CLC 1, 18, 33; DAM DRAM**
    See also AITN 1; CA 81-84; CABS 3; DLB 7; MTCW 1
Kops, Bernard 1926- ....**CLC 4**
    See also CA 5-8R; DLB 13
Kornbluth, C(yril) M. 1923-1958 .... **TCLC 8**
    See also CA 105; 160; DLB 8
Korolenko, V. G.
    See Korolenko, Vladimir Galaktionovich
Korolenko, Vladimir
    See Korolenko, Vladimir Galaktionovich
Korolenko, Vladimir G.
    See Korolenko, Vladimir Galaktionovich
Korolenko, Vladimir Galaktionovich 1853-1921 .... **TCLC 22**
    See also CA 121
Korzybski, Alfred (Habdank Skarbek) 1879-1950 .... **TCLC 61**
    See also CA 123; 160
Kosinski, Jerzy (Nikodem) 1933-1991**CLC 1, 2, 3, 6, 10, 15, 53, 70; DAM NOV**
    See also CA 17-20R; 134; CANR 9, 46; DLB 2; DLBY 82; MTCW 1
Kostelanetz, Richard (Cory) 1940- . **CLC 28**
    See also CA 13-16R; CAAS 8; CANR 38, 77
Kostrowitzki, Wilhelm Apollinaris de 1880-1918
    See Apollinaire, Guillaume
    See also CA 104
Kotlowitz, Robert 1924- ....**CLC 4**
    See also CA 33-36R; CANR 36
Kotzebue, August (Friedrich Ferdinand) von 1761-1819 .... **NCLC 25**
    See also DLB 94
Kotzwinkle, William 1938- ..... **CLC 5, 14, 35**
    See also CA 45-48; CANR 3, 44; CLR 6; DLB 173; MAICYA; SATA 24, 70
Kowna, Stancy
    See Szymborska, Wislawa
Kozol, Jonathan 1936- .... **CLC 17**
    See also CA 61-64; CANR 16, 45
Kozoll, Michael 1940(?)- .... **CLC 35**
Kramer, Kathryn 19(?)- .... **CLC 34**
Kramer, Larry 1935-**CLC 42; DAM POP; DC 8**
    See also CA 124; 126; CANR 60
Krasicki, Ignacy 1735-1801 .... **NCLC 8**
Krasinski, Zygmunt 1812-1859 .... **NCLC 4**
Kraus, Karl 1874-1936 .... **TCLC 5**
    See also CA 104; DLB 118
Kreve (Mickevicius), Vincas 1882-1954**TCLC 27**
    See also CA 170
Kristeva, Julia 1941- .... **CLC 77**
    See also CA 154
Kristofferson, Kris 1936- .... **CLC 26**
    See also CA 104
Krizanc, John 1956- .... **CLC 57**
Krleza, Miroslav 1893-1981 .... **CLC 8, 114**
    See also CA 97-100; 105; CANR 50; DLB 147
Kroetsch, Robert 1927-**CLC 5, 23, 57; DAC; DAM POET**
    See also CA 17-20R; CANR 8, 38; DLB 53; MTCW 1
Kroetz, Franz
    See Kroetz, Franz Xaver
Kroetz, Franz Xaver 1946- .... **CLC 41**
    See also CA 130
Kroker, Arthur (W.) 1945- .... **CLC 77**
    See also CA 161
Kropotkin, Peter (Aleksieevich) 1842-1921
    TCLC 36

See also CA 119
Krotkov, Yuri 1917- ....**CLC 19**
    See also CA 102
Krumb
    See Crumb, R(obert)
Krumgold, Joseph (Quincy) 1908-1980 **C L C 12**
    See also CA 9-12R; 101; CANR 7; MAICYA; SATA 1, 48; SATA-Obit 23
Krumwitz
    See Crumb, R(obert)
Krutch, Joseph Wood 1893-1970 ......**CLC 24**
    See also CA 1-4R; 25-28R; CANR 4; DLB 63, 206
Krutzch, Gus
    See Eliot, T(homas) S(tearns)
Krylov, Ivan Andreevich 1768(?)-1844**N C L C 1**
    See also DLB 150
Kubin, Alfred (Leopold Isidor) 1877-1959
    TCLC 23
    See also CA 112; 149; DLB 81
Kubrick, Stanley 1928- ....**CLC 16**
    See also CA 81-84; CANR 33; DLB 26
Kumin, Maxine (Winokur) 1925- **CLC 5, 13, 28; DAM POET; PC 15**
    See also AITN 2; CA 1-4R; CAAS 8; CANR 1, 21, 69; DLB 5; MTCW 1; SATA 12
Kundera, Milan 1929-.. **CLC 4, 9, 19, 32, 68, 115; DAM NOV; SSC 24**
    See also AAYA 2; CA 85-88; CANR 19, 52, 74; MTCW 1
Kunene, Mazisi (Raymond) 1930- ....**CLC 85**
    See also BW 1; CA 125; DLB 117
Kunitz, Stanley (Jasspon) 1905-**CLC 6, 11, 14; PC 19**
    See also CA 41-44R; CANR 26, 57; DLB 48; INT CANR-26; MTCW 1
Kunze, Reiner 1933- ....**CLC 10**
    See also CA 93-96; DLB 75
Kuprin, Aleksandr Ivanovich 1870-1938
    TCLC 5
    See also CA 104
Kureishi, Hanif 1954(?)- ....**CLC 64**
    See also CA 139; DLB 194
Kurosawa, Akira 1910-1998 ... **CLC 16, 119; DAM MULT**
    See also AAYA 11; CA 101; 170; CANR 46
Kushner, Tony 1957(?)-**CLC 81; DAM DRAM; DC 10**
    See also CA 144; CANR 74
Kuttner, Henry 1915-1958 .... **TCLC 10**
    See also Vance, Jack
    See also CA 107; 157; DLB 8
Kuzma, Greg 1944- .... **CLC 7**
    See also CA 33-36R; CANR 70
Kuzmin, Mikhail 1872(?)-1936 ...... **TCLC 40**
    See also CA 170
Kyd, Thomas 1558-1594**LC 22; DAM DRAM; DC 3**
    See also DLB 62
Kyprianos, Iossif
    See Samarakis, Antonis
La Bruyere, Jean de 1645-1696 .... **LC 17**
Lacan, Jacques (Marie Emile) 1901-1981
    CLC 75
    See also CA 121; 104
Laclos, Pierre Ambroise Francois Choderlos de 1741-1803 .... **NCLC 4**
La Colere, Francois
    See Aragon, Louis
Lacolere, Francois
    See Aragon, Louis

La Deshabilleuse
    See Simenon, Georges (Jacques Christian)
Lady Gregory
    See Gregory, Isabella Augusta (Persse)
Lady of Quality, A
    See Bagnold, Enid
La Fayette, Marie (Madelaine Pioche de la Vergne Comtes 1634-1693 .... **LC 2**
Lafayette, Rene
    See Hubbard, L(afayette) Ron(ald)
Laforgue, Jules 1860-1887**NCLC 5, 53; PC 14; SSC 20**
Lagerkvist, Paer (Fabian) 1891-1974 **CLC 7, 10, 13, 54; DAM DRAM, NOV**
    See also Lagerkvist, Par
    See also CA 85-88; 49-52; MTCW 1
Lagerkvist, Par ....**SSC 12**
    See also Lagerkvist, Paer (Fabian)
Lagerloef, Selma (Ottiliana Lovisa) 1858-1940
    TCLC 4, 36
    See also Lagerlof, Selma (Ottiliana Lovisa)
    See also CA 108; SATA 15
Lagerlof, Selma (Ottiliana Lovisa)
    See Lagerloef, Selma (Ottiliana Lovisa)
    See also CLR 7; SATA 15
La Guma, (Justin) Alex(ander) 1925-1985
    CLC 19; BLCS; DAM NOV
    See also BW 1; CA 49-52; 118; CANR 25; DLB 117; MTCW 1
Laidlaw, A. K.
    See Grieve, C(hristopher) M(urray)
Lainez, Manuel Mujica
    See Mujica Lainez, Manuel
    See also HW
Laing, R(onald) D(avid) 1927-1989 ..**CLC 95**
    See also CA 107; 129; CANR 34; MTCW 1
Lamartine, Alphonse (Marie Louis Prat) de 1790-1869**NCLC 11; DAM POET; PC 16**
Lamb, Charles 1775-1834 .... **NCLC 10; DA; DAB; DAC; DAM MST; WLC**
    See also CDBLB 1789-1832; DLB 93, 107, 163; SATA 17
Lamb, Lady Caroline 1785-1828 ... **NCLC 38**
    See also DLB 116
Lamming, George (William) 1927- **CLC 2, 4, 66; BLC 2; DAM MULT**
    See also BW 2; CA 85-88; CANR 26, 76; DLB 125; MTCW 1
L'Amour, Louis (Dearborn) 1908-1988 **C L C 25, 55; DAM NOV, POP**
    See also AAYA 16; AITN 2; BEST 89:2; CA 1-4R; 125; CANR 3, 25, 40; DLB 207; DLBY 80; MTCW 1
Lampedusa, Giuseppe (Tomasi) di 1896-1957
    TCLC 13
    See also Tomasi di Lampedusa, Giuseppe
    See also CA 164; DLB 177
Lampman, Archibald 1861-1899 ... **NCLC 25**
    See also DLB 92
Lancaster, Bruce 1896-1963 .... **CLC 36**
    See also CA 9-10; CANR 70; CAP 1; SATA 9
Lanchester, John .... **CLC 99**
Landau, Mark Alexandrovich
    See Aldanov, Mark (Alexandrovich)
Landau-Aldanov, Mark Alexandrovich
    See Aldanov, Mark (Alexandrovich)
Landis, Jerry
    See Simon, Paul (Frederick)
Landis, John 1950- ....**CLC 26**
    See also CA 112; 122
Landolfi, Tommaso 1908-1979 ....**CLC 11, 49**
    See also CA 127; 117; DLB 177
Landon, Letitia Elizabeth 1802-1838 . **N C L C**

Madhubuti, Haki R. 1942-CLC 6, 73; BLC 2;
     DAM MULT, POET; PC 5
   See also Lee, Don L.
   See also BW 2; CA 73-76; CANR 24, 51, 73;
     DLB 5, 41; DLBD 8
Maepenn, Hugh
   See Kuttner, Henry
Maepenn, K. H.
   See Kuttner, Henry
Maeterlinck, Maurice 1862-1949 .... TCLC 3;
     DAM DRAM
   See also CA 104; 136; DLB 192; SATA 66
Maginn, William 1794-1842 .... NCLC 8
   See also DLB 110, 159
Mahapatra, Jayanta 1928- .... CLC 33; DAM
     MULT
   See also CA 73-76; CAAS 9; CANR 15, 33, 66
Mahfouz, Naguib (Abdel Aziz Al-Sabilgi)
     1911(?)-
   See Mahfuz, Najib
   See also BEST 89:2; CA 128; CANR 55; DAM
     NOV; MTCW 1
Mahfuz, Najib .... CLC 52, 55
   See also Mahfouz, Naguib (Abdel Aziz Al-
     Sabilgi)
   See also DLBY 88
Mahon, Derek 1941- .... CLC 27
   See also CA 113; 128; DLB 40
Mailer, Norman 1923-CLC 1, 2, 3, 4, 5, 8, 11,
     14, 28, 39, 74, 111; DA; DAB; DAC; DAM
     MST, NOV, POP
   See also AITN 2; CA 9-12R; CABS 1; CANR
     28, 74, 77; CDALB 1968-1988; DLB 2, 16,
     28, 185; DLBD 3; DLBY 80, 83; MTCW 1
Maillet, Antonine 1929- .. CLC 54, 118; DAC
   See also CA 115; 120; CANR 46, 74, 77; DLB
     60; INT 120
Mais, Roger 1905-1955 .... TCLC 8
   See also BW 1; CA 105; 124; DLB 125; MTCW
     1
Maistre, Joseph de 1753-1821 .... NCLC 37
Maitland, Frederic 1850-1906 .... TCLC 65
Maitland, Sara (Louise) 1950- .... CLC 49
   See also CA 69-72; CANR 13, 59
Major, Clarence 1936-CLC 3, 19, 48; BLC 2;
     DAM MULT
   See also BW 2; CA 21-24R; CAAS 6; CANR
     13, 25, 53; DLB 33
Major, Kevin (Gerald) 1949- .. CLC 26; DAC
   See also AAYA 16; CA 97-100; CANR 21, 38;
     CLR 11; DLB 60; INT CANR-21; JRDA;
     MAICYA; SATA 32, 82
Maki, James
   See Ozu, Yasujiro
Malabaila, Damiano
   See Levi, Primo
Malamud, Bernard 1914-1986CLC 1, 2, 3, 5,
     8, 9, 11, 18, 27, 44, 78, 85; DA; DAB; DAC;
     DAM MST, NOV, POP; SSC 15; WLC
   See also AAYA 16; CA 5-8R; 118; CABS 1;
     CANR 28, 62; CDALB 1941-1968; DLB 2,
     28, 152; DLBY 80, 86; MTCW 1
Malan, Herman
   See Bosman, Herman Charles; Bosman, Herman
     Charles
Malaparte, Curzio 1898-1957 .... TCLC 52
Malcolm, Dan
   See Silverberg, Robert
Malcolm X ...... CLC 82, 117; BLC 2; WLCS
   See also Little, Malcolm
Malherbe, Francois de 1555-1628 .... LC 5
Mallarme, Stephane 1842-1898 NCLC 4, 41;
     DAM POET; PC 4

Mallet-Joris, Francoise 1930- .... CLC 11
   See also CA 65-68; CANR 17; DLB 83
Malley, Ern
   See McAuley, James Phillip
Mallowan, Agatha Christie
   See Christie, Agatha (Mary Clarissa)
Maloff, Saul 1922- .... CLC 5
   See also CA 33-36R
Malone, Louis
   See MacNeice, (Frederick) Louis
Malone, Michael (Christopher) 1942-CLC 43
   See also CA 77-80; CANR 14, 32, 57
Malory, (Sir) Thomas 1410(?)-1471(?)LC 11;
     DA; DAB; DAC; DAM MST; WLCS
   See also CDBLB Before 1660; DLB 146; SATA
     59; SATA-Brief 33
Malouf, (George Joseph) David 1934-CLC 28,
     86
   See also CA 124; CANR 50, 76
Malraux, (Georges-)Andre 1901-1976CLC 1,
     4, 9, 13, 15, 57; DAM NOV
   See also CA 21-22; 69-72; CANR 34, 58; CAP
     2; DLB 72; MTCW 1
Malzberg, Barry N(athaniel) 1939- .... CLC 7
   See also CA 61-64; CAAS 4; CANR 16; DLB 8
Mamet, David (Alan) 1947-CLC 9, 15, 34, 46,
     91; DAM DRAM; DC 4
   See also AAYA 3; CA 81-84; CABS 3; CANR
     15, 41, 67, 72; DLB 7; MTCW 1
Mamoulian, Rouben (Zachary) 1897-1987
     CLC 16
   See also CA 25-28R; 124
Mandelstam, Osip (Emilievich) 1891(?)-1938(?)
     TCLC 2, 6; PC 14
   See also CA 104; 150
Mander, (Mary) Jane 1877-1949 ... TCLC 31
   See also CA 162
Mandeville, John fl. 1350- .... CMLC 19
   See also DLB 146
Mandiargues, Andre Pieyre de .... CLC 41
   See also Pieyre de Mandiargues, Andre
   See also DLB 83
Mandrake, Ethel Belle
   See Thurman, Wallace (Henry)
Mangan, James Clarence 1803-1849NCLC 27
Maniere, J.-E.
   See Giraudoux, (Hippolyte) Jean
Mankiewicz, Herman (Jacob) 1897-1953
     TCLC 85
   See also CA 120; 169; DLB 26
Manley, (Mary) Delariviere 1672(?)-1724L C
     1, 42
   See also DLB 39, 80
Mann, Abel
   See Creasey, John
Mann, Emily 1952- .... DC 7
   See also CA 130; CANR 55
Mann, (Luiz) Heinrich 1871-1950 ... TCLC 9
   See also CA 106; 164; DLB 66, 118
Mann, (Paul) Thomas 1875-1955 TCLC 2, 8,
     14, 21, 35, 44, 60; DA; DAB; DAC; DAM
     MST, NOV; SSC 5; WLC
   See also CA 104; 128; DLB 66; MTCW 1
Mannheim, Karl 1893-1947 .... TCLC 65
Manning, David
   See Faust, Frederick (Schiller)
Manning, Frederic 1887(?)-1935 ... TCLC 25
   See also CA 124
Manning, Olivia 1915-1980 .... CLC 5, 19
   See also CA 5-8R; 101; CANR 29; MTCW 1
Mano, D. Keith 1942- .... CLC 2, 10
   See also CA 25-28R; CAAS 6; CANR 26, 57;
     DLB 6

Mansfield, KatherineTCLC 2, 8, 39; DAB; SSC
     9, 23; WLC
   See also Beauchamp, Kathleen Mansfield
   See also DLB 162
Manso, Peter 1940- .... CLC 39
   See also CA 29-32R; CANR 44
Mantecon, Juan Jimenez
   See Jimenez (Mantecon), Juan Ramon
Manton, Peter
   See Creasey, John
Man Without a Spleen, A
   See Chekhov, Anton (Pavlovich)
Manzoni, Alessandro 1785-1873 .... NCLC 29
Map, Walter 1140-1209 .... CMLC 32
Mapu, Abraham (ben Jekutiel) 1808-1867
     NCLC 18
Mara, Sally
   See Queneau, Raymond
Marat, Jean Paul 1743-1793 .... LC 10
Marcel, Gabriel Honore 1889-1973 . CLC 15
   See also CA 102; 45-48; MTCW 1
Marchbanks, Samuel
   See Davies, (William) Robertson
Marchi, Giacomo
   See Bassani, Giorgio
Margulies, Donald .... CLC 76
Marie de France c. 12th cent. - CMLC 8; PC
     22
   See also DLB 208
Marie de l'Incarnation 1599-1672 ...... LC 10
Marier, Captain Victor
   See Griffith, D(avid Lewelyn) W(ark)
Mariner, Scott
   See Pohl, Frederik
Marinetti, Filippo Tommaso 1876-1944TCLC
     10
   See also CA 107; DLB 114
Marivaux, Pierre Carlet de Chamblain de 1688-
     1763 .... LC 4; DC 7
Markandaya, Kamala .... CLC 8, 38
   See also Taylor, Kamala (Purnaiya)
Markfield, Wallace 1926- ....CLC 8
   See also CA 69-72; CAAS 3; DLB 2, 28
Markham, Edwin 1852-1940 .... TCLC 47
   See also CA 160; DLB 54, 186
Markham, Robert
   See Amis, Kingsley (William)
Marks, J
   See Highwater, Jamake (Mamake)
Marks-Highwater, J
   See Highwater, Jamake (Mamake)
Markson, David M(errill) 1927- ...... CLC 67
   See also CA 49-52; CANR 1
Marley, Bob .... CLC 17
   See also Marley, Robert Nesta
Marley, Robert Nesta 1945-1981
   See Marley, Bob
   See also CA 107; 103
Marlowe, Christopher 1564-1593 LC 22, 47;
     DA; DAB; DAC; DAM DRAM, MST; DC
     1; WLC
   See also CDBLB Before 1660; DLB 62
Marlowe, Stephen 1928-
   See Queen, Ellery
   See also CA 13-16R; CANR 6, 55
Marmontel, Jean-Francois 1723-1799 . LC 2
Marquand, John P(hillips) 1893-1960CLC 2,
     10
   See also CA 85-88; CANR 73; DLB 9, 102
Marques, Rene 1919-1979 ..... CLC 96; DAM
     MULT; HLC
   See also CA 97-100; 85-88; DLB 113; HW
Marquez, Gabriel (Jose) Garcia

See Garcia Marquez, Gabriel (Jose)

Marquis, Don(ald Robert Perry) 1878-1937
TCLC 7
See also CA 104; 166; DLB 11, 25

Marric, J. J.
See Creasey, John

Marryat, Frederick 1792-1848 .... **NCLC 3**
See also DLB 21, 163

Marsden, James
See Creasey, John

Marsh, (Edith) Ngaio 1899-1982 **CLC 7, 53;**
DAM POP
See also CA 9-12R; CANR 6, 58; DLB 77;
MTCW 1

Marshall, Garry 1934- .... **CLC 17**
See also AAYA 3; CA 111; SATA 60

Marshall, Paule 1929- .. **CLC 27, 72; BLC 3;**
DAM MULT; SSC 3
See also BW 2; CA 77-80; CANR 25, 73; DLB
157; MTCW 1

Marshallik
See Zangwill, Israel

Marsten, Richard
See Hunter, Evan

Marston, John 1576-1634**LC 33; DAM DRAM**
See also DLB 58, 172

Martha, Henry
See Harris, Mark

Marti, Jose 1853-1895**NCLC 63; DAM MULT;**
HLC

Martial c. 40-c. 104 .... **PC 10**

Martin, Ken
See Hubbard, L(afayette) Ron(ald)

Martin, Richard
See Creasey, John

Martin, Steve 1945- .... **CLC 30**
See also CA 97-100; CANR 30; MTCW 1

Martin, Valerie 1948- .... **CLC 89**
See also BEST 90:2; CA 85-88; CANR 49

Martin, Violet Florence 1862-1915 **TCLC 51**

Martin, Webber
See Silverberg, Robert

Martindale, Patrick Victor
See White, Patrick (Victor Martindale)

Martin du Gard, Roger 1881-1958 **TCLC 24**
See also CA 118; DLB 65

Martineau, Harriet 1802-1876 .... **NCLC 26**
See also DLB 21, 55, 159, 163, 166, 190; YABC
2

Martines, Julia
See O'Faolain, Julia

Martinez, Enrique Gonzalez
See Gonzalez Martinez, Enrique

Martinez, Jacinto Benavente y
See Benavente (y Martinez), Jacinto

Martinez Ruiz, Jose 1873-1967
See Azorin; Ruiz, Jose Martinez
See also CA 93-96; HW

Martinez Sierra, Gregorio 1881-1947**TCLC 6**
See also CA 115

Martinez Sierra, Maria (de la O'LeJarraga)
1874-1974 .... **TCLC 6**
See also CA 115

Martinsen, Martin
See Follett, Ken(neth Martin)

Martinson, Harry (Edmund) 1904-1978**C L C**
14
See also CA 77-80; CANR 34

Marut, Ret
See Traven, B.

Marut, Robert
See Traven, B.

Marvell, Andrew 1621-1678 ... **LC 4, 43; DA;**

DAB; DAC; DAM MST, POET; PC 10;
WLC
See also CDBLB 1660-1789; DLB 131

Marx, Karl (Heinrich) 1818-1883 . **NCLC 17**
See also DLB 129

Masaoka Shiki .... **TCLC 18**
See also Masaoka Tsunenori

Masaoka Tsunenori 1867-1902
See Masaoka Shiki
See also CA 117

Masefield, John (Edward) 1878-1967**CLC 11,**
47; DAM POET
See also CA 19-20; 25-28R; CANR 33; CAP 2;
CDBLB 1890-1914; DLB 10, 19, 153, 160;
MTCW 1; SATA 19

Maso, Carole 19(?)- .... **CLC 44**
See also CA 170

Mason, Bobbie Ann 1940-**CLC 28, 43, 82; SSC**
4
See also AAYA 5; CA 53-56; CANR 11, 31,
58; DLB 173; DLBY 87; INT CANR-31;
MTCW 1

Mason, Ernst
See Pohl, Frederik

Mason, Lee W.
See Malzberg, Barry N(athaniel)

Mason, Nick 1945- .... **CLC 35**

Mason, Tally
See Derleth, August (William)

Mass, William
See Gibson, William

Master Lao
See Lao Tzu

Masters, Edgar Lee 1868-1950 **TCLC 2, 25;**
DA; DAC; DAM MST, POET; PC 1;
WLCS
See also CA 104; 133; CDALB 1865-1917;
DLB 54; MTCW 1

Masters, Hilary 1928- .... **CLC 48**
See also CA 25-28R; CANR 13, 47

Mastrosimone, William 19(?)- .... **CLC 36**

Mathe, Albert
See Camus, Albert

Mather, Cotton 1663-1728 .... **LC 38**
See also CDALB 1640-1865; DLB 24, 30, 140

Mather, Increase 1639-1723 .... **LC 38**
See also DLB 24

Matheson, Richard Burton 1926- ..... **CLC 37**
See also CA 97-100; DLB 8, 44; INT 97-100

Mathews, Harry 1930- .... **CLC 6, 52**
See also CA 21-24R; CAAS 6; CANR 18, 40

Mathews, John Joseph 1894-1979 .. **CLC 84;**
DAM MULT
See also CA 19-20; 142; CANR 45; CAP 2;
DLB 175; NNAL

Mathias, Roland (Glyn) 1915- .... **CLC 45**
See also CA 97-100; CANR 19, 41; DLB 27

Matsuo Basho 1644-1694 .... **PC 3**
See also DAM POET

Mattheson, Rodney
See Creasey, John

Matthews, Greg 1949- .... **CLC 45**
See also CA 135

Matthews, William (Procter, III) 1942-1997
CLC 40
See also CA 29-32R; 162; CAAS 18; CANR
12, 57; DLB 5

Matthias, John (Edward) 1941- .... **CLC 9**
See also CA 33-36R; CANR 56

Matthiessen, Peter 1927-**CLC 5, 7, 11, 32, 64;**
DAM NOV
See also AAYA 6; BEST 90:4; CA 9-12R;
CANR 21, 50, 73; DLB 6, 173; MTCW 1,

SATA 27

Maturin, Charles Robert 1780(?)-1824**NCLC**
6
See also DLB 178

Matute (Ausejo), Ana Maria 1925- .. **CLC 11**
See also CA 89-92; MTCW 1

Maugham, W. S.
See Maugham, W(illiam) Somerset

Maugham, W(illiam) Somerset 1874-1965
CLC 1, 11, 15, 67, 93; DA; DAB; DAC;
DAM DRAM, MST, NOV; SSC 8; WLC
See also CA 5-8R; 25-28R; CANR 40; CDBLB
1914-1945; DLB 10, 36, 77, 100, 162, 195;
MTCW 1; SATA 54

Maugham, William Somerset
See Maugham, W(illiam) Somerset

Maupassant, (Henri Rene Albert) Guy de 1850-
1893**NCLC 1, 42; DA; DAB; DAC; DAM**
MST; SSC 1; WLC
See also DLB 123

Maupin, Armistead 1944-**CLC 95; DAM POP**
See also CA 125; 130; CANR 58; INT 130

Maurhut, Richard
See Traven, B.

Mauriac, Claude 1914-1996 .... **CLC 9**
See also CA 89-92; 152; DLB 83

Mauriac, Francois (Charles) 1885-1970 **C L C**
4, 9, 56; SSC 24
See also CA 25-28; CAP 2; DLB 65; MTCW 1

Mavor, Osborne Henry 1888-1951
See Bridie, James
See also CA 104

Maxwell, William (Keepers, Jr.) 1908-**CLC 19**
See also CA 93-96; CANR 54; DLBY 80; INT
93-96

May, Elaine 1932- .... **CLC 16**
See also CA 124; 142; DLB 44

Mayakovski, Vladimir (Vladimirovich) 1893-
1930 .... **TCLC 4, 18**
See also CA 104; 158

Mayhew, Henry 1812-1887 .... **NCLC 31**
See also DLB 18, 55, 190

Mayle, Peter 1939(?)- .... **CLC 89**
See also CA 139; CANR 64

Maynard, Joyce 1953- .... **CLC 23**
See also CA 111; 129; CANR 64

Mayne, William (James Carter) 1928-**CLC 12**
See also AAYA 20; CA 9-12R; CANR 37; CLR
25; JRDA; MAICYA; SAAS 11; SATA 6, 68

Mayo, Jim
See L'Amour, Louis (Dearborn)

Maysles, Albert 1926- .... **CLC 16**
See also CA 29-32R

Maysles, David 1932- .... **CLC 16**

Mazer, Norma Fox 1931- .... **CLC 26**
See also AAYA 5; CA 69-72; CANR 12, 32,
66; CLR 23; JRDA; MAICYA; SAAS 1;
SATA 24, 67, 105

Mazzini, Guiseppe 1805-1872 .... **NCLC 34**

McAuley, James Phillip 1917-1976 .. **CLC 45**
See also CA 97-100

McBain, Ed
See Hunter, Evan

McBrien, William Augustine 1930- .. **CLC 44**
See also CA 107

McCaffrey, Anne (Inez) 1926-**CLC 17; DAM**
NOV, POP
See also AAYA 6; AITN 2; BEST 89:2; CA 25-
28R; CANR 15, 35, 55; CLR 49; DLB 8;
JRDA; MAICYA; MTCW 1; SAAS 11; SATA
8, 70

McCall, Nathan 1955(?)- .... **CLC 86**
See also CA 146

Pollock, (Mary) Sharon 1936-**CLC 50; DAC;
    DAM DRAM, MST**
    See also CA 141; DLB 60
Polo, Marco 1254-1324 .... **CMLC 15**
Polonsky, Abraham (Lincoln) 1910- **CLC 92**
    See also CA 104; DLB 26; INT 104
Polybius c. 200B.C.-c. 118B.C. ...... **CMLC 17**
    See also DLB 176
Pomerance, Bernard 1940-.... **CLC 13; DAM
    DRAM**
    See also CA 101; CANR 49
Ponge, Francis (Jean Gaston Alfred) 1899-1988
    CLC 6, 18; DAM POET
    See also CA 85-88; 126; CANR 40
Pontoppidan, Henrik 1857-1943 .... **TCLC 29**
    See also CA 170
Poole, Josephine .... **CLC 17**
    See also Helyar, Jane Penelope Josephine
    See also SAAS 2; SATA 5
Popa, Vasko 1922-1991 .... **CLC 19**
    See also CA 112; 148; DLB 181
Pope, Alexander 1688-1744 **LC 3; DA; DAB;
    DAC; DAM MST, POET; WLC**
    See also CDBLB 1660-1789; DLB 95, 101
Porter, Connie (Rose) 1959(?)- .... **CLC 70**
    See also BW 2; CA 142; SATA 81
Porter, Gene(va Grace) Stratton 1863(?)-1924
    TCLC 21
    See also CA 112
Porter, Katherine Anne 1890-1980**CLC 1, 3, 7,
    10, 13, 15, 27, 101; DA; DAB; DAC; DAM
    MST, NOV; SSC 4, 31**
    See also AITN 2; CA 1-4R; 101; CANR 1, 65;
    DLB 4, 9, 102; DLBD 12; DLBY 80; MTCW
    1; SATA 39; SATA-Obit 23
Porter, Peter (Neville Frederick) 1929-**CLC 5,
    13, 33**
    See also CA 85-88; DLB 40
Porter, William Sydney 1862-1910
    See Henry, O.
    See also CA 104; 131; CDALB 1865-1917; DA;
    DAB; DAC; DAM MST; DLB 12, 78, 79;
    MTCW 1; YABC 2
Portillo (y Pacheco), Jose Lopez
    See Lopez Portillo (y Pacheco), Jose
Post, Melville Davisson 1869-1930 **TCLC 39**
    See also CA 110
Potok, Chaim 1929- .... **CLC 2, 7, 14, 26, 112;
    DAM NOV**
    See also AAYA 15; AITN 1, 2; CA 17-20R;
    CANR 19, 35, 64; DLB 28, 152; INT CANR-
    19; MTCW 1; SATA 33
Potter, (Helen) Beatrix 1866-1943
    See Webb, (Martha) Beatrice (Potter)
    See also MAICYA
Potter, Dennis (Christopher George) 1935-1994
    CLC 58, 86
    See also CA 107; 145; CANR 33, 61; MTCW 1
Pound, Ezra (Weston Loomis) 1885-1972
    **CLC 1, 2, 3, 4, 5, 7, 10, 13, 18, 34, 48, 50,
    112; DA; DAB; DAC; DAM MST, POET;
    PC 4; WLC**
    See also CA 5-8R; 37-40R; CANR 40; CDALB
    1917-1929; DLB 4, 45, 63; DLBD 15;
    MTCW 1
Povod, Reinaldo 1959-1994 .... **CLC 44**
    See also CA 136; 146
Powell, Adam Clayton, Jr. 1908-1972**CLC 89;
    BLC 3; DAM MULT**
    See also BW 1; CA 102; 33-36R
Powell, Anthony (Dymoke) 1905-**CLC 1, 3, 7,
    9, 10, 31**
    See also CA 1-4R; CANR 1, 32, 62; CDBLB

1945-1960; DLB 15; MTCW 1
Powell, Dawn 1897-1965 ....**CLC 66**
    See also CA 5-8R; DLBY 97
Powell, Padgett 1952-.........................**CLC 34**
    See also CA 126; CANR 63
Power, Susan 1961- ....**CLC 91**
Powers, J(ames) F(arl) 1917-**CLC 1, 4, 8, 57;
    SSC 4**
    See also CA 1-4R; CANR 2, 61; DLB 130;
    MTCW 1
Powers, John J(ames) 1945-
    See Powers, John R.
    See also CA 69-72
Powers, John R. ....**CLC 66**
    See also Powers, John J(ames)
Powers, Richard (S.) 1957- ....**CLC 93**
    See also CA 148
Pownall, David 1938- ....**CLC 10**
    See also CA 89-92; CAAS 18; CANR 49; DLB
    14
Powys, John Cowper 1872-1963**CLC 7, 9, 15,
    46**
    See also CA 85-88; DLB 15; MTCW 1
Powys, T(heodore) F(rancis) 1875-1953
    TCLC 9
    See also CA 106; DLB 36, 162
Prado (Calvo), Pedro 1886-1952 ... **TCLC 75**
    See also CA 131; HW
Prager, Emily 1952- ....**CLC 56**
Pratt, E(dwin) J(ohn) 1883(?)-1964 **CLC 19;
    DAC; DAM POET**
    See also CA 141; 93-96; CANR 77; DLB 92
Premchand .... **TCLC 21**
    See also Srivastava, Dhanpat Rai
Preussler, Otfried 1923- ....**CLC 17**
    See also CA 77-80; SATA 24
Prevert, Jacques (Henri Marie) 1900-1977
    CLC 15
    See also CA 77-80; 69-72; CANR 29, 61;
    MTCW 1; SATA-Obit 30
Prevost, Abbe (Antoine Francois) 1697-1763
    LC 1
Price, (Edward) Reynolds 1933-**CLC 3, 6, 13,
    43, 50, 63; DAM NOV; SSC 22**
    See also CA 1-4R; CANR 1, 37, 57; DLB 2;
    INT CANR-37
Price, Richard 1949- .... **CLC 6, 12**
    See also CA 49-52; CANR 3; DLBY 81
Prichard, Katharine Susannah 1883-1969
    CLC 46
    See also CA 11-12; CANR 33; CAP 1; MTCW
    1; SATA 66
Priestley, J(ohn) B(oynton) 1894-1984**CLC 2,
    5, 9, 34; DAM DRAM, NOV**
    See also CA 9-12R; 113; CANR 33; CDBLB
    1914-1945; DLB 10, 34, 77, 100, 139; DLBY
    84; MTCW 1
Prince 1958(?)- ....**CLC 35**
Prince, F(rank) T(empleton) 1912-...**CLC 22**
    See also CA 101; CANR 43; DLB 20
Prince Kropotkin
    See Kropotkin, Peter (Aleksieevich)
Prior, Matthew 1664-1721 .... **LC 4**
    See also DLB 95
Prishvin, Mikhail 1873-1954 .... **TCLC 75**
Pritchard, William H(arrison) 1932- **CLC 34**
    See also CA 65-68; CANR 23; DLB 111
Pritchett, V(ictor) S(awdon) 1900-1997 **C L C
    5, 13, 15, 41; DAM NOV; SSC 14**
    See also CA 61-64; 157; CANR 31, 63; DLB
    15, 139; MTCW 1
Private 19022
    See Manning, Frederic

Probst, Mark 1925- .... **CLC 59**
    See also CA 130
Prokosch, Frederic 1908-1989 ..... **CLC 4, 48**
    See also CA 73-76; 128; DLB 48
Propertius, Sextus 50(?)B.C.-15(?)B.C.**CMLC
    32**
Prophet, The
    See Dreiser, Theodore (Herman Albert)
Prose, Francine 1947- .... **CLC 45**
    See also CA 109; 112; CANR 46; SATA 101
Proudhon
    See Cunha, Euclides (Rodrigues Pimenta) da
Proulx, Annie
    See Proulx, E(dna) Annie
Proulx, E(dna) Annie 1935-...**CLC 81; DAM
    POP**
    See also CA 145; CANR 65
**Proust, (Valentin-Louis-George-Eugene-)
    Marcel** 1871-1922 **TCLC 7, 13, 33; DA;
    DAB; DAC; DAM MST, NOV; WLC**
    See also CA 104; 120; DLB 65; MTCW 1
Prowler, Harley
    See Masters, Edgar Lee
Prus, Boleslaw 1845-1912 .... **TCLC 48**
Pryor, Richard (Franklin Lenox Thomas) 1940-
    CLC 26
    See also CA 122; 152
Przybyszewski, Stanislaw 1868-1927**TCLC 36**
    See also CA 160; DLB 66
Pteleon
    See Grieve, C(hristopher) M(urray)
    See also DAM POET
Puckett, Lute
    See Masters, Edgar Lee
Puig, Manuel 1932-1990**CLC 3, 5, 10, 28, 65;
    DAM MULT; HLC**
    See also CA 45-48; CANR 2, 32, 63; DLB 113;
    HW; MTCW 1
Pulitzer, Joseph 1847-1911 .... **TCLC 76**
    See also CA 114; DLB 23
Purdy, A(lfred) W(ellington) 1918-**CLC 3, 6,
    14, 50; DAC; DAM MST, POET**
    See also CA 81-84; CAAS 17; CANR 42, 66;
    DLB 88
Purdy, James (Amos) 1923-**CLC 2, 4, 10, 28,
    52**
    See also CA 33-36R; CAAS 1; CANR 19, 51;
    DLB 2; INT CANR-19; MTCW 1
Pure, Simon
    See Swinnerton, Frank Arthur
Pushkin, Alexander (Sergeyevich) 1799-1837
    **NCLC 3, 27; DA; DAB; DAC; DAM
    DRAM, MST, POET; PC 10; SSC 27;
    WLC**
    See also DLB 205; SATA 61
P'u Sung-ling 1640-1715... **LC 3, 49; SSC 31**
Putnam, Arthur Lee
    See Alger, Horatio, Jr.
Puzo, Mario 1920-**CLC 1, 2, 6, 36, 107; DAM
    NOV, POP**
    See also CA 65-68; CANR 4, 42, 65; DLB 6;
    MTCW 1
Pygge, Edward
    See Barnes, Julian (Patrick)
Pyle, Ernest Taylor 1900-1945
    See Pyle, Ernie
    See also CA 115; 160
Pyle, Ernie 1900-1945 .... **TCLC 75**
    See also Pyle, Ernest Taylor
    See also DLB 29
Pyle, Howard 1853-1911 .... **TCLC 81**
    See also CA 109; 137; CLR 22; DLB 42, 188;
    DLBD 13; MAICYA; SATA 16, 100

Pym, Barbara (Mary Crampton) 1913-1980 **CLC 13, 19, 37, 111**
　　See also CA 13-14; 97-100; CANR 13, 34; CAP 1; DLB 14, 207; DLBY 87; MTCW 1
Pynchon, Thomas (Ruggles, Jr.) 1937-**CLC 2, 3, 6, 9, 11, 18, 33, 62, 72; DA; DAB; DAC; DAM MST, NOV, POP; SSC 14; WLC**
　　See also BEST 90:2; CA 17-20R; CANR 22, 46, 73; DLB 2, 173; MTCW 1
Pythagoras c. 570B.C.-c. 500B.C. . **CMLC 22**
　　See also DLB 176
Q
　　See Quiller-Couch, SirArthur (Thomas)
Qian Zhongshu
　　See Ch'ien Chung-shu
Qroll
　　See Dagerman, Stig (Halvard)
Quarrington, Paul (Lewis) 1953-..... **CLC 65**
　　See also CA 129; CANR 62
Quasimodo, Salvatore 1901-1968 .... **CLC 10**
　　See also CA 13-16; 25-28R; CAP 1; DLB 114; MTCW 1
Quay, Stephen 1947- .... **CLC 95**
Quay, Timothy 1947- .... **CLC 95**
Queen, Ellery ....**CLC 3, 11**
　　See also Dannay, Frederic; Davidson, Avram; Lee, Manfred B(ennington); Marlowe, Stephen; Sturgeon, Theodore (Hamilton); Vance, John Holbrook
Queen, Ellery, Jr.
　　See Dannay, Frederic; Lee, Manfred B(ennington)
Queneau, Raymond 1903-1976 **CLC 2, 5, 10, 42**
　　See also CA 77-80; 69-72; CANR 32; DLB 72; MTCW 1
Quevedo, Francisco de 1580-1645 ...... **LC 23**
Quiller-Couch, SirArthur (Thomas) 1863-1944 **TCLC 53**
　　See also CA 118; 166; DLB 135, 153, 190
Quin, Ann (Marie) 1936-1973 ....**CLC 6**
　　See also CA 9-12R; 45-48, DLB 14
Quinn, Martin
　　See Smith, Martin Cruz
Quinn, Peter 1947- .... **CLC 91**
Quinn, Simon
　　See Smith, Martin Cruz
Quiroga, Horacio (Sylvestre) 1878-1937 **TCLC 20; DAM MULT; HLC**
　　See also CA 117; 131; HW; MTCW 1
Quoirez, Francoise 1935-.....................**CLC 9**
　　See also Sagan, Francoise
　　See also CA 49-52; CANR 6, 39, 73; MTCW 1
Raabe, Wilhelm (Karl) 1831-1910 . **TCLC 45**
　　See also CA 167; DLB 129
Rabe, David (William) 1940-... **CLC 4, 8, 33; DAM DRAM**
　　See also CA 85-88; CABS 3; CANR 59; DLB 7
Rabelais, Francois 1483-1553**LC 5; DA; DAB; DAC; DAM MST; WLC**
Rabinovitch, Sholem 1859-1916
　　See Aleichem, Sholom
　　See also CA 104
Rabinyan, Dorit 1972- ....**CLC 119**
　　See also CA 170
Rachilde 1860-1953 .... **TCLC 67**
　　See also DLB 123, 192
Racine, Jean 1639-1699 . **LC 28; DAB; DAM MST**
Radcliffe, Ann (Ward) 1764-1823**NCLC 6, 55**
　　See also DLB 39, 178
Radiguet, Raymond 1903-1923 ...... **TCLC 29**
　　See also CA 162; DLB 65

Radnoti, Miklos 1909-1944 .... **TCLC 16**
　　See also CA 118
Rado, James 1939- ....**CLC 17**
　　See also CA 105
Radvanyi, Netty 1900-1983
　　See Seghers, Anna
　　See also CA 85-88; 110
Rae, Ben
　　See Griffiths, Trevor
Raeburn, John (Hay) 1941- ....**CLC 34**
　　See also CA 57-60
Ragni, Gerome 1942-1991 ....**CLC 17**
　　See also CA 105; 134
Rahv, Philip 1908-1973 ....**CLC 24**
　　See also Greenberg, Ivan
　　See also DLB 137
Raimund, Ferdinand Jakob 1790-1836**NCLC 69**
　　See also DLB 90
Raine, Craig 1944- .... **CLC 32, 103**
　　See also CA 108; CANR 29, 51; DLB 40
Raine, Kathleen (Jessie) 1908- ..... **CLC 7, 45**
　　See also CA 85-88; CANR 46; DLB 20; MTCW 1
Rainis, Janis 1865-1929 .... **TCLC 29**
　　See also CA 170
Rakosi, Carl 1903-............................**CLC 47**
　　See also Rawley, Callman
　　See also CAAS 5; DLB 193
Raleigh, Richard
　　See Lovecraft, H(oward) P(hillips)
Raleigh, Sir Walter 1554(?)-1618 . **LC 31, 39**
　　See also CDBLB Before 1660; DLB 172
Rallentando, H. P.
　　See Sayers, Dorothy L(eigh)
Ramal, Walter
　　See de la Mare, Walter (John)
Ramana Maharshi 1879-1950 .... **TCLC 84**
Ramon, Juan
　　See Jimenez (Mantecon), Juan Ramon
Ramos, Graciliano 1892-1953 .... **TCLC 32**
　　See also CA 167
Rampersad, Arnold 1941- ....**CLC 44**
　　See also BW 2; CA 127; 133; DLB 111; INT 133
Rampling, Anne
　　See Rice, Anne
Ramsay, Allan 1684(?)-1758 .... **LC 29**
　　See also DLB 95
Ramuz, Charles-Ferdinand 1878-1947**TCLC 33**
　　See also CA 165
Rand, Ayn 1905-1982**CLC 3, 30, 44, 79; DA; DAC; DAM MST, NOV, POP; WLC**
　　See also AAYA 10; CA 13-16R; 105; CANR 27, 73; MTCW 1
Randall, Dudley (Felker) 1914-**CLC 1; BLC 3; DAM MULT**
　　See also BW 1; CA 25-28R; CANR 23; DLB 41
Randall, Robert
　　See Silverberg, Robert
Ranger, Ken
　　See Creasey, John
Ransom, John Crowe 1888-1974**CLC 2, 4, 5, 11, 24; DAM POET**
　　See also CA 5-8R; 49-52; CANR 6, 34; DLB 45, 63; MTCW 1
Rao, Raja 1909- ...... **CLC 25, 56; DAM NOV**
　　See also CA 73-76; CANR 51; MTCW 1
Raphael, Frederic (Michael) 1931-**CLC 2, 14**
　　See also CA 1-4R; CANR 1; DLB 14
Ratcliffe, James P.

　　See Mencken, H(enry) L(ouis)
Rathbone, Julian 1935-......................**CLC 41**
　　See also CA 101; CANR 34, 73
Rattigan, Terence (Mervyn) 1911-1977**CLC 7; DAM DRAM**
　　See also CA 85-88; 73-76; CDBLB 1945-1960; DLB 13; MTCW 1
Ratushinskaya, Irina 1954- ....**CLC 54**
　　See also CA 129; CANR 68
Raven, Simon (Arthur Noel) 1927- ...**CLC 14**
　　See also CA 81-84
Ravenna, Michael
　　See Welty, Eudora
Rawley, Callman 1903-
　　See Rakosi, Carl
　　See also CA 21-24R; CANR 12, 32
Rawlings, Marjorie Kinnan 1896-1953**TCLC 4**
　　See also AAYA 20; CA 104; 137; CANR 74; DLB 9, 22, 102; DLBD 17; JRDA; MAICYA; SATA 100; YABC 1
Ray, Satyajit 1921-1992 .. **CLC 16, 76; DAM MULT**
　　See also CA 114; 137
Read, Herbert Edward 1893-1968 .....**CLC 4**
　　See also CA 85-88; 25-28R; DLB 20, 149
Read, Piers Paul 1941-............ **CLC 4, 10, 25**
　　See also CA 21-24R; CANR 38; DLB 14; SATA 21
Reade, Charles 1814-1884 ....**NCLC 2, 74**
　　See also DLB 21
Reade, Hamish
　　See Gray, Simon (James Holliday)
Reading, Peter 1946- ....**CLC 47**
　　See also CA 103; CANR 46; DLB 40
Reaney, James 1926- ... **CLC 13; DAC; DAM MST**
　　See also CA 41-44R; CAAS 15; CANR 42; DLB 68; SATA 43
Rebreanu, Liviu 1885-1944 .... **TCLC 28**
　　See also CA 165
Rechy, John (Francisco) 1934- **CLC 1, 7, 14, 18, 107; DAM MULT; HLC**
　　See also CA 5-8R; CAAS 4; CANR 6, 32, 64; DLB 122; DLBY 82; HW; INT CANR-6
Redcam, Tom 1870-1933 .... **TCLC 25**
Reddin, Keith ....**CLC 67**
Redgrove, Peter (William) 1932- . **CLC 6, 41**
　　See also CA 1-4R; CANR 3, 39, 77; DLB 40
Redmon, Anne ....**CLC 22**
　　See also Nightingale, Anne Redmon
　　See also DLBY 86
Reed, Eliot
　　See Ambler, Eric
Reed, Ishmael 1938-**CLC 2, 3, 5, 6, 13, 32, 60; BLC 3; DAM MULT**
　　See also BW 2; CA 21-24R; CANR 25, 48, 74; DLB 2, 5, 33, 169; DLBD 8; MTCW 1
Reed, John (Silas) 1887-1920 ....**TCLC 9**
　　See also CA 106
Reed, Lou ....**CLC 21**
　　See also Firbank, Louis
Reeve, Clara 1729-1807 ....**NCLC 19**
　　See also DLB 39
Reich, Wilhelm 1897-1957 ....**TCLC 57**
Reid, Christopher (John) 1949- ....**CLC 33**
　　See also CA 140; DLB 40
Reid, Desmond
　　See Moorcock, Michael (John)
Reid Banks, Lynne 1929-
　　See Banks, Lynne Reid
　　See also CA 1-4R; CANR 6, 22, 38; CLR 24; JRDA; MAICYA; SATA 22, 75

Reilly, William K.
  See Creasey, John
Reiner, Max
  See Caldwell, (Janet Miriam) Taylor (Holland)
Reis, Ricardo
  See Pessoa, Fernando (Antonio Nogueira)
Remarque, Erich Maria 1898-1970 CLC 21;
    DA; DAB; DAC; DAM MST, NOV
    See also AAYA 27; CA 77-80; 29-32R; DLB
    56; MTCW 1
Remington, Frederic 1861-1909 .... TCLC 89
    See also CA 108; 169; DLB 12, 186, 188; SATA
    41
Remizov, A.
  See Remizov, Aleksei (Mikhailovich)
Remizov, A. M.
  See Remizov, Aleksei (Mikhailovich)
Remizov, Aleksei (Mikhailovich) 1877-1957
    TCLC 27
    See also CA 125; 133
Renan, Joseph Ernest 1823-1892 ... NCLC 26
Renard, Jules 1864-1910 .... TCLC 17
    See also CA 117
Renault, Mary .... CLC 3, 11, 17
    See also Challans, Mary
    See also DLBY 83
Rendell, Ruth (Barbara) 1930- . CLC 28, 48;
    DAM POP
    See also Vine, Barbara
    See also CA 109; CANR 32, 52, 74; DLB 87;
    INT CANR-32; MTCW 1
Renoir, Jean 1894-1979 .... CLC 20
    See also CA 129; 85-88
Resnais, Alain 1922- .... CLC 16
Reverdy, Pierre 1889-1960 .... CLC 53
    See also CA 97-100; 89-92
Rexroth, Kenneth 1905-1982 CLC 1, 2, 6, 11,
    22, 49, 112; DAM POET; PC 20
    See also CA 5-8R; 107; CANR 14, 34, 63;
    CDALB 1941-1968; DLB 16, 48, 165;
    DLBY 82; INT CANR-14; MTCW 1
Reyes, Alfonso 1889-1959 .... TCLC 33
    See also CA 131; HW
Reyes y Basoalto, Ricardo Eliecer Neftali
  See Neruda, Pablo
Reymont, Wladyslaw (Stanislaw) 1868(?)-1925
    TCLC 5
    See also CA 104
Reynolds, Jonathan 1942- .... CLC 6, 38
    See also CA 65-68; CANR 28
Reynolds, Joshua 1723-1792 .... LC 15
    See also DLB 104
Reynolds, Michael Shane 1937- .... CLC 44
    See also CA 65-68; CANR 9
Reznikoff, Charles 1894-1976 .... CLC 9
    See also CA 33-36; 61-64; CAP 2; DLB 28, 45
Rezzori (d'Arezzo), Gregor von 1914-1998
    CLC 25
    See also CA 122; 136; 167
Rhine, Richard
  See Silverstein, Alvin
Rhodes, Eugene Manlove 1869-1934TCLC 53
Rhodius, Apollonius c. 3rd cent. B.C.- C M L C
    28
    See also DLB 176
R'hoone
  See Balzac, Honore de
Rhys, Jean 1890(?)-1979 CLC 2, 4, 6, 14, 19,
    51; DAM NOV; SSC 21
    See also CA 25-28R; 85-88; CANR 35, 62;
    CDBLB 1945-1960; DLB 36, 117, 162;
    MTCW 1
Ribeiro, Darcy 1922-1997 .... CLC 34

See also CA 33-36R; 156
Ribeiro, Joao Ubaldo (Osorio Pimentel) 1941-
    CLC 10, 67
    See also CA 81-84
Ribman, Ronald (Burt) 1932- .... CLC 7
    See also CA 21-24R; CANR 46
Ricci, Nino 1959- .... CLC 70
    See also CA 137
Rice, Anne 1941- .... CLC 41; DAM POP
    See also AAYA 9; BEST 89:2; CA 65-68; CANR
    12, 36, 53, 74
Rice, Elmer (Leopold) 1892-1967 CLC 7, 49;
    DAM DRAM
    See also CA 21-22; 25-28R; CAP 2; DLB 4, 7;
    MTCW 1
Rice, Tim(othy Miles Bindon) 1944- CLC 21
    See also CA 103; CANR 46
Rich, Adrienne (Cecile) 1929-CLC 3, 6, 7, 11,
    18, 36, 73, 76; DAM POET; PC 5
    See also CA 9-12R; CANR 20, 53, 74; DLB 5,
    67; MTCW 1
Rich, Barbara
  See Graves, Robert (von Ranke)
Rich, Robert
  See Trumbo, Dalton
Richard, Keith .... CLC 17
    See also Richards, Keith
Richards, David Adams 1950- CLC 59; DAC
    See also CA 93-96; CANR 60; DLB 53
Richards, I(vor) A(rmstrong) 1893-1979C L C
    14, 24
    See also CA 41-44R; 89-92; CANR 34, 74; DLB
    27
Richards, Keith 1943-
  See Richard, Keith
    See also CA 107; CANR 77
Richardson, Anne
  See Roiphe, Anne (Richardson)
Richardson, Dorothy Miller 1873-1957TCLC
    3
    See also CA 104; DLB 36
Richardson, Ethel Florence (Lindesay) 1870-
    1946
  See Richardson, Henry Handel
    See also CA 105
Richardson, Henry Handel .... TCLC 4
    See also Richardson, Ethel Florence (Lindesay)
    See also DLB 197
Richardson, John 1796-1852NCLC 55; DAC
    See also DLB 99
Richardson, Samuel 1689-1761LC 1, 44; DA;
    DAB; DAC; DAM MST, NOV; WLC
    See also CDBLB 1660-1789; DLB 39
Richler, Mordecai 1931-CLC 3, 5, 9, 13, 18, 46,
    70; DAC; DAM MST, NOV
    See also AITN 1; CA 65-68; CANR 31, 62; CLR
    17; DLB 53; MAICYA; MTCW 1; SATA 44,
    98; SATA-Brief 27
Richter, Conrad (Michael) 1890-1968CLC 30
    See also AAYA 21; CA 5-8R; 25-28R; CANR
    23; DLB 9; MTCW 1; SATA 3
Ricostranza, Tom
  See Ellis, Trey
Riddell, Charlotte 1832-1906 .... TCLC 40
    See also CA 165; DLB 156
Riding, Laura .... CLC 3, 7
    See also Jackson, Laura (Riding)
Riefenstahl, Berta Helene Amalia 1902-
  See Riefenstahl, Leni
    See also CA 108
Riefenstahl, Leni .... CLC 16
    See also Riefenstahl, Berta Helene Amalia
Riffe, Ernest

See Bergman, (Ernst) Ingmar
Riggs, (Rolla) Lynn 1899-1954 .... TCLC 56;
    DAM MULT
    See also CA 144; DLB 175; NNAL
Riis, Jacob A(ugust) 1849-1914 ..... TCLC 80
    See also CA 113; 168; DLB 23
Riley, James Whitcomb 1849-1916TCLC 51;
    DAM POET
    See also CA 118; 137; MAICYA; SATA 17
Riley, Tex
  See Creasey, John
Rilke, Rainer Maria 1875-1926TCLC 1, 6, 19;
    DAM POET; PC 2
    See also CA 104; 132; CANR 62; DLB 81;
    MTCW 1
Rimbaud, (Jean Nicolas) Arthur 1854-1891
    NCLC 4, 35; DA; DAB; DAC; DAM MST,
    POET; PC 3; WLC
Rinehart, Mary Roberts 1876-1958TCLC 52
    See also CA 108; 166
Ringmaster, The
  See Mencken, H(enry) L(ouis)
Ringwood, Gwen(dolyn Margaret) Pharis
    1910-1984 .... CLC 48
    See also CA 148; 112; DLB 88
Rio, Michel 19(?)- .... CLC 43
Ritsos, Giannes
  See Ritsos, Yannis
Ritsos, Yannis 1909-1990 .... CLC 6, 13, 31
    See also CA 77-80; 133; CANR 39, 61; MTCW
    1
Ritter, Erika 1948(?)- .... CLC 52
Rivera, Jose Eustasio 1889-1928 ... TCLC 35
    See also CA 162; HW
Rivers, Conrad Kent 1933-1968 .... CLC 1
    See also BW 1; CA 85-88; DLB 41
Rivers, Elfrida
  See Bradley, Marion Zimmer
Riverside, John
  See Heinlein, Robert A(nson)
Rizal, Jose 1861-1896 .... NCLC 27
Roa Bastos, Augusto (Antonio) 1917-CLC 45;
    DAM MULT; HLC
    See also CA 131; DLB 113; HW
Robbe-Grillet, Alain 1922- CLC 1, 2, 4, 6, 8,
    10, 14, 43
    See also CA 9-12R; CANR 33, 65; DLB 83;
    MTCW 1
Robbins, Harold 1916-1997 ..... CLC 5; DAM
    NOV
    See also CA 73-76; 162; CANR 26, 54; MTCW
    1
Robbins, Thomas Eugene 1936-
  See Robbins, Tom
    See also CA 81-84; CANR 29, 59; DAM NOV,
    POP; MTCW 1
Robbins, Tom .... CLC 9, 32, 64
    See also Robbins, Thomas Eugene
    See also BEST 90:3; DLBY 80
Robbins, Trina 1938- .... CLC 21
    See also CA 128
Roberts, Charles G(eorge) D(ouglas) 1860-1943
    TCLC 8
    See also CA 105; CLR 33; DLB 92; SATA 88;
    SATA-Brief 29
Roberts, Elizabeth Madox 1886-1941 T C L C
    68
    See also CA 111; 166; DLB 9, 54, 102; SATA
    33; SATA-Brief 27
Roberts, Kate 1891-1985 .... CLC 15
    See also CA 107; 116
Roberts, Keith (John Kingston) 1935-CLC 14
    See also CA 25-28R; CANR 46

See also Martinez Ruiz, Jose
Rukeyser, Muriel 1913-1980**CLC 6, 10, 15, 27; DAM POET; PC 12**
  See also CA 5-8R; 93-96; CANR 26, 60; DLB 48; MTCW 1; SATA-Obit 22
Rule, Jane (Vance) 1931- .... **CLC 27**
  See also CA 25-28R; CAAS 18; CANR 12; DLB 60
Rulfo, Juan 1918-1986 .... **CLC 8, 80; DAM MULT; HLC; SSC 25**
  See also CA 85-88; 118; CANR 26; DLB 113; HW; MTCW 1
Rumi, Jalal al-Din 1297-1373 .... **CMLC 20**
Runeberg, Johan 1804-1877 .... **NCLC 41**
Runyon, (Alfred) Damon 1884(?)-1946**TCLC 10**
  See also CA 107; 165; DLB 11, 86, 171
Rush, Norman 1933- .... **CLC 44**
  See also CA 121; 126; INT 126
Rushdie, (Ahmed) Salman 1947-**CLC 23, 31, 55, 100; DAB; DAC; DAM MST, NOV, POP; WLCS**
  See also BEST 89:3; CA 108; 111; CANR 33, 56; DLB 194; INT 111; MTCW 1
Rushforth, Peter (Scott) 1945- .... **CLC 19**
  See also CA 101
Ruskin, John 1819-1900 .... **TCLC 63**
  See also CA 114; 129; CDBLB 1832-1890; DLB 55, 163, 190; SATA 24
Russ, Joanna 1937- .... **CLC 15**
  See also CANR 11, 31, 65; DLB 8; MTCW 1
Russell, George William 1867-1935
  See Baker, Jean H.
  See also CA 104; 153; CDBLB 1890-1914; DAM POET
Russell, (Henry) Ken(neth Alfred) 1927-**CLC 16**
  See also CA 105
Russell, William Martin 1947- .... **CLC 60**
  See also CA 164
Rutherford, Mark .... **TCLC 25**
  See also White, William Hale
  See also DLB 18
Ruyslinck, Ward 1929- .... **CLC 14**
  See also Belser, Reimond Karel Maria de
Ryan, Cornelius (John) 1920-1974 ..... **CLC 7**
  See also CA 69-72; 53-56; CANR 38
Ryan, Michael 1946- .... **CLC 65**
  See also CA 49-52; DLBY 82
Ryan, Tim
  See Dent, Lester
Rybakov, Anatoli (Naumovich) 1911-1998 **CLC 23, 53**
  See also CA 126; 135; 172; SATA 79
Ryder, Jonathan
  See Ludlum, Robert
Ryga, George 1932-1987**CLC 14; DAC; DAM MST**
  See also CA 101; 124; CANR 43; DLB 60
S. H.
  See Hartmann, Sadakichi
S. S.
  See Sassoon, Siegfried (Lorraine)
Saba, Umberto 1883-1957 .... **TCLC 33**
  See also CA 144; DLB 114
Sabatini, Rafael 1875-1950 .... **TCLC 47**
  See also CA 162
Sabato, Ernesto (R.) 1911-**CLC 10, 23; DAM MULT; HLC**
  See also CA 97-100; CANR 32, 65; DLB 145; HW; MTCW 1
Sa-Carniero, Mario de 1890-1916 . **TCLC 83**
Sacastru, Martin

See Bioy Casares, Adolfo
Sacher-Masoch, Leopold von 1836(?)-1895 **NCLC 31**
Sachs, Marilyn (Stickle) 1927- .... **CLC 35**
  See also AAYA 2; CA 17-20R; CANR 13, 47; CLR 2; JRDA; MAICYA; SAAS 2; SATA 3, 68
Sachs, Nelly 1891-1970 .... **CLC 14, 98**
  See also CA 17-18; 25-28R; CAP 2
Sackler, Howard (Oliver) 1929-1982 **CLC 14**
  See also CA 61-64; 108; CANR 30; DLB 7
Sacks, Oliver (Wolf) 1933- .... **CLC 67**
  See also CA 53-56; CANR 28, 50, 76; INT CANR-28; MTCW 1
Sadakichi
  See Hartmann, Sadakichi
Sade, Donatien Alphonse Francois, Comte de 1740-1814 .... **NCLC 47**
Sadoff, Ira 1945- .... **CLC 9**
  See also CA 53-56; CANR 5, 21; DLB 120
Saetone
  See Camus, Albert
Safire, William 1929- .... **CLC 10**
  See also CA 17-20R; CANR 31, 54
Sagan, Carl (Edward) 1934-1996**CLC 30, 112**
  See also AAYA 2; CA 25-28R; 155; CANR 11, 36, 74; MTCW 1; SATA 58; SATA-Obit 94
Sagan, Francoise .... **CLC 3, 6, 9, 17, 36**
  See also Quoirez, Francoise
  See also DLB 83
Sahgal, Nayantara (Pandit) 1927- .... **CLC 41**
  See also CA 9-12R; CANR 11
Saint, H(arry) F. 1941- .... **CLC 50**
  See also CA 127
St. Aubin de Teran, Lisa 1953-
  See Teran, Lisa St. Aubin de
  See also CA 118; 126; INT 126
Saint Birgitta of Sweden c. 1303-1373**CMLC 24**
Sainte-Beuve, Charles Augustin 1804-1869 **NCLC 5**
Saint-Exupery, Antoine (Jean Baptiste Marie Roger) de 1900-1944**TCLC 2, 56; DAM NOV; WLC**
  See also CA 108; 132; CLR 10; DLB 72; MAICYA; MTCW 1; SATA 20
St. John, David
  See Hunt, E(verette) Howard, (Jr.)
Saint-John Perse
  See Leger, (Marie-Rene Auguste) Alexis Saint-Leger
Saintsbury, George (Edward Bateman) 1845-1933 .... **TCLC 31**
  See also CA 160; DLB 57, 149
Sait Faik .... **TCLC 23**
  See also Abasiyanik, Sait Faik
Saki .... **TCLC 3; SSC 12**
  See also Munro, H(ector) H(ugh)
Sala, George Augustus .... **NCLC 46**
Salama, Hannu 1936- .... **CLC 18**
Salamanca, J(ack) R(ichard) 1922-**CLC 4, 15**
  See also CA 25-28R
Sale, J. Kirkpatrick
  See Sale, Kirkpatrick
Sale, Kirkpatrick 1937- .... **CLC 68**
  See also CA 13-16R; CANR 10
Salinas, Luis Omar 1937- ...... **CLC 90; DAM MULT; HLC**
  See also CA 131; DLB 82; HW
Salinas (y Serrano), Pedro 1891(?)-1951 **TCLC 17**
  See also CA 117; DLB 134
Salinger, J(erome) D(avid) 1919-**CLC 1, 3, 8,**

12, 55, 56; DA; DAB; DAC; DAM MST, NOV, POP; SSC 2, 28; WLC
  See also AAYA 2; CA 5-8R; CANR 39; CDALB 1941-1968; CLR 18; DLB 2, 102, 173; MAICYA; MTCW 1; SATA 67
Salisbury, John
  See Caute, (John) David
Salter, James 1925- .... **CLC 7, 52, 59**
  See also CA 73-76; DLB 130
Saltus, Edgar (Everton) 1855-1921 . **TCLC 8**
  See also CA 105; DLB 202
Saltykov, Mikhail Evgrafovich 1826-1889 **NCLC 16**
Samarakis, Antonis 1919- .... **CLC 5**
  See also CA 25-28R; CAAS 16; CANR 36
Sanchez, Florencio 1875-1910 .... **TCLC 37**
  See also CA 153; HW
Sanchez, Luis Rafael 1936- .... **CLC 23**
  See also CA 128; DLB 145; HW
Sanchez, Sonia 1934- ... **CLC 5, 116; BLC 3; DAM MULT; PC 9**
  See also BW 2; CA 33-36R; CANR 24, 49, 74; CLR 18; DLB 41; DLBD 8; MAICYA; MTCW 1; SATA 22
Sand, George 1804-1876**NCLC 2, 42, 57; DA; DAB; DAC; DAM MST, NOV; WLC**
  See also DLB 119, 192
Sandburg, Carl (August) 1878-1967**CLC 1, 4, 10, 15, 35; DA; DAB; DAC; DAM MST, POET; PC 2; WLC**
  See also AAYA 24; CA 5-8R; 25-28R; CANR 35; CDALB 1865-1917; DLB 17, 54; MAICYA; MTCW 1; SATA 8
Sandburg, Charles
  See Sandburg, Carl (August)
Sandburg, Charles A.
  See Sandburg, Carl (August)
Sanders, (James) Ed(ward) 1939- .. **CLC 53; DAM POET**
  See also CA 13-16R; CAAS 21; CANR 13, 44; DLB 16
Sanders, Lawrence 1920-1998**CLC 41; DAM POP**
  See also BEST 89:4; CA 81-84; 165; CANR 33, 62; MTCW 1
Sanders, Noah
  See Blount, Roy (Alton), Jr.
Sanders, Winston P.
  See Anderson, Poul (William)
Sandoz, Mari(e Susette) 1896-1966 . **CLC 28**
  See also CA 1-4R; 25-28R; CANR 17, 64; DLB 9; MTCW 1; SATA 5
Saner, Reg(inald Anthony) 1931- .... **CLC 9**
  See also CA 65-68
Sankara 788-820 .... **CMLC 32**
Sannazaro, Jacopo 1456(?)-1530 .... **LC 8**
Sansom, William 1912-1976 **CLC 2, 6; DAM NOV; SSC 21**
  See also CA 5-8R; 65-68; CANR 42; DLB 139; MTCW 1
Santayana, George 1863-1952 .... **TCLC 40**
  See also CA 115; DLB 54, 71; DLBD 13
Santiago, Danny .... **CLC 33**
  See also James, Daniel (Lewis)
  See also DLB 122
Santmyer, Helen Hoover 1895-1986 **CLC 33**
  See also CA 1-4R; 118; CANR 15, 33; DLBY 84; MTCW 1
Santoka, Taneda 1882-1940 .... **TCLC 72**
Santos, Bienvenido N(uqui) 1911-1996 .**CLC 22; DAM MULT**
  See also CA 101; 151; CANR 19, 46
Sapper .... **TCLC 44**

See Hubbard, L(afayette) Ron(ald)
Sealy, I. Allan 1951- .... **CLC 55**
Search, Alexander
　See Pessoa, Fernando (Antonio Nogueira)
Sebastian, Lee
　See Silverberg, Robert
Sebastian Owl
　See Thompson, Hunter S(tockton)
Sebestyen, Ouida 1924- .... **CLC 30**
　See also AAYA 8; CA 107; CANR 40; CLR 17;
　JRDA; MAICYA; SAAS 10; SATA 39
Secundus, H. Scriblerus
　See Fielding, Henry
Sedges, John
　See Buck, Pearl S(ydenstricker)
Sedgwick, Catharine Maria 1789-1867 **N C L C**
　19
　See also DLB 1, 74
Seelye, John (Douglas) 1931- .... **CLC 7**
　See also CA 97-100; CANR 70; INT 97-100
Seferiades, Giorgos Stylianou 1900-1971
　See Seferis, George
　See also CA 5-8R; 33-36R; CANR 5, 36;
　MTCW 1
Seferis, George .... **CLC 5, 11**
　See also Seferiades, Giorgos Stylianou
Segal, Erich (Wolf) 1937- .. **CLC 3, 10; DAM**
　POP
　See also BEST 89:1; CA 25-28R; CANR 20,
　36, 65; DLBY 86; INT CANR-20; MTCW 1
Seger, Bob 1945- .... **CLC 35**
Seghers, Anna .... **CLC 7**
　See also Radvanyi, Netty
　See also DLB 69
Seidel, Frederick (Lewis) 1936- .... **CLC 18**
　See also CA 13-16R; CANR 8; DLBY 84
Seifert, Jaroslav 1901-1986 .. **CLC 34, 44, 93**
　See also CA 127; MTCW 1
Sei Shonagon c. 966-1017(?) .... **CMLC 6**
S<eacute>jour, Victor 1817-1874 .... **DC 10**
　See also DLB 50
Sejour Marcou et Ferrand, Juan Victor
　See S<eacute>jour, Victor
Selby, Hubert, Jr. 1928- **CLC 1, 2, 4, 8; SSC 20**
　See also CA 13-16R; CANR 33; DLB 2
Selzer, Richard 1928- .... **CLC 74**
　See also CA 65-68; CANR 14
Sembene, Ousmane
　See Ousmane, Sembene
Senancour, Etienne Pivert de 1770-1846
　NCLC 16
　See also DLB 119
Sender, Ramon (Jose) 1902-1982 **CLC 8; DAM**
　MULT; HLC
　See also CA 5-8R; 105; CANR 8; HW; MTCW
　1
Seneca, Lucius Annaeus 4B.C.-65 **CMLC 6;**
　DAM DRAM; DC 5
Senghor, Leopold Sedar 1906- **CLC 54; BLC**
　3; DAM MULT, POET; PC 25
　See also BW 2; CA 116; 125; CANR 47, 74;
　MTCW 1
Senna, Danzy 1970- .... **CLC 119**
　See also CA 169
Serling, (Edward) Rod(man) 1924-1975 **C L C**
　30
　See also AAYA 14; AITN 1; CA 162; 57-60;
　DLB 26
Serna, Ramon Gomez de la
　See Gomez de la Serna, Ramon
Serpieres
　See Guillevic, (Eugene)
Service, Robert

See Service, Robert W(illiam)
　See also DAB; DLB 92
Service, Robert W(illiam) 1874(?)-1958 **TCLC**
　15; DA; DAC; DAM MST, POET; WLC
　See also Service, Robert
　See also CA 115; 140; SATA 20
Seth, Vikram 1952- **CLC 43, 90; DAM MULT**
　See also CA 121; 127; CANR 50, 74; DLB 120;
　INT 127
Seton, Cynthia Propper 1926-1982 ..**CLC 27**
　See also CA 5-8R; 108; CANR 7
Seton, Ernest (Evan) Thompson 1860-1946
　TCLC 31
　See also CA 109; DLB 92; DLBD 13; JRDA;
　SATA 18
Seton-Thompson, Ernest
　See Seton, Ernest (Evan) Thompson
Settle, Mary Lee 1918- .... **CLC 19, 61**
　See also CA 89-92; CAAS 1; CANR 44; DLB
　6; INT 89-92
Seuphor, Michel
　See Arp, Jean
Sevigne, Marie (de Rabutin-Chantal) Marquise
　de 1626-1696 .... **LC 11**
Sewall, Samuel 1652-1730 .... **LC 38**
　See also DLB 24
Sexton, Anne (Harvey) 1928-1974 **CLC 2, 4, 6,**
　8, 10, 15, 53; DA; DAB; DAC; DAM MST,
　POET; PC 2; WLC
　See also CA 1-4R; 53-56; CABS 2; CANR 3,
　36; CDALB 1941-1968; DLB 5, 169;
　MTCW 1; SATA 10
Shaara, Jeff 1952- .... **CLC 119**
　See also CA 163
Shaara, Michael (Joseph, Jr.) 1929-1988 **C L C**
　15; DAM POP
　See also AITN 1; CA 102; 125; CANR 52;
　DLBY 83
Shackleton, C. C.
　See Aldiss, Brian W(ilson)
Shacochis, Bob .... **CLC 39**
　See also Shacochis, Robert G.
Shacochis, Robert G. 1951-
　See Shacochis, Bob
　See also CA 119; 124; INT 124
Shaffer, Anthony (Joshua) 1926- .... **CLC 19;**
　DAM DRAM
　See also CA 110; 116; DLB 13
Shaffer, Peter (Levin) 1926- **CLC 5, 14, 18, 37,**
　60; DAB; DAM DRAM, MST; DC 7
　See also CA 25-28R; CANR 25, 47, 74; CDBLB
　1960 to Present; DLB 13; MTCW 1
Shakey, Bernard
　See Young, Neil
Shalamov, Varlam (Tikhonovich) 1907(?)-1982
　CLC 18
　See also CA 129; 105
Shamlu, Ahmad 1925- .... **CLC 10**
Shammas, Anton 1951- .... **CLC 55**
Shange, Ntozake 1948- **CLC 8, 25, 38, 74; BLC**
　3; DAM DRAM, MULT; DC 3
　See also AAYA 9; BW 2; CA 85-88; CABS 3;
　CANR 27, 48, 74; DLB 38; MTCW 1
Shanley, John Patrick 1950- .... **CLC 75**
　See also CA 128; 133
Shapcott, Thomas W(illiam) 1935- ... **CLC 38**
　See also CA 69-72; CANR 49
Shapiro, Jane .... **CLC 76**
Shapiro, Karl (Jay) 1913- **CLC 4, 8, 15, 53; PC**
　25
　See also CA 1-4R; CAAS 6; CANR 1, 36, 66;
　DLB 48; MTCW 1
Sharp, William 1855-1905 .... **TCLC 39**

See also CA 160; DLB 156
Sharpe, Thomas Ridley 1928-
　See Sharpe, Tom
　See also CA 114; 122; INT 122
Sharpe, Tom .... **CLC 36**
　See also Sharpe, Thomas Ridley
　See also DLB 14
Shaw, Bernard .... **TCLC 45**
　See also Shaw, George Bernard
　See also BW 1
Shaw, G. Bernard
　See Shaw, George Bernard
Shaw, George Bernard 1856-1950 **TCLC 3, 9,**
　21; DA; DAB; DAC; DAM DRAM, MST;
　WLC
　See also Shaw, Bernard
　See also CA 104; 128; CDBLB 1914-1945;
　DLB 10, 57, 190; MTCW 1
Shaw, Henry Wheeler 1818-1885 ..**NCLC 15**
　See also DLB 11
Shaw, Irwin 1913-1984 **CLC 7, 23, 34; DAM**
　DRAM, POP
　See also AITN 1; CA 13-16R; 112; CANR 21;
　CDALB 1941-1968; DLB 6, 102; DLBY 84;
　MTCW 1
Shaw, Robert 1927-1978 .... **CLC 5**
　See also AITN 1; CA 1-4R; 81-84; CANR 4;
　DLB 13, 14
Shaw, T. E.
　See Lawrence, T(homas) E(dward)
Shawn, Wallace 1943- .... **CLC 41**
　See also CA 112
Shea, Lisa 1953- .... **CLC 86**
　See also CA 147
Sheed, Wilfrid (John Joseph) 1930- **CLC 2, 4,**
　10, 53
　See also CA 65-68; CANR 30, 66; DLB 6;
　MTCW 1
Sheldon, Alice Hastings Bradley 1915(?)-1987
　See Tiptree, James, Jr.
　See also CA 108; 122; CANR 34; INT 108;
　MTCW 1
Sheldon, John
　See Bloch, Robert (Albert)
Shelley, Mary Wollstonecraft (Godwin) 1797-
　1851 **NCLC 14, 59; DA; DAB; DAC; DAM**
　MST, NOV; WLC
　See also AAYA 20; CDBLB 1789-1832; DLB
　110, 116, 159, 178; SATA 29
Shelley, Percy Bysshe 1792-1822 . **NCLC 18;**
　DA; DAB; DAC; DAM MST, POET; PC
　14; WLC
　See also CDBLB 1789-1832; DLB 96, 110, 158
Shepard, Jim 1956- .... **CLC 36**
　See also CA 137; CANR 59; SATA 90
Shepard, Lucius 1947- .... **CLC 34**
　See also CA 128; 141
Shepard, Sam 1943- **CLC 4, 6, 17, 34, 41, 44;**
　DAM DRAM; DC 5
　See also AAYA 1; CA 69-72; CABS 3; CANR
　22; DLB 7; MTCW 1
Shepherd, Michael
　See Ludlum, Robert
Sherburne, Zoa (Morin) 1912- .... **CLC 30**
　See also AAYA 13; CA 1-4R; CANR 3, 37;
　MAICYA; SAAS 18; SATA 3
Sheridan, Frances 1724-1766 .... **LC 7**
　See also DLB 39, 84
Sheridan, Richard Brinsley 1751-1816 **N C L C**
　5; DA; DAB; DAC; DAM DRAM, MST;
　DC 1; WLC
　See also CDBLB 1660-1789; DLB 89
Sherman, Jonathan Marc .... **CLC 55**

Author Index

See also CA 104; 141; CDBLB 1890-1914;
DLB 10, 19

Syruc, J.
See Milosz, Czeslaw

Szirtes, George 1948- .... **CLC 46**
See also CA 109; CANR 27, 61

Szymborska, Wislawa 1923- .... **CLC 99**
See also CA 154; DLBY 96

T. O., Nik
See Annensky, Innokenty (Fyodorovich)

Tabori, George 1914- .... **CLC 19**
See also CA 49-52; CANR 4, 69

Tagore, Rabindranath 1861-1941**TCLC 3, 53;**
DAM DRAM, POET; PC 8
See also CA 104; 120; MTCW 1

Taine, Hippolyte Adolphe 1828-1893 . **N C L C**
15

Talese, Gay 1932- .... **CLC 37**
See also AITN 1; CA 1-4R; CANR 9, 58; DLB
185; INT CANR-9; MTCW 1

Tallent, Elizabeth (Ann) 1954- .... **CLC 45**
See also CA 117; CANR 72; DLB 130

Tally, Ted 1952- .... **CLC 42**
See also CA 120; 124; INT 124

Talvik, Heiti 1904-1947 .... **TCLC 87**

Tamayo y Baus, Manuel 1829-1898 . **NCLC 1**

Tammsaare, A(nton) H(ansen) 1878-1940
TCLC 27
See also CA 164

Tam'si, Tchicaya U
See Tchicaya, Gerald Felix

Tan, Amy (Ruth) 1952-**CLC 59; DAM MULT,**
NOV, POP
See also AAYA 9; BEST 89:3; CA 136; CANR
54; DLB 173; SATA 75

Tandem, Felix
See Spitteler, Carl (Friedrich Georg)

Tanizaki, Jun'ichiro 1886-1965**CLC 8, 14, 28;**
SSC 21
See also CA 93-96; 25-28R; DLB 180

Tanner, William
See Amis, Kingsley (William)

Tao Lao
See Storni, Alfonsina

Tarassoff, Lev
See Troyat, Henri

Tarbell, Ida M(inerva) 1857-1944 . **TCLC 40**
See also CA 122; DLB 47

Tarkington, (Newton) Booth 1869-1946**TCLC**
9
See also CA 110; 143; DLB 9, 102; SATA 17

Tarkovsky, Andrei (Arsenyevich) 1932-1986
CLC 75
See also CA 127

Tartt, Donna 1964(?)- .... **CLC 76**
See also CA 142

Tasso, Torquato 1544-1595 .... **LC 5**

Tate, (John Orley) Allen 1899-1979**CLC 2, 4,**
6, 9, 11, 14, 24
See also CA 5-8R; 85-88; CANR 32; DLB 4,
45, 63; DLBD 17; MTCW 1

Tate, Ellalice
See Hibbert, Eleanor Alice Burford

Tate, James (Vincent) 1943- ..... **CLC 2, 6, 25**
See also CA 21-24R; CANR 29, 57; DLB 5,
169

Tavel, Ronald 1940- .... **CLC 6**
See also CA 21-24R; CANR 33

Taylor, C(ecil) P(hilip) 1929-1981 ... **CLC 27**
See also CA 25-28R; 105; CANR 47

Taylor, Edward 1642(?)-1729 ..... **LC 11; DA;**
DAB; DAC; DAM MST, POET
See also DLB 24

Taylor, Eleanor Ross 1920- .... **CLC 5**
See also CA 81-84; CANR 70

Taylor, Elizabeth 1912-1975 ..... **CLC 2, 4, 29**
See also CA 13-16R; CANR 9, 70; DLB 139;
MTCW 1; SATA 13

Taylor, Frederick Winslow 1856-1915 **T C L C**
76

Taylor, Henry (Splawn) 1942- .... **CLC 44**
See also CA 33-36R; CAAS 7; CANR 31; DLB
5

Taylor, Kamala (Purnaiya) 1924-
See Markandaya, Kamala
See also CA 77-80

Taylor, Mildred D. .... **CLC 21**
See also AAYA 10; BW 1; CA 85-88; CANR
25; CLR 9; DLB 52; JRDA; MAICYA; SAAS
5; SATA 15, 70

Taylor, Peter (Hillsman) 1917-1994**CLC 1, 4,**
18, 37, 44, 50, 71; SSC 10
See also CA 13-16R; 147; CANR 9, 50; DLBY
81, 94; INT CANR-9; MTCW 1

Taylor, Robert Lewis 1912-1998 .... **CLC 14**
See also CA 1-4R; 170; CANR 3, 64; SATA 10

Tchekhov, Anton
See Chekhov, Anton (Pavlovich)

Tchicaya, Gerald Felix 1931-1988 . **CLC 101**
See also CA 129; 125

Tchicaya U Tam'si
See Tchicaya, Gerald Felix

Teasdale, Sara 1884-1933 .... **TCLC 4**
See also CA 104; 163; DLB 45; SATA 32

Tegner, Esaias 1782-1846 .... **NCLC 2**

Teilhard de Chardin, (Marie Joseph) Pierre
1881-1955 .... **TCLC 9**
See also CA 105

Temple, Ann
See Mortimer, Penelope (Ruth)

Tennant, Emma (Christina) 1937-**CLC 13, 52**
See also CA 65-68; CAAS 9; CANR 10, 38,
59; DLB 14

Tenneshaw, S. M.
See Silverberg, Robert

Tennyson, Alfred 1809-1892 .. **NCLC 30, 65;**
DA; DAB; DAC; DAM MST, POET; PC
6; WLC
See also CDBLB 1832-1890; DLB 32

Teran, Lisa St. Aubin de .... **CLC 36**
See also St. Aubin de Teran, Lisa

Terence 195(?)B.C.-159B.C. **CMLC 14; DC 7**

Teresa de Jesus, St. 1515-1582 .... **LC 18**

Terkel, Louis 1912-
See Terkel, Studs
See also CA 57-60; CANR 18, 45, 67; MTCW
1

Terkel, Studs .... **CLC 38**
See also Terkel, Louis
See also AITN 1

Terry, C. V.
See Slaughter, Frank G(ill)

Terry, Megan 1932- .... **CLC 19**
See also CA 77-80; CABS 3; CANR 43; DLB 7

Tertullian c. 155-c. 245 .... **CMLC 29**

Tertz, Abram
See Sinyavsky, Andrei (Donatevich)

Tesich, Steve 1943(?)-1996 .... **CLC 40, 69**
See also CA 105; 152; DLBY 83

Tesla, Nikola 1856-1943 .... **TCLC 88**

Teternikov, Fyodor Kuzmich 1863-1927
See Sologub, Fyodor
See also CA 104

Tevis, Walter 1928-1984 .... **CLC 42**
See also CA 113

Tey, Josephine .... **TCLC 14**

See also Mackintosh, Elizabeth
See also DLB 77

Thackeray, William Makepeace 1811-1863
NCLC 5, 14, 22, 43; DA; DAB; DAC; DAM
MST, NOV; WLC
See also CDBLB 1832-1890; DLB 21, 55, 159,
163; SATA 23

Thakura, Ravindranatha
See Tagore, Rabindranath

Tharoor, Shashi 1956- .... **CLC 70**
See also CA 141

Thelwell, Michael Miles 1939- .... **CLC 22**
See also BW 2; CA 101

Theobald, Lewis, Jr.
See Lovecraft, H(oward) P(hillips)

Theodorescu, Ion N. 1880-1967
See Arghezi, Tudor
See also CA 116

Theriault, Yves 1915-1983 .... **CLC 79; DAC;**
DAM MST
See also CA 102; DLB 88

Theroux, Alexander (Louis) 1939-**CLC 2, 25**
See also CA 85-88; CANR 20, 63

Theroux, Paul (Edward) 1941- **CLC 5, 8, 11,**
15, 28, 46; DAM POP
See also BEST 89:4; CA 33-36R; CANR 20,
45, 74; DLB 2; MTCW 1; SATA 44

Thesen, Sharon 1946- .... **CLC 56**
See also CA 163

Thevenin, Denis
See Duhamel, Georges

Thibault, Jacques Anatole Francois 1844-1924
See France, Anatole
See also CA 106; 127; DAM NOV; MTCW 1

Thiele, Colin (Milton) 1920- .... **CLC 17**
See also CA 29-32R; CANR 12, 28, 53; CLR
27; MAICYA; SAAS 2; SATA 14, 72

Thomas, Audrey (Callahan) 1935-**CLC 7, 13,**
37, 107; SSC 20
See also AITN 2; CA 21-24R; CAAS 19; CANR
36, 58; DLB 60; MTCW 1

Thomas, D(onald) M(ichael) 1935-. **CLC 13,**
22, 31
See also CA 61-64; CAAS 11; CANR 17, 45,
75; CDBLB 1960 to Present; DLB 40, 207;
INT CANR-17; MTCW 1

Thomas, Dylan (Marlais) 1914-1953**TCLC 1,**
8, 45; DA; DAB; DAC; DAM DRAM,
MST, POET; PC 2; SSC 3; WLC
See also CA 104; 120; CANR 65; CDBLB
1945-1960; DLB 13, 20, 139; MTCW 1;
SATA 60

Thomas, (Philip) Edward 1878-1917 . **T C L C**
10; DAM POET
See also CA 106; 153; DLB 98

Thomas, Joyce Carol 1938- .... **CLC 35**
See also AAYA 12; BW 2; CA 113; 116; CANR
48; CLR 19; DLB 33; INT 116; JRDA;
MAICYA; MTCW 1; SAAS 7; SATA 40, 78

Thomas, Lewis 1913-1993 .... **CLC 35**
See also CA 85-88; 143; CANR 38, 60; MTCW
1

Thomas, M. Carey 1857-1935 .... **TCLC 89**

Thomas, Paul
See Mann, (Paul) Thomas

Thomas, Piri 1928- .... **CLC 17**
See also CA 73-76; HW

Thomas, R(onald) S(tuart) 1913- **CLC 6, 13,**
48; DAB; DAM POET
See also CA 89-92; CAAS 4; CANR 30;
CDBLB 1960 to Present; DLB 27; MTCW 1

Thomas, Ross (Elmore) 1926-1995 ...**CLC 39**
See also CA 33-36R; 150; CANR 22, 63

Thompson, Francis Clegg
See Mencken, H(enry) L(ouis)
Thompson, Francis Joseph 1859-1907**TCLC 4**
See also CA 104; CDBLB 1890-1914; DLB 19
Thompson, Hunter S(tockton) 1939- **CLC 9,
17, 40, 104; DAM POP**
See also BEST 89:1; CA 17-20R; CANR 23,
46, 74, 77; DLB 185; MTCW 1
Thompson, James Myers
See Thompson, Jim (Myers)
Thompson, Jim (Myers) 1906-1977(?)**CLC 69**
See also CA 140
Thompson, Judith .... **CLC 39**
Thomson, James 1700-1748 ...**LC 16, 29, 40;
DAM POET**
See also DLB 95
Thomson, James 1834-1882 **NCLC 18; DAM
POET**
See also DLB 35
Thoreau, Henry David 1817-1862**NCLC 7, 21,
61; DA; DAB; DAC; DAM MST; WLC**
See also CDALB 1640-1865; DLB 1
Thornton, Hall
See Silverberg, Robert
Thucydides c. 455B.C.-399B.C. ...... **CMLC 17**
See also DLB 176
Thurber, James (Grover) 1894-1961 **CLC 5,
11, 25; DA; DAB; DAC; DAM DRAM,
MST, NOV; SSC 1**
See also CA 73-76; CANR 17, 39; CDALB
1929-1941; DLB 4, 11, 22, 102; MAICYA;
MTCW 1; SATA 13
Thurman, Wallace (Henry) 1902-1934**T C L C
6; BLC 3; DAM MULT**
See also BW 1; CA 104; 124; DLB 51
Ticheburn, Cheviot
See Ainsworth, William Harrison
Tieck, (Johann) Ludwig 1773-1853 **NCLC 5,
46; SSC 31**
See also DLB 90
Tiger, Derry
See Ellison, Harlan (Jay)
Tilghman, Christopher 1948(?)- ...... **CLC 65**
See also CA 159
Tillinghast, Richard (Williford) 1940-**CLC 29**
See also CA 29-32R; CAAS 23; CANR 26, 51
Timrod, Henry 1828-1867 .... **NCLC 25**
See also DLB 3
Tindall, Gillian (Elizabeth) 1938- ...... **CLC 7**
See also CA 21-24R; CANR 11, 65
Tiptree, James, Jr. .... **CLC 48, 50**
See also Sheldon, Alice Hastings Bradley
See also DLB 8
Titmarsh, Michael Angelo
See Thackeray, William Makepeace
**Tocqueville, Alexis (Charles Henri Maurice
Clerel, Comte) de** 1805-1859**NCLC 7, 63**
Tolkien, J(ohn) R(onald) R(euel) 1892-1973
**CLC 1, 2, 3, 8, 12, 38; DA; DAB; DAC;
DAM MST, NOV, POP; WLC**
See also AAYA 10; AITN 1; CA 17-18; 45-48;
CANR 36; CAP 2; CDBLB 1914-1945; CLR
56; DLB 15, 160; JRDA; MAICYA; MTCW
1; SATA 2, 32, 100; SATA-Obit 24
Toller, Ernst 1893-1939 .... **TCLC 10**
See also CA 107; DLB 124
Tolson, M. B.
See Tolson, Melvin B(eaunorus)
Tolson, Melvin B(eaunorus) 1898(?)-1966
CLC 36, 105; BLC 3; DAM MULT, POET
See also BW 1; CA 124; 89-92; DLB 48, 76
Tolstoi, Aleksei Nikolaevich
See Tolstoy, Alexey Nikolaevich

Tolstoy, Alexey Nikolaevich 1882-1945**T C L C
18**
See also CA 107; 158
Tolstoy, Count Leo
See Tolstoy, Leo (Nikolaevich)
Tolstoy, Leo (Nikolaevich) 1828-1910**TCLC 4,
11, 17, 28, 44, 79; DA; DAB; DAC; DAM
MST, NOV; SSC 9, 30; WLC**
See also CA 104; 123; SATA 26
Tomasi di Lampedusa, Giuseppe 1896-1957
See Lampedusa, Giuseppe (Tomasi) di
See also CA 111
Tomlin, Lily .... **CLC 17**
See also Tomlin, Mary Jean
Tomlin, Mary Jean 1939(?)-
See Tomlin, Lily
See also CA 117
Tomlinson, (Alfred) Charles 1927-**CLC 2, 4, 6,
13, 45; DAM POET; PC 17**
See also CA 5-8R; CANR 33; DLB 40
Tomlinson, H(enry) M(ajor) 1873-1958**TCLC
71**
See also CA 118; 161; DLB 36, 100, 195
Tonson, Jacob
See Bennett, (Enoch) Arnold
Toole, John Kennedy 1937-1969 **CLC 19, 64**
See also CA 104; DLBY 81
Toomer, Jean 1894-1967**CLC 1, 4, 13, 22; BLC
3; DAM MULT; PC 7; SSC 1; WLCS**
See also BW 1; CA 85-88; CDALB 1917-1929;
DLB 45, 51; MTCW 1
Torley, Luke
See Blish, James (Benjamin)
Tornimparte, Alessandra
See Ginzburg, Natalia
Torre, Raoul della
See Mencken, H(enry) L(ouis)
Torrey, E(dwin) Fuller 1937- .... **CLC 34**
See also CA 119; CANR 71
Torsvan, Ben Traven
See Traven, B.
Torsvan, Benno Traven
See Traven, B.
Torsvan, Berick Traven
See Traven, B.
Torsvan, Berwick Traven
See Traven, B.
Torsvan, Bruno Traven
See Traven, B.
Torsvan, Traven
See Traven, B.
Tournier, Michel (Edouard) 1924-**CLC 6, 23,
36, 95**
See also CA 49-52; CANR 3, 36, 74; DLB 83;
MTCW 1; SATA 23
Tournimparte, Alessandra
See Ginzburg, Natalia
Towers, Ivar
See Kornbluth, C(yril) M.
Towne, Robert (Burton) 1936(?)- ..... **CLC 87**
See also CA 108; DLB 44
Townsend, Sue .... **CLC 61**
See also Townsend, Susan Elaine
See also SATA 55, 93; SATA-Brief 48
Townsend, Susan Elaine 1946-
See Townsend, Sue
See also CA 119; 127; CANR 65; DAB; DAC;
DAM MST
Townshend, Peter (Dennis Blandford) 1945-
CLC 17, 42
See also CA 107
Tozzi, Federigo 1883-1920 .... **TCLC 31**
See also CA 160

Traill, Catharine Parr 1802-1899 ..**NCLC 31**
See also DLB 99
Trakl, Georg 1887-1914 .... **TCLC 5; PC 20**
See also CA 104; 165
Transtroemer, Tomas (Goesta) 1931-**CLC 52,
65; DAM POET**
See also CA 117; 129; CAAS 17
Transtromer, Tomas Gosta
See Transtroemer, Tomas (Goesta)
Traven, B. (?)-1969 ....**CLC 8, 11**
See also CA 19-20; 25-28R; CAP 2; DLB 9,
56; MTCW 1
Treitel, Jonathan 1959- .... **CLC 70**
Tremain, Rose 1943- .... **CLC 42**
See also CA 97-100; CANR 44; DLB 14
Tremblay, Michel 1942- **CLC 29, 102; DAC;
DAM MST**
See also CA 116; 128; DLB 60; MTCW 1
Trevanian .... **CLC 29**
See also Whitaker, Rod(ney)
Trevor, Glen
See Hilton, James
Trevor, William 1928-**CLC 7, 9, 14, 25, 71, 116;
SSC 21**
See also Cox, William Trevor
See also DLB 14, 139
Trifonov, Yuri (Valentinovich) 1925-1981
CLC 45
See also CA 126; 103; MTCW 1
Trilling, Lionel 1905-1975 ...... **CLC 9, 11, 24**
See also CA 9-12R; 61-64; CANR 10; DLB 28,
63; INT CANR-10; MTCW 1
Trimball, W. H.
See Mencken, H(enry) L(ouis)
Tristan
See Gomez de la Serna, Ramon
Tristram
See Housman, A(lfred) E(dward)
Trogdon, William (Lewis) 1939-
See Heat-Moon, William Least
See also CA 115; 119; CANR 47; INT 119
Trollope, Anthony 1815-1882**NCLC 6, 33; DA;
DAB; DAC; DAM MST, NOV; SSC 28;
WLC**
See also CDBLB 1832-1890; DLB 21, 57, 159;
SATA 22
Trollope, Frances 1779-1863 .... **NCLC 30**
See also DLB 21, 166
Trotsky, Leon 1879-1940 .... **TCLC 22**
See also CA 118; 167
Trotter (Cockburn), Catharine 1679-1749**L C
8**
See also DLB 84
Trout, Kilgore
See Farmer, Philip Jose
Trow, George W. S. 1943- .... **CLC 52**
See also CA 126
Troyat, Henri 1911- .... **CLC 23**
See also CA 45-48; CANR 2, 33, 67; MTCW 1
Trudeau, G(arretson) B(eekman) 1948-
See Trudeau, Garry B.
See also CA 81-84; CANR 31; SATA 35
Trudeau, Garry B. .... **CLC 12**
See also Trudeau, G(arretson) B(eekman)
See also AAYA 10; AITN 2
Truffaut, Francois 1932-1984 .. **CLC 20, 101**
See also CA 81-84; 113; CANR 34
Trumbo, Dalton 1905-1976 .... **CLC 19**
See also CA 21-24R; 69-72; CANR 10; DLB
26
Trumbull, John 1750-1831 .... **NCLC 30**
See also DLB 31
Trundlett, Helen B.

See Eliot, T(homas) S(tearns)

Tryon, Thomas 1926-1991 . **CLC 3, 11; DAM POP**
See also AITN 1; CA 29-32R; 135; CANR 32, 77; MTCW 1

Tryon, Tom
See Tryon, Thomas

Ts'ao Hsueh-ch'in 1715(?)-1763 .... **LC 1**

Tsushima, Shuji 1909-1948
See Dazai Osamu
See also CA 107

Tsvetaeva (Efron), Marina (Ivanovna) 1892-1941 .... **TCLC 7, 35; PC 14**
See also CA 104; 128; CANR 73; MTCW 1

Tuck, Lily 1938- .... **CLC 70**
See also CA 139

Tu Fu 712-770 .... **PC 9**
See also DAM MULT

Tunis, John R(oberts) 1889-1975 ..... **CLC 12**
See also CA 61-64; CANR 62; DLB 22, 171; JRDA; MAICYA; SATA 37; SATA-Brief 30

Tuohy, Frank .... **CLC 37**
See also Tuohy, John Francis
See also DLB 14, 139

Tuohy, John Francis 1925-
See Tuohy, Frank
See also CA 5-8R; CANR 3, 47

Turco, Lewis (Putnam) 1934- ...... **CLC 11, 63**
See also CA 13-16R; CAAS 22; CANR 24, 51; DLBY 84

Turgenev, Ivan 1818-1883 .... **NCLC 21; DA; DAB; DAC; DAM MST, NOV; DC 7; SSC 7; WLC**

Turgot, Anne-Robert-Jacques 1727-1781 **L C 26**

Turner, Frederick 1943- .... **CLC 48**
See also CA 73-76; CAAS 10; CANR 12, 30, 56; DLB 40

Tutu, Desmond M(pilo) 1931-**CLC 80; BLC 3; DAM MULT**
See also BW 1; CA 125; CANR 67

Tutuola, Amos 1920-1997**CLC 5, 14, 29; BLC 3; DAM MULT**
See also BW 2; CA 9-12R; 159; CANR 27, 66; DLB 125; MTCW 1

Twain, Mark**TCLC 6, 12, 19, 36, 48, 59; SSC 6, 26; WLC**
See also Clemens, Samuel Langhorne
See also AAYA 20; DLB 11, 12, 23, 64, 74

Tyler, Anne 1941- . **CLC 7, 11, 18, 28, 44, 59, 103; DAM NOV, POP**
See also AAYA 18; BEST 89:1; CA 9-12R; CANR 11, 33, 53; DLB 6, 143; DLBY 82; MTCW 1; SATA 7, 90

Tyler, Royall 1757-1826 .... **NCLC 3**
See also DLB 37

Tynan, Katharine 1861-1931 .... **TCLC 3**
See also CA 104; 167; DLB 153

Tyutchev, Fyodor 1803-1873 .... **NCLC 34**

Tzara, Tristan 1896-1963 ...... **CLC 47; DAM POET**
See also CA 153; 89-92

Uhry, Alfred 1936- .. **CLC 55; DAM DRAM, POP**
See also CA 127; 133; INT 133

Ulf, Haerved
See Strindberg, (Johan) August

Ulf, Harved
See Strindberg, (Johan) August

Ulibarri, Sabine R(eyes) 1919-**CLC 83; DAM MULT**
See also CA 131; DLB 82; HW

Unamuno (y Jugo), Miguel de 1864-1936
TCLC 2, 9; DAM MULT, NOV; HLC; SSC 11
See also CA 104; 131; DLB 108; HW; MTCW 1

Undercliffe, Errol
See Campbell, (John) Ramsey

Underwood, Miles
See Glassco, John

Undset, Sigrid 1882-1949**TCLC 3; DA; DAB; DAC; DAM MST, NOV; WLC**
See also CA 104; 129; MTCW 1

Ungaretti, Giuseppe 1888-1970**CLC 7, 11, 15**
See also CA 19-20; 25-28R; CAP 2; DLB 114

Unger, Douglas 1952- .... **CLC 34**
See also CA 130

Unsworth, Barry (Forster) 1930- ..... **CLC 76**
See also CA 25-28R; CANR 30, 54; DLB 194

Updike, John (Hoyer) 1932-**CLC 1, 2, 3, 5, 7, 9, 13, 15, 23, 34, 43, 70; DA; DAB; DAC; DAM MST, NOV, POET, POP; SSC 13, 27; WLC**
See also CA 1-4R; CABS 1; CANR 4, 33, 51; CDALB 1968-1988; DLB 2, 5, 143; DLBD 3; DLBY 80, 82, 97; MTCW 1

Upshaw, Margaret Mitchell
See Mitchell, Margaret (Munnerlyn)

Upton, Mark
See Sanders, Lawrence

Upward, Allen 1863-1926 .... **TCLC 85**
See also CA 117; DLB 36

Urdang, Constance (Henriette) 1922-**CLC 47**
See also CA 21-24R; CANR 9, 24

Uriel, Henry
See Faust, Frederick (Schiller)

Uris, Leon (Marcus) 1924- **CLC 7, 32; DAM NOV, POP**
See also AITN 1, 2; BEST 89:2; CA 1-4R; CANR 1, 40, 65; MTCW 1; SATA 49

Urmuz
See Codrescu, Andrei

Urquhart, Jane 1949- .... **CLC 90; DAC**
See also CA 113; CANR 32, 68

Ustinov, Peter (Alexander) 1921- .... **CLC 1**
See also AITN 1; CA 13-16R; CANR 25, 51; DLB 13

U Tam'si, Gerald Felix Tchicaya
See Tchicaya, Gerald Felix

U Tam'si, Tchicaya
See Tchicaya, Gerald Felix

Vachss, Andrew (Henry) 1942- ...... **CLC 106**
See also CA 118; CANR 44

Vachss, Andrew H.
See Vachss, Andrew (Henry)

Vaculik, Ludvik 1926- .... **CLC 7**
See also CA 53-56; CANR 72

Vaihinger, Hans 1852-1933 .... **TCLC 71**
See also CA 116; 166

Valdez, Luis (Miguel) 1940- ..**CLC 84; DAM MULT; DC 10; HLC**
See also CA 101; CANR 32; DLB 122; HW

Valenzuela, Luisa 1938- **CLC 31, 104; DAM MULT; SSC 14**
See also CA 101; CANR 32, 65; DLB 113; HW

Valera y Alcala-Galiano, Juan 1824-1905
TCLC 10
See also CA 106

Valery, (Ambroise) Paul (Toussaint Jules) 1871-1945 .... **TCLC 4, 15; DAM POET; PC 9**
See also CA 104; 122; MTCW 1

Valle-Inclan, Ramon (Maria) del 1866-1936
TCLC 5; DAM MULT; HLC
See also CA 106; 153; DLB 134

Vallejo, Antonio Buero
See Buero Vallejo, Antonio

Vallejo, Cesar (Abraham) 1892-1938**TCLC 3, 56; DAM MULT; HLC**
See also CA 105; 153; HW

Valles, Jules 1832-1885 .... **NCLC 71**
See also DLB 123

Vallette, Marguerite Eymery
See Rachilde

Valle Y Pena, Ramon del
See Valle-Inclan, Ramon (Maria) del

Van Ash, Cay 1918- .... **CLC 34**

Vanbrugh, Sir John 1664-1726 **LC 21; DAM DRAM**
See also DLB 80

Van Campen, Karl
See Campbell, John W(ood, Jr.)

Vance, Gerald
See Silverberg, Robert

Vance, Jack .... **CLC 35**
See also Kuttner, Henry; Vance, John Holbrook
See also DLB 8

Vance, John Holbrook 1916-
See Queen, Ellery; Vance, Jack
See also CA 29-32R; CANR 17, 65; MTCW 1

Van Den Bogarde, Derek Jules Gaspard Ulric Niven 1921-
See Bogarde, Dirk
See also CA 77-80

Vandenburgh, Jane .... **CLC 59**
See also CA 168

Vanderhaeghe, Guy 1951- .... **CLC 41**
See also CA 113; CANR 72

van der Post, Laurens (Jan) 1906-1996**CLC 5**
See also CA 5-8R; 155; CANR 35; DLB 204

van de Wetering, Janwillem 1931- ...**CLC 47**
See also CA 49-52; CANR 4, 62

Van Dine, S. S. .... **TCLC 23**
See also Wright, Willard Huntington

Van Doren, Carl (Clinton) 1885-1950 **T C L C 18**
See also CA 111; 168

Van Doren, Mark 1894-1972 .... **CLC 6, 10**
See also CA 1-4R; 37-40R; CANR 3; DLB 45; MTCW 1

Van Druten, John (William) 1901-1957**TCLC 2**
See also CA 104; 161; DLB 10

Van Duyn, Mona (Jane) 1921- **CLC 3, 7, 63, 116; DAM POET**
See also CA 9-12R; CANR 7, 38, 60; DLB 5

Van Dyne, Edith
See Baum, L(yman) Frank

van Itallie, Jean-Claude 1936- .... **CLC 3**
See also CA 45-48; CAAS 2; CANR 1, 48; DLB 7

van Ostaijen, Paul 1896-1928 .... **TCLC 33**
See also CA 163

Van Peebles, Melvin 1932-.**CLC 2, 20; DAM MULT**
See also BW 2; CA 85-88; CANR 27, 67

Vansittart, Peter 1920- .... **CLC 42**
See also CA 1-4R; CANR 3, 49

Van Vechten, Carl 1880-1964 .... **CLC 33**
See also CA 89-92; DLB 4, 9, 51

Van Vogt, A(lfred) E(lton) 1912- .... **CLC 1**
See also CA 21-24R; CANR 28; DLB 8; SATA 14

Varda, Agnes 1928- .... **CLC 16**
See also CA 116; 122

Vargas Llosa, (Jorge) Mario (Pedro) 1936-
CLC 3, 6, 9, 10, 15, 31, 42, 85; DA; DAB; DAC; DAM MST, MULT, NOV; HLC
See also CA 73-76; CANR 18, 32, 42, 67; DLB

See also CA 21-24R; CANR 12, 28, 53

Walker, George F. 1947- . **CLC 44, 61; DAB; DAC; DAM MST**
See also CA 103; CANR 21, 43, 59; DLB 60

Walker, Joseph A. 1935- .... **CLC 19; DAM DRAM, MST**
See also BW 1; CA 89-92; CANR 26; DLB 38

Walker, Margaret (Abigail) 1915-1998 **CLC 1, 6; BLC; DAM MULT; PC 20**
See also BW 2; CA 73-76; 172; CANR 26, 54, 76; DLB 76, 152; MTCW 1

Walker, Ted .... **CLC 13**
See also Walker, Edward Joseph
See also DLB 40

Wallace, David Foster 1962- .... **CLC 50, 114**
See also CA 132; CANR 59

Wallace, Dexter
See Masters, Edgar Lee

Wallace, (Richard Horatio) Edgar 1875-1932 **TCLC 57**
See also CA 115; DLB 70

Wallace, Irving 1916-1990 . **CLC 7, 13; DAM NOV, POP**
See also AITN 1; CA 1-4R; 132; CAAS 1; CANR 1, 27; INT CANR-27; MTCW 1

Wallant, Edward Lewis 1926-1962 **CLC 5, 10**
See also CA 1-4R; CANR 22; DLB 2, 28, 143; MTCW 1

Wallas, Graham 1858-1932 .... **TCLC 91**

Walley, Byron
See Card, Orson Scott

Walpole, Horace 1717-1797 .... **LC 2, 49**
See also DLB 39, 104

Walpole, Hugh (Seymour) 1884-1941 **TCLC 5**
See also CA 104; 165; DLB 34

Walser, Martin 1927- .... **CLC 27**
See also CA 57-60; CANR 8, 46; DLB 75, 124

Walser, Robert 1878-1956 **TCLC 18; SSC 20**
See also CA 118; 165; DLB 66

Walsh, Jill Paton .... **CLC 35**
See also Paton Walsh, Gillian
See also AAYA 11; CLR 2; DLB 161; SAAS 3

Walter, Villiam Christian
See Andersen, Hans Christian

Wambaugh, Joseph (Aloysius, Jr.) 1937- **CLC 3, 18; DAM NOV, POP**
See also AITN 1; BEST 89:3; CA 33-36R; CANR 42, 65; DLB 6; DLBY 83; MTCW 1

Wang Wei 699(?)-761(?) .... **PC 18**

Ward, Arthur Henry Sarsfield 1883-1959
See Rohmer, Sax
See also CA 108; 173

Ward, Douglas Turner 1930- .... **CLC 19**
See also BW 1; CA 81-84; CANR 27; DLB 7, 38

Ward, Mary Augusta
See Ward, Mrs. Humphry

Ward, Mrs. Humphry 1851-1920 .. **TCLC 55**
See also DLB 18

Ward, Peter
See Faust, Frederick (Schiller)

Warhol, Andy 1928(?)-1987 .... **CLC 20**
See also AAYA 12; BEST 89:4; CA 89-92; 121; CANR 34

Warner, Francis (Robert le Plastrier) 1937- **CLC 14**
See also CA 53-56; CANR 11

Warner, Marina 1946- .... **CLC 59**
See also CA 65-68; CANR 21, 55; DLB 194

Warner, Rex (Ernest) 1905-1986 ..... **CLC 45**
See also CA 89-92; 119; DLB 15

Warner, Susan (Bogert) 1819-1885 **NCLC 31**
See also DLB 3, 42

Warner, Sylvia (Constance) Ashton
See Ashton-Warner, Sylvia (Constance)

Warner, Sylvia Townsend 1893-1978 **CLC 7, 19; SSC 23**
See also CA 61-64; 77-80; CANR 16, 60; DLB 34, 139; MTCW 1

Warren, Mercy Otis 1728-1814 ..... **NCLC 13**
See also DLB 31, 200

Warren, Robert Penn 1905-1989 **CLC 1, 4, 6, 8, 10, 13, 18, 39, 53, 59; DA; DAB; DAC; DAM MST, NOV, POET; SSC 4; WLC**
See also AITN 1; CA 13-16R; 129; CANR 10, 47; CDALB 1968-1988; DLB 2, 48, 152; DLBY 80, 89; INT CANR-10; MTCW 1; SATA 46; SATA-Obit 63

Warshofsky, Isaac
See Singer, Isaac Bashevis

Warton, Thomas 1728-1790 ..... **LC 15; DAM POET**
See also DLB 104, 109

Waruk, Kona
See Harris, (Theodore) Wilson

Warung, Price 1855-1911 .... **TCLC 45**

Warwick, Jarvis
See Garner, Hugh

Washington, Alex
See Harris, Mark

Washington, Booker T(aliaferro) 1856-1915 **TCLC 10; BLC 3; DAM MULT**
See also BW 1; CA 114; 125; SATA 28

Washington, George 1732-1799 .... **LC 25**
See also DLB 31

Wassermann, (Karl) Jakob 1873-1934 **TCLC 6**
See also CA 104; 163; DLB 66

Wasserstein, Wendy 1950- ... **CLC 32, 59, 90; DAM DRAM; DC 4**
See also CA 121; 129; CABS 3; CANR 53, 75; INT 129; SATA 94

Waterhouse, Keith (Spencer) 1929- **CLC 47**
See also CA 5-8R; CANR 38, 67; DLB 13, 15; MTCW 1

Waters, Frank (Joseph) 1902-1995 ... **CLC 88**
See also CA 5-8R; 149; CAAS 13; CANR 3, 18, 63; DLBY 86

Waters, Roger 1944- .... **CLC 35**

Watkins, Frances Ellen
See Harper, Frances Ellen Watkins

Watkins, Gerrold
See Malzberg, Barry N(athaniel)

Watkins, Gloria 1955(?)-
See hooks, bell
See also BW 2; CA 143

Watkins, Paul 1964- .... **CLC 55**
See also CA 132; CANR 62

Watkins, Vernon Phillips 1906-1967 **CLC 43**
See also CA 9-10; 25-28R; CAP 1; DLB 20

Watson, Irving S.
See Mencken, H(enry) L(ouis)

Watson, John H.
See Farmer, Philip Jose

Watson, Richard F.
See Silverberg, Robert

Waugh, Auberon (Alexander) 1939- .. **CLC 7**
See also CA 45-48; CANR 6, 22; DLB 14, 194

Waugh, Evelyn (Arthur St. John) 1903-1966 **CLC 1, 3, 8, 13, 19, 27, 44, 107; DA; DAB; DAC; DAM MST, NOV, POP; WLC**
See also CA 85-88; 25-28R; CANR 22; CDBLB 1914-1945; DLB 15, 162, 195; MTCW 1

Waugh, Harriet 1944- .... **CLC 6**
See also CA 85-88; CANR 22

Ways, C. R.

See Blount, Roy (Alton), Jr.

Waystaff, Simon
See Swift, Jonathan

Webb, (Martha) Beatrice (Potter) 1858-1943 **TCLC 22**
See also Potter, (Helen) Beatrix
See also CA 117; DLB 190

Webb, Charles (Richard) 1939- .... **CLC 7**
See also CA 25-28R

Webb, James H(enry), Jr. 1946- .... **CLC 22**
See also CA 81-84

Webb, Mary (Gladys Meredith) 1881-1927 **TCLC 24**
See also CA 123; DLB 34

Webb, Mrs. Sidney
See Webb, (Martha) Beatrice (Potter)

Webb, Phyllis 1927- .... **CLC 18**
See also CA 104; CANR 23; DLB 53

Webb, Sidney (James) 1859-1947 .. **TCLC 22**
See also CA 117; 163; DLB 190

Webber, Andrew Lloyd .... **CLC 21**
See also Lloyd Webber, Andrew

Weber, Lenora Mattingly 1895-1971 **CLC 12**
See also CA 19-20; 29-32R; CAP 1; SATA 2; SATA-Obit 26

Weber, Max 1864-1920 .... **TCLC 69**
See also CA 109

Webster, John 1579(?)-1634(?) ... **LC 33; DA; DAB; DAC; DAM DRAM, MST; DC 2; WLC**
See also CDBLB Before 1660; DLB 58

Webster, Noah 1758-1843 .... **NCLC 30**
See also DLB 1, 37, 42, 43, 73

Wedekind, (Benjamin) Frank(lin) 1864-1918 **TCLC 7; DAM DRAM**
See also CA 104; 153; DLB 118

Weidman, Jerome 1913-1998 .... **CLC 7**
See also AITN 2; CA 1-4R; 171; CANR 1; DLB 28

Weil, Simone (Adolphine) 1909-1943 **TCLC 23**
See also CA 117; 159

Weininger, Otto 1880-1903 .... **TCLC 84**

Weinstein, Nathan
See West, Nathanael

Weinstein, Nathan von Wallenstein
See West, Nathanael

Weir, Peter (Lindsay) 1944- .... **CLC 20**
See also CA 113; 123

Weiss, Peter (Ulrich) 1916-1982 **CLC 3, 15, 51; DAM DRAM**
See also CA 45-48; 106; CANR 3; DLB 69, 124

Weiss, Theodore (Russell) 1916- **CLC 3, 8, 14**
See also CA 9-12R; CAAS 2; CANR 46; DLB 5

Welch, (Maurice) Denton 1915-1948 **TCLC 22**
See also CA 121; 148

Welch, James 1940- ..... **CLC 6, 14, 52; DAM MULT, POP**
See also CA 85-88; CANR 42, 66; DLB 175; NNAL

Weldon, Fay 1931- ... **CLC 6, 9, 11, 19, 36, 59; DAM POP**
See also CA 21-24R; CANR 16, 46, 63; CDBLB 1960 to Present; DLB 14, 194; INT CANR-16; MTCW 1

Wellek, Rene 1903-1995 .... **CLC 28**
See also CA 5-8R; 150; CAAS 7; CANR 8; DLB 63; INT CANR-8

Weller, Michael 1942- .... **CLC 10, 53**
See also CA 85-88

Weller, Paul 1958- .... **CLC 26**

Wellershoff, Dieter 1925- .... **CLC 46**
See also CA 89-92; CANR 16, 37

Welles, (George) Orson 1915-1985**CLC 20, 80**
    See also CA 93-96; 117
Wellman, John McDowell 1945-
    See Wellman, Mac
    See also CA 166
Wellman, Mac 1945- .... **CLC 65**
    See also Wellman, John McDowell; Wellman,
    John McDowell
Wellman, Manly Wade 1903-1986 ... **CLC 49**
    See also CA 1-4R; 118; CANR 6, 16, 44; SATA
    6; SATA-Obit 47
Wells, Carolyn 1869(?)-1942 .... **TCLC 35**
    See also CA 113; DLB 11
Wells, H(erbert) G(eorge) 1866-1946**TCLC 6,
    12, 19; DA; DAB; DAC; DAM MST, NOV;
    SSC 6; WLC**
    See also AAYA 18; CA 110; 121; CDBLB 1914-
    1945; DLB 34, 70, 156, 178; MTCW 1;
    SATA 20
Wells, Rosemary 1943-..................... **CLC 12**
    See also AAYA 13; CA 85-88; CANR 48; CLR
    16; MAICYA; SAAS 1; SATA 18, 69
Welty, Eudora 1909- **CLC 1, 2, 5, 14, 22, 33,
    105; DA; DAB; DAC; DAM MST, NOV;
    SSC 1, 27; WLC**
    See also CA 9-12R; CABS 1; CANR 32, 65;
    CDALB 1941-1968; DLB 2, 102, 143;
    DLBD 12; DLBY 87; MTCW 1
Wen I-to 1899-1946 .... **TCLC 28**
Wentworth, Robert
    See Hamilton, Edmond
Werfel, Franz (Viktor) 1890-1945 ... **TCLC 8**
    See also CA 104; 161; DLB 81, 124
Wergeland, Henrik Arnold 1808-1845**N C L C
    5**
Wersba, Barbara 1932-..................... **CLC 30**
    See also AAYA 2; CA 29-32R; CANR 16, 38;
    CLR 3; DLB 52; JRDA; MAICYA; SAAS 2;
    SATA 1, 58; SATA-Essay 103
Wertmueller, Lina 1928-................... **CLC 16**
    See also CA 97-100; CANR 39
Wescott, Glenway 1901-1987 .... **CLC 13**
    See also CA 13-16R; 121; CANR 23, 70; DLB
    4, 9, 102
Wesker, Arnold 1932-.... **CLC 3, 5, 42; DAB;
    DAM DRAM**
    See also CA 1-4R; CAAS 7; CANR 1, 33;
    CDBLB 1960 to Present; DLB 13; MTCW 1
Wesley, Richard (Errol) 1945- ....**CLC 7**
    See also BW 1; CA 57-60; CANR 27; DLB 38
Wessel, Johan Herman 1742-1785 .... **LC 7**
West, Anthony (Panther) 1914-1987 **CLC 50**
    See also CA 45-48; 124; CANR 3, 19; DLB 15
West, C. P.
    See Wodehouse, P(elham) G(renville)
West, (Mary) Jessamyn 1902-1984**CLC 7, 17**
    See also CA 9-12R; 112; CANR 27; DLB 6;
    DLBY 84; MTCW 1; SATA-Obit 37
West, Morris L(anglo) 1916-......... **CLC 6, 33**
    See also CA 5-8R; CANR 24, 49, 64; MTCW 1
West, Nathanael 1903-1940 **TCLC 1, 14, 44;
    SSC 16**
    See also CA 104; 125; CDALB 1929-1941;
    DLB 4, 9, 28; MTCW 1
West, Owen
    See Koontz, Dean R(ay)
West, Paul 1930- .... **CLC 7, 14, 96**
    See also CA 13-16R; CAAS 7; CANR 22, 53,
    76; DLB 14; INT CANR-22
West, Rebecca 1892-1983 ... **CLC 7, 9, 31, 50**
    See also CA 5-8R; 109; CANR 19; DLB 36;
    DLBY 83; MTCW 1
Westall, Robert (Atkinson) 1929-1993**CLC 17**

    See also AAYA 12; CA 69-72; 141; CANR 18,
    68; CLR 13; JRDA; MAICYA; SAAS 2;
    SATA 23, 69; SATA-Obit 75
Westermarck, Edward 1862-1939 . **TCLC 87**
Westlake, Donald E(dwin) 1933- **CLC 7, 33;
    DAM POP**
    See also CA 17-20R; CAAS 13; CANR 16, 44,
    65; INT CANR-16
Westmacott, Mary
    See Christie, Agatha (Mary Clarissa)
Weston, Allen
    See Norton, Andre
Wetcheek, J. L.
    See Feuchtwanger, Lion
Wetering, Janwillem van de
    See van de Wetering, Janwillem
Wetherald, Agnes Ethelwyn 1857-1940**TCLC
    81**
    See also DLB 99
Wetherell, Elizabeth
    See Warner, Susan (Bogert)
Whale, James 1889-1957 .... **TCLC 63**
Whalen, Philip 1923-..................... **CLC 6, 29**
    See also CA 9-12R; CANR 5, 39; DLB 16
Wharton, Edith (Newbold Jones) 1862-1937
    **TCLC 3, 9, 27, 53; DA; DAB; DAC; DAM
    MST, NOV; SSC 6; WLC**
    See also AAYA 25; CA 104; 132; CDALB 1865-
    1917; DLB 4, 9, 12, 78, 189; DLBD 13;
    MTCW 1
Wharton, James
    See Mencken, H(enry) L(ouis)
Wharton, William (a pseudonym)**CLC 18, 37**
    See also CA 93-96; DLBY 80; INT 93-96
Wheatley (Peters), Phillis 1754(?)-1784**LC 3;
    BLC 3; DA; DAC; DAM MST, MULT,
    POET; PC 3; WLC**
    See also CDALB 1640-1865; DLB 31, 50
Wheelock, John Hall 1886-1978 .... **CLC 14**
    See also CA 13-16R; 77-80; CANR 14; DLB
    45
White, E(lwyn) B(rooks) 1899-1985 **CLC 10,
    34, 39; DAM POP**
    See also AITN 2; CA 13-16R; 116; CANR 16,
    37; CLR 1, 21; DLB 11, 22; MAICYA;
    MTCW 1; SATA 2, 29, 100; SATA-Obit 44
White, Edmund (Valentine III) 1940-**CLC 27,
    110; DAM POP**
    See also AAYA 7; CA 45-48; CANR 3, 19, 36,
    62; MTCW 1
White, Patrick (Victor Martindale) 1912-1990
    CLC 3, 4, 5, 7, 9, 18, 65, 69
    See also CA 81-84; 132; CANR 43; MTCW 1
White, Phyllis Dorothy James 1920-
    See James, P. D.
    See also CA 21-24R; CANR 17, 43, 65; DAM
    POP; MTCW 1
White, T(erence) H(anbury) 1906-1964 **C L C
    30**
    See also AAYA 22; CA 73-76; CANR 37; DLB
    160; JRDA; MAICYA; SATA 12
White, Terence de Vere 1912-1994 ...**CLC 49**
    See also CA 49-52; 145; CANR 3
White, Walter
    See White, Walter F(rancis)
    See also BLC; DAM MULT
White, Walter F(rancis) 1893-1955 **TCLC 15**
    See also White, Walter
    See also BW 1; CA 115; 124; DLB 51
White, William Hale 1831-1913
    See Rutherford, Mark
    See also CA 121
Whitehead, E(dward) A(nthony) 1933-**CLC 5**

    See also CA 65-68; CANR 58
Whitemore, Hugh (John) 1936- .... **CLC 37**
    See also CA 132; CANR 77; INT 132
Whitman, Sarah Helen (Power) 1803-1878
    NCLC 19
    See also DLB 1
Whitman, Walt(er) 1819-1892 . **NCLC 4, 31;
    DA; DAB; DAC; DAM MST, POET; PC
    3; WLC**
    See also CDALB 1640-1865; DLB 3, 64; SATA
    20
Whitney, Phyllis A(yame) 1903- ..... **CLC 42;
    DAM POP**
    See also AITN 2; BEST 90:3; CA 1-4R; CANR
    3, 25, 38, 60; JRDA; MAICYA; SATA 1, 30
Whittemore, (Edward) Reed (Jr.) 1919-**CLC 4**
    See also CA 9-12R; CAAS 8; CANR 4; DLB 5
Whittier, John Greenleaf 1807-1892**NCLC 8,
    59**
    See also DLB 1
Whittlebot, Hernia
    See Coward, Noel (Peirce)
Wicker, Thomas Grey 1926-
    See Wicker, Tom
    See also CA 65-68; CANR 21, 46
Wicker, Tom ....**CLC 7**
    See also Wicker, Thomas Grey
Wideman, John Edgar 1941- **CLC 5, 34, 36,
    67; BLC 3; DAM MULT**
    See also BW 2; CA 85-88; CANR 14, 42, 67;
    DLB 33, 143
Wiebe, Rudy (Henry) 1934- .. **CLC 6, 11, 14;
    DAC; DAM MST**
    See also CA 37-40R; CANR 42, 67; DLB 60
Wieland, Christoph Martin 1733-1813**N C L C
    17**
    See also DLB 97
Wiene, Robert 1881-1938 .... **TCLC 56**
Wieners, John 1934-..........................**CLC 7**
    See also CA 13-16R; DLB 16
Wiesel, Elie(zer) 1928- **CLC 3, 5, 11, 37; DA;
    DAB; DAC; DAM MST, NOV; WLCS**
    See also AAYA 7; AITN 1; CA 5-8R; CAAS 4;
    CANR 8, 40, 65; DLB 83; DLBY 87; INT
    CANR-8; MTCW 1; SATA 56
Wiggins, Marianne 1947- .... **CLC 57**
    See also BEST 89:3; CA 130; CANR 60
Wight, James Alfred 1916-1995
    See Herriot, James
    See also CA 77-80; SATA 55; SATA-Brief 44
Wilbur, Richard (Purdy) 1921-**CLC 3, 6, 9, 14,
    53, 110; DA; DAB; DAC; DAM MST,
    POET**
    See also CA 1-4R; CABS 2; CANR 2, 29, 76;
    DLB 5, 169; INT CANR-29; MTCW 1;
    SATA 9
Wild, Peter 1940-............................. **CLC 14**
    See also CA 37-40R; DLB 5
Wilde, Oscar 1854(?)-1900**TCLC 1, 8, 23, 41;
    DA; DAB; DAC; DAM DRAM, MST,
    NOV; SSC 11; WLC**
    See also CA 104; 119; CDBLB 1890-1914;
    DLB 10, 19, 34, 57, 141, 156, 190; SATA 24
Wilder, Billy .... **CLC 20**
    See also Wilder, Samuel
    See also DLB 26
Wilder, Samuel 1906-
    See Wilder, Billy
    See also CA 89-92
Wilder, Thornton (Niven) 1897-1975**CLC 1, 5,
    6, 10, 15, 35, 82; DA; DAB; DAC; DAM
    DRAM, MST, NOV; DC 1; WLC**
    See also AITN 2; CA 13-16R; 61-64; CANR

40; DLB 4, 7, 9; DLBY 97; MTCW 1

Wilding, Michael 1942- .... **CLC 73**
See also CA 104; CANR 24, 49

Wiley, Richard 1944- .... **CLC 44**
See also CA 121; 129; CANR 71

Wilhelm, Kate ....**CLC 7**
See also Wilhelm, Katie Gertrude
See also AAYA 20; CAAS 5; DLB 8; INT
CANR-17

Wilhelm, Katie Gertrude 1928-
See Wilhelm, Kate
See also CA 37-40R; CANR 17, 36, 60; MTCW
1

Wilkins, Mary
See Freeman, Mary Eleanor Wilkins

Willard, Nancy 1936- .... **CLC 7, 37**
See also CA 89-92; CANR 10, 39, 68; CLR 5;
DLB 5, 52; MAICYA; MTCW 1; SATA 37,
71; SATA-Brief 30

William of Ockham 1285-1347 ..... **CMLC 32**

Williams, Ben Ames 1889-1953 ...... **TCLC 89**
See also DLB 102

Williams, C(harles) K(enneth) 1936-**CLC 33,
56; DAM POET**
See also CA 37-40R; CAAS 26; CANR 57; DLB
5

Williams, Charles
See Collier, James L(incoln)

Williams, Charles (Walter Stansby) 1886-1945
TCLC 1, 11
See also CA 104; 163; DLB 100, 153

Williams, (George) Emlyn 1905-1987**CLC 15;
DAM DRAM**
See also CA 104; 123; CANR 36; DLB 10, 77;
MTCW 1

Williams, Hank 1923-1953 .... **TCLC 81**

Williams, Hugo 1942- .... **CLC 42**
See also CA 17-20R; CANR 45; DLB 40

Williams, J. Walker
See Wodehouse, P(elham) G(renville)

Williams, John A(lfred) 1925-**CLC 5, 13; BLC
3; DAM MULT**
See also BW 2; CA 53-56; CAAS 3; CANR 6,
26, 51; DLB 2, 33; INT CANR-6

Williams, Jonathan (Chamberlain) 1929-
CLC 13
See also CA 9-12R; CAAS 12; CANR 8; DLB
5

Williams, Joy 1944- .... **CLC 31**
See also CA 41-44R; CANR 22, 48

Williams, Norman 1952- .... **CLC 39**
See also CA 118

Williams, Sherley Anne 1944-**CLC 89; BLC 3;
DAM MULT, POET**
See also BW 2; CA 73-76; CANR 25; DLB 41;
INT CANR-25; SATA 78

Williams, Shirley
See Williams, Sherley Anne

Williams, Tennessee 1911-1983**CLC 1, 2, 5, 7,
8, 11, 15, 19, 30, 39, 45, 71, 111; DA; DAB;
DAC; DAM DRAM, MST; DC 4; WLC**
See also AITN 1, 2; CA 5-8R; 108; CABS 3;
CANR 31; CDALB 1941-1968; DLB 7;
DLBD 4; DLBY 83; MTCW 1

Williams, Thomas (Alonzo) 1926-1990**CLC 14**
See also CA 1-4R; 132; CANR 2

Williams, William C.
See Williams, William Carlos

Williams, William Carlos 1883-1963**CLC 1, 2,
5, 9, 13, 22, 42, 67; DA; DAB; DAC; DAM
MST, POET; PC 7; SSC 31**
See also CA 89-92; CANR 34; CDALB 1917-
1929; DLB 4, 16, 54, 86; MTCW 1

Williamson, David (Keith) 1942- ...... **CLC 56**
See also CA 103; CANR 41

Williamson, Ellen Douglas 1905-1984
See Douglas, Ellen
See also CA 17-20R; 114; CANR 39

Williamson, Jack ....**CLC 29**
See also Williamson, John Stewart
See also CAAS 8; DLB 8

Williamson, John Stewart 1908-
See Williamson, Jack
See also CA 17-20R; CANR 23, 70

Willie, Frederick
See Lovecraft, H(oward) P(hillips)

Willingham, Calder (Baynard, Jr.) 1922-1995
CLC 5, 51
See also CA 5-8R; 147; CANR 3; DLB 2, 44;
MTCW 1

Willis, Charles
See Clarke, Arthur C(harles)

Willis, Fingal O'Flahertie
See Wilde, Oscar

Willy
See Colette, (Sidonie-Gabrielle)

Willy, Colette
See Colette, (Sidonie-Gabrielle)

Wilson, A(ndrew) N(orman) 1950- ...**CLC 33**
See also CA 112; 122; DLB 14, 155, 194

Wilson, Angus (Frank Johnstone) 1913-1991
CLC 2, 3, 5, 25, 34; SSC 21
See also CA 5-8R; 134; CANR 21; DLB 15,
139, 155; MTCW 1

Wilson, August 1945- ...**CLC 39, 50, 63, 118;
BLC 3; DA; DAB; DAC; DAM DRAM,
MST, MULT; DC 2; WLCS**
See also AAYA 16; BW 2; CA 115; 122; CANR
42, 54, 76; MTCW 1

Wilson, Brian 1942- ....**CLC 12**

Wilson, Colin 1931- .... **CLC 3, 14**
See also CA 1-4R; CAAS 5; CANR 1, 22, 33,
77; DLB 14, 194; MTCW 1

Wilson, Dirk
See Pohl, Frederik

Wilson, Edmund 1895-1972**CLC 1, 2, 3, 8, 24**
See also CA 1-4R; 37-40R; CANR 1, 46; DLB
63; MTCW 1

Wilson, Ethel Davis (Bryant) 1888(?)-1980
CLC 13; DAC; DAM POET
See also CA 102; DLB 68; MTCW 1

Wilson, John 1785-1854 .... **NCLC 5**

Wilson, John (Anthony) Burgess 1917-1993
See Burgess, Anthony
See also CA 1-4R; 143; CANR 2, 46; DAC;
DAM NOV; MTCW 1

Wilson, Lanford 1937- **CLC 7, 14, 36; DAM
DRAM**
See also CA 17-20R; CABS 3; CANR 45; DLB
7

Wilson, Robert M. 1944- .... **CLC 7, 9**
See also CA 49-52; CANR 2, 41; MTCW 1

Wilson, Robert McLiam 1964- .... **CLC 59**
See also CA 132

Wilson, Sloan 1920- ....**CLC 32**
See also CA 1-4R; CANR 1, 44

Wilson, Snoo 1948- ....**CLC 33**
See also CA 69-72

Wilson, William S(mith) 1932- ....**CLC 49**
See also CA 81-84

Wilson, (Thomas) Woodrow 1856-1924**TCLC
79**
See also CA 166; DLB 47

Winchilsea, Anne (Kingsmill) Finch Counte
1661-1720
See Finch, Anne

Windham, Basil
See Wodehouse, P(elham) G(renville)

Wingrove, David (John) 1954- ....**CLC 68**
See also CA 133

Wintergreen, Jane
See Duncan, Sara Jeannette

Winters, Janet Lewis ....**CLC 41**
See also Lewis, Janet
See also DLBY 87

Winters, (Arthur) Yvor 1900-1968 **CLC 4, 8,
32**
See also CA 11-12; 25-28R; CAP 1; DLB 48;
MTCW 1

Winterson, Jeanette 1959-**CLC 64; DAM POP**
See also CA 136; CANR 58; DLB 207

Winthrop, John 1588-1649 .... **LC 31**
See also DLB 24, 30

Wirth, Louis 1897-1952 .... **TCLC 92**

Wiseman, Frederick 1930- ....**CLC 20**
See also CA 159

Wister, Owen 1860-1938 .... **TCLC 21**
See also CA 108; 162; DLB 9, 78, 186; SATA
62

Witkacy
See Witkiewicz, Stanislaw Ignacy

Witkiewicz, Stanislaw Ignacy 1885-1939
TCLC 8
See also CA 105; 162

Wittgenstein, Ludwig (Josef Johann) 1889-1951
TCLC 59
See also CA 113; 164

Wittig, Monique 1935(?)- ....**CLC 22**
See also CA 116; 135; DLB 83

Wittlin, Jozef 1896-1976 ....**CLC 25**
See also CA 49-52; 65-68; CANR 3

Wodehouse, P(elham) G(renville) 1881-1975
**CLC 1, 2, 5, 10, 22; DAB; DAC; DAM
NOV; SSC 2**
See also AITN 2; CA 45-48; 57-60; CANR 3,
33; CDBLB 1914-1945; DLB 34, 162;
MTCW 1; SATA 22

Woiwode, L.
See Woiwode, Larry (Alfred)

Woiwode, Larry (Alfred) 1941- ... **CLC 6, 10**
See also CA 73-76; CANR 16; DLB 6; INT
CANR-16

Wojciechowska, Maia (Teresa) 1927-**CLC 26**
See also AAYA 8; CA 9-12R; CANR 4, 41; CLR
1; JRDA; MAICYA; SAAS 1; SATA 1, 28,
83; SATA-Essay 104

Wolf, Christa 1929- .... **CLC 14, 29, 58**
See also CA 85-88; CANR 45; DLB 75; MTCW
1

Wolfe, Gene (Rodman) 1931- **CLC 25; DAM
POP**
See also CA 57-60; CAAS 9; CANR 6, 32, 60;
DLB 8

Wolfe, George C. 1954- ....**CLC 49; BLCS**
See also CA 149

Wolfe, Thomas (Clayton) 1900-1938**TCLC 4,
13, 29, 61; DA; DAB; DAC; DAM MST,
NOV; SSC 33; WLC**
See also CA 104; 132; CDALB 1929-1941;
DLB 9, 102; DLBD 2, 16; DLBY 85, 97;
MTCW 1

Wolfe, Thomas Kennerly, Jr. 1930-
See Wolfe, Tom
See also CA 13-16R; CANR 9, 33, 70; DAM
POP; DLB 185; INT CANR-9; MTCW 1

Wolfe, Tom .... **CLC 1, 2, 9, 15, 35, 51**
See also Wolfe, Thomas Kennerly, Jr.
See also AAYA 8; AITN 2; BEST 89:1; DLB
152

See also CA 117; 167

Zhukovsky, Vasily (Andreevich) 1783-1852
NCLC 35
See also DLB 205

Ziegenhagen, Eric .... **CLC 55**

Zimmer, Jill Schary
See Robinson, Jill

Zimmerman, Robert
See Dylan, Bob

Zindel, Paul 1936-**CLC 6, 26; DA; DAB; DAC; DAM DRAM, MST, NOV; DC 5**
See also AAYA 2; CA 73-76; CANR 31, 65; CLR 3, 45; DLB 7, 52; JRDA; MAICYA; MTCW 1; SATA 16, 58, 102

Zinov'Ev, A. A.
See Zinoviev, Alexander (Aleksandrovich)

Zinoviev, Alexander (Aleksandrovich) 1922-
CLC 19
See also CA 116; 133; CAAS 10

Zoilus
See Lovecraft, H(oward) P(hillips)

Zola, Emile (Edouard Charles Antoine) 1840-1902**TCLC 1, 6, 21, 41; DA; DAB; DAC; DAM MST, NOV; WLC**
See also CA 104; 138; DLB 123

Zoline, Pamela 1941- .... **CLC 62**
See also CA 161

Zorrilla y Moral, Jose 1817-1893 .... **NCLC 6**

Zoshchenko, Mikhail (Mikhailovich) 1895-1958
TCLC 15; SSC 15
See also CA 115; 160

Zuckmayer, Carl 1896-1977 .... **CLC 18**
See also CA 69-72; DLB 56, 124

Zuk, Georges
See Skelton, Robin

Zukofsky, Louis 1904-1978**CLC 1, 2, 4, 7, 11, 18; DAM POET; PC 11**
See also CA 9-12R; 77-80; CANR 39; DLB 5, 165; MTCW 1

Zweig, Paul 1935-1984 .... **CLC 34, 42**
See also CA 85-88; 113

Zweig, Stefan 1881-1942 .... **TCLC 17**
See also CA 112; 170; DLB 81, 118

Zwingli, Huldreich 1484-1531 .... **LC 37**
See also DLB 179

Literary Criticism Series
Cumulative Topic Index

This index lists all topic entries in Gale's *Classical and Medieval Literature Criticism, Contemporary Literary Criticism, Literature Criticism from 1400 to 1800, Nineteenth-Century Literature Criticism,* and *Twentieth-Century Literary Criticism.*

Topic Index

Topic Index

LC Cumulative Nationality Index

LC Cumulative Title Index

Title Index

Title Index

Title Index

Title Index

Title Index

Title Index

Title Index

Title Index

Title Index

Title Index

Title Index

Title Index

Title Index

ISBN 0-7876 -3264-3

90000

9 780787 632649